ZONES OF CONTROL

Game Histories

edited by Henry Lowood and Raiford Guins

Debugging Game History: A Critical Lexicon, edited by Henry Lowood and Raiford Guins, 2016

Zones of Control: Perspectives on Wargaming, edited by Pat Harrigan and Matthew Kirschenbaum, 2016

ZONES OF CONTROL

Perspectives on Wargaming

edited by Pat Harrigan and Matthew G. Kirschenbaum

The MIT Press
Cambridge, Massachusetts
London, England

This book was set in Gentium Book Basic and Futura by Toppan Best-set Premedia Limited. Printed and bound in the United States of America.

Library of Congress Cataloging-in-Publication Data

Names: Harrigan, Pat, editor. | Kirschenbaum, Matthew G., editor.
Title: Zones of control : perspectives on wargaming / Pat Harrigan and Matthew G. Kirschenbaum; eds. foreword by James F. Dunnigan.
Description: Cambridge, MA : The MIT Press, 2016. | Series: Game histories | Includes bibliographical references and index.
Identifiers: LCCN 2015038407 | ISBN 9780262033992 (hardcover : alk. paper)
Subjects: LCSH: War games—History. | War games.
Classification: LCC U310 .Z67 2016 | DDC 355.4/8—dc23 LC record available at http://lccn.loc.gov/2015038407

10   9   8   7   6   5   4   3   2   1

Pat dedicates this book to Richard "Screaming Boy" Smart (1970–2011), stalwart gaming friend, dearly missed.

Matthew dedicates this book to John Hill (1945–2015), designer of Squad Leader *and many others.*

CONTENTS

[General William] Westmoreland's strategy had always been to use the American troops as a "shield behind which" the GVN forces could move in to establish government security. The commanding general never quite came to terms with the fact that the war was being fought at points rather than along lines. With the support or even the neutrality of the population, the enemy forces could break up into small units and go anywhere in the countryside circumnavigating the "Free World" outposts. Westmoreland was trying to play chess while his enemy was playing Go.

—Frances FitzGerald, *Fire in the Lake*

In 1961, Charles S. Roberts and Avalon Hill, the Baltimore, Maryland, company he had founded seven years earlier, published four board games with certain things in common. All four were based on historical military subjects—in fact, three out of the four concerned the American Civil War, whose centenary was that year (the other game was *D-Day*). All of them came with a sheet of die-cut cardboard counters, mostly a half-inch square and printed in two colors to represent the military units that fought in the particular battles and campaigns. All of them featured something called a Combat Results Table to adjudicate the outcome of individual battles

within a probabilistic range based on a die roll.[1] All four of the games also included a mapboard depicting some place in the real world, ranging in scope from the eastern half of the Continental United States to Nazi-occupied France to the ridges and roadways converging at Gettysburg, Pennsylvania, to the woods around Chancellorsville, Virginia. There is nothing about the game board in *Monopoly* that actually resembles the street plan of Atlantic City, but these games were different—at a glance you could see Paris relative to Calais, or where Little Round Top sat amid the fields and farms outside of a certain crossroads town. Finally, all of the maps were overlaid with the hexagonal grid that was to become wargaming's most enduring visual icon. Despite the games' differing topics and scope, each of them took advantage of this hex grid to implement a concept called a Zone of Control.

Mechanically, a Zone of Control (ZOC) is easy to explain: a combat unit's presence in any one hex is sufficient to exert some set of effects on the six hexes immediately adjacent to it. Maybe an enemy unit has to expend more movement points to enter and leave a ZOC hex (reflecting the friction of skirmishing patrols in modern warfare) or maybe the unit must immediately stop and enter into combat (reflecting what would happen when a Union and Confederate regiment found each other eyeball to eyeball across an open field). Just as important, however, a ZOC is also an artifact of the abstraction inherent in the enterprise of "gaming" war—wars and battles, after all, are not really fought on hex grids, units don't always deploy in a consistent fashion or formation, turns are not taken sequentially by opposing battlefield commanders, and so forth. Wargames at their most fundamental, regardless of medium or motivation or scope, seek to model the brutal reality of armed conflict with a set of heuristics and formulas, conventions and physical or programmable components. As a method for representing the projection of military force in a range of scales and historical epochs, Zones of Control are thus one means toward achieving the elusive compromise between gameplay and simulation, between abstraction and realism.

For us, however, the idea of Zones of Control also suggested something more. It is a conspicuously powerful phrasing, one that we felt could be put to effective use in editing a book about wargames in multiple media, formats, and player communities. Why edit such a book at all? Most all of our readers will already know that games with military themes date back to antiquity, as Jon Peterson reminds us in his opening chapter. For all of their historical variety however, wargames remain underserved by the established academic and trade literature on games and game history. Many popular writers seem content to move from a token acknowledgment of chess or Go or Chaturanga to the first-person shooter. At other times wargames are treated in a cursory manner, obligatory to mention but best not lingered over on the way to more tempting (and less bellicose) fare involving magic or meeples. Sometimes there is a

slightly more nuanced genealogy invoking the Prussian *Kriegsspiel* or H. G. Wells's *Little Wars* (1913), and perhaps a mention of Avalon Hill or Simulations Publications, Incorporated (SPI), before arriving at the presumptive finality of the digital present. By contrast, *Zones of Control* seeks to offer a richer and more granular set of perspectives on wargaming's past, present, and future, particularly in its Western contexts.

The kind of "wargames" we have in mind are generally those games that cover specific historical conflicts—wars, battles, and campaigns—as well as games grounded in recognizable real-world geopolitics. (Wargames set in fantastical or science-fictional contexts are largely, though not entirely, absent from this book.) We mean both recreational or commercial games as well as those employed by professional militaries and policymakers. We mean games that attempt to interpret and understand past conflicts, and those that seek to model and forecast potential future ones. And we mean games played on both tabletops and on screens, which is to say games in both analog and digital media. The taxonomies and genealogies here are complex, and cannot be disambiguated simply by recourse to medium and method or even the play of a particular game system. Gaming at the Naval War College at Newport, Rhode Island for example, has historically involved computer simulations, role-playing and discussion, and officers moving miniature ships around on the floor with rulers and protractors. Recreational or hobby games about naval warfare have also been published in most of these formats, indeed sometimes utilizing the same rule sets or game engines (such was the case with both Fred Jane's miniatures rules in the early twentieth century and the *Harpoon* series of today). We also follow

Peter Perla's insistence, in his *The Art of Wargaming* (1990), on using the contracted compound "wargaming" (not "war gaming") to represent the form's characteristic synthesis of topical simulation and ludic play.

Wargaming, by definition, traffics in martial subject matter. Perceived in its full historical and material diversity, however, it is not inherently militaristic. Such at least is our governing belief—readers should use what follows to arrive at their own determination. Wargaming is also possessed of deeper significance to game studies and game history than the merely topical; that is, its relevance or import cannot be evaluated simply by the extent to which one does or does not think themselves interested in games about war. Its professional practitioners will often define wargaming as a tool for abductive reasoning, a term first introduced by Charles Sanders Pierce for testing hypotheses. As contributor Rex Brynen has previously suggested, "Wargaming is much more policy- and planning-oriented than most other gaming. It also has much more rigorous traditions of design, validation, adjudication, instrumentation/reporting, and analysis."[2] In her chapter here, Sharon Ghamari-Tabrizi argues for understanding wargames as systems of inscription, rather than as mere topical playthings. The toolbox of modeling techniques and heuristics originated by wargaming has also found increasing application in other subject domains: Mark Herman has written elsewhere (2009) about the use of wargaming in strategic corporate planning, while in this volume Brynen, Mary Flanagan, and James Wallman all find ties to different kinds of "serious" games, including what Brynen has termed "peace games" for peacebuilding.

Moreover, as much as they can be games *about* history, wargames are also part *of* the history of games, as Peterson makes clear. Therefore, in their chapters here, Scott Glancy examines the methods of depicting physical conflict in tabletop role-playing game systems, and Henry Lowood finds essential connections between the emergence of computer game engines like that of id Software's *Doom* (1993) and the prior innovation of systems- and scenario-driven designs in board wargaming. Wargames have also interacted freely with the arts, sometimes in surprising ways; the contributions here from David Levinthal and Brian Conley document wargames in relation to individual artistic practice, and Esther MacCallum-Stewart surveys literary representations of wargaming in a variety of idioms.

Perhaps most important, wargames are unquestionably the most sophisticated ludic productions ever attempted in paper or predigital form, their systems and procedures self-documenting with all of their working parts materially exposed as soon as one opens the box and begins examining the often notoriously intricate rules, charts, and components.[3] (Jim Dunnigan, as we will see, calls them paper time machines.) These games thus offer the single largest extant corpus of coherent exemplars whereby the complexity (and chaos) of lived experience is reduced to ludic systems and procedures, surely a resource worth our attention and inquiry. Indeed, wargame hobbyists will often amass collections of hundreds or even thousands of titles, sometimes a dozen or more on a popular topic like Gettysburg or D-Day or the Battle of the Bulge. For the more critically minded among them, the goal is not to find the single, definitive simulation—indeed, one that merely mechanically replicated the historical outcome at each playing would be deemed a failure—but rather to compare and contrast the techniques and interpretations across the different designs, much as a historian reads multiple accounts and sources to arrive at her own synthesis of events.

This bears further comment. Although there are many commonalities among wargames, there are also enormous variations in their purposes and designs. The goals of the hobby game player and the goals of the security professional are not the same, although both might be employing very similar game systems. Contrariwise, even games that ostensibly cover the same subject matter can do so in widely divergent ways. Two examples will suffice.

Charles Roberts's aforementioned *Gettysburg* (1961) assigns varying combat and movement values to individual Union and Confederate units (Jubal Early's division, for example, rates a 4–2, making it stronger in combat than George Pickett's 3–2). This deterministic manner of assessing unit capabilities became nearly as common in wargame design as the hex map itself, but even this is not universal. By contrast, Rachel Simmons's recent design for *The Guns of Gettysburg* (2013) forgoes combat ratings altogether; with the exception of the famously tough Union "Iron Brigade," combat effectiveness is determined through a combination of position, terrain and previous combat casualties. Far from being arbitrary, this design decision reflects a particular form of historical understanding, one that assigns more value to contingent factors on the battlefield and deemphasizes the relative "quality" of the fighting men.

The venerable Avalon Hill game *Kingmaker* (1974) is designed as a multiplayer simulation of the Wars of the Roses, supporting up to seven players. Players do not take on the roles of the belligerent houses of York and Lancaster, but instead play fluctuating blocs of allied noble families, whose armies move across a map of England to control, and sometimes execute, Yorkist and Lancastrian personages such

as Henry VI and Richard, Duke of York—who are, literally, tokens. By contrast, a more recent game on the same subject, Columbia Games' *Richard III: The Wars of the Roses* (2009), is designed for two players filling the expected roles of the Houses of York and Lancaster. Jerry Taylor, *Richard III*'s principal designer, explains that the multifactional view of the Wars of the Roses expressed through *Kingmaker* was the "prevailing view among historians" in the 1970s, but that modern scholarship now leans once again toward the traditional view of the conflict as one primarily between York and Lancaster. Taylor could therefore not design *Richard III* as a multiplayer game "without doing massive violence to history"; he concedes that it would be plausible to design a three-player simulation, with the third player representing the forces of Richard Neville, Earl of Warwick, but "I've never been able to figure out a way to make a satisfactory three-player game yet" (Grant 2012).

The wargame design process therefore encodes assumptions about historical events (or contemporary real-world situations) into the mechanics of the game itself. In this they are no different from any other system of representation, since it is in the nature of a model to simplify the complexity of the world, but as Dunnigan and others frequently point out, tabletop games offer one of the most transparent demonstrations of this process. Their rules and procedures are available for all to see.

It is for this reason among others that, if there is a center of gravity to *Zones of Control*, readers will find it in the volume's preponderant attention to manual tabletop ("board") games, a decision that reverses the usual primacy of computer games in previous surveys or collections such as the landmark *Joystick Soldiers: The Politics of Play in Military Video Games*

(2010). We give space to the AAA shooters but place them in dialogue with a much broader array of design practices and ludic frameworks spanning both tabletop games and digital platforms and encompassing commercially available (hobby) games on the one hand and professional defense and national security gaming on the other.

By their very nature, manual or tabletop games account for the chronological majority of the collective record of gaming war. As well, we felt keenly that these games—particularly in their commercial incarnations from Charles S. Roberts forward—represent an underexplored area for ludology and game studies. From the 1960s until well into the 1980s, board wargaming was the single most vital area for game designers to hone their craft; as Greg Costikyan (2006) has noted, the term "game designer," in fact, has its origins at SPI, along with key industry innovations in game production and market research.[4] The conduit between board wargaming and the then-budding computer games industry—for example, between Avalon Hill and the Hunt Valley studios in Maryland—was a straight line, with many leading figures moving from one industry to the other. Moreover, the tabletop design tradition continues to this day, with a typical calendar year seeing the publication of several hundred new board wargames from the several dozen publishers serving the hobby's globalized, if niche, community. We have attempted to showcase some of this ongoing design innovation in addition to paying our respects to influential game systems. Once a board wargame could be expected to sell tens of thousands of copies, perhaps even a hundred thousand or more; today no title can command the upper end of such a market, but as recent press coverage shows (Albert 2014; Roeder 2014), there are indications board

wargaming may be making something of a comeback—a function of their ongoing topicality and agility in covering material that a major digital studio wouldn't touch, and because of a recent trend toward simplifying designs, a change from previous decades' voluminous rules sets and playing times measured in weeks or months.[5]

Tabletop (manual) gaming also remains influential in both educational and national security circles, where the strengths of its material affordances are recognized and routinely leveraged alongside computer-based simulations. As Philip Sabin argues, a manual game is accessible, teachable, and customizable in ways that most computer games are not, especially to a novice audience of nonprogrammers. Board wargames thus handily teach what we now term procedural literacy. This is a virtue not only in the classroom but also in think tanks and on field exercises, where a game that cannot be efficiently broken down and analyzed and explained is a game that is effectively useless. (These are also contexts where cost-effectiveness, rapid prototyping, and agile development are virtues.) Wargaming, in other words, is a design space where there is a strong manual and tabletop ethos that is refined and upheld to this day, and despite the notoriety of the military shooter and the investment in high-end virtual simulation environments by the Western defense establishment, we believe wargaming cannot be adequately studied without a full measure of attention to its analog fundamentals.

We also trust that now is an opportune moment for a broadly synthesizing volume like *Zones of Control*. For a long time there were only a handful of essential but well-worn texts on the subject of wargaming, variously written by analysts (Francis J. McHugh and Peter Perla), journalists (Andrew Wilson and Thomas B. Allen) or hobby luminaries (James F. Dunnigan and Nicholas Palmer).[6] These foundational studies are now joined by a new wave of books from a wider range of perspectives. In his *Wargames* (2013), the Israeli military historian Martin Van Creveld has sought a comprehensive survey of wargaming in Western contexts, encompassing not only tabletop and digital games but also gladiatorial contests, chivalric tourneys, and battlefield reenactments. Jon Peterson's opus *Playing at the World* (2012) offers readers the definitive account of the tangled genealogy of *Dungeons & Dragons* and makes clear what tabletop role-playing games do and do not owe to miniatures and board wargaming. In *Eurogames* (2012), Stewart Woods rightly foregrounds wargaming within the broader tradition of tabletop "hobby games." Philip Sabin has written two essential studies, *Lost Battles* (2007) and *Simulating War* (2012), about the historian and educator's use of wargames in both scholarly and classroom contexts; working in a media and cultural studies idiom, Philipp von Hilgers's *War Games* (2012) ties the discourses of media archaeology and the materialities of communication to the long early modern and modern histories of military gaming; Patrick Crogan's *Gameplay Mode* (2011) is the first full-length work from game studies to offer a critical framework for the digital military simulation; political theorist Richard Barbrook, meanwhile, has found in board wargames a kind of genealogy for the street-level tactics of the avant-garde Left, a history he unveils in *Class Wargames* (2014). Not all of the aforementioned authors are contributors to *Zones of Control*, but many are, and among our other aspirations for the volume we hope we can contribute by placing them and other key thinkers in close contact to one another for the first time.

We are also aware that different readers will come to these pages with different expectations. Fortunately, one of the powers of a book is to bring divergent voices and critical perspectives into tangible proximity by virtue of their sharing space beneath a common cover. (Readers, it should be said, will also find a full spectrum of political postures represented here.) Though not every contribution here will necessarily engage every reader equally, the volume is an occasion to browse and explore, or eavesdrop if you will, on the conversations (in the zones) of others. For the hobbyist, *Zones of Control* collects extended statements from many well-known designers and luminaries, but it also offers historical and critical perspectives typically absent from the pages of designer's notes or hobby 'zines. For the professional national security game designer or member of the military, meanwhile, this volume offers a crosswalk to neighboring communities in much the same manner as Connections, the small but vital wargame practitioners' conference held annually since 1993.[7] This comes at a time when there is also renewed emphasis on wargaming in the defense establishment, notably an influential memorandum calling for "innovation" in wargaming issued by US Deputy Secretary of Defense Robert Work in 2015.[8] It also demonstrates what humanistic and historical perspectives can bring to the sometimes too-presentist or positivistic objectives of a professional trained mostly outside those critical and intellectual traditions.

For the academic reader, we suggest that some of this material be regarded as primary source documentation from various communities of practice, but we have also attempted to align the volume with a number of academic fields and specializations, especially in the contributions of the longer chapters.

We have already sought to articulate what we take to be wargaming's significance to game studies or ludology. For media studies and media archaeology, wargaming offers an extended case study in negotiating medial forms, notably paper and other analog components and in relation to the digital—a negotiation carried out in terms of abstraction and representation, and the material instantiation of procedure and probability to represent the (a) "real" in the manner we have discussed. For popular culture and fan studies, *Zones of Control* offers insight into an overlooked community. For military history and war studies, this volume is an opportunity for these fields to reflect once again on the still-marginal status of games as tools for education and research, a message brought home by Robert M. Citino and Lisa Faden and Rob MacDougall, as well as Sabin.[9] Finally, for digital humanities and digital history, wargames offer numerous examples of working models, the attempt to reduce the complexity of lived (literally embattled) experience to systems of procedure and algorithms against the ground-truth of a historical record.[10]

In short, then, because wargaming deals with war does not mean that it should be shunned by ludology or a progressive scholarly establishment, nor should the diversity of its design practices and critical perspectives be homogenized for the sake of a metanarrative about Western militarism. But neither have we shied away from wargaming's implications in what Andrew J. Bacevich (2005) has termed the new American militarism. Readers will thus find discussion of wargaming's ethics and morality in the contributions from Miguel Sicart and Soraya Murray, among others, as well as an account of what has widely been regarded as one of the most progressive wargame designs in some time, 11 bit studios' *This War of Mine*

(2014), contributed by its senior writer and developer, Kacper Kwiatkowski. Patrick Crogan and Luke Caldwell and Tim Lenoir, meanwhile, bring wargaming under intense scrutiny in their respective contributions, using toolkits from the forefront of media and cultural theory. Their critical perspectives are an essential balance to the nuanced, detail-oriented historical accounts of many other contributors and the enthusiasms of individual players and designers. Crogan in particular brings the conceit of a "zone of control" fully up to date with his account of the medial battlespace undergirding contemporary autonomous warfare. And as Caldwell and Lenoir trenchantly conclude: "if our wargames cannot imagine peace, what should we expect of our future military?"

With all military histories it is necessary to remember that war is not a matter of maps with red and blue arrows and oblongs, but of weary, thirsty men with sore feet and aching shoulders wondering where they are.

—George MacDonald Fraser, *Quartered Safe Out Here*

Like John Keegan—who opened his groundbreaking book *The Face of Battle* (1976) with the same admission—neither of us have ever been in a battle, or in uniform. We are white, cisgendered American males, both the products of urban/suburban, middle-class upbringings at a time when the United States lacked compulsory military service. Nuclear war was a visceral fear brought home in countless movies like *The Day After* and, for that matter, *WarGames* (both 1983). By contrast, what conventional wars there were—Iran-Iraq, the Falklands (Malvinas), Lebanon, the so-called "brushfire" wars whose sharp imagery was a staple on the nightly network news—were geographically remote and self-contained. The Big One—a Soviet-led Warsaw Pact invasion of Western Europe—remained only hypothetical but was a prospect anticipated in countless professional and hobby wargames at the time. (Tom Clancy and Larry Bond's *Red Storm Rising*, their best-selling novelization of just such a scenario, was in fact based in part on their play of Bond's naval wargame *Harpoon*.) For Kirschenbaum, this milieu meant discovering boxed wargames on the same shelves as role playing games at the local hobby store: playing Avalon Hill, GDW, and SPI titles was part of his adolescence, coexisting unselfconsciously with Rush albums, *Dungeons & Dragons*, Tom Clancy novels, and an Apple II computer. The intricacies of wargames like *Squad Leader* (1977) or *Wellington's Victory* (1976) did not seem substantially different from these other pursuits. By contrast, Harrigan was, in the acerbic phrase of the narrator of Roberto Bolaño's *The Third Reich* (1989), one of those "adolescents more interested in role-playing games and even computer games than the rigors of the hexagonal board." Wargames were intimidatingly complex, rarely played, and intellectually aspirational, and it was several more years before he regularly began to delve into their mysteries.

We tender these biographical details because as editors of this volume we are typical of the demographic that has dominated hobby and entertainment wargaming, and to a large extent national security gaming as well. As a consequence we have exerted our own zones of control over what follows, both overtly in our editorial role but also in more subtle ways, as subjects who occupy positions of structural advantage in the social hierarchy. Our relationship to wargames, let alone war, is gendered; it is also marked by our privileges of race, class,

sexuality, and nationhood. We are mindful of William Broyles Jr.'s observation in his widely read essay "Why Men Love War" (1984) that men's fascination, indeed their capacity to *love* (his word) the brutality of war is rooted in an early and commonplace indoctrination into the fantasy of war as a game, a safe space within a magic circle where the dead get back up after being struck down. Whatever else they might be, wargames such as we treat here are often undeniably part of a progression of such masculine fantasies.

We are thus grateful to have some leading female voices to explicitly engage questions of gender, notably Mary Flanagan, Elizabeth Losh, Soraya Murray, and Jenny Thompson in their contributions. Nonetheless, *Zones of Control* is majority male in its authorship. The best that can be said for this is that it is indicative of the demographics of wargaming at large.[11] At the hobby game table, female wargamers and wargame designers remain few and far between, though there are some—including Kai Jensen, who has made major contributions to the *Combat Commander* system described herein by John Foley. In the 1970s, Linda Mosca designed several games for SPI. A singular figure is Helena Gail Rubinstein (not to be confused with the cosmetics magnate), whose game *Killer Angels*, a rigorous simulation of the Gettysburg campaign, was published by West End Games in 1984 after originating as her senior thesis at Barnard College. Sabin, for his part, notes increasing female enrollments in his wargaming courses at King's College, London. Female designers and analysts have made perhaps slightly greater inroads in contemporary national security gaming, as the contributions from Elizabeth M. Bartels, Yuna Huh Wong, and Elizabeth Losh here demonstrate, though they remain a minority voice in that space as well. Moreover, though thus far both board wargaming and national security gaming have avoided the very public ugliness surrounding the rise of women's voices that we have seen in commercial video gamer culture, they nonetheless have their own internal challenges to address.[12]

The volume's shortcomings in including non-Anglo-American perspectives are, we acknowledge, more extensive. There are board wargaming communities elsewhere in Europe besides the United Kingdom, notably France (we are thus pleased to have Laurent Closier's contribution), Scandinavia, and Poland, as well as Russia and Asia, notably China and Japan (we are pleased to include Tetsuya Nakamura). Represented hardly at all, however, are games and game designers originating in the Middle East or Southern hemisphere. Related to this, while gender surfaces as an explicit topic in various chapters, race by and large does not. Much can and should be written on race and nationality in wargaming, but the weight of the hobby's Anglo-American heritage has so far greatly limited this. It is our hope that this book can at least help to spur further writing in those areas, since we have underserved them here.[13]

We are also conscious of what we have left out from a sheer topical standpoint. We could have included chapters dedicated to high profile tabletop games about war (*Risk, Axis and Allies*) or video game franchises (*Red Orchestra, Combat Mission, World of Tanks, Kuma\War*); we could have included more material on real-time and turn-based strategy franchises (*Total War, Civilization, Panzer General*) or the vast number of miniatures gaming rule sets or flight simulators; chapters could be written on online "board" gameplay through engines like Cyberboard and VASSAL, or fan activities such as the convention and tournament scene, after action reports, podcasts,

game blogs, forum communities, and the like. Likewise, there is certainly more to be done with the 1980s efforts of Avalon Hill, SSI, and others to port tabletop hex-and-counter gaming to personal computers, as well as the current revolution in tablet wargaming and virtual tabletops. There is no chapter written strictly from the perspective of a game collector or archivist or preservationist, or one on the economics of wargames in the game industry. And so on. *Zones of Control* will, we hope, give hobbyists, academics, game designers and analysts, and other constituencies much to read, reflect on, and enjoy, but there is much more to be done, and if the book helps expose some of these neglected topics for subsequent critical and historical scrutiny, then we will be all the more gratified.

Sod this for a game of soldiers!

—Traditional

Zones of Control is organized into nine different sections (or if you prefer, "zones"), each anchored by a long chapter from an established professional or scholarly authority. Following and in dialogue with those chapters are shorter pieces from a variety of different contributors. Some are from prominent designers or other hobby or industry luminaries, some are from respected critics or journalists. Some of the shorter chapters are analytical, while others are reflective and anecdotal, serving to document the history of a particular game or project. Some are provocations, others concise case studies. Finally, some of the short pieces are artifacts of more specialized discourses that we could not fully represent in the volume but that we wanted to sample as representative of the way a particular community or constituency approaches wargaming practice.[14]

Following Jim Dunnigan's introduction, the opening section, "Paper Wars," canvases the history and practice of tabletop wargame design. The lead chapter in this section is by Jon Peterson, who discusses the history of tabletop wargaming from its beginnings to the present day. It is a superb orientation for a newcomer to the topic. Shorter chapters in this section serve to document John Curry's History of Wargaming project, which is helping to preserve the history of the field; Tetsuya Nakamura, Jack Greene, and Lee Brimmicombe-Wood then offer case studies of board wargame design for topics covering land, sea, and air, respectively; Mark Mahaffey's chapter on wargame cartography foregrounds the singular importance of the game map, the actual material underpinning of much of tabletop wargaming; finally, A. Scott Glancy explores the linkage between wargames and combat systems in tabletop role-playing games, an essential historical lineage as Peterson has also argued elsewhere (2012). The next section, "War Engines," examines the history of universal war simulators—systems that can be used to model multiple scenarios, conflicts, and modes of conflict, one of the most distinctive accomplishments of wargaming as a design practice. The lead chapter here is by Henry Lowood, who surveys and analyzes the history of this design space. Matthew B. Caffrey Jr. extends Lowood's discussion into defense and national security gaming. Other short chapters then discuss specific game engines or game systems, notably *Advanced Squad Leader* and *Combat Commander* (in the course of which J. R. Tracy and John Foley also ably illustrate how very different two game systems on the same subject can be); while Mark Herman and Ted Raicer offer similar complementary analysis for the important innovation of "card-driven" wargame systems. Finally, Troy Goodfellow presents a case

study of fan-based scenario design using computer game engines. "Operations" next turns our attention to the mathematical as well as theoretical underpinnings of wargame systems, notably operations research, actuarial tables, statistics, randomness, probability, Lanchester equations, Monte Carlo modeling, and related concepts. The lead chapter is by Peter Perla, who expands upon his classic book *The Art of Wargaming* (1990), deepening the historical discussion of wargaming to include the history of operations research. Brien Miller and Rachel Simmons then present case studies from their own design practices, ranging from a statistical model of submarine warfare to recreating the Napoleonic battlefield. Don Gilman and John Tiller and Catherine Cavagnaro follow with a pair of case studies reconstructing the design of two computer wargame systems, including the landmark *Harpoon* series. The final pair of chapters in this section shift us to professional wargaming: Nobel laureate Thomas Schelling recounts his personal history of contributions to game theory and national security gaming, while Russell Vane brings us close to a pure game-theoretical model of wargame design.

If the first third of the book is devoted to establishing the history and theoretical underpinnings of wargaming, the middle sections probe more contemporary as well as potentially more controversial topics. "The Bleeding Edge" thus examines games on contemporary and potential conflicts, paying particular attention to the digital state of the art. The lead chapter, by Luke Caldwell and Tim Lenoir, seeks to untangle the dense web of connections between military gaming in the AAA space and the so-called Revolution in Military Affairs (RMA), which has prompted so much upheaval in the defense establishment; for Caldwell and Lenoir, popular entertainment wargaming becomes a way to "premediate" (the term is Richard Grusin's) the inevitability of conflict for both the military *and* an acquiescent public. Following this, Larry Bond and Laurent Closier each offer case studies of topical and highly sensitive situations, a still hypothetical (as of this writing) Israeli air campaign against the Iranian nuclear industry, and 2004's Operation Phantom Fury, otherwise known as the Second Battle of Fallujah. Andrew Wackerfuss and Marcus Schulzke, meanwhile, address the ways in which wargames also—inevitably—propagate *representations* of war, Wackerfuss through the World War I tower defense game *Toy Soldiers* (2010) while Schulzke revisits the still enormously influential *America's Army* (2002–). Finally, two essential chapters offer careful discussions of wargaming ethics and sociopolitics in the same AAA space discussed by Caldwell and Lenoir: for Miguel Sicart, the *Modern Warfare* series, and for Soraya Murray, *Spec Ops: The Line* (2012). The next section, "Systems and Situations," further sharpens the edge, paying particular attention to wargames in resistive or countercultural contexts, including examples of nonstandard critical games. The lead chapter in this section is by Sharon Ghamari-Tabrizi, who—arrestingly—reads wargames first and foremost as writing systems, that is, as technologies of inscription, a development she centers on the RAND Corporation. Through original archival research, Elizabeth Losh further extends Ghamari-Tabrizi's insights, both in relation to RAND and to the uniquely corporatized and militarized landscape of southern California, while emphasizing the situation of the female game designer in these settings. Alexander Galloway and Richard Barbrook reveal the surprising centrality of wargaming to various forms of leftist political practice, Galloway through attention to Guy Debord's once nearly forgotten *Game of War* (Becker-Ho and Debord 2006) and Barbrook through the related contemporary activities of the London-based Class Wargames group. Finally, chapters by David Levinthal on his photography and Brian Conley on his tabletop installations document two noteworthy examples of artists adopting wargaming as their medium. "The War Room" section next examines the utility of wargames for classroom instruction and scholarly research for history, war studies, and defense. The lead chapter in this section is by Philip Sabin, who expands on ideas published in his aforementioned books to pursue the use of wargaming as a tool for historical understanding. Shorter chapters in this section, including Robert M. Citino's and Rob MacDougall and Lisa Faden's, further develop and extend that potential. Charles Vasey represents a designer's perspective as he weighs the trade-offs inherent in his craft, while Jeremy Antley uses the example of *Twilight Struggle* (2005), the most popular wargame in recent memory,[15] to explore how games themselves become artifacts *of* the very history they seek to model. Finally, Alexander H. Levis and Robert J. Elder give a glimpse into the sequestered world of professional military gaming as they discuss wargame design and evaluation in a national security setting.

The final third of the volume widens our scope still further, while also forecasting into the near-term future. "Irregularities" spotlights non-force-on-force games, including counterinsurgency simulations and games involving NGOs, noncombatants, and other nonmilitary groups. The lead chapter in this section is by Rex Brynen, who explores simulating the political, economic, and social actions taken by an armed force, collectively termed the "nonkinetic." Shorter chapters in this section discuss several tabletop counterinsurgency simulations, including the simulation of noncombatants and other elements of the "human terrain system"—and moreover, do so across both national security gaming (Elizabeth M. Bartels and Yuna Huh Wong) and the wargaming hobby (Brian Train and Volko Ruhnke); designer Ed Beach, meanwhile, reminds us that nonkinetic factors have a much longer history and explores his treatment of them in his games about the early modern era; last, James Wallman opens up the space of "cultural gaming," demonstrating how design concepts originating in wargaming can be brought to bear on a variety of other subjects and circumstances. Following this, "Other Theaters" examines wargaming in literature and film, while likewise addressing miniatures wargaming, science fiction wargaming, and actual historical reenactments. The lead chapter in this section is by Esther MacCallum-Stewart, who surveys the appearances of wargaming in many media forms, with special emphasis on Iain M. Banks's novel *The Player of Games* (1988) and Orson Scott Card's novel *Ender's Game* (1985). Bill McDonald then discusses Laurence Sterne's *Tristram Shandy* (1759), which features the first known appearance of miniature wargaming in English literature; and John Prados, designer of the Avalon Hill game *Third Reich* (1974), offers his first extended comments on Roberto Bolaño's novel of the same name, where the game serves as the novel's central structuring device. We then turn to "wargaming" in other settings, with Stephen V. Cole relating the design history of the long-running line of science fiction wargames *Star Fleet Battles* (1979–1999), and Ian Sturrock and James Wallis examining the history and gameplay of Games Workshop's *Warhammer 40,000* (1983–2014) line of miniature wargames; this is complemented by Larry Brom's reflections on his historical miniatures rules for depicting colonial warfare. Jenny Thompson

considers what "wargaming" means in the context of real-life World War I and World War II battle reenactments. The "Fight the Future" section offers a conclusion of sorts by projecting the future of wargaming. The lead chapter in this section is by Patrick Crogan, who traces a new understanding of the global map as a unified (and medial) simulation space within the context of contemporary drone warfare. Here "game" and global grid converge. Journalist and gamer Michael Peck offers a consideration of the current and future marketplace for wargames; prolific designer Joseph Miranda describes methods for modeling cyberwar and network-centric warfare; Kacper Kwiatkowski allows us a glimpse into the design process of *This War of Mine*, perhaps the first genuinely new kind of wargame we have seen in quite some time. Finally, Greg Costikyan renders his evaluation of current design limitations and his suggestions for new directions, a call further extended and sharpened by Mary Flanagan in her chapter, as strong a closing statement for the volume as a whole as we can imagine.

In "Why Men Love War," Broyles writes, "Aside from being a fairly happy-go-lucky carnivore, I have no lust for blood, nor do I enjoy killing animals, fish, or even insects." Either of us could have produced the same sentence. That great patriarch of Edwardian pacifism H. G. Wells remains perhaps the most frequently quoted proponent of the piety that the playing of wargames is redemptive because they teach us what a "blundering thing" real war is. Perhaps. Today's professional game designers and analysts similarly insist that wargaming saves lives. But we will also acknowledge something else of Broyles, who in the course of his essay confides, "Nothing I had ever studied was as complex or as creative as the small-unit tactics of Vietnam." Any wargamer who has lingered into the early morning hours optimizing the loadout on a cardboard or virtual F-16 will understand what this means. Wargames provide the means of exploring exactly those complexities, coupled with the privilege of doing so vicariously.

Wargames, in other words, are precisely Zones of Control, ordered and rationalized spaces wherein rules and procedure—sculpted out of algorithmic steps and probabilistic curves—reign supreme. This is their great appeal, and very likely their greatest liability. They have exerted a significant hold over the imagination, and not infrequently over state policy and military practice. Editing this book has been a source of great personal satisfaction for us, and we hope that readers of *Zones of Control* will come to understand something of this remarkable and continually compelling form of play.

About the Editors

Patrick Harrigan is the coeditor of the MIT Press volumes *Third Person: Authoring and Exploring Vast Narratives* (2009), *Second Person: Role-Playing and Story in Games and Playable Media* (2007), and *First Person: New Media as Story, Performance, and Game* (2004), all with Noah Wardrip-Fruin. He is a former marketing director and creative developer for Fantasy Flight Games, and he coedited FFG's *The Art of H.P. Lovecraft's Cthulhu Mythos* (2006), with Brian Wood. His work has been published by Chaosium, Pagan Publishing, Gameplaywright, ETC Press, and Camden House. He has also written a novel, *Lost Clusters* (2005), and a collection of short stories, *Thin Times and Thin Places* (2012). His website is <www.patharrigan.com>.

Matthew G. Kirschenbaum is associate professor in the Department of English at the University of Maryland and associate director of the Maryland Institute for Technology in the Humanities (MITH, an applied think tank for the digital humanities). His first book, *Mechanisms: New Media and the Forensic Imagination*, was published by the MIT Press in 2008 and won multiple awards, including the Prize for a First Book from the Modern Language Association (MLA). Kirschenbaum speaks and writes often on topics in the digital humanities and new media; his work has received widespread coverage in the media, including the *New York Times*, *Guardian*, National Public Radio, *Wired*, and *Chronicle of Higher Education*. He is a 2011 Guggenheim Fellow. But he was a grognard before he did any of that.

Notes

1. Much the same technique was then being used in classified games being conducted by the RAND Corporation.

2. See <https://paxsims.wordpress.com/2011/08/05/connections-2011-aar>.

3. This sort of thorough documentation, by definition true for commercial wargames, is much less common in policy games, where designers' notes are often variable, inconsistent, or absent; this is one reason why such games are often dismissed as a rigorous analytic method. We hope that the present volume will show the value of more robust documentation and analysis of these sorts of games.

4. He attributes the term to SPI's art director, Redmond Simonsen.

5. The classic dilemma for wargame designers is the tension between simulation and playability. Increased fidelity to detail generally means increased playing time, and there are countless examples of games that are simply too complex and time-consuming for all but the most dedicated hobbyists to play. The trend in recent years, however, is to reduce gameplay complexity, often by utilizing novel rules systems to minimize the burden on the players. (Notable in this regard is the card-driven system developed by Mark Herman; see the chapters by Herman, Ted Raicer, Ed Beach and Jeremy Antley in this volume; see also Harrigan and Wardrip-Fruin 2011.) But at what point does a simplified game system start to lose its value as a historical simulation? Do we learn more from Dana Lombardy's "monster" game *Streets of Stalingrad* (2003), which boasts a historically accurate and complete order of battle for the conflict, than from Tetsuya Nakamura's much less complex (but far more playable) *Storm over Stalingrad* (2006)? (See also Sabin 2012, 51-52.) These sorts of questions lie at the heart of *Zones of Control*. How do we model a conflict-driven world, and why?

6. Many of these, long out of print, have recently been resurrected through the efforts of John Curry,

whose History of Wargaming Project is described in these pages.

7. See <http://connections-wargaming.com>.

8. A copy of Work's memorandum is available here: <http://news.usni.org/2015/03/18/document-memo-to-pentagon-leadership-on-wargaming>. Also of note is a response from Peter Perla, "Working Wargaming": <https://wargamingcommunity.wordpress.com/2015/05/14/peter-perla-on-work-ing-wargaming/>. Taken together, the two documents are a glimpse into the state of professional US defense and national security wargaming as this book goes to press.

9. The excellent *Play the Past* group blog <http://www.playthepast.org>, as well as two recent and similarly named—but unconnected—collections, *Playing the Past* (2008) and *Pastplay* (2014) raise similar questions, and underscore the extent to which "play" is once again emerging as a rubric for historical understanding, military or otherwise.

10. See also this NEH-sponsored workshop on "Digital Methods for Military History": <http://www.northeastern.edu/nulab/dmmh>.

11. Thus it has ever been: H. G. Wells famously commended his book and game *Little Wars* to "boys from twelve years of age to one hundred and fifty and for that more intelligent sort of girls who like boys' games and boys' books."

12. In 2014 the PaxSims blog convened an online discussion dedicated to this topic. It is important reading: <https://paxsims.wordpress.com/2014/10/15/women-and-professional-wargaming>.

13. See, for example, Mukherjee 2010; and Alexander R. Galloway's work on *Special Force* and *Under Ash*, two first-person shooters played from the perspective of Palestinian subjects (Galloway 2006, 78–84).

14. A few contributors also found themselves limited in their ability to discuss classified games or developments in their field, but we are pleased they have been able to share what insights they can into the Byzantine world of the defense gaming establishment.

15. Some have argued that because of its atypicality, *Twilight Struggle* is not a "real" wargame, but we will leave such jesuitical distinctions to the message boards.

SERIES FOREWORD

What might histories of games tell us not only about the games themselves but also about the people who play and design them? We think that the most interesting answers to this question will have two characteristics. First, the authors of game histories who tell us the most about games will ask big questions. For example, how do game play and design change? In what ways is such change inflected by societal, cultural, and other factors? How do games change when they move from one cultural or historical context to another? These kinds of questions forge connections to other areas of game studies, as well as to history, cultural studies, and technology studies.

The second characteristic we seek in "game-changing" histories is a wide-ranging mix of qualities partially described by terms such as *diversity*, *inclusiveness*, and *irony*. Histories with these qualities deliver interplay of intentions, users, technologies, materials, places, and markets. Asking big questions and answering them in creative and astute ways strikes us as the best way to reach the goal of not an isolated, general history of games but rather of a body of game histories that will connect game studies to scholarship in a wide array of fields. The first step, of course, is producing those histories.

Game Histories is a series of books that we hope will provide a home—or maybe a launch pad—for the growing international research community whose interest in game history rightly exceeds the celebratory and descriptive. In a line, the aim of the series is to help actualize critical historical study of games. Books in this series will exhibit acute attention to historiography and historical methodologies, while the series as a whole will encompass the wide-ranging subject matter we consider crucial for the relevance of historical game studies. We envisage an active series with output that will reshape how electronic and other kinds of games are understood, taught, and researched, as well as broaden the appeal of games for the allied fields such as history of computing, history of science and technology, design history, design culture, material culture studies, cultural and social history, media history, new media studies, and science and technology studies.

The Game Histories series will welcome but not be limited to contributions in the following areas:

- Multidisciplinary methodological and theoretical approaches to the historical study of games.
- Social and cultural histories of play, people, places, and institutions of gaming.

- Epochal and contextual studies of significant periods influential to and formative of games and game history.
- Historical biography of key actors instrumental in game design, development, technology, and industry.
- Games and legal history.
- Global political economy and the games industry (including indie games).
- Histories of technologies pertinent to the study of games.

- Histories of the intersections of games and other media, including such topics as game art, games and cinema, and games and literature.
- Game preservation, exhibition, and documentation, including the place of museums, libraries, and collectors in preparing game history.
- Material histories of game artifacts and ephemera.

Henry Lowood, Stanford University
Raiford Guins, Stony Brook University

FOREWORD: THE PAPER TIME MACHINE GOES ELECTRIC

James F. Dunnigan

Wargames have a long history. The concept of working out battles ahead of time struck many ancient commanders as a logical way to gain an advantage. This idea was apparently reinvented many times. The concept of exploring the future in a realistic way had an instinctive appeal even before modern statistical tools like predictive analysis were developed. In the 1970s, commercial wargame designers referred to our manual games as "paper time machines," and by the late 1970s they were transferring these devices to the newly arrived personal computers. While accurate prediction was the goal of these devices, there is much to be learned in the story of how we got from an ancient insight to its modern interpretation.

Chess was an ancient wargame developed to train apprentice commanders on the finer points of battlefield operations as they existed before firearms. By the 1700s and 1800s, chess had already developed into more complex wargames that most gamers today would recognize as miniatures or manual (board) wargames. In the early nineteenth century, this new form of military wargaming, incorporating recently developed statistical tools, was quickly recognized as militarily useful and became quite popular, effective and widespread as a training and planning tool from that point through World War II.

In the late nineteenth century, simplified versions of the new military wargames began appearing for civilian use. One of the most enduring of these was a naval wargame developed in the late 1880s by Fred Jane (of *Jane's Fighting Ships* and so on). In 1913 these commercial wargames were popularized in a big way when H. G. Wells, the famed English author, published a version, *Little Wars*, that caught on in a big way and got what we now know of as miniatures wargames going. All of these nineteenth century and pre–World War II wargames were quite similar, using miniature figures (and sometimes maps and wooden or cardboard markers) and complex rules. Some caught on commercially, due to the tremendous growth in literacy and higher education that accompanied the Industrial Revolution (1760–1840 in Europe and North America). It became fashionable for members of the newly expanded educated class to wargame as a hobby. This was in large part because in Germany and Britain there was a very active effort to write books on military affairs for a general audience, and the more avid of these enthusiasts used these new wargames to gain further insights. Military professionals used more complex wargames for command and staff training as well as planning future wars, but some also used the commercial versions simply because it took less time and effort. In Europe the massive new (since the nineteenth century) reserve armies had plenty of reserve officers who, as civilians, saw the wargames as combining business and pleasure.

The two world wars killed off most enthusiasm for commercial wargames. The massive death tolls and destruction of these wars traumatized the educated classes in Europe, and by the end of World War II commercial wargaming remained active mainly in the United States. There, in the late 1950s, simpler map-based historical wargames appeared and attracted many more civilian practitioners than miniatures. The new board-type wargames were cheaper and easier to learn and play. But they were still complex and only a few percent of the population could handle them. These were the wargames I discovered during the early 1960s while serving in the army. I noted that about one in ten of the officers and troops in the field artillery missile battalion I served in either played regularly or could quickly grasp the rules and concepts of these historical games and would occasionally play.

Meanwhile, military wargaming after World War II wandered off down a blind alley. For about two decades, chess/history-based wargames were out of favor in the United States (except for the navy). The reasons for this were many; the most significant was the success of operations research (OR) techniques in supporting military operations during World War II. OR was a new tool that only became available during the 1930s and was adopted, along with the new computers, for post–World War II wargames. Another problem was the identification of the history-based manual wargames with the Germans, the major symbol of evil during World War II and a regular user of those wargames throughout the war.

Thus the popular perception that wargamers were warmongers, deranged, or worse. Some of that bad odor still lingers and has discouraged many potential users. A move away from the use of historical study to formulate future plans and policy (especially in the army and air force) turned out to be a big mistake. But with nuclear weapons and all that, the past was seen as less relevant. Russia still wargamed, but under a thick blanket of secrecy.

The traditional history-based manual wargame was replaced by computer-driven simulations of current and future events, designed using OR and more math than common sense. This caused some unfortunate results. First, OR was not capable of accurately modeling all the chaotic events that take place in combat. It took until the 1970s for this to be acknowledged as a serious problem and addressed via a return to the older history-based wargames derived from chess.

Then there was the Cold War, which created an atmosphere in the United States and Russia that made dispassionate analysis of friendly and enemy forces difficult and usually impossible for political reasons. For example, in America the Russians were the enemy and enormous US defense expenditures could only be justified if the Russians were always portrayed as an awesome threat. Realistic history-based wargames would show Russian limitations, and this was not politically acceptable. It was done anyway, but releasing the results could be a career killer. After the Cold War ended and senior members of the Soviet military staffs could speak freely, it was found that the same hostility to wargaming that was too accurate (usually by showing that the Soviets were a lot weaker than their propaganda indicated) was a career killer there as well, and the results of these realistic studies had been kept locked away until the 1990s.

By discarding military history as a tool it became impossible to catch the errors in the new OR-based combat models. The OR-based wargames created an artificial world where the possible outcomes fit the preconceived ideas of senior military and government leaders rather than known reality. With the historical approach, you could get a reality check when the game could not reproduce historical results. After the 1970s, the OR-based wargames gradually lost all credibility with the military, and much of the civilian leadership as well. Perhaps the most damaging aspect of the OR-based wargames detour was that wargaming's original purpose, officer training for combat command, fell into disuse. Instead, the "models and simulations" were given the job of finding out what future wars would require in terms of weapons and ammunition. In other words, "wargaming" was reduced to a logistics support function. These mainframe-based "wargames" were also used to justify most new weapons systems. The operations research approach had turned into a Frankenstein monster.

What had been forgotten during the first rush into using computer-driven wargames was the ancient military saying, "It's not a matter of who's better, but who's worse." Victory goes to the side that has more advantages, and playing out the maneuvers and uncertainty of warfare in a crude wargame tends to give the wargamer the edge. Many professional military personnel recognized this when they saw these board wargames in the 1960s. By the 1970s, senior people in the Pentagon began to realize this as well. As one Pentagon official liked to point out, the commercial wargames could accurately model many recent (World War II through Vietnam) battles, while the then-current Department of Defense combat models could not. That observation eventually led to

a major change in how the American military developed and used wargames.

There were other advantages to the historical approach to developing wargames. That was because this process demanded an evenhanded analysis of the situation being turned into a wargame. A wargame is a very organized look at a military situation, because a wargame must have precise rules and accurate information in order for it to portray a military situation with any degree of accuracy. Realistic wargames, be they on past battles or potential future ones, give the user a hint of what combat is like, and this provides an edge that has often been crucial.

Many military users of wargames were unaware that they were actually using OR techniques (albeit usually the simpler ones like probability and statistical analysis of terrain, weapons, and manpower) to create and use their history-based games. Many OR professionals *are* aware of this connection, which is why many in the OR field, particularly those with military experience, quickly realized the usefulness of history-based wargames during the 1960s and '70s. During and immediately after World War II, OR professionals were accustomed to examining military events from a very narrow perspective. The history-based wargames that soared to popularity in the 1960s enabled them to see combat situations in a broader context. Wargames require analysis of terrain, forces (order of battle), losses, and many other factors. Those who have used historical wargames also become familiar with the techniques used to connect real events with the same events depicted in a wargame and, as many would admit, gain a deeper understanding of a military situation.

In the 1970s the commercial wargames began to have an influence on the design and use of professional (military) wargames. At first there was an indirect influence of the hobby games as the troops bought and played them, which had a subtle and enduring impact. Military users of these wargames found that playing them for a while imparted knowledge and skills that enabled them to design their own. This sort of thing became increasingly useful going into the twenty-first century. Military users also found that the simpler techniques used by commercial wargames were more effective at simulating warfare than highly complex and heavily computerized efforts that remained in fashion until the 1990s. A common criticism directed toward professional wargames during the 1970s was the insufficient attention to historical reality, which proved to be the only way to validate the military simulations and models as accurate and therefore useful tools. With the end of the Cold War in 1991 there was less political resistance to accurate wargames.

The impact of these commercial wargames could be most clearly seen at the 1977 Leesburg wargames conference. This was the first gathering of all the major participants in Department of Defense–funded wargaming. Two other conferences were held (1985 and 1991). I was invited to all three, but the first invitation was the clearest sign that things were changing. I was clearly an outsider. This was made obvious when Andrew Marshall, a senior official of OSD (Office of the Secretary of Defense) and one of the key sources of funding for professional wargames, got up in front of the Leesburg audience and stated bluntly, "You people have never given me anything I can use."

When my turn came to speak, I pointed out that what was needed was a wargame the commander could sit down with and operate himself, preferably with no one else in the room. Having the ultimate user of wargame results actually operate the wargame would save a lot of time, get much better results, and eliminate a lot of confusion. It would also enable the commander to experiment with options that he might be reluctant to try via his staff. That was because generals were not supposed to make mistakes, especially in peacetime. This last point is important, since the sociology of senior command makes it difficult for a commander to appear ignorant of anything or capable of doing something stupid, especially in front of subordinates. But mistakes must be made to learn and develop the most effective strategies and tactics. By the late 1980s, the technology finally arrived that made my hypothetical "commander's game" possible, and by the 1990s we were seeing the "commander's game" approach taken for granted in commercial computer wargames. Needless to say, a lot of commanders were quietly buying and playing with these games on their own.

This spotlighted a major deficiency of military wargames: what commercial wargamers call the "interface." Creating a commercial wargame, be it paper or computer-based, requires that up to half or more of the effort (and budget) on the project be devoted to how the game looks (the "eye candy") and how easy the game is to use. If a game looks ugly and is too difficult to use, it won't be played and, more important, won't be bought. Because of a lack of commercial pressures, the military games often lacked user-friendly interfaces. Moreover, the people who created military games were the principal users, or computer professionals accustomed to arcane interfaces. There was never any big incentive to develop efficient interfaces so that mere commanders could tinker with these games on their own.

Another interesting development of the 1970s was that at the military academies a growing percentage of new students entered with a knowledge of commercial wargames. It would take a decade or more before these wargame-savvy officers got promoted into senior positions and made it possible for realistic and verifiable wargames to become accepted as training and planning tools. Sure enough, by 1990 wargames had become so widely accepted that they were regularly used as intended. In fact, the first wargame analysis of the Iraq invasion of Kuwait was performed the day after the invasion by using a commercial game (*Gulf Strike*) and the results of that gaming established the war plan that was actually used. These history-based wargames were used extensively during the 1990–91 Gulf War.

Another point I made in 1977 was that manual wargames require more work to use than most people are comfortable with and can be intimidating to the majority of people not comfortable with math and detailed military history. During the 1970s and '80s I repeated this observation to any number of military organizations when questioned about using wargames for training. The obvious solution was to use microcomputers. In the late 1970s I was talking about the future, but by the 1990s the future had arrived and PC-based wargames (for combat and noncombat tasks) began to proliferate. The military had been using microcomputer-based wargames increasingly since the 1980s, and with increasing success.

A lot of the wargaming activity in the military after 1975 was a result of the soul-searching and restructuring that followed the trauma of Vietnam. Commercial wargames, the paper time machine, showed up in the late 1950s and exploded in popularity just as the Vietnam War was ending. While the political rhetoric over the war was more inflamed than informed, the wargames were coolly analytical. The games on Vietnam made it clear that much could be learned from the past about such wars and warfare in general. Even non-wargamers in the army realized that studying the past and respecting the lessons found provided better ways to handle situations like Vietnam. This is a large subject that I covered in several books, notably *Getting It Right* (1993) and *Dirty Little Secrets of the Vietnam War* (1990). For the US Army in the 1970s that meant increasing use of wargames and respect for things that worked in the past (and the establishment of CALL: the Center for Army Lessons Learned). That attitude was one of the reasons why the army embraced the end of conscription and created a very different force from the one that fought Vietnam and earlier wars.

It wasn't until the US Air Force and Army made mincemeat of the Iraqi armed forces in 1991 that most people realized how drastically the American armed forces had transformed themselves in the previous sixteen years. One of the primary engines of that transformation was wargaming, in particular the history-based ones reinvented as a commercial product in the 1950s and '60s. After 1975 these wargames were welcome in the American military. Part of the post-Vietnam thinking was that if something new worked it should be widely adopted. That's what happened with wargames.

The 1990–91 Gulf War coincided with the rapid development of more and more powerful PC hardware that made mass-market wargames possible and increasingly popular. Among the key innovations here were FPS (first person shooter) real-time games. While most of these games had too many inaccuracies for military use, the military knew that they could license these games, make the needed changes and thus end up with FPS games that had training value. The military aviation community found that consumer-grade flight simulator software had become accurate enough to teach flight basics and even allow experienced pilots to experiment and practice using an "accurate enough" PC simulator.

The military has gone through many changes since World War II, and wargaming was one of them. The usefulness of wargames as a training tool led to wargames showing up in places you never expected them. Such was the case with embedded simulations. Because so many troops use some kind of computer as an interface with their weapons and equipment, it's fairly simple to add a simulation option, along with the many types of diagnostics and other forms of accessory software found in everything from rifle sights to the many systems in combat vehicles, aircraft, and ships. This fits in with the old adage that you should "train as you fight and fight as you train." Simulation software running on smart phones supplements the embedded stuff and, well, you can see where that is going because the new technologies provide the roadmap for what must be simulated next.

In the last half-century the military has had more impact on the larger world of commercial wargaming than most wargamers realize. Even during the heyday of manual wargaming in the 1970s, it was noted that "military and government" personnel were a disproportionate chunk of the wargamer market (20 percent, versus 3 percent of the general population). That continued as wargaming made its transition to computers in the 1980s and '90s. Manual wargaming is now a niche hobby, but military and government personnel are still overrepresented, because the manual games still serve as a prototyping tool for computerized sims as well as an excellent tool for training wargame designers and military thinkers in general. The military also led the way in developing "noncombat wargames," which proved a big boost to the effectiveness of all the troops who did not fight. Over 90 percent of military personnel have support jobs, most of which are similar to tasks performed by civilians. These simulations have come to be known as "serious games" and demonstrate how the basic concepts of wargames are being applied to all areas of work and life. Such games or "simulations" are becoming common and are often accepted as an expected development by a generation that grew up on simulation-type games found on PCs, game consoles, or smart phone apps. The paper time machine now casts a far wider net than in the past.

About the Author

Jim Dunnigan is the designer of more than a hundred wargames, including the classics *Empires of the Middle Ages*, *PanzerBlitz*, and *Jutland*; and publisher of more than five hundred more through his company Simulations Publications, Inc. (SPI). He is the author of more than twenty books, including *The Complete Wargames Handbook*; the former editor of *Strategy and Tactics* magazine; and the cofounder and editor in chief of Strategy Page <www.strategypage.com>. Since the 1970s, he has been a defense advisor, pundit, and general troublemaker. He writes books on military affairs, technology, and history, builds his own computers, considers risk management a splendid leisure time activity, manages software development, can conjure up simulations on anything, and enjoys problem solving as a favorite indoor sport.

I PAPER WARS

1 A GAME OUT OF ALL PROPORTIONS: HOW A HOBBY MINIATURIZED WAR

Jon Peterson

A history of wargames must begin, like a simulation itself, by defining its parameters. Wargames as considered in this chapter are not a troop exercise, but an intellectual battle which approximates the experience of command in times of war, where players control game elements that represent forces in combat.[1] A wargame has a set of rules, or "system," which determines the moves its players may attempt and the outcome when opposing forces meet in battle. Wargames are speculative, almost thought-experiments: actions may take place in real settings of the past, present, or future, or they may be located in imaginary settings with purely fantastic combatants.

A tradition of conflict simulation began late in the eighteenth century when wargames arose in the German-speaking world as a means for training army commanders. During a forty-year period of rapid innovation, these wargames leveraged advances in the military sciences to provide an unprecedented approximation of command. A second wave of invention came at the end of the nineteenth century, largely in the United Kingdom, as hobbyists repurposed these wargames to emphasize entertainment over education. Only in the mid–twentieth century did an industry begin to coalesce around wargames, one largely based in the United States, which focused on the commercial sale of prepackaged board wargames, miniature figures, dice, rules, and related paraphernalia. The ready availability of wargaming tools made a wide audience conversant with the principles of simulation, which in turn sparked a huge wave of creativity, one that ultimately inspired and informed many new categories of games: role-playing games, collectible card games, and most of all, computer games. As those all loom large in early twenty-first-century culture, they recommend the study of wargames to us as a way to explore the evolution of gaming.

To appreciate recent innovations that build on the wargaming tradition, we must first comprehend wargames on their own terms. Wargames provide us with a unique insight into the way we prosecute war, one of the most complicated and unpredictable of human endeavors, and thus the way we struggle to manage reality. It is no coincidence that wargaming began in the early modern era, which promised that all sciences, even the military sciences, could be reduced to systems with the clarity and constancy of Newtonian mechanics. If only sufficient data could be gathered and properly organized, then the outcomes of war could be determined: it would become something that can be modeled, predicted, regulated, and controlled. Everything must be measured and quantified, from the movements of the various branches of the military over differing kinds of terrain, to the accuracy of each model of gun and the expertise of gunmen, to the advantage that superior numbers bestow to a force.

Military scientists created a model of war, one which commanders leveraged in the prosecution of campaigns. The model was realized on an informal apparatus that tracked forces with maps, charts, and tokens, adjusted by planners as orders went out and field reports came in. Once the experience of actual command was reduced to operating on this

apparatus, it became possible, outside of times of war, to approximate the experience of command by exercising the apparatus as a form of training. We will see how the apparatus grew relentlessly more comprehensive: The maps showed broader scopes yet finer levels of granularity, and the focus on soldiers contracted from armies to individuals, whose activities the model prescribed for increasingly brief intervals of time. In effect, the apparatus shrank an approximation of war itself onto the surface of a table. Because it was always just an approximation, it would never tame war, never control it—but it became an ideal vehicle for commanding, in the words of H. G. Wells, "a game out of all proportion."

The Birth of Simulation

Game boards, surfaces that divide space into cells that movable pieces may occupy, date back to prehistoric times. In various shapes and configurations, they have staged race games or battle games, games where multiple pieces or only one may concurrently occupy a cell, and games augmented by casting implements of chance or those that depend solely on skill (for early games, see Parlett 1999).

Chess is the most enduring expression of a battle game where two equal opposed forces meet on a board. No information is hidden from either player, and the only surprises come from the unanticipated consequences of moves. Historians believe that Chaturanga, an ancestor of chess developed on the Indian subcontinent, modeled the warfare of its birthplace (Murray 1913). In the form that we know it, though, chess is only an abstract game of strategy: the rooks and queens of chess do not mimic the capabilities of any particular military unit, nor does the board itself represent any real or imaginary place.

While the familiar rules of chess stabilized by the mid–sixteenth century, nonetheless chess remained the subject of constant innovation and variation. In the early modern era, chess became a laboratory where inventors experimented with new game systems, expanding the board and introducing exotic pieces which moved in novel ways. Increasingly, authorities positioned chess as a means to learn real-world strategy and even statecraft: in the German-speaking world, this was articulated early on by Selenus's book *Das Schachoder König-Spiel* (1616), which makes out chess to be a "king's game," a way for rulers to better understand how to control the outcome of warfare and command their subjects. But chess armies bore little resemblance to the military of the Renaissance.

Late in the seventeenth century, the philosopher G. W. Leibniz hypothesized that "one could represent with certain game pieces certain battles and skirmishes, also the position of the weapons and the lay of the land, both at one's discretion and from history" in a game that might be played by "military colonels and captains" who would "practice it instead of the chessboard."[2] The chessboard would remain the standard for another century, although experimenters continually attempted to "modernize" chess, that is, to make the battles it depicts more realistic, where decisions in the game would more resemble the decisions commanders made in contemporary battlefields.

Hellwig

The first true departure from the principles of chess came from Johann Christian Ludwig Hellwig in his *Versuch eines aufs Schachspiel gebauten taktischen Spiels von zwey und mehrern Personen zu spielen* (Attempt to build upon chess a tactical game which two or more persons might play, 1780). Within, Hellwig uses the term *kriegsspiel*, or "wargame," to describe his invention, and this is the term by which games descending from Hellwig's work are still known to this day. He was an academic, not a soldier, though his aim was twofold: to "serve students" of warfare, but also "to provide, to those who need no instruction, a pleasant entertainment" (Hellwig 1803, 2). His invention would be used for both purposes and would spark a number of translations and imitations over subsequent decades.

As the title suggests, Hellwig's game built on the example of chess, but he reinterpreted its system entirely. He retained the pieces of chess, but he reclassified them into branches of the modern military—infantry and cavalry—and added new figures to represent artillery. Hellwig expanded the board far beyond the measure of prior chess variants, to a point where forces maneuver freely in a vast stretch of terrain. Each side starts with a huge force by chess standards, 104 pieces, but in Hellwig's recommended configuration, a board of 49 ranks by 33 files, there are 1,617 squares, so there are only pieces on around one-eighth of board at the start (compared to half in chess). And Hellwig did not object to even larger boards; he personally sold a 2,000-square model, and on boards so roomy there is no need to precisely tailor the number of troops to the dimensions of the playing field.

Furthermore, Hellwig's terrain was not the empty, undifferentiated expanse of chess. Perhaps his most influential innovation was to assign terrain types to each square, so that they might represent mountains, water, or forests. Thus, Hellwig brought to his game, and to the *kriegsspiel* that followed, a quality that chess had previously lacked: a setting. Abstract games of strategy like chess do not transpire in any particular place, but Hellwig could approximate a specific battleground with his apparatus. Crucially, he did not dictate a fixed landscape constrained to any particular battle, but instead provided tools that would permit players to design a terrain matching any historical, contemporary, or even imaginary space—to craft their own setting. It was not long before his players began implementing historical situations: in 1782, Hellwig related how pleased he was to learn that his configurable apparatus had been applied to re-create the terrain and positions of forces at the recent Battle of Krefeld.

Hellwig was however keenly aware that his game did not depict military action in an entirely realistic manner. In his preface, for example, he admits that "the game behaves such that the ratio of the length

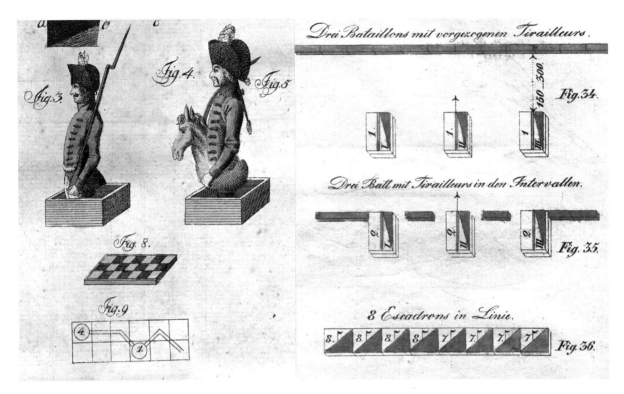

Figure 1.1
Left, pieces in Venturini (1797). Right, pieces in Reisswitz (1824).

of a day's march of infantry, with artillery in tow, versus the firing range of artillery, is roughly 4 to 3. Here, the firing range is too far" (Hellwig 1780, xiii–xiv). That is, the firing range is not realistic: guns of his era could not shoot 75 percent as far as infantry could travel in a day. Hellwig could find no way to repair this flaw without creating distortions in gameplay elsewhere, so he noted the break from realism but left it in place. Here, at the dawn of wargames, Hellwig discovered the trade-off between realism and playability, which history bore out to be among the most fundamental choices in wargame design.

The first significant work building on Hellwig was that of Georg Venturini, which appeared in the last years of the eighteenth century. Venturini recognized the problems of realism that had dogged Hellwig, and sought to rectify them by incorporating more detail into the model. Where Hellwig staged his war on a board with squares colored in to represent terrain types, Venturini took this a step further and replaced the board with a grid-overlaid map. This might sound like only a cosmetic change, but in the late eighteenth century, maps with sufficient granularity to depict a tactical situation were a novel technology born of recent advances in surveying, a huge boon to the military sciences attempting to model and control warfare. The key distinction for games is that a map has a concrete scale, a ratio between a length shown on paper and the corresponding length of terrain that the map represents: Venturini made his squares two thousand paces across. Once scale entered into the game, suddenly questions about movement distances and firing ranges became questions about the real world,

rather than questions about game design. This constrains the game system to the real-world setting: we say that scale is a tool that binds the system to the setting. This was a crucial step away from the abstractions of board games and toward a richer model of combat.

Reisswitz

Although Hellwig and his followers significantly transformed chess, it was the game of the Reisswitz family that completely dispensed with legacy systems and produced something worthy to be deemed a simulation. We know the work of the Reisswitz family today primarily through two surviving texts: the elder Georg Leopold von Reisswitz's *Taktisches Kriesgs-Spiel oder Anleitung zu einer mechanischen Vorrichtung um taktische Maneuvers sinnlich darzustellen* (Tactical wargame, or instructions for a mechanical device to show realistic tactical maneuvers) (1812) and the younger Georg Heinrich Rudolf Johann von Reisswitz's *Anleitung zur Darstellung militairische Manover mit dem Apparat des Kriegsspiel* (Instructions for showing military maneuvers with the *kriegsspiel* apparatus, 1824).[3]

To understand the origins of the Reisswitz game, one must appreciate the political situation in Germany at the time. After Prussia's humiliating defeat at the hands of Napoleon in 1806, the German people endured eight years of French occupation. During this time, the king held limited power, and the activities of the Prussian military were severely curtailed—the leadership watched its own command slip away. This led to a period of introspection in the Prussian army, where radical ideas in the military sciences were given serious consideration.

In this environment, a tutor to the king's two young sons heard of a new invention that taught military tactics. It was the creation of the elder Reisswitz, Georg Leopold. Reisswitz had grown up playing Hellwig's wargame recreationally, though an injury prevented him from pursuing a military career; when he went away to college, he re-created the game for his schoolmates. In 1809, Reisswitz read a compelling critique of Hellwig's *kriegsspiel*: that the division of space into squares, each of which could only be occupied by one piece, rendered the game unrealistic.[4] The world is not parceled into stark zones that a detachment of troops can control in this fashion. Therefore, Reisswitz discarded the gridded map of his predecessors and replaced it with a sand table, full of terrain that could be molded into whatever contours and elevations were required to accurately model real or imagined battlefields. His system represented an area thirty times smaller in scale than the maps of Venturini.

With this increasingly granular terrain scale came equally specific treatments of figure scale and time scale. Reisswitz swept away all the statuettes representing soldiers that Hellwig had borrowed from chess, and replaced them with small, nondescript wooden blocks. These blocks were chosen to occupy the exact dimensions that troop formations would on the terrain scale that Reisswitz had chosen; as such, each block represented a specific number of troops, and for smaller groupings players would deploy smaller blocks. These blocks moved on the sand table in any way that columns of troops could, in proximity or opposition to other forces without respect to any artificial grid. Reisswitz furthermore narrowed the time each turn represented from the single day of Hellwig to just a single minute. Movement and firing ranges were measured with rulers rather than by counting the vanished squares of the chessboard. Few if any vestiges of board games survived.

Reisswitz demonstrated his game for the benefit of the Prussian princes, and their recommendation caught the attention of the king. Faced with a royal command performance, Reisswitz formalized his invention, committing his system to print in his 1812 *Anleitung* and replacing the sand table with a fine wooden chest to house sculpted terrain segments that players could combine to resemble a desired battlefield.[5] The game became a favorite of the royal family, and thus the subject of fashionable attention. Beyond its value as a training tool, war on the tabletop was something the royal family could control, and a place where they could have the experience of command and even victory at a time when Prussia could not take to the battlefield. The king moved the Reisswitz apparatus to Sanssouci Palace, where it was played at night in colder times of year, with games often lasting long after the royal family would ordinarily retire.

In 1813, the Prussian people rose to liberate themselves from the French, and wargames took a back seat to the business of war. Reisswitz turned his attention to other causes after the defeat of Napoleon, and left it to his son, Georg Heinrich Rudolf Johann, to refine the family game. The younger Reisswitz served

as an artillery officer in the *Befreiungskrieg* and was well versed in the military sciences of the day. It was he who would take wargaming to the unprecedented level of a simulation.

The *Anleitung* (1824) of the younger Reisswitz augmented his father's work by adding probability and statistics. Whereas Hellwig, at the dawn of *kriegsspiel*, had stipulated that in his wargame "nothing would be left to chance," the younger Reisswitz knew from his experience on the artillery ranges, and his study of recent military literature, that chance necessarily played a role in war. During the Napoleonic occupation, Prussian statisticians had gathered massive amounts of data about the effectiveness of firearms at various ranges, which they cast as probability tables; for example, if ten capable soldiers fired a certain type of gun at a target two hundred yards away, on average, say, six could be expected to hit. Reisswitz had the key insight that these probabilities could be used to decide fictional combat in a game with implements of chance. A die could be rolled, and if the result fell within the ranges stipulated by the probability tables, then a hit has occurred, but otherwise it has not. This allowed combat in his wargame to encompass the uncertainty of real events without rendering outcomes arbitrary. It was not chance he admitted to the game, but simulation.

But this was only one technique Reisswitz leveraged to accomplish his ultimate goal: to impart to his players a close approximation of the experience of command. Dice, when used with probability, keep a player ignorant of outcomes in a way that a chess player never is: a knight cannot attempt to take a bishop but fail to do so, but on the battlefield the result of a conflict between two forces can never be completely certain. As Reisswitz put it, "only when the player has the same sort of uncertainty over results as he would have in the field can we be confident that the *kriegsspiel* will give a helpful insight into maneuvering in the field" (Reisswitz 1824, 6; translation Leeson). In order to create the needed ignorance of circumstances, the younger Reisswitz needed to do away with one more vestige of the board wargames of the past: the omniscience of players. No commanders in the field see all their troops' exact positions, let alone those of an enemy, so well as a chess player does. But there was in Reisswitz's day no practical technology for keeping competing players in mutual ignorance—without enlisting a third party.

Thus, the Reisswitz game includes a neutral referee with broad powers. First and foremost, the referee defines the scenario that will be fought, which includes choosing the terrain, the size and composition of opposing forces, and the objectives that players will vie to achieve—the referee is the final arbiter of the system, and assesses whether or not victory conditions are met. The referee is furthermore responsible for managing all secret information, such as the position on the map of all units that the players cannot both see. Players must track their own forces separately and mark suspected or discovered enemy positions on their own maps as necessary; Reisswitz recommended conducting his game on the topographic Lehmann maps used by the Prussian general staff at the time, rather than the three-dimensional terrain favored by his father. Perhaps even more significantly, players do not move their own pieces. Instead, they deliver orders to the referee, and the

referee interprets those orders and then updates the state of the game to reflect their results. This is another crucial respect in which the experience of the player approximates command in the field: they write orders and receive reports of events in exactly the manner that a Prussian officer would in times of war. They can command, but not entirely control, their troops; the interpretation of the referee may not match the expectations of a player.

Reisswitz's game was only briefly adopted by the Prussian military of his day, but it enjoyed a resurgence after the 1861 ascension of Wilhelm I—one of the two young princes the elder Reisswitz had schooled in the family game a half century earlier. Necessarily, various authors had modified and augmented the game in the intervening years. Because these games existed to educate officers in making command decisions, they needed to remain up to date; the relentless advance of the military sciences in the nineteenth century constantly threatened to make existing models of warfare obsolete. Some of those technological advances concerned the movement of troops and their efficacy in combat: railroads, for example, proved essential in the Italian War of Unification, and rifled bores radically improved the accuracy of personal firearms and field guns alike. Others changed how officers issued commands, like the invention of instant written communication at a distance through the telegraph. Wargames had to keep pace with these innovations if the model would truly capture the state of war.

Hobby Experiments

For some German soldiers, *kriegsspiel* became more than obligatory training; it was a passion. These fans

idolized the younger Reisswitz; some called him a "military Faust" (Leeson 1988, 19). Before the end of the 1820s, we learn of the existence of a Prussian club dedicated to wargames, the Berliner Kriegsspiel-Verein. One early admirer ran a club in Magdeburg—that was Helmuth von Moltke, later a celebrated field marshal, but at this time just a topographer, contributing to the development of the Prussian model of war.

Inevitably, the pursuit of simulating warfare for military education would intersect with a civilian interest in playing games that have war as their subject. Here a distinction must be drawn between simple board games that choose war as a cosmetic theme and those games that simulate command (see also Lewin 2012). By the middle of the nineteenth century, the increasing literacy, leisure time, and disposable income of the middle class provided a market for mass-manufactured games and toys that brought a little war into the home.

Branded board games hawking "improvements" on the game of checkers or chess became mainstream commercial products. While some of their designers were aware of the German *kriegsspiel* tradition,

it exerted little influence on popular games until the 1870s when, after a bellicose decade of Prussian victories under the leadership of Wilhelm I, Prussian military science suddenly became a subject of intense international scrutiny. *Kriegsspiel* of the day, such as the work of Tschischwitz, appeared in English translation for professional soldiers and even the popular press explored the curious practice of wargaming.[6]

Interest in *kriegsspiel* spread to the civilian populace of England, where some began to pursue the game recreationally. By 1873, Oxford had a Kriegspiel Club, which comprised students and teachers who competed under the original German rules. But once the central tenets of *kriegsspiel* became common knowledge, a new generation of enthusiasts re-created wargames anew, sacrificing the precision and detail of *kriegsspiel* for greater entertainment value. But beyond simple entertainment, wargames also recast warfare as something that civilians could manage and control, in a volatile world where war often starkly imposed itself on civilian life.

Stevenson

The foremost among these early experimenters was the author Robert Louis Stevenson, who began a campaign of wargames while wintering in Davos in 1881. Although Stevenson never published his rules, he did write journalistic reports on his battles that his stepson compiled for print at the end of the nineteenth century (Osbourne 1898). We know his game only through that retrospective, but the high-level system is so intuitive it requires little explanation: Stevenson played with toy soldiers, and for artillery he relied on a popgun that would propel actual projectiles to knock over enemy ranks.

Such lead soldiers had only recently become affordable, mass-market commodities, and most were of German manufacture. By the 1880s, virtually any middle-class British household with male children would possess some number of them, so they served as a convenient apparatus for wargames. But Stevenson did not squander these forces in unstructured play. He marshaled around six hundred figures and deployed them on a terrain chalked onto the floor of his attic: each figure represented one hundred soldiers in his game. Turns lasted a day, as in Hellwig, and troop movement was measured with rulers. Each turn, artillery could bombard the opposing ranks with a very literary armament: lead typesetting pieces of the letter "m" from a home printing press.

Thus it was skill with a popgun rather than probability tables derived from artillery measurement that determined the efficacy of fire for Stevenson. The experience of command in real battles typically does not extend to aiming and firing every cannon on the field, so Stevenson's game must be said to approximate something different than Reisswitz's game. Stevenson steered away from a strict simulation, and into a game that would entertain young and old alike, rendering war something as harmless as child's play.

Once Stevenson's method came to the attention of the British public around the turn of the century, a number of published systems proposed new ways of repurposing existing miniature soldier collections to fight similar competitive battles. Since the heyday of Stevenson, a native entrant to the miniature soldier business had captured much of the market for these toys in the United Kingdom: a company called Britains. Their tall, sturdy, and inexpensive figures flooded nurseries around the country and naturally lent themselves to wargames. A thinly veiled bit of advertising for Britains, in the form of a pamphlet called *The Great War Game for Young and Old* (1908), explained how to stage a competitive game with these figures, though the rules had many gaps and omissions. Those would be sorted out by the most influential of hobby wargaming rules.

Wells

Five years later, another designer—like Stevenson, an author of popular fiction—published wargame rules for toy soldiers: H. G. Wells. Whereas Stevenson gamed before he became famous, Wells had already succeeded as a novelist and social thinker when he published his *Little Wars* (1913). Nominally it described a game, but it served just as well as a polemic. Wells approached wargames with almost the opposite intention from the pioneers of *kriegsspiel*: he hoped to discourage war rather than to aid in its prosecution. Yet, like the *kriegsspiel* authors, Wells's game tries to control war, to contain it, and to explain it in a way that advanced his own agenda.

Wells's war is no modern affair; it feels a century behind its publication date—which is a curious charge to level at a futurist. Where Hellwig had attempted to modernize chess, Wells regressed wargames to a more civilized epoch, roughly the Napoleonic era of horses and muskets. By the time he wrote *Little Wars*, Wells had already predicted the advent of tanks in his story "The Land Ironclads," he had flown in an airplane and grasped its applicability to battle, and he no doubt had plotted the narrative of his forthcoming novel *The World Set Free* (1914), which prophesizes atomic warfare. In the anachronism of *Little Wars*, Wells shows us a comparatively harmless war, one confined to antique weaponry.

Nonetheless, Wells's *Little Wars* highlights the futility and arbitrariness of battle. Bombardments rain down on clusters of helpless Britains, bulky figures that are likely to topple their fellows as they fall. Worse still, when opposing forces meet they simply kill one another in equal number; only isolated forces are spared for capture. Soldiers have no capability to fire at range, and it plays as if they simply fall on one another's bayonets. Famously, Wells wrote that "you

Figure 1.2
Wells's *Little Wars* and Britains military miniatures.

have only to play at Little Wars three or four times to realize just what a blundering thing Great War must be" (Wells 1913, 100). His simulation of command tried to teach players to hate and avoid war—while still enjoying themselves.

But Wells failed to foresee that his message would arrive at an inopportune moment. The year after *Little Wars* appeared, the United Kingdom joined World War I, a miserable stalemate fought out of trenches by starving young men imprisoned in a world of barbed wire, poison gas, shells, and machine gun encampments. Wells's lesson went unheeded, and many of the young men he hoped would enjoy his game instead perished across the Channel.

Between the world wars, the wargames pioneered by Stevenson and Wells attracted a small following. In the United Kingdom, wargamers largely piggy-backed on the clubs of miniature figure collectors, notably the British Model Soldier Society, founded in 1935. Within that club, J. C. Sachs updated Wells's rules and ran an annual "Tactical Cup Challenge" as a tournament for wargamers (see *War*

Game Digest 7:1 [1971] for Sachs's rules). In the pages of the Society's newsletter, the *Bulletin*, among many articles about period military uniforms and the proper construction of dioramas, one could occasionally find reports on wargame battles conducted. But at the behest of most figurine collectors, wargames were relegated to the status of a second-class citizen.

In America, a similar group dedicated to toy soldiers, the Miniature Figure Collectors of America, convened in 1941. Even earlier, a few intrepid pioneers on the isle of Manhattan had experimented with games of their own. The industrial designer and pacifist Norman Bel Geddes staged a long-term wargame campaign in his apartment, based on a large terrain map, multiple players commanding various armies, and mechanical devices to compute combat results (Peterson 2012, 276). The science fiction novelist Fletcher Pratt also ran sessions of a naval wargame of his own invention, in which each player commanded a single ship. While Bel Geddes never published a wargame system, Pratt did produce a slim volume describing his rules in 1943, wherein he expressed, in a sentiment much like Wells before him, that "if Mr. Hitler and Mr. Stalin had had such a game available, they might not have resorted to killing thousands and disorganizing the lives of millions in order to read dispatches before their eyes" (3). But despite the aspirations of pacifists, no wargame could control war, let alone put an end to it. While Bel Geddes's game is little remembered today, Pratt's became influential once a vibrant wargaming hobby community emerged after the war.

The Diplomatic Military

Hobbyists were not the only ones who balked at the complex simulations of German *kriegsspiel*. At around the same time that the Oxford Kriegspiel Club began in the late nineteenth century, a backlash mounted in the highest military echelons of Germany against the overly complex contingencies detailed in the wargames of the time.

The most vocal opposition came from Julius von Verdy du Vernois, a member of the Prussian General Staff and thus an immensely influential figure in the German army. Verdy du Vernois argued that *kriegsspiel* rules were overly prescriptive, and that the cumbersome tables and die rolls recommended by Tschischwitz and his peers contributed little to the edification of players—remember that these die rolls nominally were conducted in secret by the referee, who then reported the results as needed to the players. Verdy du Vernois also eschewed the written order in favor of a dialogue between players and referee. Substituting a conversation for written orders also reflected the changing technologies of the time, for it was the dawn of the telephone (and soon, the radio), the beginning of an era when spoken orders could be conveyed in real time across a vast distance. The model must change its apparatus to fit the relentless advance of military technology. From the perspective of wargamers, these changes lent immediacy to the interaction between player and referee: decisions must come fast in wartime.

Verdy du Vernois set down these principles in his *Beitrag zum Kriegsspiel* (1876), and from there this style of wargaming spread to numerous later works. Farrand Sayre gives an example dialogue between a "director" and player in his *Map Maneuvers* (1908), an influential American account of wargames. That volume also details how a referee could administer a "one-sided" wargame, one with only a single player, where the referee effectively controls the forces that the player will confront. These two innovations would later inspire a whole new category of games, as we shall see.

Just as World War I showed the limits of Wells's attempt to control war with a simple game, it demonstrated the futility of controlling war with the complex Prussian model as well. Despite the extensive modeling and simulation behind the Schlieffen plan, its implementation showed that the smooth conduct of war on paper was no guarantee of real-world success. The German high command predicted a decisive victory within weeks, only to languish in a quagmire for years before an inevitable defeat. Any illusion that Prussian simulations rendered its military invulnerable was shattered.

Tactical wargames representing troops with unit counters on a board remained popular with the militaries of the twentieth century, though the applicability of these simulations to the duties of command grew more tenuous over time. Increasingly, simulating the experience of combat meant reconstructing sophisticated interfaces like those available in state-of-the-art military facilities. Electronics and early computers became factors in these models, tools that were no less expensive to simulate than to deploy in earnest.[7] While initially referees operated these tools, ultimately the machines shouldered more and more of the responsibility for executing the system and managing its state. Only later, with the advent of inexpensive personal computers, would hobby

wargaming begin to approximate, and then influence, this modern apparatus of warfare.

Moreover, the nature of warfare changed at the end of World War II, and the tools that the military employed to model war had to change as well. Total war would now be conducted with nuclear arms—no arrangement of tanks or soldiers benefited the defender when bombs targeted population centers rather than armies. A new sort of wargame would be needed to explore war in the atomic age, which lay beyond any existing doctrine of control. Now the absolutes of committing to the use of nuclear arms would drive diplomatic maneuvers rather than map maneuvers. The radical theories of thinkers like Herman Kahn, a game theorist associated with RAND, recast command in times of war; his simulations did not so much involve ordering around troops as playing through endless scenarios of nuclear brinkmanship and mutually assured destruction, thoroughly political constructs (see Ghamari-Tabrizi 2005).

By the 1950s, the operations research community began to formalize politics into games that combined strategy with diplomacy, economics, and social science. Herbert Goldhamer's "Toward a Cold War Game" (1954) combined the dialog-driven *kriegsspiel* of Verdy du Vernois with the new science of game theory in coalition-building games. Academics quickly adopted these methods for university classes, modeling structures like the United Nations with numerous independent student protagonists rather than two rigid sides of a conflict. Experiments in political gaming at institutions including Stanford and MIT in the 1950s led to the "Inter-Nation Simulation" at Northwestern in the 1957–58 school year (Guetzkow et al. 1963). This political game modeled the behavior of multiple nuclear-armed nations in times of crisis. These sim- ulations taught students the immediate conse- quences of foreign policy and decision making for national security.[8] Similar games, run as exercises

for diplomats and military commanders, demon- strated how some aspects of conflict could not be quantified, because they reflect the unfathomable depths of interpersonal relationships.

Commercial Wargaming

Wargames in the service of the military would ulti- mately reach a much smaller audience than com- mercial wargames. As the wars of the 1940s gave way to the prosperity of the 1950s, wargames began to transition from a pastime to an industry, thanks largely to the activities of three key innovators: Charles S. Roberts, Jack Scruby, and Alan Calhamer. All three took it upon themselves to self-publish wargame material at a time when no proven market existed.

Charles S. Roberts designed *Tactics* (1954), the widely-imitated progenitor of a new category of board wargames. It shipped in a box which proclaimed the contents to be "the new, realistic land army war game" and "a war game with the professional touch." Roberts structured his initial board as a large grid that Hellwig or Venturini would have recognized, but instead of chess-like pieces, he represented com- batants with colored cardboard chits. At the end of the decade, Roberts founded the Avalon Hill Game Company, which revised his *Tactics* and published a first historical simulation, *Gettysburg* (1958). It was through *Gettysburg* that wargames would reach their broadest audience yet, thanks to the upcoming cen- tennial, and the 1961 revision to *Gettysburg* granted wargames their signature hexagonal overlay rather than the ancient grid of chess. Avalon Hill's publi- cations set the initial parameters of the wargaming industry of the 1960s and 1970s.

Jack Scruby cast metal miniature soldiers and played wargames in a California group affiliated with the British Model Soldier Society. Repulsed by the discouragement of wargames material in the Soci- ety's *Bulletin*, Scruby elected to strike out and publish his own quarterly journal, the *War Games Digest*. Pre- miering in January 1957, the *Digest* created a venue where wargamers could publish rules, military his- tory, and reports on recent tabletop battles, and debate all of the above with peers. When the project grew beyond the means of a single manager, Scruby enlisted wargamers from across the Atlantic, Tony Bath and his associate Don Featherstone, to edit half of the issues. Scruby also published some of the ear- liest stand-alone pamphlets containing miniature wargame rules, and his own brand of miniatures became iconic.

Finally, Alan Calhamer produced *Diplomacy* (1959), a historical game exploring the balance of power prior to World War I. *Diplomacy* packaged a simple and intuitive conflict system together with coalition-building incentives beloved of the opera- tions research community. In order to accurately reflect the historical situation, seven players each take control of one of the Great Powers. The game is thus not a simple opposition between two par- ties, but instead a loosely cooperative game where players aspire for supremacy through alliances and betrayals. Its most striking feature is the

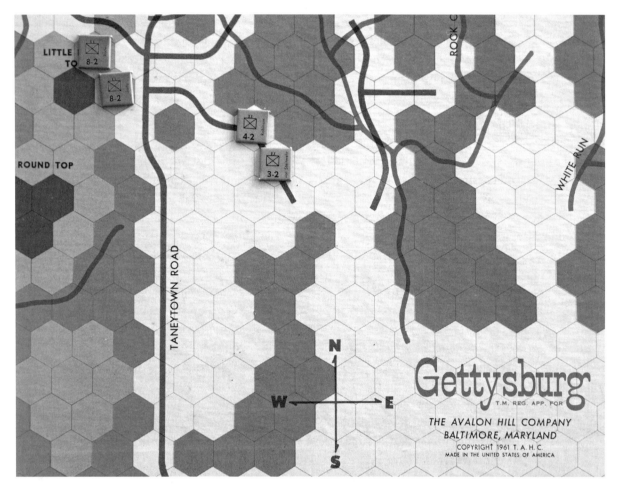

Figure 1.3
The 1961 hexagonal board of *Gettysburg*.

fifteen-minute period for diplomacy between each turn, in which players interact informally with one another, making any promises or threats needed to achieve their objectives. The open-endedness of that negotiation phase encouraged players to take on the personae of diplomats, sometimes with personalities and identities very distinct from the players themselves.

Most of the defining characteristics of wargames can be found in these earliest exemplars.[9] In *Tactics*, players may elect to move all, some, or none of their units each turn. The objective of the game, like Hellwig's 1780 *kriegsspiel*, is to occupy an enemy fortress. Combat occurs whenever, on the square grid of *Tactics*, a unit is moved adjacent to an enemy, as each unit "controls a total of 9 squares, formed in a

THE WAR GAME DIGEST

A QUARTERLY PUBLICATION DEVOTED
TO WAR GAMES AND THE WAR GAME
PLAYER

MARCH, 1957   BOOK I , VOLUME I

PRICE - $1.00

"VOLTIGEURS"

FEATURED IN THIS ISSUE:

Ideas, Rules, Uses of

THE LIGHT INFANTRYMAN

Edited and Published by Jack Scruby and Homer Delabar
P.O. Box 6 --Tipton, Calif.

Figure 1.4
The first issue of Scruby's *War Game Digest*.

square ... the square it is on and the square on each side in any direction." Although the term does not appear in the original *Tactics* rules, by the advent of *Gettysburg* four years later that nine-square area would be known as the "zone of control." When forces conflicted, *Tactics* determined the results with a die roll against a Combat Results Table (CRT), which drew on the Reisswitzian probability charts appearing in prior English-language *kriegsspiel* adaptations.

The wargame industry started small. The most successful title in the first five years of Avalon Hill, *Gettysburg*, represented a fifth of all the company's sales, or about 140,000 copies, a sum an order of magnitude less than a major board game title like Parker Brothers' *Monopoly* sold each year. For the American toy companies who eagerly marketed board games to the Baby Boomers and their parents alike, war themes remained a sensitive subject—but the nascent wargaming community proved that there was an market for these titles. Parker Brothers and Milton Bradley explored this area cautiously, with games that did not aspire to simulate the experience of command and thus fall short of the depth we expect from wargames, yet they did incorporate rudimentary military strategy.

For example, in 1957, an executive from the Miro company in France arrived at Parker Brothers to discuss a joint venture. He brought along a copy of their *La Conquête du Monde* (1957), a board wargame designed by the French film director Albert Lamorisse. Players deployed nineteenth-century troops (infantry, cavalry, and artillery) in a sprawling battle to conquer a world divided into forty-two territories. Parker Brothers bought the rights to the game immediately, and after two years of development produced their own version, *Risk* (1959). Despite its high price point, due to its large board and many wooden pieces, the title produced a million dollars in revenue for Parker Brothers in 1959 alone (Orbanes 2004, 135–36).

Milton Bradley also imported a military game from Europe around this time, though this one had roots in the early twentieth century. The French capture-the-flag game called *L'Attaque* had been sold in Europe since before World War I, and Milton Bradley had produced an early variant called *Le Choc* (1919).[10] Played on a 9 × 10 square board, *L'Attaque* is noteworthy for its one-sided standing game pieces which, like playing cards, preserve secret information by showing opponents only a uniform back, while players can see which of their own pieces represents the flag, buried mines, spies, or various ranks of soldiers. H. P. Gibson in England acquired the rights to *L'Attaque* as early as 1924 and had produced a new boxed set with updated graphics in 1957. This was followed shortly thereafter by Milton Bradley's own version of the game, *Stratego* (1961).

As the larger toy manufacturers targeted their board games to a youth audience, this ceded to the nascent wargames industry more sophisticated "adult" games with deeper levels of simulation. Parker Brothers and Milton Bradley did bring continuing innovations to the community in the 1960s; for example, when Milton Bradley revived an old pencil-and-paper title as the iconic plastic-briefcase game *Battleship* (1967), they further popularized secret information as the basis for competitive games. The smaller wargame publishers benefited from the interest in combat simulation that these games inspired in the young, but it was unclear that any of them could rise to compete with the likes of Milton Bradley without some sort of breakthrough.

The Hobby Traditions

At a time when many young Americans idealistically rejected war, wargamers countered the counterculture and came to terms with war by immersing themselves in safe simulations of it. Overwhelming, these mid-century wargames chose as their subject battles of the nineteenth and twentieth centuries, and few explored any setting after the victorious Second World War. For youths who grew up with the threat of conscription or nuclear annihilation, the anachronistic warfare of the past must have seemed quaint and safe—totally under control. Wargames showed orderly conflicts still fought by soldiers, on battlefields or ships; conflicts from the days before war became something that could incinerate all the world's cities, civilians included, at the whim of some grim button-pusher. Although the popular media painted the wargaming community as inherently pro-war, wargamers ran the gamut: some were or became soldiers, but others adhered to the philosophy of Wells, that "little warfare" encouraged pacifism.

Board wargamers were few and far between, but since wargames required at least two players, a support network was badly needed. The miniature wargame community was tinier still. Subscription to Scruby's *War Game Digest* began at forty and never exceeded two hundred, albeit many of its subscribers were prominent game designers. The miniature side of the hobby won many converts in the early 1960s thanks to books written in England by Don Featherstone, such as *War Games* (1962), or in America Joe Morschauser's *How to Play War Games in Miniature* (1962), but no amount of book learning could locate a wargame opponent.

The hobby linked itself together through four primary mechanisms: magazines, clubs, conventions, and letters. The *War Game Digest*, first among these fan-made magazines (or "fanzines"), did not survive beyond 1963, but it had many successors: Featherstone founded his own *Wargamer's Newsletter*, which became the flagship monthly of the miniature wargame community for the next decade. Avalon Hill's own magazine *The General* famously carried an "Opponents Wanted" column to connect wargamers. Many other magazines were published by clubs. Some clubs were local in scope, while others had greater ambitions, like the International Federation of Wargaming (IFW), formed in 1967. The IFW initially sponsored the most famous convention founded in the 1960s, the Lake Geneva Wargames Convention, or Gen Con, held in 1968 by Gary Gygax in his hometown in Wisconsin.

Once game fans met through clubs or conventions, personal correspondence could carry play-by-mail game moves between distant opponents, overcoming the sparseness of gamers. No game lent itself to play-by-mail quite as naturally as *Diplomacy*. In tabletop *Diplomacy*, each player secretly commits their moves for a turn to paper, and then at the turn's end, all players simultaneously reveal their moves; that is when everyone learns which promises have been honored and which have merely been a ruse. Famously, that is when the "stabs" occur that upset the balance of power in *Diplomacy*, when troops you were expecting to join your coalition to oust an enemy instead go elsewhere, and a player you believed to be an ally turns out to be a traitor. When you play the game by post, these written instructions can be mailed to a central game authority, or a "gamesmaster," who is responsible for tracking the state of play and sharing the consequences of moves. Similarly, the negotiation phase of *Diplomacy* can take the form of either private correspondence or public pronouncements sent to everyone, known as *Diplomacy* "propaganda." From the dawn of postal *Diplomacy*, in the games run in the fanzines *Graustark* (1963) and *Ruritania* (1964), propaganda unleashed the storytelling that was always latent in wargames, and made the games as much about the character a player portrays as about the armies that one commands.

As small as the hobby may have been, the core of energetic, creative people who flocked to conventions and fanzines constituted an invisible college to propose and evaluate improvements of wargames. *Diplomacy* demonstrated exceptional versatility as a platform for variants; fans transposed the game from the early twentieth century to medieval Europe, to Scottish clans, even to Middle-earth. Aspiring designers also expanded on the existing work of Avalon Hill, exploring new aspects of historical battles or shifting to adjacent actions. Amateur game design became a large dimension of the hobby, albeit not a very lucrative one. The national clubs would even distribute promising amateur game designs to their membership, though this yielded little remuneration other than esteem.

Amid this wave of innovation in the 1960s, we see an increasing focus on smaller-scale combat in miniature wargames. This narrowed the scope of simulation from armies to soldiers, and from turns representing days to mere instants. An early work along these lines was Michael J. Korns's *Modern War in Miniature* (1966), which positioned a player as an individual soldier, verbally proposing to a referee actions for a turn lasting a mere two seconds of game time. This trend reflected the changing scope of an American soldier's experience in combat, where command yielded to discretion. No longer were droves of American troops storming beaches like Normandy to wrest a foothold to confront an enemy army; now, in Vietnam, no opposing army was in sight, and small platoons struggled to ferret out enough opposition for a skirmish.

A similar narrowing of scope came to board wargames, especially in the vibrant amateur design community. For example, Mike Carr's pioneering *Fight in the Skies* (1968) modeled aerial combat down to the actions of single planes and pilots in the First World War, inspired by the exploits of the Red Baron and the recent film *The Blue Max* (1966). Similarly, Jim Dunnigan's *Tactical Game 3* (1969), published through his Poultron Press, depicted World War II combat at the level of small tank detachments conflicting on a tactical scale. It reached a broad audience, as it shipped with *Strategy & Tactics*, a widely read wargame magazine that Dunnigan's company had recently acquired. Though Dunnigan would soon found Simulation Publications, Inc. (SPI), Avalon Hill's main wargaming rival of the 1970s, Avalon Hill nonetheless regularly published his designs: a revised *Tactical Games 3* appeared under their imprint as *PanzerBlitz* (1970) and became one of their most successful titles; as of 1983, it was the only Avalon Hill game to sell more than 200,000 copies.

In the more experimental miniature community, hobbyists dared to model eras prior to Napoleon. Even before the *War Game Digest* began, Tony Bath had published medieval miniature wargame rules in the British Model Soldier Society's *Bulletin*. He ran sprawling campaigns based on a variety of unreal countries, even borrowing elements of Robert E. Howard's Hyborian Age, the setting of his famous

Conan stories, to form an ancient-setting wargame campaign—albeit one without supernatural elements. Bath's self-published ancient and medieval rules became a standard of the era.

Gary Gygax had similar interests in the medieval period, which inspired him to form a wargaming club called the Castle & Crusade Society as a subgroup of the IFW in 1970. Its newsletter, the *Domesday Book*, circulated rules for various forms of medieval warfare, from mass frays (via systems indebted to Bath) to jousting and other types of single combat. The man-to-man fighting rules brought simulation down to the individual level, modeling the likelihood that medieval weapons would hit targets protected by various degrees of armor, or "armor classes," ranging from leather through chain mail and up to plate armor. Weapons as well varied from familiar swords and bows to exotic implements like halberds and morning stars. Players consulted a combat table and, for a given weapon used against a given set of armor, attempted to roll above a target number in order to score a hit.

Gygax collected his various medieval rules ideas in *Chainmail* (1971), one of the earliest stand-alone miniature rules booklets published in the United States. Fatefully, he added a supplement to the end of the book that catered to another of his interests, fantasy. The monumental popularity of J. R. R. Tolkien's *Lord of the Rings* saga in the late 1960s created an enormous fan community around fantasy literature, and *Chainmail* became the first commercial wargame

to provide rules for modeling wizards, dragons, orcs, elves, and similar fantastic elements. The rules included systems for both swords and sorcery; when an enemy spell targets a friendly unit, defending players roll a "saving throw" on dice charts that may prevent death. To simulate the resilience of characters like Aragorn or Conan, Heroes in *Chainmail* could survive up to four hits from weapons, and Superheroes could survive eight.

Chainmail polarized the wargaming community. While many rejected fantasy as something childish and insisted that wargames were a tool for exploring history or improving skills as a commander, others recognized the possibilities that were opened up by simulating the unreal—that players could do more than just read about fantastic adventures, they could also experience them. Removing wargames from modern conflicts like Vietnam had a certain appeal for a country weary of the ambiguities and atrocities shown in the daily media—monsters like orcs are intrinsically evil, and players could slaughter them without moral quandaries.

Gygax soon learned that a Twin Cities gamer and fellow member of the Castle & Crusade Society named Dave Arneson had applied the *Chainmail* rules to a local campaign called "Blackmoor," which included a dungeon populated with monsters that small groups of adventurers could attempt to plunder. After Arneson demonstrated the work to Gygax late in 1972, the pair began collaborating on an entirely new type of game based on these principles.

Simulating the Unreal

In order to publish his new collaboration with Arneson—to be called *Dungeons & Dragons*—as well

as further wargame designs, Gygax founded a game company in the fall of 1973 called Tactical Studies

Figure 1.5
Medieval miniature wargames.

Rules (TSR), which took its name from his local wargaming club, the Lake Geneva Tactical Studies Association.

Dungeons & Dragons first proclaimed itself a wargame; the subtitle on the original 1974 box described the contents as "Rules for Fantastic Medieval Wargames Campaigns, Playable with Paper and Pencil and Miniature Figures." We can interpret *Dungeons & Dragons* as a wargame in which, in a strategic context, groups of adventurers explore a dungeon map, and when they encounter opposition in the form of monsters, a brief tactical wargame is played out in that room or hallway. Should the characters survive the encounter, they return to maneuvering on the strategic dungeon map. The earliest edition of *Dungeons & Dragons* recommends using the *Chainmail* rules to resolve those tactical battles.

While early players found in *Dungeons & Dragons* a captivating system full of innovations, the game mostly repackaged and combined existing wargaming systems into a novel and successful formula. *Dungeons & Dragons* relied on a referee-based system that Twin Cities wargamers had rediscovered from late-nineteenth century English-language imitations of Reisswitz.[11] The referee—in later editions called the "dungeon master"—creates the game world that the players will investigate. Players propose actions to the referee verbally, and "anything can be attempted" by characters: that is, the players may propose that their character undertake any action that a person in their situation might reasonable attempt. A player might say, "I try to set fire to the inn," and the referee must consult the state of the game and report the result of this attempt. A referee is also essential to dungeon exploration, as a third party is needed to both design the dungeon and to keep it secret from players as they explore.

Because effectively there is no opponent in the wargame of *Dungeons & Dragons*, this is a "one-sided" wargame operated by the referee.

Chainmail already provided a system for simulating combat down to the level of individual warriors, but *Dungeons & Dragons* encouraged a one-to-one correspondence between players and characters, where the character acts a surrogate for the player in the game world.[12] This hints at the most fundamental respect in which *Dungeons & Dragons* shifted away from traditional wargames and inaugurated a new genre. It no longer simulated the experience of command—it simulated the experience of being a person who did many things other than commanding. In the world of *Dungeons & Dragons*, a player could control only their own character, and only influence others through the persuasion of role-playing (in a manner reminiscent of *Diplomacy*) or the discretion of the referee.

While in a board wargame there is typically no persistence of individual units between game sessions, *Dungeons & Dragons* borrowed the campaign metaphor from miniature wargames to allow a player to retain the same character indefinitely. Characters also improve with experience in the game, which reviewers consistently cited as one of the most compelling and addictive aspects of *Dungeons & Dragons*. By defeating monsters and accumulating treasures, characters amass experience points which will allow them to rise in level, in turn rendering characters more powerful.

In order to increase player investment in, and identification with, a character, the system of *Dungeons & Dragons* provided a number of "life support" features to keep characters alive. The most influential of these mechanisms is "hit points," a quantitative model of the amount of damage that a character can sustain before dying—generalizing the *Chainmail* concept that a Hero can withstand four hits. As characters progress in level, the number of hit points they possess increases, making characters harder to kill; thus, the more time players invest into characters, the harder it is to lose them. Even characters who are reduced to zero hit points and killed may be restored by magic. As such, a *Dungeons & Dragons* character can go on forever; the game has no objective other than to increase the power and wealth of characters. The aim is to simulate fantastic heroism: immortal, ever-improving superiority. A clear departure from wargames, but the elements *Dungeons & Dragons* popularized became obligatory additions to future wargaming systems.

Dungeons & Dragons quickly spread through two subcultures: wargaming fandom and fantasy fandom. TSR first advertised *Dungeons & Dragons* alongside other wargaming titles it released, but savvy reviewers soon began to suggest it was no wargame. Gygax himself promoted *Dungeons & Dragons* by printing fictionalized narratives inspired by dungeon adventures, and the game quickly developed a reputation as a means of generating, and experiencing, fantasy stories (see Kirschenbaum 2009). Like many groundbreaking games before it—those of Hellwig, Reisswitz, and Roberts—*Dungeons & Dragons* inspired numerous imitators and competitors: mostly famously, and most rapidly, *Tunnels & Trolls* (1975). It was only after a number of titles based on the principles of *Dungeons & Dragons* had gone to market that reviewers began to apply the label of "role-playing game" to this new category.

The success of the fantasy setting opened the floodgates for many new wargame scenarios; it loosened the stranglehold of history on wargames.

Wargamers now freely embraced fantasy and science fiction as settings, and a dash of the fantastic quickly became a selling point. A tank wargame in the late 1970s no longer needed to provide a faithful rendition of prenuclear tactics of the Second World War—in 1977, Steve Jackson released his classic board wargame *OGRE*, which modeled far future combat where diverse military forces collaborate to take down a single, monolithic, improbable supertank. With the jettisoning of historical realism also came an appetite for novel systems that defied the traditional parameters of wargaming. A title like Eon Games' *Cosmic Encounter* (1977) embraced some aspects of *Diplomacy* but combined them with futuristic role-playing, innovative card-based combat, and zany metarules that could alter the system on the fly, permitting actions that under other circumstances would be cheating.

Unreal settings would invade much of the wargame marketplace after the release of *Dungeons & Dragons*. Some came from upstart publishers, like *White Bear, Red Moon* (1975), a fantasy board wargame by the Chaosium that first described the setting of their later *RuneQuest* (1978) role-playing game. Industry stalwarts like Avalon Hill and SPI entered the fray, though the latter, being more agile, got there first, with titles like *Sorcerer* (1975) and the more considered *Swords & Sorcery* (1978). When SPI announced its Middle-earth game *War of the Ring* in mid-1977, it became their bestselling title as of July on the strength of preorders alone, and although it periodically dropped to second place, it remained on-again-off-again their bestselling title as of April 1979. While Avalon Hill made a number of forays into fantasy, they succeeded mostly in acquisitions and outside contracts; for example, they hired the creators of *Cosmic Encounter* to make *Dune* (1979), bought

Gorgonstar's fantasy board wargame *Titan* (1980), and in the long term even acquired *RuneQuest* from the Chaosium.

The market's sweet tooth for fantasy in the 1970s did not spoil its appetite for historical simulation entirely. Traditional wargames in this period grew in both depth and breadth, though not simultaneously in the same product. The small unit actions depicted by *Tactical Game 3* inspired a number of narrow-scale successors, including SPI's *Sniper!* (1973), followed by Avalon Hill's *Panzer Leader* (1974)

and *Squad Leader* (1977), with its many expansions and scenarios. Simultaneously, other titles tried to capture the campaign-level activities of major battle theaters. From GDW's *Drang Nach Osten* (1973) there followed many of these so-called "monster games," such as the 1,400-counter juggernaut of Marshall Enterprises, *La Bataille de la Moscowa* (1975), and SPI's sprawling *War in Europe* (1976). At either the microscopic or macroscopic extreme, these games tested the limits of what could practically be modeled on a physical apparatus.

The Digital Age

Youths who grew up playing the hobby wargames of the 1960s went on to college or the military in the following decade, and there they often encountered early computers. At the beginning of the 1970s, computers remained expensive communal resources operated by large institutions; personal computers were unheard of. As early as 1967, we see in Avalon Hill's newsletter *The General* evidence of soldiers at Fort Benning, Georgia, soliciting volunteers to visit the base for "computerized wargames," surely appropriating systems reserved for military purposes. But that was no commercial venture. Around the end of 1970, Rick Loomis turned that page with a bold pronouncement in *The General* inaugurating "the computer age of wargaming" (Loomis 1970).

Loomis, founder of the game company Flying Buffalo, ran a series of for-profit computer-moderated play-by-mail wargames, beginning with *Nuclear Destruction* (1970) and most famously including *Starweb* (1976). Players would mail their orders on paper in a special format that Loomis inputted to a Raytheon 704, which would then print out individual

results for posting to each of the players. Loomis stressed how the computer was "fair and impartial"—effectively, the computer became his referee. Simulations are complex, and with the popularity of "monster" wargames they were growing ever more so. The first thing that computers promised was a simpler way to manage the many parameters of conflict: unit positions and strengths, terrain types, and so on. The most complicated board wargames now tracked so many pieces, and so many contingencies, that it was difficult for a human to conduct a game without committing errors. Wargames were getting out of control.

Sending paper mail to a computer's operator is a far cry from sitting players in front of a terminal where they could compete against others in real time—in the 1970s, such experiences were reserved for those students lucky enough to be on the systems like the intercollegiate PLATO network, where they could play homebrew graphical games including the *Star Trek* simulation *Empire* (1973).[13] By the middle of the decade, as arcade video games matured in the market, we began to see concrete proposals for enlisting computers to take over the real-time administration of competitive wargames; this was especially attractive as the computer could keep opponents ignorant of enemy positions in a wargame without requiring a human referee. But in the fall of 1976, this still looked like a distant prospect: a wargamer at MIT predicted that "hidden movement pseudo-miniatures armored battles in living color will take a while," perhaps four years, in his opinion (Swanson 1976).

Just one year later, the first personal microcomputer models targeting consumers entered the marketplace: the Apple II, the Tandy TRS-80 and the Commodore PET. With them naturally came the promise of running computer wargames. As computers lent themselves to futuristic settings, many of the early titles were space combat games. In 1978, Automated Simulations, Inc. released its first strategy title for these platforms, *Starfleet Orion*, a two-player space wargame. The following year, in a sequel called *Invasion Orion*, they tweaked the design slightly to resolve an age-old problem of wargames: the lack of an opponent. As the Automated Simulations marketing literature put it, "your opponent is included in the game"; that is, a rudimentary artificial intelligence served as an opponent to allow a pioneering single-player wargame. Computers now shared in the experience of command, simulating not just the apparatus of war but even the players.

Because of the miniscule memory of the earliest personal computers, only simple actions could be depicted, and many products targeting wargamers were at best war-themed games of strategy. A good candidate for the first true wargame on the personal computer was the debut Strategic Simulation, Inc. (SSI) title *Computer Bismarck* (1980), a

faithful translation of Avalon Hill's *Bismarck* board wargame—so faithful that legal questions were raised (see Wilson 1991). *Bismarck* on the tabletop is a limited information game in which a fleet of English ships attempts to find and sink a single huge German vessel, a scenario which would play to the strengths of computers. Avalon Hill itself eagerly entered the digital marketplace that same year through its subsidiary Microcomputer Games, which released no less than five titles in 1980 alone. Some of these early games lacked graphics entirely and actually shipped with boards and unit counters in addition to cassettes storing code: for example, Avalon Hill's *Tanktics* (1981), which calculated combat results and unit positions, instructing the player to adjust the physical board accordingly. Wargames would not peaceably relinquish their boards.

While these early computer titles adhered to the turn-based mechanic of board and miniature wargames, gradually designers rethought wargames as native to computers, especially as computing power grew continually less expensive. This paved the way for games that dispensed with turns entirely, enabling a genre of real-time wargames that behaved more like arcade game titles, or indeed like genuine warfare, as humans and computers moved game elements continuously and simultaneously. Pioneering games in this category included *Stonkers* (1983) and *The Ancient Art of War* (1984).

As consumer computer games increased in sophistication, real warfare became correspondingly more computerized. The intersection of computer wargames and war gave rise to popular anxieties and fantasies alike, both triggered by the conviction that that the apparatus of war could and would be reduced to the interface of a game. Fred Saberhagen's novel *Octagon* (1981) provides an early example

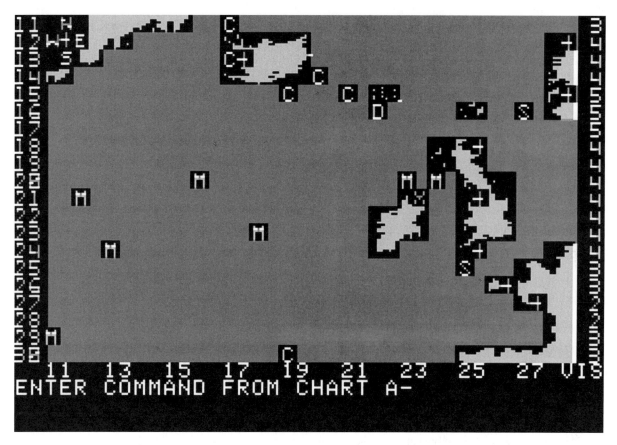

Figure 1.6
The early computer wargame *Computer Bismarck.*

of this thinking, in which a military computer joins a play-by-mail multiplayer wargame (based on Rick Loomis's *Starweb*) and finds that the optimal strategy is to dispatch a robot to assassinate other players in real life. The film *WarGames* (1983) shows a young game enthusiast who inadvertently compromises a military simulation system and directs it to play a game of "global thermonuclear war," which prompts the computer to attempt to launch real missiles. The hacker protagonist cannot at first distinguish the experience of starting a war from merely playing a game, but it is the computer's confusion that is more menacing. When asked, "Is this a game ... or is it real?" the computer mechanically replies, "What's the difference?" Ultimately, the computer learns from its own simulations the lesson that Wells hoped his wargame would impart seventy years before: "what a blundering thing" warfare is. Two years later, this anxiety was inverted in Orson Scott Card's story *Ender's Game* (1985), in which a brilliant young gamer believes that he is playing a simulation when in fact his moves are commanding a real army to victory. In that fable, a simulation truly can encompass and control warfare.

The technology of warfare has not yet evolved in quite the ways these fictions anticipated, but as the military has become increasingly computerized, necessarily the responsibilities of both soldiers and commanders correspondingly are discharged through interfacing with computers. A simulation may train a soldier to fight, but the means of conducting real combat has also bent toward the apparatus of a simulation. Ultimately, popular computer games train youths to interface with simulated conflict in ways that the militaries of today would be foolish to ignore; as Tim Lenoir and Henry Lowood say, "the entertainment industry is both a major source of innovative [military] ideas and technology, and the training ground for what might be called posthuman warfare" (Lenoir and Lowood 2003, 42). And while the killer robots of Saberhagen's *Octagon* may not assassinate unsuspecting game players autonomously today, soldiers operate lethal flying robots through user interfaces indistinguishable from simulations. It may not be obvious what is real, and what is just a game. This sort of war is truly a game out of all proportion.

Wargames beyond Computing

With the capacity to guard secret information from players, compute combat results without error, supply an opponent in the absence of a human, and even regulate a fair game without turns, how could computers not replace the boards and tabletops of traditional wargames? The 1970s are rightly viewed as the pinnacle of hobby wargames, as much of the design energy, to say nothing of the designers themselves, dedicated to wargames in that era shifted to role-playing games and computer games by the 1980s. The industry underwent significant consolidation in the process; for example, after SPI fell on hard times, TSR absorbed the company early in 1982.

For all that, traditional wargames have remained a vital force in game design, both in their influential innovations and their commercial presence. Although SPI's flagship magazine *Strategy & Tactics* fared poorly under TSR's governance, it has remained in circulation for over four decades, under the imprint of Decision Games since 1991. Nor does *Strategy & Tactics* alone saturate the market: *Fire & Movement*, a wargaming 'zine that started in the 1970s, also continues in the Decision Games family—though changes in the publishing business have recently led both of these ventures to emphasize a digital strategy over print.

Some of the greatest commercial successes of wargaming came after the heyday of the 1970s. One designer who had sometimes freelanced for SPI was Joseph Angiolillo, the founder of an independent design firm called Nova Games. Nova achieved widespread wargame industry recognition in 1980 for its *Ace of Aces*, an aerial dogfighting game with an original system based on gamebooks. One of Nova's summer releases in 1981, a World War II simulation, garnered a less warm reception from wargamers: a reviewer who saw a preview at a convention commented that the game's relationship "to the war's actual history is, at best, an abstract one" (Bomba

1981). The title was *Axis & Allies*, and like its forebear *Risk*, it spanned the entire globe, though its numerous military units comprised all manner of ships, aircraft, and even atomic bombs. While hardened wargamers may have found its simplicity underwhelming, it had no shortage of admirers. Late in 1983, Milton Bradley acquired the game, and even hired its designer, Lawrence H. Harris, to ease its transition to the popular market (which entailed the removal of nuclear weapons, among other changes). From 1984 forward, the Milton Bradley *Axis & Allies* brought the principles of wargaming to an ever-widening audience through its numerous expansions and revisions, including several computer versions.

Role-playing games as a category so dominated the hobby market of the early 1980s that, when TSR reissued Mike Carr's classic World War I aerial wargame *Fight in the Skies* under the title *Dawn Patrol* (1982), the box now called it a "Role Playing Game of WW I air combat." But as the magazine *Different Worlds* would quip, "the game is a tactical air combat game with four pages of role-playing rules in the pull-outs. *Caveat Emptor*" (D'Arn 1982). The following year, there appeared in England a game that identified itself on the box as "the Mass Combat Fantasy Role-Playing Game." In an ironic reversal of the way *Dungeons & Dragons* marketed itself as a "Rules for Fantastic Medieval Wargames Campaigns," now a wargame needed to disguise itself as a role-playing game, to the point of banishing the very word "wargame" from its cover. This new title was called *Warhammer*, and it began a lucrative franchise for Games Workshop. From humble beginnings in 1975, Games Workshop had steadily grown as a distributor for role-playing games in the United Kingdom, as well as through the strength of its signature magazine *White Dwarf*, and finally as a publisher of in-house titles. Its later-subsumed subsidiary Citadel Miniatures cast fantasy figurines to accompany its wargames, which Games Workshop still showcases in its numerous retail stores. On the strength of the *Warhammer* and *Warhammer 40,000* (1987) franchises, Games Workshop became a standard-bearer for miniature wargaming for decades to come.

By the 1990s, computers had transitioned from novel and exotic commodities to everyday household items, and the computer game market dwarfed the wargaming industry. Many gamers who purchased computer strategy titles had no inkling of their debt to tabletop wargame design. How many who bought titles in the popular MicroProse *Civilization* computer game franchise, which began in 1991, knew that it sprang from the board game *Civilization* (1980), another acquisition of Avalon Hill's? Numerous computer games have licensed and adapted *Warhammer* properties—even Blizzard's monumentally successful *Warcraft* (1994) franchise nearly adopted *Warhammer* as its setting during initial development (see Craddock 2013, loc. 3167).

The tools of simulation pioneered by wargames continually infiltrate new genres. In 1993, an innovative category of game appeared: the collectible trading card game, pioneered by *Magic: The Gathering*. *Magic* is a competitive game, typically a contest between two players, where each player draws from their own preselected deck of cards containing various creatures, spells, and lands. While the game admits of innumerable strategies, commonly players will deploy creatures and cast spells to damage their opponent: when a player runs out of life (a quantity modeled after hit points), then they lose the game. Thus, even *Magic* still simulates the experience of command, of deploying and managing squadrons of creatures squaring off against one another in a tactical situation. Its system reflects the precedent of many fantasy wargames in the tradition of *Chainmail*, perhaps most of all TSR's wargame *War of Wizards* (1975). The lucrative *Magic* franchise enabled the game's publisher, Wizards of the Coast, to acquire TSR itself in 1997.

Part of what made *Magic* so compelling was collecting the cards needed to make a powerful deck. The cards themselves were self-explanatory; most of the information needed to play with them was written on their faces, so there was rarely a need to consult rulebooks during play. These innovations made their way from *Magic* back to miniature wargaming. WizKid's *Mage Knight* series of collectible miniatures games, which began in 2000, introduced a new twist: a rotating base for miniatures that displays the health, speed, and so on of figures as they withstand damage in combat, which again keeps the rulebooks closed. *Mage Knight*'s Combat Dial (or "Clix") System spread to other titles and inspired further tabletop wargame efforts.

Exquisite paintable *Warhammer* figurines and collectible objects associated with the *Magic* and *Mage Knight* franchises helped to keep one of wargaming's feet firmly planted in the physical, rather than the virtual, world. Tabletop battles with dice, units, and terrain continue to offer a unique and compelling experience well into the computer age. While the wargame industry did not experience the rapid and enduring expansion enjoyed by other types of games, it still serves a dedicated community of hobbyists. How else can we explain the curious turn of events that after *Civilization*, which began as a board game, inspired a computer game—that then the computer game should in turn be adapted into multiple iterations of *Sid Meier's Civilization: the Board Game*? Even native real-time wargames like Blizzard's iconic *Starcraft* (1998) spawned board game versions. Increasingly, the distinctions between these categories are blurring: new projects such as *Golem Arcana* by Hairbrained Schemes integrate physical miniatures played on a board with computer tablets that manage the system and decide combat results. Nor have gamers abandoned the tabletop for their virtual diversions: Gen Con, the premiere tabletop game convention, had attendance around 1,000 in the mid-1970s at the height of the wargame boom. Gen Con in 2014 exceeded 56,000 attendees, more than doubling its 2009 attendance. Conventions will always offer something that cannot be approximated through screens.

Today, many wargames in the marketplace are backed by one of the world's largest companies. Like an ambitious conqueror, the toy conglomerate Hasbro acquired Milton Bradley (1984), Parker Brothers (1991), Avalon Hill (1998), and finally Wizards of the Coast (2003), ultimately bringing many of the commercial titles discussed in this history under a single roof. But small publishers also continue to innovate aggressively. Companies like GMT Games and Multi-Man Publishing, Inc. are heirs to the tradition of Avalon Hill and SPI, approximating the experience of command in titles that explore historical and contemporary international conflict. A title like GMT's *Labyrinth: The War on Terror, 2001–?* (2010) shows wargames still grappling with how to control warfare, miniaturized down to the tabletop—which suggests that wargames will be with us as long as we still wage war.

About the Author

Jon Peterson is the author of the book *Playing at the World*.

Notes

1. Readers interested a more expansive consideration of wargames encompassing other forms of play relating to conflict, including sporting events, gladiatorial combat, saber-rattling and even the non-lethal contests of animals are referred to Van Creveld 2013.

2. For finding this remarkable quotation, we are indebted to Philipp von Hilgers; for more on this context, see von Hilgers (2012, 28).

3. Although the 1812 work of the elder Reisswitz remains untranslated, the younger Reisswitz's 1824 work can be found in Leeson's *Reisswitz* (1989). Note that the family name is spelled inconsistently in the original German works: the father's *Taktisches Kriegs-Spiel* lists its author as Reiswitz, whereas the son is credited as Reißwitz, commonly written in English as Reisswitz.

4. For more on the evolution and system of the Reisswitz game, see Peterson (2012, chapter three).

5. These antique geomorphs were anticipated by one of the several board types Hellwig sold: "*das auf 63 verschiedene Arten verändert werden kann.*"

6. Baring's 1871 English translation of Tschischwitz's *Anleitung zum Kriegsspiel* was the departure point for many subsequent English military games. The first major American adaptation of this tradition was Totten in 1880.

7. See Perla (1990) for examples like the Naval Electronic Warfare Simulator (NEWS) of systems developed for wargaming in the 1950s.

8. For more on educational uses of wargames, see Sabin (2012).

9. The best tally of these games, especially in their formative years, is Pimper's *All the World's Wargames 1953-1977* and its *Addenda*, which is then followed by three further iterations, capturing 1978–82, 1983–89, and 1990–95.

10. See Lewin (2012, 113–4), on the earliest versions of *L'Attaque*, including the 1908 French patent. On *Le Choc*, see Lewin (157).

11. The cornerstone text for the Twin Cities gamers was *Strategos* (1880), which local gamer Dave Wesely distilled down to a brief set of Napoleonic rules called *Strategos N* (1970).

12. Phillies (1975) identified that some wargamers did command as specific characters, which he called the "Rommel syndrome."

13. Contemporary notices of *Empire* are few, but for a 1974 piece on PLATO games including *Empire*, see Nelson (1974, 27).

2 THE HISTORY OF WARGAMING PROJECT

John Curry

The History of Wargaming Project (HWP) aims to document the history of the hobby and the development of professional wargaming. With books ranging from the origins of *kriegsspiel* to classic hobby work by Donald Featherstone and current military professional wargaming, the project now has more than sixty books in print.

Wargaming has a long, rich history, but it has been underdocumented, and much important material has been lost. Books have gone out of print, and some key works can command prices of over £100 on e-trading sites such as eBay. Recently, Donald Featherstone's book on solo wargaming was offered at £115, and Paddy Griffith's book on Napoleonic wargaming was priced at over £200. These interesting and in the case of Paddy Griffith's, important—books were hard to find and out of the reach of most wargamers. Records of many military wargames have often been lost because security considerations restrict access, military officers move on, and institutional memory forgets. Part of the HWP's remit has been to collate and make this information publicly available.[1]

But the HWP has a wider significance beyond simply resurrecting old books of interest to the niche hobby of wargaming. Some of the professional wargames now made publicly available are full of concise analytical data that are invaluable to students of historical conflicts. *Tacspiel*, the American wargame from the Vietnam War era, is practically unplayable as a game without teams of umpires and analysts, but if one wants to know about the quantified realities of operational and tactical combat in the Vietnam War, it is an invaluable source of information (Curry 2011a). *Tacspiel* is an historical statement of how the American military saw the war at that point in time.

As of 2014, in the United Kingdom, the United States, and other countries, there is a resurgence in interest for professional wargaming—for practicing skills, rehearsing operations, and developing problem-solving skills among the officer corps. The HWP is a library where those concerned with such matters have been able to obtain samples of what has gone before, as the basis for future developments.

Operational analysis has long been an essential part of weapon procurement, tactical and operational developments, and war planning. The HWP has managed to make available some of the work in this area closely allied to wargaming. The key publication to date has been a second edition of *Peter Perla's The Art of Wargaming*; publishing the second edition of Perla's

work has helped highlight the relationship between the hobby and professional military games.

The Origins of the History of Wargaming Project

The inspiration for the HWP was Paddy Griffith, who formed Wargame Developments (WD) in the early 1980s as a vehicle for developing better, more culturally valid wargames for hobby and professional military use. As part of his work at the UK's Royal Military Academy at Sandhurst, Paddy Griffith (and others such as David Chandler) were using wargames as an academic technique to develop a deeper understanding of military history.[2] Paddy Griffith proposed, but never delivered, a conference session at WD's annual UK Conference of Wargamers (COW) <http://www.wargamedevelopments.org/> on the topic "Why there should be a library of wargaming, and why is there not one?"

Reading about the proposed session inspired me to start collecting (and using) some early wargaming rules from the scrap heap of wargaming history. Over the years, I had accumulated a growing archive, including some unpublished professional wargames. A casual conversation at COW in 2007 with John Basset OBE (Associate Fellow at RUSI) and Tony Hawkins launched what became the History of Wargaming Project. At their urging, I put pen to paper and published a book about one of these early wargames.

The new book was about the classic *Fred Jane's Naval Wargame*, from the early twentieth century (Curry 2008a).[3] Some wargamers were familiar with the Fred Jane game based on the summary in Donald Featherstone's 1965 *Naval War Games*, but few had seen any of the original editions of the rules, and

even fewer had attempted to re-create this game by one of naval wargaming's founding fathers. The first book in what became the HWP included the 1906 edition of the rules, a fast-play version of the rules by Bob Cordery (another member of WD), suggestions as to how to re-create the "paddles" used as firing strikers in the game, some silhouettes, and other information related to the game.

The book also contained a short set of professional military rules used by the Royal Navy for operational analysis and training. Unlike the Fred Jane game, which relied on players randomly striking paper targets to represent gunfire, the 1921 Royal Navy wargame used a gunnery table that stated the average number of hits obtained at each range in average conditions. The difference between the random hits (of the Fred Jane game) and the deterministic gunnery (a preset number of hits at certain ranges) in the professional game is a critical difference between civilian and professional wargames. Sometimes a ship's captain might carry out an ill-advised maneuver on the tabletop but still succeed, due to the random vagaries of enemy gunnery hits based on chance. Players then might take away an incorrect lesson from the Fred Jane wargame into real life, with potentially disastrous consequences. Therefore, using a deterministic combat system was seen by the Royal Navy as more likely to impart the correct training lessons. The inclusion of this short professional set of wargame rules led to a lot of correspondence with those involved in professional

Figure 2.1
Period sketch of the Fred Jane Naval Wargame being played in the early twentieth century in Portsmouth, from "The Naval War Game and How It Is Played," by Angus Sherlock, in volume 27 of the *Strand* magazine (Curry 2008a).

military wargames—much of which inquired as to when other professional wargame rules were going to be published.

As editor, I had anticipated that sales of the Fred Jane book would be at most ten copies over six months, with perhaps six of the purchasers personally known to the author. So it was with surprise that eleven copies sold within a few days of publication and I knew none of the buyers. The second book, *Verdy's "Free" Kriegspiel* (Curry 2008b), went to print shortly afterward. Emails and letters started to arrive, expressing great interest and asking to be notified when the next book in "the series" was going to be published. The wargaming marketplace assumed that the first two books were going to be the start of a major new wargaming publishing project.

Despite being in his eighties, Donald Featherstone (one of the dozen or so founding fathers of modern wargaming, who helped turn an obscure pastime into an international hobby and a useful vehicle for operational analysis and training) contacted the editor. With gushing enthusiasm, Featherstone stated that he had heard about the new series of books on the history of wargaming and asked if his work would be included.[4] Word spread through the network of those involved in early wargaming in the 1960s and 1970s. Within twelve months of Featherstone's involvement, many of the key wargaming authors had contacted me. Names such as Charlie Wesencraft, Phil Dunn, Peter Perla, and Terry Wise were keen to have their work included in this new "archive" of wargaming.[5]

The Fletcher Pratt Naval War Game

Published in 2012, *Fletcher Pratt's Naval Wargame* may have the unique distinction of being the best-selling naval wargaming book of all time (Curry 2012a). Unexpectedly, the book had an appeal well beyond the naval subgenre of wargaming; part of its market has been those interested in the wider activities of Fletcher Pratt, the well-known fantasy author and military historian.

The game had already been brought back into wargamers' awareness through the writings of Donald Featherstone. Featherstone included the rules in his 1965 book on naval wargaming, along with enticing tales of huge games with two hundred players being run in a New York ballroom during 1939–45. The cast participating in the floor-based ship battles in miniature included Isaac Asimov, L. Ron Hubbard, author Jake Coggins, Trevor Dupuy (later Colonel Dupuy of Quantified Judgment Model fame), "Doc" Clarke of the American rocket program, a certain Broadway actress who went on to star in Hollywood, and other notables.

One of the defining characteristics of the Pratt game was the core mechanic of arbitrating gunnery based on estimating the range (in inches) in order to hit. The effect of hits was calculated using a deterministic damage model (i.e., a hit of a certain caliber would always cause the same amount of damage). Ship performance was gradually degraded over a number of hits; however, a single chance hit on a turret could disable an individual gun. The game has been periodically derided; the most considered examination was by James Dunnigan (1976). The Pratt game was criticized for using a deterministic damage model, giving the players perfect situational awareness of the naval action, the absence of any campaign game, and the failure to include airpower. But incongruously, players of Pratt's game included serving naval officers, and the

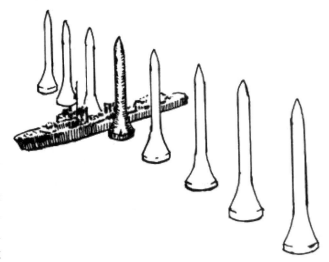

Figure 2.2

White golf tees indicated a miss, red a hit. Sketch in 1940 edition of the rules by Inga Pratt, Fletcher Pratt's wife.

American Naval War College apparently considered it of some value as a model of naval warfare. Could those involved in a World War be wrong and those looking back from future decades be right?

When I first read the 1965 Featherstone account of the game, I noted the apparent discontinuity between the rules, which looked like they were written in 1933, and the accompanying narrative about games that were clearly being run during World War II. I was skeptical that the Pratt players would not have updated the game in line with the then-current real world events. Mobilizing the resources and finances of the History of Wargaming Project, I began the hunt for the *real* Fletcher Pratt wargame. When Fletcher Pratt died in 1956, his wife (an active participant in the game) later married Pratt's chief umpire; she later passed away. Later, the umpire was about to marry a well-known US antiquarian book dealer when he too passed away, so the copyright fell to her. Working through this chain of people led me to the current owner of the copyright and to the phone call that revealed two file boxes full of unpublished material about the game. The result was a 2012 book that included the previously unpublished 1943 version of the Pratt wargame, featuring rules for limited intelligence, with scenario examples, a campaign game, air rules, and optional rules, all written by Pratt and his distinguished fellow contributors. The book was also supplemented by interviewing Commander John Bothwell, USN, who as the last surviving participant from those World War II games was invaluable in adding to the understanding of the game.

The US Army's Tactical War Game of the Cold War

A history of wargaming would have to include a number of landmark sets of rules. The key criteria for inclusion on this list would be how they inspired others to copy and change the rules to create whole series of new wargames. Examples would include the Lionel Tarr modern wargaming rules ("modern," in 1962, meaning World War II) and the Wargames Research Group's Sixth Edition Ancients, written by Phil Barker, Bob O'Brian and Ed Smith. Another such set was the American Army's Dunn-Kempf tactical wargame (1977–1997).

The intellectual inspiration for the Dunn-Kempf game came from the work of Phil Barker et al. and the WRG Wargame Rules for Armoured Warfare 1950–1985. The somewhat complex WRG rules used 1/300 scale vehicles fighting across tabletop terrain for competitive two-sided contests representing hypothetical Cold War battles. Captain Hilton Dunn and Captain Steve Kempf replaced the combat tables with classified military data, and the civilian WRG rules were modified to reflect the army's understanding of warfare. The rules were also substantially rewritten with a view to making them more accessible to the average army officer or senior NCO.

Dunn and Kempf developed the game in 1975, while they were students at the US Army Command and General Staff College at Fort Leavenworth, Kansas. They wanted to "help generate plausible and complex tactical situations for small unit commanders to have to resolve against aggressive opponents." The game was such a success that after extensive testing, the Combined Arms Center at Fort Leavenworth packaged the rules into boxed sets with GHQ "Micro Armor" tanks, terrain boards, maps and other game accessories. Five hundred Dunn-Kempf game sets were distributed throughout army commands around the world.

The original Dunn-Kempf boxed sets included a typical US "Blue" force with seventeen M60A1 main battle tanks, a mechanized infantry company with fifteen M113A1s, three 81mm tracks, two M113A1 TOW carriers, nine rifle squads, six M60 machine gun teams, and twelve Dragon teams. Additional forces were included depending on the units using the model. For example, an armored unit might have four additional TOW APCs, four 4.2-inch mortar carriers, a Redeye ground-to-air missile team, ten Sheridan M551 light tanks, etc. Units were encouraged to supplement the supplied kit with commercially bought tanks from the hobby manufacturer GHQ.

One of the secrets to the rules' success was the level of customization that took place. The terrain boards were always made to resemble the area the units would deploy to. For example, the game at Fort Irwin, California, had a terrain model for the National Training Center (NTC). The project received emails from soldiers who served in Germany and found it very useful to rehearse using the terrain board, then carry out exercises over the real terrain shown on the model.

Another important aspect of the rules was the extent to which they inspired different units to modify them to meet their own needs. While keeping the underlying rule set, the units expanded the parts most relevant to them. The US Army Infantry School (USAIS), at Fort Benning, changed the scope of the game to focus more on the infantry squad/tank platoon level to meet their needs. The III Corps Simulation Center used an "armor heavy variant" servicing the 1st Cavalry Division and the 2nd Armored Division (as well as other II Corps units)—a variant that had an impact on a significant portion of the US armored forces. This variant was also used by the 49th Armored Division (Texas National Guard) just down the road in Austin.

In addition to various units of the US Army adapting the game, the rules had a significant international impact. The Canadians produced a variant of the game to meet their own needs, with an expanded system for calling in artillery and air support. The game was also used in Australia for simulation and training, and the British Army experimented with the rules. Interestingly, the game was even played by the Russians (Curry 2008c), although one might speculate that the Warsaw Pact played the game to better understand the American view of war, rather than as training tool in its own right. The last mention of the game being used for military training was at a 1997 American Armor conference.

The Dunn-Kempf game was important, and a generation of American officers engaged with it as part of their professional development, but the story of the game was almost completely forgotten until resurrected by the History of Wargaming Project.

Too Early to Write the Definitive Wargaming History

In my view, the definitive history of wargaming has yet to be written. Jon Peterson's massive 2012 work, *Playing at the World,* has thoroughly documented the early development of fantasy role-playing, but it is not yet possible to do the same for the rest of wargaming.

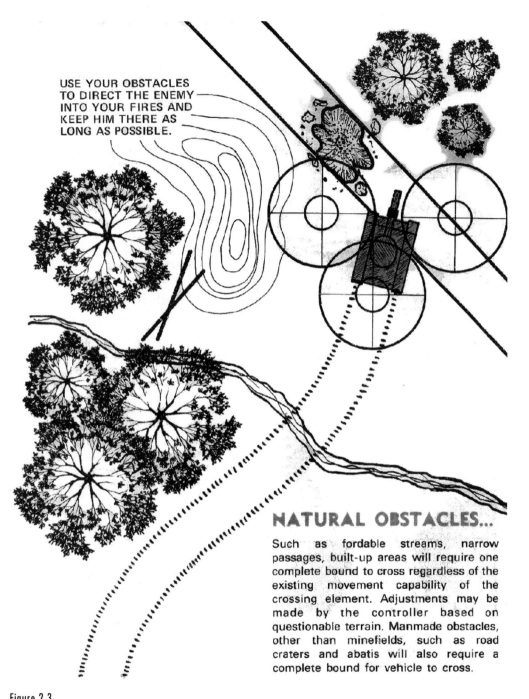

Inside the illustration:

USE YOUR OBSTACLES
TO DIRECT THE ENEMY
INTO YOUR FIRES AND
KEEP HIM THERE AS
LONG AS POSSIBLE.

NATURAL OBSTACLES...

Such as fordable streams, narrow passages, built-up areas will require one complete bound to cross regardless of the existing movement capability of the crossing element. Adjustments may be made by the controller based on questionable terrain. Manmade obstacles, other than minefields, such as road craters and abatis will also require a complete bound for vehicle to cross.

Figure 2.3

Contact!, embedded with tactical advice, was the Canadian Army derivative of the Dunn-Kempf rules. This example is from the original rule book and was drawn by Jean Michaud (Curry 2008d).

Without the History of Wargaming Project publishing *Dunn-Kempf* or the complete *Fletcher Pratt Naval Wargame*, their significance would have been overlooked. It was only in 2011 that the book *Early Wargames Vol. 1* demonstrated that H. G. Wells's *Little Wars* and Donald Featherstone's *War Games* were actually part of a succession of early wargames and were not isolated flashes of inspiration. Featherstone's classic book on wargames, for instance, was building on the work of *Sham Battles* (1929), the *Liddell Hart Wargame* (1935), and the *Captain Sachs War Game* (1940) (Curry 2011b).

A new book on early naval wargaming by the Project in 2014 set the first edition of Fred Jane's 1898 naval wargame in its correct historical context. The game was evolutionary, based on the naval games produced by Royal Navy officers, Lieutenant Castle's *The Game of Naval Tactics* (1873), Captain Colomb's *The Duel* (1880), and Lieutenant Chamberlain's *Game of Naval Blockade* (1888). These previous games and the subsequent discussions at the Royal United Services Institute in London were key in helping make the navies of the world receptive to the idea of conceptualizing a battle upon a tabletop (Curry 2014).

A forthcoming posthumous work by Paddy Griffith will discuss the important part wargaming had in ending the Cold War. The role between wargaming doyen Donald Featherstone and professional wargaming has yet to be explored. There are other significant gaps in the literature that will be filled by books over the next few years.

The Future of the Project

As of 2014, over sixty books and rule sets are now in print through the HWP. Some are second editions of the original works, with supplementary material such as new forewords and other commentary. Others are completely new works based on wargaming material uncovered in what can only be described as "wargaming archaeology"—lost books by Donald Featherstone, Charlie Wesencraft, and Paddy Griffith, and professional wargaming rules that have never been in print. Funded by book sales, the HWP has the resources to seek out missing material and bring to print even material that, while of importance to the history of wargaming, can be judged of only minority interest.

The project is not just concerned with the past. It is also attempting to document some of the current innovations in wargaming, such as committee (seminar) games, "black" games dealing with unpalatable subjects such as antiterrorist games, or games including weapons of mass destruction (Curry 2012b). Another strand of the History of Wargaming Project is creating tools for modern professional gaming—for example, the cyber domain (Curry and Price 2013)—and applying the method of matrix gaming to assist in education about international crises (Curry and Price 2014).

One of the most exciting aspects of the HWP has been the completely unexpected emergence of the hidden treasure or the conclusion to a worldwide, yearlong hunt. Recently, I received the first part of a previously unknown naval wargame from 1913. Imagine my surprise when, only two days before I sat down to write this chapter, a veteran wargamer thrust into my hands a faded typed copy of Tony Bath's *A Wargamer's Guide to Hyboria*, a work long assumed to be lost. Tony Bath was the founding father of ancient wargaming (and the Society of Ancients). He ran an early campaign involving many of the key early wargamers. Although the HWP published a book about Tony Bath's ideas for setting up a wargaming campaign and an outline of the campaign, it was assumed that no copies of Tony Bath's actual guide to the fantasy continent of Hyboria still existed. Suddenly another new book has been added to the History of Wargaming Project.

About the Author

John Curry is the program leader for the BSc in Applied Computing at Bath College, UK. He has an international reputation for his work as the editor of the History of Wargaming Project <www.wargaming.co>. He has edited and written more than sixty books on various aspects of wargaming, including *Peter Perla's Art of Wargaming: A Guide for Hobbyists and Professionals* and *Dark Guest: Training Games for Cyber Warfare*. He has worked with RUSI, the Defense Academy of the United Kingdom and is a researcher for Cranfield University and an analyst for the Wikistrat Consultancy Group.

Notes

1. A good example of this occurred in 2014, when the library at the Royal Military Academy at Sandhurst contacted the History of Wargaming Project to get details of some of the important wargames carried out at Sandhurst and the Staff College in the 1970s.

2. WD involved many of the key early UK wargamers and was a successful forum from which many innovations in wargaming emerged; rules and ideas such as DBA, matrix games, historical committee games (called seminar games in the USA), hidden scenarios and mega-games were first explored at COW or in the journal of WD, *The Nugget*. (The term "nugget" was Paddy Griffith's name for dice.)

3. Fred Jane, the inspired but eccentric founder of Jane's Information Group, had first published *Jane's All the World's Fighting Ships* as a supplement to his naval wargame (Jane 1898), making it the first-ever wargaming rules supplement.

4. Despite his status, Donald Featherstone did not assume that his name would automatically lead to the inclusion of his large number of books.

5. In fact, on several occasions the editor was reprimanded for being slow to contact authors to ask permission to include their work.

3 THE FUNDAMENTAL GAP BETWEEN TABLETOP SIMULATION GAMES AND THE "TRUTH"

Tetsuya Nakamura

Since the days of SPI, many tabletop wargame designers have pursued the goal of more accurate simulation by creating increasingly detailed game systems. For example, movement systems have been sliced into smaller and smaller time units: consider the double impulse system of *France 1940* (1972) and *The Russian Campaign* (1974, 1976), the overrun system of *The Tigers Are Burning* (1988) and other games by Ty Bomba, the friction point system of *Fifth Corps* (1980) and the Central Front series games, the impulse system of *White Death* (1979), and so on. But do such efforts succeed? I think such efforts fail because of a fundamental gap between simulation and "truth." In my experience, many wargamers and game designers believe this gap to be an issue of abstraction and hindsight.

Abstraction creates a gap because of the limit of information capacity. We cannot capture all possible information in a game; for example, we cannot include all soldiers, weapons, food and fuel supplies, fatigue levels, and so on. Therefore, in most games we must simplify and abstract (notably in such ways as including only two steps for unit reduction) to focus on the important information and round off the inconsequentialities.

The hindsight gap arises because the people living through real history did not know the results of their actions, but a player in a tabletop simulation game is aware of these results. For example, the French army believed that tank forces could not pass through the Ardennes Forest, but German Panzer forces did exactly this in 1940. In another instance, the Imperial Japanese Navy was ambushed by the US Navy at Midway in 1942 because they believed there were no US aircraft carriers there. But in a tabletop simulation game, we already know that German Panzer forces can attack through the Ardennes, and that there are hidden US aircraft carriers at Midway, so players will never fall victim to such a surprise attack.

However, even if the abstraction and hindsight issues were to be somehow resolved, would that entirely bridge the gap between a tabletop simulation game and the "truth"? For example, a tactical combat simulation game should be freer from the hindsight issue than a game on a larger scale because of the lesser amount of information known about the small-scale engagements. But this leaves the abstraction issue, and I do not believe that even increasing the level of tactical detail could resolve this entirely. To my way of thinking, even if both the abstraction and hindsight issues were resolved, we would be no nearer the truth.

The Misleading Quality of Labeling

Many wargames pursue the goal of accurate simulation through the labeling of historical elements. A good example of this is the titling of cards in card-driven wargames; these titles are generally drawn from some historical episode, but it is also present in rulebook "chrome." I call this style of design "labeling." The rules presented on a particular card will be understood by players as a specific elaboration of the card title. Similarly, rulebook "chrome" (e.g., divisional integration, artillery support or air power, command and control) is understood as being included in the rules in order to reflect particular historical circumstances. The effect of this is that players will regard such a labeled rule as providing a more accurate simulation of the truth.

But is this so? Sometimes such rules might even break the game. For example, I did not include rules for radar, VT fuses, the Japanese Long Lance torpedo, kamikazes, and other elements in my strategic Pacific War 1941–45 simulation game *Fire in the Sky* (2005), because those rules disrupted the game balance. Those rules could not be included in *Fire in the Sky* because the Japanese would be too powerful too early and the Allies too late than was the case historically. So the *Fire in the Sky* game system works better when there are no such rules attached.

To pick a different sort of example: I have often been criticized about the headquarters unit and activation chit system of my game *A Victory Lost* (2006). In this game, the HQ unit is activated when its chit is drawn from a cup of activation chits. The activated HQ unit may then activate combat units within its command range—so a single division, for example, could be activated several times by different HQs in a single game turn. The critics claim that this does not accurately simulate the historical events, but this is because they are bound by certain common wargame concepts, such as the idea that a particular unit type should be able to act only a predetermined amount during any given time frame.

I think this criticism arises from overconfidence about material factors, as well as the matter of "labeling." In *A Victory Lost*, the HQ unit and the activation chit system are labeled in the way they are merely in order to present a momentum system that encompasses not only command by headquarters, but an integrated network of command, supply status, weather conditions, soldier morale, and other nonmaterial factors and uncertainties, because in this system the chance of a combat unit's activation is also controlled by the total quantity of activation chits for a certain period. Of course, I could have used terms other than "HQ unit" and "activation chits," but it would have been difficult to indicate everything necessary in a single word or two; the difficulty is in presenting an integrated view of the various concepts, not just a matter of a particular term. So I think that no matter how well the labeling is adjusted, it can never assure a correct simulation, and overconfidence in the labeling will still lead to vacuous arguments because it promotes a superficial understanding of the game system without a sufficient understanding of the essence. I believe labeling is not required for an accurate simulation. It is only a player expectation.

Expansion and Contraction of Time and Space

Most wargamers and game designers also take for granted the precise division of time and space as a method of correct simulation. So in most wargames, each game turn equals the same unit of time; similarly, most wargame hexes represent equal quantities of space. But is this the only possible way to design a game?

In my designs I have often adjusted the scale of time and space. For example, in *A Most Dangerous Time* (2009), the distance represented by each space is large on the outskirts of the game map, but smaller at the center. In *Fierce Fight! Stalingrad Blitzkrieg* (2013), the length of time represented by a game turn is short at the beginning of the game but grows longer as the game progresses. This approach is not unique to me: In the Avalon Hill game *Victory in the Pacific* (1977), the length of the 1943 game turn is longer compared to the other turns.

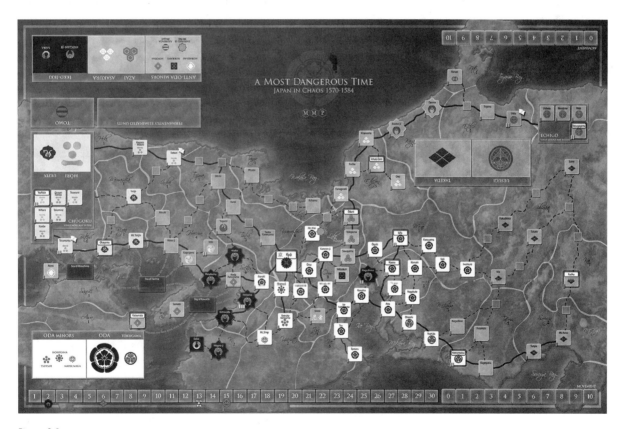

Figure 3.1

A Most Dangerous Time map.

So in a game the time and space frames can be expanded or contracted. Does this decrease its fidelity as a simulation? I don't think so. We construct our understanding of history from the depictions of history we are familiar with. For example, when we read about the battle for Stalingrad, the story probably starts with Operation Blau, and the climax no doubt features the German Sixth Army approaching the city. The early part of a book on Stalingrad will cover a large geographic area and a relatively long historical period in a small number of pages, but the scale will dilate as we read on until, as Stalingrad grows to a close, we are reading about a small geographic area and increasingly small units of time over a great number of pages. Similarly, in a narrative of Napoleon's Hundred Days, the time and map scales are wide at the beginning but focus in slowly as we approach the Battle of Waterloo.

In these cases, the authors will consciously expand or contract time and space because they wish to focus on the battlefields of Stalingrad or Waterloo. If this can be done in an historical narrative, why not in a game? Is the reason because historical writing is not a science but historical simulation design is? But even in the world of science, time and space can expand or contract—actually, the theory of relativity shows that time and space can be transformed by the viewpoint of the observer! If time and space expand and contract even in scientific thinking, why not in a game? I think they can, because correct simulation is always dependent on the player's *image* of the subject being simulated.

Truth Led by Image

I have argued that neither detailed simulation nor accurate simulation always leads to *correct* simulation. I have suggested that the player's *image* is the controlling concept in a board simulation game. Perhaps not a few wargamers have built up their own images about history by reading a chronicle of a war. Consider, for example, Paul Carell's histories or Manstein's *Verlorene Siege* (1983), both of which describe the struggle of German Panzer forces during the last period of World War II. In these sources, we read about quality German Panzer divisions first prevailing but eventually becoming overwhelmed by the quantity of enemy forces. Most wargames on the subject present this image of the situation, but is this the truth?

A historical narrative by Paul Carell is different from the truth of historical fact. But if a certain wargame simulates a Paul Carell narrative, is it not correct to call it a simulation game? If such a game is *not* a simulation game, then all fictional simulation games (such as science fiction simulations, not-impossible future conflicts in East and Southeast Asia or the Middle East, past virtual wars such as NATO vs. the Warsaw Pact, and so on) must be called incorrect simulations, and I reject such a conclusion.

I think such fictional simulation games can be accepted as correct simulations if they are presenting a reasonable *image* of the created world. Putting this in a rather extreme way, I would say that truth in a simulation board game is a product of each individual's image of history. Each individual's image of history is different and subjective; therefore, these various images create various historical truths. It is not impossible that one event is true for one person but false for another.

In my experience of game design, even if the gaps created by abstraction and hindsight could be completely resolved, the one between a simulation game and the truth never can be. This fundamental gap is caused by the subjective nature of each individual's image of history. Any particular game might be a better or worse simulation compared to another game, but neither could be called truer.

About the Author

Tetsuya Nakamura was born in Kyoto, Japan, in 1963, and began playing wargames in 1977 with Avalon Hill's *Tactics II*. He received his master's degree in history in 1990, and since 2001 has been editor in chief of *Game Journal* magazine <www.gamejournal. net>. His game *A Victory Lost* won the 2006 Charles S. Roberts Award for Best World War II Era Board Wargame and the 2006 International Gamers Award in the Historical Simulations category. His *A Most Dangerous Time* won the 2009 Charles S. Roberts Award for Best Ancient to Napoleonic Era Board Wargame. His other games include *Fire in the Sky, Storm over Stalingrad, Storm over Port Arthur, Manstein's Last Battle,* and *What Price Glory?*

4 *FLEET ADMIRAL*: TRACING ONE ELEMENT IN THE EVOLUTION OF A GAME DESIGN

Jack Greene

Scapa Flow's the place for me / When the German fleet is out at sea.

—Traditional

Most of my game designs have involved naval topics.[1] *Fleet Admiral* (FA) (1987) was no exception, being a "monster" game—a monster game is often defined as having two or more maps and is often multiplayer—on tactical naval combat in the 1912–22 period, of which the best historical example is the 1916 battle of Jutland, fought between the British Grand Fleet and the German High Seas Fleet. In 1988, I published an amateur version of some 135 copies of *FA* that quickly sold out and have become expensive collector's items. Some have said it was my best game design.

It was originally designed around the classic Jim Dunnigan formula: count the guns, the weight of the shells, and the rate of fire, and *voilà*, you have a gunfire factor (GF). For example, HMS *Dreadnought* has eight 12-inch guns capable of firing on a broadside. So you take the 850-pound shell, multiply it by eight, and give it a rate of fire of two per round, and you have a raw number of 13,600. The designer would then take an arbitrary number, say 1,000, and divide the raw number to get either 13 or 14 for a broadside GF factor.

Next take the ship's displacement, divide it by an agreed-upon number, and presto, you have Hull Factors. This was a tried-and-true method, but one that suffered from what most game designers, including myself, do too often: rely on too many English-language sources. It is difficult work, but to fully understand naval doctrine of another nation you must work in the language of that nation, as well as our native English.

For the new edition of *FA*, I thought about publishing through Compass Games in 2010, but I was not ready—actually, I had not had the necessary revolution in game design thought. But in 2012, shortly after retiring, I started rereading my library of World War I literature, starting with my longtime favorite, Arthur J. Marder's five volumes of *From the Dreadnought to Scapa Flow* (1961). Marder brilliantly covers the father of the revolutionary HMS *Dreadnought*, First Sea Lord of the Admiralty Admiral John Fisher. The First Lord was the political head of the navy, while the First Sea Lord (Fisher's position until 1910) was the professional head of the navy. Fisher stamped his presence across the period covered by my game.

I also read a great deal of new literature that had appeared since 1988. Much of this new material covered arcane topics such as World War I armaments, as treated in Norman Friedman's *Naval Weapons of World War One* (2011), or long-range fire-control methods for heavy ship artillery, as treated in Jon Sumida's *In Defense of Naval Supremacy* (1993) and John Brooks' *Dreadnought Gunnery and the Battle of Jutland* (2006).[2]

Born from this new understanding, *Jutland: Fleet Admiral II* (*FA II*)—thus its working title—is a more complex game than the original *FA*, but one in which I have focused on many of the smaller actions for play between two people; ultimately, I think the game is of medium complexity. The mammoth battle of Jutland really demands a Game Master or umpire and four to eight players (players familiar with *Dungeons and Dragons* will be familiar with the Game Master concept), but two experienced players familiar with the game and playing over a couple of sessions can refight the Battle of Jutland with its almost two hundred warships. It is also focused on just the German and British navies in this period—much more of a "rifle shot" game design than a shotgun design. In terms of game scenarios, you may play something as small as the battles of Coronel or the Falklands up to Dogger Bank and Jutland. There are additional hypothetical scenarios for major fleet actions built around the German bombardment of Yarmouth or Scarborough in 1914–15.

Naval wargames, like army tank games, often utilize rote comparisons from *Jane's Fighting Ships* or the like. They don't "look behind the curtain." For example, in the Avalanche Games' series *Great War At Sea*, the Russian *Borodino* and the Japanese *Mikasa* are both "3" for their main 12-inch armament. A great deal of this arises from the fallacy of "rate of fire + weight of shell = GF." But this is too simplistic. We have to look at range finding, crew and gun quality, and technology in general. Let me illustrate my improved understanding of this period of naval history by examining the evolution of my GFs and gunnery rules.

Admiral Reinhold Scheer commanded the German High Seas Fleet at the time of Jutland. His opposite was Sir John Jellicoe. By reading *The Jellicoe Papers* (1966), I could review Admiral Jellicoe's Grand Fleet Battle Orders for the distance between warships and the ranges for guns to open fire. These are basic concepts that a game designer must translate onto the game board.

In 1914, Admiral Troubridge, during his Court of Inquiry after the escape of the German battlecruiser *Goeben* in the Mediterranean in August 1914, commented that his Flag Captain, Fawcet Wray, a gunnery expert, told him that German "shooting is a great deal better with those Krupp guns than we can by any possibility shoot with our guns." Troubridge went on to say that German "gunnery is as good as ours, and his guns, I think, are certainly better" (Lumbry 1970, 154–65). It turns out that in 1914, the extreme ranges fired at during the Battle of Dogger Bank in January 1915 or at Jutland in May 1916 were simply not planned for. I accordingly modified the speeds and gun ranges on both sides for *FA II* and also modified data to reflect that ships were partly reconstructed in the 1914–16 period in order to fire at longer ranges. (Additionally, the British had poor shells that were not corrected until after the Battle of Jutland.) My roster sheets *on the individual battles*—a roster sheet is a listing of the warships involved in a particular scenario and their characteristics—now reflect all those changes. For example, the German battleship *König* fires at Jutland at a greater range than it does in 1914 due to improvements made over the winter.

In a letter to the First Lord of the Admiralty Reginald McKenna on August 22, 1910 (four years before the outbreak of World War One), Admiral Fisher wrote, "The [battlecruiser] *Lion* [is] as superior to the *Dreadnought* as the *Dreadnought* to all before her, and your coming 'Motor Battleship' (Queen Elizabeth class) as superior to the *Lion* as the *Lion* to the *Dreadnought*!" (Marder 1956, 337). Fisher's point was that the *Dreadnought* could bring to bear on a broadside eight 12-inch rifles, each firing a shell that was about 850 pounds, this compared to the four on the older 18-knot pre-dreadnought *Mikasa, Connecticut,* or *Borodino*. Plus, in Fisher's fevered vision, the extra speed of the *Dreadnought*, three knots, gave it a tactical advantage over the older pre-dreadnought designs—the *Dreadnought* could choose the range. It also meant a shortening of the length of the battle line: meter for meter the length of the line, with an equal number of long-range primary guns, was shorter by a ratio of almost 2:1.

The *Lion* could also bring eight guns on a broadside. But these were 13.5-inch guns firing a 1,250-pound shell (later guns of the same caliber had 1,400-pound shells); plus it could almost touch 28 knots for speed. This rapid change in ship design meant that ships became obsolete quickly. That is why the *Dreadnought*, the ship that initiated the "Dreadnought Revolution," was detached to a secondary role on the eve of Jutland, as it was really too old to fight in the battle line. Even in *FA II*'s 1914–15 scenarios, she is clearly no longer a dominating warship.

The key to this revolutionary change in naval combat was range-finding and long range firing. The "Director" is a traditional fire-control device (or devices) that had evolved rapidly in the hothouse of naval technology on the eve of World War I, allowing for accurate long-range firing. Ranges for battle could now be fought at over 20,000 yards. I included the most advanced Director in the game, and this really sets apart the British and German navies from most others. Those two nations were constantly improving their ability to fire accurately at long range from 1905 to 1916. "Exposed in his top or other position, the range-taker has a clearer view of the battle than any other man" (Baudry 1914, 27). This position was often in an armored position on the main ship's mast or above the ship's bridge. All navies carried range-finding equipment, but there were four to five levels of sophistication (and cost!) to range finding, with each level progressively superior. A new improved level could not simply be mass produced and retrofitted onto older warships, in part due to the increasing use of electrical equipment—somewhat analogous to working in an older building and wanting to use the latest electrical equipment, but not being able to because the building would require upgrading throughout. Typically, the limited amount of the latest equipment was put on the newest warships; this increased the power of a newer battleship over an older and less advanced one. So: counting guns, weight of shells fired and rates-of-fire, as we have done in the past, is simply inadequate.

The German range-finding system and equipment (used in an embryonic and earlier form by the Italian, Austrian, and US navies) was superior to the British system. The main German system was apparently installed in 1913 and updated as the war progressed. Essentially, the Germans could use their range-finders at 20,000 yards, and the British were good starting at 16,000 yards. An exception was the new British 15-inch-gunned battleships, which had improved British rangefinders. (As an aside, German range-finders were better if the target was difficult to see: The North Sea has a lot of days of poor visibility; smoke also impaired visibility, and fleet actions were coal smoke environments.)

Gunnery practice of the day held that once the range was found and the target was being straddled (i.e., the fall of shot was on both sides of the target), one went to rapid fire. Georg von Hase, on board the *Derfflinger*, later wrote:

> Now I had found the target ... the transmitting station was to give the order 'Salvoes-fire!' to the heavy guns once every 20 seconds ... While the firing was going on any observation was out of the question ... Naturally such furious rapid fire could only be maintained for a limited time ... It was not long before our salvoes fell over or short, as a result of the enemy altering course ... Each salvo was then directed afresh and this continued until the target was again straddled. And then the devil's concert began again on the order "Good, Rapid." (von Hase 1921, 148–49)

To reduce the amount of die rolling, I have incorporated all of this into the gunnery table to make it move more smoothly. This means that the player does not play the role the gunnery officer and need to determine range, rate of movement, etc.; it is simply worked into the gunnery table.

Here is an example of the GF modification process. The British 12-inch guns were not as good in construction technique as the 13.5-inch gun, and that is factored in. Admiral Bacon wrote of the 12-inch gun when he was Director of Naval Ordnance: "But what was in reality serious was that on its trials the gun proved to be inaccurate in its shooting" (Bacon 1940, 162). I could then discover in my sources when and what fire-control methods were on board; for example, the British 12-inch battlecruisers used an older system. Officers on the light cruiser *Southampton*, which operated with the British battlecruiser fleet, in May 1916 "collectively and separately came to the conclusion that the Battle Cruisers' shooting was rotten" (Gordon 1996, 46). The *Invincible*, again

as an example, had the fire-control Director on board but not installed at the 1914 Battle of the Falklands. These factors were easy to incorporate. It was not as easy to discover when other changes were made after the Falklands and before Jutland. Then, when I discovered a nugget, such as the fact that the Warrior class of armored cruisers was one of the most stable of gun platforms, I increased its GF. I try to note these "discoveries" in my designer's notes so that future players with greater knowledge can go in and retrofit my games and thus improve them.

Another factor was that the spread of a British salvo was greater with their 9.2-inch and 12-inch guns than with the 13.5, while their 15-inch guns at 12,000 yards had the least, a 200-yard spread. After the battle of Jutland, the Germans commented on the tight spreads of the 15-inch-gunned battleships. And in a letter to Jellicoe after Dogger Bank, Beatty stated that "in two places (on the *Lion*) we received very heavy bangs displacing armoured plates about 1 ft. below the water line—not losing them. I think they were caused in each case by 2 12-inch projectiles from *Derfflinger* who continually landed 2 projectiles practically in the same spot at the same time" (Patterson 1966, 131).

That is why the gunnery Combat Results Table (CRT; table 4.1) is arranged in part the way it is: When you hit, you went to rapid fire, and several hits might occur before you lost the range. No one would stay in this sweet spot for a very long time; hence, I eliminated the "acquired targets" used in a competitor's game as a needless extra step. You should *assume* a trained crew does what it is supposed to do. The CRT takes that into consideration—it is integrated into it. Also, "hits" on the Gunnery Table do not necessarily represent individual gunnery hits; they may represent several, especially for secondary armaments.

Table 4.1

Hit Table: A prototype table for determining if a Critical Hit translates into the catastrophic loss of a warship due to poor handling of ammunition

Dice Roll	1914–15	Post DB
2	G	-
3	G	BC
4	B	B
5	B	B
6	-	-
7	-	-
8		
9		G
10		B
11	G B	
12	G	B

Post DB, Post Battle of Dogger Bank; G, Germany; B, British; BC, British Battle Cruisers.

Additionally, when the German capital ships found the range, they fired on average three shells to the British two. This is why after Dogger Bank, the British battlecruisers and some battleships increased the number of shells present in the turrets and hoists so to increase the speed of loading. (This would lead to disaster for two of the battlecruisers at Jutland when unstable ammunition combined with excess "ready" ammunition stored in or near the turrets led to catastrophe.)

In both navies the pre-dreadnoughts and armored cruisers (with the exception of the armored cruiser SMS *Blücher*) lacked modern fire-control equipment, and therefore their effective gun range was substantially shorter. So the German battlecruiser *Moltke* or *Goeben* might be able to fire effectively at 14,000 yards, while the British armored cruiser *Defense* might be ineffective when firing at ranges greater than 8,000 yards because of gun and equipment limitations. Incorporating such information into the game format seamlessly is the challenge to a game designer; you do not want to encumber the game player with needless time-consuming (and mind-numbing) "bookwork."

Secondary guns were not that important against enemy capital ships, although the idea of "a hail of fire" persisted. The issue was that it had to be a hail of *large* shells. The German armor cruisers at the Battle of the Falklands scored numerous hits, but they had little impact. Especially in the battlecruiser action at Jutland, there were a fair number of German 5.9-inch hits and both sides were peppered from the small destroyer guns but this had virtually no impact on the battlecruisers or battleships.

Note that German pre-dreadnoughts had numerous 6.7-inch guns, but this was unique to them. Older battleships and all the German dreadnoughts carried 5.9-inch guns for their secondary batteries. The 6.7-inch was used to disable larger enemy destroyers, but their weight restricted the number of guns and the ammunition they could carry. Instead of some convoluted rule for this, I simply modified the Gunnery Damage Table to give a slight benefit due to the heavier weight of shell (Nottelman 2014, 43–91).

While according to Campbell, only one British shell penetrated the major armor plating of a German battleship—a 15-inch shell from the *Revenge*—failure to penetrate the heaviest armor did not translate into unsinkable. Any capital ship that was hit by twenty heavy caliber rounds was essentially out of the action, if not sunk. Slow leaks throughout, fires, loss of life, and loss of speed all added up. Do note that at closer ranges the smaller and less powerful guns would have certainly played a larger role.

There were also issues relating to poor powder and the poor handling of powder. So for example, after Dogger Bank the Germans fixed a lot of their problems; the *Lion* did as well but *did not communicate* some of those handling issues to the rest of the battlecruiser force. As a result, because the Germans clearly fired more rapidly than the British, the British battlecruisers moved more ammunition up from the magazines to the hoists and turrets, resulting in more dangerous conditions in the event of a hit. *Fleet Admiral II* reflects this situation. On the CRT you will

also find German ships losing an odd or random MF from time to time; this is due to their retention until after Jutland of their torpedo netting, the booms that are deployed at anchor. When damaged they could become entangling objects. The British eliminated them much earlier.

The gun factors reflected in *FA II* are largely guided by what people actually did. Instead of just taking rate of fire, number of guns, and weight of shell, I have assigned a modified numeric value. That is the GF. My goal as a game designer is to present the player with an accurate assessment of the issues Admirals Jellicoe and Scheer had to face—and make it a fun and playable *game*.

About the Author

Jack Greene is a graduate of Whitman College, with a bachelor's degree in history. A native of California, he has written on a wide range of naval, military, and wargaming subjects for more than a dozen magazines, including *Warship International*, *The Mariner's Mirror*, *Strategy & Tactics*, and *Command*. He has worked with Avalon Hill and Battleline Publications, was a partner in Paper Wars, and founded Quarterdeck Games. He

has designed twelve wargames. His game design *Ironbottom Sound* won a Charles Roberts award in 1982. He and Alessandro Massignani have coauthored five books. A 1990 inductee into the Charles S. Roberts Hall of Fame, he also speaks on military, political, and environmental topics at conventions and local service clubs and on local radio, including a longrunning Fourth of July radio program.

Notes

1. The lyrics to the epigraph are also rendered as: "Scapa Flow's the place for me / When you're chased by a T.B.D." A T.B.D. is a Torpedo Boat Destroyer, what we call today a destroyer. The German Navy had a very competent destroyer arm.

2. Brooks's book is a good addition to the literature, and he has a strong computer background that is useful. Part of the reason for his writing the book was to refute Jon Sumida in his brilliant *In Defense of Naval Supremacy* (1993). Both books, however, have much value.

5   THE WILD BLUE YONDER: REPRESENTING AIR WARFARE IN GAMES

Lee Brimmicombe-Wood

Air warfare games are a hardware-centered niche as characteristic as naval games, and they present the designer with unique challenges. Wargames set in the age of airpower commonly feature air as a supporting element of the surface campaign. However, there is also a genre of games that focus on air battles, separate from the context of the surface war. These modes are reminiscent of the historical tensions between airmen who believed in independent air power and those generals and admirals who sought to integrate aviation into their plans of campaign.

Airmindedness

Historically, the control of military aviation has fluctuated between those who see air power as subordinate to the surface forces and those who regard it as a means of winning wars on its own, by bombarding enemies into submission. The latter view, proselytized by "air prophets" such as Billy Mitchell and Lord Trenchard, underpinned the strategic bombing campaigns of World War II.

Strategic bombing has failed to win any war independently of surface action (Pape 1996). However, the concept of "airmindedness" survives, as articulated in the United States Air Force Basic Doctrine, which states that the airman has a perspective that the surface-bound warrior lacks. Inspired by this peculiar chauvinism, advocates of independent air power continue to churn out manifestos, such as doctrines for Global Precision Attack (USAF 2011).

Wargames reflect these perspectives on aviation, presenting it either as an adjunct to the surface war or a stand-alone subject, largely stripped of the surface context.

Air-Sea-Land

From the perspective of armies and navies, the function of air power is to support their operations. The tasks air can perform are numerous, but they include:

- Reconnaissance and surveillance
- Bombardment
- Support of surface forces
- Interdiction of surface movement
- Operations against enemy air power
- Airlift

Games focused on war in the age of airpower rarely ignore aviation; however, its treatment varies widely.

In wargames set at the tactical level, such as *Advanced Squad Leader*, air manifests as Close Air Support (CAS) and is commonly depicted as a form of artillery. Historically, CAS's unique characteristic has been its ability to throw greater explosive weight than field artillery and keep enemy troops suppressed for longer (Gooderson 1998). The mere presence of aircraft can keep heads down, and in modern counterinsurgency this is manifest in the use of flybys, or "shows of force." Some tactical rules, such as *Force on Force*, include such demonstrations as a nonlethal alternative to bombing.

The tactical land game illustrates the design problems in dovetailing air to the surface medium—events in the air happen at a vastly different scale. A jet fighter that requires miles to turn a circle cannot fit on a map made for rifle engagements. Decisions made in the air take place in seconds, whereas those on the ground may happen over several minutes. The physical and time scales are so disparate that it is pointless to represent air unit movement on a land game's tactical map.

In a naval tactical game, physical space is less problematic since ships may be thousands of yards apart. It is possible to depict aircraft threading paths between the threat rings of warships. However, the relative speeds for planes are still so fast that they will appear and be gone before the ships move any significant distance.

Aircraft that can loiter might reappear from game turn to game turn as a threat. Those with a limited weapon load will disappear after they have made their strike on a target. Either way, the appearance of air at the tactical level is usually brief and nonpersistent.

Air functions such as reconnaissance and counterair rarely show at the tactical level. These are usually dealt with at larger scales, and it is to surface operations at the battalion/army or fleet level that we now turn.

The operational-scale *Modern Battles: Four Contemporary Conflicts* (1975) shows one of the most basic approaches to aviation. Air is abstracted as "ground support points," a resource applied to critical areas of the front line to increase firepower there.

In games where aviation is treated as support, there is no flying as such. The third dimension is abbreviated to the ability to project firepower at the enemy front line or beyond. Such a treatment aggregates air forces and may not consider any differentiation between aircraft, performance or missions. This bundling into large air groups means that aviation support is doled out in a less granular manner than was historically the case.

However, operational games can distinguish between aircraft roles. The theater-level title *Group of Soviet Forces Germany* (2003) differentiates between tactical support for armies and deep strikes against distant targets. It allows for the application of strategic bombers and specialist forces for suppressing enemy air defenses.

The division-level operations of *Air & Armor* (1986) go a step further by distinguishing between aircraft types, to show the impact of different systems on the battle. The ultimate expression of this trend is *Tac Air* (1987), which gives the player command not only of ground forces, but also of air defense artillery (ADA), around whose threat rings aircraft must weave. However, ADA falls out of view in almost all games and is abstracted into the defense capabilities of large surface formations.

At operational scales the weather, which can help or hinder aviation, must be considered. Games on the Battle of the Bulge often depict those periods of the campaign in which aircraft were grounded by snow and overcast.

At the strategic level, theater-level or greater, airpower can become completely abstract. *Hitler's War* (1981) condensed aviation into a decision about investment in strategic bombing and damage to enemy production. At this level, air forces are little more than an expression of bomb lift capacity. Sight of weapon systems is entirely lost.

Unlike land warfare games, naval campaigns push air power closer to center stage. Games on the Pacific War mainly revolve around decisions to base on land or aboard carriers, finding enemy forces and then striking them from the air. In the Pacific, the use of generic "air points" looks inappropriate because of the profound differences between air systems, particularly with regard to payload and range. As a consequence many games distinguish between aircraft capabilities, with *Pacific War* (1984) assigning half a dozen attributes to its air units.

To sum up: Looking at the tactical, operational and strategic scales, airpower sits as an extra game process on top of the armature of the surface war mechanics. It has a significant effect and is present because it features in the historical narrative, but—with the possible exception of naval campaigns—it is not the focus of play. Games may well "abstract out" aviation systems while at the same time detailing surface weapon systems such as tank or ship types. It is in the nature of such games to be anything but "airminded."

Independent Air Power

Having looked at games that depict air power as a supporting partner, we turn to titles reflecting air's independent role. To a large extent these games elide the surface campaign so as to foreground aviation. A major feature of the air game is the depiction of aircraft systems; the designer rarely abstracts aircraft away, but frames them as stars of the show.

The best example of this is the genre of dogfight games, which depict battles between fighters and bombers. This is the air game in its purest form, focused on aircraft in their own medium. The surface battle rarely impinges, except through anti-aircraft fire. The dogfight game is air combat at an atomic level, with each unit a single aircraft brawling across a small volume of airspace.

The dogfight game immediately presents challenges. The first is that the battle is three-dimensional. Games take place on flat tables and altitude presents problems with physical representation. Commonly, models or counters are assigned a numerical altitude, a Z-value in a system of Cartesian coordinates. Players have to imagine how high an aircraft is.

Visually this is unsatisfying, so designers have sought other methods to incorporate the third

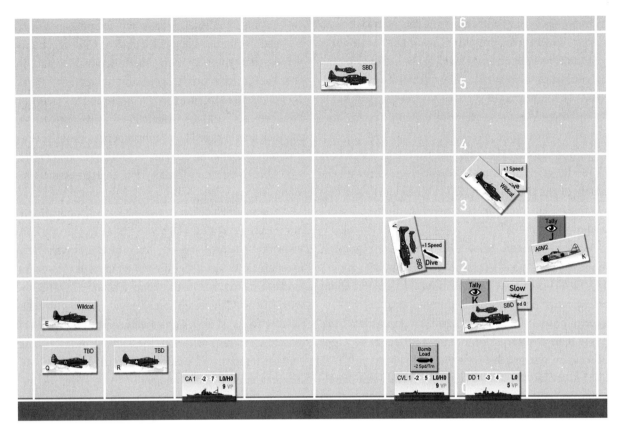

Figure 5.1
The *Wing Leader* system depicts air battles from the side. This snapshot illustrates how dive bombing can be represented.

dimension. Miniatures games use complicated systems of stands to hold aircraft models above the table. Another method is to view the battle from the side. In Mike Spike's miniatures rules, the two-dimensional battle has height and length but no breadth, losing one dimension but showcasing the all-important altitude (Spick 1978).

In addition to altitude, the orientation of aircraft is important, as they fly only in the direction they are pointed. The "Fighting Wings" series of games, such as *Whistling Death* (2003), model pitch by a twelve-point system and roll on a six-point scale. The *Birds of Prey* (2008) system uses plastic wedges

to tilt box-shaped aircraft models to the correct angles.

If this seems complex, it is nothing compared to the challenge of representing aircraft performance. Flight is dynamic, and maneuvering is the product of many factors, such as power, weight, and wing area. Performance profoundly affects scaling. In World War I, the fastest "Stringbag" fighter could fly little more than 130 miles per hour and climb hundreds of feet in a minute. In the modern era, jets dash tens of miles in a minute and climb tens of thousands of feet.

These amazing increases in performance take place at the same time as fundamentals such as pilot vision stay constant. Before the advent of radar, air combat was reliant on eyeballing foes. A fighter pilot might spot another fighter at five miles, but this is a tiny distance at high speed. The difference between closure rates of 300 feet per second in the "Stringbag" era and 3,000 feet per second in the supersonic age is profound. The time to react to an enemy drops dramatically. Sheer speed means that decisions and actions in a dogfight are resolved in mere moments.

It is no surprise, then, that scales for dogfight games trend toward large physical spaces and short timescales (indeed, timescales far shorter than it takes to execute a move in a game). The jet-era title *Air War* (1977) has a highly granular scale, with 200 meter hexes and turns just 2.5 seconds long. The jet game *Air Superiority* (1987) boasts 1/3-mile hexes and 12–15 second turns. The rationale in the latter case, born of designer J. D. Webster's own experience of fast jet operation, was that it was more reflective of pilot decision-action cycles.

Distance scales are linked not only to speed but also weapon systems. Until the 1950s, all combat took place as far as an aircraft's guns could accurately reach—maybe a few hundred yards. But the introduction of the air-to-air missile extended the reach of a fighter to miles, then tens of miles, thanks to radar and infrared guidance. Air games in the modern era must model engagements beyond visual range in air volumes a hundred miles across.

Another challenge for the designer is that motion in flight is continuous. The land-based wargame has a lot of stretch in its timescale because fights ebb and flow, with periods of relative quiet. Air fights may also have quieter phases, but aircraft continue to move. Time scaling in tactical air games is less flexible than that of surface games.

A major weakness of the dogfight genre is the representation of situational awareness, of knowing where the enemy is. Throughout history, the majority of pilots shot down were unaware of the airplane attacking them, either because they had not seen their attacker or because they were focused on another enemy. High speeds exacerbate the problem of awareness, since aircraft can fly in and out of visual range so swiftly. Veterans speak of dogfights that end abruptly, each pilot finding himself in an apparently empty sky. High speeds result in brittle formations that easily lose track of enemies and break apart.

This dynamic is difficult to re-create in tabletop games because of the god's-eye view afforded the players. Wargamers can reposition their aircraft to continue a fight against an enemy out of visual range. Efforts to get around this problem, such as double-blind games, are process-heavy and clumsy. As a result, many dogfight games fail to reproduce the way in which fights disperse formations, and rarely re-create the effect of being shot down by an unseen foe.

Problems with situational awareness are exacerbated at night. Engagements in the dark are often solitary cat-and-mouse hunts by individual aircraft, with radar sensors chasing unescorted bombers. This is an undergamed genre, although *Nightfighter* (2011) fills the gap.

The dogfight game focuses on individual aircraft. To represent large air raids a different scale is required. The raid-scale game is a genre that aggregates individual aircraft into formations.

The raid game eschews the dogfight to depict the progress of a raid through enemy airspace to its target and back again. It represents the collision between air raids and an integrated air defense system of sensors, command posts, interceptors, and surface-based anti-aircraft weapons. One of the earliest raid games was Avalon Hill's *Luftwaffe* (1971), which illustrates the asymmetry between the raider and defense. The task of one player is to force his formations through to a target while the opponent must assemble forces to harry the raiders before reaching their goal.

The scale of the raid game allows the player to wear multiple "hats." He can be the formation leader as well as the raid planner. The distances he flies over are tens or hundreds of miles, while timescales for game turns are between a minute and thirty minutes.

An advantage of the raid scale game is that it shows how different aircraft systems integrate together. In *Downtown* (2004), bombers raiding North Vietnam are accompanied by not only escorting fighters but also specialist platforms dedicated to suppressing ground defenses and jamming radar. Their opponents must arrange a layered defense of aircraft, guns, and missiles, but in such a fashion that their fighters do not get in the way of the ground defenses.

These games also feature a degree of fog of war. In *Downtown*, the exact position of missile defenses is unknown to the raiding player until missile sites start shooting. Such rules reveal another feature of air power: its ability to deceive an opponent as to the target and prevent him from massing his defenses there.

Though skies are often thought of as empty spaces, the raid game is not without terrain. Raids must be launched from bases on the ground or at sea. Enemy surface defenses may form "threat rings" that it is wise to fly around, unless the ring must be penetrated to launch an attack. And then there is the ever-shifting weather, which can limit or hinder a raid.

Unlike the dogfight game, the raid game is tied to the surface conflict. The context for a raid is a single air raid, striking or performing reconnaissance in pursuit of some higher objective. The process of selecting targets and tasking aircraft is often above the level of command in the game. To select targets you must expand the scale to operational or strategic level, where it becomes harder to divorce air action from the surface war.

As already seen, air complements the surface campaign. However, an air game with any degree of target selection or tasking would subordinate aviation to the demands of the surface war commanders.

There is an interesting wrinkle when it comes to naval operations, since aviation is intimately tied to surface ship operation and is difficult if not impossible to separate. Games such as *Carrier* (1990) are truly "joint" in that the focus is on both air and naval. The player wears hats for both admiral and carrier air group commander.

At the operational air battle scale, the focus is on matters other than raids. Operations are about:

- Building and maintaining bases
- Deploying air units to bases
- Generating air sorties
- Targeting enemy centers to be attacked
- Tasking sorties to targets

At first blush, this looks more like an exercise in resource management than in battle. Raid execution is the product, not the focus, of operations and therefore below the scope of such a game.

Because of this bean-counting aspect, the purely operational air game is a difficult sell. Furthermore, few topics lend themselves to such a treatment. It is no surprise that the handful of operational air games tend to focus on campaigns such as the Battle of Britain and Combined Bomber Offensive that were fought independently of the surface war. Furthermore, when looking at these titles—games such as *Battle Over Britain* (1983) and *RAF* (1986)—we see that they do not focus purely on operations, but mix operations with raid execution. The designers felt it necessary to hybridize the scales to sustain player interest.

Understandably, designers are nervous of the interface between air and surface operations. Creating a game that foregrounds air operations while forcing the surface war to the background risks the danger of the tail wagging the dog. We are brought full circle back to those games in which aviation supports the generals' and admirals' campaigns but does not lead them.

So is there a balance to be sought between depicting the surface war and modeling air power to a high level of fidelity? Games such as the Operational Combat Series—for example, *DAK* (1997) and *The Next War* (1978)—have gone some way down this road by depicting different aircraft systems. However, even these balk at the amount of process needed to manage detailed air operations at a theater level. The resulting game would be something of an unmanageable monster to play.

The challenge of designing an operational air game shows how hard it is to divorce the air component from the surface war. Airmindedness in gaming is to elevate a supporting arm to the center stage, at the risk of undermining the rationale for its own existence. One must conclude that, outside of the narrow confines of the dogfight and raid genres, air can only be treated as complementary to the focus of the action.

About the Author

Lee Brimmicombe-Wood is a British illustrator, game designer, and author. He is a longtime veteran of the software games industry with more than a dozen shipped titles to his credit, including *Far Cry 3* and *Killzone: Mercenary*. He also designs board wargames, primarily on air warfare topics, including *Downtown: The Air War Over Hanoi*, *The Burning Blue*, and *Bomber Command*. He lives in Ely, Cambridgeshire, with his wife and son.

6 HISTORICAL AESTHETICS IN MAPMAKING

Mark Mahaffey

I suppose it is no strange story to say I fall for wargames for their maps. Poring over Charlie Kibler's for *Stonewall Jackson's Way* (1992) for the first time, the imagination clicks open. The mind engages in a new way—suddenly present, there, within a place and time. This is the ineffable quality of the great wargame map, and it is what keeps me involved with the hobby to this day, twenty years after that experience.

That elevation into a clarified aesthetic of place and time is something a paper wargame can do as well as or better than any other medium. And it does all start with the map—the nascent blankness of Francis Tresham's *Civilization* (1982), the labyrinthine mountains landscaping Mark Herman's *Peloponnesian War* (1991), the veins of color over *Age of Renaissance* (1996), promising riches.

Great maps do not merely communicate data but also speak to our humanity, inviting introspection, empathy, and curiosity. In our day of computer-generated lines and geographically perfect maps, we attempt to control nature, to take the organic and confine it further into a narrow algorithm. As maps continue to favor scientific precision over their representational (even didactic) historical forms, the aesthetic possibilities suffer. The ability of the map to immerse, engage, and transport us is often limited. The modern mapmaker is in danger of becoming a mere technician—not even a craftsman, and certainly not an artist.

Yet, given the non-navigational nature of the wargame map, it can readily indulge these aesthetic considerations without sacrificing technical precision within its purpose. While maps are by essence abstractions, how that abstraction is applied to a given historical situation can have great effect on the experience of gameplay and the perception of the game's topic.

We will look at three cases of increasing complexity: applying that simple abstraction to the aesthetic itself, abstracting a particular mental perception of the world into the aesthetic of a map, and abstracting photographic reality to the needs of a wargame's aesthetic as faithfully as possible—and gaining the best of both worlds in the process.

Abstracted Aesthetic: A Simple Portrayal of Sengoku Japan

To fully decipher [the Bunkei-zu maps], the reader must have a background in the principles of Asian ink painting and calligraphy. This background allows a symbolic understanding of the form that can be as effective as one based on Western science, precise measurement, and geographical verisimilitude.

—Joseph Loh

The years surrounding the battle of Sekigahara in October 1600 were seminal moments in Japanese history, ending the Sengoku period and solidifying the last shogunate for Tokugawa. Matt Calkins's

game design on the campaign, *Sekigahara* (2011), used innovative and simple mechanics to address the situation. The map needed to take a similar route, representing the island of Honshu in good Asian minimalist tradition while avoiding orientalism. And so the goal here was an impression, with only the most basic attention paid to precise geography.

As a starting point, I created the first draft map with only three elements: a muted background painting of the island (without even blue tone for the surrounding water), a simple chesslike grid of the

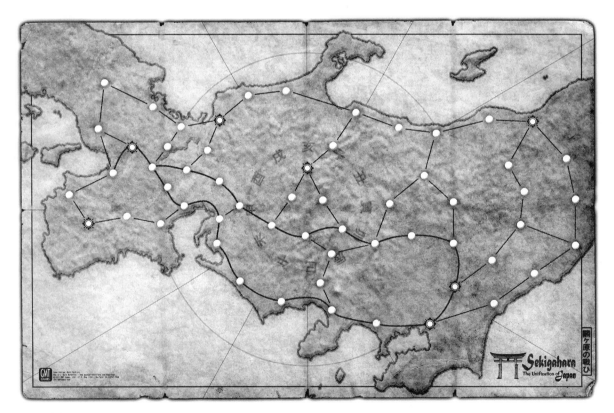

Figure 6.1
An early version of the undermap for *Sekigahara*.

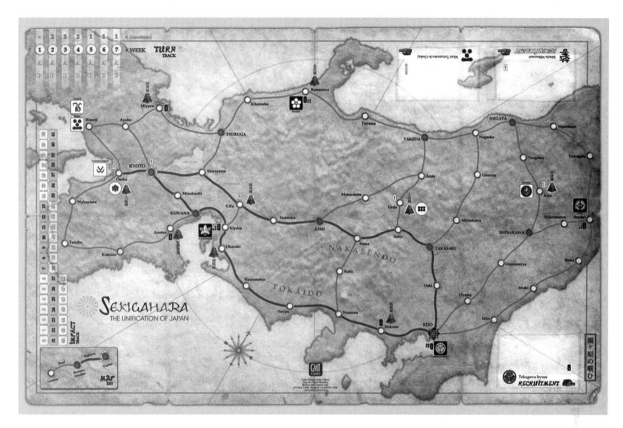

Figure 6.2
The published game board for *Sekigahara*.

connected gameplay points (lacking even names for the locations), and a construct of the twelve-point Japanese compass.

The twelve Earthly Branches are an important Eastern convention that here relate directionality to time (and mean that the four cardinal directions are further broken down into thirds rather than halves). Like maps that invert north and south or land and water in order to confront us, this compass gives the Western mind pause, presenting at a different convention in order to convey how abstract our own conventions are.

While historical and practical gameplay considerations do add labels and other material to the published map, the core aesthetic remains, and helps immerse the player in that place and time. And once the game is learned, play could even take place on the full abstraction of the earlier draft.

Abstracted Geography: A Philippine Perception of the Elizabethan World

Although the supply list for Martin Frobisher's first quest of the Northwest Passage in 1576 shows that a copy of the 1569 Mercator map was purchased for one pound, six shillings, and sixpence, most navigators ignored Mercator for nearly a century. Then they understood, as have mariners ever since.

—John Noble Wilford

As much of the world is purported to shrink, with barriers falling the globe over, the popular conception of maps remains rather myopic. Our embedded, once-young lust for navigationally perfect maps has largely been satiated, but Mercator still defines our modern conception of what a map should be, some four hundred and fifty years later. The world landscape in our minds' eyes remains constructed to sail the Atlantic along rhumb lines, a task we rarely find before us. Yet, presenting even slight deviations of perception in maps can cause surprising angst in the hobby.

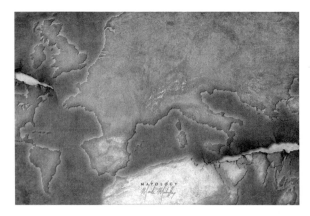

Figure 6.3
The undermap cartogram for *Virgin Queen*.

Ed Beach was working on a sequel to his earlier *Here I Stand* (2006), entitled *Virgin Queen: Wars of Religion 1559-1598* (2012). Elizabeth's reign of course included many of the great events of the late Renaissance: everything from the full politicization of the Reformation in the French wars of religion and the Dutch Revolt, up to Lepanto and the end of Ottoman dominance (Spanish, too, with the sinking of the Armada)—and add to this the continued settlement of the New World and the expansion of Western trade empires into the edges of the earth. With such a broad and eventful period of history to cover, the game has many centers of action and needs to portray many different geographical areas with differing degrees of detail.

Beach's original playtesting map was a simple modification of *Here I Stand*, using three insets to add action in the New World, the Netherlands, and Indian/Pacific oceans. However, in *Here I Stand*, the little Netherlands warranted a mere four gameplay spaces, whereas in *Virgin Queen* that count rises to a full twenty-one spaces to encompass the magnitude of the Dutch Revolt and Reformation.

What we needed was a map that would greatly enlarge the Netherlands' surface area to better reflect the relative importance of the areas during the period, while including the Indian and Pacific as far out as Australia. I quickly suggested we employ a cartogram to let gameplay flow between different geographical scales in a single contiguous map. The resulting contortion is what Beach aptly described as "the world inside Philip II's head."

This shape is indeed abstracting out how Philip II may have perceived the world: what

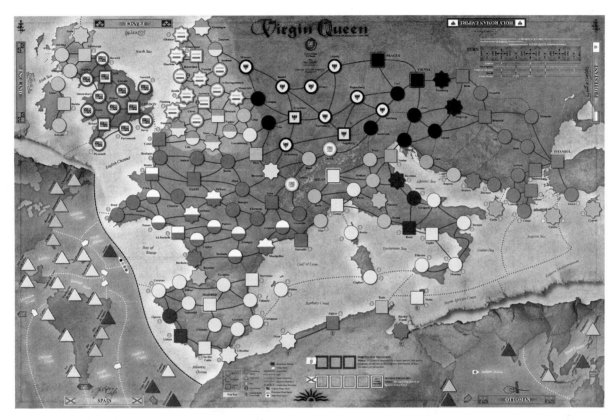

Figure 6.4
The published game board for *Virgin Queen*.

was important, what was connected, and to what degree. The map makes a historical interpretation—the illusion of a state of mind—rather than presenting the world as we have come to expect to see it.

Here again, the final gameplay elements added to the map to create the gameboard increase complexity, but the core aesthetic of the map still cannot help but to challenge the viewer and make them see the world a bit differently.

Abstracted Accuracy: A Realistic Arcadian Normandy

The poetic tradition of la douce France—"sweet France"—describes a geography as much as a history, the sweetness of a classically well-ordered place where rivers, cultivated fields, orchards, vineyards, and woods are all in harmonious balance with each other.

—Simon Schama

The great tragedy of war is all the more stark when played out against a pastoral landscape, and it doesn't get much more pastoral than the lovely farmlands of Normandy. Those ordered orchards and hedgerows define the French countryside and have remained little changed in this part of the country ever since the war—and probably long before. And so here, strangely, the very precision of the geography is the heart of its aesthetic.

Luckily, in addressing the map for Mark Mokszycki's *Operation Dauntless* (2015), a rare situation existed: the availability of actual photography of the battlefield from the time of the battle. Of course, the vast majority of warfare in human history occurred before aerial photography, and much since remains classified or difficult to access. But the RAF flew reconnaissance missions over vast swaths of Normandy, and the Royal Archives in Scotland held imagery of the entire area the map was to cover, which we were able to assemble into a complete picture.

This presented in its purest form the perennial conflict of abstracting reality into a wargame map. We could play on what amounted to a precise satellite image, down to individual trees and shell holes over the ground. Miniature wargamers sometimes use such complex terrain, but in a board game, applying this precision indiscriminately would serve more to confuse gameplay than to enhance it, given that the hex grid demanded that each of the rather large hexes in the game reflect a single type of terrain. The challenge then was to combine a detailed aesthetic of the battlefield that took advantage of the remarkable source imagery available, while maintaining a useful rendition of playable hexes for the game itself.

Once more, this evolved into an exercise in relative scale. Gameplay-critical elements (rivers, roads,

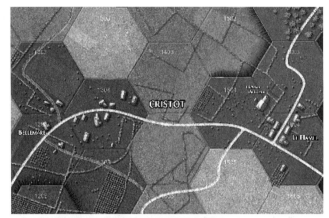
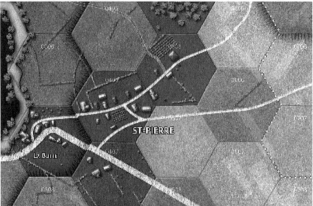

Figure 6.5
Three details from *Operation Dauntless*.

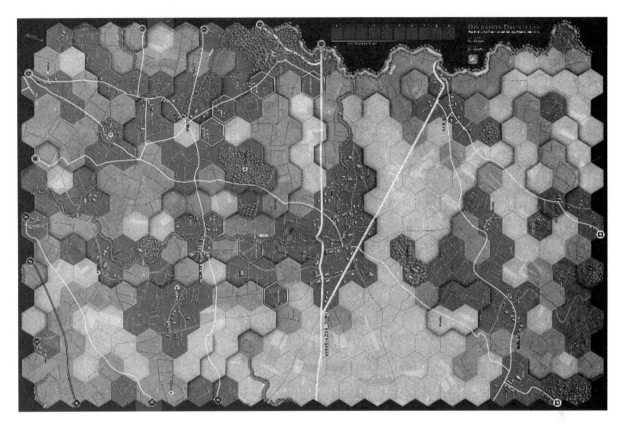

Figure 6.6
The game board for *Operation Dauntless*.

bridges, buildings, slopes, and forests) are emphasized by exaggerated scale (and allowed to morph slightly to fit to the hex grid), while aesthetic elements (individual trees, orchards, hedgerows, and fields) are shown precisely where and as they appeared.

Another feature of this map is found in the hex grid itself. Rather than slaving to a perfect grid geometry, it follows the land's underlying elevation contours, its hexsides curving to create a subtle dimensionality over the entire map and emphasize the pastoral roll of the terrain. And so the whole aesthetic of the map is meant to reflect an idealized realism, playing on our conception of the charms of the French countryside.

Comparing the modern satellite imagery of the area with the 1944 photography shows the occasional private forest denuded or village expanded, but the basic structure of the farmland and fields remains. There is a striking spot where a stone wall was removed sometime in the intervening decades, yet its outline remains subtly imprinted (or is it scarred?) onto the earth, still clearly visible from space—just as the war imprinted onto our mental conception of Normandy's very landscape, adding war's hell to those hedgerows.

Conclusion

Global thinking can only be statistical ... can only do to the globe what a space satellite does to it: reduce it, make a bauble of it ... Walk over the ground. On foot you will find that the earth is still satisfyingly large, and full of beguiling nooks and crannies.

—Wendell Berry

Through most of history, the mapmaker's task was relating spatial and ideological information rather than pure geographical precision. As mapping has become more and more utility-oriented and now even computer-based, this artistic aspect has often suffered. Given that major goals of map wargames are to evoke an historical period and to immerse the player in an experience, they provide a useful opportunity to address the basic aesthetic of a given place and time—and thus represent one of the few remaining commercial avenues where this broader tradition of mapmaking can survive and thrive.

Recommended for Further Reading

Peter Barber (ed.) *The Map Book*, 2005.

Wendell Berry, *A Place in Time*, 2012.

John McPhee, *The Control of Nature*, 1989.

Simon Schama, *Landscape and Memory*, 1995.

John Noble Wilford, *The Mapmakers* revised edition, 2000.

About the Author

Mark Mahaffey is a full-time freelance artist specializing in mapmaking for analog historical wargames. He has worked on dozens of such board games over the past decade for clients around the world, and also serves as art director for *Against the Odds: A Journal of History and Simulation*. He holds his degree in Bible and Communication from Columbia International University. His first major game design, *The Inmost Sea* (a detailed study of the battle of Lepanto), remains underway.

7 THE "I" IN TEAM: WAR AND COMBAT IN TABLETOP ROLE-PLAYING GAMES

A. Scott Glancy

Part of the evolution from wargame to role-playing game was bringing the player down from his general's-eye view of the battlefield and casting him in the role of a single actor in the thick of the action. Transitioning from wargaming to role-playing was more than just changing perspective and personalizing the danger. Role-playing meant providing the players challenges outside of combat and rules for resolving those successes and failures. Nevertheless, combat has remained at the heart of nearly every role-playing game's mechanics.

Two theories of role-playing game design and play stand out in relation to the design of combat mechanics: the closely related Threefold Model (or GDS Theory) and the GNS Theory (see Kim 2008 for a brief overview of these and other models). Both began as theories of how players express play style. Both theories hypothesize that any decision made by participants in an RPG (both players and gamemasters) will be made in the service of one of three primary goals: Game, Drama (or Narrative), and Simulation—hence GDS Theory and GNS Theory. Later, both GDS and GNS Theory were used to analyze how game designers create role-playing games, with those same three goals in mind.

"Game" (sometimes "Gamer" or "Gamerist") design goals include challenging the players in balanced and fair ways and ensuring that there are measurable means by which encounters, scenarios and even entire games can be judged as being "won" by the players. Another "Game" design goal is achieving "game balance." Game balance ensures that no weapon, character class, attribute, or skill is so powerful or important to the mechanics that it creates undue advantages. Game balance may also ensure that no encounter is beyond the characters' means of obtaining victory. Role-playing games designed with Gamerist goals in mind often have well-defined means for improving player characters, who thereby become more powerful in terms of the game's mechanics—for example, the accumulation of experience points, the improvement of skills, or the obtaining of knowledge or materials that give the player character an advantage.

"Narrative" design goals ensure that there is a story to go along with those challenges, so that the RPG is something more than a series of combats that generate in-game achievements. Rather than force the players to participate in a preset story, the Narrative goal ensures that there is well-plotted meaning that supports the events, providing motivation for participation beyond the mere Game elements of victory and advancement.

The last goal, "Simulation," does not necessarily mean creating a realistic simulation of task resolution (or combat). The goal of Simulation is to create enough internal consistency during play that it helps immerse the players into the fictional experience and suspend their disbelief. Often Simulation is not about modeling physics with the game mechanics, but modeling the fiction the game is based on. Obviously, the combat of a fictional setting like the movie *Hard Boiled* (1992) is going to be different from the combat of the equally fictional setting of the movie *Red Dawn* (1984). Sometimes it is appropriate for combat to include backflips with handguns akimbo, and sometimes it is appropriate for combat to be about your squad's volume of fire.

Combat systems have drifted back and forth along a sliding scale of complexity while in the service of the three general goals of Game, Narrative, and Simulation. At the least complex end of the scale are Abstract Mechanics; at the most complex end are Explicit Mechanics. More complexity does not necessarily mean that the combat is more realistic, but realistic combat is rarely very abstract. As of 2014, the games currently setting the trends in the RPG market tend toward the abstract end of the complexity scale.

Abstract combat was the state of the art for RPGs when TSR's *Dungeons & Dragons Basic Set* was released in 1977. Designed to simulate medieval and fantasy genre combat, including the use of magic, *D&D* divided combat up into turns called combat rounds. A twenty-sided die was rolled to determine the success or failure of attacks made during a combat round. Each combat round represented essentially one minute of time in the game, and each attack roll during

that combat round did not represent a single attack but rather the net effect of all the fighting that took place during the round. This temporal abstraction often contradicted the more explicit details, particularly where archery was concerned. Even the loss of hit points was an abstraction, as the loss did not represent actual damage, like broken bones or severed arteries, but rather an ablative reduction in the character's ability to continue fighting—and combat continued without loss of effectiveness despite characters being down to their very last hit point.

Perhaps the least realistic aspect of combat in *D&D* was the way that combat ability was controlled by character class and level and not by a character's skill—a concept that had yet to be introduced to role-playing games. Characters were defined by their character class: fighter, magic-user, cleric, thief. Certain classes were banned from using particular weapons or armor, most notably the magic-user, who could wield no weapon more formidable than a dagger and could wear absolutely no armor. Furthermore, characters of the same level would still have different combat abilities based on their character class. A sixth-level fighter would always have a better chance "To Hit Armor Class Zero" (the THAC0 rating) than any other character class of equal level. All of this was, of course, in the service of the Gamerist design goal of character balance, to ensure that no particular character class would dominate the game. Narrative and Simulation goals took a back seat.

Gamerist goals continued to be the guiding principle for combat systems into the late 1970s. The combat rules of TSR's 1978 *Gamma World* (a post-apocalyptic fantasy of retro ray guns and mutations) were so close to *D&D* as to be practically indistinguishable. The evolution of *Dungeons & Dragons* to

Advanced Dungeons & Dragons did not greatly make its system of combat less abstract, but it did certainly become more complex, with the inclusion of tables to modify every THAC0 target number based on what specific weapon type was used. While this may have been a step toward a more "realistic" way to simulate combat, as certain types of medieval weaponry were designed to be more effective against specific types of armor, it did not make the combat any more explicit. Character class, hit points, armor class, and leveling kept the combat fairly abstract.

Game Designer's Workshop's 1977 science fiction RPG *Traveller* also used a highly abstracted combat system, but with a number of Simulationist nods to more explicit and realistic combat. Combat success was determined using two six-sided dice, with skills, armor, and conditions like lighting, range, or cover used to modify the probabilities for success. *Traveller* was a game where characters were defined not by levels or character classes, but by their inventory of skills. Combat success was unaffected by character background or profession—only their skill mattered. A character generated using the Merchant background could have a higher skill with a Gauss rifle than a former Imperial Marine.

Flying Buffalo's 1975's *Tunnels & Trolls* abandoned simple turn-based combat. Under most previous systems, combat was often a matter of one side attacking, generating success and damage, and then the other side taking their turn, until one side or the other had their hit points worn down to zero. The swords and sorcery combat of *Tunnels & Trolls*, however, was a simultaneous contest of skill. Opponents had dice pools—literally, large numbers of dice, determined by which weapons the character had and adjusted by bonuses or penalties based on the character's attributes. The two combatants' dice

pools were rolled simultaneously and the results totaled. The difference between the two rolls was the damage inflicted on the one with the lower total, that number further reduced by the target's armor (which reduces damage, rather than making a character harder to hit, as in *D&D*), and the result applied as damage against the character's Constitution attribute. Multiple combatants could pool their attacks, and massed combat could be handled by applying one huge dice pool against another. While still abstracted, this system was more realistic insofar as melee combat was not about soaking up enormous amounts of physical damage. It was about skill overcoming skill.

Following the breakout hit of *Dungeons & Dragons* a number of fledgling game designers and companies deliberately moved toward far more explicit combat systems. The 1980s are characterized as a time when "realism" in combat was an overarching goal, perhaps as a reaction against the abstractions of *D&D*, and combat mechanics moved toward extremely complex means of expressing very explicit ends.

Games like *RoleMaster* (1980), by Iron Crown industries, and Chaosium's *RuneQuest* (1978) both attempted to bring a more realistic and explicit combat system to the Medieval Fantasy genre. *RuneQuest* used a set of mechanics that would eventually be simplified into Chaosium's so-called Basic Role-Playing (BRP) system. In *RuneQuest*, skills are represented as percentages, and the goal is to roll a number on percentile dice under the character's skill in order to succeed. In combat this worked the same way, with the opponent able to roll dice to dodge or parry what would have been a successful attack. A hit location table determined damage, which would have an immediate effect on combat: results could stun opponents for multiple combat rounds, disarm them, or permanently lower their chance of making a successful attack.

RoleMaster's combat was similar, but it took damage resolution to a level that many regarded as too explicit and Simulationist while sacrificing ease of play. In *RoleMaster* every single weapon had its own full-page damage table. Entire published supplements like *Arms Law* (1980) and *Claw Law* (1982) were dedicated to adding to, expanding on, and modifying these damage tables. The results of what were essentially contested combat rolls were checked against tables to determine what kind of damage would be inflicted based on what specific kind of medieval weapon was used—one table for swords, another for maces, etc. Most damage results had a small concussion point damage component that essentially represented the wearing down of an opponent without any permanent damage. The critical damage results had an immediate and almost always catastrophic effect on combat. For instance, a stun effect could leave the defender unable to parry for a number of combat rounds; this would not cause any immediate damage, but it would leave the combatant highly vulnerable to follow-up attacks. These damage effects were explicitly spelled out, with bones broken, fingers severed and arteries punctured, depending on the type of weapon and the level of success. Results degraded the opponents' ability to defend themselves until a final lethal blow could be applied. These explicit damage rolls certainly provided a level of realism, but at the cost of game time.

Even TSR attempted to create a more explicit and thereby realistic combat system with their 1980 release *Top Secret*, which simulated the spy genre. The game showed strong Gamerist tendencies, including the use of experience points to gain levels in order to increase in-game competencies. While *Top Secret*'s characters possessed so-called "Areas of Knowledge," which prefigured the use of skills in later RPGs, characters' abilities were still defined by broad character classes—an attempt to create game balance between players by forcing specialization. Nevertheless, the combat rules for *Top Secret* took a very Simulationist approach, with modifiers for ranged weapon combat and a hit location table, but a damage system still left player characters able to absorb unrealistic amounts of ballistic punishment. Perhaps the most interesting combat system in *Top Secret* was its hand-to-hand combat rules. Here the two opponents selected an attack move and a defense move, simultaneously revealed them, and then checked the results against a table. It came off as a more complex version of rock-paper-scissors, where reading your opponent's intentions became as important as the character's skills—almost like real hand-to-hand combat.

The year 1981 saw the release of Chaosium's *Call of Cthulhu*, a role-playing game set against the backdrop of H. P. Lovecraft's now-infamous Cthulhu Mythos horror stories. A period piece set in the 1920s and 1930s, modern weapons and firearms combat dominated the system. The mechanics were skill-based and used percentile dice to determine success. Today these mechanics are used by several Chaosium titles and is known as their Basic Role Playing (BRP) system.

Combat in *Call of Cthulhu* stood out for several reasons. First, no matter how much experience player characters had or what background they came from, they remained just as fragile and susceptible to physical damage as they did when they were first generated. A college professor might have just as many hit points as a member of SEAL Team 6. Character background did not affect the ability to successfully engage in combat, only the character's skill in a particular class of weapons. Skills could increase, but only by using them, so combat skills only increased by exposing characters to the extreme danger of combat. Player characters were built using the same mechanics as non-player characters, leaving the players with no mechanical advantage over the NPCs. Game mechanics allowed most firearms (and many other weapons) to kill a player character with one successful attack. This made combat extremely unforgiving. Wounds were not as immediately debilitating during play, but they healed at a rate that could render a character extremely vulnerable for the rest of a scenario. The mechanics of *Call of Cthulhu* encouraged players to engage in combat only in an emergency and only when unavoidable.

Where *Call of Cthulhu* really stood out among RPGs is that it takes into account the mental damage that can come with participating in combat. The game used a "sanity point" system for tracking a player character's mental health. Sanity points were subtracted until the character ran out and was reduced to a state of permanent insanity and removed from the player's control. This mechanic was primarily intended to show the mental damage inflicted by the extreme and unreasoning terror caused by contact with the supernatural, but as published it also covered the mental toll inflicted by combat. The rules included mental trauma damage for seeing friends and close associates die, discovering dead bodies, and even undergoing torture or extreme pain. As a power fantasy, *Call of Cthulhu* lacked the appeal of *Dungeons & Dragons*, but as a horror game it succeeded in making the players dread every roll of the dice.

For rather obvious historical reasons, games in the 1980s often used postapocalyptic settings. Here modern weapons would meet a medieval society where the players could have military-style combat without any of that military command structure getting in the way of player agency. This brought forth such titles as *The Morrow Project* by TimeLine, Ltd. and Fantasy Games Unlimited *Aftermath!*, both published in 1981, followed in 1984 by GDW's classic postapocalyptic setting *Twilight: 2000*. All three products employed very complex and explicit combat systems. *Aftermath!* boasted a two-page combat flowchart for tracking all the minute variables of resolving a single attack during a combat round and included hit location tables for standing and sitting targets. *The Morrow Project*'s combat system was notoriously difficult: ballistic damage was determined using an "efficiency factor" that was generated by multiplying the diameter of the projectile (in thousandths of an inch) by its muzzle velocity (in thousands of feet per second), divided by fifty. This efficiency factor was then compared to armor and cover, whose protection is inexplicably measured in centimeters, thereby mixing imperial and metric measurements for the purpose of generating in-game combat results. Other oddities included determining damage points before the hit location was generated.

Twilight: 2000's first edition included a number of mechanics that seemed as if they were artifacts of the game's wargaming origins. On the one hand, the game was explicit concerning all the various types of military hardware and ordnance available to the players. The fact that 9mm Parabellum ammo was not interchangeable with 9mm Makarov, or 9mm Browning Long, or 9mm Glisenti, or 9mm Largo, and all had different weights for calculating character encumbrance was included. But in combat individual bullets were replaced by the abstract concept of the "shot." A shot represented three bullets: so the Colt 1911 pistol magazine is rated as containing two shots, the M2 Baretta holds five shots, and the M16A2 assault rifle would hold ten shots per magazine. For a system so concerned with the actual weight and caliber of so many firearms and their various ammunitions, this abstraction seemed quite glaring, particularly when so many real-world magazine capacities were not divisible by three. While this appears to have been designed to simplify full automatic fire in the game, it was a bit baffling when it came to firing bolt-action sniper rifles. Players hoping for some "one shot, one kill" sniper action were forced by the mechanics to blaze away with three-round bursts of suppressive fire. This abstraction of ammunition seems like something I would expect to see in a squad-level wargame like *Advanced Squad Leader* (*ASL*) (1985). *ASL* simulates company and battalion-sized engagements involving hundreds of combatants, but role-playing combat rarely involves more than a dozen or so combatants total, including both players and non-player characters. Keeping track of the ammunition carried by individuals at that RPG level of combat complexity wouldn't seem to require that kind of abstraction in order to keep record keeping manageable.

The damage system of *Twilight: 2000* was abstract but realistic. There was a hit location table with ten possible results, but only four types of wounds: slight, serious, critical, and death. These wounds had an immediate effect on the character's ability to engage in combat, with critical wounds leading to a quick death if untreated, depending on the hit location table results. Healing in *Twilight: 2000* was particularly slow, with injuries continuing to plague characters for weeks and months. The combat system was considered so unforgiving that it actually encouraged players to avoid combat. Perhaps that was the game's most realistic aspect.

The one aspect of *Twilight: 2000*'s combat mechanics that truly stands out is the characters' Coolness Under Fire (CUF) rating. Combat rounds were divided into five segments. The lower a character's CUF, the less often he hesitated or wasted time during combat; the higher the CUF, the more segments were lost during the combat round. That lost time could be anything from fumbling while reloading a weapon to changing targets or hesitating to get under cover. This was a system that modeled modern combat on the performance of the characters, not the performance of the weapons. Sadly, unlike *Call of Cthulhu*, there were no mechanics for degrading a character's CUF rating due to combat stress. In *Twilight: 2000*, a character's CUF only gets better, not worse.

Where *Twilight: 2000* particularly bogged down was in its vehicle combat rules. Attacking rounds striking vehicles would pass through armor and interior components, with each component soaking up damage points until all the energy of the attack was spent. However, this required vehicle stats to include explicit data on the idiosyncratic interior layout of every vehicle. This emphasis on "realism" caused combat to grind to a crawl.

Perhaps the nadir of "realistic" and explicit combat systems was *Phoenix Command*, released in 1986 by Leading Edge Games. Combat rounds represented fractions of seconds. Every bullet had to be accounted for, and such factors as barrel rise, recoil, and angle of impact all had to be figured in. Each bullet had to be tracked through more than five tables of results before generating an effect that would explicitly describe the damage done to specific limbs, organs, or bones. The hit location table used three ten-sided dice to generate one thousand possible hit locations on the human body. Damage was not a matter of hit points, but a matter of a countdown clock. Based on the type of injury the character received they had a time limit for how soon a specific type of medical aid had to be delivered before the character died. The use of incredibly short combat rounds was based on the capabilities of the weapons rather than on the capabilities of the human characters handling them—humans just don't react in one-tenths of a second, even if the action of an AK-47 can. Later releases included advanced damage tables (with the aforementioned d1000 hit location table), a hand-to-hand combat system book, and multiple weapons' data books. The game's focus on the weapons rather than the characters demonstrated a design philosophy obsessed with ballistics, which jettisoned Gamerist and Narrative goals in the service of Simulating not genre, but physics.

In 1986 Steve Jackson Games began publishing their *Generic Universal RolePlaying System*, or *GURPS*. Since then the *GURPS* system has been used to simulate genre gaming experiences ranging from recreating the BBC cult TV series *The Prisoner* (1967–68) to resurrecting defunct game systems like GDW's *Traveller*. Its character generation system followed in the footsteps of Hero Games' 1981 superhero RPG *Champions*, using pools of points with which to purchase character attributes, skills and personal advantages, thus allowing complete player control over character creation. *GURPS'* combat system was, while very playable, not particularly innovative, with hit points and combat rounds as standard fare. As for *Champions*, the one thing that always stood out for me, at least as far as modeling the fiction and not the physics, was the fact that when superheroes are battling, to deliver a monologue or a sarcastic quip took literally no time at all in game terms. No matter how long a supervillain's speech was, you couldn't interrupt him with a superpunch to the face. (One has

to wonder if that rule should be changed, since the Hulk pummeled Loki mid-monologue in 2012's *The Avengers*.)

If the 1980s were all about game designers modeling physics in ways that undercut playability, in the 1990s the pendulum was clearly swinging back toward less explicit rules and the promotion of Narrative. One of the earliest contenders in this field was the *Amber Diceless Roleplaying Game*, published in 1991 by Phage Press. Combat (and all opposed contests) was decided by comparing character attributes and declaring a winner based on whoever's score was higher—unless there was cheating. Well, not cheating exactly, but that flat score comparison could be altered by either changing the type of conflict or by adding an advantage, like poisoning one's blade. Even so, this attempt to tie combat into Narrative ultimately came down to "GM fiat," where a single person's opinion—the referee's—decided the outcome of any given situation.

Games like White Wolf's 1991 *Vampire: The Masquerade* abstracted modern weaponry and concentrated on the character itself as the most important feature of the game. Their "World of Darkness" setting cast characters as various mythological creatures, from vampires to werewolves, ghosts, faerie and sorcerers. The character—its motives, drives, and supernatural abilities—became central to both the story and combat. Skills, attributes, and special abilities were more abstracted than their brethren from the 1980s, but White Wolf's mechanics were essentially dice pools with universal attributes and skills for all characters and opponents. Far more abstract offerings still waited in the wings.

Atlas Games' 1992 release *Over the Edge* surged back toward abstraction with its surreal conspiracy world inspired by the work of William S. Burroughs.

Characters were defined by four nebulous traits (three advantages and a disadvantage) that the player gets to pick. Not from a list. The players get to make up the traits, and they can literally be anything. That and a limited dice pool were the sole factors governing combat, which meant that combat was highly abstracted and Gamerist and Simulationist goals were pushed aside for an emphasis on Narrative.

Daedalus Entertainment's 1996 *Feng Shui* created a game world based on Hong Kong action movies and introduced a kind of cinematic combat never seen before. Because of the outrageous nature of martial arts movie combat, players received a bonus to their combat rolls depending on how over-the-top they described the actions they were carrying out. The more outrageous and baroque the combat maneuver, the greater the probability of success.

Atlas Games also produced a game of occult conspiracy in 1998 called *Unknown Armies*. Like *Call of Cthulhu* before it, *Unknown Armies* had mechanics for tracking a character's sanity. Staying sane in the face of supernatural horror was such an important part of *Unknown Armies* that the game tracked five aspects of mental health, but used only four attributes to define the remainder of the character's abilities. Perhaps the most interesting twist on their combat system was that players were never told how many hit points were lost. The referee just described the injury to them. If they had skills in medicine or first aid, they would receive more information as to the seriousness of the wound. But at no time were they told how many hit points were lost or how many hit points they had left. The result was certainly a less explicit system that was simultaneously more realistic. Wounds in combat became an unknown, and as an unknown they were more feared by the players.

Since the turn of the twenty-first century, RPG Gamerist goals have emphasized ensuring ease of play, with abstract mechanics and simple rules dominating the field. Narrative goals focus on the players and the referee telling the story together, with more player agency and more player participation in creating and guiding the plot. Simulationist goals focus on simulating the tropes of the genre the game is based on. Systems that give players the most control over character creation are now the standard. Task resolution is dominated by dice pool strategies and often include the accumulation and use of "plot points" or "style points" that players can use to change die results. This keeps the players in charge of the results of the action, rather letting the dice, which rarely give a damn about Narrative, to control the story. Some games even allow the player rather than the GM to define the effect of their own failure in combat, adding complications rather than subtracting damage. A player might opt to have a weapon malfunction rather than allow their character to suffer an injury. Or they might choose to suffer a specific injury, to their sword arm for example, rather than an injury to a leg, which might interfere with their ability to run away and live to fight another day. Combat is seen not as an interruption of the story, but as an integral part of it. Game systems like *Savage Worlds* (2003), *Fate* (2003), and *Cortex* (2005) exemplify this design ethic.

One of the most abstract games of recent years is 2009's much-lauded *Fiasco* from Bully Pulpit Games. Billed as "a game of powerful ambition and poor impulse control," *Fiasco* is intended as a means to create one-off scenarios of randomly generated heists, crimes, and plots that all fail spectacularly, drawing heavily from neo-noir films like *Blood Simple* (1984), *Fargo* (1996), and *A Simple Plan* (1998).

Fiasco doesn't even have a combat system or a gamemaster; in this cooperative storytelling game, the players roll dice to generate complications and failures to the story until everyone comes to a bad end.

One consistent aspect of combat in role-playing games is that it is extremely personal. Fights are anticipated to be between relatively small groups, and the Gamerist, Narrativist, and Simulationist design and play goals support this. Mass combat means slowing down the gameplay, and ease and quickness of combat mechanics is a strong Gamerist goal. Being a tiny cog is a huge war machine takes the emphasis off the player characters and puts it on impersonal events, which would undermine the Narrativist goal that the players create their own stories. And the Simulationist goals become harder to satisfy if the simulation grows to encompass events and actions outside the player characters' ability to perceive.

But one game company did find a way to bridge the intensely personal combat of RPGs and the mass combat of wargaming—sort of. During the 1980s and 1990s, the now-defunct Game Designers' Workshop (GDW) published traditional historical wargames, as well as science fiction and fantasy role-playing games. In many cases they produced companion wargames that were developed from their RPG properties. Their *Traveller, Twilight: 2000, Space: 1889*, and *Traveller: 2300* RPG lines all had companion wargames set in their fictional universes. Often these companion wargames did double duty, acting as stand-alone wargames and also as the mass combat rules for the role-playing game that spawned them. Their simplified mass combat rules allowed the players to be immersed in an epic battle but still keep the action moving. Players could experience both the mud and blood of the battle from the role-playing perspective

and the ebb and flow of the battle at the wargaming perspective.

For example, the rules for GDW's 1989 *Last Battle*, a squad-based, hexmap wargame set in the *Twilight: 2000* universe, were actually a stripped-down and simplified version of the RPG combat rules. In particular, the rules of vehicle combat were far easier to play. Many players reported using *Last Battle* to simulate mass combat while playing the *Twilight: 2000* RPG.

GDW's *Traveller* RPG and its Third Imperium space opera setting generated an enormous number of wargames. *Striker* was its miniatures combat rules for high-tech warfare. *Snapshot* was its game of boarding actions and room-to-room fighting aboard starships, and was eventually expanded into its *Azhanti High Lightning* (1980) game, which staged combat aboard a massive starship with scores of decks to fight on. *Mayday* (1978) was its small ship combat wargame, while *Trillion Credit Squadron* (1981) covered huge fleet actions between capital ships. GDW also produced even more abstracted wargames where interstellar wars, based on the history of its fictional *Traveller* setting, could be fought, including titles like *Imperium* (1977), *Dark Nebula* (1980), *Invasion: Earth* (1981), and *Fifth Frontier War* (1981).

It is worth noting that the products based on Frank Chadwick's ahead-of-its-time RPG *Space: 1889* (1988), set in alternate history of Victorian era sci-fi, were among the most successful of these wargames. While the *Space: 1889* role-playing game fell out of favor with RPG gamers, the associated miniatures and wargame rules such as *Sky Galleons of Mars* (1988), *Cloudships & Gunboats* (1989), and *Ironclads and Ether Flyers* (1990) have remained popular with wargamers, despite now being long out of print. The continued popularity of the wargames associated with *Space:*

1889 helped maintain market awareness of the setting until the new popularity of the steampunk genre led to the license being picked up first by Heliograph Games and most recently by the German game company Uhrwerk Verlag.

The one thing that stands out among nearly all of these games is the simple fact that they all wanted to present combat as "fun" and "entertaining." RPGs are escapist nonsense at heart. Very few games present combat as something to be feared and avoided, with the possible exceptions of the grimly unforgiving *Twilight: 2000* and the notorious *Call of Cthulhu*. Role-playing game designers and players almost never factor in the overwhelming mental stress of combat. Mechanics almost never govern morale, with most games leaving it to the players to decide whether they should press their attack or beat a retreat. Fantastical heroics are almost always more gameable than the gritty realism of men and women knee-deep in blood and mud. Even systems that stress Narrative goals rarely want to deal with the effects of characters suffering from the effects of PTSD—except for *Call of Cthulhu*, that is, where mental damage is considered at least as important as physical damage. Perhaps this thirty-year-old product got it right? Perhaps the most important takeaway about how to depict combat and violence in games should be to instill a desire among players a desire to avoid them when they can.

But of course, what fun is that?

About the Author

In 1998 Adam Scott Glancy left a perfectly functional career as an attorney to join up with the role-playing game publisher Pagan Publishing, the nerd equivalent of running away to join the Foreign Legion. Today he is the man in charge of Pagan Publishing (much in the same sense that the last surviving legionnaire can be said to be in command of Fort Zinderhoff), and Pagan Publishing continues to bring the best of Lovecraftian horror to gaming tables around the world. He is a contributing author on the award-winning *Delta Green* series of supplements for the *Call of Cthulhu* role-playing game and has had Cthulhu Mythos fiction published in several short story collections, including the recent *Book of Cthulhu II* and *Shotguns v. Cthulhu*.

II   WAR ENGINES

8 WAR ENGINES: WARGAMES AS SYSTEMS FROM THE TABLETOP TO THE COMPUTER

Henry Lowood

This chapter will be a lengthy but incomplete response to the question, "What can we learn from the history of wargames about games as systems?" I will focus on the history of commercial or hobbyist wargames in the United States, mostly board games produced from the early 1950s into the 1970s, but also a few computer games. Wargames—also sometimes called historical, conflict or military simulations—generally emphasize themes rather than mechanics, and simulation over gameplay. The themes can be historical or they can be speculative; they involve military conflicts that have occurred between forces that existed, might have existed, actually do exist or might exist in a future or alternative world. The thematic emphasis of wargames has been contrasted with more abstract forms of strategy games, such as "Eurogames" (Woods 2012; Costikyan 2011). One might conclude from the specific emphasis on conflict simulation that wargames have relatively lightly influenced game design generally, yet they paced the evolution of modern board game design through the 1970s, particularly in the United States. Hobbyist wargame designers such as Charles S. Roberts and James Dunnigan were responsible for an eruption of creative ideas in the United States, and their work stimulated debates about game development during the 1960s and 1970s. Along with role-playing games, wargames also played a featured role in the transition from physical to computer-based games during the 1980s, and in the increasing use of simulations by the military from the 1990s forward.[1]

The Avalon Hill Way

Your July column mentions the regular hexagon tessellation as "so familiar to bees and users of bathrooms." Perhaps you are not aware of another common use of this tessellation, that of compartmentalizing game maps, particularly what are called wargames or military simulations.

—John E. Koontz to Martin Gardner (Gardner Papers, Box 33, folder 8)

Charles S. Roberts completed a four-year stint in the Army in 1952, returning to a commission in the Maryland National Guard. While waiting for a commission in the regular army, one that never came, he pondered how to prepare for his military career while a civilian. Roberts concluded that he would "gain some more general applications for the study of the principles of war" by designing a game (Vanore 1988, 17; Roberts 1983). Most accounts of the history of commercial wargames in the United States begin with that game, *Tactics.*

Roberts's idea of a wargame thus filled a void, rather than continuing a tradition. It is perhaps surprising, but no evidence has emerged to suggest that Roberts was aware of the history of earlier wargames, such as the Prussian *kriegsspiel,* while designing *Tactics* in 1952. He simply reasoned that games could be useful in a way that books were not, because "to be conversant with the Principles of War is to a soldier what the Bible is to a clergyman," yet books can be easily read, while "wars are somewhat harder to come by." However, "since there were no such wargames available, I had to design my own" (Roberts 1983). He did not envision wargames as simulations for training purposes, however; he stressed principles rather than experiences. Decades after *Tactics,* he still believed that "when you're talking about a rifle platoon, that's what it all comes down to, and there isn't a single game that will tell you how it's done. You can't get that flavor in a game" (Vanore 1988, 18). After considering that others might be interested in his game, he began in 1954 to sell *Tactics* by mail order. He sold perhaps two thousand copies, roughly breaking even financially (Roberts 1983). Encouraged by these sales, he founded The Avalon Game Company, later renamed Avalon Hill Game Company (henceforth Avalon Hill) in 1958.

Roberts published three games under the Avalon Hill imprint in its first year: *Tactics II, Gettysburg* and *Dispatcher.* He also worked on a fourth title, *Game/ Train,* which was not published. Avalon Hill would continue to publish a variety of "adult" or family and business games; *Dispatcher* was only the first of Avalon Hill's railroad simulations, close to Roberts's heart as a historian (Rasmussen 2010). Having worked in the advertising industry, Roberts produced clever and inviting packaging and marketing. A *Tactics II* insert was typical: "Always, to play an Avalon Hill game is an exhilarating challenge ... to give one, a subtle compliment." The components were modest and even crude by today's standards for printed board games, but the company's print advertising depicted these games as sophisticated and demanding. While Roberts put games on many American kitchen tables as wargaming's first entrepreneur, he was also its first game designer, at least in the modern era, and he was prolific. He produced ten games for Avalon Hill between 1958 and the end of 1963, when he sold the company for financial reasons. Counting *Tactics* and *Afrika Korps* (1964), ten of the twelve games he designed were wargames; they defined the essential elements of this kind of game, both the set of components and the terminology to describe game mechanics and structure.

What was new about these games? A superficial accounting of *Tactics/Tactics II* includes a game board, counters, dice, printed play aids and rulebook, nothing particularly remarkable. Board games with visually similar configurations had been published in the United States since the mid–nineteenth century. *Monopoly,* first published by Parker Brothers in 1935, utilized similar components.[2] Roberts's distinctive talent was inventing game procedures through the interaction of rules with charts,

Figure 8.1
Avalon Hill's *Gettysburg* (1958).

tables and map overlays. These combinations defined the wargame. Two innovations deeply associated with Roberts's games are the Combat Results Table (CRT) and the hexagonal map grid to regulate the movement of units. Roberts introduced the CRT in the 1952 version of *Tactics.* The table's columns each represented an odds calculation corresponding to an attacker's strength divided by that of adjacent defending units; each row corresponded to "the figure thrown on the cubit," i.e., a six-sided die. After working out odds, rolling the die, and consulting the table, the result determined by the intersection of row and column was applied, usually with one or both players losing or retreating units involved in combat. The CRT integrated military simulation and procedures of play. In the rules manual for Avalon Hill's *Tactics II*, Roberts advised players that "an examination of the Combat Results

Table is imperative. As this game attempts to be as realistic as possible, the Combat Results Table reflects the fact that an attacker must have a strength advantage in order to be reasonably sure of success ... Please examine the Table very carefully" (*Tactics II*, 10). Some features of Roberts's system of combat resolution failed to catch on (e.g., indicating the side affected by a result in terms of the odds factor rather than specifying "attacker" or "defender"); nevertheless, his mechanism for combat resolution and use of an odds-based table to randomize results became a staple feature of wargames. Principles embedded in the table also persisted, such as the rule-of-thumb that an army on the offensive must achieve a 3:1 ratio of combat strengths in order to ensure a positive result.

Roberts's "invention" of the CRT indirectly led him to his second big design idea, the hexagonal map grid introduced in the 1961 edition of *Gettysburg*. The invention also illuminates Roberts's contacts with "professional" game creators, specifically the RAND Corporation think tank, a leading center for game theory and game-based research. Dunnigan tells us that there are "mechanical elements common to most" wargames that drive the specific "tactics" of playing them; "The chief among these is the hexagon grid itself" (Dunnigan 2000a, loc. 850; see also Brewer and Shubik 1979, especially 59–66; Allen 1987, especially 141–47). Before 1961, game boards for *Tactics/ Tactics II*, the first *Gettysburg* (1958) and *U-Boat* (1959) consisted of maps on which terrain features were drawn to conform to a square grid overlay. As Roberts explained in the *Tactics II* rules, "the mapboard is marked off in one-half inch squares. Each counter, representing a division or HQs [Headquarter units] fits a square. All movement is based on these squares. Units may move vertically, horizontally or

diagonally" (*Tactics II*, 7). The obvious problem with this scheme is diagonal movement. The hexagonal map grid for representing terrain and movement was the elegant solution introduced in Avalon Hill's 1961 titles *D-Day*, *Chancellorsville*, and *Civil War*, as well as the new version of *Gettysburg*.

The documentary evidence concerning Roberts's brief encounters with RAND wargamers suggests only a tenuous link between hobbyist and professional games. Lou Zocchi, whose association with Avalon Hill began in 1959, recalled that Roberts was invited to visit RAND in 1960 because the researchers there were "so impressed by *Gettysburg*."[3] After Roberts told them he had come up with the CRT on his own, he was offered and declined a position at the think tank. While visiting RAND, he "noticed that they were using a hex-pattern overlay on their maps, which diminished diagonal movement distortion," so he quietly adopted the same overlay scheme for Avalon Hill's new games in 1961 (Zocchi 2007, loc. 2650–55). According to Stephen Patrick, the resemblance of the *Tactics* CRT to a "more complex one" in use at RAND was already a cause for consternation at the think tank "in the early fifties." Roberts informed RAND's researchers that it had taken him but fifteen minutes to develop the concept, but their inquiry piqued his interest in their work, according to Patrick. Years later when he noticed photographs depicting a RAND game, his eye picked out the hexagonal grid on their game map. He immediately recognized this as the way to regulate movement in his games (Patrick 1983, 11–12; Perla 1990, 115–16). The differences between these two accounts are significant, but both connect RAND to Roberts's CRT and from there to his discovery of hexagonal map overlays. Yet there is little independent evidence to suggest that dice-driven results tables played a significant role in any RAND games during the 1950s. Roberts's CRT seems unlikely to have caused much consternation. While it is possible that Roberts took the general idea of a results table from another game such as a version of the historical *kriegsspiel* (Peterson 2012, 289) or even from RAND, one wonders why if this were the case, the details of his homespun CRT were so distinctive. As for the hexagonal map, the Gordian knot is easily cut: The photograph mentioned by Patrick probably is the one in a photoessay by Leonard MacCombe published in *Life*

in May 1959 (106). A photograph over the caption "Playing War Games" depicts two teams of RAND researchers playing out an air battle.[4] Maps on the gaming table exhibit a clearly visible hexagonal overlay. It is difficult to imagine Roberts *not* staring intently at any photograph with that image and caption and running with the idea. In any case, Avalon Hill's key design innovations seems not to have derived from any personal collaboration with the professional simulation community represented by RAND's mathematicians and social scientists.

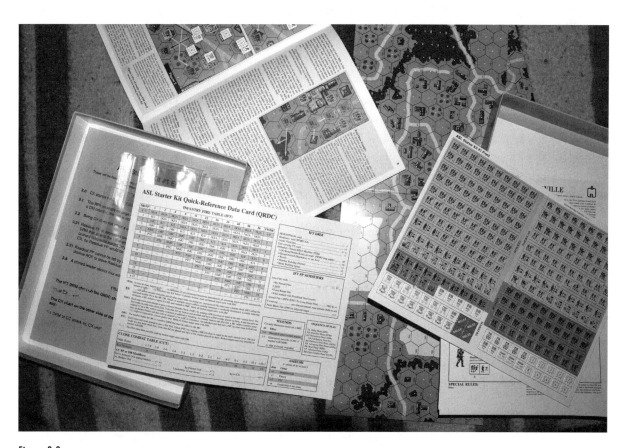

Figure 8.2
Typical wargame components: *Advanced Squad Leader*.

Roberts delivered the core components of the wargame. When Dunnigan in his handbook of wargame design specified the designer's first priorities, his list might have been an inventory of *Tactics II*: "When a game is designed, generally the first things that go into it are the map, the values on the playing pieces (combat strength and movement allowance), the Terrain Effects Chart and the Combat Results Table" (Dunnigan 1980, 34–35). In other words, Roberts's assemblage defined the field and mechanics of play. Avalon Hill also promoted wargames in two important ways that did not directly involve design. First, it created the wargame industry and built a community of players to consume its products. Prior to Avalon Hill, the dearth of hobbyist board games in the United States contrasted with the professional military's occasional embrace of the *kriegsspiel* or the many enthusiasts of military miniatures, a hobby centered in Britain. Avalon Hill filled this vacuum by developing business practices for production, distribution, and sales. After Roberts's departure from the company in 1963, Avalon Hill under the leadership of Tom Shaw hired and trained staff in areas ranging from game design and research to printing and sales, as well as working closely with players and freelance designers.[5] By the end of the 1960s Avalon Hill's bench of available designers was still short, but it had lengthened to include Shaw, Lawrence Pinsky, Sid Sackson, Lindsley Schutz, and, as we shall see, James Dunnigan. As for players, it invested in communication with and among them through its house publication, *The Avalon Hill General* (henceforth *The General*), the premiere issue of which appeared in May 1964. *The General* made players aware of other players. Its regional correspondents reported on events and club activities, and readers found "Opponents Wanted"

notices and services such as a Q&A column, news about the company, and previews of upcoming games. Some authors and correspondents appearing in the early issues later achieved star status in the game industry or related endeavors: Lou Zocchi (the Southwest editor), Jerry Pournelle, Al Nofi, George Phillies, James Dunnigan, Dave Arneson, and Gary Gygax. Game designer Greg Costikyan concluded years later that, "just as the letter columns of the science fiction pulps were instrumental in forming science fiction fandom, so the classified ads in *The General* were critical in the creation of the wargaming hobby" (Costikyan 1996). Through its business practices and publications, Avalon Hill exposed playing customers to the emerging practice of game design.

A second way in which Avalon Hill shaped expectations about game design was a shift after Roberts's departure in 1963 toward an emphasis in its marketing and magazine on historical research. During the Roberts years and beyond, Avalon Hill wargames often portrayed hypothetical or abstract conflicts (*Tactics, Tactics II, Blitzkrieg, Kriegspiel, Nieuchess*). Historical titles like *Gettysburg* and *D-Day* were always prominent in its lineup, but they offered at best rough approximations of the events depicted. In 1964, readers of *The General* may have been skeptical when they read that the company had always "specialized in designing all-skill, realistic games based on actual battles out of the historical past." The article with this claim introduced a new game on the Battle of Midway by describing a research process that included "hundreds of hours pouring [sic] over data" gathered from the Library of Congress, National Archives and other libraries. The designers sought out the help of retired Rear Admiral C. Wade McClusky, who played an important role in the battle. He was impressed by "the design staff's devotion to authenticity" and agreed to provide technical advice for *Midway*, released later that year. He also joined the company's new Board of Technical Advisors, followed in early 1965 by General Anthony C. McAuliffe, who had been consulted during development of Avalon Hill's *Battle of the Bulge* (1965). *The*

General reported that he "checked over *all* the game parts" and even discovered an error in the game's order of battle, "to our embarrassment." This was not a *mea culpa* for sloppy game development, but evidence that historical authenticity had assumed a place of prominence in quality control at Avalon Hill (Avalon Hill 1964, 1–2; 1965, 1–2).

From the Monograph to the War Engine

Dunnigan began it all in 1969 with Tactical Game 3/PanzerBlitz ...

—Rodger MacGowan, "20 Years Later and 10 Years After *Squad Leader*"

Avalon Hill's titles through the mid-1960s were *monographic* games. The *Oxford English Dictionary* defines a monograph as "a detailed written study of a single specialized topic." A monograph is not a general work "in which the topic is dealt with as part of a wider subject." Whether Avalon Hill produced games that were abstract studies of military operations, like *Tactics*, or covered historical conflicts, like *Gettysburg* or *Waterloo*, every game stood alone, covering a single conflict situation with a bespoke system, components and rules. They were fixed on a single topic. Of course, rules and components were occasionally reused in another title. Yet, even when specific rules or tables crossed over from one game to another, say, from *D-Day* to *Afrika Korps* (Martin 2001, 230), every game had its own system. It was a corollary perhaps of their monographic nature that Avalon Hill's early games were operational or strategic in scope, because the subject matter was generally a coherent battle or historical campaign. This coherence fit Avalon Hill's emphasis on playable systems and its newfound

respect for historical research based on archival documents and expert approval. An alternative model of game systems based on modularity and reusability of core components to produce a variety of scenarios, and with a more analytical approach to historical simulation, emerged in 1970 with the publication of Avalon Hill's first tactical game, *PanzerBlitz*, designed by James Dunnigan.

Unlike Roberts, Dunnigan had played wargames when he returned from the army in 1964. While stationed in Korea, soldiers in his artillery battalion introduced him to Avalon Hill's games. Back in the United States, he participated in the wargame community; he read and contributed to *The General*, wrote for a new magazine called *Strategy & Tactics*, and edited his own historical 'zine, *Kampf*. He studied games, read strategy articles, and analyzed military history. Unlike Roberts, who starting by designing a game but rarely played them, Dunnigan took apart games he played to learn how to design his own. His eclectic, skeptical, and analytical attitude toward design was summarized by the title given to his designer notes for *Tactical Game 3*: "The Game is a Game."

In 1966, Dunnigan met Shaw (then in charge of Avalon Hill), who had noticed one of his contributions to *The General*, an article in which he "blew away any pretensions to historical accuracy" in the 1965 *Battle of the Bulge* game. Shaw soon asked him to make a game for Avalon Hill (Dunnigan 2000a, locs. 2986, 4949; Dunnigan n.d.). This game, *Jutland*, was Dunnigan's first and was published in 1967. It took the game as monograph one step further; *Jutland* was a scholarly treatise in the form of a game. Dunnigan's commitment to historical simulation trumped easy gameplay. He jettisoned traditional components such as a game board and cardboard counters. Instead, he used maps and miniatures-like printed ship pieces to simulate the historical campaign at two scales—one for ship detection and the other for combat. The editors of *The General* fielded an "avalanche of inquiries" about this unfamiliar system, justifying it as flowing from "greater emphasis … on re-capturing historical accuracy than for any other game" (Avalon Hill 1967b). Dunnigan added that when asked to design the game in 1966, "I had never thought of designing a game. My interest had always been in history." Indeed, production delays were due to zealous historical research. In line with Avalon Hill's marketing emphasis on such research, Dunnigan joked about being dragged out of the Butler Library on the Columbia campus to finish the game. Between the lines, this story revealed a tense relationship with the Avalon Hill way of making games: "I had to prove a point to Avalon Hill, the delay was caused by my researching the historical data from every conceivable source imaginable, cross-indexing this information over and over again." After tangling about commitments to historical accuracy in a *General* interview about the game, Dunnigan turned the tables on Avalon Hill by prodding his interlocutor (presumably Shaw) to state the company line: "From this point on, Avalon Hill's philosophy

will be to place historical accuracy uppermost in the future design of games" (Avalon Hill 1967a). This discussion of *Jutland*'s design principles in the wargame hobby's principal forum doubled down on Avalon Hill's commitment to research as the foundation of conflict simulations.

The relationship between Dunnigan and Avalon Hill would continue as a mixture of collaboration, disagreement, and eventually competition. He created games for the company during the late 1960s. His second effort was *1914*, which Avalon Hill itself later described as a "sales success" but a "lousy game" and "too good a simulation" to be "fun to play" (Avalon Hill 1980, 9) By the time those words were published in 1980, Dunnigan's Simulations Publications Inc. (SPI) had become Avalon Hill's main competitor. When *1914* was published in 1968, he was its promising design talent, having created the company's only wargames between *Guadalcanal* (1966) and *Anzio* (1969). For Dunnigan, designing two games for Avalon Hill was instructive. He "carefully" observed their design process and concluded that there must be a "more effective way to publish games" (Dunnigan 2000a, loc. 2994). He then decided in 1969 to jump into the game industry with both feet. He gathered a group of wargamers and writers with whom he had worked on various projects. This group included Al Nofi, a likeminded wargamer/historian, and "graphic design ace" Redmond A. Simonsen, who worked out SPI's systems for production and physical component design—he coined the term "game developer" to distinguish his role from game design (Dunnigan 2000a, loc. 3009; Simonsen 1973). In July Dunnigan acquired the magazine *Strategy & Tactics* (*S&T*) from its founder, Christopher Wagner. Dunnigan, Nofi, Simonsen, and others in the SPI orbit had contributed to Wagner's *S&T*. With these pieces in place, Dunnigan began work on the two "basic concepts" behind SPI: (1) backing "games published by gamers" who controlled "all of the game development, production and marketing decisions" and (2) "publishing more games" (Dunnigan 2000a, loc. 3004; Dunnigan n.d.).

The seventeen issues of Wagner's *S&T* had provided an alternative to *The General*; it was partly a "journal of American wargaming," partly a fanzine, and at times critical of Avalon Hill fare. Yet Wagner recruited Dunnigan as a contributor because of the editor's enthusiasm for *Jutland*, an Avalon Hill game (Wagner n.d.; Dunnigan n.d.). As publisher of *S&T*, Dunnigan worked through a growing rift between his and Avalon Hill's design philosophies.[6] He later claimed that by the middle of 1969, "after doing *1914* for Avalon Hill in 1967 they lost interest in my work for a while." His games were considered "too

complicated." By 1969, he concluded that Avalon Hill had been "wandering in the wilderness" since Roberts's departure. The decision to take over *S&T* and start SPI gave Dunnigan his platform for producing more games "by gamers." His team needed to make "good, playable, realistic and authentic games" more efficiently. The first Dunnigan issue of *S&T*, number 18, was published in September 1969. It included a complete "mini-game," *Crete*, about the German airborne invasion of the island in World War II. Providing a "game in a magazine" became the defining feature of *Strategy & Tactics*,[7] with the implication that its publication schedule put intense pressure on Dunnigan and his team to create games at an unprecedented pace. An advertisement in this issue promised readers "tired of the 'one game a year' routine" no fewer than ten new games, ranging from revisions of Avalon Hill titles to new

Figure 8.3
A game in a magazine: *Strategy & Tactics*.

subjects such as ancient warfare and a facsimile reprint of an American version of the *kriegsspiel* originally published in the late nineteenth century. Rodger MacGowan, who later made his own mark on game magazine publishing and game production, remembered the promise years later: "This was unheard of. We had all become accustomed to one new release per year from AH and an occasional 'independent' title ... This ad marked the beginning of a flood of wargames" (MacGowan 1987, 34). By comparison, Avalon Hill produced four wargames between 1966 and 1969, two by Dunnigan. Efficiency in game design became a critical goal for SPI if it was to fulfill its promise to produce so many new games.

Beginning in December 1969, *S&T* began to issue a bimonthly *Supplement* as a forum for its readers. An advertisement in the first issue revealed one of SPI's methods for filling an expanded pipeline of games under development: Test Series Games. It opened with a provocative question, "Tired of the 'one game a year' routine[?] Well, you don't have to depend on Avalon Hill any longer. We have a new idea. Why not cut costs to the bone and just publish games?" The Test Series concept combined mail-order distribution, standardization of components, and user feedback in the selection and development of game titles. The prospectus for the series promised "at least" six new games per year and described thirteen under development, with another four in progress outside the series. Some of these titles had already been previewed as part of the first shot fired across Avalon Hill's bow represented by the advertisement in *Strategy & Tactics* 18. Their appearance in the *Supplement* represented Dunnigan's "solution" for the problem of producing games in volume ("Test Series Games," 1969). It is interesting to note the

number of titles that were connected to previously published or forthcoming Avalon Hill titles. Criticism, competition and collaboration between the two companies could coexist. Most of the Test Series games were battle or campaign studies, such as *1918*, *Tannenberg*, *Normandy*, or a game titled *1914 Revision*, a "cleaned up" version of Dunnigan's Avalon Hill title; these games held to monographic game design. Three Test Series titles stood out as exceptions to the monograph model: *Tactical Game 3*, *Deployment*, and *Strategy I*. These games were systems of components and rules, rather than monographic studies. *Deployment*, for example, was a "unique departure in wargames." It would provide a "wide selection of counters" to "combine different types" of military forces from the eighteenth and early nineteenth centuries in various battle scenarios. Its description promised "limitless variations." Likewise, the Test Series prospectus portrayed *Strategy I* as "based on a 'module' system of rules and components." It was designed for players "who seek variety or ... wish to design their own" games. The term was not used, but these games introduced the concept of *universal simulators* for whipping up conflict games set in any period from antiquity to World War III. They were kits for exploring vast conflict simulation possibility spaces. Dunnigan's designers would provide a few scenarios, yet such systems invited players to roll their own.

The third outlier on the original Test Series list, *Tactical Game 3*, would have the greatest impact on wargame design when published by Avalon Hill in 1970 as *PanzerBlitz*. The *S&T Supplement* described it as "Tactical Game 3 (Russia, 1944)—A new departure in games. A platoon and company level game whose main objective originally was to compare different weapons and tactical systems. Out of it all came a game that both miniature and board game enthusiasts can enjoy." After a few details about the historical setting and weapons, the synopsis emphasized its "radical new approach to historical gaming" and that it would be "the first in a series of similar games." *Tactical Game 3* was quite unlike a monographic game, but what was it? It did not portray a historical battle or campaign, but instead gave players the means to compare weapons and systems. It was not operational or strategic, but tactical, "the first game to go below the battalion level." Not a monograph, it was a system for serial production of multiple games (Dunnigan 1970, XS3).

The *Tactical Game 3* in the Test Series list was almost certainly a playtest kit distributed to a small number of testers. It followed earlier Dunnigan projects *Highway 61* and *State Farm 69*, tactical games inspired by miniatures rules and based on his historical research about mobile warfare on the Eastern Front during World War II. The new game reflected his interest in extending historical study to a more experimental, "analytical" format. For Dunnigan, "analytic history differed from the more common narrative history in that it, like the games, took a more numbers oriented and 'systems' approach" (Dunnigan 2000a, loc. 3268; Dunnigan 1970). Willingness to experiment led him to borrow rules from miniatures systems for his board game simulation, but without the "complex and tedious procedures often required in miniatures games."[8] The first version *of Tactical Game 3* consisted of rules, a rough map of the area near "State Farm 90" and two sheets of paper unit counters, some with hand-drawn silhouettes of vehicles. They provided the necessary information to play scenarios, also called

"mini-games." The nearly finished version appeared in issue 22 of *Strategy & Tactics* in July 1970.[9] The development process was nearing completion, so this was essentially a preview of *PanzerBlitz*, released a few months later as Avalon Hill's fall game for that year. Dunnigan published it as a companion to his magazine's featured game, another Tactical Game project called *The Renaissance of Infantry*. There were differences between the *S&T* and Avalon Hill versions, such as the sequence of play and combat values assigned to specific unit counters. Dunnigan addressed these changes in his Designer Notes, along with an analytical article by Steve List about the design, feedback and revision processes during playtesting, so that readers learned about the development process (List 1970; Dunnigan 1970). This version of the game did not include all of the components of *PanzerBlitz* and lacked a complete map, but it was possible to begin digesting the new game system, study a selection of the counters, and play through one mini-game. Unintentionally perhaps, the rough presentation and ad hoc nature of *Tactical Game 3* in the magazine underscored the openness of the system (Dunnigan 1970; Arvold n.d.; Dorosh 2008; Avalon Hill 1970).

Dunnigan concluded his Designer Notes for *Tactical Game 3* by expressing his wish that "*Panzer* [i.e., *PanzerBlitz*] will usher in a new era of quality in the design and presentation of historical games" (Dunnigan 1970). He might have written: quality *and quantity*. In contrast to monographic games, *PanzerBlitz* introduced the game system as a generator for multiple mini-games. Wargamers came to call these mini-games "scenarios," possibly borrowing from the term's currency among RAND's Cold War gamers to describe synopses of imagined or hypothetical political crises or military situations (see e.g., Kahn 1964, 150). Henceforth, I will call this combination of system + scenarios a "War Engine."

Games based on this design concept paced wargame development through the 1970s and 1980s, from *PanzerBlitz* to *Advanced Squad Leader*. In the *PanzerBlitz* rules, a "Note to 'Veteran' Players of Previous Avalon Battle Games" warned that it might look like other wargames, but "many of the concepts, techniques and details of play are totally unlike other Avalon Hill games." Among these differences one might have noticed that credits for game design, graphics design and playtesting named Dunnigan, Simonsen, and the staff of *Strategy & Tactics*. A more substantial one was the inclusion of a dozen situation cards, each describing a "scenario" in terms of specified arrangements of three "geomorphic" maps, unit counters used by both sides, victory conditions, the number of turns to be played, and the historical situation that would be simulated.

There was also "Situation 13," called "Making Your Own Situations." It gave players advice about how to use historical research to put together their own scenarios, noting that "you must work under the same restrictions when designing new situations" as the designers of *PanzerBlitz*. The suggestion that players use the *PanzerBlitz* engine to make their own games derived from Dunnigan's ideas about games and analytical history. In his Designer's Notes for *Tactical Game 3*, he had provocatively asserted, "How does this sound? 'Most game players are really trying to be game designers.' It's a thought I've been playing with these past few years, the idea that the 'game' itself is really not what people are interested in, at least not in the long run" (Dunnigan 1970). The point of a historical game was to test out alternative scenarios, to experiment with variables that might produce different outcomes; it was an interactive medium. Dunnigan felt that "this ability also implies that the game itself can be changed"—thus the title for his *Tactical Game 3* designer's notes, "The Game is a Game." His War Engine connected the generation of scenarios to empowerment of the player through its flexibility and accessibility. Players took up the challenge. One bibliography of articles about *PanzerBlitz* lists roughly 275 published articles, letters, variants, and replays appearing in more than two dozen magazines and other outlets over a period of about three decades. It would also become the best-selling wargame of the twentieth century, with more than 320,000 copies sold between 1971 and 1998 (Arvold n.d.; Dunnigan 1980, loc. 3056).

While *PanzerBlitz* was an Avalon Hill title, the War Engine also delivered games to the SPI catalog. Simonsen's ideas about games as a communication medium defined the roles of artwork and physical components and produced a standard format for rules presentation (Lowood 2009). The relatively consistent presentation, especially for the magazine games, helped players to deal with the increased flow of games. For example, they learned to expect a sequence of rules, procedures and cases, followed by specific details ("chrome," as Dunnigan called it) such as optional rules, design notes and scenarios, often with their own special rules. SPI defined both the game as system and a process for system design (Simonsen 1973; Simonsen 1977; Patrick 1977). The company usually described its products as "conflict simulations"; scenarios accordingly gave Dunnigan's analytical historians cases for study using SPI's systems' rules as simulation engines. Thus, the introduction to *Grenadier* (1971) described "a historical simulation of company/squadron/battery level combat in European warfare of the

Eighteenth century and Napoleonic Wars," not a battle monograph. The player then re-created specific engagements "by means of scenarios," each of which "is a complete game-simulation in itself, and simulates reality by use of the game equipment." The scenarios covered battles ranging historically from Blenheim (1704) to Palo Alto (1846), yet rarely required more than a brief paragraph of special rules to supplement *Grenadier*'s core system of rules, components and generic map.

The impact of the War Engine was twofold. First, it was an alternative to the monographic game. Second, SPI's transparency about its process highlighted innovative design practice and thus encouraged the publication of different kinds of games and simulations—and many of them. *Strategy & Tactics*, which issued between 1,000 and 1,500 copies in 1970, reached a peak circulation in 1980 of 37,000. Dunnigan estimated that fewer than 100,000 wargames were sold in 1969, mostly by Avalon Hill; in 1980, sales reached 2.2 million copies (Dunnigan 1980, loc. 3142). Another implication of SPI's emphasis on systems and scenarios was that it opened up another method for producing multiple games from a single system: inviting the player to design them. The War Engine exemplified by *Tactical Game 3/PanzerBlitz* introduced a flexible, modular approach to game design. Dunnigan concluded that by the late 1970s, players had lost their "awe" of game designers and publishers. Many decided to "do it themselves," which led to a proliferation of both games and companies that published them. In order to understand this impact of SPI's game systems, it will be helpful to compare the War Engine's "system + scenario" template for game design to the options available for modifying Avalon Hill's monographic games.[10]

Several titles in SPI's original Test Series revised, extended or applied game designs previously published by Avalon Hill. An example was *Anzio Beachhead*, published in the twentieth issue of *S&T* in 1970. Dave Williams, the designer, provided a small game on the Anzio landings of World War II that could be played as a supplement to his *Anzio* game published by Avalon Hill in the previous year. More ambitiously, Dunnigan's system of game design met the Avalon Hill monograph head on in the *Blitzkrieg Module System*, which was published as a bonus game for *S&T* 19, published in November 1969. Like Roberts's *Tactics* and *Tactics II*, Avalon Hill's *Blitzkrieg* (1965) was an abstract, fictional game about modern warfare. Designed by Lawrence Pinsky, it was a big, complex game; other than a few optional rules and modes like the fast-play "tournament version," it was also a finished game. Players intrigued by the unprecedented array of military options in the game noticed the potential for experimentation, and a few articles proposing optional rules and other variants appeared in *The General* along with dozens of strategy articles. SPI's *Module System* revisited *Blitzkrieg* not to improve Avalon Hill's game, but to morph it into a different, open system. Dunnigan and Simonsen described it as an "alternative design" or "starting point." (In this regard perhaps it was a playtest for *Strategy I*, a Test Series game.) They put together eighteen modules in the *Module System*: "They cover every aspect of the game and, if all are used, create an entirely new game" (Dunnigan and Simonsen 1969, 17). These modules were constructed so that players could use some or all of them, also picking and choosing physical components from *Blitzkrieg* or others provided in *S&T*. They were not scenarios, but rather blocks of rules, with titles like "fluid impulse" (or "rigid impulse"), "railroads," "air forces" and "weather." Players were thus given access to the engine itself, mixing rules in any combination they chose with the rules of the original game. As the title implied, the *Blitzkrieg Module System* tested whether game systems could be broken down into parts, reused and recombined. One reviewer praised SPI's modularized *Blitzkrieg* as a "major improvement" in game design over the original. He approved of its flexibility that allowed players to simulate "areas of interest" to them by adding modules to the "basic skeleton" of rules. Naturally, the reviewer suggested modifications to those modules, and players continued the discussion about changes to the *Module System* and *Strategy I* (Reddoch 1970; Bauer 1970a; Bauer 1970b). Dunnigan later explained these contributions as a natural feature of "mushware," which he defined as "what people do with complex procedures in their brain, without benefit of a computer." Players of "manual games" gladly jumped the intellectual hurdle of understanding complex rules systems and their interaction with scenario statements and physical components. Then they thought about how to modify them. His conclusion was that players "exposed to manual wargames became, whether they wanted to or not, wargame designers" (Dunnigan 2000a, loc. 161).

PanzerBlitz was published by Avalon Hill, so players may have taken its modularity as an invitation not just to make new scenarios, but also to revise Avalon Hill's other games just as the *Blitzkrieg Module System* had done. Monographic games were not particularly conducive to extension or revision, however. Yet players had since its first year filled *The General* with suggestions for variants and changes, ranging from new units and mapboards to rules modifications (see e.g., Perica 1964; Madeja

1965). One correspondent perceptively argued that Roberts's *Tactics* was an attractive target for changes, since it presented an abstract theme: "it's flexible because you needn't worry about historical accuracy" (Shimer 1965). These contributions to *The General* documented a potential for players improving and designing games. Dunnigan recognized the potential and activated it. It is hardly surprising that his transparent efforts to modularize game systems would encourage players to make or add to games. SPI's design team showed them in-house projects—the *1914 Revision* in the Test Series or *the Blitzkrieg Module System* in S&T—that taught them how to modify Avalon Hill titles.

Despite this encouragement, the fact remained that not every game was a modular system. How does one revise a published monographic game? John Edwards's *The Russian Campaign* provides the most successful example. Edwards was Australian; he became an avid player after picking up a couple of Avalon Hill games during a visit to the United States in 1968. As a new player, initially, he understood the monographic nature of these games: "Changing the rules then seemed akin to sacrilege. ... I regarded the rules as gospel, and would never have dreamed of making my own modifications." Eventually he did turn a critical eye toward the historical accuracy and playability of these games and began to fiddle with rules, orders of battles and combat factors. "Slowly but surely I was developing my own version" of Avalon Hill's *Stalingrad* (Edwards 1978; Avalon Hill 1980, 12). He corresponded with the company about his project, but it decided not to publish a new game based on his ideas. Instead, he published his "suggestions" for *Stalingrad* as "Stalingrad: Australian Style" in SPI's *S&T Supplement*. It turns out that the best way to update a monographic game is to make a new one. While praising Avalon Hill's game in the article, he noted that "many wargamers" had proposed ways to improve it, and so he did (Edwards 1970). Meanwhile, his contact with Avalon Hill led to an exclusive agreement to import and distribute its games in Australia. This business arrangement taught him that he could reduce costs by self-publishing his game at home rather than dealing with import duties and the like. He then founded a game design company, Jedko. Its first game was *The African Campaign* (1973), inspired by Avalon Hill's *Afrika Korps*. His *Stalingrad* successor, *The Russian Campaign* (*TRC*), followed in 1974.

Like computer game developers years later, Avalon Hill decided that it made more sense to join than fight players who modified their games. After redeveloping Edwards's improved treatments of subjects covered by its older monographic titles, it "introduced these playability-emphasis games to an enthusiastic American audience." Beginning in 1976 with *TRC*, Avalon Hill published Jedko games such as *War at Sea* and *Fortress Europa* that had been difficult to obtain in the United States. As it admitted in *The General*, Avalon Hill's developers found that although *TRC* "covered much the same ground" as its own *Stalingrad*, Jedko's games were "too good to ignore." Avalon Hill improved the game's graphical presentation, cleaned up the rules, and added a few "scenarios" and player aids; the result was a game that might "cover the same ground" *as Stalingrad*, but was "an entirely new game" (Avalon Hill 1976). Following Edwards's lead, Avalon Hill had replaced an old monograph with a new one. The new game begat various revisions and new editions over the years, producing a chain of connected games stretching from *Stalingrad* (1963) to Jedko's *TRC* (1974) to the Avalon Hill versions of the Jedko game (1976, 1977, 1978, and reprints), then an updated *Russian Campaign II* (1986) by Edwards for Jedko, and on to a fourth edition published by L2 Design Group (2003), followed by a *Southern Expansion Kit*, also by L2 (2004). In the company "Timeline" published in 1980, Avalon Hill acknowledged that *TRC* had driven its own *Stalingrad* "from the retail shelves," while reminding readers that an Avalon Hill developer, Richard Hamblen, edited the third edition rules with "meaningful changes." The experience of working with Jedko opened Avalon Hill's eyes to the benefits of outside developers. It also opened its wallet. When the editors of *The General* explained that *TRC* had been developed as "the initial product of another company," they added that this product was "small potatoes" compared to Avalon Hill's acquisition of Games Research Inc., the publishers of *Diplomacy* and the impending conclusion of negotiations to acquire 3M Games, the makers of a diverse line of games. In the following year, it concluded the purchase of 3M and *Sports Illustrated*'s game titles (Avalon Hill 1980, 12). The company timeline consequently dubbed 1977 the "Year of the Acquisition." Its business moves brought more than twenty-five new game titles into the Avalon Hill catalog, diversifying its contents substantially.

The example of *TRC* as Avalon Hill's model for the revision of monographic games contrasts sharply with the impact of modular systems introduced by SPI. During the early 1970s, the monograph and the War Engine followed separate paths. Six years after the release of *PanzerBlitz*, the author of an exhaustively detailed "hex by hex" analysis of its maps was baffled that Avalon Hill had not published new map

Figure 8.4
The War Engine at work: *Advanced Squad Leader*.

boards for the game system. This inattention to an obvious extension of the game's scenario possibilities was a missed opportunity, because "*PanzerBlitz* could have sold mapboards the way Barbie sold midget bikinis" (McAneny 1976, 3). That they did not—while publishing the critical remark in their house publication—suggests that Avalon Hill was not ready to jump on the War Engine, despite publishing its most influential game. Indeed, the puzzled *PanzerBlitz* expert's remarks appeared in the same issue in which the company announced its acquisitions

strategy as a primary method for adding to the product line. Avalon Hill did not build its own War Engines until the mid-1970s, publishing tactical systems like *Tobruk* (1975), *Squad Leader* (1977), and *Advanced Squad Leader* (1985), the "complete game system" that a magazine advertisement would dub the "crowning achievement" of the company's thirty-year history (Avalon Hill 1988).

There was always a connection between Dunnigan's conception of the player as designer—or at least as rules fiddler—and the launching of SPI's various design projects and innovations. These projects proved his point by showing that games could be configurable and extensible systems, and they did so in the name of raising efficiency in game design in order to publish more games. The handshakes between design efficiency and productivity on the one hand, and flexibility and modularity on the other, led to the War Engine model of game design. Building games as combinations of systems and scenarios made it possible for publishers such as SPI to produce games serially, while also encouraging players to add their own scenarios on top of the same systems of rules and physical components. And yet, I do not mean to tell a Whiggish story about how SPI's War Engine replaced Avalon Hill's monographic model. By the mid-1970s, both companies were producing games of both kinds. Dunnigan's company also produced monographic battle studies and found other ways to design efficiently. It produced "Quadrigames" like *Napoleon's Last Battles*, each one a set of four games or "folios" based on a core set of rules and linked thematically by a historical campaign. It also recycled well-received rules concepts by using them in new games. For example, Dunnigan's *Panzergruppe Guderian*, originally published in *S&T* and then by Avalon Hill as a boxed game, simulated the Battle of Smolensk in 1941. It introduced several novel aspects in the turn sequence and rules, such as an additional movement phase for armored units and a mechanism for randomly assigning combat strengths to untested Soviet units. Several subsequent games applied these design ideas in games covering other battles of World War II, so that one spoke of the "Guderian System" as a feature of this or that title. These methods for producing series of games from systems or even from specific design concepts gave SPI more tools for realizing Dunnigan's emphasis on efficiency and productivity. Competitors did not miss the point. As we have seen, Avalon Hill acquired publication rights, including those for numerous SPI titles (*Panzergruppe Guderian*, *Frederick the Great*, and others), and eventually began to produce its own War Engines. New companies might build an entire brand or product line around a single Engine. Game Designer's Workshop, founded in 1973, did just that with the *Europa* series, a massive project to deliver a series of games at one geographic scale and governed by a unified rules set. Assuming the project could ever be completed, GDW held out the possibility of combining multiple games to play out the entirety of World War II, provided one could find a table large enough for the maps. Looking back at the early days of the wargame industry, Dunnigan was satisfied that his model for design and production had spawned many game companies, "each following the SPI system to one degree or another" (Dunnigan 2000a, loc 3066).

From Paper to PC

Most of those gamers were not aware that simply playing manual games turned them into game designers, although over time most of them realized it.

—James Dunnigan, *Wargames Handbook*

There is not a hell of a lot of difference between what the best designer in the world produces, and what quite a few reasonably clued in players would produce at this point.

—John Carmack, 2002

Much recent work on the history of wargames has focused on military simulation, especially the rise and impact of the so-called Military-Entertainment Complex (e.g., Lenoir and Lowood 2005; Stahl 2010a; Crogan 2011). This chapter has been concerned with a different kind of wargaming. The professional simulation community—whether R&D think tanks like RAND or military labs—had little direct contact with Charles Roberts or SPI during the late 1960s and early 1970s. Still, it was perhaps inevitable that as with military simulation, computation would have an impact on the industry they built. Dunnigan has described the 1980s as the "conversion era" for wargames, by which he meant a general shift of energy and ideas from "manual" games to computer games. Specific game design concepts and even games also moved over to the computer. As Dunnigan put it, "By the mid-1980s, many manual [paper] wargames had been directly transferred to computers." In the early conversions, adapting manual games essentially "meant displaying a hex grid on the computer screen" (Dunnigan 2000a, loc. 3530). The first steps in this direction were hybrid games, in which software provided an opponent for a manual game. Chris Crawford introduced this approach with a game originally called *Wargy I*, first programmed in FORTRAN for an IBM 1130 computer, then published in a version renamed *Tanktics* for the Commodore PET microcomputer in 1978. Crawford remembers it as "the ONLY commercially available wargame when I first released it." A revised version for multiple systems was released by Avalon Hill in 1982, which had launched a line of computer wargames. David Myers has observed that "the main appeal of *Tanktics*—and most other computer wargames of the period—was that a game could be played without having to solicit another (human)

player." By the time Avalon Hill picked up the title, Crawford had raised that bar by programming *Eastern Front 1941* for the Atari 400/800 series of 8-bit home computers. Based on an earlier project rejected by Atari due to lack of interest in wargames, it was released through the Atari Program Exchange (henceforth APX) and may have been the best-selling software title for these machines (Crawford 1982a, 35; Myers 1990, 20).

Crawford's wargames followed a development path that resembled the movement from monograph to War Engine led by SPI. He began with monographs. *Tanktics* was a study of a single battle, and the first APX version of *Eastern Front* (1941) was a monographic study of a campaign. However, the second, cartridge version of *Eastern Front* approached the War Engine concept through the provision of a separately sold "Scenario Editor." The APX catalog for fall 1983 urged players to use this Scenario Editor to "establish your own criteria for the battles of the Eastern Front." It enabled players to "control more than a dozen factors that could alter the outcome" of their games. The utility of this tool was reinforced by other items for sale in this catalog. These included a set of three "challenging new scenarios" by Ted Farmer for the game designed to extend the war past the 1941 campaign and Stephen Hall's MAPMAKER as something "of special interest to players of the hugely popular" *Eastern Front*. MAPMAKER was described as the software Crawford had used to create the scrolling map for his game; the APX made it available to anyone "thinking of creating a strategy game" (APX 1983, 24). Together, a scenario editor and mapmaking utility certainly encouraged ambitious players to create new scenarios. Yet the system was not modular or extensible in the sense of SPI's early manual projects, such as the *Blitzkrieg Module*

EASTERN FRONT (1941)
A HISTORIC MILITARY STRATEGY GAME
FOR ALL ATARI HOME COMPUTERS

Authentic Invasion Tactics
Realistic Battlefield
Six Challenging Levels
Cartridge

ATARI
HOME COMPUTERS

Figure 8.5
Chris Crawford's *Eastern Front (1941)*.

System or even *PanzerBlitz*, because the rules system (program code) was not accessible in the same way. Manual games were not just physical games; they were also games with rules *manuals* that players read and studied. Supporting player-generated scenarios was one thing, but without providing access to the underlying game system, players could not analyze how games worked. In this sense, *Eastern Front* exemplified Dunnigan's criticism that "computer wargames plunged the games' inner workings into darkness" (Dunnigan 2000a, loc. 178). This limitation

was shared by computer wargames of the 1980s that provided scenario generators or built "universal" simulators covering different historical periods. Noteworthy efforts included the Strategic Study Group's (SSG) *Battlefront* series (1986–), Strategic Simulations Inc.'s (SSI) *Wargame Construction Set* (1986), versions of Rainbird's *Universal Military Simulator* (1987–) and more recent scenario-generating games such as HPS Simulations' *Point of Attack 2* (2004), which was issued in both a military and a "civilian" release.

Computer War Engines such as those developed by SSG, SSI and Rainbird in the mid-1980s explored and sought to extend the system + scenarios formula for wargames. In so doing they were implicitly following Crawford's prediction that "wargames on personal computers will not be just like boardgames." His vision of the "future of computer wargaming" was that game designers would strive for optimization of the "strengths of the computer" and avoidance of its weaknesses (Crawford 1981, 3). Crawford's work on *Eastern Front*, for example, had stalled initially. He restarted the project after realizing the potential that scrolling map graphics available on Atari home computers offered for a "monster game, a game with everything" (Crawford 1982b, 102). The designers of the *Wargame Construction Set* (*WCS*) and *UMS: The Universal Military Simulator* also focused on the potential computers offered as a vast simulation space, not just in terms of scale but also in terms of flexibility of representation. The influence of a way of thinking about computation with roots in Turing's Universal Machine resonated in this version of the War Engine and could be read—if faintly—in the title of Firebird's game. The game manual for *WCS*—yes, computer games had them, too—promised that players could "explore a wide range of conflict situations in military history, fantasy, and science fiction." Buyers of *UMS* read on its box cover that "from ancient battles of Classic History to the bloodiest Science Fiction fantasies, UMS lets you re-create them all with its unique 3D graphics system." Designers considered how the computer as a platform for wargames "with everything" might move them beyond the limitations imposed by cardboard counters, physical maps and game manuals.

While the possibility of a War Engine "with everything" seemed to promise unlimited scenario generation powers, the standard practice of describing the process as "editing" hinted at limitations such as those encountered with APX's "scenario editor" for *Eastern Front*. *WCS* likewise offered players access to the game's "EDITOR," which made possible map and unit editing. One reviewer, the author Orson Scott Card, considered the *Wargame Construction Set* as part of a family of computer "building" games of the early 1980s that included *Lode Runner, Pinball Construction Set*, and *Adventure Construction Set*. He described SSI's offering as "simple, elegant, infinitely variable" and focused in his short review on what it offered for game *design*, rather than how it was played (Card 1989, 12). His review underlined the ambitious vision of the limitless simulation opened up by scenario editors and construction sets. The constraints imposed by database editing as scenario generation can be illustrated by a comparison of *PanzerBlitz* and *WCS*. In the manual game, the first important set of player-created scenarios appeared in *The General* in 1974 under the apt title, "Beyond Situation 13" (Harmon 1974). These scenarios— called "Situation 13 variants" by the author— appeared in the magazine in the format of *PanzerBlitz* situation cards numbered from 14 through 25. The

scenarios each included a historical description, "map configuration" for arranging the game's geomorphic maps, setup instructions with unit manifests for both the Soviet and German forces, and a turn track. Significantly, they also included scenario-specific rules and "victory conditions." For example, Situation 18, under the title "Combined Russian Offensive: Somewhere in Russia (1944)" included a rule that "Soviet forces may not cross from one board to another (e.g., from board 1 to board 2, etc.). They may, however, fire across from one board to another" (Harmon 1974, 9). Game components were fixed by the original game, but rules were not. The scenario designer used the situation cards to provide instructions about how to deploy the existing components, but also had the option of extending or even modifying the rules by writing them in a free textual form. This was more than editing; the scenario designer (optionally) authored new rules. In the computer game, the process of creating a scenario involved using the EDITOR to create a map by selecting and placing "terrain icons," editing map colors, setting the number and type of units in a scenario, and defining the characteristics of military units, from the firepower and movement rates of friendly, player-controlled units to the selection of "aggression levels" for those under the control of the game software. The editing features provided flexibility and variability through combinations of decisions about database elements, expressed by actions such as selecting, placing, and assigning a color value to a map tile or giving a unit a numerical "firepower" rating between 1 and 99. Roger Damon, who developed *WCS*, informed players in the instructions that came with the game that "the central concept of this construction set is to first define the variables and then make them as easy to manipulate as possible. The designer's focus can turn then to wrenching a game out of the available data" (*Wargame Construction Set*, 23). The *WCS* scenario designer edited a database, without the option of writing new rules.

A second, related take on wargame systems leads us to another kind of martial game technology for computers: The game engine. Recounting the historical development of game engine technology and the first-person shooter genre would take us far afield, and I have already done so elsewhere (Lowood 2014). The question I will briefly consider here is whether the War Engine as a modular system based on systems and scenarios ought to be considered as an influence on the game engine concept—that is, a software architecture that divides engine from content. Both systems were driven into existence by daunting production schedules, at SPI and id Software respectively. Both enabled the reuse of core systems with new creative assets, such as scenario cards or game maps. These are indeed meaningful similarities. SPI and id were not working with the same technologies, but they were addressing related issues: efficiency in production, design innovation, and player creativity. It is certainly tempting to trace a recurring form of game design manifested in both the War Engine and Game Engine. This interpretive strategy might be a stretch, however. It is true enough that both SPI and id had efficiency of design in mind when they produced systems that could be reused and combined with thematic data to produce different game experiences, such as scenarios or mods. Dunnigan insists in his *Wargames Handbook* however, that manual and computer games are essentially different:

"With board wargames, you could not ignore the details of how the game did what it did. With computer wargames, you could, and most gladly did" (Dunnigan 2000a, loc. 69). In his view, a game like id's *DOOM* was a success due to superior technology. This technology, such as the game's compelling graphics and first-person perspective, were products of the engine, the secrets of which were locked away. In the terminology of the War Engine, what was left—and all that was left—to the player as designer was scenario editing, not simulation design. This was exactly why Dunnigan viewed the decline of board games as bad news. Dunnigan's and John Carmack's compatible visions aside, the transition from manual to PC games complicated access to engines and, in turn, shortened the player's field for new design content.

The designers of computer games easily repeated SPI's move away from the wargame as an authored monograph, but whether War Engines like *Eastern Front* or Game Engines like *DOOM*, the role of the player as designer was changed by an important feature: Other than their programmers, nobody had direct access to the system/engine.[11] Bringing board game and computer game designs into the same conversation about wargame systems and player-created scenarios is nonetheless a worthy exercise; doing so helps us to understand the persistent challenge of designing game systems and the relevance of "manual" wargame design for digital games. In his introduction to a collection of essays on "analog game design," former SPI game developer Greg Costikyan insisted that "digital and non-digital games are not different in essential nature." As a historian, this claim encourages me to pay more attention to tabletop games not just for their own sake, but as part of the history of digital games. One more justification from Costikyan: "As many game studies programs have discovered, tabletop games are particularly useful in the study of game design, because their systems are exposed to the player, not hidden in code" (Costikyan 2011, 13–14). I have tried to show that the Wargame Engine was an important and useful concept in game system design. If so, we have another reason to revisit the history of games on the tabletop.

About the Author

Henry Lowood is curator for history of science and technology collections and for film and media collections at Stanford University. He is also a lecturer in the Thinking Matters Program, the Science and Technology Studies Program, and the History and Philosophy of Science Program at Stanford and in the School of Library and Information Science at San Jose State University. Since 2000, he has led How They Got Game, a research and archival preservation project devoted to the history of digital games and simulations. This project includes Stanford's efforts in the digital preservation of games and virtual worlds, as well as other interactive media. His most recent book is *The Machinima Reader,* published by MIT Press and coedited with Michael Nitsche. He is currently coediting *Debugging Game History: A Lexicon for Critical Game Historiography* with Raiford Guins, also for MIT Press.

Notes

1. On military simulation and its connection to commercial games and the entertainment industry, see Lenoir and Lowood (2005) and Perla (1990). James Dunnigan has observed that the US military had "largely abandoned" wargames by the 1950s; commercial wargames "attracted the troops' attention in the early 1970s and led to a renaissance of military wargaming" (Dunnigan 2000a, loc. 196).

2. For more examples from the 1880s, see Hofer 2003.

3. He became one of Avalon Hill's early playtesters and in 1964 became the first Southwest US "editor" of *The Avalon Hill General*, the company's newsletter.

4. This photograph appears as figure 30.1 in Elizabeth Losh's chapter of this volume.

5. It is important here to note the company's close relationship with its printer, Monarch, whose owners eventually acquired Avalon Hill after Roberts's departure.

6. Dunnigan's operations appeared under a few different organizational names, with SPI the eventual wargame publishing flagship. These included Infinity Corporation, Poultron Press for magazine publishing, and Operations Design Corporation for game design.

7. As of 2014, *S&T* had published nearly three hundred wargames under a series of publishers.

8. *S&T* 23 returned the favor with the publication of *T-34*, designed by Arnold Hendricks, a version of *Tactical Game 3* for miniatures.

9. SPI published a reprint of the playtest kit several years later, with improved counter art, perhaps for collectors.

10. SPI also produced some monographic games, as did most game companies.

11. Of course, open source software leaves the engine's hood up, so to speak, but for practical purposes only to skilled programmers who understand what they are seeing. The manual game's "engine" (the manual itself) is open for all to read.

9 THE ENGINE OF WARGAMING

Matthew B. Caffrey Jr.

In wargame jargon, an engine is a program that supports a wargame. Typically, a Blue team and a Red team decide what their next actions will be, and those decisions are fed into an "engine." The software then estimates the net effect of both their actions. In reality, though, the engine of all wargaming is *need*. Necessity, or more precisely need, is not only the mother of invention but has also been the motivator for many advances in wargaming. The depth and breadth of that need is the engine for the depth and breadth of wargame use yesterday and today. Understanding how need has spawned new wargame applications in the past may help us anticipate application for wargaming tomorrow.

The depths of that need extents to the dawn of civilization. Wargames first appeared as tools to develop the minds of the children of kings and emperors, so they could defeat the children of neighboring rulers. Modern simulation wargaming began with a single set of tools used to educate the children of a single family, the royal family of Prussia. The continued need to outthink your opponents can be seen in the breadth of wargame use today. Wargames are used in dictatorships and democracies, in free market and communist economies. They are used by commanders-in-chief and fire-team leaders. This growth and evolution of wargaming sprang from many needs in many nations. In this chapter, I will discuss a few examples from recent US military history.

Losing a war is a great motivator. Prussia's loss to Napoleon was one of the causes of Prussia's invention of modern wargaming. Germany's loss in World War I helped motivate the increase in depth and breadth of interwar German wargaming. Sometimes, though, doing poorly is motivation enough. During the Vietnam War, both the US Air Force and the US Navy were very concerned by their loss ratios in air-to-air combat against adversary fighters. In Korea, the United States had believed it held a huge edge in air-to-air combat, but if it was now losing about as many aircraft as the North Vietnamese, what would happen if the United States ever fought the presumably more advanced Soviet Red Army Air Forces?

First, the US military tried to figure out what had gone wrong since Korea. A study called "Red Baron" showed that most defeats were suffered during a pilot's initial eight to ten missions. US planners concluded that our military was training its pilots how to fly but not how to fight. What air combat training that did take place was against other Americans flying the same type of aircraft and using the same tactics.

The US Navy acted first, setting up a live wargame within its Fighter Weapons School, a program better known as "Top Gun." Instructor pilots flew aircraft of similar size and performance as contemporary Soviet aircraft. They also used Soviet tactics. The impact of the course was seen quickly: The Navy's air-to-air loss ratio over Vietnam improved dramatically, while the Air Force loss ratio did not.

The Navy's success prompted the United States Air Force (USAF) to act. The USAF also established a Fighter Weapons School and also trained "aggressor" pilots to fly aircraft with similar performance and size as contemporary Soviet aircraft. Then it did more, creating a mock enemy nation on the Nellis Range, complete with adversary radars, simulated air defenses, and ground control intercept operators trained in Soviet tactics. Then the USAF created "Red Flag," which bough Air Force, Navy, and allied or friendly pilots from all over the world to Nellis Air Force Base, Nevada, to participate in what has been called the "ultimate wargame." Through Red Flag, the USAF ensured that all its combat pilots could periodically train against realistic threats. The next time American airpower engaged a hostile air force—in the first Gulf War—the loss ratio was roughly eleven to one in the favor of the United States.

This type of live wargame, pioneered by the US Navy and advanced by the USAF, has spread to other services, such as the US Army's National Training Center, and to other air forces, including the Canadian, Israeli, and Indian.

Sometimes wargames identify a need, and at other times they help anticipate how to meet that need. An early example of this is the US Navy's use of wargaming during the interwar years to identify the need

for forward bases in any future war with Japan. Because the islands where those bases needed to be were in areas controlled by Japan, the wargames indicated that the United States would need to develop amphibious assault capability to take them. Though at the time it was widely believed that modern weapons had made amphibious assault obsolete, the US Marine Corps used wargaming, along with several other methods, to develop its amphibious warfare doctrine.

A much more recent example of this two-step use of wargaming followed the Soviet invasion of Afghanistan. Since the late 1950s, the US government had been using a type of "pol-mil" (political-military) wargame to think through strategy options in the Cold War. After the Soviet invasion, a number of pol-mil wargames were conducted to examine the impacts of various actions the Soviets might take next. One Soviet option explored in was a drive by Soviet forces south from Afghanistan through eastern Iran and to the north shore of the Straits of Hormuz. The first pol-mil wargame exploring the feasibility and likely impact of such a Soviet drive concluded that such an action would be feasible and, in military, economic, diplomatic, and political terms, devastating. Since the first such wargame was played with relatively junior participants, it was repeated with much more senior players. If anything, this second wargame suggested that the consequences would be even more dire than originally estimated. As a result, the US military was directed to prepare a contingency plan to defend the north shore of the straits should a Soviet drive be initiated.

US doctrine suggests that wargaming should be used twice while developing a plan, time permitting. Once to help anticipate the advantages and disadvantages of a number of possible courses of action (typically three) and a second time when planning is nearing completion, to help identify any problems in the plan and identify options to improve it. While the first wargame tends to involve only a few members wargaming each course of action for a few hours each, the second wargame tends to be quite large, involving the subordinate headquarters who would command part of the operation if the plan was ever put into effect. Many are so large that they are named "exercises" and are reported on in the press.

In the case of planning to blunt a Soviet drive on the Straits of Hormuz, the wargame at the end of each (typically) two-year planning cycle was called "Gallant Knight." Early Gallant Knights indicated that the Soviets would be able to reach the north shore of the Straits of Hormuz faster and with more combat power than the US military could; the outcome forecast was the piecemeal destruction of American forces. However, each Gallant Knight planning cycle would conclude with lessons learned as well as an Integrated Priority List (IPL) of forces, supplies, or infrastructure that, if purchased, would likely improve the odds of the United States for victory. Gallant Knight 85 indicated that the US forces needed more ramp space to park their aircraft, the prepositioning of relatively heavy, cheap supplies (like bombs) so that America's limited lift assets could be used to get more forces into the theater sooner, and pipe to supply gas to defenders in the mountains inland from the coast, where we would be harder to dislodge. (In 1997, as a young captain, I served as an adjudicator during Gallant Knight 87. I did not learn until decades later that Gallant Knight 87 was the first time US forces were assessed as having *not* been overrun.)

The Gallant Knight series of wargames had both fairly immediate and long-term consequences.

Preparations justified by Gallant Knight laid the foundation of the Coalition victory during the first Iraq War. Arriving US aircraft had enough room to park, and due to prepositioning our limited airlift was able to get more military personnel into theater sooner because they needed to deliver fewer supplies. Even the pipe was used, to help fuel the shift of forces to the west before the air/ground counteroffensive.

Still, Gallant Knight's greatest effect may have been long-term. Its effectiveness prompted all US commands to wargame more rigorously. It had long been US doctrine to include rigorous wargaming in planning cycles. However, in practice some planning was "pencil wiped," with only the *date* of two-year-old plans being updated. It is unlikely we will ever be able to establish how widespread pencil wiping was, but in the mid-1980s the author saw one plan that still listed an aircraft as being at a base that had converted to a different aircraft six years earlier. At best, during a planning cycle the Time Phased Deployment Plan (TPDP) element of the overall plan was checked for deactivated units and updated only as necessary. Gallant Knight demonstrated how useful rigorous wargaming could be—even when they assume the wrong Red, attacking from the wrong direction. With a little help from other wargame success stories from Europe and Korea, Gallant Knight ushered in the current US emphasis on improving plans and preparations through big rigorous wargames.

Sometimes wargames answer the need to demonstrate relevance. During the interwar period, US Army airmen complained that the army was designing their wargames in order to minimize the impact of airpower. Later, through a wargame series that began in 1979, the Navy used wargaming to demonstrate the continued relevance of sea power.

During the late 1970s, factors that included diminishing hard feelings about Vietnam, news reporting on the "hollow force," an increased appreciation of the Soviet threat, especially in Central Europe, and a somewhat strengthening economy came together to produce growth in the US defense budget. A series of wargames demonstrated just how desperate the first days and weeks of a war in Europe would be and how much increased funding to the army would help. These wargames indicated that the Navy was of little if any relevance to the fight on the "Central Front"; hence, it had little or no call on any of the new money coming to defense. However, many in the US Navy, especially faculty members at the US Naval War College, felt that the US command was dangerously fixated on too small an area and over too limited a time. If war came with the Soviet Union, it would be a global war, and that war would be decided not in days or weeks but in months or years. These naval leaders needed to find a way to convince defense leaders and Congress of what they saw as obvious.

In 1979, the US Navy War College took advantage of a slow time right after graduation to conduct the first "Global" wargame. The budget was next to nothing, and many of the participants were students who had not yet departed for their next assignments. Yet, even this first Global demonstrated the impact naval forces would have on the overall course of a war with the Soviets.

Over the next decade, Global steadily increased in size, budget, sophistication, and influence. More and more members of Congress and congressional staffers gave of their time for the sake of national defense and agreed to spend two weeks in Newport, Rhode Island, in July. Actually, the Navy wargamed out a war with the Soviet Union only twice during the 1980s. Each year it would fight the war for two weeks in July, advancing the time in the wargame a few weeks to a few months. At the end of a five-year series, the Navy had wargamed the conflict from before the hostilities through to the issues related to ending the war. Both five-year cycles indicated the same thing: The Soviets could not win a short war, and in a long war they would be buried by the vastly larger output of the free world's economies.

Global also had both near-term and long-term consequences. Many credit—or blame—Global for the Navy's receiving a large share of the "Reagan buildup" increases in the defense budget. Others claim that the insights generated by Global gave US leaders increased confidence when dealing with the breakup of first the Warsaw Pact, and then the Soviet Union itself. Long-term, Global demonstrated the value to all the US services of wargames that take a overall look at how they can best accomplish their responsibilities under Title 10 of the US Code: to organize, train, and equip their forces. This appreciation led to each service establishing "Title 10" wargames during the 1990s. These wargames remain influential tools for anticipating the force needed in the future.

Finally, sometimes a service's greatest need is not insight or even money, but simply recruitment. Since the Civil War, the United States has typically met such needs through a draft; however, since Vietnam it has not been politically possible to institute one. So in the late 1990s, with individual wealth growing faster than at any time before or since, low unemployment, and budget surpluses promising continued prosperity, the US Army was finding it harder and harder to recruit soldiers. In the 1970s, the Army had lowered standards to attract more recruits, but that had not worked well the first time, and now war was even more high-tech. The Army was able to get more and more money from Congress for TV commercials, but increased funds did not seem to be producing a proportional increase in recruits. One problem was that the generation the Army was trying to recruit from was increasingly turning away from TV and toward the Web and video games.

With 20–20 hindsight, the solution seems obvious: go to where the folks you want to recruit are. Spending a hundredth of the amount it was spending on TV ads, the Army adapted a commercial computer wargame to demonstrate its mission and values and called it *America's Army* (2002–). Made available online for free, *America's Army* became extremely popular. More important, from the Army's point of view, it generated a hundred times more hits on its recruiting website than did its TV ads. (While press reports were generally favorable, some critics asserted that it was unethical or unseemly to recruit using a wargame. These same critics typically were silent on the ethics or seemliness of running recruiting TV ads during football games.)

What are the short- and long-term impacts of *America's Army*? It is hard to say. In the short term, a downturn in the economy and an increase in patriotism following the 9/11 attacks made it much easier for the army to recruit. In the long term, *America's Army* has at least demonstrated how adapting an existing commercial wargame can be done at very little cost. Such an adapted wargame retains the user-friendly interface that permitted its commercial success in the first place. Hezbollah, Russia, and China have either already produced or announced that they will produce an adaptation of a commercial wargame.

In little more than two hundred years, the engine of need has propelled modern wargames from a tool for the education of the children of one royal family to tools used by governments and militaries around the world. This spread has not been steady. Sometimes ignorance or fear of not being taken seriously—to be seen as playing children's games—has prevented needs from being met. Still, it seems likely that wargaming will become still more pervasive during the next two hundred years. Today's young adults spend far more on computer games than on movies. They do not see all games as childish. While commercial wargames make up only a small slice of the huge and rapidly growing recreational software industry, they benefit from the hardware and software advances of the total industry. There is every reason to believe that need will continue to drive the future evolution and growth of wargaming. Kings may no longer be fighting over land, but competition has endured and will continue to endure, and so will the need for games used to gain an advantage.

About the Author

Matthew B. Caffrey Jr. is the Air Force Material Command's (AFMC) integrator for Air Force Research Laboratory (AFRL) Wargaming. A retired colonel in the Air Force Reserve, he was a professor of wargaming and campaign planning at the Air Command and Staff College. He is a frequent speaker on wargaming at the German War College and the Pentagon. Coauthor of the *Gulf War Fact Book*, he has also written many book chapters and articles; his book *On Wargaming* will be published by the Naval War College Press.

10 DESIGN FOR EFFECT: THE "COMMON LANGUAGE" OF *ADVANCED SQUAD LEADER*

J. R. Tracy

Advanced Squad Leader (ASL) (1985) holds a unique place in the wargaming hobby. Nearly thirty years old, it is still going strong, with a large, ardent fan base and a smaller but no less ardent body of detractors. More a game *system* than a game, *ASL* is both respected and reviled as representing the best and worst aspects of wargaming. *ASL* itself is considered a benchmark for complexity and comprehensiveness, while its players possess a devotion bordering on fanaticism. Though its roots are firmly in the "design-for-effect" philosophy, it is viewed by many as the paragon of realism with respect to tactical World War II combat. This is born of a misguided equation of complexity and verisimilitude—*ASL* is at its heart more game than simulation, but it is a richly rewarding game, offering dramatic cinematic narrative as well as an intense competitive experience.

Squad Leader (SL) was published by Avalon Hill in 1977. *SL*'s designer, John Hill, was originally inspired to create a miniatures design and in fact *SL* shares some structural similarities with Hill's *Johnny Reb*, his miniatures rules for tactical combat in the American Civil War. Hill was striving for an impressionistic depiction of combat (see Greenwood et al. 1978), based on his interpretation of eyewitness accounts and recollections. For Hill, "Realism is in the stress and snap decisions of small unit combat" (Hill 2010). As such, *Squad Leader* featured an interleaved sequence of play, with attacker and defender acting and responding within the same player turn.

A player turn opens with the Rally Phase, as both players use leaders to attempt to motivate broken squads, as well as repair malfunctioned weapons and perform various administrative tasks. The attacking player then opens with his Prep Fire, an opportunity to soften up the opposition; however, shooting units forgo movement, so laying down too much fire leaves a player without many options for maneuver. The heart of the turn is in the Movement Phase: The attacker sets out across the hex grid, but the defender has a chance to interrupt with fire of his own from eligible units. Cagey back-and-forth feinting with diversions to draw fire from the main effort marks a high level of attacking play. After movement, the defender has a final Defensive Fire Phase. Units that moved may then fire in the Advancing Fire Phase, albeit at reduced effectiveness. Units broken earlier in the turn fall back in the subsequent Rout Phase, which in turn leads to the Advance Phase. Here, most attacking units (even those that fired earlier) are able to move one more hex, often into the location of the enemy, where matters are settled with hand grenades and bayonets in the concluding Close Combat Phase. This sequence is then repeated with the players switching roles, completing a full game turn.

Squad Leader introduced the German and Soviet orders of battle, but further expansion modules tweaked the rules for armor combat (*Cross of Iron* 1978), and added the British, French, Poles, Belgians (*Crescendo of Doom* 1979), and finally Americans (*GI: Anvil of Victory* 1982) to the system. Along with the new nationalities came added rules, and Hill's original vision of "a 'basically simple' game that could be 'gotten into' quickly" (Hill 1977) sagged under the added weight.

With the publication of *GI: Anvil of Victory*, *Squad Leader* was a popular game system burdened with a rules set spread over four separate games and modules. Don Greenwood, Avalon Hill's chief game developer and a game designer himself, saw an opportunity to consolidate and rationalize the sprawling *Squad Leader* rules set into a single volume, to "make it more playable" and "fill in all the holes" in order to "nurture an all-encompassing game system" (Greenwood 1986). The result was the *Advanced Squad Leader Rule Book* (*ASLRB*), published in 1985, alongside the first module in the series, *Beyond Valor* (1985), featuring Germans versus Soviets on the Eastern Front. Since then the system has traveled to the desert (*West of Alamein* 1988) and to the Far East (*Code of Bushido* 1991; *Gung Ho* 1992), with stops along the way for detailed treatment of individual battles (Stalingrad in *Red Barricades* [1990], Betio in *Blood Reef: Tarawa* [1999], among others).

With eighteen modules published, including more than eighty maps, thousands of playing pieces, and hundreds of scenarios, *ASL*'s breadth is staggering. The depth of detail includes treatment of seaborne invasions, parachute landings, bicycle troops, ski troops, sewer movement, and cliff climbing. Over the course of a typical game turn, a player might check for wind direction, call in artillery, lay down a smokescreen, bail out of a tank, dash across a street, search a building, fire a bazooka, create a hero, collect prisoners, ambush the enemy, and engage in hand-to-hand combat. If you read it in a book or saw it in the movies, chances are you can do it in *ASL*, on the steppe, in the desert, on an island, or in Berlin. This comprehensiveness strongly appeals to fans of the game; if you invest the time and effort to learn the system, you are rewarded with an almost unlimited ability to re-create the full spectrum of World War II ground combat. This was Greenwood's explicit goal, to "provide enough detail in one game system that players who devoted themselves to that game system could speak a common language" and "play literally thousands of games covering all types of situations while still using the same game system" (Greenwood 1986). This devotion comes at a price in both time and money; to learn and ultimately master the game requires study and practice, pushing other games aside, and the cost of the full system runs into the hundreds of dollars. As a result, *ASL* has developed a reputation as a "lifestyle game," inspiring comments such as "A lot like golf, if you start, your life will never be the same," "Greatest game/religion ever," and "A great game which was essentially the only game I played for more than a decade." For others, that immersion factor pushed them away: "You commit to playing this, or you don't play it at all" and "Kind of like law school without a six-figure salary waiting at the end of the rainbow" (Various 2001–, boardgamegeek.com).

Given the extensive *ASL* rulebook and the breadth and depth of the *ASL* universe, how does the game hold up as a model of World War II tactical combat? Some hold that it is superb: "Super-detailed tactical simulation," "It is a very realistic simulation of WWII combat," and "this is *the* WW2 tactical simulation." However, cursory examination reveals several shortcomings as a simulation. A player enjoys a tremendous information advantage over his World War II–commander counterpart, with a complete grasp of the enemy's composition and objectives in most cases, as well as exact knowledge of the positions and readiness of his own forces. Many elements of command and control are either abstracted or missing altogether; the morale state of discrete infantry squads varies, for instance, but the cohesion of the overall formation is little affected by losses. Infantry might halt or even run from the fight under enemy fire, but tanks move implacably forward, their crews unshakably committed until their vehicles are immobilized or destroyed. Offboard artillery, representing supporting batteries, is handled via a process both cumbersome and complex (even by the standards of the game!). Where do these shortcomings leave us? If *ASL* fails as a complete simulation, does it at least fulfill John Hill's goal of realism as conceived for the original *Squad Leader*?

As Hill envisioned with *SL*, a game of *Advanced Squad Leader* is full of snap decisions made under stress. The defender must either engage an approaching enemy unit or hold fire for a greater threat. The attacker must react and adjust as his assaulting force takes casualties or achieves an unanticipated breakthrough. At a higher level, success demands that those snap decisions serve an overall plan in the context of the scenario at hand. Perfect command and control yields an imperfect model, but effective coordination of disparate elements rewards an historical combined arms mentality.

For example, the scenario "A Breezeless Day" (from 1997's *ASL Action Pack #1*) depicts a German attack during Operation Nordwind in early 1945. The Germans outnumber the defending Americans two to one in infantry and vehicles but must take a town and exit the map with over half their force, a very tall order. They have the tools to do it, however. First, the infantry searches for mines. Then the JgPzVIs, super-heavy tank destroyers with frontal armor impervious to anything in the American arsenal, terrorize the American tanks. The German FlammHetzer, a heavily armored flamethrower tank, in turn chases off American bazooka teams. This clears the way for the more lightly armored assault guns to smoke and batter the infantry, until finally the panzergrenadiers move up to take and hold ground.

The possible pitfalls, however, are many: the JagdPanzers are mechanically unreliable, the FlammHetzer may well expend all its flamethrower fuel, the German infantry is brittle, and the entire armor force is turretless. All these factors are reflected in the rules, some effortlessly, some with a little overhead. The turretless nature of the German vehicles comes into play as the American Shermans are very good at shooting on the move: the US tanks dart in to take shots at the German's flanks and zip away again, while the clumsy JagdPanzers struggle to reorient themselves to meet the threat. The American armor doesn't need to survive the scenario; it just needs to keep the German armor off the GIs long enough for them to establish themselves in the town and deal with the panzergrenadiers.

All this adds up to a very interactive combined arms puzzle. While the C3I aspect of *ASL* is sketchy to nonexistent, the basic parts fit together the way they're supposed to, and without proper coordination of the various pieces it all falls apart very quickly.

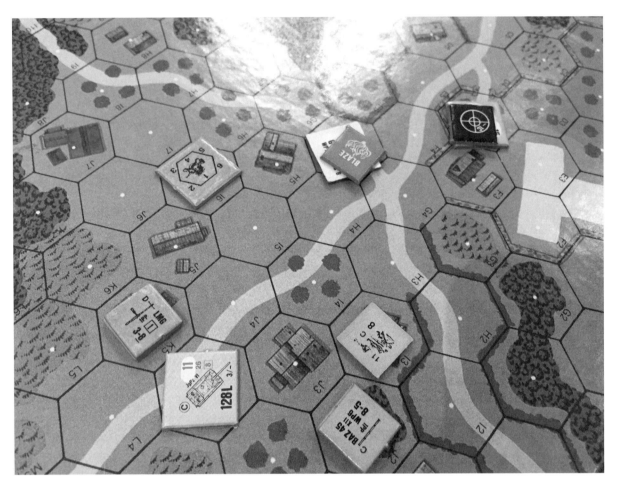

Figure 10.1
ASL, "A Breezeless Day": The hunter becomes the hunted.

Flexibility and a knack for improvisation are vital; combat is resolved via die roll, and though a given outcome may be likely it is no means certain. The occasional extreme die roll often highlights the narrative but need not define success or failure—that depends on the reaction and adaptability of the players. Adversity provides the stress, and whether a competitor thrives under that pressure determines whether he overcomes or succumbs.

Don Greenwood's "common language" of *ASL* helped create a world-spanning community, built on casual local encounters but also featuring more formal tournament play. A recent year saw nearly four dozen sizable events on four continents.[1] The popularity of tournaments in turn has generated a highly developed and competitive style of play that doesn't sit well with some players. Given the complexity of the rule set, strange edge cases and

Figure 10.2

ASL, "A Breezeless Day": Scouting out a minefield.

anomalies exist that can be exploited to advantage if the circumstances arise. For instance, assume you have a well-placed machine gun in a key building, but without anti-tank support; I might park a tank on your doorstep, drawing the undivided attention of your gunners as my infantry thunders safely past.[2] Such situations do not dominate play but falling victim to one can leave a bad taste in a player's mouth, and some have walked away from the game as a result: "Competition play has diminished the game in my eyes … tournament players have leveraged the rules in order to win" (Various 2001–, boardgamegeek.com).

In 1986 Greenwood stated, "The game glut has so saturated the marketplace that nobody is playing the same games any more" (Greenwood 1986). Twenty-eight years later, the flood of games published annually is undiminished, yet *ASL*,

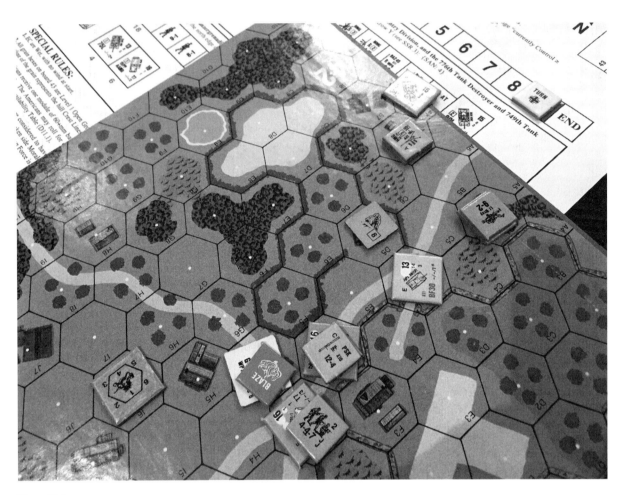

Figure 10.3
ASL, "A Breezeless Day": Dashing for the exit.

Greenwood's extrapolation of John Hill's original idea, continues to thrive and puts the lie to Greenwood's own lament. Multi-Man Publishing, licensed publisher of *ASL* products since the demise of Avalon Hill in 1999, regularly sells out its print runs of *ASL*-related products, and the flow of new material continues.[3] In a fragmented gaming market notorious for celebrating the "cult of the new," *ASL* stands out for holding the focus of a thriving population of adherents for almost three decades. Some play it for the history, some play it for its qualities as a game, some to test themselves in a competitive arena, but all interests are served by a cohesive rules set and a comprehensive breadth. Mastering the game is daunting, but the reward is substantial: the means to re-create nearly all aspects of World War II tactical combat, and a community with which to share it.

About the Author

J. R. Tracy graduated from the Massachusetts Institute of Technology in 1987. His career in finance has taken him around the world as a trader, banker, and fund manager. He has been wargaming since 1972, when he spied an ad for *Strategy & Tactics* magazine in the back of *Boy's Life*. He plays a wide variety of games in addition to *Advanced Squad Leader*, the love of his gaming life, and also playtests and proofreads for several gaming companies. He has written several strategy articles for *ASL*, appearing in *The General*, the *ASL Annual*, and the *ASL Journal*. He relentlessly carpetbombs the Internet with extensive recaps of his weekly gaming group, and shoulders the blame for many a game purchase thereby inspired.

Notes

1. See <http://aslladder.com/asltournaments.html>.

2. The infamous "VBM Sleaze-Freeze," noted here with similar gems: <http://www.ths85.net/zekesaslparadise/sleaze.html>.

3. Based on the author's conversations with Multi-Man Publishing principals Perry Cocke and Brian Youse and with Chas Argent, its chief developer for *ASL* products.

11   *COMBAT COMMANDER*: TIME TO THROW YOUR PLAN AWAY

John A. Foley

If wargaming is to "reflection" as video gaming is to "reaction," it stands to reason that the typical, effective medium for reflection has continued to be a paper vehicle, not a computer vehicle. While a computer platform certainly can be harnessed for a turn-based simulation, the simplicity of materials and the large maps of a tabletop game seem to serve the gaming purpose effectively. That a paper simulation of conflict (with maps, counters, dice, and cards) enables a reflective engagement is not the hard part for a designer; the hard part is handling time and decision making in a credible and insightful way.

Tactical wargaming comes to us from two separate strains of simulation: the "toy soldiers and cannons" world of play, with its focus on the arts-and-crafts modeling of the environment, troops, and materiel; and the "staff officer *kriegspiel*" world of play, with its focus on situational assessment, double-blind issuance of orders, and refereed outcomes. Starting in the 1960s, tactical game designs began to use hex grids and standardized terrain on paper-based maps, which eliminated the charming vagaries of miniatures rules. With the appearance of the seminal design *Squad Leader* (1977), a major leap forward occurred in tactical design: a structured, interactive turn sequence that is highly integrated with a probabilistic decision model. What you got in cardboard form was something that evoked the miniature-level view and mediated the interaction of the players with sufficient unknowns to enable an experience of command, control, and chaos.

This system and its major descendant, *Advanced Squad Leader* (1985), became the benchmark for tactical wargaming and survive healthily to this day. This design brought with it key definitions of time (the narrative of time engagement between the opponents) and decision making (the model of the command experience in the game structure). Nearly at the same time, Courtney Allen created an analogous tactical system, *Up Front*, which used a deck of cards to explore the same territory. Instead of playing on a map, players place terrain cards from their hands as their small unit formations discover or reach a particular piece of terrain. As another distinction, time in *Up Front* is not measured by a set number of turns, but rather by a certain number of passages through the governing card deck. Unlike the benchmark *Squad Leader*, space and time were placed experientially into the heads of the players by *Up Front*, leading to an impulsive experience of command in the field. Yet another system, *Ambush!*, emphasized a guided-narrative approach for solitaire play, using a map and counters coupled with an elegant mechanism by which each hex a unit enters triggers a lookup in a large booklet of numbered paragraphs, to discover what happens. The downside to this was that once a "story" was complete, players typically did not return to try the situation again.

Twenty years after these landmark designs, Chad Jensen, drawing upon his love of these previous designs, created the *Combat Commander* system for very small World War II infantry actions, finding a way to create a unique blend: a new take on a card-driven time- and decision-making experience that also played with counters on a hex grid. Currently, *Combat Commander* covers four large theater-wide modules (*Europe*, *Mediterranean*, *Pacific*, and *Resistance!*); six extensions, called "battle packs," that provide new scenarios, maps, and counters; and a variety of scenarios published in industry magazines.

Time

For a wargame player, the definition of time is central to the gaming experience, because the player continually holds the idea of real time in his or her head over against the experience of the game's paper model of time. A common goal for designers and players alike is to be able to say that what just happened in the game matches the narrative of that moment as recounted in a particular book or other reference work. When players experience those kinds of matches—during play and later in the retelling—this represents what wargamers constantly look for: the game and the subject matter are aligned (and thus enjoyable and possibly very instructive).

The time in a battle sequence can be broken down into three important layers of time: actual time, modeled time, and design time. By actual time, I mean real chronological time. By modeled time, I mean the specified time unit the designer has chosen for the time scale: depending on the game a complete game turn might represent two minutes, a day, a week, three months, and so on. By design time, I mean the discrete subphases of the modeled time, which players move through in sequence. Each of these interrelate, but how well they do in practice directly affects the experience (both the fun factor and the insight factor) for the players. I will not cover a last element of time—the time to play the game itself (playing time)—but for practical reasons it does factor into design thinking.

From a historical perspective, the challenge facing us when looking at actual time in combat comes when we try to understand past events that have some photographic (still) evidence and written evidence (primary and secondary materials), but little in the way of real-time recording of a given particular battle event. The way into this problem is to construct a model of time based on recorded measures and rates. *Squad Leader* and *Advanced Squad Leader* hold to the notion of the "two tactical minutes" as a principal structure of time, within which the minimum, necessary, and sufficient elements of battle are typically able to occur. This notion of the two minutes and what occurs in two minutes is very powerful—it serves as a bridge between game mechanisms and combat reality. It becomes a lens to structure the narrative of the experience (the gaming experience and the imagined combat experience). It should be noted that in *Squad Leader* and *ASL*, six turns, for example, formally models twelve minutes, but certain elements of "actual time" might be disregarded—such as time leading up to the start of the battle or its aftermath—such that those twelve minutes of modeled time may really represent, say, half an hour of actual time. In any case, the *ASL* design models this in formal units nominally representing two minutes each.

As another example, let's start with the subject of tactical infantry actions in the Pacific theater from 1942 through 1945, a subject that thoroughly interests me and for which I have designed a large number of scenarios for *Combat Commander*. One of the scenarios I designed, "Totsugeki!," represents a portion of the battle of Edson's Ridge, a Japanese night assault near the airfield on the island of Guadalcanal (for which my principal, but not sole, source was Richard Frank's 1990 work *Guadalcanal*). Any designer of a scenario for a tactical system faces the same questions about scope: what portion of the battle (in terms of geography and units) and what time frame to select that represents the moments of interest both in historical terms and in game design terms. Whether I am designing an infantry action for *Combat Commander* or *Advanced Squad Leader*, these questions are essentially the same. For practical purposes, scenarios for these systems typically involve a certain number of game turns, which is the requisite amount of modeled time that should enable players to engage one another through the rules to reach a demonstrative and satisfying result. Strictly speaking, the amount of modeled time represented in a tactical system maps only to a portion of the overall actual time; the time to stage at an attack line, pronounced

lulls in the action, and the aftermath of battle are not usually worth spending the playing time to simulate. In the case of this specific scenario, some ten to twenty minutes of *modeled time* represents perhaps thirty to sixty minutes of *actual time* with an expected *playing time* of three to four hours.

Design time—how the designer articulates and segments the passage through the central time unit of the design (the modeled time)—especially in a reflective, paper-based model, relies on a classic simplification, what we call the "Igo-Ugo" mechanism. First I get to do everything I can, then you get to do everything you can (while we both attempt to suspend our disbelief in how poorly this reflects the simultaneity of real events). The signal innovation in *Squad Leader* was imagining how to interleave the actions of both players using something much deeper than merely subdividing the game activities. The sequence of play embodies a representation of field doctrine, an idealization of what happens first, then next, then next, in each of the "two tactical minutes" of modeled time. We move into the realm I call design time: the mechanics by which the system walks the players through the subphases of the units of modeled time.

The *Squad Leader* design articulates the model using eight unique interleaved phases, from the Rally Phase through Prep Fire and other phases to the Close Combat Phase. The first step is to see if previously broken units can Rally to become fully capable again. The next step is for the attacker to decide which units take the opportunity to fire at full effect at the defender—this is Prep Fire—which concludes the ability of those units to take further action that turn (but which represents continuing suppressive fire throughout the time period). Next, given that this turn-long fire has started (occurred), the attacker then decides which units will attempt Movement in the face of the defender; the defender may select units to attempt to fire back at moving units: Defensive Fire. The remainder of the turn alternates between various attacking and defending functions. The point is that the attacker and defender engage in a structured dance: rally attempts by both sides, then covering fire from a fire team, the attempts to move by movement teams, the defensive response, and a last fire attempt by the attackers prior to a final advance forward and the ensuing close combat. Both sides perform this structured sequence of phases (the design time) to complete what occurs in the tactical two minutes of the modeled time.

Chad Jensen's contribution to this starts with his curiosity about the possibility of decomposing the structured narrative of the tactical two minutes. Even if military field doctrine recommends that suppressing fire from the fire team occur first, followed by the actions of a movement team, actual time in battle is substantially so chaotic after the first point of engagement that infantry activities do in fact occur in any sequence, including surprising empty periods and abruptly compressed periods.

Instead of using the sequence of play as a structure for the narrative, *Combat Commander* provides a deck of cards that primarily represent pieces of the standard structure cut up as if by scissors and drawn randomly into the players' hands. These pieces—the orders—enable one or more units to accomplish one segment of the standard structure. For example, a Fire order is different from a Movement order, and if units end up in the same hex, the close combat takes place immediately without waiting until a defined phase occurs.

Let's look at a typical hand for the Japanese attacker in the scenario "Totsugeki!" The top bar of text for each card defines what kind of order a player may issue to a unit or a group of units supported by a leader: the hand consists of two Fire orders, a Move order, an Advance order, a Revive-1 order, and a Charge order. The player turn consists of playing zero or more cards, issuing and completing a single order to each activated unit or group with a leader, and then optionally playing additional cards from the hand (amplifying the order) based on the possibilities allowed by the order type. In response, the inactive player may simultaneously play *actions* from the hand (as distinct from *orders*, which are only allowed on the active player's turn).

At the end of the activities initiated by the active player, he draws his hand back to full size and the inactive player now becomes the active player. In this manner, the Japanese player chooses what "this moment of time" is about; for example, he may decide to hold his Fire cards and use his Move card, or use one Fire card and the Advance card. The design time is not predefined into a larger regularly repeating structure; it is an available moment of possible activity. The sequence of play thus becomes what each player chooses to do with the cards available in their hands. An important side effect of this choice for design time is that a player may find himself waiting for crucial cards, and because of not having them in hand, be constrained from attempting a desired or necessary action in the game. One of the most praised (and detested) by-products of relying on a small hand of cards is that from time to time players find themselves unable to accomplish anything.

On the face of it, it does not stand to reason that a player should be unable to order his units to perform any allowed capability to match the situation, but

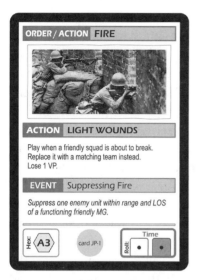

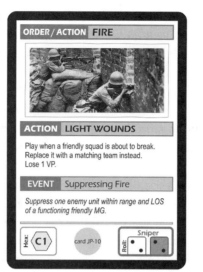

Figure 11.1

The Japanese attack hand.

historical tactical combat narratives are filled with descriptions of such inexplicable hesitations. In the case of the attack on Edson's Ridge, while the lasting image of continuous coordinated Japanese attacks comes to mind, it was often the case that separated unit groups could not communicate and they reacted (waited, moved, or attacked) without any coordination, contributing significantly to the failure of the attack. As for the US defenders, they were much better equipped from a communications perspective, but the violence of the attack put an extreme premium on strong leadership to enable the units to maintain position under fire. In one notable case, a unit commander was relieved for being a "dud," which seems like a gracious way to say that he was incapable of maintaining sufficient composure to command (and take appropriate action).

Another critical design element introduced by Chad Jensen to the card play is the use of "triggers," some of which are represented in the figure above note the Time and Sniper triggers marked at the bottom of some of the cards. Where an order or action requires random resolution, instead of rolling two dice (there are no physical dice in the game), the active player draws a card from the top of his deck and references the "roll" (the depiction of dice on each card). If one of these trigger depictions is placed next to the dice depiction, that trigger must be resolved before the order or action is resolved. An entire pass through your card deck theoretically defines the modeled time for the *Combat Commander* system (analogous to both players conducting the full eight phases of a game turn in *Advanced Squad Leader*). But in the case of the Time trigger, its appearance to resolve an order or action suddenly ends the game turn (or modeled time for the system). The player who triggered Time advances the time marker forward on the time track, takes his deck and his discard pile, shuffles them together to form a new deck, and then resolves the roll for the original order or action that required it. Both players trigger time advances this way. In this manner, not only may you be unable to accomplish what you need to do at any particular moment in time, the overall flow of time in the game may race ahead beyond your control as well.

As a final control element to the design, just because a scenario reaches its nominally specified end point (the "Totsukegi!" scenario, for example, specifies eight game turns) does not mean that the game ends. In fact, the game continues past this point for an indefinite period determined by a random die roll check for each Time trigger that occurs after the nominal end point.

It is the standard experience of a *Combat Commander* player to fret about time throughout the entire game. Formally, modeled time is much more elastic than the *Squad Leader* model, sometimes leaping forward and other times dragging on endlessly.

Design

The structured narrative of design time (in *Squad Leader*, for example) invokes a doctrinal flavor of progress through the modeled time: activities occur in orchestrated sequence. In contrast, the decomposition of the narrative of design time (as in *Combat Commander*), in which any card-defined activity can

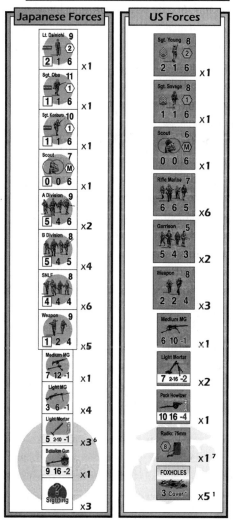

COMBAT COMMANDER

ALLIES   JAPAN

Japanese Forces
US Forces

SITUATION REPORT — scenario design by John A. Foley

EDSON'S RIDGE, GUADALCANAL, 13 SEPTEMBER 1942—
In the second major attempt at dislodging the enemy position, the Japanese maneuvered deep in the jungle to the south of the American perimeter expecting that it would be less defended. General Kawaguchi employed a complicated plan using battalions from the 124th and 4th Infantry. The terrain rendered a multi-pronged plan almost impossible to execute, however, but with sheer willpower, some of his force managed a devastating attack. During what is known as the Battle of Edson's or "Bloody" Ridge, at 2230 7th company of the Japanese II/4th Regiment launched the first of many attacks along the eastern flanks of the ridge directly at B Company of the 1st Parachute Battalion. A successful attack could dislodge or overtake Lt. Colonel Edson's command post and put the defense of Henderson Field in grave jeopardy. Amazingly, Edson orchestrated one of the greatest nighttime defenses and was awarded the Medal of Honor.

VICTORY POINT MARKER:	20 (Allied side)
TIME / SUDDEN DEATH MARKERS:	0 / 8
SURRENDER MARKER:	9
OB STATS MARKERS:	Japan — Line-4 / Attack Allies — Elite-3 / Defend
OBJECTIVE CHITS:	Open — **U** Japan — random Allies — random
OBJECTIVE CONTROL:	Japan — none Allies — all
SET UP:	Japan — last; 1 hexes deep [2] Allies — first; 13 hexes deep [1]
INITIATIVE:	Japan
FIRST TURN:	Japan

SPECIAL RULES:

1. PREPARED POSITIONS: Foxholes must be set up in objective hexes. At least one US unit must set up with each foxhole.

2. SECOND WAVE: At least seven Japanese units (and their assigned weapons) must be placed in the 1 space of the Time Track instead of setting up on map.

3. NIGHT: Night rules [18] are in effect for the entire scenario.

4. CONTROLLED WITHDRAWAL: The first Allied Move order played each turn (only) is considered a "Withdrawal". During a Withdrawal, activated Allied units may not be the target of Op Fire whenever the new hex entered is closer to the Allied friendly map edge than the one that was vacated.

5. HAIL OF GRENADES: Allied Hand Grenades actions provide +4 FP instead of +2.

6. WITHERING MORTAR FIRE: Japanese Light Mortars have +2 FP.

7. PRE-REGISTERED FIRE: At any time during the game, the Allied player may take a Commonwealth control marker from the countermix and place it into any hex of the map. This may be done up to five times and the markers cannot be moved once placed. Allied artillery attacks are always accurate when the SR is placed into a hex containing such a marker. If so, do not make a Targeting roll for that attack—instead proceed directly to the Minor Drift Check [O24.3.2.1] after placing the SR.

Figure 11.2

A *Combat Commander* scenario card, including scenario special rules (SSRs).

occur in the sequence, brings a chaotic immediacy to that modeled time. Both are cinematic, since they engender a strong, imagined, cooperative experience; this is reflected by years and years of after-action reports by players of both systems, which specifically call out how the game action plays like a movie. Both are exciting to play, but they are quite different in what they emphasize. And this is where decision making in both designs takes radical turns in different directions. In both designs, a player needs a plan, but in one of them, not only does your plan get tested heavily, but you also frequently discover, and quickly, that you have to throw your plan away. For *Squad Leader*, players can rely on things occurring at predetermined times; for *Combat Commander*, you cannot rely on very much of anything.

After players have chosen to play a particular tactical scenario, studied the orders of battle and any special capabilities or scenario rules that apply, and have reflected upon the victory conditions, they set their forces up with a plan of attack or defense and with contingencies in mind. Because all tactical scenarios include a time limit (how long game time is for the particular situation), the plans need to account for these constraints. So how players understand time (the sequence of play) directly bears on decision making: what units and capabilities to use, what sequence can effectively exploit one's strength and the opponent's weaknesses, and so on.

The *Advanced Squad Leader* rulebook is famously vast and comprehensive. The reason for this is simple: everything you can possibly attempt is presented in great detail. You have to decide whether to attempt a given action or capability or sequence, and if you so decide, you typically test the chance of whether you can actually do the chosen action, prior to seeing whether it can succeed. This two-step probabilistic approach is standard: you decide what you want to do, you roll the dice to see whether you can actually do it, and then you roll the dice to see how effective your action was. Since you know how the structured time narrative works, you can predict when you will attempt certain actions or sequences; they become a best practice for a level of play. What casts doubt on this skillful knowledge of play are the constant tests of effectiveness. The excitement of the unknown in this design is sourced in surprises inherent in a distribution of results for two six-sided dice.

Combat Commander was originally created with a motto of "90 percent of the effect with 10 percent of the rules weight" (of *Advanced Squad Leader*). Thus, the rulebook and system design does not try to account for all army types, capabilities, experience levels, materiel, and so on. Unlike *ASL*, which will devote pages and pages of rules to a very wide range of unusual firing options, the range of fire capabilities in *Combat Commander* are limited to a handful of basic rules augmented by special circumstances (called "actions") on the cards. The design offloads special rules and situations onto the cards, which means if you have the card in hand and choose to play it, you can attempt that action or capability.

Let's look back at the cards in the Japanese player hand in figure 11.1 and examine the text associated with actions: two Light Wounds, and one each of Hand Grenades, Crossfire, No Quarter, and Enfilade. While the active player may play both orders and actions during his or her turn, the inactive player may counter only with actions during the active player's turn. Rather than write a rules section about Crossfire that attempts to account for all circumstances (with the assumption of differentiated phases in a turn sequence), the design presents an action that depends on a simple precondition—"when firing at a Moving target"—that only the inactive player can use. In this manner, the player does not have to consult or have memorized an encyclopedic listing of possible responses to know when and how to take the action; he either holds the capability in his hand or he does not. This is one of the most appreciated (also disliked) features of the design, since the choices are highly constrained in advance.

Another way the design offloads special rules and situations is within the special scenario rules (SSRs). In the case of "Totsugeki!" the accounts of the attack on Edson's Ridge provide an extensive amount of detail that is not in the *Combat Commander* ruleset. The art of scenario design in this case rests in selecting the telling handful of detail and boiling it down to the fewest words.

The eight special rules shown in figure 11.2 reflect a judgment about standout dramatic elements of the Japanese attack and US defense. For instance, one of the great acts of leadership by Colonel Edson was how he managed to maintain control of his men on the ridge through his exceptional leadership, with the result that instead of breaking and retreating from the ridge positions, the men fell back in an orderly way. Special rule 4 thus breaks a standard *Combat Commander* rule to provide a special mechanism by which this kind of retreat could safely be pulled off by the US player. But without special rule 1, which forces US units to be placed more forward than a prudent player would wish (as those positions historically were that night), special rule 4 would not have the chance of being used or of feeling just right.

Another key element of the historical attack was how the Japanese staged so noisily in the jungle directly adjacent to the ridge. US troops rolled grenades down the slopes into the jungle to great effect. Note that special rule 5 does not force this kind of action specifically to occur, but when you see (as the Japanese player) that you either have long open bare terrain to cross to reach the US positions, or that you can attempt to move through the jungle to reach the US positions much more directly, then the special rule will likely be invoked—exactly as it was historically.

Special rules 6 and 7 together reference how many light mortars the Japanese were able to bring to bear during this attack and how devastating the distant 105mm artillery positions were for the US defense. Given that this is a night scenario (special rule 3), this particular scenario adds just the merest additional rules in order to paint the broad and terrifying brush of this moment in the overall two-day affair. Note that historically, this attack eventually turned into a Banzai charge-style of attack, with its terrifying aspect and results; *Combat Commander* has an event card that converts a standard attack into a Banzai charge, and this has happened on occasion when I have played this scenario. But the design choice to start with a standard attack posture placed more cards into the attacking player's hands, and more closely reflects the vigorous attacking thrusts found in the historical narrative.

Let's show how this ties together and integrate what you can know of your cards and your knowledge of the way time rapidly flows and jumps. In *Combat Commander*, if your hand of cards does not provide you with a particular option, you must either go forward with what you have or discard from your hand—waiting unhappily for what you opponent might do—and hope that your next draw will provide you with the capability you need. You have much more limited knowledge about when you can try what you need to try (as compared to *Squad Leader* or *ASL*) and in fact, there is not only an art but a doctrinal element to sound decision making (when to play, when to hold, when to discard) based on the nation you are playing (see Foley 2007). However, the primary issue you face is whether you can maintain your own composure in the face of so much uncertainty.

To return to the "Totsugeki!" example, let's look briefly at what the Japanese player faces in the scenario. The player has a more numerous force at the point of attack, but cannot start immediately on map with all of it—special rule 2 breaks the attack into waves, which is how it occurred that night—and has the daunting task of making headway across open terrain. Night movement rules restrict movement, visibility, and hand flexibility but give players the ability to place starshells for illumination. If the player chooses to move through the lower jungle, it will consume a huge amount of game time and overly concentrate the force into the gully. If the player chooses instead to doggedly proceed forward into the open ground (and thus move much faster), his units will be broken and eliminated much more quickly.

Players who hold onto their cards too long and who stick with a decided approach too long can sometimes feel frustrated and believe that they cannot master the system at all. Players who adjust, discovering that they must decidedly cast aside their cards and plans (for indeed, the system is designed to upset your plans) are more frequently rewarded with the ability to win, possibly even on the very last card play—which, given good play, is a common outcome in this system. Repeatedly I have found that

the Japanese player has to try just about anything and everything opportunistically in the hope that the right combination of illumination and infiltration occurs, allowing an unbroken unit to appear suddenly in the midst of the US positions. This scenario is one of my favorite for illuminating the nasty dilemma that players face in Combat Commander: you must survive the constant feeling of losing the situation completely by striving constantly and inventively within constraints ("I do not have the right cards") and chaos ("three Time triggers in ten minutes of play").

The excitement of the unknown in this design is sourced in surprises inherent in holding only a few of your seventy-two cards at any one time. Since you do not know how the narrative flow will go, you face chaos more directly; instead of competing against the other player with emphasis on a doctrinal model, you are competing against the other player with emphasis on maintaining your own gamer's morale. Years of results have shown that effective *Combat Commander* players are frequently able to throw away their original plans ruthlessly and intuit a more effective path through chaos. When you need to use Movement orders but don't have any, perhaps you should still push forward with the more limited but special Advance orders instead of merely waiting ... or perhaps you should wait.

It occasionally happens in playing a Combat Commander scenario that both players suffer a temporarily severe run of bad cards; this is the notable "maintain your own morale" moment. The normal course of play typically has the player suffering the absence of the right card for the given moment, but he usually has other things he can and should do, even if it means waiting for a short while. In a simple sense, the design levers persistently take your footing out from under you. With your planning wrenched from your hand, you must flexibly reframe your approach, and as all *Combat Commander* fans know (and say), never, ever give up. Things change in the most dramatic ways, and this is perhaps one of the most-loved aspects of the design.

About the Author

John A. Foley is an operations science manager (process visualization, analysis, and improvement) currently at Alcatel-Lucent, prior to that holding various positions in Lucent Technologies and Bell Telephone Laboratories in product management, program management, software engineering and architecture, software techniques research, human factors engineering, and technical writing. He has been a wargamer since 1965. He was among the earliest contributors of support materials for the *Advanced Squad Leader* system in the 1990s. Since then he has been the developer for published wargame designs and series by Rick Young, Chad Jensen, and John Butterfield. He has designed battle packs for Chad Jensen's *Combat Commander* system and published articles in GMT's *C3i* magazine.

12 *EMPIRE OF THE SUN*: THE NEXT EVOLUTION OF THE CARD-DRIVEN GAME ENGINE

Mark Herman

Wargames have their origins in extending and focusing the chess mechanic through a historical lens. This transformation of chess into historical simulations left a legacy of giving the players perfect to near-perfect information about the location and capabilities of their opponent's forces. This characteristic of wargames is orthogonal to a military leader's experience of pursuing their objectives while managing risk with imperfect information.

As a designer, I always strive to develop game systems that allow the players to compete in a plausible historical narrative that allows for the suspension of disbelief and offers insight into a period's dynamics. Back in the 1990s, I was wrestling with these challenges while attempting to design a game on the American Revolution. At some point during the process I hit on the notion of using cards as the activation mechanism for army movement, political activity, and singular significant events. In a nutshell, cards were the mechanism that allowed a player to drive the action in the game. The result was *We the People*, published by Avalon Hill in 1994, which created a new game genre, the card-driven game (CDG).

In my original concept, a hand of cards would offer a player a series of choices between using operations to move their armies or compete for the loyalty of the populace, as well as periodically allowing significant personages, via events, to weigh in for their cause. The pivotal CDG concept presents a player with a decision trade space between military and political activity. Prior to the CDG concept, the assumption was that this trade space was bounded by the kinetics of moving, supporting, and fighting your forces, with all other political effects treated as a free good. The reality is that any senior decision structure can only handle some finite number of priority issues; the CDG concept acknowledges this limitation of senior decision maker bandwidth and the finite number of issues that can be implemented at any given time. Even in an era of large military staffs, one only has to reexamine the months of meetings, plans, and effort required to conduct the US troop "surges" into Iraq and Afghanistan to see the veracity of this concept.[1] This player decision space around using a card to conduct political-military activities or to use the historical event has become the general definition of a CDG.

Evolving the CDG for Twentieth-Century Warfare

While a game system arguably cannot be copyrighted (this has caused lawsuits in the past), game methodologies can be patented.[2] One of my early decisions was to allow this intellectual property to become public domain, opening up the hobby's design aperture by not pursuing this path. Many CDG designs followed the look and feel of *We the People*, using a point-to-point movement system with named leaders who were activated with the cards. (I often choose point-to-point maps in my pre-twentieth-century designs because of the advantages they bring in depicting land forces tightly tied to geography for movement and supply. When one considers twentieth-century situations and the advent of airpower, this map technique is less appropriate and is often used incorrectly.)

After publishing the *For the People* CDG (a strategic-level American Civil War game) in 1998, I focused on a sequel to my 1985 *Pacific War*, published by Victory Games. The resulting *Empire of the Sun* (GMT Games 2005) design took the earlier operational level *Pacific War* concepts to the strategic level of warfare.

When doing any design, it is important to define its character by answering several canonical questions. This list of questions morphs based on the design and circumstances, so the following list is not meant to be exhaustive, but representative of my general thought process.

- Role: Who do the players represent? Are they specific individuals? Do they represent a collection of leaders with their staffs at a level of warfare (e.g., strategic, operational, or tactical), or are they a blend of several levels?

- Decision Space: Based on who the player represents, what is the universe of decisions and challenges that I want them to face during the game?

- Intelligence: What kinds of information will be available to the player for decision making?

- Player Objectives: How is victory defined? How does a player win?

- Physical Simulation: How will the design handle time and space factors? How will a player's resources kinetically interact with the map and the opposing forces?

- Orders of Battle: What is the granularity of the simulation? Said another way, what are the smallest force quanta in the game? What kinds of forces are being represented and how detailed will they be in the simulation?

- Conflict Resolution: How are the kinetic and psychological factors represented in combat? How is the chaos of war captured in the simulation?

- Logistics: How will logistics impact player decisions and force capabilities? At what level of detail will logistics be modeled?

- Historical Narrative: How do the elements of the design fit together to offer historically plausible narratives in an unscripted environment?

- Playing Time: How long, on average, will it take to play the game?

Using this type of structure, I set out to design a strategic-level World War II game. What follows is how I intermixed these issues for the birth of this design.

Game Engine

I wanted the players to be the important theater commanders in the Pacific. Specifically, I wanted the players to represent Nimitz, MacArthur, Yamamoto, Mountbatten, and their supporting staffs. I specifically did not want the players to control the decisions made in Washington, London, and Tokyo, but to respond to guidance and the resources allocated to the Pacific Theater. I also wanted to divorce this design from the choreography of a carrier battle by avoiding tactical detail, as that was not the decision space of a theater commander. I wanted a laser focus on running the military campaigns, not the battles.

So, when one considers the kinds of decisions a Nimitz made during the war, it is clear that he and his staff were constantly balancing intelligence, geography, force disposition, logistics, and enemy reactions in order to prosecute their strategy. While I had not explicitly decided to use my CDG engine for this design, it rapidly became clear that it was an ideal mechanic for seamlessly integrating these factors. What was different is they way in which I would use an individual card to portray a package of player choices.

In *Empire of the Sun*, a single card's value represents the amount of time available for movement, integrated with the quantity and types of forces that can be logistically supported (see figure 12.1).

Early in the design process, I moved away from an area or point-to-point depiction of geography due to the importance of airpower and the need to easily calculate aircraft ranges. By using a traditional hexagon map with an equal area map projection of the theater of operations, aircraft and naval range calculations became both accurate and intuitive. This allowed for simple time and space calculations and their conversion into force movement, while emphasizing the historical importance of critical air bases and ports (e.g., Truk).

Radio traffic analysis and code breaking were important factors that drove decisions during this conflict. I chose to incorporate this important feature through the same card mechanic, by associating intelligence security with the card value. Large long-range offensives are harder to hide from enemy intelligence and subsequently have a higher chance of being detected and reacted to by enemy forces. The reason for this is that larger operations generate the need for more coordination and subsequent radio use that is detectable by enemy intelligence systems. Even if the codes used to transmit the information remain unbroken, the sheer volume of radio traffic is usually enough to tip off the enemy. This notifies the enemy that something is up and allows them to focus their air reconnaissance assets on a smaller geographic area, increasing the probability that they will detect their opponent's forces as they approach their objectives. In this manner, a single card play could integrate a campaign's objectives, intelligence operations, and logistics, plus time and space factors.

VADM Kondo
Conquest of the Dutch East Indies

Activation: South or South Seas HQs only.

Logistic Value: 7

Float Plane Tactics: Japanese CA naval units add 2 to their attack strengths for the duration of this Offensive.

Operation Watchtower
Guadalcanal Invasion

Activation: Any HQ.

Logistic Value: 5

Intelligence: Surprise Attack

Conditions: A maximum of one ground unit may be activated for this Offensive.

Figure 12.1

These are examples of military events. The upper left value is the card's operations value; this is a measure of time, with 1 being the shortest and 3 being the longest. This value determines the amount of time all forces will have to move on the map. The letters and numbers (e.g., OC:5 EC:7) next to the operations value represent the intelligence value; this is the implication of using the card in a limited or full manner (i.e., as an operation or as an event); the higher the intelligence value on the card, the greater the chance that the enemy will penetrate the information security for the offensive activity. This simulates the various intelligence systems, such as radio traffic analysis, used during the war to divine enemy intentions. Below the graphic and the title used for narrative and historical inspiration is the event information, which sets the parameters for the offensive with regard to command arrangements, logistical support, and other conditions and bonuses derived from the historical event.

Kinetic Factors in an Air and Naval Campaign

At the theater commander level, Pacific War strategy for both sides was driven by the need to support operations with land-based air power and mobile fleets. One of the key decisions that a player in *Empire of the Sun* constantly considers is how to use his military infrastructure (airfields and ports) to support his ability to generate combat power with his air and naval assets.

Part and parcel of the deployment decisions is asking how the opponent's forces impact those decisions. The game captures the impact of land-based air through various systems, most notably how air units are based to project zones of influence (ZOIs) representing reconnaissance, and their effect on movement and intelligence. A corollary to the importance of air forces was where to position the respective fleets to support those operations. Harder to depict are the second order effects of air power on military operations. It is easy to capture the kinetic abilities of air forces (e.g., bomb results), but the ability to show the nonkinetic effects of air power on enemy decisions has tended to be elusive in game designs, if not entirely omitted. During World War II the ability to operate a port within range of enemy airfields was expensive in terms of lost assets, while having a profound impact on operational tempo.

A good example of this phenomenon in the European theater was the siege of Malta. In this case the Allies chose to bear the cost of defending the island from an aerial siege, but while doing so, Malta's ability to react to enemy operations was severely curtailed. A comparison of Axis logistic flow to North Africa is inversely proportional to the health of

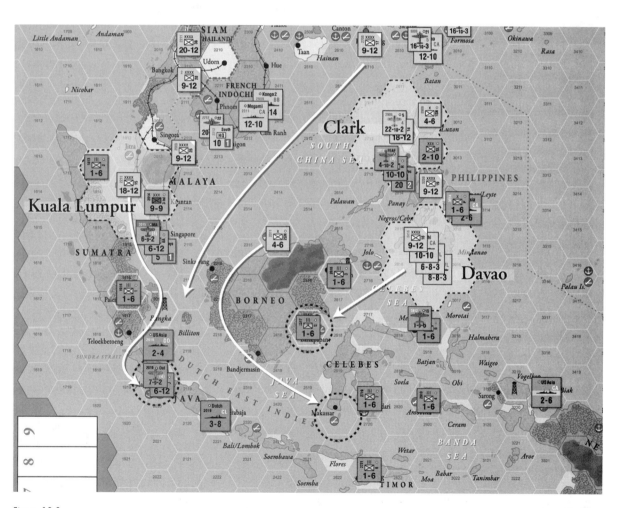

Figure 12.2

Empire of the Sun map detail.

British air and naval assets operating from Malta. The data shows that when Malta was subjected to intense Axis air bombardment, the island was unable to interfere with Axis supply convoys in the central Mediterranean Sea. During these periods Axis forces in North Africa received a larger proportion of the supplies intended for their use. When other Axis commitments reduced the air pressure on Malta, a larger proportion of Axis supply convoys were sunk in transit.

The subtlety for a game design is how to capture the impact of enemy air power on a particular base, whereby the player can choose to withstand a Malta-like aerial siege or decide to redeploy assets outside of harm's way. The Japanese were faced with a similar set of decisions regarding the viability of Rabaul and Truk as fleet bases. As the Allied drive—up the Solomon Islands, into New Guinea, and across the central Pacific—gained momentum, their forward deployed air units forced the Japanese to decide how, and from where, the Imperial Japanese Navy would support their defensive perimeter strategy. *Empire of the Sun* portrays the impact of Allied air power on this Japanese decision through the application of its battle hex concept: A unit that is attacked must remain to fight the battle, preventing it from participating in another simultaneous battle. This allows an offensive player to use his air power to effectively neutralize the ability of an enemy base to generate combat power over the course of a particular operation, while allowing the base to continue to generate offensive combat power while its assets remain viable. (Historically, the Japanese fleet abandoned Truk when Allied air power threatened it.) This overt and subtle portrayal of air dispositions reflects theater strategy during the war.

Deck Construction

With a view to how the air-naval campaign would portray player decisions, the final major piece was how to construct a deck of cards to bring all these factors together. Deck construction is an art, but it does follow well-understood probability principles. While it is possible to guess at the right number and types of cards, the number of hand combinations is so large that only calculating the possible card distributions makes any sense (an 84-card deck has 5.429 billion unique seven-card hands; *Empire of the Sun* has two separate 84-card decks).

For *Empire of the Sun*, I gave each player his own, unscripted deck, meaning that all cards are available from the opening turn. The use of temporally segregated decks (e.g., early or late war) reduces replayability and gives the players more knowledge than their historic counterparts. I favor unscripted decks, but they are much harder to build, as you have to account for a greater number of hand distributions. In *Empire of the Sun*, each player's deck has various functions that have to be consistently and randomly delivered to the players each turn. For example, it is important that a certain number of military offensives and reaction cards are present in each hand to allow the desired operational tempo, player interactions, and historical opportunities. While every card can be used for its operations value in logistics, the event categories offer logistic efficiencies that separate skilled from less skilled players. The important categories are: military offensives, political events, and planned counteroffensives, plus unique resources and capabilities. The goal of deck building is to ensure that over a year of game conflict (i.e., one complete game), a player will have a desired distribution of these different categories of cards.

Victory

The last key challenge in the game was how to deal with the victory conditions. The historical reality is that the Japanese never had any chance of winning the war; except right after Pearl Harbor, the United States devoted approximately 20 percent of its overall resources to the Pacific War, so once Germany was defeated it was only a matter of time until Japan's demise. The design challenge was how to define Japanese victory to remain faithful to the historical events while still offering a challenging player experience. The Japanese intellectually, if not emotionally, understood that they could not defeat the United States in a long war. But they felt that if they could make the United States pay a prohibitive cost for its inevitable counteroffensive, they could coerce a negotiated settlement from the Allies that would allow Japan to "legalize" some of its key conquests. As unrealistic as this notion appears in historical hindsight, it was the ultimate solution to this design issue. I was also persuaded from my research that although the United States would inevitably solve the design and engineering issues required to create an atomic weapon from nuclear theory, it was not a foregone conclusion that it would necessarily occur on the historical timeline. The more important historical factor was the highly secret nature of the Manhattan Project, which kept knowledge of its existence from the military planners. Consequently, the Allied player must play the game with the historical mindset that they will probably have to invade Japan to end the war. This ensures that the rationale for the late war campaigns on Iwo Jima and Okinawa occur organically without special rules.

Closing Remarks

At some level, this chapter is a motorcycle ride through an art gallery, but hopefully it has conveyed some of the thinking behind my design for *Empire of the Sun*—or any of my games, for that matter. What I enjoy about CDGs is the ability to introduce interesting historical details without encumbering the design with unnecessary game systems. For me, *Empire of the Sun* was an opportunity to revisit the CDG genre and fight the Pacific War in an afternoon.

About the Author

Mark Herman has designed more than sixty commercial wargames on topics ranging from the Peloponnesian War to tactical warfare in antiquity, the American Revolution, the American Civil War, World War I, World War II, modern warfare, and science fiction. He is a member of the gaming industry

Hall of Fame and has won numerous domestic and international awards for his designs and articles. He is the coauthor of *Wargaming for Leaders*, numerous anthology chapters, and an upcoming book on game design.

Notes

1. Later CDG designs extended this trade space franchise from a hand of cards to each individual card, although at times I think this feature has become dogmatic and sometimes misapplied. The historical reality is that, prior to the invention of the Prussian General Staff system, senior leaders' bandwidth was even more restricted than today. Many CDGs fail to acknowledge this by using a rote application of the method without accounting for the historical bureaucratic structures that support such decisions.

2. See *Wizards of the Coast LLC v. Cryptozoic Entertainment LLC et al.* and Wizards of the Coast US Patent 5,662,332, on trading card games.

13   THE PATHS OF GLORY LEAD BUT TO THE GAMING TABLE

Ted S. Raicer

The year 2014 marks the centenary of the outbreak of the First World War (known until 1939 as the Great War), a conflict now little known to the general public but widely understood by historians to be the foundation of our world today. Even a partial list of the consequences of World War I is staggering: the Russian Revolution and the rise of Communism, the emergence of the United States as a world power, the rise of fascism, Nazism, and Japanese militarism, World War II, the Cold War, the fall of Europe's vast colonial empires.

But despite its historical importance, World War I gaming was mostly relegated to the fringes of the commercial wargame hobby during its first Golden Age (the 1970s and '80s). Apart from David Isby at SPI, no designer specialized in Great War games, and many of the games produced dealt with air or naval combat, despite the fact that World War I was overwhelmingly a land war. Even by the mid-1970s, with scores if not hundreds of games in print, you could count the number of World War I land games on your fingers, with digits to spare. This situation remained largely unchanged into the 1990s, at which point my own designs helped spark a new interest (one could hardly say "revival" of interest) in the subject.

One reason for the lack of popularity of World War I games into the 1990s was simply that most designs (Isby's excepted) were not very good. ("World War I games don't sell," I was told by Avalon Hill when I tried to sell them my first design. To which I wanted to reply, "Well, not the ones you've published, anyway.") But the real underlying cause of the gaming public's lack of interest was the myth of the Great War as a static struggle in the trenches, which reduced a conflict of tremendous geographic scope and military variety to the stalemate of the Western Front in 1915–17. The five World War I games I published in *Command* magazine from 1992 on helped break that stereotype, and by the time the decade ended the war was, if not a hot topic for wargames, at least a warm one.

Nevertheless, the popularity of my last design of that decade took everyone, including me, by surprise. Published by GMT Games in 1999, *Paths of Glory: The First World War, 1914-1918* (known to most gamers simply as *PoG*) was an instant hit, swept every available hobby award, and has been reprinted three times (a fourth reprint is in the works). It has been published in French, German, Spanish, and Chinese versions and has a website in Polish dedicated to it. Nowadays it is even linked to from most websites talking about

Stanley Kubrick's classic movie *Paths of Glory*. In the relatively small pond of the wargame hobby, it turned out to be a monster fish. Why?

Credit in the first instance must go to game designer Mark Herman, who allowed me to borrow the idea of a card-driven wargame (now known in the hobby as CDGs) from his game *We the People* (1994), which was both about the Revolutionary War and revolutionary in its design. *We the People* gave its opposing British and American players a hand of randomly drawn cards. Some of these were used to conduct military or political operations on the point-to-point map board, while others contained historical events (the Declaration of Independence, French intervention, Indian massacre, and so on) that affected the course of the war. The CDG system accomplished multiple design goals in a simple, elegant fashion. As in any card game, having a hand of cards allowed for a certain level of advance planning, while lack of knowledge of the opponent's hand introduced an element of fog of war, and the random nature of the draw Clausewitz's "friction" ("In war everything is simple, but the simple things are difficult"). The use of the cards for events allowed the game to cover a broad range of political, economic, diplomatic, and other factors that are often completely abstracted out with minimal rules overhead.

My initial reaction to this amazing design was that it would work very well for an American Civil War game, but it turned out Mark had already had the same thought, so as someone already known for World War I games, I decided to consider whether I could adapt the CDG system for the Great War.

The challenges were considerable: *We the People* was designed for a war between two nations (with help from a third) using small armies that engaged in nonlinear campaigns, in which your entire force on the map might be concentrated in a couple of spaces, and the action revolved around whether to move from, say, New York to Philadelphia or Boston. The Great War involved five great powers (and two minor powers) from the start, with others entering later. Millions of men were mobilized—several times the entire population of the thirteen colonies in the Revolutionary War—and the opening campaigns involved lines of armies moving together over hundreds of miles of front. A straight adoption of Mark's system was clearly not going to work, but I was determined to use as much of it as I could, if only because a Great War CDG promised to be a hard sell, and the *We the People* system an obvious selling point. (At the time I assumed *We the People* was a big hit for Avalon Hill because I enjoyed it so much; I'm no longer sure if that was actually the case.)

So, for starters, in addition to the use of cards, a point-to-point map gave *We the People* players a familiar entry point into *PoG*. The basis of any wargame is its representation of military formations and terrain. A wargame map is inherently abstract: Your map is your game board, like the 8×8 square in chess, and once you place any sort of grid over a map to regulate the movement of your military units you are faced with choices that involve abstracting geographic reality. You are deciding what terrain was militarily significant at your chosen scale and how to depict it in the context of your design's rules. But there is no question that a point-to-point system involves more abstraction, and more designer choices, than a traditional hex grid.

This was complicated by my desire to include the Near East theater (Egypt, Palestine, the Caucasus, Iraq) as well as covering the entire European theater from Paris to Minsk and Riga to Salonika, all on a

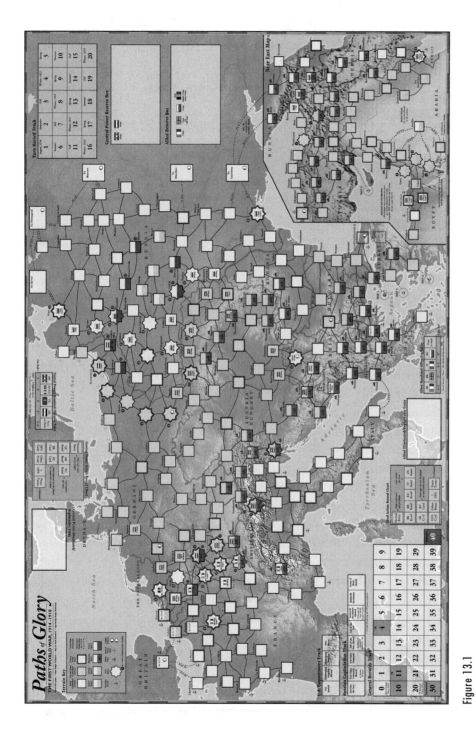

Figure 13.1

Paths of Glory map, showing Europe and Near East insert.

single standard 34″ × 24″ map. This would require either increasing the scale of the European theater to present a very limited number of spaces or doing the Near East map at a different scale. I chose the latter because I wanted to model operations in France and Russia with sufficient detail to give a sense of the almost-Napoleonic maneuvers attempted by both coalitions in 1914. The limited logistical capabilities of the Near East theater allowed me to narrow the lines of movement so that a few well-chosen chokepoints could stall an enemy advance, making up for the fact that the larger scale meant units were actually marching a greater distance when moved.

Despite the inherent abstractness of a point-to-point system, the *PoG* map actually contains a fair amount of detail: swamps, mountains, forests, deserts, and man-made fortifications. Each space was named, but because each space covers a much bigger area than a single city or town, the specific names were chosen for historical flavor, not precision. Setting the exact arrangement of the map spaces was largely a matter of trying to model, at the strategic level, the major campaigns of the war. For example, to re-create the actions of the German First Army in 1914, I had to draw map connections that would allow it to destroy the Belgian forts at Liège, force a retreat of the British Expeditionary Force from Belgium, then advance through Cambrai and Amiens. At that point, in order to stay in touch with the rest of the German line, the First Army turned inward (southeast) to the Marne, and then when the Allies counterattacked in September, it retreated to the Cambrai space, where it entrenched. Later in the war, the ability to attack the Cambrai space from multiple spaces can encourage Allied assaults (the Somme) just as the similar vulnerability of the Verdun space makes it a likely target of German

attacks. All of this involved a lot of trial and error through playtesting.

PoG was not my first strategic World War I design. I had already published *The Great War in Europe* and *The Great War in the Near East* in *Command* magazine, which could be combined into a campaign covering the same theaters of war as *PoG*, but with a traditional hex-based system and on a very different scale: three maps instead of one, and divisions instead of *PoG*'s armies and corps. These earlier games used a random chit draw system to introduce various historical events into play, and I adapted many of these into the events in *PoG*'s cards. Since practical cost considerations limited me to a deck of 110 cards, it was clear I could not include all the events I wished to if I followed *We the People*'s course of separating out cards allowing operations from those providing events. It would also be fatal in the linear campaigns of World War I for a player to be stuck with several event cards and unable to respond as enemy operations broke open his front. But once I decided on dual-use cards, where each one would allow either operations on the map or an event (but not both on the same play), I quickly decided to take things even further, and added two additional options for a single card play: strategic movement and replacements. The former would allow a player to move units long distances by rail or by sea, and the latter would allow the player to "call up" troops to replace losses as needed.

Because each card can usually only be used for one purpose each card play (or "round") the player would constantly have to prioritize. Perform operations on the map or use an event to bring in reinforcements or provide a special tactical advantage, such as poison gas? Move units from front to front by rail, or call up replacements for your worn-out armies? This tension was intensified by having the play of most events remove that card from the game, and by having the most useful events provide the highest level of operations, strategic movement, and replacements. Trade-offs, always trade-offs, and the sheer number of choices ratcheted up the tension to levels some players actually found headache-inducing!

In *We the People* (and his subsequent CDGs), Mark Herman has favored a single deck. This has some advantages, particularly regarding the element of surprise and the reduction of card counting and deck management, but it has the flaw of increased randomness—a lack of narrative coherence. The events of the war tumble out unconnected from each other and create a game narrative in which the different distinct periods of a typical conflict blur together. Instead, in *PoG* (and my subsequent CDGs) I chose to give the Central Powers and the Allies their own card decks, and then divided those into three periods: Mobilization, Limited War, and Total War. This prevented the Germans from randomly developing the shock troop (Stosstruppen) tactics of 1917–18 in the early days of the war, since those cards are in the Total War deck.

I then tied the player's use of his later Limited War and Total War cards to the increase in his War Status, itself raised by the play of certain events. For example, the Allied Mobilization Deck Blockade card not only provided a victory point to the Allies each year but also increased the Allied War Status. And the combined War Status of the two sides, marking the war's growing intensity, was tied to the play of cards bringing in the United States and threatening Tsarist Russia with revolution and withdrawal.

I now had the game's CDG engine in working condition, but how to integrate it with the varied and changing nature of actual World War I land campaigns? In *We the People*, Operations Points (OPS) had been played to activate leaders (generals) on the board and the forces stacked with them. The better the leader, the fewer OPS points were required. Such a system would be out of place given the vastly larger armies, linear fronts, and frankly generally mediocre generalship of World War I. Instead, each OPS point would be allowed to activate a single space, so that depending on the card played, one to five spaces could be activated. This would allow for a historical level of activity and coordination, while ensuring a player could never do everything at once.

I had insisted for years that World War I was not just the trench stalemate of western memory, but, of course, it did include that trench stalemate. The actual movement and combat system would have to allow for both mobile operations and deadlock. So first, to slow the action down to levels that fit World War I and not the blitzkrieg of World War II, I separated out Movement and Combat as types of activity. When you activated a space through OPS points you marked it for Move or Combat, not both. The attacker was now only able to strike at a target space he had moved adjacent to in a previous round, and this gave the other side warning of where a blow might fall, and so a chance either to reinforce it or to withdraw first. To this I added card events allowing the construction of trenches, which gave the defender the option of ignoring retreat results in combat at the cost of additional troop loss. But I made entrenching a particular space a matter of a die roll, giving the French, British, and Germans a greater ability to dig in than the Russians and Austrians—which, along with the shorter front line in France/Belgium, makes a trench stalemate far more likely in the west than the east.

Next I had to deal with the matter of supply. On the strategic level the ability of the various powers to raise and maintain armies was dealt with through the play of reinforcement event cards, and the use of cards for replacements. Battlefield supply was another matter. The traditional "trace through friendly hexes (spaces) to a supply source" was fine, but raised the question of what the penalty would be for an army caught out of supply. Controversially, I decided to make the penalty drastic indeed: an inability to perform operations, and permanent elimination if still out of supply at the end of a game turn. But this drastic penalty had the desired effect: As with their historic counterparts, the players became paranoid about open flanks and breaches in their lines, and would shut down all other activity to protect their lines of supply. This prevented the game from producing a series of encirclements and pocket battles which would be more 1939–41 than 1914–18. Among experienced players, checking supply first each round became second nature, and in practice few units are actually lost to attrition.

Finally, I faced the question: What constituted victory in World War I? From early on in the war both coalitions expanded their ambitions, until they eventually required the complete defeat of their opponents to meet their goals. But apart from marching into Paris, Berlin, or Vienna, no one had any idea of what it would take to force an enemy surrender. Instead, battles were fought to secure ground for tactical, operational, or strategic reasons, or because annexing that ground was part of a nation's war aims. So I decided on a victory point system based on the control of certain spaces, but affected by the play of certain card events, which would raise or a lower a nation's morale, and thus affect what it was willing to accept to "win."

The combination of all these design elements, using a relatively simple set of rules thanks to the CDG engine, produced extremely complex effects. Despite months of testing, with six choices of card play per side per turn and the need to balance events, War Status, replacements, and actual campaigning, there was every possibility that *PoG* would collapse once it was released into the hands of thousands of players. But though there were problems (for example, the rules for the Allied invasion of Gallipoli had to be altered to lower Allied chances to more historical levels) the game held up, and became my most successful design.

In today's market, where scores of wargames are released every year, it is a mark of *PoG*'s success that some gamers have played it enough to develop an expertise far beyond that of the designer. In fact, over the years these "*PoG* sharks" forced me to respond to their play, as they developed rather ahistorical strategies for winning, chief among them withdrawing German forces to the Rhine and focusing their campaigns on Italy and the Near East. While this was not historically impossible, it was certainly improbable, and I introduced a "historical variant" to the game that I believe solved most of these issues. The sharks themselves went further, and have over the years designed and refined a tournament version. Many players, less experienced and perhaps cutthroat, still prefer the original, more open version of the game, and as a designer one always has to remember that the game must work for the far larger number of casual players and not the sharks alone.[1]

After *PoG* was published, interest in World War I gaming continued to grow. I published several more Great War designs and was joined by a range of other designers, producing games of both monster size and complexity and pocket games playable in an hour or two. World War I will likely never be as popular a game topic as its bigger child, World War II, but it is no longer a neglected corner of the wargame hobby. *PoG* has helped people understand that the Great War consisted of much more than stalemate in the trenches, and in many cases it has led players to a deeper exploration of the history behind the game. In this way, *PoG* has played at least a small part in the increased interest in the conflict one hundred years on. "The paths of glory lead but to the grave." Or, sometimes, to the gaming table.

About the Author

Ted Raicer was born in 1958 to parents who served in World War II. Raised in Rahway, New Jersey, he took an early interest in military history through studying the Civil War, and his love of English literature later led to a broad interest in European history, particularly the two World Wars. His father bought him his first wargame in 1969 (Avalon Hill's *1914*), and by the mid-1970s he was a dedicated hobbyist. In 1991 he published his first game, *1918: Storm in the West*, for the late lamented *Command* magazine. A string of award-winning World War I games in *Command* followed before the publication of his most famous design, *Paths of Glory*, by GMT Games in 1999. *PoG*, as it is generally known, has been through three additional printings, with another on the way, and has been published in French, German, Spanish, and Chinese editions.

Note

1. For those interested in the tournament aspects of *PoG* play, see <http://www.boardgamers.org/yearbook/pogpge.htm>.

14 A NEW KIND OF HISTORY: THE CULTURE OF WARGAME SCENARIO DESIGN COMMUNITIES

Troy Goodfellow

Computer wargames have been, for most of their history, roughly identical to their board-and-counter cousins.[1] The distinguishing factor in how they have been played is usually not design, setting, or audience, but speed.[2] A computer can calculate the results of combat, track weather effects, and referee the rules with consistency and accuracy. This speed means that even monster games like *Gary Grigsby's War in the Pacific* (2004) can be completed at a pace hundreds of times faster than a similar board-and-counter game. Add in the ability to substitute a computer opponent for a human one, and the speed of play transforms how regularly and easily a gamer can complete and understand a new wargame.

This speed has major consequences. Since the game can now be completed more quickly and more often, players can more easily detect flaws or ways to exploit a game's AI or core rule set. Frequent exposure to the same setting and same maps means that a designer often cannot simply make a game about one battle if they want to sell many copies; multiple scenarios or a campaign mode (whether in chained scenarios or set piece encounters) become essential for all but the largest-scale wargames. Computer wargames therefore become more polished (or more

complex) and have a greater variety of battles and tactical puzzles.

Though we can see the influence of editing and player-driven scenario design in some of today's board wargames (the *Command and Colors* series, for example, is modular), for the most part, board wargames are limited by fixed maps and limited army selection. But since most board wargames (especially the larger ones) are played rarely, this is not a problem for most people. Their enjoyment of a board wargame is hardly likely to be exhausted from seeing too much action.

The speed difference means that since the dawn of computer wargaming, designers have sought to prolong the life of their games through editing tools. Games would be sold with an in-game kit that would enable the player to make their own battles, their own armies, and sometimes their own maps.[3]

The classic early wargame *The Ancient Art of War* (1984) was an abstract affair that avoided true history, but it had quasi-historical settings and a wide range of AI generals, each with a different play style. Players could create their own battles, designing the map, setting fort locations, and deciding the composition of enemy troops (admittedly limited to archers, knights, and barbarians). Robert Smith's *Encyclopedia*

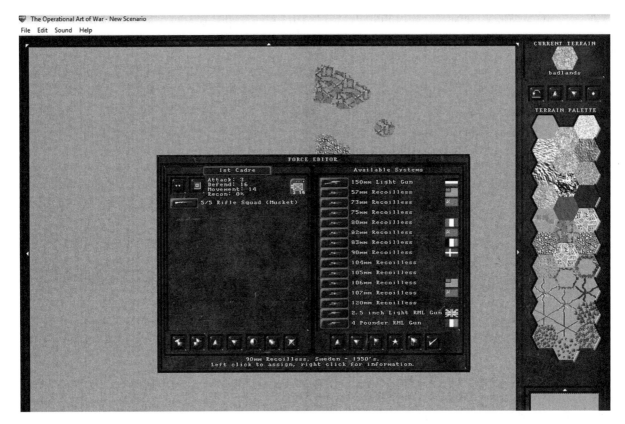

Figure 14.1
With patience and a good order of battle, some editors, like the one in *Operational Art of War III*, promise unlimited creativity.

of War: Ancient Battles (1988) came with dozens of different historical armies but only four battles; any enjoyment beyond this point came from generating battles randomly or designing them yourself in the editor. No Battle of Plataea? Use the Spartan army and Persian army, grab your pocket Herodotus, and make it yourself.

Ezra Sidran's early Universal Military Simulator games from 1987 and on were neither universal nor a simulator and left out some important parts of "military," but they aimed to let the player make any battle from any time in history while including

a handful of battles from various points in history, presumably to show off the flexibility of the design.

From today's vantage point, it would be easy to jump to the conclusion that these editors were included so that players could swap new scenarios or army configurations, thereby multiplying their own efforts by working with others. But it is important to remember that there was no reliable file sharing economy when these games were conceived. There was no Internet; bulletin board systems were usually local, limited, and idiosyncratic; and though many of these games included hot-seat multiplayer (i.e., playing the game against an opponent in the same physical space as you), there was certainly no guarantee that you would find a motivated opponent nearby, even in the golden days of computer wargaming when fans of the genre were overrepresented among PC early adopters.

Editors must have primarily been included, therefore, not to promote sharing of ideas and scenarios, but to prolong the lifespan of a wargame. Sharing was certainly not discouraged, and, even if it were, the lines of communication between designers and players were sporadic at best.

But this lack of reliable communication often meant that there was little feedback about the quality of the editing tools. Even today, wargame editors are often fussy; data entry, placement of units, modifying terrain, and so forth, have never come easy, and a good scenario can be a tedious mixture of research, mistakes, and trying over again—unless you get discouraged.[4] For early wargames, the lack of reliable player-driven conversation meant that tips and advice could not be easily shared either. It is to our great detriment that a decade of user-created wargame scenarios has been lost, like so much of the electronic ephemera of that era.

The Golden Age of user scenario design can be laid at the feet of two games: *Harpoon* (1989) and *The Operational Art of War* (1998). These games would see an explosion of player interest in trying out historical or hypothetical situations, newly empowered by the rise of university computing networks and the availability of home Internet.

Harpoon predates the Internet, of course (see Don Gilman's chapter in this volume for a detailed history of this seminal naval wargame). For our immediate purposes, the first computer version was released in 1989, just as the Cold War itself was fading into history and *Harpoon*'s conjectures of the Red Navy

duking it out with Nimitz carrier groups were fading with it.

But a rerelease in 1997 revived *Harpoon*, its expansion packs (full of alternate timeline scenarios, like a revived Russian monarchy, as well as likely flashpoints in the Middle East and Indian Ocean), and its scenario editor. Suddenly, the Internet was full of user-created content that either wrote new histories or modeled recent historical naval/air encounters. Despite the possible variety, however, most scenarios tended to be large ones. Given new toys and new ways to show off how much they knew, the archetypal player-designed scenario for *Harpoon* would have hundreds of aircraft, as many carrier groups as the fiction would permit and, if possible, a nuclear submarine bristling with ballistic missiles.

The relative peace of the oceans during this period of history was an essential missing constraint on scenario designers. Canada and Spain might mobilize warships in a battle over cod, or American ships in the Persian Gulf might be harassed by small Iranian craft. But modern/near-future warships and planes meant that most scenario designers were limited only by their imaginations, with few concrete ideas of what modern naval war would look like. As we saw with recent Ukrainian conflict scenarios designed for *Command: Modern Air/Naval Operations* (2013) and *Operational Art of War*, once games draw subject matter from the current era, news headlines and hypotheticals drawn from foreign affairs or what-have-you become sparks to generate new scenarios.

The most popular scenarios would be multicarrier duels in the North Atlantic or variations on the first *Harpoon*'s concluding scenario, the defense/attack of Iceland. Even those settings least likely to have major fleet engagements, like the Indian Ocean, would take any excuse for the British and French or American and Russians to square off. New databases and maps were built by players for the game so they could find new settings for grand duels between China and whomever, if the current peace in the seas represented in *Harpoon* was not quite enough.

Norm Koger's *Operational Art of War* games,[5] an evolution from his *Wargame Construction Sets*,[6] tried to model all warfare from the 1930s to the current day—an ambitious undertaking, but one that proved to be very popular with amateur scenario designers. Unlike a game focusing on current day events, players had the entire twentieth century as their playground; though battles included with the game started in 1930, much of the equipment available in the editor was designed to equip armies that might have outdated weapons, more suitable for World War I or earlier (the Abyssinian War, for example).

Again, popular user-created scenarios tended to be large—maps were expanded, unit size adjusted to either fit the larger geographical scope or fill out entire fronts. Why make a better version of El Alamein when you can do the entire African Front as it stood in 1942? If you can edit in reinforcement and replacement schedules, then a longer-term campaign like Barbarossa or all of the German invasions of 1914 become almost feasible. The operational level of the game is pushed to a strategic level, with the strategic decisions being made off-stage or contingent to how the map responds to player action.[7]

This tendency to larger scenarios that push the limits of the simulation and the assumptions of Koger's model can be seen in many of the scenarios included in the most recent version of the game, *Operational Art of War III*. This newly packaged version in 2006 included 130 of the "best scenario designs of the last five years," probably marking the first time that a retail product has used its inclusion of user-created content as a major selling point.[8]

"The Great War 1914–1918" by Fiero Falloti dubs itself a "monster scenario," but the scenario "Global Conflict 1988" by Haris Riris (designed for play-by-email) best typifies the monster scenario ethos. It has 20-kilometer hexes and covers all of Europe and the Middle East as far as Iran. Most of Europe is dotted with tiny cities, each worth something in the way of victory points, making the game's size even more intimidating since an odd kind of arithmetic comes into play as you win or lose cities.

Though of course the selection available in this final retail version tends to reflect more modest aims in all, the online depositories of scenarios demonstrate a willingness of players to push a wargame system as large as they possibly can. "European Theater of Operations," "Europe 1939," "Soviet Union 1941," even one dubbed "World War 2," show that many scenario designers are interested in division-level combat, even though Koger's equipment-based modeling of war outcomes tends to break down at the higher command levels; summing up the number of tanks and machine guns that a squad has is one thing, but the more that dubious math is stretched along a wider front, the more assumptions that the scenario designer is forced to make about supply, frontage, and spacing—or else neglect these matters altogether and toss the idea of simulation out the window.

Editors in the hands of many players became more than ways to fill in the gaps of a scenario list. Given the choice to design a scenario about a small section of a front or to make a game that is an entire theater, many gamers chose to go big. Editors offer the chance for players to become game designers, in the limited sense that they are using someone else's rules to design games that they've always wanted to have.

The tendency of many players to use editing and design tools to expand more than refine has been

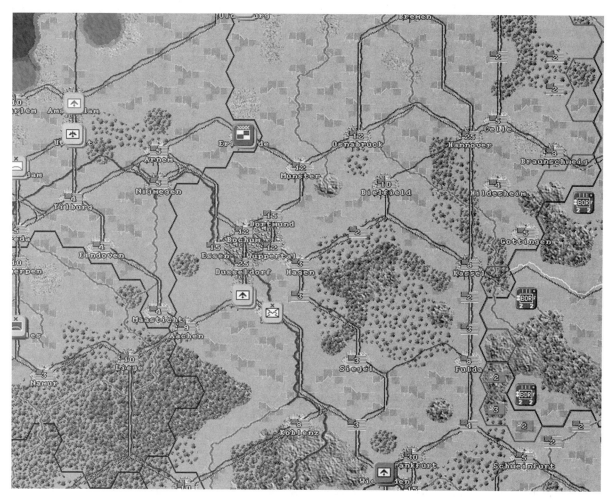

Figure 14.2
The "Global Conflict 1988" scenario for *The Operational Art of War III* made every location count for something.

noted in other games. Soren Johnson, the designer of *Sid Meier's Civilization IV* (2005), has dubbed player modifications that try to do too much "double-your-pleasure" mods, since they presume that if something is bigger, then it must be more satisfying.

As the skills and tools for general modification have become more common, the most skilled amateur designers have been pulled into modding instead

of scenario design. A quick look at the Steam Workshop[9] additions for any of the recent *Total War* games shows great attention to more realism, better AI or even more colorful uniforms, but no new historical battle scenarios for the tactical wargame that Creative Assembly uses to sell the franchise. Player attention is drawn to the strategic layer, where all battles that occur are the outcome of player

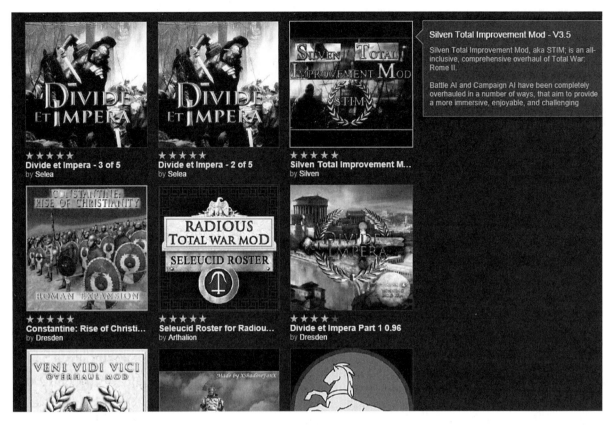

Figure 14.3

Overhaul mods of *Total War: Rome II* are consistently popular for players.

decisions; the historical scenarios are an after-thought, even though the *Total War* games have been used in television programs to reenact or illustrate historical battles.

Part of the reason for this is that Creative Assembly tucks the editor away from most people. You need to add a line to the executable file or use another workaround to get into this mode. "Custom battles" can be generated, but these are just two army lists thrown together on a generic battlefield. Still, user-created content has thrived for the *Total War* series almost since its birth; it's just that the users have moved beyond making accurate versions of

Gaugamela—they want "Total Realism" mods that change how armies develop and are recruited.

One especially interesting trend in custom scenarios is the tendency of players to not design a battle that someone else has made. Though professional designers see no problem in revisiting Gettysburg or Tannenberg, community designers give each other a wide berth. The largest depot of *Age of Rifles* scenarios (the wargamer.com Games Depot), for example, has only one version of Fredericksburg, one version of Khartoum, and one version of the Alamo, each from different scenario designers.[10] The official Slitherine forums for their ancient/medieval miniatures wargame *Field of Glory* (2009) have few competing versions of Cannae or Bannockburn. Most designers seem to steer clear of offering or defending varying interpretations.

The core difference between professional wargame designers and scenario designers, of course, is that scenario designers are all working within the same system and not designing competing ones. However, given the number of possible variants based on timing, sources, or interpretations of movements and army capabilities, it is disappointing that scenarios are not used better by amateur designers, many of whom have extensive historical knowledge, to argue about our understanding of the history itself.[11]

About the Author

Troy Goodfellow is a veteran strategy game critic who has been published in many major video game magazines and websites. His blog, Flash of Steel, has hosted long form essays and criticism for a decade

Instead, the culture of sharing and commenting on the Internet has led to these sorts of debates being hashed out in forums or reviews. Scenario builders will iterate on their designs within weeks if there is serious dispute about how a battle is being constructed. On the official forums of *Unity of Command* (2011), for example, scenarios are often labeled with version numbers or updates to distinguish themselves from early interpretations of historical encounters, an example of how the very terminology of software development has permeated user-created content.

Editing and creating scenarios for wargames will always be a niche within a niche. Still, it has become such an accepted part of the genre that almost every wargame developer forum supports or welcomes links to battles created by users.

and he founded the strategy focused podcast Three Moves Ahead in 2009. Troy now works for Paradox Interactive.

Notes

1. Here I will confine my discussion to "wargames" properly understood, not general strategy games. Though titles like *Civilization V* (2012) and *Europa Universalis IV* (2013) and similar grand strategy games are interesting, they present different issues. By "wargame," I mean one with an historical or quasi-historical setting, with strong emphasis on tactical deployments and movements in battle with little player control over production of extra units or diplomatic policy. Some games, like Creative Assembly's *Total War* series, have wargames inside the strategic layer and historical battle elements.

2. Generally speaking, computer wargames still move in turns or phases (though there are major real-time and WEGO games), still use a hex- or tile-based system, even though computers can track real geography and spacing, and are marketed to and designed for educated older men with military and history backgrounds. As with all generalizations, there are notable exceptions and these trends wax and wane throughout the history of the genre. But the two most notable Eastern Front games of the last five years, *Gary Grigsby's War in the East* (2010) and *Unity of Command* (2011) stick to traditional presentation and ideas.

3. I am distinguishing editors from modifications. "Mod" is a term best used to describe a player-driven change to core aspects of a game by introducing new elements (magic, licensed universes) or new rules to a game that fundamentally transform its nature. Changing *Unity of Command* to invade Romania is a question of editing (the equipment is already there); changing it to invade Hoth is a question of modding (new units, rules and maps will have to be made, and that means changing some programming code).

4. I made the Battle of Paraiticene in *Rome: Total War* (2004) for my own amusement. This is a relatively light wargame, but I never ventured to make another battle after that experience. The best scenario designers have a reservoir of patience that escapes me.

5. *Operational Art of War I: 1935–1955* (1998), *Operational Art of War II: Modern Battles 1956–2000* (1999), and *Operational Art of War II: Flashpoint Kosovo* (1999) were the major titles, all published and developed by Talonsoft, with the entire collection being released as *Century of Warfare* in 2000. The game has been published, distributed, and updated by Matrix Games since 2006.

6. The first game, simply called *Wargame Construction Set* (1986), was similar in design and intent to the *Universal Military Simulator* games. Players were given tools and a few battles to use as models so they could design and test their own encounters. The second WCS game, *Tanks*, focused on armored warfare. The final game in the trilogy, *Age of Rifles: 1846–1905*, established the core idea for *Operational Art of War* by assuming that you could successfully model a wargame by simply knowing the capabilities of the equipment available to the units. The wealth of information available to players, as well as the fertile period covered by *Age of Rifles*, made it exceptionally popular with scenario designers. It also had a relatively simple interface, since a unit's battlefield strength was, taking training and experience into consideration, a function of unit size and weaponry.

7. *Operational Art of War* allowed for events to be triggered by date, status of victory points, and so on. This proved to be a very popular innovation for large scenario builders.

8. Also worthy of note is that the most popular full modified conversion of the game is a nineteenth century set of units and weapons, designed mostly so people could fight US Civil War battles, or, commonly, the entire war itself—with some violence to Koger's model, but great fidelity to the equipment.

9. Steam Workshop is a part of Valve's video game storefront Steam and is full of player additions, modifications, and customizations for those games that are open to the Workshop tools. Since its introduction in 2012, it has become a one-stop shop for changes and customization to a wide range of war and strategy games.

10. This is not necessarily evidence of designer reticence in covering the same ground, but it could also be evidence of how small and communal the network is.

11. See Philip Sabin's *Lost Battles: Reconstructing the Great Clashes of the Ancient World* (2007) for a compelling case for how game and scenario design can settle or resolve conflicting interpretations of sources and military theory.

III OPERATIONS

15 OPERATIONS RESEARCH, SYSTEMS ANALYSIS, AND WARGAMING: RIDING THE CYCLE OF RESEARCH

Peter P. Perla

Actual war is a very messy business. A very, very messy business.

—Captain James T. Kirk, *Star Trek*

Let me tell you a story. Partly it is a story about how what we today call defense analysis came to be. It is not the complete story; indeed, the complete story may be beyond our poor ability to relate or to comprehend. This simple version of the story is woven from three main strands: what we have come to term *operations research*, *systems analysis*, and *wargaming*. (In this context, however, I use the term *wargaming* to refer to its "serious" uses by the military and defense-analysis communities, rather than the hobby uses described earlier in this book.) Each of these strands, at one time or another, has been seized upon by decision makers as the key tool for understanding the critical realities of warfare—to make predictions about the future direction of war so that today's decisions would lead to tomorrow's success.

The rest of the story is this: war is too complicated and too critical for us to bet our future on the process or product of any one of those tools. The best we can do is to use all of our tools in an integrated way in order to understand the past, investigate the present, and prepare for the future. Decision makers need to learn how to learn—to learn about how to deal with an uncertain and unpredictable future; to learn about how to understand its complexities; and to learn about how to make good decisions today and tomorrow in spite of those complexities, uncertainties, and unpredictability. To do that, researchers, analysts, and professional wargamers must learn to use operations research, systems analysis, and wargaming, complemented and supplemented by a deep understanding of history and current experience, in a continuous cycle of research to educate, advise, and support those decision makers.

Operations Research: Quantifying Experience to Plan Action

There are two theories, however, evolved by Mr. Lanchester to which I may safely draw attention. The first

he has called the N-Square Law, and it is, to my mind, a most valuable contribution to the art of war. It is the scientific statement of a truth which, although but dimly perceived, has been skillfully used by many great captains, both Naval and Military, but it is now for the first time stated in figures and logically proved.

—Maj-Gen. Sir David Henderson, KCB,
Aircraft in Warfare

The physical sciences have had a long and checkered relationship with the practice of the military arts. The mythic role of Archimedes in the defense of Syracuse against the Roman war machine, and his death at the hands of one of its legionaries, is one of the earliest stories. Because military force is a highly distilled application of physics and chemistry, the harnessing of scientific knowledge and engineering expertise to create, produce, and apply better and more destructive weapons has been at work from pre-biblical—probably prehistoric—times. The application of scientific techniques to the higher levels of warfare, operations and strategy, took some halting first steps in the geometric formalisms of Jomini's analysis of Napoleon's methods in *Précis de l'Art de la Guerre* (1838). Despite the criticisms and ultimate discrediting of that work, the lure of applying scientific and quantitative reasoning to the problems of military operations proved to be overwhelming.

At the height of the slaughter on the Somme during World War I, one of the legendary foundational pieces of modern scientific analysis of warfare made its appearance. Written by British engineer Frederick W. Lanchester, *Aircraft in Warfare: The Dawn of the Fourth Arm* (1916) proposed some simple mathematical models of combat in the form of two sets of simultaneous equations, which became known as the linear and square laws.

Lanchester characterized the linear law as representative of ancient combat, in which battle could be thought of as a series of individual duels. In this case, a numerical advantage could not be exploited fully because it was difficult for more than one warrior to engage a single enemy simultaneously. In this case, a side with a qualitative advantage in the skill of its individual fighters could offset a numerical advantage of its enemy. This is seen most clearly in the basic equation of the linear law. It is a linear equation describing the state of the combat in terms of the number of losses on both sides at any point during the combat and on the effectiveness of each side at defeating its opponent. The *state equation* takes the form

(Effectiveness of Blue) × (Blue losses) = (Effectiveness of Red) × (Red losses).

If both sides fight to the finish, then the Blue army will win (that is, have at least one survivor when Red is wiped out) as long as

(Effectiveness of Blue) × Initial (Blue army size) > (Effectiveness of Red) × (Initial Red army size).

On the other hand, Lanchester characterized his square law as representative of modern warfare, in which effective long-range firearms would allow several soldiers to concentrate their fire on a smaller number of the enemy. In this case, the relevant state equation analogous to that above takes the form

(Effectiveness of Blue) × [(Initial Blue strength)^2 – (Current Blue strength)^2] =

(Effectiveness of Red) × [(Initial Red strength)^2 – (Current Red strength)^2]

In this case, Blue wins the fight to the finish if

$$(\text{Effectiveness of Blue}) \times (\text{Initial Blue strength})^2 > (\text{Effectiveness of Red}) \times (\text{Initial Red strength})^2$$

In this case, the size of the army plays a disproportionate role in determining the winner because its effect is squared while the effect of the individual fighting power is not. Quantity has a quality all its own.

Lanchester's discussion of the principle of concentration and this N-Square Law looks very like the mathematical equations later common in the operational research of the Second World War. Though he supported his "law" by an insightful analysis of Lord Horatio Nelson's battle plan for, and the actual course of, the battle of Trafalgar, Lanchester's analysis was largely of the a priori type; that is, he derived his mathematical relationships from deductive reasoning, rather than basing it on inductive analysis of data from actual battle outcomes.

Before Lanchester, the primary emphasis of scientific support to warfare lay in the creation of new weapons. What made Lanchester's work so groundbreaking was the fact that his "law" pointed to how technology could better be used in combat. Lanchester's equations argued that if one side in a fight could concentrate a large fraction of its killing power against a smaller fraction of the enemy force, it would achieve greatly superior results than spreading itself out to engage all the enemy forces at once. Indeed, focusing on aircraft, the core subject of his book, Lanchester argued from the basis of the square law for the fundamental importance of numbers in air operations, whether against aerial or terrestrial targets. In the latter case, he argued that an attacker should force the anti-aircraft defenses of the enemy to disperse their fire over a large number of simultaneously attacking aircraft rather than send smaller numbers of aircraft in sequential attacks, which would allow the defenders to concentrate their fire against those smaller numbers. This principle remains a core tactical concept of air and missile combat today, that of saturation of the defense.

Scientists Go to War

Soon after the start of World War II, P. M. S. Blackett, "widely regarded as 'the father of operations research'" became involved in the organized application of scientific principles of study to support military operations (McCloskey 1987, 454). Blackett was a professor of physics at the University of Manchester when called upon to support the war effort more directly. He organized small groups of scientists to conduct what he called "operational research." His earliest work was for the Army, in support of the pressing business of improving the anti-aircraft defense of London under the German bomber blitz of 1940. He later moved to RAF Coastal Command and the Admiralty to deal with a range of other military issues, including the Battle of the Atlantic against the German U-boat menace.

Blackett wrote two fundamental and important reports in 1941, which he later updated and included in his 1962 book *Studies of War*. He proposed assigning scientists to support operational military staffs to provide the operators with "scientific advice on those matters which are not handled by the service technical establishments" (Blackett 1962, 171). The data to support their analyses included the usual reports provided to such staffs, such as weather, after-action reports, and similar administrative information. The basic methodology used by the scientists revolved around "variational methods."

These methods were common tools in scientific fields such as biology and economics, which were characterized by the study of complex phenomena based on only limited amounts of relevant quantitative data. This state of affairs he contrasted with the situation in physics, "where usually a great deal of numerical data are ascertainable about relatively simple phenomena." As a result, Blackett saw the object of operational research to be the eminently practical one of helping operators to find "means to improve the efficiency of war operations in progress or planned for the future. To do this, past operations are studied to determine the facts; theories are elaborated to explain the facts; and finally the facts and theories are used to make predictions about future operations" (177).

In addition to Blackett, the first generation of operations researchers counted among their number several other future Nobel laureates in hard science, including E. A. Appleton, A. H. Huxley, J. C. Kendrew, and C. H. Waddington. They supported real operations by applying the thinking of real scientists. Their practitioner's view of science was centered on learning from experience. But that experience was organized and codified by an appropriate and rigorous "combination of observation, experiment, and reasoning (both deductive and inductive)" (199–200).

Once the United States entered the war late in 1941, American scientists involved themselves in the war effort as well, and were soon learning from and cooperating with their British forebears. Philip Morse and George Kimball later documented some of the principles and techniques of the American effort in another classic of operations research literature, *Methods of Operations Research* (Morse and Kimball 1946). In its original edition, Morse and Kimball

define operations research (OR), as the Americans would call the field, using precisely Blackett's words quoted earlier.

Another prominent American practitioner was Doctor Charles Kittel. Kittel is credited with one of the most widespread definitions of the field: "Operations research is a scientific method for providing executive departments with a *quantitative basis for decisions*. Its object is, by the analysis of past operations, to find means of improving the execution of future operations" (Kittel 1947, 150; emphasis in original).

Morse and Kimball elaborated on some of the foundational ideas of the technique, explaining that "certain aspects of practically every operation can be measured and compared quantitatively with similar aspects of other operations. It is these aspects which can be studied scientifically" (Morse and Kimball 1951, 1). Because even the smallest military operations are extraordinarily complex in their execution, the first step in the analytical process was to "ruthlessly strip away details" so as to identify "very approximate 'constants of the operations'" and to explore how those constants varied from one operation to another. The key point Morse and Kimball make is that such constants "are useful even though they are extremely approximate: it might almost be said that they are more valuable *because* they are very approximate" (Morse and Kimball 1946, 3; emphasis in original).

This important distinction between practical utility and theoretical precision they termed "hemibel thinking." A bel represents a factor of ten in a logarithmic scale, and a hemibel is the square root of 10, or about a factor of 3. Morse and Kimball argued that getting within a factor of 3 of some theoretical "actual" value for operational data and constants was good enough. This was so, they argue, because there is usually a large discrepancy between the theoretical optimum of any operation and its actual outcome.

> If the actual value is within a hemibel (i.e., within a factor of 3) of the theoretical value, then it is extremely unlikely that any improvement in the details of the operation will result in significant improvement. In the usual case, however, there is a wide gap between the actual and theoretical results. In these cases, a hint as to the possible means of improvement can usually be obtained by a crude sorting of the operational data to see whether changes in personnel, equipment, or tactics produce a significant change in the constants. In many cases a theoretical study of the optimum values of the constants will indicate possibilities of improvement. (Morse and Kimball 1946, 38)

As an example of this sort of thinking, Morse and Kimball presented some data related to submarine sightings of merchant ships during patrols. The data table they presented is given in table 15.1 (Morse and Kimball 1956, 2164).

They rounded all the numbers to one or two significant figures, "since the estimate of the number of ships present in the area is uncertain, and there is no need of having the accuracy of the other figures any larger." The operational sweep rate (Q_{op}) tabulated here is a calculated figure encapsulating the efficiency of the sweeping force. The difference between Q for regions B and E is considered insignificant because it is less than a hemibel. But that between B and D is greater than a hemibel and demands further investigation. This investigation "shows that the antisubmarine activity on region B was considerably more effective than in D, and, consequently, the submarines in region B had to spend more time submerged and had correspondingly less

Table 15.1

Contacts on Merchant Vessels by Submarines

Region	B	D	E
Area, sq. miles, A	80,000	250,000	400,000
Avg. no. ships present, N	20	20	25
Ship flow through Area per day, F	6	3	4
Sub-days in area, T	800	250	700
Contacts, C	400	140	200
Sweep rate, Q_{op}	2,000	7,000	4,500
Fraction of ship flow sighted by a sub, C/FT	0.08	0.2	0.07
Sightings per sub per day	0.5	0.6	0.3

time to make sightings." The analysis thus suggested that it would make sense to transfer subs from region B to region D (assuming no constraints about doing so). Furthermore, additional calculations comparing the operational sweep rate to its theoretical maximum showed that "no important amount of shipping is missed because of poor training of lookouts or failure of detection equipment. ... The fact that each submarine in region D sighted one ship in every five that passed through the region is further indication of the extraordinary effectiveness of the submarines patrolling these areas" (Morse and Kimball 1956, 2165).

Thus, the core of operations research is its strong emphasis on learning from experience. This scientific perspective is a source of both strength and weakness in the approach. The scientists themselves could gain only limited direct experience of war—especially the chaos of combat. For the most part, they had to rely on secondhand reports from the military. As a result, the scientific experience of the OR practitioners had to find a modus vivendi with the practical experience of military commanders and staffs. Fortunately, the hard school of real war, and the reality of the relationship between the scientists and the operators helped prevent a strictly mechanical and scientific view of operations from dominating actual combat decisions. The founding practitioners of operations research were sensitive to the prerogatives of the military command, and sensible about their supporting role; as a result, they delineated a sharp dividing line between their own responsibilities and those of the commanders. Both sides came to recognize that the results of an operational analysis formed only part of the basis for executive planning and decisions. The operations researcher had the responsibility of recommending the course of action that his scientific and quantitative analysis concluded was best (if such did in fact exist). But it was the executive officer's job to incorporate that recommendation with others from different sources, particularly qualitative ones such as his own knowledge and experience, to make the final decision.

Blackett cautioned the OR analyst to avoid splitting hairs too finely when advising action based on his analysis:

> Though the research workers should not have executive authority, they will certainly achieve more success if they act in relation to the conclusions of their analysis as if they had it. I mean by this that when an operational research worker comes to some conclusion that affects executive action, he should only recommend to the executives that the action should be taken if he himself is convinced that he would take the action, were he the executive authority. It is useless to bother a busy executive with a learned résumé of all possible courses of action leading to the conclusion that it is not possible to decide between them.

Silence here is better than academic doubt. (Blackett 1962, 203)

There is a sense of balance here, one that is critically important because, unlike the physical sciences with which most of the original practitioners were familiar, the operations of war are subject to the often chaotic and unpredictable behavior of human beings and their creations. There is also the seed of danger here, a seed that would bear fruit later as the postwar analysts' desire to believe the analysis provided the best, if not the only, basis for action would lead to their forgetting the wisdom of hemibel thinking.

During the war however, despite the delicacy of the relationships and the sometime tension between scientists and warriors, the sheer intellectual quality of the original operations researchers, and their astute ability to work within the military establishments of World War II, helped them produce both well-supported and practical results. A litany of OR contributions to the Allied war effort would be out of place here, but a couple of examples might illustrate the general shape of those efforts.

The course of anti-U-boat operations in the Bay of Biscay is a prime example; it is described by Morse and Kimball in the "How to Hunt a Submarine" article referenced earlier (Morse and Kimball 1956) and is also discussed in fuller detail in a book by currently practicing OR analyst Doctor Brian McCue (2008). During much of the war, the vast majority of German U-boats operating in the Atlantic had to cross the bay as they moved to and from their bases in France. Long-range Allied bombers conducted ASW operations against them. A key measure of effectiveness (MOE) developed by the OR analysts was the number of sightings made by the Allied aircraft. By monitoring changes in this MOE over time, Allied scientists were able to detect when German countermeasures—in the form of radar warning receivers—were becoming effective. This in turn led to equipping Allied aircraft with different, less detectable, radars. The competition between searchers and submarines was tracked and abetted by the MOEs developed and monitored by the OR analysts.

Another example illustrates how an analyst's willingness to question common operational practice—coupled with some basic arithmetic applied to carefully collected operational data—could make a significant contribution. This is what happened in the case of Cecil Gordon's work for Coastal Command in early 1942 (Budiansky 2013, 203–206). Operating a fleet of aircraft requires careful juggling of the amount of time aircraft spend in each of four possible states: actually flying missions; serviceable (ready to fly) but not flying; being serviced by the maintenance and repair shops; and waiting to be serviced. Common RAF practice was that at least 75 percent of all aircraft were to be ready for action (flying or serviceable) at all times.

Gordon looked at this policy and decided that it was responsible for unnecessarily limiting the number of flight hours that units could produce. After much debate, in which Prime Minister Churchill himself became involved, Gordon was allowed to conduct a test of his ideas using an operational squadron. He demonstrated that a better policy was to "fly enough to ensure that the maintenance shops were fully employed at all times. To get more flying hours, in other words, you had to *increase* the breakdown rate. That would mean more aircraft needed repair at any given time, but the total throughput of the maintenance shops would increase" (Budiansky 2013, 203; emphasis in original). Indeed, Gordon's test squadron

nearly doubled its flying hours. What's more, the data analysis also revealed that routine inspections of working systems "in many cases *increased* breakdowns, apparently the result of disturbing components that had been working fine" (Budiansky 2013, 206). The result was that the new flying policy recommended by the scientists was implemented across Coastal Command.

These and other wartime successes convinced scientists, civilian administrators, and the military establishment alike that the new science of operations research should be expanded upon to address the increasingly complex problems of an uncertain peacetime. (Not to mention their application to nonmilitary fields, which I will not consider here.)

In the afterglow of that wartime success, Morse and Kimball argued that the increased mechanization that characterized World War II had created the conditions that allowed operations research to come to prominence, and presumably to flourish in an increasingly mechanistic future.

> Another reason for the growing usefulness of the application of scientific methods to tactics and strategy lies in the increased mechanization of warfare. It has often been said, with disparaging intent, that the combination of a man and a machine behaves more like a machine than it does like a man. This statement is in a sense true, although the full implications have not yet been appreciated by most military and governmental administrators. For it means that a men-plus-machines operation can be studied statistically, experimented with, analyzed, *and predicted* by the use of known scientific techniques just as a machine operation can be. The significance of these possibilities in the running of wars, of governments, and of economic organizations cannot be overemphasized. (Morse and Kimball 1946, 2; emphasis in the original)

But overemphasized it was. The temporary wartime expedients evolved into permanent peacetime positions within the defense establishment unlike anything seen before. In the past, civilian scientists had been called upon to provide peacetime advice to the Army and Navy by serving on such committees as General Boards, but now civilian scientists, soon to be known by the sobriquet "analysts," became an integral part of the nascent "military-industrial complex." As the Cold War with the Soviet Union shifted into high gear, and the administration of President John F. Kennedy took office in early 1961, a new kid appeared on the block, the "whiz kid." And the whiz kids brought with them a new idea; it came to be called systems analysis.

Systems Analysis: Applying Economics to Build Consensus

The contribution of analysis was so clearly positive that military officers urged its continuation into peacetime, when, paradoxically, defense analysis is largely deprived of its empirical footing. In the absence of evidence that might falsify their hypotheses, analysts have too often felt free to propound the hypotheses as truths.

—from "The Defense Debate and the Role of Analysis," CNA 1984

President Kennedy's new Secretary of Defense, Robert S. McNamara, introduced both new faces and new ideas to the department. Among those new faces was Charles J. Hitch. While working at the RAND Corporation during the 1950s, Hitch had developed new ideas about applying concepts from economics to defense matters. When he was appointed assistant secretary of defense (comptroller), a position he held from 1961 to 1965, he found himself in a position to implement many of those ideas. Together with his colleague and collaborator Roland McKean, Hitch had articulated the foundations of the new field of systems analysis in a 1960 book titled *The Economics of Defense for the Nuclear Age*. They described systems analysis as "*a way of looking* at military problems ... [as] economic problems in the efficient allocation and use of resources" (Hitch and McKean 1960, v; emphasis in the original).

They argued that

Economy and efficiency are two ways of looking at the same characteristic of an operation. If a manufacturer or military commander has a fixed budget (or other fixed resources) and attempts to maximize his production or the attainment of his objective, we say that he has the problem of using his resources efficiently. But if his production goal or other objective is fixed, his problem is to economize on his use of resources, that is, to minimize his costs. These problems may sound like different problems; in fact, they are logically equivalent. For any level of budget or objective, the choices that maximize the attainment of an objective for a given budget are the same choices that minimize the cost of attaining that objective. (Hitch and McKean 1960, 2)

The Systems Analysis Paradigm

Hitch and McKean argued that their way of thinking economically about the problems of defense was the single best way to integrate all points of view so that discussion and agreement could be reached on common terms—that it is nothing less than a lingua franca of defense decision making. Systems analysis became the means for building consensus about the details of defense programs, once some general decisions were made, primarily by congressional budget decisions, about how many resources should be committed to defense. In this view, the goal of rationalizing choices about military matters devolves into decisions about efficiency. Furthermore, Hitch and McKean argued that there were only three "interrelated and interdependent" approaches to achieving the sought-for efficiency:

1. The improvement of institutional arrangements within the government to promote efficiency. ...

2. Increased reliance on systematic quantitative analysis to determine the most efficient alternative allocations and methods.

3. Increased recognition and awareness that military decisions, whether they specifically involve budgetary allocations or not, are in one of their important aspects economic decisions; and that unless the right questions are asked, the appropriate alternatives selected for comparison, and an economic criterion used for choosing the most efficient, military power and national security will suffer. (Hitch and McKean 1960, 106)

The systems analysis philosophy embodied in item number three above thus did not inherently depend on the quantitative techniques of item two. Rather, the approach required only five key elements, which together form what may be called the systems analysis paradigm:

1. One or more objectives to accomplish.

2. Alternative approaches to achieving those objectives.

3. Costs of resources used for each of the alternatives.

4. A model or models, defined as "abstract representations of reality which help us to perceive significant relations in the real world, to manipulate them, and thereby predict others. ... In systems analyses models of one type or another are required to trace the relations between inputs and outputs, resources and objectives, for each of the systems to be compared, so that we can predict the relevant consequences of choosing any system."

5. A decision criterion, which "is frequently the central problem in designing a systems analysis" (Hitch and McKean 1960, 106–107).

Hitch and McKean argued that systems analysis "is *a way of looking at problems* and does not necessarily depend upon the use of any analytic aides or computational devices." Nevertheless, sometimes such tools "are quite likely to be useful in analyzing complex military problems, but there are many military problems in which they have not proved particularly useful where, nevertheless, it is rewarding to array the alternatives and think through their implications in terms of objectives and costs." In any case, such quantitative analyses "are in no sense alternatives to or rivals of good judgment; they supplement and complement it. Judgment is always of critical importance in designing the analysis, choosing the alternatives to be compared, and selecting the criterion" (Hitch and McKean 1960, 118–120).

One of the earliest—and perhaps splashiest—examples of how McNamara intended to apply systems analysis to Defense decisions may be found in his 1963 decision not to agree with the Navy's recommendation that its next aircraft carrier (which would become the CV-67) should be nuclear powered. McNamara initially rejected that recommendation as being based on "inadequate information," leading McNamara to request "a full study of the whole 'nuclear-propulsion' question" (Murdock 1974, 80–81). The Navy's response "merely listed the advantages of nuclear propulsion and recommended adoption. McNamara again rejected the analysis, listing the failures of the study, notably "the failure to weigh added cost against added effectiveness." Turning to the Center for Naval Analyses (CNA) to provide an analytical argument the Secretary might accept, the Navy was disappointed when the CNA study failed to support their case. So the Navy did its own in-house study, attempting to play the cost-effectiveness game—but not very well. The new Navy study "listed the factors determining effectiveness, ranked both types of propulsion for each factor, weighted the factors (for example, 'other factors,' which included the 'advancement of technology,' constituted eight percent of total effectiveness—the nuclear carrier was 1.25 times better on 'other factors') and concluded that a nuclear task force was 1.21 times better that a conventional force and cost only 3 percent more." McNamara was not impressed. He "carefully destroyed the final Navy effort to justify nuclear propulsion. He concluded that since his information was inadequate for a decision on the future of nuclear propulsion, expedience dictated the choice of conventional power for the time being."

This incident shows that

> McNamara's insistence on a cost effectiveness approach is clearly demonstrated, as well as his initial unwillingness to let the military provide the analysis. The Navy's inability to do so (reinforced undoubtedly by the suspicion that analysis would not provide a rationale for the desired position) led McNamara to reject the consensual judgment of the military. This example illustrates McNamara's determination to make "rational"

decisions—a determination which resulted in an increased reliance on the Systems Analysis Office. Whether the OSA's greater role brought more analysis into the making of decisions is another question. (Murdock 1974, 81)

Systems Analysis under Attack

Despite the emphasis systems analysis theoreticians placed on judgment and perspective over quantitative techniques, systems analysis practitioners soon came to apply more and more frequently the sort of a priori mathematical modeling and analysis that is anathema to practitioners of traditional operations research. As early as 1943, Blackett had warned against such methods:

> One possible method of procedure is to attempt to find general solutions to certain rather arbitrarily simplified problems. In times of peace, when up-to-date numerical data on war operations are not available, this method may alone be possible. This procedure is to select, out of numerous variables of a real operation of war, certain important variables which are particularly suitable for quantitative treatment, and to ignore the rest. Differential equations are then formed and solutions obtained.

> Certain results obtained by this method are of great interest. An example is Lanchester's N^2 Law. ... But it is generally very difficult to decide whether, in any particular case, such a "law" applies or not. Thus it is often impossible to make any practical conclusions from such an *a priori* analysis, even though it be of theoretical interest. (Blackett 1962, 179)

Some thirty years later, J. A. Stockfish echoed Blackett in his book *Plowshares into Swords: Managing the American Defense Establishment* (1973). He argued that model-building designed to treat combat and evaluate existing and, especially, conceptual weapons systems is used (or more accurately, abused) in the bureaucratic setting. This abuse occurs because models and model building tend to become equated with the scientific method itself. But scientific endeavor also requires that models (or theories) be validated, which necessitates recourse to empirical methods. It is this latter part of the scientific method that is largely absent in the existing military study and evaluation system. (Stockfish 1973, 190)

A fundamental problem that plagues analysis of future hypothetical systems and combat is the lack of real operational data to form the basis for developing the underlying principles of a priori models of future operations. Even more important from a scientific perspective, there was no way to *disprove* the theories and conclusions embodied in the models. Not surprisingly, alternate solutions to the problem emphasize one or the other of these issues. Stockfish identified "a basic philosophical difference" between those he called "structuralists"— analysts who sought more and more detailed microscopic "realism" to overcome the perceived structural shortcomings of their models—and the empiricists, who argued that

> a "realistic theory" is a contradiction. The purpose of theory is to distill from the mass of data that constitutes "reality" the facts and variables that are relevant. The criteria for evaluating theory is relevance, and the hallmark of relevance is predictive value. Without independently derived evidence to support the assertion that follows from theory, the most sophisticated theory (or model) will still be judged against common sense. (Stockfish 1973, 199–200)

There seemed to be a sort of hubris inspiring many of the postwar (and sadly, current) generation of systems analysts. (I call them the true believers.)[1] Such analysts had come to believe that their a priori models—implemented on more and more powerful computers but spun from whole cloth with virtually no real data to calibrate and test them against—could solve ever more complex problems, not only of military operations but also of human motivation, and the effects of culture (see also Alt et al. 2009). The care with which Hitch and McKean had originally described their ideas was not always visible in the way these other and later practitioners of the art of systems analysis spoke about and used it and its results. By the 1980s, the whiz kids and their philosophy had lost much of their charm.

Even bureaucrats such as R. James Woolsey, a former undersecretary of the Navy and later the director of Central Intelligence, argued that the approach had, at best, outlived its usefulness. In 1980, Woolsey left the Department of Defense; in his book of that year, he pointed his finger squarely at the analysts who, to him, seemed to have fallen into an almost mindless pattern of doing calculations primarily to spark debate about the calculations and to build a consensus about just what inaccuracies everyone involved could agree upon as the basis for moving forward, regardless of their relationship to anything even vaguely real.

> Over the course of the last two decades, planning military forces, particularly for the navy, has become a matter of concocting [such a great word!] rather elaborate scenarios for specific geographic areas of the world. These scenarios are boxed in by innumerable assumptions, and force options are created and then tested in the scenarios using complex computer simulations— campaign analyses and the like. ... The interesting question about ... most scenario-dependent navy force planning, is not "Why don't we do this

slightly differently?" but "Why are we doing this *at all?*" (Woolsey 1980, 5–8; emphasis in the original; interpolation mine)

Woolsey suspected that the entire process was more about the interests of those who managed it than about the truly substantive issues. He even found it at times counterproductive: "it has fostered the idea that we can predict the scene and nature of future conflicts, even if we do not plan on being the ones who start them, and that we should not proceed with weapons programs until there are agreements about such scenarios and such analyses" (ibid.). He argued that the fundamental raison d'être of systems analysis—helping to define the future DoD programs—was, or had become, bogus. As

> a tool for designing forces, tools of marginal analysis frequently are themselves useful only in a rather marginal way. ... The lead time for weapons design and production is vastly greater than our ability to forecast where war might occur or even what countries, such as Iran, might or might not be on our side. (ibid.)

Woolsey's words reflected the existence of a growing debate about the roles and practice of defense analysis. About the same time as his book was published, the General Accounting Office (GAO) released its own report on defense analysis, *Models, Data, and War: A Critique of the Foundation for Defense Analysis* (GAO 1980). In the cover letter releasing the report, the Comptroller General of the United States wrote, "This report critiques the management and use of quantitative methodology in the analysis of public policy issues, focusing on the inherent limits of the methodology as a tool for Defense Decision, and the essential role of human judgment in any such analysis."

Operations Research Strikes Back

Four years after the attacks of Woolsey, the GAO, and others, the Center for Naval Analyses—the direct lineal descendant of World War II's first US operations research organization—formally entered the lists of the debate. CNA presented the OR counterattack against the dominance of systems analysis through two essays in its annual reports for the years 1984 and 1986. These essays, entitled respectively *The Defense Debate and the Role of Analysis*, and *Systems Analysis in Perspective*, threw down a gauntlet challenging the largely deductive approach that had come to characterize systems analysis, and calling for a renewed emphasis on the inductive approach that had originally characterized operations research.

The 1986 *Systems Analysis in Perspective* prominently featured an extract from Elting E. Morison's essay *The Parable of the Ships at Sea*. I have always found this story fascinating, and it is worth reproducing at length Morison's capsule summary of his main point.

> Things went on well enough for the men in the naval service as long as they worked with familiar and limited means. Then gross and continuing expansion of the means threw them into a considerable confusion. At first it was simply a matter of trying to figure out how all the new apparatus worked, but then the uncertainty over the novel means extended to the ends. What were they to do with all these things that so enlarged their own capacities? For some time they hoped to solve this problem of ends by making the means work better—improvement in the technology, as it is now called. But that simply added to the confusion. Then Mahan explained what the purpose of a navy that had all these new things should be. Given such a defined and recognized

end in view, the men in the service then found they had a way to put all the forces and materials that had distracted them into a sensible system that served the intended purpose. It was a system they could manage in an informed way. (Morison 1977, 151)

Spelling it all out: If you know the kind of war you want to fight you don't have much trouble designing and controlling the machinery. Building on Morison's point, the CNA essay argued that "the power of an organizing idea magnifies the apparent power of analysis. Once the ends of defense are clear, the selection of means becomes amenable to analysis" (CNA 1986, 17).

But there is an important paradox here—a solid consensus on a policy and the programs to implement it can be helpful to defense planning, but also it can be potentially fatal when that consensus gets it wrong.

> In sum, a war might unfold in many ways, but it will unfold in only one way. Before the fact, it is impossible to know how one or another piece of hardware will affect the outcome. For war is decided by men and luck; the machinery is almost incidental. Of course, it is better to have the machinery than not. But in war, the demands of the immediate situation and the user's ingenuity will determine how well a particular weapon is used. (CNA 1986, 12–15)

The forty years since Morse and Kimball had argued that man-plus-machine warfare behaves more like a machine had seen the industrial-style warfare of World War II replaced by the threat of nuclear annihilation on the one hand, and guerilla-style "wars of national liberation" on the other. To CNA and other operations analysts who considered themselves lineal descendants of Morse and Kimball, it seemed as if the masters might have got

it wrong. But if wartime uncertainties dominate and overwhelm our ability to predict them using any models and techniques we can hope to create, what do we do? "Denied the solace of a 'rational' approach to defense planning, how do we attain a military posture that is robust enough to deal successfully with an unpredictable future?" (CNA 1986, 17).

CNA argued that there were two answers to this question. The first of these was consistent with both Morison's parable and the systems analysis philosophy. That approach was "to forge a consensus about the ends of defense and about a military strategy compatible with those ends. But such a consensus is hard enough to reach in wartime, let alone in the demipeace we have 'enjoyed' since World War II." The second answer was "to design organizations [and] institutions ... capable of rapid, effective learning and adaptation to changing internal and external conditions" (Ackoff 1977, 39).

The essay concludes with a statement that, in the wake of the 9/11 terror attacks, is all too much on point: "This paradigm may be unsatisfactory to those who seek certainty in an uncertain world. But it is better than the false certainty offered by analysts and critics of analysis who would fine tune the future with inadequate tools and visions" (CNA 1986, 17). Of course, neither answer alone is sufficient, just as neither operations research nor systems analysis alone can solve all defense problems; we must pursue both lines at once, and in a complementary fashion. No real progress can be achieved without the building of consensus. But if we are to avoid the dangers of agreeing to be precisely wrong, that consensus must take a clear-eyed view of the limitations of operations research and systems analysis when applied in the real world.

We must recognize, as Jim Woolsey did, that the systems analysis "revolution" (if we may be so bold as to call it that) was about more than simply quantification; it was about more than applying some of the scientific (and pseudo-scientific) principles of the World War II operations researchers to the dangerous new world of the Cold War. It was about using a formal approach to thinking about problems in order to help articulate policy decisions and build consensus using a new language, a language of economics.

Unfortunately, too often the conversation devolved into an "irreconcilable clash of competing theories of combat" (CNA 1986, 11). But, as Woolsey himself put it, "the intellectual tradition that has produced program analysis and systems analysis, is an important one. It is a tradition reaching back probably before, but certainly to, Locke, Mill, Adam Smith, Ricardo, and the roots of modern economics. But that tradition may not have cornered the market on reality" (Woolsey 1980, 14). Indeed.[2]

Wargaming: Living Stories to Create Experience

This is not a game! It is training for war! I must recommend it to the whole army.
—Prussian Chief of the General Staff Karl von Muffling, on watching a demonstration of the Reisswitz *kriegsspiel*

And so at last we come to wargaming. As the third principal tool or approach or philosophy of thinking about defense issues, it continued a slow but inexorable coevolution with both operations research and systems analysis. Wargaming's modern roots can be traced at least as far back as the Prussian 1824 *kriegsspiel* of the elder and younger Reisswitz (see Jon Peterson's chapter in this volume). Since then it has experienced cycles of popularity and obscurity throughout the past two centuries.

Reisswitz's *kriegsspiel* grew out of a tradition of board games representing essential aspects of warfare for the education and edification of the nobility and warrior classes. But it went one step further. Unlike the abstractions of chess and other such games, *kriegsspiel* attempted to represent real military operations on a detailed topographical map of

real terrain, such as might be used during actual military operations. Reisswitz emphasized that the game presented the players with a realistic basis for making tactical and operational decisions. Furthermore, he created a system of rules and charts that purported to determine the results of those decisions and the activities of the military units involved based on actual experience and data from field trials. The Prussian, and later German, army leadership saw such value in these sorts of games for educating staff officers and leaders, as well as for studying potential conflicts, that the various forms of *kriegsspiel* became major elements of their system. The successes they enjoyed in the wars of the late nineteenth century sparked interest and imitation in other Western nations, as well as Japan (see Perla 1990 for a fuller discussion of the history of *kriegsspiel* and military wargaming).

From its initial emphasis on tactical decision-making, wargaming by military professionals expanded into operational and strategic dimensions. Naval wargaming, too, developed in the post-Mahanian days at the end of the nineteenth century, experiencing an important period of development at the US Naval War College in Newport, Rhode Island. Prior to World War I, all the major European powers wargamed out the various war plans. For example, the Russians played out their initial campaign plan for the invasion of East Prussia. In an incident to be repeated many times in the future of wargaming, the Russian game strongly indicated the difficulties they would face with two widely separated armies, commanded by generals who were disinclined to cooperate with each other, against a more agile and concentrated German force. Ignoring the insights the game might have given them, the Russians followed the plan to the disasters at Tannenberg and the Masurian Lakes in August 1914.

Wargaming continued to be used as a method of exploring potential future conflicts between the world wars, and even during World War II. As discussed later, the US Navy made extensive use of wargaming between the wars to help develop the tactics and operational concepts that would prove successful in the Pacific War against Japan. After that war, new techniques developed to take advantage of electronic systems and computers to develop more and more complex games, in the hope of creating more and more realistic environments to explore and test new warfighting concepts, including concepts for nuclear warfare.

Unlike operations research and systems analysis however, wargaming did not enjoy much attention from academics beyond some small groups of hobbyists until the near-simultaneous growth of political-military gaming and hobby board wargaming during the 1950s (see Peterson 2012). Because of its less-than-academic origins, however, wargaming's credibility remained somewhat suspect, especially among analysts weaned on the McNamara SA orthodoxy.

Part of the reason for this almost deliberate disdain for wargaming among many analysts was their tendency to view wargaming as nothing other than poor, unrigorous analysis rather than a distinct tool. The standard DoD "official" definition didn't help matters: "a simulation involving two or more opposing forces using rules, data, and procedures designed to depict an actual or assumed real-life situation" (JCS 1987, 28). Instead of that definition, I proposed the following in 1990: "a warfare model or simulation whose operation does not involve the activities of actual military forces, and whose sequence of events affects and is, in turn, affected by the decisions made by players representing the opposing sides" (Perla 1990, 164). The key elements of this definition are to be found in the words "players" and "decisions."

Wargaming is not in itself analysis—although it draws on analytical techniques. It is also not real—although good games strive to create the illusion of reality. Neither is wargaming duplicable—although you can play a game repeatedly, no two games can ever be identical. A "wargame is an exercise in human interaction, and the interplay of human decisions and the simulated outcomes of those decisions makes it impossible for two games to be the same" (Perla 1990, 164). As a result, wargaming does not pretend to—indeed, is simply not able to—address all problems associated with defense, as systems analysis claimed to do. Its focus is on human interaction, human knowledge, and human learning.

The essence of wargames is found in their basic nature. They are about people making decisions and communicating them in the context of competition or conflict, usually with other people—all the while plagued by uncertainty and complexity. Through these processes, the players live a shared experience and learn from it.

Modern "professional" wargames take many forms and use many different instrumentalities. Seminar wargames exhibit some surface similarities to the hobby game *Dungeons & Dragons*: game controllers present players with situations and call for them to decide what to do; actions and outcomes are discussed and debated and the situation updated to advance to the next critical decision point. Other types of games can look very like a commercial hobby board game. The hypothetical war in the Central Front of NATO as played out in a series of Navy Global War Games during the 1980s was represented by a large paper map with an overlay of hexagons and a set of unit counters that would have been familiar to any wargame hobbyist of the period. Rather than simple paper combat results tables, however, controllers used minicomputer combat models to adjudicate battle outcomes.

Whether played as seminar-style discussions or rigidly controlled tabletop or computerized map games, modern professional wargames continue to serve as both educational and training tools and as analytical research resources. In every case, however, wargames are helping their creators and participants to learn something useful and important about the decision-making environments they represent. Those environments cover the range of issues facing defense today.

In the past few years, games designed and conducted by my colleagues and me at CNA have ranged from explorations of the broad shape of the US defense program over the next thirty years to the types of systems and tactical concepts that the US Marine Corps might need to develop to face hybrid-warfare threats in the Middle East and elsewhere. We have done games to explore the broad scope of logistical issues that might arise in a potential major war

with a peer competitor fifteen or thirty years in the future, and we have applied wargame techniques to explore political-military issues in Africa, as well as problems associated with managing and sharing water resources in south Asia.

Regardless of their form or subject, games motivate players to become engaged in the simulated world of the game. They provide the players some immediately applicable education in terms of facts and analysis, and they encourage the players to act on those facts to make decisions and to deal with the consequences of those decisions. These activities, in turn, help the players learn about themselves and about how they make decisions by allowing them to practice decision-making in a protected environment, or "safe container" (Brightman and Dewey 2014). Games help us organize information in meaningful and memorable ways; they help us see how and why things happen as they unfold before our eyes. Games help us explore what I call the five knows: what we know, what we don't know, what we don't know we know, and (the most difficult ones) what we don't know we don't know, and what we know that ain't so—all through the mechanisms of discovery learning.

Learning games are all about change. Their goal is to change the learner—at least, to change the learner's mind. Those of us who design and use games build a synthetic, working world, and help the players enter that world and bring it to life. Most of all, we help them change that world through their decisions and actions, and in the process they change themselves (the educational use of games) and us (the research use of games).

Recent scholarship has emphasized the idea that the proper source of insight from wargaming is beyond the mere decisions made by the players.

Based on social science research that seems to indicate that most humans are poor judges of how they would behave if a hypothetical situation became real, Professor Stephen Downes-Martin at the US Naval War College has argued that using game decisions as the key information source for wargaming insights is an unreliable one (Downes-Martin 2013). Pursuing this line of thought, Naval War College professor Hank Brightman and student Melissa Dewey proposed that the true source of useful information and insight available in a game derives from the conversation among the players as they communicate by both word and action (Brightman and Dewey 2014). Indeed, "Wargaming is an act of communication" (Perla 1990, 183).

In all its varied dimensions, wargaming works to create a shared synthetic experience among its participants. To do so effectively, it draws on the inherent human propensity for telling, and learning from, stories. Its power derives

> from its ability to enable individual participants to transform themselves by making them more open to internalizing their experience in a game. … [Indeed,] gaming, as a story-living experience, engages the human brain, and hence the human being participating in a game, in ways more akin to real-life experience than to reading a novel or watching a video. By creating for its participants a synthetic experience, gaming gives them palpable and powerful insights that help them prepare better for dealing with complex and uncertain situations in the future … [and] is an important, indeed essential source of successful organizational and societal adaptation to that uncertain future. (Perla and McGrady 2011, 112)

As a vibrant hobby wargaming community, who understood wargaming intuitively and based on their own experience, grew and expanded its reach in the last half of the twentieth century, it produced new generations of policy, systems, and operations analysts familiar not only with the techniques of wargaming but also with their important strengths and dangerous weaknesses. Most importantly, the growing community of professional DoD wargamers has begun to demonstrate the inherent power and persuasiveness of combining the full range of information and tools available into what I have termed the cycle of research (Perla 1990, 273–290). This cycle integrates systems analysis, operations research (particularly through its analysis of exercises and real-world experience), and wargaming into an active collaboration to paint a more complete picture of the problems we face in the future, and to identify more creative potential solutions to those problems.

Creating the Cycle of Research

Alone, wargames, exercises, and analysis are useful but limited tools for exploring specific elements of warfare. Woven together in a continuous cycle of research, wargames, exercises, and analysis each contribute what they do best to the complex and evolving task of understanding reality.

—Peter P. Perla, *The Art of Wargaming*

In his book The *Logic of Failure* (1986), German psychologist Dietrich Dörner explores human decision-making in complex and uncertain situations. He argues that there is "no universally applicable rule, no magic wand, that we can apply to every situation and to all the structures we find in the real world. Our job is to think of, and then do, the right things, at the right times, and in the right way" (Dörner 1986, 287). I argue in *The Art of Wargaming* that analysis, exercises, and wargaming, while sharing some common characteristics, are distinct tools for studying and planning for potential future conflict. When that latter book was published, our practical experience of real warfare was too limited to include the non-exercise aspects of operations research in my concept. Today, however, we are in the unenviable position of having an extensive body of operational experience and research to factor into our thinking—and into the background, context, and databases of our other tools.

Just as there is no "universally applicable rule," neither is there a universally powerful tool. We cannot continue to make wise decisions in face of the increasingly complex world we must navigate if we rely on only one of our tools—or even on all of them but in isolated "cylinders of excellence." Instead, we need to apply all our tools—operations research, systems analysis, and wargaming—to address those aspects of our problems for which they are best suited. Then we need to integrate and interpret their results to paint a more complete picture of both the problems and their potential solutions.

This cycle of research approach is one that has worked in the past. During the 1920s and 1930s, the US Navy integrated an extensive program of analysis and wargaming at the Naval War College with an equally extensive program of large-scale fleet exercises, titled for the most part "Fleet Problems" (see Nofi 2010). The process the Navy used followed this prescription:

> Ideas developed or problems encountered on the game floor were analyzed by students and often tried out in the Fleet Problems, usually after some practical experimentation in the fleet and during routine exercises. Likewise, questions that arose during the Fleet Problems were often incorporated in an NWC game, of which there were some 200 in the period. As the process developed, the rules for both the Fleet Problems and the NWC wargames were continuously revised and updated. This kept the gaming process honest, because, as Rear Adm. Edward C. Kalbfus, President of the Naval War College, cautioned in 1930, "we can make any type of ship work up here, provided we draw up the rules to fit it." (Nofi 2012, 296)

The results of this tightly spun cycle of research included most of the operational concepts, tactics, and systems employed by the US Navy so successfully during the war against Japan. Perhaps even more importantly, the process helped produce the mindsets and habits of thought used by the men who led and fought during that conflict.

A similar, though less widespread, dramatic, and influential example is one I actually participated in during the heyday of the Cold War in the mid-1980s. Based on ideas generated in the fleet, CNA conducted a series of technical analyses designed to explore the potential tactical advantages the Navy might gain against the Soviets by operating aircraft carriers from within fjords in north Norway. Other analyses tried to quantify the effects such operations might have on defeating a Soviet attack in the region by providing close air support and battlefield interdiction to support defending NATO forces. The idea captured the imagination of Vice Admiral Henry "Hank" Mustin, then the commander of US Second Fleet and NATO Strike Group Atlantic. To explore the full range of operational and strategic implications of adopting such an aggressive forward stance, VADM Mustin sponsored, and played himself, during a wargame at Newport. I was privileged to participate in that game as an observer/analyst.

VADM Mustin also directed at-sea exercises to explore the practicality of such fjord operations, and to identify requirements to make it work and obstacles to its success. Partly as a result of the game and the exercises, CNA and others embarked on more studies and analyses under the umbrella term "Targets that Count," to explore what other Soviet targets carrier air wings might be able to attack or hold at risk from those areas to enhance deterrence or apply warfighting pressure.

Creating an integrated cycle of research like those described above does not happen automatically or by magic—there is no "magic wand" available to conjure with. It requires an integrated approach in which

> each of the tools strengthens and supports the others. Analysis provides some of the basic understanding, quantification, and mathematical modeling of physical reality that is required to assemble a wargame. The game presents some of the data and conclusions of the analysis to its participants and allows them to explore the implications that human decision-making may have for

that analysis. It can illuminate political or other non-military, non-analytical assumptions and points of view, raise new questions, and suggest modifications to existing or proposed operational concepts. (Perla 1990, 290)

Exercises, and to some extent real-world operations, provide the military opportunities to test the concepts with real people and real systems in real environments. When studied and analyzed carefully and rigorously, such exercises and operations can be used "to measure the range of values that mathematical parameters may actually take on, to verify or contradict key analytical assumptions, and to suggest even more topics for gaming, analysis, and follow-on exercises, thus continuing the cycle of research and learning" (Perla 1990, 290).

So it can be done; the cycle can be created and used. But it requires some person, some group, or some organization in a position of authority and influence to make it happen and to make use of its output to affect current and future decisions, concepts, and plans.

Riding the Cycle of Research to Interactive Planning

Most planners ride into the future facing the past. It's like trying to drive a train from its caboose. ... Top-down planning is usually initiated when senior executives go into hiding in the Bahamas. ... Bottom-up planning is taken no more seriously than promises made in church.

—Russell L. Ackoff, *The Corporate Rain Dance*

So, where does that leave us?

Analysis is fundamentally about providing scientific, and especially quantitative, advice to support decision makers. Those decision makers may be

operators in the field, conducting real actions against real enemies, or preparing for that real possibility; or they may be Pentagon bureaucrats concerned more about what to buy in the next budget—whether tools for future operations or balancing support for current operations with investments for the future. Making such decisions entails thinking about that unknown (and sometimes unknowable) future as well as our own organization and its overarching operating environments.

Two related but distinguishable approaches came into existence to help decision makers address these issues: "classic" operations research and "modern" systems analysis. Operations analysis (as it is also called) typically relies on real data from real-world operations to identify alternatives and recommend changes in tactics and perhaps in technology that should help to improve performance of operations in the field. Systems analysis, on the other hand, was created as a shared language using precise terminology and supplemented by mathematical models to build a shared paradigm for mustering and evaluating evidence, and to facilitate the formation of a consensus on issues not subject to the harsh tests and dictates of real-world performance data.

Wargaming is not analysis in the same sense as OR and SA. Unlike OR and SA it is not so much about the reductionist disassembling of problems into their component and quantitative parts. Instead, it is about the holistic integration of problems and the human beings who have to confront and act to overcome them. Wargaming is, or at least can be, predictive, but not in the absolute sense. It doesn't tell us the future with certainty, but rather it shows us its possibilities. In a presentation given at the Connections conference in Baltimore several years ago, Professor Robert "Barney" Rubel of the Naval War College described this idea in terms of wargaming being "indicative"—of the potentials inherent in situations and of the hidden relationships that a game, especially a series of related games, can help us discern.

Here is where most of the classic forms of modeling and simulation fall down. They cannot forecast outcomes that are not already embedded in the underlying mathematical constructs of the model or simulation. At best, such techniques pick apart and illuminate outcomes that are consequences of what we already know well enough to embed in the models. They do not, in fact, generate new knowledge, but they can reveal the sometimes complicated, overlooked, and surprising consequences of old knowledge.

Wargaming is a far better tool for going beyond old knowledge and exploring unforeseen consequences. This power of gaming to illuminate dark corners of future possibilities makes it especially important in light of the concept of the Black Swan. Popularized by Nassim Nicholas Taleb in his eponymous book (2007), a Black Swan is an event with three defining characteristics: (1) it is unpredictable; (2) it has massive impact on the course of events; and (3) after the fact, we can convince ourselves that we could have foreseen it if only we had been more astute. Black Swans became connected to the infamous concept of "unknown unknowns" described by former Secretary of Defense Donald Rumsfeld. Wargames can be an effective tool for exploring Black Swans and other such off-axis paths toward the future because what is possible in a wargame when played most productively goes beyond what is possible in a closed model—because in a wargame one or more working human brains are engaged in conflict with others, and those brains generate a wealth of ideas that go beyond those created by modelers working in more static environments.

Wargames frequently help us identify where and how we can make improvements to what we plan or do and one of the most important of those improvements lies in learning how to adapt to change. We can see this highlighted in the use of wargaming by the Naval War College during the interwar period. An important—if not perhaps the most important—outcome of that long series of games was that the students and future leaders of the wartime Navy learned adaptive techniques. In a famous letter to the

Naval War College after the war, Admiral Chester Nimitz stated that "the war with Japan has been [enacted] in the game room here by so many people and in so many different ways that nothing that happened during the war was a surprise—absolutely nothing except the Kamikaze tactics toward the end of the war; we had not visualized those" (quoted in Wilson 1968, 39).

It was not so much that War College gamers had gamed out everything the Japanese ultimately did in the war, but rather that the officers who would ultimately lead the US Navy during that conflict had had to adapt to changes in how the Japanese systems modeled in the games worked, in the tactics the different players used, and in the relative effectiveness of weapons as represented by changing model inputs. Remember that not everything the War College gamers did during that series of games was correct in the sense of representing actual Japanese tactics, strategy, or capabilities. (A prime example is our consistent underestimation of the Long Lance torpedo and how the Japanese would use it.) But by changing assumptions from game to game and year to year, the students were forced to learn how to discover crucial facts and adapt to them, not only to specific events, but also in general terms.

Another of Rubel's examples from the interwar period was the development of the US Navy's carrier doctrine and capability. The wargames at Newport showed Admiral Reeves, War College president at the time, the importance of putting large numbers of aircraft over the enemy fleet in short periods of time. But the operational doctrine used by the Navy's experimental carrier, USS *Langley*, limited her to operating only about a dozen aircraft at a time. Reeves passed the game's insights to Admiral Moffet, chief of Naval Aviation, and Moffet arranged for

Reeves to take command of *Langley*. Very quickly Reeves and his team developed the arresting gear and barrier combination that allowed *Langley* to operate more than fifty aircraft at a time. Thus, one of the crucial steps toward developing the carrier techniques that helped win the war in the Pacific can trace its lineage to Naval War College gaming. By communicating the results of those games effectively to the key decision makers, the games and Reeves's experiments helped Moffet shape the future.

The history of wargaming is full of examples like those above. It is clear that wargaming creates the opportunity for analysts, operators, and decision makers to have synthetic experience of rare events so that we may become more open to considering them in our thinking, operating, and planning. But just as reality limits our view of possibilities by our limited real experiences, a single wargame can also produce a "cognitive lock" on the specific events of that game. Participants may become just as vulnerable to overestimating the likelihood of the occurrence of game (or gamelike) events in the real world because of the immediacy of the gaming experience.

This danger argues for a broader and more formal application of gaming to decision making, one that operates in full partnership with modeling and simulation as part of the analyst's toolkit. It is only by incorporating wargaming as an equal partner with operations research and systems analysis that we can exploit the capabilities of all three techniques to the fullest in our quest to learn, adapt, and avoid the pitfalls of a complex and uncertain future.

Such a combination, the cycle of research, is a necessary and natural element for applying what management scientist Russell Ackoff called "interactive planning." Ackoff described this type of planning as one based on the belief that the future of an organization is largely under its own control. "It depends more on what we do between now and the future than on what has happened up until now." That the future depends on decisions yet to be made. This type of planner "focuses on all three aspects of an organization—the parts (but not separately), the whole, *and* the environment. He believes that often the most effective way of influencing the future of an organization is to change its environment. He may not have as much control over the environment as he does over the organization, but he uses as much as he has up to the hilt" (Ackoff 1977, 38–41).

Ackoff contrasts interactive planning with reactive and preactive planning. Reactive planners try to fix the problems within an organization so that it can become again what it was once during the "good old days." Preactive planners try to forecast the future and create "programs" based on their forecasts. Unfortunately, future forecasts can only be truly accurate when that future is fully determined by the past. "It turns out, then, that the only conditions under which the future can be predicted accurately are the determined ones that nothing can be done about. Then why forecast?" (ibid.)

Unlike those far more typical approaches to planning, in which planning is the exclusive job of the planners, interactive planning encourages all elements of an organization to participate in the planning process. They do so by articulating how things would be if they could "replace the current system with whatever they wanted most ... subject to only two constraints: technological feasibility and operational viability." It also focuses on learning and adapting to change. The process "is built on the realization that our concept of the ideal is subject to continuous change in light of new experience, information, knowledge, understanding, wisdom, and values ... it is an *ideal-seeking* system, unlike a utopia which pretends to be beyond improvement" (ibid.).

The cycle of research is—dare I say it—an ideal means for implementing such an interactive planning system. Implementing an organization-wide cycle of research integrates all our tools in the process of understanding reality and making decisions. Within DoD, the Planning, Programming, Budgeting, and Evaluation System (PPBES) pays lip service to the idea of involving all elements of the organization by soliciting inputs from operational commanders, program sponsors, and others across the geographic and specified commands, the services, and the defense agencies. But the system is a bureaucratic one, not an interactive one.

What appears to be needed to make it more interactive and more effective at integrating the relevant facts and points of view is a way to bring together the operational and system perspectives—not only OR/SA analysts, but also the operators and the technical experts—in a way that will allow them to share and learn from each other's perspectives. Wargames can play a central role in this process. Within the safe circle of a game, all perspectives can engage in focused conversation to expose all options and perspectives, build a shared experience and understanding, and create the catalyst for new ideas. From the wargame, the participants can take that shared overarching experience back to their own bureaucratic niches, and carry out their distinct duties with that shared view, that "organizational intent," if you will, in mind. The cycle of research thus begun can gather energy as those individual persons and organizations conduct new analyses, new exercises and experiments, and new wargames, all focused on seeking to reach the current ideal and adapting that ideal to circumstances as they change.

We have all the pieces. If only we would stop seeing OR, SA, and wargaming as competitors for influence over decision makers instead of complementary tools to help them make better decisions. P. M. S.

Blackett organized a group of scientists to create operations research and help win the biggest war ever fought. Robert McNamara introduced systems analysis as the lingua franca of the defense debate and helped overhaul one of the largest bureaucracies in the country. It remains to be seen whether and how interactive planning and the cycle of research can take us forward into the future.

About the Author

Peter P. Perla has been involved with wargaming, both hobby and professional, for over fifty years. A lifelong interest in military history and games of strategy led him to the world of commercial wargames before his teen years. As a youngster, he had already published articles in the hobby press before becoming an undergraduate mathematics major at Duquesne University. After earning a PhD in probability and statistics from Carnegie-Mellon University with his thesis on Lanchester mathematical combat models, he joined the Center for Naval Analyses in 1977 as a naval operations research analyst. By the early 1980s he had worked on several navy campaign studies, designed naval games, documented existing Navy wargames, and led a study to define the principal uses of wargaming and to identify some of its fundamental principles. Over the next few years, he conducted and led research projects on a wide range of issues of

importance to the US Navy and Marine Corps. In addition, he participated in a nearly a dozen classified major Navy wargames, including the Global War Game. In 1990, the US Naval Institute published the first edition of his book, *The Art of Wargaming.* This book became a fundamental international reference on the subject (including a Japanese-language edition), and a standard text at US military schools. Since that time, he has continued his work on Navy wargaming, and has branched out into analysis and gaming for other US government agencies, including the Centers for Disease Control and Prevention, the Department of Health and Human Services and the US Army's Training and Doctrine Command. He is regarded as one of the nation's leading experts on wargaming and its use in defense research. The History of Wargaming Project published a second edition of Dr. Perla's book, including new material, in 2011.

Notes

1. At a workshop on wargaming and analysis held by the Military Operations Research Society in 2007, I

was surprised to hear one of these true believers express his sense of frustration that "just when we had finally developed accurate models of conventional warfare, the emphasis had shifted to irregular warfare and counterinsurgency." I must have missed the memo. In the face of the grossly inaccurate predictions that such "accurate" models had produced about coalition casualties during Operation Desert Storm, I thought his assessment just a bit disingenuous. For example, Air Force academic Phillip

Meilinger reported that "prewar estimates, which had gone as high as 20,000 US casualties during the ground offensive, were dramatically reduced to fewer than 300" (Meilinger 2003, 212).

2. For one example, see Immanuel Kant's work dealing with subjectivity and relativism as a major intellectual alternative (Kant 2003).

16 THE APPLICATION OF STATISTICAL AND FORENSICS VALIDATION TO SIMULATION MODELING IN WARGAMES

Brien J. Miller

Consider the challenge: A designer has deep interest in a battle or campaign and sees in it an opportunity to explore the whys and wherefores of how the battle was fought or how the campaign came about, and how it culminated in a victory for one side or draw for both. Most often such interest begins from reading various histories.

Our designer now sits down to make a series of foundational decisions—size, scale, complexity—and does so by asking questions such as these: How much area does the map have to cover? What were the names, types, and equipment of the various organizational units that fought? How many men? What were the roles of the leaders? Did the terrain affect the outcome or perhaps channel the initial contact? So many questions upon which key initial design considerations will be based, and once based, will be harder and harder to change as the design evolves.

Moreover, assume that our designer wants to create an underlying simulation that hews closely to the mechanisms and the dynamics of the event under study. However, he also wants to ensure that there is a competitive game in it: a mix, which, if successful, will reveal a compelling story, one that will ultimately provide well-founded insights to its players as

to how history unfolded and how it might have gone otherwise.

The challenges that our designer faces are numerous and often interrelated, ranging from fitting the game to a product format that caps map and rulebook sizes and the number of playing pieces to evaluating functional performances of units, successes or failures of leadership, and logistics. Add to this a myriad of odd or special circumstances, such as the occurrence of unusual events, the nature of which could range from having a dramatic effect on the core design to simply being unique flavoring, and the design could begin to flounder from a lack of clarity.

The logical answer is to understand the simulation/game as a model—in fact, a series of models structured within an overall model. The question then is to understand the nature of models, what distinguishes good ones from not so good ones, and techniques for creating a dynamic model capable of abstracting details and revealing key processes.

A wargame, regardless of medium, is nothing more than a model, and, as George Edward Pelham Box (1919–2013), British mathematician and professor of statistics at the University of Wisconsin, once observed, "All models are wrong, but some are useful." The question, as Box himself posed, is, "How wrong does a model have to be to not be useful?" (Box and Draper 1987).

Useful models tend to exhibit three criteria (derived from George Box, as cited in Odlyzko 2010):

- They contribute to a rational understanding of the subject under study.
- They often provide a basis for extrapolation of conditions worthy of further investigation.
- They tend to be efficient in the use of parameters for the generation of output. (In short, they meet the Ockham's razor test: the principle of parsimony, economy, or succinctness used in problem solving devised by William of Ockham [c. 1287–1347].)

However, in order for a model to be truly useful it has to pass two tests: *verification* and *validation*. Only when a model has passed these two tests can we begin to say that the model is *credible* or useful for its intended purpose.

Verification is defined simply as a model working as intended. That is, the model's systems and subsystems operate as the design team expects them to. However, *validation* is the key to making a model useful. Validation focuses on determining whether a model is an accurate representation of the system under study. A model is said to be valid when the decisions or output of that model are similar to the real world construct or event that it represents. It is only when a model and its results are accepted by the users as being valid that a model is deemed *credible*.

For models that represent existing constructs, such as a model of a working V-8 engine, simulation engineers can make exacting measurements with which to construct the model and can furthermore experiment with that model in conjunction with the real engine in order to bring the model's performance in line with the real system under study.

When models represent repeating events such as business processes, the modeler can make continuous ongoing observations in order to align the model to the process flow under study. However, when the event is a one-time occurrence, especially one that has taken place sometime in the distant past, the challenge of constructing a "valid" model vastly increases. When those events are historical, and subject to subjective viewpoints and analysis based on limited data, the quality of which varies widely, then the challenge may be insurmountable.

This chapter examines two approaches that can be utilized when designing game and/or simulation models of historical events—statistical and forensic analysis—and will show how they can improve validation of a model and thereby improve the model's credibility.

The Problem of Historical Events

In their simplest form, wargames are models of historical events presented in a game format with the underlying understanding that the model is based on reasonably sound operational theory applicable to the conditions surrounding the occurrence. However, historical events are one-time affairs, often far more dynamically complex than can be perceived in even the best of written histories. While modern conflicts are the subject of deep operational studies using extensive metrics, events of conflicts in the past, even conflicts as recent as twenty years ago, can be subject to dispute. The further back in history we go, the more difficult it is to effectively establish criteria by which to evaluate them. Moreover, historical evaluations are often subjective in nature, written from perspectives with significant interest in portraying specific motives and outcomes.

Even when histories are well composed and provide the best information possible, because of the one-time nature of historical events, modern-day evaluators are often left with the assumption that the outcome of a battle or campaign reflects, more or less, the most likely outcome given the inability to discern the probable range of actual outcomes.

Figure 16.1 shows an example of just such a problem that poses challenges to validating a model. The figure assumes that, given perfect knowledge and a perfect model, if we were to run an event n times,

that we could establish a probable range of event outcomes. Then, if we were to look at some historical events against their probable range of outcomes, we would, in a number of cases, find that the actual outcome was outside of the standard deviation, perhaps even excessively so.

Thus, without being able to see or estimate probable range of outcomes it is not unreasonable to assume that in numerous cases the *outcome that did happen* was judged by historians to be inside of the standard deviation. But if it was not, and if a model were to be made based on upon that assumption, it would invisibly inhibit that model's validity and wrong conclusions might ensue.

To explore a few examples, it is probably reasonable to be highly confident that the outcome of the Battle of Little Bighorn,[1] in which a US force of approximately 650 troopers was annihilated by a

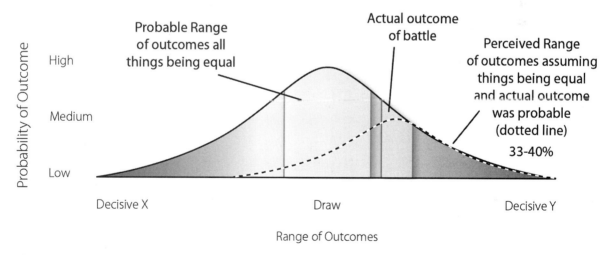

Figure 16.1
Event outcome perceptions.

force of perhaps 2,500 Native American warriors was very close to the center of its expected outcome. Less so might be the battle of Crécy.[2] Here, approximately 10,000 to 15,000 English troops decisively defeated a French force of upward of 25,000 troops, including heavily armored cavalry. French disorganization and rashness, combined with a strong English defensive position, resulted in a battle that altered territorial possessions on continental Europe for centuries and provided assumptions about medieval combat that have remained until this day. But was that battle's outcome actually in the expected range of all possible outcomes, or did French failures so skew the result that understanding the actual nature of medieval combat from it is impossible?

If we were to build models of each battle above with the assumption that combat would ensue, but allow for variations in the approach, we might likely find that while the outcome of Little Bighorn would in fact, be validated—that is, the action's outcome was within the expected range of outcomes—the historical result at Crécy might not be so. A rested and organized French force could very well result in an expected outcome range different from what has been heretofore supposed by many.

I should note that we are not here to argue the outcomes of these battles, but rather to understand that resulting wargame designs, in order to be considered credible by players, would, given no other way to view it, have to favor Native American and English victories in these respective battles. However, in the case of favoring a victory of the English at Crécy, the outcome might very well be out of the nominal expected range; thus, a game designed to reproduce that result would be based on an incorrect assumption, even if users/players expect that as the usual conclusion.

Ultimately, we seek valid models even if the result yields outcomes contrary to common tradition. We do this because a good model lets us explore and test results beyond just what happened at Crécy or Little Bighorn, and they do this because a good model is based on validated assumptions. When a historical game's process or results fly in the face of convention, players will only consider it credible if the designer goes to lengths to demonstrate why the model is valid.

In short, not validating a wargame model leads to a bias, and a biased model is insufficient to properly explore and truly understand the dynamics of the event under study. Worse, biased models contributes to mythologizing rather than analyzing.

The question, then, is: What tools allow us to improve validation?

A Statistical Approach

Statistical validation of models in the engineering and scientific worlds is not news. These methods have been a cornerstone of most validation efforts ranging from simple data aggregation to the more complex data analyses such as Bayesian inferencing and data topology. However, in the realm of historical models—that is, models based on historical events—applying statistical approaches can be fraught with difficulties due to the substantial lack of data. Even when there is significant data to be mined and evaluated, historical model validation often runs into preconceived notions based on rarely questioned subjective perspectives.

One such example is Winston S. Churchill's famous quotation about the U-boat war of World War II. Churchill, then the former Prime Minister of Great Britain, wrote in his six-volume history *The Second World War*, "The only thing that ever really frightened me during the war was the U-boat peril" (Churchill 2005, 529). This quotation has led to subjective historical evaluations declaring Germany's World War II U-boat campaign as a "near run thing" (as the Duke of Wellington one said of Waterloo) in which over six years, nearly a thousand U-boats nearly choked the shipping lanes of Great Britain to exhaustion, cutting off vital supplies of food, fuel, and raw materials, and nearly bringing the nation to its knees.

The statistics however, vibrantly disagree.

By March 1943, the Allied efforts in convoying, advances in technologies such as radar and sonar, aggressive deployment of ASW-capable small vessels trained in multiunit ASW tactics, and the immense power of the shipbuilding industry in the United States had all but effectively ended the U-boat war. Even Grand Admiral Karl Dönitz, the German U-boat commander, admitted such in an often-ignored 1943 memo that essentially conceded that the U-boat war was over.

Clay Blair Jr., in his two-volume, highly detailed books on the U-boat war (1996; 1998; follow-up to his book *Silent Victory*, on the United States campaign in the Pacific) pointed out that the U-boats were never as effective as some historians maintain. Blair's assessment was that the U-boat war was not a "close run thing," but rather "one more suicidal enterprise foisted on the Germans by Hitler." With a 75 percent rate of U-boat loss, most of which occurred after Dönitz's March 1943 turning point; and realizing that in all but one month of the entire war, more new replacement merchant tonnage was launched than lost; and given the statistical fact that 98 percent of all shipping sailing from America to England reached their destinations (a quantity of shipping well sufficient to maintain the island nation's survival), how could it be elsewise?

This assessment was foreseen by a little-known but seminal work published in 1965. In *The Attack Submarine: A Study in Strategy*, Robert Kuenne proposed a series of economic analyses leading to statistical models that evaluated both the American Pacific campaign and the German Atlantic campaign in order to project probable strategies for the growing American nuclear submarine fleet during the Cold War. Kuenne's work and Clay Blair's extensive books detailing American and German operations formed the genesis for my solo tabletop (war)games/simulations *Silent War: The United States' Submarine Campaign Against Imperial Japan* and *Steel Wolves: Germany's Submarine Campaign Against British and Allied Shipping: Vol. 1 1939–1943*.

The challenge of course was overcoming the perception of gamers (users of the model as defined above) who come to the German submarine campaign under the impression left by Churchill's lone quotation. The only effective way to overcome preconceived notions was to build a solid model based on statistical findings and validated against the data. Without doing so, preconceived perceptions could lead users to believe the model was not credible.

To accomplish this, codesigner Steve Jackson and I began by compiling an enormous array of data

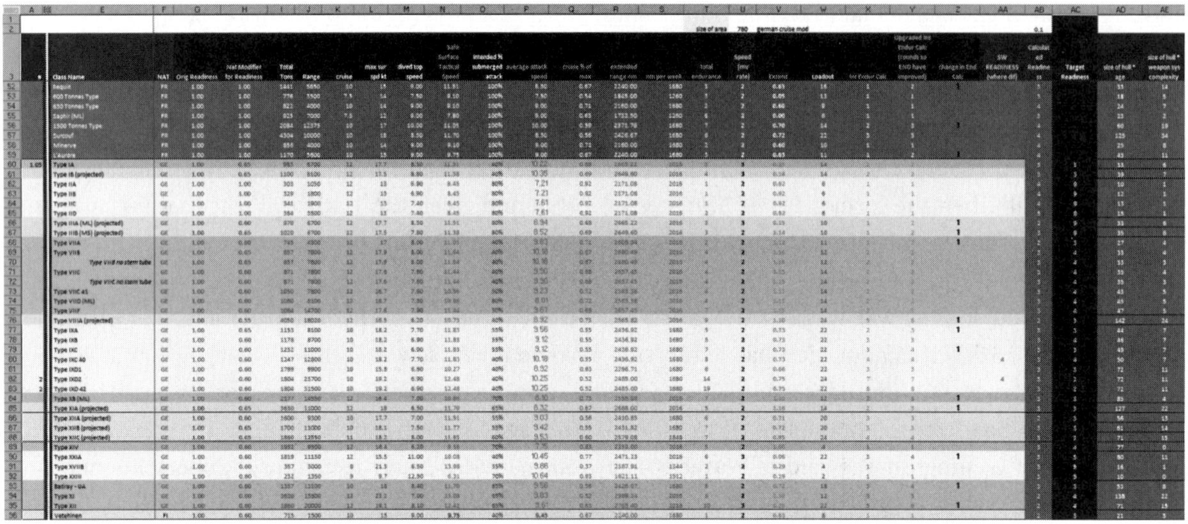

Figure 16.2
Submarine master data.

from well-established sources on the submarines used during the war. The process began with creating a statistical model of the various classes of submarines.

Figure 16.2 shows just a small portion of the Submarine Master Data set used to calculate both *Silent War*'s (2005) and *Steel Wolves*' (2010) submarine models. This portion of the spreadsheet recorded data for nationality, readiness factor, national modifiers for readiness, total tons of the submarine, maximum range and cruise speeds, maximum surface speed, and maximum diving speed.

The data in this section provided input to formulas used to derive such values as cruise speed as a percentage of maximum speed for various speed brackets, fuel bunkering, extended range in nautical miles given fuel consumption per various speed brackets, and calculating effective nautical miles traversed per week based on the map scales using

various movement rates. Other portions of the dataset recorded such information as diving depth, rate of dive, tactical turning rates, size of hull, and percentage of hull devoted to various systems such as propulsion. From this data we calculated maneuverability and survivability as well as other factors used in further calculations. These values integrated external factors such as speed of ASW ships, rate of fall of depth charges, and other details that help put various information into context. Last, we recorded weapon loadout (quantities of torpedoes and types of decks) and tactical employment information such as the number and types of tubes fore and aft, known reload rates, and combat systems capabilities represented by the German and American target data computers then in use. All told, over fifty-five separate factors, either recorded or calculated, comprise this dataset for 138 submarine classes built from 1920 through 1945, covering all nationalities, not just German and American.

Of the fifty-five factors, thirteen are used on the actual playing piece, eight of which are the result of extensive calculations done in the Submarine Master Dataset. Figure 16.3 shows the front and the back of the submarine playing piece: one side represents the submarine's tactical capabilities (left image) while the other represents its transit and in port values (right image).

It should be noted that one of the game's "playability" features is that it requires no separate pencil and paper recording of information. All information in the game is recorded on data tracks, printed on the map or, more important, subsumed into the game as part of a probabilistic determination. The most obvious of these latter model components is a submarine's endurance rating, which is a combination of torpedo loadout[3] and other consumable aspects of the submarine. As a patrol progresses and as more combats take place, probability that the submarine will have expended all of its torpedoes and/or consumed all of its other sustainability

resources increases until the player fails an endurance roll, at which point the submarine must return to base. The tracking of individual torpedoes is not required using this statistical approach.

However, the submarine models are only the start. The actual core of the game revolves around composing a vast amount of historical patrol data, including ships and tonnage sunk, into a playable format by which the game's users can resolve search, contact, and any ensuing combat. This is known as the area activity system (AAS), which generates the various area activity charts (AACs): the zones in the ocean space where submarine operations took place.

To build the AAS statistical models we collected actual patrol data of every submarine for every patrol conducted by the United States between December 1941 and August 1945 (for the Pacific game), and every submarine for every patrol conducted by Germany between September 1939 and June 1943. This data included length of patrol, patrol results, torpedoes fired, ships and tonnage sunk, and whether the submarine was lost on that patrol (and the cause,

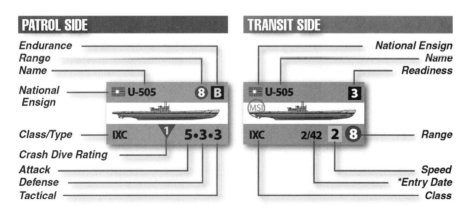

Figure 16.3
Submarine playing pieces showing values used.

when known) or whether it had to return to base, and the reason for that return to base.

The sources for this information were the appendices provided by Clay Blair Jr. in his various volumes, actual patrol records from the United States Navy archives, and the extensive two-volume set *U-boat Operations of the Second World War* (1997–8), by Kenneth Wynn. This data was augmented by searches on the Internet and cross-referenced with more detailed single-ship information found in various other books and publications too numerous to mention here.

The information collected was entered in spreadsheet form and imported into a database program, the list view of which is shown in figure 16.4. Where boats patrolled in more than one area on the same patrol, separate entries were made, resulting in geographic scatter diagrams that allowed us to determine how we would break the North and South Atlantic, as well as portions of the Indian Ocean, into the various sea zones, which then would become the basis of the AACs. The 692 records indicated in figure 16.4's list view represent the patrols for 1939 and the first half of 1940. All told, through 1943

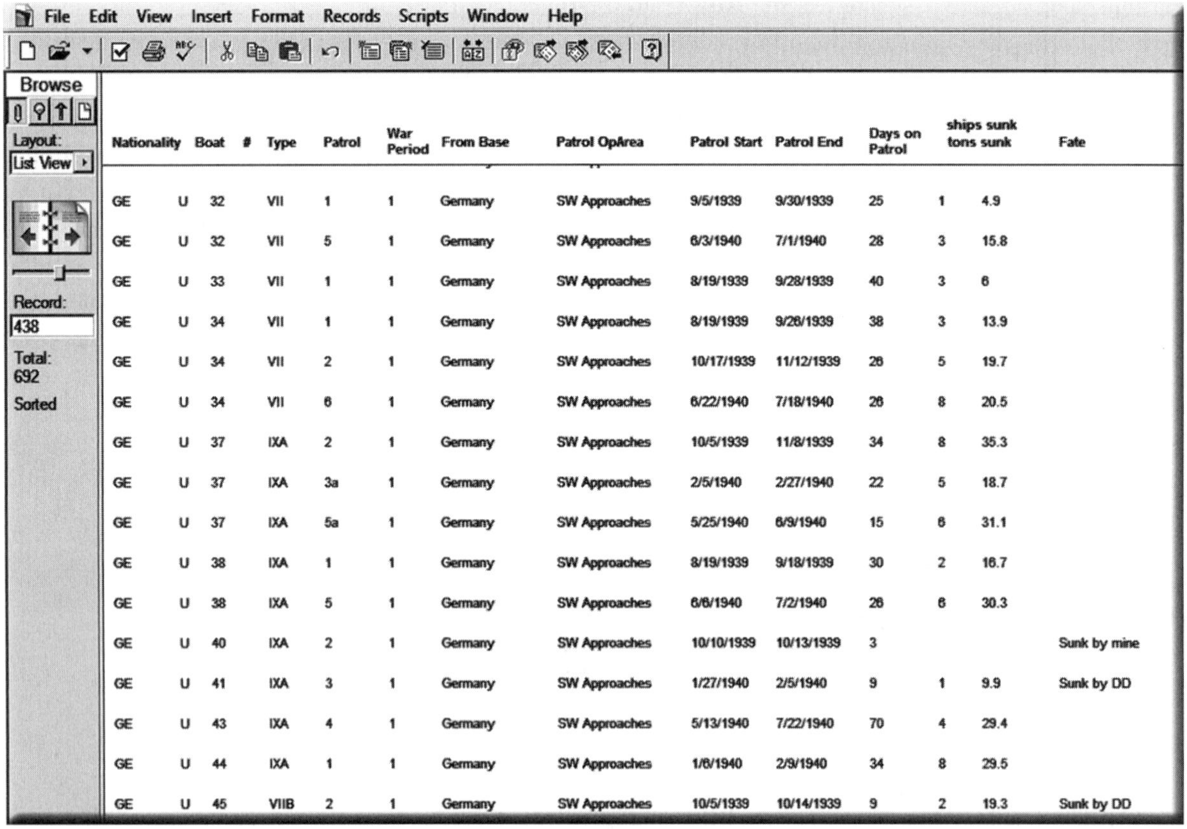

Nationality	Boat	#	Type	Patrol	War Period	From Base	Patrol OpArea	Patrol Start	Patrol End	Days on Patrol	ships sunk	tons sunk	Fate
GE	U	32	VII	1	1	Germany	SW Approaches	9/5/1939	9/30/1939	25	1	4.9	
GE	U	32	VII	5	1	Germany	SW Approaches	6/3/1940	7/1/1940	28	3	15.8	
GE	U	33	VII	1	1	Germany	SW Approaches	8/19/1939	9/28/1939	40	3	6	
GE	U	34	VII	1	1	Germany	SW Approaches	8/19/1939	9/26/1939	38	3	13.9	
GE	U	34	VII	2	1	Germany	SW Approaches	10/17/1939	11/12/1939	26	5	19.7	
GE	U	34	VII	6	1	Germany	SW Approaches	6/22/1940	7/18/1940	26	8	20.5	
GE	U	37	IXA	2	1	Germany	SW Approaches	10/5/1939	11/8/1939	34	8	35.3	
GE	U	37	IXA	3a	1	Germany	SW Approaches	2/5/1940	2/27/1940	22	5	18.7	
GE	U	37	IXA	5a	1	Germany	SW Approaches	5/25/1940	6/9/1940	15	6	31.1	
GE	U	38	IXA	1	1	Germany	SW Approaches	8/19/1939	9/18/1939	30	2	16.7	
GE	U	38	IXA	5	1	Germany	SW Approaches	6/6/1940	7/2/1940	26	8	30.3	
GE	U	40	IXA	2	1	Germany	SW Approaches	10/10/1939	10/13/1939	3			Sunk by mine
GE	U	41	IXA	3	1	Germany	SW Approaches	1/27/1940	2/5/1940	9	1	9.9	Sunk by DD
GE	U	43	IXA	4	1	Germany	SW Approaches	5/13/1940	7/22/1940	70	4	29.4	
GE	U	44	IXA	1	1	Germany	SW Approaches	1/6/1940	2/9/1940	34	8	29.5	
GE	U	45	VIIB	2	1	Germany	SW Approaches	10/5/1939	10/14/1939	9	2	19.3	Sunk by DD

Figure 16.4
Submarine patrol list view.

over 5,000 patrols were tracked, with each patrol having a location origin, date started, date ended, total days on patrol, and ships and tonnage sunk. The fate of the submarine is noted if it was lost on the patrol.

From the list view we generated a set of visual statistical analyses that allowed us not only to break down the sea zones into AACs, but to begin to compose each AAC's war breakout data, which forms the basis of the search and contact process used in both games.

To aid us in evaluating the data from a visual point of view, a geographic image of the data was created showing the operational areas we were considering for use in the game. Figure 16.5 shows this submarine patrol geographic view. In it, statistics were displayed for all the areas recorded as patrol targets with the displayed data (such as the 1.75 value shown in the Southwest Approaches) representing the average number of attacks per day that resulted in at least one ship sunk. This visual display allowed us to manually slide time forward and backward by clicking

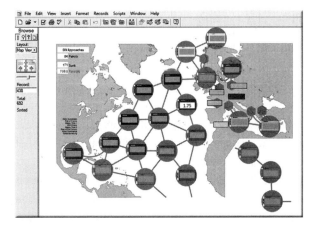

Figure 16.5
Submarine patrol geographic view.

through the date range; this allowed us to visually see the tempo of the actual campaign played out onscreen. This analysis technique greatly enhanced our ability to grasp the dynamics of the campaign while allowing us to dig deeper into data of interest, greatly informing the modeling of each AAC.

The result of this effort, combined with known key Allied events such as the introduction of convoys, the deployment of new ASW technology, the entry of the United States into the war and other such occurrences, resulted in identifying five "war periods" with sufficiently altered probabilities such that they could be represented as separate activity periods in the game. These war periods were identified as WP1 through WP5 and carry the game through to early 1943. As an example, WP1 is the opening of the war through the capitulation of France.

Once we had an effective understanding of the flow of submarine operations in the various war periods and the resulting contacts with surface targets, regardless of whether the contact resulted in a sinking or not, we exported the calculated data set into a spreadsheet designed to generate the actual Area Activity Charts that would appear the game. This data resulted in not only the AAC, as shown in figure 16.6, but also generated the actual contact table used to determine what type of contact—loner, convoy, or task force—the submarine encountered.

In figure 16.6, we see the AAC on the left broken into white, yellow, green, blue, and red boxes, which indicate the likelihood of a contact, with white being no contact and the various colors indicating increasing likelihood of a contact. If the result of a die roll on an AAC was a colored box, the player moves to the contact table shown on the right and rolls again to determine what if any surface ships he sighted. In the final version of this table, we manually inserted

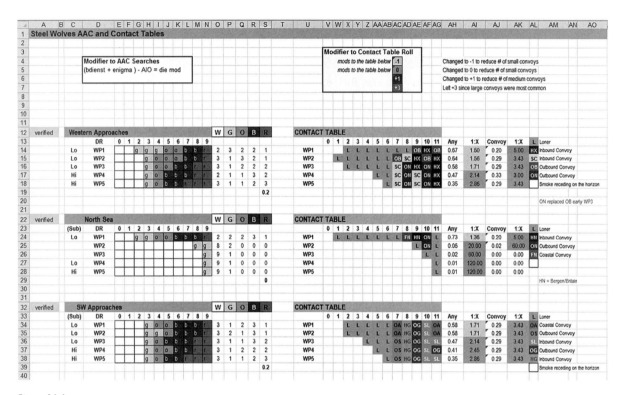

Figure 16.6
AAC and Contact Table calculator.

the historical convoy designations that a submarine would probably contact in any given area to the contact table probabilities. This was the only manual insertion of data during this stage.

The spreadsheet contains the statistical information about both the AAC and the Contact Table. This information was used during integration and final testing to adjust each table based on test results. Using these tables allowed us to map results against historical data as well as predictive data-derived algorithms based on Keunne's work in *The Attack Submarine*. This part of the effort permitted us to assess whether or not players (and thereby the models used by the game's players) were able to achieve nominal

historical results, as well as to see if they could better the historical results where predictive models indicated that the actual campaigns fell short of their effective potential.

Figure 16.7 shows the final playing board (map) used in the game for the same three areas shown in figure 16.6. As can be readily seen, the final published map shows different values than the original design spreadsheet shown in figure 16.6. Changes came about during three phases. The first occurred during integration, when we brought together the various systems and began testing (playing) them together. One example of how this phase of integration affected the final design occurred when

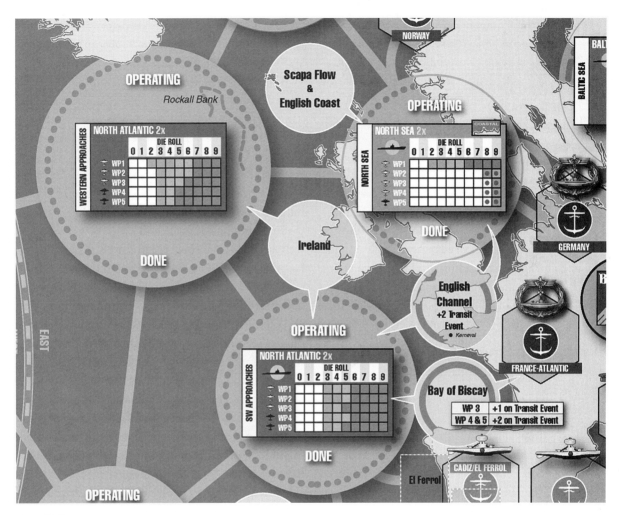

Figure 16.7
Final production map for *Steel Wolves*.

integrating movement system with the abstract AACs in *Silent War*. The raw data strongly suggested a long endurance range for the various submarine classes. However, during integration we found that submarines were effectively exceeding historical one-week cruise ranges. The issue lay in a combination of how we arranged the AACs on the map, how

we connected those AACs, and an overly optimistic cruise speed estimate based originally on a combination of submarine design data and optimistic trial data. The result altered some connectors and induced a 15 percent reduction in range values. Once these changes were introduced, play reflected nominal historical results.

Once all the components were integrated we launched the second phase, a series of multiple blind tests in which the game was sent out to several players who recorded each action for each submarine taken every turn and would play eight to twelve turns before sending in results. This initial "alpha" test, lasting about five months, revealed gaps in wording, procedure sequences, and general playing mechanisms which had to be worked out and fixed before moving to the next phase.

We then repeated the process, this time focusing on patrol results; this was the "beta" phase in which validation of the models based on tracking ships and tonnage sunk, as well as submarines lost, became the focus. During beta we recorded the results of approximately twelve test players against historical data and used statistical models to project trends and analyze player results. As we did so, we were able to detect locations where we would see anomalies building, such as having less contact with enemy's forces than historically occurred or an increased rate of sinkings compared to our baseline data. This allowed us to evaluate both the original submarine data—that is, the data used to determine the combat factors on the playing pieces—and the enumerated data as reflected on the map. Where we saw localized deviations we assumed it was map error, and where we saw deviations across multiple areas but restricted to one or two classes, then we assumed basic submarine data to be problematic.

This process went on across eighteen months and ultimately included "de-blinding" the game, allowing players to compare results directly. This allowed us to very carefully refine the data in the game as well as to modify modeling as needed. Finally, at the end it allowed us to assess what a nominal game could result in and provide us with statistical guidance on

where to set the goal post that determined whether the players achieved marginal, substantial, or decisive victory based on their accomplishments.

It also permitted us the ability to introduce perhaps the most-detested rule players must face in the game: career longevity. If the player does not achieve a certain tonnage sunk by a certain date, the game ends for them—because historically, if submarine commanders failed to achieve certain results they were relieved of command. No rule has garnered so much wailing and gnashing of teeth by the players as this career longevity rule, but at the same time it is well within reach, because it was statistically set. Many players simply reset the game and begin again.

It should be noted that the process of integrating data into the game system was both iterative as well as recursive. We began the design with some notional models in mind based on what we termed our "going-in" perceptions about how the campaign's dynamics worked; as we accumulated data, we adjusted our models to reflect what our validated findings told us. Elements of the submarine models, such as nominal transit times, torpedo performance and torpedo firing practices, and propulsion and diving capabilities as they related to tactical performance were brought into line with the probabilities depicted by the dataset. This occurred across all models, including refit and replenishment activities vital to maintaining the campaign.

As we integrated the various models into an aggregated game system, the data allowed us to streamline play by abstracting portions of patrol activities into more readily playable game functions that ensured we remained tightly coupled to the statistical data, while still allowing players to relate their game play to the simulated experience of commanding a submarine campaign.

All of this of course raises the question: Who validates the validation? Both games took nearly five years each to produce, the first year solely devoted to incorporating the data into the various model systems, while the following four years were devoted primarily to continual testing and refinement. For testing, we employed both human players as well as predictive computer-based algorithms using spreadsheets to establish first and foremost whether the game system could actually track to reasonable historical performances, and then to assess what balancing might be needed to move the games from an exercise in statistics to a functional gaming experience. Both titles employed three test teams of four to five people each, during the first several rounds of which none of the teams knew of the existence of the others. Where the game systems produced unusual results we first explored the possibility of misplay, caused either by a failure on our part to adequately describe the game processes or by player error, and only then considered errors in the data or the interpretation and/or use of the data.

The road was not always smooth during integration and testing. Both games experienced unusual skew. The Pacific game experienced significant skew in the war's final years, 1944 and 1945, when historically more than two hundred US submarines roamed a nearly empty Pacific Ocean. On the Atlantic side, the game experienced an early 50 percent reduction in both ships and tonnage sunk despite the fact that each individual engagement produced the correct expected range of outcomes.

In the Pacific game's case, the problem was simply linear testing. It was very difficult to test the entire game through into its final years, and starting a game in those late years using the historical situation (such as the submarines deployed and ships and tonnage

sunk in January 1944) only masked the problem. In the case of the Atlantic game, the issue lay in that the fundamental transit calculations had been based on the Pacific game, whose distances are vast compared to the area around the British Isles. Here, we discovered that the system as designed—that is, designed to emulate a week's worth of effort in the Pacific—was underproducing effective contacts by 50 percent. The fix was simply to allow U-boats who were in close-by British waters two entire search and contact phases inside one turn. That time, normally used for transit in the Pacific, was effective patrol time in British Isles waters. This one change fixed the entire German campaign. The validated data showed us the way.

In regard to the Pacific Game again: after publication, we discovered a wording error in the rules, which effectively gave a single patrol a week's jump on returning to base. This increased the turnaround rate at various bases by 15 percent, allowing submarines a faster return to hunting areas. We had to fix that issue in the game post-publication, which, with the larger base of players—now nearly six thousand copies sold, compared to the original fifteen testers—finally allowed us to find. Once fixed, game results, which we tracked courtesy of player feedback, settled right into the validated expected outcome track.

Last, prior to publication of the Atlantic campaign, the question at the heart of the historical matter came to the fore. Could a player, in fact, achieve a historical interdiction of Great Britain sufficient to "knock England out of the war?" The answer as derived by the game system in its pure validated data form was simply "no." Between the tonnages added to the merchant fleet and the ever-increasing deadliness of antisubmarine operations, the game indicated that the Germans would have had to more than double their sinking rates at every point in the war prior to the end of the Battle of Britain (October 1940), in order to achieve the critical mass of losses that would interdict England. For the final publication, in order to "make a game of it," we had to introduce assumptions that the Battle of Britain was actually effective in terms of destroying strategic supply, and that British strategic supply was far more vulnerable to shipping losses. Even given these adjustments, interdicting the British Isles is nearly impossible and if not achieved by the end of the Battle of Britain, it is doomed to failure.

As to the primary cause of the German failure: while there are several, one of the major ones was the inability of Germany to turn around U-boats quickly in port and ready them for the next patrol. A submarine campaign is all about effective torpedo tubes at sea, and the Germans fell far short of this goal, taking, more often than not, twice to three times the amount of time their US counterparts did in the Pacific. Couple that with the selection of the wrong type of U-boat for a war that would extend the operating zone far beyond British waters and you have the germination of the campaign's failure.

Thus, through the eyes of validated data generating carefully modeled systems, it wasn't as much of "a close run thing" as perhaps Churchill thought, and players now accept the more apparent truth of the German submarine campaign.

A Forensic Approach

For campaigns and battles in which significant data, statistics, or other usable information exists, a statistical approach works well. However, for events not so well recorded, or recorded with clear errors and ambiguities, an effective statistical approach is virtually out of the question. This is particularly true when we begin to look at battles prior to the twentieth century and is exceptionally true when we look at battles in the medieval period or earlier. In some of these battles, not only is the number of participants questionable, but the very location of the battlefield itself is also unknown, making empirical statistical evaluations nearly impossible.

In cases where we can put together reasonable estimates of force sizes and examine probable locations, the forensic method of validation can be useful. Over the latter half of the twentieth century dedicated academic and martial practice studies experts have begun to reassess and evaluate various fighting techniques that existed in Europe from the Romans onward, particularly for the medieval and Renaissance periods. These studies have provided very reasonable estimates of key aspects of combat, such as how much space various soldiers in various periods took up in both close and open orders. They have allowed us to understand how formations may have moved and dispersed, and they have allowed us to understand and evaluate mounted combat (cavalry) as well how as both gunpowder and non-gunpowder artillery operated.

Simply put, the forensic approach asks the question: given our knowledge of knowable conditions, what can we predict about the unknowable conditions? It is generally accepted that there are two types of "unknowable" conditions: knowable unknowables, and the unknowable unknowables. The focus of forensic evaluation is to establish a rational basis-of-estimate for filling in the gaps in the know-able unknowables.

In two game systems for which I employed just such a method, *Order of Arms* (covering the period 1000 to 1525)[4] and *Eagles of the Empire* (covering the Napoleonic Wars from 1805 to 1815), forensic information was used to estimate probable troop strengths. For *Eagles*, forensics involves understanding the physics of charging horses and the movement of linear infantry lines. We have significant information in regards to that period and thus we generally do not have to guess at troop strengths (although for some battles it is still an unknown for certain units). For later historical periods, forensic questions focus on effective movement rates, the effect of concentrated musket fire on troops, and other such cause-and-effect questions, including topology questions (i.e., how landforms affect troop activities and battles in general). For battles in earlier historical periods, achieving a reasonable estimate of the number of troops present is a worthy accomplishment alone, along with understanding how the combatants fought the battle at the time.

The battle of Tewkesbury,[5] fought during the English Wars of the Roses, is a good example in which forensics aided in validating models of period combat. For years the exact location of the battle was in question, and the numbers provided by the scribes of the time unreliable. Using forensic reasoning, the noted British historian Alfred Higgins Burne (1886–1959), in his book *Battlefields of England*, disputed the long-held assumption of where the battle was fought, suggesting instead a new battlefield based on measurements of how much space various troops took up in various formations, and aligned his suggested battlefield to the reported number of formations present. This in turn provided a reasonable guide for

estimating the most likely strengths present. His efforts effectively relocated the battle.

While such activity does not necessarily guarantee accuracy, it does provide limits at both the low and high values based simply on what could fit where. This, coupled with the known sequence of events at the engagement (itself potentially questionable), then provides insights into the fighting, now based on reasonable estimates of numbers involved and any effect terrain may have played on the outcome of the battle.

Such forensic studies also allow us to explore key moments at such battles. It is recorded that at Tewkesbury, a hidden group of two hundred House of York spearmen on the right flank of the Lancastrian line routed a major formation comprised ostensibly of upward of two thousand men. On the face of it, such a rout seems unlikely, even given surprise. However, it appears that the right side of the Lancastrian line did in fact disintegrate from just such an assault. Forensic measurements and careful modeling strongly suggest that while two hundred spearmen could have hidden in the likely area from which they were reported to have launched their attack, the area in which the Lancastrian right wing stood simply does not effectively accommodate two thousand men, given the presence of the other two Lancastrian formations. The area we assume to be the location of the Lancastrian right actually accommodates somewhat less than half of the reported number, based strictly on measurements of space and occupancy. That two hundred spearmen launching a surprise attack against nine hundred Lancastrian troops could rout the troops at a key moment is a much more likely event than the routing of two thousand. This is not to say that those numbers as reported during the battle (or as written by the victors shortly thereafter,

Figure 16.8
Mortimer's Cross: Topology is a key element of the game.

as most likely happened) are wrong per se, but topological and forensic evidence strongly suggest questioning the historical account to a degree.

Similar analysis was conducted for the *Mortimer's Cross* test play map (figure 16.8); this map was developed specifically to isolate the non-mounted knight rules and test them to assure that they work as intended. Eventually, this map and its playing pieces will be included in a future multiple-battle game for the *Order of Arms* system.

The point here is that there is a great opportunity throughout historical simulation game design to use even the most rudimentary forensic rationales about what may or may not have happened. Where forensic rationales can be tied to measurable elements and those measurable elements mapped successively to various models within the game system, then the game system becomes more credible, particularly when the users/players understand the approach being used, even if that approach may result in a gaming simulation contrary to otherwise traditional histories. Validation via forensic methods provides confidence in the model being used and improves credibility.

Finis

Returning to George Edward Pelham Box's question, "How wrong does a model have to be to not be useful?" we can now hazard an answer. It has to be wrong enough for a user/player not to find it credible. However, the assessment of credibility itself has to be informed by validated data that yields reliable functional models of events for credibility to be given. In many cases, given no other indicators upon which to judge a game, users and players of historical simulations may rely on anecdotal evaluations of historical events—that this or that other event was "a near run thing," as their basis of judgment.

However, as we can see, having only anecdotal evidence should raise the flag of skepticism (at least of the historical validity) in the user or player of any game without a transparent basis of validation. It is well possible that the pure gaming value may exceed any shortcomings a game, as a historical simulation, might have. Regardless, informing users of the value of validation will encourage both players and designers to raise the standard of validation of any products touted for their historical insights.

That validation takes work and effort there is no doubt. It can consume a significant portion of a design's development cycle. Nevertheless, a validated model that users and players can rely on both for enjoyment as well as learning advances all causes and ensures that following generations of players will treat historical simulations as not merely toys of their fathers, but tools of their time for looking into our common history.

About the Author

Brien J. Miller is a senior aviation and engineering transportation program manager with over twenty-four years of experience in designing real-time and simulation systems for the FAA, NASA, and the US Navy, including the Navy's first artificially intelligent tactical trainer. A former US Navy lieutenant, he has been involved in wargame design since the early 1970s and has designed and/or contributed to more than thirty commercial titles, including *Silent War: The United States Submarine Campaign Against Imperial Japan 1941–1945*, which won the prestigious *Games Magazine* Game of the Year award. He is an active participant in medieval warfare research, in particular medieval mounted combat. He resides in Maryland on his horse farm.

Notes

1. Fought June 25–26, 1876, between an allied force of the Lakota, Cheyenne, and Arapahoe, led by Sitting Bull and Crazy Horse; United States force led by George A. Custer.

2. Fought on August 26, 1346, near Crécy in northern France between England (with the Holy Roman Empire) led by Edward III, and France (with the Genoese, plus mercenaries) led by Philip VI.

3. Loadout is the term for weapon inventory; it can refer to all weapons or to a specific weapon type. For World War II submarines we use the term to refer to the torpedoes carried.

4. *Order of Arms* is an upcoming (2015) game series designed by Brien J. Miller and developed by Matt Kirschenbaum that portrays battles of the medieval period from Hastings to Pavia with particular focus on mounted combat. The first game will be Fornovo 1495, the second Tannenberg 1410, and the third title probably a multibattle set of smaller battles including Mortimer's Cross (1461) and Bouvines (1214).

5. Fought on May 4, 1471, between the "red rose" House of Lancaster, led by the Duke of Somerset, Margaret of Anjou, and Edward the Prince of Wales; and the "white rose" House of York, led by Edward IV and Richard of Gloucester. It was the decisive battle of the war, in which the House of York triumphed and claimed the throne of England.

17 GOAL-DRIVEN DESIGN AND *NAPOLEON'S TRIUMPH*

Rachel Simmons

I would like to start this discussion of the design of *Napoleon's Triumph* (2007) with some passages from Jim Dunnigan's *The Complete Wargames Handbook* (1992):

> Most wargames start with a map ... a hexagonal grid [is] superimposed on it [and] is used to regulate movement and the position of units. ... The game designer analyzes the terrain in each hex ... Each type of terrain has a different effect on movement and combat ... In wargames, tactics are also affected by certain mechanical elements common to most games. The chief among these is the hexagon grid itself. (Dunnigan 1992a, 17ff)

The first and most significant thing about this set of quotations is that it can exist at all. That the design and play of a wargame can be discussed in a completely generic way, without regard to the period, location, or scale is itself a remarkable thing. No such completely generic guide to the design and play of other genres, such as euro, card, or abstract games, is possible. Why is that? What makes the wargame genre different from the others?

I would suggest that it starts with applying the hex grid to the map. Dunnigan uses the word "superimposed" to describe this, but I think the word "imposed," with its implications of forced

submission, would get to the heart of the matter better. There is no organic connection between the hex grid and battlefield terrain, and the grid can easily reduce the terrain of an actual battlefield to a set of (often not very significant) "modifiers" to the powerful geometry of the hex grid itself. The power of the grid does not end with its effects on terrain: it also profoundly affects the combat model as well. In his book, Dunnigan goes on to describe basic wargame tactics in terms of the grid alone, in a completely abstract and generic way, with consideration given to neither scale nor period. The subject, whether it is a tactical game on the battle of Waterloo or a strategic game on the Eastern Front in World War II, just doesn't matter. The hex grid is thus the generic foundation that underlies most wargames, and which makes a generic wargame design process possible.

This ability of the hex grid and the rules based upon it to overpower the ostensible subject of a game, to reduce an enormous variety to an unvarying sameness, is, I think, the great weakness of the hex and counter system. And yet that has been its greatest strength as well, and does much to account for its remarkable fecundity and, paradoxically, even creativity and originality. The hex and counter system, precisely because of its ability to reduce varying subjects to sameness, meant that there was a common vocabulary used to describe a wide variety of subjects, yet that vocabulary was capable of change. A new game might be almost entirely derivative from some other game, yet it could still introduce a new idea, a new rule, a new subsystem. And that new idea was an addition to a growing common vocabulary, an expansion of it. And so, over time, this vocabulary grew richer and richer, and games became more varied because they expressed different parts of that vocabulary. And of course, it wasn't just designers that were learning that expanding vocabulary; players were learning it as well, allowing them to learn highly complex games with surprisingly little effort, because even if the game as a whole was new, the parts from which it was made were not, because players knew them already from other games that came before.

Yet no matter how much that vocabulary expanded, there remained ideas it could not express, things that it could not say. (A trivial but memorable example is SPI's 1973 game *Sniper!* with its weirdly distorted buildings with 60° and 120° corners, because hex grids don't really do 90° angles too well.) In the early 1980s, during the last years of my first incarnation as an (almost entirely nonprofessional) wargame designer, I was involved with a Napoleonic miniatures group. I had designed a set of miniatures rules for them based on Frank Davis's game on the battle of Waterloo, *Wellington's Victory*. (More than any other wargame, I dearly loved that design. The title of *Napoleon's Triumph* is homage to it.) I had tweaked them and tweaked them to deal with this or that perceived shortcoming, and yet it finally reached the point where I just couldn't think of any way to make them do more of what I wanted. Within the vocabulary of that set of rules, the best I knew of, I just couldn't

think of anything I could do with them that would get any closer to saying what I wanted to say. There were fundamental shortcomings and limitations that I just couldn't overcome. There was nothing more to do. And so I stopped doing anything.

More than twenty years passed before I would design or attempt to design another wargame. The motive for my return and subsequent design of my game on the battle of Austerlitz, *Napoleon's Triumph* (along with its predecessor, *Bonaparte at Marengo*) was actually visual. I felt the urge to design a game that would use the visual symbology of nineteenth-century period battle maps, which I thought quite beautiful, and which would look like such a map in play. I came to call this appearance "The Look," and achieving it was one of the most important considerations in the design process for *Napoleon's Triumph*. It was because of this that I could not use a hex and counter design. The imposed geometry of the grain of the hex grid with its 60° angles would overwhelm the geometry of the long thin lines of the armies with their terrain-following subtleties that I wanted to express. Cardboard counters posed a similar visual problem in that their printed surfaces can look attractive when viewed from directly above, but their sides, where the raw cardboard edges are exposed, are an eyesore, which made counters not acceptable on a purely visual level.

While achieving a certain visual appearance was the initial driving force behind *Napoleon's Triumph*, there was also the matter of a twenty-year-old set of unresolved frustrations from my Napoleonic miniatures days. The details do not require mention here, but a commonality to many of them was playing time. Everything just took too darn long. I had come to conceive of a game as being like a machine to translate the player's decisions into physical reality. An important measure of the quality of the machine was its efficiency. The path between intent and reality should be as short and direct as possible. Chess was my model of an efficient game/machine. If you watch a chess game, most of the playing time is just the players thinking: once they decide what to do, it is the work of a moment to actually pick up a piece and move it. Further, a player typically makes fewer than fifty moves over the course of the whole game. There could hardly be less physical work involved. Another important point is that chess also has no place in it for unimportant moves: The game never wastes the players' time. Wargames, by contrast, viewed as machines, are typically very inefficient. Not only do wargames tend to have large numbers of pieces whose moves and activities individually contribute little to the game's outcome, becoming significant only in aggregate, but wargames also tend to have mechanisms that add physical work to the process beyond moving pieces on the board: Over and over again, dice are rolled, tables are consulted, counters are stacked and unstacked, markers are placed and markers are removed. (With my eye on playing time, die rolling had become particularly odious to me; whenever I saw a die go off the table, requiring that it be found and fetched, which was far too often, I just wanted to scream.) By removing all this guff but leaving in the good stuff, what I hoped to achieve was a sort of concentrated essence of wargame.

The two goals stated above (achieving The Look and efficient gameplay) were common to both *Bonaparte at Marengo* and *Napoleon's Triumph*: so much so that in many aspects it is more accurate to view them as a single design effort performed in two stages rather than as two separate designs. However, in the process of designing *Napoleon's Triumph*, the subject of which was battle of Austerlitz, a new goal was developed to set alongside the first two: that the game had to not just have an Austerlitz map and order of battle, but that it had to have the quality of Austerlitz-ness. Austerlitz, in which Napoleon lured an Austro-Russian army into a carefully laid trap and then destroyed it, seemed to me to have its own quiddity, its own essence, that made it what it was: a unique historical event and not just an instance in a class of events. Whereas in the design of *Bonaparte at Marengo*, I had the idea that the choice of battle was incidental, that my real design project was a Napoleonic "system," in the design of *Napoleon's Triumph* the choice of battle was not incidental; it was essential to what I was doing. And so, to set alongside the two goals of The Look and efficient gameplay, I added a third goal: subject specificity.

In discussing how the pursuit of these goals translated into the actual game, probably the place to start is the game's most distinctive visual element: the thin, rectangular wooden blocks used to represent the opposing armies. While there is a subgenre of wargames called block wargames that had been using square, rotatable blocks decades before *Napoleon's Triumph*, they had nothing to do with the design of my blocks, which were not based on them, but on the block shape used in the much older nineteenth-century German *kriegsspiel*. My purpose in selecting this shape was not functional but aesthetic, in that it was what was required to give my game The Look. Also present was a second class of pieces new to *Napoleon's Triumph*: metal flag stands labeled with stickers to represent corps commanders. These pieces, quite striking in play, are a departure from the cartographic tradition that dominates the visual design of the rest of the game. They instead borrow from the tradition of miniatures wargaming, and are there to take visual advantage of the fact that I was designing a three-dimensional game rather than a two-dimensional map.

Any discussion of the pieces can hardly avoid my use of color: red for one army (the Allies) and blue for the other (the French). This choice comes from the tradition of military cartography and is foundational to The Look, and as such the choice is a hill I am willing to die on—and through the years there have been many people willing to kill me there for it. There is a strong contrary expectation among many players that the colors be based on uniform colors (red for British, blue for French, white for Austrians, etc.). But there is a reason for the use of blue and red in military cartography, and that is that these colors permit high contrast with each other and with the map. Consistent with this end, the map art has no rich, saturated colors, and is mostly various shades of light green, with light blues, browns and grays here and there for different terrain types. Taken in itself, the map is visually quiet, even dull, but it is not intended to be taken by itself, but as the background against which the strong, highly saturated blue and red of the armies can and do pop.

Of course, the map design has a functional role as well as an aesthetic one. With regard to function, hexes could not be used for reasons previously mentioned. But what to do instead? It was of course possible to have no regulatory layer on the board, something that miniatures games have long done. This approach, however, carried with it what I call the tyranny of small differences, in that typically there are huge distinctions between almost identical distances like 15/16 of an inch and 17/16 of an inch, resulting in a fussiness that is very dislocating to the sense of period—no Napoleonic commander ever worried about whether the enemy was ninety-nine yards away or a hundred and one yards away.

Further, the constant measuring and remeasuring is painfully slow, completely incompatible with making efficient use of the players' time.

After some consideration, I settled on an area design. While hexes in a grid system are basically units of distance, the areas in *Napoleon's Triumph* are basically units of time: the size of an area represents roughly how far the forces of the armies could move in an hour. Difficult terrain was represented by small areas and open terrain was represented by large areas. Further, the boundaries between the areas followed a military analysis of the terrain. In defining them, I looked first for the sorts of features that Napoleonic armies preferred to defend, with ridges, hills, streams, and towns topping the list. Where these features existed, I put area boundaries. After these, additional boundaries were added as needed to keep the areas at the sizes to reflect movement rates. In this way, the area design was, as much as possible, grown organically from the underlying terrain of the battlefield, rather than being an arbitrary grid imposed upon and overpowering it.

While the physical design was driven by the goal of achieving The Look, the design of the victory conditions was driven mainly by the goal of subject specificity. The main design problem was that Austerlitz was essentially a French trap, into which the Allies were lured. This was bad for gameplay in two different ways: first, the game could not simply play out as the historical deception over and over again without being a pretty terrible game, and second, the Allied player in the game knows what the historical Allied commanders at the battle did not, that an Allied attack on the French stood little chance of success. Yet I felt strongly that if I did not have French deception and an Allied attack, I did not have the essence of Austerlitz. After months of working on the

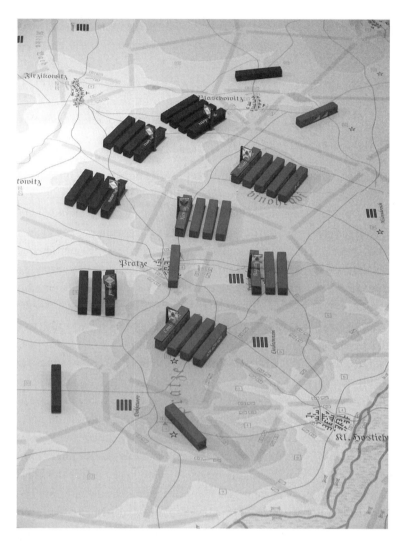

Figure 17.1
Napoleon's Triumph in play: "The Look" of nineteenth-century battlemaps in game form.

problem, I finally found a solution that was both simple and drawn naturally from history. First, I allowed both sides the freedom to substantially and secretly depart from the historical arrangement of forces. (In the game, players normally can see where the opposing blocks are, but not their type or strength.) Thus,

neither player in the game knows where the other player has put his strength. Second, I let the French player bring on as discretionary reinforcements the two French corps that Napoleon concealed from the Allies. If the French player never introduces those reinforcements, the Allies have to take terrain behind the French lines to win. This ensures an early Allied attack. Once the French player introduces them, however, the objectives flip and it is the French who have to take objectives behind the Allies to win. (Either side could win by inflicting sufficient losses on the enemy army.)

Movement and command in the game are closely intertwined with each other, and the design of both was very much dominated by the goal of mechanical efficiency. By not requiring a couple hundred pieces a turn to be moved by counting off distances and movement points through a hex grid, the map's area design went a considerable ways toward making movement efficient, but the problem did not end there. The key to making this process more efficient was the direct modeling of command at the corps level. (Of course, the command system was historically how the actual commanders were able to move their armies as well; sometimes game design problems echo historical problems in interesting ways.) The game gives each player a small number of three or four independent commands, each of which allow a single piece to be moved. But this is grossly inadequate to move the armies on the battlefield; for almost all movement the players depend on five to eight corps commands, each of which can move up to eight pieces together as a single corps group from one area to another. Because the design of the physical pieces is such that a single player movement generally suffices to move an entire corps, a player will typically only have to make a hundred or so physical moves over the entire course of the game.

The design of combat in the game is driven by a combination of the goals of subject specificity and mechanical efficiency. Subject specificity is primarily a matter of atmosphere and feel. Modeling the battle of Austerlitz is fundamentally about deception

and bluff. While limited intelligence and the way the objectives are handled do much to achieve that at a strategic level, this basic "feel" permeates the game at a deeper level, down to the way combat is modeled. Resolving an attack in the game was consciously designed to have a poker-like feel, in which the players alternately have to decide whether to give up or increase the stakes, an escalating test of nerves that continues until the attack is ultimately resolved. In terms of mechanical efficiency, this process might at first seem to be actually highly *inefficient* in that attacks can require as many as a dozen steps to resolve. But that apparent inefficiency masks three things. First, efficiency is a measure of translating player decisions into reality, and each step in the combat procedure represents a player decision, none of which require much physical effort to make real (no lists of modifiers to be consulted, no dice to be rolled, no tables to be consulted, no markers to be placed). Second, because attacks in the game are actually a type of move, the number of attacks in the game is restricted by the same command limits that restrict movement, so that even if resolving an attack can be time-consuming, there can't be many attacks in the game. Third, the combat system gives a lot of game result bang for the player effort buck: Attacks in *Napoleon's Triumph* can be just brutal, with a single high-stakes attack taking the losing army as much as a quarter of the way toward demoralization.

Although *Napoleon's Triumph* has been a highly successful game that has attracted a great deal of attention and acquired a devoted following, it has had little or no effect on the game design world as a whole, which has gone on pretty much exactly as it did before. (Compare and contrast with how card-driven play has become widespread in the hobby.) I think this is because it is too much of an outlier for its design elements to be integrated into the general vocabulary of hex and counter wargames, and too subject-specific to be easily turned into a "system" for a set of similar games. Yet, I think I am still satisfied with the results, in that *Napoleon's Triumph* is a good demonstration of just how unconstrained in its possibilities the idea of wargaming is by the reality of what currently exists. If it inspires any imitation, I hope that it will be imitation in the form of some design breaking away, not only from what wargaming in general is but from what I've done as well.

About the Author

Rachel Simmons is a transgender woman who publishes under the name Bowen Simmons. A very active gamer in her teens and early twenties, she enjoyed board wargames, fantasy role-playing, and miniatures. She largely stopped gaming at about the same time she began a twenty-year career as a software engineer. In her forties she returned to gaming and began publishing a small series of games on specific nineteenth century battles: Marengo (1800), Austerlitz (1805), and Gettysburg (1863). They are respectively titled *Bonaparte at Marengo*, *Napoleon's Triumph* and *The Guns of Gettysburg*. Her games are noted for their numerous departures from the traditional features of board wargames.

18 *HARPOON*: AN ORIGINAL SERIOUS GAME

Don R. Gilman

Harpoon (1981) was first created as a tabletop (miniatures) tactical naval and air wargame (referred to as the *Paper Rules* or *Paper Harpoon*). It was envisioned by Larry Bond, then a lieutenant junior grade in the US Navy, as a tactical training tool for the wardroom of his destroyer. In 1975, the standard US Navy training aid was a classified tabletop product called *NAVTAG*. Since it contained classified data *NAVTAG* had to be kept under lock and key when not in use. *Harpoon* was deliberately designed using unclassified information so that it could be easily distributed and played without security restrictions.

The *Paper Harpoon* game was published commercially in 1981. The *Paper Rules* were (and are) focused on small numbers of naval combatants in order to allow the game to flow with the minimum amount of bookkeeping. This product, in its fourth edition, is still in print by the Admiralty Trilogy Group and is now coauthored by Captain Christopher Carlson, USNR (Ret) and a host of contributing writers, designers, and researchers.

Harpoon 1 Products

Differences between the *Paper Rules* and *Harpoon 1* (1989) were basically scope and medium. The scope difference was focused on the scale of the engagements: the *Paper Rules* focused on a handful of ships and aircraft executing one battle lasting a short period of time; the computer *Harpoon 1* allowed for fleet-on-fleet encounters and could execute theater-level simulations over several days of battle. Another key difference was that the computer game could be played solo, while the paper game required two players (if not an umpire).

The computer medium allowed for several features that may have been the first of their kind. One was that the product line consisted of a single-player commercial retail product, an online multiplayer product, and a professional military product. Other unique features included the "Staff Assistant" (a programmed assistant that made suggestions and appeared onscreen as a subordinate officer), "BattleSets" (collections of themed scenarios and databases tied to a map and time period), time compression[1] (allowing the game to be played in real time but also allowing the game to be sped up during the long periods of transit and search), a high replay value (made possible by randomized orders of battle and starting locations), fog of war (initial contact data was rarely ever complete as to type, location, or speed), sophisticated Victory Conditions (layered with conditional logic and two levels per side), and, what is now considered de rigueur, modding. (In *Harpoon 1*, modding was limited to user-created scenarios and the database of platforms and systems.)

The development cycle was very challenging, starting with Applied Computing Services (led by Don Gilman) and then Digital Illusions (led by Gordon Walton), resulting in *Harpoon 1* being published in 1989 by Three Sixty Pacific. *Harpoon 1* would run on Macintoshes with 1Mb of RAM and either black and white or color displays. The PC version was targeted to IBM PCs with 640Kb of RAM and a CGA (320 × 200, four-color) display.

In 1991, Kesmai Corporation signed an agreement to produce a dial-up modem multiplayer version of *Harpoon 1* (Harpoon OnLine) for online services (Gilman 2012), and in 1993 beta testing started on the GEnie online service. The product went live in 1997 to a limited following. Three Sixty updated the *Harpoon 1* product to v1.3, which allowed for the creation of the *Harpoon* Designer Series BattleSets. These new BattleSets featured player-created content and updated databases. The final version was called *Harpoon Commander's Edition* (updated by Anthony Eischens and Brad Leyte).

Over the years *Harpoon 1* was also published by Alliance Interactive, iMagic, Advanced Gaming Systems Inc. (the spin-off of the original Applied Computing Services, also managed by Gilman), and finally Matrix Games.

Harpoon II/3 Products

Three Sixty Pacific's technical team conducted maintenance on the *Harpoon 1* product and from that experience felt they could do better, especially considering the more powerful systems now available to home users. Starting in 1994, the team (led by Carl Norman) targeted home systems such as PC-compatible computers with the Intel 286 16-bit chips and Macintosh IIs with Motorola 68020 chips. Video displays were at least VGA (640 × 480 in sixteen colors) and computers usually had one to two megabytes of RAM. This product featured multiple, resizable windows, a full world map, and included all the editors (see below). *Harpoon II* (1994) was updated in 2001 as *Harpoon III*,[2] by Jesse Spears, and later versions were called *Harpoon 3* (2002),[3] which included multiplayer capabilities developed as a side effect of the original *Harpoon 3 Professional* work (see below). *Harpoon 3* was also renamed *Harpoon 3: Advanced Naval Warfare* when published by Matrix Games in 2006 (Gilman 2012).

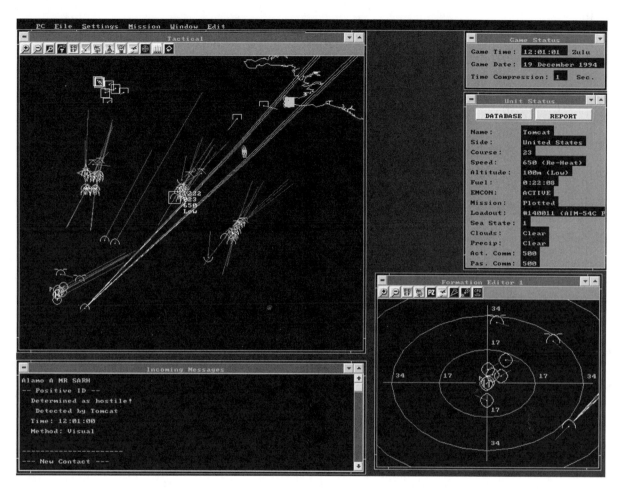

Figure 18.1
Harpoon 3 Basic Display.

H3 Pro/H3 MilSim

Harpoon 3 Professional (*H3Pro*) was developed in 2000 for the Australian Department of Defense (ADOD) as a PC-only product. In the mid-2000s, Northrup Grumman and the ADOD cooperatively worked with AGSI to further enhance *H3 Pro*. This version appeared in 2009 as *H3MilSim*[4]. This final version was packaged as a single-player desktop analysis tool, a server and a client, and included enhanced editors. It contained features that were intended for use by professional military customers and not made available to the public.

The Final Compilation: *Harpoon Ultimate Edition*

In 2011, Matrix Games bundled twenty-two PC versions of the commercial *Harpoon* products onto a single DVD and sold them as *Harpoon Ultimate Edition*. This bundle featured the final *Harpoon 3* and *Harpoon Commander's Edition*. This even included the 1988 *Harpoon 1* demo which runs on an open source virtual machine.

Harpoon Functionality

In *Harpoon*, the player assumes the role of a formation commander tasked to accomplish a scenario's Victory Conditions (VC). VC might be as simple as destroying a certain number or type of enemy units, or might include elements such as the length of time a unit stays in a specified rectangle (i.e., time on station), limits on friendly casualties and so on. Scenarios specify start time, duration, location (map), weather conditions, player's side, and VC. They feature a variety of different platform classes within four major unit types: ships, submarines, land bases, and aircraft. The player's span of control ranges from a single vessel up to hundreds of aircraft and dozens of ships and subs with supporting land bases.

Harpoon features a user interface that captures the flavor of a NATO Combat Information Center (CIC). The key display is the Naval Tactical Data System (NTDS), which had been carefully designed over several decades by the NATO countries to provide workable situational awareness for large fleet battles occurring above, below, and at sea level simultaneously (Graham and Dick 1996). NTDS had design constraints that included displaying a lot of data (some of it uncertain), with limited processing power and limited displays; the ability to quickly and clearly indicate friendly, enemy, surface, subsurface, and unknown types of units was vital for a simulation of *Harpoon*'s scope.

In *Harpoon 1*, the player was aided by a user interface element called the Staff Assistant; this was the image of an officer acting in the role of the player's aid: the "competent subordinate." The simulation's generated messages to the player were crafted to be in the voice (audio and/or a text message) of the Staff Assistant. The player operated from four fixed windows on the screen: a Strategic map, an

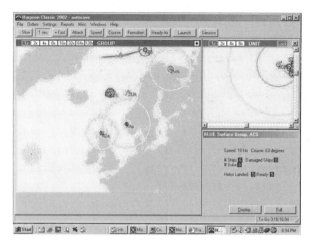

Figure 18.2
Harpoon Classic 2002: Strategic Map hidden.

Operational map, a Tactical map, and a Reports area. The Strategic map showed the overall map for the given scenario, with two rectangles showing the relative size and placement of the Operational and Tactical maps. The Staff Assistant image and reports would appear in the Report window (see figure 18.2).

Sound effects included aircraft, helicopters, missiles, torpedoes, and explosions for any unit anywhere on the map! This was a concession to customer's expectations, somewhat like the sounds made by spaceships in *Star Wars*. Each air, surface, and subsurface platform also had a series of informational displays that included a hand-drawn picture of the platform, platform data (e.g., size, speed, age, description), sensor ranges, typical weapons data (airborne units had lists of typical weapon loadouts and ranges), and in the case of ships, the firing arcs for the weapon systems.

Harpoon II and *Harpoon 3* still used NTDS displays but had more colors and an unlimited number of map windows. Displays of units were scanned line

drawings, photographs or videos, and the sound effects were much richer (albeit no more accurate than offered by *Harpoon 1*). The Staff Assistant was not actively presented, nor were BattleSets featured (although they still existed). The database in these products was much more detailed, so their platform displays were more detailed but less graphical.

The tools that allowed this detailed data to be manipulated in both product lines (*Harpoon 1* and *Harpoon 3*) were the Scenario Editor and Database Editor, both built from the same software code as the game engine. The Scenario Editor allowed for selection of a map, data sets, and some weather conditions. Generally, the player would select one or more starting points for different groups of units and then populate the groups. The player could design the scenario, assigning groups to appear on the map during game play in several different locations. Players could play either side of created scenarios, but it quickly became "best practice" to designate in the scenario description which side a human player should take in order to test his or her prowess against the computer player.[5]

The ability for a player to use the Scenario Editor to craft a complete scenario in *Harpoon 1* was fairly rare in computer gaming in the early 1990s. The closest product was Microsoft's *Flight Simulator*, in which you could select a map, weather, an aircraft and a flight plan. Given that *Harpoon 1* was designed to be data-driven from the outset, it was quite easy to polish the editors for a commercial release, but not bundling the editors at the outset was a business decision. The publisher, Three Sixty, published a Scenario Editor product in 1991; after a few releases the editors shipped for free with the games to allow players to develop their own scenarios or to modify the scenarios shipped with the game. This occurred at about the time the modding of first-person shooters such as *Quake* took off, proving that games that allowed player created content sold more units and had a longer product lifecycle—the *Harpoon* series was active from 1989 to 2013.[6]

The databases for both products were organized into annexes that contained hundreds of ships, submarines, fixed wing aircraft, helicopters, guns, bombs, torpedoes, depth charges, mines, missiles, and rockets. Some annexes detailed sensors such as radar, sonar, infrared detectors, passive radar detectors, and magnetic anomaly detectors. There were annexes addressing collections of weapons in magazines, and the combination of those magazines with fire control systems, arcs of fire, reload rates, and number of trackable targets. All of these data were combined into mounts which were specific to each class of ship, submarine, or land base. Bases were a new class of unit specific to the computer version; effectively immobile ships, they were capable of handling aircraft operations including magazines, refueling and self-defense, and they operated aircraft via runways.

By making players more productive in modding the database, the more content they would produce, thus adding life and value to the product. About 1990, Jon Reimer created a Microsoft Access–based editing tool for both *Harpoon 1* and *Harpoon II* products; in time, Advanced Gaming Systems purchased the rights to the editors and renamed them in his honor. Figure 18.3 demonstrates the Reimer Editor in use with *Harpoon 3* data from about 2005.

Maps were another type of data. For *Harpoon 1*, that meant hand-digitized navigation charts. The source maps were from the Defense Mapping Agency at a scale of 1:5,000,000. No real land altitude nor water depth data was captured, as the computers of the time

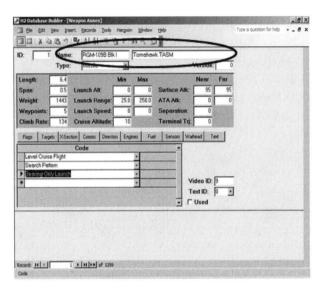

Figure 18.3
Reimer Editor with *Harpoon 3* data. (Note that the editor didn't have the header text changed from "H2," which refers to *Harpoon II*.)

simply did not have the memory for holding that amount of data, let alone for processing navigation and search data against a real map. A fractal algorithm was developed by Rob Brannon to artificially contour the coastline and seabed so that submarines could not go to maximum depth when close to the shoreline. By contrast, *Harpoon II* used digital data from the CIA World database. This massive multi-megabyte database allowed for real-world contours both above and below sea level. Due to the improved hardware requirements, *Harpoon II* could process most search and navigation in the game map. The *Harpoon 3 Professional* products went further and allowed for the importation of simple visual references in the form of geometric lines and points from mapping software systems (e.g., ESRI GIS software), with the final version (v3.11) allowing for the lines to be processed as real map features and thus impact game play.

A BattleSet is a collection of scenarios, set in a specific geographic area during a short time period, and featuring a set number of countries. Typically a BattleSet would have a backstory or theme that would drive the background stories in each of the scenarios.[7] The business rationale behind this was to allow the publisher to continue to sell inexpensive add-ons to the game without having to develop, ship and market a new game. Over time, bundles were introduced, and the editors allowed players to make their own BattleSets.

The *Paper Harpoon* rules were published in a rulebook that provided details on game turns, scales, and abstractions from the real world (e.g., 30 seconds of real time was one tactical combat turn). These were supplemented by various search, movement, and combat charts found on the *Harpoon* Reference Charts, and in many areas were the basis of the computer code. Combat outcomes provided damage points (when applied to a ship) or units destroyed (e.g., when applied to aircraft, since aircraft were always in small groups). One set of charts covered damage effects. Sensor outcomes would provide different levels of information based on the type of sensor and how it was used. A player might get detection of an enemy (yes or no), identification of a detected unit (nationality of an emitting radar, or the radar model, or the exact unit type), and/or location (bearing and range; or bearing, range, speed and direction). One aspect of the paper game's damage model was the concept of "critical hits": when a weapon strikes and damage is inflicted on a vessel, there is a chance of critical systems being knocked out—a "mission kill" even though the damaged vessel is still afloat. Using a ratio reflecting the amount of damage received, the *Paper Harpoon* player rolled on a table appropriate to the type of vessel hit (aircraft carrier, ship, or submarine).

Note that the computer products ran in real time (or faster than real time) while the tabletop rules worked in player turns. This distinction resulted in changes to the movement, search, and to some extent the combat models as implemented in all of the computer *Harpoon* products.

The computer *Harpoon* products basically kept the search values for the *Paper Rules* sensors and platforms (*Harpoon 1* much more so than *Harpoon II*, and *Harpoon 3* attempting to move back to the values from the *Paper Rules*). Given the potential for dozens of ships and hundreds of aircraft and missiles, detection had to be fast so as to not tie up the computer; therefore the computer products would execute a search no more than once every thirty game seconds—incidentally matching the *Paper Rules* tactical turns. Every unit could potentially detect specific types of target energy emissions if they were fitted with the appropriate sensor, and each target could emit or reflect energy in specific ways (e.g., radar emissions, radar reflection, acoustic emission, sonar emission, sonar reflection, magnetic, visual, infrared, and hydrostatic). Solving this vexing calculation problem was key to having a realistic but playable product.

Consider that scenarios regularly featured a hundred or more aircraft per side, each potentially firing two to eight missiles apiece, while dozens of ships could fire torpedoes and missiles at each other simultaneously. Now consider that many of the missiles and torpedoes had their own sensors; coupled with the other platforms this might result in a thousand searches occurring simultaneously. On an 8-bit Intel 8088 processor, it would take *days* to run the sensor searches for that many sensor-equipped units, if left to a brute force approach.

The solution was a processor and RAM-efficient algorithm and data structure that allowed real-time performance and accurate results. This algorithm sorted the objects on their latitude (the *Harpoon 1* maps were always wider than taller), then longitude every thirty seconds of game time. The search routine would "walk" the latitude list left to right (i.e., west to east), comparing the current unit to all units to the right (east) whose latitude was within the maximum sensor range then for the current searching unit (so an AWACS at low altitude, for example, wouldn't be searching ~300nm but only ~90 nm). If a target was inside the boundary, the longitude (or "Y value") was also compared. If the target unit was in the "box," then the sensor mask would take over.

The matching of a target's energy type to the searching unit's detectors was handled by a sensor bit mask. If a unit was moving through the water, the flag (or bit) would be true for acoustic noise. Likewise, if the searching unit had a hydrophone, the corresponding bit would be true. When compared using Boolean logic, any matching flags would then kick off a more computationally "expensive" range calculation.[8] If the units were within actual maximum sensor range, then the detailed search routine would be called to finalize actual detection. This detailed routine took into account technology differences, relative bearings (e.g., a bow mounted sonar cannot detect an acoustic target directly behind it, nor can a fighter aircraft's search radar detect a target on the left wing), acoustic conditions (e.g., shallow water,

location of the thermal layer), etc. The sensor/signature masks filtered out most potential matches (e.g., a radar not detecting submerged submarines, and sonars not detecting jet fighters).

This process was repeated down the latitude list before any movement or combat results were processed. The resulting detections would update a data structure linked to the detecting unit, detailing the type of detection, time, and just how much information was shared with the player. This processing executed in real time for most scenarios, and the uncertainty provided a true "fog of war" experience for the players.[9] Today, one would leverage the massive parallel processing capability of graphics cards, sometimes with several thousand simple vector graphic engines running in parallel within the Graphics Processing Unit (GPU).

A third set of models addressed computer-unique problems, such as taking the unit's location from the internal mapping system (expressed in x/y integer coordinates) to both a real-world latitude/longitude and the x/y location on the computer screen given the current window locations, zoom level and the player's computer resolution. These calculations were also done using only integer math for most of the products. The concept of a distance unit was used to represent one nautical mile at the equator. Lookup tables were used for trigonometry functions and interpolation was used on 32-bit integers to finalize calculations. In time, most of these calculations were upgraded to floating point.

The Market

The 1989 computer game market was dominated by "strategy" and "simulation" products. This was

probably because the first programmers capable of creating games wanted to play those titles, and the computers were (just barely) capable of creating "acceptable" simulations on those topics using mostly map-based displays. This was before the Internet and the advanced video cards that make First Person Shooters so engrossing. There were no smart phones, and the home computer market demographic was generally male, middle-class, educated, and interested as much in learning as playing. By 2014 the market was quite different, and the computer *Harpoon* products would not have been viable in their current form if launched today, because they take too much thought and too long to play on a PC.[10]

Starting with the advent of the Internet, the *Harpoon* community became very active in establishing online resources for the trading of scenarios, tutorials and the underlying databases. Key sites included Harpoon HQ, HarpGamer, and various forums on gaming-centric websites, plus a few troll sites (including that of one particular troll who had been thrown off of everyone else's sites, forums, and communities). Modding of the *Harpoon* products was inspired by the same desires that other gamers have when they mod first person shooters; AGSI supported their efforts by a clarification in the AGSI copyright promoting user-created content for free distribution (but not for sale).

Some players put in their own platforms and/or adjusted values provided by AGSI. Others modified the original work of others without permission (such as the aforementioned troll). The slighted parties felt that AGSI should take legal action to stop the "theft." This was not going to happen for several reasons. First, the original and copied products were not sold, so there were no damages to claim. Second, the accused infringer was not in the United States, and many times neither was the slighted party. Third,

AGSI didn't have $500 an hour to spend on attorneys who knew international copyright law. This was not taken well by the slighted parties (and emboldened the troll).

Some of the more prolific editors felt that the only way to correct errors (real or perceived) in the computer games was to modify database values. In some cases AGSI and Bond/Carlson agreed, while in other cases they did not. When bugs were fixed in the software there was resistance to changing the customized databases and their matching and finely tuned scenarios.[11] Some of these "errors" had to do with the performance of systems that had been tested in combat fewer than five times. After an evaluation against the reference standards used for the paper game, AGSI would confer with Bond/Carlson. It is important to note that, given the few air/naval combat incidents of the last quarter century, the Bond/Carlson models have been validated in every real-world instance to date.

AGSI had a quality engineering objective shared by Bond and Carlson: When something was broken, it was fixed. Given the age of the code base and the sheer number of developers who touched it, *a lot was broken*. Most of AGSI's code changes were bug fixes. This was not what the modders wanted when they had invested so much in custom databases and scenarios. But giving in to the demands would alienate AGSI's programmers, and not giving in would cause conflict in the community.

AGSI partnered with the Australian firm REPSIM to market the military product (*H3 Professional/H3 MilSim*) and even raised the price to a "respectable" amount to represent the extra development and support costs for the extra features. AGSI made several small military sales to professional military trainers and analysts in countries that included Australia,

Colombia, Japan, and Norway. Defense contractors included Thales, Northrop Grumman, and the US Navy.[12]

Over twenty-plus years, occasional letters, emails, and online postings from former military professionals shared how they used the *commercial* product in their official jobs, often without their supervisors being aware of it. Some used the products for education; others reported that they used the product to do desktop analysis before engaging in various wargames on mainframes (e.g., at the US Naval War College) or with actual forces in the field (i.e., actual ships and planes conducting wargames in the real world) (Gilman and Bond 2006). The RAND Corporation used the system to evaluate a Taiwan vs. China engagement (Shlapak et al. 2000). One admiral claimed that he was influenced to join the Navy right out of college because he played *Harpoon 1*!

The bitter irony is that in the end, the original design objectives were reached in three markets: commercial, online multiplayer, and military. However, the financial objectives were never quite realized, due to the multiple publisher bankruptcies and the inability of the military to adopt a $50 "game" even though their multimillion dollar systems only accomplished a fraction of the same functionality.

About the Author

Don Gilman started gaming with Avalon Hill's *France 1940* while in school. His first publication credit was material for Avalon Hill's *Flat Top* in *The General*. He started writing for *The Journal of WWII* (later *20th Century*) *Wargaming* as a reviewer and tournament designer/judge. He has been playing the *Harpoon* system since 1981. His computer gaming contributions include: *Orbiter*, *PT109*, *Sub Battle Simulator*, and *The Shard of Spring* (all in the 1980s). He created many of the design elements of the original *Harpoon* in 1989, and again for the current *Harpoon 3 Professional/H3 MilSim*. He works for ViaSat as a Software Engineering Project Manager and is the veteran of five start-ups, three of which were gaming firms.

Notes

1. Gordon Walton has suggested that this feature made *Harpoon* the first Real Time Strategy (RTS) game!

2. The change from *Harpoon III* to *Harpoon 3* occurred when Jesse Spears's firm stopped publishing the product and AGSI took over. No material changes occurred to the code at that time.

3. Trivia: *Harpoon 4* was the ill-fated attempt to make a new product from scratch. This version also killed several companies before an incomplete version was scrapped by Bond, Carlson, and Gilman in the 1990s.

4. The subtitle *H3Pro* was added back in 2013 due to a possible trademark conflict regarding the term "MilSim."

5. Trivia: During development, the code that comprised the opponent's logic was called "Chekov," after the *Star Trek* character. Since the developers

were American and the game shipped with a Battle-Set called "GIUK Gap" (featuring the US vs. the former USSR), it seemed fitting that the opposing computer force was named for a Russian character from a TV show the developers loved.

6. As of 2015, the game was still being sold by Matrix Games.

7. While the ability to have units move through scenarios was desired, that feature was never built in any of the versions.

8. Range was calculated through geometry: the hypotenuse of a triangle formed by the x and y distances, i.e., the square root of the sum of x squared plus y squared.

9. The core search algorithm ended up being reused in a different programming language in the cleanup of underwater waste located at the Department of

Energy Oak Ridge National Laboratories, Kerr Hollow Quarry facility (Schrock 1989; Blank 1991).

10. Gilman did develop a new vision for *Harpoon* utilizing social media, mobile devices, role-based play, and cloud services, but there was no interest from a funding, licensing, or publishing perspective.

11. This eventually caused quite a massive rift in the *Harpoon* community. One group's members were specifically told that if they thought they could do better, they needed to build their own game; after about ten years they shipped *Command: Modern Air/Naval Operations* in 2013.

12. A custom BattleSet was created for the US Naval Institute, which led to *Harpoon* acquiring one very notable fan: Admiral Sir John "Sandy" Woodward, commander of the British task force that retook the Falklands in 1982.

19 THE DEVELOPMENT AND APPLICATION OF THE REAL-TIME AIR POWER WARGAME SIMULATION *MODERN AIR POWER*

John Tiller and Catherine Cavagnaro

Imagine you are in a room with a dozen other US Air Force captains, conducting a team exercise with *Modern Air Power.* There are five teams, each at a computer, with specific responsibilities. Your team's charge is air superiority. The F-15s feature long-range air-to-air missiles, and, should enemy fighters appear, your job is to destroy them. The Strike Team calls out, "Enemy aircraft in quadrant F3!" You vector the F-15s for the intercept, transitioning to after-burner thrust, using enormous amounts of fuel but now flying at supersonic speed. Once in range, your air-to-air missiles streak through the air, reaching the enemy fighters within seconds and scoring two hits. Another salvo, two more hits, and the threat is eliminated. As the fighters slow to subsonic speeds, you see that fuel is at a critical minimum. Fortunately, the Air Mobility Team has positioned KC-135s nearby and you vector the fighters to intercept them for air-to-air refueling.

Since 2005, *Modern Air Power* has been used in the curriculum at the Air Force's Squadron Officer College, with more than 21,000 students having experienced this wargame in multiplayer games against the AI. It is key that in this use the accurate representation of air power doctrine be presented to the students, as well as enforced through rules. In exercises lasting all day, students in teams are divided up by mission responsibilities such as air superiority, strike, CSAR (Combat Search and Rescue), air-to-air refueling, and air mobility. They are graded via a sophisticated spreadsheet-type assessment form both for individual mission performance as well as overall score. One interesting aspect of the current scenario, in use since 2013, is that the students are tasked with nuclear deterrence, having to eliminate enemy ground and air nuclear assets in a set amount of time. Failing that, they are "treated" to a video of a nuclear explosion on their screens as their airbases and strategic targets come under attack.

The development of *Modern Air Power* commenced in 2001 with the goal of developing a real-time air power wargame simulation for commercial as well as military applications. The intent was that this should be a "thinking" game that presented the player with a top-down, third-person view of a campaign area, as opposed to the more conventional first-person flight simulator interface. In this way, the interface may be likened to one in which a person might view an air war from the screens of an Airborne Warning and Control System (AWACS) aircraft monitoring developments at a distance. Traditionally however, air combat is thought of as being in the first

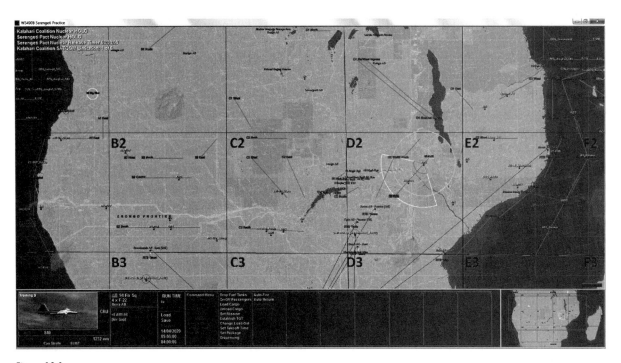

Figure 19.1
Screen shot of the current *Modern Air Power* scenario in use at the Air Force's Squadron Officer College.

person—most people would design an air combat game with a traditional "dogfight" approach. However, for multiple reasons described in this chapter, this approach would not have supported the many varied objectives of this development.

The user playing *Modern Air Power* deals with multiple assets at a given time: mostly airborne, but also surface assets such as ships and ground units, as well as air defense assets. The play modes supported by *Modern Air Power* include: single-player against the Artificial Intelligence, multiplayer team play against the Artificial Intelligence, and both single and multiplayer against each other over a network.

It is key in the multiplayer approach that players on a given side are allocated specific assets and can only control those assets during play. This compels players on a team to coordinate with each other in an operationally organized manner and thus enforces air doctrine during play. This is in contrast with other wargames where users have the ability to "lasso" units to form ad hoc groups that they then command in what might be considered swarm tactics. It is key in *Modern Air Power*, particularly in its use for professional military education, that more rigorous command and control rules be enforced to correlate with and reinforce the student's classroom instruction.

The focus of the engine development was air combat in the age of the guided missile; this began historically with the Vietnam War and continues to the present. The historical air war over Vietnam was the first game released, and covered the years 1965–72. This was followed by a game considering the historical air wars of the Middle East involving Israel, from 1956 until today. A third game (under development as of 2014) covers the air wars involving Iraq, including not only Desert Storm but also the Iran vs. Iraq air war.

These releases are currently sold online by John Tiller Software; as in other games sold by John Tiller Software, these three games form a series, each sharing a common game engine but specific with respect to setting. A key aspect of the discussion of *Modern Air Power* is to understand how the commercial development supported and in turn was supported by effects in research and education. The success of *Modern Air Power* in the commercial arena made it essential that it supported a user-friendly interface as well as some other "soft" features, such as attractive graphics and realistic sound effects. These features are often undervalued when implemented but are dearly missed when they are absent. For example, turning off the sound effects in most computer wargames would probably be judged to be a diminished experience by most players.

While *Modern Air Power* includes features such as close-range dogfighting and conventional bombing, the emphasis of the game engine development is on those features reflecting air combat in the modern, near-modern, and near-future eras. This means fairly detailed implementations of features such as:

- guided air-to-air missiles involving both radar and infrared guidance;
- radar and other sensors, including specialized features such as Doppler and Over-The-Horizon (OTH) radar;

- an effective representation of stealth and various ISR features such as Electronic Intelligence (ELINT);
- implementations of future advanced weaponry, including High Powered Microwave (HPM) and High Energy Lasers (HEL);
- an implementation of cyber assets and cyber warfare that interacts with the kinetic effects in the game engine.

These features distinguish modern air combat from that of previous eras. Sensors, detection, and guidance are the predominant issues. While eyes (the principal sensor of the early days of air combat in World War I) still apply, and radar (the key development of the air war in World War II), is still crucial, the sophistication in the use of most of the electromagnetic spectrum dominates modern air power considerations. One key design issue relative to this sophistication is in the representation of all of these aspects to the player via a single display. *Modern Air Power* makes significant use of color-coding in the representation of various areas on the display, including visual, radar, weapon, IR, and ELINT ranges all displayed in a coherent manner. For example, when a weapon is selected, its maximum range is indicated by a red arc showing both the distance the weapon can travel as well as the angle it can engage an enemy aircraft. Likewise, the maximum flying range of an aircraft is shown as a black circle which continually shrinks in size as the aircraft flies.

More complicated is the representation of cyber aspects, as these represent an entirely separate "world" where the issues of space and time do not apply. *Modern Air Power* displays cyber actions on the map using an easily recognizable color-coded computer icon together with a rather retro sound effect from the days of dial-up modems. (This sound effect probably makes little sense to younger users.) For example, a player might decide to conduct a cyber probe of an enemy installation. If successful, this provides the player with otherwise unknowable information. Another option might be a cyber attack. This can be disruptive to the enemy installation and can only be defeated by a cyber defensive act by the enemy.

Starting about 2003, development of the *Modern Air Power* engine had reached the point that the Squadron Officer College at Maxwell Air Force Base became interested in using this wargame in the curriculum for their 2nd Lieutenant students. Prior to this, SOC had no good asymmetric wargame, since this would necessitate a competent Artificial Intelligence computer opponent. Fortunately, at that time the Air Force Office of Scientific Research (AFOSR) initiated funding and became interested in *Modern Air Power* and other wargame simulations by John Tiller Software for the purpose of doing research into AI. This effort resulted in several new approaches to AI and how it might be structured (Rushing and Tiller 2011). Additionally, AFOSR has an interest in determining how these simulations might be used to explore the future use of its advanced weaponry under development. Since that time, John Tiller Software has had regular research funding for this purpose and developed a number of research papers looking at AI research as well as the potential for advanced weaponry such as HPM and HEL to alter future warfare.

One key objective in this research is to better understand the impact of such future weaponry and how it might affect future Air Force doctrine. For example, in one key investigation, it was found that UAV-mounted HPM weapons could restore air superiority balance in the face of enemy swarm tactics. As this investigation progressed, it suggested optimal doctrine for both American and enemy assets when these assets were deployed. As such, this research provides insight into how such advanced weaponry can affect future combat and suggests at least a few iterations of how the standard countermeasure sequence might progress. Having such insight before actual combat could provide military leaders with a definite advantage.

In 2012, Captain Daniel House (USAF) used *Modern Air Power* in support of his MS thesis at American University. In that work, Captain House considered how a military version of the Virgin Galactic suborbital SpaceShipTwo might be used in support of deep strike missions by an air force. He used scenarios developed in *Modern Air Power*, based on research he had done on possible suborbital spacecraft configurations together with various levels of an Integrated Air Defense (IAD) and combined these scenarios with conventional strike scenarios using current aircraft technology such as the F-15, B-52, and B-2. His results demonstrated that the suborbital spacecraft concept does indeed provide an effective deep strike capability with benefits far in excess of what can be achieved even with advanced aircraft. This work by Captain House demonstrates how a user-friendly yet accurate wargame simulation can assist in developing initial concepts of future military capabilities. This offers a real opportunity to engage multiple audiences—those with the skills and inclination can apply user-friendly commercial wargame technology to investigate advanced topics, and those with limited computer wargame experience will enjoy a user-friendly environment.

Several years ago, we commenced research with the goal of considering the wargame outcomes being generated by John Tiller Software simulations and to develop a better understanding of those results. This research began by considering a mathematical formulation for the concept of the "tipping point" (Cavagnaro and Tiller 2011) and later transitioned into the topic of risk assessment. Together, this research has the potential to provide air force planners with advanced tools in the assessment and planning of future air operations. This research can also provide critical analysis to military planners in providing insight into questions such as these:

- In the deployment of military assets, are there "tipping points" in the outcome? That is, are there instances where insufficient allocation might result in drastically negative outcomes? Likewise, are there instances where increasing allocation has diminishing returns?
- Similarly, are there tipping points in the outcome relative to the enemy's allocation of assets? That is, while the current situation may be acceptable, is there an unrealized tipping point that occurs if the enemy should increase their deployment of a particular asset? Obviously, knowing that now rather than by experience is critical to military planners.
- In the face of uncertain intelligence about an enemy, their assets, and their intentions, how sensitive is our estimation of an outcome to that uncertainty? Is the outcome particularly sensitive to our uncertainty or not? If it is deemed to be sensitive, then devoting additional effort into intelligence gathering with the goal of reducing that uncertainty could be warranted.

John Tiller Software has continued to use *Modern Air Power* and other wargame simulations in support of research for the Air Force Research Lab and Air Force Office of Scientific Research. This research has benefitted from the parallel commercial development and has also resulted in new commercial features arising from that research. In 2013, Thomas Hussey of the University of New Mexico studied the benefits of the use of civilian wargames for the military. In his report, Dr. Hussey provides evidence that the features and user-friendliness of "serious games" may well provide very cost-effective benefits to the military and enhance existing in-house simulations, which may be more detailed but also more costly to use and harder to maintain. This is very attractive to a military that is currently transitioning to a much leaner procurement environment; as budgets come under pressure, the cost of custom simulations has precluded many organizations from using them. Having an off-the-shelf application that provides some preliminary analysis capability allows military researchers to spend their limited funds on areas where civilian development can't support them, especially when issues of secrecy and classification are applicable.

In 2013, John Tiller Software initiated the porting of some of its wargame simulations including *Modern Air Power* to the Android and iPad mobile platforms. This transition is possible because mobile devices have reached the point at which they can now be considered genuine computers and are capable of supporting software at a certain level. These ports are smaller versions of the more robust PC versions, but do effectively run smaller scenarios. Given the failure of some attempts to merge these two technologies into a single interface, it appears that individual interfaces must necessarily be supported. So far, these apps have been quickly tested by the public and have generated considerable interest among more

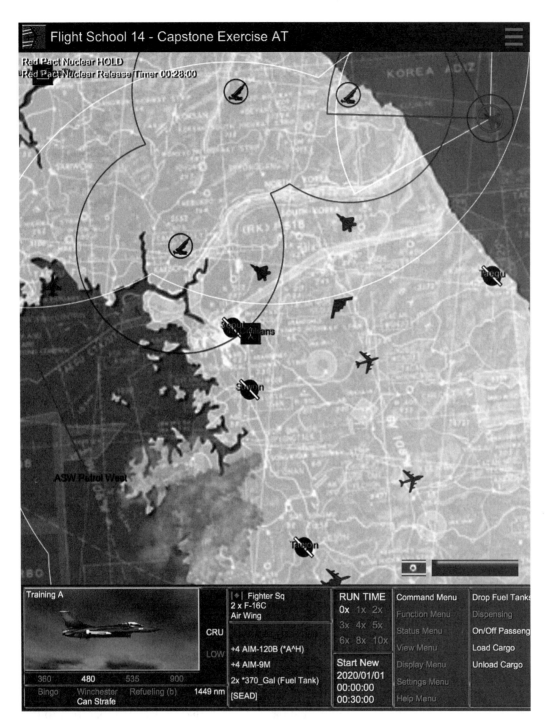

Figure 19.2
Modern Air Power iPad display.

serious gamers. This blossoming of mobile technology is fascinating, but how things will eventually develop remains uncertain; the industry is still coming to grips with how mobile technology and desktop technology will evolve. The impact of this on game software development is an unresolved issue.

In conclusion: research, design, and development over the past ten years have resulted in a sophisticated computer wargame with a number of significant characteristics:

- a user-friendly interface supporting a number of commercial releases of the game engine;
- a detailed representation of modern air operations that supports advanced research into doctrine and advanced weaponry;

- a sophisticated Artificial Intelligence capability that supports not only human player versus AI play modes but also batch simulations possible of generating aggregate results for research.

Together, these represent a unique combination of commercial, research, and educational interests in wargaming. In modern computer game development, there are two main commercial areas: high-end million-dollar developments utilizing sophisticated 3D graphics and effects, and serious niche developments that have more fidelity. *Modern Air Power*'s niche has the space for multiple developments, as described earlier, and can support a greater effort than a single application could.

About the Authors

John Tiller started developing professional computer wargames in 1995 with Talonsoft and the award-winning *Battleground* series. Since then, he and his company John Tiller Software have developed more than seventy computer wargames and published with multiple companies such as Matrix Games and HPS Simulations. Most recently he has transitioned to self publishing through the John Tiller Software Store. Wargames developed by John Tiller are known for their accuracy and user-friendliness and have been utilized for multiple military research and education projects; clients include the Air Force Squadron Officer College and the Air Force Office of Scientific Research.

Catherine Cavagnaro is professor of mathematics at Sewanee: The University of the South. She has jointly authored and published research papers on the mathematical analysis of wargames, including the concepts of risk and tipping points as part of research supported by the Air Force Office of Scientific Research. In addition to mathematical research, she is a flight instructor, holding the top certificate issued by the FAA, and operates her own aerobatic school. She has published multiple articles on flying in aviation magazines.

20   RED VS. BLUE

Thomas C. Schelling

Back in 1957, I spent a summer at the RAND Corporation in Santa Monica, California, talking to people on the subject of limited war. Then I spent eight months in London, helping to establish the International Institute for Strategic Studies, and spent a lot of time in London and in Geneva, discussing what was the fairly new subject of limited war. Then I went back to RAND for a year and discovered that RAND had two kinds of wargaming going on, neither of which I liked.

One was a purely military—call it tactical—kind of wargame, in which it was decided to have China attack Taiwan or something of the sort. And what I didn't like was that this was a limited wargame, which meant that limits were attached in advance. The main limit was "no nuclears." I thought that was a severe limitation, partly because you weren't allowed to consider such things as: Do you change the readiness status of your strategic nuclear force? If you're in a crisis and the crisis gets worse, what do you do with your strategic forces? Do you enhance their readiness? If so, do you enhance their readiness in a conspicuous fashion to signal something to the adversary, or do you do it as inconspicuously as possible so as not to warn them and not to alert them? But more important, I thought, in any serious limited

war the danger of escalating to the nuclear level is bound to be a major preoccupation of the adversaries, and if you know in advance that the war can't escalate to the nuclear level, that terribly inhibits the kind of signaling you can either engage in or look for. So I thought, the important thing is to explore how, during the course of a crisis, including a crisis that erupts into military activity, how are limits arrived at? How do you signal your readiness to observe limits? What kinds of limits look as if they might be adopted by both sides in a military engagement? In other words, where do the limits come from? How are they arrived at? How are they recognized? What kinds of limits might survive? And, I thought, this is as important as anything else to study in a limited war, and the RAND technique didn't allow that.

The other thing I didn't like was that the RAND social science department had done some so-called political games, diplomatic games, in the course of which the participants engaged in what they called "role-play." Somebody would be the Secretary of State, somebody would be the Secretary of Defense, the Secretary of the Treasury, the White House National Security Advisor, and so on. Everybody was expected to play the role that had been assigned to him, and if you were assigned the role of Foreign

Minister of the Soviet Union, you displayed your talent by speaking the way you thought a Foreign Minister of the Soviet Union would participate in a cabinet-level discussion. And what I wanted was for the participants to be truly, personally engaged in the decision making, not to play a role, but to engage in the discussion: What do we do next? What do we think they're about to do next? Where is this likely to end up?

Therefore, I wanted everybody on a Red team or a Blue team to be fully personally engaged in the argument of, "Where do we stand and what do we do next and how do we read what the adversary is doing?" And that's what led me to decide that I would like to help design a game in which the limits weren't attached in advance and in which everybody was responsible for the decision that came out, and not merely for playing a role.

When I got back to Harvard University, I teamed up with a fellow from MIT, Lincoln Bloomfield, and we designed a game. Originally, we made it an Iran game. Many readers probably don't remember, likely because they weren't born yet, that there was a time when Iran and the United States were allies, and we were committed to the defense of Iran against the Soviet Union. So we designed a game in which the Soviet Union began to encroach on the northern border of Iran and threatened to come in and go all the way to the Persian Gulf. And the United States, which was in the process of having a carrier task force in the Persian Gulf, including a contingent of Marines available for establishing a beachhead, started this little war on the border of Iran. We had a Red team and a Blue team, and both teams consisted of Americans—both teams consisted of the same *kinds* of Americans, with the idea that if misunderstandings arose between the Red team and the Blue team, you couldn't

blame it on the lack of a common language or a common culture; you knew that the people who should be best able to understand each other misunderstood each other, and that's one of the things that's worth exploring here.[1]

So we had a Red team and a Blue team. We had seven-member teams, Red and Blue, and we had a five member control team. I chaired the control team. The technique was this: we began with a scenario that led up to a crisis of some kind, maybe military activity, maybe the stationing of forces north of the border, maybe insinuating some forces into Iran, and with that scenario to begin with, each team had to decide what it would do, but it also had to analyze for us what it thought was going on, what it thought the danger was, what the adversary was likely to do. Then they had to decide what they were going to do, and that took on several forms: What will they do unconditionally and promptly, what will they do with some delay, and what will they do conditionally based on what the adversary does ("If they do this, we'll do that")? Then they gave that to the control team—actually, they would spend about four hours developing their analysis of the situation and deciding what they would do, not just what they would do anyhow, but what they would do *if* the adversary did certain things that they might anticipate. And then the control team would spend a couple of hours projecting the original scenario forward, to take into account what these two teams had decided, including what each had said it would do conditionally on what the other side did, so you had to mesh the two things and see where that was going to take them, within the next few days or weeks or however long it would take to get some activity. Then we would give the scenario back to the two teams and they would have another three or four hours to go through the same procedure, deciding: Now what do we do? And now what do we think they're doing? And what will we do unconditionally and what will we do if and only if they do certain things? And this went on until, along about Sunday afternoon (we did this on a Friday/Saturday/Sunday) the control team made one last projection of the scenario, and then we had a postmortem session, in which each team got to see the other team's documents and discover how badly they had been misunderstood or how badly they had understood, and what the outcome of this was.

One thing we noticed, even in that game, was that there was a tendency for the little war to peter out. It didn't escalate. It sort of toned down, and the control team had to learn how to introduce something that would stir things up. An analogy might be that in the Ukraine recently, somebody shot down Malaysian Airlines flight 17, killing 298 people. This is the kind of thing that looks as if nobody quite knows for sure who authorized that or who did it—and that was the kind of thing that the control team could interject if it had to, to keep the crisis bubbling up.

Anyway, one participant in that Iran game, on my control team, was Walt Rostow of MIT, who became President Kennedy's appointment as assistant secretary of state for policy planning. In the summer of 1961 I was about to go to RAND to spend the summer, and a good friend of mine, Charles Hitch, who had been head of economics at RAND when I had spent a year there, had become assistant secretary of defense comptroller. He lived in Washington, and he invited me to dinner, and he invited Walt Rostow, and the two of them started talking about the Berlin crisis, which was the crisis du jour at that time, and Walt described for Charles the game in which he had participated with me. They both decided that it

would make sense to invite me to cancel my trip to RAND and stay in Washington to design a Berlin game. And I said, "I can't do that, I've rented a house and my children are looking forward to the beach and I have to go to Santa Monica. But I can probably spend the whole summer designing a Berlin game just as well as I could do it here in Washington, and then I'll come back, and if it looks good we can try it out."

So I went to RAND for the summer and recruited Alan Ferguson to help me design a Berlin game. We had to compose a scenario that would get something started, and we selected from among the RAND personnel people to be the Red team and the Blue team. We tried it out and it looked good. Everybody who participated said, "Gee, I learned a lot." And we would ask: What kind of things did you learn? And they said: we learned a lot about how you have to evaluate what's going on in order to decide what to do and how to anticipate what the other side will do if you do one thing or another thing or another thing. Essentially, they learned something about the nature of decision making in a crisis. So we decided, okay, sounds as if the game is good for something.

So I went back to Washington, and at this point I engaged the interest of Paul Nitze, who had become assistant secretary of defense for international security affairs, and I already had Walt Rostow in the State Department, and the two of them sponsored this game. We gathered a team that was fairly high level: we had the deputy strategic analysis guy from the White House, we had an assistant secretary of state, we had I think a deputy secretary from the CIA, we had several military officers from at least the Army and the Navy (I don't think at that time we had a Marine, although later on in another game we did have a Marine), and we had Air Force because we wanted somebody who understood SAC operations, which we thought would become important in the game.[2] We went by helicopter up to Camp David for the weekend, got there about noon, and began the game: all of Friday afternoon and evening, all of Saturday, all of Sunday morning. Sunday afternoon we had the postmortem, and everybody was astonished at how little they had understood of the nature of decision making in a crisis. They had thought that they would understand what the adversary had in mind. They thought it was comparatively easy to signal what you took seriously and what you didn't take seriously. If you wanted to threaten something, not verbally but by your actions, how did you choose the action that would indicate how serious you were or how ready you were to escalate? It had been an educational experience for these people in the nature of decision making, of analysis and planning, in a comparatively small-scale military engagement with the prospect of escalating into something a lot bigger.[3]

Everybody, as I've said, was astonished at how poorly they had signaled to the adversary what they took seriously, how badly each side had read the other's behavior and interpreted how far they were willing to go or what they took seriously, and how many things that were of no significance they spent a lot of time analyzing. At one point, the Blue team decided that in response to some air combat activity they would bomb an airfield in East Germany used by the Soviet Air Force. And the other team, the Red team, spent more than an hour analyzing exactly why that particular airfield had been chosen. Well, it turned out that particular airfield hadn't actually been chosen—the Blue team just said: we will pick an airfield and bomb it in order to let them know that this is how we respond if they introduce aircraft into

this altercation we're having, and it was up to the control team to pick any old airfield. There were a lot of things like that, which I would say both stunned and amused the Red and the Blue teams during this postmortem. But one of the things that puzzled them was that the control team had had to use a lot of ingenuity to keep the crisis going. I'll come back to that later as a phenomenon that requires explanation, and it made us wonder: Does this happen in a real crisis? Or, *could* this happen in a real crisis? Or is it maybe a peculiarity of, not Soviet-American hostilities, but of hostilities between two American teams, one doing its best to achieve what it takes to be objectives of the Soviet Union and the other trying to promote US objectives?

The enthusiasm that this gained was such that two weeks later, Paul Nitze and Walt Rostow decided that they would do another version of it, and this time it was easy to get participants because the team members of the first game had advertised how much they had—I won't say "enjoyed" it—but how much they thought they had learned from it, how ignorant it turned out they had been about how you make decisions in a crisis. So we had a second game, and again the control team had to use a lot of ingenuity to keep the antagonism active. To do that, we had to introduce plausible events that didn't impute too much to either the Blue team or the Red team, but accidents, so we could always invent some activity on the part of the East Germans (which the Red team didn't control and hadn't anticipated) in order to keep all this going.

We then had a third game in which very much the same phenomena occurred. Not the same activity on the ground, but the same effort on the part of both Red and Blue teams to signal in advance what they would do. What do we take seriously? How do we read the other side? And it was just amazing during the postmortem how poorly each team recognized how it had signaled its intentions. Things they had done that they thought were strikingly significant may have passed almost unobserved on the other side, and things they had thought were strongly threatening weren't so recognized on the other side. And most of the contingencies that they had anticipated and said, "If this happens, this is what we will do," didn't arise, partly because most of those contingencies were things that involved the adversary reacting to what this team had done; the Blue team thought, "Maybe the Red team will do this," and it turned out the Red team would only do "this" in response to an equivalent move by the Blue team, so the contingency didn't arise and each side was astonished that it hadn't been perceived.

Now, I spent a lot of time trying to figure out how this phenomenon arose—namely, that it's hard to keep the dispute going—and if it could possibly be true in the real world as well as in the game. This tendency was strikingly observed by everybody, including all of the staff people of the Joint Wargames Agency, who were involved in, well, call it "staff work," which made them fully acquainted with what went on. All of them recognized how hard it was to keep the crisis going.

I later came to the conclusion, which I published somewhere, that the reason for this tendency of the crisis to slow down was that each team's projected response, each team's planned actions, could be rated along several dimension: one was hard versus soft (or dangerous versus not so dangerous); another was immediate or delayed; and a third was conditional or unconditional.

Usually the members of the team were of various motivations, ranging from very hawkish to somewhat dovish, and each team's decision had to be a compromise between those who wanted to do very aggressive things and those who thought it was better to do comparatively mild things in the hope that it wouldn't escalate. The way a compromise was adopted was that it was agreed that: all the easy things we will do at once, unconditionally; things that are a little more difficult and dangerous and aggressive, we will postpone; and things that are really aggressive and dangerous, we will only do in response to what the enemy does. As a result, what each team saw the other doing was only what had been decided upon to do immediately and unconditionally; those things each side decided to do only conditionally based on what the adversary did didn't really get responded to, because they weren't seen.

It's almost as if I said, "You can slap me once and I'll contain myself; slap me a second time and I'll get mad; slap me a third time and I'll pull out my gun and shoot you." And unless you slap me three times, you'll never know how dead serious I was if you slap me too much. And that was the way these teams responded. They never saw the more aggressive readiness of the other side to escalate to a higher level of violence. I asked a lot of people to keep in mind, the next time we had a crisis like a Berlin crisis, to see whether that phenomenon occurred within the US team (which was all they could observe), but I don't know how that came out. So to me, after fifty years it's still an hypothesis that the nature of decision making in a crisis depends a lot on the way that the executive committee, or whoever's in charge, reaches a compromise in what to do next.

The Joint Wargames Agency decided that they would like to involve even more senior people than we had involved. We had one game, a combination of four military crises, all stimulated by Cuba: one in Portuguese Angola in Africa, three others in the Western Hemisphere. And this time they had two levels of activity. Each team, Red and Blue, consisted of high, but not the highest levels, of government. And then, each Red and Blue team, what you might call the active part of the team, briefed a senior team for an hour, which then approved or changed what the active team had decided on.

I didn't particularly like that version, because I thought the most active people at the—I hate to say "lower level," because it was high level, just not the highest level—I thought they wouldn't feel quite as responsible for what they did if it was going to have to be approved by a higher level. And I thought the higher level would never get the experience of having to try on its own to read what was happening on the other side, to read the evidence of what the adversary intended, and what the adversary responded to. Anyway, that was the way it was, and I didn't control that.

And so we had these four games going on, and in the postmortem, there I was, forty-two years old or something like that, chairing it. We had the chairman of the Joint Chiefs of Staff, the commandant of the Marines, two assistant secretaries of state, the deputy director of the CIA, the attorney general of the United States—Robert Kennedy—and the director of the US budget, and it was a very successful session. And when it was over, Kennedy came up to me and said he thought this kind of activity could be used in evaluating and deciding on strategy for desegregating schools in the South. I thought, that's never occurred to me. He said, "Do you think we could talk to the president about that?" And I said, "I'm willing." That was Halloween of 1963, and within three weeks the president was dead and it never came off,

but I was struck by how somebody wholly new to this kind of thing—not wholly new, he'd been involved in the Cuban crisis of the year before, so he had some (a lot) of experience, personal experience in how an executive committee arrives at crucial decisions—but the idea that he could perceive that this had potential relevance outside of the military sphere struck me as an acute observation and probably a good one.

I've mentioned this "Why no escalation?" and the nature of compromise, and how each team was surprised at how poorly it was understood, even poorly understood by Americans on the Red team or Americans on the Blue team, who shared the same language and same culture, and all of whom were either political appointees or fairly high-level Civil Service or Foreign Service people. They just couldn't read each other's signals. I mentioned how they focused on comparatively unimportant events, thinking they were critical, like that airfield that they hadn't even picked.

One of the interesting things is that the Red and the Blue teams had been allowed to send verbal communications. They could have said, "If you'll hold your peace, we'll hold our peace; if you escalate to this level we're bound to counteract in this fashion." But there was almost never any verbal communication. All communication was by significant acts, and each side failed to recognize that its most significant acts weren't going to be visible because they wouldn't be prompted by what the other side was doing. Now, in all of the games I had to do with, we never allowed individual members of the team to send any communication to the other side. All verbal communication had to originate with the whole team. And one of the reasons that there may have been so little verbal communication was it would be so difficult to agree on what to say.

I'll digress for a moment. In 1961, President John F. Kennedy appointed John J. McLoy to be the White House arms control advisor. McLoy set up eight committees, and I was made chair of a committee on war caused by accident, miscalculation, or surprise. We gathered all the proposals for arms control of any kind that had surfaced in the Executive Branch. One of them went under various nicknames, of which the main one was "the red telephone." The red telephone was a precursor of the concept of the hotline, referring to a landline, including an undersea line, rather than radio, which could be interrupted or intercepted or disturbed. And one of the things that had showed up in all of the discussions of the hotline was that it was important (as the Cuban crisis was going to prove) in a crisis that the president of the United States be able to communicate quickly and directly with whoever was in charge on the other side. (As if Khrushchev and Kennedy had any language in common that they could speak over the telephone.) Well, we recommended a hotline, and we recommended that it shouldn't depend on the president either being able to communicate directly with the Soviet premier, or that if he could—if they spoke the same language—whether he would want to. Because if the Soviet premier makes some kind of threat or offer, you want to think it over and discuss it with your team; you don't want the president to be improvising on the telephone.

I had been on several committee online cablegram conferences between Washington and NATO headquarters, and it turned out that every time a message came in, we sat around the table and discussed it for an hour or two and then had to compose our response. And that required having somebody who had taken good notes write what our response should be, and then it goes around the table and everybody gets to correct our response. And finally, after about three hours, we sent a reply, and then we didn't expect a reply to our message for another three hours because they had to do the same thing at the other end. (These were all English-speaking people, who had the same vocabularies, so that the hotline wasn't really a telephone.) It turned out that one of the members of that team, Henry Owen, was a member of the State Department policy planning staff. Later he was an ambassador-at-large. He was in Moscow in some negotiations with a Soviet delegation, and he persuaded the Soviet delegation that the hotline was their idea. And pretty soon we had the hotline, which took the form of Cyrillic alphabet teletypewriters being installed in the State Department and the Defense Department, and Roman alphabet teletypewriters being installed in the Kremlin. And every day, the US government sent a message like "the lazy dog jumped over the crazy fox," so that every letter of the alphabet would have to be correctly recorded at the other end, and that was just to make sure that every day the teletypewriters were in good operation.[4]

I think all of the participants in these games said that the main thing that came out of them was their own education. It wasn't that the games gave them any basis for predicting how a Berlin crisis or a military engagement in East Germany would turn out, or what would happen if they blocked the autobahn from which we supplied Berlin. It wasn't that they learned what might happen, but they learned what it's like to be trying to make decisions with all of that uncertainty, and all of that critical feeling that things could escalate. We had thought, when we designed the game, that a crucial part of the decision making in the game would have to do with the status of the Strategic Air Command. Would it go on a higher state of alert? If so, would it do so as conspicuously as possible, so that the adversary would take the warning, or as inconspicuously as possible, so it didn't look as though we were preparing a preemptive attack or anything of that sort?

A year later, during the Cuban crisis, the *Boston Globe* had photographs on its front page of B-52s on runway alert at Logan Airport, suggesting that Boston had become one of the most urgent preemptive targets if the Soviets wanted to attack the United States. And the question arose: Was that a wise move, to make it look to the Soviets as though a preemptive attack couldn't succeed, or was that a stupid move that obliged them to hit major US cities and sites like Newark, La Guardia, Idlewild (as it was then called), Logan Airport, and other large city airports because there were, apparently, no SAC airbases of any kind big enough other than the few bases where the strategic aircraft were already located? Well, it turned out that in none of these games did anybody pay any attention to the status of our strategic arsenal. Nobody thought of using the status of SAC as a signaling device. Nobody thought of the question: If this should escalate to nuclear weapons on the battlefield, where do we want our SAC aircraft to be? In this way it suggests that it's possible to become so preoccupied with what you might call the local theater of the crisis that you forget that your worst preoccupation should be escalation to the nuclear level—which should be perpetually on your mind.

It's a little like what happened at the outbreak of US engagement in World War II. There was widespread expectation across the US government that the Japanese were going to attack. Possibly in the Philippines, where we had troops on the Bataan Peninsula, headed by General MacArthur; we thought

they might be going to attack Singapore, which they did. We thought of all kinds of things (they were already at war in China, as you remember). But it never occurred to anybody that the Japanese were capable of attacking the US battle fleet at Pearl Harbor. And I think the intellectual error was this: if they had asked, given an attack on American troops in the Philippines, what can the Japanese expect as the outcome of the war? Because the answer would have been: if the battle fleet at Pearl Harbor is left intact, the Japanese can't win this war. Therefore, if you postulate that the Japanese will launch an invasion of Southeast Asia, then you had to consider the possibility that they knew that they had to attack Pearl Harbor in order to do that. Do we think they conceivably could find a way to reach Pearl Harbor by surprise? And with the technology of launching surface-level torpedoes? And I think, in some ways, in 1941 the thinking about being prepared for a Japanese invasion didn't go to the question, "What would be a prerequisite for them to be willing to start a war with the United States?" Attacking Pearl Harbor would then look almost essential to their prospects for victory.

And, I think, in these wargames, nobody was ever thinking about: If it should escalate to the level of nuclear weapons, even very local tactical weapons in East or West Germany, where do we want SAC to be? In what defense mode do we want SAC to be? One of the primary objects of study was the question, during a small hot war in East Germany, where do we want SAC to be, in what state of readiness, in what location? We already at that time had airborne alert, which took care of part of the problem, but still, if you thought nuclears were going to be introduced, the status of SAC should have been on everybody's mind. But they were so preoccupied with the local theater that it never occurred to them that the location of the navy or the status of SAC should have been on the menu.

In this Iran game, during the postmortem, everybody agreed that we never even came close to seeing either side introduce nuclear weapons. And I interjected that the truth was that the Red team indicated under what circumstances it would use nuclear weapons: very locally. I don't think they were going to use them to hit US naval vessels or anything, but I think they had planned to use them against airfields in northern Iran from which US forces might refuel and attack them, or something of the sort. And the Blue team had spent a lot of time discussing (and then rejecting, but nevertheless discussing) the possibility of doing some of the things for which the Red team had said, "If they do that, we will use nuclears." So at this postmortem I said, you can't say we never got close to seeing nuclear weapons used, because the Blue team almost did what the Red team said would cause them to use nuclear weapons. Therefore, we were close to seeing—we didn't see it, but we were close to it—a decision on the Blue team that would have prompted nuclear use by the Red team. Doesn't that mean that we were at least close to using nuclears? The chairman of the Red team, Richard M. Bissel, deputy head of CIA, sort of smiled and said, "Tom," he said, "I'm not sure we meant it."

About the Author

Thomas C. Schelling is Professor of Economics, emeritus, at the University of Maryland and Professor of Political Economy, emeritus, at Harvard University. In 2005, he was awarded the Nobel Prize in Economics for "enhancing our understanding of conflict and cooperation through game-theory analysis." He has been elected to the National Academy of Sciences, the Institute of Medicine, and the American Academy of Arts and Sciences. In 1991, he was President of the American Economic Association. He received the Frank E. Seidman Distinguished Award in Political Economy and the National Academy of Sciences award for Behavioral Research Relevant to the Prevention of Nuclear War. He has held positions in the White House and Executive Office of the President, Yale University, and the RAND Corporation. Most recently, he has published on military strategy and arms control, energy and environmental policy, climate change, nuclear proliferation, and terrorism.

Notes

1. Sometimes you learn a lot of a factual nature in a game like this. I remember an interesting thing: the US had jet aircraft in the Persian Gulf in that Iranian game, and in order to strike targets over the border in the Soviet Union, the planes didn't carry enough fuel. And the question was: how could these naval aircraft refuel themselves in order to go on to targets either just inside the Iranian border or just over the

border? A lot of thought went into how you can deploy jet fuel somewhere north of Tehran so the planes can reach targets and get back to the aircraft carriers, and finally it occurred to somebody to raise the question: what do Iranians use for fuel? Cooking fuel. Heating fuel. It gets cold in Iran in the wintertime, and people have to cook their meals. But it turned out that all of this was done with kerosene, and there were huge tanks of kerosene, which the jets could all use as fuel. That was an incidental discovery that came out of the game.

2. I'm reminded that, during the Cuban crisis of 1962, a group of people, all of whom I knew, gathered in the office of Assistant Secretary for International Security Affairs McNaughton. Somebody said, "This Cuban crisis sure demonstrates how realistic Schelling's games are." And somebody else responded, "No, Schelling's games just demonstrate how unrealistic this Cuban crisis is." And in the Cuban crisis, if you've read any of the verbatim descriptions of the Executive Committee's deliberations, it looks as if they were in about the same predicament as the people I witnessed in these games. I think one thing the Cuban crisis illustrates is that it matters an awful lot how you compose the team. The chairman of the Joint Chiefs elected not to participate in the Executive Committee. It contained the secretary of the treasury, the attorney general, and the head of CIA, but the chairman of the Joint Chiefs said, "I'm chairman of the Joint Chiefs, I want to maintain the integrity of my independence, of the politics of this thing." As a result, I think the Joint Chiefs couldn't understand how seriously the Kennedy administration was taking this crisis. And I think that a very important motive on the part of the president was that he might be coerced into

something he didn't want to do because the Senate was in continual consultation with the military leaders. If the Joint Chiefs had their own representative on the Executive Committee, they could have learned from a reliable source how seriously this was being taken. So that I think it matters who's on the team.

3. We also observed in the Berlin crisis, whenever the fear was that Soviet tanks would invade West Berlin, people had to anticipate where they would enter, what routes they would follow, and so forth. And by the time the game was over, everybody on the Blue team and most of the people on the Red team had virtually memorized the streets of Berlin, just because they had to study the streets in order to figure out where the Soviet tanks were going to come from, and where they could stop them. And as a result, even years later when I spoke to some of the participants, they still had a pretty good mental image of the street layouts of Berlin.

4. I had the pleasure of receiving a Nobel Prize in Economics back in 2005. I had long since given up (although a lot of my friends and colleagues thought I might deserve a Nobel Prize) any thought of the possibility, because you're not allowed to receive it after you die, and I thought I was getting so old that I would have already have received it if they had any intention of giving it to me—otherwise they ran the risk that I would be dead by the time they did, and they were giving it to a lot of young economists. (My wife sort of anticipated it, but that was just in case.) But at ten minutes of seven in the morning I got a phone call from Stockholm, and I was told that the news release had gone out two hours earlier, announcing that I was to receive a Nobel Prize in Economics. Five minutes later I got a call from

Colombia, and five minutes after that I got a call from Slovakia, from news people in those countries, and all day long I got phone calls. And when I was in Stockholm to get this prize, I raised the question, "Why did you wait so long to let me know?" And the answer was that they couldn't find my right telephone number. I said, "Tell your intelligence agency that I don't think much of their ability, because all they have to do is consult a Washington, DC, telephone directory, and there's my name and there's no other Schelling in Washington." That suggests that they just didn't have a hotline.

21 HYPERGAMING

Russell Vane

Wargaming with a deep knowledge of Hypergame Theory (WHT) is very effective in guiding tabletop exercises using subject matter experts as players. I have found that human knowledge workers (the subject-matter experts) are more capable of being redirected dynamically than simulation software.[1] WHT is a powerful way to evaluate a situationally derived decision landscape and prevent surprise. For the United States, which often has a number of favorably valued choices, preventing surprise leads to highly valued outcomes.

This chapter provides a very short introduction to game theory, then discusses what hypergame theory is, and as a step-by-step example applies WHT to the first Gulf War.

Introduction to Game Theory, Its Exciting Ideas, and Its Shortcomings

Game theory is an important quantitative technique used to discern the value of collecting information on people's choices. Invented in the 1930s and first completely outlined by John Von Neumann in 1944, the idea is profound: Is there a strategy mix that is unpredictable yet delivers the best "repeated play" value of a known game? A known game is one where all the possible choices for both players are known and all of the outcomes of player choices are known as well. By best repeated play value, I mean that over a very large number of observed choices, player performance could not be improved. Both sides of a two-player game can play that well; the intersection of both players' play is called the Nash Equilibrium Mixed Strategy (NEMS).[2] (Gamers will also call these the "minimax" or "maximin" strategies.) And such work generalizes for even more players.

Furthermore, game theory can help determine the "expected value" of the game, which was not as obvious before game theory was invented. An expected value of any game is the "average" payoff—the weighted sum of the payoffs for choices divided by the number of choices made. In the child's game rock-scissors-paper, for example, the value of the game is zero: we expect to win one-third of the time, draw one-third of the time, and lose one third of the time. Further, in rock-scissors-paper, the NEMS is 1/3 rock, 1/3 scissors, and 1/3 paper; in any given game instance, no one can predict what each player will do, yet this mixed strategy yields the highest mathematical result in repeated play.[3]

The concept of the value of the game helps strategists decide when to add a new choice to a game or even when to stop playing the game. Strategists often will not play games that have negative value to playing; such games are losing situations that are weighted against them. (Modern casino gamblers appear to reason differently.)[4]

Game-theoretical reasoning may be even more useful for insurgency or terrorist situations than when it was originally invented. For instance, if the Taliban is collecting historical information about NATO's actions at a forward operating base in Afghanistan and is trying to decide whether to place a bomb along a frequently used route, then NEMS seems a very valuable tool. The bomber has to guess at the local NATO commander's strategies, because NATO forces may do something different every day. Armed with the knowledge of how many roads there are and an estimation of the cost of emplacing a bomb, there is a real cat-and-mouse game occurring. In analyzing such situations, planners calculate their own mixed strategy and that of their opponents.

As exciting as these results are, there are practical concerns that the theory has trouble addressing. Situations rarely achieve the kinds of steady states that would reduce them to known games. A bomber is killed, which changes the cost of building bombs; a new kind of armored vehicle is delivered to the operating base—even a change in either side's perception of acceptable losses should be analyzed. Issues such as these are better addressed by hypergame theory.

Introduction to Hypergame Theory

Hypergame theory was first formulated in Bennett and Dando's 1979 article on the successful 1940 German campaign against the Allies. They proposed that because of each military's experiences, goals, and means, the Germans and the Allies visualized the conflict differently from what game theory's assumption about the consistent alignment of beliefs would suggest.

This simple idea, that even players playing a completely revealed game (such as chess) would see and reason about the contest very differently depending on past experience, resonated with me during my early doctoral studies, which were aimed at applying artificial intelligence techniques to strategy generation. I had observed that chess masters would play much differently against unranked adversaries than when playing other chess masters. The idea blossomed; it actually seemed likely that every nontrivial game was rarely played by both (or more) players in exactly the same way.

For example, a player's understanding of the situation and options might vary in a number of ways:

- differences in player knowledge and expertise;
- differences in player starting situation assessment;
- differences in player ongoing assessment capability (evidence processing);
- differences in player understanding of strategy projection (what beats what?);

- differences in player information (both at the strategy commitment phase and during the operations);
- differences in robustness and resilience of each player's strategies;
- varied player constraints because of time;
- differences in player creativity (what tricks can be added, such as feints, hidden reserves, denial and deception operations).

When considering such variation in options and perceptions, an average person's analytical ability is rapidly outstripped. Few players are capable of considering more than two to five courses of action in a few diverse situations without using tables to organize such data. (Rules of thumb for redressing this limitation are scattered among the literature.) Thus, hypergame theory has to be supported by transactional memory (any artifact created to help humans remember, retrieve, and use information); I chose to extend the usual game-theoretic form.

Hypergame theory combines features of game theory and decision theory into a common table framework to help assess the impact of evidence, opponent knowledge, game knowledge, and contextual knowledge in order to analyze future competitions.

An Example of Descending the Diagonal

To enrich the number of possible strategies considered, I suggest a technique called "descending the diagonal," which represents expanding a game to consider more possible strategies. Using a larger matrix than whichever table might actually be used to solve a competition helps analysts bound problems about the future. The rationale of the process is to consider a strategy (a row or column in the matrix) as already chosen and then to design an antistrategy (its nemesis). (This is very similar to many game theoretic ideas from the 1950s.) After the nemesis is devised, we come up with the strategy which beats it, and so on. This is a kind of, "If you do this, then I'll do this to beat you" analysis.

To make these considerations more concrete and similar to Bennett and Dando's cited work, let us examine in a step-by-step way the considerations that could have occurred in formulating a battle strategy for the Allies in the first Gulf War. As a quick review: About 500,000 US forces and considerable allies assembled in Saudi Arabia to liberate Kuwait after the Iraqi invasion of 1990. The Iraqis have occupied Kuwait and have pillaged some of it; they have set up a defense and now await an Allied attack (or will watch the Allies give up and egress). The Allied air force has gained air supremacy.

Please note that this scenario favors the Allies; they will recapture Kuwait and damage the Iraqi forces to reduce Iraqi adventurism in the next decades. Ultimately, Allied planners want to unbalance the game to win a *great* victory, not to just prevail. The Iraqis are the Column Player, and the Allies are the Row Player.

In all of the following tables, the relative assessment number at the intersection of a Row choice and a Column choice summarizes an expert opinion of the range of results.

Because both sides are committing to a battle, only one number is recorded from the Allied (Row) point of view; this is for ease of table creation and decluttering of the visual representation. For the rest of this explanation, and consistent with zero-sum game theory, we will consider Column's outcome to be the negative of Row's, so we need not record it. Beware of choosing zero-sum automatically in actual problem solving sessions—adversaries often share some values, or both want to avoid an outcome (such as a nuclear exchange).

The entries in the table represent levels of game victories, where draw (0), marginal victory (1), strategic victory (2), and decisive victory (5) are given relative weights of success. Each side's semantic definition of the result varies, so a –2 for the Allies is approximately 10,000 personnel killed or seriously wounded and enhanced Iraqi military prestige. A 0 might represent fewer casualties for the Allies and less-retained Iraqi military strength, or a combination thereof. Please note: the "focus" in table 21.1 is where Row is trying to lessen Column's result.

In the Column, "Defend" is a frontal defense, evenly distributed. In the Row, "Frontal Attack" is an unweighted assault across the frontlines. The result of these two strategies is that the Allies will take a significant number of casualties, hence the –2 result. They will accomplish the mission of ejecting the Iraqis from Kuwait.

Row needs a better approach. The Row player tries to improve results by adding rows. As in all military engagements, Row could maneuver left or right,

thereby adding two more rows, as we see in table 21.2. Since the Allies (Row) start south of the Iraqis (Column), heading northward, we will use geospatial labels; thus, "go left" becomes Main (Attack) West, and "go right" becomes Main (Attack) East. Expert opinion assesses that with either of these approaches the Allies will slightly lessen their casualties.

The "focus" is where Column is trying to worsen Row's outcomes. Note that the focus is on the worst result for the Column player, in this case –1, which occurs in two rows. Both must be evaluated.

Likewise, the Iraqis can also add columns (see table 21.3). Column could Defend (Weighted) West or Defend (Weighted) East. Defend West was designed to damage a Main West attack and would yield more Allied casualties, so it is assessed as a –3 for the Allies. Likewise Defend East is designed against Main East.

The strategy and antistrategy reactions are beginning to appear on the diagonal; this is the concept of "descending the diagonal." Currently, this analysis favors Column objectives.

Noting the double focus in table 21.2, the Column player will examine those rows that yield better results. Practically, this must be done sequentially. So: (1) When two approaches seem to give the same outcome, start with the one the current player (in this case Column) believes will be the most fruitful;

Table 21.1
Initial situation

	Defend	
Allied Frontal Attack	Row: -2 Column: (-(-2)) = 2	
	focus	

Table 21.2
Adding more rows

	Defend	
Frontal Attack	-2	
Main West	-1	focus
Main East	-1	focus

Table 21.3

More columns

	Defend	Defend West	Defend East	
Frontal Attack	–2	–1	–1	
Main West	–1	**–3**	0	
Main East	–1	**0**	–3	
		focus	focus	

Table 21.4

Dominant row added

	Defend	Defend West	Defend East	
Frontal Attack	–2	–1	–1	
Main West	–1	–3	0	
Main East	–1	0	–3	
Envelop Vertically	2	0	0	focus

(2) If it isn't, the planner will shortly discover why the other is more promising.

Table 21.3 shows nine possible combinations of strategies and probable outcomes. A strategy to mitigate outcomes is emerging in the table, but all of the entries in the table must be assessed before completing the analysis. Notice, for instance, that Row's Main West would achieve success and break through the Iraqi line with fewer casualties when matched against Column's Defend East (0).

It becomes apparent as the analysis proceeds that the Allies can accomplish the mission by attacking frontally, but will receive unacceptable levels of casualties. In doing this, Row will miss opportunities to fake out Column or to win big. To win big, Row must add another row that effectively deals with these static defenses. Table 21.4 adds another row and creates a dominant row strategy, one with the highest value outcome in every column.

Fortunately for Row, there is an effective attack against the current three defenses. Envelop Vertically means to deploy airborne or air mobile troops to hit opponents in the rear. The expected value of the game has gone from negative to positive. The other rows are worse. Column can play either weighted defense (Defend West or East) to gain a

drawish result (represented by a 0 result), but they can no longer expect to win.

In table 21.5, Column has added a defense in depth labeled "Defend with Reserves" to get a valuable result against Envelop Vertically. The continuation of analysis (down the diagonal) has stimulated a new strategy for Column. This changes the status of the previously dominant strategy—it is now just another row. This is common: rarely is a strategy dominant at the end of the analysis; there are few strategies that work well regardless of what an opponent does.

In table 21.6, Row considers a wide maneuver to the west of Column's forces: Envelop West. It is an even better dominant strategy, and it shows why the Allies are likely to win. Indeed, we know after the fact that even in the most pitched battles in the war the Allies quickly broke the enemy. If somehow Row could get Column to configure its defense in the wrong way then Row would do even better.

Two Column counterstrategies are possible: Screening and a Republican Guard Counterattack. Again the previously dominant strategy (Envelop West) is reduced by Column's new strategies.

Note in table 21.7 how the original three rows work pretty well against the last two columns. This is

Table 21.5

Additional column

	Defend	Defend West	Defend East	**Defend with Reserves**	
Frontal Attack	−2	−1	−1	**0**	
Main West	−1	−3	0	**0**	
Main East	−1	0	−3	**0**	
Envelop Vertically	2	0	0	**−3**	
				focus	

Table 21.6

Row adds Envelop West

	Defend	Defend West	Defend East	Defend with Reserves	
Frontal Attack	−2	−1	−1	0	
Main West	−1	−3	0	0	
Main East	−1	0	−3	0	
Envelop Vertically	2	0	0	−3	
Envelop West	**3**	**1**	**5**	**1**	focus

often why our first strategies in our tables are rarely useless. In our minds, we think that if our opponent does something else, then they will be in a worse situation. So as Row generates new strategies, it is important to continue to assess all rows and columns, not just the diagonal focus which is driving new strategy creation.

To prevent Column's Counterattack option, Row needs to signal that they are going to attack frontally (a value of 4 in row 1). In the actual operation as the air campaign kicked off, Allied forces started to move their rearward ground forces closer to the Iraqi front lines, signaling that the Allies were about to attack across the front.

Last, we consider the effects of a deception strategy. If we can raise the likelihood of the enemy

choosing the best column for our actual choice then we will have earned a great victory. In table 21.8, one can see how the US Marine Corps feint could influence the Iraqi generals. If they thought they could give the Allies a bloody nose on the beach, without having to expose their forces to air attacks by moving, that lure might become compelling. The Iraqis may also have been influenced by the position of the valuable Iraqi oil fields near the coast or a commonly held notion that forces committed to a wide sweep would get lost in the desert. The feint (Invade Beach) is shown by the −3 in the Defend East column.

Findings

In real life, we are rarely certain that we have scanned even most of our options. A coping strategy for addressing this realization by planners and actors was discovered by Herb Simon in 1956 when he labeled the use of "tried-and-true" methods of addressing known problems as "satisficing."[5]

Table 21.7

All of Iraq's options

	Defend	Defend West	Defend East	Defend w/ Reserves	Screen	Counterattack
Frontal Attack	−2	−1	−1	0	1	4
Main West	−1	−3	0	0	1	1
Main East	−1	0	−3	0	1	1
Envelop Vertically	2	0	0	−3	−2	−2
Envelop West	3	1	5	1	−1	−2
			deceive			

Military strategists have an entire staff looking for opponent patterns or lazy thinking, while investigating anomalous outliers that might signal the invention of a new option by the opposing player.

What we are really doing is systematically eliciting from a game situation all of the players' strategies that deliver the big wins and big losses. These might be called the "wild ideas" of brilliant strategists, rather than what we expect. By determining a larger landscape of possibilities, we are actively attempting to prevent surprise by our opponent. Risky, high payoff strategies are generated during initial planning; these extrema lie outside of what we would actually ask warriors to do, but they act as a "type" for reasoning. Then we can dampen such wild ideas' radical nature and lessen some of their vulnerabilities. We can always attack more slowly, for instance, relying less on our inspiration and completing our projection by acting in a more deliberate manner to ascertain the enemy's situation more accurately.[6]

A strategist may waste time by developing new options, but one cannot make the value of the game worse by doing so. Developing a repeatable method, such as descending the diagonal, for finding significant rows or columns is highly desirable. An unknown strategy played as a surprise can destroy the predictive power of a strategy mix from original game theory.

Game theory helps one most when a strategist has run out of new options and players are pretty much restricted to competing in generally known games. Hypergame theory helps best when there is a new game or in a situation where there are significant structural advantages to one side. WHT promotes the concept that both players are creative and resourceful, and may even be deceptive. WHT is a more open approach to the process of examining what might happen in the future based on our possible choices than are scenario-based wargames. While WHT can still benefit from calculating the game-theoretic expected value of a game, that value is highly unlikely to be delivered by a small subset of the WHT well-examined situation/game. Instead an approach of modeling opponents from WHT yields repeatedly better results (Vane 2000).

Last, if we note the salient features of opponents' plans, we can do whatever we can to delay our decision until their strategy is betrayed by intelligence

Table 21.8

Invade Beach feint

	Defend	Defend West	Defend East	Defend w/ Reserves	Screen	Counterattack
Frontal Attack	−2	−1	−1	0	1	4
Main West	−1	−3	0	0	1	1
Main East	−1	0	−3	0	1	1
Envelop Vertically	2	0	0	−3	−2	−2
Envelop West	3	1	5	1	−1	−2
Invade Beach	**1**	**2**	**−3**	**−1**	**−2**	**−1**

collection (also called indicators and warnings). At that point, game theory isn't even needed, because we know the enemy strategy.

In conclusion, hypergame theory is a valuable tool that combines many aspects of decision theory and game theory to address new outcomes, new strategies, differences in player planning capability, and evaluations of deception. In a way similar to Bennett and Dando, using an abstraction of a recent world contest provides a context for exploring how hypergame theory can evaluate the future. Combining wargaming with hypergame theory can develop valuable strategies to educate warriors and support intelligence collection.

About the Author

Russell Vane has been serving in the US wargaming shop assigned to attack IED networks since early 2008. He earned his doctorate from George Mason University in 2001 with the dissertation "Using Hypergames to Select Plans in Competitive Environments." Thereafter he wrote numerous articles on the futures of artificial intelligence, intelligent augmentation and applying hypergame theory to sense-making and decision making, including "Planning for Terrorist-Caused Emergencies" for WinterSim 2005. He coinvented a patent for General Dynamics for Cognitive Automation, awarded in 2010. From 1980 until 2000, he applied his master's degree in computer and information science to delivering numerous defense- and weather-related systems. He coauthored *The Arab-Israeli Wars* with W. Seth Carus for Avalon Hill Company in 1977. In the late 1970s, he served as an Armored Cavalry officer after earning Airborne and Ranger tabs.

Notes

1. WHT is useful in many varied situations. Since 2008, I have field-tested the WHT approach more than a hundred times, supporting the US military's counter-IED efforts.

2. A Nobel Prize was awarded in 1994 for contributions to game theory to three researchers and later to John Nash (inventor of the Nash Equilibrium Mixed Strategy), subject of Sylvia Nasar's book (and subsequent film) *A Beautiful Mind*.

3. While many practical studies of repeated play games have occurred, the most well-known is the famous "Prisoner's Dilemma."

4. One of the most significant findings of game theoretic reasoning occurs when one or more choices are available to a player, but these choices are not part of the NEMS mix and should not be used. A player can increase the value of his/her play by simply excluding those choices.

5. "Evidently, organisms adapt well enough to 'satisfice'; they do not, in general, 'optimize'" (Simon 1956, 129). "A 'satisficing' path, a path that will permit satisfaction at some specified level of all its needs" (136).

6. Adding a new row or column can radically alter the expected value of any game. I have shown elsewhere (Vane 2000) that the expected value (EV) of a zero sum game with M+1 rows and N columns always yields a game value to Row that is equal to or better than an [M row × N column] game. Likewise, an [M row by N+1 columns] game always yields a game value to Row that is less than or equal to an [M row × N column] game. Symbolically, the finding is:

$$EV(M+1, N) \geq EV(M, N), \text{ better for Row.}$$

$$EV(M, N+1) \leq EV(M,N), \text{ worse for Row.}$$

IV THE BLEEDING EDGE

Luke Caldwell and Tim Lenoir

In a 2012 YouTube video (Call of Duty 2012) featuring Brookings Institute fellow Peter Singer and retired US Marine Lieutenant Colonel Oliver North, we are told that the future of warfare is rapidly approaching and that we are simply not ready for it. While many of these technologies "sound like they are things out of science fiction," like lasers and autonomous robotics, Singer assures us that "the weapon itself is getting more independent"— for better or worse. Oliver North, infamous for his role in the Iran-Contra scandal, rejoins with a "nightmare scenario" in which a "hacker breaks into our system that controls satellites, UAVs—even the launch of missiles" and uses our technologies against us. The video cuts quickly to a grainy Guy Fawkes mask and lingers a moment. "I don't worry about a guy that wants to hijack a plane," continues North. "I worry about the guy that wants to hijack all the planes." Singer caps off our paranoia with: "the future is not as far off as most people think ... *We're not ready for it*" (ibid.).

Watching this clip is more than a little confusing. It seems on the one hand official and grounded in the authority of its experts: one a retired Marine with a history of running illegal clandestine operations, and the other one of the foremost experts on the future of warfare. However, it remains unclear from the content itself what purpose it fulfills: it seems like a documentary promo about the future of war, but it also has a certain cinematic flair to it. Instead of the more detached and objective perspective of reporting or documentary filmmaking, what comes through loud and clear is an attempt to interpolate the viewer into the military machine: these technologies "allow *you* to blow things up," hackers break into "*our*" control systems, and "*we*" are simply not ready for this rapidly approaching future. The clip only identifies itself in the last few seconds with a large splash screen that claims: "The future is black ..." followed by a logo situating it within the *Call of Duty* franchise (ibid.). Perhaps we are not ready for the future of warfare, but with the help of the game *Black Ops II* (2012) we might just get there.

While this docu-trailer provides a convincing backdrop to the *Black Ops II* gameworld, it is thoroughly entrenched in a military discourse about how high technology will revolutionize the strategies and conduct of future wars. This discourse and transition has come to be known in military theory as the "Revolution in Military Affairs" (RMA). In this chapter, we argue that wargames like *Black Ops II* have increasingly become a vector for naturalizing the ideas and predictions offered by the military under the banner of the RMA.

We will first look at how US military and media interests have aligned to provide consumers experiences that interpolate them within speculative futures largely outlined by military theorists and argue that this interactivity has the effect of producing subjects that see the RMA as natural and inevitable. We will then trace the gradual integration of these proposals about the future threat landscape, military technologies, and strategic doctrine throughout the history of video wargaming. We argue that the military shooter has evolved from a genre primarily concerned with the reenactment of historical wars to one obsessed with the techniques, technologies, and predictions of the RMA. As these games further integrate scenarios grounded in documents like the Defense Quadrennial Reviews, they help manufacture consensus around their anticipated threats, propose investments, and promote their ratification in future legislative budgets. We conclude with a discussion of some of the contradictions embedded within the RMA and its representation in popular wargaming. We raise questions about the role of peace and nonviolent resolution to conflict within an ideological apparatus constructed to make warfare cheaper and last longer, and that simultaneously glorifies and condemns violence as the ultimate solution to problems. We issue a call to reimagine the ways that violence is justified and incentivized in gaming—because if our wargames cannot imagine a future of peace, why should we expect our military?

Premediating the Future of Warfare

That a fictional game like *Black Ops II* should attempt to ground itself in contemporary military developments is as unsurprising as it is uncontroversial today. Much has been written on the enmeshed relationships between the US military and the entertainment industry—the military-entertainment complex—and how the interactivity of gaming serves as a vector for subjectivation. Early works examining the military-entertainment complex from the perspective of media effects were particularly alarmist, claiming that militarized content in entertainment conditions people to have lower inhibitions for committing real acts of violence (see e.g., Grossman 2009). Other works by Tim Lenoir and Ed Halter have focused on the exchange of expertise and training platforms between the military and the commercial game industry, and how militaries have developed and marketed game platforms as recruiting and training tools (Lenoir 2000, 2002, 2003; Lenoir and Lowood 2005; Halter 2006). Finally, works by Roger Stahl and James Der Derian have focused on how the military-entertainment complex constructs support for militarism and militaristic ideals, effectively short-circuiting civil discourse about the conduct of warfare (Stahl 2010a; Der Derian 2009).

While much can and has already been said about how games like *America's Army* (2002–) have bolstered military recruiting or how the military uses simulation platforms like *Virtual Battlespace* (2002) in training, we would like to focus here in the spirit of Stahl on the constructive power of popular wargaming. *America's Army* and other simulation platforms certainly function well as vectors for official military values and conduct, thus making them invaluable recruiting and training tools (Mead 2013), but what interests us most here is how popular wargaming distributes a commodified and franchised vision of militarism through Western entertainment. Rather than being strictly in line with official military codes of conduct, popular wargames like *Call of Duty* glorify the tools and technologies of war while obscuring safeguards that limit and constrain military conduct during wartime. Unhinged from the restrictions and constraints of law, bureaucracy, and codes of conduct, popular wargames often articulate scenarios that line up with worst-case visions of future warfare offered by politicians and military strategists looking to frame future public investment. In most cases, these games empower their players to confront a force of overwhelming evil with cool guns, gadgets, and brazen disregard for the chain of command, international law, and human rights. Instead of creating subjects who want to join the military, popular wargames naturalize a future in which war is always the correct solution to international problems and prescribes public investment in novel tools and "cool" technologies that allow warfighters to kill more effectively. This story, in short, is about how popular wargames participate within politico-economic realities that help solidify the ideological grounds that will anchor wars of the future and encourage players to imagine and invest in a future of constant and inevitable war.

Stahl, in particular, gives us a useful theoretical framework to proceed from. In *Militainment, Inc.* (2010), he argues that in the aftermath of 9/11, militaristic rhetoric has pervaded the social field such that it engages consumers on an interactive level. In contrast with the military public relations of Operation Desert Storm, where the public was dazzled by the spectacle of a "clean war" hidden behind images of laser-guided munitions and the green glow of night-vision goggles, the military of the new millennium is integrated into every aspect of social life. While the strategy of spectacular war disengaged civic debate and protest by making the sterile image of war seem more real than war itself, its downfall grew out of the inability to completely engineer all media representations of the war. The early stages of Desert Storm maintained the ruse of a "clean war" by literally burying countless bodies and burnt-out vehicles beneath the sand with "Armored Combat Earthmovers" to keep them out of media circulation (Sloyan 2002). Maintaining such control over the war narrative, however, was precarious and the brutality of war made its way into public view after Coalition air power slaughtered hundreds if not thousands of retreating Iraqi soldiers trapped on a major highway. The leak of these images soured public support and inspired President Bush to cease hostilities the following day.

The strategy of interactive war, however, approaches the relationship with mass media more proactively and has enjoyed far greater long-term success. Rather than tenuously placing the civilian and military in different social realms and connecting them only through the thin veneer of military public relations, interactive war brings about their merger by making war fun. In the post-9/11 world, militarism is ever present in social life, from children's toys to video games to the many firefights recorded and broadcast for all on YouTube. For Stahl, under the interactive war paradigm, we become "Civilian Soldiers" through our entertainment and are conditioned to accept foundational assumptions about the conduct of war that are ultimately depoliticizing and benefit the Department of Defense (DoD).

As militarism has become increasingly interactive and has spread deeply into all forms of entertainment, depictions of potential threats have also become more speculative and oriented toward possible futures than toward recreating or justifying the past. In his book *Premediation* (2010), Richard Grusin locates this transition in the collective shock of 9/11, which he argues imprinted a massive collective trauma on US culture writ large. In order to protect us from such a shock again, media have become obsessed with predicting various futures so that if one of those futures comes to be, we will not be caught unprepared. In his words, "Premediation works to prevent citizens of the global mediasphere from experiencing again the kind of systemic or traumatic shock produced by the events of 9/11 by perpetuating an almost constant, low level of fear or anxiety about another terrorist attack" (Grusin 2010, 2). Whether this fear circulates through the near omnipresence of the figure of the terrorist in post-9/11 media or through consistent reinforcement of terrorism as a significant and ongoing threat, mass media reminds us what is important by virtually exposing us to possible realities that would be too costly to actually experience. In so doing, these premediated futures coalesce into an affective unconscious that is always anticipating the threats of the future.

In what follows, we extend the work of both Stahl and Grusin to show how popular wargames from roughly 2006 onward have helped construct and distribute a commodified vision of militarism that appropriates many ideas, technologies, and scenarios from theorists of the RMA. While Stahl sometimes overemphasizes the centralized role of military public relations in engineering discourse about the military, making his account sometimes read as a conspiracy theory, connecting his theory of interactive war with Grusin allows us to emphasize how premediation functions within a culture industry that constructs national consensus around vested political and economic interests. Rather than being a conspiracy through and through, the military-entertainment complex is fueled by a nexus of coinciding interests between the military and the entertainment industries. What emerges in this picture is a relationship of productive resonance between the military and entertainment industries, with game companies reaping huge financial rewards and the military having many of its foundational assumptions about the future branded as cool and inevitable. Downplayed in this relationship are alternative perspectives that reveal war as the horrific business it is, show the long-lasting negative consequences of war, or advocate for alternate solutions to international conflict. Before turning to the representation of the RMA in wargames, we will first work through some of its core ideas, assumptions, and implementations.

The Revolution in Military Affairs and the New American Way of War

In late February 2014, Secretary of Defense Chuck Hagel, facing serious budget reductions, recommended shrinking the US Army to its smallest size since 1940. His proposal called for shedding

120,000 soldiers over the next few years and reinvesting some of those savings in improved training and technology for the remaining soldiers. While such a suggestion predictably sparked claims that this would cripple US warfighting ability, Hagel's suggestion is the culmination of a decades-long transition that argues that a smarter, more flexible military, supported by superior information technology is both fiscally responsible and strategically necessary for the wars of the future (Cooper and Shanker 2014; Simeone 2014).

Since the widespread integration of computers into the conduct of war during the Cold War, military theorists have been trying to predict how information technologies will revolutionize the wars of the future. This discourse has come to be known as the Revolution in Military Affairs (RMA). While our purpose is not to get bogged down in a comprehensive genealogy of these debates—within which there are many disagreements and conflicting visions—what we would like to present here is an overarching summary of how RMA ideas have given rise to what military historian Max Boot has called "a new American way of war" that is grounded in "speed, maneuver, flexibility ... precision firepower, special forces, and psychological operations" (Boot 2003). In essence, we would like to focus on how technological and organizational change has moved the US military from one based on size, attrition, and overwhelming land power to the lean and flexible military represented in Hagel's recent proposals.

Schematically, RMA discourse generally encompasses developments in three different yet interconnected domains: technological change, organizational adaptation, and the perceived threat landscape of the future. That is to say, RMA theorists generally engage questions about how new technologies change the organization and operation of the military and how the technological and organizational changes of potential enemies will change the way future wars are conducted. Rather than a strictly academic exercise, these predictions embody the constructive power of premediation that we would like to highlight. By anticipating virtual futures, these theorists influence technological investments that aim to exploit or prevent these predictions.[1] Accordingly, these statements hook into a vast defense economy and are made with an eye toward the health of a military-industrial complex that must remain strong and innovative to help fuel the strategic dominance of the United States.

Tellingly, the RMA rose as a discourse in the context of significant budget cuts. Following the winding down of the Cold War, Congress imposed budgetary restrictions on the DoD that affected both manpower and procurement. Over the course of the decade from 1991 to 2001 the budget for the Department of Defense was cut by 24 percent, falling from $382.5 billion (in constant 2001 dollars) to $291.1 billion (Cohen 2000, B-1). In terms of combined active military and reserve personnel in the DoD, there was a reduction from 3,200,000 personnel on the eve of the first Gulf War In 1990 to 2,062,000, or an active force 35 percent smaller in 2001 on the eve of Operation Enduring Freedom (ibid., C-1). Procurement for new systems declined from a highpoint of $97.7 billion in 1990 to a low of $45 billion in 1996 and 1997, a reduction of 54 percent (ibid., B-1). Citing the necessity of procurement for the RMA, Secretary of Defense William S. Cohen (1997–2001) was able to restore this budget to $60.3 billion, still only 62 percent of its post–Cold War height. Faced with these cutbacks, Cohen and others advanced the RMA as a means for extracting the greatest efficiency from their investments.

As budgetary concerns loomed, the strategic advantage afforded by information technology was also revealed through the wars of the 1990s. The successes of Operation Desert Storm and the Kosovo War showed that information technology was signaling a new era of warfare in which US casualties were minimal and victory was decisive. Leveraging the new Global Positioning System (GPS), precision-guided munitions (PGMs) provided the capability to strike enemy positions with accuracy from long ranges. Experimental systems like the Joint Surveillance Target Attack Radar System (JSTARS) also allowed management of the battlefield from high in the sky and fed troops on the ground information far forward of their position. In short, networked information technology allowed for dominance on the battlefield by providing improved command and control over weaponry at great distances, far superior intelligence, surveillance and reconnaissance capabilities (ISR), and faster, more coordinated responses to real-time intelligence.

In the latter half of the 1990s, theorists such as John Arquilla and David Rondfelt began to suggest that the military itself depart from its centralized, bureaucratic mode of organization and fully embrace the networked management structures and technologies of the information society (Arquilla and Ronfeldt 1997). Admiral William A. Owens, vice chairman of the Joint Chiefs of Staff, argued that US forces need to become a "system-of-systems" and allow networked forms of organization to provide redundancy and flexibility in the face of new challenges (Owens 1996). Vice Admiral Arthur Cebrowski and John Garstka branded this theory as "network-centric warfare," emphasizing more localized responses to

threats and bottom-up self-organization based upon information sharing (Cebrowski and Garstka 1998). Such suggestions were already in line with many of the budgetary constraints facing the Pentagon through their emphasis on smaller, more independent squads supported by sophisticated information collection and sharing infrastructures.

A final precursor to the wholesale adoption of the RMA was a reevaluation of the kinds of threats facing the United States in the future. The strategists of the RMA argued that the evolution of the threat landscape in twenty-first-century international politics called for a transformation in the type of warfare the US forces should prepare to conduct in the future (Gunzinger 2013; Krepinevich 1992; Metz and Kievit 1995). From 1993 through 2006, the DoD's force planning scenario looked to past conflicts for analyzing force preparedness. They assumed the US should maintain the ability to conduct two major regional conflicts on par with Desert Storm in different parts of the globe, as well as conduct multiple proxy wars and counterinsurgencies (Gunzinger 2013). The events of September 11, 2001, and the ensuing operations in Iraq and Afghanistan, however, signaled a change in the projected threat model of twenty-first century warfare away from state-based actors to asymmetrical, nonconventional threats. RMA advocates accordingly lobbied for heavy development of tactics and technologies like Special Operations Forces (SOF), long-range missiles, and unmanned aircraft for striking targets where physical access was limited.

While the Global War on Terror provided the final impetus for the institutionalization of many RMA ideas, these changes made inroads in a piecemeal and fragmentary form until President Obama took office in 2008. Under Obama, many programs implemented sparingly by his predecessor—such as cross-border Special Forces raids, drone assassinations, and cyberwarfare—became the status quo (Turse 2012). Early successes of the war on terror, like the removal of the Taliban from power and the storming of Baghdad, were attributed to the power of the RMA and the efforts of Secretary of Defense Donald Rumsfeld in transforming the military for the information era. As Rumsfeld claimed in his 2002 Annual Report, these victories

> were the direct result of a new style of warfare. ... The battle for Mazar-i Sharif—which set in motion the collapse of the Taliban regime—demonstrated the potential of highly networked joint operations. By linking AC-130 gunships, Predators, Global Hawks, and JSTARS, Operation Enduring Freedom has demonstrated that high pay-offs result from early network-centric warfare concepts of operations. The Special Operations Forces on the ground, as well as sophisticated overhead reconnaissance systems, served as a network of sensors that provided a picture of the battlefield. (Rumsfeld 2002)

Such initial optimism was not just limited to the war in Afghanistan and extended to Iraq as well. As Max Boot notes, compared to the first Gulf War, the taking of Baghdad in 2003 required half as many troops, produced fewer than half as many casualties, took a little over half as long, and cost only a fourth as much (Boot 2003). If these wars had stopped at this point, they might have been considered dramatic successes and would have unquestionably enshrined the RMA in the military apparatus.

As the insurgencies in Iraq and Afghanistan blossomed and pronouncements of victory were retracted, flaws were revealed in this initial strategy. While SOF and flexible armor divisions were effective in toppling governments, they proved less

adept at finishing the task. Amid souring public opinion and renewed budget scrutiny, the policies advocated by Rumsfeld and the visionaries of the RMA finally crystallized into the new American way of warfare centered around smaller organizational units that use modern information, communications, and robotics technology to mount the kind of agile campaign seen in Afghanistan in 2001-02. DoD planning documents such as the 2006 Quadrennial Defense Review emphasized investment in longrange smart missiles, drone aircraft and other unmanned systems, integrated intelligence gathering and surveillance systems, and systems of defense for communications systems as necessary pieces of the new warfighting requirements (Department of Defense 2006, 31–32).

New methods of acquiring, analyzing, and distributing information that could help units make more strategic decisions became increasingly important for cutting through the fog of war to allow assets to respond locally to highly networked and flexible threats. Reflecting on his experience as Commander of US Forces in Afghanistan, General Stanley A. McChrystal summarized this transition:

> In bitter, bloody fights in both Afghanistan and Iraq, it became clear to me and to many others that to defeat a networked enemy we had to become a network ourselves. We had to figure out a way to retain our traditional capabilities of professionalism, technology, and, when needed, overwhelming force, while achieving levels of knowledge, speed, precision, and unity of effort that only a network could provide.
>
> The idea was to combine analysts who found the enemy (through intelligence, surveillance, and reconnaissance); drone operators who fixed the target; combat teams who finished the target by capturing or killing him; specialists who

exploited the intelligence the raid yielded, such as cell phones, maps, and detainees; and the intelligence analysts who turned this raw information into usable knowledge. (McChrystal 2011)

Such synergistic coordination between specialized teams evokes Owens's concept of the military as a "system-of-systems" that self-synchronizes and adapts according to changing flows of information (Owens 1996). Importantly, prior to being in charge of US forces in Afghanistan in 2009, McChrystal led the highly secretive Joint Special Operations Command (JSOC), leading to the expansion of RMA Special Operations tactics into the larger command.

As normal forces began operating more like Special Forces, the latter also expanded dramatically under RMA guidance. Since the birth of the Global War on Terror, Special Operations Forces (SOF) have conducted continuous worldwide counterterrorist and counterinsurgency operations against al Qaeda and other irregular forces. The number of SOF deployed overseas before the War or Terror was approximately 2,800, and quadrupled annually until 2012. During the surges in Iraq and Afghanistan, that number reached around 12,000 and has remained constant since (Thomas and Dougherty 2013, x). To meet increasing needs in both Afghanistan and Iraq as well as other missions consonant with the War on Terror, the US Special Operation Command (USSOCOM) increased in size from 38,000 in 2001 to 63,000 in 2012, and saw budgetary increases from $2.3 billion in 2001 to roughly $10.4 billion in 2013 (Thomas and Dougherty 2013, x–xi; McRaven 2012).

Providing intelligence, surveillance, and reconnaissance (ISR) capabilities to an increasingly networked and flexible military has also prompted significant and game-changing investments in robotics and Orwellian surveillance systems. The number of Unmanned Aerial Vehicles (UAVs, or drones) owned by the Pentagon has skyrocketed from 167 in 2002 to 7,500 in 2010 (Gertler 2012, 2), and yearly UAV investments have increased from $284 million in 2000 to $3.3 billion in 2010 (ii). From 2001-2013 the Pentagon is estimated to have spent over $26 billion researching, acquiring, and operating drones (13), which have gone from representing 5 percent of all military aircraft in 2005 to nearly one-third in 2012 (Ackerman and Shachtman 2012). Equipped with sophisticated sensors and powerful cameras, these drones provide such overwhelming amounts of information that the military has had to develop new infrastructure to deal with the spike in bandwidth needs. A lone Global Hawk requires bandwidth on the order of 500 megabits per second, a number that is five times larger than "the total bandwidth of the entire US military used during the 1991 Gulf War" (Gertler 2012, 17).

Longer-term plans for institutionalizing network-centric warfare within the traditional forces would also see significant investments during the War on Terror. The massively ambitious Future Combat Systems (FCS) and Objective Force Warrior programs, for instance, were launched in 2003–2009 with contracts awarded to Boeing and SAIC for $200 billion aimed at creating a "system of systems" networking all elements of the US armed services in a battlefield environment to enable unprecedented levels of joint connectivity and "battlespace" awareness. The program, which was canceled under the austerity measures implemented by Secretary of Defense Robert Gates, aimed to equip fifteen of the Army's roughly seventy combat brigades with new robots and hybrid diesel-electric manned vehicles connected by a secure communications network and equipped with high-tech sensors.

At the individual warfighter level, the Objective Force Warrior program attempted to tie soldiers into this network as both consumers and producers of information. Soldiers mounted on infantry carriers would have full access to all information on the network by way of their vehicle. When dismounted, a special heads-up display would seamlessly integrate necessary information on a data screen for them to access remotely. Featuring sensors at overlapping scales (platoon, company, battalion, and brigade levels), the system would allow tactical leaders to launch UAVs and smart munitions to critical points on the battlefield and peer through the fog of war by collecting massive amounts of information—all without being observed by the enemy. As nodes in a sensing network, soldiers and intelligent machines would transmit information upward to those with greater vision of the entire battlefield, making them function effectively as flexible nodes within an expanded network.

While the FCS was never fielded, such technologies will inevitably find their way into future products such as the Tactical Assault Light Operator Suit (TALOS) being researched by DARPA and SOCOM. Expected to incorporate specialized lightweight armor with a robotic exoskeleton and 3D augmented-reality displays (Hoarn 2013; McDuffee 2014), the soldiers of the future and the wars they will fight are becoming more machinically mediated and networked than ever before.

The RMA in the History of Wargaming

In *Premediation*, Grusin makes the claim that media coverage following the event of 9/11, because of its repetition, reach, and affective power, has indelibly inflected and reshaped the real event. Rather than following Baudrillard or Žižek in claiming that digital mediation dematerializes the real, Grusin argues that this mediality is added to the event and, in being added, shows how media are "agents or aspects of governmentality in the management and mobilization of populations" (Grusin 2010, 25). In what follows, we will argue that a similar phenomenon is taking place with the naturalization of the new American way of war through wargaming. Put simply, rather than remediating conflicts and modes of warfare from the past, as they did prior to 2006, post-2006 wargaming has so strongly premediated ideas of war that the ways people think about war—including those who invest in and wage them—are inevitably reframed. Until around 2006, commercial video games can be seen a sideshow to the contemporary conduct of warfare, and looked instead to the past for their inspiration. Now they are the real show, engaging and premediating the future. In what follows, we will trace some of the steps that brought us here.

Simulation, Realism, and Ludic Constraints

Computer wargaming audiences have always been hooked on realism. This brand of realism, however, is quite peculiar and focuses almost exclusively on the detailed depiction of actual (or seemingly realistic) combat weapons, vehicles, tactics, historically accurate scenarios, and other instances of graphical and mechanical representation. In awarding high marks to a game, reviews routinely applaud this brand of realism—fidelity to physics and so-called hard factors—in addition to technical features like the game mechanics and playability that make it fun. What we would like to stress here is how realistic game mechanics and scenarios are often at odds with a rich and entertaining gaming experience. Put simply, war is not intrinsically fun and requires significant rebranding in order to create the kind of consumer experiences gamers have come to expect and support.

Analyses of the military-entertainment complex often express consternation with games like the US Army's *America's Army* (2002–) and Bohemia Interactive's *ARMA* (2006) series (which we will refer to as simulations) because they were either intended to be, or were slight modifications of, military training tools. For many, including Stahl, they represent a dangerous leakage of militarism into everyday life because of their desire to communicate specifically military values, procedures, and tactics to players. Yet if we look at the circulation of such simulators in comparison to popular titles from the *Call of Duty* (*COD*) franchise, these simulators that adhere to a strict interpretation of realism are niche products that lack a widespread following. While *America's Army* has enjoyed a high level of success for simulations, with more than thirteen million players registering over its eleven years running (Anderson 2013), *COD 4* alone sold over thirteen million copies as of 2009. Collectively, *COD*'s *Modern Warfare* (2007, 2009, 2011) and *Black Ops* (2010, 2012) series have sold approximately 108,700,000 copies since 2007. Other popular franchises like *Battlefield* (2002–2011;

40.57 million sales) and *Medal of Honor* (1999–2012; 37.31 million sales) have also enjoyed significant successes in comparison to these simulations as well.[2] Not to be dismissive of the relative followings that simulations like *ARMA* and *America's Army* have, in what follows, we assume that popular wargames shape expectations about warfare in ways that simulations cannot, simply by virtue of their greater circulation and popularity. We argue that it is the *selective realism* of popular wargames that has helped not only turn them into highly successful commodities and franchises, but has also helped to construct a cultural imaginary in which the new American way of war is seen as desirable, effective, and natural while eschewing the many problems and contradictions that accompany it.

This selective realism in popular wargaming articulates a series of ludic constraints necessary for translating something as tedious, varied, and complicated as war into a fun and standardized mass experience. On a general level, ludic constraints inspire deviations from realistic mechanics—for example, in the ways characters can move, how much gear they can carry with no impact, with weapon ballistics, or how much damage characters can withstand—and from much, if not all, military tactical and strategic training. Wargames often give rise to "run-and-gun" styles of play that reward fast reflexes more than caution, strategy, and teamwork (Bayer 2006). These deviations are prompted by the simple fact that realistic representations in these areas make the game experience less affectively compelling, less widely consumable, and very difficult to master.

Ludic constraints also impact the personal, social, and geopolitical narratives chosen by wargames in their pursuit of giving the player reasons to kill wave

	Sales
COD - 2003*	1,750,000
COD 2 - 2005*	2,500,000
COD 3 - 2006*	1,250,000
Modern Warfare - 2007	17,700,000
World ar War - 2008*	11,000,000
Modern Warfare 2 - 2009	24,500,000
Black Ops - 2010	29,700,000
Modern Warfare 3 - 2011	29,830,000
Black Ops 2 - 2012	24,200,000
Ghosts - 2013	14,500,000
Total	139,600,000

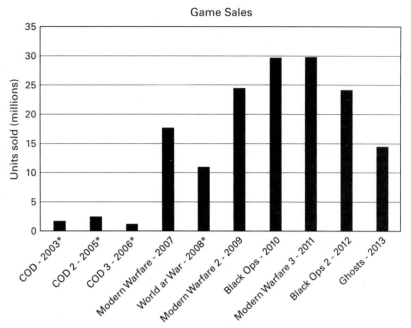

Figure 22.1

Call of Duty units sold in millions ("Call of Duty Franchise Game Sales Statistics" 2014). Asterisk, games with historical orientation.

after wave of bad guys. Both simulations and wargames play out against a backdrop of ideological commitments that shape the greater cause for "why we fight," such as the fight to preserve freedom, democracy and "our way of life." They also simulate the tension and human drama of the firefight in a struggle for valor, victory, and the preservation of brothers-in-arms. Yet when commitments to realistic scenarios and military values come into conflict with heightened drama and cool game mechanics, simulations and wargames typically choose one emphasis over the other. Rather than capturing the complete experience of war, popular wargames must contend with their embeddedness in a representational regime tasked with making the horrors of war

cool, honorable, exciting, and eminently consumable as entertainment. To this end, the techniques, technologies, and worldviews promoted by the new American way of war have formed a nexus of coinciding interests that reinforce and popularize one another: game companies can ground their narratives and game environments in premediations of future conflict, making them seem cutting-edge and "authentic," thereby circulating military ideas in extreme forms and branding them as cool, effective, and inevitable.

What is important about this nexus of interests, however, is that it doesn't necessarily follow a centralized propaganda model, moving from the Pentagon outward into culture. These games and narratives are first and foremost born from market research, branding, and commodification efforts from within the entertainment industries. As with the military, the revolution in military affairs forms a strong business model that brings significant financial returns.

Wargaming: From Remediation to Premediation

Just as the RMA was gradually integrated into US military planning in a piecemeal and fragmented form, the same is true for its integration into popular wargaming.[3] From the late 1990s up through the invasion of Iraq in 2003, the most popular commercial wargames remediated past wars, mirroring military force planning of that period. Acclaimed franchises of this period, like *Medal of Honor*, *Battlefield*, and *Call of Duty* (*COD*), focused almost exclusively on World War II. The *Medal of Honor* series created by Steven Spielberg in 1999 stuck with the World War II formula for longest, finally departing from it in 2010 with their thirteenth release. Early *Medal of Honor* (Electronic Arts) games were inspired by Spielberg's work on *Saving Private Ryan* (1998) and aimed to give an interactive experience that evoked the real history as genuinely as the movie. Game missions grew out of historical research and were widely perceived as authentic representations of the many facets and fronts of the war.

The *Battlefield* series also originally focused on World War II with *Battlefield 1942* (Electronic Arts 2002). In addition to being able to use weapons of the historical period, players could also operate a wide variety of historically inspired vehicles through battle maps that took inspiration from the major conflicts and theaters of World War II. The *Battlefield* series allowed for greater customization of the gameplay experience than previous titles by allowing players to inhabit one of five combat roles, each with particular strengths and weaknesses. For example, Anti-tank roles gave one the ability to attack vehicles effectively, but not regular infantry, while Scouts allowed greater surveillance capacities and long-range engagements, but not effective close-quarters capabilities. Medics could heal teammates and Engineers could repair equipment but were both less suited to engage than the Assault class, which sported strong firepower. Balancing these different capabilities promoted a strong sense of cooperation and teamwork that previous shooters had not.

As *Battlefield* contributed to a sense of synergy between specialized forces in multiagent combat, *Call of Duty*s 1-3 (Activision 2003–2006) continued the focus on World War II and helped move the single-player wargaming experience away from a "lone wolf" style of play to one in which the player works as part of a team controlled by artificial intelligence. By placing the player within a team rather than having them explore an open world to complete missions, *COD* maintained a strong grip over how one could progress through the game. This allowed for constructing the single-player experience as a compelling narrative rather than just providing an historical context to imbue play with meaning. In *COD* campaigns, the narrative follows you throughout the whole experience, heightening emotion and drama as if it were an interactive movie that only progresses through your contributions.

That World War II provided a starting point for three of the most successful wargaming franchises can be partly explained by simple social and institutional networks—Electronic Arts published both the *Medal of Honor* and *Battlefield* series and the creators of *COD* worked on *Medal of Honor* games prior to forming their competing studio (Infinity Ward)—but the extreme narratives of World War II also helped justify the entertainment value of interactive war. One of the prime ludic constraints of popular wargaming is providing a believable context that explains why the player should kill wave upon wave of enemies without feeling like a psychopath. Without a clear reason to kill, the violence of shooters becomes banal and reveals war as an unentertaining and traumatic enterprise.[4] The moral clarity that accompanies a mission to defeat the Axis powers provides that justification and opens the experience to positive affects of virtue and heroism. In the aftermath of the events of 9/11 and the rapidly expanding Global War on Terror, the figure of the terrorist became a fitting substitute for the Nazi and now occupies that position of absolute evil.

Early attempts to consider modern warfare were tentative in breaking from the older paradigm of large-scale land warfare and still presented foreign nations and coalitions as the primary threats to international peace and security. *Battlefield 2* (2005) broke from an historical orientation to imagine a new world war between the United States, China, and an emerging Middle Eastern Coalition (MEC). The game features territorial invasions by the United States and Western allies into the Middle East and China as well as Chinese and MEC invasions into the United States.

But while *Battlefield 2* enjoyed moderate success with approximately 1.5 million copies sold, it was not until *Call of Duty 4: Modern Warfare* (2007) that the power of the new paradigm of warfare was made clear. As *Battlefield* integrated new geopolitical rivals like China and Middle Eastern powers into their narratives, *Modern Warfare* exploited fears of terrorists in control of nuclear weapons to provide an epic and affective narrative. Featuring an odd coalition of Middle Eastern zealots and Russian "ultranationalists," *Modern Warfare* imports Cold War paranoia into widespread concerns about nuclear proliferation and asymmetric warfare brought about by the Global War on Terror. Amid increasing public discontent with an expanding war in Iraq and repeated failures to turn up the weapons of mass destruction that were its justification, *Modern Warfare* makes players experience the effects of WMDs firsthand. Playing as a Special Forces Marine in a Middle Eastern country, your character dies a slow death along with 30,000 other Marines and countless civilians when a radical leader nukes his own city to repel a US invasion. The campaign concludes with an intense fight through a Russian nuclear facility taken over by extremists in order to self-destruct several ballistic missiles already en route to the east coast of the US.

In addition to exploiting discourse around terrorism and nuclear proliferation, *Modern Warfare* also shows the start of a trend that, in RMA fashion, demonstrates a strong preference for Special Operations units rather than standard infantry or armored forces. Campaign missions are split between a member of the Marine Special Forces (who dies in combat) and members of an elite British Special Air Service (SAS) commando squad that performs clandestine raids across the Middle East and Russia. Modern weaponry augmented with specialized silencers, scopes, and other accessories as well as modern UAVs and other forms of networked air support give these flexible squads the edge they need to dispatch far more numerous enemy forces.

Modern Warfare also revolutionized the multiplayer experience to include a leveling system that traded players' investment in the game for increased avatar customization. Previously, multiplayer wargames often provided standardized roles from which players could choose. While *Modern Warfare* maintained five standard classes for inexperienced players, one of its most profitable innovations was a leveling system that gradually unlocked weapons and perks as players gained experience points. Rather than using one of the preset classes, players above level five could customize their own loadouts to use better weapons as they earned them and tailor their avatar for their own style of play. This provided additional incentives for players to keep playing and unlock gear that made them more effective killers. *Modern Warfare* also popularized "killstreak" rewards that gave access to performance boosts and sophisticated RMA weapons for killing a certain number of opponents without being killed.

The changes introduced by *Modern Warfare* were dramatic and revolutionary for subsequent wargames. Collectively, the first three *COD* games sold approximately 5.5 million copies, while *Modern Warfare* leapt forward and sold 13.5 million alone. *COD* returned to a World War II scenario the following year with *World at War* and saw their sales drop by 2.5 million, indicating that the context of modern warfare provided something important for wargaming audiences that a historical treatment did not. Integrating customization into the multiplayer leveling system also placed the tools and technologies of the RMA into focus as an important way to incentivize

players and secure their loyalty. Cool guns outfitted with an array of scopes or silencers and each imbued with distinctive characteristics contributed to a growing sense that success in warfare is a matter for high technology to decide. *Modern Warfare* also helped solidify commandos and small tactical units as the primary element for creating an epic war narrative. Not only were commandos in tune with the evolution of the modern military but they also provided a powerful context for character development and allowed players to step into the shoes of a "realistic" supersoldier.

Stepping off from *Modern Warfare*'s successes, two sequels continued the narrative to record sales. *Modern Warfare 2* (2009; 24.5 million sales) and *3* (2011; 29.8 million sales) moved increasingly toward clandestine special operations with the creation of Task Force 141, an elite multinational counterterrorist unit. The sequels feature Russian sneak invasions of the US mainland and Europe, nuclear explosions in Washington, DC, and poison gas attacks throughout Europe. In *Call of Duty*, modern warfare is characterized by the power of asymmetric terrorist threats and shows the impotence of traditional forces in the conduct of this new warfare paradigm.

Battlefield 3 (Electronic Arts 2011; 16.75 million sales), meanwhile, continued in the spirit of the *Modern Warfare* series, exploiting fears of nuclear terrorism as well as showcasing the power of the RMA. The single-player campaign features a small squad of US Marine Special Forces tasked with "finding, fixing, and finishing" an Iranian insurgent group in possession of Russian "suitcase" nukes, one of which is detonated in Paris and the other en route to New York City.

In addition to featuring a similar multiplayer leveling and customization system as the *Modern Warfare* series, *Battlefield 3* also foregrounds an aesthetic that thoroughly evokes the RMA. Loading screens trace the outlines of soldiers and equipment in glowing neon networks and are accompanied by synthy electronic bass lines that seem far more at home in the Disney franchise *Tron* than in military conflict. Objectives and other information appear in the same form throughout the game on your heads-up display (HUD), differentiating teammates and targets within the game environment and providing other useful directions.

Later games in the *Medal of Honor* franchise also attempt to exploit the new American way of war, first in an historical context and later in the near future. *Medal of Honor* (Electronic Arts 2010; 5.82 million sales) is loosely based in Operation Anaconda, one of the first operations in Afghanistan to utilize large numbers of conventional US forces rather than SOF and undoubtedly one of the battles Rumsfeld and McCrystal had in mind when they observed that large footprint styles of warfare weren't going to be as effective for wars of the twenty-first century. Players split their time between operatives of SEAL Team Six conducting stealth raids to great effect and traditional forces that are routinely ambushed by overwhelming insurgent forces. Large-scale tactical maneuvers routinely fail in the game, producing heavy casualties, while commando tactics are held up as an answer.

The game's sequel *Medal of Honor: Warfighter* (Electronic Arts 2012; 2.76 million sales) follows the same group of SEALs out of a declared warzone into the properly "global" war on terror. Now operating under the secretive Joint Special Operations Command (JSOC), the player carries out sabotage operations and hostage rescue missions, conducts night raids, and repeatedly operates in conjunction with foreign Special Forces units in areas as diverse as Pakistan, the Philippines, Bosnia, and Somalia. Largely autonomous from the lumbering military bureaucracy, their lean and flexible forces are able to take down a powerful terrorist network by becoming a network themselves.

Like their World War II predecessors, these rebranded *MOH* games repeatedly emphasize their "authenticity." The evolution of the franchise from World War II to the war on terror was accomplished through a glorification of the most elite Special Forces units. Much is made of so-called "Tier 1 Operatives": members of the most prestigious SOF units like Navy SEAL Team Six (the squad responsible for the high-profile Bin Laden raid) and the Army's DELTA Force. *MOH 2010* paid actual Tier 1 Operatives to consult on the project to lend the narrative credibility, but *Warfighter* went even deeper in its pursuit of authenticity. As the latter's website touts, the narrative was written by "active U.S. Tier 1 Operators while deployed overseas and [was] inspired by real world threats" and promises to connect "gameplay missions with a dotted line to real world incursions" (Electronic Arts 2013). Pursuit of such authenticity, however, proved dangerous and led the seven Navy SEALs involved in the project to receive formal letters of reprimand from superiors for revealing classified information and violating "the unwritten code that SEALs are silent warriors who shun the spotlight," fining them a month's pay and effectively killing their chances at promotion (Martin 2012; Ackerman 2012). Caught between a military culture that relies on secrecy, discipline, and sacrifice, and an entertainment phenomenon that turns them into celebrities, these SEALs exemplify the uneasy balance between the actual military and its circulation as entertainment.

Warfighter's search for authenticity also crossed into troubling territory with merchandising and branding strategies that connect players to real weapons manufacturers in disturbing ways. Since the widespread popularization of wargaming in 2006, in-game weapons have started carrying additional branding that points to their actual manufacturer rather than just a generic model number or fictional name. A .50 caliber sniper rifle therefore becomes a Barrett M82 or an assault rifle becomes a TAR-21 made by Israel Weapon Industries. While such name changes were made to heighten realism, they also open games to legal action under trademark law that wouldn't be the case with fictional names. Real weapons manufacturers now regularly license the representation and brand name of their weapons to game companies in exchange for fees, revenue sharing, or even just promotion and endorsement (Parkin 2013). Such licensing agreements also give manufacturers some control over how their guns are represented both on the level of mechanics and within narratives. Barrett firearms, for example, disallows the use of their weapons by "individuals, organizations, countries or companies that would be shown as enemies of the United States or its citizens," and requires that 3D models "perform to the standards that our rifles do in the real world" (Parkin 2013). Licensing agreements such as these have been increasingly enforced in AAA wargames since 2006, but *Warfighter* takes this branding to a new extreme. In addition to extensive weapon branding, they also feature branded weapon attachments and scopes from a number of manufacturers and, controversially, provided links on their blog where players could purchase real-life weapons from the game (Medal of Honor: Warfighter 2014; Smith 2012).

Another series of franchises integral for naturalizing the tools and technologies of the RMA is distributed by Ubisoft under the moniker of *Tom Clancy*. Successful franchises such as *Ghost Recon* (2001–2014; 16.28 million sales) and *Rainbow Six* (1998; 14.69 million sales) have perhaps most consistently focused on the RMA and the worldviews of the war on terror. Focusing exclusively on small commando squads, these franchises leverage the high technology of the RMA to resolve terrorist threats. *Rainbow Six* features an elite counterterrorism task force called "Rainbow" pitted against highly organized and financed terrorist masterminds attempting to inflict mass causalities through bombings or chemical attacks. Game mechanics place *Rainbow Six* firmly within the sphere of the RMA by leveraging advanced imaging technologies as core game mechanics. Players can easily switch between multiple visualization modes, including night vision, thermal, and sonar vision, each impacting gameplay in its own way and allowing Rainbow to defeat far more numerous foes.

The *Ghost Recon* series displays an even greater affinity for the RMA within the context of fighting terrorism. *Ghost Recon: Advanced Warfighter* (Ubisoft 2006; 1.9 million sales) was one of the earliest tactical wargames to feature the technologies of the Future Combat Systems (FCS) and Objective Force Warrior (OFW) programs under military development. The player is placed in charge of "Ghost Recon," a highly secret group of US Army DELTA Force operatives that specialize in accomplishing controversial missions unseen. Missions unfold throughout Mexico City and foreshadow the urban settings envisioned by US military strategists. Ubisoft's summary of the game echoes the spirit of network-centric warfare in future US Special Forces operations, fully decked out with the technologies of the military's planned Future Combat Systems:

> In 2013, the U.S. Army will implement the Integrated Warfighter System (IWS), evolving what we know as the modern soldier. IWS combines advanced weapon systems, satellite communication devices and enhanced survivability into one fully integrated combat system ... Following an insurgence in the heart of Mexico City, the U.S. Army's most elite Special Forces team is deployed to the center of the conflict to regain control of the city. Greatly outnumbered but fully equipped with the IWS, this elite team is the first and last line of defense on the battlefield ... Using a fully integrated combat system with cutting-edge weapons and revolutionary communication systems, gamers embody the soldier of the future. Based on actual U.S. Army research, the Ghosts give gamers a realistic view of how war will be fought in the next decade. (Ubisoft Entertainment 2005)

To achieve this network-centric style of play, *Ghost Recon* created a communication device called the "Cross-Com," which allowed soldiers to receive visual and auditory feeds from drones and other players and projected it on the soldier's visor.[5] Subsequent games in the franchise bring other futuristic technologies into play, like sensor grenades that automatically tag and track enemies and quadcopter surveillance drones. The increase of situational awareness these RMA tools brings allows for more effective command of your squad and brings domination to the battlefield.

Cyberwarfare and Beyond

As both battlefield and economy have grown increasingly reliant on information networks, attention has been drawn to defending and exploiting computer

A final game that is perhaps one of the most important expressions of the RMA in popular wargaming is COD's *Black Ops II* (Activision 2012; 27.2 million sales). Jumping between the 1980s and 2025, the narrative of *Black Ops II* (*BO2*) presents a stark contrast between pre- and post-RMA warfare: in the '80s you ride on horseback with the mujahideen in Afghanistan blowing up tanks with RPGs and combing the desert with an AK-47; in 2025, you operate high-tech drones, have scopes that give you X-ray vision, and commandeer enemy equipment with a few taps on a combat smartphone. In the future, everything is driven by sophisticated electronics and *BO2* illustrates the danger of this state of affairs even as it simultaneously glorifies it. Dependency on electronics opens the modern world to the cyberattacks of a populist group protesting international inequality and worldwide Navy SEAL raids aim to reestablish order.

While little has been said thus far about cyberwarfare under the RMA, we will turn there now to provide an example of how the appropriation of the RMA in modern wargaming is not benign but rather helps to construct consensus around expectations of future warfare in both popular opinion and in the military. After looking briefly at the discourse surrounding cybersecurity and cyberwar, we will return to *BO2* as an example of how problematic assumptions are amplified through their integration in epic narratives.

systems to maintain or gain strategic advantage. While worries about the security of national networks have been present since the development

Figure 22.2

Call of Duty: Black Ops II: The past and future of war provide a juxtaposition that glorifies the technologies of the RMA.

of the Internet, they reached a fever pitch in 2010. In the Quadrennial Defense Reviews from 1997–2006, the word "cyber" only appears fifteen times and in vague and general terms (1997: zero times; 2001: five; 2006: ten). In QDR 2010, "cyber" appears seventy-three times and forty-five in 2014, indicating a significant shift. QDR 2010 announces the creation of a new military command, the US Cyber Command (USCYBERCOM), to work as a military wing of the NSA to protect and secure DoD networks and critical national infrastructure. While much of the official language surrounding the creation of USCYBERCOM characterized it as defensive in nature, QDR 2010 also vaguely indicates more, saying that the military "will prepare to ... conduct full spectrum cyberspace military operations" in the future (US Department of Defense 38).

In an article justifying USCYBERCOM, then-Deputy Secretary of Defense William Lynn III argued that cyberspace requires special focus. Indeed, in a move typical of discourse around cybersecurity, Lynn conjures "cyber-doom" scenarios that clarify the need for the militarization of cyberspace: "A dozen determined computer programmers," he claims, could "threaten the United States' global logistics network, steal its operational plans, blind its intelligence capabilities, or hinder its ability to deliver weapons on target" (Lynn 2010, 98–99). He then claims that other nations and shadowy hackers know this and are in the process of developing capabilities like these to target not only government computers, but also "critical civilian infrastructure," like "power grids, transportation networks, or financial systems" (100).

Mike McConnell, former NSA Director (1992–1996) and Director of National Intelligence (2007–2009) added to the doom and gloom, claiming in a 2010 op-ed that we are already in the midst of a cyberwar that we are losing. Writing in the aftermath of a cyberwargame simulation called Cyber Shock Wave, where participants brainstormed solutions to an imagined cyberattack that left "40 million people without power; 60 million cellphones out of service; [and] Wall Street closed for a week" (Nakashima 2010), McConnell claims that we are woefully unprepared to defend against cyberwarfare at all: "For all our war games and strategy documents focused on traditional warfare, we have yet to address the most basic questions about cyber-conflicts" (McConnell 2010).

With such dire warnings coming from top defense officials, it is no surprise that cybersecurity has received significant funding since 2010 and is currently one of the strongest growth areas for defense contractors.[6]

But while most discourse around cyberwar has been rationalized through appeals to defensive use, 2010 was also a year that revealed the partial and ideological nature of this story. In 2010, a malicious computer worm called Stuxnet was found targeting industrial control units at the Iranian nuclear facility in Natanz. Developed by the US and Israel under the top secret program Olympic Games (2007–2010), Stuxnet infected computers controlling centrifuges used for enriching Uranium—precisely the type of infrastructural attack that government officials had been warning could happen (Sanger 2012). The worm masqueraded as legitimate software and modified the windows kernel (installed a "rootkit") to prevent detection. In addition to physically damaging over one thousand centrifuges, what makes Stuxnet so impressive is that it managed to infiltrate a facility without any external network connections (it was "air gapped"), giving an air of magic to its accomplishments (Langner 2013).

The successes of Stuxnet showed both the power and threat of cyberweapons and USCYBERCOM was constructed to defend against the world the US military helped create.

Cyberwar and Video Games: Press X to Hack

As hacking has come into focus as a national issue, it has become a central narrative device for television and film. Nearly every TV show dealing with politics, crime, law, or technology now has a resident hacker that can bend the digital to their whim: hacking firewalls, phones, and emails, cracking encryption, and hijacking surveillance systems all happen with little effort. Rather than showing the process of hacking, narratives generally only show the surface effects, the results of their technological wizardry. The hacker is usually a supporting character that is integral to moving the plot forward, but much of what they do is obscured behind an impenetrable wall of technobabble and awkward social skills. Put simply, the hacker is a magician that defies easy identification.[7]

For this reason, the hacker has not found a ready place in much of modern wargaming. While hackers are occasionally supporting NPCs, such as in the Tom Clancy *Splinter Cell* franchise, it is difficult to interpolate the player into the subject position of the hacker—to make *you* become the hacker. One of the first wargames to attempt this within the context of cyberwar and the RMA is *Black Ops II*.[8] *BO2* effects a key transition that subsequent wargames are likely to follow: while previous games offered onscreen tips such as "Press X to Interact," *BO2* began offering "Press X to Hack." By pressing X and tapping a few buttons on your avatar's sleeve, you can open locked containers and doors, activate enemy drones to defend you, or hijack other

enemy equipment. Hacking is easy and ubiquitous in *BO2*.

In addition to small game mechanics like this, the campaign narrative of *BO2* engages deeply with cyber-doom scenarios that echo those of government officials. The primary antagonist of *BO2* is Raul Menendez, a charismatic yet largely anonymous leader of an international populist movement against economic inequality. Menendez launches a false flag cyberattack against Chinese financial institutions for which the United States receives blame. In response, the Chinese prepare for war and cut off supply of rare earth minerals to the United States—a serious problem since US military might is reliant on drones and high-tech weapons that require these resources. Menendez then develops some sort of quantum computing device that is so powerful that it can break all encryption in an instant. Using this, he takes control over the entire US drone fleet and sends it to attack US cities. After wreaking havoc and killing many, Menendez eventually turns the drone fleet against itself, destroying it in a populist gesture of restoring a level playing field.

BO2 grapples with the danger of becoming too dependent on the technical developments of the RMA. In some levels, you orchestrate defense with fully autonomous killing machines that can distinguish good guys from bad. In others, you are tasked with destroying these same machines as they are turned against you. Such folded narratives are endemic to the network society as it enables the flow of power, yet amplifies the possibility and potency of disruption. As Activision itself experienced while marketing *BO2*, control in the network society can so easily turn into its opposite. Recall that in the docu-trailer we reference at the opening of this chapter, Activision flashes the Guy Fawkes mask that has become a symbol of the hacktivist community Anonymous as an example of cyberterrorism. Offended at the comparison, Anonymous promptly launched #OpActivision in response, threatening to overwhelm game servers with junk Internet traffic when the game launched and eventually leaking personal information on Activision CEO Eric Hirshberg with a note claiming, "We are not the enemy but, well you want it you got it [*sic*]" (Yoder 2012). As a story of the difficulties of control in the network age, this seems only fitting.

The Fantasy of Absolute Access and the Future of Cyberwarfare

With *BO2*, cyberwarfare comes front and center in a ludic form that equates it with magical powers. Combined with the cyber-doom scenarios that plague cyberdiscourse, these magical powers craft a formidably pessimistic mythology around the kinds of security we can expect from digital systems. In 2014, for the second year in a row, Director of National Intelligence James Clapper testified before Congress that hackers are the greatest threat facing the nation—a threat greater than global terrorism or the proliferation of weapons of mass destruction (Mazzetti 2014). When hackers are framed as sha-mans who can conjure the keys to digital systems with the press of a button, certain solutions like mass surveillance and militaristic deterrence rise to the top while the fundamental problem—poor programming—remains.

This fantasy of absolute access underpinning both political and media representations of hacking also obscures how difficult real hacking is—something the military has observed acutely when trying to develop their own cyber capabilities. When NATO forces con-sidered launching cyberattacks to disrupt Libyan air defense systems in 2011, they estimated it would have taken a team of programmers at least a year to design an effective cyberweapon (Nakashima 2012). To close the development gap between traditional and cyberweapons, the DoD created a new DARPA program called "Plan X" in 2011 and gave them $110 million to develop foundational strategies and capa-bilities for the conduct of cyberwarfare. While the program is not directly tasked with creating offen-sive cyberweapons, its goal is to make the conduct of cyberwarfare as easy as its representation in TV and video games.

The first step in this process is to develop plat-forms that allow officers to conduct cyberwar with-out requiring sophisticated technical knowledge about networks and computer systems. As project creator Dan Roelker puts it, "Say you're playing *World of Warcraft*, and you've got this type of sword, +5 or whatever. You don't necessarily know what spells were used to create that sword, right? You just know it has these attributes and it helps you in this way. It's the same type of concept. You don't need the techni-cal details" (Shachtman 2013).

In order to translate the technical details into a form that can be utilized by nonspecialists, DARPA turned to Frog Design, an interface design firm that worked on past design projects like the Sony Walkman and the Apple IIc, for a prototype interface for this cyberwarfare platform for dummies. The prototype runs on a Samsung SUR40 Touch Table, what *Wired* calls "a kind of 40-inch, multi-person iPad" (ibid.), and features intuitive visualization of network topology and information flow, and touch-based targeting and weapon deployment. Massive Black, a conceptual art studio that has worked on gaming projects ranging from *BioShock* (2007) and *League of Legends* (2009) to *Risen 2: Dark Waters* (2012) has also been contracted for interface design. Under their guidance, a weapon interface was designed as a playbook "like Madden Football. You might have a running play, a passing play, a fake ..." Since much of network conflict involves running the same programs repetitiously, they aim to "build a template and then just allow a planner to look through all the different plays they have" to simplify the process (ibid.). Each weapon features an easily recognizable icon and indicates the risk and power associated with its use. Every time an exploit is used, it reduces the effectiveness of that exploit in the future, so weapons are ranked and categorized according to the investment in them to allow operators to weigh the potential risk against the potential gain. Selecting a "play" instructs a computer to begin compiling the exploit for the targeted system and you can fire when ready.

While this interface could allow for more intuitive conduct of cyberwarfare, it also only addresses one half of the puzzle. Cyberweapons are only effective if you know where to point them. A second dimension to Plan X is the development of network mapping tools to categorize access points and vulnerable systems worldwide. These maps will indicate which exploits will work and where. The trouble with such a map is that it must be constantly updated. If Microsoft pushes out a Windows update that seals a critical vulnerability, these tools must be able to constantly provide updated information without alerting the target that they are under attack.

At the time it was demonstrated to the press in 2013, Plan X was more of a video game than a cyberwarfare platform: it was just an interface that displayed fake information and didn't actually weaponize anything. Since then, however, defense heavyweights like Raytheon and Northrop Grumman, along with smaller companies like Data Tactics, Intific, Apogee Research, and Aptima have received nearly $74 million in contracts.[9] With this kind of power and money behind it, Plan X may ultimately succeed in making "Press X to Hack" a reality.

The folly of such pursuits only becomes evident when we break through the rhetoric of cyber-doom scenarios and jettison the mythology that hackers are already magicians with access to anything digital. Rather than the biggest threat to Western society, the magical hacker is a projection of the US government's own desires. We now know that the US government is the largest investor in the market for unreported computer vulnerabilities ("zero-day exploits"). Rather than incentivizing researchers or hackers to disclose these vulnerabilities to vendors so that software flaws can be patched, governments worldwide are purchasing them for hundreds of thousands of dollars and hoarding them for offensive use (Menn 2013).

What gets lost in this militarization of cyberspace is the circulation of alternative solutions to the problem of cybersecurity that are not merely more of the same. Under the reins of the military, even cyberdefense sounds an awful lot like cyberoffense.

Defensive strategies of preemptive attack, global surveillance, and deterrence-based legal regimes obscure the fact that the real problem is primarily one of poor programming or uninformed users. Instead of spending millions on exploits, the government could be funding development of open-source software to help make computers more secure rather than less secure. The government could also launch digital literacy campaigns to help people realize that they shouldn't click on strange links or wire money to that promising Nigerian prince. But such simple and effective solutions eliminate a strategic cyber-advantage and fail to stimulate the burgeoning economy around cybersecurity the same way that billions of dollars in defense contracts do. Such alternative solutions, if they come at all, could empower users to take their security and privacy into their own hands rather than placing it trustingly in a militarized overclass of cyberwarriors.

RMA Futures and the Naturalization of Constant Warfare

Belief in the inevitability of conflict can become one of its main causes.
—Donald Rumsfeld, in Errol Morris, "The Certainty of Donald Rumsfeld"

While much of the RMA seems like common sense fiscally, technologically, politically, and strategically, it also gestures toward a future in which warfare becomes a constant reality void of any particular meaning. James Der Derian coined the phrase "virtuous war" to capture the sentiment that the increasing virtualization of warfare acquires the character of virtue in US public discourse. Keeping our troops out of danger through virtual mediation—whether through training them in high-tech simulators or placing them behind the joysticks of a UAV—shapes public perception of the morality of warfare far more than the violence with which warfare is conducted (Der Derian 2009). Taken to the extreme, however, the virtualization of the RMA might introduce more problems than it solves and could turn virtuous war into its opposite. In their early analysis of the costs and benefits of the RMA, Metz and Kievit point to the possible negative effects of technologized war on traditional core values of the military:

> The second order effects of the RMA ... warrant additional study. It is possible, for instance, that the RMA might lead to methods of warfighting incompatible with the ethos and tradition of the U.S. military. One example concerns training ... [if] all training becomes simulation or wargaming, can armed forces still be disciplined and bonded into effective units? Will they need to be? The answer to both questions may be "no." In fact, if warfighting is done from a computer terminal, it may not be necessary to have distinct military forces instilled with discipline and personal bravery. In any case, the implications of this should be explored before the point of no return. (Metz and Kievit 1995, 27–28)

Metz and Kievit recommend consideration of Orson Scott Card's novel *Ender's Game* for a valuable perspective on these issues.

A second conflict the RMA raises for military values cuts to the foundation of what it means to show valor and sacrifice. In February 2013, the military unveiled a new award, the Distinguished Warfare

Medal (DWM) to recognize people who made "extraordinary" contributions during combat operations. Eligibility for the DWM did not require that this contribution involve personal valor or sacrifice or even proximity to the area of conflict. Drone pilots and cyberwarriors who made a considerable impact on the war effort were therefore eligible along with traditional military forces. Critics from both political parties immediately revolted, claiming that placing people who conduct war from a distance and soldiers on the front lines in the same category was disrespectful to the sacrifices, dangers, and valorous efforts of real soldiers. Other critics argued that rewarding drone pilots and cyberwarriors with commendations obscures the morally questionable character of the type of war they conduct. As a result, only two months after it was announced, the DWM was scrapped (Lexington 2014). A significant ideological divide must therefore be crossed before virtual soldiers are seen with the same reverence as their predecessors. Since the virtue and sacrifice of the soldier are central to wargaming narratives as well, it will likely be quite some time before cyberwarriors form compelling protagonists.

A third issue that the RMA raises—perhaps the most important—is that war itself becomes less targeted and starts expanding rather than dissipating. As technologies like UAVs, techniques like cyberwarfare, and groups like Special Forces reduce the risks of conducting war, finding peace becomes increasingly difficult. Not only is warfare becoming too easy to conduct on a continual basis, it also increasingly takes on the character of policing rather than specific military interventions with determinable objectives.

Amid a widely publicized military pivot toward Asia, US forces have been slowly spidering southward into Africa as well. Since 9/11, the US military has been involved in forty-nine of the fifty-four nations in Africa, constructing facilities and bases, developing logistics infrastructure, training militias, and building alliances (Turse 2014). According to the Congressional Research Service, the United States has spent $2.2 billion from 2006 to 2014 training and equipping foreign services in forty different countries to carry out the war on terror in our stead. These proxy conflicts are often guided by Special Operations Forces and some receive continuing Pentagon support in the form of intelligence and logistics (Schmitt 2014). As the war on terror becomes increasingly global and dispersed, the United States is increasingly finding others to fight and die for its national objectives, all the while maintaining the illusion that the new American way of war is actually one of peace and stability.

As war is outsourced to proxies, is dissolved into bits of information, and is conducted from a distance via remote control, we start losing sight of why we are still at war. In an interview following his retirement as the nation's longest-serving Director of the NSA, General Keith Alexander made a startling claim: despite over a decade spent fighting the war on terror, the number of worldwide terrorist attacks is only growing. According to the START Program at the University of Maryland, the number of terrorist attacks grew from 6,771 (causing more than 10,000 casualties) in 2012 to over 10,000 (causing more than 20,000 casualties) in 2013 (Schwartz 2014). War, it seems, has become a perpetual-motion machine that simultaneously generates the conditions that justify it: a war against terror generates more terrorists, defense against cyberwar requires the constant conduct of cyberwar, and steps toward peace are seen as a road map to war. All roads lead down the same path.

A recent bipartisan analysis of the US UAV program raises the danger that targeted killings and cross-border raids may raise the prospect of a war without end. The study warns that "the increasing use of lethal UAVs may create a slippery slope leading to continual or wider wars" because the "seemingly low-risk and low-cost missions enabled by UAV technologies may encourage the United States to fly such missions more often, pursuing targets with UAVs that would be deemed not worth pursuing if manned aircraft or special operations forces had to be put at risk" (Stimson Center 2014, 31). The same can be said for the turn away from large-scale land invasions to targeted special operations incursions and the use of cyberwarfare. These transformations expand war significantly from an exceptional circumstance that is legally declared and regionally bounded to one that is diffuse, global, and without regard for territorial sovereignty. As these techniques become standard practice in the militaries of the future, non-Western regimes will no doubt adopt these precedents as justification, predictably arousing outrage and declarations of war in response. Again, overly burdened to imagine a future of peace, war brings about its future realization.

As Iraq once again descends into civil war and defense officials warn the public to prepare for another *two decades of war* (Page 2014), the virtuousness of war is eroding into a state of apathy and malaise. Wars under the RMA remain virtuous so long as we can remember what we are fighting for, but this war has been going on for so long and with such questionable gains that the importance of fighting has long lost focus. Wargames, for better or worse, try to remind us why we fight. They force us to confront the most extreme projections circulated by the military-industrial complex and petition us to defeat them, all while rewarding us with money and points for killing wave after wave of people that, for some reason, deserve it. Wargames from 2006 to the present—and certainly into the future—popularize the prospect of this new American way of war by making it interactive and cool, yet the banality that haunts the war on terror also stalks wargaming. As first-person shooters imagine all kinds of new technology with which to kill, nearly no thought is spent on providing game mechanics to deescalate conflict. The ability to disable or capture enemies is displaced in favor of headshots and multi-kills with awesomely lethal weapons. The banality of wargaming again rears its head in the popularization of multiplayer deathmatch modes that strip out even the geopolitical rationale for conflict and turn fighting into a sport, conducted only for reasons of competition and, if you are good enough, domination.

As wargames increasingly engage military capabilities of the future, they also premediate and naturalize expectations for future investments. As Peter Singer mentions in an interview about his role advising on *Black Ops II*,

> There is no one definitive future. There are a multitude, an infinity of potential futures that might happen. There's the goal of identifying trends that are happening right now that will shape the future. ... One of the main pathways is that science fiction creates the expectations that shape that world. ... These games are incredibly popular, particularly among young teens, but also those already serving in the military. This isn't a predictor of the future, but one of the things that will help shape people's expectations about what kind of technology might be available and "might be" quickly becomes "should be." (Snider 2012)

This shift in expectations from "might be" to "should be" is the productive side of premediation. Just as the representation of hacking in entertainment heavily inflected the goals and desires of DARPA in creating Plan X, so too will the wargames of tomorrow frame discourse around military strategy, tactics, and investments. Thus, we leave off with a challenge and a call: If our wargames cannot imagine peace, what should we expect of our future military?

Perhaps the RMA and war on terror will save lives in the long run. But perhaps how to save virtuous American lives is the wrong question. A better question might be: can the RMA and modern wargaming bring about peace? Maybe the conduct of warfare shouldn't become easier while the cultivation of peace remains so hard. In our view wargames can bring about both futures. On the one hand, like current wargames they can celebrate military violence for its own sake. Or it might just be possible to create wargames that can complicate, contextualize, or challenge the new American way of war, effectively situating it in a critical, more reflective mode. The latter approach offers great potential for challenging the otherwise inevitable militarism of the future.

About the Authors

Luke Caldwell is a PhD candidate in the Program in Literature at Duke University and a Beinecke scholar. His work examines the naturalization of cyber and information warfare under digital capitalism and contemporary manifestations of the military-entertainment complex.

Tim Lenoir is University Professor and the Kimberly Jenkins Chair for New Technologies in Society at Duke University. He holds appointments in Art, Art History & Visual Studies, Computer Science, and the Literature Program. Lenoir is faculty director for the Program in Information Science + Information Studies (ISIS), and he is codirector of the GreaterThanGames humanities lab at Duke, a multidisciplinary lab focusing on the development of transmedia alternate reality games. He has published in the area of science and media studies and designed *Virtual Peace: Turning Swords to Ploughshares* <www.virtualpeace.org> in 2009–2010, a training and simulation game-based learning environment for workers and students in the field of peace and conflict resolution; and with students from the GreaterThanGames lab he has recently developed an app for Android and iPhone for CPR instruction and emergency response for the Duke Heart Center.

Notes

1. For example, Metz and Kievit summarize one of the goals of RMA analysts as "providing a blueprint for technology acquisition and force reorganization" (1995, vi).

2. Unless otherwise specified, game sales statistics were gathered from VGChartz (2014).

3. While science fiction shooters like the *Halo* series (Microsoft Game Studios) could be seen as proto-RMA wargames, their fantasy context leads us to exclude them from our definition of popular wargames.

4. *Spec Ops: The Line* (2K Games 2012) is a great example of the violation of this tenet to make a critical argument about the banality of interventionism. As the player moves further into the game, it becomes apparent that the only reason for continuing is to make sense of the violence already committed—despite the fact that these reasons only evaporate at an ever-increasing pace.

5. Technology like this was reportedly used by SEAL Team Six during the Bin Laden raid, to great effect (Ackerman 2011; Trimble 2011).

6. The government is estimated to spend between $13 and 14 billion for cybersecurity in 2014 alone and this number is projected to rise 7.6 percent compounded annually (Slye 2012; Sternstein 2013). The military investment in USCYBERCOM has also followed this trend, despite significant budget reductions. When USCYBERCOM was created in 2010, it was initially staffed with nine hundred soldiers and support staff and funded to the tune of $120 million. Four years later, it has grown 500 percent to 4,900 people and their budget has increased to over $500 million (Garamone 2010; Fryer-Biggs 2014).

7. See, for example, Abby and McGee from *NCIS*, Huck from *Scandal*, or Finch from *Person of Interest*.

8. Earlier hacking games that do not engage with the modern idea of cyberwarfare have been skipped over here, but have been highly influential nonetheless. Games like Introversion Software's *Uplink: Hacker Elite* (2003) and the many mods that followed in its wake created the genre of "hacking simulators," but these remain distinct from the militaristic use of information warfare under the RMA.

9. Since receiving these contracts in mid-2013, Data Tactics has been acquired by L-3 and Intific by Cubic Corporation, both defense giants looking to expand their cyber expertise.

23 CREATING *PERSIAN INCURSION*

Larry Bond

One of the most important foreign policy issues of the Middle East concerns the possible existence of an Iranian nuclear weapons program. Given the drumbeat of statements from Iranian officials like President Ahmadinejad threatening to destroy Israel, the Israelis have every right to be concerned.

Israel might try to use military means to remove the Iranian nuclear weapons capability, triggering certain retaliation by Iran. Thus, logic demands that the Israelis act preemptively, before Iran could respond with an atomic weapon. Educated opinion predicts that such an attack would take the form of airstrikes on critical nuclear installations.

Can the Israelis mount such an attack? Would it be successful? How could the Iranians retaliate? What would the political effects be, not only on the belligerents, but on their supporters and the rest of the world?

The Goal

I first suggested the idea of a game exploring the Israel-Iran issue in the summer of 2009 to my publisher at Clash of Arms, Ed Wimble. Ed was enthusiastic about the idea, as was my coauthor, Chris Carlson. We added a third designer, Jeff Dougherty, to the team, because we believed his expertise would help in modeling the political issues in the game. All three of us agreed completely on the basic concept.

Persian Incursion (2010) would not consider whether Israel should attack, or under what conditions they might decide it was necessary. The starting premise was that the Israeli leadership had already made the decision and had ordered the IAF to execute an air campaign against Iran.

Our goal was not to find out whether such a strike was justified. The game limited its scope to exploring the complex question of how such an attack might be carried out and its military and political effects, and that was quite enough to take on.

Although we use the term "game," it was not play-balanced so that each side had an equal chance of winning. Instead, we wanted a tool that allowed the players to "bang the rocks together" and find out what happens. We did not expect the simulation to show whether an attack would succeed or fail. It was hoped, through repeated plays, to discover any dominant factors in the conflict. Since the Israeli and Iranian leaderships were asking the same questions in the real world, presumably those factors were foremost in their thinking about the issue.

The Start

We envisioned an Israeli campaign to destroy the Iranian nuclear program as operating on two levels simultaneously: military and political. While any military campaign would be relatively short, it would not be a single strike like the Israeli raid on Iraq in 1981 or Syria in 2007. The target set was just too large.

Even if the first airstrike was a resounding success, within twenty-four hours Iran's leadership would call out to the world community for support and sanctions against the Israelis. Some countries would be more than willing to offer the Iranians different levels of support. Even the United Nations (UN), which has criticized the Iranians for their lack of compliance with nuclear safeguards, would have to acknowledge that in this case, the Israelis were the aggressors. We decided that in addition to the two players, the other countries that could influence the conflict and the UN would be represented as nonplayer actors.

We could model the airstrikes and the defenses using *Harpoon*, a modern tactical wargame Chris Carlson and I created, first published in 1981 and now in its fourth edition. Designed to be played manually with naval miniatures or counters, each player takes on the role of a formation commander controlling the actions of surface ships, aircraft, and submarines.

Development began in 2008 and continued until publication in the summer of 2010. It was designed as a standard two-sided game, and while the format began as a miniatures supplement, it morphed several times until it became a board game using both counters and cards.

While the first edition covered hypothetical North Atlantic Treaty Organization (NATO) and Warsaw Pact conflicts, the Falklands War, which happened shortly after the first edition was published, showed that the game could be adapted to cover modern naval combat in any part of the world. Published supplements now cover not only the Falklands, but hypothetical actions in the Pacific, as well as Cold War scenarios. At the time development on *Persian Incursion* began, the *Harpoon* systems annexes included data on over one thousand different ship and sub classes, hundreds of aircraft types, and all their associated sensors and weapons. Mature and full-featured, *Harpoon* had the data and rules needed to create scenarios simulating Israeli airstrikes on different targets in Iran, as well as other military actions by both sides that might be part of the conflict.

The political modeling would be addressed using a card game. For this purpose, we recruited Jeff Dougherty, an experienced designer who had created other card-based wargames. (Jeff also made many contributions to other parts of the game; it is fair to say that the three designers each created 60 percent of the final product.)

So that the players could take political as well as military actions, we created a card deck with actions and events drawn from many other conflicts. These could be actions taken by the player, such as an appeal to the UN, or an espionage operation, or they could be random events like a scandal. The cards were drawn and laid out in a moving "river" that constantly changed from one turn to the next, modeling both the randomness and ephemeral nature of a political opportunity. Each turn the players could spend accumulated points to use one or more of the cards. The results of the cards were also points that could be used to influence the countries that were involved in the game, or the players' own populations.

Our first challenge was to integrate these two different formats. It was understood that the military strikes could not decide the issue alone. The outcome would have to be decided in the political arena. That meant the results of the airstrikes had to be transferred to the political arena.

We had already decided that support from the other countries to the two belligerents would be modeled using military, intelligence, and political points. These represented resources either accumulated by the two players or provided by other countries to the players. The points could be used by the players to take different actions in the game. The number and type of points given to Israel and Iran would vary depending on each country's level of support. The airstrikes would also generate political points for the players.

Analysis and Initial Discoveries

As we gathered information and began the mission planning for the Israeli airstrikes, geography showed us how closely tied together the political and military aspects of the game would be.

Israel has no common border with Iran, so the Israeli Air Force (IAF) would have to overfly either Turkey, Iraq, or Saudi Arabia to reach its target—or more properly, targets. The overflight would not be a solitary event. Postulating a one-week campaign, not only would combat planes be flying the route every day, but aerial tankers and possibly combat search and rescue missions to recover downed pilots would also be using the same airspace. And what about damaged Israeli aircraft? Could they divert to fields along their flight path if they couldn't make it all the way back to their home base?

Israel would have to essentially rent an air corridor for at least a week over one of these three Muslim countries or the campaign wouldn't happen. That had to be included in the game's setup.

We modeled the different nonplayer countries (Saudi Arabia, Turkey, Jordan, Russia, China, and the United States, along with the United Nations) using "attitude tracks" that showed their level of affiliation/support for one side or the other. These were all the countries that could directly affect the conflict by supporting or restraining the players' cause. At the start of the game, each county would have a value, expressed as a number between 10 (for Israel) and –10 (for Iran). The "attitude values" for each country would be provided in sets, reflecting different political scenarios. These sets would include Israel coming to an accommodation with each of the three countries, as well as other political situations. The players could also create their own mutually agreed-on starting set.

Another big issue was the uncertainty of much of the information we found. While a surprising amount of material about orders of battle and capabilities was available, rumored arms sales were mixed with propaganda and speculation. Had the Iranians purchased modern Pantsir SAM systems from the Russians through Syria? That would represent a significant increase in Iranian short-range air defenses. We knew which mark of GBU precision-guided bomb the Israelis had purchased from the United States—the GBU-28B—but what if they also secretly bought the newer GBU-28C, in anticipation of the campaign? Having greater penetrating power, it would halve the number of bombs that would have to be dropped to destroy the underground enrichment halls at Natanz. The Israelis have done that type of thing in the past.

Writing fiction (*Red Phoenix*, *Dangerous Ground*, *Shattered Trident*, etc.) has taught me a few tricks that authors like to use. If your plot has a problem with no clear answer, write it into the story. Instead of trying to decide which rumors were true, we gave the players points at the start of the game that could be spent on different upgrades to their forces. Some were real-world rumors of weapons sales; others were actions each side might reasonably take in anticipation of a conflict.

Allowing for a variable setup in both the political and military aspects not only resolved the problem of uncertain information, but it also kept the game from being dated too quickly. Obviously the political situation would change, probably as soon as the game went to press. Players could create their own sets of political attitudes for each country; they could also add new "upgrades" as new rumors appeared or existing ones were confirmed or debunked.

It would also further the exploratory purpose of the game, as players tested different combinations of political and military situations. By using different political and military setups, they could determine which factors dominated the conflict in many or even most cases.

Finishing the Design

Initially, we considered every possible action that each side might take, and made sure that the game included the rules the players would need to perform them. As we worked with the design, we discovered several actions that did not need to be included and removed them from the game.

For example, the principal Iranian military threat to Israel comes from Iran's ballistic missiles. The Iranians have a large number and are experienced in their use from the Iran-Iraq war. Israeli aircraft could try to destroy these missiles and their launchers. This would remove them as potential carriers of a nuclear weapon or, if Iran started using conventionally armed missiles during the air campaign, reduce the number of missiles reaching Israeli targets.

In addition to researching the Iranian missile order of battle, we looked at Coalition "Scud hunting" results during the first Gulf War. The results were not encouraging: only forty-one of the many launches were actually spotted, and of those, only eight (20 percent) were converted into a kill—and this was after the missile had been launched. While Iran doesn't have an infinite number of transporter-erector-launchers, killing them one at a time after a launch was not attractive. The coalition also had many advantages Israel would not; Israel would be working at arm's length, without the advantage of overhead E-3 and JSTARS radar surveillance.

Striking the missile magazines was out of the question. Each of the missile brigades had more than a hundred hardened shelters for their weapons. Even with perfect weapon performance, it would take several squadrons just to make a dent in one storage area. Better to destroy the ability, and desire, to make a nuclear bomb.

Other player options we considered and discarded included Iranian ballistic missiles with "dirty" or CBW warheads, Israeli ballistic missiles armed with conventional instead of nuclear warheads, and a long-range one-way Iranian retaliatory airstrike against an Israeli city. Dirty bombs would not have the destructive effects of a nuclear weapon but would have risked Israeli nuclear retaliation. Israeli ballistic missiles with conventional warheads didn't have enough destructive capability to effectively destroy the Iranian nuclear facilities, and the Iranian one-way airstrike was not only judged unlikely, but it also would be annihilated long before it reached any target in Israeli territory. It would be seen as a political loss for Iran, a demonstration of its military ineffectiveness.

While we allowed the Iranians to attempt to "close the straits of Hormuz," as they have threatened to do, we abstracted the process, concentrating not on the means or military results but on the political effects, which was after all, Iran's goal. Simulating the actual closing of the straits with missiles or air attacks would require a game of its own, with no connection to the air campaign, and its effect on the political situation could be described simply as either resulting in international pressure on Israel to stop its air campaign (the Iranian goal), or international backlash against Iran for its attacks on merchant ships (which is what happened the last time they tried it in 1987, during the Iran-Iraq war). It might even pull the United States and other countries into the war on the Israeli side.

We also added more variability to the game by giving the Israeli player an additional strategic option, striking Iran's oil industry. In spite of strenuous efforts to diversify its economy, Iran's primary source of foreign income is oil. Its arms, purchased from China, North Korea, and Russia, are paid for with oil or oil money. Iran also has a modern industrial society that depends on oil to run. And it is vulnerable. Iran has still not repaired all the damage its oil industry suffered during the Iran-Iraq war. With foreign technical assistance gone after the 1979 revolution, Iran has had to learn new skills or buy them abroad. Although an oil producer and exporter, Iran still has to import refined products.

We added refineries and oil terminals to the target set, along with their defenses, which were much weaker than those around the nuclear facilities. We developed simple criteria for determining if the Iranian economy had reached the breaking point, at which point they would sue for peace.

Winning the War

After many discussions, we also arrived at the all-important victory conditions for an air campaign against the nuclear facilities. After all, if the Israelis level the Natanz enrichment facility or the Arak heavy water reactor, or anything else, the Iranians can just rebuild. It may even be easier to build and better than before because they now have the experience and expertise from constructing the first one.

What the Israelis must do is convince Iran's leaders that they will never be able to finish the bomb. Iran has gone to amazing lengths to construct a nuclear weapon, suffering international sanctions that are adversely affecting its economy, and spending precious money and talent that could have been used, for instance, to recapitalize its still-crippled oil industry.

Our analysis and common wisdom, confirmed by early playtests, showed that the IAF could destroy any part of the nuclear infrastructure and that the Iranian air defense system could at best hope to knock down a couple of aircraft, if its operators were smart and lucky. But that might be enough.

In an air campaign against Iran, expectations would set the bar for the Israelis very high. Of course, they could blow up any part of Iran they could reach. The question was, what price would they pay in lost aircraft and pilots? In our game, those losses were translated into political points for the Iranians. If the price was too high, Israel could flatten every nuclear facility in Iran and still be the loser.

In short, Israel not only had to win, but win big, and win easily. They had to demonstrate that they could not only destroy any installation that Iran built, but that they could come back and do it again, any time they wanted, and Iran couldn't do a thing to stop them.

The precision-guided bombs on Israeli aircraft were really aimed at the minds of the Iranian Supreme Leader and the rest of the leadership. After spending all that time and talent, they had to look at the smoking craters and say, "There's no future in this." That doesn't mean that the Iranians will change their attitude—just that they won't try to build a nuclear weapon, which is the narrowly defined goal of the Israeli campaign.

Unless the Iranians came to that conclusion, unless they were convinced that the time and treasure invested on developing a nuclear weapon was a complete waste, the Israeli air campaign would fail. In contrast to the Israeli necessity to win big, all the Iranians had to do was not lose.

After Publication

Persian Incursion was published in the summer of 2010 and consisted of a box containing a forty-seven-page rules booklet, a forty-three-page briefing booklet, a thirty-seven-page booklet called "Target Folders," a 22″ × 17″ map, two decks of fifty-five political cards each for the two players, cardboard counters, aircraft data cards, and dice. In addition, we produced a sample rules booklet as a PDF available for free download.

The game was well received both by the gaming and the professional community. It was reviewed by the magazine *Foreign Policy*, and more recently *The Economist*. The response from people in the professional "pol-mil" community was mixed. They liked the game and were interested in playing, but they often had no background in air warfare. They understood that allocating resources (aircraft) to different targets was important, but some wanted the resolution of the attacks abstracted even more than the simplified combat and damage rules we had adapted from *Harpoon*.

To support these requests, we created two different products. The Quickstrike rules allowed players to run the air missions as before, but they resolved the actual weapon drops more quickly. A set of even more simplified strike rules appeared later, designed for people who found the airstrike planning process too daunting or time-consuming.

The military community saw the game primarily as a training tool. For example, *Persian Incursion* was tested by the Army War College as a vehicle for teaching the staff planning process. They concentrated on the military part of the game, with the players responsible for organizing and executing airstrikes, like a real-world air staff. We produced an expanded damage form and a summary of Iranian SAM sites to support the military community's interest. All of these supplements are available for free download at the Admiralty Trilogy Group website.

All three designers have been gratified by the reception the game has received. It not only serves as a validation of our work, but it also encourages us to continue to support and update the game. The April 2014 issue of *The Naval SITREP* includes an article by Jeff Dougherty updating the game, and we intend to produce a second edition of *Persian Incursion* that will not only include the most current data but will also address the interests of the different professional communities.

It also encourages us to look for other places or situations where this political-military hybrid model could be applied. Political factors have always been a part of, and the most important part of, warfare, but in this age of high-speed and high-density communications, the political factors appear when the war starts, not just at the truce table.

About the Author

After earning a bachelor's degree in quantitative methods, Larry Bond worked as a computer programmer for two years before being selected for Officer Candidate School in Newport, Rhode Island. He served as a surface warfare officer in the US Navy until 1982, then worked as a naval analyst for defense consulting firms. He coauthored *Red Storm Rising* with Tom Clancy and has teamed with several different authors to write eighteen novels: five with Pat Larkin, starting with *Red Phoenix*; eight with Jim deFelice, *The First Team* and *Red Dragon Rising* series; six with Chris Carlson, including the Jerry Mitchell series; and his latest book, *Lash-Up*. Five of these have been *New York Times* bestsellers. He has also codesigned the Admiralty Trilogy series games, which include *Harpoon*, *Command at Sea*, and *Fear God & Dread Nought*. All three have won industry awards. He now writes and designs games full-time. His website is <www.larrybond.com>.

24 MODELING THE SECOND BATTLE OF FALLUJAH

Laurent Closier

Phantom Fury (2011) is a tactical simulation of the battles that took place in Fallujah, Iraq, at the beginning of November 2004. Generally speaking, wargames based on contemporary conflicts are rather rare because their designers are confronted by many constraints, such as the difficulty of finding trustworthy sources on the succession of events, the actual effectiveness of combat tactics and equipment (weapons, C4I, etc.), the fact that those who participated in the conflict may still be alive, the integration (or not) of ethical considerations in their design choices, or anticipating that the audience's (players') reaction will discredit a game that goes off the beaten path even before it is published.

Choosing this battle for my first wargame as a designer was not a matter of vanity or provocation, but simply because the opportunity presented itself. By the simple grace of my professional reading, I discovered the article "Lessons Learned: Infantry Squad Tactics in Military Operations in Urban Terrain During Operation Phantom Fury in Fallujah, Iraq," published in the *Marine Corps Gazette* in September 2005 (Catagnus et al. 2005). Within these pages, every aspect necessary for creating a simulation was placed at my fingertips. All that was left was to transcribe them as a list of rules. It was the beginning of a long journey that would last nearly two years.

First Objective: Publication

From the beginning, I worked on my game with the hopes of publishing it. Therefore, it was out of the question to make it a two-player game, especially given the fact that three-quarters of the potential buyers/players would be American, some of whom may have even been veterans of the Iraq War. For me, it was unthinkable to propose that they "kill" their cardboard comrades. From there came the first important design decision: It would be a solitaire game. The strategic level and the abstraction of a game such as *Labyrinth* (2010) make playing the jihadist side "comfortable." But *Phantom Fury* would not have the same feel, given the tactical perspective and the pathos it could engender. The tactical scale also allows the players to more easily identify with the troops they manipulate, reinforcing the immersive aspect of the game and attaining the same extreme nature as FPS (first-person shooter) and TPS (third-person shooter) video games. I had to be sure that my approach to the battle, and its translation in terms of a game system, would not offend. The very nature of war-themed board games reassured me that *Phantom Fury* would be nothing like *Six Days in Fallujah*. That type of game, like other FPS/TPS, provokes an instinctive approach by stimulating the player's senses through shocking images and an up-tempo soundtrack. But nobody reads a twenty-page rulebook before turning on their game console. The rules of a wargame clarify the designer's thought process as well as the relation between cause and effect resulting from players' choices. Players will then be more likely to accept the game if they understand, even if they do not share, the designer's point of view. While gradually designing *Phantom Fury*, I decided that war-themed board games could address any conflict in history, even those that are the most delicate from an ethical or moral standpoint. *Liberia: Descent into Hell* (2008) is an example of such a board game.

The moral aspect can also appear when it comes to the question of managing the wounded. It is a major factor in modern combat, but it is rarely simulated in board games. Choosing to represent wounded soldiers with a game piece (before they have been evacuated from the battlefield), makes them potential targets just like the active soldiers. Therefore, leaving it up to the player—or the game system in the case of a solitaire game—to deliberately attack the wounded could add tension to the game.

Publication means production. Initially, the game board was randomly built with thick cardboard tiles to create a surface of four lines and six columns, each tile representing a specific form of terrain

(urban, dense urban, mosques, suburbs, industrial areas, ambiguous landscapes) with many locations (courtyards, the ground floor, additional floors), as would be the case in the final version. From a design perspective, it was an easy choice to make. The use of abstract levels for each zone flowed naturally from the historical sources. The player would then choose a scenario, which indicated the construction of the game board; for example, sixteen urban tiles, one mosque tile, four industrial area tiles, and so forth, to be placed randomly. I quickly abandoned this extremely onerous system because of an editorial suggestion and decided that a historical map offered the advantage of reinforcing the game's realism.

However, finding detailed aerial photos of Fallujah was, without a doubt, the hardest task. In the end, blurring the map details allowed the functional elements to come alive (as well as to facilitate the reading of those elements). Regarding the playing pieces, the tactical scale imposed the use of silhouettes. But the biggest handicap of my project was the fact that it was written in French. It was impossible for me to submit my game as such to an American publisher. In 2009, there was only a single wargame publisher in France (Hexasim), and its managing editor seemed to find the subject too delicate for his taste. But then I met Thomas Pouchin, a graphic designer who was immediately interested in remaking the map for *Phantom Fury*. A couple months later, Nuts! Publishing was created, and Thomas joined them with my project in hand. So, as chance would have it, I did not need to promote my game in order to find a publisher. *Phantom Fury* innately possessed all the ingredients (tactical scale, modern combat, solitaire play) that Nuts! Publishing needed to instantly market the game.

Second Objective: Simulation

Another war-themed board game at the same tactical level and with a relatively similar theme had just appeared when I started working on design. Thanks to its graphics and gameplay, *A Day of Heroes* (2008), met with a great deal of success in the eyes of gamers familiar with tactical combat and tense situations. The setting of the game (Mogadishu in 1993) made it possible to "relive" the events described in Mark Bowden's book *Black Hawk Down* (1999). I had mixed feelings regarding *A Day of Heroes*, which gave the impression of being inspired instead by Ridley Scott's 2001 film of *Black Hawk Down*. For me, the succession from *event* to *book* to *film* to *game* introduced too many filters, and I wanted my end result (the game *Phantom Fury*) to be as faithful as possible to the original events (at least as much as possible for a wargame). Furthermore, I wanted to avoid the romantic aspect of *A Day of Heroes*: pieces representing named protagonists, a game seeming to glorify US special forces (Delta Forces and Rangers), and Ramboesque scenarios (battles lasting hours in which the protagonist is outnumbered 10–1). I wanted to accentuate the didactic aspect, and I hoped that *Phantom Fury* would be perceived as a modest tool for understanding modern urban combat such as took place in Fallujah. As a result, I chose to base the game in a more general and neutral background (the hero pieces are unnamed and there are no pieces representing the NCOs), without visibly dramatic effects (so the management of wounded soldiers was abstracted), and I centered it on common soldiers (or "privates").

But did the creation of a specific tactical game on the battle of Fallujah justify itself? Was it not possible to use an existing system to simulate this fight? The article in the *Marine Corps Gazette* emphasized the importance of terraced roofs; controlling these roofs allows one to counter the enemy's retreat and to clear the building through the technique of "flooding," or taking possession of a building with a swift and decisive invasion. Tactical wargames normally treat roofs as a supplementary upper floor (with a few exceptions, such as the possibility of starting a fire there with a mortar), but by itself that was not reason enough to redraft rules for the "flooding" technique. However, in Fallujah, the third dimension brought more than just clear lines of sight. This dimension allowed for the execution of specific tactics and influenced ways of evacuating the wounded— the easiest evacuation being to start the attack from below because the evacuation involved moving downstairs, and the hardest evacuation attacking from the roof and escaping by climbing back up the stairs. I needed to come up with original rules in order to simulate, as faithfully as possible, the chain of events of these assaults in a three-dimensional environment.

Tactical wargames often impose detailed and complex rules to integrate technological aspects of modern combat. In my case, I wanted to avoid this trap by rendering the use of the combatants' individual weapons abstract—explosives and rocket launchers are the only exceptions. History shows that a combat unit's actions are related more to its experience and the pertinence of its tactical maneuvers than weaponry. In the case of Fallujah, the Marines were instructed in urban combat prior to the attack. Their level of experience being homogenous, the only thing left to account for was the number of soldiers in a squad in order to determine its "combat value" in the game. Each playing piece is therefore extremely

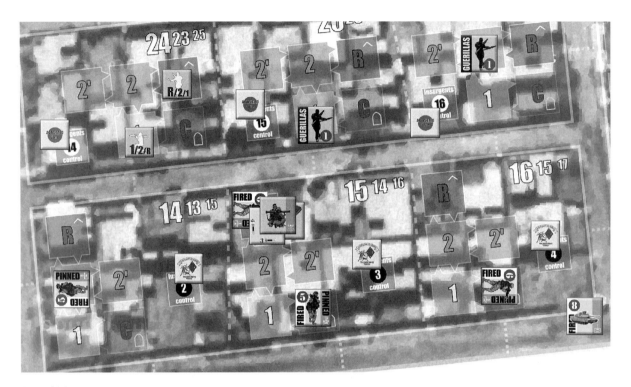

Figure 24.1
Detail of *Phantom Fury* game board and pieces.

simple: One value (related to the number of fighters) characterizes the squad or insurgent group.

The quality of a solitaire game resides in the capacity of its artificial intelligence to transcribe the behavior of the enemy battle forces. Thanks to the analysis provided by the article in the *Marine Corps Gazette*, modeling the insurgents' actions (guerilla warfare or stubborn defense) was relatively easy. The slight minor complexity of the AI unfolds naturally in the insurgents' basic tactics. Slight innovation was influenced by the addition of random events to improve the narrative aspect of the game.

Finally, using only a single source to create a game is an error to avoid at all costs, unless it is a document that offers a precise and objective synthesis of the situation to be simulated. The *Marine Corps Gazette* article met these particular demands. It got me off the hook about any possible justification concerning the credibility of my game design in relation to my nonmilitary, non-American roots. I do not know if my game has been played by American soldiers who have served in Iraq or not, but I have not received any criticism to date regarding the treatment of this battle in my game.

Phantom Fury: What's in Its Future?

I did not think that a game modeled on the Battle of Fallujah would be adaptable to other battles. Certain gamers have asked me if I would adapt it to Grozny, to Afghanistan, or even to the Gaza Strip. Each time my response has been "no." But in 2013 a Canadian gamer proposed an expansion of *Phantom Fury* for the Afghan conflict. After having seen his impressive work, I decided to join him in the development of his project, called *Strike of the Sword*, in order to make it an entirely separate game in preparation for an edition with Nuts! Publishing. This new adventure is in progress, and I hope it will come out soon.

About the Author

Laurent Closier was born in 1969 in a small town in central France. After studying mechanical engineering and computer science, he joined the Ministry of Defense in 1992, where he currently works in the field of missile threats. His passion for board wargames dates to the early 1990s, with the discovery of *Advanced Squad Leader*. In 1996, he created the fanzine *Le Franc-Tireur*, dedicated to *ASL*. *Phantom Fury* (2011) is his first game as a designer (two other games have since been published in the magazines *Vae Victis* and *Battles*). He has never been attracted to computer or console games, since he considers gaming to be a social activity whose central point is a pleasant time sitting around a table with other players.

25 PLAYING WITH TOY SOLDIERS: AUTHENTICITY AND METAGAMING IN WORLD WAR I VIDEO GAMES

Andrew Wackerfuss

Even as the one hundred-year anniversary of World War I arrives, options for refighting the conflict on video screens have remained remarkably limited. Game companies have likely avoided the war in part because of its legendary reputation for invalidating the very concept of individual heroism that their audience demands. In a war of industrialized attrition, combatants quickly learned that their individual actions rarely influenced the outcome of battle, which instead resolved for impersonal, material, and industrial reasons. This strong historical memory of the war, while not universal by any means, has inhibited World War I's cultural value in the context of an American culture dedicated to depicting warfare as a heroic contest that offers a chance to display virtues and defeat evil.[1] World War I therefore makes a poor video game by the standards of AAA first-person combat simulators, which gamers evaluate based on requirements of challenge, accuracy of simulation, and seeming authenticity of experience. Because of this internal logic, World War I games have faced the challenge of building an "authentic" war experience by confining their simulations to the air, where

heroic and seemingly realistic combat could still be positively portrayed, or by ignoring authenticity itself in favor of surrealism and fantasy (see Wackerfuss 2013).

In recent years, however, a new genre has emerged that has opened up space to offer both interesting gaming and authenticity of memory. The genre of tower defense perfectly matches World War I: the conflict's static nature matches the genre's structure, while the player's perspective encourages focus on the war's psychological legacy of vast, impersonal destruction. One of these games, Signal Studio's *Toy Soldiers* (2010), became among the most popular titles on the Xbox Live arcade (XBLA) marketplace due to its innovative combination of first- and third-person gameplay, evocative period details, and a surprisingly astute metacommentary on the nature of wargaming itself. This chapter will discuss how *Toy Soldiers* combined these features to achieve commercial success, garner critical acclaim, and convey the historical memory of World War I to a new generation far removed from that war's important legacy.

Origins and Features of Tower Defense

Tower defense partisans often locate the origins of their genre in user-made modifications of several real-time strategy games popular in the late 1990s and early 2000s. In truth, an earlier game, Atari's 1990 title *Rampart*, first developed many of the genre's elements. But it was only with the rise of mods for *Age of Empires* (1997), *Starcraft* (1998), and particularly *Warcraft 3* (2002) that tower defense games became widely known. In the mid- and late 2000s, tower defense games found popular platforms in web browser and touchscreen games, which eventually solidified the genre into the following form.

Tower defense games present players with a map on which they will place static defensive turrets in order to eliminate waves of enemies progressing from an entry point to an exit point. Towers generally will provide a variety of capabilities or features, and will vary in their effectiveness against different enemy types. Any enemy successfully breaching the end gate will damage the player's overall life total, eventually ending the game once too many get through. Killing enemies will earn the player currency to add and upgrade towers, and defeating all waves will advance the player to the next map. Enemy pathing can take one of two forms. In a basic model, enemies emerge from one point and progress along a set path or maze, advancing along a predictable route. Sometimes, multiple start and end points are used. Alternately, many games present a more open map that does not route enemies through a preset maze. Players must then use wise tower placement in order to block direct approaches and channel enemies through fortified lines. The latter form has become more standard in modern tower defense

games, as it offers more interesting gameplay and allows players freedom to adapt the map to their preferred strategies.

Having coalesced around this basic formula, the tower defense genre grew in popularity as its own mode of gaming. It has produced many successful browser and mobile games, and eventually broke through into the AAA market as well, taking advantage of the XBLA marketplace's ability to deliver titles directly to gamers' consoles. Though the basic gameplay remained the same, prominent AAA tower defense titles have displayed a variety of interpretations and moods, including the cartoony *Plants vs Zombies* (2009), the absurdist and self-referential *South Park Tower Defense Let's Go Play!* (2009), and the lush sci-fi scenario *Defense Grid* (2008). All these saw great success. *Toy Soldiers*, however, broke all records not only for tower defense games but also for downloadable games in the overall XBLA marketplace. According to one independent estimator of XBLA sales, *Toy Soldiers* sold over 200,000 copies in its first month of March 2010, a figure that represented almost one-third of XBLA's total earnings and contributed to a higher volume of sales overall (see Lemne 2010). It continued to succeed through expansions, sequels, high earnings, and critical acclaim. These accolades established *Toy Soldiers* as the leading example of both tower defense and World War I gaming, demonstrating the natural synergy between tower defense and World War I. Much of this success came from the game's ability to match structure and tone, with both elements working together to build a less problematically "authentic" simulation of a certain type of war memory.

Structures of Conflict: Tower Defense, Gameplay, and World War I

As the earlier summary of genre conventions indicates, tower defense games seem structurally well poised to depict World War I, a conflict notorious for its static and defensive nature. *Toy Soldiers* mobilized this synergy to achieve what had previously proven difficult for makers of World War I games: to create a real-time battle simulation that simultaneously upholds the military truisms of the war while also preserving interesting gameplay. It must be said that the seeming truism of a static World War I has often shifted under scrutiny, with modern scholars recognizing that many campaigns, especially in the east, featured far more mobility. However, the cultural memory of the trenches' unique horrors continues to overpower historians' attempts at revisions, making *Toy Soldiers* a document of the war's psychological reality even as it declines to reflect its more nuanced empirical experience.

Toy Soldiers presents players with a series of battlefields that include several standard features of the tower defense genre. The level begins with an overhead flyby of the terrain, which shows players both the general layout of the battlefield and the key features that will determine their strategy (i.e., point of enemy wave entry, locations where players can place their defensive towers, and exit gate that must be defended). Players begin with a set amount of money that they will use immediately to create their initial defense. Then, at the sound of a horn, the first enemy wave begins. Tower options mirror the most important defensive weapons of the era, including:

- Machine guns. Machine gun nests offer the most common and cost-effective means of eliminating enemy infantry. Many players will rely primarily on these towers to defeat waves of enemies, the same role these units played in the actual war. Some players may even find that they rely on these units with near exclusivity. They are cheap to build, quick and efficient to upgrade and repair, and, just as in the real war, offer an astonishingly effective method of area control and infantry annihilation. If destroyed, they are also easily replaced.

- Artillery. Another important type of tower reproduces the other key weapon of the historical war: long-range artillery that fired indirectly at massed enemy formations. In *Toy Soldiers*, players may only place artillery in specialized, larger slots dedicated for long-range fire, a limitation that reproduces concepts of layered defense that dominated that era's strategy. Players may therefore place these guns only near their end of the map, or at times along the sides, where the guns will remain generally safe from harm but still capable of dominating the main battlespace.

- Antiaircraft guns. In many levels, players will also encounter waves of enemy biplanes, which pose particular threats to backline artillery that otherwise could avoid attack. Players may therefore place antiaircraft guns in the long-range tower slots in order to defend against this threat, which cannot be countered by any other ground unit. In practice, however, players often choose not to use these towers, for reasons again mirroring historical logic: aircraft were a psychologically significant but militarily marginal side of the conflict. Players therefore often choose to focus on towers more effective against the main threat from the ground.

- Gas turrets. The use of gas turrets as units similar to the machine gun nests represents one of *Toy Soldiers'* only significant structural departures from period military weaponry. Both machine gun and gas towers are relatively inexpensive frontline defensive structures, with the machine guns filling the role of rapid long-range fire while the gas towers dispense a small zone of local area effect damage. The sickly green color of the cloud marks it as chlorine gas, the first effective gas weapon of the war. The color also signals to experienced video game players the weapon's adherence to gaming's general tropes of poison damage, as a form of indirect and passive damage usually indicated by the color green. This depiction of gas towers, however, marks the developers' most major revision to general accuracy in historical weaponry. In the real world, World War I armies developed chemical weapons as offensive tools to break fortified lines. They used artillery shells or gas-dispensing canisters to clear low-lying and tightly packed enemy trenches, causing defenders to die or flee so that their own armies could occupy the evacuated space. For obvious reasons, using gas defensively would risk disaster by flooding one's own lines with poison. Gas was therefore something that special attacking units carried to the enemy, rather than a weapon that kept the enemy from approaching (Heller 1984). In this way, *Toy Soldiers* deviates from its otherwise accurate representation of the war's general structure, a departure necessitated by the desire to include such an iconic weapon in a game whose genre is essentially defensive. In order to meet player expectations that a World War I game would include gas, the nature of that gas had to change to meet the structural conventions of tower defense.

- Barbed wire. One final type of defensive fortification transcends the preset limitations on where players may place their structures. Unlike towers that actively kill the enemy, players may place barbed wire on any open spot of ground, where it will slow enemies so that they may be mowed down by the other towers. It thus offers a cheap and effective means of zone control. It can, however, be easily destroyed by enemy armored units, as well as artillery and mortar fire from both sides. In this respect, players much constantly refurbish and extend their barbed wire nets, lest they eventually dissipate altogether. This project consumes player resources in two ways: the money to build the wire, and the time and attention it demands from players who must also juggle several other priorities at any given time. Barbed wire therefore creates interesting gameplay by increasing challenge, as well as by allowing players to discover and develop ways to shape the battlefield according to their personal strategies. In other words, the dynamic closely mirrors the historically accurate experience of fortification during the war. The massive trench system that developed by the end of 1915 was not a natural state of being; it was instead a constructed battlescape that required constant attention, investment, and personal risk by troops seeking to build their own defenses while undermining the enemy's. The developers' implementation of barbed wire therefore perfectly balances historical authenticity and interesting gameplay, prompting players to acknowledge the active, constructed nature of the World War I trench systems while also offering opportunities for stimulating challenge.

Figure 25.1
Repulsing a wave of enemies in *Toy Soldiers*, the interior wall of the toybox visible in the background.

All these structural elements combine to represent the experience of World War I in a way that evokes many of the most important elements of the war's historical memory. As players watch from above, waves of enemies crash against their own massed formations, channeled through barbed wire into predetermined "paths of glory" that end in slaughter. Players thus replicate the war experience primarily as generals, filling the same role as the distant figures of godlike detachment depicted in the 1957 Stanley Kubrick film called, yes, *Paths of Glory*. Just as those generals sat in elegant Parisian salons, moving figures on maps and sending men to the slaughter, so too do players sit in comfortable living rooms and command thousands of virtual soldiers to their deaths. World War I, quite authentically, becomes a contest of detached material attrition, divorced from the individual cost. Tower defense games like *Toy Soldiers* therefore offer the perfect vehicle to convey the war experience, not in spite of their avoidance of first-person heroism, but because of it.

Mood, Imagination, and Play: What Is Being Simulated?

This chapter has thus far avoided discussing the visual, auditory, and other aesthetic depictions of war in *Toy Soldiers*, which in themselves present a novel and innovative approach to wargaming. When starting up the game, what was hinted in the title becomes immediately clear: the game does not actually take place in the trenches, but rather in a child's toybox. Title and loading screens show the players period-inspired advertisements for the toy sets they are about to play with, putting gamers in the mindset not of a soldier in the trenches, but a child in the bedroom, collecting and imagining warfare while not directly taking part. Musically, the soundtrack does not feature the type of heroic, orchestral score generally expected for first-person heroic epics but instead mobilizes period-authentic music that might be played on a living room phonograph in the 1920s. Once in the game, it becomes clear that the units themselves are toys rather than people. They do not bleed when blown up, but rather fly high into the air as if flung by a child's hand. (Game stats even gleefully track the record heights attained by blasted units.) The map itself, upon further examination, turns out to be a diorama built for play. One can see over the edges into the bedroom, where bookshelves and other artifacts of a child's room show that a larger world of reality exists outside the realm of play.

The meta-setting also appears in the ability to take control of single units for a period of time, an element that not only adds interesting possibilities for gameplay, but also furthers the game's commentary on the nature of play itself. Players may assume control of units in order to move them around the battlefield, a feeling similar to how a child would grip and move toys around the bedroom. In practice, most players will choose to control the biplane or the tank, the two technological wonder weapons that captured participants' imaginations as possible escapes from the brutal nature of trench warfare. While it can be fulfilling to take control of a machine gun nest and mow down endless waves of enemies, in practice these units function perfectly well unattended. Players therefore feel encouraged to find methods of more meaningful participation through the air and armored units, making them more attractive options for a first-person experience—just as in reality.

In prizing play over replication, *Toy Soldiers* succeeds in simulating a cultural type of World War I experience because it chooses to avoid representing the war itself. Instead, it re-creates the experience of playing at war, a popular activity for boys too young to join the fighting themselves. These boys, the prime consumers of the toy soldier industry in the late nineteenth and early twentieth centuries, dealt in war as an idealized construct that shielded them from its worst physical and psychological effects. Historically, that dynamic had a sinister side: scholars of fascism note that while the Nazis often portrayed themselves as representatives of the front experience, one of their most important demographics were in fact youths who had just missed participation, and who therefore retained idealized notions of heroic warfare that their fathers or older brothers had discarded when faced with reality. Critics of the militarization of present-day American culture have expressed concerns that a similar dynamic has begun in the United States, in that video wargaming and warlike films dominate

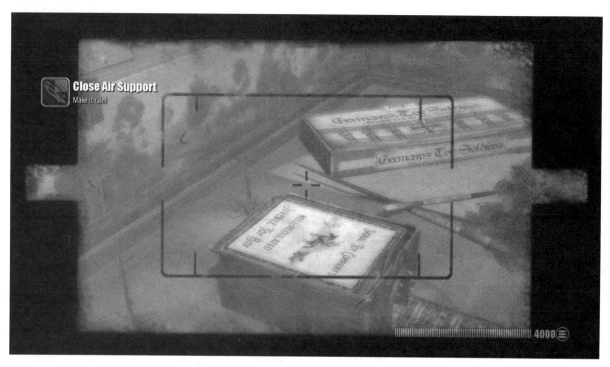

Figure 25.2
Aerial view of toy sets, with one repurposed as a train tunnel.

the culture but only 1 percent of the population serves in the actual military. That disconnect looms large behind every video wargame—even if most refuse to admit it. When the industry and its audience prize a first-person experience of supposed authenticity, they usually measure it according to how games create the most naturalistic environments, the most realistic-looking blood spatters, or the most accurate simulations of ballistic physics. Dozens of World War II titles have sought audiences through these technical feats, yet few acknowledge those elements they fail to even attempt. Video games inherently lack the ability to replicate fully battlefield conditions of deafening noise, nauseating smells, slow rot of disease, and direct existential

terror. Games thus fail to convey a truly authentic war experience even as they claim to seek that as their goal. Their false authenticity, critics fear, contributes to the militarization of any culture that believes it knows war, but in fact knows only the game.

Ironically, this danger minimizes in games depicting World War I, which history remembers as so horrible as to defy any realistic attempt at simulation. Critics of militarized cultures may well see less to fear from *Toy Soldiers*, which wears its artificiality on its muddy green sleeves. Games like these show American culture as self-aware, ironic, and indeed postmodern in its embrace of the constructed and artificial over the superficially real. *Toy Soldiers* thus allows a culture to have its hardtack and eat it too, playing at war while acknowledging the gulf between play and reality in a way that honors the historical memory of a terrible war.

About the Author

Andrew Wackerfuss is a historian with the US Air Force, stationed with the Air National Guard History Office at Joint Base Andrews, Maryland. He holds an MA in German and European Studies and a PhD in history from Georgetown University, where he continues to teach night classes in European history. He is the author of *Stormtrooper Families: Homosexuality and Community in the Early Nazi Movement* (2015) and of what he hopes to be an essential philosophical guide to a postapocalyptic world, *Thus Spoke Zombiethustra: A Book for the Living Undead.*

Note

1. On the strains of psychological reaction to the war, see Leed (1979, 1–32). On the militarization of American culture, see Andrew Bacevich's example of the film *Top Gun* (Bacevich 2013, 113–116). Applied to video games, see Stahl (2010a, 91–112) and Mead (2013).

26 AMERICA'S ARMY

Marcus Schulzke

America's Army (*AA*) (2002–) is a revolutionary military first-person shooter (FPS) that marks a new era in wargaming because of the way it was produced and the interests it was designed to promote. *America's Army* was created by the US Army in an explicit effort to extend the Army's influence through the video game medium. It was, by the developers' own admission, meant to attract potential recruits, discourage unsuitable recruits from joining, present a positive image of the Army, and provide the army with a forum for engaging in "strategic communication" with civilian audiences (McLeroy 2008).

Despite its explicit persuasive goals, *America's Army* has been extremely popular. This probably owes much to the fact that it can be downloaded and played for free while still offering a gameplay experience that is similar to that of other military FPS. Since the game was first released in 2002, it has been updated with dozens of expansions and two sequels that have enabled *AA* to compete with the latest commercial FPS. By the summer of 2013, over thirteen million people had played the game, accumulating around 260 million hours of combined gameplay (Anderson 2013).

AA's persuasive intent, the civil-military links it established, its contribution to the growth of the military-industrial complex, and its ability to attract a large audience have made it a catalyst for concerns over the expansion of military influence. I will argue that much of the criticism the game has attracted is deserved and that *AA* can be accurately characterized as propaganda because it attempts to influence players with the help of highly stylized and often misleading depictions of military service and war. However, I will also urge restraint when criticizing *America's Army* by calling attention to the lack of empirical support for some of the more serious charges that have been raised against it and by arguing that the game's propaganda function has some redeeming benefits. Most important of all, *AA* provides greater insight into the US Army and its goals at a time when the Army has undergone the profound disruptions brought about by the end of the Cold War and the initiation of the War on Terror.

Joining the Virtual Army

AA's effort to influence players is evident from the first moments of the game. Like many FPS, *America's Army* opens with training missions that are designed to familiarize players with the game's controls and the various weapons that are available. However, unlike other games in the genre, these missions are modeled on real training exercises and teach players about weapons that American soldiers currently use. Throughout training, players learn about and use digital models of real weapons, such as the M16A2 assault rifle and the Mark 19 grenade launcher. They also learn about the Army's institutions and culture through the comments made by virtual drill instructors and the messages posted on the game's loading screens. After completing Basic Combat Training, players can go through specialized training programs that display the range of employment opportunities the Army offers; these include medical, airborne, and Special Forces training. The game's goal of giving players a sense of what it is like to become an American soldier is therefore explicit and frames the game narrative.

The core element of gameplay in *America's Army* is multiplayer combat between two opposing teams of players in a variety of settings, including forests, deserts, cities, airfields, and towns. One of the gameplay elements unique to *AA* is that players can only be American soldiers during the multiplayer battles. Every player sees his or her own avatar and those of teammates as American soldiers. Opposing avatars are shown wearing nondescript black uniforms, though the opposing players controlling those

avatars likewise see themselves as the American soldiers. This visual trick allows players on both teams to perceive themselves as Americans, despite their opposition, and ensures that all players will be fighting for the US Army.

During the multiplayer battles players are bound by strict rules of engagement (ROE) that dictate how they can use their weapons and who they are allowed to target. Players who attack civilians or teammates are penalized and repeat offenders can be sent to a virtual prison cell in Leavenworth. The values of the US Army—loyalty, duty, respect, selfless service, honor, integrity, and personal courage—serve as a scoring system and a mechanism for enforcing the ROE. *AA* incorporates seven different scores, corresponding to each of the Army values, and these rank players based on things like achieving mission objectives and saving wounded teammates. This scoring system indicates that the Army has extremely high ethical standards and that soldiers consistently meet those standards.

The loading screens displayed between multiplayer battles offer a persistent reminder of the game's underlying purpose. Some show recruitment videos or present facts about the Army's institutions and culture. Others display some of the Army's latest technologies, such as the Atlas robot, and special training programs like Elite Engineer Training. Finally, these screens direct players to other Army resources, such as the game's website, which features comic books, information about "real heroes" of the wars in Afghanistan and Iraq, and information about joining the Army.

Interactive Propaganda

America's Army is among the most controversial video games ever produced. It has inspired its own sub-genre of critical commentaries that raise serious ethical and political concerns relating to the game's efforts to influence civilian gamers (Schulzke 2013a). The most common criticism of the game is that it is propaganda (e.g., Delwiche 2007; Höglund 2008; Ottosen 2009; Salter 2011), and there is a great deal of evidence to support this charge. *America's Army* is accurately described as propaganda not only because of the clear efforts at persuasion discussed in the previous section but also because it relies heavily on stylized and misleading information to achieve its persuasive goal.

AA strives to show soldiers adhering to strict ROE, living according to US Army values, and acting professionally. This attention to ethical precepts creates the impression that the US Army is a relatively benign force—except to enemy combatants—and that its soldiers perfectly embody the organization's values. There is no acknowledgment that soldiers are sometimes guilty of misconduct or that the Army's ethical precepts may be problematic. The game further suggests that soldiers are able to effectively wage wars without ethically compromising themselves in any way, so long as they follow the ROE. This is implausible given the prevalence of accidental attacks on civilians and allied soldiers in contemporary wars, which take place even when soldiers attempt to act ethically (Schulzke 2013b).

AA's selective presentation of violence facilitates the construction of an ethical army. Whereas other military FPS tend to be extremely graphic in their representations of violence, especially when showing the corporeal effects of weapons, the combat of *America's Army* is sanitized. Wounded and dead avatars bear little evidence of their injuries and, because there is no game narrative linking the multiplayer battles, players are not forced to confront the long-term costs of war, such as the loss of teammates or the enormous destruction inflicted by modern weaponry. As Roger Stahl correctly notes, this is to be expected, since "a game that seriously approached the horrors of battle would probably undermine the recruitment effort" (Stahl 2006, 124).

The propaganda function of *AA* is heightened by the way the game avoids considering alternative viewpoints on military service or on American military operations. The American soldier's perspective is the only one that can be represented and the game consistently seeks to make players understand war from that perspective. The game likewise fails to consider the possible nonmilitary solutions to the conflict scenarios that frame the multiplayer battles or to raise the possibility that military operations could destabilize the countries in which they are carried out. This tacitly suggests that military force is a morally justifiable and politically expedient way of achieving foreign policy objectives.

Interpreting *America's Army* as a propaganda game raises the questions of what this propaganda is meant to achieve and how effective it is in influencing players. The game is explicitly designed to promote military service and to attract high-quality recruits. However, many commentators argue that the game goes beyond this and that its underlying function is to make players more comfortable with how the US military shapes global politics. Peter Mantello argues that *America's Army* "advocates a form of global humanitarian interventionism that justifies any breach of another country's sovereignty, the legal justification to conduct extrajudicial killing and a narrative which brutalizes and demoralizes its faceless victims" (Mantello 2012, 272). Similarly, Salter and Dyer-Witherford and De Peuter (2009) express concern that *AA* could legitimize American empire and military interventions that violate state sovereignty.

Other commentators call attention to what *AA* may do to players. Stahl (2009) says that *America's Army* and other interactive war media transform players into "virtual citizen-soldiers" who identify with the American military and its operations. By Stahl's account, *AA* and media like it make players more compliant and less politically engaged, thereby hindering the formation of a critical citizenry. Similarly, Ian Shaw says of *America's Army* and several other games that "video games are vital in linking a brutal colonial present with the intimate spaces of

the home computer, thus facilitating mass cultural participation" (2010, 798). Moreover, he maintains that the simulated war players take part in is one that is oversimplified and presented in terms of American interests.

Concerns that *AA* may promote American imperialism or that it may produce a more complacent citizenry are plausible. However, it is important to be cautious about these kinds of claims and to avoid implying that the game actually succeeds in its efforts to influence players. The game's effects on players' attitudes about the Army and about uses of military force have not been subjected to systematic empirical testing and therefore remain uncertain. Future research into audience reception could clarify *AA*'s impact, but at present no studies appear to be capable of providing the empirical evidence that is needed to determine whether the game is successful in its persuasive efforts. For now, the ethical and political implications of *AA* are best assessed strictly based on what the game's content reveals about the US Army's propaganda strategy.

Learning from Propaganda

Although *America's Army* can be fairly characterized as propaganda because of its unwavering support for the US Army and its efforts to generate player interest in military service, the game's deep biases allow it to offer insight into how the service sees itself and how it wants to be seen by audiences. Thus, the game's propaganda function not only raises the risk of promoting militarism but also provides a lens through which to analyze the Army and its ideology. This is an extremely

important dimension of *AA* that deserves greater investigation because it is all too often neglected in studies of the game that take a purely critical perspective.

Many critics have objected to *AA*'s sanitized violence and its emphasis on values, interpreting these as elements of a disingenuous attempt to make the US Army appear more ethical. However, these can also be interpreted as reflections of what the Army hopes to become in the future. The values and ROE presented in *America's Army* were not created for the game. Rather, they were devised as part of the Army's ongoing project to improve soldiers' ethical awareness and were incorporated into the game to publicize this effort. The inclusion of values and ROE in *AA* signal the end result the Army hopes to reach, thereby creating an aspirational version of the organization and its members that civilian gamers may inspect and evaluate.

America's Army not only displays the Army's aspirations but also reveals uncertainty about its future mission. The use of nondescript enemies in the game is extremely important in this respect. Many games designed to persuade their players provide more details about the enemy forces, and may even identify them by name. For example, Hezbollah's games *Special Force* and *Special Force 2* simulate the organization's battles against Israeli soldiers in a way that demonstrates the organization's intense opposition to Israel and its likely future operations. By contrast, *AA* is reluctant to explicitly name enemies or to link them to a geographical area.

The lack of clear enemies in *AA* facilitates the game's propaganda function. As Robertson Allen points out, "The erasure of a differentiating enemy race was deliberate, for it aided in the construction of an anonymous enemy who was potentially anywhere and applicable to any situation" (Allen 2011, 49). Nevertheless, while it may be true that some of the game's developers meant for the enemy avatars to create a pervasive sense of threat, one can also interpret the lack of identifiable enemies as being a sign of that the developers do not know who the US Army will be fighting in the future. The faceless enemy avatars and fictional settings betray a sense of profound anxiety from an army that has lost

the Cold War–era certainty about its enemy and the form its wars would take. The game thus provides a digital manifestation of the Army's continuing effort to redefine itself and to adjust to new kinds of operations.

Its ethical aspirations and its uncertainty about the future are brought together in *AA*'s effort to depoliticize the US Army and its soldiers. As Ian Bogost points out, the game's refusal to consider the political dimensions of the conflicts it simulates indicates that the army soldier "is an apolitical being" at least in principle (2007, 77). The game's presentation of apolitical soldiers who have no concern for, or even much awareness of, the political dimensions of the wars they fight is a central part of the Army's ethical identity. Soldiers are supposed to be thoroughly depoliticized in an effort to subordinate them to civilian control. The game establishes the absolute political disengagement of its soldiers as an ethical ideal in the Army's purified version of itself, thereby affirming the Army's goal of being a neutral instrument of foreign policy at a time when controversial wars in Afghanistan and Iraq have risked politicizing it.

The depoliticized depiction of the Army likewise provides additional evidence of the Army's uncertainty about its future missions and enemies. This is most obvious in the latest version of the game, *America's Army: Proving Grounds*. Whereas earlier versions of the game released during the wars in Afghanistan and Iraq were set in fictional conflicts against enemies who were labeled "terrorists" and "insurgents," *Proving Grounds* is presented as a prolonged training mission throughout which the US Army is redesigning itself and preparing to counter prospective threats while politicians decide when and where American military forces will be committed. The game thus establishes the certainty of war in the near future and the need to continue adapting, though without being able to identify how it should adapt.

Conclusion

As I have argued, *America's Army* is video game propaganda because it strives to influence players with self-serving and often extremely deceptive ways of presenting the US Army and its soldiers. The game emphasizes its moral purity, downplays the consequences of war, presents an attractive view of military service, makes armed force appear to be a fairly unproblematic foreign policy tool, and conceals information that might conflict with these themes. Nevertheless, I have also argued that there is some value in the game's propaganda function, which should not be neglected by critical studies of the game. Specifically, *AA* allows players to explore the Army's ideal version of itself and its operations, thereby offering insight into the Army's institutions, culture, and identity—as well as the disruption these are undergoing in the aftermath of the Cold War and the Army's most recent deployments in the War on Terror. The challenge for future research on *America's Army* will be to monitor the development of these themes, to uncover new dimensions of the game, and to account for the hitherto neglected audience perspective.

About the Author

Marcus Schulzke is a Postdoctoral Research Fellow in the School of Politics and International Studies at the University of Leeds. He received his PhD in political science from the University at Albany, State University of New York, in 2013 with a dissertation on the ways in which soldiers make ethical decisions during counterinsurgency operations. His primary research interests are security studies, contemporary political theory, and the political dimensions of new media. He has published research on a wide variety of topics in each of these fields, as well as work on politics and religion, applied ethics, and video games.

27 WE THE SOLDIERS: PLAYER COMPLICITY AND ETHICAL GAMEPLAY IN *CALL OF DUTY: MODERN WARFARE*

Miguel Sicart

Who would have expected a multimillion-dollar, mainstream blockbuster video game to be able to be *serious*? When the newest iteration of the *Call of Duty* series was announced in 2007, the prospect of a high budget game about "modern warfare" was not very promising. In fact, I feared the worst: another example of excellent action gameplay wrapped in a pseudopropagandistic narrative that tried to glamorize modern warfare.

Surprisingly enough, I was wrong. *Call of Duty: Modern Warfare* did have a tendency to fetishize the military, but it also delivered a carefully crafted narrative that questioned the nature of "modern warfare." Don't get me wrong: *Modern Warfare* is a militaristic shooter, an adrenaline rush that combines outstandingly crafted action gameplay with a semirealistic depiction of weapons, tactics, and military lingo. But it is also a narrative-driven game that proposes a different discourse about warfare. This narrative was not presented as conventional cut scenes, but as authored sequences with limited player agency. The careful combination of limited agency with authored narrative made *Modern Warfare* stand out as a popular yet thoughtful militaristic video game.

Modern Warfare's economic and creative success led inevitably to a sequel, a title that pushed the techniques pioneered in *Modern Warfare*.[1] However, it did push too far, and one of its central gameplay sequences became an example of militaristic shooters gone wrong. In *Modern Warfare 2*'s infamous "No Russian" level, players were forced to witness, or participate in, the slaughter of innocent civilians in an airport. The level created controversy, but it failed to generate the same kind of thoughtful interpretations that the previous game had. Still a great computer game in terms of its gameplay design, *Modern Warfare 2* failed to create a nuanced emotional experience for players.

Military games, and particularly first-person shooters, are as popular a product as they are criticized for being vehicles for propagandistic discourses. Most of these critiques are right. Many military computer games are propaganda devices that use the medium of games to promote epic stories of misunderstood heroism (see Breuer, Festl, and Quandt 2012). These games do not question the origins, context, or role of politics in wars, trivializing the real consequences of war by turning everything into a visual roller coaster representing basic cops-and-robbers gameplay. Video games can be excellent instruments for propaganda (see Chomsky and Herman 2010) because we can decouple the pleasures of the core loops (shoot-hide-reload-shoot) from the fictional context used to communicate these loops (war in the Middle East). The fictional element of the game attracts us, but the core loops engage us, and then we stop seeing the fiction and its messages as rhetorical acts, but instead as justifications for our actions. But there are alternatives to this approach.

In this chapter I will be looking at these two titles to provide an account of how they tried to create an emotional/reflective bond with the player, and why *Modern Warfare 2* fails at this. These two games share a particular design approach to narratives, which I define as "authored agency." Authored agency was used to create a frame of interpretation designed to engage players morally. This player complicity will be subject to an analysis, using virtue ethics and my own theory of ethical gameplay, to explain why *Modern Warfare* succeeds at creating player complicity through authored agency, while *Modern Warfare 2* fails at doing so, despite the use of similar techniques.

This chapter has a broader mission, though. Militaristic computer games are, together with sports games, the last bastions of classic AAA productions, and can be defined as the games for the core audience. In fact, these games are often defining not only what AAA and the games industry are for a broader audience, but also the image and culture of new hardware. Modern consoles are often sold on their lavish graphics, which are often illustrated with explosions and gore. This is an obvious problem in times of illegal, unethical wars—that our mainstream entertainment glorifies the visual appearance of war without questioning its meaning, impact and role in society.

However, I believe that if we are able to articulate alternative, richer ways of designing and interpreting militaristic computer games, if we dare to address our unethical war times, with wars forged by lies and strategic global surveillance, from a reflective entertainment perspective, we will be able to not only reach a broader audience and perhaps contribute to change their worldview, but also to enrich the cultural presence of games and their role in configuring our understanding of the world around us. We can make even militaristic computer games devices for moral reflection, if we dare to engage players beyond the pleasures of conflict, in reflective practices of gameplay.

Military games will always be popular, because they appeal to our core interest in agonistic play, and because war has a strong cultural, social, and rhetorical effect in our culture. However, not all games need to be propagandistic tools. We can reclaim military games as reflective devices, as instruments for critically engaging with the importance and effect of war, and its consequences. These games might not teach us lessons, but they could give us arguments, ideas, or emotions to deal with the impact of war. We will not lose battles playing these games, but we can, to the extent we demand them to be expressive, win culture wars.

Two Instances of Complicit Play

Modern Warfare does not hide its cards. A game about war, developed in the period of the Iraq war, it sets its stage immediately. We are in the Middle East, in a land ravaged by civil war. Our character is a prisoner in the hands of an irregular army that controls a city. Without us, as players, being able to do anything about it, we are thrown into a car and driven across a city. We can move our heads, observe. Something will soon happen, we hope. We will be saved, or we will soon have control and the means to protect ourselves. But nothing happens; we just cross the city until we reach a stadium. We are dragged to a pole, bound, and shot. We die.

The starting sequence in *Modern Warfare* is a reinvention of the narrative introduction pioneered by *Half-Life*: a narrative introduction with limited agency helps us to recognize environments and get used to basic movement controls and the setting of the game. However, in a clever twist of this design paradigm, *Modern Warfare* does not give us agency over a hero, but over a victim. We play the dead, in this game of war.

A different type of experience awaits us in *Modern Warfare 2*. Early in the game, we have to play a sequence where, together with three other characters, we load our weapons and put masks on while going up on an elevator. One last warning before the doors open: "No Russian"—meaning we should not say a word in that language. Once the doors open, we can see our target: the civilian users of an airport. We walk through the terminal, gunning them down. We walk: the game does not allow us to run, or hide. Our only choice is not to shoot or to shoot, but only to shoot civilians; our weapons are ineffective against our murderous colleagues. Of course, that is because we are an agent infiltrated in a terrorist cell and we don't want to blow our cover. However, we need to walk through the horror, the chaos, the massive murder of civilians. The sequence then turns into a firefight with the police, after which our terrorist partners,

who knew about our actual identity all along, execute us.

"No Russian" has a similar structure to the scripted sequences in the first title: players are given a relative amount of agency that is not related to the control they have over the flow of events or the meaning of their actions.[2] Players can witness the massacre or participate in it, but they cannot stop it.

These types of limited agency sequences have become a hallmark of the *Call of Duty* series. If *Half-Life* innovated by scripting us as almost-passive spectators to our arrival in the game setting, *Call of Duty* modified that paradigm in order to confer a stronger emotional punch. Instead of using limited agency to present the plot and the location, as in *Half-Life*, *Modern Warfare* uses these sequences as pivotal plot points that change both the story being told and its meaning.

There are a number of reasons why this might be the case. First, *Modern Warfare* is a game designed to test our reflexes and coordination. Once we get good at the game, the world in which we play becomes devoid of its meaning and we are just shooting "enemies," the narrative becoming nothing else than a wrapping. In order to give more meaning to the narrative, the designers of *Modern Warfare* occasionally vary the pace of the game to introduce sequences that frame player actions. By doing so, the designers ensure that even the most engaged players who might otherwise ignore the narrative could get a feel for the story.

Second, by modifying player agency and its meaning, the designers of *Modern Warfare* could experiment with the degree of emotional involvement of players, giving them reasons to think about the meaning of their actions. Instead of streamlining a roller coaster of action sequences, the first *Modern*

Warfare game gave players reflective pauses to engage with the narrative domain of the game. For some precious minutes we could have limited agency in the world, but we did not have to engage in the conventional, mechanical activities of conflict gameplay: we just had to watch and play, we just had to observe. In *Modern Warfare*, these sequences end up in death, because that's where their draw their dramatic power from: limited agency that leads to death.

It is a convention in computer games that players should be empowered to act and do within the game world whatever they need to do in order to win. To design games is to design activities that players engage with and that pose sufficient challenge such that we can lose, but that can be won by learning new skills. All actions available to players should have a meaning oriented toward the completion of goals and overcoming challenges.

This classic game design wisdom is challenged in those sequences in which players are only given limited control over the game. We as players can look around and move, but that is the extent of our potential interactions. And we do so in order to witness the unfolding of critical sequences of the narrative. In these sequences the purpose is to slow down the pace of the action so we can reflect, think, and be affected. These sequences break the rhythm of gameplay, the cybernetic loop between input, feedback, and output.[3]

The designs of these sequences share some principles:

- Agency is restricted to movement and vision: All the player can do is move around, often at a slower pace than usual, and look at the environment. Interaction with the environment is not possible.

- Short duration: The sequences are short to avoid player frustration.
- Narrative dimension: All sequences have a meaning in the plot of the game, usually giving rise to one of the major plots in the narrative.
- In terms of gameplay design, understood as the design of the flow of action, processing and feedback to the player, these sequences remove the capacity for the player to produce input, yet they still operate within known patterns of interactive narrative development.
- These sequences present an "authored narrative" to the player. It is irrelevant whether the player wants to accept it or not. These sequences open the possibility for a particular interpretation of the game narrative by forcing players to adopt a limited interactive spectatorship position. The player becomes an NPC, forced to observe the development of the world in motion.

I shall call these design devices instances of "authored agency." Authored, in the sense that the constraints to player agency have a clear intention, closely tied both to the narrative of the game and to an intended experience. The use of "authored" here does not necessarily reflect on the presence of a designer as author; it here refers to a conscious limitation of the interpretations that can be assigned to a particular sequence.

As I have mentioned, in these sequences player agency is limited in relevant ways, often to only movement. Besides the narrative elements, this is where we can see the authorial imprint that seeks a particular interpretive mode: by limiting the agency capacities of players, the interpretive process is directed toward specific meanings. In "No Russian," we can only walk, not run. We are forced to have the agency of witnesses. In the opening sequence of *Modern Warfare*, our agency as players is as restrained as that of the character we are playing. We are therefore as helpless as he is.

One could claim that all games have authored agency, because designers create mechanics for players to use in their experience of a game world with the goal of creating particular experiences. However, the widespread use of this concept would not really help us better understand game design. Therefore, I propose to use authored agency to describe those situations in games in which player agency is restricted for expressive purposes—to create frames of interpretation and emotional experiences directed from an authorial presence in the game.

The concept of authorial agency helps explain how *Call of Duty: Modern Warfare* contributed to broaden the expressive palette of military computer games. Through the use of authored agency, the developers of *Modern Warfare* attempted to engage players in emotional experiences.

Complicity, War, Play

Engaging with the "No Russian" sequence is a voluntary act. We need to explicitly agree to play this sequence. And playing the sequence requires strong willpower; it is a gruesome, gratuitous succession of brutal, unjustified murders. It can easily become a very discomforting experience. Arguably, however, the goal was not to promote violence, but rather the opposite: "No Russian" can be read as a critique of the very concept of (secret) wars and heroic sacrifice. This interpretation is suggested by its authored agency; we are forced to spectate or participate in an event we cannot stop in order to create a reflective, moral experience in players.

I will call this consequence of authored agency "player complicity." Player complicity defines a type of interpretational and experiential gestalt created when players are forced to submit to an authored agency sequence. The purpose of creating player complicity is to engage players as reflective beings in the activity of playing the game, to tease out the ethical player and force it to interpret the experience of the game.

Player complicity can be seen, then, as a device for engagement: engagement in the emotional sense—creating a particular response to a sequence that is pivotal as far as plot is concerned—but also engagement as an interpretive mode, in which players are given the opportunity to reflect critically about their play experience. The success or failure of authored agency should be measured by the level of player complicity.

From an ethical perspective, player complicity means that when playing, we become complicit with the moral system we engage with, as well as with the fact that, as players, we also have values we play with. Playing is engaging with a game that has its own values, and negotiating ways in which we can reconcile the values presented in it with the values we want to live by. Player morality is negotiated in the wiggle space between the ethics inscribed in the game as an object, the ethics in practice of the game as an experience, and the player as a moral, embodied being with a history and values of her own. Player complicity is a way of directly invoking the player capacity to interpret these values, to read the game from a moral perspective. Player complicity is a challenge to the conventions of interpreting and experiencing a game, a challenge that is designed to take place through particular gameplay structures, like authored agency.

It is this complicity that allows us, as players, to experience the kind of fringe themes often present in games without necessarily running into risks to our moral integrity. Complicity is a type of interpretational opening, a challenge to subvert our expectations and to experience the game using our own moral sense. By becoming complicit with the kind of experience that the game wants us to enjoy, we are also critically open to whatever values we are ourselves going to enact. And the degree of our complicity, the weight we will give to our own values and not to those of the game, will determine our moral behavior in the game.

The use of player complicity in the militaristic context of the *Modern Warfare* games, then, allows us to read them also as moral experiences. That interpretation will be the focus of my argument that player complicity succeeds in *Modern Warfare*, while *MW2*'s "No Russian" fails.

A Moral Experience of Played War

Before analyzing the authored agency of *Modern Warfare* and *Modern Warfare 2* from an ethical perspective, we need to frame what we mean by "ethics" and what its relationship with gameplay is. To do so, I will quickly summarize here my own theory of ethics and games as a framework for analysis.

The first important distinction to make is the one between ethics and morality. Even though I have used these two concepts casually up to now, they are actually specific concepts that we need to have clearly defined in order to use them appropriately in our analysis. Briefly, morality is a public system that defines how we should behave with ourselves and with others, and what are our notions of good and bad, the desirable and the undesirable. Morality is based on a general set of heuristics that can derive from religion, law, or philosophy. The branch of philosophy that asks questions about the nature of good and bad, and that develops heuristics that are then turned into moral practices, is ethics. Colloquially put, ethics is theory, morality is practice.

When looking at games, I argue that we need to take as our analytical starting point the ethical bases of players and of the game. All players come to the game with an assemblage of different ethical systems that govern different instances of their lives. The actions they take in the game, their specific moral understanding of a game, is partially derived from those ethical systems. However, it is only *partially* derived from it, because games also have ethical systems inscribed in them—sometimes consciously, as part of the design of a gameplay experience. When we talk about the morality of a game, we should be referring to the way the act of playing that game by a moral agent configures those ethical inscriptions into particular moral discourses.

If we want to look at the ethics of computer games, then, we should look at the ways the ethics of a game and the ethics of players fuse into the morality of the gameplay experience, understood as the specific, phenomenological interpretation of a game by a particular individual or group of individuals. I am taking here what ethicists might call a constructivist approach (in the tradition of Aristotelian ethics; see Bynum): there are no *a prioris* in the morality of the gameplay experience; the experience itself is configured as a moral experience, constructing the morality of the game(play) experience as we play it. That is, we cannot say that a game is ethically wrong, but we can say that the experience of a game by a moral agent is wrong. Violent games, to use a classic example, are not *necessarily* ethically wrong (they may be tasteless, but that is an aesthetic judgment), but they can yield experiences in which a moral subject is harmed (for instance, by being exposed to a cultural taboo or to a sequence that triggers a trauma), and therefore they *can* be ethically wrong. We can only make these judgments about the experience of play, not about the game as a cultural object.

My approach to the ethics of games is a hermeneutic one: players approach a game with their ethics and interpret the ethics of the game from that perspective; the moral experience a result of that process of interpretation. This hermeneutic process is filtered through the values of the player outside of the game experience. It is not only the game we play and our ethics as players that define the moral gameplay experience, it is also who we are as moral subjects who engage with a game.

Any ethical analysis of a game, then, needs to define the ethics of players and the game before making any analysis. And to define those ethics, we can use classic philosophical theories. In my case, I am mostly a virtue ethicist, in the classic tradition of Aristotle (see also May), and deeply influenced by Brey (1999) and Verbeek's (2007) philosophy of technology. I argue that ethics can be seen as a constellation of values that we want to live by, all guiding us toward developing and fulfilling the best of our potential while respecting others and their well-being—and that this moral development cannot be isolated from the experience of technology as a mediator (such as ubiquitous computing) or as a medium, as computer games are in this case. In the case of games, my argument is that when we play games, we interpret the values of a game through our own values as players and embodied beings, and we develop the practices of play, the actual morality of gameplay, by developing a sense of who we want to be as players, and what values we want to foster by that experience.

From this perspective, let's look at the types of experiences that *Modern Warfare* proposes, and how they can create ethical gameplay experiences.

In *Modern Warfare*, authorial agency sets up a particular mode for the interpretation of the game. To make a virtue-ethics interpretation of these sequences, we need to see them as laying the foundations for developing a certain understanding of the virtues the game wants to foster in players as creative, engaged, moral beings. The reason why authored agency works in the context of militaristic games, and particularly in the case of the first *Modern Warfare* game, is that it breaks the pleasures of agonistic play, of skill-based combat gameplay, in order to make us, players, take a step back and reason about our own agency in the game. Instead of overpowering us, authored agency disempowers us without making us pure spectators. We are spectators, but we still get to participate. We are reminded of our actions as complicit with the narrative of the game. Authored agency creates complicity, and complicity develops a critical view on the narrative and the actions of the game. This critical view allows designers to address complex topics, and to engage players in the narrative of the game not just as a succession of events that they trigger with their actions, but as a story they are helping to unfold. Complicity involves players moving beyond the consumer role into that of the critical interpreter, who has more at stake in the experience of the game than just playing it. In other words, players can understand this military game not as mass-produced propaganda discourse, but as a thoughtful reflection on the role of soldiers, and their vulnerability, in modern warfare.

Therefore, I argue that the first *Modern Warfare* constructs a fictional world in which players are not heroic, superhuman soldiers, but human warriors, heroic but not invulnerable to combat that is beyond their control. Unlike in many other games, *Modern Warfare* makes players realize that their actions take place in a larger context, that they are just pawns, vulnerable to the brutality of war. Furthermore, by authoring agency on key sequences of the game, players can take a reflective step back and contemplate their actions. The game lets us foster a critical view on the actions we take, and on the nature of war and conflict. As a spectacle of war, *Modern Warfare* actively refuses to become an epic work. This is not *The Iliad* or a John Wayne film. It is a complex intervention in the discourse on war, an appropriation of a medium, maybe even a daring intervention in the core rhetorical structure of the most popular core genre of the AAA game industry.

This critical view is closely tied to the sequences with authored agency. These are sequences focused on the aftermath of the actions we take, or that lead into to the game's story—the sequences happen on the margins of the main narrative, framing it. We are not direct participants in the major events that drive the plot; our position in the narrative is that of a pawn that makes the story. And by being complicit, we as players can reflect about the meaning of the game, both as an experience and as a cultural artifact embedded in a particular sociocultural time. Complicity challenges us to be reflective, moral beings. And in the context of militaristic games, this means questioning the very nature, meaning and role the games play in our understanding of the mediated imagery of modern warfare.[4]

The failure of "No Russian" is precisely a failure of complicity. Unlike *Modern Warfare*, in which the authored agency sequences occupy the fringes of the narrative we play, "No Russian" puts us directly in the action. Complicity is not used as a way of distancing us from the narrative. The ambition of "No Russian" is high: to create complicity not with the story but with the actions themselves—to distance players from the narrative and give them instruments to reflect about the narrative through those actions. Hence the fact that players must participate in the terrible actions that lead to the main narrative of the game. Unlike in *Modern Warfare*, players do not encounter these actions as active spectators but as participants. This should theoretically lead to a more intricate development of moral complicity, but it does not.

It does not because in order to develop a critical understanding of the game, player agency needs to be closely tied both to the narrative and to the player autonomy in interpreting this narrative. In "No Russian," player autonomy is very limited, yet the actions are central to the narrative development of the game. We are tasked to be passive observers in a situation in which there are few reasons to justify that passivity. Our character is of course framed as an undercover agent, but even in that case, as players that construct our moral values by playing the game, we need to be able to play by them.

In "No Russian" there is a dissonance between the requirements of the scene as authored agency, and the way moral values at play are developed. We are forced to be spectators on a sequence that demands action, particularly if we want to build our moral being as a player. We are not allowed to create our values if we want to stop the assassination. No matter what, we observe, and that position is a gimmick, a trick of authored agency. Complicity in "No Russian" fails because we are placed in an uncomfortable middle ground that does not help develop a critical understanding of the game actions. "No Russian" does not lead to reflective engagement with the narrative of the game, and therefore it does not give us sufficient interpretational cues to read it as a moral experience.

Authored agency can create complicity that opens a game for interpretation, for the creation of a moral hermeneutics of the game. But for that moral hermeneutic to take place, we need to create a liminal space, an opening in the authored agency that allows us to reflect. If that space for reflection is occupied instead by direct action, as in "No Russian," complicity will fail.

The design of complicity for ethical reflection is complicated, and it does not require an absolute limitation of agency. However, in the case of authored agency techniques, complicity has to be designed as a consequence of limited agency that allows players to contemplate the experience of the game from a moral hermeneutic perspective.

The success of *Modern Warfare* in creating complicity through authored agency, and the failure of "No Russian," can be seen as a way of understanding the cultural role of military computer games in their capacity as expressions of the intersection of propaganda and entertainment. If we want to perform moral readings of military games, we can observe how they fail to create player complicity with the worlds they create. This is my core argument: if we want military games to be instruments for reflective engagement, and not just cheap thrills that are tone-deaf to the state of world affairs[5], developers need to look at the expressive possibilities of player complicity. Player complicity should be nothing new for a developer—it is, after all, a modality of engagement. But it is crucially different in that it subverts expectations and engages players not only as consumers, audiences, or input providers, but as complex moral beings.

We Were Soldiers

In this chapter, I have argued that there is a way of vindicating military computer games as devices for reflection, and that some franchises, despite their partial glorification of military conflict, have created experiences that are open to more nuanced interpretations.

I have argued here that player complicity can be an instrument to design "moralized" military game experiences. If developers treat their players as moral agents, and if they give them the spaces to act or reflect upon their actions from a moral perspective, then we will be fulfilling some of the promises of the medium.

Player complicity needs not be a consequence of authored agency. A game like *Spec Ops: The Line*[6] offers a variety of design methodologies to engage players in this kind of experience, from manipulating their agency to breaking the fourth wall. The key is to acknowledge that to interpret these games as moral products that play a role in the configuration of our discourses and understanding of our world, we need the players' complicity. And this complicity can be a consequence of deliberate design choices.

About the Author

Miguel Sicart is a game scholar based at the IT University of Copenhagen. For the last decade his research has focused on ethics and computer games, from a philosophical and design theory perspective. He has two books published: *The Ethics of Computer Games* (MIT Press, 2009) *and Beyond Choices: The Design of Ethical Gameplay* (MIT Press, 2013). His current work focuses on playful design, the subject of *Play Matters* (MIT Press, 2014). He teaches game and play design, and his research is now focused on toys, materiality, and play.

Notes

1. In fact, *Modern Warfare* is a franchise now readying its fourth iteration. In this chapter I will not analyze *Modern Warfare 3*, even though it shares some of the design traits I describe here.

2. In *Modern Warfare* there is at least one other sequence designed with authorial agency techniques: "Shock and Awe," in which the players die after a helicopter crash following a nuclear detonation. (I write more about "Shock and Awe" in Sicart 2013).

3. This loop can be viewed as similar to Boyd's OODA (observe, orient, decide, act) loop, a mainstay concept in operations research and military science. See also Peter Perla's chapter in this volume.

4. See also Patrick Crogan's chapter in this volume.

5. While writing the final version of this chapter, I found the perfect example of the game industry's tone-deafness when it comes to military games. The August 2014 shooting of Michael Brown, an unarmed black man, by a white police officer in Ferguson, Missouri, gave rise to escalating protests and revealed the increased militarization of US police forces. Only a few months earlier, EA had announced *Battlefield Hardline* <http://www.battlefield.com/hardline>, a shooting videogame where players can play as heavily armed police officers fighting heavily armed criminals. The dissonance between the state of affairs in US politics and the way the video game was marketed speaks for itself.

6. See Soraya Murray's chapter in this volume.

UPENDING MILITARIZED MASCULINITY IN *SPEC OPS: THE LINE*

Soraya Murray

Locate and rescue Army Colonel John Konrad and his 33rd Infantry Battalion: this is the deceptively uncomplicated objective of *Spec Ops: The Line* (2012), designed by Yager Development and published by 2K Games. Konrad, a decorated war hero, is somewhere deep in the heart of postapocalyptic Dubai. As Martin Walker, motivated by the loyalty of a life-debt to Konrad and committed to leave no man behind, you are to find him and his men, then radio for evacuation. Along with operators Adams and Lugo, you explore the ruins in search of the source of a distress signal. The ensuing scenarios combine ecological catastrophe and issues of moral culpability with a recognizable military narrative. Over the course of fifteen chapters, the game elicits intense visions of the worst of war, including civilian casualties, chemical and remote warfare, massacre, blight, torture, bare life, and extreme psychological breakdown. Walt Williams, the lead developer, created a storyline that he describes as initially inspired by Joseph Conrad's 1899 novella *Heart of Darkness*. Accordingly, *Spec Ops: The Line* has been widely referred to as the *Apocalypse Now* of video games, since it generally employs themes around the psychological cost of war and presents an ignoble vision of conflict.[1]

Spec Ops: The Line is visually gratifying, narratively rich, and eminently playable. At first glance, one might mistakenly presume this game to be a hawkish military shooter, and perhaps not even the most exemplary of what the genre has to offer. However, in its departure from typical genre conventions, it challenges the industry to deliver more thought-provoking content. Toward illuminating its iconoclasm, this chapter considers the game's troubled mythic construction of the normative (i.e., white, heterosexual, male) American soldier under the duress of inglorious conflict, against a racialized backdrop of an Arab megacity in ruins.

Normative Soldiers, Good and Necessary Wars

Criticism of wargames circulates around their pedagogical role at inuring players to militarized vision and violence, as well as their parallel uses as simulations for recruitment and training (see, e.g., Payne and Huntemann 2009; Dyer-Witherford and De Peuter 2009; Gagnon 2010; Mead 2013). While there is

Figure 28.1
Walker and his men enter Dubai.

much sociology-based debate in the popular media of the direct connection between enacting violence in a game and doing the same in the lived world, less studied is the critical cultural approach that games may enlighten. Nina Huntemann draws connections between post-9/11 anxieties and the potential benefits of catharsis that thematically related games may demonstrate relative to that traumatic event. While she does not advocate for making generalizations around how a player may respond to the content of games like the *Kuma\War*, *Metal Gear Solid*, *SOCOM*, *Splinter Cell*, and *Rainbow Six* series, Huntemann does suggest a correlation between a phobic post-9/11 response and ideological constructions around masculinity as embracing warlike and jingoistic

worldviews, or engaging in revenge fantasies (Huntemann 2009, 223–36). Tanine Allison (2010), elucidating present-day anxieties through World War II historical military shooters, analyzes an ideological sleight-of-hand in which such games point to a moment firmly constructed in history as good and necessary, and then nest contemporary conflicts within that sensibility. A player may then reenact the presented scenarios until they are surgically executed and perfected. This is achieved by presenting a system of missions that function within the formal structure of gameplay as goals and rewards, with no lived-world repercussions.

Even if the current wars in Iraq and Afghanistan do not fit the model that is propounded by these games—a war of precision aiming and firing in which enemies are clearly located and there is no collateral damage—these games still reflect the fantasy of what modern war is: clean, precise, fast-paced, and with quantifiable success. Video games present war as something that can be controlled and mastered, without post-traumatic stress disorder or real death. (Allison 2010, 192)

This seems to resonate with a contemporary political affective moment that for some heralds the death of "traditional America"[2] or generates fears around the erosion of the American way of life and its moral firmament, which was more stable in the historical configuration of World War II as a "good war."

It is true that most military shooters presume the heroic and moral rectitude of their protagonists, and that they may appeal to a player's desire to feel a certain way about their soldier-heroes. However, *Spec Ops: The Line* proves an exception to Allison's characterization of "good" military masculinity by presenting compelling missions that beg for successful and efficient achievement on a game-mechanical level, while on a narrative level grating against the character's (and by extension the player's) presumed sense of righteousness and moral culpability. In this, *Spec Ops: The Line* uniquely departs from its genre conventions (Payne 2014).

Matters are complicated by Walker's gradual mental breakdown and delusions, not to mention the duplicitous aims of those with which he comes into contact. In one mission completed at the behest of a CIA agent named Riggs (Chapter 10, Part 2, "Stealing Water"), he agrees to collaborate in protecting the last remaining water supply in Dubai from the rogue 33rd Battalion. Too late, Walker learns the truth: that Riggs in fact depended upon controlling or destroying the supply, thereby killing all witnesses, so that the ugly truth about the 33rd would not be learned by the world. When, inevitably, the last of the water is destroyed by Riggs, Walker can only stand by and watch, knowing he's conferred a death sentence to both the remaining soldiers and the refugees. In fact, the vast majority of missions in the game are executed against soldiers bearing the same uniforms as your own, or in flagrant disregard for the original humanitarian mission of the 33rd. Early on, confusion obfuscates this truth, and missions are undertaken with seemingly earnest intentions. However, this does not last, and before long the combatants have transitioned from a nebulously described assortment of Arabs to very specific targets who were initially the objectives of a rescue operation.

Mirroring as Self-Criticality

The cinematic referentiality of the game mobilizes semantic and syntactic elements of contemporary war films to lend it authenticity. The game is replete with military clichés that are self-consciously generic to the critical viewer. Gregarious banter at the introduction of the core team of characters creates a sense of a preexisting bond. A strong physical

manifestation of elite training is conveyed through the practiced, efficient execution of commands. Stylized renderings of one-dimensional supersoldiers depict them banding together on a mission. Each of the Delta team soldiers is normative in the sense of embodying a cocksure, rugged, militarized manhood. However, as the narrative unfolds, these tropes turn in on themselves as the player begins to question Walker's thinning rationalizations for violence, and his perpetual straying from mission—as well as his team's persisting loyalty. Players begin to want to distance themselves from the very character with which they should most identify.

Load screens didactically signal critique with phrases like:

> "Do you feel like a hero yet?"
> "You are still a good person."
> "You cannot understand, nor do you want to."
> "This is all your fault."
> "What happens in Dubai stays in Dubai."

These are messages charged with a kind of reverse polarity to the action of the game, which is itself dubious. These undermine the presumption that one plays from a central position of good, or as the hero of the narrative. Particularly, the latter-most phrase makes reference to a popular advertising slogan, "What happens in Vegas, stays in Vegas," which suggests letting go of one's inhibitions in the sequestered party zone of "Sin City." In the case of the game's fictive Dubai, it is not pleasure but an orgy of violence that is to remain behind—which configures the central figure as villain. In an interview, Williams, lead writer of *Spec Ops: The Line*, insists that anything there purely for shock value

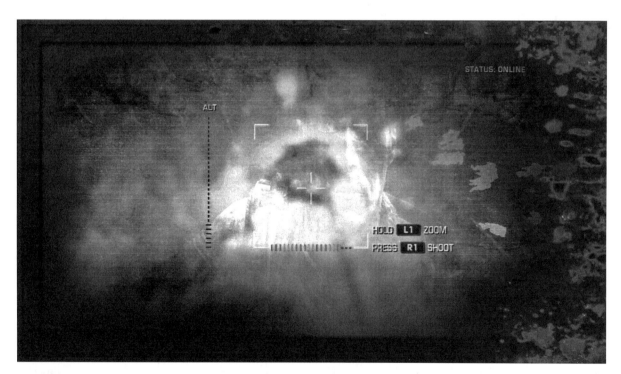

Figure 28.2
Walker's face reflected in the in-game camera monitor for mortar controls.

was removed. He wanted all moral dilemmas to be realistic. The game, he asserts, asks the player to "hold a mirror up to [himself] and say, 'Why am I playing this game the way that I am playing it?'" (McAllister 2012)

This notion of self-reflection appears as a leitmotif in *Spec Ops: The Line*, through the repeated use of reflective surfaces. The literal and metaphorical use of mirroring as an analogue of self-criticality, or in other words, looking at oneself in the mirror, invokes culpability and lack of ethical clarity, as well as moments of revelation that interrupt the character's coherent sense of self. The most potent example of this is in the pivotal white phosphorus assault in Chapter 8, "The Gate," during which Walker uses incendiary warfare on American 33rd soldiers that far outnumber his team. If the player wishes to continue, there is no viable alternative but to play through Walker's choice. This comes at roughly the middle of the game, after a geographic descent that generates an aesthetic vision of this place as ever more hellish, treacherous, and unconscionable. This incident is imaged in a very sophisticated use of visual signifiers to conjure the act of playing the game in relation to the excessive cruelty that will take place—and which mirrors recent lived-world events. The controls for the white phosphorus mortars are not unlike those used for game play: a case containing toggles, buttons, and a screen. First, despite the outspoken protest of Lugo, your team launches a camera device that will provide a bird's-eye view, to be observed on the monitor within the player screen. Most poignantly, Walker's face is imaged in the reflective surface of the camera monitor, so that the player sees simultaneously an onscreen "self" and the remote "bomb-vision" of white phosphorus charges deployed at "your"

command. Initially, the enemy "army" is viewed from this distancing militarized logic, reduced to little more than roaming white marks. Given the battlefield advantage of the "high ground" and the superior weaponry, the slaughter below is thorough, and impersonal in its remoteness. The playability feels easy compared to other elements of gameplay. But the actual damage—chemically burned soldiers writhing on the ground in pain and frozen in grisly death poses—is agonizing to survey later.

Worse yet is the collateral damage of noncombatant refugees, many of them women and children, who have suffered the same fate. A close-up of a charred woman and child, huddled together, her hand held over the child's eyes, drives home the not-so-subtle message.[3] Here women and children are configured not as having agency, but as passive victims. While women imaged in *Spec Ops: The Line* are initially a moral *motivation* for the ensuing conflict, they can no longer figure into Walker's savior-hero fantasy. Importantly, they function as civilian victims of excessive force used by a supposed hero. Internal fighting flares again when Lugo reacts to the horror, claiming they've gone too far this time. The question of who exactly has gone too far may point to Walker, Adams, and Lugo on one level; to the game designers, who painfully conjure the recent use of this weapon in Iraq by both Saddam Hussein and the United States; and the US military itself, which has defended its use of white phosphorus as not being in violation of chemical warfare prohibitions on account of its official classification as "incendiary" (US used white phosphorus in Iraq 2005).[4]

It is crucial to note as well that gameplay is also limited in the continuum of decisions it allows. That is to say, while moral quandaries are presented,

Figure 28.3
Woman and child victims of white phosphorus mortar attack.

gameplay does not permit the player to opt for a more morally sound path. It is not possible to play as "good" or "evil" Walker. In one scenario (Chapter 9, "The Road"), for example, one must choose between shooting a man who stole water out of desperation—a grave offense—or the soldier who killed the thief's family in an attempt to apprehend him. Under threat of sniper fire, one must decide: shoot soldier or civilian, attempt to free them by shooting their ropes, attempt to shoot the snipers, or simply try to run.

While some nuances of narrative result from the varying options, none of them profoundly impact the trajectory of the story or major outcomes. Still, the game was generally praised for seeking to integrate moral questions into the shooter genre, and for its subversive narrative. This is likely due to its effective mobilization of a tension between the core mechanic of the military-themed shooter, and the fact that shooting often means butchering civilian noncombatants and brothers-in-arms.

Mobilizing Ludonarrative Dissonance

Walt Williams, lead developer of *Spec Ops: The Line*, spoke at the 2013 Game Developers Conference in San Francisco, which he seized as an opportunity to do a wrap-up of the game and his team's intentions. He spoke precisely about the tools they used to intervene in the typical genre conventions of military action shooters, which operate on ludic and narrative levels. He identified the role of "ludonarrative dissonance," or in other words, the oppositional friction between the stated narrative contract of the game and its mechanical contract. This term was initially constructed by Clint Hocking as a way of characterizing a flaw in a game, whereby the message contained within the narrative is somehow contradicted by actions undertaken in game play, or perhaps in the point-scoring system. For example, Hocking (2007) critiqued the purported narrative of self-sacrifice in *Bioshock* (2007) while the gameplay itself, through its opportunism and violence, ultimately sends a message of self-interest. In his presentation, entitled "We Are Not Heroes: Contextualizing Violence through Narrative," Williams summarized how the core game mechanic of *Spec Ops: The Line* shapes the limitations of what the player can do:

> Our genres are defined by action, and that action is how you are going to be interacting with the world. It's going to be how you overcome obstacles, how you effect change, how you progress in your goals. If it is a platformer, you are going to do that by jumping. If it is a shooter, you are going to do this by killing someone with a gun. (2013)

A shooter requires shooting, plain and simple, so it is not as if Walker, our main character, is going to do much else. But instead of being a flaw of the game design, this dissonance between the ideals of a humanitarian mission and the use of excessive violence can be maximized, the apparent hypocrisy mined as constitutive of the main character's transformation. As one critic opined, "as the game goes forward, it becomes weirder and weirder that he's killing so many people" (Hamilton 2013).

Still, the heteronormative male shooter trope is also undermined in the narrative. Watts writes of this, particularly the frustrated "'masculine' satisfaction accompanying gameplay mechanics of dominating one's environment using violence and aggression" (Watts, 256). In *Spec Ops: The Line*, Captain Walker performs his role of supersoldier, seeking to dominate every scenario with military might. However, as the game progresses, he and his team physically transform from a well-oiled and surgically accurate unit to burned, bloodied, traumatized aggressors. Their psychological breakdown mirrors this, but in particular, Walker's verbalizations to his men shift from jocular confidence to stern aggression, then finally psychotic rage.

This transition from supersoldier to mass murderer occurs across the arc of fifteen chapters of gameplay. In the early portions of the game, the narrative models hackneyed homosocial relations in terms of the mythmaking of soldiering as an unconditional, loving bond between men. This depoliticizes the image into a band-of-brothers myth, which functions through its focus on the individual and interpersonal relations, rather than larger political forces at play in the circumstances of soldiers in battle (Dyer-Witherford and De Peuter 97–122). But as key characters of *Spec Ops: The Line* become more exhausted, injured, filthy, surly, hopeless, and morally bankrupt, verbal cues by the primary character move from clichéd war film dialogue to unhinged bloodlust. Walker mutates into a menacing figure, a terrorist who imposes his ideology and will onto others in pursuit of unsanctioned objectives no one else shares. Through this, the image of the ideal soldier as embodiment of righteous justice is tarnished, which makes it harder for the player to sustain identification.

This is particularly heightened in Chapter 14, "The Bridge," near the end of the game. By this time, one teammate, Lugo, has been eliminated; both Adams and the player character Walker are injured and under extreme duress. During this challenging mission, you face a large number of enemies in a courtyard that has been converted into a chain of bunkers with snipers, stationary machine guns and elite soldiers. Slowly pressing forward from one stronghold to the next, Walker's verbal abuses can be heard as he berates Adams to encourage him to fight. In one exceedingly perverse moment, you engage your long-dead operator Lugo in combat—a nightmarish delusion that he has returned as a fully armored and armed "heavy" to avenge his own death. Overhearing the verbal commands of your adversaries, it is clear from the nature of their agitated comments that you embody death itself for them. Though they greatly outnumber you, they are audibly terrified. The only option during this scenario is direct, meat-grinding brutality; it is not possible to progress using stealth or any other strategic avoidance of violence. Game critic Brendan Keogh in his compelling, book-length documentation of his experiences and insights while playing *Spec Ops: The Line*, excellently captures the inevitable conclusion drawn by players at this point:

> Yet again, through the pervasive fear of the 33rd in this final stages, *The Line* manages to comment on something prevalent in all video games: the unreality of how much death and destruction the player brings along with them. *The Line* doesn't offer an alternative to this—it never offers alternatives—but instead it treats that death and destruction (and the player who brings it) as it should be treated: monstrous, impossible, terrifying, wrong. (Keogh, loc.2278–82)

Walker's metamorphosis under the duress of battle from the beginning to the end, and his mounting rationalizations that become tantamount to dementia, agitate a deep-seated longing for the stability of that normative male role. But it is stripped away and eroded throughout the game until what remains is psychopathy and the figure of hero as menace who uses pure, excessive violence as a destructive form of expression. Walker is effective in the execution of his elite training, but his motivations are flawed and his ultimate endeavor to save lives is utterly impotent at this point. This is brilliantly underscored in the verbal articulations of Walker's insanity and aggression that are so overblown as to alienate the player from his cracked interiority.

Conclusion

With little exception, the protagonists of first- and third-person military shooters assuredly fight on the side of right, and the games are designed to encourage affinity in the player for the player character. In blurring the ethical boundary between soldier and mass murderer, *Spec Ops: The Line* indicts the idealized notions of militarized masculinity established at the beginning of the game and recognizable from long-established genre conventions. In this, "the line" that is crossed may refer to excessive use of the core mechanic, specifically shooting and other forms of heinous violence, as a part of the game progression. Consequently, the enacted fantasies of full-spectrum dominance remain technically fulfilled but morally frustrated. As a player, this frustration results largely from feeling dragged into Walker's insanity and self-righteous military display, without having any real power to choose otherwise, within the scope of options the genre compels.

This encapsulates the "wicked problem" of the game: how to keep playing and remain willing to partake in the insanity, how to make enjoyment of a shooter possible, despite the ethical self-scrutiny that the game invites (Sicart 2013, 111–16). While cinematic elements and the signifiers of military shooters initially present a conventional vision, *Spec Ops: The Line* deftly exploits morally condemnable tactics as a strategy for confounding players' expectations that their character represents the good (Sadd 2012). This troubles the implicit rules of the military shooter genre by sullying the gratification that would usually accompany a well-executed mission. When it is ultimately learned that John Konrad is long dead, and his voice heard throughout the game is a mere projection of Walker's delusion, the decimation of the militarized male protagonist is complete. What remains is the psychological and ethical ruin of a Western soldier-ideal, whose time has passed and whose prescribed role as a protector/gatekeeper against the backdrop of an Arab heart of darkness is defunct. The moral high ground of rescue is collapsed; the steady foundation of the righteous ends justifying a violent means is shattered. Walker's victory can only be seen as pyrrhic, in the sense that the emotional trauma and collateral damage of the battlefield far outweighs the gains. As for the question of whether the game itself effectively makes an ethical critique, it does model the relationship between the raw brutality of military conflict in its immediacy, and the sense-making that takes place to narrativize it later. The friction between these two things is virtually impossible not to contemplate through gameplay, thanks to the dissonance between *Spec Ops: The Line*'s primary mechanic of shooting, and its legitimizing narrative of militarized humanitarianism.

About the Author

Soraya Murray holds a PhD in art history and visual studies from Cornell University. An assistant professor in the Film and Digital Media Department at the University of California, Santa Cruz, she is also affiliated with the Digital Arts and New Media MFA Program and the Center for Games and Playable Media. She is an interdisciplinary scholar who focuses on contemporary visual culture, with particular interest in contemporary art, cultural studies, and new media art. Her writings have been featured in print and online publications such as *Art Journal, Nka: Journal of Contemporary African Art, CTheory, Public Art Review, Third Text, ExitEXPRESS, Gamesbeat,* and *PAJ: A Journal of Performance and Art.*

Notes

1. *Apocalypse Now* is widely known to be a loose interpretation of *Heart of Darkness*.

2. Bill O'Reilly, American television host of *The O'Reilly Factor* on the Fox News Channel, discusses this, but it is common terminology used by conservatives to speak about what they believe to be a break from "traditional" America, especially in the wake of President Barack Obama's 2012 reelection.

3. Even as of the game's release in 2012, it is extremely rare to see children imaged in military conflict games, and even rarer for the player-character to be able to hurt or kill them.

4. White phosphorus is a key ingredient in flares, used to illuminate areas, or to create smoke. Because it comes from an "incendiary" device, namely flares, it has not been officially categorized by regulating bodies, such as the Organisation for the Prohibition of Chemical Weapons (2005), as a chemical weapon. Its status is undefined, and thus it skirts regulations.

V SYSTEMS AND SITUATIONS

29 WARGAMES AS WRITING SYSTEMS

Sharon Ghamari-Tabrizi

In 1959, the strategist Herman Kahn (1960, 294) argued that the best way to compel the Soviet aggressor to back down was to appear "slightly mad, intemperate or emotional." The US should adopt the pose of being fanatically committed to irrational war-aims. "If we wish to have our strategic air force contribute to ... deterrence," he suggested, "it must be credible that we are willing to take one or more ... actions. Usually the most convincing way to *look* willing is to *be* willing" (287). By the mid-1960s, Kahn reversed himself on the inexorability of fighting, surviving, and reconstructing society from a nuclear war in the near future. He confessed, "Like the people in Washington, like most people, like you, I don't really believe in it." The existential reality of nuclear war in one's lifetime struck him as being "akin to a religious issue" (quoted in Herken 1985, 205).

Wargaming contributed to Kahn's belief in the certainty (or improbability) of near-future nuclear war. For nearly everybody working for the Pentagon in the 1950s and '60s, the rationale for wargaming was straightforward:

The requirement to prepare for potential conflicts with weapons of a radically new sort, where previous experience gives little guidance, impose[s] the necessity for developing a substitute for experience; and simulation is precisely a technique for creating synthetic experience (Sterne 1966, 66).

Wargames are synthetic experiences—substitutes for real life. But what are the categories we can use to identify and embed them into context? The problem of determining which stream of past life in which to anchor wargames is not trivial. Certainly they are training exercises and drills that develop group loyalties, discipline, message handling, and decision making. But wargames can also be located within the sensorium of the combined effects of the entertainment, communication, and transportation technologies of any historical moment. In other words, wargames can be positioned alongside movies, radio, and television, carnivals, fairs, amusement parks, and thrill rides. Wargames are venerable elements in curricula, indoctrinating newly promoted military personnel into fresh roles and responsibilities. But they have also been used for experiments in group organization and dynamics, as well as individual and group creativity. Wargames are training mechanisms for inducing specific modes of embodied attention, concentration, and endurance. Yes, they teach by doing, but they can also be slotted into the history of reading and writing.

For the last twenty years I have been thinking about the various constellations within the civilizational endowment into which the historian can assign the wargame. A wargame exhibits kinship with the multi-sensory stimulation of mass entertainments; it is a specimen of the routinized labor of the soldier, sailor, airman, astronaut, ICBM missileer in a given time and place; it can be summoned as evidence for the blurring between the *echt*-real and its simulacra. Just what realities does the wargame attempt to represent? How shall the historian reconstruct the threads that gave rise to the transient verisimilitude of a discrete moment in the past?

Since I regard embodiment, feeling, and thinking to be inextricably interdependent, I begin by assuming that perceptual and affective knots combine to make wargames realistic for defense analysts, strategists, weapons designers, and trainees in some interval in time. I have found this to be a useful starting place whether I was combing archives, as I had done in my Herman Kahn book, or interviewing contemporary wargame designers, as I had done from 2003 to 2006. I also assume that reports of what counts as realistic in wargame design, play, and interpretation will be historically inflected, and therefore can be located in social space and time. That is to say, I assume that statements about the verisimilitude of a wargame can be anchored in a specifiable matrix whose associations and commonplaces will suggest what contemporary actors might mean by its realism.

The Reality Effect of Wargames

The bomber dove and opened fire on the men on deck. Passing over the ship, it banked, pulled up, then began to climb rapidly. A marine blasted his machine gun at the receding plane. The officer struggled to be heard. "Next to standing up and actually taking it," he screamed, "this is the nearest thing possible to standing on the deck of a destroyer and getting dive-bombed and strafed." It is 1943 and we are standing at the front of the "Hell-on-Wings" theater in the Norfolk Naval Training Station. Near us are several curved panels that make up an enormous cinema screen, speakers near us amplify the sound more loudly than we have ever heard, and directly in front of the screen, we see a young man braced against an electric light gun. When he pulls the trigger, a burst counter records his shots, calculates how many simulated bullets have been fired, and how many shots hit the target. Standing next to us is a civilian also observing the scene. He exclaims how "startlingly realistic" it all is. The reporter (Shalett 1943, 25) marvels, "It creates within a small blacked-out room the illusion of aerial bombing and strafing and steels our men to stand up and fight the surprise and frightfulness of such attacks" (see also Taylor 2013).

The inventor of "Hell-on-Wings" claimed that his trainer accurately reproduced the sights, sounds, and vibrations of warfare. Writing in the *Journal of the Society of Motion Picture Engineers* in 1946, Fred Waller declared that his Flexible Gunnery Trainer "correctly [simulates] conditions of firing in a way that otherwise could only be found in actual combat" (quoted in Taylor 2013, 26).

While Waller's trainer reproduced the battle conditions of World War II, duplicating the information processing machines of a combat command center became a chief preoccupation of designers of immersive simulations in the early Cold War. In early 1951, several RAND Corporation psychologists built a replica of the Tacoma, Washington, Air Defense Direction Center (ADDC) as well as several early warning (EW) stations in a large back room in a Santa Monica billiard hall. They re-created all of the hardware an air defense crew needed: "Information-gathering equipment (radar sets), the communications net (radios and telephones), information storage aids (central displays and written records), and its response equipment (interceptor aircraft and their weapons)" (Chapman et al. 1959, 254).

> Each of the ADDC sections had one or more simulated radar scopes (PPIs) ... The EW stations also had simulation input devices. Simulations of internal and external communications included the intercom within the ADDC, telephone lines between it and the EW stations, telephone lines between the ADDC and an adjacent ADDC, a headquarters center ..., the civil air traffic agency, the interceptor bases, and radio links to the interceptor aircraft. (Parsons 1972, 165)

In 1958, the Naval War College debuted an immersive training environment called NEWS (the Navy Electronic War Simulator). The NEWS gave the trainees experience in rapid, accurate information processing. The journalist observing its operation echoed his hosts' declarations that the simulator was true-to-life:

> [The] training device ... enables the Navy to play realistic war games in the era of supersonic aircraft and 20,000 mile-an-hour missiles.... It can carry the speed, radar characteristics and firepower of two fleets of twenty-four units each in

its memory section. Commanders in 20 command posts receive their information via radar and voice circuits just as they would in combat. (Fredericks 1958, 96)

With the introduction of high-speed jet bombers, even faster missiles, and digital computing, the tempo of information processing speeded up. Simulating combat became easier. In 1961, an operations researcher pointed out how close the wargame was to the real thing:

> The enemy bomber, no longer even a dot in the sky, becomes a blip on a radar scope, a counter on a plotting board, or even a number on a vertical screen. The "fog of battle" becomes a blur of numbers on a tote board or a battery of blinking lights at the computer console. ... The colored pins in the maps of the game room are hardly distinguishable from those of the command post. The computer output of the simulation can certainly emulate the clickety-clack of the teletype or even the cathode-ray tube of the radar. These results surely look real. (Thomas, 460)

Inevitably, these immersive role-playing games attracted criticism for being too real. In 1964, RAND analyst Robert Levine objected to the assumption that role-playing was credible. "As representations of decision-makers ..., it is difficult to say what they represent or what differences with the real world should be allowed for." Ambiguities in game design made it hard for players to gauge the difference between the gameworld and reality. The problem was that

> game-players never seem quite sure whether they are supposed to be positive or normative representations of decision-makers; game-players generally have both an imperfect knowledge of the decision-makers they are representing, and ... a very imperfect intuition of the way in which the

decision-makers feel the various pressures on them; and game-players do not have the time to think systematically and objectively of the ways they differ from real decision-makers. (Levine et al. 1991, 47–48)

What was it about these gameworlds that made them so convincing? In 1968, Roland Barthes suggested that gratuitous particulars were the key to the "reality effect" of Flaubert's novels. That is, the author's painstaking specification of particulars that do nothing to advance the plot convey a sense of reality in literary fiction. A superfluity of details gives rise to the reader's sense that the world of a novel is the same as hers. Correspondingly, the masses of accurately reproduced details furnished in immersive wargames *do* contribute to the conviction that the gameworld is "startlingly realistic" (Barthes 1985).

But in order to make sense of the gamer's confidence in the simulation's accuracy and reliability, let us extend the reach of the reality effect of the gameworld to the excitation of a gamer's somatosensory systems. What we want to pinpoint are the sensory inputs that prompt the subjective conviction that a wargame "feels real." To help us understand this, we turn to the work of Jonathan Crary.

In his 1999 book *Suspensions of Perception*, Crary argues that in the late nineteenth and twentieth centuries, visual, auditory, haptic, vestibular and kinesthetic sensations were subject to ceaseless reform and refocus. "Mobility, novelty and distraction became identified as constituent elements of perceptual experience" (30). Simple acts of perception required endless "adaptation to new... speeds and sensory overload." One marks the passage of time—as subject and as historian—with the perpetual

adjustment of one's cognitive and perceptual powers. Crary remarked, "The management of attention depends on the capacity of an observer to adjust to continual repatternings of the ways in which a sensory world can be consumed" (33).

In order to grasp how the immersive role-playing wargames of the twentieth century felt real to its operators, let us step away from the social and technical worlds of the military and jump social and temporal space back to the first decade of the twentieth century. Tom Gunning's (1990, 231) notion of the cinema of attractions examines the reality effect in mass entertainments such as the circus, vaudeville, carnival, fairground, and amusement park.[1]

Gunning is particularly interested in *non-narrative* cinema of the first decade of the twentieth century. These attractions combined motion picture displays with realistic theater sets. In "Hale's Tour," for example, someone could be seated in the replica of a railway car, look out her window, and behold a train speeding into a tunnel or across a bridge. "Not only did the films consist of non-narrative sequences taken from moving vehicles (usually trains), but the theater itself was arranged as a train car, with a conductor who took tickets, and sound effects simulating the click-clack of wheels and hiss of air brakes" (Gunning 1990, 231).

The physiological, nervous, and psychological excitation of the spectators was provoked by the potent sensory prompts of film-based attractions. "Like the devotees of thrill rides at Coney Island, the spectator of early film could experience the thrill of intense and suddenly changing sensations" (Gunning 1993, 11). The aesthetic key to non-narrative films was *attraction*. An attraction, "whether of the cinema, the sensational press or the fairground," fixed the spectator's attention directly on the visual pleasure offered by the technical apparatus itself, rather than the more customary pleasure in storytelling, that is, in guessing the possible plot points of an unfolding narrative and identifying with the story's characters (Gunning 1994, 190).

What significance do cultural historians such as Gunning and Crary attribute to the pleasure in attractions? They are training technologies: they teach their users how to extract the pleasure in their operations. Not only must perception—how to look at a film—be learned, trained, and habituated, but the right kind of attention must be cultivated. Crary (1999, 1) defines cognitive and perceptual attention as "a disengagement from a broader field of attraction, whether visual or auditory, for the sake of isolating or focusing on a reduced number of stimuli."

Within the domain of entertainment, Gunning shows us how spectators learned how to see the cinema-based attractions in the right way in order to find pleasure in them. If we widen our gaze to include other technologies, we can extend the argument: as a result of ordinary interaction with communication, entertainment, and transportation technologies, the encompassing technical surround induces historically distinct, alterable modes of foregrounded attention.

If this is true, then it seems reasonable to suppose that as an ensemble, the technologies of mass entertainment, communication, and transportation are the perceptual referents underlying the felt sense that immersive role-playing wargames are realistic. To the degree that the gamer is long habituated to the technical surround of the culture, having consumed the entertainment media of his generation—rollercoasters and carousels, cinema, radio and TV; having routinized the visual, auditory, and kinesthetic experience of transportation technologies—streetcars and buses, trains, planes, automobiles, bicycles, skateboards, motorcycles; having naturalized communications media—photography, cinema, telegraphy, telephone, radio, television, time-shared computers, personal computers, cell phones—to that same degree will the multimodal sensory stimulation of the wargame appear consonant to him. That is, the immersive simulation will be *as real* and *as mediated* as his mundane sensorium. Thus, the convergent conditions of the technologies that combine to produce the reality effect of wargames will remain constant, even though any particular simulation that once struck its users as being lifelike may appear laughably contrived to later observers.

"So what?" I hear you say. "How does this alter our understanding of immersive role-playing wargames?" By itself, this idea does not account for the subjective experience of the gamer's verdict that the simulation *feels real*. For this, we need to look more closely at the historically inflected nature of the gamer's decisions and feelings prompted by the simulation.

The Historicity of a Compelling Experience

Let's unwind the spool a little more. We stopped in 1964 with Robert Levine's objections to the sloppy equivalence between the thoughts and feelings of the wargamers and the actual inner experiences of political and military decision makers. What's the next station in our history? In the late 1960s and early 1970s, wargame designers concentrated on modeling combat and logistical processes as though they were physics problems. They abandoned political-military crisis scenarios to the seminar room (Ghamari-Tabrizi 2005, chapters 5 and 6).[2] Also in these years the majority of wargames were displaced from tabletop terrain models to the battlespace conditions that successive generations of mainframe computers and software languages could accommodate.[3] Eventually annual iterations of wargames resulted in baroquely embellished, opaque congeries of hand-me-down programs, shortcuts, and modeling assumptions. By the middle 1970s, we begin to see the public expression of professional dissatisfaction with the hopelessly unintelligible black box of computer modeling.

For example, in 1975, RAND analyst John Stockfisch blasted the spurious findings of much of the Army's conventional combat simulations. He declared that most defense analyses were grossly wrong. They were characterized by "inadequate empirical endeavor, an apparent misuse of what empirical data there are, and a large-scale production of pseudo-data" (6). Game designers neglected or refused to test their assumptions empirically. "We have a situation where arbitrary or postulated numbers are inputs for a theoretical model." Stockfisch concluded that "at best" a computer-based wargame was "a computational exercise with a limited or murky empirical foundation" (77).

While role-playing exercises seemed to have been eclipsed by quantitative models in these years, by 1977, it was clear to wargame professionals that *both* kinds of wargames were troublingly erroneous: the highly aggregated model was unintelligible due to its lack of transparency and empirical validation,[4] and the thick description of the immersive gameworld presented a confusing mishmash of multiple foci and empirical uncertainties.

A discussant (Reiner Huber in SRI International 1977, 80) at a Department of Defense conference in 1977 captured the tension between these two approaches. He pointed out that "many people want high resolution [i.e., immersive role-playing games] because they think that high resolution models better reflect reality than higher aggregated models." They believed that because the high-resolution models were crammed with details, it was "more realistic." The problem was that the details complicated the game until "he can't understand the model any more."

This 1977 conference was a milestone in the history of wargaming which would ultimately swing simulation back toward role-playing simulation. The host of the event, Andrew Marshall, the Director of Net Assessment in the Office of the Secretary of Defense, remarked to the audience, "I have felt that the current modeling or indices that people have are not really descriptive of almost any military balance that I really know of, including the strategic balance" (18).

Marshall confessed that he had been disappointed for many years with the lack of transparency of virtually every model he had encountered. A day or so later, the only commercial (i.e., hobbyist) wargame designer present at the conference responded to Marshall. The game designer Jim Dunnigan argued that professional wargamers needed to discipline their urge to proliferate details (141–148). The gameplay enabled by the models was forbiddingly intricate. He suggested that game designers radically simplify their models and reorient toward greater human involvement. The wargame "has to be presented in a way that the user will be tempted." The temptation Dunnigan had in mind was the urge to play with the game and try things out. He cautioned, "Don't underestimate the power of play" (137). Right now DoD had a warehouse of data, but nobody wanted to go near it. The trick was to stimulate interest. How do you get them to want to play with the data? "You can get them to use it more if you make it enjoyable. But if you're turning the people off, or if you're not turning them on ..., you're not going to get this interest in the models and what they can do" (140).

Marshall was intrigued. He offered Dunnigan a consultancy helping to rejuvenate senior-level wargames. For the first time in the history of Pentagon gaming, the services of an entertainment professional, a designer of hobby games, was sought by the American defense community.[5] Marshall hoped that Dunnigan's notion of fun, of tempting presentation and simplified game design, might solve his problem with the unintelligibility of simulations.

What is also significant about Marshall's recruitment of Dunnigan was that the hobby subculture's orientation toward gamers' pleasure began to play a role in designing a high-level military gaming space. Hobby gamers emphasized the virtues of dynamic process and playability; Marshall's unorthodox alliance with Dunnigan signified a shift toward recognizing once more the importance of human factors in defense simulations. In particular, wargame designers became ever more sensitive to the requirement for emotionally appealing game scenarios and rules. This would become a central concern in the 1990s and thereafter (see e.g., Stanney, Mourant and Kenney 1998, 327–351).

Now let's leap ahead to the Institute for Creative Technologies (ICT) at the University of Southern California. In 1999, the Army Research Laboratory sponsored the establishment of the ICT as an official University Affiliated Research Center. ICT's director, Richard Lindheim, had worked as a television producer at Paramount. He hired entertainment professionals such as game designers, programmers, artists, filmmakers, and screenwriters, as well as computer scientists with expertise in artificial intelligence, natural language recognition, and virtual reality.

I spent all of 2004 at the ICT as an ethnographic observer. Everyone there declared proudly that what was being created at ICT was new. On a return visit in July 2010, ICT staff persisted in claiming the revolutionary significance of blending entertainment with pedagogical technologies for military training. Not only did they assert the newness of combining narrative with training, they frequently invoked the power of "Hollywood storytelling techniques."

During my year at ICT I gradually shifted my attention from looking at the production of the elements of a wargame's verisimilitude as the source of simulation realism to what ICT employees repeatedly, hypnotically, echoed was the key to their efforts, namely, the creation of a "compelling experience." Even as of the time of this writing (August 2014), on the front page of ICT's website inside a graphic box headed "What we do" the text reads, "Compelling stories, characters and special effects. The University of Southern California Institute for Creative Technologies applies this winning Hollywood formula to benefit service members, students, and society at large."

I attempted to probe the nature of what seemed to be self-evident. In many different contexts I asked people to tell me more about the compelling experience of a wargame. I asked about their approach to narrative:

- How did you originally translate the training objectives laid out in the project requirements document into a story-driven simulation?
- Conversely, how did you map the fully fleshed out story back onto the training objectives when you were speaking to Army personnel?
- How did you translate the cognitive demands of the training objectives into prompts and triggers for the right behavior and emotion in the user?
- Specifically, how did you fix emotional cues to plot points?

I asked about the emotions the designers sought to elicit in the trainee:

- What are the emotional cues you are trying to create in this simulation?
- How do you know if you have succeeded in triggering a response?

I asked how the simulation attracted and held the trainee's attention:

- What are the sensory prompts you have added to intensify the user's emotional response?
- How do you know the simulation is sticky enough to block out competing stimuli in the user's present?
- How do you know it stimulates the user's emotional and cognitive energies?

I asked how they evaluated the effectiveness of the simulation:

- How do you know that this narrative is engrossing, instructive, and memorable?
- Do you test specifically for the "compellingness" of the simulation?

I wanted to learn how they understood the *appeal*—visceral as well as narrative—of their simulations. My inquiry had turned into a reflection on what counts as "compelling" for entertainment and Army professionals in the first decade of the twenty-first century.

Since everyone at ICT blandly or dogmatically declared that their projects were a new way to teach and train Army troops, naturally enough I wondered if it was possible to determine if and what was actually new in the emotional cues and plot decisions of ICT's computer games, movies, and immersive environments. If I compared their simulations with earlier ones, would I be able to detect the *historical inflection* of these solicitations of the spectator?

The approach to the question seems to move in two parts. First, I wanted to extract people's basic assumptions about what works to solicit the attention of a spectator; then, I wanted to see if it was possible to isolate formal or affective elements of an appeal or cue that could serve as indexical markers of a historical period, present at one moment but not at another. Naturally enough, there would be a continuity in some elements. But surely there would also be elements of spectator solicitation that appeared historically distant, obsolete, and unlike those identified by my ICT informants as being particularly effective prompts for spectator engagement.

To clarify my own thoughts, I started to think about simple solicitations as such. This means the solicitation of Americans en masse, not just military personnel. What sprung to mind was the imploring sidewalk fundraiser or petitioner who tries to catch the eye of every passerby. Surely the starkest model of solicitation is the barker. Before radio jingles and movie trailers, there was ballyhoo:

pitchmen for fairs, amusement parks, circuses and carnivals, vaudeville, burlesque, and variety shows (see Reichenbach 1931 for a richly detailed account of the inventions of entertainment marketing).

While I experience the patter of pitchmen as auditory assaults even when they are graphically inscribed, Gunning is interested in the "aggressive *visuality*" of advertising, marketing, and merchandizing in the first three decades of the twentieth century. For Gunning (1994, 195), *every* domain of consumer culture that solicits passersby could be folded into a single encompassing framework in reference to which early cinema should be allied. After all, consumers learned how to find pleasure in visual display not only in attractions such as world fairs and amusement parks, but also in commercial spaces such as shop windows of department stores, billboards, posters, print advertisements, and the covers of books and magazines. Gunning's analysis of visual pleasure, the tension between attractions and narrative in film, emotional and visual appeals in advertising and promotion might help us to discern what *is* historically new in the simulations produced at ICT.

Learning How to Read Wargame Documents

In 1912, US Navy Captain McCarty Little famously observed that the wargame "offers the player the whole world as a theater" (Little 1912, 1219). Suppose we consider this remark literally and thought about wargames as though they were stage plays in theaters of old; what difference would that make to our understanding?

The literary manager, or dramaturge, of a repertory company, observed Bert Cardullo, is "the guardian of the text" (1995, 10). It is her job to learn about the social, political, economic, cultural, and personal milieu that enfolded the playwright in the course of composing a classic work. The dramaturge's role is "to ensure the theatrical transmission of the playwright's vision" when a director decides to transpose a script into dramatic performance.

Leon Katz, the formidable professor of dramaturgy at the Yale School of Drama, outlined in exacting detail the topics a dramaturge should learn in order to assist the director of a classic play. She will write a detailed report, the dramaturge's protocol, which contains the following:

(a) the historical, cultural, and social background of the play;

(b) relevant biographical information concerning the playwright, plus a history of the writing of the play and an assessment of its place in the author's oeuvre;

(c) a critical and production history of the play, including a report on the textual problems (if any) of the original and an assessment of the major translations (if the play was written in a language other than English);

(d) a comprehensive critical analysis of the play, including the dramaturge's suggestions for a directorial-design concept for a new production;

and (e) a comprehensive bibliography of materials on the play: editions, essays, articles, reviews, interviews, recordings, films ... (Katz 1995, 13–14).

What is the value of such extensive research? The playwright's "language, stage conventions, and world-view" can most finely be understood if a thorough reconstruction of the circumstances of the play's original production were responsibly undertaken. That is, if, theater historian Joel Schechter (1976, 89) points out, "the director wants to work true to the original text." The German word for this method of historically informed performance is *werktreue*.

What would we gain if the historian adopted the dramaturge's protocol as a template for assessing a historical wargame? For one thing, the notion of *werktreue* cautions us against assuming that we can pick up a wargame document and easily grasp its significance. We must recognize that in the unfolding of gameplay from game documents something happens in the minds, hearts, and bodies of the players in a socially locatable place, time, and setting. The game is not just a design for strategic interaction, it is a dynamic interpersonal event. Thinking like a dramaturge helps us remember the force of RAND analyst Robert Specht's observation in 1958, "A war game teaches both intellectually and emotionally—it is an experience one lives through" (149).

In order to attempt to reconstruct the possible thoughts, feelings, and behaviors of players immersed in a wargame, let us consider further Crary's notion of the historicity of attention. First, we might want to orient toward the focal points of a game document: What are points of condensation and foreshortening in any aspect of gameplay? What are areas for exploration? What is taken for granted? More interestingly, what would we as contemporary readers of historical game documents regard as universal constants in gameplay? In other words, what might be elements of thinking, deciding, and communicating within the wargame that strike us as being similar across time? Only then

might we be able to alight on textual clues that locate a wargame as belonging to a long-ago time and place and not now.

Having identified the elements of familiar gameplay, could one espy in wargame documents historically inflected traces, zeitgeist markers of the actual experience of gaming in an immersive environment? Since emotionally intense experience was precisely what the Cold War wargamers believed made their simulations feel real, and since this is also a mind-state associated with ICT's "compelling experiences," I wondered if I could differentiate zeitgeist markers in wargames from two different historical periods.

A word about how I'm thinking about zeitgeist markers. It is impossible for me to think about a historical moment in terms of the atmospheric generalities the word *zeitgeist* usually conveys. What I'm looking for are traces in game documents that reveal the historicity of the forms of attention and perception enjoined by the game technologies, scenarios, and gameplay—forms of attention and perception that appear to us as being *unlike* our own. These traces might be common to Americans accustomed to everyday entertainments, communications and transportation technologies. Or they might be peculiar to a cohort of military personnel in a specific milieu.

The Babbage Archive at the University of Minnesota has extensive holdings from the RAND System Research Laboratory, the RAND System Research Division, and the System Development Corporation. In particular, it has an extraordinarily rich collection of documents related to the immersive simulation experiments that formed the core of the group's theoretical and practical interests from 1950 through 1965. I was overjoyed to find transcriptions of an audio record of their earliest experiments in 1950–52. This was exactly what I was looking for: a detailed soundprint of how participants in the simulation learned how to use their instruments, make timely decisions, and work together as a group under stress within a highly realistic immersive environment (Ghamari-Tabrizi 2012).

The setting was a replica of an Air Defense Direction Center linked to several Early Warning stations circa 1951. It had some elements that were historically new. Learning how to read distributed messages in the air defense network involved learning how to ignore most data streams. This enjoined a split cognition: operators had to learn what to ignore, what merited close attention, and how to refocus their attention after bouts of boredom and reverie. Determining the optimal flow of information for a single team and a single member of a team was as much a matter of instrument display design as it was a matter of a new kind of literacy. The experiments had a dual focus. The scientists wished to test the conditions of information saturation as well as discover techniques that could train operators to read their radar consoles accurately and vigilantly under conditions of increasing stress and boredom.

While we regard the subjective experience of information overload as something that characterizes the present and immediate past, psychologists began to experiment with this in the early 1950s. Articles about information overload and information processing under stress appeared in 1960 (see e.g., Miller 1960; Jay and McCornack 1960). By 1964, information overload began to be articulated to and by educators (see e.g., Miller 1964; McLaughlin 1967). By 1968, urged on by a feeling of national and planetary crisis and the need for radical curriculum reform, futurists argued, "We must educate so people can cope efficiently, imaginatively, and perceptively with information overload" (Michael 1968, 108; see also Drucker 1968 for discussion on new learning in the knowledge economy).

Would the transcripts of the conversation among trainees in this simulation offer clues about their airmen's *thinking, feeling,* and *acting* about the blips crowding their screens? Could their recorded behavior be tied to decision-making practices that arguably differ from the present? It is an interesting problem. Attack and defense are so primal, the decision making is so basic—*is this a threat or not?*—it is hard to see how something as transient as the technical-cultural surround within a military simulation could contain *zeitgeist* markers. But this is what I am looking for. Can we find behaviors, speech, emotional cues or prompts in this Cold War setting that parallel, or do not parallel, the story-and-character cues of ICT's training games, movies, and environments?

If I can show how the habitus of the technical-cultural surround leaves traces in the social and cognitive means by which operators sort information in a defense simulation, I would be able to say something useful about zeitgeist markers in simulations, past and present. What I have in mind is not something as facile as finding in the transcription a bit of slang or reference to a popular movie or song. What I am thinking about are stimuli entering into the simulation as inputs that require a response, emotional and cognitive, from the user that could be regarded as being historically inflected. *How am I supposed to feel about this? Is this important or irrelevant? Is there something I'm supposed to see in this confusing pattern?* An exacting study of the possible answers to these questions might surface traces of zeitgeist markers in an old wargame.

Making Learning Fun: Adapting Entertainment Technologies for Education

In the late 1980s and '90s, educators seriously promoted the need for "making learning fun" (see e.g., Malone and Lepper 1987; Parker and Lepper 1992; Reiber 1996). Their enthusiasm for new media established the ground for ICT simulationists' belief that they were uttering common sense in their claims for the newness of their work. For example, in 2003 the president of the Federation of American Scientists, Henry Kelly, stated matter-of-factly that "new technologies can make learning more productive, compelling, personal and accessible" (Learning Federation 2003, 6). Interactive simulations have "the potential to reshape learning," he opined. The problem in American education was outdated pedagogy: "reading texts, listening to lectures, and participating in infrequent—and usually highly scripted—laboratory experiences." New media, on the other hand, could improve student motivation, learning, and retention because new media was *compelling*. "It can provide accurate compelling simulations of physical phenomena and virtual environments for exploration and discovery. These can be used to illustrate complex concepts through the ancient art of talking and showing and can be used to build challenging assignments and games" (Kelly 2005, 34; 2008).

Paging through any number of professional journals of education, we can spot repetitive claims for the power of new media to improve learning. Let the following stand in for countless others: "Video games allow learners to immerse themselves in highly interactive and engaging experiences. Such experiences can lead to contextual learning of complex activities and the development of understanding, skills, and innovativeness" (Foster and Mishra 2009, 34).

Not only are digital media thought to be more enthralling than paper texts, lectures, and instructor-led class discussion, strong claims are made that the learning style of people thirty years old and younger differs considerably from previous generations. From years of playing with digital games, traditional activities such as lectures, classroom discussion, and meetings are intolerably dull (Prensky 2001, 59).

Advocates for the historical difference of so-called "digital natives" (i.e., young people who cannot learn in classrooms, but *can* pay attention and exert significant cognitive effort in interactive and narratively based learning situations) also claim that in the contemporary world, visual literacy is as important or even more significant than prose texts. As irrefutable evidence they point to the nearly universal adoption of PowerPoint multimedia presentations in public addresses (see e.g., Duncum 2004; Childers et al. 1998; Darley 2000; Unsworth 2001 on visual and multimodal literacy).

To boil down the characteristic thesis of the late 1990s through the first decade of the twenty-first century, the staff at ICT emphatically insisted that learning is more effective when it is experiential, graphically dynamic, event-based, and when didactic material is embedded in a story.

There are two points to consider. If we regarded ICT projects in the dramaturgical vein, into what technical-cultural continuum would we slot ICT story-driven simulations? Just as we noticed the continuity between the technologies within the immersive simulation and the ordinary technologies of daily life, here too, in order to situate ICT's wargames, we must step outside of the military world and regard them as one entry in the catalog of edutainment games and interactive websites widely available in the culture. I could not find a single point on which Army enthusiasts for games, immersive simulations, and interactive movies differed from eager adopters from other standpoints in the social landscape.

Given the availability of edutainment, the dramaturge of the future would want to know about the reception of these wargames. She would want to know how educators as well as Army trainers assessed the effectiveness of story and game-based training. She might look at the arguments offered by Army advocates for the use of serious games and immersive environments for training. She might also look at the reception and critical analysis of ICT's simulations, interactive movies, and games.[6]

As expected, I found that there was *no* consensus among the educational psychologists evaluating ICT projects. In fact, there was distinct friction between a USC educational psychologist who collaborated with ICT staff, Richard E. Clark, and Army psychologists conducting independent evaluations of ICT games and simulations. Clark, who directed the Center for Cognitive Technology at USC's Rossier School of Education, plays two significant roles in this story. He was a consultant to ICT, advising producers on the best way to cleave to the learning objectives in the Army's requirements documents, even as they fleshed out their stories and characters. He also rebuked overenthusiastic Army advocates of new media for training. His critical stance appears to have had the effect of curbing some of ICT simulationists' more intemperate claims for new media's revolutionary powers (see e.g., Clark and Feldon 2005; Kirschner et al. 2006; Clark et al. 2010).

This is not the first time entertainment media has been adopted by educators. I was curious to drop back in time. What I was looking for were claims made for the specific difference that the introduction of each new media would make. I wanted to see what claims were made, and whether specific claims for earlier entertainment technologies were being recapitulated by advocates for contemporary new media. Could claims for instructional technology be a resource for finding zeitgeist markers in wargames?

While textbooks and lectures may very well be soporific for digital natives, this has been true for generations of drowsy, indifferent pupils. The possibly greater appeal of using motion pictures in the classroom was recognized early in the twentieth century by educators and publicists. In 1909, the cinema trade journal *The Bioscope* published a declaration of the usefulness of films as instructional technologies ("Education and the Bioscope: Can Moving Pictures Be Used in Schools?" (quoted in Savage 2006, 8). The following year, the film distributor George Kleine published and distributed the nation's first catalog of instructional films, *Catalogue of Educational Motion Pictures*.

In 1913, Thomas A. Edison predicted, "Books will soon be obsolete in the schools. Scholars will soon be instructed through the eye. It is possible to teach every branch of human knowledge with the motion picture. Our school system will be completely changed in ten years" (Smith 1913, quoted in Savage 2006, 8).

Nearly as soon as moving pictures were invented, they were used for advertising and publicity. The Edison Company produced a filmed advertisement for Admiral Cigarettes in 1897; Biograph made filmed announcements of Shredded Wheat Biscuits and Mellin's Baby Food around 1903 (Savage 2006, 6). By 1919, the notion that visual culture supplanted speech had become a truism among advertisers and publicists. Hence in an article entitled "Selling goods by illustrated lectures," E. P. Corbett, an employee of the National Cash Register Company (quoted in Savage 2006, 8) confidently asserted that "It has been proved that 87 percent of what we know is learned through the sense of seeing. Only 7 percent of our knowledge is gained through the sense of hearing."

Edison was dyslexic, so it is no surprise that he famously repeated his "books are obsolete" remark in 1922: "I believe that the motion picture is destined to revolutionize our educational system and that in a few years it will supplant largely, if not entirely, the use of books" (quoted in Cuban 1986, 9). Indeed, in the 1920s there was a brief efflorescence of pedagogical ideas, methods, and training techniques in visual literacy (see e.g., Freeman 1924; Johnson 1927; Dorris 1928; Weber 1928; see also e.g., Eliot 1913; Dewey 1925; Roark 1925; Collings 1931; Johnson 1938; Hurd 1945 for efforts to shift learning from passive absorption to active doing in these same years).

A survey of fads for new media in classrooms will show us a repeated pattern: exaggerated claims for the difference in student learning new technology makes; enthusiastic assessment that new media does improve motivation, attention, and learning; followed by later sober reevaluations. We can see this played out in articles about introducing films into classrooms (see e.g., Dench 1917; Ellis and Thornborough 1923; Cromwell 1926; Hollis 1926; Arnspiger 1936; Jordan 1937; May 1937; Hoban 1946) as well as the attractions of comic strips and cartoons as instructional aids (see e.g., Wilson 1928; Gay 1937; Tuttle 1938; Sones 1944; Zorbaugh 1944). Once stable receivers, transmitters, and local broadcast networks had been established, educators experimented with educational radio (the best resource for this is Saettler 2004, especially the chapter "Emergency of Educational Radio: 1921–1950," 197–222).

The Army was a major investor in the overlapping fields of instructional technology, educational psychology, and instructional design. During World War II, the military heavily experimented with instructional technology (see e.g., Witty 1944 and Hound et al. 1949 as basic resources). "During the past decade," one observer remarked in 1956, "research in audiovisual communication has increased largely because of the research programs being conducted by the Armed Services" (Allen 1956, 125).

After the war, educators continued to explore the usefulness of audio-visual instruction (see e.g., Miles and Spain 1947; Svenson and Sheats 1950; Kendler and Cook 1951; Church 1952; Lumsdaine 1953). Communications research compared the staying power of instructional films with classroom lecture and discussion (see e.g., Gibson 1947; Smith and Ormer 1949; Hoban and Ormer 1950; Carpenter 1953; Harris and Buenger 1955). Just as there had been eager experiments with educational radio in the early 1930s, with the advent of television came efforts to measure it against regular classroom teaching (see e.g., Rock et al. 1952; Jackson 1952; Boehm 1954; Kanner et al. 1954; Godfrey 1967, monograph 3; Hooper 1969).

Last, we come to the vogue for role-playing educational games that bloomed in the 1960s and persisted well into the 1970s.[7] Right here we can find ideas that are continuous with contemporary ones as well as themes that strike me as viable zeitgeist markers.

In order to appreciate the themes that characterize the educational games in the 1960s, we must put some elements into place. First is the recognition of the importance of multidisciplinary scientific and engineering teams that worked so effectively during World War II. Of special importance to this genealogy is the development of operations research (OR) during the war (see e.g., Shrader 2006; Fortun and Schweber 1993; Rau 2000; and Peter P. Perla's chapter in this volume). OR was an analytic method for probabilistically modeling the interaction of variables in order to find an optimum or minimum solution. After the war these techniques migrated into economics and other social science disciplines (Mirowski 1999; Heims 1993). In America, OR morphed in the postwar years into systems analysis. Systems analysis soon diffused into more disciplines and sectors of the economy, aided by the availability of digital computers (Haigh 2001).

Among the more remarkable offshoots of systems analysis were various attempts to regularize social science and military forecasting. Systems analysts at the RAND Corporation experimented with quantitative models, multidisciplinary seminars, and role-playing games. Two RAND personnel, Olaf Helmer and Herman Kahn, would become particularly identified with future studies (Kahn, Bell, and Wiener 1968; Bell 1964).

In 1967, Helmer published a paper outlining his recommendations for the methods the social sciences should adopt when considering society in the future. First of all, the futurist must "adopt ... a systems approach as a basic principle," work in interdisciplinary teams, and make use of the "indispensable tool" of role-playing games (1–3). Along with other RAND colleagues, Helmer valued role-playing games for the two unique experiences they imparted to players. First, they were especially potent *communication* techniques; role-playing games would teach players how to talk across disciplines by showing them how to consider a problem "through the eyes of persons with backgrounds and skills different from their own." Second, they demonstrated the value of thinking about a problem as a *system*. Not only must the player step away from his settled point of view, but by working in a team, he must also "consider many aspects of the scene that might normally escape his attention when he works in isolation. Thus the game ... has an integrating effect that induces a systems viewpoint in the participant" (Helmer 1967, 3).

Multidisciplinarity appeared to have been a significant factor in the scientific and technical achievements of World War II. Another had to do with the fact that these teams tinkered with different combinations of interacting variables in a dynamic system. This gave rise to the notion among wargamers that games not only facilitated insight into a problem when it is regarded as a system, but also that they enhanced the creativity of its participants. The general idea was expressed by two wargamers in 1965 (Barringer and Whaley, 451): "Gaming stretches the limits of one's imagination, of one's notion of the plausible and the possible."

RAND analysts' claims for the merits of role-playing games were clustered around the themes of systems thinking, creativity, novel experience, and multidisciplinary research. For the scientists and engineers who participated in OR and systems analysis during the war and the decade afterwards, there arose the idea that where any authentically avant-garde research and innovation was taking place, its participants felt exhilarated (Ghamari-Tabrizi 2005, 46–60). As reports of RAND's novel organization of R&D tied to genuine technical and scientific innovation circulated throughout the 1940s and '50s, educators, businessmen, psychologists, sociologists, and philosophers became interested in the experience, social setting, and meanings of play, fun, and creativity.

Articles in scholarly journals explained why it was important for Americans to have fun. William Menninger (1948) himself argued that regular recreation was part of mental hygiene. Play, fun, and creativity were tangled together in nostrums for robust mental health (see e.g., Rogers 1954; Lowenfeld 1957; Barron 1963).

In the mid- and late 1950s, the National Science Foundation sponsored three major conferences devoted to identifying "creative scientific talent." The author of a report (Taylor 1959, 102) concluded, "It is hoped that concurrent attacks on problems of creativity will be undertaken by researchers in industry, government, universities, and school systems" (see also e.g., Taylor and Barron 1963). His wish was amply satisfied by the scores of articles and books about creativity that began to appear in the 1950s and swelled in the 1960s. Most pertinent to the fashion for educational games were works promising to enhance creativity in their readers. Books were published which showed readers how to "utiliz[e] ... your creative potential" (see e.g., Osborn 1953; Interdisciplinary Symposia on Creativity 1959; Allen 1962). Naturally enough, the business press found the topic appealing, publishing articles such as "Operational Approach to Creativity" and the indubitably attractive title *Creativity and Innovation* (Gordon 1956; Haefele 1962; Cummings 1965).

Educators were keen to know how this research could help them "motivate the creative process" in their classrooms (Institute of Contemporary Art 1957; MacKinnon 1961; Parnes 1963, 331; Torrance 1965; Taylor and Williams 1966; Heist 1968). In the stampede for fomenting creativity in the nation

there were only a handful of dissenting views. In 1960, for example, Jacques Barzun published an article disdaining the "cults" of research and creativity (see also e.g., Kiell 1961; Kraft 1966; 1967). On the whole, Americans were eager to stimulate creativity in themselves, their children, their businesses, and their classrooms.

A few years after RAND analysts began experimenting with operational role-playing wargames, the technique began to be transposed. The forerunner of a business simulation originated at RAND in 1955, "Monopologs" was a simulation of an Air Force supply system. The following year, the American Management Association produced "Top Management Decision Simulation." In 1957, the "Business Management Game" was produced for a private consulting firm. That same year the game "TOP Management Decision Game" was used in a class at the University of Washington. In an article in the *Harvard Business Review* the management game designer explained how his simulation could impart an invaluable skill to players: "It forces an over-all point of view" (Andlinger 1958a, 125). Indeed, the integrative experience afforded by the game was precisely the quality singled out by a vice president of Sylvania's Electronic Systems Division, who remarked, "[The game] ... forces me to do more thinking about the interrelated aspects of my position" (McDonald and Ricciardi 1958, 140).

The vogue for business simulations and games took off. From 1957 on, business schools adopted simulation games as part of their curriculum. A 1962 survey (Graham and Gray 1969) of 107 AACSB member schools showed that 71 percent used games in at least one required course. J. M. Kibbee estimated that in 1961 there might have been as many as one hundred business games circulating in business schools and management firms (Kibbee et al. 1961; also see e.g., Hamburger 1955; Rehkop 1957; Malcolm 1959; Ricciardi 1957; Andlinger 1958b; Moore 1958; Schrieber 1958; Jackson 1959; Kibbee 1959; Dale and Klasson 1962; Dill and Doppelt 1963; Elliott 1966; Roberts and Strauss 1975).

The fashion for role-playing games was eagerly adopted for use in K–12 schools and universities (see e.g., Robinson 1966; Cherryholmes 1966; Attig 1967; Carlson 1967; Coleman 1967; Boocock and Schild 1968 for representative samples). "Games change what goes on in the classroom," wrote a prominent promoter (Boocock 1967).[8] By the end of the 1960s, it seemed clear to many educators that role-playing games were particularly good at teaching people how to think about a problem in terms of relationships: of part-to-part, part-to-whole, and parts in a system interacting dynamically. These ideas seemed to be a sign of the times. One educator remarked, "As our society becomes more complex, and linkages more diverse, it becomes conceptually necessary to develop holistic viewpoints" (Marien 1970, 1).

Another sign of the times at the end of the 1960s was a widespread feeling that Americans confronted a planetary crisis. In an article published in 1969 in *Science*, John Platt cried out, "It has now become urgent for us to mobilize all our intelligence to solve these problems if we are to keep from killing ourselves in the next few years" (Platt 1969, 1121). The complexity of social, political, and ecological problems overwhelming the readers of *Science* was menacing and lethal. "The task is clear. The task is huge. The time is horribly short. ... Today, the whole human experiment may hang on the question of how fast we now press the development of science for survival" (see also e.g., Kahn and Weiner 1961; Boulding 1964; Brand 1968–72; Meadows et al. 1972; Toffler 1970).

A cluster of themes mark the historical moment at the end of decade: an urgent feeling of crisis tied with systems thinking. We can hear this in Buckminster Fuller's predicament of 1969: in the atomic age, one must choose either utopia or oblivion (Fuller 1969a).[9] Environmental pollution, population pressures, nuclear brinksmanship demanded "creative" responses to worldwide threats to human survival. In 1969, the theologian Martin Marty remarked that since people considered the past "useless," Americans must now think of their present and future as requiring a thorough exploration of "the creative possibilities of the moment" (Marty 1969, 12).

We do see some continuities between the clusters of ideas about innovations in education, creativity, play and games, and systems thinking in the 1960s and more contemporary notions of the specific powers of interactive computer games, films, and immersive environments. Let's take a look at these. We can do no better than take a look at Marshall McLuhan's ideas about the effect of new media technologies on education.

In the 1950s and '60s, Marshall McLuhan, a Canadian communications theorist, highlighted the importance of the multimodal sensory stimulation engendered by communications media. Since all communications media taught its users how to perceive them, he argued that educators should offer students "sensory situations for the training of perception" (McLuhan and Parker 1968, 5; see also McLuhan and Carpenter 1960; McLuhan 1961; Grosvenor 2012). In 1967, McLuhan co-authored an article on "the future of education" in a popular American magazine. Several of his desiderata find counterparts in contemporary ideas. Innovation is necessary; schools must "create a new kind of learning environment"; students should experience the feelings of play in their classrooms; the interactivity between student and instructor, whether teacher or instructional technology, should be fun. With these reforms, he predicted, "the school experience can well become ... rich and compelling" (McLuhan and Leonard 1967, 25).

While there are a great many similarities, there are substantive differences between contemporary enthusiasms for games for training and the curricula, experiences, and claims made for the usefulness of games in the 1960s and early 1970s. In the earlier period, role-playing games were wholly social group activities. Instruction via machine such as "programmed instruction" was individualized. Contemporary educational media enthusiasts (Johnson and Johnson 1970; Hill and Nunnery 1971; Weisgerber 1971) point to the unique customization afforded by computer-based learning; however we can find discussions of "individualized" technology-assisted learning in 1970 and 1971.

So what can we alight upon that differs palpably between contemporary games and earlier ones? Whereas contemporary educators emphasize the student's self-directed exploration of the subject matter within the learning environment of the game—touted as the medium's uniquely adaptive "interactivity"— in the 1960s and '70s, pedagogical objectives oriented toward the living adaptive cybernetic system. Educational game enthusiasts argued that the difference between games and any other instructional technology was that gameplay teaches the student how to grasp the problems addressed in the game-world as a complex whole.

In 1957, Marshall McLuhan suggested that new media offered "new languages with new and unique powers of expression" (McLuhan and Carpenter 1957, 26). In 1974, a professor of urban planning argued that games could be "the means whereby appreciations of complex wholes may be more quickly and more reliably told to others" (Duke, 135–6). Richard Duke suggested that the role-playing game was the ideal communication medium for the exigencies of the moment. In a historical present characterized by "complexity, future orientation, thoughtful consideration of alternatives, and inevitable recognition of the nature of systems," traditional forms of expression based on "the burden of strict sequentiality of the written and spoken language" were no longer adequate. Society needs "flexible ... conceptual tools which will let the participant view new and emerging situations, having no precedent, in a way that permits comprehension" (137). The "new language form," he suggested, was the role-playing game.

Suppose we took this literally. Wouldn't it be interesting to think of the wargame as a gestalt inscription, uniquely capable of communicating holistically? (Rhyne 1972). Alongside learning how to read *into* the wargame document, would it make a difference to our scholarship if we considered the wargame as a writing system?

The Wargame as a Writing System

Let us circle back to McCarty Little's observations of 1912. He not only likened the wargame player to the actor in a play, he characterized the naval chart game as an *inscription system*. "We must not overlook the fact that the game is a convention just as is the chart or printed page, or indeed language itself; and if we wish to use either, we must learn to think in it." But what kind of writing system was it? "The war game is a cinematographic diagram; and it is as important to us to be able to read it as to read a chart or book" (Little 1912, 1219–1220).

Writing systems are not neutral graphic records. They are "emotionally loaded," observed Florian Coulmas (1991, 226), "indicating ... group loyalties and identities." Role-playing wargamers strongly believe that *playing* a wargame rather than *reading about* one is the best way to learn how a wargame trains, educates, rehearses, and surprises soldiers and civilians working in the armed forces.

What I want to argue, ultimately, is that wargames are gestalt inscriptions. In the heyday of 1970s futurism, Richard Duke described games as a language in which non-sequential ideas could be expressed. This idea resonates with something the Internet thinker Jaron Lanier (2010) once described as "post-symbolic communication." Several years ago he prophesied that a hundred and fifty years from now, games would be compact semiotic packages exchanged as "tokens" of communication. He suggested, "Children [will] discover an alternative to the use of symbols; they [will] invent the content of a shared environment at a conversational rate instead of using tokens like words to refer to contingents that aren't present."

What might Lanier be pointing to? Let's think about two girls who adore several genres of storytelling. Let's imagine twelve-year old twins who devour Young Adult novels that have to do with romance and friendship. They love different subgenres: vampire romance, psychic and occult romance, time travel romance, fantasy worlds populated by demons and fairies where animals and humans can communicate, cyberpunk science fiction, and psychic

detective stories whose heroines are fifteen-year-old girls. These girls read about three YA novels a week and swap them with their friends. Now let's imagine them sitting at their usual table during lunch. Since the group of seven girls have overlapping tastes, and each girl has read most but not all of the same books, our girls will describe their current favorite character and plot with reference to the titles and genre features of books the others know. "It's like *title of subgenre A*, but with *characters from subgenre B* along with this *plot point from subgenre C*." Thus when Lanier says, "I have ... found that some of our most cherished uses of abstraction, such as categories, are not necessary when one has fluent control of concreteness," we can imagine the rapid back-and-forth that can take place among genre devotees.

Suppose we regard wargames as semiotic packages—multimodal, multisensory writing systems of wholes, gestalts, systems? The pivot that will allow the imagination to swing back and forth between the present and the various old presents I've been looking at is *how people think about the gestalt of simulated experience*—its totality, the foreground of various sensory and technological prompts for attention, and the cognitive and emotional responses from participants to these prompts. We can capture the points of decision and emotional response in that set of actions, reactions, thoughts, feelings, moods that typically fall under the heading of "interaction within the simulation." The zeitgeist markers found *within* the simulation are consonant with the intertexts of entertainment, communication, transportation technologies in the culture at large that together make up the historically inflected sensorium. Against the background of the sensorium shared by others, we must insert the specific routines practiced by the groups of men (and later, women) operating the complex equipment in a simulation that mimics the tactics, techniques, and procedures for warfighting.

We assume that the felt worlds and repertoires for saying and unsaying, noticing and ignoring differ from 1951. Certainly the materiality of reading digital displays has altered: the practice of peering into a flickering instrument face and deciphering graphic symbols as well as words—with speed—is ubiquitous and unremarkable today. In 1951, the radar console display competed only with the television screen as an information appliance with a lookalike visual appearance. The legible surface of the world's screens has multiplied, giving us a different notion of volume, surface, depth, solidity.

It is incontrovertible that the mostly unnoticed tempo of everyday experience has speeded up in more than a half century. If we look at all of the sectors that make up the bodily sensorium, the velocity of transportation, communication, and entertainment technologies have increased, conditioning our bodies in definite ways. Not only is the tempo of the circulation of ideas, goods, fashions, and news faster, experience fragments coded in writing systems disseminate ever more rapidly through communications media. The pop culture term for these fragments is "meme." A meme, according to Wikipedia (as of 2010), is "a unit of cultural ideas, symbols or practices, which can be transmitted from one mind to another through writing, speech, gestures, rituals or other imitable phenomena. ... Supporters of the concept regard memes as cultural analogues to genes." The concept has taken off as a descriptor for a notion rapidly circulated on the Internet. Whether packaged as the customized genres of branded products and services, remediations of stories into toys, games, commodities, or films, or as Internet memes, the

notion that concretized bits of experience could be chopped into fragments always available for recombining into new ideographic constellations appears to many to characterize the present.

Is rapid recombination a zeitgeist marker of the present? Would this have bewildered the young men tensely passing messages to one another in the air defense simulation in 1951? Certainly in 1951 recombination was available to be noticed. We could point to the recombinations of fragments that jazz and classical musicians and composers were exploring. We could look to the prose and poetry of Gertrude Stein, Samuel Beckett, and James Joyce, whose works could be found in bookstores and metropolitan and university libraries. We could look to the fact that prewar works by surrealists, Dadaists, and expressionists were known to educated people. But did these formal styles show up in the lifeworlds of ordinary people? In the postwar world, we could point to the influence of lowbrow amusements such as pulp magazines and comics on avant-garde artists (this is the thesis of Earl 2009; see also Earl 2012). The young men in 1951 would have had daily exposure to the modernist graphic arts of magazine covers, paperback fiction and comic books, posters, record album covers, and advertisements—all of which featured combinations of fragments (see Remington 2003, 83–135, for a discussion of "the creative forties"; see also Wild 2007). These trainees lived in Los Angeles, the automobile city, whose architecture and urban spaces were decisively influenced by modernism in the postwar period.

What are we left with? Something about speed ... something about the multiplication of digital inputs. Of course, there are differences between the lifeworlds of the trainees absorbed in the wargame in 1951 and those of the first decade of the twenty-first century. The superficial marks are easy to spot. I am looking for something particular. I'm hunting for traces in the wargame document that prompt cognitive and affective responses in the individual and in the group that reflect the historical matrix of the sensorium of the masses *as well as* the habitus of the warfighter. It is *the bundle of these responses* that I want to isolate and historicize.

Fred Turner (2006; especially 2013), is a careful scholar of the rise of the experiential stimulation of American bodies and minds in the mid- and late twentieth century. In response to a draft of this chapter he pointed out that I had not defined the common experiences of the mediated sensorium that wargamers shared with other Americans. Nor had I specified how the simulations cultivated occupation-specific reflexes and cognitions in the simulation trainees and gamers—patterns of thinking, acting, and feeling that they did *not* share with civilians. He urged me to consider whether "the general experiences of the crowd explain the responses of military and think-tank folks? What was their specific *habitus*? And how might it connect to the larger world of fairs and movies? There's a missing middle here and without it, I

think your search for historically specific elements of realism may go unfulfilled."[10] This is a reasonable objection. In order to substantiate the approach I outline here, I would have to find recordings or transcriptions of gameplay, identify plausible zeitgeist markers, and then trace them out in two directions: first to the general sensorium of the social-cultural matrix they share with other Americans; I would also have to argue that the statements and behaviors I find in the archive attest to a definite cognitive, affective, and gestural repertoire of the operators of complex weapons systems of that time and place. I think there *must* be a period style in wargaming, as there is in every human activity.

Wargames inscribe richly ambiguous totalities. I invite everyone reading this chapter to find ways to decipher the dynamic worlds they record and (attempt to) orchestrate. Surely they mean more than they say. Those of us who study them can contribute to a history of perception, distraction and boredom, the history of emotions, the history of embodiments, the history of educational technology, the history of labor and masculinity, as well as the history of reading and writing.

About the Author

Sharon Ghamari-Tabrizi is a historian of science with an interest in how new scientific, medical, and technical knowledge practices are formulated, justified, and stabilized. She is the author of *The Worlds of Herman Kahn* (Harvard University Press, 2005). Her website is <www.sharonghamari.com>.

Notes

I gratefully acknowledge the last-minute assistance from librarians Sandhya Malladi and Kimberly Hunter of the Muis S. Fairchild Research Information Center at Air University at Maxwell Air Force Base, Alabama. They stepped in at the last moment to track down long-forgotten sources.

1. I am indebted to Lauren Rabinovitz for drawing my attention to Tom Gunning's work. For a consideration of the bodily sensorium of early twentieth-century motion simulation entertainments see Rabinovitz 2004; 2006; 2012).

2. See also <www.strategypage.com> for more on the design problems of role-playing wargames.

3. Separate from wargaming as such, training simulators remained a mainstay of Air Force, Army, Marine Corps, and Navy crew instruction. Descendants of Edwin Link's original flight simulator of 1929, these man-machine systems were complex stand-alone apparatuses into which the trainee climbed and practiced the choreographed routines for operating various weapons systems such as airplanes, tanks, and ICBM missile silo double-key launch procedures. (For an overview, see Shrader 2006; Parrott 1963; Barnes 1963; Armed Forces Management 1963; Ray 1966; Unique Simulator for SAC Crews 1967; Allen 1977; Rhea 1980; Gadomski 1980.) The simulators were used in every service throughout the 1960s–80s. They were exceptionally expensive, often as costly to purchase as the weapon system they supported. With the advent of networked computers, by the early 1990s the Pentagon shifted funds from maintaining behemoth simulators to networked simulation systems that could be transported, miniaturized, and ultimately deployable at the desktop or en route to a mission (Frost and Sullivan 1980; Tapscott 1993; Bettner 1994).

4. Stockfisch was not alone in expressing these criticisms. By 1980, the commonest complaints against analytic models could be compressed into the following: "The use of a few simple, static measures of force effectiveness; their application to a narrow range of military forces having common exchange parameters; the presumption of a few rather shallow and highly stylized scenarios focusing on force exchanges; and the absence of much of the complexity and reality of allied and adversary perceptions or motives" (Graubard and Builder 1980).

5. Before the encounter between Dunnigan and Marshall, various attempts had been made previously to introduce modified commercial wargames into the curriculum of the service schools and war colleges, as well as to endorse playing commercially available games on base during off-duty hours (see Morgan 1990 for a brief overview of service wargaming for an audience of hobby gamers).

6. I read especially deeply in the available Army Research Institute for the Behavioral and Social Sciences (ARI) reports from 2000 to 2008. The ARI is tasked to evaluate the immersive simulations, interactive movies and games produced by ICT. For evaluations of ICT projects see Beal and Christ 2004, as well as Zbylut and Ward 2004. For discussions of games for training see Morris and Singer 2002; Belanic et al. 2004; Orvis et al. 2005; 2007; and Cianciolo et al. 2006. For immersive environments see Lampton et al. 2001; Pleban and Salvetti 2003; Weiland et al. 2003; Campbell et al. 2004; Jones and Mastaglio 2006; Singer et al. 2006; and Knerr 2007.

7. Charles and Stadsklev (1973) describe and analyze seventy social studies games designed for K–12 grade students. The second half of the book lists more than 250 other social science games, as well as game bibliographies and other resources on the development of educational games in the previous decade (see also Gordon 1970; Shaftel and Shaftel 1967; Stoll and Livingston 1973).

8. The boom in educational games continued well into the 1970s (see e.g., Shirts 1970; Avedon and Sutton-Smith 1971; Wentworth and Lewis 1973).

9. *Utopia or Oblivion* (1969a) is less known than his other work *Operating Manual for Spaceship Earth* (1969b). We can note the influence of his participation in Navy wargames in his youth in his "World Game" at Southern Illinois University in 1969 (see Anker 2007).

10. He also pointed out (in a September 10, 2014 email to the author) that from the point of view of the theorists and designers of simulations in the post–World War II period, "the power of such environments grew from their ability to solicit engagement from active audience members—members who in turn would acquire the holistic vision of their leaders by so doing, and thus be empowered." That is to say, for Turner, role-playing games and simulations *for civilians* were intended to cultivate in the players strong feelings of individual agency.

PLAYING DEFENSE: GENDER, JUST WAR, AND GAME DESIGN

Elizabeth Losh

Although the "military-entertainment complex" is often imagined as the monolithic expression of an organizational culture of masculine command and control, the actual work practices involved in developing wargames are remarkably polymorphous and complex, and female interaction designers, project managers, and digital artists are often active participants in fostering potentially subversive forms of exploration and engagement. This chapter focuses on Southern California as an area of what AnnaLee Saxenian has termed "regional advantage," where the development of military games has flourished west of the I-405 freeway for over a half century, from the RAND Corporation to the Institute for Creative Technologies. By using the approach of feminist science and technology studies, it is possible to consider how gender is enacted in local laboratories of game design that attempt to represent just war in remote geographies of conflict through procedural rule-based systems. It may be obvious that gender and sexual identity play an important role in these battlefield simulations, but it may be less obvious that the deliberative and dialogic processes of iterative game design in which these simulations are composed also reflect dynamics around gender identity and the positioning of difference.

In their classic book on craftwork and tacit knowledge in the field of reproductive medicine, *The Right Tools for the Job* (1992), Adele Clarke and Joan Fujimora assert that "rightness," "tools," and "jobs" are all situationally constructed. Participants in labs must constantly improvise with doable problems and ad hoc arrangements and cope with sometimes unworkable disciplining tools. Labor practices require enrolling allies, analyzing cryptic texts, and participating in routines that adapt to constraints, opportunities, and resources. Designing computer simulations for military training in collaborative work groups involves many of the same characteristics of similarly technoscientific occupations, and now that many of these wargames involve partnerships with 3D animators, interaction designers, sound engineers, and others from digital entertainment industries, more tacit knowledge from the fields of media arts and computer science may be required for success.

This is not to say that there are not strong masculinist biases in the culture of the armed forces that favor paradigms of command and control, and computational media are often designed accordingly. Work in surveillance studies on drone warfare, which exploits the sensorium of earth-observing media devices and the scope of more granular aerial views, analyzes assumptions about moving objects to be targeted and how these protocols of screening should be operationalized in theaters of combat. Such interfaces with real-time interactivity can be presented as the ultimate god game (see Patrick Crogan's chapter in this volume). Furthermore, specialized apparatuses for reconnaissance and weaponized engagement often utilize features from existing commercial consoles and controllers that are already familiar to gamers. It may also be fair to posit that mass-market games that involve first-person shooting mechanics or the avatars of soldiers can serve as implicit recruiting tools. In the case of *America's Army* (2002–)—which was actually funded by the US military to make basic training and deployment seem more desirable—this implicit function becomes explicit. As Sut Jhally points out in the documentary *Joystick Warriors* (2013), "One of the functions of popular culture is to bridge the divide between the public and the military; to provide a kind of fantasy that connects the two." Moreover, male and female game designers may have completely different experiences when joining soldiers to participate in wargame activities—based on how they are told by superiors to engage with the enemy—and thus may bring radically different perspectives about appropriate types of situated interaction in combat back to the game design milieu, as designers in a mixed-gender team developing *ELECT BiLAT* discovered, when female designers were expected to use "soft skills" with a local imam while male designers experienced sadistic interactions toward captured prisoners of war.

With women serving in the vast majority of army occupations, it is surprising that the possibility of assuming a female subject position in military training games with human characters is often minimized during the state-sponsored design process. For example, although initially there were plans to create a parallel version of the game *Tactical Iraqi* with a female protagonist (Major Kate Jones), game developers gave up on pursuing a version with a female mission leader. Researchers cited cost and design issues, the demographic features of the typical service person, and the social dynamics of what could be called "military drag," in which those who put on a uniform assume its masculine gender position in order to be treated as authority figures bearing lethal force. Female military personnel using language-learning games may even be encouraged to use the grammatical constructions in a foreign language usually assigned to a male speaker.

In *Tactical Iraqi* and other games based on recent US missions abroad, female figures are often generic nonplayable characters (NPCs), much like the stock characters Anita Sarkeesian derides in her Feminist Frequency work about the misogynistic tropes of commercial games. Female NPCs in military training games are generally to be tactfully avoided or mollified through participation in elaborate ceremonies that display cultural competence but involve primary interaction with rituals of hospitality, not the personhood of the woman, because excessive familiarity with women might jeopardize the mission.

In games in which women may have meaningful albeit minor social roles, such as Na'eema, the suspicious doctor in *ELECT BiLAT*, or Munaa, the sentimental girls' school principal in *Tactical Iraqi*, the inner lives of women remain inscrutable and resist the player's advances, and their scripted comments do little to subvert gender norms. Female military game characters generally reprise traditional roles dating back to epic narrative conventions, in which women can only serve as goal, as guide, and as obstacle. In other words, female agents can redirect the trajectory of the hero or misdirect him from his goal, but they cannot participate as central agents in the pedagogical drama in their own rights. Even when women play fellow soldiers, such as Faris, an Arabic-speaking Chaldean Christian who also happens to be a US reservist in the same platoon as the player's character in *Tactical Iraqi*, they can only make suggestions.

Anxieties about changing norms around masculine coming of age have certainly shaped military game design as well. Colonel Casey Wardynski, who would later help develop the game *America's Army*, was at RAND's Pardee Graduate School when he started to consider the implications of data indicating that young men seemed no longer to value the opportunities for leadership, travel, and community service that the army had traditionally offered and saw service among ground troops as lowest in prestige among all branches in the military. In rebranding the army with a compelling video game experience, Wardynski hoped that players might identify with their virtual soldier avatars and eventually become more open to enlistment. The targeting of hardcore gamers and a young male demographic with the *America's Army* product, which was touted at trade shows like E3, reinforced the view of warfare as a site of acquisition and dominance.

The confluence of instrumentalism and machismo represented in simulation culture can be read as the logical manifestation of what Tim Lenoir has called "the military-entertainment complex" (2000). This term obviously suggests the same hegemonic power of the "military-industrial complex" that was described by Dwight Eisenhower in 1961 as an immense bureaucracy based on a "formalized,

complex, and costly" program of joint research and development that was capable, as Eisenhower warned, of undue influence by virtue of its size and scope. For Paul Virilio, Eisenhower's military-industrial complex represents "scientific futurology" (Virilio 2000, 31), "triumphalism" (33), and ultimately "mass destruction" (55). As Lenoir suggests, the military-entertainment complex that supplants the military-industrial conflict of the Cold War world also seems to exemplify important aspects of our current "post-human state" and a "fundamental shift in our notions of material reality" (Lenoir 2000, 290). Although Lenoir presents a compelling account of a symbiotic genealogy in which the history of gaming, computer graphics, and interactive media cannot be untangled from that of defense industry technologies for contemporary warfare, I am going to tell a somewhat different and less linear story about big tech and shared resources that is messier both in presenting organizational culture and in depicting the ethical questions around participation in conflicts that supposedly promote democratic institutions.

The game development that takes place in studios funded by the military involves iterative, collaborative, interdisciplinary, and sometimes combative processes of deliberation in which partisan conflict, philosophical disagreement, political debate, and spitballing about the implications of different identity positions of gender, race, and class all invariably take place. As Manuel Castells has noted, the culture of software development is actually composed of a number of potentially divisive networked subcultures that include "the hacker culture," "the techno-meritocratic culture," "the virtual communitarian culture," and "the entrepreneurial culture" (Castells 2001, 37) in a sometimes volatile "intersection of big science, military research, and libertarian culture" (17).

Based on her own fieldwork studying the Gamelab studio, Alice Daer has argued that game design is an intensely rhetorical process in which often contentious and complicated processes of deliberation are key to maintaining the artistic and political norms of the workplace. Daer observed how designers negotiated disagreements and maintained flattened hierarchies in ways that represented certain ideals of the creative classes.

> They considered themselves part of a team of interesting people who make interesting things in interesting ways, and each member of the team was expected to be an equal contributor. They believed that they could maintain that approach by focusing together on the challenge of building games that explored novel ideas, actions, and contexts that enabled players to have experiences they might not ordinarily get from other games ... Gamelab's games were not quite a performance of an idea: they were ideas in action, opportunities and spaces for thinking and doing. The games they produced were therefore working instantiations of their collaborative and intellectual style of making games. (Daer 2010, 110)

Daer presents a vision of game development workplaces as rhetorical spaces in which different possibilities are explored with attention to the process as well as to the product.

In other words, many game designers building military simulations at sites like the Institute for Creative Technologies still primarily identify as game designers and claim to think like game designers rather than generals or studio executives. Although Lenoir may be correct that the ICT "seeks to merge the military's interests in interactive simulation technology with shared interests in technology of

academics and the film industry" (Lenoir 2000, 333), at the level of individuals interacting at a job site, these interests are hardly monolithic, and the designers' habits of interaction may reflect an interest in depicting a heterogeneity of attitudes rather than merely propagate mass indoctrination by foreclosing possibilities.

These game designers also recognize that military engagement may involve ethical quandaries for those who play as soldiers on the battlefield, much as Miguel Sicart, in *The Ethics of Computer Games* (2009), has posed the "moral assassin" as an archetypal hero in consumer game plotlines. Although there may be a wealth of procedures that can be ported from conventional armed forces training manuals into the rulesets of game engines, the gap between the playable simulation and the ramifications of real-world policies can create tensions about acceptable and unacceptable conduct each time the player enters a scenario. As I have argued in my work on war crimes in *World of Warcraft* (2005–), despite the amount of attention that has been paid to how violence is *represented* in digital environments, up to this point surprisingly little has been devoted to how it is *rationalized* (Losh 2009). In political and sociological discourses about violent commercial video games with algorithmic rewards, for example, the cultural conversation between policy makers, researchers, and other authority figures tends to ignore the possibility that the rules governing conduct in such stylized aggression can be understood as part of a longer intellectual history around just war doctrine.

Evidentiary claims that condone just warfare or forbid war crimes are frequently deployed by players in the forums of multiplayer environments for massive role-playing games. Although the hyperbolic and sometimes vulgar terms of these debates may seem very different from the refined discourses of Aquinas or Grotius, players often engage in extended discussions about when, where, and how it should be permissible to apply asymmetrical force to the avatars of other players. For example, the norms around competition and cooperation in raiding in *World of Warcraft* can be interpreted to produce a range of positions that vary on a continuum from zero-sum thinking to self-sacrificing radical generosity. Even

vengeful discourses about whether those who engage in rule-breaking activities can be subjected to ambushes, humiliation, or vigilante justice at least recognize that both sides potentially have certain basic rights in armed scenarios and that might alone might not make right. The existence of "friendly fire" prohibitions in many commercial games, as Sicart has asserted in *The Ethics of Computer Games* (2009), also seems to indicate that representing just war doctrine is a strongly encoded practice.

From Duels to Microworlds: The RAND Corporation

It is significant that the public was sometimes appalled by the apparent violation of conventional just war philosophies at the RAND Corporation, where traditional doctrine seemed to be supplanted by amoral number-crunching computer models extrapolating from elaborate mutual destruction scenarios about thermonuclear war. Cartoonists and columnists particularly delighted in mocking corpulent RAND strategist Herman Kahn, who often made headline-grabbing pronouncements about the winnable apocalypse. RAND (an acronym for research and development) had split off from Douglas Aircraft in 1948 to become an entity devoted to hyperrational computer simulation and supposedly nonpartisan analysis. By 1959, according to one history of the corporation, RAND had started to cultivate a "very close and intense ongoing relationship with the Advanced Research Projects Agency (ARPA), which supported much of the computer-science research" (Ware 2008, 2). ARPA (or DARPA, as it became in 1972 to recognize the primacy of "defense") was also interested in applying game theory to policy questions related to new weapons

of mass destruction. Although game theory was recognized by the company's mathematicians as a valid approach, the value of running actual wargames that were time-consuming and clouded by subjective experiences and multiple variables was often subject to debate within RAND, according to Kahn biographer Sharon Ghamari-Tabrizi. Playing wargames at the Santa Monica think tank did eventually progress from being "regarded both as synthetic histories and laboratory experiments" to being "used to generate operational data" (Ghamari-Tabrizi 2005, 169). Ghamari-Tabrizi argues that the power of gaming to stimulate creativity, teach both intellectually and emotionally, and convey otherwise tacit knowledge was frequently lauded (162). For example, games were considered a way to produce a capacity for intuition in which players might develop a "feel" for how to respond in a particular situation.

Although war strategy games have a long history of producing prototypes that includes many examples discussed in this volume, RAND was quickly recognized as a pioneering firm that capitalized on

Figure 30.1
RAND Corporation gameplay in *Life* magazine.

access to both analog and digital computers, along with a liberal supply of board games, card games, and dice games. For example, a 1959 spread in *Life* magazine titled "Games, Brass and Overtime" shows two teams of employees intently playing a territory board game with hexagonal segments in which the game play of competitors is obscured by a low wall, much like the conditions for the classic game *Battleship* (1931). Among the abstractions of the mock air missile battle being staged on the two boards, star-shaped pieces represent enemy bomb bursts.

One of the first simulations produced by the company in the 1940s was apparently a mechanical contraption called the "pinball machine," which simulated very large bombing runs in which targets already destroyed might be inefficiently hit multiple times. As one witness described it, the pinball machine "lights lights, rings bells, and adds up your score automatically" (Ware 2008, 91). The observer went on to waggishly point out that round bomb craters were perfect squares, that square city blocks were represented by spherical balls, and that instead of throwing bombs at a target the device threw targets at a bomb. Ironically, commercial arcades would go on to buy a number of mechanical devices that simulated the effects of violently destructive bombing campaigns, including Mutoscope's *Atomic Bomber* (1946), which promised "'chain-reaction' sales" in its 1946 advertising and was still getting attention in 1954 for offending peace-loving Swedes at Stockholm's Coney Island. In *Atomic Bomber* the player views a scrolling panorama through a bombsight and waits for crosshairs to align with the target.

As the gaming efforts of RAND proliferated in the mid-1950s, debates about the differences between games and simulations were hashed out in public forums, such as the 1955 first national Symposium on War Games, where participants agreed that it was the "experience of dynamic play" that was tantamount (Ware 2008, 153). RAND also expanded its repertoire from wargames to role-playing crisis games. RAND's interest in this newer form of gaming was "leaked" to the public in a 1963 *Steve Canyon* comic strip, after creator Milton Caniff was invited to participate in one of these Pentagon-sponsored exercises himself (160). In the syndicated comic, the fictional hero participates in a Blue team/Red team exercise that pits the United States and its allies against "red bloc" nations. An outspoken, pearl-earring-wearing female character who waves a cigarette holder, "Miss Calhoun," plays along with fellow "persons of importance." Soon, however, she becomes a figure of fun, after she naively asks, "When will our decisions be put into effect by the government?" This comment marks her as one without the sophistication necessary to distinguish a simulation from reality.

Simpler game scenarios from the period involved two players rather than two teams, and the stockpiling of weapons was often an important metric in the success of gameplay. For example, the earliest "Gaming" pre-1970 bibliography (RAND Corporation 2000a) from RAND records a 1964 publication by Michael Intrilligator called "Some Simple Models of Arms Races," which is described as follows:

> A simplified study of the complex structure of arms races in the real world by the assumption of two contenders, each having one policy variable: weapons stocks. With such simplification, arms races are studied by means of reaction curves that indicate optimal weapons stocks, given the weapons stocks of the opponent. The ratio goal and Richardson models are formulated in terms of reaction curves. Allowance is made for the neglect of strategy and constraints by these models.

Figure 30.2
Steve Canyon comic strip with crisis gameplay.

The analysis is suggested only and does not consider the many dimensions of policy. (RAND Corporation 2000a)

Although the abstract contains a disclaimer about the nuances of policy and its implications, this fundamental model of a two-player game that could be structured as a race or duel was a relatively common one during the early days of RAND.

Specifically, between 1950 and 1970, no fewer than a dozen papers were written about duels to model how different information and resource conditions might generate different outcomes. There were papers on both "silent" duels and "noisy" or "loud" duels, on duels with continuous firing and on one-bullet duels, and on duels involving bombers, fighters, and machine guns. Obviously, a duel is a

Figure 30.3
Female operator of analog computer/coverage machine at RAND.

very masculinist way to imagine how conflict might be staged between aggressors/defenders. A duel assumes there is no collateral damage and presumes that honor is a stable category marked by respecting the norms of a strong gender divide. In the visual ephemera generated by RAND leadership, we also see many examples of everyday sexism in official communications, including hypersexualized illustrations of busty women and muscular men in Kahn's humorous memorandum "Ten Pitfalls of Modeling." There were also more subtle manifestations of male privilege in the game development environment at RAND. For example, pictures of the company's putting green only show use by male players. (There were also shuffleboard courts on the RAND campus.)

Despite the dominant corporate culture, women were important actors in RAND's strategic initiatives. They appear in photos from the company's institutional history as operators of physical analog computers, including "coverage machines," as punch card operators reviewing duplicates for errors, and as smiling senior programmers. Although RAND lists authors' first names only by their initials, many women have been identified through cross-referencing by RAND archivists. Even among the earliest published studies on gaming from RAND, names like Annette Heuston and Jean Rehkop Renshaw indicate that women made important contributions. For example, Heuston and Renshaw jointly published a 1957 paper on *Monopologs*, an inventory management game about the Air Force's supply system, in which they described reasons for iteration in the design process and how a game was eventually developed in which a player could generate "his own demand patterns."

As artificial intelligence and computational linguistics became more important for RAND's modeling of expert systems, more sophisticated ways to think about game environments emerged. At the same time, constructivist theorists were advocating for microworlds that emphasized the spaces and places for learning. Such microworlds also used more stable software platforms—including commercial, off-the-shelf components—and required less knowledge of code by operators, which made them popular to use in game design. For example, one research brief praises a microworld as "a computer-based learning tool that enables an individual to interact with a specific environment much in the way that a flight simulator enables a pilot to practice a wide range of aerial maneuvers." RAND also broadened its imagined user base beyond the elite who would play as powerful generals or diplomats with a god's-eye perspective on the action to include logistics training for lower-level staff in lower-stakes positions to improve performance more generally.

Virtual Humans and the Body at Risk: The Institute for Creative Technologies

As the influence of situated learning theorists studying communities of practice such as Jean Lave and Etienne Wenger percolated into military culture, the purpose of rehearsal in military games and simulations began to change. Much as education more generally was recognizing the importance of peripheral participation, identity work, reputation systems, and social dynamics, military training was moving away from the model of the autonomous learner. Embodied interactions became more important than abstracted simulations, and the signature computational media products developed by the Institute for Creative Technologies reflected this transformation.

The ICT was founded in 1999 with a five-year US Army contract to the University of Southern California. In one RAND press release about touring their high-tech installations, the ICT is described as "a high-powered collaborative effort between the US Army and Hollywood that was established to use entertainment, games, and immersion techniques to improve training, rehearsal and analysis for the military." But ICT designers claimed to eschew passive spectacles. Although the two wargaming facilities were minutes away from each other on the Pacific Coast Highway, ICT and RAND were very different entities. The ICT courted media attention much more directly and had fewer security restrictions. Some of its technological infrastructure, such as an elaborate light stage for producing more photorealistic simulations, could even be repurposed for rental by Hollywood studios to refine their own digital effects for blockbuster films.

The dynamics of gender play in the theater of combat also seems to have been a more explicitly debated aspect of design philosophy at the ICT than it was at RAND. After all, in imagining military doctrines of prevention and preemption for both generals in the war room and soldiers in the field, it is often necessary to create gendered scenarios around victimhood and war crimes that require specific representations of violence involving embodiment and affect. Recent scandals about sexual harassment in the military have also brought questions about justice and the body at risk closer to home for designers of training games and simulations.

ICT designer Jacquelyn Ford Morie produced particularly vivid simulations for the institute. "Dogs bark, water trickles, and people you can't see murmur in the distance" in Morie's mission simulator set in an abandoned mill complex in war-torn Bosnia (Chaplin and Ruby 2005, 211). To create a particularly immersive experience, Morie designed a scent necklace that emitted odors at specific times in the scenario. She has also been part of the feminist game collective Ludica, which protests the "hegemony of play" promulgated by the commercial games industry and presents research on the importance of reciprocity, dress-up, and cooperative learning for participants in gaming of all genders. Other feminist developers of games and simulations who published with the ICT included Magy Seif El-Nasr and Nonny de la Peña.

Women were also project leaders at the ICT. For example, Diane Piepol headed up development of *Cultural and Cognitive Combat Immersive Trainer* (*C3IT*), a 2006 simulation about an IED investigation that requires the participant to question potential witnesses, informants, or suspects at a market without violating expectations about propriety, respect for women, and the privacy of domestic concerns.

Despite her personal pacifism, Morie is unapologetic about having worked on designing virtual reality systems for the military for the better part of a quarter-century:

> I worked on how to train people better, so they don't die, so they didn't make stupid decisions and so they were as prepared as possible. I was doing research; I wasn't supporting war. I don't believe that you are ever going to get rid of war, but you can train people culturally and promote situational awareness, so they don't knee-jerk trigger-happy shoot a child that runs across the street.[1]

In this interview Morie described how other women joined development teams at the ICT, particularly women trained in computer animation and visual systems, although they remained a miniscule fraction of the leadership group. Toward the end of the interview session, she admitted that it could be "really frustrating to be a female at the ICT," particularly when she felt constrained by its "boys' network." Even though Anita K. Jones of DARPA was a prominent participant at the early organizational meetings that would contribute to the founding of the ICT and lead to the publication of seminal documents, such as the 1997 volume on *Modeling and Simulation: Linking Entertainment and Defense*, it could also be challenging to design female characters with existing skins that no one "would get freaked out about," given the repression of sexual politics in

military life, even after a series of scandals reached the media and were aired in senate hearings.

Morie proposed an education program based upon the "Enhancing Sexual Harassment Training for the 21st Century Military" white paper that included scenarios set in a bar or nightclub. Morie explained how she didn't want to do something about "training women to stay out of harm's way" that reinforced a blame-the-victim mentality. In the simulation, the player's 3D avatar either witnesses sexual harassment in process and must choose how to intervene or hears a victim's confession and must decide on how best to respond. Morie wanted to make virtual worlds part of the experience of "every incoming recruit," but she acknowledged that it was probably "way too early" and too ambitious in tackling the reporting structure. Knowing that "gaming the system" is

Figure 30.4
Early prototype for sexual harassment virtual role-playing scenario.

common in role-playing scenarios, she had hoped to "use all the gesture recognition and voice prosody" and really measure "if they were paying attention," with "quantifiable metrics on their performance" (see note 1).

Although no longer using commercial virtual worlds like *Second Life* (2003), the ICT continues to develop sexual harassment training tools with its suite of virtual humans. The ICT also continues to create other military training simulations that use elements of gaming interfaces and technologies, such as the Emergent Leader Immersive Training Environment (ELITE) and the Immersive Naval Officer Training System (INOTS) for instruction, practice, and assessment focusing on the interpersonal communication skills for junior leaders in the US Army and US Navy. As a platform for a particular game mechanic, ELITE has been a particularly generative site for role-playing scenarios involving sexual harassment training. The ELITE simulation had always been a way to rehearse "real-world issues such as financial troubles, post-deployment readjustment and alcohol-related performance issues." Now more recent office counseling scenarios involving training for interpersonal skills with active listening in conjunction with the ICT's life-sized virtual humans "address issues around sexual harassment and assault" with instruction, practice, and assessment.

Since 2006, the ICT has also produced UrbanSim, which is a game-based training software system for mission leaders that can be downloaded from the MilGaming website and used by squad leaders. In many ways, the ICT's wargames are now explicitly designed to appeal to the military's middle management and emerging leaders, a demographic more likely to be accustomed to navigating game worlds and more open to training activities. Many of these

simulations also use first-person point-of-view for the interactions with virtual humans, so that the conflict between representing embodiment and presenting more abstracted games about opportunism or mastery of resources is resolved in favor of a more meaningful situated performance.

As was the case at RAND, much of the pressure on designers during the development process of launching a military game focuses on achieving verisimilitude. As ICT Project Director Julia Kim explained in an interview, being able to "up our fidelity" through "connections to military folks" that provide "reference materials and interviews" can be critical for success, because "details matter," from the particularities of uniforms to landscape features.[2] Earlier ICT games and simulations that were dependent upon running without glitches on laptops in the field were sometimes stymied by the technical limitations of graphics and memory capabilities even though, as Kim explained, "rather than perfectly simulating virtual characters as means to an end" ICT wanted to focus on "what's good enough" to serve the purposes of education as distinct from training.

Marisa Brandt, who did fieldwork at ICT studying the virtual reality environment *Virtual Iraq*, which is used to treat veterans' posttraumatic stress disorder, describes how there are still pressures to make the design of games or simulations more elegant and the procedural rhetorics more comprehensible and streamlined. As Brandt explains, in "the economy of design in VR therapy systems, reality is schematized, stripped down to an operationalized model of the world; in it, each element, be it physical or social, reflects an assumption about how to elicit and promote the control of unhealthy behavior … But variation among these systems reveals the diversity of opinions about how best to use existing VR technology to intervene in subjectivity" (Brandt 2014, 526). For Brandt, these logics of algorithmic efficiency also reveal particular ideological operations. In this case, the territory to be mastered is the landscape of a disordered mind, and VR therapy provides the simulation environment for rehearsal to regain control over disordered cognitive processes.

The development of military games in Southern California continues to change, as the ICT works to meet the needs of a "realist" just war doctrine rather than a "hearts and minds" just war doctrine, according to Kim. After efforts to promote democracy in Iraq and Afghanistan energized the dynamics of civil war, military designers of games and simulations are interested in pursuing rehearsals of realpolitik in computational environments rather than a performance of ideals divorced from reality. In particular, the ICT is developing a series of turn-based strategy games about counterterrorism with a political scientist at the Naval Postgraduate School in which the gameplay is "nation-agnostic." Michael E. Freeman hopes that these games, in which there are always trade-offs and no single right strategy, will provide more accurate preparation for real-world negotiation and policy making in which dealing with dictatorial police states is a fact of life. Unlike the ICT's therapeutic VR systems, in which players actually see counselors or advisors who project an embodied ethics of care, the game is exclusively based on text instructions. Freeman is also developing another ICT game with a similarly agnostic framework about "dark networks," which recognizes the fact that illicit networks can protect both drug cartels and underground railroads to freedom.

In considering these ways to algorithmically model just war and playing defense during its seventy-year history in Southern California, it is difficult to assert that the military-entertainment complex is monolithic—or even marginally consistent about applying its doctrines about aggression the same way over time. Choosing female military game designers as a way to explore the ambiguities of playable simulations might be just one way to tell a more complex story about the rise of command-and-control computational media and new forms of information warfare. However, even if we shun supporting state-sponsored games with a god's-eye perspective of surveillance and mastery, patriarchal authority structures may still be reinscribed in certain kinds of playable systems. For example, cultural competence games like those built by the ICT can promote extremely patronizing speech acts in which a white male from the Global North presumes a position of knowledge based on very little information. Such games use crudely designed game engines that do little to address persistent microaggressions. At the very least, there are potential problems designing military gameplay as a disembodied experience, particularly when the performance of gender requires a greater repertoire of skins and scripts with which to work. As Judy Wajcman observes, technofeminism is about more than just women and computers. It is about design choices and what those design choices say about power.

About the Author

Elizabeth Losh is the author of *Virtualpolitik: An Electronic History of Government Media-Making in a Time of War, Scandal, Disaster, Miscommunication, and Mistakes* (MIT Press, 2009) and *The War on Learning: Gaining*

Ground in the Digital University (MIT Press, 2014). She writes about the digital humanities, new forms of learning, institutions as digital content-creators, the discourses of the "virtual state," the media literacy of policy makers and authority figures, the rhetoric surrounding regulatory attempts to limit everyday digital practices, and communities that produce, consume, and circulate online video, videogames, digital photographs, text postings, and programming code. She is director of the Culture, Art, and Technology program at Sixth College at UC San Diego, where she teaches courses on digital rhetoric and new media.

Notes

1. Personal interview with Elizabeth Losh, May 14, 2014.

2. Personal interview with Elizabeth Losh, July 6, 2014.

31 DEBORD'S NOSTALGIC ALGORITHM

Alexander R. Galloway

"I await the end of cinema with optimism," Jean-Luc Godard announced in 1965. And indeed the end was near. "The cinema seems to me to be over," was Guy Debord's blunt assessment by the spring of 1978. Much happened in those intervening years, with the progressive explosion of the middle to late 1960s engendering a crisis and retrenchment in the early to middle 1970s. The transformation was evident in a number of events and pseudo-events: student revolts in Paris and elsewhere, the French Left's flirtation with Maoism and other militancies, the oil crisis of 1973 and 1974, a painful renovation in the economic base of developed societies coinciding with the rise of information networks, and the concomitant changes in the role of the individual in society.

Guy Debord never recovered from the crisis of the 1970s. His late life was beset by chronic illness brought on by an ever-growing gluttony in food and drink. He deserted the capital city and grew more introspective in his work, mixing manifesto with memoir. By March 8, 1978, Debord's former glory as a radical filmmaker and author had faded. "The cinema seems to me to be over," he wrote in a letter. "These times don't deserve a filmmaker like me" (Debord 2005, 451).

These times were times of crisis. On March 16, 1978—eight days after Debord's dalliance about the cinema being "over"—the world awoke to a dramatic turn of events. The longtime prime minister of Italy, Christian Democrat Aldo Moro, had been kidnapped during a brazen intervention by the Red Brigades, a revolutionary communist group. In Italy, the progressive militancy of the 1960s had metastasized during the following decade into an actually existing low-level guerrilla war. Moro was held for fifty-four days. During that time, Moro appealed to the Christian Democrats to acquiesce and negotiate with what both the newspapers and government officials alike called terrorists, that newly evolved form of political actor so closely associated with the late-modern period. Held in secret and sentenced to death in a so-called people's trial on or about April 15, Moro received little solidarity from his former government colleagues, and sensing the imminent culmination of events, the presumed future president of Italy stipulated that no Christian Democrat leaders should be present at his funeral. There were none.

Moro's body was discovered in the trunk of a red Renault R4 hatchback; he had been shot ten times. Wistful was the police report, as quoted in the *New York Times* of May 10, 1978: "The cuffs of his trousers

Figure 31.1
Aldo Moro kidnapped by the Red Brigades.

were full of sand as if he had been walking on a beach or been dragged across rough soil shortly before his death."

The decade of the 1970s was long in Italy. It "began in 1967–68 and ended in 1983," recalled Antonio Negri, the man scooped up by the police in April 1979 and indicted for the Moro events, then exonerated, then indicted again and hounded in various forms for the next twenty-plus years.[1] "In 1967–68, as in all the developed countries, the student movement took to the barricades. However, the breadth and impact of this part of the movement was not as extensive as in other European countries: in Italy, the student May 1968 was not a particularly significant moment" (Negri 1998).

Much has been said about Debord being at those May barricades, certainly in spirit if not also in the flesh, with Situationist graffiti festooning the pediments of respectable French society. But a frontline militant he was not, and Debord soon left Paris to settle in one of the hexagon's more remote outposts, the rural Auvergne. There he stayed for much of the rest of his downhill life, watching the passing parade from a safe distance. The new social movements of the 1960s, having swollen in importance, were soon met by an iron fist and eventually crushed by the freshly transformed post-Fordist economies of the middle to late 1970s. If the 1960s represented a certain triumph, the 1970s was a decade of defeat. "The first to be defeated were the social movements," remembers Negri. "Having cut themselves off totally from the representatives of the traditional left ..., the social movements were thus dragged into the abyss of an extremism that was becoming increasingly blind and violent. The kidnapping and killing of Aldo Moro was the beginning of the end" (Negri 1998).

Although Debord had declined to engage significantly with Negri or Moro, he had indeed monkeywrenched with the Italian political scene by helping Gianfranco Sanguinetti write his August 1975 hoax pamphlet *The True Report on the Last Chance to Save Capitalism in Italy*, as well as translating the text from Italian to French. Contrast this with other French philosophers who were much more vocally involved with the Italian situation, such as Gilles Deleuze, who intervened with his September 20, 1977, tract against repression of Italian leftists, "Nous croyons au caractère constructiviste de certaines agitations de gauche" (*We Believe in the Constructivist Quality of Leftist Militancy*). Deleuze also published two short pieces in 1979 lobbying for Negri's freedom, and would later more formally affiliate himself by writing the preface to the 1982 French edition of Negri's influential book on Spinoza, *The Savage Anomaly* (Deleuze 1977, 149–150; 2003, 155–161, 175–178). When he did finally address Moro and the Red Brigades, in his 1979 preface to the fourth Italian edition of *The Society of the Spectacle*, Debord spat on the guerrilla movement, claiming that the Red Brigades were in fact unknowing pawns of the state Stalinist forces. Writing to Sanguinetti before the killing, Debord predicted that Moro would be "suicided" by his own government, thus allowing the state forces to consolidate power (known in Italy as the "historic compromise") around the common fear of terror and anarchy.

"Italy epitomizes the social contradictions of the whole world" (Debord 2007, 96), warned Debord. Moro was an emblem of the newfound asymmetrical conflicts plaguing developed nations, from France's Algerian uprising in the 1950s, to scores of militant splinter groups, bombings, and airplane hijackings. The tactics are called "asymmetrical" or "unconventional" because they no longer resemble the customs of so-called civilized, oppositional conflict, in which professional armies meet in known theaters of conflict to thrash out victory in blood and arms. With his life obscured today by the romantic mist of apotheosis, it is easy to forget that Debord was something of a fading violet when it came to actual conflict. He preferred the mischievous potshot to the Molotov cocktail. But the raw heroic drama of militancy forever excited him. Like many political thinkers, it was the thrill of revolution that was so seductive, of the possibility that this depraved life might one day be cast off and refashioned anew. "I am very interested in war," Debord confessed unapologetically in his late autobiographical work, *Panegyric*, amid glowing citations from Carl von Clausewitz on the emotional intensity of going to battle. "I've thus been studying the logic of war. And I even had some success, already some time ago, in realizing the essence of these processes in the context of a simple chessboard" (Debord 1993, 69–70).

While his fascination with war was not ironic and indeed perhaps uncritical, it is plausible to assume that Debord knew of Frederick Engels's famous assessment of Clausewitz, contained in a 1858 letter from Engels to Marx. Clausewitz's approach to philosophy was "odd," cautioned Engels, but "*per se* very good." More than anything else, war resembles commerce, he told Marx. "Combat is to war what cash payment is to commerce; however seldom it need happen in reality, everything is directed towards it and ultimately it is bound to occur and proves decisive" (Marx and Engels 1929, 241).[2]

So as Moro lay in the trunk of the Renault R4, Guy Debord was at his rural home playing board games and toying with the idea of fashioning one of his own. The backdrop of European militancy in the 1970s makes Debord's penchant for playtime all the more delicious. One such game was *Djambi*. A distinctly late-modern game, it is played on an extruded chessboard of nine by nine squares. It proceeds, not bilaterally as chess, but multilaterally with four players. The game tokens are not modeled on the medieval court of kings, queens, knights, and bishops, but instead on the various political actors that make up our advanced liberal democracies: the news reporter, the provocateur, the activist militant, and the assassin. If the Moro events were to be distilled and simulated in the form of an intellectual diversion, as chess did for feudal skirmishes—and of course in doing so anesthetizing the player from any immediate knowledge or experience of political realities— *Djambi* would be it.

"Thanks for Djambi," Debord wrote on May 7, 1978 to his friend and benefactor Gérard Lebovici in a letter otherwise disdainful of the game. "As long as the only goal of the game is to eliminate all the others, there can exist but one absolute mode of winning, which can't be shared in any way, to the point that in this game of trickery, you can't trick anyone. The rules suffer from a contradiction between the game's totalitarian goal and its representation of the struggles of an 'advanced liberal democracy'" (Debord 2005, 462). The ridiculous subtext of *Djambi* was clear to Debord: How could a board game ever correctly model the types of complex political dynamics encircling France, or Italy, or what Lyotard in his book on postmodernity would soon call "today's most advanced societies"? What is to be done, when the power elite goes global in order to hide itself from the base of society? What is to be done, when control and organization are no longer hierarchical or repressive, but instead have migrated into flexible, rhizomatic networks?

In fact at that moment, Debord was intensely focused on trying to work through the challenges of advanced liberal democracy, and particularly how armed struggle could be simulated in the form of simple parlor games. The cinema was over, he had concluded. A new format was required. So in the winter of 1977, after having been a filmmaker and author, Debord did something rather unconventional for a leftist intellectual: he formed his own company for making games.[3] Not chess exactly, but a variation of his own design, dubbed first in his notes

the "Kriegspiel" and later more formally *The Game of War*.

"I insist on the opportunity to throw the Kriegspiel into the stunned world as soon as we can," Debord wrote to Lebovici. "It's quite obvious that its time has come" (Debord 2005, 451).[4] In January 1977, the two founded the company Strategic and Historical Games and set out to produce an edition of the game. Debord's *Game of War* is a Napoleonic chess-variant played by two opposing players on a game board of 500 squares arranged in rows of 20 × 25 squares; by comparison, a chess board is 8 × 8, while a Go board is 19 × 19. Like chess, *The Game of War* contains game tokens of varying strengths and speeds that one must maneuver across a grid landscape in an attempt to wipe out one's enemy. Unlike chess, one must also maintain "lines of communication" that crisscross the terrain, keeping all friendly units within transmission range of one's home bases. (Debord reportedly also finished a naval warfare game called *Jeu de la bataille navale*; however, the game was never committed to paper and is now lost.) "The surprises of this Kriegspiel seem to be inexhaustible," he confessed later in his memoir *Panegyric*. "It might be the only thing in all my work—I'm afraid to admit—that one might dare say has some value" (Debord 1993, 70).

In his letters and notes Debord referred to the game as the "Kriegspiel," borrowing the German term meaning "wargame." But when the game was fabricated and released in France, Debord officially titled it *Le jeu de la guerre*. A short discussion on the most appropriate translation of the game comes in Debord's letter of May 9, 1980, to Lebovici. After reviewing the English proofs, the last question remaining was the English title: *The Game of the War* or *The Game of War*? "We must choose the more

Figure 31.2
Guy Debord, *The Game of War.*

generalizing and glorious title," he insisted. "Even if *kriegspiel = wargame* is the most 'linguistically' exact, it doesn't fit at all historically. *Kriegspiel* connotes 'a serious exercise by commanders,' but *wargame* connotes 'an infantile little game played by officers'" (Debord 2006a, 55–56).

With the assistance of Lebovici, Debord produced the game in a limited edition of four or five during the summer of 1977. The edition included an 18 × 14 1/4-inch game board and player tokens fashioned in copper and silver metal. The game was fabricated by a certain Mr. Raoult, a Parisian artisan whom Debord

trusted implicitly, referring to him as the "intrepid Raoult," and admiring him for his "politeness, rationality, and capacity to recognize what is essential in the matter at hand" (Debord 2005, 426; 2006a, 26–27). By the end of June 1978, after a setback due to poor health, he finished drafting a written copy of the game rules. "I am sending you soon the rules for the Kriegspiel," he wrote to Lebovici. "Its main section, given over to a juridico-geometric writing style, has cost me innumerable headaches" (Debord 2005, 466). As illustrated also in his jab at *Djambi*, Debord was thus intimately aware of the true reality of games, that they are a conjunction of two elements: the "juridical" element, meaning the spheres of politics and law, and the "geometrical" element, meaning the realm of mathematical processes and spatial logics. This was no longer an intervention in spectacle or in narrative, as were his films, but now an intervention at the level of a "juridico-geometric" algorithm, that is, at the level of a finite set of rules that, when executed, result in a machine able to simulate political antagonism.

The game board is divided into a northern territory and a southern territory, each with a single mountain range of nine squares, a mountain pass, three forts, and two arsenals. In addition each faction has nine infantry, four cavalry, two artillery (one footed and one mounted) and two transmission units (one footed and one mounted). Each combat unit has an attack and defense coefficient, and may move either one or two squares per turn depending on the type. The forts, arsenals, and mountains are welded to the game board, and thus immobile. The combat and noncombat units are mobile and may be positioned in any desired formation before the beginning of a match.

Arsenals radiate lines of communication vertically, horizontally, and diagonally. In addition, transmission units propagate any line of communication aimed at them. All units must remain in direct connection with their own lines of communication, or be adjacent to a friendly unit in communication. If stranded, a unit goes out of communication and becomes inert. The lines of communication are immaterial constructs, and thus have no game token to represent them. Instead, they must be mentally projected onto the game board by each player. Like the "knight's tour" in chess, the lines of communication are in essence a network of patterns superimposed onto the basic grid of squares, helping to determine where and how each piece may move. As the game unfolds, these patterns can and will shift, adding to the complexity of possible games and possible strategies.

The metal game of 1978 is stunningly modernist in its formal simplicity and reduction of ludic function into plain, abstract shapes. The cavalry units, far from aping a horse, are represented by a tall wire spike, mounted on a hexagonal base, while the infantry are represented by an upright, snubbed peg, affixed to a square base. To indicate their communicative duties, the transmission units sport a crisp flag, protruding at ninety degrees. The artillery emblem is equally spare: a horizontal hollow tube to indicate a cannon barrel. The most representational design is reserved for the mountains and the forts, the only two elements not aligned to a faction: the mountains are hulking chunks of metal, appealingly chiseled to bring out miniature crevices and peaks; the forts resemble gallant storybook parapets, hexagonally cut for the North faction, and solidly square for the South. The mountain passes have no representational form at all, but are merely the absent spaces residing at gaps in the mountains. None of the pieces displays any sort of ornament, or additional engraving or color. All of them conform to an extremely muted, almost ascetic, formal design.

The game proceeds in turns. A player may move up to five units each turn, followed by a single attack against an enemy unit. An attack is determined by summing all the offensive power in range of an enemy target square, then subtracting this number from a summation of all the defensive power supporting the same target square. Offensive and defensive power emanates from a unit in a straight line vertically, horizontally, or diagonally. If the offensive

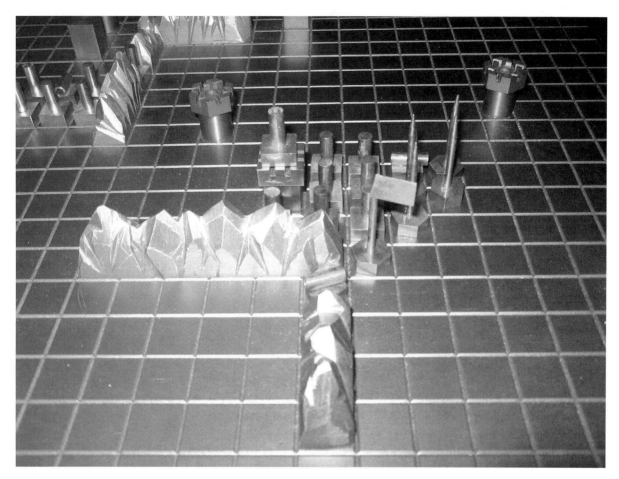

Figure 31.3
Guy Debord, *The Game of War.*

power is less than or equal to the defensive power, the unit resists. If the offensive power is two or more, the unit is destroyed.

Like the lines of communication, which require a certain amount of mental energy to be maintained in the imagination of each player, the combat mechanic for the game requires a nontrivial amount of player arithmetic, particularly as multiple units are involved in attack and defense at any given moment.

A player wins the game by either destroying all enemy combat units or destroying the enemy's two arsenals. (Although not mentioned in Debord's rulebook, it is possible to deduce one additional win state: a player wins if the enemy's two relays are destroyed and all enemy combat units are offline.) Alternately, if both sides agree to quit, the game is a draw.

While stressing the symmetrical quality of Clausewitzian warfare, Debord at the same time noted that the terrain of the game board should be asymmetrical. Here is revealed Debord's talent for game design. His aim was to achieve balance through asymmetry, such that the game would not lapse into predictable strategies and styles of play. Thus, while certain approaches are better than others, there is no "optimal" overall formation in the game. Instead, one plays through a series of compromises, always having to adjudicate between "contradictory necessities" (Debord 2005, 352). For each offensive movement of aggression, one's rear flank becomes that much more vulnerable. This dialectical tension was part of what Debord aimed to achieve with the game. Thus, the two mountain ranges in the game are arranged asymmetrically: North's mountain cleaves the terrain sharply between east and west, inhibiting lateral movement but leaving a cramped passage across the top; South's mountain is a wall expelling downward advances and making any penetration into its territory difficult. But more important is the placement of the arsenals. South's two arsenals are split wide apart and held flush to the baseline, while North's two arsenals are staggered closer to the middle. This makes for two very different styles of play. South must run a split defense, or else sacrifice one arsenal and bunker down with the remaining one. North, on the other hand, can use the terrain to its advantage, gaining protection from the mountains (which block fire) plus a defense boost from the mountain pass in range of its westerly arsenal.

Ten years after the game first appeared in limited edition, it was mass-produced on cardboard with wood tiles. In that year, 1987, Debord and his wife, Alice Becker-Ho, also published a book devoted to the game. An unconventional text, the book consists of more than a hundred annotated diagrams showing snapshots of the game during each round of a complete match played by the duo. At the end are appendices containing the game rules and strategy tips. In 1991, Debord ordered all his published works destroyed, including this book. But after Debord's death and under Becker-Ho's stewardship, the French publisher Gallimard reissued the book in 2006 as *Le jeu de la guerre: Relevé des positions successives de toutes les forces au cours d'une partie*. After remaining untranslated for twenty years, an English edition of the work appeared a year later from Atlas Press, translated by Donald Nicholson-Smith, an ex-Situationist with whom Debord had kept in touch over the years.

In 1986, as his publishing house was suffering hard times in the wake of the death of Gérard Lebovici, Debord suggested a scheme to Floriana Lebovici, Gérard's widow, to relieve the publisher's debts by commercializing *The Game of War*. It was merely a business matter, Debord wrote, like *Monopoly*. "Or is my judgment of the strategic, and thus economic, value of this Kriegspiel distorted by a certain indulgence? We shall see" (Debord 2006a, 448–449). But while Debord and Lebovici had originally formed a company around the game, Strategic and Historical Games, it is unclear how serious they had ever been about making the game commercially viable. Debord never trusted Kessler, the intellectual property lawyer hired to assist with the game. "You worry me greatly by bringing up 'strange things about Kessler,'" he wrote in 1985 to Floriana Lebovici. "Of anyone in the world, Kessler is in the best position to swindle us" (Debord 2006a, 306). In the end, the game was never commercialized in any serious way.

While distilled to a simple essence, Debord believed that *The Game of War* represented in game form all the necessary principles of war. He did admit however that three things were missing from his near perfect simulation: climate conditions and the cycles of day and night, the influence of troop morale, and uncertainty about the exact positions and movements of the enemy. "That said," he continued, "one may assert that the [*The Game of War*] exactly reproduces the totality of factors that deal with war, and more generally the dialectic of all conflicts" (Becker-Ho and Debord 2006, 151). Debord's ambitions for the game were grandiose. By evoking the "dialectic of all conflicts," he was appealing backward to the power of 1968 and the days of the Situationist International, but also forward to the game's future potential in training and cultivating a new generation of militants.

But the game was missing more than just climate conditions. In fact, viewed against the silhouette of Debord's other work, it is surprisingly square. The spirit of "wandering" or "hijacking," from the Situationist days, is absent in the game. There is no mechanism for overturning society, no temporary autonomous zones, no workers' councils, no utopian cities, no imaginary landscapes of desire, no cobblestones, and no beach, only grids of toy soldiers fighting a made-up war in a made-up world.

It prompts the question: Why was this game relatively unadventurous, while Debord's other work so experimental? Can this be explained away through an analysis of media formats, that Debord had a certain panache for radical filmmaking and critical philosophy, but lapsed back into the predictable habits of the bourgeois parlor game when he tried his hand at game design?[5] Did Debord simply lose his radical zeal late in life, his Hegelianism finally winning out over his Marxism? Why, when the guerrillas were staging assassinations in Italy, was Debord playing with toy soldiers in France?

Was there a link between Moro's killing and Debord's late work? Of course not, nothing more than a coincidence of dates. Yet this very incompatibility frames in stark relief a crisis within the work: Why an objet d'art instead of a cobblestone?

A number of explanations are possible. For example, it is possible that the abrasively anachronistic Debord was simply restaging the same Trojan Horse logic he had used many times before. He was well known for masquerading inside the very thing he found most repulsive. For example, Debord took up the "reactionary" form of cinema precisely in order to criticize that same medium of spectacle. Perhaps now he was merely making a "reactionary" game in order to explode the logic of play from within.

Alternately, it is plausible Debord never intended the game to be a theoretical proposal, and therefore should not be evaluated as one; the game existed simply to train militants. Thus if, in Debord's view, *any* tactical training helped unlock radical consciousness, then it mattered little that *The Game of War* stresses Clausewitz (instead of Sun Tzu) or the legacy of the Napoleonic wars (instead of Parisian street revolts).

Debord admitted that the game was bound to an historical period: "This doesn't represent wars of antiquity, nor those of the feudal period, nor modern warfare refashioned by technology after the middle of the nineteenth century (railways, machine guns, motorization, aviation, missiles)" (Becker-Ho and Debord 2006, 149). In other words, the game refers to warfare as it was practiced in the early and middle modern periods up to about 1850. The "classic equilibrium" of the eighteenth century was his model, a mode of warfare best represented by the Seven Years' War, and characterized by symmetry, regularity, professional armies, the preciousness of personnel, and the importance of supply stockpiles (Debord 2005, 351). So *The Game of War* is indeed historically specific. But it is historically specific for a century long past, not the century in which Debord was living. (As Philippe Sollers quipped later, Debord wasn't interested in the twentieth century.) In comparisons made between the game and chess, he accentuates the question of historical specificity. He positions chess firmly in what the French term the "classical" period, consisting of kings and corporal fiat, while *The Game of War* belongs to a time of systems, logistical routes, and lines of communication. In chess, "the king can never remain in check," but in *The Game of War* "liaisons must always be maintained" (Becker-Ho and Debord 2006, 165–166). Spatial relationships between pieces are indeed paramount in chess, the "knight's tour" serving as a classic mental projection of pattern and recombination. Debord preserved this spatial relationship approach, but he stepped it up a notch. The "liaisons" in *The Game of War* are not simply the projections of possible troop maneuvers, but a supplementary layer linking far off fighters back home. In this sense, the chess king is an intensive node, one that must be fortified through the protection of its allied footmen. But Debord's arsenals are extensive nodes; yes, they too must be protected, but they also serve as the origin point for a radiating fabric of transmission. The body versus the liaison—this is not unlike the sorts of historical arguments made about the shift from early modernity to high or late modernity (i.e., the "disciplined" modern body as opposed to the postmodern "line of flight"). Chess presents a set of challenges in proximity to a consecrated corpus, a prize, but *The Game of War* is a game of decentralized space itself, the assets of war strung out in long lines and held together by a tissue of interconnection.

Seen in this light, the game seems less nostalgic for bygone eras. The key is the network of lines of communication, a detail of game design entirely lacking in a game like chess. Superimposed on the game board, the lines simulate the communication and logical chains of campaign warfare; Debord's rules stipulate that all pieces on the board must stay in contact with a line, else risk destruction. (Even Go, a game that is largely about spatial patterns and relationships, lacks the concept of an extended ray or any sort of network phenomenon.) "This 'war' can be fought as much on the plane of communication as that of extensible space," writes McKenzie Wark on *The Game of War* (Wark 2008). Thus, while perhaps tenuous, a sympathetic reading of Debord would be to say that the game's communication lines are Debord's antidote to the specter of Napoleonic nostalgia. They are the symptomatic key into Debord's own algorithmic allegory—or allegorithm, if the term is not too clunky—of the new information society growing up all around him in the 1970s. In short, Debord's *Game of War* is something like "chess with networks."

Chess required intense strategy, but it was ultimately too boring for Debord. *The Game of War* "is completely contrary to the spirit of chess," he explained. "Actually it was poker I was trying to imitate. Less the randomness of poker and more the powerful sense of battle" (Becker-Ho and Debord 2006, 166). Chance has no place in *The Game of War*; after an opening coin toss to determine who moves first, the game plays out dice-free.

But ultimately what attracted Debord to *The Game of War* was not an argument about historical periodization. In his view, a game can only ever be about general principles, and thus abstract war simulations like chess were more apt than the actual historical reenactments of specific Napoleonic campaigns.

Knowing precisely how Prussia fell was uninteresting to Debord. But knowing the abstract, general rules of antagonism, that was the key. Still, "abstract and general" did not mean "theoretical" for Debord. He considered theory to be an inferior form, one beholden to passing fancy, to perpetual obsolescence. This is why Debord was so enamored with war. "War" for Debord means "not theory" (just as for Napoleon war meant "not ideology").[6] War is that thing that is not vague. It springs from the heart and from a sensible and practical empiricism. It finds presence in the execution of things. War is the opposite of the absolute. War is *contingency*—that special term so dear to late twentieth-century progressive movements.

"I'm not a philosopher," Debord confessed to Giorgio Agamben. "I'm a strategist" (Agamben 2006, 36). Or as he put it in *In girum imus nocte et consumimur igni*, his final film, which was produced concurrent with the game: "no vital periods ever began from a

Figure 31.4
The Charge of the Light Brigade (1936), Michael Curtiz, director.

theory. What's first is a game, a struggle, a journey" (Debord 1999, 26).

In *In girum*, Debord incorporated footage stolen from Hollywood scenes of epic pitched battles. One such film sampled by Debord was Michael Curtiz's *The Charge of the Light Brigade* of 1936, a movie adapted from the Tennyson poem of the same name, which itself mythologized the notorious and bloody defeat of the British Cavalry in 1854 during the Crimean War. What does it mean to hijack such horse-mounted heroics and crosscut them with footage of *The Game of War*? As Debord wrote later with only a hint of irony, "in a very heavy-handed and congratulatory way, *The Charge of the Light Brigade* could possibly 'represent' a dozen years of interventions by the Situationist International!" (Debord 1999, 66). This "representation" takes center stage in *The Game of War*, in the form of the cavalry game tokens, the most powerful units in the game due to their elevated speed and special "charge" ability resulting in compounded, focused damage of up to 28 attack points. Through the game he was able to relive, in a mediated environment, the types of heroic monumentality attained in his previous interventions. But what a cruel narrative arc, that what started on the streets of Paris must end in an abstract plane of combat coefficients and win-loss percentages. "The SI is like radioactivity," he joked in a letter to one of his Italian translators. "One speaks little of it, but detects some traces almost everywhere. And it lasts a long time" (Debord 2006a, 45–46).

A game is a machine, but a book is never a machine. Of this Debord was certain. "No matter how often one would want to replay them," he wrote in the preface to the 1987 book devoted to the game, "the operations of game play remain unpredictable in both form and effect" (Becker-Ho and Debord 2006, 7).[7] In

Debord's view, there is a stark difference between *The Game of War* and the pastime of military reenactment, wherein a specific historical battle is restaged with little unpredictability in its outcome. The reenactment of a specific historical event was uninteresting to Debord. His desire was not that of a nostalgia for a past event. Rather, he sought to model, in a generic and universal way, antagonism itself. "Those who are well-versed in strategy," he wrote, "will see in operation here an actual model of warfare."

The 1987 book is a meditation on losing. But who lost the match, Alice or Guy? Unfortunately, no explicit answers exist in the text as to who played the North faction and who played the South. But one may say with precision: Debord played the South. He is the one who perishes in the end.

But how is it possible to make such a claim? To explain it I must detour slightly toward a matter of some delicacy. It concerns a number of mistakes that exist in the Becker-Ho and Debord book of 1987, mistakes that largely persist in both the 2006 French reprint of the book and in the 2007 English translation, *A Game of War*.[8] In addition to a few minor graphical errors, the book contains one patently illegal move, plus five additional moves that, while more subtle in nature, are also illegal given a proper interpretation of the game rules.[9] The first illegal move concerns turn 9′ (turns are numbered 1, 1′, 2, 2′, 3, 3′, etc.). A southern infantry unit moves to position I17. However, infantry can only move one square at a time, and thus the book would require that one of the infantry units move two squares. The five additional illegal moves are as follows: the K15 infantry in move 14′; the L12 cavalry in move 17′; the I9 infantry in move 35′; the J10 infantry in move 36′; and the J14 infantry in move 46′. In each of these instances, the unit in question would be thrust out of

communication during the course of the player's turn. However, according to the game rules, noncommunicable pieces are inert and cannot move. Thus, there is an impasse: in order for these five moves to be legal, one would have to overlook one of the game's rules governing the "online" and "offline" nature of units. So, assuming that all game rules must be followed, these five moves must be marked illegal.

There are two final details worth underscoring. First, all of these mistakes are committed by the same player, the southern player; North commits no fouls. Second, (almost) all of these mistakes remain unremedied through multiple authorial and editorial stages: Becker-Ho and Debord's original playing of the match in question; Debord's documentation of the match and his writing of the annotations contained in the book; then three subsequent rounds of editorial oversight, in 1987, 2006, and 2007. Yet after all that, roughly one out of every eight full turns documented in this book contains an error. How could this be? How could so many mistakes pass through five rounds of scrutiny? Would we forgive him if *Society of the Spectacle* contained a nontrivial mistake in logic on every eighth page? What can explain this blindness?

Let me stress in passing that the identification of these mistakes is not meant to be a mere schoolmarm act of one-upmanship, pointing out that Debord and Becker-Ho failed to publish a typo-free book. It is much more than that. What must be understood is that the identification of these mistakes reveals a very different sort of textual "fact" than one might reveal in the identification of a typo, a misspelled word, or even a minor grammatical blunder in a work of literature. These mistakes are not orthographical or even simply syntactical in nature. They are algorithmic. Which is to say, they deal not with a relatively localized condition of correct writing (in, for example, the case of a misspelled word), but with the correct execution of rule-bound action. The correct execution of rules is rarely ever localizable; it implies dramatic repercussions in the diachronic progression of the artifact in question, be it a game or other action-based text. Traditional texts are not executed—I will happily allow the Derrideans in the room to blanch at such a claim—and therefore the status of a fault in an algorithmic text is of a very different order than the status of a fault in a traditional text. For example, a false move or an incident of cheating in a game will essentially invalidate the game from that point onward. As any schoolchild knows, cheating taints a game to such a degree that any outcome will "not count." One is obligated to "start over." Thus, I would not think it too dramatic to assert that the Becker-Ho and Debord book of 1987, in some basic sense, does not count. We must call for a do over. (But is this not in the end the most Derridean claim of all, that the text is, in some actual, demonstrable way, flawed to the core?)

Let me summarize: first, there is a hypothesis on the table (that Debord played the South), and second, there is a set of exegetical observations (that the Becker-Ho and Debord book of 1987 contains a number of nontrivial mistakes). But where does this lead?

A common assumption that people make when learning of the mistakes in the *Game of War* book is that Debord must have played North. The argument goes roughly like this: since Debord was the game designer and had been playing the game, or some form of it, since the middle 1950s, he would be so intimate with the game rules that he would not break any of them. This line of reasoning locates Debord as the northern player, and Becker-Ho the southern.

While such an argument is somewhat persuasive, I want to offer a different argument that strikes me as ultimately more persuasive. I want to suggest that instead of relying on a psychological rationale (what Debord did or did not know, what he did or did not intend, etc.), it is more productive to rely on a structural—or we might even say an algorithmic— rationale. The mistakes are not so much a red herring as they are decoys for what is actually happening. Instead of a style of mind, therefore, let us speak instead of a style of code. Let us speak of algorithmic and structural aesthetics.

Important to this algorithmic aesthetics is the concept of optimization, that is, the notion that in any rule-based system there is always an optimal state of affairs in which the structure at play is exploited to the fullest. In the case of *The Game of War*, optimal troop formations are identified by crystalline shapes such as lattices, ladders, X-formations, crosses, and wings. The reason for this is straightforward. The game rules (which are an algorithm of a certain sort) define states of affairs. In particular, they define things like attack coefficients and defensive coefficients, plus the commutativity of these power coefficients to both friendly and enemy players across the grid of the game board. Since attack and defense propagate in straight lines, the game tends to privilege formations with strut shapes, such as lattices and crosses. These structures can be described as crystalline in the sense that they offer a highly organized, local microstructure (for example, a cross) that may be iterated multiple times to create durable material forms. "Crystal" aesthetics, then, is an aesthetic of the superego: it mandates optimal material behavior through the full execution of rules. If an algorithm is sufficiently simple, the point of maximal exploitation may be known. If a gamer is sufficiently experienced with the rules of a game he or she will learn the point of maximal exploitation and, since it is in his or her interest, will enact these techniques of optimal exploitation as often as possible. For example, in *The Game of War*, this crystal aesthetics appears via unit formations in the shape of crosses, ladders, and wings. Figures 31.7–8 demonstrate the southern player's affection for such formations. The same southern formations are also seen in figures 31.5–6, which derive from the "Explanatory Diagrams" section of the game rules (which we know were authored by Debord, not Becker-Ho), in which the southern player is the "protagonist," even if only for purposes of explanation. The northern player displays none of the same tics anywhere in the book.[10]

The hypothesis, then, is less to indicate precisely that Debord played the south side and Becker-Ho played the north. And there is little value gained in trying to demonstrate that he was a more skilled player than she, or vice versa. This would amount to little more than petty intramarital speculation, and to what end? The hypothesis is that both the south player and the author of the game rules are the same person, because they both display the previously described crystalline style of game play. Debord is that player and hence played South.

So, in the end the mistakes (turns 14′, 17′, 35′, 36′, and 46′) are something of a red herring. In identifying play styles, it is much more important to identify higher-level algorithmic skill (knowledge of how rules can be exploited for optimal game states) than it is to worry over small, largely technical mistakes.

But does this not lead to a new contradiction, that the very same crystalline player, who knows the optimal troop formation throughout the course of the

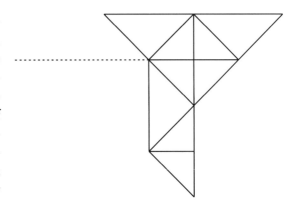

Figure 31.5

Visualization of combat relationships for the southern player in Guy Debord's *Game of War*, "Explanatory Diagrams, Figure 5" (Becker-Ho and Debord 2007, 33).

match, and who displays a "macho" algorithmic affect, is the same player who repeatedly makes small mistakes (turns 14′, 17′, 35′, 36′, and 46′)? How could this be? Wouldn't this seem to invalidate the notion that the crystalline player is an algorithmic agent first and foremost?

The answer requires a sense of how algorithmic knowledge works. The answer lies in the fact that it is possible for a single individual to be skilled at upper-level knowledge of pattern formation and rule-bound behavior, while still failing at more demanding, highly technical execution of those operations. Programmers often work in this manner: most programmers have a cultivated sense of algorithmic knowledge, and yet even the most skilled programmers are unable to identify certain bugs that for the machine are trivial to identify. There are machines and then there are machines. In the case of Debord, we have a crystalline player who is adept at the level of game play (that is, the programmer's level), but who, like most of us, is never truly a machine at the level of the Real.

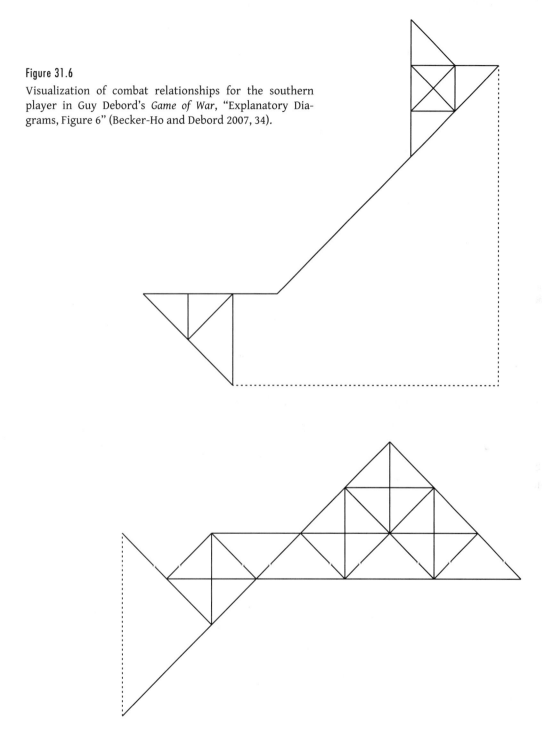

Figure 31.6
Visualization of combat relationships for the southern player in Guy Debord's *Game of War*, "Explanatory Diagrams, Figure 6" (Becker-Ho and Debord 2007, 34).

Figure 31.7
Visualization of combat relationships for the southern player in Guy Debord's *Game of War*, "Turn 22" (Becker-Ho and Debord 2007, 83).

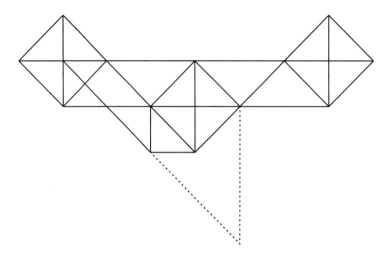

Figure 31.8
Visualization of combat relationships for the southern player in Guy Debord's *Game of War*, "Turn 44" (Becker-Ho and Debord 2007, 127).

So Debord plays the South. He is the one who loses in the end. But he doesn't just lose; worse, he throws in the towel, punishing himself with a stern lecture on the necessity of better strategic knowledge and planning. The final annotation of the match appears at the moment of South's concession:

> The South ceases its hostilities. It's time now for him to reflect on the operations of the campaign, recalling the unchanging theories of war, in order to understand the string of circumstances, the assumptions, and maybe also any relevant mental traits recognizable in his command, that this time led the North to victory. (Becker-Ho and Debord 2006, 127)

What are these relevant mental traits? Has he gone mad? Or worse—has she? One wonders if Debord ever really won anything, or if the entire history— the Situationist International and all the rest—was always leading up to this end and this end alone. First

cinema and philosophy, and finally the bourgeois parlor game.

Certainly, the domain of simulation and modeling is always something of a bitter pill for progressive movements. This is the root anxiety lurking beneath the surface of Debord's game. The Left will always be deceived in the domain of abstraction. This is not to say that Spirit or the *logos* are by necessity contrary to progressive political movements. Nevertheless, the lofty realm of rational idealism has always been something of a hindrance to those suffering from the harsh vicissitudes of material fact. And here one must revisit a long history indeed, of traditionalism versus transformation, of philosophy versus sophistry, of essence versus process, of positivism versus dialectics, of social science versus "theory," and so on.

Progressive art movements are very good at beginnings, but terrible at endings. As Debord said in 1978 amid his losses (the death of the SI, the "end" of the cinema, his expanding waistline and vanishing sobriety): "avant-gardes have but one time" (Debord 1999, 47).

We might say something similar about leftist cultural production in general: (1) the Left is forever true in the here and now, always in the grip of its own immediate suffering, but (2) it will forever be defeated in the end, even if it finds vindication there. This is why Debord can occupy himself with both "struggle" and "utopia." It is also a window into why Debord became obsessed late in life, not with street revolt, but with the sublimation of antagonistic

desire into an abstract rulebook. It is not that the past is always glorious and the future antiseptic. Quite the opposite, both past and future are internally variegated into alternately repressive and liberating moments. For the Left, the "historical present" is one of immediate justice won through the raw facts of struggle and sacrifice. In short, the historical present is always *true*, but forever at the same time *bloody*. But the future, the utopian imagination, is a time of complete liberation forged from the mold of the most profound injustice. In short, utopia is always *false*, but forever at the same time *free*.

About the Author

Alexander R. Galloway is a writer and computer programmer working on issues in philosophy, technology, and theories of mediation. Associate professor of Media, Culture, and Communication at New York University, he is the author of several books on digital media and critical theory, mostly recently *The Interface Effect* (Polity, 2012). In 2008, he released *Kriegspiel*, a computer-based re-creation of Guy Debord's 1978 *The Game of War*.

Notes

1. Negri was a victim of Italy's draconian Reale law of 1975 and antiterrorist laws of 1979 and 1980, which among other things suspended habeas corpus, allowing for preventative detention of suspects for a period of three years and three months without trial.

2. I thank Richard Barbrook for bringing this letter to my attention.

3. Of course, play was at the heart of Debord's work since the beginning. "The situationist project was ludic above all else," writes one of his biographers. "Debord's life revolved around games, seduction and warfare, provocation and dissimulation, labyrinths of various kinds, and even catacombs where the knights of the lettrist round table played a game of 'whoever loses (himself) wins'" (Kaufmann 2006, 265). Debord's interest in games coincided with his self-imposed exile to a small town in the center of France after the events of 1968. "I have long tried to lead a life of obscurity and evasion so that I may better develop my experiments in

strategy," he confessed in 1978. "My research results will not be delivered in cinematic form" (Debord 1999, 50). One may assume that "not in cinematic form" is a reference to the new ludic form of the Kriegspiel; a footnote reminds us that this was Debord's last film.

There is also an interesting overlap between the Situationist International and the work of Johan Huizinga, author of *Homo Ludens: A Study of the Play Element in Culture*. Constant Niewenhuys in particular was inspired by Huizinga, as evidenced in a late interview with Benjamin Buchloh in which the former Situationist architect aims to reconcile Huizinga and Marx: "It is not so difficult, I should think, to make a link between Huizinga and Marx.... Huizinga, in his *Homo Ludens*, was speaking about a state of mind, not about a new kind of humanity; of human being, but in a certain sense a state of mind, of certain temporary conditions of human beings. For instance, when you are at a carnival, a feast, a wedding party. Temporarily you become the *homo ludens*, but then the next day you can be the *homo faber* again" (Constant 2001, 24–25). The final phrase refers to the forward of Huizinga's book in which he evokes, first, the classical notion of *homo sapiens*, followed by the modern, industrial (and one may assume, although Huizinga resists using the name, Marxian) notion of *homo faber* or "man the maker" (Huizinga 1950). Yet, Huizinga's politics were more ancien régime than progressive revolutionary, a detail often overlooked in the frequent connections made between Huizinga and Situationism.

4. In fact, Debord had tinkered with the Kriegspiel in some form or another since the 1950s. The first recorded mention of the game dates to 1956, where, in a text on the "Project for an Educational Labyrinth," Debord mentions the game by name, and describes it as a mixture of chess and poker (Debord 2006b, 285).

5. McKenzie Wark calls the game "Debord's 'retirement project'" (Wark 2008). Tom McDonough says something similar about Debord's mature work: "We might say that Debord was born into this class [the petty bourgeoisie] and, at the end of his life, returned to it." In McDonough's assessment the late Debord is "marked by the deployment and consolidation of a normative—if not archaic—conception of selfhood" (McDonough 2006, 42, 40).

6. Napoleon was responding at the time to the recent coinage of the term "ideology" by Destutt de Tracy in 1796. Napoleon spat on the concept, calling ideology a "diffuse metaphysics" responsible for "all misfortunes which have befallen our beautiful France." These quotations are cited without reference in Williams (1976, 154).

7. The generative quality of games coincided with Debord's penchant late in life for autobiographical introspection. This new intuitive, unpredictable media format became a useful figuration of the self. "With his 'war game' Debord formalized his rules for living. It was his most *autobiographical* work, the only one that would be recognized as a work, because it was inexhaustible" (Kaufmann, 267).

8. Over and above the fact that there exist bona fide mistakes in the Becker-Ho and Debord book, there also exist deviations and mistranslations in the available English editions. First, the title and format of the book changed in translation: in the original French publication, the documentation of the match appears first, followed by the rules in appendix form; the English publication reverses

the priority, with rules first and the "record of a game" second; the French title is *The Game of War*, the English *A Game of War*. Additionally, the two existing English translations of the game rules—Donald Nicholson-Smith's translation for Atlas Press and an inferior translation bundled at the end of Len Bracken's biography of Debord—both misstate details. Whereas Debord indicated that a charge consists of any number of cavalry in a contiguous, straight line and immediately adjacent to the enemy, Nicholson-Smith has no fewer than "all four" cavalry in series, while Bracken allows for noncontinuous series. Bracken also mischaracterizes the combat mechanic when he states that, after successful destruction of the enemy, "the destroyer must occupy the empty square." In fact, Debord stipulated the opposite, that it is not obligatory to occupy the empty square, nor could it be, given how movement and attack function more generally in the game. Bracken inverts another rule when he states that communication units can destroy arsenals by occupying them (they cannot) (Bracken, 240–249;

Becker-Ho and Debord 2007, 11–26). I thank Adam Parrish for first discovering some of these discrepancies. In fact, the publication of 1987 contained, by Debord's own admission, five mistakes in placement of pieces during various points in the game. Many of the mistakes were only pointed out by readers, one of which he acknowledged in a letter of March 9, 1987 (Debord 2006a, 458–459).

9. I gratefully acknowledge the contributions of Stephen Kelly and Jeff Geib, who first pointed out some of these mistakes to me and helped refine and clarify in my mind the manner in which these mistakes appear in the book. Those wishing a more detailed summary of errata should consult <http://r-s-g.org/kriegspiel/errata.php>.

10. The highly structured, crystalline forms displayed here are even more interesting when compared to the unstructured, wandering topographical forms featured in much Situationist work. See, for example, Debord's famous map from the late 1950s titled "The Naked City."

Richard Barbrook

The invasion streams eastwards and reaches its final goal—Moscow. ... But, all at once, instead of the chance happenings and the genius which hitherto had so consistently led ... [Bonaparte] to the predestined goal, an innumerable sequence of reverse chances occur—from the cold in his head at Borodino to the frosts and the spark which set Moscow on fire—and, instead of genius, folly and baseness without parallel appear. The invaders run, turn back, and run again, and all the chances are now not for ... [Bonaparte] but always against him.

—Leo Tolstoy, *War and Peace*

On March 2, Class Wargames launched the 2014 season of the Ludic Science Club with a public participatory performance at Furtherfield Commons in London's Finsbury Park of our hacked version of the 1812 "Crossing the Berezina" scenario from Richard Borg's *Commands & Colors: Napoleonics* (expansion #2 2013). A couple of years earlier, we'd successfully adapted this wonderful military simulation to celebrate the world-historical victory of the Haitian Jacobins over the French Bonapartists at the 1802 Battle of Fort Bedourete (Barbrook 2014, 232–236, 321–322). Now, for this event at this celebrated London avant-garde art gallery, we were going to use Borg's game to re-create the only time that Carl von Clausewitz and Antoine-Henri de Jomini—the two most influential theorists of Napoleonic warfare— had faced each other in combat. During the nineteenth century, their writings would come to define rival pedagogies within the military academy. For the admirers of Clausewitz's *On War*, his dialectical philosophy elucidated the political ambitions which were realized through the brutality and chaos of the battlefield. In contrast, Jomini's *The Art of War* taught that the armed struggle was primarily a set of technical skills that defined the professional officer corps.

However, in November 1812, these two soldier-scholars had yet to publish their canonical texts of military theory. Instead, they were both participants in the final drama of Bonaparte's disastrous attempt to invade Russia. On one side of the Berezina River in Belarus, Clausewitz was serving as a staff officer in the tsar's army, which was in hot pursuit of the heathen defilers of the motherland. On the opposite bank, Jomini was an aide-de-camp to one of Bonaparte's marshals along with the bedraggled remnants of the retreating French army (Bassford 1993, 5; Clausewitz 1995, 206–212; Zamoyski 2004a, 458–480). In their famous books, both of them would draw upon this dramatic confrontation to theorize the difficulties of defending river crossings against a determined enemy. On that day in 1812, much to the chagrin of Clausewitz, Jomini and the rest of Bonaparte's army were able to escape from the encircling Russian forces (Clausewitz 1993, 522–540; de Jomini 2010, 226–232). Much to our delight, in the scenario booklet for *Commands & Colors: Napoleonics* (2010), Borg laid down this challenge to the players of his game: "Can you change history?" Class Wargames was going to investigate whether Clausewitz and the Russians could prevail in the Crossing of Berezina this time around.

As we laid out the wooden blocks and terrain features on the board, I explained the special rules that we had added to the scenario which came with the Russian expansion set for Borg's game. In the original version, the two armies were compelled to advance toward each other to secure victory. However, we decided that it would be much more interesting if the goal of the French army was to escape off one side of the board, while the Russians' task was to stop them. Adding to the fun, Clausewitz and Jomini were also added as special pieces that could activate units without needing a command card.[1] Once the deployment for the Berezina scenario was completed, Richard Parry—with Vagelis Makropoulos as his aide de camp—took on the role of Mikhail Kutuzov directing the Russian army. As their opponents, James Molding—with Tim Martin as his advisor—became Napoleon Bonaparte leading the French forces. In the opening moves of the game, the Russian team adopted a twin track strategy of advancing on their left flank to cut off the enemy's escape route while their right harassed the invaders' rear guard to slow down their move across

the bridge. While fending off these attacks, the French generals focused on getting as many units on their left flank over the Berezina River as quickly as possible. Once the bridge was destroyed, those regiments that failed to make it would be lost and count toward the Russians' tally of victory banners which decided the outcome of the game.

When we first tried out our remix of the Berezina scenario a week earlier, the Bonapartists had triumphed with ease. However, on this occasion, their contradictory imperatives of holding a defensive line and moving units off the board proved to be fatal. As the Russians advanced over the hill toward the bridge, the retreating French left suffered heavy casualties in the subsequent firefight. While Jomini, one cavalry, one artillery, and two infantry regiments did eventually make it across the Berezina, three units were destroyed before it was blown up. With the Tsarists accumulating victory banners, the Bonapartists tried to counterattack with their right flank forces. Unfortunately for them, their enemy had a command card that launched a cavalry charge, one that destroyed the French cuirassier unit in one devastating blow. In their next move, this Russian mobile reserve pounced on the now-exposed Imperial Guard regiment, which was soon reduced to one block. Luckily for them, the French possessed a command card that enabled this shattered unit to exit off the board. However, this nifty maneuver only delayed the inevitable. After a brief exchange of musketry between Clausewitz's and Jomini's infantry regiments, the Tsarists concentrated their firepower against the Bonapartist artillery. Thanks to impressive dice rolls, both batteries were eliminated and the game was won. This time around, the Russians had prevented the

Figure 32.1

As Clausewitz and the Tsarists close in, Jomini and the Bonapartists make a last doomed attempt to escape across the Berezina.

invaders' army from escaping across the Berezina River. Bonaparte—the usurper of the 1789 French Revolution—died a defeated man in Belarus. As Borg had promised, history could be changed on the game board.

In early twenty-first century England, this desire to rewrite the past is often associated with Tory nostalgists who fantasize about the wrong side winning the decisive battles and political crises that shaped the modern world (Evans 2014). It would have been much better if Charles Stuart had crushed his Parliamentary opponents, the slaveowners' rebellion had triumphed in the American Civil War, and the Kuomintang had thwarted the Maoist peasant revolution (Adamson 2003; Sears 2001; Waldron 2001). As his contribution to these reactionary reveries, Adam Zamoyski has imagined that Bonaparte's victory over the Russians in 1812 would have united Europe into one federal empire and thereby prevented the disastrous wars that devastated the continent during the early twentieth century (Zamoyski 2004b). Not surprisingly, when we refought the Crossing of Berezina for our Ludic Science Club, Class Wargames had no intention of endorsing this Tory delusion that the crucial role of contingency and choice within political-military conflicts refutes the materialist conception of history, especially in its Marxist variants (Ferguson 2003; Evans 2014, 47–89). On the contrary, our group took its inspiration from the leading theorist of the Situationist International: Guy Debord.

Back in 2007, we originally set up Class Wargames to promote the playing of this New Left prophet's long-neglected *The Game of War* (1977). During the hard times of the 1970s, having helped to catalyze the May 1968 French Revolution, Debord made a tactical retreat to an Auvergne cottage where he spent long hours devising this iconic horse-and-musket simulation (Becker-Ho and Debord 2007; Debord 1991, 33–34). Yet for his hagiographers, their hero's enthusiasm for wargames is usually nothing more than a slightly dubious eccentricity that provides quirky titles for their books or exhibitions (Hussey 2001; Guy and de Bras 2013). Most of them instead concentrate on praising Situationism as the avant-garde art movement that wrote the tactical manual for punk rock, culture jamming, and relational aesthetics. Fortunately, the more enlightened also admire Debord for his searing critique of the media-saturated societies of modern capitalism. Participatory creativity was the avant-garde premonition of cybernetic communism (Bracken 1997; Hussey 2001; Jappe 1999; Kaufman 2006; Marcus 1989; Merrifield 2005; Wark 2011).

From the outset, Class Wargames' strategic objective has been to go beyond these artistic and political understandings of Situationism by celebrating Debord's fascination with military history and military theory. Coming from the homeland of the Sex Pistols and Banksy, we began our campaign of ludic subversion by gleefully reenacting the first avant-garde iteration of the International: issuing fiery Marxist communiques mocking neoliberal orthodoxies, making our film about *The Game of War* with telling clips sampled from other movies, performing in emotionally evocative locations like the Winter Palace in St. Petersburg and enabling the players of this horse-and-musket simulation to savor a brief moment of participatory creativity (Barbrook 2014, 28–108). As Pussy Riot's 2012 "Punk Prayer" provocation proved so well, these art tactics can still be stunningly effective against culturally conservative regimes, such as that of Vladimir Putin in Russia (Riff 2012). Unfortunately, as the Situationists themselves emphasized, the mass media and the art world in the West are adept at turning avant-garde weapons against their inventors (Debord 1981, 18–20; Vaneigem 1999). Outraging conventional taste, remixing appropriated material, user-generated content and social networking have long been incorporated as clever business techniques within the information economy. The Sex Pistols are now a heritage icon of English cultural innovation (Stallabrass 1999, 67–68; Bourriaud 2002, 79–104).

In response, Class Wargames is committed to proclaiming the New Left politics manifested in *The Game of War*. To the casual observer, Debord's simulation looks like a simplified version of an Avalon Hill or

SPI recreation of a Napoleonic engagement, with its infantry, cavalry and artillery pieces. Yet, for its inventor, *The Game of War* was a ludic lesson in Situationist politics. When Debord had been a rebellious youth in 1950s France, the Left was dominated by the uptight politicians of the Social Democratic and Stalinist parties. Despising these old-school operators, many radicals of his generation were attracted by the romantic image of the revolutionary warrior intellectual: Leon Trotsky, Mao Zedong, and Che Guevara (Fields 1988; Bourseiller 1996). In its early years, the Situationist International had mimicked the intensity of a Bolshevik sect with its ideological splits, membership purges, and, in Debord, a maximum leader. However, after having witnessed the collective power of the people during May 1968, Debord realized that the elitist style of politics now had to be abandoned. In a smart move, Debord dissolved the International in 1972 to prevent its admirers from coalescing themselves into a Situationist version of the vanguard party (Debord and Sanguinetti 1985). As his next turn, he then published his ludic antidote to the temptations of Bolshevism: *The Game of War*. By adopting a Napoleonic theme, Debord deftly connected the 1917 Russian remix of the modernizing revolution with its original 1789 French version (Barbrook 2014, 254–257). In both countries, the leaders of the oppressed had become the new oppressors. Through their republican dictatorship, the Jacobins had anticipated the Bolsheviks' totalitarian rule. Above all, Bonaparte was the prototype for the twentieth century's charismatic men in uniform who saved the revolution by destroying it. The Left's greatest enemies were too often drawn from among its own ranks (Barbrook 2014, 112–229).

The Situationists had the hard task of ensuring that the rebels of the May '68 generation didn't make the same mistakes as their illustrious predecessors. Artists, activists, and academics can make an important contribution to struggle for human emancipation, but they are effective only when their efforts are closely combined with those of the working class as a whole. Inventing *The Game of War* was Debord's inspired remedy for the New Left's unhealthy fascination with Trotsky, Mao, and Che. In Debord's game, the four cavalry pieces symbolize the vanguard units of the insurrectionary army. By engaging in simulated horse-and-musket warfare, its players learn that their mounted regiments—like the Situationist International during May '68—must be sacrificed when necessary to break through the opponent's defenses. On Debord's miniature battlefield, victory over the enemy requires the skillful and combined direction of its infantry, cavalry, and artillery units. From this ludic experience, Left militants would come to understand that vanguard intellectuals are expendable pieces within the class struggle. If everyone can play at being Bonaparte on the game board, then no one will become a new Trotsky, Mao, or Che in real life.

In the early twenty-first century, Debord's ludic message has not lost any of its relevance. The Soviet Union may be long gone, but the Bolsheviks' elitist politics still haunt the Left. Ironically, among the 2011–2012 Occupy movements in the United States and Europe, their firm ideological rejection of formal hierarchies empowered a small group of highly networked individuals who coordinated the street protests and online activism of the spontaneous multitudes (Gerbaudo 2012). In such circumstances, *The Game of War* becomes not only a history lesson about these revolutionary vanguards but also a training tool for democratizing the skills of political leadership so far monopolized by the few. By moving pieces across the board, its players are engaged in a practical critique of intellectual elitism within the Left. They are understanding that it is their intelligent actions, not their ideological fervor, that will transform the world. Rejecting the postmodernists' obsession with the cultural question, Debord proudly proclaimed that, "I'm not a philosopher, I'm a strategist" (Agamben 2002, 313).

Crucially, in its rules and layout, his horse-and-musket simulation was designed as a ludic abstraction of Clausewitz's *On War*. For Lenin and Mao, this classic book of dialectical theory had anticipated the militarization of the social revolution in Eurasia. The vanguard party was the general staff of the people's uprising (Kipp 1985; Mao, 266–268). Countering this Bolshevik recuperation, the players of *The Game of War* are learning the five key tactical and strategic principles of *On War*: coup d'oeil,[2] psyching the enemy, concentration of forces, outflanking the enemy, and hot pursuit. While competing to destroy each other's arsenals, the rival teams are turning Clausewitzian theory into Situationist practice (Barbrook 2014, 230–341). In this way, *The Game of War* is a ludic prophecy of cybernetic communism. When every Red partisan is learning to fight like Bonaparte, the dispersed forces of the Left will be able to unify into the collective skillful general and then prevail over the capitalist enemy on the spectacular battlefield.

Since our foundation in 2007, Class Wargames has championed this seductive vision of ludic subversion. From Belo Horizonte in Brazil to Irkutsk in Russia, we have hosted participatory performances of *The Game of War* and other political-military simulations. Through our publications, films, xenographs, and website, we have proselytized for the Left to embrace the Situationist antidote to its sterile theoretical problems and tired ideological disputes. The practical skills of collective leadership are there to be learned on the game board. When the Ludic Science Club met to play the 1812 Crossing of Berezina, our objective was to continue Debord's emancipatory mission by experimenting with a new détournement of *Commands & Colors: Napoleonics*. Like our 1802 Fort Bedourete scenario, we had devised this reenactment as an interactive history lesson in the dramatic course and consequences of this famous battle. Best of all, as well as marking the beginning of the end of Bonaparte's empire, playing the Crossing of the Berezina also contributed to our collective study of Jomini's and Clausewitz's military theories. During that afternoon at Furtherfield Commons, the Russian generals were definitely more skillful in implementing the five practical principles of *On War*, which they had learned from *The Game of War*. They had made better use of this difficult terrain divided by an impassable river, they constantly intimidated the enemy with their self-confidence, they launched deadly pincer attacks on both flanks, they focused their firepower for the decisive blow against the Bonapartists' rearguard and they kept up relentless pressure until the Tsarist victory was achieved. Although more literal in its design than Debord's simulation, we had proved that *Commands & Colors: Napoleonics* could also be successfully deployed as a teaching tool for Clausewitz's *On War*. On that spring afternoon at Furtherfield Commons, the Ludic Science Club had fulfilled its key Situationist objective. The skills of collective generalship were being practiced on the game board. In the coming struggles for a truly human civilization, cybernetic communists must know how to fight and win against neoliberal capitalism.

¡Hasta la victoria, siempre!

222

About the Author

Richard Barbrook teaches at the Department of Politics & International Relations of the University of Westminster, London, England. He is a founding member of Class Wargames and his book about their adventures, *Class Wargames: Ludic Subversion Against Spectacular Capitalism*, is published by Autonomedia: <www.classwargames.net>.

Notes

1. This new version of the Berezina scenario for *Commands & Colors: Napoleonics* can be downloaded from the Class Wargames website: <www.classwargames.net>.

2. Coup d'oeil is the ability to know instinctively how to deploy troops to maximize their effectiveness in a particular terrain of combat (see Clausewitz 1993, 127).

33 WAR GAMES

David Levinthal

In 2013, the Corcoran Gallery of Art in Washington, DC, held a forty-year survey of my photographic artwork, entitled *War Games.* The exhibition focused on images that I had created of war and conflict utilizing toy soldiers and miniatures. In addition to providing a chronological overview of my work, the exhibit also showed how both my process and my vision had been refined and defined in that period.

While my work with miniature military figures began when I was in graduate school at Yale, the genesis was much earlier. As a young child, I had been given a large set of Britains lead soldiers, which turned me into an avid young collector. Of course, back then I had no idea that taking these beautifully painted soldiers out of the box and playing with them greatly diminished their value. However, the play value and enjoyment were enormous.

Carefully dividing the linoleum floor of my bedroom into distinct countries, I would battle endlessly with my metal armies. Later, perhaps around the age of ten, I discovered the Avalon Hill military board game *Tactics II* (1958)—I have never been clear on whether there was a *Tactics I*. I spent the next several years avidly honing my skills on games such as *D-Day* (1961), *Afrika Korps* (1954), and especially *Stalingrad* (1963). With *Stalingrad* I became a master of directing a successful German offense and equally adept at mounting a winning Russian defense. These were my finest hours.

Years later, in 1972, I started to photograph small 1/72 scale plastic military figures, juxtaposing them with simple wooden blocks to re-create a vision of the world of childhood play. The soldiers were unpainted and taken straight from the box, and the backgrounds and environments were intentionally simple. I soon began to introduce additional elements, such as blue paper to create a river and HO scale telephone poles and buildings, all found at a local hobby store, to add a small sense of quasi-realism.

As I photographed these very small figures, I saw that when they began to fade slowly out of focus the images started to take on a more and more realistic feeling, one in which there almost appeared to be a sense of momentousness infused into these inanimate figures.

Shortly after graduating in 1973, Garry Trudeau and I embarked on what was to become a three-year project that eventually became the book *Hitler Moves East*, published in 1977. The book was a re-creation of the Eastern Front in World War II. At the time of our

Figure 33.1
Untitled, from the series *Hitler Moves East* (1973); 8 × 10 inches; Kodalith.

work, there was little visual consciousness in the West of this aspect of the war. In fact, in 1978 the BBC released a twenty-part documentary series entitled *The Unknown War*, illuminating the massive conflict that took place in Russia and Eastern Europe.

As I continued to work on the book, my photographs of toy soldiers became more and more realistic as I attempted to simulate the documentary images that I was looking at in my research. The toy soldiers themselves became more sophisticated as well. Instead of the small static plastic figures that I had started with in graduate school, I found highly detailed figure models in a larger scale that I could assemble and paint in a great variety of poses, providing me with an almost unlimited range of possibilities. Most of these model figures were of German soldiers, since there were virtually no models available of Soviet troops or equipment.

The 2013 exhibition at the Corcoran gave me the opportunity to reflect back on this early work, and the transformation that took place as the photographic work for *Hitler Moves East* progressed.

Looking at the cover image of the book, a photograph of a German motorcycle and sidecar advancing directly at the viewer through a staged wheat field, one can see how dramatically the work had changed over time. This image, which became one of the signature pieces from the series, draws its power both from the larger scale of the figures, which allowed me to focus more closely on them, and the seeming reality of the set.

I had grown a small 3 × 3 foot patch of grass with a small rising terrain to simulate the vast Russian steppes. The paleness of the grass grown indoors when photographed created a virtual flowing field. Placing the motorcycle in the midst of this scene, and then photographing through it with a narrow depth of field created the perfect blend of detail and implied motion. The ambiguous spray-painted background created a sense of space and distance combined with a feeling of a battle-filled sky.

While the toy motorcycle itself was not an especially accurate model, there was one specific detail that helped to transform the photograph: The goggles of the driver and the blurred headlights of the motorcycle combined with the hunched-over position of the soldier seemed to create an overwhelming sense of reality.

Perhaps the single most iconic image from *Hitler Moves East* is that of a group of soldiers on the crest of a hill, in which one of the soldiers appears to be flying through the air from the force of an explosion. Once again I utilized my faux Russian steppes as a ground. Assisted skillfully by Garry Trudeau, I placed four figures in the scene. Sticking a thin pin into one of the soldiers, Garry placed our "flying soldier" at the top of the hill, with the pin blending perfectly into the grass. Just behind the hill we sprinkled what turned out to be a more than sufficient quantity of theatrical explosion powder. Triggered by a burning cotton ball, a significant and very loud explosion ensued, leaving me with a very opaque but transcendently beautiful negative. I have always been very grateful for Garry's expertise with explosives, which he must have acquired at an early age.

Early in my career, I was often asked why I was choosing to simulate photographs that already existed. Part of our goal in creating *Hitler Moves East* was to play with the idea of fantasy and reality, and to try and blur the line between them. We might juxtapose a photograph of a detailed diorama next to an image of a plastic soldier with a visible seam running down the front of his body, providing a visual clue to the origin of the photographs. Thus, it was a great

Figure 33.2
Untitled, from the series *Hitler Moves East* (1975); 8 × 10 inches; Kodalith.

Figure 33.3
Untitled, from the series *Hitler Moves East* (1975); 8 × 10 inches; Kodalith.

surprise that when the book first appeared I would find it placed in the history section of bookstores. On more than one occasion I was also asked how I was able to obtain these "documentary photographs" that I must have obviously manipulated.

Over thirty years later, in 2009, I returned to the subject of war with the book *I.E.D. War in Afghanistan and Iraq*. This, along with *Hitler Moves East*, served as "bookends" for the *War Games* exhibition.

One of the things most fascinating to me was that the toys and models from the war in Iraq were being produced in real time. Unlike approaching a war from a historical perspective, as I had done with *Hitler Moves East*, I was now creating images based on events that were currently happening, using photographs and videos virtually streaming in real time. The toys and models that I found available followed the same time frame. For example, as the military moved from the Humvee to the Stryker, so too did the toy companies immediately follow suit. Models and figurines of everything from civilian contractors to Iraq and Afghan civilians, Muslim clerics and insurgents, both dead and alive (one box of plastic figures of Sunni insurgents was labeled "The Bad Ones"), became quickly available for use in dioramas.

It was quite an eerie feeling to be creating these scenes of a war that I could see every day on the television screen. That visual accessibility had a significant effect on my work. Seeing the many images of combat taking place at night with the greenish hue of night vision goggles caused me to try and recreate a similar feel in my work. After many trials, it turned out that the simplest approach worked the best: one dollar's worth of green cellophane over a $4,000 lens.

From my perspective, the difference between *Hitler Moves East* and *I.E.D.* is that the early work on *Hitler Moves East*, done mostly during the period of 1974–75, represented an early exploration fueled by youthful enthusiasm and excitement. Successfully creating the Russian steppes with grass filler seeds and potting soil was a cause for celebration. Snowdrifts of Gold Medal flour were blown across the scene with the aid of a can of compressed air. Theatrical explosive powder seemingly lifted a toy soldier into midair. I used the flames from a burning plastic building as the sole light source for a photograph. When I look back on these photographs, I see a raw power in them. To me they will always remain my most significant work, because they led to everything that followed.

By the time that I began my work on *I.E.D.*, I had been working for over thirty years creating dioramas to photograph. With *I.E.D.* there were new problems to solve, such as simulating tracer rounds (multiple Mini MagLites waved around by my five-year-old son). But the goal was much the same: to place the viewer visually and emotionally into the scene. To do this, I often brought the viewer close into the image, utilizing a macro lens, which allowed me to both magnify and soften the images using a very narrow depth of field. This technique allowed me to create a greater sense of space and ground than what actually existed.

One of my early photographs from my ongoing Vietnam series, taken in 2010, shows a helicopter photographed against an *Apocalypse Now*–like background. Utilizing a silk fabric with metallic highlights I created the sense of tracer fire and burning by simply backlighting the material and casting the helicopter mostly in shadow in front

Figure 33.4
Untitled, from the series *Vietnam* (2010); 61 × 79 inches; pigment print on paper.

of the material. Once again, the viewer is brought into the scene by showing only part of the helicopter.

The final two pieces in the exhibition were made in 2012, and represented a significant change in my approach. I began to attempt to do two things simultaneously: Broaden the scope and plane of photographs, and at the same time draw upon iconic historical imagery directly. These two photographs, *Fall of Berlin* and *Custer's Last Stand*, have become the first in what is now an ongoing series with the working title *History*.

In both of these photographs, and particularly *Custer's Last Stand*, I used many more figures than I would normally have used in the past. Previously I would often take advantage of the suggestion,

Figure 33.5
Fall of Berlin (2012); 61 × 79 inches; pigment print on paper.

created in my photographs by the use of the soft focus, that there was more occurring in the image than what was actually there. In the Custer photograph, I found for the first time that I was able to create multiple instances within the complete scene of groups of figures going in and out of focus, and that combining these various "mini-scenes" within the larger complete image created a greater and more powerful whole. I have continued to try to develop and refine this technique as I move forward with this new body of work.

Figure 33.6
Custer's Last Stand (2012); 61 × 79 inches; pigment print on paper.

About the Author

Writing in the *New York Times* about the photographer David Levinthal, Charles Hagen said, "What distinguishes Mr. Levinthal's work is his interest in emotionally charged historical material. But the real force of his images comes not from his choice of subjects but from the way he tells their stories." Levinthal is the coauthor, with Garry Trudeau, of *Hitler Moves East*, originally published in 1977. *Dark Light*, a ten-year survey exhibition of his work, was organized in 1994 by The Photographers' Gallery

Figure 33.7
The Charge of the Scots Greys (2013); 61 × 79 inches; pigment print on paper.

in London, and traveled throughout the United Kingdom. In 1997 the International Center of Photography in New York presented the first retrospective "David Levinthal work from 1977 to 1996." He has received a National Endowment for the Arts Fellowship and a Guggenheim Fellowship. His work is included in numerous museum collections including the Whitney Museum of American Art, the Museum of Modern Art, the Metropolitan Museum of Art, the Gene Autry Western Heritage Museum, and the Menil Collection.

Brian Conley

Thousands of Americans, usually men, belong to gaming communities that play out historical battles with miniature soldiers on handmade dioramas, a hobby that began in the mid-1950s, at the time of the Cold War. Gamers may stage the battles of Hittites and Babylonians, the Napoleonic Wars, or World War II, beginning from historically accurate circumstances and representing both sides in the given conflict. Their games are not reenactments, however, because events proceed not only according to the demands of military strategy but via rolls of the dice. Play thus yields ahistorical, counterfactual outcomes.

This activity could be seen as an exploration of alternative realities, possible worlds. Yet historical wargamers take great pains to establish realistic conditions for their play. By assigning values to particular dice throws, the gaming rulebook accounts for variables in ballistics, terrain, weather conditions, fatigue, injury, and so on, a blending of computation and happenstance that speaks to the intensely technical yet profoundly random conditions of battle. Deeply psychological phenomena also take hold in the midst of game play, just as they would in actually life-threatening circumstances. Indeed, gamers report that they enter a "magic cir-cle" in which the diorama comes alive with all the stress, elation, calculation, exhaustion, and uncertainty of combat. Needless to say, however, when the game is over, no injuries have been sustained, and no world-historical balance of power has been shifted.

At the moment of this writing, in September 2014, the US military has pulled out of Iraq except for personnel staffing and guarding the embassy in Baghdad. President Nouri al-Malaki has spent years alienating its Sunni majority. The Sunni insurgent group ISIS is hoping to establish a new caliphate, and to that end it has captured the city of Mosul, taken towns along the Tigris and Euphrates rivers, and surrounded Baghdad. All this presents yet another kind of "possible world"—a reality not envisioned in the 1997 *Statement of Principles* generated by the Project for a New American Century (PNAC), which, well in advance of the 9/11 attacks, argued for the strategic importance of invading Iraq. Several authors of this document, including Donald Rumsfeld and Paul Wolfowitz, later found themselves in positions from which they could help to implement—in real time, with real combatants, in real places—the hypotheses that had been generated years before under think-tank conditions.

Figure 34.1
Miniature War in Iraq (2010), installation.

Figure 34.2
Miniature War in Iraq (Dice Throw) (2007), video still.

The use of models, maquettes, and game boards in formulating military maneuvers and training soldiers goes back to early forms of chess and perhaps to ancient times; tabletop wargamers' play and elite geostrategic planning exhibit significant structural similarities derived from their shared historical sources. Inevitably, such modeling circumscribes and distances the messy, contingent facts of full-scale political and/or armed struggle. The map is not the territory, and, after all, any form of representation foregrounds some aspects of reality while bracketing others. Still, relations between processes of strategic modeling, gaming, and propaganda should not be overlooked. As consumers of news in globalized culture, and as citizens taking part in the American electoral system, we depend on media sources that are increasingly corporatized, expensive to sustain, and restricted in their support for in-depth investigative reporting—in other words, our information sources are, like wargames, distanced, filtered, and allied to entertainment formats. Yet our political choices can only be as grounded as our news is "factual" and "real."

Military planning, politics, and media are not alone, moreover, in their reliance on gaming structures. Other disciplines have their own discourses of the counterfactual. In psychology, counterfactual thinking can lead, on one hand, to obsession over missed opportunities; on the other, it serves an important function in teaching patients to self-correct maladaptive behavior. In epidemiology and other health sciences concerned with disease control, researchers seek to predict the spread of illnesses under diverse potential conditions. Analytic philosophy discusses the truth-value of counterfactual statements and the use of modal logics in relation to possible worlds. As an artist with a background in all three of these areas of study (I earned a bachelor's degree in psychology and studied the philosophy of science before getting a PhD in analytic philosophy), speculation about diverse epistemological structures and the ways in which knowledge is established and given transitive form

Figure 34.3
Miniature War in Iraq (Confrontation) (2007), video still.

have remained among my primary interests. Art is distinct from social science and philosophy in that it privileges "uselessness" and sensuality for their own sake, and I was drawn to make art in part because I value its ability to realize possible worlds in physical, deliberately crafted objects, to make irrational postulates visible and sensually appealing. Art embraces its own falsity and nonconsequentiality, foregrounding nonrational thought and demarcating free-play zones.

It is with such ideas in mind that I developed a project titled *Miniature War in Iraq* (2007), along with a second iteration titled *Miniature War in Iraq ... and Now Afghanistan* (2010). Part game and part thought experiment, encompassing performance, sculpture, video, and photography, *Miniature War* investigates what might be called interlocking "magic circles," discursive spaces in which, at times, we lose our bearings in the seductive intensity of our involvement. Artistic practice neither denies nor apologizes for the status of its objects as unreal. Yet despite its fascination with vicarious experience, *Miniature War* was not entirely unreal either. An uncomfortable connection to real violence was self-consciously built in to the project through the melding of current events in Iraq with gameplay in the United States, and the incorporation in the installation of streaming online footage from the conflict, as well as via the participation of Middle Eastern researchers who, during the performance, were communicating live with individuals in Iraq.

Miniature War in Iraq took shape in the following way: at Games Expo in Las Vegas in March 2007, I collaborated with a group from the Kansas City–based Heart of America Historical Miniature Gaming Society to play/fight recent battles from the war. An onsite Arabic-speaking research team that had

traveled with me to Las Vegas investigated competing versions of events then unfolding on the ground, culling information from the *New York Times* and Al Jazeera, militant Islamic websites, US military sources, American soldiers' selfies and combat videos, and real-time exchanges with Iraqi bloggers. The researchers selected an event to be played, and handed off that scenario to the gamers. Guided by resources such as Google Maps, and using their standard kit of materials—which includes model buildings and trees, toy cars and trucks, sand, and other props, as well as mass-produced cast-metal soldier-and-civilian figurines, many of which are designed for use in scenarios from the Crusades—the gamers proceeded to build a tabletop diorama representing the setting of the selected events. For the first day of play, the scene was a village and date-palm grove in the Zarga region near Najaf. On the second day, the diorama was reconfigured to become a Baghdad neighborhood.

The 2010 performance, *Miniature War in Iraq ... and Now Afghanistan*, occurred in New York City. The engagement in Afghanistan has been the longest war in US history. President George W. Bush launched Operation Enduring Freedom against the Taliban in the first week of October 2001. Two years later, for reasons consonant with the PNAC plan, American forces were diverted from their focus on the Taliban and Al Qaeda by the occupation of Iraq. I was prompted to produce my project's second iteration when, nearly a decade into the quagmire, the newly elected Barack Obama sent thirty thousand additional troops to Afghanistan. The surge resulted in the war's deadliest single year—and, in the present, the country remains unstable.

Miniature War as it opened in New York was an installation comprising the game table as it had been

Figure 34.4
Miniature War in Afghanistan (Crossing) (2010), performance.

left at the close of the final Las Vegas game, along with a video documenting the 2007 game in play, plus an array of Web-based and hardcopy materials gathered by the Arabic-speaking research team, whose computers—monitors still screening the online footage culled in 2007—sat at the edge of the tabletop diorama. On the walls hung photographic portraits of several of the mini soldier figures, heroically enlarged to a scale at which imperfections in casting and painting loomed grotesquely. One month later, toward the end of the New York exhibition's run, the diorama was reorganized, and a game master from

the Heart of America society joined with visitors to the gallery and local artists to play a new, Afghanistan-based game. Working live alongside the players, Pashto- and Dari-speaking researchers selected and documented a scenario from then-recent events in Kandahar.

For this performance, the table itself was also reconstructed. While American and Iraqi combatants in the 2007 game were relatively equal in their ballistic and logistical capacities, each side in the 2010 game had distinct powers and deficits. Because the diorama was so large, any given player could only reach a third of the way toward its center. But the table had been cut into four puzzle-like parts and placed on wheels, so that each section could be positioned independently. Only Taliban players were allowed to pull the table open to move soldiers and materiel in the interior. The Americans, however, could overfly the entire scene: A performer (as it happened, a young woman) was suspended in a harness above the table, holding a model drone in one hand and with the other controlling an electronic joystick that allowed her to cruise back and forth above the diorama.

Figure 34.5

Miniature War in Afghanistan (Toy Soldier) (2010), color photograph mounted on aluminum.

Historical gamers approach and retreat, at one and the same time, from the violent situations that absorb them; they enjoy the visceral drama of battle but their games are by definition limited, pretend. In order to do their jobs, meanwhile, military planners must believe that by playing out their hypotheses via projections and metrics they will be able to predict the consequences of various battle plans. They are confident that their modeling and framing will deliver actualities on the ground. When online communities coalesce around a particular multiplayer game—or when friends devote hours to a first-person-shooter game—a mood takes hold that blends intimate enmeshment and consequence-free distance, engagement and detachment, in not unrelated ways. Such psychological effects can also be experienced by a viewer who is not playing the game, yet participates vicariously—as do noncombatant partisans in any conflict, as well as spectators watching other kinds of games. Not least among these uneasy meldings of approach and retreat is drone warfare, in which a specialist in Nevada, say, may be engaged in remote-bombing a target in Tora Bora—a (partial) dephysicalization of deadly force that, in many ways, functions in synergy with the apparatus of highly aestheticized computer games designed for entertainment.

Nevertheless, there is also a difference between virtual and analog wargaming. In three-dimensional analog games, the manipulation of objects in real time is paramount—as against the virtual feats that a videogame avatar, or a drone operator, can accomplish. Players roll the dice and move the playing pieces by hand; they reach across the table, crane their necks for sightlines, crouch to measure distances, and so forth, yet all the while they tower gigantically above the fray. This tension is

Figure 34.6

Miniature War in Afghanistan (Drone) (2010); performance.

emphasized in the *Miniature War* video of the 2007 game in play, where all we see are the godlike hands of players reaching in from out of frame to gather up or knock over figures, upend vehicles, or dismantle buildings. The magic circle of absorptive involvement is made tangible in *Miniature War*, even as it is exaggerated to an extreme, almost caricatural level.

If this video draws attention to the fantasies of deus-ex-machina mastery inherent in both miniaturization and military planning, other parts of the installation seek to dramatize other aspects of the information system that surrounds us. The online research teams used sources of all kinds, from the US State Department or the *Washington Post* to insurgents' video posts. Is such official or eyewitness documentation more real than the three-dimensional, vividly detailed diorama or the monumental photographs—which suggest a cross between billboard advertisements and posters eulogizing fighters as martyrs? Are screengrabs from the Internet or data retrieved from wire service reports more real than the physically immediate actions of the players, or the excited responses of the gallery audience? Perhaps. But in what ways, exactly? And where, in all this speculation, is the reality of individual people shot at, bombed, burned, maimed, suffering from PTSD or haunted by memory? These are questions that *Miniature War* hopes to provoke.

Propaganda is a magic-circle machine, but its goal is to entice audiences to suspend disbelief, to accept the exaggerated or counterfactual as real. Art, in contrast, constantly reminds the viewer that representation, information-relay, even "truth" are inextricably bound up with projection, theatricality, and all the shifting formulas of "as if." Art insists on its identity as a game. At the same time, because *Miniature War* intersects with events that have had literally bloody consequences, the project also seeks to expose our understanding of faraway war as inescapably partial and therefore degraded.

But the magic circle is not only a space where misinformation and projection can hold sway. It is also a zone of imaginative empathy. In a game about World War II, one group of participants might have to play as Nazis; in a scenario derived from Vietnam, some players would have to fight as Viet Cong. When players take on these "enemy" roles, they plunge in with full conviction, urgently feeling what it is like to be something, or someone, that they themselves probably abhor. In the same way, in *Miniature War*, some gamers were required to play as Iraqi insurgents, Taliban fighters, or al-Qaeda operatives and to strive wholeheartedly to win the day—which they did. I would argue that this relinquishing of identity on the part of the player, which the viewer witnesses and in which he or she vicariously takes part, holds an important potential for opening up an imaginative frame of reference beyond the game itself. In this sense, there is no righteous position from which to play the game. Art freely admits its power as a magic-circle generator, and this means, I believe, that art can reflect in unique ways on even such dire and tragic human events as war. Using a set of conceptual tools not available to journalists or academics, art can cast the spell of the counterfactual while still insisting on the immediate.

About the Author

Brian Conley's practice as an artist encompasses multiple media, from radio performance to sculptural, research-based, and collaborative installations and is concerned with the roots of social violence, the origins of language, and the possibility of meaningful communication even across radical divides—for example, between human and animal. He cofounded *Cabinet* magazine and participated in the startup of a remote-teaching art program and communication hub for Iraqi artists in the diaspora as well as those in Baghdad. He has exhibited internationally, including at the Whitney Museum of American Art, ArtBasel, and MassMoCA, as well as producing commissioned works at the Wanas Foundation in Knislinge, Sweden, and the ArtPace Foundation for Contemporary Art in San Antonio, Texas. Conley holds a PhD in philosophy and an MFA in studio art from the University of Minnesota. He is a professor and acting chair of the Sculpture Program at the California College of the Arts in San Francisco.

VI   THE WAR ROOM

35   WARGAMES AS AN ACADEMIC INSTRUMENT

Philip Sabin

I have been an academic in the Department of War Studies at King's College London for thirty years, and an increasing focus of mine during that long period has been designing and using wargames as an instrument of education and research. Simulation and gaming are very much growth areas in higher education as a whole, and there is an increasing literature about their utility to engage students in an interactive learning process (Crookall and Thorngate 2009; Kebritchi and Hirumi 2008; Lean et al. 2006; Moizer et al. 2009). There have even been entire recent special issues of the journal *Simulation & Gaming* devoted to the use of such techniques in the specific academic field of international studies (Boyer 2011; Brynen and Milante 2013). Rex Brynen and other scholarly contributors to this volume give a good sense of the popularity of such exercises, even when they reach such heights of ambition as Rex's own very intensive weeklong peacebuilding simulation involving over one hundred students (Brynen 2010). Where my own experience differs is that I focus not on the widely used and easily understood techniques of "pol-mil" gaming, with its emphasis on negotiations, role-playing, and seminar discussions, but instead on much more structured models of actual armed conflict, more akin to the various recreational wargames discussed in many chapters of this book.

Academics are certainly no strangers to formal models that try to capture the dynamics of real conflicts within numbers and formulas. Operational analysis and mathematical modeling are flourishing academic fields, and "game theorists" have long tried to analyze human decisions with reference to simpler analogical situations such as the "prisoner's dilemma" (Biddle 2004; Haldon et al. 2010; Shubik 2002; Morse and Kimball 1959; Schelling 1960). However, wargames of the kind discussed in this chapter fall uncomfortably in between these rigorous and rather arcane mathematical models and the much freer and less structured role-playing in international studies classes. Apart from the many sociological studies of the impact of violent video games (e.g., Anderson, Gentile, and Buckley 2007), and the occasional rather plaintive article urging the use of hobby wargames in history teaching (Glick and Charters 1983; Corbeil 2011), one would scarcely know from the scholarly literature that wargaming of this kind even existed.

As the Venn diagram in figure 35.1 makes clear, wargames are designed and played much less by academics than by two other groups, without which they would not exist at all. The first group consists of the many private enthusiasts who for over half a century have seen wargames as an intriguing supplement to books and films as a safe vicarious means of exploring the dynamics of armed conflict. The specific wargames discussed in this book are only a tiny fraction of more than ten thousand different hobby game designs, played with computers, cardboard counters, or model figures, and covering between them almost every recorded conflict in military history (Sabin 2002; Halter 2006; Dunnigan 1992b; Martin 2001; Lewin 2012; Hyde 2013). The other key group that has underpinned the development of modern wargaming techniques consists of military officers and defense analysts. Ever since the Prussian army embraced von Reisswitz's *kriegsspiel* system two centuries ago, various forms of wargames have played a significant role in military training and war planning (Allen 1987; Perla 1990; von Hilgers 2012). Defense wargaming and simulation have become increasingly computer-based in recent decades (Wilson 1969; Hausrath 1971; Smith 2009), but manual techniques also persist, and the defense community forms the main target audience for the major international conferences of more than one hundred wargame professionals that I have co-organized at King's College London since 2013. (The proceedings of these Connections UK conferences are available at <http://www.professionalwargaming.co.uk>.)

In this chapter, I will draw on my own experience to explore the potential and problems of using

Figure 35.1

Techniques used by different groups to study armed conflict.

wargames in the more unfamiliar context of academia. First, I will discuss what wargames can contribute to supplement more traditional means of scholarly study. Then I will assess the relative merits of manual and computer wargames, and explain why I make more use of the former. Next, I will talk about my long experience of getting my postgraduates to design wargames for themselves on conflicts of their choice. I will proceed to consider the practical obstacles and trade-offs that impede wider academic employment of wargaming techniques. Finally, I will discuss why wargames evoke such stigma in scholarly circles, and suggest how this stigma might best be overcome.

The Contribution of Wargames

War and games might appear to be utterly dissimilar activities, but in fact they share certain characteristics that go back as far as the days of medieval tournaments and the gladiatorial contests of ancient Rome (Cornell and Allen 2002; van Creveld 2013; Huizinga 1970, chapter 5). My favorite articulation of this relationship is Carl von Clausewitz's claim (before the rise of *kriegsspiel*) that "in the whole range of human activities, war most closely resembles a game of cards" (Clausewitz 1976, 86). Adversarial games artificially generate the kind of stark conflictual relationship that is so characteristic of war, but that is relatively rare in other kinds of human interactions. As a result, games can mirror some of the distinctive dynamics of war, in particular the action-reaction contest that develops as each side tries to get the better of an active and thinking opponent. Edward Luttwak has written vividly of the "paradoxical logic" that characterizes war and games, with antagonists often deliberately choosing "inefficient" approaches such as attacking through the poor terrain of the Ardennes forest in 1940 and 1944, in order to surprise their opponents and catch them unprepared (Luttwak 1987).

So what can wargames add to the millions of books and research studies about war, which already do a pretty comprehensive job of capturing these interactive conflict dynamics through the safe vicarious media of words and maps? The key difference is that books about past wars only report on what happened on the single occasion when the conflict happened for real. Wargames, by contrast, bring certain very limited and selective aspects of the conflict "back to life" and allow it to be refought as an endlessly replayable game of "glorified chess" (Dunnigan 1992b, 13). Wargames about potential future conflicts offer the much greater attraction of allowing defense planners to experiment safely with strategies and options *before* doing anything for real, but here the absence of even the single historical precedent available when modeling past

conflicts makes it commensurately harder to know if the wargame accurately reflects what might happen in the real world (Sabin 2012, 130–132 and chapter 4).

One key contribution of wargame modeling in either case is that it forces users and designers to engage systematically with questions that are all too easy to neglect when simply reading or writing about the conflict situation concerned. Wargames by their very nature are less concerned with stories and anecdotes and more focused on the deeper underlying dynamics of the situation. What was or is the strategic and political geography of the entire theater (not just the part where fighting happened to occur historically)? What alternative options were or are available for force deployments? What were or are the antagonists actually trying to achieve militarily and politically? What was or is the relative importance of influences such as numbers, quality, morale, leadership, culture, intelligence, logistics, terrain, weather, and time? How plausible are alternative outcomes to the contest, and what might trigger such divergence? Wargame modeling is an incredibly ambitious enterprise in that it seeks to create in miniature a laboratory within which human conflict in all its complexity may be represented and experimented upon, but if it succeeds even slightly in this endeavor, it may raise questions that would have been overlooked had analysts restricted themselves simply to writing about known facts.

A second key contribution of wargames stems from the decision element. Mathematical modeling of force capabilities is supplemented in wargaming by the equally important element of interactive player decisions to determine what strategies are actually pursued. The players themselves benefit from a unique form of *active learning*, since instead of merely reading or hearing about the choices available, they must weigh up the options and decide for themselves, and then make follow-up choices once they see the response of their active opponents. This is a very powerful way of giving players an intuitive understanding of the force-space-time dynamics in the actual conflict, as well as of key military dilemmas such as how to balance attack and defense across key sectors and whether to reinforce success or salvage failure. From a research perspective, seeing the decisions that players make across repeated plays of the game, and their consequences in terms of game outcomes, offers useful experimental information that supplements any single real historical precedent and allows better informed discussion of variability and contingency.

This leads on to a third key contribution of wargame modeling, namely that it provides much stronger feedback as to the limitations of the designers' and players' understanding of the situation. Traditional scholarly media such as books and lectures focus on the one-way transmission of information and ideas to a more or less receptive audience. Wargames, by contrast, are complex interactive devices that usually fail badly when first tested, and that need to be refined through a process of iterative correction that provides very useful feedback as to the deficiencies in the initial design assumptions (Berg et al. 1977, 44 and 52; McCarty 2004, 256). Anyone can draw blocks and arrows on an unresponsive map, but it takes days and weeks of very instructive testing and iterative refinement to get the player-guided actions of units in a wargame to resemble even vaguely those of their real-life counterparts. Not only that, but it is far more evident from their active choices and discussions whether the players themselves really understand the dynamics of the modeled situation than it is from sage nodding in a traditional lecture hall, and so it is easier to identify where further discussion is required.

I build on these particular contributions of wargames by using them as a judicious supplement to more conventional educational methods of lectures, seminars, debates, private study, and essay writing across the range of my undergraduate teaching in military history. Students use over a dozen different wargames to study the intertwined military and political characteristics of the Second Punic War, the operational and strategic dynamics of World War II, and the shifting tactical and operational features of air warfare over the past century (Sabin 2012). My most ambitious use of wargame modeling as a scholarly technique was in my 2007 book *Lost Battles*, which seeks to cast new light on the vexed controversies over how to reconstruct individual Greek and Roman land battles by developing a common wargame system with which three dozen such contests may be refought, thereby allowing proposed individual reconstructions to be tested against generic overall patterns and against sensible player choices through a process of "comparative dynamic modeling" (Sabin 2007). I will return shortly to my other equally ambitious use of wargames as an educational device, but first I will discuss which medium for wargaming offers the greatest academic benefits.

Manual vs. Computer Wargames

The microchip revolution has transformed wargaming as it has so many other areas of modern life over the past few decades, and many people understandably think that any form of "simulation" now inevitably involves computer systems. Recreational video games, including military first-person shooters like the *Call of Duty* series, now have a bigger turnover than Hollywood films, and are played by significant proportions of the population (Halter 2006). As I mentioned, professional military wargaming has been dominated by computers for decades (Smith 2009; Mead 2013). However, as the present book makes abundantly clear, manual wargaming is far from dead—in fact, more different manual wargames are being published today (albeit in diminished volumes) than ever before (Chupin 2011). I will now assess which type of wargame offers the greater payoff for academic purposes (an issue I discuss at greater length in Sabin 2011).

Computers come into their own for their ability to conduct rapid calculations and apply programmed rules automatically. This allows them to run complex and detailed models at speeds entirely unattainable by other means. Academics have sometimes used this for "agent-based modeling" of the actions of thousands of individual entities using artificial intelligence routines, as in John Haldon's research project on Byzantine logistics (Haldon et al. 2010). I use similar capabilities within commercial computer wargames by having top-down map-based representations of air raids in the Battle of Britain and Vietnam play out automatically in real time on the projector screen while I discuss with my students the tactical interactions and intelligence issues involved.

The other area where computers shine is in portraying complex virtual 3D worlds from a real-time first-person perspective. Here again, it is in my air warfare teaching where this is most relevant, and I use various commercial combat flight simulator games to allow single students to take control of a fighter plane in dogfights of different eras while the rest watch. The beauty of this vivid way of bringing air combat tactics to life is that it takes only tens of minutes even for multiple iterations of the simulation, allowing the majority of the class to proceed along more conventional lines so as to consolidate the insights gained. I need to choose the games carefully and avoid the many distorted "arcade" portrayals of the subject, and even with more credible simulations, it is important to make clear to students such unavoidable artificialities as the absence of g-forces and of the life-and-death stakes that make real pilots more cautious than our virtual pilots invariably are!

Although I am entirely familiar with other commercial computer wargames that cover other aspects of my military history modules, I do not use them in class, for a variety of reasons. There are not actually that many credible computer wargames that still run on modern operating systems and avoid the arcade distortions so prevalent in the mass entertainment market. Those that do exist tend to be obsessively detailed and time-consuming representations with hundreds of units (see <http://wargamer.com>), very far from the "pick up and play" character of the first-person simulators. The costly suites of networked computers used in military wargaming are less readily available in an academic context, so it is far from easy to give multiple students simultaneous direct involvement in the game. Not only that, but the computer displays which have such advantages in portraying fast-moving real-time 3D images are less comparatively attractive for showing units on a strategic map. Large physical maps and counters have more tactile appeal, are better suited to the human eye's combination of central acuity and breadth of vision, and allow competing players to engage with one another face to face instead of by staring at a screen.

Published manual wargames have their own severe limitations as vehicles for academic study. Although they are less infrastructure-dependent, far more numerous, and less prone to arcade distortions than mass-market computer games, they are still primarily entertainment products rather than scholarly endeavors, and many of them are poorly researched and documented and offer only questionable and superficial reflections of the conflicts they purport to simulate (Sabin 2013). A much bigger problem is that the many published manual wargames that do offer a credible and worthwhile simulation of real conflict dynamics are at least as complex, detailed, and time-consuming as are serious computer wargames. With hundreds of counters to set up, and with rulebooks dozens of pages long to be mastered and applied manually, it is readily apparent that most commercial board wargames are even less suitable for class employment than are their computerized counterparts (as is evident from the thousands of reviews and images at <http://www.consimworld.com>, <http://grognard.com>, and <http://boardgamegeek.com>).

What swings the balance decisively in favor of manual games, in my own view, is *design accessibility*. Very few strategic studies scholars or students have the programming expertise to do much more than play computer games as they come, warts and all. Manual games, in contrast, expose their rules systems as a necessary component of learning to play them, and if one disagrees with their assumptions, it is fairly simple to tweak the rules or scenarios to accord better with one's own judgment. I already emphasized in the previous section that visible and flexible systemic modeling of conflict dynamics is a key part of the distinctive contribution that wargames can make to our understanding of war. This contribution is significantly weakened if the game system is concealed within an unmodifiable "black box" of computer code.

Although worthwhile published manual wargames are almost all too complex and detailed to play in class, this is not a necessary characteristic of manual wargames per se. Some published board wargames take the form of small "microgames" (Nordling 2009), though they are of very variable quality and utility. Based on the examples and ideas in the many hundreds of manual wargames of all sizes that I own, I have designed my own smaller and simpler microgames with only a few dozen counters and a few pages of rules, which are precisely tailored to highlight the conflict dynamics which I want my students to grasp. It is these personal designs that underpin the great majority of my academic wargaming. Almost all of my designs are available online for free download (Google "Sabin consim") or are in my two latest books: *Lost Battles*, which I have mentioned already (Sabin 2007), and my recent *Simulating War*, which contains the rules and components for eight other complete wargames (Sabin 2012). I will discuss shortly the practical problems with using even such simple tailored wargames in an academic context, but first I will outline the most significant educational innovation that the invaluable design accessibility of manual wargames has allowed me to develop over the past decade and more.

Teaching Wargame Design

Among the most important insights of wargaming guru James Dunnigan about manual wargames is that "if you can play them, you can design them" (Dunnigan 1992b, 252–253). Having seen the truth of this aphorism myself through my own wargame designs, I decided to make it the centerpiece of a new elective module for our MA students, in which they design their own simple wargames on conflicts of their choice, from ancient times to the most recent wars. The aim is to help the students to develop a deeper understanding of their conflict's dynamics than they would gain simply by writing a conventional essay, while also teaching them about conflict simulation as a methodology in its own right. A further key benefit is that successful wargame design requires a very rich mixture of intellectual skills, ranging from focused research and analytical creativity to legalistic clarity and graphic design, as well as the teamwork needed to help test and refine one another's developing projects. It is precisely these skills that are in prime demand for a wide range of modern careers.

The module has been running since 2003, and over a hundred students have now completed it and produced individual simulation projects. Around half of these projects have been posted online for free download for the benefit of future students and others (again, Google "Sabin consim"), and a few have gone on to be published as hobby wargames. I am especially pleased that the gender balance of the students has not been as stereotypically male-dominated as one might expect for such a wargame course (van Creveld 2013, chapter 7). As figure 35.2 shows, seven of the fifteen students on my latest module were female. The course has evolved significantly through experience and student feedback, and several lessons have emerged that I will now set out for the benefit of anyone else thinking of starting such a module (as Richard Barbrook from section V of this book did a few years ago).

One lesson is that such a module requires an unusually large commitment of time, both from the students and from the teacher. Designing wargames is a prolonged and iterative process, and my module stretches across two full terms, during which the students spend significantly longer on this course than on their other equivalent modules. This is not necessarily a problem as long as they are warned up front, since (as Rex Brynen has found with his own intensive peace-building simulation), modern students are actually keen to be challenged and stretched in return for their high fees. The greater teaching time required to supervise and mark wargame projects compared to conventional essays or dissertations is a bigger problem in today's increasingly pressurized and efficiency-conscious university environment—even a full class of sixteen students is a big strain, and any more would be impractical in my view.

A second lesson is that the initial understanding of the students is extremely variable. Some of them

Figure 35.2

My MA students learning to play simple published wargames.

are experienced wargamers, but most (despite being very intelligent and accomplished in traditional essay and exam techniques) find it a real struggle even to *play* simple wargames at the start of the course. Some have a lot of trouble with practical matters such as understanding the difference between battalions and divisions, making sense of basic statistics and probability, or using graphics software to create the maps and counters. I have found that the key to tackling this variable understanding is to make maximum use of teams of four students, each working on broadly related simulation projects. The more experienced team members can help the others grasp the basics, while the less experienced students can perform in return the equally vital service of helping their overambitious colleagues to simplify their own designs and produce intelligible games that can be played within the crucial two-hour time constraint. Those with prior wargaming experience usually start out by trying to retain too much of the detail and complexity of

published wargames, and it is often the neophytes who are better at focusing on the essentials and abstracting peripheral details.

A third lesson is that most students find it as hard to grasp abstract design theory as they do to understand wargame rules. Not until they actually play specific games for real do things become clear. By far the most common request in student feedback has been for more time playing and experimenting with games instead of just talking about the design issues involved. Now that the design theory from my early course lectures has been set out in full within my latest book *Simulating War* (which is very much the textbook for this module), I can afford to talk less and leave more time for the students to try things out for themselves with the help of my own teaching games and the simplest published manual wargames. Nothing could illustrate better the point I made earlier about the utility of wargames as an active learning technique. Students now routinely opt to get together in their teams outside class to play various wargames, including their own evolving designs, and so supplement the inevitably limited class time itself.

A final lesson is that the students need to be shown that wargaming is not just a recreational pastime, but also something that has real professional utility. Although the published wargames I lend to the students to help with their own designs are perforce hobby games, I acquaint the students as much as possible with my own academic and defense wargaming activities, and we always have a guest session with one or more defense wargame professionals to reinforce the point. Former students on the course often return to help their successors, and they can attest further to the utility of their studies in their own careers. I will return in the final section of this chapter to this key issue of the credibility of wargaming as an academic activity.

Unlike in hobby wargames, my students are required to devote around half the words in their simulation projects to historical analyses, design notes, and reflective essays that explicitly attest to the research effort and learning experience involved, and I will conclude this section with a few telling extracts from the most recent reflective essays:

- "All in all, these 7 months were an intense experience for me and this project is until now one of the most challenging yet rewarding ones I was confronted with throughout my academic career. The balance between theory and practice, research and designing a conflict simulation game enabled me to understand the particular operation I chose through so many different methodologies."

- "After 15 iterations of the rules, my game fits within the constraints set by the course, but only barely. However, I am quite happy that these limitations were set. They forced me to make maximum use of the counters and map, abstract the rules and concentrate on the essentials. This produced a more refined end product that I am quite pleased with."

- "Designing a conflict simulation has been a fantastic exercise in discovering how easily first impressions of a battle can be broken by game design and how it can then help form a better understanding as you are forced to re-evaluate all that you thought you knew."

- "The main thing I liked about the module was that I felt my progress. The first time I read the WWII game rules I did not understand anything, even after having spent three hours with them. Now I am able to grasp rules of all my classmates' games after reading them once and I am also able to critically reflect on their mechanics. The very visible learning curve was one of the main reasons why I was so highly motivated and why I thoroughly enjoyed this module."

- "Throughout the entire course I have felt constantly exposed to new material and approaches to warfare I had thought beyond the realm of academia, or simply not thought of at all. Conflict Simulation rapidly overtook my other subjects as prime example of 'what it is I'm doing' during my masters, as I found explaining the simulation of warfare through physical board games and die rolls far more universally understandable than the flood of literature the average postgraduate is inundated with. A major problem with the medium's value, however, lies in the inherent complexity that must be incorporated in order to simulate something resembling battle of some form."

Practical Obstacles and Trade-offs

As the last comment mentions, there are significant practical challenges associated with creating and using wargames in academia to give a worthwhile reflection of real conflict dynamics. I would highlight three interacting constraints that limit what it is practical to achieve, namely *time*, *expertise*, and *resources*. I will say something about each constraint in turn, and then discuss how I have sought to tackle the associated obstacles and trade-offs within my own academic employment of wargaming techniques.

Time is a problem because (as I have said) the great majority of published wargames except first-person computer simulators take a long time to learn and play. Whereas one can skim quickly through books and articles to get the gist of the argument, or highlight only the key points during a lecture or conference address, this shortcut is not easily available with wargames. Enthusiasts and military users are often prepared to spend days playing an individual wargame (Perla 1990), as are some academics for whom the game (typically a pol-mil simulation) is a one-off centerpiece of an entire course (Brynen 2010). However, my own preference is to use multiple different wargames to cover diverse aspects of conflict, and to do so as a supplement to traditional scholarly techniques such as debates and seminar discussions. Time is hence at a premium within crowded conference schedules or within the standard weekly two-hour classes of a taught module.

Expertise is an equally important constraint because those who have never played wargames before find it difficult to understand even simple versions just by reading the rules rather than by practical hands-on instruction. My MA course shows that this barrier can be overcome in time, but newcomers without such support find the complexity and unfamiliarity of wargames utterly offputting. Humanities students and scholars find it even harder to comprehend explicit mathematical models of conflict constructed by analysts like Stephen Biddle (2004), but at least they can grasp the verbal conclusions that such authors draw—manual wargames, by contrast, demand that the system be understood properly in order to play them at all. As I have said, some

computer wargames (especially first-person simulators) can be "picked up and played" with much greater facility, but only experienced computer programmers can modify or create them.

Resources are a further significant limit on academic wargaming. It is almost unknown for scholarly libraries and archives to hold any of the many thousands of wargames that have been published over the past six decades. Preserving the loose-leaf maps and hundreds of separate counters in board wargames, or maintaining or emulating the rapidly dating hardware and software needed to run successive generations of computer wargames, are significant challenges and disincentives in their own right. Although it would be easier in principle to preserve the many thousands of issues of specialist magazines commenting on this growing corpus of wargames, the lack of scholarly interest in the technique means that such collections that survive are almost all in private hands. Digitization of magazine archives (as at <http://www.wargamedevelopments.org/nugget.htm>) has made their study more practical, and John Curry (<http://www.wargaming.co>) is doing wonders in preserving and republishing key wargaming books and rulesets (as he describes in part I of this book), but most wargames are accessible only to those who have already collected them or who are willing to buy used copies while the secondhand market endures (Sabin 2012, appendix 2; <http://www3.telus.net/simulacrum/main.htm>).

These three constraints of time, expertise, and resources interact to make it very challenging to give individual students, conference participants, or fellow scholars a rich and realistic decision experience through the use of wargames. If simulation were not an issue and all that mattered was to run a challenging abstract game, then one could simply distribute plenty of cheap chess sets and have everyone play one another. Likewise, if player decisions were not required, one could simply select a realistic computer wargame and have it run automatically while everyone watched and discussed the unfolding representation (as I actually do in my Battle of Britain and Vietnam air war classes). The problem lies in *combining* simulation with decision dilemmas, since it takes very clever game design to embody realistic decision options and trade-offs within a wargame on a particular conflict, without making the resulting game system too complex and time-consuming for users to grasp and employ it effectively at all (Sabin 2012, 117–124), and without unduly encouraging unrealistic behavior aimed at exploiting the artificial game system itself (Frank 2012).

My own response to this challenge has been on several levels. First, I have spent decades amassing my own personal collection of more than a thousand published wargames and an even larger number of issues of specialist magazines. Based on this enormous archive, I have honed my design skills through repeated iterations so that I can create tailored wargames that capture key conflict dynamics as simply and accessibly as possible. (For example, my *Lost Battles* system evolved through a series of related designs stretching back for over twenty years [Sabin 2007, xix].) It is these personal wargame designs that I use in my academic work, for instance in 2014 when I created a simple centenary *kriegsspiel* of the 1914 campaign in France and Belgium (available at <http://professionalwargaming.co.uk/2014S.html>) for use at a World War I counterfactual conference I organized at Windsor Castle with my colleague Ned Lebow and on a couple of occasions later that year. I make my designs as widely available as possible through my books and websites, and I receive a steady stream of messages from academics all around the world who have been inspired thereby to employ wargaming techniques for themselves.

The second level of my response has been to develop wargaming expertise among my postgraduate students. To make up for the lack of wargames in the college library, I lend each of my master's students a few wargames from my personal collection on topics related to their own chosen conflict, and I use my own design experience to help advise them how to create their own simple wargame simulations. In return, some of my master's and research students act as teaching assistants to help me to run wargames in my various BA modules, as well as in wider events such as the 1914 *kriegsspiel* just mentioned. I run a practice session with my assistants before each class or event, in which we play through the game together to ensure that they understand the nuances of the rules and the tactical situation. The ultimate example of synergy between my postgraduate and undergraduate teaching is that the wargame that we use each year to study Hannibal's campaigns in my BA ancient warfare module started out in 2006 as the MA class project of my student Garrett Mills, before being redesigned and published under our joint names in 2008 (Sabin 2012, 145–160).

The third level of my response to the challenge of reconciling realistic decision involvement with system accessibility is to employ an approach of "guided competition." Since students and conference participants alike are almost all nongamers who would feel at sea if left alone even with the simple games of my own design, most of my games are run by facilitators whose role is to help apply the detailed rules, to keep the games moving quickly, to advise the students against egregious tactical errors, and to lead initial

Figure 35.3

My BA students being helped to play one of my own wargame designs.

discussion of how far the simulation reflects real conflict dynamics. Having postgraduate assistants available as facilitators allows me to run three or more simultaneous games as shown in figure 35.3, while I myself move between them to maintain an overview and keep things running smoothly. With six to eight players per game, the opportunity for individual decision experience is obviously diluted, but having teams of around three people command each side does have the significant benefits that those with a stronger grasp of the system can help their colleagues and that decisions need to be debated explicitly—a key educational advantage. A final plenary session in the class or conference as a whole allows the

experience from the individual games to be shared and the issues to be debated with reference to the real conflict that we are trying to study.

The final way in which I reconcile decision involvement with system accessibility is by designing some wargames that are so simple and quick that I can leave players to run them for themselves in multiple one-on-one contests after all. I have done this several times over the years, and the best example is the drastically cut-down version of my 1914 *kriegsspiel* with just one rather than four pages of rules, which I ran with several dozen participants at a British Army wargaming workshop in 2014 (as shown in figure 35.4) and again at our Connections UK conference at King's College (<http://www.professionalwargaming. co.uk>) later that year. The game system needs to be *really* simple, and I need to spend significant time at the start of the session explaining the rules and running through an illustrated example for the group as a whole. This makes it vital that the game itself can be played quickly, especially since it is preferable to have the players immediately swap sides and play the game a second time to get the most benefit from their initial investment in learning the system. My 1914 mini-game proved a great success in its intended role of giving players a quick hands-on introduction to wargame dynamics and showing that wargames can still capture key strategic dilemmas without being impossibly complex.

These are only my own responses to the practical challenges of using wargames in an academic context. Other approaches are entirely feasible. For example, George Phillies, a physicist at Worcester Polytechnic Institute in Massachusetts, has published several books and a freely available YouTube lecture series on wargame design, focusing on classic commercially published board wargames from

Figure 35.4
British Army officers playing my 1914 mini-game one on one.

the 1960s (Phillies 2014; <http://www.wpi.edu/ academics/imgd/news/20134/174110.htm>). Scholars who are already familiar with wargames will be able to devise their own ways of overcoming the practical obstacles and trade-offs I have discussed. What is much more difficult is for those with little or no prior experience of wargaming to develop wargame courses or activities, as military officers and academics working with military students are sometimes asked to do. My MA course shows that the necessary skills can be learned with the proper input of time, expertise, and resources, but wargaming cannot simply be "picked up" swiftly by unsupported browsing of the literature as some other subjects can. What is needed for proper professional institutionalization of wargaming is much more structured hands-on education by existing experts, and here a key obstacle is the skepticism of many nongamers (especially in academia) about the value of the technique as a whole.

Stigma and Skepticism

I discussed at the start of this chapter the failure of wargaming proper to attain anything like the scholarly respectability of approaches such as mathematical modeling, operational research, game theory, simulation, or pol-mil gaming. Even those books and academic courses that focus squarely on the military conduct of particular battles or wars almost never mention the existence of detailed wargame simulations of the conflicts concerned. Martin van Creveld is one of very few nongaming scholars who have written about the various forms of wargames, and he treats them as sociologically interesting objects of curiosity rather than as potentially useful techniques of enquiry (van Creveld 2008; 2013). Rob MacDougall and Lisa Faden discuss this attitude further in their own chapter later in this section. As Pierre Corbeil wrote recently, "the power of the game as a tool for the study of possibilities has not been adopted by the historical profession as it exists in the universities of the world" (Corbeil 2011, 419). Why should this be?

One reason is simple ignorance, due to the very low profile of serious wargames in wider society. Professional military wargaming is a sensitive area cloaked by security restrictions, to the point where a student of mine could find few practical details of US Army wargames conducted prior to the 1991 Gulf War even after interviewing the key participants. I myself have not been allowed access to most tests of a planning wargame that I am helping to design for the UK defense ministry. Recreational wargames are unclassified, but they are sold by specialist outlets and reviewed in specialist magazines, so they have very little visibility outside the hobby community. One famous historian told me recently that he was not necessarily prejudiced against wargames—he simply knew almost nothing about them. Air historian Alfred Price wrote that, "I had a rather fuzzy pre-conceived notion that wargamers were grown-ups who played around with kids' toys, and tried to make out that they were making some serious contribution to military understanding in the process" (Spick 1978, 7).

This leads on to a second problem, namely the widespread perception in society as a whole, and even among some self-conscious hobbyists themselves (McGuire 1976), that wargaming tends to attract childish nerds. Jane McGonigal has written perceptively of the stigma attached to the words "game" and "play" (McGonigal 2011, 19), and scholars have coined the term "serious games" to try to offset the negative connotations involved (Abt 1970; Smith 2009). The word "wargame" has precisely the opposite effect, since it suggests that the tragic sacrifices of armed conflict are being reduced to a mere "game." There are even suspicions that some wargamers are closet militarists with an unhealthy admiration for Nazi military prowess (Smelser and Davies 2008, chapter 7). Small wonder that wargamers are usually very reticent about their activities, and make extensive use of euphemisms. As Jim Dunnigan wrote, "A wargame is a playable simulation. A conflict simulation is another name for wargame, one that leaves out the two unsavory terms 'war' and 'game'" (Dunnigan 1992b, 236). (On the vexed terminological distinction between simulations and games, see Klabbers 2009.)

A third reason for wargaming's image problem is that it is seen primarily as a recreational activity for private enthusiasts instead of as a valid scholarly tool like game theory. Academics are often uncomfortable engaging with "popular" works in their field, since they are seen as lacking the objectivity and specialist rigor of proper scholarly studies (Overy 2010). As I have said, many published hobby wargames amply merit such suspicions, because of their poor simulation and arcade distortions. Some defense wargamers such as Robert Rubel have called for greater professionalization within the military wargame community (Rubel 2006). However, it is far from clear that wargames ever can approach the attempted "scientific" rigor of works of operational analysis like those by Stephen Biddle and David Rowland (Biddle 2004; Rowland 2006). Even if they exploit every scrap of available real-world data, wargames contain so many subjective choices in their mechanism and structure that skeptics will always be able to challenge their assumptions and dismiss them as guesswork and invention. Veteran US defense wargamer Peter Perla is very clear that "designing a wargame is an art, not a science," and he suggests that "game design has no real formalisms. Instead it is dominated by individual style and fashion, and in that respect is more like painting than other arts" (Perla 1990, 183–184).

The fourth reason why wargames attract such skepticism lies in the variability of their outcomes. Wargames offer a powerful means of exploring the role of contingency within war and conflict, but such "counterfactual" speculation is a very controversial technique in scholarly circles. Although there have been several recent works of popular history that have explored "what if?" questions, especially regarding World War II (e.g., Tsouras 2002; Showalter and Deutsch 2010), and although some prominent historians such as Andrew Roberts, Jeremy Black, and Niall Ferguson have championed this counterfactual approach (Roberts 2004; Black 2008; Ferguson 2000), most historical scholars remain doubtful and prefer to focus on what actually occurred (Collins 2007). My colleague Ned Lebow (with whom I organized the World War I centenary conference at Windsor Castle) has written thoughtfully and eloquently in theoretical defense of carefully framed counterfactual speculation (Lebow 2010), but eminent historian Richard Evans has gone beyond the usual attitude of silent skepticism and written an entire book articulating the contrary view (Evans 2014). For those who think it pointless to ask "what if" history had gone differently, historical wargames founded on this very premise of contingent variability are unlikely to hold much attraction.

The variability of wargame outcomes attracts skepticism for other reasons as well. Whereas automatic computer simulations can be run thousands of times to generate a statistical spread of outcomes, wargames with human players are more time-consuming to repeat, and so there are understandable fears that individual results may be unrepresentative. A particularly sore point lies in the use of dice as a quick abstract means of modeling detailed uncertainties (Rubel 2006, 119–120). In real war, bad luck such as orders going astray is impossible to challenge and clearly attributable in hindsight to a specific causal chain, but an unlucky die roll in a wargame seems abstract and arbitrary by comparison, and raises uncomfortable parallels with games of pure chance such as Snakes and Ladders. In my *kriegsspiel* games in 2014, I deliberately used limited intelligence rather than die rolls as the means of generating uncertainty and random variation, since it was more acceptable to the officers and academics involved. My other wargame designs are more open because I specifically want players and facilitators to have full visibility of the interactive dynamics involved, but the use of dice is a constant credibility problem, despite being fully justified in simulation terms to avoid unrealistically chesslike calculations by the players (Sabin 2012, 117–120).

After many years of experience in using and promoting wargaming techniques within academia, I now have a pretty good idea of the reaction from the scholarly community. Academics who are themselves recreational wargamers (from a wide range of subject disciplines) tend to be very supportive, and relieved that they can admit their interest and discuss the problems and possibilities of wargame modeling as a scholarly technique. My books have sold several thousand copies each, and have spawned flourishing Yahoo discussion groups with hundreds of members and many more words in their thousands of posts than there are in the books themselves (<https://groups.yahoo.com/neo/groups/lostbattles>; <https://groups.yahoo.com/neo/groups/simulatingwar>). I have given lectures on my simulation studies at universities in several countries, and I have become increasingly involved in discussing, promoting, and designing wargames within the professional defense community. However, nongaming scholars, especially in military history, have paid very little attention to my work. Most seem not even to have noticed it, or have dismissed it as some strange enthusiast aberration. Only in journals such as *Simulation & Gaming* or in books like the present one are games of this kind really taken seriously in the academic environment, and nongaming scholars are very unlikely to read such sources in the first place or to be persuaded easily even if they do. My extensive use of wargames as an educational vehicle has been accepted without too much trouble, thanks to positive student feedback and a predilection in the university system for novel methods of assessment. I won a King's College award in 2009 for innovative teaching, and one external examiner praised my MA module for providing "fascinating assessment and a welcome change to the usual chore of essays." It has been a very different story as regards research. My *Lost Battles* book has made little impact among professional ancient historians, and when I proposed a similar study of ancient naval battles as part of a major interdisciplinary research grant application, my contribution was dismissed by one reviewer as "just wargaming." King's College has not risked submitting my various articles on wargaming (Sabin 2002; 2011) to our national research evaluation exercise for fear of a similar reaction, nor did it submit my latest book (Sabin 2012) despite a thirty-seven-page bibliography and a scholarly review that said, "If I had to recommend one military history book I have read this year it would be Philip Sabin's *Simulating War*" (<http://smh-hq.org/smhblog/?p=516>). It is lucky that I was already a full professor before I started publishing seriously about wargaming, since in the current

academic environment it is difficult even to keep one's job with research this controversial, let alone to get appointed or promoted. I am very conscious that, when I retire, my modules will probably be replaced with more conventionally taught ones, and wargaming at King's will disappear with hardly a ripple.

So is there any way to rescue academic wargaming from the stigma and skepticism and to set it on a more secure foundation? To my mind, the only practical way forward is to build on and expand the small core of scholars who are already knowledgeable about and sympathetic to wargaming. There will always be many academics who remain irredeemably skeptical (with considerable justification given the many problems and limitations of the technique), but there are also surprising numbers of scholars who do find wargames interesting and enlightening but who have been hiding their light under a bushel hitherto for fear of ridicule or of being accused of "bringing their hobby to work." The more that they see other academics using and writing about wargames, the more emboldened they may be to join in and to try something for themselves. With even nongaming academics sometimes being asked now to run wargames for military students, we may at last be approaching the day when wargaming experience is something to be mentioned proudly on a CV instead of tactfully concealed from skeptical appointments panels.

As regards the best way of showing anyone from students to professors what wargames have to offer, I am convinced that there is no substitute for actually playing games so that people can see for themselves. That is why I am so keen on designing simple and accessible wargames that can be played within a very short time. The initially skeptical Prussian chief of staff was famously converted and persuaded to give his full backing to the original *kriegsspiel* when he actually saw it in operation (Perla 1990, 26). I have lost count of the number of times that players of my own wargames have had similar revelations, and registered their amazement that a few dozen counters and a few pages of rules can reproduce real campaigns and reflect real military dynamics and dilemmas. Books like this one are all very well as far as they go, but the more people who are directly exposed to serious but accessible wargames, the less pervasive will be their image as trivial and childish diversions or impossibly complex and time-consuming pastimes for obsessive nerds.

About the Author

Philip Sabin is Professor of Strategic Studies in the Department of War Studies at King's College London. He has written or edited fifteen books and monographs and several dozen chapters and articles on a wide variety of military topics, as well as designing several published wargames. His current research specialism is the analytical modeling and simulation of the key dynamics of armed conflict, as reflected in his two recent books *Lost Battles* (2007) and *Simulating War* (2012). He has decades of experience in using wargames to teach military and civilian students, including through his MA module in which students learn to design their own wargames on conflicts of their choice. He has close links with the armed services, lectures internationally on wargaming and other military topics, and is co-organizer of the annual Connections UK conference for wargames professionals.

LESSONS FROM THE HEXAGON: WARGAMES AND THE MILITARY HISTORIAN

Robert M. Citino

War is a serious business, and so is the writing of war. For that very reason, most professional military historians tend to shun the commercial wargame as a legitimate tool of knowledge and research. Oh, they may have one or two hidden away in the closet, or they may admit to having played them in graduate school, but most scholars "put away the things of a child" as they come of age, and the notion that a commercial wargame has anything significant to teach has never found much purchase within the community of military historians.

The scholarly rejection of wargames is a shame, however, since military simulations can offer valuable lessons to even the most knowledgeable and accomplished scholar, lessons that no other medium can teach so effectively.

A Personal Journey: Epiphany in The Game Hut

If I may be allowed a personal remembrance, let me take the reader back in time and place to Bloomington, Indiana, in the late 1970s. Home to a world-class university and an excellent research library, Bloomington was also my residence as a graduate student in European history. While I was interested in military affairs in general, and military history in particular, Indiana University didn't really have a military history program at the time. The post-Vietnam hangover was in full swing and history departments nationwide were embarking on their great transformation, moving away from traditional military history—or, indeed, military history of any sort—toward concerns more aligned with the trinity of race, class, and gender. I am not sure if Indiana was offering a single dedicated military history course in European history during the years I was there.

I became a military historian anyway, and for that I have two circumstances to thank. First, I was fortunate enough to be studying under a pair of wonderful professors, Barbara and Charles Jelavich, two scholars of towering achievement and open-mindedness to even their most wayward student, and they encouraged me to follow my military history muse. Barbara Jelavich even became my *Doktormutter*, supervising my dissertation on German defenses against Poland in the Weimar period and offering sage advice throughout the process.

The second factor that turned me into a military historian was the presence in Bloomington of a small store called The Game Hut. A fellow graduate student and I were playing the game *Risk* (1959) one afternoon, when he mentioned that there was apparently a store in town that sold games. "Like *Risk*," he declared, "but more detailed." We decided to check it out—graduate students will try anything, as long as it means not having to sit down and work on their dissertations.

Walking into The Game Hut in 1979 was like an epiphany. Wargames (or "conflict simulations," as I soon learned to call them) were everywhere, dealing with every conceivable historical topic. The shelves sagged (I mean that description literally) with bookshelf and boxed games (from the Avalon Hill Game Company), games that came in strange flat plastic trays (Simulations Publications, Inc., or SPI), and big, thick games in oversize ziplock bags (GDW). The topics were all over the map, but World War II and the American Civil War seemed to dominate. Napoleon (about whom I, like most American college students then and now, knew next to nothing) was also big, as were games on a future war between NATO and the Warsaw Pact. I even found a game on alternate history, SPI's *Dixie* (1976), a simulation in which the South had won the Civil War and the two sides were having a second go at one another in the twentieth century. *Dixie* was the first wargame I bought. It regularly makes "worst game of all time" lists, but to me it represents my youth, and I have invested it with a warm, rosy glow.

Finally, there were the people—the store's proprietors and their clientele. They were a fascinating bunch. They would talk your head off about almost anything, and they could absolutely throw *down* on the precise details of this or that historical campaign—order of battle, commanders, terrain features. Like all graduate students, I wasn't as smart as I thought I was, a lesson I learned when a fellow shopper in The Game Hut corrected my grievous mispronunciation of "Coutances."

And so I was off. I bought dozens, and eventually hundreds of wargames, and soon they filled every nook of the two-room apartment I shared with an extremely patient wife. Sure, I was buying games, but I could justify my newfound obsession on scholarly grounds. I was then deep in the research and writing of my dissertation, and just beginning to realize how crucial wargames (*kriegsspielen*) had been to the German army as it planned its campaigns. The *kriegsspiel* wasn't a "game" to be won or lost, so much as a command exercise that sought to pose the German officer with the same kind of decisions and dilemmas he would have to face in combat. In fact, a great deal of my dissertation (which in 1987 became my first book, *The Evolution of Blitzkrieg Tactics*) described these German wargames of the 1920s, and I would return to the subject again and again in my scholarly career (most directly in 1995's *Path to Blitzkrieg: Training and Doctrine in the German Army, 1920-1935*). I have been fortunate to have a fruitful publishing career, and I have spent a great deal of it discussing games and simulations as planning tools.

Lessons Learned

As I delved deeper into the world of wargames, I began to perceive them less as game and more as war.

I came to view simulations as a useful interpretative tool for the military historian, certainly not by replacing archival work or the necessity to develop a firm grasp on the secondary literature (which is monstrously large in military history), but rather by augmenting and reinforcing these basic activities.

Three areas stand out. The first is the obvious one: the utility of the wargame as a visual and tactile representation of the real-life event. Indeed, it is not even necessary to play the game to completion in order to gain this benefit. Simply setting the game up, arranging the maps, and deploying the at-start orders of battle for both sides can be enough to tell a researcher a great deal about the battle, campaign, or war under investigation.

For example, one fact that tends to be underemphasized in histories of the fighting in North Africa in World War II is the sheer size of the theater—approximately six hundred miles from Rommel's initial base at El Agheila across the chord of the Cyrenaican bulge to the Egyptian border, and a great deal longer than that for road-bound infantry marching along the Via Balba, the one paved highway in Libya. And no visualization of that simple fact matches sitting down to play a wargame on the North African theater. Consider Avalon Hill's venerable game *Afrika Korps* (1964). With its two maps laid out end to end, with the Germans deploying at one end of a long table, and with General Rommel's objectives, Tobruk and Alexandria, lying far to the east, *Afrika Korps* teaches a lesson the moment you set it up, and does so in a way that merely reading about the campaign cannot. You can see at a glance that the theater is huge, that the commitment of force on both sides is relatively tiny, that you can maneuver anywhere you want to but often to little effect, and that conquest of terrain—mainly empty desert—matters little outside of a few key strategic points: all solid evocations of the actual event.

Or consider Germany's 1942 campaign in the Soviet Union. A number of companies have published games on *Unternehmen Blau* ("Operation Blue"), the campaign toward Stalingrad and the Caucasus oilfields. *Drive on Stalingrad* (1977) by SPI was the first one I played, a long time ago, and once again the mere act of setting up the game drove home crucial lessons. *Drive* was a multimap extravaganza, and it highlighted all the problems present from the start in the German operational plan. A key player in Blue was General Hermann Hoth's Fourth Panzer Army. Hoth's start line lies in the far north, and with a simple calculation you can count the number of turns it will take him to seize his first objective, the city of Voronezh, then to wheel ninety degrees to the south, clear the entire vast bend of the Don river, cross the river, and head eastward to Stalingrad. Even if there had been a complete absence of opposition, Hoth's ride to Stalingrad (and thence to the oilfields of the Caucasus, since that was the German schema in 1942), would have been an *anabasis* of epic proportions: from Voronezh to Kalach (400 miles), then Kalach to Rostov (225 miles)—with both legs necessary to clear the Don bend—and then another four hundred and fifty to the oil city of Grozny: nearly eleven hundred miles in all as the crow flies. But of course he faced opposition the whole way, and armies don't move as the crow flies—they head one way, double back, launch one time- and energy-consuming flanking movement after the other. All of these gyrations may well double the original length of the journey. Moreover, Hoth would have to use most of his limited fuel and kinetic energy in a drive almost due south—not heading east at all, which is where one would expect to be heading when fighting Soviet armies. And *Drive on Stalingrad*—a famously flawed design that was nearly unplayable as originally issued due to problems with the rules and apparently limited playtesting—shows all these problems at first blush. A single glance at the game map will give even a player with an underdeveloped coup d'oeil the shivers.

A second fruitful use of wargames is that they can help to illustrate the various levels of war: tactical, operational, and strategic. Of all the ideas a professor needs to get across to students in a military history class, the notion that there are three interlocking levels of military activity and analysis, and that the adversaries are waging war on all three of them simultaneously, may well be the most difficult to teach.

But wargamers quickly learn to recognize the concept of "level," and again they can do so merely by looking at the map. A game in which the map represents a few acres or square miles, with the two hostile armies already in contact, or that consists of geomorphic maps that can be fit together in various ways, is bound to be tactical. Here SPI's old "Pre-Seventeenth Century Tactical Game System" (1976), or PRESTAGS, comes to mind, as well as Avalon Hill's highly successful game *Squad Leader* (designed by John Hill and released in 1977). A game in which the map represents a region or province, with the armies beginning the match out of range of one another, a situation that offers both sides a great deal of opportunity for pre-battle maneuver or advance to contact, is operational. Here the exemplar, for a person of my generation at least, is SPI's *Panzergruppe Guderian* (included in *Strategy & Tactics* 57 [1976]), a study of the German drive on Smolensk and points east in 1941. The fight at Smolensk saw the Soviets, even in defeat, blunting the German blitzkrieg for the first time, with an incalculable impact on the rest of the campaigning season. The game spawned a whole series of

descendants, such as *Cobra* (1977) (*Strategy & Tactics* 65; designer B. E. Hessel) dealing with the successful American offensive that shattered the German defenses in Normandy and led to the Allied breakout, and *Kharkov* (1978) (*Strategy & Tactics* 68; designer Stephen B. Patrick), a simulation of the huge but abortive Soviet offensive in 1942. Finally, games in which the map embraces entire countries or continents, with the players having to allocate resources of some sort to build their forces, thus simulating the economic aspect of military power, are strategic. The dominant strategic game at the time that I was haunting The Game Hut was *Third Reich* (Avalon Hill 1974; designer John Prados), a complex and addictive simulation of World War II in Europe in which the player earned "Basic Resource Points" based on the territory he controlled and then had to purchase new forces. Essentially, success in conquering and exploiting led to economic success, a step forward in simulation technique, since previous wargames had all but ignored economics. The very next year, SPI published *World War I* (1975; designed by James Dunnigan), a simulation of World War I in Europe in which the front rarely moved an inch—that is to say, a hexagon—either way, but the players spent a great deal of time budgeting and juggling "Combat Resource Points," addictive in its own way, but never reaching the popularity of the World War II version.

One piece of advertising boilerplate within the wargaming industry is to tell the potential buyer whether the game is tactical, operational, or strategic. The approach makes a certain amount of sense, since different personalities prefer different levels: some love the nitty-gritty of a tactical level infantry assault, while others want the sweeping maneuver associated with operational level campaigning. But indeed, this traditional disclaimer is almost always unnecessary, since the experienced wargamer soon develops an intuitive understanding of these things.

Certainly, wargames are not perfect in this area. All too often, games conflate and confuse the levels, so that the players have to make decisions that should by rights be reserved to the president or national command authority, while also worrying about battlefield logistics, and then forming up their poor bloody infantry for an attack on a ridge. But the best designers of commercial wargames over the years—Dunnigan, Prados, John Hill, Ty Bomba, Joseph Miranda, Ted Raicer, and others—usually invest a great deal of thought and care into pegging the game's level.

By contrast, many scholarly military historians give no thought at all to the issue, with individual books and articles ranging all over the place from the tactical to the grand strategic. The US Army's official histories of World War II, the famous "Green Book" series, are perhaps the worst offenders, with the scene shifting from the Oval Office to the Supreme Command in the field to a grunt earning the medal of honor for battlefield heroism, often on the same page.

Third and finally, wargames succeed like no other medium in squaring the ultimate circle of military history, what we might call the "Jomini-Clausewitz conundrum." Wargames are Jominian at their core. They quantify, order, and prescribe military activity. Players take turns, and the turns break down into segments or phases that proceed in a strict order. In ninety percent of wargames, movement takes place first, with combat following. Military units have ratings, usually numbers, denoting their attack, defense, and movement capabilities. The notion that war is a science, a measurable object that unfolds according to strict, fixed principles—the essence of Jominianism—is even visible on the standard simulation map, with its hexagons, its color-coding, and its notations for terrain, slope, and elevation.

And yet wargames have, from the start, incorporated one classic Clausewitzian artifact: the die. Used to determine combat outcomes, it serves as a randomizer, a trickster, an imp, reminding the player of the essential uncertainty of war. Go ahead: set up an attack on a crucial hex, carefully count out your three-to-one combat superiority, have armor in the spearhead and artillery in support, with bonuses for divisional integration and engineers, and then roll a 6. Attacker eliminated.

Most wargamers feel, at first, that this is unfair, that it invalidates all the careful planning they did, and that their hard work has gone unappreciated. But this is precisely the point that Clausewitz made in *On War*. In war, "everything is very simple, but the simplest thing is difficult" (Book I, Chapter 7). Uncertainty reigns. Fog settles in, and nothing is as it seems. War does not take place in the quiet of a study or laboratory, but in the realm of danger, and thus is inherently unpredictable. "Let us accompany a novice to the battlefield," Clausewitz writes:

> As we approach, the thunder of the guns grows louder and alternates with the howling of the cannonballs, which begin to attract the attention of the inexperienced man. Rounds begin to land close around us. We hurry up the hill where the commanding general holds forth with his large entourage. Here cannonballs and shells burst so frequently that the seriousness of life begins to punch through the young man's fantasy image. Suddenly someone we know falls—a shell explodes, leading to instinctive movements among the group. You start to feel that you are not as calm and collected as you were. Even the bravest become a bit preoccupied (Book I, Chapter 4).[1]

Indeed, we might write these same words, in a figurative sense, to describe a first-time wargamer who has just seen his carefully planned assault on Cemetery Ridge or Omaha Beach go badly awry, even after he lined it up precisely, thanks to a random die roll.

If there was an arc to the process of game design over the years, it was to increase the Clausewitzian side of the equation. Random events tables, for example, can be very effective in simulating off-battlefield developments, often in the political realm, that utterly disrupt the combatant commander's plan for the front and are more or less dumped into his lap without premonition. One good early example is *The Crusades*, a Richard Berg design that appeared in *Strategy & Tactics* 70 (1978). A die roll of 1 meant that a random event had occurred, followed by another die roll that directed the player to a chart. For the Third Crusade, for example, one likely result might be:

> Philip Goes Home: Remove the King of France plus Philip, Comte de Flanders; William de Les Barres; Peter de Courtney; Dreux de Mello; and Aubrey Clement

and suddenly, carrying out that Third Crusade gets a whole lot more difficult! Designer Joseph Miranda also used such technique to good effect. In *Franco-Prussian War* (*Strategy & Tactics* 149 [1992]), he offered "Political Events" markers, chosen randomly from a cup, that could profoundly affect the course of the game, from Austrian intervention (Bismarck's nightmare) to the Paris Commune to a democratic uprising in Prussia (highly unlikely by this time, in fact, but an interesting construct nonetheless). In doing so, Miranda returned the Franco-Prussian War as we have come to know it—a pushover and a sure victory for Prussia—back into what it actually *was* at the time: a nail-biting gamble and a mass of questions for all concerned. All in all, rule modules like these force the gamer to confront Clausewitz's famous dictum that "war is merely the continuation of policy (*Fortsetzung der Politik*) by other means."

Clausewitzian notions of chance and uncertainty found their way into wargames in a multitude of ways beyond politics, however. Once again, the game *Panzergruppe Guderian* (1976) was in the forefront, including "untried units" on the Soviet side, which could vary wildly in strength, and which remained unrevealed until a German unit attacked them. Miranda dove a fathom deeper into Clausewitz in *Franco-Prussian War* (1992) by including a mandatory "Fog of War" rule and by making movement, rather than combat, dependent on the roll of a die. The varying possibilities (the unit may move as intended, it may not move at all, it or may even move "impetuously" toward the nearest enemy unit and attack it) made it nearly impossible to carry out a plan from the beginning of the war to the end, a problem that would have felt very familiar to army commanders of the nineteenth century.

Conclusion

In Book I, Chapter 1 of *On War*, Clausewitz describes war as "a matter of calculating probabilities" rather than a scientific and systematic activity. "Only one single element is necessary in order to make it [war] a game (*Spiel*)," he writes, and that is "chance" (*Zufall*). Chance, he says in his distinctive manner, "is the element that war lacks the least."

Certainly, it is easy to scoff that they're only games. Commercial wargames can be fun to play, not that there's anything wrong with that. In 1990, designer Ty Bomba—who does alternate history better than anyone—gave us *Mississippi Banzai*, a game of a nightmarish future in which America has lost World War II and the Imperial Japanese and German militaries are duking it out over St. Louis. Resembling a version of Philip K. Dick's famous novel *The Man in the High Castle* on steroids, *Mississippi Banzai* is a great deal of fun to play, and I would play it forever if I did not have to hold down a steady job. But wargames can also serve as heavyweight research tools, and that same designer, Bomba, was also the one who gave us *Balkan Hell* (*Command Magazine* 35, 1995), a simulation that offered the best orders of battle available for the just-concluded war in Bosnia, including previously obscure intelligence on Croatian, Bosnian, and rebel Serb forces alike.

Beyond the informational content or fun quotient, however, wargames offer the operational military historian a means to interpret past events, to unpack the calculations that go into planning a campaign and then to analyze the reasons for success or failure. Wargames allow for compelling analyses of time, space, and force dilemmas; they clearly delineate the tactical, operational, and strategic levels of war; and they allow the player to appreciate the truths inherent in both Jomini and Clausewitz, rather than establishing a false dichotomy, choosing one and rejecting the other. In the end, war itself is a violent, bloody, and unpredictable game, with time-honored Jominian principles serving as the "rules" and Clausewitzian *Zufall* interfering as the randomizer.

So, may I offer the following advice to any military historian seeking to learn more about a battle, campaign, or war of the past? Get serious: play a game.

About the Author

Robert M. Citino is an American historian at the University of North Texas. He is a leading authority on modern German military history, with an emphasis upon World War II and the German influence upon modern operational doctrine. He has previously taught at Eastern Michigan University, West Point, and the US Army War College. He is a fellow of the Barsanti Military History Center, former vice president of the Society for Military History, and a consultant for the Department of the Army. He has also appeared as a consultant on the History Channel.

Note

1. Translations from Clausewitz are my own.

37 SIMULATION LITERACY: THE CASE FOR WARGAMES IN THE HISTORY CLASSROOM

Robert MacDougall and Lisa Faden

Do wargames belong in the history classroom? Does the question even need to be asked? Today's innovative thought leaders know that games aren't just games. They're multimodal platforms for synergizing twenty-first-century imaginations in a brave new world of constant—

Hold on. Can we dispense with the sales pitch? This is the third chapter in the sixth section of a book about wargames. We're all gamers here, right? We know how to talk about games when evangelizing to nongamers.[1] We've seen the TED talks, written grant applications, made the case for games to skeptical parents and stuffy old deans. There's a standard protocol. Since we are history teachers, we start by bemoaning the state of history education today. We get in a few digs at boring lectures and textbooks, toss out a depressing statistic about how few children can identify George Washington or the Battle of Hastings. Then we invoke the future, with talk of "digital natives" and high technology. Finally, we reveal that games are fun.

Games *are* fun, and a lot of the standard pitch is true. But sales pitches rarely bring us toward deep understanding. And it is high time to move beyond a simple "Games are great!" vs. "Games are bad!" debate. This chapter tries to face the question squarely and honestly: What can simulation games, and wargames in particular, bring to the history classroom? How do they align and how do they clash with the fundamental goals of history education? Really investigating these questions requires thinking deeply about history as well as games. There is a rich literature on historical thinking and the civic purpose of history education, but it has rarely been connected to conversations around game-based learning. By engaging with that literature, we can go beyond simple pro- or anti-game manifestos and grasp the real promise of games and simulations for history education. But we can't do that until we ask, why teach and study history in the first place? What is the history classroom for?

Why Teach History?

Conversations on *how* to teach history remain superficial until we really dig into the question, *why* teach history? What is the purpose of history education? There is today a rich body of scholarly work that poses exactly this question. The answers can take us down at least four different paths: history as heritage, history as disciplinary knowledge, history as education for democratic citizenship, and multiliteracies.

One traditional model of history education sees history as heritage. In this approach, the reason we teach history is to remember and celebrate the achievements of the past (Hamer 2005). Most typically, the heritage to be embraced is the story of the nation-state, a narrative intended to promote social cohesion and national pride. But groups within the nation can also take a heritage approach to history, with their own celebratory or didactic narratives about the past. The problem with this model is that it asks learners to accept historical narratives uncritically and renders invisible important questions about which version of history should be learned.

The history as disciplinary knowledge model is perhaps best known through the work of cognitive psychologists like Sam Wineburg and Peter Seixas, who have spent more than two decades exploring the proposition that rigorous historical analysis, which they call "historical thinking," offers unique intellectual benefits. In this disciplinary approach, the goal is to teach students to think "like a historian": to critically examine primary sources, weigh the truth claims of conflicting accounts, and construct interpretations of past events. Under this model, history is not a narrative to remember but a set of skills and practices to cultivate.

Other educators locate the value of history in its contributions to a vital democracy: history education makes good citizens. This citizenship model emphasizes the role that history can play in helping students engage with diverse cultural traditions, develop their understanding of the common good, and illustrate strategies for bringing about positive change. Keith Barton and Linda Levstik assert, "Discussions about how to promote social well-being and how to care for the public realm are at the heart of participatory democracy, and ... history has an important role to play in preparing students to take part in such deliberation" (Barton and Levstik 2004, 38).

A fourth way of thinking about history education comes from developments in the study of literacy. Literacy scholars have come to understand reading as a broad practice of meaning-making. In this framework, the "texts" we "read" are not only the printed word. They can be visual, verbal, digital, procedural, or kinesthetic (including games). The goal of multiliteracies education is to teach students to read, produce, and interpret texts in multiple modalities (New London Group 1996). Applying this model to history education, history becomes a source and a subject of all kinds of texts to critically examine or create.

Each of these four models has its own implications for what history is taught and how, but the models need not be mutually exclusive. The disciplinary knowledge model suggests many of the skills and practices we want to teach our students. The democratic citizenship model explains *why* we want our students to obtain these skills. And the multiliteracy model directs us to ask: How will our students communicate what they learn, and how can history education develop their capacity for deep reading and self-expression? Even the history as heritage model has a place, not in its simple, uncritical mode but in a more multifaceted form. To embrace something as part of one's heritage—literally, the things we inherit from the past—means to see it as valuable or meaningful to one's own present. The heritage model obliges us to make history relevant to our students, and teach them to read and interpret the many heritages they will be offered.

The Allure of War

Having laid out several goals for history education (without imagining that that question is fully settled), we can judge the value of wargames in the classroom with far more clarity than such conversations usually attain. Instead of simply choosing to be for or against games, we can ask, does this tool serve for these purposes? How do the affordances of wargames as learning exercises align with specific teaching goals?

There are reasons to be skeptical about wargames in the history classroom. For one thing, wargames are about war. Certainly, games can simulate a million other things, but wargames are our topic here, and we should not pretend that violent combat is not the most popular subject of simulation games by some margin. Why is this focus on war a problem? Our concern here is not about copycat effects. We are not worried that students will decide to invade Russia after playing *Axis & Allies*. Our concern is about the place war already holds in school and popular history.

War stories dominate popular history and most history classrooms as well. "Many people understand war as the principal marker of historical periodization," observes Alan Filewod in a study of wargames and reenactments. "For many, history *is* war" (Filewod 2012, 21). The claim that traditional military history has been pushed aside in favor of social or cultural histories may be true at the university level, but is not borne out in high schools and elementary schools. Our own studies in the United States and Canada show that wars and battles are the dominant subjects in many history classrooms, especially in terms of class time, if not stated curricular goals (Faden 2014). Such a focus might make sense in a military college, where wargames and simulations have an obvious and powerful role to play (Sabin 2012, 31–46), but should a fourth-grade history classroom look like a course in strategy and tactics?

None of the models for history education described earlier demand or support a lopsided focus on combat and war. Yet it persists, less for intellectual or ideological reasons than because military history is easy to teach. "War makes rattling good history, but peace is poor reading," wrote Thomas Hardy. Wars are historical turning points. They make contingency visible and change real. Combat creates high stakes and human drama. And good teaching materials on war are readily available. Working teachers know that on a day-to-day basis, the history they teach is shaped as much by the materials available at hand as by any state-sanctioned curricula, and far more than by the current fashions of academic history. Teachers of war have no shortage of readings to assign, dramatic films to show, historical sites to visit, or stirring stories to tell. Wargames may engage students with military history, but the average history teacher doesn't need much help making military history engaging. What they need is help making every other aspect of history as vivid and exciting as the history of war.

Why Historians Mistrust Simulations

Setting aside the allure of war, there are deeper reasons for history educators to be wary of simulation games as teaching tools. If "historical thinking" means learning to think like a historian, then it is worth asking what professional historians think about games and simulations as representations of the past. The answer is: not much.

The other social science disciplines—economics, sociology, political science—generally embrace the modeling of social phenomena. They try to distinguish between dependent and independent variables, to make generalizations that will be applicable in many places and times, and ultimately, to uncover the laws of human behavior. Models and simulations are appropriate tools for this work.

But historians work differently. We believe in contingency and context above all else. We prize specificity and attention to detail. All generalizations are inaccurate, says the historian, including this one. Other social scientists are trained to value parsimony—the idea that the simplest explanation is the best. Historians frustrate their colleagues in other disciplines by refusing to offer short or simple answers. Our best explanations for historical events weave a tapestry of causes, rooted in prior conditions and specific contexts. We insist on complexity, even at the cost of clarity (Gaddis 2002, 53–70).

So most historians mistrust simulations. We think the world, and human systems in particular, are too complex to be modeled in this way. We don't believe, as a rule, in social science's ability to predict the future. And we worry about what happens when states or policymakers put undue faith in reductive models and expect—or worse, try to force—the real world to conform.

Yet simulations have become an essential part of today's intellectual technology, a basic tool of modern business, politics, and foreign affairs. They are not likely to go away anytime soon. Catastrophic failures of models and simulations in the twentieth century—think of Soviet collectivization, or America's struggles in Vietnam—have not warned away twenty-first century policymakers, only fuelled demand for more elaborate simulations. "Washington is already SimCity," Paul Starr warned, in an essay about the influence of simulations on government policy written twenty years ago (Starr 1994). If we are all to live in SimCity, one goal for history education must be to hold the models up to reality, to point out all the ways the hex map is not the territory, to tell the stories of when and where the black boxes failed.

The Cure for Simulation Fever

Does this mean that wargames do not belong in the history classroom? On the contrary. It suggests a crucial role for them to play (and play is the operative word).

Media theorist Sherry Turkle (1997) has described two ways to respond to the spreading influence of simulations in our politics and culture, both unsatisfactory. Some treat simulations as oracles, blindly accepting their predictions and decrees. Others distrust them entirely, rejecting simulation out of hand. Games scholar Ian Bogost observes that many of us feel pulled toward both reactions simultaneously, a condition he calls "simulation fever" (Bogost 2006, 108–109). Both Turkle and Bogost call for a third response: the development of simulation literacy. We must become, and help our students to become, active and critical readers of this increasingly pervasive medium. "We come to written text with centuries-long habits of readership," Turkle writes (1997, 82). The habits she has in mind, Turkle adds, are the historians' classic heuristics for engaging with written sources, precisely the questions that history teachers teach their students to ask: "Who wrote these words, what is their message, why were they written, how are they situated in time and place, politically and socially?" One goal for education in the twenty-first century must be "to interrogate simulations in much the same spirit ... to develop habits of readership appropriate to a culture of simulation."

How do you interrogate a game? By playing it, and playing with it, critically and reflectively. You try out a strategy and see what happens. You take on a role, but only lightly. You fiddle with the inputs and watch the outputs. Then you back up, discard certain roles or assumptions, and play again. Eventually, you come to understand the rules of the simulation. Maybe you try to break them. Your failures become learning moments, as do the game's failures ("That phalanx sunk my battleship?!?"), exposing gaps between the simulation and your own understanding of the world.

This playful stance—neither hostile nor deferential, but creative, curious, actively seeking to learn and be amused—is crucial. Playing, we would argue, is a smarter and healthier thing to do with simulations than either submitting to them as oracles or rejecting them as lies. Certainly, it is wiser to play a game than to use it to dictate policy or plan a war. Play, as long as it is critical and reflective, is the cure for simulation fever. It is the first step toward simulation literacy.

Gaming Agency and Structure

So: games can teach simulation literacy. This is a good reason for making games part of the twenty-first century classroom, and it fits strongly with the goals of multiliteracies education. But it is not an especially strong case for using games in the *history* classroom. We still need to ask: which goals of history education can wargames or simulation games support?

Simulation games can engage some of history's fundamental questions, combining the cognitive skills emphasized by the history as disciplinary knowledge model with the civic dimensions of the history as citizenship approach. For instance, games and game design foreground the question of agency and structure, an issue that has been at the heart of historical thinking for more than a generation. Agency is a magic word for modern historians. It can be defined, loosely, as the capacity of individuals to make meaningful choices in their lives. Structure is agency's counterweight: everything which limits those choices or their significance. The great project of the "new social history" that emerged in the 1960s and 1970s was to uncover the agency of ordinary people. Where structure ends and agency begins has been a maelstrom of historical debate ever since (Johnson 2003).

Wargames can help teachers and students engage this debate. Agency as a concept is often slippery and abstract. But games make agency and structure explicit. The line between structure and agency is ultimately analogous to the line between a game's rules and the choices of its players. A top-down strategy game in which players command the movements of large armies and battalions, but roll morale checks to see whether individual units scatter or retreat, locates agency in a very different place than a first-person shooter in which players take the roles of individual soldiers following orders provided by a computer or prewritten scenario. Game designer Sid Meier once defined a game as "a series of interesting decisions." In a historical simulation game, the players take on the roles of those who made interesting decisions. The rules of the game define the structure that constrained those decisions. "Play can be defined as the tension between the rules of the game and the freedom to act within those rules," write Douglas Thomas and John Seely Brown (2011, 18). Play, in other words, explores the boundaries of agency and structure—and "the ability to make interesting decisions" is about as succinct a definition of historical agency as we are likely to find.

Thus, teachers can use games and game design to engage questions of historical agency in ways that are accessible and concrete. Who are the players in this game? Who were the historical actors in this conflict? What meaningful choices did they have? What could they control and not control? There are thought-provoking historical arguments embedded in the rules of all our games. Once, military history was largely a chronicle of grand strategies and campaigns. Generals and kings were the only actors believed to have real agency. Wargames adopted the same top-down perspective. Today, the most popular simulations of war are first-person video games, offering immersive identification with a single front-line combatant. Is it a coincidence that role-playing games grew out of 1:1 scale wargames in the 1970s (Peterson 2012), the very same years in which the new military history was discovering the agency of individual soldiers? Well, yes, probably. But it's still interesting.

Wargames are also sites for exploring and debating historical memory. As Andrew Wackerfuss reports in this volume, first-person video games set in World War II are common and extremely popular, but game designers have struggled to create similar games about World War I. Ted Raicer's chapter in this book makes a similar point regarding tabletop games, astutely attributing the difficulty to popular understandings of World War I as a long, static stalemate. Most of us do not believe that individual soldiers in the trenches of the Great War possessed the same kind of agency as their counterparts in World War II. That is a significant historical judgment embedded in game design. By contrast, almost all video games about the Vietnam War are first-person shooters. Top-down strategy games about Vietnam are rarely seen. This says much about the nature of that war and also, undoubtedly, about the influence of war movies on collective memory. A top-down perspective might seem appropriate for modeling the war in Vietnam, in which the United States military placed tremendous emphasis on strategic air power. But on film, the Vietnam War is almost exclusively depicted through images of infantrymen on foot patrol. And World War II, called the "Good War," seems amenable to gaming in almost every genre. What are the links between game design, historical agency, and our more generally positive memories of this war? Critical gameplay, and better yet, critical game design, would be a fascinating way for students to grapple with these issues.

Contingency and Causality

History also involves the study of contingency and causality. Almost every schema of historical thinking highlights these concepts as crucial yet difficult to teach. Here is another place where wargames and other simulations can play a helpful role. Though simulations inevitably simplify, they can still illustrate contingency and causality in a more vivid, dynamic way than most written texts. "Causality itself," argues evolutionary psychologist John Tooby, "is an evolved conceptual tool that simplifies, schematizes, and focuses our representation of situations" (2012, 34). Historical events always have multiple causes. Indeed, multiple layers of causality are acting and interacting at each and every moment. Yet we speak and write and even think as if historical events had only one or two identifiable causes. Why was there no socialism in the United States? What "caused" the First World War? The social scientist's search for independent variables is an extreme version of this, but historians' narratives must also highlight one or two knowable factors, or else become unreadable jumbles. We know our narratives are simplifications, but language and grammar make it difficult to express the true complexity of historical causation.

Simulations also simplify, but not as much—or at least, in different ways—than the written word. They are designed to model complex systems. Their procedures and algorithms build multiple layers of intersecting, interacting causality.[2] Their branching outcomes are contingency in action. As players become familiar with a simulation, they come to understand the interplay of factors it is modeling, often in a tacit way that is difficult to put into words. Jeremiah McCall makes the case: "a simulation can place students at the center of complex systems where a variety of variable factors ebb and flow simultaneously in ways that cannot readily be represented in other media" (2011, 13). This is a significant addition to the historian's toolbox: the ability to describe the past in a dynamic, multidimensional way that does not reduce the complexity of causation to a cartoon of single causes. It belongs in the history teacher's toolbox, too.

Conclusion

If all this sounds a little highfalutin for high school or middle school classrooms, that is because these things are difficult to put into words. Much of the learning that comes from play is tacit or unspoken. You can't tell people how to ride a bike or throw a football—you can try, but they won't learn until they actually do it again and again. Wargames and simulations may be less physical, yet their deepest lessons also lie beneath or beyond words. Spelled out in prose, these concepts sound abstruse. Through play and praxis they become clear.

This is why games in the classroom complement, but will not replace, reading, writing, and discussion. The things that games are good at teaching are the very things that written texts are not. There's no need to make a binary choice between games and books. Ideally, students using wargames in the history classroom will use written sources to critique and complement the games they play, and use games to do the same with the written works they read.

Of course, the games we play need not all be wargames. History teachers can make great use of simulation games about social movements, or global citizenship, or political economy. When those games do not exist, we can get our students to design them. Game design is a powerful and underexplored strategy for teaching and learning. But war will remain part of history, and as long as it does, there will be a place for wargames in the history classroom.

The key to using games effectively and appropriately in the history classroom is, ultimately, the same as using any other tool. We have to articulate what we are doing in the first place—not only asking "why games?" but also "why history?" Then we have to build outward from those goals, creating games and activities whose procedures are the kinds of critical thinking we want to cultivate, whose moving parts are historical ideas themselves.

About the Authors

Robert MacDougall is an associate professor of history at the University of Western Ontario and associate director of its Centre for American Studies. He studies the history of information, communication, and technology. He is the author of *The People's Network: The Political Economy of the Telephone in the Gilded Age* (2014). A longtime player and sometime designer of tabletop board and role-playing games, he is interested in all varieties of playful historical thinking.

Lisa Faden is Research Specialist and Education Coordinator at the University of Western Ontario's Centre for Education Research and Innovation. She taught high school history in US public schools for ten years before completing her doctorate in education, focusing on history education and representations of national identity in Canada and the United States. Her academic interests include history and professional education, critical pedagogy, and qualitative research methodology.

Notes

1. Even a book as thoughtful and worthwhile as Jeremiah McCall's *Gaming the Past* (2011)—by no means the kind of puffery we are satirizing here—frames its case for games in the history classroom as a set of "talking points" for use on nongaming skeptics (8–21). The assumption seems to be that there are gamers and there are nongamers, and that only the former, who already know they want to use games in the classroom, would ever read the book.

2. Tabletop wargames are no less algorithmic than computer games. As Matthew Kirschenbaum puts it, tabletop games "function as paper computers," with their quantitative model "embodied in cardboard and charts" and "materially exposed for inspection and analysis" (2009, 359–360). Philip Sabin agrees, and he makes a strong case for the value of tabletop games over computer games in classroom settings (Sabin 2012, 22–30; see also 2007).

38 THE AMATEUR DESIGNER: FOR FUN AND PROFIT

Charles Vasey

A work of art is never finished. It is merely abandoned.

—E. M. Forster

Style: The Designer as Dilettante

Professional wargame designers (manual or computer) labor at their desk day after day to earn a crust. But by far the greater proportion of recreational board game designers only do so in their spare time, often for little more than a hobby income. This division between journeyman (or artisan) and dilettante (or hobby) designer has profound effects on the way games are designed and which games are designed. I belong to the ranks of the Amateur Designer.

At the start of a design, the journeyman would be handed down a design task by his employers or commissioners, but most amateurs will select the topic themselves and then match it to the publisher later—resulting in many a stalled project and some dreadful games. The key here is the flow of incentives. The artisan designer designs for hire, albeit with the professional aim of doing a good job. The amateur designs because he likes the topic or game system, albeit with the aim of making a few quid sometime maybe. To some amateurs the sheer pleasure of appearing in print is enough (amateur Amateurs, as we might call them).

Because the key issues for the amateur are the topic and rules system, the range of amateur games is wide. They may clump around certain topics where a system or popular book inspires several designers, but they can also include many comparatively little-known topics or previously unconsidered treatments. For example, a visit to Boardgamegeek.com and a search for the word "Waterloo" brings us forty-seven games (and that is not all the games on the topic; some will not have the word in the title). The Battle of the Bulge or Kursk may similarly produce large numbers. However, the English Civil War yields but one named board game (though there are others, at least two of which were designed by me). The Russo-Polish War of 1920–22 has much fewer, and many are Polish.

One notable French designer has more than fifty games, but barely a French defeat among them. The amateur marches to the beat of a different drummer.

Since the chief input for the amateur designer is inspiration, the designs can cover a wide range of treatments, from History Lite (where a game system has some history sprayed onto it) to History Heavy (where a game is hacked out of a history book, often with lots of detail). The ludic treatment (that is, the play element) can contain a surprising amount of history, although often only if you agree with the interpretation of the designer, and the heavy treatment often results in the game being an adjunct to further reading rather than a frequently played item.

There is also my favorite kind: the Art House Game, in which the nature of the topic is brought out without the big budget. How does that differ from History Lite? Chiefly in increasing the history count without increasing the word count. To produce Art House requires one to know the topic well enough to reduce it to its basics—I discuss some of these techniques below—and to transmit that intellectual effort to the player/reader/user. One does this not just to appear dreadfully clever but because one has to interest the busy gamer in a topic he has not gamed before; he must therefore be persuaded into your web. Fortunately wargamers read large amounts of history and tend to have catholic tastes; there can be few topics that do not attract a number of interested parties. Cynically, of course, applying a patina of learning to one's games means they sell to those who like to appear learned, but they all count one way or the other. Additionally, the correct intellectual credentials can enhance the pleasure a gamer derives from the game. A simple game need not be simplistic but it better be prepared to demonstrate that it is not.

Given this interest in the new and the need to reduce history to a lovely thick sauce, the amateur designer can be a prey to topic drift. He may start designing Game A (at Scale A and Topic List A) only to realize that the subject demands not just, for example, a catalog of battles but a treatment of how the armies were raised for those battles. The designer plays other designs and reads more books. Time passes. There are no deadlines. Years become decades. The design is willed to the eldest son to complete. The designer has become Il Divo; he voyages rather than designs, hoping one day to reach the distant shore.

These amateur voyagers are a great irritation to gamers who Just Want The Game, but are a boon to all others as they spend both powder and blood in producing new methods and new insights. But only when they can. As each game struggles out of its long gestation I wonder how many more each designer will manage before the Grim Reaper turns up to help develop the last one. (I like a good laugh as much as the next man.)

Style: The Designer as Autodidact

One of the downsides of the amateur designer buoyed on the wings of inspiration is that he can be an Enthusiast. He loves his topic, he loves his books, he loves his rules, he loves the chrome and the extra set of cards. He loves the initial design, and the advanced version, and why not add a few more turns. The

Enthusiast enjoys one hour of the game and therefore believes he will enjoy two hours twice as much. Rather than face the difficult task of reducing all that detail to a viable system he may just add more details and "leave God to sort them out." After all, to some gamers a complex or detailed game may have more transferable intellectual value (giving a shiny patina of scholarship to its owners, like a large library) than a shorter game based on an inspired and rigorous analysis. "Never mind the quality, feel the width."

Even if our amateur designer can control his enthusiasms he is seldom a trained historian or skilled in forensic analysis of evidence. He is a self-trained amateur designer who is a self-trained amateur historian. We designers need to admit early on that our games do not cover the "Wars of Louis XIV" but the "Wars of Louis XIV as analyzed by Hatton, Lynn, Rowlands, Wilson, and Stoye." By admitting this we lift ourselves on the shoulders of giants.

After borrowing from historians we can then borrow freely from other designers. We get points not for innovation (though it is nice if that happens) but for exploiting innovation in interesting and appropriate ways.

Palette: We Paint Not Light but the Impression of Light

In the 1970s we all used the Avalon Hill Combat Results Table and one needed only three things: a map, an order of battle and factors for your unit. If you wanted to be different, you had more units and a bigger map. This pointillist approach still has its advocates, especially with the tech-heavy modern game. But I believe the Amateur Designer needs to consider more impressionistic approaches, remembering always that Seurat used pointillism as part of his neoimpressionist work—the two can meet at the extremes. The impressionist style of design recognizes (as noted above in connection with Art House Games) that with less popular topics one cannot overstay one's welcome or demand too much of the gamer: one must instead give them the core of the topic in a system that shows it off at its best and do so before the light changes. By doing this we also lift the gamer up from the task of forming every company and positioning every battery. We show them the battle from perhaps the elevation of Napoleon (both physically and hierarchically). We

also confound the tedious argument that we need not struggle to put realism into our games, since a game played in safety is inherently an unrealistic model of war; here we see that we are giving just the impression of war, perhaps placing the gamer at a key point and seeing how he handles this impression of the stress. Of course, in the search for the intellectual camouflage lots of detail may be helpful, but it carries a fearful cost. Pascal's remark that "I would have written a shorter letter, but I did not have the time" comes to our rescue.

All of this prompts us to the very hard point of how much reality or history is enough reality or history. The answer must depend on our subject and our audience: it is always a subjective answer, but I suggest that it should be sufficient to make the issues found in reading a good history book manifest in playing the game, yet not so much as to make a good hard puzzle become too much like real work. This intersection of pleasure and pain is a key design decision.

In my design *England Expects*, I wanted to show why France and Britain tussled over naval control: maritime trade. But equally the gamer wants to command fleets, not convoys. Accordingly I had to give the impression of trade. I lifted a general level of trade statistic across the period. I then lifted a rough measure of the size of the various merchant marines. I bodged the two together. The trade was the demand level the merchant fleets serviced, and the total trade you carried gave you victory points (it would generate excise income). Now after each turn (a year) one simply matched up demand to the remaining merchant fleets (after privateers and frigates have done their worst) and parceled out the trade to Britain, France and the neutrals. Unless

France could protect its merchantmen it began to lose its share of trade. But what's this? Those pesky Americans pinching their share of our trade! One began to understand the War of 1812. This process is fast but rewards the player who harries the enemy trade routes. It gives the impression of what was a long and detailed process—it takes us into their mindset.

At all times we Amateurs must remember, and take heart, from the principle so splendidly illustrated not by an impressionist but by a surrealist: when Rene Magritte painted a picture of a pipe in *The Treachery of Images*, he reminded us that "*Ceci n'est pas une pipe.*" Ours is a picture of war: "*Ceci n'est pas une guerre.*"

Palette: Puzzles, Patterns or Narrative—What Is Fun?

If our game is to include the impression of its topic it must yet also be a game—it must be ludic. But what does that mean? To some gamers, even those seeking a historical context, the game must provide equal chances of victory and those victories cannot be reached by a single vital piece of randomness (the lucky dice roll). Although not all gamers would state the model in those bald terms, there is sufficient truth there to apply to nearly all gamers. It is a matter of degree.

In this section's subheading I have suggested three types of gaming fun—a topic handled in greater detail by more exact minds than mine. We can present puzzles (how can Napoleon defeat Wellington), we can ask the gamer to identify patterns (one defeats an entrenched enemy by combining fire and movement) and we can present narrative (placing the gamer in the same place with the

same metadecisions as his heroes). In practice we will try all three, but it does seem to me that the order in which I have presented the three fits best the standard nonimpressionist game (the impressionist approach requires perhaps more narrative). It also strikes me that each method contains elements of the others, like a series of Venn diagrams. For the puzzle to work, it needs to have, I suggest, a historical answer.

Not all games require and not all gamers enjoy the more pared-back contest of, say, Go or chess. Wargaming must also cater for the gamer returning from a stressful job to play a game—a game, not just a contest. This means that the designer needs to place a number of bells to be rung to generate our Pavlovian response. There is a challenge certainly. There must also be some historical context. Wargaming and reading are closely related; the gamer expects to see certain factors present and suspension of disbelief will fail if they are missing. Some gamers (a large majority, I suspect) will want to see a game where both sides have an opportunity to move and attack. As with the Noble Art, ten rounds in which one boxer covers up followed by two rounds in which he wins makes for a contest of skill—and a dreadful spectacle. To return to the importance of institutionalizing intellectualism, the designer needs to make the winner feel he has won by being cleverer, not by being luckier.

The function of a good game is to celebrate the role of the smart-arse. Yet in so doing the designer must be careful that in being intellectually acceptable one must avoid being too overtly intellectual. The Anglo-Saxon world is perhaps alone in having phrases like "too clever by half." One must instead depend on the Shaker view: simple, yet elegant, with clean lines.

Palette: Armatures for the Working Day

The Amateur Designer faces constant demands on his time, and his design time must be hacked from his free time. Look for similarities. I suggest that he should therefore borrow from the work of others: OCR in a set of rules, and then adjust as you go. Start with their map and counters, then remeasure. There is no shame in this unless you stop before you have finished your design.

A typical design structure can be strengthened early on by not just seeking similarities. Compare and contrast is a powerful method to tweak your design. Why did Louis XIV not renounce the Spanish Will and avoid years of costly war? Were his judgments based on something other than your present victory conditions? If so, change your present victory conditions. If Plan A failed, what was Plan B? Marlborough wanted a coastal landing and a drive toward Paris. Might that have worked? Does your game allow it?

Making laws or sausages, said Bismarck, is something the public should not see. It is an interesting question whether gamers should see games in design. This is an important part of marketing your game, as the potential purchasers begin to savor your ideas. But are you giving away too much? Will the game's value be compromised? It could be, but by careful exposure of the historical ideas behind the design you can have the best of both worlds and the benefit of engaging with others who are passionate about that topic. They will share ideas with amazing freedom.

Rule one of Drafting Club is that there are no more rules in Drafting Club. The different styles of drafting rules all have advantages and disadvantages, often at the same time to different people. In general though, be careful about punctuation; lawyers often avoid its use with good reason. Commas particularly have an exciting and adventitious private life. Remember that the most difficult concept will have occupied your time the most; you may therefore forget how hard it was to grasp and not explain it in necessary detail. Do not hide rules in examples. Acquire two friends to review text: a Wrecker (someone whose joy is wrecking rules by being deliberately precise when you were not) and a Slow Fellow (someone who moves item by item without ever bounding ahead). They are of immense value.

The atelier for designers: All designers benefit from a team of friends and allies that provide skills:

knowledge of the game topic, of graphic design, a grasp of ergonomics, the ability to see if behind the analysis lies a game, and behind the game lies history. Then there are the unsung foot soldiers of design: the playtesters. May you be blessed with good ones.

Palette: The Storyboard and the Spreadsheet (and What Ifs)

There is no more powerful tool in building your design into a model that speaks to historical fact than the storyboard. I use this term to cover a series of events recorded to give the pace and pattern of the original topic. Just as a film director blocks out the scenes in advance to arrange his shooting schedule, so we record them in retrospect to understand the rhythm of war. For us a storyboard is a breakdown of historical events in game terms based on turn length and map scale (and any other measure that you consider of value). This will test the relationships between time and space: movement values and terrain features. It will indicate whether all your units are in motion at one time, or whether only some; this in turn may indicate a limited number of key "movers and shakers"—a consideration in modeling command. If your game can fit the storyboard then you are on the right track. Of course, you do not want it to be unable to deviate from the storyboard, but the player will demand some relationship between the two.

There can be no easier method of building a storyboard than good old Microsoft Excel with its ability to add columns and rows and sort and resort them as you work into your historical texts. I might, for example, decide to do a storyboard on British Naval operations. I might start with a series of fleet positions at various dates, drawn from an academic work. I would record this to give me not only the raw number of vessels, but their stations and their size

(how large a fleet could be maintained away from major bases). I might notice over time that never more than X vessels operated out of Y. This will give me a view as to the logistic capability of that area. My columns might be dates, my rows locations (ports or stations) and the cell data might be numbers of ships. As I notice key changes, I might highlight the cell and direct my research there. If I suddenly decide to add a station, I simply insert a row. This spreadsheet flexibility can be vital if, for example, you started your storyboard on the basis of monthly turns and then decide to move toward seasonal turns. Try doing that with a notebook and pencil! Be prepared to accept such changes as, for example, your initial geographical divisions may not fit the actual movement of the historical armies.

The storyboard can also point you toward the useful concern about who your players represent. In a Napoleonic game one player often represents the coalitions against Napoleon. One might term him "Britain" and allow him access to other states as they become available. Or one might go for a multiplayer solution, for which see Mark McLaughlin's *The Napoleonic Wars* (2002). Recently, working on a game on Louis XIV (*The Sun King*), I had assigned the role of opponent to the Maritime Powers (the uneasy alliance of the Netherlands and England, starting with William and Mary). But from 1672 to 1688 England was either a secret or active ally of Louis, and until 1672 the Netherlands, while uneasy about French strength, was neutral. So perhaps his enemy was the Austrian Habsburgs, yet although there was no love lost they avoided active combat for a long time, keeping their eyes on the Ottomans. Can one really have a player who is actually playing another game at the same time? Perhaps Spain (the target of Louis's attempts to recover his wife's lands) was the best opponent, yet it was pretty much powerless militarily and not the center of any form of diplomatic initiative—it was too passive for the role. Perhaps the role was a "spirit of the age" where various states periodically opposed the Sun King (encouraged by the inveterate Louis hater Francois Lisola). In the end, the storyboard told me one thing: there was no second player; it had to be a solitaire game.

Once your model is working, you can consider the degree to which you can provide for counterfactuals (events that did not happen but might have). Some degree of counterfactuality will exist in all games that are not replays of the historical events. Battles that were lost may be won, fortresses that were held may fall; you need to be able to consider at least first-degree counterfactuals. Where counterfactuals occur you will need to consider what alternative resources were available to the actors at the time. Such features as alternative leaders, alternative supply points, alternative funding levels and sources may all be needed. The difficulties with counterfactuals arise when one pushes out from the first-degree counterfactual. I can suggest that if Carlos II of Spain had died in the 1670s, then his illegitimate half-brother Don Juan José de Austria might become king, thus neatly forestalling a Spanish succession crisis. But since Don Juan José died in 1679, this prompts one to wonder who his successor might have been (a second-degree counterfactual). With each diversion a chain of new possibilities open up, all of which you will need to consider. Fortunately, in some cases the counterfactual might have reverted back toward the factual if the original had a strong enough imperative; this might save you valuable time. It could also keep your game in that difficult zone beyond actual events, but not too far beyond them.

Conclusion

My title is "Fun and Profit." By using these techniques, I believe one can produce a game that others will want to play and which will carry something of the historical spirit that first interested you. I believe that that process need not be unremitting slog and that the journey can be as much fun as the destination. Good hunting!

About the Author

Charles Vasey is the designer of *Chariotlords*, *Flowers of the Forest*, and *Unhappy King Charles!* among other wargames. He practices as a chartered accountant via his firm Charles Vasey & Co. and, between 1972 and 2005, regularly reviewed for *Military Modeling* magazine in the UK and was the publisher and editor of *Perfidious Albion* magazine.

39 STRUGGLING WITH DEEP PLAY: UTILIZING *TWILIGHT STRUGGLE* FOR HISTORICAL INQUIRY

Jeremy Antley

Clifford Geertz suggests in *Deep Play: Notes on the Balinese Cockfight* that the role of cockfighting in Balinese culture mirrors the role *Macbeth* holds and continues to play for Western audiences: namely, that we each see in these art forms what a respective culture's "ethos and private sensibility ... look like when spelled out externally in a collective text" (1972, 449) That a cockfight or *Macbeth* can play such an important role in establishing and displaying cultural sensibilities is due to their inherent magnetic power that pulls together the values, contradictions, and viewpoints intersecting those sensibilities. The collective and connective text embodied through ritualized expression, as seen in a Balinese cockfight or the dramatic recreation of *Macbeth*, actively places those sensibilities on display and in doing so helps maintain those sensibilities within that cultural group.

It is not a stretch, then, to suggest that what Geertz found to be the complex cultural associations tied to the idea of deep play can be carried over to another cultural form, wargames. Many disciplines embrace the study of games, of which wargames are only a subgenre, while some, like history, are only just beginning to sketch out a methodology sufficient to interact with games as source materials (Antley 2012;

Christiansen 2013; Sabin 2012). These efforts are important because games, and especially wargames, blend together textual, material, and procedural elements in order to situate themselves along the cultural axis of the society they reflect. Their absence in more mainstream historical inquiry is something that can and should be rectified.

Identifying potential stumbling blocks for the meaningful integration of games into historical thinking reveals two lines of argumentation. The first, which relates to counterfactual thinking facilitated by games, strikes at the heart of what history holds dear at an epistemological level. Some feel that counterfactuals found in games dabble too much in conjecture, clouding accurate comprehension of historical events and/or eating up precious classroom time for too little gain. The second, which states that games give players too much interpretative authority, calls into question the pedagogical role of the instructor. With their emphasis on the player as producer of knowledge, games undercut the instructor's authority as a gatekeeper of interpretation.

In an article on counterfactual thinking inspired by the computer game *Europa Universalis II*, Tom Apperley roundly condemns both arguments. He suggests that the presence of coherent chronological narratives in historical thinking imposes "a notion of teleological inevitability that fails to acknowledge past contingencies" (2014, 188–89). Acknowledgment of the counterfactual potential, Apperley states, "allow[s] people to imagine a different world where strange and unfamiliar mappings and trajectories of time and space have been produced. This allows the 'what-if' to challenge deeply held certainties, and opens the historical dynamics of power to question" (190). Indeed games, and especially wargames, allow "thinking with history," as Carl Schorske put it, "linking or dissolving static elements in a narrative pattern of change" (1998, 3) The reason for this is simple: wargames are synthesized reflections of the past situated in the present mindset of their creation.

Recognition that games form a particular and distinct collection of cultural ethea suggests that we investigate *how* games situate themselves along the culture of the community that feeds and sustains such ethea. Games, and especially wargames, utilize three axes in their presentation and play: material, textual, and procedural. Examining a popular wargame that centers on a period (the Cold War) still alive in recent memory, GMT's *Twilight Struggle* (2004), demonstrates how these three axes interact and combine within the form of the wargame to create a cultural reflection of the event portrayed.

Twilight Struggle is a two-player wargame depicting the hegemonic battle for global influence between the United States of America and the Soviet Union during the period from the end of the Second World War to the fall of communism in Russia and East Central Europe in 1989–90. Over the course of ten turns, subdivided into three distinct eras (Early War, Middle War, Late War), players are dealt hands of cards that are used either to re-create famous events of the Cold War or to place influence points among countries grouped into geopolitical regions. To win, players must capitalize on the play of region-specific scoring cards that are interspersed in *Twilight Struggle's* deck. These scoring cards act like a snapshot, documenting the hegemonic saturation each side possesses in that region; the higher the level of control, the more victory points are awarded to the player. Once a player reaches twenty victory points, the game ends with an ideological victory for that superpower.

Twilight Struggle also includes separate "Defcon" and "Military Ops" tracks that measure aggressive actions undertaken by each superpower. Players can attempt to remove an opponent's influence in a country by conducting coups that add points to the Military Ops track, or they can engage in less hostile realignment efforts that do not provide military ops points. Failure to maintain a certain level of military ops awards victory points to one's opponent at the end of each turn, making coups a destabilizing yet necessary activity each side must undertake. As the Cold War "heats up," either through coups or the play of events, the Defcon meter degrades and prohibits further coups/realignments in certain geopolitical regions; Defcon Four, for example, restricts activity in Europe, while Defcon Three and Two restrict activity in Asia and the Middle East respectively. If a player's action reduces Defcon to level One, the game immediately ends in nuclear war.

While this is a rather simple description of how *Twilight Struggle* operates, it nonetheless conveys the outlines of an argumentative position embodied in its mechanic design. Players win by convincing nation-states to embrace their ideology. Geopolitical regions open up as the game turns progress into the Middle and Late War periods, mimicking the historical development of events in which Africa, and later Central/South America, became increasingly important. Nuclear tensions rise and certain regions become off-limits as the result of increased global aggression and meddling via coup attempts. With little more than cards, a map, and some relatively simple feedback mechanics, *Twilight Struggle* manages to distill the zeitgeist of the Cold War.

Traditional historical methodology, however, is almost at a loss when interpreting *Twilight Struggle* as a reflective Cold War artifact. Breaking down the various elements of *Twilight Struggle* along the three axes mentioned above—textual, material, and procedural—is a progressive step toward building a methodological bridge between wargames and the discipline of history.

To begin, let's examine the textual axis. Wargames represent some of the most complex textual artifacts found today, their rules ranging from a few simple pages, as with the solitaire game *We Must Tell the Emperor* (2010), to literally a binder full of paper in the case of *Advanced Squad Leader* (1985). *Twilight Struggle* hits the sweet spot for wargames of medium complexity, with a rulebook totaling a mere eleven pages. While full of content that can be classified as strictly procedural, rulebooks for wargames often include designer notes and historical background on the materials used in the game. Designer notes are especially useful for the historian because they serve as a thesis presentation regarding the wargame's purpose and design.

The designer's notes for *Twilight Struggle* contain several informative nuggets of perspective. The game's designers, Ananda Gupta and Jason Matthews (see the deluxe edition, 2009), write about the influence of previous card-driven games like *We the People* (1994) or *Paths of Glory* (1999) upon their own game,

cluing readers in on the ludic historiography that formed the backbone of their design decisions. Gupta and Matthews also note the influence of electronic games like Chris Crawford's PC game *Balance of Power* (1985), on their decision to make nuclear war, a constant and often accepted threat in older Cold War games, a fail state that immediately ends the game. While other games carved out ludic space for nuclear exchange, *Twilight Struggle* clearly moves away from this horrendous possibility and states directly that such an outcome is anathema to the desired win state of the game. This ties into the larger question of the point of view of *Twilight Struggle*, something detailed in the designer's notes:

> *Twilight Struggle* basically accepts all of the internal logic of the Cold War as true—even those parts of it that are demonstrably false. ... Not only does the domino theory work, it is a prerequisite for extending influence into a region. Historians would rightly dispute all of these assumptions, but in keeping with the design philosophy, we think they make a better game. (*Deluxe Edition* rule book 2009, 31)

While opponents of counterfactual thinking are likely to read this and declare *Twilight Struggle* to be full of gross inaccuracies, it must be remembered that ideas like the domino theory and even the value of a limited nuclear exchange once held cachet among intellectuals, politicians, and military planners. Historians would not dismiss a period source that advocated these ideas outright; they would instead bring those materials into a larger synthesis that critiques these ideas. Therefore, finding these elements overtly stated in the designer's notes provides the historian another avenue to ask *why* these ideas were so popular and *why* they continue to capture a share of popular understanding today.

Beyond rulebooks and designer's notes, another source of textual materials for wargames are online forum posts. As of September 2014, the two largest online forums are Boardgamegeek and Consimworld; here one can find player questions on rules and designer insights on game mechanics not covered in the rule book notes, as well as rules/design suggestions to correct perceived imbalances or inauthentic results derived from various games' procedural play styles. Forums allow the text of the game to interact with the text of the players, yielding collisions of interest and interpretation. They reveal the nature of the player as much as the nature of the game discussed, and for this reason forum threads are an invaluable source with which to judge the *vox populi* surrounding not just the game but the sensibilities and cultural ethos built into the game as well.

One such Consimworld thread demonstrates how forum posts manage to blend questions over game mechanics with rationales that go beyond the purely mechanical. Created on June 19, 2004, this *Twilight Struggle* forum <http://talk.consimworld.com/WebX?14@@.1dcfda60> currently boasts over 14,000 posts. Early, prerelease topics tended to focus on specific mechanics within *Twilight Struggle* and how closely they tracked with historical events or methods of superpower intervention. This was especially true for the question of how *Twilight Struggle* handled both conventional and proxy wars between the United States and the Soviet Union. "There is no system for handling open non-nuclear warfare between the superpowers," wrote codesigner Ananda Gupta. Wars in *Twilight Struggle* would be modeled using event cards, not independent design systems. The decision to exclude a conventional war option was simple: "Basically we divided into two cases: either the superpowers are waging proxy wars

or they blow up the world" (forum post 27, July 6, 2004).

Not everyone was satisfied with Gupta's rationale. One forum user expressed concern that players could not engage in direct conflicts outside of those dictated by card events (Johnson 2004). His suggestion was to make proxy/conventional wars into a specific game system and replace the war cards in the event deck with alt-history variations. Another user commented that "wars sound so luck-dependent," before adding that a more robust system utilizing covert political markers "would seem less abstract ... than fulfilling a certain number of mil ops each turn" (forum post 113, July 14, 2004). Gupta responded first, noting that both he and Matthews tried out various mechanical systems allowing the players to engage in proxy wars but that this yielded "wild ahistoricity" (forum post 86, July 4, 2004). Matthews (forum post 114, July 14, 2004) asserted that proxy wars rarely came down to levels of superpower involvement, as success lay in other factors such as troop quality and local conditions. Ultimately, he concluded, "*Twilight Struggle* ... really does focus on the core nature of the Cold War—a political struggle that held the threat of world-consuming violence in its back pocket."

Many similar threads concerning the intersection between game design and the fidelity to—or possible variance from—the historical record exist in the larger forum corpus. What the above selection demonstrates is that wargames are a natural conduit of Geertz's "deep play,'" a nexus through which questions of design and the expression of an ethos blend together. While some questioned the premise of a Cold War game lacking robust military components, Matthews and Gupta pushed back and made a case for why their political-themed focus precluded more jingoistic elements. Online forums create for wargames more than just an argumentative space; they foster an analytical space that blends popular sensibility and point of view into design critique and exploration.

The various components of *Twilight Struggle*, which exemplify the material axis in wargames, provide yet another blended space to examine. *Twilight Struggle* is a tour de force of material culture, the various components assaulting players' visual and emotional senses through evocative design. Even in static isolation, the game components used in *Twilight Struggle* convey associative meanings set among Cold War sensibilities and ethea. These components are of two sorts: the event cards held by the players, and the game map upon which those cards and players interact.

Event cards combine images from popular period media or news reports with procedural game text in a mutually reinforcing, symbiotic manner. "Blockade," for example, is a Soviet-themed Early War card that represents the attempted 1948 blockade of West Berlin by the West, while "Marshal Plan" is a US-themed Early War card that provides game effects (specifically, the free placement of US influence in Western Europe) indicative of its namesake. Neutral Events, like "Olympic Games," are assumed not to be inherently advantageous to either player. The increasing prominence and role of China during the Cold War is abstractly modeled through the use of a specific "China card." The USSR begins the game in possession of the China card, but once it is used for operations (such as placing influence or conducting coups/realignments) the Soviet player must pass the card to the US player. This player in turn must pass the card back to the Soviet player once it is used, and so forth.

Mechanically, the use of cards as the primary driver of action on the board provides players with the sense of watching actual Cold War events unfold, in addition to the tension of not quite knowing what the other superpower is capable of playing. Thematically, the cards combine images with game text that play with sensibilities related to Cold War reflection—albeit in often quite nostalgic terms. The most obvious example is the "Duck and Cover" card, featuring an image of Bert the Turtle, the iconic character from a 1951 civil defense film shown in US schools across the country. Selection of card imagery, in addition to the pairing of an event to a procedural game effect, projects tremendous associative power which, if done successfully, draws upon the theme of the game even as it reinforces it. In the case of *Twilight Struggle*, the use of event cards lets players create a fleshed-out narrative with minimal active prompts.

The other prominent component of *Twilight Struggle*, the game board, also utilizes associative imagery and design to promote player immersion. As what is perhaps the primary component of many games, the board must serve two roles. First, it should act as a functional display of the game's operation, and second, it should draw the player into the larger theme through use of aesthetic elements.

Countries, in a literal embodiment of the Cold War theory, form domino-shaped spaces linked together like a spider web across a geopolitical map. Framing the geopolitical map are various tracks measuring abstracted game systems. The Space Race is one such track, containing milestones such as launching an Earth satellite or achieving lunar orbit, and the turn track, depicting famous US and Soviet leaders, is another. Victory Points, Military Ops, and the Defcon tracks can be found on the bottom half of the board. Even here little design cues pull players into a Cold War mindset. The Defcon meter goes from "5" to an ominous mushroom cloud where we would expect to

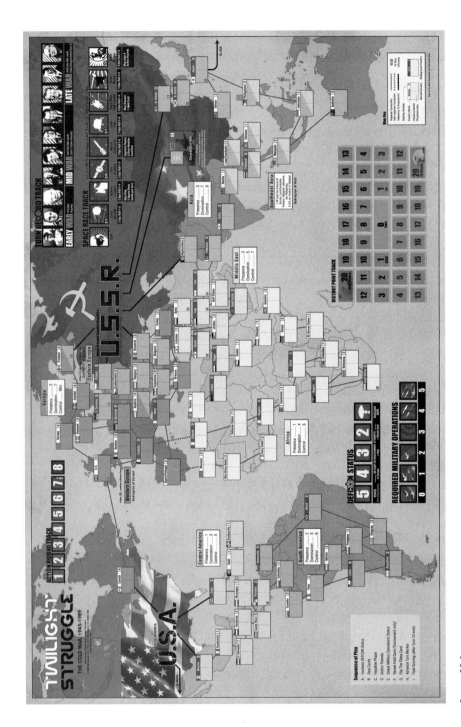

Figure 39.1

Twilight Struggle map.

find the "1." The Victory Points track shifts from a dark red shade at –20 VPs, indicating a Soviet victory, to a dark blue shade at +20 VPs, indicating a US victory, with the intervening numbers taking on reduced gradients that eventually coalesce into a blend at the "0" mark.

Taken together, the board and event cards create a materialistic, skeletal frame upon which the player-driven construction of narrative can attach and mold itself. While *Twilight Struggle* is at its core an area control game, what sets it apart from being marked as a *Risk* clone is the combined effect of material aesthetics and design mechanics meant to embrace a particular point of view tied to the Cold War zeitgeist. Invocation of famous events on the cards or a map portraying "domino" countries provides players of *Twilight Struggle* with narrative cues to frame and contextualize their play. These cues also suggest that while analyzing the material culture of wargames provides a thoroughly satisfying examination on its own merit, the nuances of wargame design cannot be appreciated without actually *playing* the game in question. This leads us to the final axis to be discussed: the procedural.

Ian Bogost, in his work *Persuasive Games: The Expressive Power of Videogames* (2007), establishes the concept of procedural rhetoric, or the way in which procedural, rule-based representations produce their own sort of rhetorical persuasion aimed at the player. Even though Bogost's analysis focuses on video games, the ideas presented are easily ported over to the rule-based procedure found at the heart of tabletop wargames. While video games handle complex operations or calculations thanks to a dedicated processor, tabletop wargames utilize abstracted systems in order to make the larger design both playable and representative of the desired effect. In *Twilight Struggle*, design mechanisms involving event cards, coups, Defcon degradation, and even the progression through game turns could all be interpreted through a pure textual reading of their procedure and effects, yet only when these mechanisms become kinetic—when they are actually brought about through the process of play—can an observer truly *feel* their combined effects.

Many reviewers of *Twilight Struggle* note how the game actively re-creates a sense of tension assumed to be inherent in the Cold War period. Much of this is due to interlocking design systems creating feedback for the players to act upon. The use of event cards provides players with hidden information and gives each one a sense of foreboding, of not knowing what the other superpower is capable of executing. It is a viable strategy, for instance, to drive the Defcon as low as possible, as high-level tensions ironically make the actions of your opponent somewhat more predictable given the restrictions imposed by the Defcon meter. Many of the interlocking design mechanisms of *Twilight Struggle* produce a reinforcing game theory effect upon play, reflecting theories prevalent in other Cold War cultural artifacts, such as novels (Belletto 2011). It is only through examination of the actual play of the game that one can observe and critique the procedural rhetoric embodied throughout the entire design.

Take the idea of domino theory being embedded in both the map and rules design. Since players may only place influence in countries connected to those already possessing some of their influence, an actual domino effect occurs, whereby the failure to check an opponent's progress in one country can allow them to spread their influence throughout a region. The China card is a highly abstracted method of representing the Communist state, yet its high value (and increased worth if used in Asia) allows the game mechanic to take on narrative weight; since the China card must be passed to your opponent after play, careful timing of its use means that the card, and by extension the subject of the card, takes on enhanced prominence.

Perhaps of most interest is the way the card-hand mechanic, in which players are dealt fresh hands of cards each turn and then play them in alternating fashion, echoes strategic thinking of the period that centered on insights derived from game theory. Players must strategize not only the play of their own hand but also all possible reactions arising from what their opponent might play.

There are alternative ways one can come to terms with procedural rhetoric without actually engaging in play, such as watching tutorial or "Let's Play" videos, and while these methods are superior to a strictly textual or material analysis, they pale in comparison to actual play. In relation to the textual or material, the procedural axis is the least tangible in terms of static analysis. When engaged in the act of play, however, the procedural becomes the most expressive axis felt by the player. While the material and textual provide the boundaries and accouterments of a game, the procedural is what elevates these passive forces into active elements that combine and facilitate the act of "deep play." For *Twilight Struggle*, the procedural axis is essentially the active embodiment of the sensibilities and ethos built into the textual and material elements purporting to represent the Cold War.

Returning to Geertz's analysis, parallels between what he identified as deep play and the three interpretive axes of wargames—textual, material, and procedural—suggest that there is more involved with the play of wargames than might otherwise get credit. As the analysis of *Twilight Struggle* demonstrates, there are many cultural and argumentative threads intertwined among the materials, rules, and actual play of the Cold War game. While not purely a textual source, *Twilight Struggle* does, like many wargames, embrace textuality. Yet it does so in a context that foregrounds and backgrounds that textuality against a synthesized view of the past constructed through procedural and material frameworks. It is, in effect, both a secondary source about Cold War history and a primary source about modern reflections on the Cold War experience. Because of this, *Twilight Struggle*, and by extension the wargame genre as a whole, holds tremendous promise as an investigative source for use in historical scholarship and pedagogy.

About the Author

Jeremy Antley is a doctoral student of history at the University of Kansas, currently finishing his dissertation on the immigration of Russian Old Believers to Oregon in the early 1960s. With an avid passion for both criticism and games, Jeremy has written on diverse subjects ranging from the moral implications of playing a drone strike card game to modern narratives of progress encoded in medieval settings found in fantasy games like *Skyrim*. His writing can be found on his own site, Peasant Muse, and at Play the Past, a site featuring investigations of games and culture.

Alexander H. Levis and Robert J. Elder

The Global 2000 Wargame

The Global wargame has been held annually at the US Naval War College in Newport, Rhode Island, since 1979 (Hay and Gile 1993; Gile 2004). It serves a multitude of purposes, primarily as "an opportunity to investigate ideas and concepts that may vary from current strategy or policy wisdom" (Hay and Gile 1993). The Global wargame, the largest annual wargame run by the US Navy, is at the flag-officer level and challenges the participants with complex scenarios for which there are no easily identified effective courses of action.

Exercising effective Command and Control (C2) has always been, and will always be, a challenging undertaking, as proven by the degree of training and experience necessary to conduct it successfully. However, even well-trained officers are facing new challenges as the scope of military operations has expanded into operations other than conventional war. The overall mission success may well hinge on a combined set of military, political, and social objectives. The focus of the Global 2000 wargame was the exploration of netcentric operations, that is, the military activities undertaken by forces that are thoroughly interconnected (or netted) (Watman 2001) so that information sharing and collaborative processes are enabled.

The Global 2000 wargame of August 14–25, 2000, included about six hundred participants (invited players, military from all services, civilians, guests, and gaming staff). The players were organized into several groupings: Blue represented the United States, Brown represented an ally of the United States, Red was the adversary, and Green was the adjudicating team. The teams were given a challenging problem and they had to develop suitable campaigns to address it. The game was structured in three phases. At the beginning of each phase, the Green team described the then-prevailing geopolitical and military situation. The Blue, Brown, and Red teams would then develop their courses of action and make their moves. On the morning of each day of a particular phase, the consequences of the moves of the previous day would be announced and the current situation described. The teams would then work on their next move. The process was repeated each day until all three phases were carried out. At the conclusion of the game there was a plenary session where the issues and the approaches were discussed and lessons from the game noted.

The command structure used by the Blue team in Global 2000 consisted of a Coalition Joint Task Force and several subordinate component commands. A Blue's Red Assessment Cell (BRAC) supported the command structure; it consisted of intelligence analysts and subject matter experts. The BRAC provided the Blue Commander with assessments of possible or probable Red reactions to Blue's actions. These possible reactions spanned a wide spectrum of areas other than purely military, although, as the wargame progressed, the focus narrowed to essentially purely military operations. The process for utilizing the BRAC was as follows: the Commander and his immediate staff would issue "Inquiries" to the BRAC on a particular topic each day during the early morning briefings, and the BRAC would prepare responsive reports ("assessments") in a timely manner—before noon of the same day. The output of the BRAC provided to the Commander and his staff had a very concise format and content, usually not more than one page long. These reports were reviewed by the BRAC chief and others prior to their release; they were then disseminated throughout the command structure via the Global game's intranet and other mechanisms. The intent of the assessments was to transmit findings and recommendations succinctly and directly, since the workload at the higher levels of command precluded an in-depth review of lower-level products.

The team from the System Architectures Laboratory of George Mason University was assigned to support the BRAC through modeling, simulation, and analysis. The initial inputs to the modeling suite used were the Desired Effects (or move outcomes), the Candidate Actions (or tasks to be undertaken during the move), and timing information. A suite of models was used to develop, analyze, and evaluate alternative Courses of Action (COAs), a timed sequence of coordinated tasks. The results were used by the staff as the basis for recommending specific candidate COAs to the Blue Commander.

In addition to the use of models, a formal representation of the wargame's operational or functional view of its architecture was developed. The Commander of the Blue forces had several Component Commands under him as well as several other standard staff offices, including Intelligence (see figure 40.1). The BRAC, which was responsible for trying to think like the adversary and suggest or predict possible or probable Red reactions to Blue actions, was a unique feature of Global 2000.

Figure 40.2 illustrates the information flow between the organizational elements. A basic Command Node (say Blue), consisting of a Commander and his Subordinates (i.e., the Command Staff of Blue), is responsible to the Higher Authority (HA), and has a set of Resources that it commands.

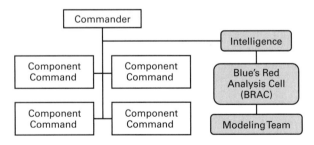

Figure 40.1

A partial representation of Blue's Command structure.

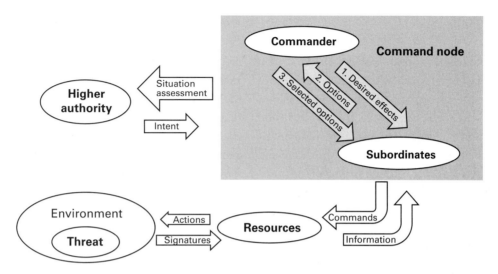

Figure 40.2

Operational Node connectivity description.

The Resources interact with the Threat (say Red) within the Environment as defined by the scenario. Resources can both act against the Threat as well as gather information about the Threat and the Environment. It is only through the Resources that the Command Node can gather any information about the Threat and the Environment and can only act on the Environment/Threat through commands sent to its Resources.

Participation of the System Architectures laboratory team in Global 2000 provided an invaluable opportunity to test the theories, tools, and techniques of using multiple models (see the following section) in an operationally realistic environment and led to a research program on multimodeling and metamodeling, discussed later in this chapter.

Several observations were made and lessons were learned from that experience, among them these two: (1) The multimodeling capability was used by the command staff as a primary tool for developing and/or evaluating proposed courses of action. The results were of significant utility in three different analyses conducted before and during the Global wargame. (2) The information needed for the execution of the models was primarily derived through interaction with Intelligence analysts and/or subject matter experts, not only in the BRAC but also from game participants and invited guests in general. This was a labor-intensive process but was doable in a timely manner. Current technology-enabled information sharing capabilities make this task much easier and faster.

Modeling Challenges

No single model can capture the complexities of a multiperson wargame such as the Global wargame of the Navy or the corresponding Unified Engagement wargame of the Air Force, in which individuals and groups play diverse roles. The games include multiple teams that are organized in different ways and interact with each other through formal procedures. When multiple models are used, often expressed in different modeling languages, to capture and support different aspects of a wargame, it often becomes necessary to have these models interoperate. However, each modeling language, while it offers unique insights, also makes specific assumptions about the domain being modeled. For example, social networks (Carley 1999) describe the interactions (and linkages) among group members but say little about the underlying organization and/or command structure. Similarly, organization models (Levis 2005) focus on the structure of the organization and the prescribed interactions such as the chain of command but say little about the social/behavioral aspects of the members of the organization. Timed Influence net models (Wagenhals and Levis 2007; Mansoor et al. 2009), a variant of Bayesian net models, describe cause-and-effect relationships and can be used to assess the decisions made and the courses of action that were executed during the wargame but say little about the decision makers and operators themselves.

In order to address the modeling and simulation issues that arise when multiple models are to interoperate, four layers need to be addressed. The lowest layer, the Physical one (i.e., hardware and software) is a platform that enables the concurrent execution of multiple models expressed in different modeling languages and provides the ability to exchange data and also to schedule the events across the different models. The second layer is the Syntactic layer, which ascertains that the right data are exchanged among the models. The Physical and Syntactic layers have been addressed through such developments as the C2 Wind Tunnel (C2WT) (Hemingway et al. 2011; Karsai et al. 2004) by Vanderbilt University in collaboration with UC Berkeley and George Mason University. (It was so named in reference to the physical wind tunnels used by aeronautical engineers, in which scaled models of aircraft and other aerodynamic surfaces are tested.) The C2WT is an integrated, multimodeling simulation environment. Its framework uses a discrete event model of computation as the common semantic framework for the precise integration of an extensible range of simulation engines, using the Run-Time Infrastructure (RTI) of the High Level Architecture (HLA) platform. The C2WT offers a general solution for multimodel simulation by decomposing the problem into a model integration task and an experiment or simulation integration task. The specific model federates (the different modeling languages) implemented in an instantiation of the C2WT depend on the domain. Some domains in which the C2WT has been used are discrete piece manufacturing, surveillance, and reconnaissance, as well as wargaming. The specific models used depend on the application being studied.

Once the technical means to execute concurrently interoperating models expressed in different modeling languages is achieved, a third problem needs to be addressed at the third (Semantic) layer, where the interoperation of different models is examined to ensure that conflicting assumptions in different modeling languages are recognized and form constraints to the exchange of data. In the top layer, the Workflow layer, valid combinations of interoperating models are considered to address specific issues. Different issues require different workflows and may also require domain-specific workflow modeling languages (Levis and Jbara 2013). The use of multiple interoperating models is referred to as multimodeling (or multiformalism modeling), while the analysis of the validity of model interoperation is referred to as metamodeling. Such an approach has been used since the mid-1990s to model a wargame as it is being designed in order to explore the possible outcomes of potential courses of action and at best compute the probability that a certain outcome will occur; it has been used to explore the different outcomes and not to predict what outcome will occur. It has also been used, in the same wargames, to conduct real-time analyses and explorations of the decisions made and actions taken during the wargame.

Multimodeling

Current military operations need, and future operations will demand, the capability to understand the human terrain and the various dimensions of human behavior within it. Behaviors in the human terrain context extend across the spectrum from adversaries to noncombatant populations, to coalition partners, and to government and nongovernment organizations. As the type of missions that current and future commanders must address has expanded well beyond those of traditional major theater combat operations, the need to broaden the focus of models that support planning and operations has become critical. Actions taken by all agents, together with the beliefs, perceptions, intentions, and actions of the people involved in an area of operations interact to affect the outcome of a coalition operation, a disaster relief plan, and/or a peacekeeping effort. No single set of models and tools can support the operational commander addressing the challenges of conducting nonconventional warfare missions. For example, while there are many models using diverse databases, none can address the complexities of coordinating kinetic and nonkinetic operations (e.g., Information Operations) when the adversary is embedded within a complex noncombatant population. The realization that operations take place in a contested cyber environment has made the concurrent use of interoperating models even more necessary.

In the last fifteen years, a suite of modeling tools has been developed at the System Architectures Laboratory of George Mason University and the Center for Computational Analysis of Social and Organizational Systems of Carnegie Mellon University that addresses different aspects of modeling the development, evaluation, and execution of courses of action. These tools enable the consideration of integrated kinetic and nonkinetic actions in diverse environments. A subset of the currently available suite of tools, shown in figure 40.3, has been used to support different wargames.

Caesar III (Levis et al. 2008) is a tool used to model and analyze the organizational structures of Blue as well as adversary forces. It has an interface

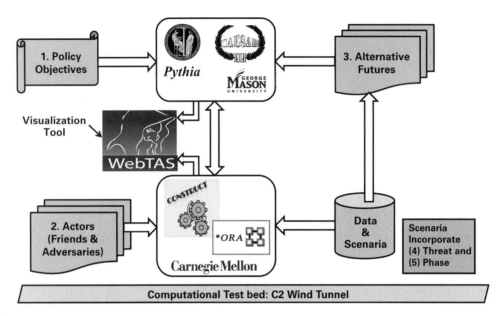

Figure 40.3
Modeling tools using different modeling languages applied to wargame design.

that allows the user to define the organization members and graphically specify their interactions: whether they receive and share information and whether they issue or receive commands that restrict their options for action. Behind this graphical modeling interface is a Colored Petri Net engine (CPN Tools) (Jensen and Kristensen 2009) that generates and executes a discrete event dynamical system model. The Timed Influence Net application Pythia (Mansoor et al. 2009) is used to develop Courses of Action and compare their outcomes. Timed Influence Nets are a special form of Bayesian nets that model cause-effect relationships where the link between a cause and an effect is expressed in terms of the strengths of the influences the cause has on the effect occurring. ORA (Carley et al. 2009) is an application for the construction and analysis of social networks and enables social

network analysis through a wide variety of measures. Construct (Lanham et al. 2014) is an agent-based modeling tool through which the dynamics of the interactions among different agents representing the organizational entities can be analyzed. In addition, WebTAS <http://www.issinc.com/government/products/webtas-enterprise>, a visualization and timeline analysis tool developed by the Air Force Research Laboratory, which provides access to data from multiple databases and can receive streaming live data from sensors, has been integrated into the C2 Wind Tunnel to enable visualization of data and show results on maps. Each of these C2WT federates corresponds to a different modeling language and uses a different simulation engine.

Given a set of policy objectives for a particular wargame, given a set of actors and a set of data and associated scenarios, a set of alternative futures is defined. This information is used to model the organizational structures, model the desired effects and the set of admissible actions or tasks available to the players, and model their interactions. Execution of the models either separately or as interoperating models enables the simulation of the wargame during its design phase and the assessment of the actions taken in real time during the actual wargame.

Metamodeling

Effective multimodeling requires that the modeling languages used, the models themselves, and the supporting data do not contain assumptions that invalidate the specific model interoperation. This leads to the need for metamodeling analysis.

Metamodeling analysis indicates what types of interoperation are valid between models expressed in different modeling languages. Note that model interactions can take a wide variety of forms: (1) one model runs inside another; (2) two models run side by side and interoperate (the interoperation can be complementary, in which the two run totally independently of each other, supplying parts of the solution required to answer the questions; or supplementary, in which the two supply each other (offline and/or online) with parameter values and/or functionality not available to either individual model); and (3) one model is run/used to construct another by providing design parameters and constraints or constructs the whole or part of another model. These are all aspects of the need for *semantic interoperability*.

The underlying premise is that two models can interoperate (partially) if some concepts appear in the ontology of both modeling languages. By refining this approach to partition the concepts into modeling language input and output concepts and defining the concepts that are relevant to the questions being asked by the game players and expressed by the modelers, it becomes possible to determine which sets of models can interoperate to address some or all of the issues of interest, and which sets of models use different input and output concepts that are relevant to those questions.

The technical approach used to understand modeling language semantics, so that multiple models can interoperate, has been to use concept maps <http://cmap.ihmc.us> to describe the characteristics of the set of modeling languages and data that are available. The information contained in the concept map of each modeling language is then formalized as a refactored ontology expressed formally using the Unified Modeling Language (UML) <http://www.omg.org/spec/UML/2.4.1>; an enriched ontology is then generated as the union of the refactored ontologies of the modeling languages being used (Levis et al. 2012). This multimodeling and metamodeling approach was used to support a recent wargame, described in the following section.

Concepts and Analysis of Nuclear Strategy

A wargame was held over a two-day period in 2011 in support of the Strategic Multi-layered Assessment office of the Department of Defense. Its purpose was to explore four nuclear policy objectives: (1) prevent proliferation of nuclear weapon technology and capabilities; (2) assure friends and allies; (3) deter potential adversaries; and (4) maintain global and regional strategic stability. To support this wargame, the multimodeling approach was used. Generic models were developed prior to the game because the actual scenario for the game was not available until game time. Once the actual scenario information became available, the generic models were instantiated for the specifics of the scenario during the first move of the game and were run during the conduct of the game; proposed moves by the various teams were encoded and the models were run to provide data suitable for analyzing and evaluating each move. Three different Blue teams worked in parallel but independently to address the issues. The actions of each team were modeled and analyzed using different instances of the modeling suite.

The models were developed using a suite similar to that in figure 40.3 to address the five dimensions of the problem: Policy Objectives, Actors, Future Environments, Threat, and Operational Phase. The Time Influence Net model was used to decompose policy objectives into high-level effects; these effects were subsequently analyzed to identify actions and subactions that would contribute or detract from achieving these high-level effects. The effects reflected perceptions of a decision maker or decision-making team. One set of actions (those of the adversary and the environment) was derived from the scenarios to reflect the threat and phase; these generally run counter to the desired effects. Other actions reflected a proposed course of action (COA) to influence the adversary to behave favorably relative to the desired effects. Subject matter experts worked with Time Influence Net modelers to assign conditional probabilities (strengths of influence) to the cause-effect relationships, as well as to estimate the relative start time for actions taken to influence the adversary, create effects, and achieve desired objectives, and the time delay for each action to contribute to an effect or subeffect. The visualization tool WebTAS was used to display key events as a function of location and time.

The models did not address the question of defeating a nuclear adversary except in the context of *deterring* that adversary from pursuing nuclear-related behaviors that might threaten US national interests and those of the US allies. This led to development of a modeling system (figure 40.4) based on examination of cause-effect relationships involving both potential adversaries and friends or allies during the development of a crisis, with a primary focus on nuclear-related actions derived from traditional military strategy. Since most nonmilitary strategy elements vary significantly based on actors and regions, these elements were described only as diplomatic, informational, or economic. Core beliefs were treated as scenario inputs for the generic Timed Influence Net model; these can be refined when specific actors are provided during the examination of regional issues using region-specific models.

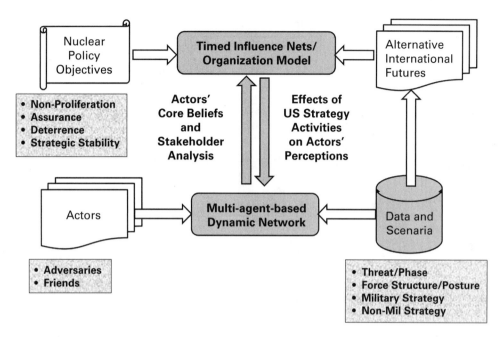

Figure 40.4
The multimodeling process for the Nuclear Strategy game.

A typical example of the type of results developed in real time is shown in figure 40.5. Blue Team B proposed three different Courses of Action (COA) in response to a regional challenge. Each COA was simulated using the modeling system and the results were assessed in terms of four measures that reflect their effect on the game's nuclear-related objectives: (1) promote favorable decision calculus by the adversary; (2) prevent nuclear proliferation and use; (3) achieve strategic stability; and (4) strengthen regional stability. Furthermore, the models enabled, through sensitivity analysis, tracing back and identifying which COA actions led to the differences in the results. Since the analysis was done in real time, the modelers were able to suggest adding or deleting actions that could increase the probability of achieving individual objectives. The low values in the probability of achieving the desired effects is a reflection of the complexity of the game scenario.

Conclusion

There are many models that support specific aspects of military wargames, such as combat models and space models. However, a need emerged for using interoperating models expressed in different

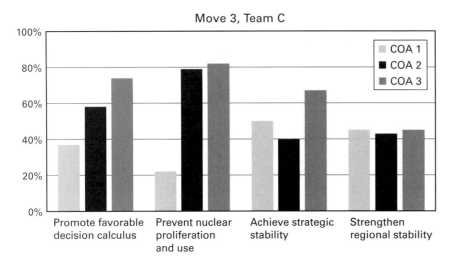

Figure 40.5
Effects of COAs on game's objectives.

modeling languages as the flag-level wargames started addressing courses of action that not only include kinetic and nonkinetic actions but also diplomatic, informational, and economic actions and the environment was not an isolated battlefield but possibly populated by noncombatants. This need has led to basic and applied research on multimodeling and metamodeling to ensure that the model interoperation is valid. This approach has evolved over the last fifteen years and has been used in selected multiperson military wargames.

About the Authors

Alexander H. Levis is University Professor of Electrical, Computer, and Systems Engineering, and has headed the System Architectures Laboratory in the Volgenau School of Engineering, George Mason University, since 1990. From 2001 to 2004 he served as the Chief Scientist of the US Air Force at the Pentagon. From 1979 to 1990 he was a Senior Research Scientist at the MIT Laboratory for Information and Decision Systems. He was educated at MIT, where he received BS (1963), MS (1965), ME (1967), and Sc.D. (1968) degrees in mechanical engineering, with control systems as his area of specialization.

Robert Elder joined the Volgenau School of Engineering at George Mason University as a research professor following his retirement from the Air Force with the rank of lieutenant general. He holds a doctorate in engineering from the University of Detroit. He served as the Central Command Air Forces Deputy Commander for Operation

Enduring Freedom and later as the Air Operations Center Commander and Deputy Air Component Commander for Operation Iraqi Freedom, as well as commander of Eighth Air Force and US Strategic Command's Global Strike Component. He was the first commander of Air Force Network Operations and led the development of the cyberspace mission for the Air Force. He also served as Commandant of the Air War College.

VII IRREGULARITIES

41   GAMING THE NONKINETIC

Rex Brynen

During America's counterinsurgency wars in Afghanistan and Iraq, a new terminology entered the military lexicon: that of "nonkinetic" action. In contrast to "kinetic" efforts to destroy an enemy through the employment of weapons, nonkinetic actions are those political, economic, and social measures an army might use to secure its objectives in ways that do not involve directly trying to kill the enemy. This might include anything from political engagement with local officials, to facilitating the provision of water, sanitation, and health services, all the way up to building the general capacity and legitimacy of a host country itself. Naturally, the growing attention devoted to use of these sorts of instruments in war also had its effect on wargames too.

This chapter will examine "gaming the nonkinetic" through the lens of three different groups. The first of these will be the *national security*

community, predominantly the military but also including the intelligence community and policymakers more generally. Wargames here serve the purposes of analysis and of individual and institutional capacity-building. The second perspective to be explored will be that of *wargaming hobbyists*, for whom gaming is primarily about social interaction and entertainment. For this group, interest in such issues has grown as the nature of contemporary conflict has changed. Finally, attention will turn to those in the *conflict resolution, humanitarian assistance and development communities*. Here gaming has become increasingly important as a training and educational tool. These are not wargames properly, in that they do not intend to model the dynamics of war. However, they are serious games wherein war provides the essential backdrop to the decisions that players make.

Gaming to Win: Nonkinetic Dimensions in the National Security Community

Within the military, wargames typically have as their primary purpose analysis, education, or experiential practice (Burns 2013). Modern wargaming made its first appearance in the Prussian military in the early

nineteenth century, and its initial focus was entirely upon the tactical and operational employment of lethal military force. In large part, this reflected the warfare of the day, wherein nonkinetic action was almost entirely irrelevant to the outcome of battles and campaigns. It also reflected the extent to which, as von Hilgers (2012) has argued, the emergence of modern wargaming was intimately linked to the evolution of military science and a belief in the mathematical computability of warfare. Early *kriegsspiel* thus focused heavily on the size of formations, the rates of march and fire set forth in drill manuals, and the estimated accuracy and lethality of weapons. The social and political dimensions of warfare were both harder to quantify and much harder to represent within rigid rules.

Of course, at the strategic level both military theory and diplomatic practice recognized—as it had always done—that warfare took place in a political context, and for political purposes. The influential Prussian military theorist Carl von Clausewitz (1976, 87) himself had famously declared that "war is merely the continuation of policy by other means," a "true political instrument," and that military means "can never be considered in isolation from their purpose"

(see also Waldman 2013). The industrialization of modern warfare also meant that factors of economics, transportation, and logistics mattered greatly in both the planning and conduct of military campaigns.

Despite this, wargaming was relatively slow to adapt to the importance of the nonkinetic. It is true that civilian transportation networks were addressed within German wargaming prior to the First World War, notably in the development of Germany's deployment plans and opening moves for the Western (and possible Eastern) Fronts (Zuber 2002). However, prewar planning and wargames lacked any attention to diplomatic and political factors, with the political situation written into the scenario rather than determined by players and their decisions. This failure to explore alternative political contexts and responses may have come at a price when war came, since the actual configuration and forces arrayed against Germany was rather different than those presumed in many of these wargames.

The Rise of Pol-Mil Gaming

After the war German military planners sought to address this shortcoming—and, roughly a century after the invention of modern military wargaming, the political-military dimension was substantially integrated into the game and gameplay itself for the first time. In particular, some German interwar games assigned foreign ministry personnel to assume the roles of key diplomatic actors (Perla 1990, 41–42). The Japanese also made some limited use of the technique. In the United Kingdom, United States, and elsewhere, however, wargames were still only used to explore or teach about kinetic military operations,

narrowly conceived. Moreover, no country really explored how nonkinetic actions might contribute to military and political success.

It was during the post–World War II era that such "pol-mil" wargames became fully established, in the United States in particular. There were two major reasons for this.

The first was the growing sophistication of operations research (OR), which had matured substantially during the Second World War in both the United States and the United Kingdom. Operations research confirmed that many of the kinetic aspects of war could be quantified and modeled. Over time, this was expanded to other areas that lent themselves to quantification, such as force structure, defense acquisition, and emerging technologies. Advances in computational power also contributed to the sophistication of OR. However the rise of sophisticated modeling also highlighted the extent to which many aspects of human decision making could not be easily captured in algorithms, despite considerable efforts over the years to do precisely this. Instead it required games that put humans in the loop, not only in military roles (as had been the case since the dawn of modern wargaming) but in political ones too.

A second and even more important reason for the development of pol-mil wargaming was the emergence of a Cold War era characterized by political competition, proxy wars, and nuclear deterrence. On the one hand, the specter of mutual nuclear annihilation through miscalculation heightened the urgency of understanding crisis behavior. On the other hand, the importance of influence, proxy conflict, subversion, and irregular warfare all underscored the need to factor political dynamics into national security gaming.

A key pioneer of this was the RAND Corporation, which starting in the mid-1950s sought to examine the political elements of national strategic decision making through role-played games. Such crisis games were also increasingly used by scholars starting in the late 1950s, partly for research purposes, but also as an educational tool. Some early examples of the latter—for example a series of games held at MIT in 1959 (Bloomfield and Padelford 1959)—significantly influenced the work done by RAND and others, and vice versa. Several key scholars of the time participated in both.

The purpose of these games was not so much to evaluate policy choices or forecast political-military futures, but rather to provide experiential insight into "the pressures, the uncertainties, and the moral and intellectual difficulties under which foreign policy decisions are made" (Goldhamer and Speier 1959, 79). The US Joint Chiefs of Staff Joint Wargaming Manual (1969) describes such games thus:

> Whereas conventional war games may be used to validate organizational, equipmental, and doctrinal concepts through careful measurement of material, time, and distance factors, politico-military games are intended to educate and inform the players regarding possible interactions between political, economic, psychological, sociological, and military factors. Like war games, some PM games conducted in government are intended to help identify possible future problems and potential opportunities and to provide scenario material for refining operational plans and intelligence collection requirements. Also within government they have additional values: they enhance interagency rapport, they inform action level and senior officials regarding prevailing attitudes and philosophies, and they supplement other interagency study efforts.

> PM games feature the illumination of problems from the pseudo-perspective of an enemy or ally in a simulated conflict atmosphere. They provide a sense of personal involvement, the element of competition, and, most importantly, an unrestrained, thought-provoking environment.

Most pol-mil games took the form of seminar or freeform games (Jones 1985), in which the two sides were presented with a written scenario. The teams then met to discuss their options, with players often assigned to role-play particular organizations or individuals. The teams then decided upon these and reported the to the control group or "white cell," which then adjudicated outcomes and advanced the scenario to the next turn. Adjudication could either be by qualitative expert judgment, through use of a formal computational model, or some combination of the two.

Although there was spirited behind-the-scenes debate among those that conducted pol-mil games as to their cost-effectiveness and whether some might attribute too much weight to their findings (Levine et al. 1991), they nonetheless did generate insight into the uncertainties of crisis behavior. In many such games actors tended to perceive each other's signals poorly. Strategic decisions, moreover, were often driven as much by the need to reconcile competing views within an actor as by the dynamics of communication and deterrence between hostile parties (Schelling 1987; Brynen 2014a). In short, as Allison would argue in his classic study of the Cuban missile crisis (Allison and Zelikow 1999), domestic and bureaucratic politics and organizational procedures had a great deal to do with how states behaved in crisis—and, potentially, in war. Decision-maker idiosyncrasies mattered too, highlighting the limits of treating conflict or war as a mechanistic process.

By the 1960s, and up until the present, crisis games became fairly commonplace within the American national security establishment for both analytical and educational purposes, with participants drawn from the military and intelligence communities, the State Department, and others (Wilson 1969; Allen 1987). Games were also sometimes conducted for senior Congressional staff and even members of Congress (McCown 2008). Outside the United States, such crisis games were much less used. The Soviet Union wargamed, too (Perla 1990, 156–158), but these games appear to have focused on the military implementation of Soviet policy, rather than treating political decision making itself as a variable. Most other countries typically lacked the resources, think-tank community, or degree of national power to sustain many pol-mil games.

Gaming Nonkinetic Actions

For the most part bringing politics and policymaking into wargaming in these ways fell well within the Clausewitzian conception of war as a tool used to pursue policy goals, and the consequent view that the use of military force must be calibrated to the scope of those broader objectives. However, other aspects of the nonkinetic lie outside Clausewitz's notion of war as wholly as a physical act of violence, "an act of force to compel our enemy to do our will" (Clausewitz 1976, 75)—and, indeed, similarly outside the comfort zone of many militaries. Specifically, the end of the Cold War, and even more so the post-9/11 era of US-led intervention in Afghanistan and Iraq, increased the salience of military operations short of full-scale war, such as peacekeeping and stabilization operations, counterterrorism, counterinsurgency (COIN), or humanitarian assistance and disaster relief. Addressing these required wargames that addressed the political, military, economic, social, information, and infrastructural dimensions of a situation ("PMESII" in Western military jargon), and the diplomatic, information, economic, as well as military (DIME) dimensions of national power and policy. It also required examining the various nonkinetic actions that military forces might take.

The US military's 2006 handbook of counterinsurgency doctrine FM 3–24 (US Army 2006) underscored this, highlighting the central importance of building the political legitimacy of the host government, an endeavor in which "political factors are primary" (US Army 2006, 1-22). As a consequence, "the conduct of COIN is counterintuitive to the traditional U.S. view of war," in that "sometimes, the more force is used, the less effective it is," and "sometimes some of the best weapons for counterinsurgents do not shoot." (US Army 2006, 1-26–1-27). While subsequent versions of US counterinsurgency doctrine (US Army 2014) refocused somewhat greater attention on the conduct of armed operations, it retained the idea that legitimacy was key and that nonkinetic actions were an essential part of building this. Similarly, the US military's main doctrinal guide on stability operations FM 3–07 (US Army 2008) highlights a long list of key tasks that a stabilization mission would need to undertake or support, including disarmament and reintegration of former combatants, supporting reestablishment of the rule of law, restoring or providing civil services, assisting displaced populations, providing emergency food and other emergency humanitarian assistance, supporting public health and education programs, governance reform and capacity building, and economic development and employment generation. As none of these kinds of actions could take place in a vacuum, there would also need to be considerable attention to the "human terrain" of social groups, culture, tribal or ethnic identities, religion, demographics, social and economic dynamics, and local politics. Since most elements of a stabilization operation would be carried out not by the military directly, but rather by other agencies, international organizations, nongovernmental organizations—and, of course, the host country itself—operations of this sort inevitably involve especially complex interagency and coalition interaction and coordination.

All of this needed to be addressed in professional wargames if they were to be used effectively for decision support, analysis, education and training for contemporary national security challenges. Initially, however, there was a "huge vacuum of [military simulation and serious game] tools to address this new threat" (Smith 2009, 154). As one survey of professional wargamers noted:

> As we look to the future, however, we face some "wicked problems" in which the overlap of various political, social, economic, military and other types of issues creates a denser thicket of uncertainties that we have to sort through … It is not clear just how well we actually understood the issues associated with conventional warfare (as opposed to our ability to convince ourselves that we did), but it is not hard to agree that our understanding of irregular, or asymmetric, or fourth-generation warfare is lagging behind our need to know more about it. (Perla and Markowitz 2009, 56)

Military wargaming has sought to adapt. One end of the spectrum has seen the development of complex computational models such as the Peace Support Operations Model, a computer-based model of stabilization operations developed by the UK Ministry of Defense to support force development, campaign planning, and military training and education. PSOM is a "faction-to-faction, turn-stepped, cellular geography, semi-agent-based model that was designed initially to represent a range of civil and military aspects of Peace Support Operations," using "a human-in-the-loop representation of the leadership of all major factions"—in short, a computer model whereby the actions taken by human players are used as input, and then converted into effects via PSOM's embedded algorithms, thereby providing some or all of the setting for the next turn of a game (Body and Marston 2011, 69–70). In addition to addressing intelligence and "kinetic" military action, the model addresses such dimensions as the effects of collateral damage, information operations and strategic communications, humanitarian aid, infrastructure, human capital, population attitudes, security sector reform, governance and legitimacy (Appleget 2011; Body and Marston 2011; Strong 2011; Warren and Rose 2011; Gaffney and Vincent 2011; Talbot and Wilde 2011). As does the United Kingdom, the United States also uses PSOM (largely for teaching counterinsurgency), and Canada, Australia, and others are evaluating its potential utility.

Much more commonly, nonkinetic elements have been introduced into traditional wargames and military exercises through the addition of players representing other agencies. Scenario design and the "injects" used to introduce developments in the game may also be designed to explore political, social, and economic dimensions of the conflict. The adjudication of nonkinetic actions and effects may be carried out qualitatively by members of the white cell (with or without input from subject matter experts), or some aspects of the economy and aspects of the human terrain may be modeled computationally using much more limited models than that found in PSOM. An example of this overall approach can be seen in the Swedish military's annual multinational Viking stabilization training exercises, involving dozens of nonmilitary agencies (Brynen 2014b).

Existing digital wargames and simulations have also been modified to include more nonkinetic and civilian elements, albeit often as backdrops rather than as foreground scenario elements. Bohemia Interactive's *VBS2* ("Virtual Battlespace") and now *VBS3* combat training simulations—widely used in Western and other militaries—have been designed to incorporate civilians with realistic appearances and (user-programmable) behaviors.

US engagement in Afghanistan and Iraq led to the development of a number of purpose-designed game-based educational software designed to teach mission-critical nonkinetic skills in the military. While the development costs of these can be quite high, from the military's point of view software-based games have several educational advantages. They facilitate standardized teaching across multiple, worldwide locations. Indeed, they can even be made available more broadly via the US military's milgaming web portal (US Department of Defense 2010). Such games are often less dependent on the availability of skilled facilitators, compared to manual wargames and role-play exercises. They can also be self-guiding and provide structured feedback within the game itself.

One example of this is *UrbanSim*, a training game developed for the US Army by the Institute for Creative Technologies at the University of Southern California (Wansbury et al. 2010; Mockenhaupt 2010; Peck 2011). This is superficially somewhat similar to the popular computer game *SimCity*, except the focus here is learning effective population-centric counterinsurgency operations wherein the goal is "a safe, secure, and prosperous population that is the cornerstone to self-sustainment and a functioning Host Nation government" (McAlinden et al. 2008) In *UrbanSim* a single player takes command of US forces in a simulated town, where they seek to increase the local level of security. While the use of force is part of this, of even greater importance the simulation's emphasis on the complex nonkinetic aspects of such operations, including mentoring host country security forces, intelligence collection, information operations, improving essential services, increasing local employment, strengthening governance, and respecting local sensitivities. Students are encouraged to learn and manage a variety of intertwined lines of effect, engage in social network analysis of their area of operations, and understand the importance of unintended and second- and third-order effects of their actions. The simulation includes in-game tutorials and a series of learning modules, as well as opportunities for post-game debriefs with instructors.

Another training game produced by ICT is *ELECT BiLAT*, a bilateral negotiations simulator in which players must interact with 3D simulated local leaders in order to achieve their mission—namely, to discover why a project built with US aid is not being used by the locals (ICT 2012; Losh 2010; see also Elizabeth Losh's chapter in this volume). It is, in essence, a computer game to prepare warriors for war, but with no kinetic warfare in it whatsoever—a very different thing than nineteenth-century Prussian wargames.

Wargames in the military, especially those that take the form of digital simulations, must often undergo some process of verification and validation. Verification is to assure that the model does what it is supposed to—that is to say, that the original concepts have been correctly implemented in the simulation or game design. Validation is assuring that it simulates what it is supposed to represent with the desired level of fidelity and accuracy. A wargame might be expected to incorporate the concepts and relationships put forward in military doctrine—for example,

by treating close air support in a way that matches expectations and approved practices. A game in which the effects of weapons or the course of conflict failed to resemble its real-world counterpart would fail validation.

This is difficult to do with the myriad aspects of contemporary warfare. Certainly some things, such as the technical performance of weapons systems or the capabilities of logistics systems, might be known quite well. When wargames and military simulations address the vast social complexity of nonkinetic actions and effects, however, things become much more difficult. The sheer number of variables that might be considered is overwhelming.

All wargames, of course, face a trade-off between accuracy and parsimony, and must also adapt the employment of models to suit particular analytical or educational needs—focusing on some areas and abstracting or even ignoring others (Sabin 2012). However, modeling nonkinetic dynamics in wargames faces the additional hurdle that the causal relationships between these many variables are often poorly understood, as is the relationship between them and military outcomes. Does increased employment reduce local grievances and hence undermine support for insurgents, as most COIN doctrine suggests? Or does it increase the amount of resources available for diversion to the insurgent cause and create opportunities for symbiotic and parasitical fundraising? Research on the issue suggests this is a rather complex relationship, and not what military planners might presume (Cramer 2010; Berman et al. 2011). In many cases, scholars are simply not agreed on the causal dynamics at work.

The 2007 US troop surge in Iraq provides a further illustration of these analytical and modeling challenges. Some interpretations credit the subsequent (temporary) downturn in violence in the country to augmented US troop strength, possibly combined with the adoption of new COIN tactics. Other analysts however, argue that the critical element was the somewhat earlier "Anbar Awakening," whereby local engagement encouraged Sunni tribes to cooperate with the United States against jihadist groups. Still others emphasize the importance of the widespread sectarian violence that followed the February 2006 al-Askari mosque bombing, which reduced the prevalence of mixed neighborhoods and pushed former Sunni insurgents into a more cooperative relationship with US forces. Of course, all of these factors were probably at work. However, the failure of the national security community to agree on why violence temporarily declined by over 300 percent between mid-2006 and late 2007 (see Iraq Body Count 2014) highlights how difficult it is to wargame conflicts of this sort with any sort of confidence.

In the context of such analytical uncertainty, wargames and other military simulations tend to look to doctrinal answers to cause and effect: if doctrine suggests a certain relationship between kinetic and nonkinetic actions on the one hand and outcomes on the other (for example, the emphasis in FM 3–07 and FM 3–24 on defeating insurgency through government legitimacy, and building legitimacy through employment and government services),

then that is what, in the military's view, the game ought to depict. "It depends" or "we don't know" are not the sorts of messages military training usually tries to impart.

Games built on the asserted certainty of doctrine may be less effective—and indeed, even counterproductive—in encouraging military personnel to question prior assumptions and treat each individual case in its own social and political merits. Yet, inculcating a critical and questioning attitude may be essential. As work on Afghanistan and Iraq has clearly shown, local conflict dynamics are often rather different from what Coalition forces have perceived them to be on the basis of their prior planning and training (Ledwidge 2011; Martin 2014). Unintended second- and third-order effects may particularly confound soldiers whose training (whether game-based or otherwise) has prepared them for rather simpler cause and effect. This problem, moreover, is not confined to military personnel; growing research suggests that international organizations and NGOs, critical partners in peacebuilding, stabilization, and counterinsurgency efforts, may also suffer from a failure to fully appreciate complex webs of causality or the extent to which their perceptions and subcultures can generate unintended and perverse consequences on the ground (Aoi et al. 2007; Auteserre 2014).

Gaming to Play: Nonkinetic Dimensions in the Wargaming Hobby

Like their professional military counterparts, wargame hobbyists have also been alert to the role of political, social, and economic factors in military conflict. However, the hierarchy of gaming requirements for the hobbyists is rather different than for

professionals. Specifically, in contrast to the primarily analytic, experiential, or educational purpose of professional military wargames, commercial hobby games need to be enjoyable—this being, after all, the primary purpose for which they are purchased and played. For some players enjoyment may derive from a game's representation of military history or potential future conflict, and the apparent fidelity with which this is depicted. Others, however, may prioritize the gameplay experience—and especially its social aspects, as Woods (2012) has shown—over realism. In the latter case, warfare may simply provide the thematic setting for a game whose mechanics are not terribly representative of actual conflict. These differences continue to fuel a "what is a wargame?" debate between fans of consims (conflict simulations emphasizing historical accuracy) and euro-wargames (who prefer less complex games with elegant and engaging game mechanics, as in the broader category of "Eurogames").

Wargamers also generally favor the recreation of active warfare rather than nonkinetic operations. It is noteworthy, for example, that after more than six decades of United Nations peacekeeping and more than seventy UN peacekeeping missions, the hobby website Boardgamegeek lists only two games substantially devoted to the topic—*Somalia Interventions* (1998) and *Global Challenge* (2001). Of these, the latter was developed for the Dutch armed forces and had no substantial commercial distribution. Several of the wargames published in recent issues of *Modern War* magazine also illustrate the point. *Somali Pirates* (2013) largely eschewed depicting the rather pedestrian initiatives (improved communication and coordination, the outfitting of commercial ships with antiboarding devices and pirate-proof citadels, the deployment of armed private security personnel onboard ships, securing the agreement of regional states to prosecute captured pirates, and the development of agreed standards and best practices) that have characterized counterpiracy efforts in the Indian Ocean, in favor of an imagined future of

heightened military naval, air, and ground operations. *Kosovo: The Television War* (2014) does not depict the war that was actually fought in 1999 with its humanitarian crisis and political constraints, but a much more kinetic "what-if" scenario of a major land campaign.

That being said, however, hobby wargames do often integrate significant nonkinetic elements into game design. Economic production, resource management, and even technological investment, for example, are key elements of many strategic-level hobby wargames.

In many wargames players also need to engage in diplomatic and political efforts to secure the support of potential allies, the attitudes of which are tracked and adjusted within the game. *Liberia: Descent Into Hell* (2008), for example, has players track the attitudes of regional countries, foreign aid donors, naïve NGOs, and even various criminal elements.

Political, social, and economic events often enter games through random events or other mechanisms. Card-driven games (CDGs) lend themselves particularly well to depicting nonkinetic events.

The influential board game *Twilight Struggle* (2009) is a case in point. The game examines the Cold War, with players primarily involved in the nonkinetic effort of extending (political, economic, and military) influence so as to bring neutral countries into their geostrategic orbit. The players' cards depict historical events ranging from brushfire wars and major crises to the "Voice of America," shuttle diplomacy, grain sales, and even the election of Pope John Paul II. Each card has an associated game effect. Because these effects are unique to each card, the game itself need not feature generalized rules for all the many nonkinetic actions and effects depicted. Instead players simply need read the card when played and follow the individual instructions as to that card's individual effect. The cards also act as a narrative device, describing an unfolding alternative history in which many real-world events occur, but not necessarily in the same order or with the same consequences.

Not surprisingly, this sort of mechanic has been used to explore other political-military conflicts. *1989: Dawn of Freedom* (2012) examines efforts to overthrow or preserve communist rule in Eastern Europe, building political support and engaging in power struggles. *Labyrinth* (2010) uses a CDG mechanism to depict key elements of the post-9/11 "Global War on Terrorism" from drone strikes and the Patriot Act to theological debates within Islam. While the game contains many kinetic elements—the jihadists undermine governance through attacks and organize terror plots, while US troops can be used to disrupt terrorist cells and even overthrow

Islamist regimes—the game also centrally hinges on a nonkinetic "war of ideas." The COIN series developed by Volko Ruhnke and GMT Games uses a rather different card-based system to explore insurgency and counterinsurgency in Cuba (*Cuba Libre!*, 2013), Vietnam (*Fire in the Lake*, 2014), Columbia (*Andean Abyss*, 2012), and contemporary Afghanistan (*A Distant Plain*, 2013). Once again, nonkinetic elements figure prominently both in the cards used by players and the basic actions they may take. These, depending on the game, include such things as raising funds through casinos or drug smuggling, drug eradication, extending government control through the expansion of civilian policing, governance and patronage—as well as traditional kinetic actions such as sweeps, patrols, and air strikes. For many players, winning the political support of the population is key, and military force is only one of several means by which to do this.

Wargaming the Politics of Insurgency and Revolution

As the preceding discussion has already suggested, nonkinetic elements often figure prominently in the gaming of insurgency, counterinsurgency, terrorism, and revolution. This is hardly surprising. Guerilla doctrines place heavy emphasis on securing popular support—the people being the "sea" within which the insurgent "fish" swim, in Mao's classic analogy. Similarly, as we have also seen, contemporary Western COIN doctrine places considerable emphasis on political legitimacy through improving governance and service delivery.

One compilation of current insurgency- and terrorism-related manual wargames maintained at Boardgamegeek by Tom Grant <http://boardgamegeek

.com/geeklist/6478/insurgency-and-terrorism> listed some fifty or so such games, a number which has grown by perhaps a dozen since then. It should be noted that this is only a very small proportion of the over ten thousand manual wargames listed on the website—clearly, insurgency is less popular than more traditional military conflicts. Of those insurgency-themed games he lists, moreover, almost half seemed to be largely focused on the clash of military forces. This is often the case for Vietnam War games, such as *Hearts and Minds* (2010)—which, despite its title, does little to model Vietnamese attitudes. On the other hand, several COIN-themed games with a heavy emphasis on nonkinetic actions do currently rank among the top-rated wargames of all time, with *A Distant Plain* currently ranked thirty-sixth, and *Andean Abyss*, *Labyrinth*, and *Cuba Libre* all placing in the top fifty.

In addition to games already mentioned, several others stand out for original game mechanics that address political, economic, and social dynamics. *Vietnam: 1965–1975* includes a system whereby South Vietnamese units and leaders are assigned a factional affiliation and regime loyalty rating, and may even support a military coup. US strategy therefore includes not only predominantly kinetic elements but also attempts to stabilize the regime by influencing the composition and attitudes of the ARVN officer corps. Brain Train's *Algeria* (2006) highlights the importance of propaganda, urban protests, and counterinsurgent intelligence collection alongside kinetic action. His design, used in modified form for teaching about COIN at the Central Intelligence Agency, was also adapted for the US Department of Defense as the foundation for "Algernon," a person-in-the-loop wargame exploring irregular warfare (Ottenberg 2008). This was used to help refine wargame scenarios, as well as to train analysts. Joe Miranda's design for *Nicaragua* (1988) included an innovative system that linked the political program adopted by the government and guerillas (Marxism-Leninism, Social Democracy, Liberal Democracy, and Oligarchy) to the attitudes of key social groups (Peasants, Intellectuals, Workers, the Church, Indians, Samocistas, and the Middle Class), and included psychological warfare as a key part of the conflict. Although it depicted a *Star Wars*–like universe of rebellious planets rather than any real-world insurgency, *Freedom in the Galaxy* (1979) deserves particular attention for its representation of the importance of demonstration effects and identity politics in revolutionary political

mobilization, as well as its ability to fully integrate cadre-level covert actions into a much larger strategic game.

Modern War magazine has produced several games that address recent or possible (or unlikely) near-future conflicts. Several of these, such as *Decision Iraq* (2013), use a Joseph Miranda-designed combat system. This distinguishes between kinetic (regular military) attacks, guerilla warfare, and "civic action"—the latter representing efforts at such things as political influence and service delivery. Each uses a different combat results table, and some units have advantages when performing guerilla warfare and civic action. Others of Miranda's games of modern insurgency show how varied the approaches to the topic can be. *Battle for Baghdad* (2009) certainly includes nonkinetic actions and even actors (it includes a "nongovernmental organizations" player), but is in many ways a Eurogame-type multiplayer abstraction that does not bear close resemblance to the actual conflict in Iraq. *BCT Command Kandahar* (2013), although not necessarily based on actual battles in Afghanistan, gives a much better sense of counterinsurgent campaigns, including planning and the importance of civil-military cooperation. The objectives being pursued by players can also vary from turn to turn, thereby depicting the challenges of operational planning amid higher-level strategic uncertainty.

Nonkinetic dynamics also figure prominently in military coups. However, very few games have focused on this as a central element of the design (Train 2011), and most of these have done so for entertainment rather than simulation purposes. A rare exception was SPI's *The Plot to Assassinate Hitler* (1976). Although this drew heavily from SPI's traditional kinetic games in its depiction of political intrigue—it used a hex map to depict both spatial and abstract relationships, units were rated for attack and defense, and even exerted zones of control—it nonetheless was innovative in many respects. Indeed it might have been too innovative, for it was never very popular among wargamers.

Digital War and Politics

Thus far, this chapter's examination of wargaming the nonkinetic has largely focused on nondigital wargames. What do war-themed computer and video games add to the picture?

Issues of economic production certainly figure in many real-time strategy (RTS) games, and are centrally important to the entire genre of 4X (eXplore, eXpand, eXploit and eXterminate) digital games, such as the *Civilization* series. Many modern first-person shooter (FPS) digital games are set in scenarios that include political intrigue, insurgency, and humanitarian crises. Rarely do they ever explore this in any dynamic way—instead it is largely used as part of the narrative setting in which players blow things up. Indeed, they might try to blow too much up, with the International Committee of the Red Cross having complained that many FPS games fail to reproduce the constraints imposed on military action by international humanitarian law (ICRC 2013). A rare exception is *This War of Mine* (2014), a FPS-like game in which players assume the role of civilians trying to survive, rather than combatants trying to kill (Sterrett 2014).

Some digital wargames have been very sophisticated in their modeling of subtle political relationships in warfare. The medieval grand strategy game *Crusader Kings II* (2012) is perhaps the best example of this: while kinetic warfare is a key element of the game, political intrigue, family relationships, strategic marriages, and building coalitions are even more important. A typical game might well involve the simulation of tens of thousands of key aristocrats and other individuals, their attitudes to each other, and the relationships between them. *Tropico*—not a wargame at all, but rather a series of lighthearted "banana republic" simulations in which players assume the role of the dictator of a fictional Latin American island republic—models the political preferences of factions and individual citizens and their corresponding response to government policy. Under certain conditions, rebel groups may form and launch attacks, or the military may attempt a coup.

Both of these represent in many ways a commercial entertainment application of the sort of computational agent-based modeling used by social scientists, some national security simulations, and serious games like *UrbanSim* to understand how the aggregate behavior of individual actors shapes larger systems and processes. Similar sorts of approaches are increasingly found in political and geopolitical simulators such as *Masters of the World* (2013), in which both states and individual decision makers respond dynamically to the actions of others.

The massive growth of the digital gaming industry has had substantial impact on the evolution of professional military wargaming and simulation, as well as on the wargaming hobby. The computational power available to the average computer or video gamer has increased exponentially, and with that has come much greater ability to model complex situations. There have also been corresponding improvements in the realism of animation, graphic imagery, and virtual reality. Within the military, many increasingly understand wargaming in largely digital terms. Why, after all, use paper and cardboard when so much can be done with software?

This technological revolution also presents challenges, however. If a designer is not careful, too much simulated complexity can easily overwhelm a player, who may be unable to conceptualize the vast array of causal relationships at work and hence become frustrated in trying to decide upon an optimal course of action. Most hobby gamers, wargamers and video gamers alike, want to play God to some extent, with the ability to make armies clash and determine outcomes through their choice of strategy and tactics. They do not want to be fully embedded in a realistic messy social, economic, and political environment where it is difficult to rapidly

effect clear and significant change. From an instructional perspective, software hides relationships within the black box of computer code, making it difficult for a player to know, understand, or critically assess the assumptions upon which a model is built. The increasing realism of graphic imagery can be beguiling, enticing users to forget that the virtual world in which they immerse themselves might be based on dubious analytical assumptions (Turkle 2009). Finally, some professional wargamers have expressed concern that contemporary digital games and gaming culture create expectations of immediate gratification, and encourage players in serious games to enter a sort of "win at all costs" gamer mode that can interfere with the learning process (Perla and Markowitz 2009, 83; Frank 2012). None of this invalidates the very great contribution that digital gaming has to make to the simulation of nonkinetic aspects of war, but it does raise some issues that will need to be addressed as digital entertainment has ever greater impact on serious gaming for professional purposes.

Gaming for Peace: Peacebuilding, Humanitarian, and Development (War)Games

Recent years have seen a growing use of games to address such topics as peacebuilding, humanitarian assistance, and longer-term development in fragile and conflict-affected countries (Hockaday et al. 2013; Brynen and Milante 2013). Most such games are educational or experiential in nature, intended to build the capacity of groups and individuals to address complex challenges. Often, they seek to highlight the operational difficulties of operating in real or potential warzones in ways that do not put participants at risk. As with professional wargaming, it is far better

to develop skills and learn from mistakes in a simulated conflict environment in which no one actually dies.

The genealogy of most such efforts however, generally does not trace its roots through wargaming as either a hobby or profession. Instead, the primary conceptual influences have been military and disaster-response exercises, negotiation role-play, and a broader growing attention to e-learning and digital games.

In the case of the former, many humanitarian agencies have developed training programs for personnel that mirror field exercises by militaries, police, and emergency services. These often take the form of "skill drills" in which participants are asked to apply their acquired knowledge in situations that resemble some of the difficult conditions they might find in the field, including political tensions, hostile militias, coordination problems, and even feckless officials or NGOs that complicate operations (for a typical example, see McCabe 2013). Usually such exercises are at least partially pre-scripted to assure that participants are exposed to all of the required training components. They thus have less of a "game" element to them, in that the choices made by participants may not fully determine sequences or outcomes. Such exercises also often serve a networking function too, bringing stakeholders together to "gain a better understanding of individual personalities and how they can better work together in the event of a real emergency" (Hockaday et al. 2013, 3).

International institutions involved with peace and stabilization operations have also adapted traditional military command and map exercises (Brynen 2014b). The United Nations uses the fictional country of Carana as the basis for an array of exercises and training modules for peacekeepers and other UN personnel. This includes maps of the country, and full descriptions of its history, economy, society, and politics, with training modules addressing a range of topics including conflict analysis, mission planning, civil-military coordination, protection of civilians, and sexual and gender-based violence. Carana-based exercises have also been used, in modified form, by the African Union to develop an African Standby Force with the capacity to mount regional stabilization missions. The emphasis in such exercises is often on planning aspects, and much less upon interaction with an adaptive adversary.

Negotiation exercises have long been used to train law and management students, and are now often used for training about conflict management and resolution (Kumar 2009; USIP n.d.; PILPG n.d.). In some cases, role-playing games have even been used to help humanitarian agencies plan for the future (Brynen 2013a), or in an effort to assist those actively engaged in conflict to find a mutually acceptable political compromise. These sorts of games typically bear far more resemblance to role-playing games than to any hobby wargame, although the fundamental focus remains one of conflict and conflict resolution. The World Bank also uses the same basic approach to teach staff about development in fragile conflict-affected countries, basing its own role-playing in the same fictional setting of Carana used by the UN and others. Perhaps the largest and most complex simulation of this sort is the week-long "Brynania" simulation, used for more than a decade at McGill University (Brynen 2010). In it, more than a hundred students play the roles not only of governments and insurgents, but also aid workers, journalists, and civil society organizations.

The growing focus on e-learning (Wills et al. 2011), not surprisingly, has also had its impact on gaming conflict resolution, humanitarian assistance, and development in conflict areas. "Country X" (2009), for example, is an educational game developed at Columbia University in which students seek to avert violence and mass atrocity by taking various preventive measures (Harding and Whitlock 2013). Educational software in this area can take the form of multimedia "choose your own adventure"-type games, in which the player's choices determine the subsequent vignettes they face. This format has also been used for advocacy and awareness generation. The web-based game *1000 Days of Syria* (2014), for example, explores the current civil war in Syria. Because such multimedia educational tools have become commonplace in business, several software packages now exist to support authoring and publication. Free online applications are also available to enable the authoring of simpler text-based "adventures" too (Brynen 2013c).

Why has wargaming had so little to do with the evolution of serious games designed to address the mitigation, effects, and recovery from war? There are likely several reasons.

As previously suggested, many hobby wargamers favor the kinetic over the nonkinetic in their games, both out of an interest in military history and hardware, and perhaps because some of the ludological characteristics of such games (competition, conflict, clear winners and losers) too. Indeed, there is some evidence to suggest that players of historical tabletop wargames tend to have slightly higher social dominance orientation (Vela 2013), a psychological measure of preference for hierarchy that has been shown to correlate with nonaltruistic, power-seeking behaviors.

A second set of reasons has to do with the interaction—or lack thereof—between these different communities. Many professional military and national security gamers are wargamers too, and more than a few commercial and hobby wargame designers have worked in or with the military. By contrast, anecdotal evidence suggests that hobby wargamers are a very small proportion of personnel in the development and humanitarian communities. The vast majority of UN peacekeepers these days come from the developing world, where hobby wargaming is much less common, and military wargaming may be less developed.

Humanitarian workers, if they have any experience with serious gaming, are much more likely to be familiar with medical and disaster simulation and field exercise. While military and national security gamers have increasingly called upon humanitarian and other nonkinetic subject matter experts in the conduct of wargames, there has been only limited effort to cultivate ongoing networks and lasting relationships. The annual Connections and Connections UK interdisciplinary wargaming conferences stand as a rare exception to this, and have sought to engage with those involved in gaming nonkinetic aspects of conflict (Brynen 2012; 2013a). They have also encouraged professional wargamers to think about how they might game nonkinetic military operations such as humanitarian assistance and disaster relief, a process that has given rise to one game (*AFTERSHOCK: A Humanitarian Crisis Game*) now used for teaching university students, humanitarian aid workers, military officers, and peacekeeping personnel. (PAXsims 2015).

The peacebuilding and humanitarian community has also largely focused on gaming as a teaching and learning technique, rather than using it as a tool for analysis. Partly this is for practical reasons—aid agencies and nongovernmental organizations can rarely spare the time and resources to do sophisticated analytical gaming. However, it also likely arises from lack of familiarity with the techniques of serious analytical gaming, another area where greater professional interaction across wargaming communities might yield significant benefits.

Conclusion

As this chapter has shown, depiction of the nonkinetic dimensions of conflict has become increasingly common in modern wargaming.

In the case of professional wargames in the national security community, this has reflected recognition of the importance of politics in national security decision making, the importance of social, economic, and political context in contemporary military operations, and of the role of nonkinetic actions in achieving military and policy objectives. Military gaming, however, has encountered difficulty in trying to represent the complex and often only partly understood dynamics at play. At times it has responded to this by asserting doctrinal confidence rather than necessarily encouraging the sort of critical and questioning attitude that might best prepare both soldiers and policymakers for future wars in unknown places. As former US Secretary of Defense Robert Gates recently noted (2014), too much confidence in the predictability of war is a dangerous thing: "For too many people—including defense 'experts,' members of Congress, executive branch officials and ordinary citizens—war has become a kind of videogame or action movie: bloodless, painless and odorless. But my years at the Pentagon left me even more skeptical of systems analysis, computer models, game theories or doctrines that suggest that war is anything other than tragic, inefficient and uncertain."

Within the wargaming hobby, most gamers still show a strong preference for the kinetic aspects of warfare—destroying tank battalions, it seems, is simply more fun than airdropping relief supplies, tangling with host country corruption, repairing electrical grids, or having tea with a tribal leader. However, there have been a number of innovative manual wargames published, especially in recent years, that substantially address nonkinetic issues. Quite apart from their play value, these offer a repertoire of mechanics and ideas to inspire future game design, in keeping with Jim Dunnigan's oft-cited Second Rule of Wargame Design: "plagiarize" (Dunnigan 2000b, 147). Digital gaming also offers new possibilities to simulate complex nonkinetic dynamics, although it also presents some potential pitfalls in doing so.

Finally, there has been increasing attention by those most involved in the nonkinetic aspects and consequences of war—namely humanitarian and development workers, and those professionally involved in conflict resolution—to the contribution that serious games can make to training, education, and institutional capacity-building. Very little of this has drawn upon professional military wargaming, however, and even less from the wargaming hobby.

Analytically, this points to the interesting role that knowledge communities and game genealogies play in the use and play of games. Practically, it suggests that considerable benefit might be had from greater interaction between gamers of all sorts interested in these kinds of issues.

About the Author

Rex Brynen is Professor of Political Science at McGill University, and coeditor of the conflict simulation website PAXsims <www.paxsims.org>. He is author, coauthor, editor, or coeditor of eleven books on

Middle East politics, conflict, and peacebuilding, including *Beyond the Arab Spring: Authoritarianism and Democratization in the Arab World* (2012). In addition, he has worked as a member of the policy staff of the Canadian Department of Foreign Affairs, as an intelligence analyst for the Privy Council (cabinet) Office, and as a consultant on conflict and development issues to various governments, United Nations agencies, and the World Bank.

42 INHABITED MODELS AND IRREGULAR WARFARE GAMES: AN APPROACH TO EDUCATIONAL AND ANALYTICAL GAMING AT THE US DEPARTMENT OF DEFENSE

Elizabeth M. Bartels

One way to approach game design is to treat the game as an instantiation of a particular model describing an aspect of conflict. By this understanding, a game designer seeks to build out a "sandbox" that allows players to inhabit an artificial world whose actors, environments, and rules align as closely as possible with those of the model, whether conceptual or formal.[1] This approach to game design is particularly effective when working with practitioners, because it allows a firmer connection between their intuitive, experiential understanding of key problems and more abstract understandings provided by academic models and theories. This chapter briefly describes this method of game design and discusses how it can be operationalized for both educational and analytical purposes.

To illustrate how this approach works in practice, I explore examples of games created to support the US Department of Defense's College of International Security Affairs (CISA) by the Center for Applied Strategic Learning (CASL) at the National Defense University (NDU). The college aims to educate midcareer national security professionals from the United States and partner nations about counterterrorism and irregular warfare at the strategic level. By picking games done for the same organization, both studying how states can better combat irregular threats in West Africa, I hope to focus attention on how understanding games as instantiations of models will change the game's form depending on the game's purpose.

To start, it is important to understand how this definition of gaming differs from other common definitions used by US government gamers. Games are most often defined as a "warfare model or simulation not involving actual military forces, in which the flow of events is affected by and, in turn, affects decisions made during the course of those events by players" (Perla 1991). However, it is often more helpful to see a game as an instantiation, or a representation in a concrete case, of a model rather than as a model in and of itself. Because of games' strong narrative content, it is rare to see a game that is divorced from the specificity of time and place. This context means games usually cannot be generalized in the way many models are. To draw on a metaphor from the social sciences, a game is less the equivalent of a scholar's model of conflict than it is the case study the author uses to illustrate or test his or her model.

Instead, I argue that a game is an instantiation of a model in which key independent variables (or inputs), dependent variables (or outputs), or both are human decisions. Based on this rendering, games can also broadly be conceived as having three elements: environment, roles, and rules. The environment describes the tangible or intangible landscape that will be affected by the model. The actor (or more often actors) are the decision-making entities attempting to affect the environment, which the game's players will represent through the roles that are assigned to them. Finally, the rules lay out the causal mechanisms by which the actor can make decisions and how those decisions will impact the environment.

This reconception of the relationship between games and models is important not only for game designers, who should be cautious when making claims that treat their game's finding with more authority then they would a single case, but also in shaping participants' relationship with the game. Regardless of whether a game is analytical or educational, game design should seek to create a space where participants can interact with a model in a specific and concrete way. Interaction is a particularly valuable aspect of games when used with audiences whose understanding of a phenomenon is based on experience rather than abstract modeling. This is sometimes known as "metis" knowledge (Scott 1990): knowledge that is implicit and learned through personal experience.

If the purpose of the game is educational, the designer aims for participants to interrogate and absorb the model by demonstrating first, how a world described by a model would work, and second, how that artificial world parallels reality in ways that make what is learned in the game helpful in real life. Based on this premise, all game design choices aim to align the key elements of the game's environment, player roles, and rules of play to the key aspects of

the model: environment (or context), actors, and mechanisms. In practice, this usually involves the game designer selecting a real or fictitious example of a phenomenon of conflict and describing each element in a way that is consistent with the model.

To give a concrete example, the educational game "Connected Shadows" depicted a current irregular conflict according to some of the theories taught at CISA. The classroom model emphasized two basic types of violent non-state actors: those with a large base of popular support who use violence as a means to a political goal, and those with little support who rely on violence as a goal in and of itself. The model then focuses attention on the role of grievances, particularly those rooted in political, economic, social, historical, and geographic inequalities, and the role they serve in motivating the population to take up arms. Next, the model focuses on the desired end goals of both the national government and the non-state actor(s), how each actor seeks to achieve them, and what tools are available. This is intended to reveal not only the strategy of each actor, but also when the actions of either actor are not being effectively countered by the other. Finally, the public narrative of both the threat group(s) and government are analyzed. Based on this assessment, a strategy is then designed to counter the threat group by identifying and countering the enemy's center of gravity, correcting the policies fueling grievances, ensuring the government is countering the strategy of the insurgents, and developing an effective counternarrative.

Connected Shadows was built to instantiate this model by presenting a case study of irregular warfare in the Sahel region of Africa examining political violence in Mali, Algeria, and Nigeria. Connected Shadows was run as a seminar-style game, meaning that game play consisted of discussions between players without the assistance of formal mechanics such as dice, cards, boards, or specialized computer interfaces to reproduce the dynamics of the model. Instead, the model was manifested in the information about the environment given to the students, the instructions that laid out the rules of the road for each section of the game, and the descriptions of the roles students were to assume during the game. Students then played the game by assuming their assigned role and engaging in debate to determine collective analytic conclusions and desired actions. These were then formalized in a PowerPoint briefing that could be shared with other groups.

Prior to the exercise, students were assigned to focus on Nigeria, Algeria, or Mali and given a substantial primer on their assigned country and how it has been impacted by ongoing conflicts. While these documents included several maps and a short description of the geography of the country, far more attention was given to describing key social structures, political institutions, economic conditions, and historical narratives. Additionally, information in each section was carefully tailored to highlight the same issues that the CISA model emphasized as important to understanding the conflict. For example, the discussion of Malian politics focused on dynamics seen as being important to fueling conflicts, such as the substantial political role of the military and limited franchise for Northern minority groups, rather than presenting the political situation in the way a general article would. Thus, the read-ahead materials not only established an environment in which decisions were to be made, but they also primed students to be aware of the issues seen as particularly salient to a grievance-based model of political violence.

On the first day of the game, students were presented with their roles and the rules of the game in a series of memos. These documents laid out a series of fictitious security incidents in each country that was depicted as a catalyst for the governments of Algeria, Mali, and Nigeria to each undertake a systematic review of their strategies to counteract threats to their government. These documents also informed students that, for the purposes of the game, they had been selected to advise a strategy review of their assigned country based on their personal experience and previous education. They were tasked to produce an analysis of the conflict and recommend courses of action to respond to violence using the CISA model.

During the first day of the exercise, students worked in small groups to prepare a briefing of their assessment of the conflict and their recommended course of action for their assigned country. To a casual observer, each seminar room must have looked like a slightly out-of-control classroom, with faculty observing from the sidelines while students debated and built out briefing slides to convey their analyses and recommendations.

The second and third day of gameplay proceeded in roughly the same way, with one major change. On the second day students were ask to change the role they assumed. Whereas on the first day students filled the role of advisors to the government, on the second day they changed roles to advise the leaders of the threat groups challenging the government. Thus, rather than use a predefined scenario or group of subject matter experts to determine what would occur next, students themselves served as the game umpire and determined what the threat group would do as a result of their initial actions as the government. On the third and final day of the exercise,

Figure 42.1
Students collaborate to develop a presentation of recommendations.

students switched back to playing the role of advisers to the government and were able to update and finalize their strategy based on what students playing the threat group in the previous move projected would occur. Students then presented their findings to panels of faculty members for feedback.

While compared to a traditional role-playing game, board game, or the more rigid worlds of video or computer games, the events described above may seem extremely unstructured. However, each element of gameplay was designed to closely mirror the environment, roles, and rules highlighted in the CISA model of irregular warfare. This was particularly evident in the way the key environmental factors of the model were represented in the game. Whereas a game focusing on a more conventional warfare environment would primarily represent physical geography, CISA's model of irregular warfare is primarily concerned with the social structure and preferences of the population (known as a population-centric perspective in military circles).

Thus, where a conventional World War II battle game might present the environment as a map describing the hills, roads, and forests of a geographic area, the environment of Connected Shadows focused on building out a view of the society of each country through written documents.

The same parallelism between CISA's model and its instantiation in the environment of Connected Shadows can be seen with regard to roles. Over the course of the exercise, students took on the role of both major actors in the model: the national government and the organization(s) using violence to undermine the government. The game's level of analysis and motivations were also consistent with that of the original model. For example, as the government, students were asked to recommend a whole-of-government strategy, rather than advising a single subunit of the government, in line with the model's belief in the importance of an integrated national approach. Similarly, game materials presented the motivations of non-state users of political violence as deeply rooted in grievances. This depiction of the threat group's motivation primed students to focus their analysis (regardless of perspective) on a grievance-based model of conflict causation rather than considering competing models.

Finally, the rules of the game were perhaps the most direct instantiation of the CISA model of any element of the game. Students were asked to complete their analyses using the same prompting questions that faculty used in class to cue analysis of conflict. These questions focused students on determining the nature of the threat to the state, the role that grievances played in motivating participation in violence, the areas in which non-state actors' actions were not met by the state with effective countermeasures, and the role of narrative in shaping popular support. Furthermore, rather than an outside team determining the effects of player teams' strategies, players determined the results of their own actions when they took on alternative roles during the second and third day of play. These game elements were designed to more fully embed the players in the model to increase their understanding of the rules it proposed.

In contrast to the educational model of Connected Shadows, if the purpose of the game is analytical, the designer helps participants instantiate their own (often mental and underarticulated) models in the game to improve and disseminate understanding of a phenomenon. While the structure of game elements may be similar to those of an educational game, the purpose of an analytic game is to open a space for critique so that the model instantiated in the game can be refined based on the participants' experience. Therefore, the goal of an analytical game designer is to provide a point of comparison for participants' intuitive mental model of a particular aspect of conflict, which they may not be able to articulate directly. When done in a group, this can be a particularly useful way of highlighting differences between participants' understanding of the problem by creating a common reference point in which the participants are not directly vested.

One example of this approach is "Scattered Lights," which was used as part of CISA outreach to current strategic practitioners. This game allowed for established experts to challenge both the school's framework (described earlier) and their own understanding of current topics of interest to the policy community. A team of American, French, and Nigerian security professionals that were concurrently assessing Mali sought to improve shared understandings of the problem on the ground, available tools, and approaches to managing the conflict. This exercise was run at the same time as a student seminar-style game that looked at irregular conflict in Mali; the student game was very similar in structure and content to Connected Shadows. However, at the same time the students were working on their assessments of the conflict and recommended actions for both the government and the violent non-state actors, the practitioners engaged in a shorter exercise that focused on developing options for international support.

While the basic setup of Scattered Lights had many of the same elements as Connected Shadows, when used with an expert audience their purpose was rather different. While the game materials provided structured information regarding the environment, roles, and rules, the game design team assumed that the most critical information that would shape experts' game play was their existing mental models of both Mali and their understanding of irregular warfare more generally, which had been build up throughout their professional careers.

At the beginning of the exercise, the expert group was asked to take on the role of the international stakeholder community to develop a strategy, including a desired end state for Mali and what the international community could do to assist the government in reaching that state. Both the roles and rules given the group paralleled what students were assigned. However, the experts' rules and roles were less directive in order to allow them to critique, add to, or alter the model's understanding of key actors when needed. To ensure that this looser structure did not translate into unproductive discussion, a

Figure 42.2
Students debate their irregular warfare strategy.

member of the game design team facilitated the discussion. When participant discussion revealed that they disagreed with the way the game depicted a element of the environment, roles, or rules, the facilitator was able to prompt participants for a more complete explanation of how they felt the issue worked, and solicit input from other experts to determine how widely held the alternative model might be.

This model of game design effectively reverses the process of the education model: Instead of the designer teaching a model by instantiating it in a game, the participants effectively teach the game designer their mental models through their discussion. Over the course of the game, players instantiated a new model, first implicitly though the understandings shared by players in the discussion. This understanding was then formalized in written documents complied by the game designers to document the new model.

In the case of Scattered Lights, expert participants' collective understanding touched on key aspects of the environment, roles, and rules. For example, participants felt that the environment needed to be regional rather than national, because of the greater importance they placed on the transnational nature of key drivers of conflict. The group of experts also identified many international actors as worth analyzing more fully then the classroom model definition of roles suggested. Finally, the exercise revealed that while participants generally shared the classroom model's view that non-state actors' use of violence is rooted in political, economic, and social grievance, the experts treated the capacity of the government to resolve these longstanding issues as an open question, rather than a stated necessity. Combined with other findings, these assessments created an alternative vision of how irregular warfare occurs and how the state counters it.

Treating games as a sandbox can also allow more concrete reporting after the game. Because the game is designed to instantiate a specific model, reporting after the event can evaluate how well the game was able to depict specific elements of the model based on the evidence of student behavior. For example, following Connected Shadows, game designer analysis focused on evaluating how student products deviated from what was expected. By contrast, reports from Scattered Lights focused on where participants' mental models deviated from the model taught in CISA classrooms. Because Scattered Lights was run several months prior to Connected Shadows, game designers were also able to use the experienced participants'

discussion to update and refine materials in advance of Connected Shadows. Furthermore, while both Connected Shadows and Scattered Lights were only run once, under other circumstances an iterative approach could be used to continue to refine and improve both games.

Regardless of whether the purpose of the game is education or analytical, the author has found treating games as instantiations of models, rather than as models in and of themselves, to be particularly helpful when working with practitioners, who have a great deal of "metis" knowledge learned through personal experience. This character can make it very hard for students to leverage their knowledge in the classroom, either because of the difficulty of connecting abstract theories to their lived experience or because the students cannot articulate how their experience-based mental model differs from the theory being presented in order to offer meaningful critique. Thus, using games to present abstract models as experience provides students with a more comparable parallel to their existing base of knowledge. For analytical games, where the goal is to formalize the knowledge the participants have gained though experience, treating game design as an instantiation created more flexibility to allow participants to contribute their understanding without risking an unstructured, and thus unproductive session. As a result, while the purpose of the game changes many design choices, the core principles of instantiating models serves a useful role in both contexts.

Box 42.1

Exercise Concept

1. **Purpose**: To examine violent non-state actors and national policies to counter violent extremists.

2. **Objectives**: This exercise serves as the beginning-of-year activity for the International Counterterrorism Fellowship Program and the South and Central Asia Program. It is intended to allow students to utilize models of insurgency and terrorism in order to:

   - Analyze a range of threat types, to include "roots of conflict" and the Ends-Ways-Means of the threat group(s), to prepare a Strategic Estimate of the Situation.
   - Consider the effects of regional and global phenomena on national conflicts.
   - Develop a Strategic Course of Action to address threats using all instruments of national power and adapt the plan to unfolding events.
   - Develop and brief policy options appropriate to senior leaders at the national and international levels.
   - Assess incoming students' understanding of instruments of national power, whole-of-government strategy, operational art, and campaign planning.

3. **Methodology**: For this Kickoff Exercise, CISA students are tasked to offer threat assessments and policy recommendations based on a hypothetical scenario. The scenario, combined with this briefing book, will represent the "exercise world," which will outline what the situation will look like for exercise purposes. As a rule of thumb, *do not fight the scenario*. Artificialities are included for a purpose.

Students will be divided into three groups, each of which will represent a "world." These groups will then run through the exercise in parallel. Within these groups, students will be further subdivided into three "country teams" focusing on Mali, Algeria, and Nigeria,[2] respectively. *If you have received this guide, then you have been assigned to represent the country of Algeria.* Teams are free to communicate with the other country teams in their world and are free to organize in whatever way they find helpful. However, each of the nine country teams will be required to appoint two Briefers, who will be responsible for reporting out the team's work. This position will rotate to other team members in subsequent "moves."

During Moves 1, 2, and 4, students assigned to the three Algerian country teams (one to each "world") will act as an advisory committee to the Government of Algeria. Between each move, the scenario will evolve, requiring new analysis in subsequent moves. At the onset of each move, students will be provided with a scenario update and tasking. They will then craft a statement of their understanding of the problem and proposed response they believe the Government of Algeria should pursue.

During Move 3, students will change to "Red Team" roles and act as leadership figures of the groups that threaten Algeria. As such, they will respond to the product that has been previously developed by a different world's Algeria group by proposing reactions from the threat groups.

After all four moves, two individuals selected by each group will brief the group's recommendations. At the end of the first three moves, students will brief other student teams. At the end of Move 4, students will brief the final product, which represents the culmination of the groups' efforts, to a panel of CISA faculty and leadership.

About the Author

Elizabeth Bartels is a doctoral candidate at the Pardee RAND Graduate School and an assistant policy analyst at RAND. Prior to joining RAND, she was a senior associate at Caerus Associates and a research analyst at CASL. Her work as a national security educator and analyst has focused on the operational and strategic levels of irregular and asymmetric conflict. Past projects have analyzed urban operations, insurgency, terrorism, cyber security, and Middle Eastern politics. Her current research focuses on the use of social science research design methods to improve wargame design and analysis. She received a bachelor's degree in political science from the University of Chicago and holds a master's degree in comparative political science from MIT.

Notes

1. While this is a common trope among game designers in informal conversation, there is relatively little work from national security gamers that formalizes this design principle. Passing references to this philosophy can be found in Lenoir and Lowood (2003) and Perla and McGrady (2009).

2. While many other countries play a critical role in the security of the region, we have selected these three as representative of three very different challenges and three different roles that West African nations have taken up.

43   CHESS, GO, AND VIETNAM: GAMING MODERN INSURGENCY

Brian Train and Volko Ruhnke

The last fifty years of commercial board wargaming pose the following mystery: Why have the most common sorts of wars been the least commonly gamed? Insurgency—internal war, guerrilla war, irregular war—has been the most widespread form of warfare throughout history (Kilcullen 2010, ix). Yet, a hobby that prides itself on astute historical exploration has shied away from the topic, instead delving ever deeper into dissection of a relative handful of "conventional" wars. Why should that be so? Does that tell us anything about warfare, or about ourselves as students of war? And is that a good thing or bad?

This mystery confronts the two of us personally. We have designed of a number of commercial board games about modern insurgencies, and we are doomed constantly to ponder what it might be that has led us to wander off in another direction than the rest of the tribe. In this chapter, we address some of the history of this phenomenon, the challenges posed by the topic of insurgency itself, the difficulties or points for attention for those who design games on modern insurgencies, and the possible insights that these games may generate for those who would play them.

Children of the COIN

The predominant mode of armed conflict since the end of World War II has not been formalized inter-state, force-on-force warfare. Instead, it has been a range of activity captured by the general term "irregular warfare," especially counterinsurgency (COIN). As relevant as these contemporary conflicts may be to our lives and the interests of our nations, civilian market wargames devoted to exploring and understanding them are relatively uncommon.

Professional military gaming, which started two hundred years ago as a training aid for officers, spawned the civilian hobby in the 1960s. As middle-class Americans acquired both more spare time and higher levels of advanced education, their mass culture also sponsored popular interest in military history and current affairs. Therefore, there has always been a modest overlap between the two wargaming worlds; one can find examples both of civilian games being used by the military and of civilianized versions of military games repackaged and released onto the civilian market.

Whatever the medium, wargames produced for a professional military audience are different in their intention, focus, and execution from those produced for the civilian market. Military wargames can have as their objective the testing of new theories, tactics, equipment, or procedures, or analyzing the cause and conclusion of hypothetical courses of action or conflicts. They are more educational than aesthetic in function. In contrast, a civilian wargame is primarily an aesthetic object: its purposes are to serve as a pastime or frame for friendly social engagement, to provide relaxation through regulated competition, or to be enjoyed as a uniquely interactive form of art or complex puzzle. Military wargames often focus on "getting the numbers right," but the extent to which a civilian wargame may have been carefully researched may have nothing at all to do with its actual reception. Unlike participation in a military wargame, this is, after all, a voluntary exercise for the player.

The American military has a large amount of historical experience of counterinsurgency, though documentation of its many "small wars" is much less complete than those of its participation in formal, state-on-state wars. Even as the formal methods of operations research that had proven so useful in World War II percolated into professional military wargaming, it was not until the early 1960s that the American military received its first serious games on counterinsurgency. In 1963, the Advanced Research Projects Agency commissioned a game called "AGILE-COIN" that was used in training Army and Special Forces officers to remind them of the political consequences of military actions. About the same time another game called "TACSPIEL," actually an adaptation for counterguerrilla operations of a larger-scale game modeling conventional combat, began to be used for officer training (initially for officers and staff in the newly forming Air Cavalry squadrons).

Meanwhile, *Viet Nam*, the first civilian-designed COIN game and one of the first commercially available wargames, appeared in 1965. It was meant for team play, and players could win either a diplomatic victory or a military victory. Rules included simultaneous and hidden movement, a government stability index, world opinion, terrorism, ambushes, air strikes, and psychological warfare—all in a four-page rulebook. This was an early start on the subject, but of the thousands of civilian-market manual wargames published since 1965, there are very few that deal primarily with the problems of modeling irregular warfare, in any historical period.

So why has so much less commercial gaming taken on insurgencies than the world wars? We feel that there are two main difficulties with the topic that explain this scarcity: the sensitivity of the subject matter itself, and the way that the complexity of the subject matter is reflected in games on it.

The Sensitivity of the Subject

First, there can be difficulty with the concept of wargames themselves, whatever the type of war depicted. Wargames evoke strongly negative reactions, especially when they appear to transgress existing and popularly held moral codes or political agendas, or even concepts of fair play. In order to avoid such a reaction, perhaps, wargames will rarely if ever feature game mechanics representing terrorism or genocide, though these are common features of actual warfare.

Wargames and Our Culture

As artifacts of the culture that produced them, wargames serve in the continual exercise of historical revision and socially useful amnesia (Antley 2013). People have romanticized warfare for as long as there has been rhetorical language, image, and metaphor to cover up its sordid reality. Like all human creative endeavors, a wargame is not and cannot be a neutral object. The designer, through the processes of research, conceptualizing, testing and production of a game, must make a series of choices of what to include in his design and what to leave out. Because a wargame is a commodity meant to be consumed (that is, bought and played, or at least studied), the artwork, images, and content are chosen to entice the player/customer, who is at least implicitly presumed already to have done much of the romanticizing in his head.

It is somewhat ironic that wargames attempt to portray the species at its most illogical and atavistic through a rational framework of consistent logical regulations and mathematics and a prim concern for only what is thought to be "militarily significant." Thus, designers of World War II wargames participate naturally in the process by assembling detailed and complete orders of battle for the Axis forces, including units of the Einsatzgruppen and lawless SS brigades and divisions, whose main historical achievements were murder and ethnic cleansing—yet there is nothing for these units to do in these games except to be thrown into the front line as cannon fodder. Yet what would be thought of a designer who did write rules that gave realistic roles to such units?

Even after decades of militarizing influences at work in Western popular culture (or perhaps because of them), the general public appears far from coming to grips with current conflicts beyond a superficial level. Even after 9/11, with the explosion of books, magazine articles, blogs, and websites devoted to counterinsurgency and terrorism, there has been no parallel increase in the demand for intellectually demanding games on the subject.

Instead, popular interest in mass-market games about current wars has been mostly confined to modifications of tactical-scale, first-person shooter video games that, for the most part, fail to convey the background and complexity of these conflicts, or to "militainment" games and recruitment tools like *America's Army* (2002–) or *Prism: Guard Shield* (n.d.). Even among civilian video games, negative public reactions to certain examples point to a selective vision of war. *Six Days in Fallujah*, which was to be the first video game to focus directly on the Iraq War and was developed with extensive input from US Marines who were in the battle, was held from release after negative public pressure on the publisher, Konami. It remains unpublished. The online version of the 2010 release of *Medal of Honor* was to have allowed players the option of assuming the role of the Afghan Taliban, but this was later changed into a generic "Opposing Force" when public groups, the media, and senior officials of several NATO governments condemned the possibility of playing that enemy role. The 2012 video game *Spec Ops: The Line*, as an exception to the rule, tackled the corrosive moral and psychological effects of irregular warfare, as the players become complicit in war crimes and lose their sanity; it did not do well commercially, however, because players found it boring.

The Difference for Insurgency Board Games

All this is natural, and we do not mean to imply that games about insurgency somehow soar above or are immune to cultural influence, market taste, and the impulse to romanticize. However, because terrorism and other such violence against noncombatants is central to outcomes in internal wars, these aspects of all war tend to feature explicitly in even hobby board games about insurgency or civil war.

The 2008 board wargame *Liberia: Descent Into Hell* featured game mechanics for bribery and seduction, child soldiers, torture, cannibalism, hostages and drugs. All of these were material features of the 1989–97 Liberian civil war, supported by the designer's research and documented within the game. Yet the game was attacked in online forums such as Boardgamegeek.com as an exercise in sensationalism, trivialization, and racism.

Comments discussing and reviewing *Andean Abyss* (2012) and *A Distant Plain* (2013), two games in the COIN series by GMT Games, revealed player discomfort with the activities of some factions, for example the right-wing paramilitaries and drug-running cartels featured in the former, and questions of NATO complicity in corruption and the ethics of drone warfare in the latter. (In fact, the entire question of corruption and the role or aspirations of organized crime in insurgencies has been barely touched on in civilian games, except in GMT's COIN series and other games by the authors of this chapter.) The flawed yet seminal 1977 COIN wargame *South Africa* attracted

some controversy because of its central assumption that no victory was possible or permissible for the minority white government, which, given the game's infinite length, would eventually fall to the black Communist-sponsored insurgent.

Adding to the challenges of meaningfully but tastefully representing internal wars, simulating modern insurgency crashes full on into the delicacy of recency noted above with Iraq or Afghanistan video games. It should not surprise us that the board game hobby appears far more comfortable with the fun of representing Hitler or Stalin in World War II than with playing games about wars from which

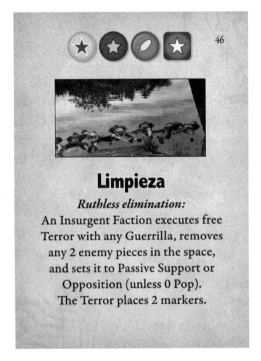

Figure 43.1

A playing card from GMT Games' COIN series board game *Andean Abyss*, depicting terror and some of its effects in 1990s Colombia.

our friends and family members have just returned—or not returned. Some gamers recoiled at the early advertising from GMT Games for *Labyrinth: The War on Terror 2001-?* (2010) in the belief that the company was seeking to exploit the 9/11 tragedy commercially.

One exhibit in favor of the contention that recency of topic alone—not just the nature of internal war—is a challenge to the acceptance of modern insurgency is some of the reaction to Nick Karp's 1984 game *Vietnam 1965-1975*. As late as the 1990s, US observers questioned the perceived insensitivity in making and playing a game about events that hurt so many American families so deeply. Yet now, gaming Vietnam appears increasingly accepted, as the strong demand for the reprint of Worthington Games' *Hearts and Minds: Vietnam 1965-1975* by Vietnam veteran John Poniske and for GMT's COIN series volume on the conflict, *Fire in the Lake* (2014), attests.

So, even for some hardcore *grognards,* the distaste with recency alone is enough reason to stay away from a game like *A Distant Plain*, at least for now. For others, paradoxically, that delicacy is the fun, by the following logic: our fun in board wargaming is in some measure about learning or experiencing history. History is interesting because it is relevant to us today. How much more relevant are recent and current wars than ancient ones? Recent conflicts are not only an appropriate topic for games, but perhaps the most appropriate. And most of those recent wars are insurgencies.

Board wargamers, of course, are a small subset of the general public; a smaller subset of them have sufficient interest to play complex games on current or irregular warfare topics; an even smaller subset of designers have interest in creating such games; and the smallest subset of all is the number of publishers willing to risk considerable money and effort producing and distributing such unlikely products. ... But this does not form an incurable economic death spiral: games on touchy, current topics continue to appear, and sometimes even flourish within their niche audience.

The Complexity of the Subject

The other obstacle to greater numbers and acceptance of civilian games on insurgency is the very complexity of the subject itself. Counterinsurgency has been called the "graduate school of warfare," and for a wargame to be more than a superficial depiction of COIN, it must respect as many as possible of the following points of complexity. For this wargame to be also a playable exercise, its mechanics must address these points in practical ways, and we have supplied examples of solutions from past COIN games.

Multipolarity/Factionalism

Many irregular war situations feature shifting loyalties and utility of civilian government, tribes, classes, foreign powers, or military formations. As international insurgency expert David Kilcullen notes, "counterinsurgency is always more than two-sided" (Kilcullen 2010, 31).

A good way to treat factionalism is to have more than two players, who will then supply a lot of randomness and complexity in a game just through natural human obstinacy and deviousness. Each game in the COIN Series, for example, accommodates up to four players, each player representing a faction very different in its methods and objectives from the others. When fewer players are available, the game system provides flowcharted algorithms to operate the spare factions and thereby keep the multiparty nature of the depicted conflict in view.

Other games that cover internal wars but are designed for two players commonly feature a number of factions that must be recruited into a player's coalition: *Chad: The Toyota Wars* (1991) features two main and twelve smaller factions, *Liberia: Descent into Hell* (2008) combines eight factions with fourteen ethnic groups, and *Nicaragua* (1988) has seven "social classes" that must be lobbied for support. The courting of foreign powers for assistance, from economic aid to outright intervention, constitutes a subgame in these three games as well. The internal politics of the government and how it can interfere with the military struggle can be shown simply, as in *Greek Civil War* (2014), in which the counterinsurgent player must adopt a particular deployment scheme for the army as demanded by the civilian government; or through the intricate mechanism of assigning branch, corps, and division commanders and balancing political factions to avoid coups d'etat in *Vietnam 1965–1975*.

Nonlinear Combat Results, Randomness, and Friction

Insurgencies are primarily contests of political will and psychology, and many COIN games use some form of semi-arbitrary political support or "national will" point scale to gauge a player's overall position. Gains and losses on these scales are the effect of a very wide range of player actions, and are unpredictable in their magnitude. In some games, these political points can be deliberately expended to mobilize new units or conduct other actions, representing the use of political capital. In *Algeria* the French player, who has near-infinite material resources compared to the insurgent enemy, must contend instead with the limited amount of patience the government in Paris is willing to extend in continuing to fight the war. Also, a game may feature combatlike but nonkinetic operations that have no immediate military or material result but have strong political and psychological effects. For example, *Tupamaro* (1996) features several nonkinetic actions, such as Propaganda and Riot/Strikes, to which the Government player had to react lest he lose further support.

A game design needs to include randomness and unexpected consequences. Causes are never tied neatly and linearly to effects. An interesting problem is modeling the concept of "cascading effects," where a change in one part of a system will have unanticipated results in unexpected other parts, which leads to the idea of the "black swan" event. Besides the periodic random events that are a feature of many wargames, other more recent games like *BCT Command Kandahar* (2013) and *Third Lebanon War* (2014) use the concept of "Chaos Cards" or "Cascading Effects": certain events in the game such as overkill or collateral damage may result in further, unanticipated events that may work against one player or for the other. *Tupamaro* features Intimidation missions that directly attack the morale of the Army, Police, and Politicians, which serves to restrict their activities and eventually provoke severe follow-on organizational crises.

Friction, manifesting as poor command and control and interfaction coordination, is also an important part of COIN games. *Somali Pirates* cleverly balances the vast power and technical sophistication of the "Coalition" antipiracy force by the political stances of their national governments—hence, the Coalition player has a lot of potential power, but can mobilize only one faction (nation) of it at a time. In *Tupamaro* and *Shining Path* (1995), the Army and Police have separate budgets and differing levels of competency, and frequently cannot cooperate on missions. A player whose forces consist of allied factions may find they do not work well together, or at all: in *Beirut '82: Arab Stalingrad* (1989), the Christian Phalange faction may or may not cooperate with its nominal ally the Israeli Defense Forces; in *Vietnam 1965–75* large sections of the South Vietnamese Army are chronically ineffective due to incompetent or disaffected leadership. *Labyrinth: The War on Terror 2001-?* presents jihadism as a global insurgency; the player controlling it must roll a die for almost every action by any of his far-flung and often only locally motivated terrorist cells. In *A Distant Plain*, such friction is precisely the point of including multiple player roles. The complex and ambiguous relationship between the players posing as the Coalition and as the Government of Afghanistan—who must manage a joint account of resources toward their divergent tastes—has been described as being "like a bad marriage."

Flexible Treatment of Time and Space

Insurgencies tend to last longer than conventional wars (about ten years on average, according to a 2010 RAND Corporation study of eighty-nine modern insurgencies). Some insurgent movements, like the Sendero Luminoso of Peru or the FARC of Colombia, are well into their fourth or fifth decade of armed opposition to government. Consequently, COIN games, at the operational and strategic level, tend to have a relaxed attitude to the amount of time a game turn encompasses, and the amount of activity a player can complete during each turn. The GMT COIN series of games refines this further with the concept of Propaganda Rounds, which represent an inevitable break in the action as the combatants regroup, assess their position, and take into account some longer-term effects of sustained fighting. Tactical-level COIN games, meanwhile, are presented with the same time/space dilemmas as games on conventional wars.

Sometimes one can dispense with a geographical map entirely: in *Tupamaro*, since almost the entire insurgency took place within a single city of 1.5 million people over four years, the physical locations and movements of the antagonists at any one time did not matter. The game map was an abstracted representation of the city of Montevideo divided into nine Social Sector Areas (e.g., University, Government Ministries, Shops). These did not represent physical areas of the city but more conceptual areas of economic and social activity. In the game, there is little or no physical movement of units on the map except to deploy them to and from various areas.

Fog of War

Asymmetry of information is a marked aspect of war generally, and insurgencies specifically. Often the counterinsurgent marks his triumphs more through intelligence breakthroughs than actual battles. Indeed, it can be a breakthrough for

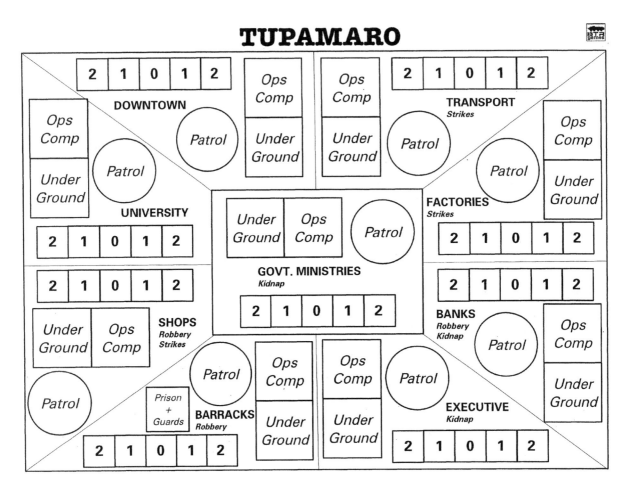

Figure 43.2
Mapping the social sectors of insurgency: *Tupamaro* game board by Brian Train.

a government to realize it has a genuine military emergency on its hands, as many times in history the initial stages of an insurgency have been treated as a matter for the police.

An essential problem with many civilian wargames is that they are near-perfect information exercises—perhaps their greatest departure from military wargames and the greatest criticism that can be lodged against them in their claim to simulate anything like actual warfare. Therefore, this is a fundamental problem when designing a COIN game, and many different methods have been used to address it. Often the insurgent is given an inbuilt intelligence advantage in that he may tell the counterinsurgent player when to take his turn (*Algeria, Tupamaro*), or inspect his force arrangements with impunity. For his part, the counterinsurgent player will find himself chasing inverted counters that may be dummies ("Political Sections" in *Vietnam 1965-1975*), attempting to locate insurgents in an area only to have them evade (*South Africa,* or games in GMT's COIN series where counterinsurgents must first Sweep an area containing guerrillas before Assaulting them), or conducting missions to assemble fragments of intelligence that may give him a transitory advantage (*Algeria*). These are simple methods of addressing the issue; even more satisfactory but involved ones include simultaneous pre-plotted movement (*Insurgency* [1979], *Dien Bien Phu* [1973], *Viet Nam*) or even a game with a third-party umpire to keep both players in the dark!

Changing Nature of the Conflict and Combatants over Time

Though it's showing its age, the Maoist doctrine of "protracted people's war," with a three-stage

progression of low-level engagements in remote areas to larger areas of control and more decisive military battles is still a model that can be used to conceptualize the ebb and flow of insurgencies. In a conventional wargame, as one side gains the upper hand the other loses units and is forced back into its rear areas; in a COIN game the insurgent may not be physically dislocated but may be forced into situations in which he is politically remote from his objective, and his forces may not be reduced in number or strength but dispersed more and more finely.

COIN games can also exhibit considerable variation in force structures over the course of a game (*Nicaragua, South Africa, BCT Command Kandahar*). Insurgent forces may include political/training cadres, several grades of progressively more mobile and better equipped and trained guerrillas, political front organizations, networks of auxiliaries that give more direct support, and so on. This permits the insurgent to change strategy over time, moving back and forth between periods of covert organizing and overt kinetic action. Meanwhile, as time advances and efforts are made, the counterinsurgent forces can become better trained or organized to fight the guerrillas. For example, in *Tupamaro* and *Shining Path* the security forces start at Recruit level (cheap to mobilize but inept, so that when used on missions they cost political support for the government), but can be trained to Line and eventually Elite levels.

Asymmetry of Methods

The antagonists in an insurgency are quite unlike each other in terms of resources, structure and capabilities, much more so than in a conventional war setting. This quality should permeate the design as completely as possible, and permit players choices in resolving dilemmas and contrasts such as firepower vs. dispersion (building up, breaking down or otherwise reorganizing units, as in *Algeria, Vietnam 1965-1975, Nicaragua, South Africa*), adopting a hierarchical organization vs. a cellular/decentralized network (an important theme in *Third Lebanon War*), different kinds of mobility (air mobility vs. tunnel movement, etc., as found in many Vietnam games), and building force structures for different missions from varied unit types.

This asymmetry may go far enough to convince players that they are in effect playing two different games on the same map. Not surprisingly, historians have applied such a gaming metaphor to asymmetry in counterinsurgency—in the common observation about strategy in the conflict over South Vietnam, for example, that the United States appeared to be playing chess while North Vietnam was playing Go. This concept, as applied to the Afghanistan conflict, inspired one of the present authors to design *Guerrilla Checkers* (2010; see sidebar) as a very simple physical expression of the metaphor.

In a less abstract example, GMT's COIN series depicts asymmetry of means in other ways, through dissimilar operations menus for each player. Only some of the choices—"Training" and "Rally," "Patrol" and "March," and so on—can be recognized as different flavors of basic activities such as building forces, maneuvering, and striking the enemy. Even these flavors are quite distinct in mechanics however, and many other activities—eradicating drug crops, suborning local officials, and so on—are entirely unique. The burdens of this method of depicting asymmetric means are that players must learn a new menu for each role, that they must learn to anticipate what several other distinct suites of capabilities might do to their own position, and the game development must test out and balance all these dissimilar menus to ensure that reasonable decisions result in a roughly historical array of tactics and result in an enjoyably tense contest. Such are the challenges of the "graduate school" of wargaming.

Asymmetry of Objectives

Who wins an insurgency? More to the point, how does one win, and when? In general terms, the counterinsurgent is attempting to defend or preserve a state of stability and social order, whether it is just or unjust. The insurgent seeks to overturn that order, and he may consider it a victory of sorts as long as he continues to exist and fight in that cause. But the insurgent does not have chaos and disorder as his desired end state: he wishes to substitute a different stability and order of his own, after the necessary struggle to remove the government from power. So the insurgent must advance his position toward that end goal.

So, insurgencies are contests of physical preponderance, political will, and psychology. An insurgency game quantifies these aspects through various metrics. But in the ambiguity of concepts like "political will," in the measure of insurgent progress in the eye of the beholder, and in the multiparty nature of insurgency as discussed before, there is no reason the definition of victory for one player should be exactly the same as for another, or even stay the same over the course of a game.

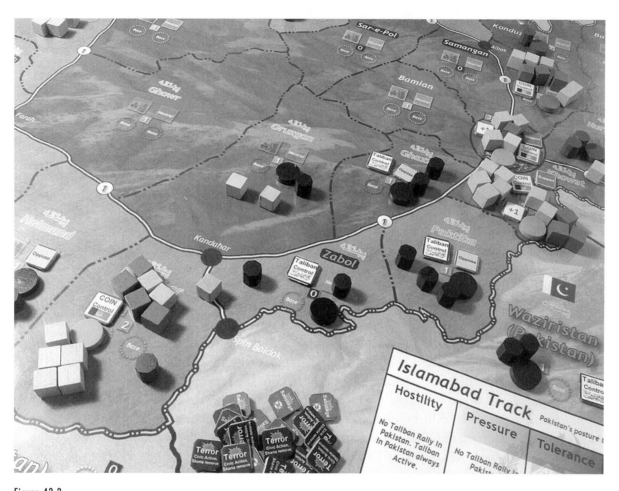

Figure 43.3
Asymmetrical operations menus and victory conditions from GMT Games' COIN series board game *A Distant Plain*.

The COIN series uses a different combination of victory conditions for each player (in addition to the different routes to achieve them discussed above) to put a point on the overlapping rather than always directly opposed goals of the multiple factions in the insurgencies depicted. In *A Distant Plain*, for example, each faction pursues a set of two objectives: one in direct opposition to another faction's objective, and a second objective independent of the other factions (though always opposable somehow). The diversity allows the shifting politics of internal wars to flow naturally from the players' pursuit of their assigned goals, hopefully providing the players insight into the political dynamics of the conflict through their own strategies.

In *Third Lebanon War*, the Israeli player can choose between a "Counterforce" or a "Countervalue" strategy. The former proposes that the IDF will give priority to destroying Hezbollah's military capability; the latter represents the "Dahiya Doctrine," in which heavy air and ground firepower will be used against civilian infrastructure that facilitates Hezbollah military operations, as a form of collective punishment. In the game, if the IDF player selects the latter strategy, he will gain Victory Points for inflicting Collateral Damage results—but because these events generally favor the Insurgent, he will be making his military task harder with each event.

A suggestion for a further variation on modeling objectives in counterinsurgency arose during a discussion the authors had while doing a podcast some time ago. A player's victory point-garnering objectives should be hidden from the other player, as well as his progress toward victory; for the ultimate effect, a player's "real" strategy could even be hidden from himself! We were discussing the Vietnam War: in the early 1960s, during the "advisory period,"

some officers in the US Army realized that a strategy based on pacification (that is, emphasizing political stability, local security in rural areas, and prioritizing civilian/paramilitary law enforcement efforts over regular conventional forces) might have been the way to make headway against the National Liberation Front guerrillas, and said so years before the commitment of large numbers of troops in 1965. But doctrine, and senior leadership, called for big battalions, large sweeps, high mobility, and massive firepower to reduce the enemy by attrition, so that was how it was done in 1965–68. Later there were changes, but not necessarily because the Army commanders knew they were doing it wrong. The point is that they were "playing the game" of the Vietnam war but didn't know *and couldn't have known* the true victory conditions.

One of the present authors has experimented with this notion, but to our knowledge no published game has yet implemented such metalevel "fog of war." However, a nod to such uncertainty over one's own goals can be found in Joe Miranda's *BCT Command Kandahar*, in which the victory conditions may change

Table 43.1

A Distant Plain factions and victory conditions

Faction	Opposed incentive	Independent incentive
Taliban	Raise opposition to the government	Build insurgent infrastructure
Coalition	Raise support for the government	Get out of Afghanistan
Government	Consolidate military control	Strengthen patronage network
Warlords	Keep military control divided	Amass wealth

Government   Warlords

Government

COIN Operations

Train (3.2.1) + any Special Activity?
Purpose: Augment Government forces and Support.
Location: Any Provinces or Kabul.
Cost: 3 Resources per space.
Procedure: At Kabul and each COIN Base space, place up to 6 Govt cubes, from map if none in box. Then, if desired in 1 Training space, replace 3 Govt cubes with 1 Govt Base or, if COIN Control, buy Civic Actions.

Patrol (3.2.2) + any Special Activity?
Purpose: Protect LoCs.
Location: Any LoCs or Kabul.
Cost: 3 Resources total.
Procedure: Move any Govt cubes into or along adjacent LoCs or Kabul, stopping at Sabotage. Then, in each LoC, Activate 1 Guerrilla for each cube there and, if desired, free Assault on 1 LoC.

Sweep (3.2.3) + Transport?
Purpose: Enter area, find enemy (not on final card).
Location: Any Provinces or Kabul.
Cost: 3 Resources per destination space selected.
Procedure: Move any Govt Troops onto adjacent un-Sabotaged LoCs if desired, then to adjacent spaces. Activate 1 Guerrilla per Govt cube there. 1 Resource to Warlords per entered LoC with any Guerrilla.

Assault (3.2.4) + Transport or Eradicate?
Purpose: Eliminate enemy forces.
Location: Any spaces.
Cost: 3 Resources per space.
Procedure: In each space, remove 1 Active Guerrilla or Insurgent Base for every 2 Govt Troops (Bases last). Kabul or LoC—Remove 1 piece per any 2 Govt cubes. Mountain—Remove 1 per 3 Govt Troops. +6 Aid per Taliban Base removed.

Victory (7.0)
Coalition: Total Support plus Available Coalition pieces exceeds 30.
Taliban: Total Opposition plus Taliban Bases exceeds 20.
Government: COIN-Controlled Population plus Patronage exceeds 35.
Warlords: Uncontrolled Afghan Population exceeds 15 and Warlords have more than 40 Resources.
After final Propaganda: Closest to goal wins (7.3).

Special Activities

Govern (4.3.1) max 2 spaces
Purpose: Add Controlled Population or Patronage.
Accompanying Op: Train or Patrol.
Location: 1 or 2 COIN-Control spaces with Support or ? Population.
Procedure: If no Returnees there, place Returnees -1Pop. Or, if no Coalition Base there, transfer Pop value from Aid to Patronage and set to Neutral.

Transport (4.3.2) 1 space to 1 space
Purpose: Relocate Troops quickly.
Accompanying Op: Any.
Location: Any 1 origin space to 1 destination.
Procedure: Move a group of Govt Troops onto/along a chain of LoCs (or Kabul) if desired, then into an adjacent space. Stop at Sabotage. Pay 1 Resource to Warlords per entered space with any Guerrilla.

Eradicate (4.3.3) max 2 spaces
Purpose: Destroy Warlord Bases, gain Aid, Patronage.
Accompanying Op: Train, Patrol, or Assault.
Location: 1 or 2 Provinces with COIN Control, Government cubes, and any Warlord Bases.
Procedure: Each space, +3 Aid, +1 Patronage, remove 1 Warlord Base, shift 1 level toward Opposition, and—if *Pashtun*—place a Taliban Guerrilla.

Warlords

Insurgent Operations

Rally (3.3.1) + any Special Activity?
Purpose: Augment or recover friendly forces.
Location: Any Provinces or Kabul.
Cost: 1 Resource per space.
Procedure: Place 1 Warlord Guerrilla or replace 2 with a Warlord Base. *If Base and not Pashtun*—instead may place Guerrillas up to Population plus Bases or flip all Warlord Guerrillas there Underground.

March (3.3.2) + any Special Activity?
Purpose: Move Guerrillas (not on final card).
Location: Any spaces.
Cost: 1 Resource per non-LoC destination (LoCs 0).
Procedure: Move Warlord Guerrillas into adjacent spaces. *If destination is a LoC or Pashtun, and if moving plus Taliban Guerrillas there exceed 3,* Activate the Guerrillas.

Attack (3.3.3) + Suborn?
Purpose: Eliminate enemies (Coalition to Casualties).
Location: Any spaces.
Cost: 1 Resource per space selected.
Procedure: Activate all Warlord Guerrillas. Roll a die—equal to or less than the number of Guerrillas removes 2 pieces (Coalition to Casualties, Govt cubes before Coalition, Bases last). If *"1"*, place a Warlord Guerrilla.

Terror (3.3.4) + Suborn?
Purpose: Neutralize support or economic activity.
Location: Spaces with Underground Warlord Guerrillas.
Cost: 1 Resource per Province or Kabul (LoCs 0).
Procedure: In each selected space, Activate 1 Underground Warlord Guerrilla.
If *Province or Kabul*—add a Terror marker and set any Support or Opposition to Neutral.
If *un-Sabotaged LoC*—place Sabotage.

Victory (7.0)
Coalition: Total Support plus Available Coalition pieces exceeds 30.
Taliban: Total Opposition plus Taliban Bases exceeds 20.
Government: COIN-Controlled Population plus Patronage exceeds 35.
Warlords: Uncontrolled Afghan Population exceeds 15 and Warlords have more than 40 Resources.
After final Propaganda: Closest to goal wins (7.3).

Special Activities max 1 space

Cultivate (4.5.1) max 1 space
Purpose: Add a rural Base.
Accompanying Op: Rally or March.
Location: A Province selected for Rally or as a March destination. If must have Population >0 and more Warlord Guerrillas than Police.
Procedure: Place 1 Warlord Base there.

Traffic (4.5.2)
Purpose: Gain immediate Resources.
Accompanying Op: Rally or March.
Location: Spaces with Warlord Base and no Coalition.
Procedure: Each selected space, add +1 Warlord Resource per Warlord Base. *For each space with Taliban Control, also add +1 Taliban Resource; for each with COIN-Control, also add +1 Patronage.*

Suborn (4.5.3) max 3 spaces
Purpose: Neutralize enemy or hide Insurgent forces.
Accompanying Op: Any.
Location: Any of up to 3 spaces.
Procedure: Each space, pay −2 Resources to remove 1-3 Government cubes, 1 Government Base, or 1 Taliban Guerrilla, or to flip any or all Guerrillas there Underground.

A distant plain

A distant plain

Figure 43.4

Insurgency, terror, and frenemies in modern Afghanistan: Coalition, Government, Islamist Taliban, and opium-cultivating Warlords in *A Distant Plain*.

during play, in this case representing guidance from higher-level leadership and back and forth between commanders within the province. In the game, each player holds three Objective Cards that give conditions for gaining Victory Points; however, these cards are revealed during play, and may also change during the game, randomly or by request.

COIN Gaming and Systems Thinking

In sum, a decent game design on an insurgency must take on the interplay of overlapping but not identical incentives in its victory conditions and dissimilar capabilities to pursue those incentives in its conflict mechanics. Players must learn, keep track of, and exploit all these ambiguous relationships and asymmetrical capabilities. And all that must be tested and developed to ensure that the game is nevertheless balanced, easy enough to learn, and fun to play. So why should we go to all this trouble?

We should do so because it is so relevant to our lives. If insurgencies are the commonest of wars today, how are we ordinary folk to understand them? Insurgency is a classic example of a complex adaptive system, in which the dynamic relationships among entities yield the outcome rather than the aspects or measures of any given participant. Insurgency is an environment full of stable and unstable equilibria, system shocks, phase changes, snowballs, and feedback loops. For example, guerrilla presence in a province enables an insurgency to undertake coercive and non-coercive actions to erode popular confidence in the government, adding to the government's incentive to move military forces into that province to root out the guerrillas and provide protection for civic action investments, those military forces then helping to restore public confidence but also tending to produce combat operations and misdirected fire that harms the local population and yields popular resentment against the government and recruits for the guerrillas.

Recall, for example, the ball-of-yarn model of Coalition strategy in Afghanistan famously shown to General Stanley McChrystal in the summer of 2009, with interwoven arrows of relationships curving this way and that among "Population Conditions and Beliefs," "Narcotics," "Tribal Governance," and dozens of other major and minor aspects (Bumiller 2010). We are all struggling to understand insurgency as a system.

Unless we are personally involved in the fighting (and at a high level of authority), how else are we to understand (much less forecast) such a complex interplay of incentives and capabilities than to try it out from the inside, through a game? How else can we improve our systems thinking but to construct a model of the system, climb inside it, and play? If insurgency and internal war have a future on our planet—and sadly, they surely do—then board games about them should remain a key bit of kit in the thinker's bag, perhaps more than they have been.

The results, even with a highly simplified model such as that presented in GMT's COIN series, are worthwhile. In the interactions of ordinary hobbyist players, board games have proven a laboratory for exploring and understanding the behaviors of the

Guerrilla Checkers

©2010 Brian R. Train

Equipment

- Checkerboard or 8 × 8 square grid
- 6× checkers or large pieces for the Counterinsurgent (COIN) player
- 66× small pieces for the Guerrilla player (flat glass beads or buttons: Go stones might be too big, depending on the size of the squares on the board; look for something about the size of M&M candies)

Setup and description of play

The COIN player places his pieces on the marked squares. The Guerrilla player starts with no pieces on the board, but begins the game by placing one piece on a point (corner of a square) anywhere on the board, then a second piece on a point orthogonally adjacent to the first piece.

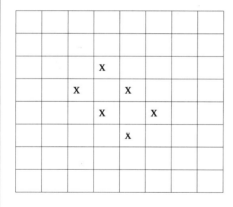

Moving and capturing

- The Guerrilla player does not move his pieces. Instead, he places two and only two pieces per turn on the board, on the points (intersections) of the squares. The first piece must be orthogonally adjacent to any stone on the board; the second piece must be orthogonally adjacent to the first piece placed. He may not place pieces on the exterior board edge points (i.e., any place it is impossible for him to be captured). He captures an enemy piece by surrounding it (i.e., having a piece, or an exterior board edge point, on each of the four points of the square the piece occupies; note that this makes the edge of the board very dangerous for the COIN player). He removes the piece.
- The COIN player either: moves one piece per turn, one square diagonally in any direction; or makes captures with one piece by jumping over the point between two squares into an empty square, removing Guerrilla pieces as he goes. He is not forced to capture if he does not want to, but if he starts capturing he must continue to make captures for as long as it is possible for him to do so, along the path he chooses.
- Players may not pass.

Victory

The player who clears the board of all enemy pieces at the end of his turn wins. The Guerrilla player loses if he runs out of pieces.

Notes on tactics

Guerrilla player: Remember the words of Mao Zedong:

- "The enemy advances, we retreat." It's okay if you lose lots of pieces in a turn (and you will); as long as you have one left, you are still in the game. Play where the enemy can't get at you right away.
- "The enemy camps, we harass." Exploit unit boundary confusion by playing between enemy pieces when you can; he can't jump you there.
- "The enemy tires, we attack; the enemy retreats, we pursue." Your forces do not move but they "flow":

think of your pieces as an ever-growing web to trap the enemy. Deploy lines of pieces to hamper his movement and trap him; he has to move next to you before he can jump you.

COIN player:

- You have the tougher job—you can mow them down but they will keep coming back!
- Watch for any mistakes the enemy might make; if you can completely clear a whole corner of the board

of enemy pieces, it will be a while before he can return there. But you must do a complete job.

- Be careful of the edge of the board; any piece left there can be eliminated with only two enemy pieces, or even one in the corners, if there are enemies nearby. Don't run into such an ambush.
- The Guerrilla will always be setting up thin walls and traps for you; watch where he puts these. If he makes too large a "string," you can reduce his forces to almost nothing in one move.

quasi-allies and "frenemies" that inhabit internal wars such as the current one in Afghanistan.

We can apprehend these complexities more readily via insurgency games because they are more vivid in the multiparty and asymmetric nature of an internal war than in more typically gamed conventional conflict. However, all wars are such complex adaptive systems! Any serious study of any conventional, outwardly two-sided war will reveal that is a multiparty contest underneath, riven by bureaucratic, personal, intra-alliance, and many other rivalries, and that understanding the war is impossible without exploring the varied relationships within it. And we can design or modify wargames on conventional topics to explore them. To pick just one example, *Road to the Rhine* (1979), a classic

design about the Western Front in World War II, emphasizes availability of supply and can therefore readily be adapted as three-player contest in which allied British and US players experience the tug of war over limited resources.

And not only our conversations and mutual understanding of current affairs such as Afghanistan or historical go-to settings such as World War II can benefit: all endeavors by large numbers of human individuals—all our own lives—are complex adaptive systems. Yes, you and we, dear reader, share overlapping but distinct incentives and capabilities. So experimenting with asymmetry through gameplay—whether in insurgency or another human activity—teaches us about ourselves.

About the Authors

Brian Train has been publishing wargames and writing articles on military-related subjects since 1993. His special interests in game design are irregular warfare and "pol-mil" games. In many cases, he was the first (and in some cases still the only)

person to have designed games on such subjects or situations as the Chinese Cultural Revolution, the Finnish and Greek Civil Wars, the Algerian War, the Cyprus Emergency, the Uruguayan and Peruvian guerrilla wars, and so on. In his spare time, he is an

Education Officer in the British Columbia Ministry of Advanced Education. He likes asymmetry and is years old.

Volko Ruhnke has designed and published numerous commercial board games, scenarios, and variants, many on modern political-military topics. His work has repeatedly won industry awards, including a total of five Charles S. Roberts Awards. His published designs and codesigns include GMT Games' *Labyrinth—The War on Terror* and its ongoing COIN series of board games about insurgency and counterinsurgency in countries such as Colombia, Cuba, and Afghanistan. The series' most recent volume, *Fire in the Lake,* deals with insurgency in Vietnam during the main period of US engagement (1964–72). By day, he works as an intelligence analyst and educator.

44   IRREGULAR WARFARE: THE *KOBAYASHI MARU* OF THE WARGAMING WORLD

Yuna Huh Wong

Irregular warfare (IW) is the *Kobayashi Maru* of the wargaming world—the no-win test in *Star Trek II* that plunges eager young Starfleet Academy midshipmen into impossible, public, and highly stressful situations for the entertainment value of seeing how badly they fail. (I won't insult the geek cred of anyone reading a book on wargaming by reminding him or her that James T. Kirk was the only one to pass the test—by cheating.) The whole affair seems designed to crush a person's spirit and inflict a lifetime of self-doubt, rather than to impart any moral, confidence, or useful instruction. The situation is not quite so deliberately cruel when it comes to IW wargames, but IW wargames truly are a test of how one confronts an impossible problem. It's not a matter of *if* one fails; merely how badly you fail and at what point you realize it, and how you recover, or at least continue.

The IW Problem

Understanding IW involves understanding the conflict dynamics simultaneously faced in a given area and their interrelated connections with other conflicts, from the local level to the international. What is driving the insurgency in Afghanistan? What is causing this most recent wave of international terrorism? What does the Syrian civil war have to do with renewed Sunni-Shia conflict in Iraq and how does that relate to Iran? As complex as these types of questions seem, they are actually the ones where we know the most and have the most experts to consult.

Gaining insight in IW also means getting a handle on the whole range of IW-related actions and goals that the United States and its partners are trying to execute to affect the conflict dynamics. It would seem the most obvious thing in the world that if anyone would understand the activities of the US government, it would be the US government. But the US national security apparatus is so vast and complex that people can spend their entire career without a good grasp of how other agencies perceive the world, define their mission, and conduct their activities. Nor are there a ready number of experts who are up-to-date on the dynamics within the government, because former members of the bureaucracy begin to have dated information as soon as they leave.

Achieving a basic understanding of just the Department of Defense is hard enough. Fifteen years after I started dealing with DoD in various professional capacities, I still encounter entire communities of people within DoD that I have never run across before. There is even a book, *Assignment Pentagon: How to Succeed in a Bureaucracy* (Smith 2007), that tries to explain the Pentagon and its bewildering ways to career officers who have been part of the military their entire adult lives. Truth is stranger than fiction. I can only imagine how opaque and impenetrable it must look to those completely on the outside. I've had the experience of trying to explain organizational dynamics to a highly intelligent and accomplished outsider helping us on a study. She furiously took notes and sent them to me afterward, at which point I realized that nearly all of it was wrong. During the wars in Iraq and Afghanistan, too, enormous amounts of data on DoD activities were not captured or were extremely difficult to find after the fact. This is despite the tremendous effort spent on generating briefings, e-mails, and reports and compiling databases.

Compound this steep learning curve across DoD, State Department, USAID, the sprawling number of intelligence agencies, law enforcement agencies, and other US government organizations involved in IW, and add White House national security staff and Congressional dynamics. This is because one of IW's unique features is the extent to which DoD must interact with other agencies in the US government. This does not even take into consideration the other partner and host nation actors that the US government is supposed to be working with. Theoretically, someone should be able to understand what is going on, but the practical challenges can be enormous.

Another aspect of understanding IW is trying to understand what happens to conflict dynamics when the US government takes action. The difficulty here is in understanding what actual impacts are caused by US activities. What is the effect of State Department public diplomacy programs in areas of the world hostile to the United States, if any? What is the effect of development programs in Afghanistan on the insurgency? What would happen to the dynamics in Syria if the United States were to intervene? These types of questions are the most difficult to answer. Even though the United States has been heavily involved in a wide spectrum of activities continuously since 9/11, the answers to these types of questions are not clear—nor in some case are they even knowable. Despite the amount of research that has been directed at questions such as these, the level of complexity and structural uncertainty in these types of cause-and-effect questions is extremely high. And it is this last set of questions that makes IW wargaming so very difficult: How to depict all this in a game?

The US government is not the only actor attempting to change the situation in the way they prefer. There are other nations, international organizations, host nation actors, and local actors who are all reacting to the United States and to each other, all trying to change the course of events in their favor. Rather than thinking of a static environment waiting for US action and direction, it may be better to think of a pile of crabs trying to climb on top of each other, with the United States being one more crab that has arrived late to the scene.

Examples of IW Games

If this were the movies, an IW game might involve several stiff generals in a cavernous, high-tech room full of photogenic young staff and wall-sized computer screens. There would be computer-generated battle graphics moving around, and video of Godzilla/Megatron/zombies/terrorists. The scrappy hero or heroine, dissed earlier by at least one general, would suddenly discover the enemy's single point of failure. The generals would urgently call the President of the United States, and the military would go on to implement the solution and save California/Autobots/mankind/Americans.

Clearly, real life is not like the movies. There so many types of wargames going on within DoD that it is extremely hard to make generalizations about them. And my handful of wargame experiences makes me hesitate to suggest that there is such a thing as a typical game. Here though, are a few examples of some types of games:

Game #1: I was an observer who mostly came for the "hot wash" after the game. It was a very large game at a posh facility involving many active duty officers, a few retired generals, and ambassadors. The food was memorable. It was mostly a planning exercise where people discussed issues and problems. As far as I could tell, nobody "played" the bad guys—bad guys were simply part of the background scenario but did not have any actions during the "game." Nor was there any indication that people faced consequences in later turns from decisions they had made earlier. This was not really a wargame but a Bunch of Guys (and Gals) Sitting Around a Table (BOGGSAT). So nobody really got the full advantage of unexpected insights that wargames are supposed to offer.

However, it was typical of DoD "wargames" that I would put into the category of Important People Came to My Huge Event Therefore It Was Awesome and the General Is Pleased.

Game #2: I was an analyst for another "IW game" that was really a planning exercise and not a wargame. Again, the adversary was static and had no life in the event after the briefing. There was a scenario, but then the military officers simply began to plan, and to discuss what type of specialists they might or might not need. Nothing in the event was designed to let them test out their plan against someone pretending to be other actors. The organization hosting the game put repeated pressure on the planners to accept the types of specialists they suggested; instead of asking if someone with such-and-such a skill was required, they would ask, how many? I ran into the colonel in charge a few days later. He kept fishing for compliments, so I finally mollified him by earnestly saying, "The general seemed pleased." This one I put in the category of Cooking the Books to Get Results That Support My Solution But Without Realizing It Because I Know Nothing About Wargames.

Game #3: I was an observer to an "analytic" game where the point was to use the wargame results to feed further quantitative analysis using a computer simulation. It was a counterinsurgency game depending mostly on die rolls, with rather binary actions that players could make. This one was much more of a game than games one and two outlined above, but I thought the commercial insurgency games by Brian Train were far superior in their understanding of important counterinsurgency dynamics (you know, like the political side of things). This was actually a game though, and involved the simulated use of forces rather than real ones, with one side being the insurgents and making moves that the US forces in the game had to respond to. I have lots of problems with using computer simulation for IW analysis, so I personally put this game in the category of Games that Feed Computer Models Because It's Become Like *The Matrix* Where People Exist for the Sake of the Machines.

Game #4: This was one of two games where I was the sponsor's rep. There were a table of US players, a table of UN players, a table of international actors, a table of players for host nation #1, and a table of players for host nation #2. The US table had instructions on a strategy they were to try to implement. I'd asked the game to be designed to give host nation players a big say in events, rather than having a static population, as was typical in most IW games I'd seen up to that point. The United States was supposed to work with the United Nations to do humanitarian assistance and engagement with the two host nations and to try to help with conflict in the area. Internal politics within the two host nation countries outran the strategy that the United States and United Nations were trying to implement. The United States managed to piss off both host nation governments royally and never understood why. The United States also inadvertently helped trigger a coup rather than help reduce any conflict. I thought it was quite realistic. I like to think that this one belongs to the category of IW Games Where You Actually Let the Host Nation Screw with Your Carefully Crafted Approach.

Life Cycle of a Wargame

The life cycle of a DoD wargame typically begins with the sponsor. The sponsor decides there should be a game and pays for or secures funding for the game. It is also in the sponsor's name that participants are invited and the game is played. But even in this beginning phase, which seems straightforward enough, dealing with IW games can be tricky. Others have written about the challenges of getting the sponsor to articulate what it is that they want to accomplish in the game—a prerequisite for making sure that a wargame is on track.

As with study sponsors, wargame sponsors even in normal times have trouble explaining what it is that they want to accomplish. Having been the sponsor's rep in the life cycle of a wargame, I can say that this is because establishing wargame goals is challenging. It is not because your IQ drops precipitously between being an analyst and being a sponsor or sponsor's rep. Those who labor to design and conduct wargames probably think so, but I urge more sympathy. Some of the uncertainty and confusion is because the role is unfamiliar to the person who must suddenly commission a wargame. Even if you have been involved in professional wargames before, involvement may have been infrequent enough that you don't really understand what is and is not possible with wargames.

This was certainly true for me the first time I had to do this. The first time we proposed a wargame for our IW project, nobody batted an eye, either in our leadership or the Pentagon committee who approved funding after a series of meetings. Wargaming is simply something that DoD does. Asking why you have a wargame is as baffling as asking why we live in North America. What do you mean why? We just do. But the first question that has to be answered in wargaming is: Why do you want a wargame, as opposed to something else? This moves wargames from the category of standard operating procedure to one of specific purpose and design. Peter Perla at the Center for Naval Analyses (CNA) had to confront me with this question for the first time in my life, poor man, but thankfully the acquaintance survived.

But once you get some notion of what wargames do and do not do, I think the most difficult thing about sponsoring an IW wargame is that the discussion on objectives naturally leads to thinking about the game's limitations and trade-offs. This is logical, since you cannot accomplish everything but must prioritize what you absolutely want. But the paralyzing moment in IW games comes when you have to make choices, and you hesitate because you realize *that you don't know enough about the problem to be confident about what you are taking off the table.* Wargames can offer insights on complex problems—but if you understood enough about a complex problem to make informed choices about a wargame's purpose and objectives, you would not need a wargame in the first place. You don't know what you don't know, but the first step is already to constrain the set of answers you may get. What if you are leaving out the most important thing but don't know it?

The next stage in the IW wargame—wargame design—is the next impossible test. With so many structural uncertainties, and such a complex problem, how ought a game be designed? Designers working on historical games of revolution or insurgency have the benefit of knowing how things turned out in retrospect (see, e.g., Brian Train's *Algeria* [2000] or Ed Beach's *Here I Stand* [2006]). A historical perspective helps to identify the major factors that appear to have had the most significant consequences.

In contemporary IW situations, it is pretty much impossible to know which way things could potentially go. It was unclear during the worst days of the 2003–11 Iraq War that there would one day be a Sunni Awakening that would drive the Sunnis from al-Qaeda and into cooperation with US forces. A commercial board game, *Battle for Baghdad* (2009), eventually emerged and was designed so that the Sunnis might or might not turn from al-Qaeda, and might or might not side with the Americans. But this is because, in hindsight, we are able to tell that the Sunni Awakening was a pivotal point in the war. A whole range of strategic, geopolitical, and technological factors—all subject to change when confronting contemporary or future scenarios—are written in stone for a past case.

Wargames for actual national security purposes, as opposed to those for entertainment, are of more use if set in the present or future. IW games introduce complex phenomena and then try and project them out into the future. How valid are the starting assumptions? How valid is the scenario? Are the key aspects of the problem properly scoped and given enough room for play? Does the game mechanism represent the best one for the problem? Are the roles the correct ones? How should complex dynamics be reduced to a manageable game that can be executed coherently in a few days? All of these demand such a level of expertise in very specific IW contexts, and highly specialized knowledge about game design, that it really does start to become an impossible problem. It is not a matter of *if* an IW game design is wrong, but a matter of *how* wrong, and if the effort can still be useful to the sponsor and participants.

A significant part of game design is the problem of adjudication. Stephen Downes-Martin at the Naval War College (NWC) asks the question of who is fit to adjudicate a highly complex phenomenon like IW (see Downes-Martin 2013). Who really is expert enough to understand what outcomes would arise from player moves in a game about Syria? Adjudication is futures thinking, and the more complex the judgment, the easier it is for it to go awry. This is the third part of understanding IW, where there is the most uncertainty and where years of DoD-funded studies have only made progress in certain areas. But adjudication is a critical piece. If the adjudication in IW games is wrong, merely echoing back doctrinal expectations, negative learning can take place in a game and nobody would truly be aware of it. There is the heightened danger of learning the wrong lessons from a wargame about counterinsurgency, but feeling that these were legitimate insights because the shared socialization that comes out of a wargame can be such a powerful and memorable experience. Peter Perla talks about the power of story living in a game, but if the incorrect story was lived and remembered, that too has effects when the players take mental models from the game into future decisions.

Another difficulty for IW wargames lies in securing the correct roles and the correct players. Determining what roles get to make independent decisions in a game (such as DoD, or a certain insurgent group) is to pass judgment on what actors in real life have the most impact on the IW dynamics. Have too many roles, and the game gets unwieldy. Have too few, and you will miss important decision makers, institutions, and social groups.

An IW wargame's credibility also comes from the level of expertise that the invited players bring to the table. Who are the right players in an IW game? People experienced in one war tend to take that experience into another situation, whether it is warranted or not. For example, when I watched a group of army officers playing a counterinsurgency game, their conversation and understanding of cause and effect reflected their experience in Iraq, down to what had happened in specific towns; even though it was a game in a totally different geography, they were recreating a stylized version of Iraq in their game. We see how the US experience in Bosnia set the mental map for many going into Iraq and Afghanistan, the 1991 invasion of Iraq set the expectations for those going into the second invasion, and aspects of the Iraq war approach were copied and pasted into Afghanistan. There is a tendency on the part of even those with IW experience to misunderstand the shape and significant dynamics of a brand-new situation, and to bring along the understanding that made them experts on the previous war.

Another set of problems with recruiting the right experts for an IW wargame is that DoD IW games tend to be classified. Because this automatically precludes anyone without a security clearance, it can often mean that the very best experts on the topic cannot be invited to a game. Game participants must come from within the US government or its contractors, which introduces the danger of creating an echo chamber if invitations and viewpoints are not well managed. Even within the US government, there is also an imbalance of who is available to come to multi-day wargames. DoD dwarfs the rest of the US government and runs so many games that other parts of the government can have a hard time sending people to every game where non-DoD participation is desired. This has the potential to skew the perspective brought to the table.

All these issues compound by the time you arrive at the next stage in the life cycle of a wargame: analyzing the results. Analysis for IW games is greatly complicated by the importance of qualitative developments in the game, over quantitative outputs that are more characteristic of games designed to examine conventional war. Although many formal qualitative analysis techniques are available, they are rarely used in wargame analysis. Nor do most typical DoD wargame analysts have the right background to be familiar with them.

So this is the area where I have spent more of my energy in the two games where I was the sponsor's rep: experimenting with applying qualitative methods to wargame analysis. In one game we tried out a rapid, team-based ethnographic approach to notetaking to study game adjudication, keeping Stephen Downes-Martin's comment in mind that the adjudicator is a super player in complex games (Beebe 2001; Downes-Martin 2013). In the second, we had someone skilled in narrative analysis at the host nation table, and realized later that structured forms of narrative analysis could be extremely valuable in understanding the dynamics between host nation factions, the transitional government, the United States, the United Nations, and other international actors during a game.

If there are any conclusions to take away from this chapter, it is that IW wargaming is an impossible problem, but that there are sometimes real benefits to failing. And by failing, I mean that you should be aware of the shortfalls in both the design of the game itself, and the unmet objectives or unintended consequences of US actions in the game. When you fail, you can ask yourself what went wrong. If you walk away impressed with the vastness of what you didn't even realize you were clueless about, then the *Kobyashi Maru* does actually have value. But if you don't realize IW wargaming is an impossible test, you'll draw all the wrong conclusions.

About the Author

Yuna Huh Wong is an operations research analyst for the US Marine Corps. She was the methodology lead for a Pentagon-level irregular warfare study that ran for three years and incorporated wargames and other methods. Research interests include wargaming, the use of expertise, and futures methods. She holds a BS in political science and a BS in economics from MIT, an MA in political science from Columbia University, and a PhD in policy analysis from the Pardee RAND Graduate School, where her dissertation was on noncombatants in urban operations and in military models and simulations.

A MIGHTY FORTRESS IS OUR GOD: WHEN MILITARY ACTION MEETS RELIGIOUS STRIFE

Ed Beach

Wargames have traditionally focused on modeling the military operations of the combatant nations. But all wars are influenced by factors outside the military arena. In this chapter, I describe a set of conflict simulations that I designed that expand their focus to examine warfare in a broader historical context. These three games, two tabletop and one digital, track simultaneous military and religious conflicts within their multilayered game worlds. The application of the same design approach used in the tabletop games to the digital medium demonstrates the wide applicability of these mechanisms. Furthermore, although religion is the focus, the design techniques I present here can be used equally well to simulate any outside factor that impacts a military action.

Is Paris Worth a Mass?

Sixteenth-century Europe was a rich period for military conflicts with strong religious overtones. This time of religious warfare arose from the Protestant Reformation, a schism within Western Christendom that brought the fledgling Protestant nations into direct conflict with European states that wanted to retain their traditional Catholic heritage. The board games *Here I Stand* (*HIS*) (2006) and its sequel *Virgin Queen* (*VQ*) (2012) model the intersection of the religious and military conflicts of this century. In either game, each of the six players portrays a single ruler prominent in this period. The asymmetric lineup of powers included ensures that some powers will be most involved in the religious struggle, while others are most keen to gain glory through traditional warfare. The game mechanics employed by these board games allow conflicts in both the military and religious spheres to be simultaneously represented.

In *HIS* and *VQ*, the key towns of Europe are drawn on a point-to-point grid, as is common for all games in their card-driven wargame (CDW) genre. When political control of a CDW space changes (typically through military conquest), the new owner gets to place one of his control markers on the space to depict that town's updated status. In *HIS* and *VQ*, these control markers serve a dual purpose. The nationality of the marker is still used to portray political ownership. However, the back side of each counter has a white interior. When a marker is on this white side it means that, regardless of which power enjoys political control, the townspeople of that space are now following the reformed, Protestant faith. This distinguishes these spaces from those with markers on their front (fully colored) side, which indicate places where the inhabitants have remained faithful to the Catholic Church. These dual-purpose markers allow the game system to track two layers of conflict (political and religious) on a single map.

The mechanics for battle and seizure of political control of spaces in *HIS* and *VQ* are similar to those used across the CDW genre. However, these games contain two new mechanics that model the religious struggles of this time. Powers involved in the religious conflict are allowed to play their cards (or trigger events off the cards) to undertake actions that result in conversion attempts (CAs). These religious conversions are most likely to succeed in locales close to historical religious leaders (such as Martin Luther or John Calvin) and in spaces adjacent to towns that have already flipped to the desired religion. Success in a CA changes the religious influence of that space; players can mark this new state by flipping the existing control marker to its opposite side. Once a religious power has swayed the people of a space to their preferred faith, they may then go a step further and undertake a rebellion. These actions represent the raising of troops willing to take up arms and fight to

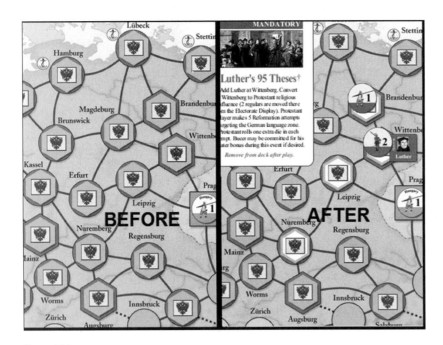

Figure 45.1

Here I Stand opens with the publication of Luther's ninety-five theses. In this game, the citizens of Brandenburg, Wittenberg, Leipzig, and Nuremberg choose to follow the Protestant faith (shown by flipped control markers on their white side); Protestant troops rise up to protect Brandenburg and Wittenberg.

defend the newly established religion. (Historical examples of such a rebellion include the German princes who formed the Schmalkaldic League in Germany and the Huguenot forces in France.) The Rebellion action is our first example of a religious mechanic triggering a result that spills over into the military conflict.

HIS and *VQ* are at their best in these moments when the political and religious spheres collide. For *HIS*, this occurs most frequently in Germany. The Hapsburg player, taking on the traditional role of the Holy Roman Emperor, must keep the six electorates of Germany under his political control. Even though the Hapsburg player is unable to take any direct religious actions, his armies provide strong modifiers to efforts by the Papal player to flip spaces back to Catholic religious influence. It is common in the later stages of a *HIS* game to see Hapsburg armies moving into Germany at the same time as Papal religious envoys. Such a combined operation is the best way for these two powers, one military and one

religious, to work together and jump-start the Counter-Reformation.

In *VQ*, the religious struggle takes place in four distinct areas: France, the Netherlands, and Scotland (areas where the Protestant player is trying to displace the traditional Catholics) and England (where the Catholics are trying to reestablish their faith after having been expelled by Elizabeth I's Protestant reforms). Establishing a strong religious presence through CAs before undertaking a political rebellion is especially critical in each of these regions. If the Catholics are successful enough in England, they can rebel against Elizabeth and place Mary Queen of Scots on the English throne. And if the Huguenots can establish a strong enough presence near Paris, the Protestant player may declare that control of Paris is indeed worth a mass. Just as occurred historically, that declaration allows Henry Navarre to lead his Huguenot armies into the French capital, a move that often leads directly to Protestant victory.

Taking Gods and Kings onto the World Stage

I led the design team implementing a similar multilayer system to model religious and military conflicts in the PC computer game *Sid Meier's Civilization V* (2010), which introduced a detailed religious system with its 2012 expansion pack *Gods and Kings*. When playing *Civilization V*, your nation is able to create one of history's great world religions. You then reap rewards for spreading your religion's belief structure as far and wide as possible. This section looks at how a multilayer conflict model was again used, though this time in altered form to leverage the advantages of a digital implementation.

Religions in *Civilization V* consist of a set of five gameplay boosts themed on historical religious thought or institutions. Known as "Beliefs," these boosts can provide a benefit either to the owner of a city or to the founder of the religion. Because the benefits of most Beliefs scale based on the percentage of the game world following that religion, a player who founds a religion is rewarded for spreading his faith as far and wide as possible.

The game map for a typical *Civilization V* session contains several thousand hex tiles. Although the political owner of each of these spaces can change on a tile-by-tile basis, that level of granularity was too detailed for a secondary system like religion. Therefore, religious control is tracked on a city-by-city basis. However, detail is added by tracking the religious affiliation of each citizen living in a town. Based on the total religious pressure received from nearby religions the population of a city is divided among competing faiths. For example, a city of population 8 could find its citizens split as follows:

- 4 Buddhists
- 2 Catholics
- 1 Zoroastrian

- 1 atheist (i.e., a point of population not yet committed to a religion)

If half or more of the population is committed to a single religion, the benefits of that majority religion apply in all the tiles associated with that city (so, in this example, Buddhist beliefs would be active). Such a detailed breakdown of religious affiliation is easily possible here on the computer, but it would be a nightmare to track for a tabletop game.

Conversion actions that change religion affiliation are present in this game world, much like in *HIS* or *VQ*. Now the agents of religious change are on-map

Figure 45.2

In a screenshot from *Sid Meier's Civilization V*, a Celtic Missionary approaches the Ethiopian capital of Addis Ababa. This unit is able to spread its faith into adjacent cities, perhaps establishing Catholicism as a more dominant religion in Addis Ababa than its current Eastern Orthodoxy.

units purchased by players with an ample supply of the Faith resource. The most common unit, the Missionary, has a Spread Religion action that applies pressure to an adjacent city. These actions are typically powerful enough to cause several citizens of that town to change to that Missionary's associated religion.

One difference between this digital implementation and its board game cousins can be clearly seen in the mechanic that represents the impact of religious ideas creeping into nearby locales. In *HIS*, the existing presence of your religion in each adjacent space provides an extra die roll to each conversion attempt. This mechanic represents both the historical tendency of new religious ideas to spread from town to town and provides players with an incentive to establish and maintain their religion in key geographic chokepoints. In the digital version, however, the computer is an excellent tool for providing a "slow drip" pressure from the presence of your religion in a nearby town. So in *Civilization V,* each Missionary's Spread Religion action is not boosted by adjacent cities following his faith. Instead this adjacency pressure is modeled by simply adding a small increment of pressure to all cities within ten tiles as the game advances from turn to turn.

Civilization V also exhibits numerous areas where the political and religious arenas interact. Political control is strictly required to operate the second religious unit, the Inquisitor. The players use these units to remove the presence of unwanted foreign religions from any city that they control. In addition, they block CAs by enemy Missionaries in a town they are protecting. However, an Inquisitor is of no use in foreign lands, so supporting them by maintaining political control of a region is paramount.

Some of the religious beliefs that can be selected for your religion are also directed at enhancing military action:

- Defender of the Faith: helps you defend cities following your religion.
- Just War: helps you capture cities following your religion.
- Holy Warriors and Religious Fervor: allow you to spend the Faith resource to purchase military units (instead of its typical use for religious units and buildings).

Finally, the political climate of the game is affected by the level of religious strife. Foreign leaders take offense to your conversion activities in their lands, ramping up tensions and perhaps initiating a war. Since religious units are not able to defend themselves when faced with a military unit, the most effective way to stop enemy proselytizing is by declaring war and capturing the enemy religious units directly. *Civilization V* players quickly learn how far they can push their missionary efforts without having an active military presence to back up their spiritual forces.

Conclusion

The common simulation mechanic present in these three games is the tracking of political and religious control on independent layers of the game map.

Most transactions in the game world occur within just one of these layers: battles and sieges decide political control, while the outcomes of conversions and debates decide the religious victor. However, in all three of these games, mechanics have been included to ensure that the two layers interact directly. Modeling these linkages makes it possible to simulate the key historical turning points that make these multidimensional conflicts so fascinating to study. Since religion was a fertile historical battleground throughout the Middle Ages and Renaissance, it worked particularly well in the titles discussed as a nonmilitary factor that helps to bring these game worlds to life. However, the mechanic described has no specific tie to religion: the technique of isolating nonmilitary conflict onto another game layer and providing discrete points of interaction between layers can be utilized to model any sort of nonmilitary conflict.

About the Author

Ed Beach is a lead game designer and programmer working for 2K/Firaxis Games. He headed up the development of the *Civilization V* expansion packs *Gods and Kings* (2012) and *Brave New World* (2013), a nominee for strategy game of the year. He has been involved in the design, production and/or programming of numerous computer games, including *Cleopatra*, *Tropico: Paradise Island*, *Emperor: Rise of the Middle Kingdom*, *Civilization III: Conquests*, *A Force More Powerful*, and *The Battle for Middle-earth*. In his spare time he designs historical board games. Over the past fifteen years, he has led the development of the Great Campaigns of the American Civil War series. He has also designed two award-winning games set in Renaissance Europe, *Here I Stand* and *Virgin Queen*. He is a graduate of Dartmouth College, where he majored in computer science and Russian language and literature. He is also a runner, travel enthusiast, and the pitcher on the Firaxis softball team.

46 CULTURAL WARGAMING: UNDERSTANDING CROSS-CULTURAL COMMUNICATIONS USING WARGAMES

Jim Wallman

A cultural wargame is a conflict simulation that places the social, demographic, and cultural aspects of the participants in a conflict at the center stage of a game. This is in contrast to games where the focus might be on hardware, logistics, maneuver, or kinetic combat.

A cultural wargame might use a range of different game structures, including some that look very like conventional operational military games. The key difference is one of focus. So, in a typical cultural wargame, players are briefed with their background and objectives that reflect their culture. These might reflect organizational infighting ("Your primary objective is to achieve promotion"), social factors ("Whatever happens, you must ensure that the Nervii tribe do not gain more honor or status than your tribe"), or personal factors ("You need to make money out of this conflict"). These are all distinct from the "pure" problem-solving found in many wargames, in which the task is to optimize operational outcomes or most efficiently maximize the effective use of resources. This distinction is useful when designing games that replicate "wicked problems" or issues where military operations are conducted in a complex human terrain.

Many cultural wargames are designed in the form of seminar games (e.g., "Barwick Green"—see later in this chapter), but the principles have also been applied to large multiplayer map games (e.g., "Crisis in Binni," "Sengoku," "Crisis in Britannia") and games using game boards and counters (e.g., "Henchmen").

A cultural wargame works by deliberately placing the participants in the position of an unfamiliar culture, with rules and procedures and objectives that reflect that culture specifically and then expose them to a scenario that places strains on their assumptions and challenges them to respond *culturally* to the crisis. This has educational and developmental outcomes. So, the cultural wargame can be characterized thus:

- It exposes hidden assumptions in players, and in exposing those assumptions challenges preconceptions.
- It has distinct roles and perspectives.
- It includes cooperative as well as competitive interaction.
- Nonkinetic nonviolent objectives and outcomes are typical; human terrain and soft factors tend to dominate.

- The "rules" are variable and closed—in this context, "closed" means not available to the players but instead operated by the facilitation or control team.

- The game is very likely to include a high premium on societal factors.

Organizational Cultures

I have spent many years developing wargames for diverse audiences.[1] These have ranged from designs for school educational settings all the way through to games for leadership development of senior two-star leaders in the diplomatic, military, and defense fields. In between these two extremes have been games for military training establishments, the UK Ministry of Defense, museums, corporations, and charities—and of course, for recreational wargamers. Many of those games have used the technique of cultural wargaming, especially with the more senior players.

One of the opportunities created by working with such a variety of audiences is to be able to compare a wide range of organizational cultures and attitudes to wargaming. Within the defense sector, for example, there is considerable interest in reflecting human terrain and soft factors, in particular looking at how, in a future war context, military forces can engage with civilian populations and governments, given that the shape of conflict in the twenty-first century is increasingly being conducted within such complex human terrain.

One of the most common insights from facilitating wargames for organizations in the commercial and the third (i.e., charity) sectors is that they are often most concerned with issues related to organizational functionality and communication. These are not always obvious at the outset, but it comes up again and again in the debriefing and gathering insights stage of games.

There have been three main strands of organizational interest that the cultural wargaming technique has been useful in addressing:

- Team development, in particular addressing intercommunication and how to approach hidden agendas. A cultural wargame can expose the effect of those personal agendas on a situation without it being explicitly about the players' real jobs. With careful debrief and facilitation, the game can give an opportunity for constructive insights.

- Personal development. In the context of developing personal leadership and negotiation styles, cultural wargames can create an environment where the participants reflect on their patterns and style—and ask themselves, "Why did I do that?" This is possible in a conventional wargame as well, but in a cultural wargame there is a greater emphasis on intercommunication, and so there are usually greater opportunities for useful and reflective interactions.

- Understanding different cultures. By framing the game materials and in particular personal briefings for each player, some understanding of a different culture, or even the effects of a clash of cultures, can develop. Of course, this might also be achieved by reading material on different cultures, but in the case of a cultural wargame, by interacting within the game environment, the emerging gameplay gives the players an opportunity for "learning by doing," in greater depth and this will help to embed that understanding.

In developing a cultural wargame, we look at the key questions that explore motivation and decision making within the game. As the game unfolds, we find that in the majority of cases a player's actions were based on either a set of assumptions that were untested, or on some underlying assumptions about the other players, their attitudes, or their behaviors. And in interrogating these assumptions we find that they are very often culturally influenced. Every society has its rules, taboos, norms, and conventions. In the wider context, an organization is a microcosm of society as a whole. However, it isn't always fully representative of that wider culture and can easily become a specific, self-selected, subset—in some ways even blind to alternatives or different perspectives.

Perspectives on Other Cultures

My wargame designs for educational and recreational audiences have, over many years, expanded on this theme: looking at familiar subjects and historical periods through the lens of another culture or civilization. I quickly discovered that these approaches and methods are, and have been, eminently transferable to the "serious" world of professional wargaming. To give some examples of what I mean:

- A game on the Vietnam War entirely from the Vietnamese perspective. This game turns around ideas of how the cultural norms in Western culture, in particular how "the other" is viewed. In this game, the interactions between the various nationalist, rural, and regional groups and the South Vietnamese and North Vietnamese governments are played out, looking in particular at political, economic, and social objectives. The involvement of the United States and its allies is treated as an uncontrollable external factor that intervenes semirandomly, often with tremendous force.
- A game on the 1941 invasion of Malaya from the Japanese perspective. This campaign was, and still is, regarded as a terrible disaster for the British Empire, often seen to have been overmatched by a ruthless and efficient enemy skilled in jungle warfare. Turning this story around shows the confusion, lack of capabilities, and genuine uncertainty on the Japanese side, as well as their assessment of how a colonial power might resist. From this perspective one can examine crucial differences in understanding and attitude and see how outcomes are less certain when viewed from the "other side of the hill."
- A game set in the world of J. R. R. Tolkien's *The Lord of the Rings*, but from the orcs' perspective. In the books, the orcs are an unspeakably evil species, in effect an *untermenschen*, and have absolutely no redeeming features. But what would it be like to represent these ultimate outcasts? What are their motivations, objectives, and society like? This game tests assumptions in a challenging way and looks at how behavior and communication are thoroughly defined by preconditions and cultural assumptions (in this case, that "orc" is equal to evil).

This "countercultural" gaming exposes players to some key experiences and can, on a good day, not only fundamentally challenge their understanding of the scenario but also create some profound reflections on the nature of their own culture.

Spoken and Unspoken Assumptions

In a cultural wargame we use the scenario to expose assumptions. These are grouped into four types and then reflected in the game structure and team/player briefings at one level or other.

- Spoken assumptions. These are the obvious: given hierarchies, professional skills, organizational habits, and rituals that underpin how we work. This is typically modeled in the visible game structure and understood by all.
- Implicit assumptions. These involve what you think you know about the other. These are reflected in player-specific team briefings and in some cases form a key part of the background to the game and for the players. Playing the game can be a vehicle for gaining insights into players' own implicit assumptions.
- Unspoken assumptions. Language, rules, and acceptable behavior are all present but deliberately not always made explicitly clear because it is assumed that "everybody knows." This is a fertile area for development through the game medium because different players or teams of players will be given (or bring with them) a set of "everybody knows" unspoken assumptions.
- Hidden assumptions. These are assumptions you don't know you are making. These have the potential to make all of the above useless; they are possibly the most interesting type of cultural

assumption and one that is amenable to being brought out as an outcome from the game. Good facilitation and postgame debrief will help players reflect on and identify those hidden assumptions—and in the context of developing team communications, this is often the most valued takeaway from the game. Carefully setting game briefings and objectives create opportunities for these hidden assumptions to enter the emerging gameplay.

Built into every wargame, every scenario, and (I would argue) every participant are both spoken and unspoken cultural assumptions. Military audiences have readily identifiable spoken assumptions: their hierarchies, professional skills, organizational habits, and rituals; these are generally known to all parties and can be easily accessed. On the other hand, the unspoken assumptions are both more interesting and more likely to cause friction. Unpacking these unspoken assumptions is a challenge, but it can be managed by the imaginative use of a wargame in the right setting, and in a cultural wargame this is an explicit outcome or insight from a given game. Additionally, one may want to expose participants to cross-cultural communication from the operational environment: things such as working with allies, engaging the political environment at the village level, or interacting with the more general human terrain in the game.

"Barwick Green: An Everyday Tale of Country Folk"

This is a game and scenario that I have run as a non-theater-specific example. It is deliberately rather fantastic in order to illustrate the point.

Game Structure

This is a map-based seminar game. It is facilitated by "Game Control," one or two entities who represent all the external factors and create, in the minds of the players, the game environment by adding to descriptions in the briefings, introducing key events (following a set of event guidelines), and ruling on the outcomes of interactions or players' actions. Gameplay takes place with a large reference map of the village and its environment, and ideally with some breakout space for private discussion between the main players.

Scenario

At some undetermined time in an alternative present day, England is undergoing a bitter quasi-civil war. Outside the big cities the rural villages are run by

Figure 46.1
Berwick Green map and counters.

traditionalists who hold on to ancient rituals and beliefs (such as belief in the Church of England, listening to or watching the BBC, drinking tea, and eating fish and chips), and these are often infiltrated by the violent extremists from the Albion First Movement and the National Freedom Front. UN forces have been deployed on peacekeeping in the County of Borsetshire, with troops patrolling the various villages. The game focuses on the tiny fictional village of Barwick Green.

Player roles:

- Local wealthy landowners.
- Local tenant farmers.
- Pub landlord.
- Smallholding farmers.
- Local notables: the vicar, the chair of the Women's Institute, a local middle-class busybody, a village policeman, a shopkeeper.
- UN peacekeepers.
- UN translator/civil advisor.

The villager players (some of them in teams) are all aware of their place in the economy and society of the village. They have personal status, which they are encouraged to guard jealously. They need to work to make some in-game money (the game system has players generating income via the "day job"), although the game's background of unrest and insurgency has an impact on their income. Taken altogether, these factors create a working environment and set an important part of the context.

Some of the villagers have private sympathies with the extremists. However, there are no village players briefed to be part of the extremist faction at the start of the game. The UN players do not know this, and might make assumptions that the village contains active insurgents—this last bit is important, as the core scenario model is of an otherwise peaceful village placed in an unusual, challenging, and potentially stressful new situation.

Into this peaceful village scenario comes a UN military force. This force does not need to be played, but it can add to the scenario when it is; it can also easily be run by Game Control. Where the game participants are military in real life, then the incoming force must be one utterly unfamiliar to them—say, UN troops from Bangladesh, Nigeria, or Angola, for example. In some cases—for example, if this is being played outside the United Kingdom—the basic cultural assumptions will be unfamiliar. In one game played in the United States, an American player playing one of the villagers had to have it explained that everyone didn't own a pistol and no civilians have automatic weapons legally in the United Kingdom (although farmers might have a shotgun).

Issues that arise from the peacekeepers might include:

- Repeatedly getting people's names wrong, especially mispronouncing them.
- Misunderstanding the role of the Church of England.
- Not paying attention to the established social hierarchy.
- Ignoring the economic necessities of the village; e.g., some people need to travel to the nearby town to work, farmers need to congregate at market.
- An unspoken assumption that all the villagers are untrustworthy or extremists.
- Issues around gender and particularly the roles of women as leaders in society.

The villager players get to explore the concerns, objectives, and daily life in a village and test these assumptions against what they think might be the motivations and objectives of the UN forces.

If the UN peacekeepers are played, they will have objectives based in their home culture, including attitudes to women, alcohol, music, and religion and their own social norms. For example, a predominantly Muslim peacekeeping force might have to take particular measures to keep their troops out of the pub. Care is taken with these briefings not to resort to simple cultural stereotyping; however, the UN briefing gives depth and can be educational for players unfamiliar with an alien culture.

Usually, in this sort of game, the villager players quickly become frustrated at their lack of power and how they are marginalized and (unintentionally perhaps) treated with disrespect. In many games like this, some players quickly become militant, as one would expect, though it is also the case that players engage with their roles so that conflict and tension among the villagers is as important as between the villagers and the UN.

Typically "Barwick Green" takes about half a day; there are longer versions that can run for a couple of days, with a more complex scenario and additional injects such as rural council meetings and activities by extremists. These specific crisis points can deepen the game considerably, but the game doesn't need to be long or especially elaborate for the point to be made; it can achieve some really good outcomes in just a couple of hours.

Outcomes

The outcome and insight debrief of a game such as this is essential, as participants will often reflect on their own communication practices, especially if they are explicitly invited to do so. Open questions such as, "How did you feel your decisions/actions affected the interplay between the villagers and the UN, and how might that have been different?" start meaningful conversations about cultural difference, assumptions, and most important, perceptions of the other.

Typical outcomes and insights from a game like "Barwick Green" include:

Figure 46.2
Berwick Green map and character cards.

- Modeling cultural difference. The players are challenged and given the opportunity to draw

insights about how they approach cultural difference.

- Drawing out participants' hidden assumptions.
- Observing and extracting insights into individual negotiation approaches and options analysis.
- Making the familiar unfamiliar, which generates opportunities for explicitly exploring "perspective bias."

Through games like "Barwick Green," the cultural wargame, either as a stand-alone game or as a key component of a conventional wargame, has a great deal of utility in reflecting the social and human terrain aspects of a wargame scenario. In its use of different perspectives and its careful development of roles and briefings, it brings out insights that might be much harder to achieve using other techniques.

About the Author

Jim Wallman is a professional game designer specializing in manual games for developing insights, strategy, and team development and for education, with more than twenty years of experience in the field. He has designed and delivered map wargames at the political, strategic, and operational level for the UK Defense community; board games for the British Army; more than forty published sets of sand table wargaming rules; and command and decision games covering issues such as equipment development, political crises, strategic planning, and civil disorder. He has worked extensively with the corporate, public educational, and voluntary sectors, in particular designing and implementing games for senior leadership development and analytical wargames for the UK Ministry of Defense. His background and training is primarily in the social science and history fields, with a particular interest in the practical application of positive psychology to game structures.

Note

1. See <http://www.pastpers.co.uk> for my ludography.

VIII OTHER THEATERS

Esther MacCallum-Stewart

But first let it be noted in passing that there were prehistoric "Little Wars." This is no new thing, no crude novelty, but a thing tested by time, ancient and ripe in its essentials for all its perennial freshness—like Spring.

—H. G. Wells, *Little Wars*

There is a long-standing tradition of wargames told through the medium of storytelling. The Brontë sisters were inspired by a box of toy soldiers, and created the Angria stories and the Gondal Saga from subsequent games with them. Anne and Emily Brontë continued to work on the Gondal Saga throughout their lives and Emily produced over seventy Gondal poems. Poems like "The Prisoner" tell specific moments from the Saga, but often hint at far more developed backstories:

> The captive raised her hand and pressed it to her brow:
> "I have been struck," she said, "and I am suffering now;
> Yet these are little worth, your bolts and irons strong;
> And were they forged in steel they could not hold me long."
> (Emily Brontë, 1845)

Although Charlotte Brontë destroyed a great deal of the work after their deaths, what does remain suggests a richly developed world subject to war, political intrigue, and overthrow. One hundred and fifty years later, the first *Dragonlance* series (1984–1985) by Margaret Hickman and Tracey Weis, and Tom Clancy's books *The Hunt for Red October* (1984) and *Red Storm Rising* (1986) mimic this structure by retelling, respectively, an *Advanced Dungeons & Dragons* campaign and aspects of the games *Harpoon* and *Convoy* (see LaGrone 2013).

The *AD&D* games were played by the authors and their friends from TSR in the early 1980s; the *Dragonlance* books were released consecutively with several *AD&D* modules of the same name and went on to become a successful franchise. "Dungeon crawl" novels are still popular, and echoes of these can be seen in many fantasy series including Jim Butcher's Harry Dresden books, in which the characters clearly become stronger as they progress through the novels, and even more directly in Jen Williams's *The Copper Promise* (2014), in which the main characters clearly mimic an adventuring party moving through various encounters and ultimately fight an epic battle against an invading horde of dragon people: "Even the trio of central characters bear the hallmarks of a tabletop fantasy RPG: a fighter/mage (Lord Frith), a paladin (Sir Sebastian) and a thief (Wydrin, aka 'the Copper Cat')" (Webb 2014).

This first aspect of wargaming literature demonstrates how objects or game systems can be used to create stories, echoing Bruno Faidutti's statement about wargames being a site of suspenseful reenactment (2007). War and combat underpin the narrative throughout: the forces of darkness threatening to overwhelm Krynn, a war against faerie and humanity, an invading army. However, how do players reach this point? For the Brontës, toy soldiers led to an obvious act of paidia, subsequently re-created through poetry and writing. Hickman and Weis needed a more regimented existing structure, the *AD&D* rules, in order to give their war story voice; around this evolved a rich narrative in which warfare plays an integral part, both as part of the metanarrative, and through individual moments such as skirmishes between the player characters and other adversaries.

This in turn leads to the first of the transitional wargame literatures, the "example of play." In tabletop role-playing games, it is common for an example of play to be written as a script, with stage directions indicating the points at which game rules come into effect. The text is meant to demonstrate to players how they might integrate role-playing with the more technical aspects of combat. The *Call of Cthulhu* rulebook has a cringeworthy example of this, where the fictitious players mix actions interchangeably between role-play, ludic play, and the representation of themselves as players or their characters:

> The KEEPER continues: Shuffling into the room is a ghastly parody of a man. It stands almost eight feet tall, with deformed, twisted extremities. Its face is a mass of wrinkles. No features are visible. Its sickly brown-green skin is loose and strips of decaying flesh flap from its limbs. It drips the filthy brown water seen earlier. You three try Sanity rolls for 1/1D10 points each.
>
> JOE: I made my roll successfully.
>
> CATHY: I blew it, but Jake lost only 3 Sanity points.
>
> PAULA: Uh-oh! I'm really scared! I lost 9 points. (*Call of Cthulhu*, 1981, 88)

Gary Fine sees this sort of construction as integral to building a shared fantasy of the gaming world, and helps establish what he calls the idioculture—the culture that develops between small groups in order to help them negotiate unique social cues—of each individual group (Fine 1983; Fine 1979, 734). Fine differentiates wargames from role-playing games since they lack such developed levels of personal involvement, are more tied to history, and are not as ludically flexible. Regardless, the emphasis on the historicity of the role-playing gameworld, which often contains warfare and is frequently referred to using military terminology (e.g., "campaigns" are lengthy story arcs), shows that there is considerable, although often blurred, crossover between the two. Jon Peterson argues persuasively that this was not a coincidence: it derives from Gary Gygax and Dave Arneson's roots in wargaming, and resulted from their use of such terminology in *Chainmail* and early versions of the *D&D* handbooks (Peterson 2012, 203–205).

Although the example of play given above is fictitious, Matthew Kirschenbaum notes a clear stylistic similarity between write-ups of wargame battles and actual war reportage. Wargame accounts posted online often have disclaimers in front of them "lest an unwary Web surfer, Googling for grist for a term paper, mistake a wargame after-action report for an authentic account of a victorious Japanese navy or a triumphant Napoleon at Waterloo" (Kirschenbaum 2009, 357). These after-action reports are written in the style of war reportage, detailing each action, giving statistical information, tallying up casualties, losses, equipment and munitions in an abstracted manner, as if written from afar. In the case of the Gondal Saga and the *Dragonlance* books, a more detailed, personal context overlays this type of account, adding depth and compassion through characterization and individual responses. The examples of play are a sort of halfway house whereby statistical information or ludic detail is inserted to provide guidance for players and to encourage them to develop their role-play in response to this.

H. G. Wells's 1913 *Little Wars* is regarded as a core moment in the development of wargaming (see Jon Peterson's chapter in part I of this collection). It combines these modes of wargame literature in the short pamphlet that explains how to play the game. Before the rules of the game are explained by Wells, *Little Wars* contains thirteen pages of introductory text which detail how the author invented the game and honed the rules, largely through playtesting with friends. This serves as an early version of a development diary, as well as justifying the importance of wargaming to the prospective audience. After the detailed and rather discursive rules section, the book has an "example of play," a long description over another eight pages of "The Battle of Hook's Farm." This could perhaps be described as inventive reportage— the author supplements his commentary with subjective statements wryly analyzing each competitor's moves:

What Red did do in the actual game was to lose his head, and when at the end of four minutes' deliberation he had to move, he blundered desperately. He opened fire on Blue's exposed centre and killed eight men. (Their bodies litter the ground in figure 7, which gives a complete bird's-eye view of the battle). (Wells 1913, 27)

Little Wars uses these different techniques to engage its audience, drawing in those familiar with the author's work into the unfamiliar territory of gaming, and providing them with a number of different access points through which to appreciate the game.

The examples given here are important not because they represent defining moments in the historicity of wargaming or wargaming literature, although some do this as well, but for their varied nature and for the diversity of writing formats represented within them. The Gondal Saga is a series of imaginative retellings of paideic play, while *Little Wars* and the "example of play" in *Call of Cthulhu* are imagined descriptions of a series of ludic rules for a game. H. G. Wells deliberately takes this in three different directions: the narrative at the beginning draws in readers familiar with his writing, the rules explain the game, and the example of play balances both together. The *Dragonlance* series and *The Copper Promise* extend the reportage aspect into a more imaginative domain: they are retellings of tabletop role-playing games after the event, which narrativize the adventures of the participants in a fictional context and contain warfare as an undertone in the background. All of these texts are legitimate examples of wargaming literature, despite their differences. At the core of each example lie fundamental differences in the way that "play" and "game" are understood, and as such, they not only epitomize the multifarious issues surrounding these terms within game studies, but are a fair expression of the diversity of narrativized wargaming.

Importantly for the purposes of this chapter, each example engages with war in different ways. *Dragonlance* tells the story of a long, drawn-out campaign, in which war takes second place to the development of character. H. G. Wells uses *Little Wars* to justify his fascination with simulating battles through play, as well as presenting a series of rules to readers who he assumes are totally unfamiliar with the then nonexistent genre. The example of play in *Call of Cthulhu* is also instructional, attempting to detail a short combat sequence through the eyes of a typical role-playing group. While this example might seem furthest from "wargaming," it still carries elements of reportage and showcases a single moment within a larger battle.

My argument here is that it is difficult to separate each formation when looking at literary accounts of wargames. These complex representations all encapsulate one or more ways of representing wargaming in literature, but they also suggest rather fuzzy edges. While tabletop games contain extensive campaigns that often lead players into war, they might not always be termed "wargames." However, as Wells has shown, the difference between a wargame and a tale of a wargame is not always clear-cut. It is worth remembering this when thinking about texts such as Tom Clancy's *The Hunt for Red October* or Ernest Cline's *Ready Player One*.

The latter book contains core plot elements devoted to *Dungeons & Dragons*, the video game *Joust* and the film *WarGames* (1983). *Ready Player One* is a tale of protagonist Wade's journey to find the secret at the heart of the MMORPG/virtual world the OASIS—but at the same time, the signifiers of wargaming in video, paper, and filmic format throughout the book not only place Wade into a situation where he must play his way free from each scenario but also suggests a more direct war against the villainous employees of the ISP IOI; at the end of the book, Wade and his friends use giant retro-mecha to fight IOI. It is this sort of complexity, whereby wargame, wargame narrative, and narratives that contain wargames overlap, that must be taken into consideration when considering the narrative potential of this subject.

The Evolution of Wargame Narratives

I have deliberately taken an expansive view of the term "wargame" for several reasons. Literature (and other media) use rather generalized and nebulous criteria to define this term, criteria that shift from text to text. This chapter examines these texts critically rather than attempting to categorize them within a framework of "better" and "best" representations of wargames and wargaming—an entirely reductive activity that does not allow for effective critique. The mode and semiotic meaning of "wargame" is constructed according to need by these texts, and this moves beyond literary depictions alone, as many of the different perspectives elsewhere in this collection clearly demonstrate. It is not therefore a productive activity to follow this avenue; rather, we must examine how literature and popular media use the term, and what subsequent meanings these texts produce.

As Kirschenbaum has argued, board wargames have a lot to teach about how narrative is created in games and "help us to understand the role of process and procedure in stories and games" (Kirschenbaum 2009, 369). In addition, they have a rich history of their own as reportage, literary texts, and fan-produced artifacts. Literary and popular texts also refer to wargaming as a common trope, including using them as a central theme, as an adage or plot device, as extended or short metaphor, or simply as a throwaway reference. Why are wargames used so pervasively as tropes in popular culture, yet why are these depictions so limited? Furthermore, many of the texts used here suggest that the difference between a wargame and a tale of a wargame is not always clear-cut. This chapter therefore examines some of these examples but also asks if it is possible to move beyond these constructions.

In what follows, I will unpack some of these ideas and argue that wargaming literature occupies a number of different positions within popular media. Thus, the two ideas—of seeing literary elements in wargames through playing them as a narrative and consuming their narratives retrospectively arc able to live cohesively together.

Although gaming continues to become a more developed leisure activity and engages more people in both physical and virtual contexts, this has translated slowly into popular culture representation, which often still presents gaming—perhaps because of feelings of threat or unease—as problematic and artistically stunted. The social stigma of playing games means that they are referred to vaguely within other texts, lest authors be seen to have too much of a close relationship to them, or to alienate readers with details they might not know. Direct references to games are often seen as a marker of geek culture, rather than as signifiers in their own right; for example, the discussion of *Settlers of Catan* in Benedict Jacka's novel *Chosen* (2013) demonstrates the unity and domestication of a group of characters who were antagonistic in the previous book in the series—but *Chosen* is clearly aimed at a very specific urban fantasy niche.

This chapter thus examines the popular and literary representations of wargaming, but it also questions what this literariness means and how it manifests in popular culture, as allegory, metaphor, and subject. Rather than list the repetition of wargaming tropes in popular culture, I discuss some of the motivations for this. Wargames are often used as signifiers to suggest fairly broad tropes: the villain who plays chess is a clever tactician who will almost certainly be caught out in the end by the hero; the soldier who takes part in a team game before the war begins is doomed from the moment he picks up his cricket bat (see also Clover 1992 for the "final girl").

Ideas of sportsmanship, playing by the rules and cheating become dominant thematic elements. Here, a more vague idea of what play entails is used to suggest that warfare in general is not a "fair" activity, engaging with a more emotive ethos of war and conflict that usually positions it as wrong. These ideals are confused by the contradictory ideas that war is definitely not a game but that, like games, warfare is an ultimately futile, immature activity. Elsewhere, physical wargames such as LARPs, reenactments, or Airsoft often connote deviance and criminality. This chapter unpacks some of these ideas, asking whether popular culture has any inclination to portray wargaming and its participants in a more nuanced light.

I then examine how games can be used to suggest or discuss warfare in literature and other popular culture. First, I examine how chess is used as a quick-and-dirty signifier to connect metaphors of warfare and games. Chess provides a familiar example for the reader, although surprisingly it is also rather semiotically bland, rarely moving beyond this binary connection or making in-depth situational arguments. Despite this, wargame-as-chess metaphors have become important cultural signs.

Next I discuss the rather fleeting examples of wargames in literary texts that have been used to discuss social, political and cultural constructions. (Although one might expect wargames to be a pervasive feature of science fiction texts in particular, they are rarely the focus.) Notable examples occur through the creation of fictitious war/sociopolitical games such as in the HBO series *Game of Thrones* (based on

George R. R. Martin's long-haul fantasy series *A Song of Ice and Fire*), the worldsphere of Orson Scott Card's *Ender's Game* and the Global Thermonuclear War "game" in the 1983 film *WarGames*.

Finally, the last two examples in this chapter show how depictions of wargames can move beyond simplistic representations. Here, games are used to reflect the adversarial nature of political machinations, but develop in novel ways. In Roberto Bolaño's *Third Reich*, the Avalon Hill game *Rise and Decline of the Third Reich* takes center stage as the author uses protagonist Udo Berger to explore the potentialities of a German playing the Third Reich in a World War II wargame, unpacking ideas of nationalism, sanity, and obsession. In Iain M. Banks's *The Player of Games*, the game of Azad not only underscores the central argument of the book but is also narratively a game so powerful that it determines who rises to power and shapes an entire empire. In these novels the ideas of wargaming and "war as a game" are used more subtly, and perhaps point to more sophisticated means of representing wargames in future media.

"All Part of the Plan": The Metaphor of Warfare

References to wargames in popular culture are often vague or simply refer to games or gaming culture in general; so, for example, it is common for the act of game playing to be mentioned as an indication of manipulation, or for a central character to be seen playing a wargame (usually chess—see the following) to demonstrate their devious nature. Similarly, children or young adults are often shown playing wargames (usually FPS titles), to connote their abstraction from society, lack of social graces or violent tendencies. Wargames are rarely mentioned

in a positive context; they are often used instead to suggest that their players have skill or intelligence but possess underlying sociopathic or degenerative tendencies. An interesting example of this comes from the TV show *CSI: New York* (2004–13). In the episode "Fare Game" (2006), a man is shot at a graveyard and yet no bullet is found in his wound. The trail leads to a group of people who are playing an ARG called *WaterGun Wars*, in which they are given targets who they then have to stalk and "kill" with water pistols (the series calls *WaterGun*

Wars a "wargame," whereas to a more critical eye the game seems more a combat-based ARG or PvP game). The prize for being the last contender is $100,000, but it rapidly develops that the contestants don't really know how their targets are being selected; instead, they receive instructions and "hits" from an organizer known only as the "Supreme Commander." The detectives track down contestant and suspect Jordan Stokes, first seen watching a preview of the game *Hitman* through a shop window. In fact, the game is a red herring and the murder involves out-of-work actors (those rascals!), but the implication throughout is that the participants are greedy and rather paranoid (one contestant hires an office to entrap other contestants and adds glass powder and security lasers to his windows). Although the "violent video game" trope is not trotted out here (it makes several appearances in other *CSI* episodes), the "wargame" is seen as a peculiar, antisocial activity, and attached to a type of gaming that might appear unusual to a casual onlooker.

A related trope deploys wargames in a more omnipotent manner: characters in books or series might be trapped within the "game" of an adversary and forced to play by specific "rules" in order to escape. Examples of this include the 1982 film *Tron* or the 2010 *Sherlock Holmes* episode "The Great Game." In *Tron*, the initial plot revolves around the fact that all of protagonist Kevin Flynn's programs have been plagiarized by villain Ed Dillinger, thus resulting in Flynn's quest for proof within the virtual world of the ENCOM system. Within this world, "users" are forced to play martial games until they are destroyed, thus ensuring that Dillinger's acts are never exposed to the world outside the game. In *Sherlock*, the allusion is more bland and refers to both Sherlock Holmes's

habit of declaring in the short stories that "the game is afoot!" and the plot, in which Holmes must solve a number of cryptic riddles sent via text message before an allotted time runs out. "The Great Game" also demonstrates a further common trope: wargames in which the villain cheats or adds a new, unforeseen element, as the puzzles set by Moriarty conclude when Holmes manages to solve the final riddle only to find that Moriarty has strapped explosives to Watson which he plans to detonate regardless of Holmes's actions.

Cheating or playing "unfair" seems to be tied to a literary semantic idea that suggests that war itself is unjust and cruel. Wargames in literature fall particularly foul of this, as it makes for a strong twist if the game proves to be something other than it pretends to be, or is being played by different rules. *Ender's Game*, which I will return to, is a very strong example of this—in it Ender ultimately discovers that the game he has been playing has been a real war all along—but more generally this trope is used in a variety of different literary texts to suggest that villains perhaps understand the viciousness of warfare better than the more "sporting" protagonists. In the MMORPG *World of Warcraft*, the Medivh or "Chess" encounter within the Karazhan raid forces players to adopt the role of chess pieces and fight against the opposite army, controlled by Medivh himself. The encounter is fairly easy, since it does not rely on a player's equipment or ability other than to move pieces around the board and attack the opposing side, but Medivh periodically cheats by moving pieces incorrectly or attacking the players in unexpected ways. Here, Medivh is specifically positioned as a villain because he bends the rules of chess unfairly, thus showing that not only is he unchivalrous, but deviant.

One of the most direct examples of this trope occurs in the 1987 James Bond film *The Living Daylights* (1987), during the final encounter between Bond and villain Brad Whitaker. Whitaker's deserted mansion is filled with waxworks of his own likeness wearing the uniforms of famous tyrants, including Adolf Hitler, Napoleon, and Genghis Khan. Whitaker is using a wargame table with automated figures and special effects such as miniature explosions to reenact the Battle of Little Round Top "as I would have fought it." He tells Bond that Gettysburg would have incurred a further 35,000 casualties if Grant had been in charge since

"Meade was tenacious but he was cautious." After Bond knocks Whitaker off his feet by activating a remotely controlled drawer in the wargame table, he explodes a statue of the Duke of Wellington next to him, knocking Whitaker onto another diorama. Later, when asked what happened, Bond says grimly, "He met his Waterloo." Although rather comic, the obvious parallel between playing at war and moral turpitude are clearly made here. Whitaker isn't just a megalomaniac, he's one with a deranged sense of how war should be fought "well," inspired by the dehumanizing use of miniatures instead of people.

Chess

Napoleon the Great, who had a great passion for playing chess, was often beaten by a rough grocer in St. Helena. Neither Shakespeare, Milton, Newton, nor any of the great ones of the earth, acquired proficiency in chess-playing. ... A game of chess does not add a single new fact to the mind; it does not excite a single beautiful thought; nor does it serve a single purpose for polishing and improving the nobler faculties.

—C. Munn, S. Wales, and A. Beach,
"Chess-Playing Excitement"

It would be impossible to write a chapter of this nature without referring to the vast usage of chess as a metaphor for conflict within all forms of popular literature, which also includes the long tradition of war chess variants.[1] As a game with an already-abiding cultural footprint, viewers are familiar with the game and its semiotic meanings. Surprisingly however, the examples tend to be very similar, and present rather bland expressions

which are not often used in much depth. The quotation at the top of this section is extremely unusual in that here chess is seen as a negative activity for those with weak minds (rather unfairly pillorying grocers) and tyrants (Napoleon). However, the underlying precept that chess is a military activity played by strategists remains, and this underpins most examples of the game's appearance in popular culture.

A number of distinct tropes emerge from within this formation; here I examine the ones that specifically deal with warfare or conflict.

Chess as Power Struggle

Chess is played between two antagonists, usually at an early stage in the proceedings before other power plays or actions have come into effect, or when one of them has been caught and safely imprisoned. This gives the two a chance to meet and establish some of their dominant characteristics without real conflict between the two taking place. Magneto and Charles Xavier play chess while Magneto is locked in his glass prison at the end of the first *X-Men* movie (2000). The game foreshadows the fact that Magneto will escape at the start of the sequel, and the game is visible in the background as he does so (2003).

Conversely, "chess as power struggle" is used when antagonists have become so adversarial that they can only communicate through a game, with the suggestion that conflict in real world situations would be socially inappropriate, possibly violent. In *X-Men: Days of Future Past* (2014), a much younger Magneto and Charles Xavier play chess again as they attempt to find common ground from which to rebuild their formerly amicable relationship.

A Game Like Chess

Again, many examples of this exist, but it is usually fantasy or science fiction worlds that take these to useful extremes when reflecting on warfare. Three-dimensional chess (*Star Trek*), Thud! (the Discworld novels), and Cheops (*Dune*) are all used similarly to chess to reflect the importance of tactical thought in "real" situations, to show superiority, and to reflect on the specific marital makeup of each situation.

Thud! began as a 2002 real-world game based on the Discworld novels and ultimately became the topic of a novel of the same name (Pratchett 2005); Pratchett reverse-engineered the history of the game to echo that of chess, and the cover of the book shows the main protagonist trapped between life-sized stone pieces that look rather similar to

those of the Viking Game (circa 400 CE), standing on a black-and-white-checkered game board. The interplay between the characters and the Thud! pieces suggests a melding of Discworld life and game, in which the two come to represent elements of each other; this neatly summarizes the tone of the book itself.

Cheops is perhaps one of the most ludicrous chesslike games, being "nine-level chess with the double object of putting your queen in at the apex and the opponent's king in check" (Herbert 1965, 588); however, it is a useful example since it neatly encapsulates the internecine warfare and gendered power struggles that take place in the Dune books, demonstrating "as in chess, so in life."

Chess to Signify Conflict Elsewhere

Players play chess to take their minds off an ongoing conflict or to foreshadow one about to take place. Tavi from Jim Butcher's *Codex Alera* series (2004–9) plays chess ("ludus") on several occasions, including during a battle, when he is asked by opposing general Nasaug to allow his people to collect their dead. The two play ludus while this happens, and the game is used to imply Nasaug's tacit support for Tavi against the insane ritualist Sarl. In the 1982 film *The Thing*, MacReady pours whiskey into a computer chess game, foreshadowing the frustration with technology and science he will feel when dealing with the later conflict with the Thing. Other famous examples occur in *Star Trek*—which often includes tri-dimensional chess in recreational scenes during which the crew discuss the events going on or defeat visitors who express more martial agendas—and the Holochess game played by Chewbacca and

R2-D2 in *Star Wars*. It is of course advisable to let the Wookie win.

Chess Players are Really Smart ... or Rather Stupid

Mastery of chess signifies a complex, often deviant mind, and many of literature's greatest minds play chess to demonstrate to readers just how clever they are. Interestingly, this form of chess is often played against an absent or nonexistent opponent. Sherlock Holmes plays chess with himself, and Lord Vetinari of the Discworld novels plays Thud! remotely with a friend in Uberwald; Thud! is also used to contrast the oppositional viewpoints of Reacher Gilt and Lord Vetinari in *Going Postal* (2004).[2] In the Harry Potter books, Wizarding chess is additionally a signifier of empathy, since the players must gain the trust of the pieces. Hermione is terrible at it, but Ron is very good indeed and consistently beats Harry throughout *Harry Potter and the Philosopher's Stone* (1997). All three heroes have to collaborate in the "real" version at the end of the book, with Ron telling them what to do and ultimately sacrificing himself in order for Harry to win. Here, the differences between cleverness, wisdom and empathy are seen as complementary types of intellect.

Chess is sometimes played by people who do not understand the game or what it symbolizes, and proceed to either make up their own version or play the game with different rules. Players either become engrossed with these rules or give up on the game, usually after an argument. Here the effect is often comedic, but can also symbolize differences between opponents or a character's lack of tactical prowess. In *Going Postal*, Crispin Horsefly's misunderstanding of Thud! signifies his stupidity. A 2001 episode of the sitcom *Friends* (7.20: "The One with Rachel's Big Kiss")

begins with Phoebe and Joey apparently playing intently, using a competition timer. "We should really learn how to play the real way," says Joey, but Phoebe counters, "I like our way," moving a pawn like a checkers piece and triumphantly announcing: "Chess!" This fleeting scene is a typical use of chess to make a quick point, building on the "nice but dim" nature of Joey and the eccentricity of free spirit Phoebe. As a rather stupid beefcake and a pacifist, neither, it is implied, would be particularly good at either tactics or "real" chess.

Human Chess

Probably the most famous version of human (or anthropomorphic) chess is the game that takes place in Lewis Carroll's 1871 novel *Through the Looking Glass* and forms the majority of what plot the book contains. *Through the Looking Glass* is the key origin text for the trope of human chess and includes an image by Carroll of the "moves" played by each character on a chessboard. The motif of human chess (or chess played by omnipotent rulers) remains popular: it is an early visual signifier in Patrick McGoohan's 1967–68 TV show *The Prisoner*, and helps to set the tone for the series. In Scott Lynch's 2007 novel *Red Seas Under Red Skies*, nobles play a variant of human chess wherein every time a game piece/person is captured, the opponent is allowed to enact any punishment except death upon them. Both examples imply heavily that the human pieces are ultimately powerless "lions" led by uncaring "donkeys," and draw attention as well to the disparities between class and power during conflict (see also Taylor 1974).

Chess is therefore a popular and useful symbol of war in popular culture, providing a quick shorthand to explain a number of concepts, character motivations, or potential responses. However, to continue in this vein would simply create a long list, rather than a critical examination. Studying chess as a referent to war, or within war literature itself, makes it clear that many examples exist—however, after first examination, there is not really much to them. For this reason, this chapter now turns to media texts that specifically deal with the wargame as a central narrative theme.

WarGames

The 1983 film *WarGames* is a Cold War thriller produced at the height of the "Star Wars" project in the United States. David Lightman (Matthew Broderick) is a typical slacker teen, more interested than playing video games than studying. When he breaks into an unlisted computer called WOPR, its AI "Joshua" gives him a list of options of games to play, ranging from chess and backgammon to "Theaterwide Biotoxic" and "Global Thermonuclear War." Out of boredom, and to impress his girlfriend Jennifer Mack (Ally Sheedy), he chooses the last option, unaware that the computer has now started a simulation at NORAD that convinces the military that the Soviet Union is about to launch a nuclear attack.

The film contains several major themes, expressed largely through Lightman's playing of Global Thermonuclear War, and the consequences of doing so. These include the now familiar unease about the growing role of video games (the graphics used to depict the NORAD war room are deliberately very similar to those of 1981's *Galaga*, which Lightman is seen playing in the first scene of the movie), a paranoia that distinguishing between real war and a simulation/game is becoming increasingly difficult (NORAD is repeatedly fooled by Lightman and then WOPR), a tension between traditional forms of learning and self-taught digital native behaviors (both Lightman and Mack get "F" grades in their biology class, which are subsequently changed by Lightman when he hacks into the school database), and an underlying fear about the political situation of the time.

Although Matthew Broderick learns to become a more responsible adult (this is, after all, a children's film—although Wikipedia seems to think it is also a "Cold War thriller"), by ultimately tricking the computer into a stalemate situation, *WarGames* clearly warns viewers of that perennial social fear: that games will turn us into an unthinking society that pays little attention to the subtleties of our real-world lives. This has little to do with the wargame aspect of the film, but it is interesting that this message shares equal weight with a warning against the perils of video games; as a result of Lightman's choices, both at the beginning of the film when he chooses the interesting option (a poor decision), and its conclusion, in which agrees to play "a nice game of chess" with WOPR (a good decision), the film rather drearily seems to suggest that conformity and a lack of experimentation are desirable social assets. Indeed, although the conclusion by WOPR that "the only winning move is not to play" is an obvious comment on the "game" of war, it also suggests that Lightman himself should stop playing and return to a more conformist lifestyle. The film is a cultural touchstone because it manages to transmit contemporary unease around issues such as teenage disaffection, the interchange between "real" and "virtual" war (still a perennial worry), and the intrusion of the military into daily lives while also appearing to be an early teen flick. Yet *WarGames* is neither teenage coming-of-age movie nor thriller, hovering

somewhere between both. Although the film ends with a conformist solution, the central plot still resonates today—in Ernest Cline's 2011's novel *Ready Player One*, part of protagonist Wade's first challenge is to enact the entirety of the film as though it were a game.

Ender's Game

Orson Scott Card's 1985 novel *Ender's Game* is excessively dystopian, and it has caused considerable controversy and disquiet among scholars and critics (Kessel 2004; Radford 2007).[3] In the book, Ender, a young boy from a violently dysfunctional family, is trained from a young age to become a military general as part of a group of children who have been closeted from the rest of the world. The children play a series of martial games, which are both physically demanding and tactical, and take place via computer simulation in rooms rather similar to the X-Men's "Danger Room." The harsh training program extolls bullying and violence in order to determine strong leaders; girls are relatively unsuccessful because, it is implied, they are genetically weaker. As the greatest hope in his group, Ender is systematically taught to distance himself from others in order to become a more ruthless tactician and commander, and during the course of his training, he kills two other children (although is unaware that he has done this). The book concludes with one final game against the enemy, an intelligent insectoid race called Buggers. At the climax of the game, Ender realizes that the enemy Buggers are behaving as if they were a hive mind. He isolates

and destroys the queen. Retrospectively it is revealed that the game was in fact real, and Ender's murder of the queen has implemented a genocide of the Bugger race; every Bugger in the vicinity died at the same moment as their queen. Ender is horrified by what he has done, but the government considers him a war hero. Later books in the series chart Ender's attempts to reconcile himself to these events.

Card's depiction of a real event dissembling as a wargame points to one of the perennial background tropes of science fiction: the expression of politicized ideologies within a fantastical narrative. As with *The Player of Games* (see the following), *Ender's Game* demonstrates that once again, despite being a core component of the novel, the game is not really the thing. Rather, it is a metonymic plot device demonstrating the underlying manipulative nature of the civilization concerned. In the dystopian world of *Ender's Game*, it is Earth's military forces who mercilessly exploit Ender and encourage him to annihilate the Buggers; in *The Player of Games*, the Azadians reflect some of the worst excesses of humanity, and are thus ultimately destroyed—and not necessarily for the good—by the utopian agenda of the Culture.

A Song of Ice and Fire (*A Game of Thrones*)

Barquiel L'Envers rested his chin on one fist. "Will you teach me to play the game of thrones? I think not, Delaunay."

—Jacqueline Carey, *Kushiel's Dart*

George R. R. Martin's sprawling political epic deals with the machinations of a series of dynastic families and their struggle to rule the land of Westeros. Written over a period of nearly two decades (and incomplete at the time of writing), *A Song of Ice and Fire* (1996–present) makes frequent reference to the "game" of politics, and by telling the story from a split narrative point of view presents each character as a player within it. Characters can easily be likened to pawns, queens, knights, and religious leaders (bishops). Martin deliberately portrays his characters with nuanced strengths and weaknesses, and allows readers multiple perspectives on the same events. The frequent betrayals, assassinations, and conflicts among these characters mean that the reader perceives each as potentially disposable, as mere pieces in a grander conflict, and the various factions in the novels clearly echo the representation of traditional factions in war and wargaming.

The title of 1996's *A Game of Thrones*, the first book in the series, uses a relatively common construction from fantasy literature to describe political intrigues; Jacqueline Carey uses the same term in 2003's *Kushiel's Dart* to describe politicking in the D'Angeline court, and Robert Jordan uses the phrase "Game of Houses" in the *Wheel of Time* series (1990–2007; posthumously Jordan and Sanderson 2007–13); Raymond Feist and Janny Wurts use "Game of the Council" in the *Empire* series (1987–92). In all of these long-haul series, machinations between ruling families underscore the central plot arcs.

A Song of Ice and Fire has been adapted by HBO into their most popular television series to date, renamed *Game of Thrones*; the change of name places a stronger emphasis on intrigue and warfare than the more ambiguous "ice" and "fire." *Game of Thrones* retains the emphasis on split narratives, although it frequently edits Martin's chronology in order to present a more coherent narrative to the viewing audience—for example, one or two characters may figure heavily in the same episode in order to make their story more memorable and cohesive, whereas the same events may have been interspersed throughout several books of the novel series. *Game of Thrones* visualizes its global conflict using various means, notably in its opening credit sequence. In this, the viewer takes a bird's-eye flight across a steampunkish clockwork map; as the camera approaches each stronghold or location, the building assembles itself, unfolding or growing accordingly. Marked on each building is the sigil of the house or faction that controls it. The map changes according to which locations are featured in each episode, and to reflect the current status of the buildings; for example, in some series, the fortress of Winterfell is a smoking ruin—although the surviving characters are represented by a world tree still growing in the ashes. This opening sequence directly connects a wargame-style map with the action of *Game of Thrones*. The (invisible) characters are rendered unimportant within the grander scheme of a larger game, and the buildings and terrain become tactical pieces to be captured or destroyed. The bird's-eye view of the camera as it sweeps across the map suggests a player who perhaps controls the map or acts as an omnipotent, dispassionate observer.

Game of Thrones therefore portrays a sophisticated response to wargaming, one which demonstrates a knowing relationship with the viewer. It does not matter if a particular viewer does not pick up on the wargame map metaphor—the credit sequence is still visually impressive and iconic (it won a Creative Arts Emmy Award in 2011) and encodes other strong metaphors, such as the encapsulation of the whole world within an orrery. During the series, the viewer also sees incarnations of the map in physical form at Stannis Baratheon's fortress, and on paper at Winterfell and King's Landing. Various characters, most notably Robb Stark, Stannis Baratheon, and Tywin Lannister, are seen manipulating wooden or pewter figures on war maps.

The suggestion that the players are pawns or pieces within a game fits nicely with the themes of both show and books, and makes the references to wargaming less crude and overt. The books and series stay true to this theme; despite the nuances of most characters, and a blurring of obviously "good" and "evil" characters, the political landscape is nonetheless played out as a cutthroat, aggressive game. Following naturally on from the books, Fantasy Flight Games have also released a number of *Game of Thrones* board and card games.

The Third Reich

Roberto Bolaño's posthumous *The Third Reich* (2010; originally published in Spanish as *El Tercer Reich*, 1989) contains one of the most complicated depictions of wargaming in literature, first because it depicts an actual game, Avalon Hill's 1974 *Rise and Decline of the Third Reich*, and second because Bolaño depicts the obsessive nature of the protagonist Udo by tying the narrative of the game tightly to the overall structure of the novel, becoming more detailed as Berger spirals toward madness. Berger, who always plays the German side, embarks on a game in the second half of the book with El Quemado, a burned man and itinerant hobo who may or may not be the devil. As Berger becomes more engrossed in the game, so his behavior becomes more disassociated from the real world, subject to erratic and seemingly hallucinatory episodes.

It is clear that many reviewers of *The Third Reich* don't know how to interpret the gameplay within the book. Giles Harvey describes it as "like *Risk*, only much more complicated" (Harvey 2012), and Nicholas Thomson as "a strategy game much like *Axis and Allies*" (Thomson 2013). It's likewise clear from these examples that reviewers are not generally comfortable with discussing, or indeed, understanding, the intricacies of the game—if they are even aware that it is a real game. Anthony Paletta argues that this leads to incorrect descriptions of Berger's gameplay as "obsessive": "That's not inaccurate, but it's a sort of obsession rendered by a clear kindred spirit, with a detail of gameplay description impossible to anyone who wasn't deeply familiar with the topic" (Paletta 2012). This in itself is interesting, suggesting that critics are more willing to go down the stereotypical route of "games as dangerous obsession" than really trouble themselves with the nature of Berger's play (he is a wargaming champion accustomed to playing intensive, lengthy campaigns). There's also an assumption in their rather trivializing examples that this type of game isn't really worth investigating in more depth; this despite the intensity of the gameplay descriptions of *Third Reich* within the novel.

The Player of Games

The idea, you see, is that Azad is so complex, so subtle, so flexible and so demanding that it is as precise and comprehensive a model of life as it is possible to construct. Whoever succeeds at the game succeeds at life; the same qualities are required in each to ensure dominance.

—Iain M. Banks, *The Player of Games*

One of the most prolific writers to feature wargames is Iain Banks (or, while wearing his science fiction hat, "Iain M. Banks"), whose caustic utopianism forms a dramatic contrast to the political and social mores of books such as *Ender's Game*.

Banks uses games in several of his books, including 1987's *Consider Phlebas* (Damage), 1993's *Complicity* (*Despot*), and 2007's *The Steep Approach to Garbadale*, which features a family who have become rich through the sales of the board game *Empire!* Most of these games are themed around conflict in some form; *Despot* is loosely based around the video game *Civilization*, and Banks frequently described its inclusion in the book as a justification for the huge amount of time he spent playing it. *Despot* anticipates the complexity of later god-games such as *Civilization IV* (2005) and *Europa Universalis* (2000), and protagonist Cameron delights in playing an aggressive, immoral leader throughout the book: "*Despot* is a world-builder game from HeadCrash Brothers, the same team that brought us *Brits*, *Raj* and *Reich*. It's their latest, biggest and best, it's Byzantinely complicated,

For a more in-depth discussion of Bolaño's novel, I refer the reader to John Prados's chapter in this volume.

baroquely beautiful, spectacularly immoral and utterly, utterly addictive" (Banks 1993, 51).

Cameron is less immoral as he likes to think, however, and as his life starts to collapse (a result of making the right decision a moment too late), someone hacks his game and destroys his carefully built world. In *The Steep Approach to Garbadale*, *Empire!* is a game of conquest and strategy, mirroring the rather unscrupulous nature of the Wopuld family. Arguments over the nature of the game, and whether to allow a buyout which will almost certainly result in *Empire!* losing its core ethos, reflect the numerous conflicts and family secrets they hold. As a further example, in *Consider Phlebas*, the utopian society the Culture has been at war with the Idirans for many generations. Reflecting the constant presence of violence and conflict are violent and antagonistic games such as Damage, where players bet the lives of other people against each other.[4]

However, the most famous of Banks's wargames is Azad, from 1988's *The Player of Games*. The protagonist of the book, Jernau Gurgeh Morat, is a renowned game player from the Culture (Morat means "game player" in the Culture's language, Marain). Bored of playing the same games and their lack of challenge, Gurgeh is recruited by Special Circumstances, the covert arm of the Culture, to play Azad, a game so complex that forms the basis of an entire society, in which those who perform well in periodic Azad tournaments are allocated positions of power according to their relative proficiency and play style.

Gurgeh's preparation and playing of Azad takes place over the majority of the book, which explores elements of morality and ludus in society, as well as commenting more generally on the nature of societal structure and ethics. Banks's socialist approach can be seen in the way that Gurgeh ultimately wins the game by playing more like the utopian, inclusive Culture than by assimilating the aggressive, reductionist tactics of the Azadians. As the book continues, Azad as a society is gradually exposed as deceitful, corrupt, misogynist and elitist. It is suggested that the Emperor of the Azadians may not actually have won his way to ascendency, but instead has fixed matches in order to reach the top. To avoid the xenophobic shame of an alien winning the game, later Azad tournament matches are staged so that Gurgeh is apparently knocked out quickly and decisively, although he continues to play subsequent games. When Gurgeh is about to win the final game (and therefore become Emperor himself), the current Emperor cheats in order to keep his position. It is also suggested through this act of cheating that constructive interpretation of the rules, chicanery, assassination and political behind-the-scenes wrangling has been responsible for the placement of players throughout the games—however, this is an aspect of "play" that Gurgeh does not realize until this moment.

Gurgeh's blindness to concepts such as ownership or gender bias initially prevent him from understanding how to win, but ultimately allow him to use unexpected tactics against his opponents. His participation in Azad and his subsequent "win" causes the xenophobic Empire to collapse; exactly what the Culture had in mind: "Azad—the game itself—had to be discredited. It was what held the Empire together all these years—the lynchpin; but it made it the most vulnerable point too" (Banks 1988, 296).

The Player of Games epitomizes some of the issues with representing fictional games through nonvisual media. There are several apparent contradictions in the game rules as presented, as well as areas in which the game is simply not explained very clearly, although this may be authorially deliberate. Instead, the reader is given fleeting glimpses of the game and basic details such as the fact that it takes place on three large, terrainlike boards and that the pieces are genetically engineered, "part vegetable, part animal": "It was only when he started to try to gauge the pieces, to feel and smell what they were and what they might become—weaker or more powerful, faster or slower, shorter or longer lived—that he realized just how hard the whole game was going to be" (Banks 1988, 104). Azad is both a two-player and a multiplayer game during different stages of play. Gurgeh plays two rounds against large groups of ten players, but alternates between two-player iterations of the game that appear to take the same form. Near the end of the book, when he has progressed to the last stages of the game, his penultimate round is against two other people. Of course, this is within the remit of a complex wargame, and many board games can be played by between two through six players—however, it is very unusual for games which involve two players to be successful with as large a group as ten people. Perhaps inevitably, artists Mark Salwowoski and Richard Hopkinson both drew their covers of *The Player of Games* to suggest an alternate variant of chess.[5]

Conclusion: "The Only Winning Move Is Not to Play"

The most memorable quote from *WarGames* seems to reflect an underlying message about representing wargames in popular culture and literature: playing games is bad, and mixing war and games is even worse. Many of the examples in this chapter have shown games to demonstrate moral bankruptcy, deceit, ulterior motives and degenerate personalities. Although wargame literature does exist in forms such as the example of play or post-game reportage, the majority of popular and well-known examples of wargaming show it in a negative light. Thousands of examples exist for chess, and the cultural meme that links playing games with poor socialization or a twisted understanding of reality is taken to extremes when wargames are used to connote dangerous situations or power struggles. It is therefore difficult not to see the use of wargames in popular culture as a rather negative trope. They are not seen to disabuse traditional moral panics about games, tied as they are to undercurrents of violence or deviance; in most texts the reference is rather lazy, included to make a simple, trite point. Finally, as with Iain M. Banks and the fantasy writers who discuss variants of the "game of thrones" within their work, there is a generic element to representing wargames; it is used to suggest political situations or relationships, but rarely drawn further into actual descriptions of functioning games themselves. Bolaño's *The Third Reich*, with its detailed hex-by-hex play, is the only meaningful counterexample of which I am aware.

Matthew Kirschenbaum has suggested that wargames can be read as narratives, and this brief overview of wargaming writing has shown that it also provides a valuable foundation for different types of prose. As a trope it seems culturally pervasive but not particularly exciting. Perhaps not playing is indeed the better option—or more optimistically, we can develop readings of alternative sorts of texts, such as "after action" reportage and play examples as more complex ways to position wargaming in popular culture. It would be heartening to think that as games in general become more culturally accepted, their representation in popular texts will increase in complexity.

About the Author

Esther MacCallum-Stewart is a Research Fellow at the Digital Cultures Research Centre, University of the West of England. Her work investigates the ways that players understand narratives in games and she has written widely on representations of warfare in gaming, gender, role-playing, and sex and sexuality in games.

Notes

1. The website *Chessvibes* once hosted a video montage of several hundred examples of chess used in film and television series, spanning everything from domestic drama to space opera (and sometimes both);

this has since been removed for copyright infringement. But see also TVTropes <http://tvtropes.org/pmwiki/pmwiki.php/TabletopGame/Chess>. Some chess variants were actually called *kriegsspiel*: see Wikipedia's excellent page on this subject <http://en.wikipedia.org/wiki/Chess_variant>.

2. In the same book, when the characters Death and Granny Weatherwax have to play Thud! against each other—in a nod to Ingmar Bergman's *The Seventh Seal*—they both decide to play cards instead.

3. *Ender's Game* has disturbed critics because of the unrepentant cruelty of the novel, as well as the Final Solution enacted upon the Buggers. Card's underlying homophobia (implied in the racial nickname for the Buggers, but expressed more specifically elsewhere) is throughout his writing also accompanied by suggestions of racial superiority and misogyny. "Whereas most exciting controversial novels include one or two hot-button topics at most, Card's novel is composed of nothing but a half-dozen hot-button issues wrapped in a *bildungsroman*" (Broderick and Di Philippo 2012, 16).

4. Also note Azad's "wagers of the body," whereby players use different types of mutilation as a betting tool.

5. Although Azad is an "impossible" game, in 2014, a group of players attempted to make a version of the game at the 72nd Worldcon (Loncon 3) in London, in honor of posthumous Guest of Honor Iain M. Banks. A group of game developers (including Steve Jackson, the inventor of *GURPS* and *Munchkin*), Banks experts, and fans took part in a breakneck game-jam as part of the convention. The games produced were lighthearted versions of the "Board of Form" and the "Board of Origin," one spreading across the convention floor and another using a baffling array of pyramid-shaped pieces, fruit, and playing cards with the names and possible ideologies of Culture ships and characters. Small children were recruited by players to build war machines in exchange for bananas, and organizers role-playing adjudicators around the edge of the Board of Origin motivated the spectators to get involved, change the rules as they went along and heckle the players. The result was chaotic and ridiculous, more like a game of "Mornington Crescent" than anything serious, but it did show the potential of Azad to inspire development and creativity.

TRISTRAM SHANDY: TOBY AND TRIM'S WARGAMES AND THE BOWLING GREEN

Bill McDonald

Queen: *What sport shall we devise here in this garden,/To drive away the heavy thought of care?*

First Lady: *Madam, we'll play at bowls.*

Queen: *'Twill make me think the world is full of rubs./And that my fortune runs against the bias.*

—*Richard II*, III, iv

The devotion to nonsense, and enthusiasm about trifles, is highly affecting as a moral lesson: it is one of the striking weaknesses and greatest happinesses of our nature.

—William Hazlitt, *Lectures on the Comic English Writers*

Tristram Shandy *is as much an act of pure play as any novel ever written, but as with other kinds of games, it is play that makes us strenuously rehearse some of the vital processes by which we must live in reality.*

—Robert Alter, *Partial Magic*

All I wish is, that it may be a lesson to the world "to let people tell their stories their own way."

—*Tristram Shandy*, IX, xxv

Veteran readers of Laurence Sterne's *Tristram Shandy* (1759–67) will pity anyone attempting an overview or summary for those who have yet to enter its six-hundred-plus page labyrinthine playground. Ostensibly an autobiography, the novel is famous for its narrative arabesques, compulsive digressions, learned wit, associative stops and starts, hilarious non sequiturs, plotlessness, parody and satire, childish and adult bawdy humor, intertextual mazes, bizarre catalogs, sentimental orations, deliberate misquotations, paralysis and impotence, pleonasm, long sections in Latin or French, philosophical conundrums, and its inability to arrive at the birth of its eponymous hero and narrator before its third volume. So it is a relief to avoid the quagmire of a full account and focus, as best as *Tristram* allows, on the specific subject given me for this chapter. That subject is 1.5 roods of English turf, located just beyond the vegetable garden of Captain Toby Shandy, uncle to our narrator, brother to his hyperrational father, and veteran of King William's Nine Years War against Louis XIV and the French (1688–97). My goal is likewise narrow, though difficult to contain: to explore the world of the wargames conducted by Uncle Toby on his bowling green, whenever possible foregrounding the turf itself. So, happily eschewing summary, I will take Tristram's own advice about beginning to heart—"first I write the first sentence—and trust[ing] to Almighty God for the second" (VIII, II)—and get right to it. And there is no book I would rather revisit in 2013, Sterne's tercentenary year.

Toby's bowling green has several facets, both historical and imagined. It is a distant descendant of England's medieval bowling greens, of which Southampton's, which dates from 1299, is the oldest survivor. Bowls' general popularity in the succeeding centuries was great enough to merit censure from several English noblemen and kings; though relishing the game themselves, they forbade commoners to play it on the grounds that it distracted them from honing their archery and other useful war skills. A legal ban against the game was on the books, if irregularly enforced, from Henry VIII's day all the way to 1845. Henry's statute forbade "artificers, labourers, apprentices, servants & the like … to play bowls at any time except Christmas." Since Anne Boleyn was among the game's many fans, he may have had several motives. Later, city officials also took exception to the wagering that grew up around the game, necessarily ignoring the fact that several of their rulers, notably James I and Charles I, were high-stakes bowls gamblers (Sarudy 2013).

Many bowling greens were set up near English taverns in Sterne's time, so that customers could take their well lubricated competitiveness outside.[1] Eighteenth-century bowling greens were typically square, flat of course, and laid out slightly below the surrounding turf, with a gravel border and, often, low hedges that set them apart from the rest of the garden. However, Toby's "tall yew hedge … rough holly and thickset flowering shrubs" (II, v)—note the two sacred plants—isolate his bowling green completely, making it in effect a *hortus conclusus*, a sanctuary and playing field for the two men. Bowls must have been played on it at some point, but neither

Tristram nor Toby makes any mention of its particular history. So in the novel the bowling green never serves the purpose it was designed for, but becomes instead a blank canvas, an earthen Etch-a-Sketch, upon which Toby and his loyal corporal and companion Trim re-create the sieges of the latest continental struggle. No doubt Tristram's readers also enjoyed the joke of having a bowling green, forbidden to ordinary soldiers in the name of military training, be the site of wargames run by two wounded veterans.

Part two of the bowling green's etiology necessarily covers some familiar ground for *Tristram Shandy* aficionados. For readers yet to have that pleasure, I will present it chronologically, a straight-line narrative path the novel systematically avoids. Toby's lifelong commitment has been to serving England in the field ("I was born to nothing, quoth my uncle Toby … —but my commission" [IV, iv]), a service he dearly loves. That service came to an end in 1695, at King William's siege of the Flanders city of Namur. While either lying (IX, xxviii) or, more probably, standing (II, i) in a traverse trench before the city walls, preparing to attack, Toby suffered "a wound to my groin" from a large piece of stone broken off by, ironically, an English shell striking the parapet of Namur's hornwork fortification (I, xxi; II, i; IV, xix). The wound damaged both his pubic bone and his ilium (as for any further damage to his groin's soft tissue, we have to wait and see). Toby is repatriated to England, where his merchant brother Walter rents a London house and takes him in. But his wound will not heal: the bone "exfoliates" (I, xxv; II, v)—casts off infected cuticle very slowly in the form of leaves or scales—leaving Toby, like Amfortas, largely bedridden and "suffering unspeakable miseries" (I, xxv). Well-intentioned Walter decides that a talking cure can aid his brother, and invites all visitors to climb the stairs to Toby's sickroom to hear his battle story. Company does provide some relief, but—typical of most any action or rational plan in *Tristram Shandy*—soon paralyzes Toby because he cannot tell his story without first explaining all the fortifications, as well as the cross-trenches, dykes, and drains in the battle-field. The complexities of correctness and inclusion repeatedly overwhelm him, and three months of this treatment only worsen his condition.

So Toby devises a new plan: showing, not telling. He procures a large, detailed map of Namur's fortifications and the surrounding topography so that he can point out to visitors the "exact spot" where he received his wound. This, together with reading a book on military architecture, does make him more articulate, and more exact. But his rapidly accumulating knowledge of that "spot" soon becomes entwined in such a maze of technical fortification terms, elaborate outworks and crisscrossing natural features that his health remains at risk.[2] Over the ensuing three years he reads everything he can on the seemingly inexhaustible topics and subtopics of military strategy, and acquires maps of "nearly all" the important fortified towns in France and Italy (VI, xxi). Tristram terms this Toby's "hobby-horse," the subject he will ride on any occasion and apply to any circumstance. But the wound remains.

So Corporal Trim proposes the decisive final step: that they return to the Shandy homeland in Yorkshire and re-create on the Captain's bowling green the siege of Namur. Here is a longer quote to give Shandeans and non-Shandeans alike a feel for this decision, and for the novel's prose:

> I think, quoth Corporal Trim, with humble submission to your Honour's better judgment,—that these ravelins, bastions, curtins, and hornworks, make but a poor, contemptible, fiddle-faddle piece of work of it here upon paper, compared to what your Honour and I could make of it were we in the country by ourselves, and had but a rood, or a rood and a half of ground to do what we pleased with: As summer is coming on, continued Trim, your Honour might sit out of doors, and give me the nography—(Call it ichnography, quoth my uncle)—of the town or citadel, your Honour was pleased to sit down before,—and I will be shot by your Honour upon the glacis of it, if I did not fortify it to your Honour's mind. ... We might begin the campaign, continued Trim, on the very day that his Majesty and the Allies take the field, and demolish them town by town as fast as—Trim, quoth my uncle Toby, say no more. Your Honour, continued Trim, might sit in your arm-chair (pointing to it) this fine weather, giving me your orders, and I would—Say no more, Trim, quoth my uncle Toby—Besides, your Honour would get not only pleasure and good pastime—but good air, and good exercise, and good health,—and your Honour's wound would be well in a month. Thou hast said enough, Trim,—quoth my uncle Toby (putting his hand into his breeches-pocket)—I like thy project mightily;—And if your Honour pleases, I'll, this moment, go and buy a pioneer's spade to take down with us, and I'll bespeak a shovel and a pick-axe, and a couple of—Say no more, Trim, quoth my uncle Toby, leaping up upon one leg, quite overcome with rapture,—and thrusting a guinea into Trim's hand,—Trim, said my uncle Toby, say no more ... (II, v)

His goal is explicitly, if zanily, therapeutic; by showing the exact spot and by constructing the walls and fields around it, Toby can put his mind—the ongoing source of his incurable wound—to rest. And returning to the scene of the wound, or rather to its simulacra, does work for Toby, sort of. His wound heals, though he still requires a crutch and experiences some pain (III, 24), presumably because of the damage to his ilium. But his hobby-horse now rides off in a new direction, unrelated to physical injury, as suggested by Trim. They will follow the numerous sieges of the War of the Spanish Succession (1702–13), and re-create on the bowling green each successive investment as reported in the government's *Gazette*. They take seriously the military meaning of "retirement," stepping away from the main lines but not ceasing to be soldiers. So now they wait for each new siege to begin, dig out the relevant map, and set to work recreating on a largish scale the war's progress in France. Their emphasis falls on the process of constructing each site accurately, with Toby giving the orders and Trim carrying out the construction: architect-commander and engineer. But they must also, like expert gamers, develop detailed strategies—gun placements, for example—to flesh out what their reports do not narrate (e.g., V, xix). And given the size of the bowling green, a lot of work (and of Toby's £120 a year) is required. The success (or failure) of the siege, including the destruction of the model with a shovel (e.g., VI, xxxiv) is honored, but their underlying purpose is to re-create, and at the same time to sustain their relationship: on to modeling the next siege! Their simulacra are also, themselves excepted, free of any model soldiers: human-free fortifications in which no death reenactments take place. In Roger Caillois's well-known typology, Toby and Trim avoid games of (1) *agon* (competition), (2) *alea* (chance) and (4) *ilinx* (literally, a whirlpool: unbalancing, thrill-seeking, confusing) for his third category: mimicry: imitation and simulation (Caillois, 14ff). Poor Tristram is clearly mired in the fourth category ("we live among riddles and mysteries—the most obvious things have dark sides" [IV, xxvi]).[3] Their wargames are pure pleasure, honorific, celebrative ... part of the "whimsical theatre" of the Shandean family (III, xxxix).

And unlike the actual theater, and nearly all games, this one need not come to an end.

Now for the specifics. Toby Shandy's bowling green is big. Forced into cramped quarters throughout the novel—the claustrophobic, smoked-filled rooms of Shandy Hall, the snug living room of Widow Wadman, Toby's "neat country house"—most readers have underestimated its size: a "rood and a half of ground to do what they would with" (II, v). At three-eighths of an acre, it is just a little smaller than Toby's adjacent kitchen-garden, and its more than sixteen thousand square feet offer protogamers Toby and Trim considerable space for large-scale modeling: no tidy tabletops for them. "Fate" and "Nature" have conspired to give it just the right balance of compost and clay for shaping outworks and prospering in every weather (VI, xxi). They follow only the sieges, not the general progress of the war. And Tristram is explicit in his "sketch" of the terrain: each map was "enlarged to the exact size of the bowling-green." First Trim, who does all the construction, lays out stakes and packthread, then meticulously constructs the fortifications and ditches that comprise the site.[4] Accuracy is paramount, and camaraderie essential; neither man plays on the bowling green alone.

Because the whole green is taken up with the fortified town, the besiegers' trenches regularly have to move into Toby's garden. The captain spends all day—no surprise, given the scope of the constructions—sitting and "chatting kindly with the corporal upon past-done deeds" while he works (VI, xxi) and no doubt relishing the "voluble" Trim's replies (II, 5). And when the *Gazette* reports that Marlborough's forces have breached a town's defenses, Toby marches into his bowling green and right up to the ramparts, reading the report of the

Figure 48.1
Toby and Trim take the field. (Engraving: *The siege of Namur by Captn. Shandy & Corporal Trim. Tris: Shan.* by Henry William Bunbury, 1772; published 1773 by J. Bretherton; British cartoon prints, Library of Congress.)

success "ten times over" as Trim fixes the British colors to the wall.[5] So three interweaving narratives take shape on the bowling green: the latest official report of each siege's ebb and flow; the visual construct of the current investment; and the verbal recollections of "past deeds," presumably ones involving the two men. The three together create a permanent state of military exaltation, fueled by war storytelling, that easily incorporates each new theater into its enchantment. Their work, like

Sterne's novel, is always beginning again, but without succumbing to change or paralyzing self-consciousness; Toby and Trim never lose the sense of immediate and permanent presence in their gaming. Questions as to its significance or its self-deceptions simply do not arise once they step inside its borders. War has been effectively transferred to the private sphere even as its scene has moved from foreign or royal land to private property (elaborated in Lanham 1973, 79ff).

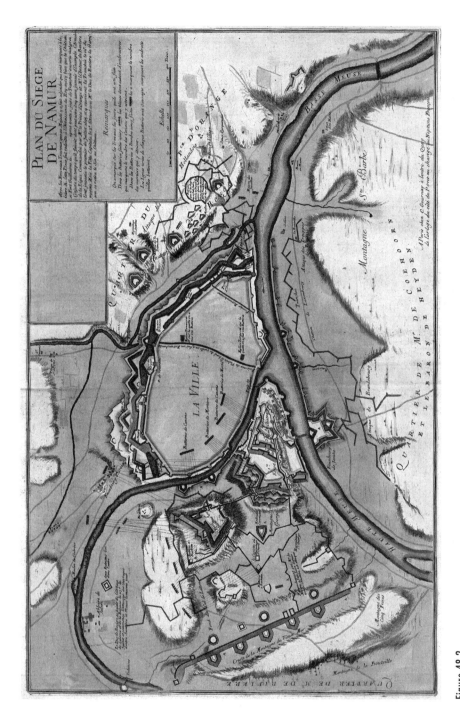

Figure 48.2
The siege of Namur.

Over the years refinements are added (Tristram compares their immersion in the game to that of "connoisseurs" [I, xxviii]) and the strict adherence to realism liberalized a little. First come four drawbridges, then gates with portcullises (later converted into a set of small mounted cannons), then a sentry box for protection against the weather and to hold war conferences, and finally Trim (not Toby) suggests a generic Low Countries town, built by a Yorkshire carpenter, whose freestanding houses can be moved around to re-create the geography of each invested city: "Surely never did any town act so many parts, since *Sodom* and *Gomorrah*, as my uncle *Toby's* town did" (VI, xxiii). A church is added soon afterwards, and the Shandy houses raided for brass that could be recast as cannon; the rules of their game evolve, as does the cost: Walter loans his brother £100 (VI, xxxii). Note that neither the Protean town's specific architecture nor the cannon appear on the siege maps; they require memory and imagination in order to maintain realism's strict illusion. This becomes more the case as time passes; the bowling green's initial role as a virtual fractal of Namur and succeeding sieges loosens its aesthetic to include "armaments" that seem less realistic, though not to either Toby or Trim. When Turkish pipes are re-cast as siege cannon, their tobacco haze (like smoke pellets in a Lionel steam engine) may require great suspension of disbelief from the reader to "see" cannon fire, but not from our two principals. Both are also delighted by the pair of heirloom jackboots, survivors of Marston Moor, cut up to resemble large-bore artillery pieces (III, xxii), that seem well outside the model realism with which they began: invention freed from form. In short, accurate reconstruction and imaginative immersion do not conflict for them. All of these serve to "keep up something like a continual firing of the imagination" (VI, xxiii) that became vital to the entire hobby-horsical project.

They also have no nostalgia about either visiting or memorializing any particular site, goals of many wargame enthusiasts. When the siege is lifted, they are eager for the next one to begin. Outsiders may ridicule the whole enterprise—the fate of every gamer?—but its elevating effect never alters for its players. On the single occasion when Trim deliberately breaks the illusion, reminding a Toby already made "listless" by the war-ending Treaty of Utrecht, that they are in fact on English soil not at the Dunkirk they have been modeling, the Captain actually "rallied back the ideas of those pleasures, which were slipping from under him ..." even as they destroyed their model (VI, xxxiv–xxxv).[6] They feel no need to explain.

It is at this point that most modern commentators turn to psychology to account for Toby's blinkered behavior: sublimation, substitution, compensation, repression, antisocial behavior, fixation all have had their day. Representative is one of Sterne's strongest readers, Richard Lanham: "The whole of Toby's character is a purity of feeling bought *at the price of obsession.* ... Toby is deluded. His delight in war is uncritical, naïve, illogical" (Lanham 1973, 84, 81). Commentators all gravitate toward a theory of character that splits Toby's actions and his "real nature," a conscious/unconscious binary that we moderns cannot resist making all-powerful. The theory indeed has some merit in parts of Tristram's world: in Walter's machinations, for example, or Tristram's own flight from death. But Toby is much closer to the Momus glass exemplum given in I, xxiii: a transparent character, visible all the way down, with matching surface and depth, precisely the kind of character, like Don Quixote, that we find hard to take at face value. For most of us worldliness and irony triumph over sentiment. Further, some have overgeneralized, seeing Toby as hopelessly ignorant, but it is mainly women's anatomy and his brother's philosophizing that mystify him. His arcane knowledge of all matters military, including its history (VIII, xix), shows clear intelligence, and several of his asides reveal a reservoir of common sense (e.g., IV, xxix). Away from the bowling green he can demur, even satirize, and regularly signals the presence of surprise, cant or absurdity by whistling (never actually singing) his favorite tune, "Lillabullero."[7] Most readily associated with the Don, Toby occasionally plays a Panza-skeptic to his brother's quixotic quasi-philosophical flights (see Alter 1987, 93). So Tristram's account of his uncle—all we have, after all—allows for a little post-Freudian speculation if we must, but mainly points us instead in another direction: Toby's sentiment. Tristram tells us that he will use Toby's fortifications hobby-horse to characterize him, and so he does, but beneath that metaphoric toy creature Tristram tells us is Toby's "real nature." Toby is a character we can know completely, the magical gift novels have always offered us in our readerly isolation.

It is also helpful to approach Toby's real nature in a wider cultural field, a bowling green of our own devising. Many interpreters have elaborated on Toby's pivotal representation of masculinity's evolution in eighteenth-century England. He models the change from the heroic, aristocratic male hero as figured in classical and early modern societies to the sentimental good man who instinctively feels the misery of others, feelings that generate a natural ethic. The wounded soldier was a perfect archetype for the shift, and the end of Gray's "Elegy in a Country Churchyard" perfectly encapsulates the new

standard: "gave to misery all he had, a tear." Toby marks the shift from greatness or "excellency" to goodness (III, xxxiv), from "Captain" to "Uncle," as the male ideal: from the field of action to the relational and domestic scene (see Staves 1989, 84). Contributing to this conversion, Tristram rarely tells stories of Toby's actual combat experience, concentrating instead on the feelings it produces after he is sidelined by his wound. Volume VIII, xix comes closest, with its brief, piecemeal account of Namur. He has been a courageous soldier in battle—"I fear nothing ... but the doing a wrong thing"—and odds on has killed or wounded an enemy. But he gives no account of actually shooting or bayoneting anyone, only of bravely "marching up to the mouth of a cannon" (V, x) or recreating, with great emotion, an advance upon the French trenches to "receive their fire and fall in upon them ... horse and foot ... helter skelter" (V, xxi: see also V, xxxii). Such bravery, as Tristram tells us, is not alien to love, and creates in him, years later after Toby's death, "the secret spring of sentiment or rapture" (IX, 24). Toby has now retired from the field, but without surrendering the feelings that made it meaningful.

Next, Toby has been an obsessive reader from his youth, when he spent his pocket money on the English romance of Guy of Warwick and sobbed his way through the *Iliad* and the many popular imitations of Spanish chivalric tales (VI, xxxii) that monopolized his attention. This makes him a direct descendant of Don Quixote (of which more in a moment). He has also been a lifelong reader of the Bible—the siege of Jericho understandably is the "most interesting" to him (IX, xix)—and his Christian theology is "natural," flowing directly from his core sentiments. The man of feeling is more open to God, and has little use for religious law or convention: only feeling, not the right action but the right reaction, matters. It has undeniable, if not measurable, value.[8] "Pity is akin to love," Tristram tells us (VI, xxix), where pity does not have the condescending, problematic overtones it has for us today. So Toby's patriotic and personal feelings flow together seamlessly, and the bowling green is one site where they are perfectly enacted; he stages the battles for the same reasons he went to war: "for the good of the nation" (III, xxii) and to serve his country so that, as he says, "quiet and harmless people, with their swords in their hands, to keep the ambitious and the turbulent within bounds … answering the great ends of our creation" (VI, xxxii). Later, during his siege of Widow Wadman, he tells Trim that "the knowledge of arms … that we have practiced together on our bowling green, has no object but to shorten the strides of Ambition … and whenever that drum beats in our ears, I trust, Corporal, we shall neither of us want so much humanity and fellow-feeling as to face about and march" (IX, x).

Ronald Paulson argues that Toby's books of military science and history have seamlessly replaced his chivalric romances—"an eighteenth-century Quixoticism in which real events (the siege of Namur) are appropriated into the 'romance' world of fortification" (Paulson 1998, 152). I would add that the *Gazette*, with its accounts of contemporary sieges, has supplanted both. Together with the Bible, it is now Toby's main reading, the equivalent of a sports page for a committed fan. Unlike the Don, Toby does not renounce his books.

The comic irony evoked by "for the good of the nation" and the rest of Toby's speech remains in force, but does not erase the valued feelings that inspired it; doubleness, as Jonathan Lamb (1989) has convincingly shown, remains the watchword of *Tristram Shandy*. Of course his model building can be—and most often is—taken for impotent parody of the real thing, if viewed through the conventional heroic lens.[9] But seen in light of Toby's history as soldier and reader, another angle of vision seems more central to our interests. For what Toby and Trim demonstrate every time they essay the bowling green is the love and camaraderie that filled them when they came under fire, or that sustained them through the flux and swampland of King William's unsuccessful 1690 siege of Limerick (V, xxxviii).[10] This camaraderie includes, for them, the strict preservation of rank as ordering their friendship, not interfering with it. Companions for twenty-five years (VI, vi), Trim was wounded in the knee at the horrific battle of Landen in Flanders (1693: more than 28,000 casualties, 19,000 of them on the English Allied side), and nearly died of sepsis—though his leg now stands up to his demanding labor on the bowling green. He became Toby's servant and loyal companion afterwards. Historians and psychologists of war from Thucydides to John Keegan tell us that soldiers may fight for country, but most fundamentally for their fellow soldiers. Veterans returning from Iraq or Afghanistan frequently say that they see the civilian world they are supposed to reenter as flat, even meaningless, in comparison to the intensity and bonding of the battlefield. It is precisely this void that Toby and Trim, without self-conscious reflection, fulfill and preserve on their "little circle of pleasures," the bowling green. To quote from Toby's illogical yet affecting "apologetical oration" in defense of ongoing war, "if his heart is overcharged, and a secret sigh for arms must have its vent, he will reserve it for the ear of a brother, who knows his character to the bottom [as no woman can], and what his true notions, dispositions, and principles of honour are" (VI, xxxii).[11] All this to say that their wargames have a strong ethical as well as pleasure-giving character, sustaining the love and fellow-feeling that they experienced in battle. Self-consciousness about their project would be destructive, a kind of curse; ethical knowledge rooted in sentiment is natural, intuitive. Toby and Trim have unified, virtually conjugal spirits, and care little if others find them quaint, or ridiculous. The open artificiality of what they do disturbs them not at all.

Of course, from a worldly point of view they are alienated men, with their comic, aborted love affairs and their ignorance of much of society. But satire and sentiment often go hand-in-hand in Augustan England, and nowhere more richly than in *Tristram Shandy*. In the most revealing of these combinations for us, Toby and Trim's mock-epic diminutions are reversed: they partake of what Jonathan Lamb (1981) has called the "comic sublime," a Cervantik-derived eighteenth-century celebration of the eccentric but sincere individual who stands apart from society, and whose greatness can only be discerned in small deeds. By 1740 Don Quixote, Lamb shows, had become a model of nobility rather than madness in English culture; Tristram praises him as embodying the "highest idea of the spiritual and refined sentiments" even if he is repeatedly defeated, and "whom I love more, and would actually have gone further to pay a visit to, than the greatest hero of antiquity" (I, x). Lamb (1989) concludes, citing Longinus's *On the Sublime* —a text that Sterne read first to intensify the oratory of his own sermons—that the comic sublime "includes almost every irregularity, from digression to syntactic breakdown. ... As long as they are warranted by pressure of feeling any failure in the order of words, even speechlessness itself, may be powerfully

expressive" (Lamb 1981, 121): Toby's limits and greatness in a nutshell.

So what Toby loves about the bowling green is the soldierly bonding, the experience (sublime) of advancing fearlessly on and, like ideal sex for others, an experience that can be repeated again and again without losing interest: the miracle of satisfied desire that keeps on being satisfied and renewed. It is a magical, Edenic site, mortality-transcending (for a time): fictive yet sustaining. Toby's experience of war included the ugly (the Limerick siege) so he is anything but naïve about its horror. He does not deny that it is terrible, and death-producing (VI, xxxii). But the *meaningful* parts of war are (1) love of country enacted; (2) disruptive rulers or nations curtailed; (3) love of fellow men enacted to overcome fear of death (narrator Tristram's bogey-man); and (4) "the great ends of our creation" served. Toby exemplifies the ethical heroism of sentiment and the comic sublime, even as the novel does not deny his childlike aspects or urge us all to set up a bowling green. Rather we are to imitate his feeling as best we can or (re)discover its central place in our own hearts. As Lanham has it, "They must remain wholly within the game to teach a lesson to the world outside it" (Lanham 1973, 44). The love and loyalty that Toby and Trim practice on their field of play might well be the goal of gamers everywhere: signifier and signified are one. Wargames paradoxically become the site for the practice of love.

> And I believe, continued Trim, to this day, that the shot which disabled me at the battle of Landen, was pointed at my knee for no other purpose, but to take me out of his service, and place me in your honour's, where I should be taken so much better care of in my old age—It shall never, Trim, be construed otherwise, said my uncle Toby (VIII, xix).

Stepping back now, the campaigns re-created on the bowling green have also been compared to the literary game of writing *Tristram Shandy*, first by the author himself: "the life of a writer ... was not so much a state of *composition*, as a state of *warfare*" (V, xvi: italics in original). Tristram's nine volumes in as many years each constitute a new beginning, with an uncertain number of chapters and actions that shift like the fortunes of war. These new volumes parallel Toby and Trim's multiple sieges, each a new beginning or fresh chapter in the war's progress. The two soldiers comprise, in effect, a two-headed artist—designer and craftsman—constructing new simulacra via a realist aesthetic that gradually includes more overtly make-believe innovations. They face similar difficulties as Tristram in shaping their earthen sculptures, returning again and again to a metaphorical blank-page bowling green that requires design, labor, dedication. And Tristram perhaps senses the similarity when he vows, with great feeling, that "thy fortifications, my dear Uncle Toby, shall never be d'molished" (III, xxxvi).

It is an analogy fruitful in both directions, however, and focusing on the differences will enable us to see a little further into our bowling green. First, Toby and Trim do not imitate life directly—after all, they are leaving the war out of war—but rather incarnate stable, objective documents that present the external world in capsule form: architects' fortification maps and the government's own *Gazette*. Labyrinths of trenches that once befuddled Toby's battlefield narratives now can be laid out, controlled, "well seen" as sieges conducted from a general's overview, not a bewildering maze of trenches. As a consequence our old soldiers have a more sure-handed control over the time and space separating them from actual siege-fields than does their chronicler, who fights

endless, and usually losing, battles against a much larger field of unruly time-space and the unpredictable flow of associations that fill his mind. The bowling green suggestively allegorizes their more simple consciousness, one that necessarily reinvents the world but without anxiety.

But what is it that Toby and Trim actually control? Seen from the point of view of the *Tristram Shandy* project, their realism aligns them with the mimetic practices of Sterne's novelistic competitors: Richardson, Fielding, Smollett, and company. Throughout the novel Tristram has parodied literal realism, for example detailing herky-jerky movements that paralyze his characters.[12] The bowling green contributes to this parody but in a broader way, giving us a tightly confined, strict mimesis within the sprawl of *Tristram Shandy*'s pages. It was realism that forced Toby to extend his parallel siege-lines into his vegetable garden. So its high hedges and isolation allegorize realism's limits: sticking with maps, written reports, and "chatting" about old war adventures ironizes the new realism's claims to be the best truth-telling mode. Only by arbitrarily bracketing the constant associations of the mind that comprise Tristram's subject matter can realist narrators arrive at their allegedly omniscient, truthful accounts of the world. They do not have a way of determining when they have told the reader enough or fully explained an action. Still more important, for *Tristram Shandy* it is the relationships between mental connections and imaginings that are most real, not the relationships between events. In sum, the bowling green represents the artificiality, the lack of reality in conventional realism, and is in turn encapsulated neatly as a fenced-in field of pleasure within the much more complicated, unmanageable linguistic and gestural universe of the novel. The comic sublime the bowling green wonderfully sustains comes at a price, in Sterne's view: not only their hermetic isolation but their artificial narrative mode. Toby and Trim's moral sentiments may awaken our authentic natural selves, as they did Tristram's (III, xxxvi), but as noted already their pastoral fantasy world does not. So the bowling green both dramatizes the ethical power of sentiment and the artistic limitations of the realism used to generate it—a message that may carry weight for gamers of any age.

Carrying out all the implications of this parody, we can say that Toby and Trim have, like gamers, only themselves to please. With each new volume Sterne must again face anxiety over the wider world's reception of his work, an anxiety reflected in his several dedicatory letters and in Tristram's dozens of asides on the fate of his project. Toby and Trim have no such anxiety because they wish no audience beyond themselves: any outsiders—the Widow Wadman or her maid Bridget, just to mention two—disrupt their sublimity. Tristram wants his story to reach the world, bring him fame, and fatten his pocketbook; Toby and Trim's achievement would be undermined, reduced to laughingstocks, by any audience or notoriety.

Moving past both the bowling green and Tristram's labyrinthine struggles, there is the larger game masterfully played by Sterne himself. He writes through and around his narrator Tristram, inserting dedications and introductory letters in his own voice, satirizing and sympathizing with his alter ego. And his game includes the many great players who came before him: Montaigne, Burton, Swift, the Scriblerus Club, and especially Rabelais and Cervantes, the designers of the texts that undergird his own and

appear in his pages in many forms.[13] Toby and Trim have their sources too, of course, but both those are clear, relatively uncomplicated and easy to read; the texts of Rabelais and Cervantes are daunting and vast, and any direct reproduction of them risky (though Tristram occasionally chances it, as in the end of volume V, xxix). These two are to be honored and perhaps even equaled, even as competing novelists are surpassed; there is certainly money and fame to be earned and competitions to be won on this literary field.

Finally, nearly all *Tristram Shandy* readers would agree that in the novel's last three volumes Sterne incarnates his own increasingly desperate attempts to elude death from tuberculosis. Tristram's flight across the continent mimics his own attempt to escape its grasp: a serious game indeed. And while novel writing may not prevent death—"Sterne did not live to continue the book" is the final footnote in James Work's groundbreaking edition (see Stern 1940)—it did give Sterne a bowling green upon which to metamorphose his dread into great comic art that endures. Fritz Gysin summarizes Toby in language that might well be applied to Sterne himself: "Toby seeks shelter from an 'immediate' or 'domestic' reality in order to be able to concentrate fully on another, a more distant but to him more relevant kind of reality, which he then imitates, transforms, and thus masters by way of playing" (Gysin 1983, 121). "Transformation" is the operative word, and one shared ultimately by Toby, Tristram and their creator: imitation alone is not enough, and while following the mind's associations risks great confusion, it is only by bravely following that radical reality that he can transform it into significance. The game is worth playing.

About the Author

Bill McDonald taught at the University of Redlands Johnston Center for Integrative Studies from 1969 until his retirement in 2005. He was professor of English and humanities and the first holder of the Virginia Hunsaker Chair in Distinguished Teaching. He has coauthored two volumes on the Johnston Center (1989, 2004), a book on Thomas Mann (1999) and, with Johnston faculty colleagues and former students, published an anthology of criticism and teaching strategies for J. M. Coetzee's novel *Disgrace* (2009). His academic fields include the history of the novel, international modernism, literary theory, ancient Greece, and interdisciplinary studies in the humanities.

Notes

1. Sterne's contemporary George Washington was an avid player from boyhood, and Mount Vernon sported two of them as "suitable for the intelligentsia & ranking army officers." Bowling-Green Fence and Park in Lower Manhattan remains a city landmark today.

2. This mimics the associative pattern of the book, continuously broadening out, losing control of storylines, wandering off into innumerable byways.

3. David Illingsworth (2007) offers a lively discussion of Tristram's plight.

4. Mark Loveridge shows that early eighteenth-century science "often took the form of obsessive modeling, of taking all-pervasive universal patterns and trying to re-create them in the smaller world of man" (Loveridge 1983, 94).

5. In this Tristram suggests that Toby satirizes, consciously or otherwise, the pomp of Louis XIV, famous for his extravagant entrances into cities.

6. The corporal has always been more alert to the fiction-fact distinction than his captain, as befits a Panza-character and one whose actual given name—James Butler—contrasts with his fictive nickname, Trim (II, v).

7. The refrain (later the title) of a piece of political doggerel written in 1687 by Lord Thomas Wharton to satirize the appointment of General Talbot as lord lieutenant of Ireland. The point of view is that of an Irish peasant. The rhyme influenced popular sentiment during the Glorious Revolution of 1688. The lily was the emblem of William of Orange's Irish supporters against the Catholic James II, and the words "lilli bulero bullenala" are a deliberate corruption of the Irish "An lile be leir e ba linn an la" ("the lily was triumphant and we won the day").

8. Once the target of condescension, even abuse, sentiment's made something of a comeback in recent decades: several scholars have illuminated its strong roots in the secular thought of Shaftsbury and Hume, even the physiology of Hartley and others, and show how it has come forward forcefully in the modern era; it no longer can be patronized as an eighteenth-century phenomenon (see Mullan 1988, 201ff).

9. Representative is Martin Price: "his elaborate operations on the bowling-green are an end in

themselves—a reduction of warfare to a harmless game. ... [T]he bowling-green ... is a world he can control and reshape at will ... there warfare becomes a purely tactical game, abstracted from cruelty and suffering" (Price 1987, 24–25). While it is a little distance from my narrow subject, the preponderance of the textual evidence supports the view that Toby was *not* maimed sexually by the Namur projectile. Trim explicitly denies it (IX, xxviii), and both Walter and his wife consider his proposed marriage a real possibility.

10. Sterne spent much of his boyhood following his father's nomadic military career, including time served in Ireland: no doubt his own strong sentiments for Toby and Trim have roots in this history.

11. Madeleine Descargues (2006) works out with impressive clarity the layers of *Tristram Shandy's* double attitude toward war, including Toby's use of phrases taken from Robert Burton's diatribe *against* war in *The Anatomy of Melancholy* (see also, e.g., the Florida Edition: Sterne 2003, 700). Descargues shows that the novel contains "no consistent message about and against war" (249).

12. Sterne's earliest commentators—for example, Horace Walpole in a letter of 1760 to Lord Dalrymple—saw his novel as a satirical sally against realism's dependence on chronology (cited in Keymer 2006, 55). Keymer's essay gives an excellent account of the full novel's complex place in the emerging genre, but I must stay within the bowling green's narrow literalism.

13. One of the ironies uncovered by recent scholarship: Sterne's translation of Rabelais toned down some of that writer's bawdy excesses; the original might well have proved too much even for our liberal clergyman.

John Prados

In the category of life following art, we have the board game *Third Reich* (1974) and the novel *The Third Reich* (1989). I designed the board game (the full title is *Rise and Decline of the Third Reich*) in 1973 and sold it to the Avalon Hill Game Company, which published it for the Christmas season in 1974; Don Greenwood developed the game for Avalon Hill. As the name suggests, *Third Reich* took an all-Europe perspective on World War II and was pitched at the strategic level. It can fairly be said that *Third Reich* wrote the book on strategic-level board games. In its various editions, *Third Reich* sold more than a half million copies and is still remembered fondly by many gamers today.

At the time I designed that game, there was another major wargame company, the New York outfit called Simulations Publications (SPI), headed by its top designer, James F. Dunnigan. I was a freelancer beginning to contribute articles and games to SPI publications and had sold Dunnigan a Vietnam game and article package. SPI had a practice of holding Friday evening sessions where gamers volunteered to playtest products under development. In search of more assignments, I'd adopted the practice of dropping by SPI from time to time, usually on a Friday afternoon, staying into the evening to see what games

were under development, hanging out with my friends among the staff, and always making a point of exchanging notes with Jim. At any rate, Dunnigan had a strategic World War II title of his own in the pipeline, and I saw it being tested. The game felt all wrong to me—not enough granularity, plus a lock-step process at the same time. It was as if a tactical game of a single battle, with its fixed order of appearance, had been elevated to the stratosphere of strategic events. At one of my drop-ins with Jim I offered him some suggestions to open up that game. He was not receptive. A couple of weeks later, at dinner with a former SPI person, I related this story, and my friend encouraged me to go for it—do my own World War II strategic design. I jawboned the basic design concept over the next half hour or so. *Third Reich* was born at The Symposium, a Greek restaurant near Columbia University in New York. Then I went off to make it all real.

The essential insights flowed from the game's origins. There would be diplomacy in the world of multiple players; some of their countries had yet to enter the war, and many minor lands were at peace, open for players to declare war and attack. The perspective of the player had to be that of a national leader. Someone at that level should control an economy and select what kinds of capabilities to acquire. Historicity could be injected by limiting the universe—which I called the "force pool"—to the set of forces the nations actually built. Combat mechanics would be true to the era of armored warfare; hence the selection of corps as the unit of representation. I wanted players to *choose to make* moves that were historical because the game made them logical, not because special rules obliged them to do certain things. I also differentiated between levels of play—offensive versus attrition options, one in which players would act in detail, the other in which losses of troops and territory would be minor and based on overall strength in combat—and among fronts. The combination of the fronts (Western, Mediterranean, and Russian), and the need to pay for Offensive Options obliged players to consider their strategies.

As suggested earlier, *Third Reich* was and remained enormously popular. Unknown to me, among the game's aficionados was a young Chilean who had migrated to Spain, Roberto Bolaño. He had ambitions to become a writer. Some consider Bolaño the most fearless Latin American novelist of his generation, publishing fifteen works of literature before his death in 2003. After Bolaño's passing, his executors found the manuscript for a sixteenth novel among his papers. The book, written in 1989, had never seen the light of day. It turns out the novelist did more than just play *Third Reich*—he wrote a novel about it. The manuscript, translated from the Spanish by Natasha Wimmer, was published in the spring of 2012 by Farrar, Straus and Giroux as *The Third Reich*. The other books won prizes; *The Third Reich* made a game into a literary symbol.

All of which brings us to culture and the iconic aspect of all this. The manuscript, we are told, was among his first. Apparently Bolaño used this project to learn how to structure and pace a lengthy work of fiction. Literary specialists tell us that plot devices and themes Bolaño used in his best-known works, *2666* (2009) and *The Savage Detectives* (2008), were prefigured or rehearsed in this text.

The story concerns Udo, the German national wargame champion, who takes his girlfriend on vacation to a Spanish seashore village. Udo's family had gone there on holiday when he was a child, but he also has an ulterior motive: to develop a perfect strategy for *Third Reich*. Udo and his girlfriend meet other German vacationers and make friends with some of the locals, including an odd fellow Udo inducts into his inner sanctum. "I drew a map of Europe, North Africa, and the Middle East," the protagonist recounts, "and with the aid of many arrows and circles I illustrated my decisive strategy to win at *Third Reich*." Sound familiar? As did so many gamers like him, Bolaño spent endless hours attempting to conceive a "perfect strategy" for the simulation. Whole magazines of the time were filled with commentary on optimal strategies for use at various stages in the game, or for the play of various countries, since in *Third Reich* the possibilities for the different countries represented were quite asymmetrical. But Udo's quest for the perfect strategy was problematical: while there were typically main lines of game events that unfolded fairly reliably, the free-form character of play ensured that the game was endlessly surprising. This became one of the secrets of its success.

In *The Third Reich*, the game becomes metaphor for the vicissitudes and violence of life. One of Udo's new German friends disappears without a trace. The Spaniard who becomes his opponent looms with odd menace over the board of Europe; he turns out to be getting covert advice from the hotelier, who warns Udo of dire consequences if the Spaniard should win. The possibility of murder is not excluded. Udo's girlfriend, in a classic evocation of the "wargame widow," leaves him and goes home. But Udo perseveres. The game becomes the hinge upon which the author pins the trajectory of action in his book. Descriptions of

game events at various stages of the chronology of *Third Reich* serve to prime Udo for events in the novel, and sometimes the game events take center stage.

It is clear this is all real. The game events cited in *The Third Reich* are all episodes that reliably occur in the board game. The evolution of the game Bolaño writes about is a logical progression and recognizable

Figure 49.1

"France defends the classic front line of Hex 24s and a second line of defense along the hex 23s. Of the fourteen infantry corps that by this point should be present in the European Theater, at least twelve should cover hexes Q24, P24, O24, N24, M24, L24, Q23, O23, and M23."

from the simulation. It is also clear that Bolaño used the third edition of *Third Reich*, published in 1981, the first edition to have an alphanumeric system for identifying specific hexagons. Referring to the Spring turn of 1940, he writes, "France defends the classic front line of Hex 24s and a second line of defense along the hex 23s. Of the fourteen infantry corps that by this point should be present in the European Theater, at least twelve should cover hexes Q24, P24, O24, N24, M24, L24, Q23, O23, and M23," and so on.

Udo discusses—this is supposed to be his journal—optimal placement of the British Expeditionary Force ("In any deployment the strongest hex will be the one where the English armored corps is located"), possible German countermeasures (including an invasion of Britain), and the ideal German offensive maneuver. It is clear from the novel that its author understood tactics in the game. For example, *Third Reich* had a mechanic that permitted armored units to flood through opposing lines if they achieved a "breakthrough" against infantry-type units, which lacked zones of control. The second-line defense referred to in the preceding quotation was a standard tactic against breakthroughs. Using German parachute troops for a lightning invasion of Britain was another popular—and much discussed—gambit. Elsewhere Bolaño refers to a perfect strategy for the game proposed by then-Avalon Hill stalwart Robert Beyma, a real person of that era who actually did write about this game. There can be no doubt that Roberto Bolaño was actually writing about *Third Reich*—and from the perspective of a real gamer with actual experience.

Some aspects of the novel are more difficult to comment upon, at least for a gamer from this side of the pond. Bolaño has an entire European gaming infrastructure, with national championships, game conventions, fanzines, its own gurus, and much more. From here in the United States I always knew a strong game culture had evolved in Europe—and certainly their conventions were huge—but I knew nothing of gurus or championships, and only a little about fanzines. But as a general proposition the setup has a ring of authenticity. In the States it is quite true that *Third Reich* became a staple at game clubs—and the era from about the mid-1970s to, say, the early 1990s was the heyday of the American clubs. Bolaño himself refers to one American game magazine, *The General*, which was Avalon Hill's mouthpiece, as well as to other wargames, including *World in Flames*, *Russian Campaign*, *Russian Front*, *Fortress Europa*, *Cobra*, *France '40*, *Panzer Armee Afrika*, and *Panzerkrieg*. These are all authentic game titles from that same period. Taking the novelist's construction of the European game scene as authentic, it would appear that in the United States the evolution has been a little bit the reverse. That is, in America we had a strong club movement, and the meet which now happens every summer called the National Boardgaming Championships did not yet exist. The push to create national championships took off in the late 1980s and 1990s, just as the clubs were losing steam. We still have clubs, of course, and I am a big fan of them—I had one when I lived in New York—but as a national trend the clubs are nothing like they used to be.

Another commonality is the communications network of gaming. The novel's protagonist has begun to sell game articles to the magazines, give lectures—his carrying *Third Reich* along on vacation is for the purpose of compiling remarks he expects to make at a game con—and place items in the fanzines. There was a network like that in the United States, or perhaps more broadly in the United States and Britain, in the 1980s. It ranged from fanzines like Charlie Vasey's

Perfidious Albion to straight strategy game mags like Fire & Movement or Campaign and crossover "adventure gaming" products like the publication of that name or the TSR Hobbies product The Little Dragon. The list would include The Gamer, Command, The General (named in Bolaño's novel), Moves, Ares, and Strategy & Tactics. A number of these outlets paid, either in credits (game companies did this a lot) or in cash. It was possible as a freelancer to earn some money here. As a game designer it was certainly possible to make a living from the hobby, as I did through the 1970s and into the '80s, when I sold my first book, The Soviet Estimate (1986). I am less certain of the possibilities for someone like Udo, a player. The tournaments didn't have purses, the zines paid a pittance, and so on. In this respect, Udo's ambition may have been just that—a hope for a bright future of gaming. On the historical gaming side, at least, it did not turn out that way, but at the time it was a reasonable expectation.

Finally, one chapter of The Third Reich consists solely of commentaries on Udo's favorite World War II generals. This is not a pastime only of gamers, but gamers were (and are) avid enthusiasts for assorted historical characters, weapons systems, tactics, and the like, ready to debate the merits at the drop of a hat. I'd wager there are few gamers of the World War II era who've never argued the relative quality of the Tiger tank over the Panther, or the skills of Field Marshal von Manstein.

The unresolved lives that recede into the future are familiar to the board gamer who has experienced the "wargame widow." Other things fit less well, such as the mystery of Udo's German acquaintance, who dies in the book. A mystery, wrapped in a metaphor, and all about board games. Beyond being an amusing read, the Bolaño novel furnishes an indicator that board games have entered the cultural milieu in a new and intriguing fashion.

About the Author

John Prados is a senior fellow and project director for the National Security Archive in Washington, DC. He is the author of twenty-one published books on aspects of national security, intelligence, military, or diplomatic history, including The Family Jewels: The CIA, Secrecy and Presidential Power; Islands of Destiny: The Solomons Campaign and the Eclipse of the Rising Sun; and Vietnam: The History of an Unwinnable War, the last the winner of the Henry Adams Prize in History.

Other recent works include Normandy Crucible, and How the Cold War Ended. Prados's books Unwinnable War, Combined Fleet Decoded, and Keepers of the Keys were each nominated for the Pulitzer Prize. He is also the designer of many award-winning board games, including Third Reich. He holds a PhD in Political Science (International Relations) from Columbia University.

Stephen V. Cole

In 1975, my senior year of engineering school, I was already a published game designer (having published the magazine *JagdPanther* since 1973) and had been to the first Origins convention. One afternoon, while watching *Star Trek* reruns, I was playing *Jutland*, a 1967 game about World War I battleships that tracked damage by marking off rows of little boxes. Inspired, I grabbed a pad of graph paper, which every engineering student had, and began working out how I would design a starship combat game. Going beyond *Jutland*, which simply "turned off" a gun turret for every few damage points, I established boxes for each system on the starship (weapons, power, tractor beams, transporters, shields, and so on)—the first time anyone had done this.

The ship was laid out in a pattern that more or less followed the "actual" ship seen on television: a round saucer, a secondary hull, and two engine nacelles on pylons. The weapons were located where they were seen on the screen, and the various official and unofficial blueprints that had been published showed the location of some other key external features such as the bridge and shuttle bay. Everything else was fitted into any convenient places in the overall framework. The idea of a "ship diagram that looked like a ship" was intended to make the player feel that he really

was driving a starship. Previous games on various subjects had largely just handled checkboxes as rows and columns with no particular effort to look like a tank, airplane, or warship.

The state of graphic arts in 1975 was nowhere near what it is now. Game graphics were made using thin black tape, a razor knife, rub-on lettering, and a sheet of paper with blue grid lines. Each ship was about two feet square and took a day or two to complete. The arrival of computer graphics in the early 1980s would change everything, but that was still in the future.

The movement system started from air combat games like *Richthofen's War* (1972) but quickly moved far beyond that, providing for the simultaneous movement of dozens of ships, small craft, missiles, and torpedoes. Previously, air combat games moved one aircraft at a time through a series of maneuvers (usually out, turn around, close back in). I wanted my players to be able to fire at any point during the movement of the units, and for the units to move at the same time. The game was playtested with one ship against one ship for three years before anyone tried to fight a larger battle, and all of the core elements were hardwired into the system based on what players could handle with one ship. Shortly after

FEDERATION HEAVY CRUISER

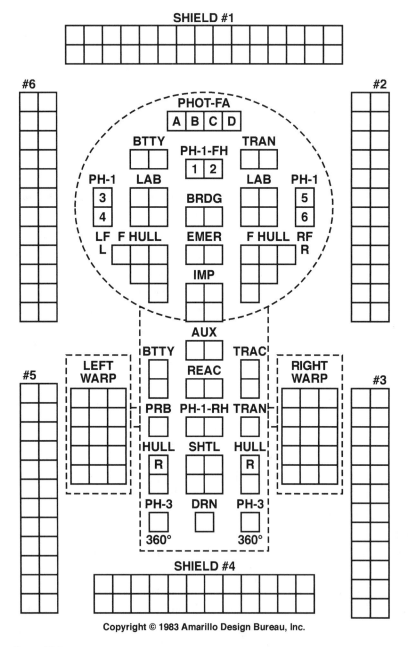

Figure 50.1

Federation Heavy Cruiser ship diagram.

publication, however, players were engaged in ten-on-ten battles without difficulty.

Within twenty-four hours, I had invited a gaming buddy to test the first rough design of what led to *Star Fleet Battles* (*SFB*) (1979), which already included the new concepts of energy allocation, damage allocation, and proportional movement. Under that system, ships paid for a speed and moved during a proportionate number of the turn's thirty-two impulses, spread out during the turn.

Hand-drawn copies with roughly typed rules were a favorite at the office of *JagdPanther*, but everyone knew we did not have any legal basis to publish the game, so it remained only a private amusement. It continued to grow, with new rules, ships, and scenarios. I had been a casual fan of the TV series but now started buying whatever books, manuals, drawings, and technical information I could. By the spring of 1977, *JagdPanther*, never designed to make a profit, had closed down after paying all of its bills, and I took up a new interest—Leanna Williams, marrying her that fall. But the wargaming bug would not die.

My gaming buddy and former *JagdPanther* partner Allen Eldridge and I began thinking in 1978 of forming a new game company. We looked into the industry for a workable business concept. We found two ideas that appealed to us: pocket games (pioneered by Metagaming) and—a first for the industry—no sales to anyone but wholesalers, just to reduce the workload. We sought advice from many people in the game and hobby industries, and decided that to get into the wholesalers we would have to offer four games on the first day. By the spring of 1979, we had plans well in hand. The name "Task Force" was a military term for a mixed organization of combat forces, one that had featured prominently in some game concepts. The term had stuck in our minds and became the company name.

One evening, I was chatting with my friend and mentor Lou Zocchi about industry practices and trends when I mentioned that it was a shame we could not print the "*Star Trek* game I designed in college" because there would be no way to get a license for such a small project. Lou Zocchi put us in contact with Franz Joseph Schnaubelt, the engineer who designed the *USS Enterprise* for Paramount and published the *Star Trek Star Fleet Technical Manual* (1975). Franz Joseph, as he was popularly known, had licensed Lou Zocchi to do his *Star Fleet Battle Manual* (1977) and the original plastic starships (which sparked a hundred lines of miniatures by dozens of companies). Franz agreed to license Task Force to do a "sort of *Star Trek*–like game" within strictly defined limits. Franz had no part in the actual game design, and all of his input came from his book rather than from himself.

At the time the game was designed, electronic games were at the level of a screen of "periods" with a "K" to indicate where the Klingon ship was located, so there was no influence from that source. Since then, several computer games have been based on *Star Fleet Battles* (legally or otherwise), including the best-selling *Starfleet Command* series.

The pocket edition of *Star Fleet Battles* appeared (with three other pocket games) at Origins 1979. Task Force stumbled into a major bit of luck, in that the dominant game publisher of the day had upset the entire industry by selling games at wholesale terms to individual gamers. The retailers and wholesalers were outraged by this policy, which undercut their own sales. A near-riot erupted at Origins in front of the dominant company's booth, demanding that the company stop the practice and preferably end all direct mail orders. The president of that company told the wholesalers, "Nobody sells only to wholesalers!"—only to hear Allen Eldridge (in the booth next to theirs) announce, "That's how we do it!" A few wholesalers who had already been contacted by Task Force confirmed that this was true. Delighted, every wholesaler in the industry (and every retailer at Origins) signed up to carry Task Force Games products on the spot.

Task Force Games, recognizing we had a winner, sold out of the pocket game in a month and reprinted it as a boxed game with added materials. We followed this in 1980 with three "expansions," which was a concept almost unknown in the industry to that date. Unfortunately, the demand for new *Star Fleet Battles* materials quickly exceeded what could be properly tested and what could be made to work well inside the existing game system, and *Star Fleet Battles* began to pick up unpleasant nicknames such as "Errata Wars." I responded by periodically producing entirely new editions of the game that incorporated all of the previous errata, addenda, updates, corrections, and so on.

Allen Eldridge and I increasingly disagreed as to the best way to run Task Force Games, wanting to pursue very different business models. In 1983, we decided to split the company in half. I took *Star Fleet Battles* to my new company, Amarillo Design Bureau. The two companies were "married" by a network of contracts, but relations between the companies varied over time from best buddies to barely speaking. During this time, the strategic (World War II in space) version of *Star Fleet Battles*—named *Federation & Empire* (1986) because I liked the Isaac Asimov book *Foundation and Empire*—came along, and with it I had the idea to brand the pair of games as the "Star Fleet Universe." Over time, the universe came to include

role-playing games (*Prime Directive*), card games (*Star Fleet Missions*, *Star Fleet Battle Force*), tactical ground combat (*Star Fleet Marines*), and more space tactical games (*Federation Commander*, *A Call to Arms: Star Fleet*, and the SFU version of *Starmada*). Also included was a line of miniatures.

A magazine, *Captain's Log*, was created to support all of the games (new ships, weapons, and extensive tactics) and produced a considerable amount of fiction and background. *Star Fleet Battles* created the concept of players submitting "tactics articles" to advise other players how to win (and the entire Star Fleet Universe expanded that concept: every game has its own tactics forums). *Captain's Log* always opens with a piece of fiction that becomes part of the history of the Star Fleet Universe. In the fiction, the reader discovers the background for various abstracted scenarios for the wargames.

By 1987, Paramount had finally noticed Task Force Games and its "sort-of *Star Trek* game" and, finding it legal, offered TFG a "sort-of *Star Trek* license" which remains in place today (and never expires). We got such a good license because *Star Trek* was effectively dead at that point, and the only new material being published was fan fiction and our games. We continued to expand the Star Fleet Universe. When Paramount started doing movies, we noted that there were some differences, and "canon *Trek*" and the Star Fleet Universe have continued to diverge. While canon *Trek* constantly updates and revises its technology, changing long-established principles, the Star Fleet Universe has remained very nearly consistent from 1979. We have a very different map from any of the several "canon" maps. Both canon *Trek* and SFU have added many new empires, none of which appear in both places (we have Lyrans, they have Cardassians). Canon *Trek* moved beyond "The

Original Series" into new time periods eighty years later, but the Star Fleet Universe remained focused primarily on the twenty years after Jim Kirk romanced the women of the galaxy. Canon *Trek* has no drones, cloaked ships cannot use their shields, and the Romulans and Klingons use very different weapons than they do in the Star Fleet Universe. The Star Fleet Universe has fighters and carriers, and our gunboats are much larger than canon *Trek*'s runabouts.

Task Force changed owners in 1990 and again in 1994 (when another new *SFB* edition was released) and finally closed its doors in 1999. At that point, Amarillo Design Bureau incorporated, bought the license and all of TFG's rights under the "marriage" contract, and became the publisher as well as the designer. The result was yet another edition of *SFB* and *F&E*, along with many other product lines for the Star Fleet Universe.

ADB has been in the forefront of social media such as Facebook and Twitter. We reach out to a broad audience, including Trekkers and cosplayers. Our audience includes all ethnic groups; it also spans the globe, with a sizable minority (five percent) not having English (American or British) as their native language. Women comprise five percent of the fans of our products. This is probably a reflection of the diversity of population found in the original source material.

Playing wargames allows players to understand that there are overall principles of tactics and technology that apply to every situation, in the real world or the many worlds of science fiction and fantasy. Probably the best line I ever wrote was that "wargames teach you to work together pleasantly with someone who is trying his best to kill you."

The Philosophy of *Star Fleet Battles*

The basic concept was to "simulate" starship combat, not just do a spaceship game. Being a registered professional engineer and having also had advanced military training (as well as having read over a thousand history books), I knew how major military and mechanical systems worked. There was to be no "roll a die and move that many squares" in this design. While "luck" had a role in the game (since a die roll of 1 produced more damage than a die roll of 6) this was really not luck at all, just real-world statistics for the probability of a weapon striking a moving target at long range.

My designs reflected the *Star Trek* source material at every turn, even when the source material was contradictory or not based on reality. Doing the math

based on the speed of light, the number of 10,000-kilometer hexes the ships are moving through, and the definition of "warp factor," each turn in *SFB* represents an impossible 1/30 of a second, during which the ship can turn, fire weapons, load shuttlecraft, fight Marine boarding actions, and do no end of other things. While absurd from a technological point of view, this scale matched the action seen on television. Obviously, the television show was written based on dramatic effects and needs, and the game (intended for fans of the show who wanted to drive their own starships) had to reflect that. (Actual naval battles take far longer than a television audience will watch.)

Power was always a key element. The *USS Enterprise* generates thirty-six "points" of power: fifteen boxes each in the left and right warp engine, four boxes in the impulse engine, and two reactor boxes. It costs one point to move one hex, one point to fire a phaser, 1/5 of a point to operate a transporter, one point to keep the crew alive, two more to power the shields at basic levels, a point to run the targeting scanners, and so forth. There is never enough power to do everything, and a key element of gameplay is prioritizing what needs to be done. This mirrors the actions of starship captains on the screen, who were always giving orders like, "Divert power to shields."

With virtually no hard data regarding the power of the weapons, I used my engineering skills to calculate the probability of a hit and the rate that the energy in a weapon would be lost over the distances involved. No element of the design was ever done for political or ideological reasons; everything was based purely on engineering and the need for good game design. We worked from the premise that if the game isn't fun to play and doesn't scare the players half to death, it won't be successful.

Having studied aerial combat games such as *Richthofen's War*, I knew that a critical element of the design was the ratio of how fast the ships could move versus how often (and how far) they could fire. If the ships moved too slowly (compared to rate of fire and range) the game would have no maneuver, only pounding on the enemy, which would require that weapons have lower hit probabilities. I went the other way, with ships that move about twice as far per turn as they can seriously hurt each other. (A typical World War II battleship could fire at least twenty times while covering the distance the shells fly.)

Die Roll	PHASER-1 0	1	2	3	4	5	6-8	9-15	16-30
1	9	8	7	15	5	5	4	3	2
2	8	7	6	5	5	4	3	2	1
3	7	5	5	4	4	4	3	1	0
4	6	4	4	4	4	3	2	0	0
5	5	4	4	4	3	3	1	0	0
6	4	4	3	3	2	2	0	0	0

Figure 50.2
Phaser weapon table.

Seeking weapons had existed in *Star Trek.* For instance, the Romulans launched a seeking plasma torpedo at the *USS Enterprise*, and the ship survived only because the torpedo ran out of steam. That torpedo went into *SFB*, but we added more kinds and sizes of plasma torpedoes because the engineering design of the multitude of ships needed them. (Real world warships don't all carry the same size of weapons.)

The semiofficial blueprints mentioned that the Klingon ships carried target-practice drones (never seen on any screen) that could be used to deliver nuclear warheads to the enemy. Drones of many types and sizes became elements of the game design and are used more to scare the enemy into or out of certain areas than to actually damage the target. Those same blueprints showed that the Klingon ship had a lot of phasers that it had never fired on television, so these became less efficient phaser-2s that were the same weapons as the Federation phaser-1s but had less accurate fire controls and a shorter range. The long-range photon torpedoes never required Captain Kirk to get in range of the Klingon phasers.

Geography drove the technology to some extent. Empires "west" of the Federation (Klingons, Kzintis) use drones and disruptors; empires "east" of the Federation (Romulans and Gorns) use plasma torpedoes. The Federation, in the center of the strategic map, uses the superb photon torpedo. Everybody uses phasers, which are the universal "gun" weapon.

Some non-television elements were added to the design to improve the game. Overloaded weapons (twice the power, twice the damage, limited range) were a non-television concept that I added to force combat to shorter ranges and keep the ships from endlessly poking at each other for hours without actually damaging each other. Shuttles were given a small phaser because without that, there was nothing for them to do. The phaser wasn't enough, so later rules allowed shuttles to be loaded with energy and electronics (wild weasels) so they look to the stupid robot brain of a missile like the ship itself, to carry several drones (scatter-packs), and to deliver suicide bombs.

Star Fleet Battles is the ultimate in "complicated" games, with several hundred pages of rules and hundreds more pages of starship data, scenarios, and charts. Even so, there were several places where deliberate decisions were made to simplify concepts, physics, and rules; otherwise, the game mechanics would exceed what players will put up with. Moving targets are no harder to hit than motionless ones, and die roll modifiers to reflect if the target were moving toward you or across your front were rejected. Gravity has no effect unless you wander too near a black hole, and "orbiting" isn't really done in a way that has anything to do with space satellites.

While television is simplified due to the time available to develop stories (e.g., Klingons are mean, move on) the entire Star Fleet Universe included extensive background, geography, and economics to show that even the bad guys had their warm sides and soft spots. The Klingons, being a military dictatorship, are mired in corruption. The Romulans are divided into "great houses" that combine aspects of mega-corporations and political parties. The Gorn legislature never wants to spend money on the military. The Tholians are "reclusive" because they consider humans, Klingons, and Romulans to be little more than bacteria. Only a few Tholians arrived here from another galaxy, and they spend most of their time avoiding wars that they don't have the strength to fight.

Star Fleet Battles, like some tactical games that appeared back in the 1970s, is a "scenario-based" game system. You have the rules, but you play specific scenarios, each of which defines the starting position of a set number of ships and their objectives for the battle. This is not a limiting factor, however, since the basic scenario can be adapted by players to use any ships they want, and the eight hundred published scenarios cover every imaginable military and political situation (but we keep finding new ones). You can rescue a freighter from a minefield, drive a monster away from a colony planet, or fight your way through the enemy fleet to destroy their supply base and force them to retreat.

As the game grew, I invented an alphanumeric rules system. Movement rules are "C," while seeking weapons are "F," and so forth. This allowed future expansions to add new rules to the appropriate chapter and kept all of the direct-fire weapons under "E" regardless of what product they were published in. *Star Fleet Battles* became the first wargame in which players were expected to cut their rulebooks apart and shuffle the pages from several products into one combined rulebook. This concept was continued into *Federation & Empire* and other games and was later copied by other companies, as, for example, in *Advanced Squad Leader* (1985).

The original game included individual ship diagrams; the weapons charts were in the rulebook. Players later showed me pages they had "taped together and photocopied" in which the ship was on the right half and all of the tables for its weapons were on the left. This concept was adopted immediately, and now more than three thousand ships are in the game. While television only showed cruisers, real navies have a myriad of larger and smaller ships, as well as older ships kept in service with refits, brand new ships just coming into service, and failed designs kept in service to get some value from the money wasted. With only so much budget, a navy must buy some small ships because there are so many small jobs that need doing.

Star Fleet Battles, like most wargames, is purely military (other than a few civilian ships used as targets in campaigns), but the whole point of a military is to protect the civilians who actually produce the money and develop the resources that pay for the military as a "necessary business expense." The larger Star Fleet Universe (which includes many games reflecting the same database) includes RPGs that focus more on what the civilians are doing. The Star Fleet Universe, like *Star Trek*, prides itself on the diversity of its characters, with plenty of female and minority captains commanding its starships. (For that matter, plenty of women and young people are involved as staffers, playtesters, and players.)

Star Fleet Battles has published more player-created material (new ships, empires, weapons, scenarios, tactics, fiction, history, art, and no end of other things) than any other game system, and the other game systems of the Star Fleet Universe also publish extensive customer submissions. Some customers have designed entire products and gone on to open their own game publishing companies; Amarillo Design Bureau, Inc., prides itself on promoting creativity and rewards those outside designers who truly add something new and unique. This publishing philosophy has kept the players involved and the game system fresh, and is used in all of our product lines. Players are recognized for their contributions with not just the usual free copies and mentions in the books, but with medals and campaign ribbons posted on the company website.

About the Author

Steve Cole, the president of Amarillo Design Bureau, Inc. (ADB) <www.StarFleetGames.com> has been around the wargame industry for a very long time. The son of a building contractor and a reserve engineer colonel, he studied engineering, graduating from Texas Tech in 1975. He played his first game (*D-Day*) at a church party in 1963 and published his first game (*MP44*) as part of *JagdPanther* magazine in 1973. He ran *JagdPanther* from 1973 to 1976, founded Task Force Games in 1979, then founded ADB in 1983. He has more than one hundred published game designs and has won three Origins Awards and a Gaming Genius Award. Best known as the designer of *Star Fleet Battles*, he would rather be known for other games he designed, most especially *Prochorovka*. He has designed tactical (*Federation Commander*) and strategic (*Federation & Empire*) board games, RPGs (*GURPS Klingons*), and card games (*Star Fleet Battle Force*). His book *Running a Game Publishing Company* is available for free at <www.starfleetgames.com/book>.

Ian Sturrock and James Wallis

Games Workshop is the behemoth of the tabletop wargaming field. It is not just the largest company in the industry, but the genes of its games, its miniatures ranges, its imagery, and its marketing are felt virtually everywhere in modern wargaming. As of mid-2014 it had 1,753 employees across four continents, annual revenue of £123.5 million ($187.1 million), and a worldwide network of more than four hundred shops that sell nothing but its own products. Games Workshop also supports two magazines, a weekly and a monthly, and a fiction publishing arm, the "Black Library," that has several *New York Times* bestsellers to its credit. Its shares are traded on the London Stock Exchange (symbol: GAW) and at the time of writing it has a market cap of around £184 million ($278.8 million). In a field of comparative minnows, how is it possible for this one whale to have evolved?

Games Workshop did not start out as a wargame company. It was founded in the mid-1970s as a company creating high-quality wooden boards for classic games. In 1976, it acquired the exclusive license to distribute *Dungeons & Dragons* in the UK, and it began to morph into a specialist games distributor and retailer. In 1977, it launched *White Dwarf* as a role-playing game magazine, mostly supporting games

that it distributed, and in 1978 it opened its first shop. A year later, Games Workshop entered into partnership with Bryan Ansell, a wargame designer and sculptor who had previously founded Asgard Miniatures, to create the jointly owned company Citadel Miniatures. All of these moves were important components of the company's later success, but it was this last one that would prove to be the foundation of its future.

Citadel's early ranges included miniatures licensed from larger American producers such as Ral Partha, as well as its own lines of generic fantasy and science fiction figures, and ones based on tabletop RPGs that Games Workshop had either developed (*Judge Dredd*) or had the UK rights for (*Runequest, Traveller, Paranoia*). During the heyday of fantasy role-playing in the early to mid-1980s, after having experimented with publishing a selection of original board games and role-playing games, in 1983 Games Workshop took the slightly sideways step of releasing *Warhammer*, a fantasy wargame co-designed by Bryan Ansell, Richard Halliwell, Rick Priestley, and Graham Eckel.

The first edition of *Warhammer* comprised three books in a cardboard box, including the wargame rules that have remained fundamentally unchanged ever since, creature lists, rules for the use of magic, and a rudimentary set of role-playing rules. Although it did not contain any figures in the box, in a foretaste of GW's cross-promotional strategy to come it did include Citadel stock codes for the characters and races described.

A second edition of *Warhammer* followed a year later in 1984, with more lavish production and cardboard counters in the box, and then a third edition in 1987 alongside the first release of its far-future brother-title *Warhammer 40,000* (*40K*). This moment also marked a shift in the company culture. Founders Ian Livingstone and Steve Jackson had sold their interest in Games Workshop to Bryan Ansell in 1985, and as the popularity of RPGs waned in the mid- to late 1980s he refocused the company around the *Warhammer* products and brands, notably Citadel's range of miniatures, as well as relocating it from London to Nottingham. *White Dwarf*'s content became increasingly dominated by the twin games until the only non-*Warhammer/40K* content to be found was

coverage of Games Workshop's other miniatures-based games: *Advanced Heroquest*, *Blood Bowl*, *Mighty Empires*, *Dark Future*, and others. It was also around this time that *White Dwarf* stopped printing advertisements for any products other than Games Workshop's own.

Ansell ran the company until a management buyout in 1991 led by former TSR (UK) staffer Tom Kirby. Three years later the company floated on the London stock market with an initial share price of 115p ($1.74), valuing it at £35 million ($53 million). Kirby has been CEO, chairman or both ever since, and the company's direction has remained largely unchanged. Its first computer game licenses were released in the early 1990s, its fiction-publishing arm the Black Library launched in 1997, and in 2001 it entered into a major licensing deal with New Line Cinema to produce miniatures and wargames based on the *Lord of the Rings* movie trilogy, and more latterly the *Hobbit* trilogy too. But Games Workshop remains pointed in one direction: Total Global Domination.

Three Unique Things

To understand Games Workshop's success, you need to understand three things about the company that make it unique. These are: the "Games Workshop Hobby," the company's structure and its extraordinary vertical integration, and the meaning of "Total Global Domination."

The phrase "total global domination" has rung through the last twenty years of Games Workshop history. It appears in many of the annual reports to shareholders from 1994 onwards, and it used to appear on the cover of the retail staff handbook in embossed silver letters. In the 1990s and early 2000s,

the company's years of explosive growth, the idea of total global domination sounded less hubristic than today, but when questioned on it, Tom Kirby told one of the present authors, James Wallis, in August 2014, "Global is still the strategy. The march is more Mao than Sousa."

"Total global domination" sums up much of Games Workshop's business model, although annual reports and the company's website describe that model in a few more words: "We make the best fantasy miniatures in the world and sell them globally at a profit and we intend to do this forever."[1]

Despite the possible hyperbole of these two phrases together, Games Workshop's perception of itself is as a global company but not as a major global brand. It perceives itself as a niche business, and its tactic is to "consciously and deliberately pursue a niche market model" (Games Workshop 2014, Strategic Report section). "The Games Workshop business model ... is predicated upon the desire to own (lots of) miniatures. ... Out there in the world is the gene that makes certain people (usually male) want to own hundreds of miniatures. We simply fill that need," wrote Tom Kirby in the Chairman's Preamble to the company's 2005–2006 annual report. Its market, it believes, is self-selecting: they will find their way to Games Workshop because Games Workshop's products are better than anyone else's. Linked to this—we hesitate to say because of it—is the fact that Games Workshop spends no money on advertising or publicity for its products, brands, or shops. When it preaches, it preaches to the converted and hopes that some of their friends will overhear the message.

Everything that Games Workshop does or sells is based around the concept of what it calls "the Games Workshop Hobby." This is a combination of four linked activities: collecting miniatures, painting miniatures, modeling (converting miniatures or building dioramas) and playing games using a miniatures collection (Games Workshop Group PLC 2000–2014a). To sell the components of this hobby to its customers, the company has evolved a vertically integrated structure of extraordinary efficiency.

All the products that Games Workshop sells are designed and created in-house (with the sole exception of the tie-in novels from its subsidiary the Black Library, written by freelance authors). It owns and operates the manufacturing facilities making its metal and plastic miniatures (printing is outsourced, but everything else is in-house.) Its products are sold through mail order and its own website (*Warhammer Monthly* and the now-weekly *White Dwarf* magazines function as de facto catalogs), as well as its own global chain of Games Workshop-branded shops. Additionally it runs its own distribution network to independent hobby retailers, and tries to avoid Internet discounters by insisting that resellers must have a "bricks-and-mortar" presence in order to stock its products.

As a result, Games Workshop's control of how its products are presented, sold, and priced is almost total. The integrated production structure ensures that costs are controlled, and the majority of profits are kept in-house.

Games Workshop's stores are spread worldwide but are mostly in Europe and the United States, with more than a third in the UK. Some are survivors from the company's chain of general game retailers set up in the 1980s, but most are more recent creations and have only ever sold the company's own products. To think of them just as game stores is a mistake: Games Workshop's term for them is "hobby centres," and their role is crucial. As well as product, stores typically have an area set aside for painting with regular demonstrations, and a table set up with an active game of *Warhammer* or *40K*. They are recruitment centers and clubhouses as much as they are retailers; new players can learn the games and the basics of the hobby here, while existing *Warhammer* fans come to play against familiar or new opponents, to meet other players, to pick up new painting and modeling techniques, and to buy miniatures and support materials for their collection and their games: paints, terrain, army books, novels, and magazines.

The company's magazines serve a similar purpose as the shops; they are aimed at the existing collectors and players, but are visible to the outside world. Their content is entirely about Games Workshop products, mostly covering recent and forthcoming miniatures releases. Some people may be surprised by their success: In 2013, White Dwarf was selling 80,000–100,000 printed copies a month, which puts it at the same level as New Scientist and Vanity Fair. Recently relaunched as a weekly, its digital edition is normally near the top of the Apple charts on the day of release.[2]

In recent years a fifth arm of the hobby has evolved: moving Games Workshop's intellectual property outside tabletop wargames and into other media, notably computer games produced under license, board games produced under license, and novels and stories published by the Black Library. Games Workshop does not consider this a core part of its eponymous hobby but it contributes a significant share of the company's revenue, although it took a major hit at the end of 2012 when Games Workshop's major licensee for computer games, THQ, declared bankruptcy.

At the heart of the licensing and everything else it does lies its intellectual property. It has three core brands: Warhammer and Warhammer 40,000, both of which it owns outright, and Lord of the Rings/The Hobbit, which it produces under license from New Line Productions. Everything it sells is connected to one of these three brands, or to the hobby activities that grow out from them. The company defends its intellectual property vigorously, to the extent of closing down fan websites and making legal threats against a novel called Spots the Space Marine for alleged trademark infringement. Actions of this type have caused negative press for the company, along with accusations that it is out of touch with its fans and players. Tom Kirby is bullish on the subject: "If we do not try to protect what we own, the law sees us as not valuing it so we lose it. It is a tricky situation to be in. How much is too much? But then, why do these people think it is OK to steal from us?" (personal communication, Tom Kirby to James Wallis, August 2014).

The Three-Act History

That, then, is a rough picture of the shape of Games Workshop in the twenty-first century, but it does not explain how it got there.

Like a good screenplay, the history of Games Workshop falls into three acts, with "reversals" happening at each of the act breaks. The first act is the Livingstone/Jackson years, building the business as a game distributor with a chain of retail shops, and the founding of Citadel. The reversal is the launch of the first two editions of Warhammer in the early and mid-'80s and the corresponding leap in sales of Citadel's fantasy ranges, which tripled as a result (personal communication, Bryan Ansell to James Wallis, August 2014).

The second act, the Ansell years, covers the pivot away from general games to focusing entirely on the company's own products, based on its own intellectual properties. There's no question that the pivot was based on the success of Warhammer and its miniatures at the same time that sales of RPGs, previously the company's backbone, were declining worldwide. Bryan Ansell has described the merger of

Games Workshop and Citadel as a "reverse takeover" (ibid.), and longtime senior GW staffer Alan Merritt is reported as having regretted that the company kept the Games Workshop name rather than the Citadel one.

The second act ends with the 1991 management buyout—not with the flotation on the stock market, as some might expect—and the third act is all of Tom Kirby's years of leadership. Ansell's tenure had repositioned Games Workshop as a miniatures-based business with its own retail chain, but at this stage it was merely a successful business. The decision to refocus the company on miniatures was based on the success of the early *Warhammer* releases but also on one other crucial aspect: Bryan Ansell's passion for miniatures and wargames. It was what he loved and what he wanted to make and sell. Ansell was not a board gamer or a role-player, nor was he a natural businessman—Tom Kirby describes him as "a capricious autocrat who understood miniatures almost transcendentally" and adds, "We follow the miniatures vision slavishly, but nothing else" (personal communication, Tom Kirby to James Wallis, August 2014). In particular, the presence of the retail chain—which, it can be argued, was central to Games Workshop's market penetration and brilliant vertical integration—was almost a fortuitous accident.

Once in charge, Kirby shook the company by the scruff of the neck, integrating all aspects of the company's activities, focusing on core business and creating the vision of the Games Workshop Hobby. The flotation in 1994 removed the company's existing debt and provided more cash for expansion and growth. For its first two years as a PLC Games Workshop was growing at around 30 percent year on year and the stock price soared. At the same time the focus of the products narrowed even further: some new big box games emerged but they were set in either the *Warhammer* or *40K* worlds (*Warhammer Quest* and *Mordheim; Gorkamorka* and *Necromunda*) and were designed with expansions and more miniatures sales in mind. The main games and their armies were structured to put a fresh focus on new releases and upgrades. Bryan Ansell told James Wallis that, "What we did with *Warhammer* was to create something like a playground, while the current version is more like a route march," a statement that makes an uneasy companion to Kirby's earlier description of the march to total global domination being more Mao than Sousa. It should also be remembered that Mao's Long March was a retreat.

Is it possible that another wargame or hobby game company could rise to anything like the size of Games Workshop? The general opinion is no, but for differing reasons. In interview Kirby is customarily forthright: "The words 'idle' and 'feckless' keep getting in the way. Here's one version: I'm sure there are others. We are focused on being a successful company with longevity; they are focused on their private obsessions. Pretty designs, clever mechanics, proving us wrong, copying us, or whatever else."

From our own analysis, we think Games Workshop's success is and will remain unique. It comes from the tripartite combination of a direct route to market via the company's own distribution and retail chain, followed by a visionary director who created two startlingly commercial gameworlds and assembled the talent to best exploit them, and last a CEO whose vision of an integrated company providing an integrated hobby has proved to be a success. Combine that with first-mover advantage, and the result is very hard to follow. It would be extremely hard for another company to replicate that model, and impossible for a miniatures company to reach anything like the same size or market without the shops, the magazines and the two gameworlds that might have been designed to press every button in a teenage boy's mind.

Hobbyists have been predicting Games Workshop's imminent decline and bankruptcy since it began to focus on miniatures and Warhammer in the late 1980s, but the company has sailed on regardless. The most recent annual report (Games Workshop Group PLC 2014) does seem to indicate that while its turnover is largely stable, increased retail prices have led to decreased unit sales and lower profits. However, Games Workshop's share price has always been volatile, and it is impossible to judge whether this is another blip or an indication of a more long-term problem in the company's strategy.

Even if the skeptics are correct and the company's fortunes are faltering, its track record is still remarkable. To have sustained a hobby game business of this size for this long is unprecedented. TSR Inc., publisher of *Dungeons & Dragons*, lasted twenty-four years before being bought by Wizards of the Coast, which itself was only independent for nine years before it was bought by Hasbro Inc. Games Workshop is forty years old and has spent more than half its existence as a publicly traded company.

And if the future does prove to be dark, Games Workshop will surely be prepared for it and will not go down without a fight, because as every *Warhammer 40,000* player knows, and as we will explore in the rest of this chapter, "In the grim darkness of the far future, there is only war."

Warhammer 40,000

Warhammer 40,000 (*40K*) is GW's flagship game. GW's business model requires they "defend our intellectual property rigorously against imitators" (Games Workshop 2000–2014), although that property was itself influenced by other science fiction, fantasy, and pop culture artifacts. Until the company's relatively recent spate of cease and desist letters and lawsuits, there was no controversy in recognizing that the *40K* setting drew on many much-loved previously existing elements, allowing fans to play wargames incorporating all of them.

This excerpt from the cross-examination of GW sculptor Jes Goodwin, during the 2013 *GW vs. Chapterhouse* court case, is telling; they refer to a sentence in *The Art of Warhammer* (Gascoigne and Kyme 2007):

> Q. Well, let's look at the rest of the sentence. "Taken from *2000AD* and Michael Moorcock novels and real history all put into a big pot and regurgitated by us." Do you see that?

> A. Yes.

> Q. Isn't that what Games Workshop did?

> A. That's a very, very simplistic reading of it, yes.

40K is a dice-based, miniatures wargame, set in the forty-first millennium. Players can be generals of armies—chapters of elite Space Marines or regiments of Imperial Guard defending humanity and its Emperor; enemy factions—Chaos Space Marines who once served the Empire but have been corrupted; their allies the Chaos Daemons; or aliens ("xenos") such as the H. R. Giger-esque Tyranids, elf-like Eldar and Dark Eldar, aggressive Orks, anime-inspired Tau, or undead robot Necrons.

The game is played between two players, using armies of 28mm-scale miniature warriors, vehicles, and monsters, across a 6' × 4' table enhanced by scale models of terrain. Tape measures are used to determine distances for movement, shooting, and

Figure 51.1
A hard-fought battle between the Imperial Fists and Blood Angels at HATE (Hackney Area Games Club), London, UK. These are both space marine armies—not an unusual sight, given the popularity of space marines, though they are on the same side in the "fluff" (i.e., the material that forms the *Warhammer 40K* background).

charging. Each attacker has a number of attacks, and rolls one die per attack to see if he hits, then picks up all the "hits" and rerolls them to see how many wounds they inflict. The defender then rolls an "Armour Save" for each wound, typically removing any models who fail their save. The traditional "Igo-Ugo" game turn format is used, so the active player makes decisions during his turn, with the passive player relegated to making a few defensive dice rolls, or sometimes deciding which casualty to remove or defensive option to use. The current seventh edition of the game (2014) also allows the passive player to react by rolling dice to fire weapons as "Overwatch" against charging troops; this concept of reacting to the active player stems from Avalon Hill's 1985 *Advanced Squad Leader.*

Influences on *Warhammer 40,000*

Unhallowed knowledge brought the Dark Time, and fire from the sky, and death to men in ten times a thousand dreadful ways. So I say this to you: Seek not to know, for to know is to sin. Ask not how, nor how much, nor how many. He who disturbs the mysterious ways of the Universe is heretic, an enemy of God and Man. And he will burn.

—Robert Gilman, *The Navigator of Rhada*

In *The Navigator of Rhada*, Robert Gilman presents a far-future setting in which high technology is the domain of a priesthood, guarded by Inquisitors, millennia after a near-mythical Golden Age that was destroyed by that very technology. The Golden Age concept is as old as Plato; the associated trope of forbidden technology, dating back to that idealized past, and frequently controlled by a Catholicism-like religious order, was common in 1960s science fiction, famously in Walter Miller's 1960 *A Canticle for Leibowitz*. Gilman's Rhada cycle though, along with the *Dune* series, clearly inspired *40K*'s long-ago apocalypse, complete with conscious, deadly robotic warriors that turned on their creators and shattered the Golden Age. *Dune* has a "crusade against computers, thinking machines, and conscious robots" in its distant past (Herbert 1965, 594).

Echoes can be seen in *40K*: technophobic religious extremism, and an Imperium that reunited human colonies scattered in the dark times. The *40K* era is "a time of superstition, in which a great and unfathomable technology has been enslaved to the forces of mysticism ... to the ordinary humans ... scientific thought represents an abhorrent perversity; a corruption of honour and religious virtue," due to fear of the forces of the distant "Dark Age of Technology" (*Warhammer 40,000: Rogue Trader*, 132).

Gilman's name inspired that of Roboute Guilliman, the founder of *40K*'s iconic Ultramarines chapter of Space Marines. Obfuscated names as tributes to inspirations was common for the Games Workshop design team during the 1980s and 1990s; examples include "Sly Marbo," a lone jungle fighter based closely on the *Rambo* films starring "Sly" Stallone, and "Pedro Kantor," named for Pete Cantor, one of *40K*'s playtesters. The designers borrowed names and concepts from myths and other sources; to briefly examine one Space Marine chapter, the Dark Angels: the Primarch "Lion El'Jonson" is named after Lionel Johnson, a nineteenth-century English poet whose "The Dark Angel" (1892) inspired the *40K* Dark Angels' guilt and secrecy, as well as their name; the most high-ranking characters are Azrael and Sammael (originally Hebrew angels of death), and Belial and Asmodai (Hebrew demons). Angelic mythology is more widely referenced, with all Space Marines described as "Angels of Death."

Britain's weekly *2000AD* comics were a significant influence, particularly *Nemesis the Warlock* for its Catholic, alien-hating human Empire, "Terminator" soldiers, sorcery, and Chaos as opponents, and Gothic styling. The elite police of *40K*, the Adeptus Arbites, were modeled on *Judge Dredd*.

Tony Ackland described creating the Gods of Chaos, the game's antagonists: "Whereas Michael Moorcock's Elric stories were the main source of inspiration for Bryan [Ansell], I leaned more towards H. P. Lovecraft" (Jafnakol 2014). Ansell, owner of Games Workshop during the development of much of their IP, explains: "Moorcock was an influence and inspiration ... in my case Jack Vance and Clark Ashton Smith were equally important" (Jafnakol 2013). Recognizing influences, the second edition of *Warhammer Fantasy Battles* was "Dedicated to Phil Barker, Donald Featherstone and Michael Moorcock, whose fault it all is." The rules were also influenced by tabletop RPGs: "*Rogue Trader* and *Warhammer* both grew out of the role-playing boom of the late '70s and early '80s—in their original forms they were open format role-playing style games played with miniatures" (Hoare 2011).

Early *40K* concepts and especially monsters were also influenced by popular films of the 1980s. The antagonists of the *Alien* franchise became "Genestealers," fast, deadly denizens of abandoned starships who combined their victims' genetic material with their own to create "hybrids" and were eventually retconned to be part of the Tyranid hives. Although not initially a playable force, the Tyranids and Genestealers went from being pure antagonists to a viable army for players with the 1995 Tyranid Codex. The skeletal humanoid robotic creatures the Necrons (introduced in 1999), while drawing on Egyptian iconography and the cosmic horror of H. P. Lovecraft, were based visually on the *Terminator* franchise, their unstoppable toughness represented by the "We'll Be Back" rule, in an homage to Arnold Schwarzenegger.

Music was another inspiration. Ansell heard death metal band Bolt Thrower's first music via John Peel, and a collaboration between the *40K*-obsessed musicians and GW began: *Realm of Chaos*, the band's second studio album was released on Earache Records in 1989, and featured cover and booklet artwork from the artists at Games Workshop. In fact Games Workshop briefly had a record label (Warhammer Records) and their wargames magazine *White Dwarf* released a "Thrash Rock Special" (#95, November 1987), including a free flexi-disc record from thrash-metal band Sabbat. Though the company no longer markets to any particular musical subculture, the thematic connection remains: "At both the tournament and Games Workshop stores, bands like Black Sabbath, Tool and Metallica are pumped on high volume speakers to the majority long-haired, scruffy, heavy-metal band t-shirt wearing attendees. The fiction of the *40K* universe aligns well with this broader contextualisation within heavy-metal culture" (Harrop et al. 2013, 5).

Softcover to Slipcase

The seven editions of *40K* (1987–2014) demonstrate an evolution from narrative-driven, campaign-oriented, skirmish-level (ten to thirty models in each "army") game to a competitive, still narrative-

Figure 51.2

As well as the tanks, warriors, and terrain that should officially be on the table, it is common to see a rulebook or two opened up for reference, as well as scrap paper to note down army composition, psychic powers, and special abilities.

friendly, all-inclusive rule set capable of handling anything from 500 points on each side (perhaps twenty to seventy models) to a massive battle involving 10,000+ points of tank formations, ranks of monstrous creatures, hundreds of infantry models, and several days' worth of playing time.

Looking at the physical books, it is clear that the first edition is a hobby game, if a well-presented one. Its full-color cover shows beleaguered Space Marines making a last stand, bolters firing in all directions, grim resolve on every face, tattered banners clutched in armored fists. This is probably the most common theme in *40K* art. Of the 282 pages, most contain rules, but 96 pages are devoted to background ("The Age of the Imperium"); these do mix in rules information—for example, game statistics for the creatures they describe. There is limited use of spot or full color; most pages have at least one illustration, but the interior design looks cluttered to a modern eye.

The new seventh edition looks like a luxury coffee table product. It comes as three hardcover books, with over 400 full color pages, in a heavy-duty slipcase. Covers and interiors are impressively designed but remain cluttered. Book III contains game rules. Book I is devoted to collecting, painting, and modeling miniatures, and Book II is background. The shift in focus from pure wargame to "The Games Workshop Hobby—Collecting, painting, modelling and gaming … with the best model soldiers in the world" (Games Workshop 2000–2014) is evident. GW's concept of the "Games Workshop Hobby" is supported by Harrop, Carter and Gibbs's analysis; the game is just "one of a broad variety of inextricably interlinked practices engaged in by players" (2014).

The blurb of each book gives an insight into the core of the game, which has not significantly changed. First edition (*Warhammer 40,000: Rogue Trader*) is the experience of commanding "the forces of the Imperium or any one of the many enemies ranged against its borders … in the nightmare future of the fortieth millennia." The seventh edition, published in 2014, is the experience of commanding "the heroes and villains of *Warhammer 40,000* in a galaxy where there is only war."

The core dynamics (Brathwaite and Schreiber 2008) have always been open-ended, and determined by the players (or Games Master, where present). The rules explain how to play, but offer a variety of optional ways to win. In the first edition, the Games Master may use Victory Conditions (e.g., "the Space Marines must slay all of their opponents" (*Warhammer 40,000: Rogue Trader*, 66), or Victory Points (VPs), different in each scenario, to determine the winner; in the sample scenario included, the Space Marines gain VPs via the "survival" and "destruction" core

dynamics, whereas the Orks primarily gain VPs by recovering the treasure buried beneath the battlefield (a variant of the "territory" core dynamic) (*Warhammer 40,000: Rogue Trader*, 66).

In the seventh edition, various mission types facilitate a variety of core dynamics. The main variations are "Maelstrom of War," in which core dynamics change at the start of each turn, and "Eternal War," in which core dynamics are determined at the start but afterward remain static (*Warhammer 40,000*, 129). Core dynamics can include "survival," "destruction," and "territory." Certain units are more effective when it comes to territory (in the form of "Objectives"), at the expense of effectiveness in survival and/or destruction. As an alternative, a "Creating Your Own Missions" section (*Warhammer 40,000*, 128) supports first edition-style Victory Conditions and flexibility; such missions are also published in magazines and supplements. The core dynamic in every edition of the game is "building": players design their own armies from a points-based list. The variation in core dynamics, especially in Maelstrom of War, brings some balance; it is not possible, for example, to rely on a powerful shooting army to wipe the opponent out (as could have been done in fifth or sixth edition), because an opponent bringing troops to hold territory can accumulate enough VPs to win even if destroyed by the end. This makes self-balanced rules: "The idea is to build in counters to the game so that even if some things end up more powerful than you expected, the game is resilient enough that players can deal with it" (Sirlin 2008a). Maelstrom of War does reduce agency to mere interactivity, perhaps reducing *40K* to a good game rather than a great one, given that the way the victory conditions alter is not under either player's control.

The biggest change from the first to seventh edition is the increased scale. The rule sets are similarly complex, both needing thorough readthroughs and practice games to attain mastery. The first edition's complexity is in the special actions taken by individual soldiers, such as hiding, discovering hidden troops, driving, etc. The seventh edition abstracts those concepts, focusing on units of five to thirty troops, vehicles (with an undefined "crew" treated as part of the vehicle), and larger units such as Flying Monstrous Creatures, Squadrons, and Lords of War. The legacy of skirmish rules remains, with individual soldiers having most of the same characteristics (Strength, Toughness, Ballistic Skill, Weapon Skill, etc.) as in the first edition.

This skirmish-scale legacy is problematic from a game balance perspective, as well as being clunky compared to the elegance of Eurogame-style rules. The game is theoretically playable at anything from a few hundred to tens of thousands of points (with an individual soldier costing perhaps five to forty points), but in practice it is difficult to design a balanced army during much of that point range. Under 1,500 points it is hard to create an army capable of defeating a "horde" army of light infantry but also capable fighting an army of small numbers of powerful armored units. At higher points levels (2,500 and up), the power of some army builds is such that victory can seem random (the first player to go has chance to wipe out most of the enemy army with just one volley). Most tournaments run to 1,500 to 2,500 points, reducing the utility of the rule set, yet even so limited, games can seem unbalanced. Games Workshop conducts minimal playtesting, and the more open-ended and asymmetric a rule set is (certainly a feature of *40K*'s multi-faction, points-based army design system), "the more it needs to care about balancing the fairness of the different starting options" (Sirlin 2008b). So competitive tournaments seem dominated by armies that exploit

imbalance: "'Cheese' describes the player practice of finding gaps, or over interpreting the rules, in order to allow uncharacteristically or unfairly powerful units or actions" (Harrop et al. 2013).

Every iteration of the game is a competitive one, with the expectation that it will end with a defined winner and loser, but a cooperative, collaborative culture is recommended by the rulebooks, and seen among players. A 2013 interview with *40K* players found that the combination of the social aspects and the capability of players to rationalize the loss of a game as a happy experience due to the other aspects of the hobby (painting, modeling, creating a "fluffy,"—i.e., characterfully themed—army, etc.) seemed to provide a "protective" effect ("*W40K* as a strategy game provides players with a framework for finding positive experiences in loss through the value of their strategic play, a value separate from necessarily winning the match" [Harrop et al. 2013]) against the potentially negative psychological effects of competitive games (e.g., "In a competitive relationship, one is predisposed to … have a suspicious, hostile, exploitative attitude toward the other" [Morton Deutsch, quoted in Kohn 1986, 143]).

The first edition gives little guidance as to the spirit of the game, but it demands a Games Master along with two or more players, recommending that in advanced play, the Games Master should create a detailed, flexible narrative campaign in the cooperative play style of the tabletop role-playing games that were Games Workshop's main line of business during the 1970s and 1980s (Ewalt 2013, 9). The seventh edition is more explicit: "the rules are just the framework to support an enjoyable game" (14). Even tournament players "felt it was important to bring a list that was fun for other players to play against" (Carter et al 2014, 13).

The Battle at the Farm

The first edition introductory scenario pits Orks against Space Marines in a short but bloody battle. For most players this was their first experience of *40K*. Since "meaning emerges when a text is actualized or practiced" (Bizzocchi and Tanenbaum 2011), one of the present authors, Ian Sturrock, played through and a performed close reading of the scenario for this chapter.

The Games Master (Ian) and one player (Kyle) had played *40K* fifth and sixth editions, and related games such as *Space Hulk*, and were familiar with the setting. The other player (Bridie, mother to Kyle) had not played any *40K* game, but was aware of the background. All three participants had played many Euro-style board games and tabletop roleplaying games.

Preparing for the game, we were struck by the highly androcentric nature of the scenario (and the game in general). All the Space Marines were male, portrayed as superhuman soldiers—stronger, larger, and faster, reminiscent of Mulvey's "more perfect, more complete, more powerful ideal ego conceived in the original moment of recognition in front of the mirror" (1975, 12) The opposing Orks, though not even mammalian according to the game's background, are depicted as powerful and savage males, so any combatant on either side is "free to command the stage, a stage of spatial illusion in which he articulates the look and creates the action" (34). No women were represented in the scenario, and of 249 illustrations and photographs depicting humanoids, only eleven (less than 5 percent) contained any women. All eleven were background illustrations; none were photographs of miniatures, emphasizing the androcentric nature of the battlefield (and thus

of agency within the setting). Of the humans shown, all appeared Caucasian. Three photographs of actual players depicted white males.

Turn 1

Bridie: "I am scared!"

Kyle advanced his Orks forward fearlessly, largely ignoring the few bits of cover on his side of the board. Bridie checked that her Missile Launcher marine could see some Orks, with Kyle turned away so as not to reveal the Marine's hiding position if the Missile Launcher could not see him. It could, and shot at five Orks, but scattered off-target, only hitting one.

Turn 2

The Orks advanced again. Kyle expressed frustration at their slowness, and his lack of options. In the fifth and sixth edition rules, which he had played many times, as in the seventh edition, Orks and other infantry move faster inherently (six inches rather than four inches, in the Movement Phase), and can choose to give up their shooting for a turn so as to move faster still (Run Move); neither of these are possible in the first edition. Two of the Marine squads moved into cover. Two squads also shot, killing three Orks.

Turn 3

The Orks moved forward. Kyle checked their weaponry, and elected to shoot bolt guns and a bolt pistol, saving the plasma pistol (which can only fire every second turn) for a sure shot at closer range. He caused no casualties. Bridie said, "I think I'm getting the hang of this," firing but missing. "My missile launcher is fucking useless," she laughed. Kyle replied, "My everything is fucking useless!"

Turn 4

Having lost eight of his initial twenty-one Orks, with no enemy casualties and no prospect of getting into close combat this turn, and with fewer Orks left than there were Marines, Kyle elected to retreat, shooting on the way. He hit and killed one Marine en route. Bridie by now was more confident, playing with her Marines as though they were action figures, or perhaps people, moving them a pace at time with sound effects: "bom bom bom bom." She was also rolling dice all at once, like a veteran player.

> The same dice that 'hits' is re-rolled to 'wound'; these dice do not simply replicate the complex statistical capacity of machines, but each die becomes imagined as a physical representation of the fictional action it seeks to resolve; each die represents a bullet, and the result of the roll represents that bullet's performance. The bullets which miss are discarded, and those which hit are re-rolled to determine if they wound." (Carter, Harrop, and Gibbs forthcoming, 10)

Four more Orks died. "I'm sorry Kyle, I'm really sorry. Not just losing so badly, but losing so badly to your mum. You've gotta see the funny side really." "Yes. It's hilarious."

We were struck by how unbalanced the game seemed. It is common practice in historical wargames to create unbalanced scenarios, in which one side is likely to overwhelm the other, but also to balance that situation with victory conditions skewed the

other way (for example, an outnumbered defender might "win" the scenario by surviving for a certain amount of time). The victory conditions for this scenario do not reflect that; indeed, Ork victory is harder to achieve than a Marine one. Positional advantage can be significant in any wargame, and would usually be considered in balancing a scenario; the Marines gain a significant boost by being the defenders, with positional advantages of "Cover" and "Hiding." The Orks are forced to make a slow advance from the table edge toward the farm, with little cover. We calculated the strength of both forces using the first edition points-based system, and determined the Ork force to be underpowered (215 points to the Marines' 452.5).

Little wonder this game was quite the massacre. It seems to have the expectation that it is winnable for the Ork player, but we were unable to see how, giving the impression that this scenario had not been playtested, and the force costs probably not even worked out by the designers.

Imagining the perspective of an inexperienced gamer, or a fan of other games trying to determine if 40K has sufficient depth to hold their interest, this level of imbalance will be offputting. As Bridie put it, "The whole thing just seemed incredibly pointless. I don't know if it was just the way it played ... I'm not saying my tactics were amazing, but ..." Kyle was disappointed at the poor performance of the Orks, but also frustrated, as a gamer, at his lack of options. If a game is "a series of interesting choices" (Meier, quoted in Juul 2011, 19), this was no game; Bridie found it pointless due to the obvious dominant strategy (stand behind cover and shoot), and Kyle found it pointless due to the ineffectiveness of his forces (the only significant decision he made was when to give up).

Using a game design analysis lens, there is no problem with the game per se, since the introductory scenario was not actually designed according to the rules. The slow movement, and relative lack of options, would in most games be outweighed by the other options this skirmish-level wargame/narrative RPG hybrid offers over later editions. As with an RPG, there is an expectation that the Games Master will balance things to keep the game fast-moving, interesting, and enjoyable, but this is explained in the Advanced Gamer section and is thus is nonobvious to new players (*Warhammer 40,000: Rogue Trader*, 238).

Considering the game with an eye on accessibility, representation, and inclusivity, the unbalanced starter scenario is even more problematic. We have already seen the hobby's art depicting primarily white males, or nonhuman males. Adding the requirement to read and master a lengthy rulebook is a barrier to entry. A starting scenario with little strategy, despite complex rules, increases the likelihood that new players will decide the wargaming hobby is not for them, particularly if they fail to recognize the Games Master's intended role of providing balance where the rules or scenario do not.

The Battle at the Farm, Rebooted

For our seventh edition close reading, we replayed the Battle at the Farm scenario, updated for seventh edition and with properly balanced forces, based somewhat on a reboot of the scenario found in the 2008 fifth edition. Ian played the Space Marines and recruited Kyle as his opponent. No Games Master was necessary.

Turn 1

The Orks moved 6" and then ran instead of shooting. Kyle was very happy at how much further they had moved than the last game. Ian moved his Marines behind the fences of the ruined farm and fired, killing a couple of Orks with his Bolters and damaging the Deff Dread (a large, armored "walker" vehicle) with his missile launcher. As this was our first game with the newly released seventh edition, we needed to check a couple of rules during the turn, but this was done quickly and easily.

Turn 2

After moving, the leading Orks were already touching the farm's fences, immediately giving a much more dynamic feel to this game than the first edition one. They opened fire ineffectively. The Ork Mek (mechanic) failed to repair the Deff Dread. The Marines retreated slightly, and opened fire, again ineffectively.

Turn 3

The Deff Dread advanced, the Mek moving with it and this time effecting a repair. Kyle was pleased: "Yes!" The Orks opened fire. The Tactical Marines' armor shrugged off the damage, but the Veterans were not so lucky, with three of them dying. Usually this would necessitate a Morale Check, but they are a Fearless unit and so could not rout. The Marine shooting damaged one unit of Orks quite severely, forcing a Morale Check, which the Orks initially failed. The Orks had a

"Bosspole," enabling their leader to kill one of his own number to prevent the others from fleeing, allowing a reroll, which succeeded.

Turn 4

Feeling that he sensed victory, or at least blood, Kyle declared a "Waaagh!," a once-per-game special move that made his units Fearless for the turn, and allowed them to both run and attack in Close Combat, usually an impossibility. With a 1d6 roll for each unit's Run, in inches, he rolled two ones and a two. One of his units successfully charged into Close Combat, but only after taking three casualties from their victim's bolters shooting in Overwatch. "This is the worst Waaagh! This is almost as bad as the time Abaddon the Despoiler turned into a Chaos Spawn!" Fortunately his luck turned, with the Orks acquitting themselves well in Close Combat, killing the last of the Veteran Marines as well as several Tactical Marines, at a cost of some dead Orks. The Burnas (flamethrower-armed Orks) were still far from the fight, due to being in the same unit as the Mek; the Deff Dread was likewise somewhat distant. Ian was able to immobilize it, with a shot from his still-unengaged missile launcher.

Turn 5

The Mek repaired the Deff Dread, enabling it to move again. At this point Ian agreed to concede: most of his Marines were dead or engaged in close combat (where they are less effective, point for point, than Orks), and the others would soon be attacked by the Dread and Burnas.

Seventh edition seemed enjoyable, dynamic, dramatic, and full of options, despite our limited test. It is not perfectly balanced for competition, but is designed for flexibility in creating "a shared experience" and "evoking the imagery and feel of the 41st Millennium" (*Warhammer 40,000*, 4). For competitive play, tournament organizers alter the rules (Robbins 2014), or rely on a mixture of peer pressure and "soft scores," whereby points given by players for good sportsmanship, or by tournament organizers for "fluffy" and/or well-painted armies, allow a less competitive army to win the tournament even if it lost in battle. The former approach (rules tweaks) is common in the United States, the latter in Europe and Australia (Carter et al. 2014).

As for representation and inclusivity, again the game is androcentric, with eighteen illustrations in the main art book (8 percent) depicting one or more females out of a total of 223 showing humanoids. This is a rise since 1987, and all of the females were combatants: either the Sororitas (an all-women faction similar to Space Marines), or Daemonettes (female-formed demons), or female warriors among the predominantly male Eldar and Dark Eldar forces (an elfin, humanoid species). The background fiction mentions women serving in the Imperial Guard, but none are depicted in the rulebooks, and no female Guardsmen miniatures are made by GW. Two illustrations appeared to show a non-Caucasian human, Kor'sarro Khan (*Warhammer 40,000*, 37, 39) from the White Scars Space Marines (depicted as Mongol-style raiders).

In conclusion, although recent editions' emphasis on "forging a narrative" has alienated some highly competitive players (e.g., a well-regarded writer on *40K* tactics wrote that the game, "already on life support, [was] made into a mockery" [Stelek 2013], and ceased playing or writing about it), the game has always been intended to be played in that friendly, narrative manner. In the terminology of GNS Theory (see A. Scott Glancy's chapter in part I of this volume)—intended to classify tabletop RPGs, but also applicable to *40K* due to its RPG roots—it is primarily narrativist ("expressed by the creation, via roleplaying, of a story with a recognizable theme") rather than gamist ("expressed by competition among participants"), despite its gamist trappings of "victory and loss conditions" (Edwards 2001). As the work of Carter et al. shows, many participants recognize and enjoy this narrativist element. *40K* has always had a significant barrier to entry, though, in that the rules are complex and demand a considerable degree of mastery. The potentially inelegant nature of those rules, especially with more and more elements bolted on to what was once a small-scale skirmish game, may increase that barrier, especially to a more sophisticated, Eurogame-playing audience. Likewise, the lack of representation of women and minorities is likely to form a further barrier. Finally, the vast universe of "fluff," though massively appealing and immersive to hardcore *40K* fans, may serve to increase the mastery requirement for any players wishing to take the narrativist approach to play that is apparently expected in the rules—though the various armies may be sufficiently iconic to obviate this problem somewhat (even a new player can recognize the primitive Orks and heroic Space Marines, and associate each faction with meaning of their own).

Conclusion

Games Workshop is a unique case. No other hobby game company has built and sustained such an empire, let alone one based solely on two closely related intellectual properties. There are many reasons why it has grown to dominate the field: its first-mover advantage, its vertical structure, its vision of the "Games Workshop Hobby," the commercialization of its imagery and fluff to spread the awareness of its gameworlds, its squeezing of profit margins, and many more. No single one can explain the company's continued success, except for one final point that this chapter has barely touched on: its miniatures. For three decades, Games Workshop has consistently employed the best figure sculptors, has pioneered new molding techniques in white metal, plastic and resin, and uses its own technology and plants to manufacture its products. The result is a range of figures of a quality that is both exceptional and distinctive. When Tom Kirby says, "We make the best fantasy miniatures in the world," he means it, and without that commitment to excellence in its most visible product Games Workshop would be a footnote. Whether on the cover of *White Dwarf* or in the windows of its shops, Games Workshop's figures have always been its best advertisement, for its games and for miniatures gaming in general.

Figure 51.3
Batch painting a squad of Inquisitorial Henchmen so as to save time, and putting some finishing touches to some Death-wing Terminators.

About the Authors

Ian Sturrock is a tabletop role-playing game designer and Game Studies lecturer. He wrote the award-winning *Slaine* and *Conan* RPGs for Mongoose Publishing, among many other things. He teaches and researches at the University of Hertfordshire and runs Serpent King Games, a small-press RPG publisher. He started wargaming with Avalon Hill's board wargames in the early 1980s, and these days enjoys painting, collecting, and even occasionally gaming with miniatures for *Warhammer 40,000*, *Infinity*, and *Song of Blades and Heroes*.

James Wallis is a game designer and author with fourteen books to his credit. He is best known as the founder/director of Hogshead Publishing Ltd., the largest publisher of role-playing games in the UK in the 1990s, but he has also been a TV presenter, magazine editor and *Sunday Times* journalist, and an award-winning graphic designer. His game designs include the storytelling games *Once Upon a Time* and *The Extraordinary Adventures of Baron Munchausen*. These days he runs the games consultancy Spaaace, lectures in game design at London South Bank University, and lives in London with his wife and 1d4–1 children.

Notes

1. See <http://investor.games-workshop.com/our -business-model>; with slightly different phrasing, this text also appears in Games Workshop PLC 2006, Chairman's Preamble.

2. Information obtained through personal communication between James Wallis and a former senior Games Workshop employee in early 2014.

Larry Brom

I have been asked why an American such as myself wrote *The Sword and The Flame* (*TSATF*), a game set during the high-water mark of the British Empire. I have always been a great fan of nineteenth-century Britain and Queen Victoria's military. When I read the stories and poems of writers like Rudyard Kipling, how could I not be? In the late 1960s or the early 1970s, there were no colonial rules that allowed even a slight possibility that natives could win against Her Majesty's troops. Why should I play a game like that? So I wrote *TSATF* as I did.[1]

I never collected miniature soldiers. Playing games with the little guys has always been most important to me. My cousins and I threw rocks at 54mm Britains, Mignots, and Elastolin figures in the back yards of our Chicago neighborhoods. Throughout my childhood, spending Saturdays in my neighborhood movie theater was a ritual, and there I came to love the classic adventure films of the time: *Gunga Din*, *The Lives of a Bengal Lancer*, *The Four Feathers*, *Drums*, *The Adventures of Robin Hood*, and *The Charge of the Light Brigade*, to name just a few. This wonderful combination of cinema and history was something I happily absorbed, remembered, and later used when I wrote *The Sword and The Flame*. The game's title is taken from a Rudyard Kipling poem, "The Widow at Windsor," and the title of this chapter is from Kipling's "Tommy" in *Barrack-Room Ballads*.

I enlisted in the US Marines when I was eighteen, made the landing at Inchon in 1950, and was wounded in combat in Korea. After I returned stateside I got married, began raising a family, and started a career as a folding carton structural designer. And still the thrill of wargaming stayed with me. The periods I was most interested in gaming were the era of British colonialism encompassing the years 1878–84, featuring Pathans, Zulu, Boers, Egyptians, and dervishes. The battles of Isandlwana, Rorke's Drift, Majuba Hill, Tel-el-Kebir, and the Siege of Khartoum—these were what fired the imagination and called out for miniature gaming!

As an adult, I became seriously interested in gaming in the early 1960s with the advent of Holgar Ericson's 25mm (not very well-) painted SAE (South African Engineers) wargame figures. I made the discovery of these "gems" in a North Carolina toy store, when I went in to purchase some doll furniture for one of my daughters' birthdays. Those amazing figures, resplendent in their orange boxes (about sixteen or seventeen infantry figures to a box) and costing about $2.50 per box, almost bowled me over. Strangely, the store had among its sets of mainly

American Civil War troops one box of British colonials in scarlet tunics and white pith helmets, and four boxes of charging Zulu warriors. These five boxes were the start of this whole "colonial" madness. (By the way, I did get the doll furniture too, for those of you who were wondering, but I can't recall the color or price.)

I now had the figures and the interest, but what about rules for playing a game? To this point the only published set of gaming rules I had ever seen was a copy of H. G. Wells's *Little Wars*, from around 1913. I was a subscriber to Jack Scruby's publications, with their many homegrown rules and game concepts, and in 1965 I joined Doug Johnson's *Colonial Society Bulletin* (later *Savage and Soldier*), which offered additional colonial gaming ideas. Then, in the late 1960s, I came across a set of colonial game rules from England in a magazine or perhaps a booklet. I have no idea what they were titled, but they were a well-crafted little set in the classic style of British game rules of that era. I had acquired more colonial figures by this time, so I coerced my one gaming friend into having a go at colonial gaming. We eagerly played four or five games with this wonderful new rule set, having great fun, but then realized that neither of us wanted to be the native force!

Where was the challenge? Once the forces of the Empire were formed and ready and the dervishes or Zulu got in range, it was all over. Historic, but discouraging. No wonder no one played colonials: no one was doing rules, and there weren't many figures available. Shortly thereafter, my friend moved out of the area, and with no one to game with I concentrated on building more mainstream armies—ACW, Napoleonic, and Franco-Prussian—and developing my own rules for each period.

It was now the early 1970s, and more and more rule sets for miniature wargaming were available. Most of these were from Britain and a few from the United States. So I purchased a goodly number, played games with a few, and read all of them. Slowly, in my view, it became apparent that something was lacking. But what? Most of these rules were well-crafted, offered some interesting mechanics (like "saving throws," which to this day still mystify me), introduced morale, required some form of command control or influence, and utilized masses of modifiers and myriad other concepts to make tabletop games more "realistic."

Then came the revelation: I wasn't having any fun! I was too busy with the game mechanics, thumbing through pages and cross referencing chart A.1 with C.2-e. Then and there I decided that I would design my own rules for my own enjoyment. And I would go back to my first love, British colonial troops. I already had small armies, so all I needed were some rules.

All the rules I was aware of, as well as the ones I had written, were subjected to serious scrutiny based on what I thought I wanted to do with toy soldiers on a game table as a hobby and to have some fun. After some months, I settled on the five things I desired from a set of rules, none of which existed in the ones I knew of in the early 1970s: enjoyment, playability, drama, excitement, and historical flavor. With *The Sword and The Flame*, I was going to attempt to introduce new ideas and what I considered to be a very workable and creative system for miniature gaming. I decided on five basic functions: setup, movement, firing, hand-to-hand combat, and morale.

After scanning all the rules I knew of, and confirming that none of them made any reference in their "Introductions" or "Designer's Notes" to these factors (and most of today's rule sets don't either), I determined that I was out of the mainstream of miniature gaming and always would be. So I would just design rules for myself using the above criteria, and relax and enjoy the hobby.[2]

Early in 1978, the late Craig Taylor, formerly of Heritage Models in Dallas, and then with Yaquinto Games, contacted me about my possibly writing an introductory set of game rules for the colonial era, to be issued with miniature figures for the same period. After more back-and-forth on the phone and in letters, I signed an agreement and started on the rules in June 1978.

Because these rules were designed thirty-five years ago, I am hard pressed to remember the exact reasoning and thought processes involved in the creation of the rules as they evolved, other than that I always kept my five main considerations uppermost in mind. I will highlight three issues that I was determined to address in this, my first published rules attempt. These were:

1. Eliminating alternate movement (you move, I move) and firing (you fire, I fire).
2. Injecting excitement into the hand-to-hand combat (most games didn't have it).
3. Not allowing preset movement distances (e.g., "infantry move 6 inches," "cavalry 12 inches," etc.).

I knew from the start there had to be some form of random factor in the movement and sequence of the game. Most games at that time used alternate movement. How wonderfully choreographed this can be! While my opponent is moving his troops, I leisurely watch every troop disposition and calmly plan the countermoves I will make when it's my turn. There

are no surprises, no hurried response from me, and no excitement.

I toyed with a number of techniques. How about an initiative roll (quite common now, but not in the 1970s)? Perhaps the player with the high roll would move first? Maybe not only did the high die move first but the player moved that number of units as well? Then I tried creating "movement" cards by writing the name of each player's units on small cards, shuffling them into a deck, turning them over, flipping the top card, and moving that unit.

This was the procedure I was going to use when one of my daughters asked, "Dad, instead of going to all that trouble, why don't you just use a deck of cards?" Now, I'm no fool, I know a brilliant idea when I hear it, and so my famous "random move card innovation" was born! Prior to 1979, movement was accomplished by one side moving a set distance depending upon the troop types and then the other side responding with a set distance of movement, after being able to observe the opponent's move. Opponents always knew the distance various troops would move; no excitement and no randomness. It still exists today in many successful forms. But not in *The Sword and The Flame*, thanks to a young girl's common sense. The card deck also addressed and answered the random firing issue: same technique, same randomness. I was well on my way to the rules concepts I wanted.

I have always believed that the most exciting moments in any miniature wargame should be the hand-to-hand combats. These represent the culmination of all our planning, maneuvering and evolutions on the tabletop—to close with the enemy, drive him from his positions and exert our moral superiority over his forces and win the day. But the dullest combats I have ever participated in or seen are those where wonderfully painted figures or units, with colors flapping in the breeze, close with an enemy. The tiny soldiers should be shouting and screaming. Their bayonets or swords should be flashing. But then everything comes a halt while the gamers resolve the combat phase. This often goes something like this: count the number of figures or units, consult the charts for point values, calculate a dozen plus or minus modifiers, and eventually come up with a number value. Then each player rolls one multisided die, and the highest number wins the melee with one die roll.

Where is the suspense, where is the drama? There is none! All the game systems that I have designed settle the close combat by pitting figure against figure or stand against stand.[3] The opposing players roll six-sided dice with very simple modifiers and the high total wins. This continues until each pair of opponents has fought. After the dust has settled, only one side still has figures or stands "on their feet." It requires a lot of die rolling, but this game mechanic adds a tremendous amount of excitement.

In our hobby of gaming with miniature figures we are pitting our skill, concepts, knowledge, and luck against an opponent in simulated combat on a tabletop. My theory of eyeball-to-eyeball confrontation by rolling many dice for individual combat resolution is the closest we civilized beings will ever come to actually crossing swords, bayonets, or tomahawks. And talk about suspense and drama! At any convention, if one game table suddenly erupts in loud cheers, groans, and finally exultation, the high probability is that a melee matching man for man or stand for stand has just culminated. I know this because that's what happens at my games. In fact, I will guarantee it at my games.

Measured movement distances are probably the strangest aspect of gaming rules that have been generally embraced. The idea that two armies or forces on any given tabletop will always all move exactly the same distance has always been incredible to me. I won't even address historic justification that this is a fantasy, but will merely discuss the issue within the framework of wargaming. Some gamers, of course, are control freaks and love preset movement distances. It is absolutely wonderful during a game to have enemy cavalry on your flank and by firing a battery at them (you had to measure the range, of course) you know they are 48″ away. Since they are cavalry in line and move 12″, you smugly know that you have four turns to prepare for their attempt at outflanking you. What an exciting challenge! No risk, no drama, and it's a piece of cake. But not for me. I favor some form of random movement distances in all the games I design and play in order to offset this artificial concept.

Once I had incorporated these concepts into the rules system I was formulating, I was close to completing the first draft of the rules. What remained was the tedious detail, the formatting and integration of all the charts and other necessary minutiae required for the creation of a workable, playable rules system that reflects the designer's vision of battle in a particular historical period. And throughout all these phases of fashioning the rules framework are the endless and repetitive playtests, playtests, and more playtests. This is the key to a workable, playable set of rules, and the correct group of playtesters is essential. I was extremely fortunate to have the Jackson, Mississippi, War Game Society at my beck and call (ha!). This group was the most stubborn, opinionated, argumentative gathering of gamers the world has ever known and could tear apart any set of rules in two turns or less, but if you could hang in there with them, their revisions and suggestions were almost magic.

The first rough manuscript was submitted to Mr. Taylor on July 3, 1978, for his review. After lengthy dialogues between us, a second draft was submitted on August 28 of that same year. The third (final) draft of the rules was sent to Yaquinto on January 22 (shades of Isandlwana!), 1979; sometime that summer, the rules were produced and released to the gaming community.

As I mentioned earlier, movies have always been my inspiration for gaming, as well as for writing rules. The most appealing part of wargaming to me has always been the visual aspect, and I call my approach to gaming "Hollywood wargaming." I wanted to get the same thrill and visual spectacle that I got from a movie screen when gaming with my toy soldiers on a tabletop. I still enjoy looking down at a beautiful table and seeing all the troops lined up.

And like a movie, gaming is not to be taken too seriously. Many years ago, at a small convention, I was putting on a game with the US Cavalry vs. Apache Indians. I had painted my troops to resemble Hollywood films, with yellow kerchiefs around their necks. A very well-known author and historian (whose name I've forgotten) came over to me in the middle of the game. He was smoking a pipe and was wearing a vest, cravat, and corduroy trousers. The rest of us were a bit more casual. He pulled the pipe from his mouth, and said to me, "You know, of course, the Army in the West *never* wore yellow kerchiefs," smiling in a rather condescending way. I stood up from rolling dice, looked at him, and said, also smiling, "Well, if it's good enough for John Wayne, it's good enough for me." He didn't know what to say, so he turned around and left.

If you have read through all of this, maybe you have a feeling of how and why I created *The Sword and The Flame*. I have always been very pleased with the mostly positive response to them and appreciative of all of the stalwart gamers who were willing to take a chance on a rogue set of rules and have played, endorsed and enjoyed them through the years. You realize, of course, that if you play colonial games and embrace my slightly different approach to gaming, you are a renegade, an outlaw, and outside the mainstream of miniature wargaming. But have courage, my comrades—we are a force to be reckoned with, and our numbers are growing.

I've been wargaming for over sixty years, in many periods, but have never come across the caliber of camaraderie and enjoyment that I've experienced with fellow colonial gamers. For many years we were dismissed. Only if you played Napoleonic, American Civil War, or World War II games were you taken seriously. However, all these years after *The Sword and The Flame* was published, the number of colonial games continue to grow, and *TSATF* is still being played. I can't explain why a certain type of gamer is attracted to *TSATF*, but I know you couldn't ask for a finer group of gamers. My closest friends have always been wargamers, many of them friends of thirty-plus years. My philosophy is to *have fun* with your gaming and the hobby. Try to find a likeminded group of people to game with. Read history, view films, and check out the various groups on the Internet. It's a wonderful time to be a wargamer. So roll the dice, move the troops and enjoy yourselves. The game has just begun!

About the Author

Larry Brom was born in Chicago in 1930. His six and a half years in the Marine Corps, coupled with a life-long love of military history, influenced his interest in wargaming, but he was always quick to tell people that what is done on a game table bears little or no resemblance to actual combat: we are playing a game, not being shot at; our lives are not in danger. In 1979, he published the first version of *The Sword and The Flame* colonial-period miniatures rules for Yaquinto Games. Larry Brom died in 2015 as this volume was going to press.

Notes

1. I have recently discovered that an ancestor of mine, Trooper Robert Kincaide of the Natal Mounted Police, survived the battle of Isandlwana and died in South Africa in the late 1930s. I didn't know this when I decided to write *The Sword and The Flame.*

2. I had written other sets of rules for gaming with toy soldiers. *Before I Was a Marshal I Was a Grenadier* is set in 1805–15, during the Napoleonic Wars. *Glint of Bayonets* is for battles in the American Civil War. I was always an avid reader of anything Napoleonic, and prior to writing *The Sword and The Flame*, I gamed mainly Napoleonic and American Civil War. Ed Mohrmann, my gaming partner in the early 1960s, and I developed *Before I Was a Marshal* as a simple alternative to the very complex Napoleonic rules available then.

3. A stand can hold several numbers of figures but is usually treated the same way as individual figures are treated. It simply makes for a quicker game.

53 WAR RE-CREATED: TWENTIETH-CENTURY WAR REENACTORS AND THE PRIVATE EVENT

Jenny Thompson

To do it for real, you'd get killed. It's not like playing tennis, you know. You can play tennis for real and not get hurt. But if you want to try to get a sample of what war was like without getting killed, this is about as close as you're going to be able to do it.

—Luke Gardner

Reenactors who belong to the twentieth-century war reenacting hobby, which includes the reenactment of World Wars I and II and the Vietnam War, agree wholeheartedly that they can never "relive" the wars of the past. But as the above quote from one reenactor makes clear, they seek a "sample of what war was like."[1] As a group, reenactors share a (usually lifelong) fascination with war. And they share a desire to move beyond the limitations of war portrayals found in books, television, and films. It is only through a three-dimensional, real-time reenactment that they can connect with history in a way that is otherwise unavailable to the passive consumer of the war story.

Reenactors, who belong to units across the United States, participate in a variety of types of public events, such as air shows, parades, and mock battles.[2] Such events (dubbed "dog and pony" shows by one reenactor) can be fun, but most reenactors agree that public events are separate and distinct from true reenacting. Some reenactors are reluctant to perform in mock battles staged for the public since they view such events as strictly public entertainment—neither historically accurate nor true reenactments.

The heart of this grassroots hobby lies in the "private event"—a reenactment that usually takes place over the course of a weekend. Held on a variety of sites, from private land to state parks to federal military installations, private events range in size from twenty to well over fifteen hundred participants. Reenactors either camp in the field or make use of onsite cabins or barracks. Most importantly, these events are free from the public gaze. *No outsiders or spectators are allowed.* Thus, reenactors are free to strive toward one of their primary goals: achieving authenticity both in appearance and in terms of the portrayal of history itself.

Reenactors admit that their hobby is, in a sense, "a game," and they sometimes jokingly refer to it as "playing army." But they shy away from treating reenacting as kids' play. In fact, reenacting is serious business. Through the course of the seven years in which I conducted ethnographic research on reenactors, I learned that while the hobby is a voluntary, and often pleasurable, activity, it is a highly structured undertaking. Despite the fact that it operates without a single official governing body or set of standard rules, reenactments are not only well-organized but they also follow a similar pattern. The ways reenactors shape and experience their private events, the choices they make, the rules they impose, and the debates they engage in reveal just how seriously they approach their pastime; and it is in the setting of the private event that the hobby comes into true light. This is reenacting in its purest form.

Most reenactors drive long distances, their cars and trucks packed with equipment, food, and other gear, to reach a remote site for a private event. There, they join other members of their units, commanded by their "officers." While each unit employs its own rules and regulations, all reenactors are also subject to the rules and administrative procedures of the event hosts. Safety briefings, planning meetings, and ammo inspections are all essential components of a private event. Event hosts,[3] who procure or govern the event site, must secure insurance coverage for events and oversee the registration of participants.

A private event involves various activities: arrival and unpacking; registration; the setting up of camps and barracks; visits to the flea market, where vendors sell militaria; eating and drinking; socializing; and, of course, mock combat.[4] Usually, the combat portion of an event takes place over the course of a full day, beginning early in the morning. In World War I events, units take position in their designated trench sectors.[5] In World War II events, action is far-ranging. Units and vehicles, if present, are deployed in fields or wooded areas. Vietnam War events are often built around small units patrolling on foot. In all types of events, combat consists of small-scale engagements conducted by individual units or perhaps only several reenactors. And no matter the war being reenacted, participants face the impending action knowing little if anything about what will happen.

During a World War I event, I stole into the French trench sector at nighttime. Flares illuminated no-man's-land, and I watched in awe as reenactors hurried to and fro, walking ghostlike through the black trenches. When the French commander saw me, he kneeled down and whispered, "Just be careful." After a dramatic pause, he warned, "You never know what will happen."

Indeed. I was quite surprised to learn that reenactors do not attempt to replicate actual historic battles in their private events. Unlike a public battle, which is almost always "scripted," a private battle is "open-ended" or "free-flowing." This means that soldiers who were historically vanquished in a war, such as the Germans, are not always defeated in a reenactment. "Can the Allies force the German Army out of Italy, or will reinforcements reach Kesselring in time to blunt the Allied advance?" one event announcement asked. "Join us for the Italian Campaign 1998 and find out for yourself!" (*Italian Campaign* 1998).

Although reenactors may argue that they are "re-creating" history, their battles are designed so that anything essentially can happen. And even though events are given specific historic titles such as "Duel on a Dutch Levee" (based on Operation Market Garden) and "Elbe River" (Eastern Front), they are set only within general historical time frames and locations. "The time frame for this event," read one event announcement, "is September–October of 1944. The area is eastern France, Belgium or Holland" (*Odessa* 1997).

These basic time frames and places give reenactors a chance to enact what they call "scenarios"—small- or large-scale dramatic sequences within an overall event itself. "We're talking about night attacks, individual raids where two or three guys can go out and try and get in the enemy lines," reenactor Paul Donald said in an interview, describing some of the likely scenarios in a World War I event. "We're talking about firing machine guns and mortars. ... If there's an attack at the right-hand line they can call up reinforcements from the left-hand line. You can actually go out and set up a scenario where you fake an attack on this end, the enemy draws their reinforcements down there and then you get them at the other end." Like others, Paul stresses the variety of opportunities reenactors have to take action.

"We are bound," one World War I reenactor said, "only by our creativity and knowledge of World War I in the creation of our scenarios" (Aylward 1993, 5). Using a combination of creativity and knowledge, reenactors are free to act regardless of history's actual outcome. (In fact, many reenactors even assert that the word "reenacting" is a misnomer.) What they choose to do in an event is shaped more by their sense of what "could have" happened historically rather than what actually happened in a given time and place.

Reenactors prefer these open-ended battles with only the slightest script used to frame the action, since attempting to replicate historical events is largely viewed as "counterproductive" (Call 1997).[6] Ironically, it is only in the absence of a predetermined historical script that they believe they can achieve any degree of authenticity. "Scripted scenarios are okay (if not required) for public events," one reenactor explained, "but they are the kiss of death for a tactical event" (Tilden 1997). Since reenactments are limited in scope, trying to recreate an actual battle would "cheapen the actual event by presenting a lame-o parody" (Samuel 1997). Thus they design events according to their own capabilities. For example, World War I events lack an important element of real combat of the Western Front: artillery. "Big battles of World War I of course are hundreds and hundreds and hundreds of guns and masses of infantry," reenactor John Loggia explained in an interview, admitting that reenactors lack those essential components of combat. But he rationalized such a discrepancy, stating, "The kind of sector that we're portraying is maybe a semi-active one away from where a big battle would be going on."

Whatever action reenactors decide to take during an event depends less on what happened in history and more on the fact that "sometimes they might want to stir things up and sometimes they don't," as John said of his own unit members. The freedom to decide whether to "stir things up" is vital. Commanders may plan an attack or a certain scenario in advance—at one World War I event, the Germans planned a surprise twilight surrender to the Allies en masse—but they don't inform the enemy of their intent. "I don't believe in letting the Allies know when we will attack," one reenactor stated. "This way neither side knows what to expect and it will be more realistic" (Henry 1993, 5).

As much as an event is open-ended, however, reenactors are not supposed to "run around" without a purpose. "You can't do something and not have any knowledge about it, if you want to do it correctly," reenactor Fred Legum explained in an interview. "You can't just go out there and flub about." Thus, they are expected to "implement the appropriate period tactics for a given situation." In short, they try to use historically authentic tactics, such as ambushes, trench raids, gas attacks, or tank battles. A lot of reenactors find that having a tactical mission or a plan for a scenario makes the action more interesting. Reenactor Greg Grosshans told me in an interview that this helps them avoid "mindless running around in the woods shooting at one another." Unit members are also expected to follow orders and pursue assigned objectives. "Being given realistic goals for units of similar size that were actually given to historical units is good," one reenactor commented. "No one should be out there without orders, but leave the scripts to people on a stage" (Mason 1997).

Aside from performing tactically in period fashion, reenactors are also expected to behave with "some degree of control" (Harris 1999). From being told by event hosts where to park to being told by unit commanders what to wear and carry, event rules and guidelines are profuse, beginning with the inevitable safety inspection. "Remember," one event announcement instructs, "No pop-up flares, no military grenade or artillery simulators, no shotguns, no weapons with inoperative safeties, no affixed bayonets, no red flares, and *no live ammo!*" (*Duel* 1996).[7]

Next come the rules of engagement: "Do not aim and fire directly at individuals within twenty yards of you. Blanks can be dangerous at close range. If in doubt, aim and fire your weapon straight up, or when in close combat inside the trenches, just yell, Bang!" (Robb 1996, 7). Unit commanders also issue orders regarding period behavior in the field. "Don't talk about anything anachronistic unless it's absolutely necessary! (i.e., someone is having a heart attack)" (Gardner 1994).

Even when not in combat, behavior is subject to restrictions: "Please do not stand on the battlefield and become spectators and/or take pictures of your fellow reenactors. [This] distorts what we are trying to accomplish" (Johnson 1996). Finally, they are instructed about more personal conduct: "No use of controlled substances. No disorderly conduct. No drunkenness" (W2HPG).

While reenactors may be expected to "have respect for the rules" and to conform to safety guidelines, in an open-ended, all-volunteer grassroots hobby, the rules themselves are constantly subject to revision and debate. After all, in a game where participants are "free" to decide their own course of action, determining the limits of that freedom can be complicated. More overtly worded rules (no live ammo) are accompanied by others that are more open to interpretation (i.e., reenactors must "die" when shot). And indeed, a major area of concern is the failure of reenactors to "take hits" (fall to the ground and feign death when "shot"). Another concern is the exercise of authority: "officers," after all, are either self-appointed or promoted from within individual units, hence the difficulty, at times, of getting reenactors to conform to the wielding of authority from others. Further, while the vast majority agree that they are attempting to portray a "common" or "average" soldier's war experience (most reenactors portray privates), they must reach some agreement on just what that experience entails. Most agree that they should avoid representing what they consider to be war's "exceptional" aspects. Luke Gardner's order to his men that "John Wayne stuff has no place here" underscores the general aversion to rendering war a la the "Hollywood mentality." Surviving a battle or performing a feat of great heroism is generally frowned upon. "The idea is not so much to kill Germans," Luke said, "but to avoid being killed yourself" (Gardner 1993). Hiding from the enemy, often more than attacking, consumes a great

Figure 53.1
Hiding from the enemy, Battle of the Bulge reenactment, 1995.

majority of their time. "We try to put ourselves in the most horrific situation we can and it's usually trying not to get shot or get spotted, which is what I think a lot of it was," reenactor Fred Legum explained in an interview. "During war you tried to stay clear and stay hid as much as you can because ... you don't want to be where it's really hot all the time."

To be sure, real soldiers try to avoid being killed. But most reenactors think they must suffer and inflict large numbers of casualties—for authenticity's sake. In the words of a World War I reenactor, "Everybody dies!" Unlike their attempts to control the portrayal of violence in public events, in private they freely and repeatedly kill each other as well as die themselves many times in a single event. "Trigger time"—or combat—lasts until one side or another (or both) is overrun. This might take three hours, or it might take twenty minutes. They then retreat, regroup, and either break for a meal or begin another scenario.

Interspersed within combat scenarios, they spend a good deal of time performing rather mundane activities, such as standing in formation, marching, drilling, assembling equipment, digging foxholes, fortifying trenches, and inevitably, waiting around. They also conduct "noncombat scenarios" such as patrols, wire cutting parties, intelligence missions, and guard duty. They capture prisoners and interrogate them. They write up commanders' orders. They study maps and captured intelligence. They string out phone lines and operate radio systems. They sit in their camps, bunkers, and trenches. They open lonely soldier packages. They eat, talk, write letters, conduct mail call, and, especially at World War I events, sing. Women reenactors either fight as soldiers or serve alongside units as correspondents.

They also serve as nurses and Red Cross and Salvation Army personnel, tending to the wounded, cooking, or knitting. And all reenactors engage in a variety of other activities, such as posing for photographs, bartering at the flea market, and talking with each other about contemporary subjects.

In all types of private events, the same kind of scenarios are replicated over and over. But a reenactment is never complete. No one ever decides, "Well, we successfully re-created the Battle of the Bulge, let's call it quits." Instead, an event's open-ended structure allows for a kind of reenactment of

Figure 53.2
View of no-man's-land from a World War I German post; Great War Association (GWA) site, 1997.

Figure 53.3
Troops in the woods, Battle of the Bulge reenactment, 1994.

reenactments ad infinitum. One reason for an event's repetition lies in the fact that they do not enact any specific historical narrative. "We don't reenact any particular thing," reenactor Paul Donald said. "But we do re-create a time period and live in it." Reenactor Hank Lyle explained in an interview: "I think it gives us a chance [to say], okay, this could be anywhere in France, and given the same tools that they had we're given a chance to explore those bits of history, those time frames, those years."

Reenactors explore those bits of history using period tools (uniforms, equipment) that provide a tangible link to the past. In doing so, they try "to experience the life of a soldier," as reenactor Richard Paoletti said in an interview with me, "just an average soldier." And most are unconcerned with issues beyond the narrow scope of that experience, including victory or defeat. A majority—more than 70 percent—look upon winning in an event as either somewhat unimportant or not important at all.[8] Many find winning irrelevant, since their highest standard is not victory but authenticity. "Who cares who wins?" one reenactor asked. "Reliving history should be our number one concern; otherwise we are just expensively dressed paint ballers" (Johnson 1996). Others admit how hard it is to tell who wins a given scenario, since so many die and it's often so confused. "In every reenactment everyone ends up dying, so to say that one side won a battle and the other side lost is very difficult," Greg Grosshans explained. "The end of a reenactment is usually just spent recounting different instances in the scenario where one guy shot another guy or you were able to sneak up on someone or, you know, little surprise things."

Ultimately, these "little surprise things" constitute the substance of the private event. And no detail is too trivial. Haircuts, shoes, language, weight, gender, rifles—these are just some of the details of their portrayal that are ceaselessly and often mercilessly debated. And there, in a sense, the game of reenacting really begins, and its site shifts beyond an event's physical boundaries. Now, the game is played out over the Internet, the cell phone, and in person as reenactors discuss, debate, and disagree over what precisely constitutes authenticity in terms of defining those details. In many ways, these debates are just as critical to the hobby as is the action in the field.

Thus, reenacting proves to be a form of voluntary recreation whose very substance lies in the continuous debate and refinement over the details of the game itself. Because there is no "official" reenacting organization that lays down the rules and enforces them, reenactors must engage in a war, as it were, over defining what precisely constitutes the authenticity of a common soldier's war experience. Reenactors may have claimed control over the portrayal of the war story by moving it into the realm of their private events, but there, the battle to define the nature of that portrayal has only begun.

About the Author

A graduate of San Francisco State University, Jenny Thompson has an MA in American Studies from the George Washington University and a PhD in American Studies from the University of Maryland. She has taught courses in American history and culture at the University of Maryland and at Roosevelt University in Chicago. Her work focuses on twentieth- and twenty-first-century American history and culture, the cultural history of American wars, and the history of images. Her publications include *War Games: Inside the World of 20th-Century War Reenactors* (Smithsonian Books) and *My Hut: A Memoir of a YMCA Volunteer in World War I* (editor). Her essays and reviews have appeared in various anthologies and publications, including the *New York Times.* She currently serves as Director of Education at the Evanston History Center and works as a consultant on a variety of public history projects.

Notes

1. All reenactor names used here are pseudonyms. All the interviews with reenactors cited here were conducted by the author.

2. Twentieth-century war reenactors can be found in countries other than the United States.

3. Event hosts are reenactors themselves. World War I reenactors on the East Coast own and run their own event site, the Caesar Krauss Great War Memorial site near Newville, Pennsylvania. The one-hundred-acre site, complete with an intricate network of trenches, is run by a reenactor organization, the GWA.

4. For some reenactors, the combat portion of an event is the least interesting. In fact, reenactors span a wide spectrum in terms of their interests in war (some are more interested in uniforms and vehicles, for example; others in "camp life" or other war-related aspects).

5. Some World War I events take place on sites without trenches.

6. During the course of my research, I was a member of several online newsgroups focused on reenacting; this quotation and some others here are drawn from online discussions that took place in those groups.

7. Serious violations of safety regulations are grounds for ejection from an event.

8. This is based on a written survey I conducted of more than three hundred reenactors.

IX   FIGHT THE FUTURE

54 WAR, MATHEMATICS, AND SIMULATION: DRONES AND (LOSING) CONTROL OF BATTLESPACE

Patrick Crogan

The organizing principle of the technical object is in this object qua tendency, aim and end.

—Bernard Stiegler

This chapter will reflect on aspects of the expansion of military drone usage by Western powers in the "war on terror" over the last decade or so. Theorists approaching drones from different fields such as Gregoire Chamayou and Derek Gregory have argued that the systematic and growing deployment of unmanned aerial vehicles puts into question established cultural, political, legal, and ethical framings of war, peace, territory, civilian, and soldier in the societies on behalf of which these systems are deployed. Animating this profound undoing of cultural and geopolitical moorings is what Chamayou in *Théorie du drone* calls the "tendency inscribed in the material development of the [drone] weapon-system" (Chamayou 2013, 230).[1] I will explore the nature of this tendency inherent in drone materiality and technology, concentrating on the virtualizing, real-time digital developments in remotely controlled and increasingly automated robotic systems.

The projection over the inhabited world of a simulational model of the contested space is a constitutive part of this tendency. In the military logics and technologies powering this projection, the inhabitants of the spaces of concern in the global war on terror are better understood as environmental elements or threats in what Robert Sargent has called the "problem space." This is his term for the environment or situation the simulation designer seeks to model conceptually as a key prerequisite to programming the simulation so that it can provide an effective means to seek experimentally for a solution (Sargent 2005, 135). In a similar "experimental" manner, in Afghanistan and elsewhere a specifically designed spatiotemporality is enacting a performative reinvention of the lived experience of both inhabiting and contesting the control of space in time.

If, as these writers have shown, this projection of and over "enemy territory" has clear precedents in European colonialist strategies and procedures, what is unprecedented today is the digitally enabled expansion and intensification of this spatiotemporal reanimation of the world. This reanimation must be understood as a key contributor to a transformative and troubling pathway toward the automation of military force projection across the globe. I will analyze the nature and implications of this reanimation of the world in digital modelings of the enemy in and as milieu, a milieu as tiny as the space around a single "target" and as large as the world, existing both in a brief "window of opportunity" and within a permanent real-time of preemptive, pan-spectrum surveillance.

In this chapter I will first spend some time tracing the sources of this performative military-technological tendency back to the part-mythical, part-historical origins of Western civilization in ancient Greece. I will argue that the contemporary intensification of a technical and conceptual, military and digital projection of the battlefield "problem space" finds there its progenitors in the origins of geometry and mathematics, in strategic and tactical innovations and their philosophical, aesthetic, and political accommodation in the classic foundations of Western society. Stretching back into prehistory, wargames with pebbles were already playing a part in building these foundations. As John Onians has proposed, their proto-simulational techniques and artifacts for imagining territory and contesting control over it offered models and means for conceptual developments in geometry and mathematics (Onians 1989). This dynamic between the material, technical and the conceptual in the production of a zone of control continues to animate traffic between wargames, simulational forms and the implementation of robotic weapons systems in real geophysical conflict zones today.

In examining contemporary and envisaged drone deployments I am also concerned with what they can reveal about the technical tendency animating them. Tracing them back to the beginnings of Western culture shows that the material course of drone "advances" shares key features with wider trends in global digital technocultural becoming. "We"—"we" living in and enjoying the benefits (as well as suffering the toxifying effects) of today's real-time, online, ubiquitous media environment—perhaps too readily treat this environment as more or less distinct from and unrelated to the lived experiences of those in the contested spaces subject to military supervision and intervention. Documentaries such as *Unmanned: America's Drone War* (2014) make it clear that many of those living under drones share much of "our" experience of the global media environment. This commonality of experience and aspirations—however unequally distributed—is also fundamental to the ethics of the humanitarian and social justice activism concerning drone use in targeting killings. This activism insists on the continuing legitimacy of human rights protections for noncombatants and agitates for adherence to the existing legal definitions of the spatial and temporal limitation of military conflict (see Stanford International Human Rights & Conflict Clinic and the Global Justice Clinic of New York University 2012).

And there is a third, increasingly apparent dimension of the commonality of technical tendency and material lived experience that draws together drones and contemporary digital technoculture in the emerging global future. It is perhaps most apparent in developments toward commercial deployment of automated systems for security, surveillance and other uses (such as Amazon's delivery drone gimmick) as well as in their regular appearance in the latest releases of AAA shooters such as the *Battlefield* and *Call of Duty* franchises. But inasmuch as drones are also a leading-edge innovation in the computerization and online networking of manufactured objects in general, they can be seen as overflying a generalized implementation of automated, permanent, real-time surveillance and regulation of lived experience that is unprecedented in human history.

The scale, historical scope, and diverse overlappings of the technical tendency "inscribed in the material development of the [drone] weapon-system" represent a challenge to critical thought. In what follows, I will set out an approach to thinking "tendentially" about military drones with an eye on the wider technocultural dynamics with which they are composed. In the course of this I will need to consider longer and shorter wavelengths of this tendential development toward the reinvention of war—which is also the reinvention of peace—and how these wavelengths overlap and crystallize today in the poststrategic, postpolitical potential of drone deployment by the United States, Israel and other "advanced Western powers." The materialization of a tendency is never its complete realization, and it offers other possibilities and other anticipations of the tendency. This gap of incompletion between the actualized devices, procedures, and systems and the tendency is the space and the time for reflection, review, critique, and renegotiation. If today it seems to be ever the shorter and smaller, it is nonetheless critical to inhabit it with a less operational mode than that described in Sargent's principles of simulation design. A properly critical engagement is less concerned with improving the validity of the conceptual modeling of the "problem space" of the real world and more concerned with how the problem space has been defined, according to what logics, what questions, and supporting what inherent tendency. It is through posing and answering these questions that the possibility of altering its course arises.

Tendency, Composition, and Ethnocultural Development

The expansion of drone operations is my principal concern and I will examine it in detail in subsequent sections. As their highest profile representatives (in the mainstream media as much as in wider academic and political debate) the unmanned aerial vehicles known commonly as drones can stand in for the wider gamut of robotic weapons developments across the armed forces and security agencies. These include the Samsung SGR1 armed machine gun system permanently monitoring the zone between the two Koreas, the bomb-disposal robots (such as the Cobham tEODor) used on the ground in Iraq and Afghanistan, and the various experiments in remotely operated naval surface and submarine devices. The SGR1 and similar automated targeting and firing systems like Raytheon's Phalanx CIWS (Close-in Weapon System) and its land-based variant the C-RAM (Counter Rocket, Artillery and Mortar), are sometimes excluded from categorization alongside the unmanned vehicles, understood to be part of the preceding "generations" of automatic weapons such as the "smart" missiles using infrared, radar or laser guidance. As M. Shane Riza argues in reflecting on an encounter with the C-RAM, however, the lines are blurred between automatic and autonomous weapons, and it is necessary to pay attention to the extent to which the automation of target acquisition and weapons fire has already become endemic in the warfighting conducted by the militaries of the advanced powers even before the recent phase of unmanned systems (Riza 2013, 2–4).[2]

As a further development of the doctrine and implementation of "air superiority," it is no surprise that drones are at the forefront of developments (and debates) concerning the expansion of auto- mated and remotely operated weapons. As Philip Lawrence noted in *Modernity and War*, control of the skies is a key principle of total war in the modern industrial age, an age in which "control of the future" has become the "watchword" (Lawrence 1997, 62). As Chamayou points out, the drone's eye in the sky sees all, adopting the prescient perspec- tive of God, reaching out over the territory of the enemy in a preemptive precondition for the desired total control of the enemy threat (Chamayou 2013, 57). To anticipate and interdict the enemy's capacity to act represents the key strategic functions of air- power: surveillance and strike. As I will examine later, the use of drones has expanded rapidly over the last decade and evolved in such a way as to put the coherence of this strategic goal in question through a rapid implementation in simulational, semiautomated systems that are largely (but not unanimously) supported by a rationalizing volun- tarism in military and political circles.

It is important to understand this expanded implementation of remote and automated weapons systems, however, as continuing developments that were set in train by earlier trajectories of tech- nical and cultural-political compositions of dis- courses, practices, and inventions. For it is in the dynamics animating the composition of these that a material tendency finds its motive force. In *Technics and Time 1*, Bernard Stiegler characterizes history as the product of a composition of human and techni- cal forms. Stiegler's conception of the central role of technical development in human history draws on André Leroi-Gourhan's notion of the constitutive role played by the technical tendency of "exterior- ization" in the evolutionary process of "hominiza- tion" through which human beings arrived at

their most successful, globally extended form (Stiegler 1998, 62). The human evolves through a process of technical developments that export functions and capacities that were "interior" to the pre-human biological genetic organism. At a certain (for Stiegler unlocatable but nonetheless attained) threshold, this process formed a new dynamic that takes becoming human beyond a strictly natural evolution to an ethnocultural becoming that pro- ceeds in tandem with this exteriorizing technical tendency.

Human history subsequently develops and diver- sifies through a series of "adjustments" vis-à-vis the technical in the dynamics driving the various spheres or systems of human society such as the political, the religious, and the economic. Their complex interplay unfolds on the basis of the technicity of the human as technical, exteriorized becoming. Stiegler employs Bertrand Gilles's notion of adjustment (and malad- justment) between systems by way of formulating an account of the challenges posed by the sophistication and reach of industrial and increasingly complex and automated modern technology (Stiegler 1998, 41–43). In the industrial age of standardized production and the emergence of technology as the application of "scientific," rational principles to manufacturing processes, the technical system becomes increasingly dominant because of the speed of its innovation, the impact of its enhanced productive capacity and the ensuing global spread of its influence. As both con- cept and material form(s), technology is in this regard a specific historical (and Western European) develop- ment of technics. Technics refers in Stiegler's work to all those techniques and artifacts exterior to any individual consciousness and upon which its individ- ual development as part of a collective, cultural identity is based. Culture is in this regard always a "technoculture" of sorts inasmuch as it is transmitted and evolves on the basis of this exterior archive and resource. The becoming technological of technics represents, however, a radical globalizing shift in the dynamics of this technocultural evolutionary process for the West and across its colonial extension.

Drawing on Gilbert Simondon's philosophy of technology, Stiegler qualifies this preeminence of the technological in modernity with a sense of the deeply compositional relations through which each sphere of existence develops in relation to the others (Stiegler 1998, 65). As the being (or becoming) who anticipates, the human plays a crucial role in the ongoing advance of the technical tendency as technological innovation and this means the human (via its other spheres of existence and concerns) retains a key potential to inflect its course. Stiegler's analysis of the contemporary moment, however, is that we are witnessing a troubling destabilization of the balance of the composition of human and technical becoming. The complex, technologically framed scenarios in which the human anticipates the future of technology tends today to limit the extent to which nontechnological experience can inform or qualify that anticipation. Stiegler asks in what metastable, "organological" arrangement of human biological and technocultural "organs" and instrumentalities is this anticipation of things to come properly fostered? And what happens when its stability unravels? (1998, 78–81).[3]

Stiegler's approach to this questioning deserves a more careful unpacking than I can provide here, but what is key to grasp is that it treats the technical as both a sphere of existence with its own dynamic and as inherently composed through and with the other spheres of human existence. The classic either/or of the technological determinism debate—technology as determining or as culturally and historically produced and rationalized—appears in this light as a misreading of the complex co-constitutivity of the technical and the cultural. The "what invents the who just as it is invented by it," argues Stiegler in summarizing his position on the origin (and future) of the human and the part played by technics (177). This reposes the dilemma of technological determinism as one concerning the nature, politics, and ethics of the adjustments made by the cultural, political, and other systems to their composition with technological developments. The key question becomes how to adopt and modify the course of the tendential unfolding of new configurations of ethnocultural becoming.

I will argue that the radical overturning of political and cultural notions and practices of "territory" already recognizable in the trajectory of drone deployments indicates that a reconfiguration of the very conditions of human-technical evolution is on the horizon of their "material tendency." In Stiegler's view, the "human" in this composite term does not refer to a stable or transcendental entity, but to a contingent and at best metastable organization and promise of a particular kind or kinds of social and individual existence. It has to be argued over and argued for today. For instance, the legal activism against remote-controlled killings makes it readily apparent that the program of drone use is heading in a radically different direction to the project announced in declarations and conventions on "human rights." As the human rights-focused *Living Under Drones* report demonstrates, the life of those who have to live under the ever-present surveillance and imminent threat of Hellfire missile strike posed by drones is reduced to one of survival.

The social and cultural activities and practices that make life worth living as a human being are suppressed by a permanent threat from the air (Stanford International Human Rights & Conflict Clinic and the Global Justice Clinic of New York University 2012).

Tracings: Mathematics, War, and Technics in the Seat of Western Civilization

The contemporary Western involvement in Afghanistan and Pakistan incorporates two contrasting projects that share a common heritage as Western European in character. On the one hand, there are the ongoing legal and human rights agencies' efforts agitating for a truly global realization of the human rights of a humanity whose universality was first proposed as a key theme of Enlightenment philosophical humanism. On the other hand, there is the experimental techno-militarist expansion of a (no less universalizable) operational battlefield in which human rights are increasingly irrelevant and provide no practical orientation for those acting on and within its limits. Each of these projects has key philosophical, political, scientific, and technical roots in ancient Greece. The legacies of ancient Greece represent for us today a wellspring of scientific, philosophical, and cultural-political advances of abiding significance for the West. These advances also had a history—strictly speaking a prehistory—of technical, ethnocultural, and political developments in Egypt, Assyria and the Mesopotamian region more generally. These included the invention of geometry in Egypt and the invention of writing and the gradual emergence of phonetic alphabetic scripts in Assyria.[4] Nonetheless, ancient Greece names a singular period of transformations that crystallized in a philosophical and technocultural program, carried forward and modified by the Romans, whose significance for the subsequent histories of Western

European ethnocultures is indisputable. Since the sixteenth century CE, this history is also a global history of European colonization of the "new world" and its aftermath, right up to today's postcolonial, global world order.[5] If, as I am proposing, the drone program is at the avant-garde of the West's passage toward another technocultural (and technopolitical) shift in the wake of the long and catastrophic twentieth century of global war and social and economic reinvention, it does so in part as an inheritor of certain key compositions of technical, scientific and cultural-political development that characterized the "miracle" of ancient Greece.

John Onians makes this abundantly clear in "War, Mathematics and Art in Ancient Greece" (1989). He shows how the constant conflict between the Greek city-states was a significant driver of those developments in mathematics, art and architecture, philosophy, and politics so central to the legacy of ancient Greece. Indeed, he argues, war must be understood as the dominant motive force of their achievement (40). In contrast to the relatively more stable (internally at least) Egyptian or Persian civilizations, the status and significance of the advances in Greek philosophy, politics, mathematics, architecture, and sculpture must be thought of in relation to the importance of military considerations in securing or expanding the territory of the competing Greek city-states. Onians provides a variety of examples of linkages between advances in military techniques and technics and the conceptual and theoretical developments of Greek mathematics, art, and philosophical and political thought.

I am most interested here in tracing two of these linkages between military technics and conceptual "discoveries": that which goes from the development of the phalanx battle formation to the formulation of abstract, mathematical laws of order and proportion; and the related dynamic connecting a proto-simulational modeling of the politico-strategic real with mathematical formalization and philosophical speculation. Between them, they mark a decisive turn toward the conceptual and technical complexes of automation and simulation I wish to examine in the deployment of drones.

The phalanx was a key tactical discovery of Greek military commanders for organizing the armed foot soldiery, the *hoplitai* (hoplites), into an effective rectangular formation maximizing the defensive capacity of the form as it maneuvered and engaged enemy units. It predates the celebrated philosophical and mathematical advances that were to follow in the classical period from the fifth to the fourth century BCE; by exactly how long is the subject of debate among scholars of ancient Greece, a debate that may be interminable given that the developments in question span the threshold of the pre- or protohistorical periods and the beginnings of recorded history. Researchers rely on different source materials to develop competing hypotheses concerning the nature, significance, and historical trajectory of the phalanx and its relation to the development of the Greek *poleis* (city-states) in the classical period. These sources include archeological evidence, geographical survey data, artistic and mythopoetic and dramatic texts (subjected to philological and literary analysis), and the non-contemporary accounts of later historians and philosophers of Greek and Roman antiquity. The scholarly orthodoxy—subject to revision and challenge in recent decades—has it that the phalanx developed quite rapidly in the seventh century BCE as a revolutionary transformation of eighth century mass battle tactics, associated with a new double-handled, heavier shield design (*hoplon*), and that this new approach to fighting land battles based on tight formations of armed infantry was adopted by most or all of the major Greek city-states in their frequent battles over territory and conflicting colonial aspirations (Hanson 2013).[6]

Training and discipline were required to maintain the phalanx's effectiveness in battle as the shield's substantial weight and method of holding it—by inserting the left forearm through a strap to grip a handle on the right side—indicate that the individual *hoplite* depended on the shield held by the warrior to his right for protection on his spear-carrying right side. The discipline was celebrated in Homer's *Iliad* with metaphorical allusions to the fence and tower-like qualities of the battle formation in which the soldiers had become perfect compositional elements of a unified architectural entity (Onians 1989, 43). The earliest extant records of Homeric poetry are from the eighth century BCE, but the canonic texts may have crystallized in their enduring forms over the subsequent centuries (Snodgrass 2013, 89–90). While Homer's mythic poetry relates accounts of battles from a legendary, heroic Bronze Age past, it has been interpreted by some classicists as reflecting the already mass character of Iron Age warfare of the archaic period preceding the classical period. Anthony Snodgrass discusses this recent movement to read the Homeric texts in terms of the context of their production. While skeptical of reading the *Iliad* and the *Odyssey* as fully coherent and consistent fictional portrayals of the historical state of warfare at the time of the writing down of the oral narrative tradition, Snodgrass states that at the least they provide a clear indication that mass war and formation fighting were significant features of conflict in the time the *Iliad* crystallized prior to the historical accounts of phalanx warfare in the fifth century and later (86).

For Onians, the Homeric allusions to the disciplined, architectonic character of the phalanx of tightly formed soldiers in the *Iliad* illustrates key combat-forged virtues for the subsequent development of Greek civilization and culture. In a similar vein, he proposes the "Geometric" style of eighth century BCE funerary pottery be renamed "Military" style since "the qualities they reveal"—armed men reduced to a repetitive patterns of shields and spears—"are precisely those valued in a war situation" (Onians 1989, 40).

In the fifth century Pythagoras and his followers inherited this appreciation of the value of "geometricality" passed down in the cultural tradition from a number of sources, including the pre-Socratic, cosmological writings concerning the foundational role *eris* (strife, conflict) plays in the universe and in human affairs. Pythagorean mathematics developed a metaphysics of polarized forces locked in *eris*, the secret ordering of which could be formulated and utilized.[7] The primacy of number as a material cause of entities in the world, and the importance of mathematical patterns and order in the *kosmos* were central to Pythagorean doctrine and its philosophico-political practice. Onians tells us that *kosmos* (order) is a cognate term with *kosmeo*, "I arrange" or "I marshal," and *kosmetor*, "supreme commander" (45). The configurations of important Pythagorean number patterns—mystical

entity-principles derived in the uncovering of the cosmic order—resemble the phalanx and other "foundational" military groupings: the rectangle principle develops into a phalanx-like structure of rows of dots, while the *Tetragonos* corresponds to an alternative square tactical formation from around the same period (the fifth century). The most revered pattern, the *Dekas*, takes its name from that for a basic company of ten soldiers first mentioned in the *Iliad* (ibid.).

The "harmonious" order of the Pythagorean cosmos conceptualized in the musical movements of the planetary spheres is a further confirmation of the military inspiration for this mathematical conception of reality: *Harmonia*, daughter of the god of war Ares, was a term associated in Homer and Hesiod with the use of music in war and military training, and as a figure for the close linkages required in the phalanx and other battle formations (46). Onians asserts that "*Kosmos* and *harmonia* are two of the key terms in the Pythagorean program of reducing the universe to numbers primarily because they had long been associated with numerical order on the battlefield" (48). He goes on to discuss Pythagoras's ill-fated venture in Croton—the city he chose as a base for his community—to train three or six hundred (both numbers having associations with the phalanx formation) male youths through an instructional regime incorporating military, political, and mathematical training aimed at improving the lot of the city following a recent military defeat (49).

Similar ventures will be undertaken or at least proposed by subsequent philosophers. Plato's utopian *Republic* sets out the program of training for an ideal philosopher-warrior "best at philosophy and best equipped from birth for war" (Plato 543A). A metaphor—or rather, a Pythagorean translation of the aim of such training from Simonides, a contemporary of Pythagoras—is cited by Plato in *Protagoras*: "It is difficult for a good man to come into being, square [*tetragonos*] in hands and feet and mind, wrought without blame" (Onians 1989, 53). Training is the craft of shaping what is "wrought"—and here I would gloss Onians's comment by noting that training is a kind of *tekhne*—that is, craft, technique, and skill in the fashioning of technical artifacts. Crafting the "good man" aims at an outcome corresponding as close to the ideal mathematical entity of the square as possible.

Tekhne is dedicated here to the ideality of the shape it struggles to bring into being imperfectly. Simonides's comment typifies what Stiegler characterizes as the metaphysical development of the ancient Greek thought of technics in this period inasmuch as it removes from view the dynamics of technical development and the part they play in the very conceptualization of experience. *Tekhne* is not central to the key questions about the true nature of experience or being inasmuch as it concerns "means and ends" in the transitory, imperfect realm of material existence. What counts is the animating principle of the ideal form (Stiegler 1998, 1).[8]

The tendential analysis I am proposing here on the basis of Stiegler's approach to technics sees the animating force as a compositional dynamic involving an interplay between material, technical developments and the "discovery" of abstract and generalizable concepts. Onians describes the way this movement toward the ideal realm of mathematical order, regularity, and abstract perfection in Pythagorean and later philosophical work on the application of metaphysical principles was accompanied by a conceptual movement that envisaged the human element as a building block in larger structures reflecting the ideal order. Onians's evidence for this is aesthetic as much as it is textual, and he claims this is a major current of classic proportionality in Greek art and architecture (such as the Parthenon) that also resonates in literary and philosophical works. This relation of material forms and Greek thought can be explained readily in the terms of the Western philosophical tradition whose origins and influences are in question here as the necessarily imperfect, material exemplification of the transcendental ideal forms sought after by the fathers of Western philosophy. Beyond Onians's acute demonstration of an influence that is soon glossed over or "repressed" in the course of Western history and culture, I find here a key instance of a tendential composition of material and conceptual development, a decisive mutual evolution of a technical tendency developing across tactical, strategic, architectural, and aesthetic domains and a conceptualization of war, the warrior and their relation to the *polis* as community and state.

The ability of the citizens both to equip themselves with the "hoplite panoply" of armor and weapons and to make themselves available to participate in the training for and conduct of mass formation warfare was central to their increased participation in the political assemblies and juridical institutions that replaced the dynastic monarchies of the major Greek city-states of preceding eras. In Victor Davis Hanson's defense of the longstanding orthodox interpretation of the significance of the *hoplitoi* in the emergence of democratic forms of government in ancient Greece, the "revolution in military affairs" that led quite rapidly to the spread of phalanx warfare in the seventh century was a key causative force in the overturning of aristocratic monarchic rule across the Greek world (Hanson 2013). Dependence on larger numbers of soldiers drawn from the nonaristocratic and largely agrarian "middling class" of the *poleis* (who could afford the money and time to fight in the growing ranks of the phalanxes) translated into political challenges to aristocratic rule and in time to various kinds of timocratic or more inclusive democratic political structures, in all of which the right and obligation to fight was instrumental (259). The weight given to the hoplite revolution in Greek political transformation, the demographic constitution of the Greek communities and of their armies, the historical timing of the emergence of phalanx-based combat, and even the nature of phalanx tactics are some of the subjects debated in recent challenges to this orthodoxy (Krentz, Foxhall, and van Wees 2013).[9] Evaluating these respective positions is beyond the scope of this chapter (and the expertise of this author). That political constitutions across Greece incorporated greater numbers of nonaristocratic members of the community, and that these members became increasingly central components of the frequent and long-lasting conflicts between the *poleis* in the late archaic and classical periods is not in dispute. Following Onians's lead, it is enough for my purposes to cite one of the major sources of the orthodox position, Aristotle, who in his *Politics* asserts that "once the *poleis* grew and those with hoplite armor became strong, more people shared in government" (Aristotle 4.1297b20–24, cited in Hanson 2013, 259). While arguments continue as to precisely how to interpret Aristotle's sociology of Greek political history, this is further evidence of the perceived significance of military developments for Greek civilization in the classical period.[10]

In the classical sources Onians mobilizes, the soldier is prepared by *tekhne* for conversion into an artifactual state. Through rigorous physical training and behavioral and intellectual habituation he learns to adopt an instrumental role as an element in larger structural formations that (ideally) will realize a harmonious architectonic materiality. Submission to this process entailed a willingness to submit to the potential sacrifice of life in return for a political citizenship that took various forms at different times in the course of the major Greek *poleis* in the first millennium BCE. From this perspective the celebrated Greek origins of Western democracy—reference point for the subsequent emancipatory, democratic movements of European modernity seeking to universalize political citizenship—can be thought of here as the negotiation of a right to rise above the condition of artifactual component of the state when not required for its military operations to expand or preserve itself. With the development of automated robotic weapons systems, the promise of a perfected artifactuality of the soldier implies the redundancy of this foundational negotiation between the modern democratic state and its citizens. I will return to this implication of a movement beyond this legacy of a political negotiation of the state's power to wage war.

Alongside this mathematically conceived artifactual conversion of the citizen-soldier into an architectonic element of state power is an imaginative technical practice of conversion that begins before Greek mathematics but contributes to the mathematical transformations of war (and the ancient Greek *polis*) noted above. Today it is readable as a proto-simulational conceptualization of the technical and strategic implementation of war as governed by mathematical abstraction. Onians observes that it "is also surely likely that pebbles were used to show young men the different formations of the battlefield long before they were used to illustrate points of mathematics, as is suggested by their established use in board-games which simulated battles" (Onians 1989, 45). The becoming geometric, compositional element of the warrior in Pythagoras and Plato passes from pebbles to dots to the conceptual space of the mystical number patterns. In Onians's conjectural reconstruction, the pebbles find their way, via a graphical translation into dots, from material forms for wargaming and training to symbols in a transcendental plane of number and shape.

These pebbles and board games evidence a simulational—as distinct from a more symbolic—representational technics as seen in other games and ludic artifacts from other civilizations with histories stretching back into prehistory. According to archeological evidence, mancala ("pit and pebble") games appear early in ancient Egypt before spreading southward to West Africa and westward to Asia (Parlett 1999, 217). The Chinese beginnings of Weiqi (Go in Japan) recede into legend but are generally situated around the second millennium BCE (Parlett 1999).[11] Each of these traditions of games bears witness in different ways to the playful modeling of the labor of living and surviving through a process combining material and conceptual work. This modeling work involves a miniaturization and a selective representation of more complex spatiotemporal phenomena such as the seasons and seasonal variation, the nature and intentions of the enemy, movement in space, and the unpredictable concatenation of natural and human-authored events.

The abstract realm—of the imagined battle against the enemy conducted through the calculation of choices between possible moves—is conjured through and hence dependent upon the material realm in these ethnoculturally diverse compositions of experience and technical forms. The production of and play with the "pebble-representatives" in the prehistorical Greek wargames Onians mentions is such an exteriorization of experience through technical form and gesture. As Stiegler explains in a commentary on the development of number as a transcendental concept, no concept emerges in the absence of such an exteriorization (Stiegler 2011, 48–51). Immanuel Kant forgets this when discussing the transcendental realm of number (and by extension of mathematics), even as he himself writes the material marks that represent the transcendental concept.[12] These marks, Stiegler reminds us, have a material history of emergence, from objects to single marks to symbols representing larger numbers and the relations between different values. Onians proposes just such a history leading from game "counters" (as they are known today in their generic, arithmetical guise) to dots with a mystical numerical significance in the Pythagorean cosmology. Philip Sabin notes that "one can find instances as far back as Thucydides and Polybius using mathematical calculations to explore the relationship between the numbers, depth, spacing and frontage of troops within a battle line" (Sabin 2014, 5). Writing about the history of wargames in Germany from the medieval to the modern period of computer simulation, Philipp von Hilgers acknowledges that it was an ancient Greek achievement "to think strategies and numerical figurations together" (Hilgers 2012, 8).[13]

The inside and the outside—thought and technics—are born and develop together. Making things is dedicated to a future outside the maker where it will have significance, worth, and thus be worthy of being remembered, reflected upon, and reproduced. With the pebble game, this means being worthy of replaying for fun and/or for the lessons learned. This game for soldier-boys is already a future-directed, proto-simulational modeling of a "problem space" but is not yet subject to formalizing procedures based on mathematical regularities and algorithms making it repeatable across domains of practice and experience. Today's board game and computer simulations of battle continue to develop iterations of their ancient pebble ancestor for fun and/or for the lessons learned—from amateur boardgaming practices, to serious military simulation and gaming, to the more commercial video games such as the *Total War* series. These wargames, with a "mathematical modeling of reality" as a fundamental component, have revisited the ancient battlegrounds of Greek and Roman antiquity to replay historical conflicts, have tested the hypotheses of the hoplite orthodoxy concerning phalanx tactics, and have utilized the inferential power of computer simulation to stage hypothetical conflicts between anachronistic military forces and orders of battle (Sabin 2014, 4).[14] Simulation-based research on (and play with) historical, contemporary and future conflict continues today and continues to play a significant role in military and strategic-political spheres as well as in commercial and popular entertainment.

These board games and computer simulations are the nearest descendants of the ancient practices and artifacts of simulating war in a contemporary technoculture that is at the other end of the tendential trajectory of the mathematical translation of specific material practices to more widely applicable conceptual formulations (and materializations). As Onians so compellingly demonstrates, these formulations were discovered and developed substantially for their potential to order and regulate the course of war as a (or possibly *the*) fundamental contingency of existence for the ancient Greeks. This tendency of Greek thought is readable in the passage from the game space and its playing pebbles via the Pythagorean (and subsequent Greek) mathematical transformation of geometry into an abstract, conceptual space of numbers and their formulaic relations to each other. Geometry, the measuring of the earth developed by the ancient Egyptians, became the protoscience launching Western science. Archimedes, whose inventions served the defense of his native Syracuse against the invading Romans in the third century BCE, symbolizes this dynamic between military technical development and conceptual elaboration as much as he does the advance of mathematics as foundational technique and analytic method informing geometry, astronomy, architecture, and the other knowledges of the world. And, as Hilgers has shown, in the early nineteenth century mathematically innovative wargaming practices in Germany dovetail with (among other things) the major cartographical enterprise that will eventuate in the systematic, mathematically accurate surveying and mapping of the territory of the prospective German nation first surveyed and rendered as a battle space (Hilgers 2012, 55). The dynamic between abstract concept and practical application continues and intensifies in the heart of European modernization. "Mathematics," argues Hilgers, may be distinguished by its abstractness, but it nonetheless requires forms of evidence and visibility" (91).

Postwar Technoscience: Computerized Battlespace

This tendency toward the demonstration in practice of an expanding activity of conceptualization reaches a new level and is realized on an unprecedented scale in the twentieth century with the rise of scientific and increasingly mathematical innovations in military technologies and techniques. Tracing this tendency through the intervening eras is a task beyond the scope of this chapter, but its modern technoscientific course received key bearings both from the emergence in eighteenth-century Europe of the modern sciences (from out of the domains of philosophy and theology) and their mobilization to accelerate and multiply the ramifications of the technical discoveries that led to the industrialization of production toward the end of that century. Hilgers's account, cited earlier, of the role of wargames in aspects of these developments is no small contribution to an analysis of the course of this material-conceptual dynamic.

The industrialization of production has also entailed the industrialization of destruction and has thus been central to the course of Western modernity's global expansion in the twentieth century.[15] The century of industrial modernization was also that of the two global conflicts, of the emergence of "total war" as industrial project requiring "total mobilization," of the rise of the global superpowers, and of the prospect of global thermonuclear war. In the post–Cold War period, global geopolitical conflict has been characterized by what James Der Derian calls the "postwar warring" of the industrial powers—a blurring of military and security operations with actions supporting other agendas and agencies in a context where "war" as state versus state and armed forces versus armed forces no longer occurs

(Der Derian 2001, 59). The "asymmetrical" conflicts that have ensued in Iraq, Afghanistan, the Palestinian occupied territories, Somalia, and elsewhere continue the legacy of this century of globalizing modernization.

Onians is right when he says that "mathematics was not exclusively military in character" and that it soon "acquired a life of its own" in later cultural contexts (Onians 1989, 62). This is still true, but if it is a mistake to forget or repress its connections to military practices and motivations in imagining a more pacific and idealist (and idealized) history of the ancient Greek "miracle," Onians concludes with the speculation that it is perhaps "an unconscious recognition of the military relevance, not just of Greek mathematics, but of Greek art too, which has guaranteed them their continued authority" (Ibid.). Indeed, but in the light of my concern with the composition of conscious (and unconscious) interiority with exterior technical material dynamics, the relevance of military concerns to mathematics (and art and architectural works), however sublimated in histories of science and civilization, remains decisive in their mutual becoming in the ongoing history of the Greek legacy.

Moreover, this relevance is heightened in the explicitly strategic-political postwar reorganization of the relations between science and technological innovation that Andy Pickering (1995) has characterized as the emergence of a military-led technoscience. This reorganization has produced material and conceptual "inventions" that lead directly to the developments in the contemporary technical tendency that drones instantiate and intensify. Above all, these are the simulation of the conflict and the virtualization of its conduct, along with the possibility of automating the latter.

In his work Derek Gregory has traced developments in aerial bombing and surveillance that lead from World War II to the counterinsurgency and antiterrorist operations in which drones play a significant part today in the air over what he calls the "global borderlands" (Gregory 2011a, 2011b). Drones act either in support of other attacking units through their ability to provide the persistent monitoring of targets or as a "hunter-killer" platform combining reconnaissance and strike capabilities. Vietnam was crucial to these developments for the emergence of three constitutive elements of contemporary "armed overwatch": the systematic deployment of "remotely piloted aircraft, real-time visual surveillance and a networked sensor-shooter system"—as yet not integrated in a larger operational complex (Gregory 2011a, 2). In this regard the principal achievement of the post–September 11 military actions of the United States and its allies is to have attained such an integration, one which is conceived and implemented as a unified sphere of spatiotemporal coordination achieved by real-time networked digital communications.

The unified sphere of war operations was envisaged in post-Vietnam military doctrine. It emerged tendentially as a conceptual consolidation of the most technologically sophisticated, computerized military "advances" of the US-led campaign. The spectacularly unsuccessful prosecution of the geopolitical strategy of the containment of communist expansion in Vietnam spawned the so-called "Revolution in Military Affairs" that sought to rethink military operations in an explicitly systemic and informational manner. Military commander in Vietnam (1964–68) General William Westmoreland's

vision of war in the age of computers, articulated in a report to the American Congress in 1970, is often cited as the catalyst for this revolutionary movement toward an era of "smart weapons" and real-time command and control networks. Westmoreland predicted that "enemy forces will be located, tracked and targeted almost instantaneously through the use of data links, computer assisted intelligence evaluation and automated fire control" (Chapman 2003, 2). The paradigm shift is exemplified in the subsequent redefinition of the theater of war as a "battlespace." Tim Blackmore states that this three-dimensional, volumetric space incorporates land and sea (on the surface and below), the air above and the space above that, and the spheres of signals and communications, information and mediation (Blackmore 2005, 3). Achieving victory in operations in battlespace becomes a question of attaining "full-spectrum superiority" across all of the spatiotemporal dimensions of "air, land, maritime and space domains" and the "information environment (which includes cyberspace)" (Department of Defense 2014b, 113).

Battlespace is a conceptual elaboration of the "abstract and technical" distancing of the enemy other and the enemy territory Gregory identifies in his analysis of the electronic surveillance technologies and sighting techniques that emerged in the conduct of the air war over Vietnam (Gregory 2011a, 2). In this regard, he discusses the "pattern bombing" of Viet Cong–dominated regions of South Vietnam, the area bombing of forests (with defoliants) by B-52s and the subsequent damage assessment analysis. At 25,000–30,000 feet in the air, the bomber crews executed a highly impersonal, familiar technical exercise, as instruments of the command and policy decisions of others (5). Photo interpreters read images of the results in terms of holes in the ground and target boxes: "Throughout the targeting process the language of patterns, areas, circles, holes and boxes erased people from the field of view; bombing became a deadly form of applied geometry" (4).

This applied geometry became increasingly "virtual" with the "electronic battlefield" established in 1967 to interdict the supply of Viet Cong forces along trails running from North Vietnam to the south along the border with Laos. Operation "Igloo White" established a large sensor field over the "Ho Chi Minh trail." The seismic and acoustic sensors dropped by parachute listened and felt for the movement of vehicles and people along the trail and their signals were monitored in an electronic map screen at a command center in Thailand from where air strikes were ordered in and then monitored live. The Assessment Officers at the Infiltration Surveillance Center in Thailand looked for trails of lights from the sensors indicating the passage of a potential target along the trail. These "target signatures"—"abstract geometries" of "lines on screens" and "boxes on maps"—traced the movements of people via these ephemeral electronic signals until they disappeared. Their last moments were played over the PA system in Thailand and later for the "Electronic Battlefield Subcommittee" of the Senate's Armed Services Committee (8).

Gregory points out that today's "drone wars" evidence the unification of Vietnam War-era developments (in real-time surveillance, networked sensor fields and remote piloting of aircraft) in a single operational system. The key difference is that "the 'viewing screen' now occupies a central place and has become indispensable for those who wage remote war" (9). As an instance, or acceleration, of the Revolution in Military Affairs, however, it is

equally fundamental to the nature and implications of its implementation that this systemic integration is "powered" by the computer microprocessor revolution (Chapman 2003, 3). The digitization of what were analog electronic networks of reconnaissance, surveillance and the coordination of strike aircraft represents a profoundly significant alteration in the mathematical-technical abstraction of war in this real-time, global assemblage of elements. The integration of diverse elements is facilitated by the translation of phenomena and procedures for analyzing and acting on them into databases and algorithms inscribed in binary code. As Paul Edwards has argued, in the Cold War technoscientific matrix out of which computer hardware and software emerged, the promise of digital computerization was to contain the world of dangerous contingency within the parameters of programmable routines (Edwards 1996). If analog networks of reconnaissance, analysis, and communications made real-time "dynamic targeting" possible in Vietnam, the expansion of global digital networks led toward a computational pursuit of this promised incorporation of what is external and contingent in an integrative digital spatiotemporality. It is in this light that Edwards discusses Operation Igloo White as model for the computerized enclosure of the world desired by military strategy and Cold War political doctrine (15–20).

I have elsewhere analyzed the development of flight simulation (and virtual reality) technologies in this period as a launchpad for the materialization of this ambition by emphasizing how the modeling of the battlespace served an anticipatory logic of developing a preemptive mastery of the territory and its potential threats (Crogan 2011). Today's "drone wars" represent the contemporary stage of the materialization of this tendency in a process that radicalizes this simulational modeling of the enemy's potentiality. It alters the nature of war and peace in the manner I identified at the outset of this chapter as a symptomatic but highly problematic trajectory of the West's global technocultural expansion.

Drones and Mathematical Materializations: Simulation, Virtualization, and Automation

It is important to emphasize—as Gregory does in his analysis of the lines of descent leading to the contemporary remote-controlled military operations in Afghanistan and elsewhere—that tracing the lines of these tendential developments is neither to affirm faith in the promise of total incorporation and control of the enemy, nor of the earlier rhetoric of "progressive" or "beneficial bombing" realizing an increasingly rational and efficient conduct of war (Gregory 2011a, 1). On the contrary; I will suggest at the conclusion of this chapter that a better candidate for a "futurology" of global military-led security operations is Paul Virilio's speculations, dating from the 1970s, concerning the "territorial insecurity" which develops as the "reality projected by the system" dedicated to attaining this total control (Virilio 1976, 37). For his part, Gregory's detailed analysis of a botched joint USAF and Special Forces operation in Uruzgan province in 2010 that led to the deaths of many Afghani civilians (and to the prosecution of members of the team remotely operating the drone involved in the attack) forcefully demonstrates the large distance between the promise and the reality of a fully integrated and systematically coordinated militarized modeling of battlespace (Gregory 2011a, 2011b).

The efforts to realize this incorporation of contested territory in a "system of systems" capable of full-spectrum superiority nonetheless transforms the conduct and conceptualization of war (Chapman 2003, 3). I am emphasizing the simulational character of this, by which I mean it evidences the application and extension of a process that corresponds to Sargent's influential account of the simulation design cycle I cited at the outset of this chapter. I argue that essential features of the simplification and abstraction of phenomenal complexity that characterize the simulational modeling of a "problem space" able to be defined and resolved—or rather whose problems can be anticipated and controlled—through software-based "solutions" are manifest in many aspects of drone deployments.

The use of drones such as the MQ-1 Predator (first deployed with Hellfire missiles in 2001) and MQ-9 Reaper (since 2007) as hunter-killer systems combining surveillance and strike depends on such a process of abstraction and simplification to execute strikes on designated targets (Gregory 2011b, 207). Drone operations proceed on the basis of the systemic coordination of numerous computer-based systems, including those for the coordination of remote vehicle piloting between the Nevada-based pilot and sensor operators and the "Launch and Recovery" crews (responsible for takeoff and landing) at bases in the contested geographical territory where the drones are stationed, for the pilot's interface setup (screens and sensor outputs, joystick, throttle and other input devices) in the ground control station and the drone's translation of this remote user input into aerial maneuvers, for the communications linkages and video/sensor feeds between ground control with other elements engaged in joint operations, tactical command positions in the battlespace and strategic command centers situated in the United States and elsewhere, the smart weapons systems and their communications with these other networks of command and tactical elements, and so on.

The computerization of systems supporting targeting is a key feature of this complex system of systems for conducting remote war, and one that displays most vividly the simulational logics emerging in these operations. Gregory is right in identifying the centrality of the visual video feed from the remotely operated vehicle for targeting and execution as a key transformation from the Vietnam-era developments in remote control warfare. The "immersive" involvement of the ground crews in the digitally enabled battlespace occurs as a juxtaposition of intimate proximity and extreme distance. As Gregory states, the remote "pilot and payload" team are located both eighteen inches from the video monitor and at around six to seven thousand miles from the contested territory (Ibid., 207). Many of the crucial ethical, political, and psychological themes explored in response to the expansion of the UAV program turn on the issues and implications of this paradoxical combination of proximity and distance. Gregory characterizes this combination as an uneasy ensemble of "near-sighted" and "far-sighted" vision that creates as many uncertainties as it resolves concerning the accuracy of its tactical implementation and the effectiveness of its strategic and political goals. The video game–like "immersive capacity" of the remote drone operator interface places them virtually in the battlespace occupied by allied soldiers and pilots. It connects them to

a community mediated by real-time audiovisual monitoring of the enemy. This network of screens amounts to a "political technology of vision," one that "renders our space familiar even in 'their' space—which remains obdurately other" (Gregory 2011a, 12).

This confusion of near and far perspectives is repeated in the US domestic sphere (and its global diffusion) in the proliferation since the first Gulf War in 1991 of what Roger Stahl has analyzed as "militainment" (Stahl 2010b). Stahl examines the trend toward a more intensive and "interactive" experience of combat in video games, embedded reporting and reality TV, and more recently via online video sharing of footage of firefights captured by helmet-cams, of drone strikes, and so on. This experience of war as increasingly immersive entertainment corresponds with and indeed occasions a movement away from a deliberative social or political engagement in the far-flung operations against terrorism and the enemies of US interests. For Stahl, miltainment's contradictory movements ever closer to the action but away from a political means for collectively negotiating its significance generate cultural-political tensions. I would characterize these disturbances of the body politic (and the collective visual imaginary of the "virtual citizen-soldier") emanating from the commercial media sphere as symptomatic of the destabilizing impetus of the technical tendency at whose leading edge drone operations develop today (Stahl 2010b, 110).

If "eyes on" the target via high resolution video imaging is crucial both for the surveillance capabilities of drone vehicles and to the positive identification required for authorization of a strike, it is important to recognize that the video image is part of a larger flow of sensory data feeding the reconnaissance and targeting operation. The drones themselves supply multispectral image data—infrared, daylight, and image-intensified video. Developments are well underway in the operational implementation of wide-area composites of multiple high resolution surveillance scans to form a kind of tiled mosaic of detailed video scanning of the contested territory—"Gorgon Stare" and ARGUS-IS are two such projects (Gregory 2011b, 193). The persistent flow of datafeeds from these various sensors is treated by video analysis software designed to selectively identify key information required for intelligence analysis and targeting processes. These "highly formalized" procedures—that is, statistical, algorithmic programs for making usable an overwhelmingly enormous database of pixels—set out to "distinguish 'normal' from 'abnormal' activity in a sort of militarized rhythmanalysis that is increasingly automated" (Gregory 2011a, 10).

This cutting-edge "big data" software development includes the NVS system (National System for Geo-Intelligence Video Services) being produced under the direction of arms manufacturer giant Lockheed-Martin. According to Paul Richfield, NVS will filter, sort and produce video-on-demand reports through software agent functions comparable to Netflix's user profiling of preferences and related searches (Richfield 2011). Reports combine various statistics concerning the full-motion video playback and resemble financial reporting on MSNBC or watching a football game on ESPN. Like all database processing software, the generation of useful reports depends on the quality of the metadata produced through the indexing of video data according to relevant categories. The allusion to ESPN is more than illustrative: Chamayou notes that the US Army licensed a version of the video analysis software ESPN uses in its football coverage to aid research and development of its drone-supported counterinsurgent targeting (Chamayou 2013, 61). The software is especially good for collecting and cataloguing videos associated with a particular player from a massive archive of game coverage, and this dovetails with the desire to map and characterize the past actions of individuals identified as insurgent or terrorist.

Chamayou comments that this turn to professional sports coverage seems to fulfill Walter Benjamin's prediction that future war (in a dystopian, fascist future) will replace categories of warrior and war in favor of sporting terminology (Chamayou 2013, 62). From our perspective on these developments as a continuation and exacerbation of the military-mathematical tendency of Western technoculture, this adoption is one of many indications of the digital extension of the game space of pebble counters on a little field of circumscribed action to a more generalized simulational space.[16] The analysis of enemy "play-moves" is now subject to a formalized procedurality that seeks to render less incalculable the complexity of events in real geophysical space on the basis of a ludic, abstracted, simplified, and delimited game space. Moreover, this software processing of the pattern of the enemy-as-player is becoming increasingly automated. Projects such as the Defense Advanced Research Projects Agency's (DARPA) "Mind's Eye" are working on Artificial Intelligence to analyze and annotate video automatically. The envisaged "visual intelligence" would be able to learn to recognize and classify actions between elements (people, vehicles and so forth) in a video sequence (Defense Aerospace.com, 2011). Beyond machine vision developments in pattern recognition and object identification, the ambition of this project is to automate a cataloguing of actions and relations between objects. The ever-growing flows of multispectrum video scans from battlespace will necessitate the implementation of such programs able to "automatically translate the aggregations of pixels into nouns, verbs and propositions" (Chamayou 2013, 62).

Systems and software such as NVS and Mind's Eye will be added into the suite of statistical and analytical software delivering the "militarized rhythm-analysis" Gregory describes. These include "Geotime," which gathers and visualizes various forms of surveillance data such as satellite monitoring and mobile phone signal tracking. Mobile phone tracking, made possible by the "spectrum dominance" over the communications sphere of battlespace, has become a significant contributor in the intelligence analysis supporting the targeting of individual "insurgents" in the deployment of drones to support or execute targeted assassinations. It has also been at the center of some of the more infamous mistaken strikes, such as the alleged killing of an election campaign team in northern Afghanistan by a joint operation relying on cell phone tracking to identify the target (Gregory 2011a, 13). According to Kate Clark, the special forces team came to believe the Taliban deputy leader of Takhar had switched phones and adopted an alias when in fact the phone they tracked in order to locate the target and execute the strike was still in the hands of its original user, a former Taliban figure well-known in democratic Afghani politics (Clark 2011, 2).

The US military have rejected the claim that this strike was a catastrophic case of mistaken identity. Wherever the truth resides, Clark's detailed investigation shows both that it is widely held to be so in Takhar province and in Afghanistan more

generally, and that "technical intelligence" from phone tracking was central to the special forces operation. The phone tracks are an important part of what is known as "pattern of life" analysis used across the drone operations of both the US Air Force and the Joint Special Force operations they are involved in and by the CIA's targeted assassinations in northern Pakistan and elsewhere. A person's activities, associations, and electronic communications with others can be compared against a "normal" civilian set of routines and social exchanges for people in the surveilled territory in order to identify unusual "patterns" or associations. Such abnormal patterns indicate potential targets for further monitoring or possible assassination. The individual identified with such a pattern may find themselves graduating from the database of potential targets—the "Disposition Matrix"—to becoming a "nomination" on the "kill-list" under consideration in the Pentagon and ultimately by the US President (Becker and Shane 2012).

It has been claimed that strikes based on pattern of life analysis represent a significant component of drone-based hunter-killer attacks on individuals who are only known as potential threats through a process reliant on software-based analysis (16). These targeted individuals no longer need to be identified except as a certain kind of deviation from a norm established through the statistical modeling of sets of data drawn from full-spectrum monitoring of the battlespace. Their names and lived reality are less relevant than this conceptualization of them as potential threat known as a "signature target" as opposed to a "personality"—the signature refers to the particularity of their abnormal data pattern of movements, habits and web of associations that marks them as a threat (18).

In their "anonymity" and "abstraction" the signature targets "are ghostly traces of the target signatures that animated the electronic battlefield" of the Ho Chi Minh trail (Gregory 2011a, 13). Moreover, they register the systemic transformation of this Vietnam-era experiment in remote warfare: from a dynamic targeting procedure responding to "signature" analog traces of the movement of (presumed) enemies, to the programmatic generation of a pattern from data processing that is used to produce the targets *in advance of their threatening movement or action*. As Chamayou notes, this technical procedure instantiates a promise to "predict the future and be able to modify its course through preemptive action" (Chamayou 2013, 66).

The simulational character of this procedure is striking. It repeats the rationale offered for SIMNET's development in the 1980s as a comprehensive, computer simulation-based training system enabling a precocious mastery of the contingent complexity of future conflict: to use history to anticipate and prepare for the future. As Lenoir and Lowood demonstrate, the networking of military simulation enabled the collective training of joint force elements in a distributed but unified battlespace based on detailed archives of terrain, military units, and prior operations. SIMNET developer Jack Thorpe expressed the desire to make an interactive training vehicle that would use history to prepare for the future (Lenoir and Lowood 2005, 19). In analyzing these SIMNET developments in *Gameplay Mode* I posed a question about the effect of this modeling of the terrain and the enemy and its future impacts on battlespace. Lenoir and Lowood had already indicated that simulational systems were finding their way closer—in both spatial and temporal terms—to ongoing operations through

battlefield deployment of systems aiding tactical planning (20). In this regard I would say that the emerging practices of increasingly automated and schematic generation of targets represents a radicalization of this preparatory logic that drove simulation ever closer to the conduct of war. The modeling of the enemy as a set of behaviors is no longer limited to the realms of a hypothetical operational scenario—however close its correspondence to envisaged operations. This modeling of enemy-as-pattern is now performatively rather than hypothetically enacted in targeting decisions. The anticipatory impetus of simulational technologies have overtaken the very processes spawning military actions in a creeping barrage of increasingly automated data-scraping and scenario modeling.

In a similar manner the digital simulation of space supporting the planning of attacks has found its way out of the hypothetical mode of simulation with the digital implementation of "joint fire areas" or what were known as "killboxes." These are names for a procedural designation of physical space enabling the coordination of elements engaging targets within a specified area that is both temporary and scalable according to the nature of the target and the conditions and constraints of the operation. As Chamayou explains, the killbox describes a process as much as a space: "one opens, activates, freezes and then closes a killbox" (Chamayou 2013, 83). The killbox is a zone of temporarily and flexibly realized virtual space: virtual inasmuch as it comes into existence digitally thanks to the real-time technologies of modeling, monitoring, measurement, and transmission. It puts into practice the redefinition of traditional geographical and strategic-political territory projected in the theory of battlespace. Killboxes can in principle (and in their virtuality as digital diagrams) be opened anywhere in the world, and be as small or as large as required, rendering irrelevant traditional geopolitical limitations such as national borders, city walls, and geophysical boundaries such as mountain ranges, rivers and so forth. Chamayou speaks about the killbox's combination of precision measurement and flexible delineation enacting a dual principle of the "globalization and homogenization" of space (86).

It is in the technological implementation of procedures such as the killbox (and its more recent iteration as the "joint fire area") that the redefinition of the theater of war as "battlespace" is concretized in the manner of the technical object: that is, as the ongoing materialization of a tendency that demands critical-theoretical as well as legal-humanitarian attention.[17] This is made clear in the history of the "killbox" concept that Chamayou dates to a 1996 USAF report scoping the future use of unmanned aerial vehicles in zones of "autonomous operation" (326). Today's remote operations involving UAVs are semiautonomous, requiring the coordination of teams across the globe. They employ a virtualizing principle and procedure, by which I mean a mediation of space and time via an interface that translates and transacts actions back and forth between actual and virtual, physical and digital. "Classic" questions of digital technoculture concerning the impact of real-time communications and telepresence on subjective experience, cultural identity, and social-political structures are posed by the virtualization of missile strikes in a way that brings into focus the long history of the military motivations of technological and technoscientific advances.

The drone is, in this regard, a materialization of the tendency to fashion an artifactual warrior identified by Onians in ancient Greek philosophy, literature, and material culture. As weapons system it repeats the contradictory, dualistic treatment of the citizen-soldier in the origins of Western democracy— the composition of political subject and pure object of the State's strategic-political will is mirrored in the virtual, globally distributed composition of the military personnel with the drone weapon platform. If the seeds of democracy are to be found in the warrior's negotiation of the rights and responsibilities that are entailed in a conditional, intermittent acquiescence to a state of artifactual instrumentality of state violence, however, this was on the basis of his commitment to the life or death stakes of the collective struggle. In drone operations, this composition is undergoing a disorienting disintegration. The tendency is most apparent in the use of drones as both targeting support and target elimination.

The military personnel—at least those "at home" in the USAF base in Nevada, or in the strategic command centers far from the drone in flight over its target—are still part of the military machinery, but less as warriors than as operators of a technological system for the preemptive resolution of environmental problems that threaten to impede its effective functioning in coordinating its many elements in the global battlespace. Tensions within the US military evidence this ambiguous status of the drone operators in Nevada.[18] At the same time, as Gregory has shown, their virtualized spatiotemporal involvement in joint operations via video feed with forces on the ground, voice communications, and chat windows can involve them intensely and intimately in a vicarious experience of the warrior's exposure to risk (Gregory 2011b, 198ff). Those who suffer psychologically from this unprecedented involvement and experience of the carnage of industrial, high-tech killing have stretched the boundaries of the definition of posttraumatic stress disorder in that exposure

via proximity to the risk of death is a central diagnostic criterion (Chamayou 2013, 155). The contradictions multiply.

Conclusion

The tendency of this materialization of a digitized, preemptive modeling of global "problem space" is toward an automation of lethal robotic systems. Its proponents, such as the controversial AI scientist Ron Arkin, suggest that this would resolve the various legal and practical contradictions of virtualized war through automation of both the deliberation and execution of the preemptive processing of the enemy. Advances in AI would deliver a superior application of rational decision making better equipped to function in the extreme circumstances of life-or-death conflict than human consciousness with its emotional and instinctual baggage (Arkin 2010). Arkin's claims for AI capable of making correct and ethical combat decisions is echoed in scoping documents such as the *U.S. Air Force's Unmanned Aircraft Systems Flight Plan 2009–2047*. The vision of a "path to autonomy" is clearly mapped out, where robots will conduct operations supervised by personnel "on the loop" rather than in the loop, once "legal and ethical questions" have been resolved by "political and military leaders" (United States Air Force 2009, 41).

This promise of the future of automated global warfare bears something of the transcendent, universalizing ambition of the Pythagorean incorporation of military procedures and principles in the pursuit of a *kosmic* harmony of close-fitting and well-ordered elements. A confidence in the future technological realization of the mathematical incorporation of the world in a system of global monitoring and

preemption of rationally identified and precisely actioned anomalies is to be expected in the rhetoric of its proponents and those hoping to advance the fields of AI and robotics to support its implementation. The technical realization is, however, never only an instrumental process of approximating some transcendent, mathematical ideality. The "legal and ethical questions," and with them technocultural and political implications of the pursuit of such a trajectory from remote to automated war will inflect and detour the flight path to autonomy. It is already doing so. The technical and conceptual composition of the West's globalizing future course is already materializing what Virilio thematized as a paradoxically essential accident of the Cold War effort to impose a global system of military oversight ensuring the anticipation of security threats (Virilio and Lotringer 1997). This accident is the emergence of a generalized countertendency toward an insecuring of territory, both in the homeland and in the distant border zone of what was the global chess game of the nuclear superpowers. This insecuring undermines the ostensible Western geopolitical program of the spread of stable, democratic government, material security and economic development, individual liberty and rights.

Today these "global borderlands" undergo a post–Cold War continuation of these efforts to secure the territory. The accident continues to unfold beyond the end of the nuclear standoff through the technoscientific tendency to pursue what Virilio characterizes as an ever more extreme and nihilist projection of a computerized, ubiquitous, real-time, automated integration of the social and political realms within a closed, militarized world order (Virilio 1997, 167–172). In a similar vein, Gregory proposes that the military adventures in remote counterinsurgency at the borders of the West's zones of control in Afghanistan and Pakistan will produce a "vortex": "If the battle space is now global, and if the United States claims the right to use lethal force against its enemies wherever it finds them, then what happens when other states claim the same right? And when non-state actors possess their own remotely piloted aircraft?" (Gregory 2011a, 15).

Chamayou captures best, perhaps, the systemic dimension of this contradictory production of the very opposite of the secured geopolitical world future projected with and through the current deployments of drones. He criticizes the remote conduct of counterinsurgent operations, citing military strategist David Kilcullen's condemnation of these as the misuse of an effective tactic that threatens the very strategy of counterinsurgency inasmuch as this depends on the building up of relationships and sympathies between armed forces and local inhabitants on the ground (Chamayou 2013, 100–103). Chamayou sees here the victory of an anti-terror doctrine over a counterinsurgent one. Moreover, "dronified anti-terror" can be understood as employing a perversely strategic logic whose pursuit implies its own failure as strategy. The fact that drone operations tend to produce the conditions for the recruitment of more radicalized extremists—the core of the counterinsurgent strategists' critique of their use—becomes the rationale for their expansion and technological "improvement." The system

incorporates its inherent contradiction in what Chamayou characterizes as an "endless spiral" that is unable to "decapitate the Hydra that it itself permanently regenerates by the productive effects of its own negativity" (108).[19]

As in Newsgaming's elegant and prophetic critical game, *September 12th: A Toy World* (2002), the remote eradication of targeted terrorist threats is also the guarantee that the threat in general is never eradicated; in fact, it is central to the systemic perpetuation and exacerbation of threat. In this critical simulational intervention in the post-9/11 context of renewed military mobilization in the United States, the player's only move in response to the appearance of terrorist icons moving among the general population of a generic Middle Eastern town is to launch a missile from her aerial (drone-like) perspective. The missile destroys terrorist and civilians indiscriminately, however, and the more strikes the player orders the more terrorist icons are generated.[20]

Playing *September 12th* quickly evokes the sense of the paradoxical counterproductivity of pursuing such a military-technological approach to global terrorism that one gains from reading the more substantially elaborated figurations of Chamayou's spiral and Gregory's vortex. These geometrical figures trace the uncertain future of a Western technocultural tendency whose envisaged automation of security within a digitally integrated, virtualized spatiotemporality is anything but assured. Instead of securing the global borderlands, the projected implementation of a mathematically conceived and regulated *kosmos* will make everywhere a borderland of uneasy transactions between the virtual and the physical, the simulated and the actual, the state of war and the state of peace, the "life worth living" and the anomalous pattern of life.

About the Author

Patrick Crogan teaches at the University of the West of England, Bristol, and is a member of the Digital Cultures Research Centre there. He wrote *Gameplay Mode: War, Simulation and Technoculture* (University of Minnesota Press, 2011) and has published numerous articles on relations between the digital and the military in contemporary simulational technoculture in journals such as *Theory, Culture & Society* and *Angelaki*, and in books including *The Illusion of Life 2: More Essays on Animation* (Power Publications, 2008), *The Pleasures of Computer Gaming: Essays on Cultural History, Theory and Aesthetics* (MacFarland and Co., 2008) and *Homo Ludens 2.0* (Amsterdam University Press, 2014).

Notes

1. Translations from Chamayou are my own.

2. This applies also to those able to access the advanced weapons systems of the advanced industrial economies, as was brought home (once more) by the downing in July 2014 of the Malaysian Airlines commercial flight MH17 over the contested territory of the Ukraine by what many believe (at the time of writing) was a SA-11 (Buk) surface-to-air missile developed by the former Soviet Union's military-industrial complex.

3. The tool is the *organon* in ancient Greek and Stiegler plays on this to argue for an approach to technology and culture that acknowledges their intrinsic interconnection. Organology is also in part Stiegler's response to Simondon's call for a "mechanology" to understand technological becoming; Stiegler insists on thinking the technological in composition with human becoming to develop an appropriately historical and political account of technology.

4. See Stiegler's analysis in *Technics and Time 2: Disorientation* of these progenitors or what he characterizes (in respone to Assyriologist Franz Bottero's account) as moments of "conception" prior to the "birth" of Greek civilization (2009, 47–53).

5. Chamayou (2013) and Gregory (2011a, 2011b) spend considerable time analyzing the continuities of contemporary military operations with the history of European colonial involvements in the region. In this regard, see also the experimental video project *Airminded* (2014) produced by the Ontofabulatory Research group in a collaboration led by Rob Coley, available at <http://antipodefoundation.org/2014/01/28/intervention-airminded>. This project traces historical and geospatial continuities connecting distant cultures and communities through the Lincolnshire-based Royal Air Force operations in Afghanistan and Pakistan in the twentieth century and today.

6. The controversies over the "Grand Hoplite Narrative" include "gradualist" revisions of the "revolutionary" character of the arrival and spread of the phalanx formation, as well as more profound challenges to the orthodox account of the significance of the phalanx for an understanding of the social and political transformations in classical

Greece *poleis* away from dynastic monarchies and toward more democratic political arrangements of various kinds (Viggiano 2013). I will return to this briefly in what follows, inasmuch as the debates touch on my observations here concerning the relationship between war and technical and conceptual tendencies still animating Western technoculture today.

7. Onians lists some of these Pythagorean polarities: "Limited and Unlimited, Odd and Even, One and Many, Right and Left, Male and Female, Square and Rectangular, Light and Dark, Straight and Curved etc" (1989, 45).

8. *Tekhne* has no "self-causality" for Aristotle and hence has no dynamic of its own (Stiegler 1998, 1).

9. For his part, Stiegler (engaging with other philological and philosophical scholarship) attributes the Greek innovations in democratic political forms in large part to the invention of a nonmilitary technology, linear orthographic writing, inasmuch as it enabled the kind of analysis, critique and reform of legal constitutions and judgments that writing affords, and that this was now accessible to all those able to read and write (2009, 39–41).

10. In his afterword to his and Gilles Deleuze's *Anti-Oedipus: Capitalism and Schizophrenia*, Felix Guattari cites the phalanx as a privileged example of the concept of the "machine" mobilized in their reinterpretation of culture and history in this and subsequent works (Guattari 2013). The phalanx is a combination of elements (the hoplite warriors), each a machine comprised of soldier and arms (the hoplite panoply) and the phalanx is itself a machine element in larger machines, right up to the Greek city-state machine. A fundamental point of this characterization is to circumvent a conventional historical analysis of the political and cultural causes and influences leading to and from the phalanx and to instead posit the significance of the combination of human and non-human, material, technical and strategic and conceptual elements as an ensemble that drives history and events. As an arrangement of equal elements (in machinic "phyla"), the machine's dynamic is not reducible to a human-centered narrative of ideas and their projected materialization, nor to an account of tools as means to human-authored ends. In this Deleuze and Guattari's "machine" corresponds to Stiegler's efforts to think the constitutive role of technical developments in human becoming (further evidence of the debt they each owe to Simondon's philosophy). Stiegler's more "anthropocentric" (to be understood here minus the assumption concerning the essential stability or inevitability of the *anthropos*) concerns with the possible ethico-political dimensions of the future of the technical tendency offers me a better basis on which to approach critically the developments in automated and unmanned systems I am concerned with in this chapter.

11. The most well-known and studied war board game in a European context, chess, traces its predecessors to Persian sources in the sixth century CE which in turn look further back to the Indian game chaturanga (Parlett 1999, 278). As with the "hoplite controversy," identifying the origins of this and the older games is provisional and subject to different interpretations of archeological finds and later literary allusions. For instance, there is archeological evidence suggesting an even earlier appearance of a mancala game in Sri Lanka as far back as the fourth century BCE, but Parlett follows Murray's earlier *History of Board-Games Other Than Chess* in preferring to

start the story in the Egyptian "Empire Age" of 1580–1150 BCE (Murray 1952, 159).

12. Stiegler deconstructs the Kantian "schematism" whereby certain concepts (such as number) mediate between the empirical contents of and the transcendental structures of consciousness, asking "in what sense is a number like one thousand *possible*, as a method conforming to 'a certain concept' for the consciousness of which it is the object, *without an image*? The answer is clear: in *no* sense" (2011, 51; emphasis in original).

13. Hilgers's approach, influenced by Friedrich Kittler's materialist media and cultural theory, is not unlike Stiegler's thought of the composition of cultural, political, and technical tendencies. He analyzes the role played by the material and technical practices of wargames in the transforming cultural-political context of an emerging German nation-state in the center (geopolitically and in terms of cultural, philosophical, and scientific developments) of Europe. Hilgers's insightful account places wargames not only as significant contributors to the European history of conflict and cultural transformation, but as major conduits for the advances in mathematics in the West that led to its preeminent role in the modern military-technological complex driving key innovations of World War II, a state of affairs that will extend into the postwar technoscientific transformation of culture into global technoculture.

14. The *Total War* game engine has been used in television series to animate historical reconstructions of famous battles (as in the History Channel's *Decisive Battles* in 2004) and to stage replays of historical engagements as a competition between contestants (*Time Commanders* 2003–2005; see e.g., the "Battle of Leuctra" episode at <https://www.youtube.com/watch?v=Id9GRHA2bzE>).

15. As Manuel De Landa demonstrated, the standardization of mass-produced items gained its "impetus" from advances in French and American weapons manufacture. The standardization of rifle production during the US Civil War was influential in the development of the assembly line system of production and its generalization via Taylorist "scientific" principles (1991, 31).

16. Key moments in the history of this extension of wargaming, from chess to *kriegsspiel* to computer-simulated gaming and simulation practices are covered in considerable detail in Hilgers (2012) and in other chapters in this volume. In "Wargaming and Computer Games: Fun with the Future," I argued that *kriegsspiel* crystallized a simulational practice that advanced the notion of the applicability of a rationalizing logic and mathematical procedure to the conduct of that most unpredictable affair of warfare (Crogan 2008). The formalization of principles for the abstraction and miniaturization of terrain, and the algorithms for calculating movement, unit damage and so on are progenitors of the battle simulation software pervasive today across the military-entertainment complex.

17. The human rights and legal challenges to the expansion of targeted assassinations by drones and US special forces has focused on the way they abandon the legal and conventional delimitation of the theater of war as they identify and pursue targets in the "global battlefield" (see e.g., Human Rights Watch 2010; Stanford International Human Rights & Conflict Clinic and the Global Justice Clinic of New York University 2012). War becomes a "manhunt" in

Chamayou's thesis, conducted by the hunter on the basis of a unilateral claim to the right to pursue a suspected threat to the homeland or its citizens anywhere it can be found (Chamayou 2013, 107–108).

18. Chamayou discusses the controversy over a proposition to award service medals for "bravery" to drone operators (2013, 145).

19. Chamayou cites another commentator on military strategy, Joshua Jones in this regard. Jones likens the drone operations aimed at tallying up lists of eliminated terrorist threats to the failed "body count" strategy in Vietnam, saying that "the kill list never gets shorter, the names and faces are simply replaced" (Jones 2012).

20. *September 12th* can be played on Newsgaming's website at <http://www.newsgaming.com/games/index12.htm>. Among others, I have written about the eloquence of its "procedural rhetoric"—to cite a term from one of Newsgaming's founders, Ian Bogost's analysis of the critical potential of ludic and simulational forms (Bogost 2007). See Crogan 2011, 146–148.

Michael Peck

"What are you talking about?"

Bafflement spread across the face of the gray-haired man in the camouflage uniform. He was the US Army colonel in charge of designing some of the army's computer simulations, and I was there to talk to him about wargames.

I had recently started writing for defense magazines, and as a wargamer, I had made it a point to write as much as I could about how the military uses games for training or planning. Naturally, I had assumed that officers who work with simulations would know of historical wargames. Surely he must have played, or at least seen, the classic wargames like *PanzerBlitz* (1970) or *D-Day* (1961)?

He hadn't. It was then that I realized that if soldiers didn't know what historical wargames are, neither would almost anyone else.

This was back in 2004, and in the last ten years, the situation has only become worse. Many times, I have pitched ideas for historical wargaming articles to editors who have never seen these games. Many times, I have had to explain that these are not Xbox video games or *Risk*.

And yet, the most amazing thing has happened. For more than a decade, I have written numerous pieces on historical wargames for a variety of mainstream publications, from *Foreign Policy* magazine and Slate.com to Jewish newspaper *The Forward* and various defense magazines. I am not just flattered. I am perplexed. These are not game magazines. Their focus is on weighty issues such as foreign affairs or national defense. Why should they care about replaying the Crimean War?

Answering this question is vital to the future of historical wargaming, because the brutal fact is that historical wargaming is fading. One estimate puts the number of wargamers at just 50,000 to 100,000 worldwide. Many games sell just a few hundred or a few thousand copies. Paper wargame publishers like GMT insist on five hundred preorders before printing a game—and many games wait years before they reach that figure, if ever.

How could there be scarcity amid such abundance? There seem to be plenty of wargames out there, an avalanche of game boxes and screenshots depicting tanks and guns and battleships. But this is only true if one defines wargames—like many nongamers and casual gamers do—as any game that has some vague connection with warfare. By that standard, a first-person shooter game in which soldiers are killed and then respawn into life thirty seconds later is a wargame, or real-time strategy games where your troops capture an enemy tank factory that promptly starts churning out your tanks.

Perhaps these are wargames in the broadest sense, but they are not historical wargames. They do not really try to simulate those factors that explain why history occurred the way it did (or why future conflicts can turn out the way they might)—games that are willing to add realism at the expense of simplicity.

That sphere of wargaming is disappearing. Historical wargame forums echo with the laments of players who own huge game collections yet cannot find anyone to play them.

To survive, and, more important, to thrive, historical wargaming must be able to attract new blood. I don't pretend to have all the answers, but I can offer a few thoughts based on my experience writing for mainstream audiences.

Foremost, the most pressing challenge for historical wargaming is to let people know that these games even exist. When I entered wargaming as a junior high school student in the 1970s, there was a slim but not insignificant chance of meeting someone else who knew of these games. My college had a gaming club that mostly played wargames, and there were several local hobby shops that stocked them.

Now many college gaming clubs play video games or abstract strategy games (Eurogames), and many of the hobby shops have closed. The average person is extremely unlikely to encounter—or meet anyone who has encountered—a serious simulation of the Peloponnesian War, the Seven Years' War, or Korea.

Wargaming forums bubble with solutions for reinvigorating the hobby, usually along the lines of making wargames smaller, faster and simpler. If only we could improve the games, then new players will come, the reasoning goes. These solutions may or may not help, but they miss the point. Making a game simpler accomplishes nothing if prospective players have never heard of it.

How we can let the world know that historical games exist? By writing articles, or perhaps by using games in the classroom. But then the question becomes, why would anyone play them? AAA videogames might enjoy $50 million budgets to pay for the finest graphics. No computerized historical wargame can compete with that. Nor can paper wargames compete with Eurogames, or role-playing games like *Dungeons & Dragons*, on accessibility and social interaction.

So historical wargaming must appeal on a different level. Fortunately, it has several appealing attributes. One is current events. For example, I have written articles for mainstream publications on *Persian Incursion* (2010), a paper wargame of a hypothetical Israeli aerial strike against Iranian nuclear facilities (see Larry Bond's chapter in part IV of this volume), *Combat Mission: Shock Force* (2007), a computer wargame of a hypothetical NATO invasion of Syria, and *Labyrinth* (2010), a political-military board game of the Global War on Terror (see Brian Train and Volko Ruhnke's chapter in part VII of this volume). No major videogame studio—let alone stockholders—is going to sink $50 million into games that meaningfully simulate these topics.

Wargames can also link past history to the present. During Scotland's recent vote on independence, I wrote a piece on *Hammer of the Scots* (2002), a game of England battling Scotland in the thirteenth and fourteenth centuries. On the seventieth anniversary of D-Day, I wrote a roundup of wargames simulating that battle. On the anniversary of the Cuban Missile Crisis, I did a piece on a wargame on that subject, written from the perspective of a survivor of a hypothetical nuclear war. When France sent troops to fight rebels in Mali in 2013, and the inevitable jokes about French fighting prowess appeared, I looked at five wargames in which the French fought well. The possibilities are limitless.

Another draw is that historical wargames offer a unique insight into history. When I write a game article or pitch an idea to an editor, I don't emphasize that historical games are fun. Instead, I mention that they have rules for logistics, or command and control, or combined arms warfare. Not in any great detail, but enough to convey the idea that these games are a window into the past unmatched by any other form of entertainment or education.

That leads to another powerful hook, which is that historical wargaming is hands-on history. It puts you in the shoes of commanders like Napoleon or Patton and confronts you with many of the challenges that they faced.

This brings up wargaming's secret weapon: the human imagination. That is what lured me, as a budding twelve-year-old gamer in 1975, when I saw an advertisement that described wargames as paper time machines. Imagine that! A time machine that takes you back into history!

Yet historical wargaming has become ossified in many ways, a mature hobby that too often focuses on minutiae such as whether the game depicts the correct model of tank or fighter plane. Those aspects are important to an historical simulation, but they don't stir the imagination.

Historical wargaming will never appeal to everybody. But it will appeal to some, and that's enough. It is a window into the past. Now is the time to open the curtains.

About the Author

Michael Peck is a writer who has covered hobby wargames for publications including *Foreign Policy* *Magazine*, *Slate*, *The Forward*, and the *Military Times* magazines.

Joseph Miranda

One day back in the 1990s, I was driving with Keith "Kirk" Schlesinger to Connections, the US Air Force–sponsored conference on wargaming and simulations. As we motored from Kirk's home in Ohio down to Maxwell Air Force Base in Montgomery, Alabama, I kicked around ideas for a topic on which I was to give a presentation. My original idea was to talk about wargaming and insurgency. After all, I had recently designed a couple of insurgency wargames for *Strategy & Tactics* magazine: *Nicaragua* (1988) and *Holy War: Afghanistan* (1991). Insurgency added an additional level to warfare, mainly in the psychological-political realm, and I had worked out some unique systems to model all this. But given the then-recent fall of the Berlin Wall, it seemed that communist-era insurgency tactics were not very high on the agenda. Anyway, I was perusing a glossy book called *Mondo: A User's Guide to the New Edge* (Rucker et al. 1992), a compilation of magazine-style articles dealing with the cutting edge of cybernetics, and came up with a better topic: Why not design a wargame on how these emerging technologies would revolutionize warfare?

As we drove through Kentucky and Tennessee, I jotted down ideas for how to model everything from network access attacks to virtual reality. But what to call all this? Kirk suggested a term for this new form of warfare: "data conflict." This was the first time I heard a term for what is now commonly called "cyberwarfare."

I gave my talk at Connections and then went on to design a board game called *Crisis 2000* (1997), developed by Kirk, and originally published by One Small Step (updated as *Crisis 2020* by Victory Point Games in 2007). *Crisis 2000* is set in the near future, with the United States as a battleground for rival factions, each armed with both conventional military and advanced cybernetic technologies.

Data conflict superseded traditional psychological operations (PSYOP) as new technological frontiers opened. I used standard wargame mechanics, with some twists. Units had two combat factors: one for conventional armed military tactics, the other for data conflict. Each type of combat had a different range of outcomes. Conventional warfare eliminated enemy units if successful. Data conflict caused enemy units to defect; it included the exploitation of technologies such as the emerging Internet, and can be projected forward to nanotechnology and other ways to revolutionize operations. Units were printed on both sides of the game pieces, the front being pro-Government, the reverse pro-Rebel; when a defection was inflicted, you flipped over an enemy unit, and it came over to your side. (Government and Rebel were defined in different ways depending upon the scenario.)

Potentially, data conflict was much more powerful because you were not only taking a unit out of the enemy order of battle, but also adding it to your side. But there was a catch: data conflict took place at the start of a player's turn, before units moved. Armed conflict took place after movement. This meant that the enemy would always have an opportunity to counterattack or withdraw before being hit with a defection attempt. It was a neat and simple way to work in the asymmetry of the two tactics.

The game order of battle reflected emerging force structures. You had an array of high- and low-technology forces, special operators, and insurgents. A special unit was the cybernaut, a cadre trained to utilize cybernetic warfare and other future technologies. Think of them as anticipating the various military and intelligence commands conducting cyberwar today.

There was more. Players had access to Crisis markers. These markers represented specialized technologies and major events, things like media access, virtual reality, advanced weaponry, and alliances with everyone from the Pentagon down to urban militias. Crisis markers provided enhancements to various types of combat, as well as being the triggers for Black Swan events such as cyberterrorist attacks. Critically, *Crisis 2000* shows these events as deployable playing pieces, making them as tangible as weapons systems.

This gets back to my thesis that warfare takes place on multiple levels. You have the conventional military level, with combat units and such. But there are other levels which deal with a wide range of psychological and cybernetic systems. Look at current Pentagon doctrine, with its emphasis on full-spectrum warfare.

As noted, I did a couple of wargames dealing with Cold War–era insurgencies. *Nicaragua* was a very systems-oriented game, dealing with Sandinistas, Somocistas, and Contras. It included models for national will, psychological warfare, insurgent front organization, social groups, and counterinsurgency operations. All this is realistic, but it tended to produce a mathematical model that can become predictable—something that has both its advantages and disadvantages in a wargame.

Holy War: Afghanistan simulated the Soviet war in that country (1979–89), one of the major Cold War conflicts, and one which did much to unravel communism. For *Afghanistan*, I went in for a more effects-oriented design. Each player had a pool of Political markers, representing various factions involved in the conflict as well as outside intervening powers. Players drew these markers at random, based on their overall level of support from the populace. The random draw reflects the chaotic nature of the conflict, with factions coming and going. You find yourself running a shifting coalition and thinking in terms of how your military operations can get the political balance in your favor. It was easier to apply some chaos theory principles than to come up with complex models which would have gotten you to the same point.

As for popular support, an easy enough mechanism can quantify it. You have an index running from zero to one hundred, with each increment representing one percent of the population supporting one side or the other. Then it's a matter of determining the impact that game actions have on it. For example, a successful military attack might shift the index ten points in your favor—and then enemy media exploitation of collateral damage shifts it twenty to the other side! It gets back to the issue of political will, which has been a decisive factor in most conflicts, especially in the politically charged world of the Cold War.

Today, with the Internet, the political front is everywhere, and just about everyone with access to a computer terminal or cell phone can be a virtual combatant. There are multiple players, with networks emerging, conducting campaigns, then dissolving and reforming.

A design that brings some order out of chaos is *Battle for Baghdad* (2009), for Modern Studies Conflict Group (and I must give a shout out to Mike Anderson and John Compton for the work they did in developing this one). *Battle for Baghdad* is a seminar-style game covering the struggle for control of the Iraqi capital in the years following the US/Coalition military victory of 2003. The game map shows Baghdad divided up into various zones (Sadr City, the International Airport, and so on). Players deploy tokens that represent mobile combat units and static infrastructure. You can have up to six players, each with a different set of capabilities and each having a different set of objectives. Warfare is asymmetrical, both tactical and strategic, and you have to be concerned about not only your own objectives but also blocking the other players. Each faction has its own strength. For example, the United States can bring to bear strong military forces, while the Sunnis and Shiites can infiltrate across the map.

One mechanism that proved useful was cards. The game has two decks: "Arab Street" and "Arms Bazaar." The Arab Street generates various events in specified Baghdad neighborhoods, representing things like an uprising breaking out in Sadr City to a demand for garbage pickup in the Green Zone. You then have to get your forces into the right place at the right time to deal with them. The Arms Bazaar gives you weapons, tactics, and special actions you can take to gain the edge when it comes to fighting it out. The cards also add in actionable opportunities such as petroleum booms, elections, and surges.

This points up an advantage of board wargaming, where the physicality of the cards does much to enhance player experience. The cards are also a neat way to display many different factors, from precision-guided weapons to media exploitation of collateral damage. Having a hand of cards facilitates organization of information, and the card graphics do much to enhance the quality of play. You can think in terms of playing certain options as opposed to referencing a rulebook.

Having a group of players sit around the table makes for a social occasion, especially since the game allows the formation of alliances (as well as backstabbing). Often, it is how people interact that can be decisive, a point to be considered when using games for training. That human dimension is important.

Then it was off to the Horn of Africa for *Somali Pirates* (2012), published in *Modern War* magazine (Decision Games). One player controls assorted Somali rebel factions, the assumption being that they are making a united effort to gain control of the country, supported by income from pirate operations in surrounding waters. The other player commands various Coalition contingents.

If you look at the military lineup, the Coalition appears to have the edge: plenty of warships, aircraft, high-tech ground forces, and special operators. But there are a couple of catches. One is that Coalition contingents represent forces from various powers: US and NATO combined joint task forces, the Somali

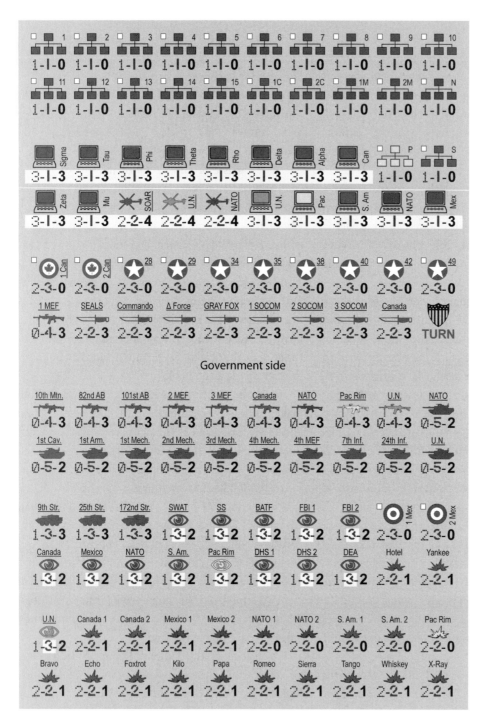

Figure 56.1

Crisis 2020 counters, front and back.

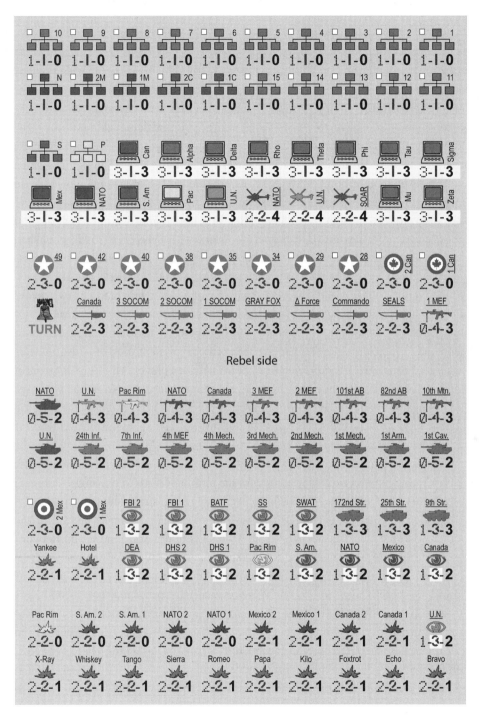

☐ 10	☐ 9	☐ 8	☐ 7	☐ 6	☐ 5	☐ 4	☐ 3	☐ 2	☐ 1
1-1-0	1-1-0	1-1-0	1-1-0	1-1-0	1-1-0	1-1-0	1-1-0	1-1-0	1-1-0
☐ N	☐ 2M	☐ 1M	☐ 2C	☐ 1C	☐ 15	☐ 14	☐ 13	☐ 12	☐ 11
1-1-0	1-1-0	1-1-0	1-1-0	1-1-0	1-1-0	1-1-0	1-1-0	1-1-0	1-1-0

		Can	Alpha	Delta	Rho	Theta	Phi	Tau	Sigma
☐ S	☐ P								
1-1-0	1-1-0	3-1-3	3-1-3	3-1-3	3-1-3	3-1-3	3-1-3	3-1-3	3-1-3
Mex	NATO	S. Am.	Pac	U.N.	NATO	U.N.	SOAR	Mu	Zeta
3-1-3	3-1-3	3-1-3	3-1-3	3-1-3	2-2-4	2-2-4	2-2-4	3-1-3	3-1-3

								2 Can	1 Can
☐ 49	☐ 42	☐ 40	☐ 38	☐ 35	☐ 34	☐ 29	☐ 28		
2-3-0	2-3-0	2-3-0	2-3-0	2-3-0	2-3-0	2-3-0	2-3-0	2-3-0	2-3-0
TURN	Canada	3 SOCOM	2 SOCOM	1 SOCOM	GRAY FOX	Δ Force	Commando	SEALS	1 MEF
	2-2-3	2-2-3	2-2-3	2-2-3	2-2-3	2-2-3	2-2-3	2-2-3	0-4-3

Rebel side

NATO	U.N.	Pac Rim	NATO	Canada	3 MEF	2 MEF	101st AB	82nd AB	10th Mtn.
0-5-2	0-4-3	0-4-3	0-4-3	0-4-3	0-4-3	0-4-3	0-4-3	0-4-3	0-4-3
U.N.	24th Inf.	7th Inf.	4th MEF	4th Mech.	3rd Mech.	2nd Mech.	1st Mech.	1st Arm.	1st Cav.
0-5-2	0-5-2	0-5-2	0-5-2	0-5-2	0-5-2	0-5-2	0-5-2	0-5-2	0-5-2

2 Mex	1 Mex	FBI 2	FBI 1	BATF	SS	SWAT	172nd Str.	25th Str.	9th Str.
2-3-0	2-3-0	1-3-2	1-3-2	1-3-2	1-3-2	1-3-2	1-3-3	1-3-3	1-3-3
Yankee	Hotel	DEA	DHS 2	DHS 1	Pac Rim	S. Am.	NATO	Mexico	Canada
2-2-1	2-2-1	1-3-2	1-3-2	1-3-2	1-3-2	1-3-2	1-3-2	1-3-2	1-3-2

Pac Rim	S. Am. 2	S. Am. 1	NATO 2	NATO 1	Mexico 2	Mexico 1	Canada 2	Canada 1	U.N.
2-2-0	2-2-0	2-2-0	2-2-0	2-2-0	2-2-1	2-2-1	2-2-1	2-2-1	1-3-2
X-Ray	Whiskey	Tango	Sierra	Romeo	Papa	Kilo	Foxtrot	Echo	Bravo
2-2-1	2-2-1	2-2-1	2-2-1	2-2-1	2-2-1	2-2-1	2-2-1	2-2-1	2-2-1

Figure 56.1
(continued)

Transitional Federal Government, the Chinese with their new power projection navy, and in an expansion set, the Russians. There are even private military contractors. To mobilize a contingent, you have to pay Netwar Points, the game currency. Having more Netwar Points than the other guy can give you victory at the end of the game. Lose too many points, and your effort collapses. It's the dilemma that has been common in modern warfare: win the battle but lose the war. The Netwar Index represents the overall support you have mobilized for your efforts, a combination of popular backing in Somalia, political will back in the home country, and favorable coverage in the global media (both conventional and alternative, the latter including the Internet).

Political support has been a major factor in many conflicts. In the past, it was largely a matter of good leadership backed up by organization and psychological operations (that is, propaganda). But today the Internet provides another front. And it's a front in which just about everyone can engage. In some ways, it has superseded the Cold War–era reliance on physical infrastructure such as radio and TV broadcasting and public demonstrations. The perceptual battle is resolved on the virtual front of Internet communications, blogs, homemade video postings, and much more across the spectrum.

The Netwar Index of *Somali Pirates* represents the strategic end of the spectrum. But there is also the tactical end. You have combat units, rated for both their kinetic combat strength and their capacity for asymmetrical warfare. The former is used to destroy enemy forces, the latter for special operations such as terrorist spectaculars, pirate attacks, and targeting high-value enemy targets.

Players can purchase Netwar markers, representing infowar, tactical advantages, ISR, UAVs, black

ops, and other factors not usually appearing on the order of battle. These are a development of *Crisis 2000*'s Crisis markers. Again, they make virtual technologies as quantifiable and deployable as an armored brigade. They are part of your arsenal, and their use at the right time can be decisive (though the game system does provide for the occasional blowback, so there is no sure thing).

I went in for a much more granular design on cybernetic warfare with *Cybernaut* (1996), published by One Small Step. *Cybernaut* pits Netrunners—Internet-based insurgents—against a globalized network security agency. The game map has two levels. One is the Realworld, showing various urban complexes around the globe. The other is the Cyberspace Display, an abstract representation of a future Internet. The idea was to get players thinking in terms of multiple levels of operations. For example, you have insurgent characters who are good at combat in the Realworld but are not as capable as others when it comes to netrunning.

Cyberspace has multiple levels, and the idea is that Netrunners have to penetrate to the highest to gain various objectives—which can be anything from triggering a revolution to melding one's mind into the Net itself. The Netrunners are opposed by network security teams—agents who track down threats in the Realworld—and various defensive programs within Cyberspace (the programs use terminology then common in cyberpunk fiction). Passive programs block access, while aggressive programs go after network intruders, attacking them with disabling feedback pulses.

To penetrate Cyberspace, Netrunners need to gain enhancements to their capability for cybernetic interface (called "wetware" in the game). This means interacting in various Realworld environments to pick up programs and gear. This in turn means taking risks while navigating the mean streets of the near future, though on occasion you can pick up allies along the way (for example, you can gain control of nanotechnologies, which let you enhance certain abilities). This gives gamers the opportunity to engage in a simulation of Internet-based warfare that can be learned and played in short order. Right now I am considering doing an update to *Cybernaut*.

While I have worked mainly in board wargaming, I have also been involved in the design of computer simulations. One such project was done for the US Air Force, called *Cyberwar XXI* and produced under the aegis of Hexagon Interactive. This started off as a simulation of the impact of emerging weapons systems in a hypothetical Persian Gulf conflict. It included extensive rules for the utilization of cybernetic warfare options to exploit the impact of high-tech weaponry, as well as to open new fronts that let you win without having to cause a lot of physical destruction. The game also tied in various concepts of systems warfare, with operations against enemy command control and infrastructure. I was inspired, in part, by some talks given by Colonel John Warden at Connections on airpower and nonlinear warfare. *Cyberwar XXI* also included cybercadres, units representing teams of cybernetic warfare specialists as well as other full spectrum operators. Again, this gets Netwar forces into the order of battle.

Designing computer simulations provides some different approaches than board wargaming. A computer program can handle many of the details, such as calculating complex psychological factors, as well as providing artificial intelligence agents to run the opposition force. On the other hand, board games provide a human dimension as players interact with each other. Another advantage of board games is that players can easily make changes to them; this allows for them to be continually updated as well as modified for user end purposes.

The recent conflict in the Ukraine led me to design *New World Order Battles: Kiev*. This is part of a series of wargames to be published in *Modern War* magazine, of which I am the editor. The games in the system show actions from the Gulf War into the near future on the grand tactical level; maneuver units are generally battalions. There are the standard rules for combat, with additional systems for hyperwar tactics. Hyperwar-qualified units can use a special combat results table that gives enhanced results. They can also conduct "rolling attacks," allowing them to fight continuous actions, much as in the US-British drive upcountry during 2003's Operation Iraqi Freedom. This reflects the higher pace of operations—a superior OODA Loop, to use John Boyd's term—which comes from modern networking systems and superior training. A force that has a higher command control level is going to be able to accomplish more before the enemy gets his act together. This can be seen during campaigns such as Desert Storm and Operation Iraqi Freedom, where Coalition forces could seize operational objectives before the Iraqis could respond.

But there's a downside. Players have the ability to launch Netwar attacks against the other side. These attacks can "crash" opposing hyperwar units, depriving them of their special capabilities. You suddenly have a twenty-first-century brigade trying to slug it out with Cold War–era tactics. The system gets you thinking in terms of the implications of future technologies. They work great until they crash, at which point you are going to have to improvise. A lower-tech foe might then be able to gain the upper hand.

You can see how all this has played out in the last couple of decades. Information operations and cyberwar have become major instruments of national security. Asymmetrical warfare is a major factor in current operations. The ISIS offensive in Iraq is one example, with fourth-generation insurgents overcoming a well-armed government foe (though perhaps this situation will change). Another example is Russian president Vladimir Putin's actions in the Ukraine, combining paramilitary forces with regulars to seize objectives such as the Crimea. And to return to data conflict, the US role in the Anbar Awakening and the subsequent surge in Iraq shows the value of converting potentially hostile forces to your side.

All these designs show the many fronts that can be simulated via wargaming. It's a matter of applying proven systems with radical new ideas. Best of all, you can set up these games on your kitchen table and play them out, learn lessons, and perhaps apply them in the real world.

About the Author

Joseph Miranda is currently the editor in chief of *Modern War* magazine. *Modern War* covers contemporary and near future military affairs, and includes a wargame in each issue. He has designed more than two hundred published wargames and has been on the design team for several computer simulations. His designs have included various historical, hypothetical, and near-future topics, with current work in netcentric and cyberwar operations for the commercial market and various defense-related agencies. He is a former editor of *Strategy & Tactics* magazine and has been a featured speaker at various professional simulations conferences, such as Connections. Miranda is a former US Army officer, and he has developed and taught university courses in counterterrorism.

Greg Costikyan

I want to conduct a thought experiment with you, but to do so, I must transport you to a different time and place: specifically to the year 1979, and the offices of Simulations Publications, Inc. (SPI), then the world's second largest publisher of board wargames after Avalon Hill.

SPI is, for its time, a technically advanced company; grossing less than $2 million a year, it nonetheless owns its own minicomputer, an IBM System/3 (and in fact its president, Jim Dunnigan, was featured in an IBM advertisement vaunting the utility of its minicomputers to small businesses). It is used primarily for accounting, but a handful of games can be played on it, and we do, because, of course, we are gamers.

In 1979, we are on the verge of the microcomputer revolution, and we know it. The Apple II is out there, there are rumblings from the CP/M community—clearly it's only going to be a few short years before home computers are widespread. And as wargamers, we want wargames on computers, obviously. Wouldn't that be fine? Inevitable, too. There are only three markets for games in the United States: the arcade, with its blaring twitch nonsense; mass market boardgaming, which sells old perennials and crappy games based on movie or TV licenses; and the

hobby market, where wargames and role-playing dominate. Only the latter has the kind of geeky, complex, intricate games that can truly benefit from computing power—games, moreover, that appeal to smart people, and surely early adopters of home computers will be smart people.

So let us, in 1979, dream about the wargames of the future. What will they be like? What amazing things are in store?

Oh sure, we could simply take some of our existing board games and do computer versions of them, displaying hexes on a screen and (what's a mouse?) using key commands to move them about and order them to attack, but what would be the point of that, really? You can do that on a table, without thousands of dollars of hardware. No, surely the wargames of the future will take advantage of the unique capabilities of computers to advance the state of the art, to do something quite novel and different.

Well, what might that entail? Let's start by thinking about the drawbacks of board wargames and how computers might redress them.

For one thing, those hexes. Board wargames adopted hexes because they produce less distance distortion than a square grid, but it's a kludge, of course; the real world is not gridded, and instead has continuous position and motion. In principle, you could do a board wargame in which you measured distances and moved units around accordingly (and indeed, that is precisely what you do in miniatures wargaming), but that would be a bit of a pain. Still, a computer wargame should allow us to break free of the grid; performing distance calculations is trivial, after all, for a computer.

And that has another great advantage. In a hex-based wargame, every unit occupies one hex, but that's not how real-world units behave. In close urban warfare, a regiment might occupy a handful of blocks; urban conflict can suck in a huge number of troops in a very restricted area, as at Stalingrad. Conversely, a regiment might occupy miles of a front in a rural area. In other words, units do not occupy hexes; units are squishy. They can concentrate on a small objective, or they can expand out—not infinitely, because with an extended line you want each man or squad to remain in contact with the next up the line—but over a long distance. A digital wargame also allows us to break free of the tyranny of cardboard counters; it allows us to treat units in a more flexible and realistic way.

For that matter, the whole hex-and-counter metaphor exists only to make it possible to simulate military conflict in a board game. It is hardly the only metaphor people have used when portraying military history. Consider the *West Point Atlas* books: they typically show what is going on by drawing a front line and dividing it into unit sectors, with arrows showing attacks and such. A digital game could totally adopt that metaphor, and it would be an excellent one for simulating, say, the Eastern Front in World War II. You could imagine assigning units to sectors, perhaps sliding sector boundaries up and

down the front line, pulling units back into a reserve, but having the whole metaphor be the line, the army group and the units assigned to it, and the outcome of battle not be a unit moving into a hex but the line moving forward or falling back.

That's only the first and most obvious alternative metaphor for portraying military conflict. Surely there can be many others, and surely the imaginative game designers of the beautiful digital future will invent wholly novel and interesting ways of doing so.

Another thing board wargames do badly is fog of war. Naturally—you and your opponent are sitting at a table, staring down at the board, and how could you hide anything? Oh, a handful of games try. In *Quebec 1759* (1972), your units are wooden blocks that face you, *Stratego*-like, and your opponent doesn't know their strength until they attack. Or in *Panzergruppe Guderian,* all the Russian units have question marks in place of their combat strength, and only when they attack are they flipped over to show their real value—neither player knows their strength until then (an arguably realistic feature, since the Russians were basically throwing raw recruits into the face of the Nazi advance). But fog of war in a board game is hard; fog of war in a digital game is easy.

And not just fog of war in the sense of "we can't see over that ridge." Imagine yourself in command of a US regiment in Pennsylvania in the Civil War. You encounter some Rebs. Is this just a regiment of Southerners—or is this advance guard of the whole damn Army of Northern Virginia? You are faced with a dilemma; the right response to their presence depends critically on the answer, but you cannot know. Thus, all board wargames are inherently unrealistic because you know too much when you sit down to play; if this game is called *Gettysburg*, you know full well that you're about to explore the most important single battle of the Civil War. But historically, the actions of both sides on the first day of that battle can really be understood only by realizing that *they* didn't know this was the big one.

Imagine instead a game that re-creates that kind of uncertainty; a game of Civil War battles, say, but with the conditions of each new game procedurally generated at the inception of play, so that, like actual commanders, you never quite know what you are stepping into. Wouldn't that produce novel and interesting insights into the nature of command, and the conditions of the war the game simulates?

For that matter, if we have learned anything from World Wars I and II, it is that at the beginning of a war, no one knows squat, because technology changes so quickly in the industrial era that assumptions based on conditions from the previous war are bound to be wrong. At the inception of World War I, most everyone thought the war would be short and over soon. "Home before the leaves fall," right? It came as a huge surprise that machine guns gave enormous advantage to defense, that industrialized nations could sustain vast armies in the field for years even as a whole generation was ground to hamburger, that Europe was to embark on what amounted to siege warfare on a continental scale. At the inception of World War II, only the Nazis (and Charles de Gaulle) had realized that the combination of tanks deployed en masse, with air support, could smash the defensive lines of yesteryear. That far from a world of siege warfare, we were now in the world of the blitzkrieg, a war of vast sweeping movements and advances at a speed never before seen in history.

So ... when thinking about the next war, the hypothetical war in the 1980s (in the future from

1979), a conflict between NATO and the USSR, about all we can really conclude is that it probably *won't* be like World War II. And yet, that is more or less what NATO is planning for. How will our World War III be different? It's impossible to say. Perhaps the anti-tank weapons fielded by infantry are now enough to blunt tank offensives, and we're back to trench warfare. Perhaps the dominating weapon of the World War III battlefield will be the helicopter. That is hard to know without actually fighting a war, but a good simulation should, perhaps, account for all these possibilities. You can't do that in a board game, but in a digital one ... What if the relative effectiveness of weapons and units are procedurally determined at the start of play, but unknown to the player until discovered? What if every game was different, because the conditions would be different? Perhaps with the option for the player to decide on conditions before starting a game, to explore all kinds of "what-ifs."

Another advantage of computers, of course, is their ability to perform complex calculations that would be impractical in a board game. Board wargames typically use a combat-ratio resolution table: express the attacker's strength as a ratio to the defender's, find this ratio on a table, roll a die, and cross-reference the die roll and ratio to determine the result. But this inherently reduces a unit's effectiveness in combat to a single, unitary number. To be sure, we do things such as giving certain units benefits in some types of terrain, but we are still expressing something that, in reality, is a very complex thing—the effectiveness of a unit in combat—as a single unitary number. By comparison, theorists like Trevor Dupuy (1979) have written whole books exploring the mathematics of military effectiveness in different conditions, taking into account things like the firepower and speed of weapons, training and combat experience, morale, effective manpower, posture, and terrain to provide heuristics for determining a unit's effectiveness. It would be absurd to have a board game that tried to do all this, to have players solve problems in calculus each time they resolve an attack. But you could do so in a computer game, surely. The difficulty wouldn't be in performing the calculations; the difficulty, rather, would be in surfacing the reasons for the results to the players, making it clear that the outcome was because of casualties in a previous attack, or ineffectiveness in this kind of terrain, or whatever the critical factor was in this situation. It's a UI problem, in other words; the underlying complexity of the system isn't a problem in itself.

So yes, doubtless our future wargames will have extremely complex algorithms under the hood, providing much more realistic and sophisticated simulations of war.

The ability to perform complex calculations will have another impact, too; in the realm of board wargames, we have pressed up against the limits of what is reasonable or feasible. SPI publishes a monstrosity called *Campaign for North Africa* (1979) that is so complex that it does things like track individual pilots in the North African campaign, deal with water consumption by individual battalions, and require you to site prisoner of war camps and keep them supplied. So much recordkeeping is required that when you play it, you must photocopy multiple forms and spend much of your playing time recording and updating the data involved. Indeed, when it was playtested at the SPI offices, manila folders with forms were thumbtacked to the playtest room walls, and some wag added another form: a "Form for Requisitioning Forms." It is a game of unprecedented

depth and complexity, but also a complete chore to play; you have to be kind of nuts to do so, really. But we could totally do that in a computer game: record lots of data, update it frequently, perform complicated calculations. You can imagine a production system in which a whole economy is updating frequently under the hood, or a game in which we get away from the turn-based metaphor and have things moving in real time, updating changes in morale and the like continuously. You can even increase the scale, if you had a fast enough machine: simulate the entirety of World War II at this level, instead of just North Africa. The result might still be very complex and hard for people to wrap their heads around, but it would be playable in a way that *Campaign for North Africa* is not.

What about multiplayer? Hard with microcomputers, to be sure, but in 1979, I was playing *Empire* multiplayer on the Vaxen at NYU, and it was pretty cool, for a pure text game. Modems exist. Someday there will be big multiplayer games, surely. Just imagine what that could be like. Imagine playing the entirety of World War II with thousands of others. Maybe each player commands a battalion, and you have to coordinate with your regimental and divisional commanders, and they with the army group, and they with the high command. Wouldn't that be a blast?

Very well, then, let us put ourselves into cold sleep and fast-forward to the twenty-first century. How are we doing?

What kind of wargames do we have? Well, let's take a look at today's bestsellers list. Two *Call of Duty* (series 2002–) titles and *Battlefield 4* (2013). Fire 'em up! Oh, I'm a single soldier running around with a gun. Health packs fix me up when I take damage. Single bullets apparently just chip away at my health instead of sending me screaming onto the ground and groaning for a medic. Well, *this* is realistic. Not.

Consider some key elements you might expect to be handled in a game of squad-level tactics, which is more or less what these are:

- Chain of command. A squad is led by a sergeant, who typically takes orders from a first lieutenant in command of several squads. In other words, in a group of eight or so soldiers, one would be giving the orders; FPS games are typically chaotic firefights with any coordination among the avatars either based on rudimentary AI or, in a multiplayer game, among players communicating via voice chat. Chain of command is hardly a focus.
- Terrain and cover. Most stationary models provide cover, so there's some element of this here, but proper use of screening terrain, slope enfilades, and so on, are hardly a major element in play.
- Combined armed tactics. Nope.
- Unit coordination, enfilade, and covering fire. While this is feasible, it almost never happens, due to the lack of focus on chain of command, and the chaotic nature of interplayer communication.
- Improvised defenses, whether entrenchments or things like sandbag barriers and razor wire. Also nope.
- Supply and ammo constraints. Definitely nope.

By nature, the common tropes of the FPS mitigate against a sense of realism or even verisimilitude; no, there are no magic health packs that can patch you up in mid-firefight in the real world. No, being hit with a bullet doesn't erode your health a little but still allow you to keep fighting on. No, if you happen to find a dropped weapon somewhere, it's unlikely to be fully loaded. No, dead people do not respawn.

These aren't wargames; they're first-person shooters laminated with a thin veneer of war. They teach you squat about history, or strategy, or the nature of military conflict. Not saying anything against them as games qua games; but while war as a theme may be marketable, war as simulation, war as history, war as a strategic discipline, is nowhere to be found. Simulation and realism, or at least verisimilitude, is part of the aesthetic of the wargame; it's not the whole thing, of course, because we still want our games to be fun, but if something is just ridiculous, if it's gamey, if it actually breaks the fourth wall that allows us to suspend our disbelief and pretend that we are experiencing military conflict vicariously, then it has no place in a wargame. Which these are not.

Maybe we're looking in the wrong place. One of the top ten grossing mobile games of the year is *Clash of Clans* (2013). Let's try that. Consider what a player's village looks like, at least if he has some understanding of how this game works. Every building is surrounded by walls, because walls slow attackers down, and having walls everywhere gives your defensive towers more time to wear down the attackers, benefiting your defense.

But from a simulation perspective, this is madness. No medieval fortification ever looked like that; how can the defenders communicate and support each other when attacked? In other words, this is gamey; "walls everywhere" falls out of the nature of *Clash of Clan*'s system, but it violates any sense of historicity. Arbitrary systems force players into strategies that have no connection to anything real. It may be fun to play, but ... this is no wargame. Again, there is nothing more than a military veneer atop an arbitrary game.

All right, maybe *Clash of Clans* wasn't the right mobile game to look at. How about *Boom Beach*? That at least looks more like a wargame, with little soldiers and landing craft, and graphics made to look something like what American marines—you—might see in the Pacific Theater in World War II. And *Boom Beach* does offer one element of player volition that *Clash of Clans* lacks: if your units start doing something dumb, you can fire a flare to designate a preferred target for them.

But beyond that, it's the same essential scheme as *Clash of Clans*. Soldiers attack but don't defend, islands are defended by defensive towers. And combat is basically rock-paper-scissors: flamethrowers are effective against Riflemen, who deal good damage but have low hit points, but not against Heavies, who do less damage but are meat shields for your other troops. Is this realistic? Let me put it this way: a .45 bullet through your brain will kill you. Doing lots of push-ups will not get you "more hit points" and save you therefore. Yes, some design thought has gone into making this a "balanced" game with a variety of possible strategies, but verisimilitude and simulation value were tossed out the window before the first line of code was written.

What about real-time strategy? Firing up *Age of Empires III* for the first time is undoubtedly a "wow" moment: beautifully rendered soldiers and sailing ships and siege engines. Elephants! There is certainly a level of historical research shown here, in the loving attention paid to period detail. And our surmise about the ability to move away from turn-based games to real-time motion was evidently correct. The surprise here is how beautiful a modern

videogame can be; in 1979, with its black and white bitmaps and 64k machines, the graphics of twenty-first century machines would have been almost inconceivable.

Yet, from the very inception of play, you know this is a war-themed game, with no real concern for simulation. The resource gathering and base building elements are bogus and irrelevant. The multiplayer game is an economic rush, with victory going to the player who masters the interface best. Terrain has almost no effect; there is no command hierarchy, no use of formations, no field fortifications—all critical elements of warfare in the ancient world.

Well, this is mass-market stuff, and mass-market stuff is always lowest common denominator. Let's take a look at things actually marketed as wargames. And so we find ourselves at the Matrix Games site, where we find ... games with hexes. And units in hexes. Good lord, really? All these years later? Why even bother? Okay, I get it: wargamers got older, had trouble finding the time to get together with others to play, and the computer is always there; the ability to pick up and play for a bit on your own schedule has value. But how ... jejune, simply to re-create the tabletop experience in a digital game.

Are there any games that break the hex mold? Why yes, a few: *Gary Grigsby's World at War* (2005), for instance, quite a good game really, but you know, curiously reminiscent of *Axis & Allies* (1981). Better and more realistic than that game, but your units are basically plastic soldiers and aircraft carriers; there's at least a stab at simulation here, but the board game antecedents are very clear.

Turn-based strategy games, like *X-COM: UFO* and *Jagged Alliance 2* also don't use hexes. They are, however, directly modeled on simultaneous-movement board games, like *Sniper!*, in which players write down orders for their units, reveal them simultaneously, then resolve the results of the turn.[1] Similarly, in turn-based strategy games, you give orders to your units, editing them until happy, then committing, and then you watch opposing units respond in real time to the actions of your characters. This has the advantage of getting rid of the "Igo-Ugo" dynamic, which certainly improves realism, but at the expense of turning the chaos and terror of war into a curiously chesslike strategy game, in which you ponder and plan your moves, then watch the chaos in real time. Obviously, this isn't how combat actually works.

What about *Hearts of Iron* (2002)? This is more promising: it has the kind of scale and complexity I was imagining, with an underlying economy and system requiring enough continuous calculation that you could not reasonably re-create this game in paper form. This is clearly the most impressive attempt we have looked at yet, but it is also far from a good simulation. You can play as Romania and conquer the world—that's absurd. There is clearly an initial design intent to simulate World War II conflict, but no real desire on the part of the developers to pull back when the implications of their systems take them up entirely silly paths. Doubtless they tell each other that it's just a game. True, of course, but historicity should count for something.

What else have we got? Well, there's *World of Tanks* (2011). Here at least there's attention paid to the characteristics of the many different armored vehicles available in the game; you can get a real sense of the different between a Panzer and a T-34. But it is far from a sophisticated simulation of armored warfare—it's mostly a bunch of people

tooling around in tanks and blasting each other, a sort of first-person shooter variant with tanks. Fun in its own way, but it never really makes you think like an armored commander, nor to feel like you're an ongoing part of a desperate military struggle. Still, props to the game for trying something novel, and something you do need a 3D world and a first-person view to provide.

And then there's *Total War: Rome II* (2013). Here at last is something that is recognizably a wargame and does something that would have been difficult or impossible to do in a tabletop game: vast numbers of individually animated soldiers moving in formation according to flocking algorithms, with you as commander able to issue them orders essentially as quickly as you can click around. It can be visually stunning (but generally isn't, since you keep the view zoomed out far enough that you can see what's happening on the battlefield as a whole, rather than zooming in to marvel at the havoc), and the ability of units to adopt different formations (locking shields and such) gives a real sense of Rome at war. There is a real attempt at simulation fidelity as well, with things like flanking attacks and unit morale playing critical roles, though it is certainly possible to quibble (field entrenchments were a major element in Roman warfare, and are given short shrift here). The strategic game is risible, bearing no relation to the actual concerns of the Roman aristocratic class or its economic support, but this is perhaps forgivable, since it is really just meant as a mechanism for setting up the conditions for the next battle, and the moment-to-moment play during battle is quite convincing. To be sure, there are elements important to ancient warfare it does not address (the need to signal or send messengers to units to give them commands, say), but any simulation has to focus on the elements it wants to draw out most deeply, and gloss over others; trying to simulate everything is a fool's game.

In other words, surveying the modern genres that have some connection to war, they divide into two camps. One set, which I have claimed are not wargames, are war-themed, but their essential gameplay does not derive from a simulationist impulse, nor do their designers feel any need to create artifacts that express something about historical reality. We have *Doom* (1993) and *Quake* (1996), and so some developers decide to take the conventions of the first-person shooter, and apply a war theme to them—hey presto, *Battlefield: 1942* (2002). We have *Dune II* (1992) and *Warcraft* (1994), and designers decide to apply a military theme—thus we get *Age of Emipres III* (2005). And so forth. Nice games, but not wargames in a meaningful sense.

The other set do derive from a simulationist impulse: hex-based wargames, turn-based strategy, grand strategy games like *Hearts of Iron*, and real-time battle games like *Total War: Rome*. And yet, of these, only *Total War* is, from the perspective of 1979, an impressive and novel accomplishment, though *Hearts of Iron* certainly stands as an example of a kind of game that we could have predicted, but could not have implemented in tabletop form.

All in all, you look at thirty-five years of development and think: Well, there have been a handful of novel and exciting developments here, but fundamentally it all seems rather disappointing. There has been so little effort to break the mold, to imagine how digital technology can enable wholly novel game styles, to experiment and find new metaphors for simulating war. It is as if videogaming were not an art form at all, as if products rarely get developed if they

have any design risk, as if commerce and not creativity rule the world.

Oh, wait …

Well, that explains that.

What else could we do? You could take some of the ideas I suggested at the beginning of this chapter and run with them: the front line as the metaphor, the use of procedurally generated battle conditions to simulate the uncertainty of conflicts at their inception, pushing the edge with fog of war. What about playing as Erwin Rommel, leading from the front at El Agheila—a first-person view game, but not a shooter (or if it becomes one, your bodyguard has let you get too damn close to the British)—observing what's going on, issuing orders, your presence improving the morale of the men? What about a massively multiplayer game set in the sixteenth century, with players the monarchs of everything from the Ottoman Empire to the tiniest German polity? What about a World War I game that depicts squad-level combat in a realistic way, as your men drop like mayflies in a withering hail of machine gun bullets and cry out piteously for help, their agonizing cries continuing until you yourself die on the barbed wire and can hear them no longer (a surefire bestseller, that one).

It is not like interesting ways to represent military conflict in digital form are hard to think of, nor that we have remotely rung the changes on the possible. There is a huge design space to explore here—and one we were essentially unable to explore, in the era when all development had to be AAA and aim at millions of unit sales. But in the world of indie development, exploration and experimentation at lower budgets, aimed at a niche audience of players, are entirely feasible.

So get to work.

About the Author

Greg Costikyan has designed more than thirty commercially published board, role-playing, computer, online, social, and mobile games, including five Origins Awards winners; is an inductee into the Adventure Gaming Hall of Fame; and is the recipient of the IGDA's Maverick Award for "tireless promotion of independent games." At present, he is a senior game designer at Boss Fight Entertainment. He is the author of *Uncertainty in Games* (MIT Press, 2013). He has lectured on game design at universities including the Copenhagen ITU, Helsinki University of Art & Design, RPI, and SUNY Stony Brook, and his writings are used in game studies course across the globe. In addition to academic publications, he has written on games, game design, and game industry business issues for publications including the *Wall Street Journal Interactive*, the *New York Times*, *Salon*, *Game Developer Magazine*, and *Gamasutra*. He founded the NYC chapter of the IGDA, and is the author of four published science fiction novels. His personal website may be found at <www.costik.com>.

Note

1. In the case of *X-COM: UFO*, explicitly so; Julian Gollop says he was inspired by *Sniper!* (1973).

CIVILIAN CASUALTIES: SHIFTING PERSPECTIVE IN *THIS WAR OF MINE*

Kacper Kwiatkowski

This War of Mine (*TWoM*) (2014) is a videogame developed by 11 bit studios S. A. for PC, with versions planned for other platforms. I am responsible for part of the game's design, story, and writing. The game is based on an original concept by the company's CEO, Grzegorz Miechowski, and is developed under the direction of Michał Drozdowski (design director), Przemysław Marszał (art direction), and Bartosz Brzostek (technical direction). The leaders are Rafał Włosek (lead designer), Dominik Zieliński (lead artist), and Grzegorz Mazur (lead programmer). The story and writing were handled by Maciej Skóra, Wojciech Setlak, and myself, with contributions from the rest of the design team.

TWoM aims for a different approach than most of the games utilizing war settings: it focuses on the civilians affected by the conflict and their struggle to survive. In the chapter, I will explain the team's approach to this premise and how *TWoM* differs from other wargames. I will also break down the process of designing the game to present the means used to achieve this specific goal.

Portraying War in Fiction

War has been present in video games since the beginning of their history. It is worth noting that even the first widely known video game had "war" in its title: *Spacewar* (1962).[1] However, in this chapter I will discuss only the wargames inspired by modern and historical conflicts, passing over explicitly fantastic settings. In this formulation, the first notable title is most likely *Tank*, a simple arcade game released in 1974. Since then, war-inspired games have evolved along with the whole industry, spawning countless different genres and utilizing various settings, themes, and levels of fidelity. Some of the most popular genres include real-time strategy games (e.g., *Company of Heroes* 2006), real-time tactical games (e.g., the *Commandos* series [1998]), grand strategy games such as the *Total War* series e.g., *Shogun* [2001]), or shooters (e.g., the *Call of Duty* series [2003]), to name a few. However, despite all this diversity, the games have been homogenous in their focus on certain military aspects, with the player always directly involved in the conflict in one of a few conventional roles: a soldier (or more specifically, a "hero-soldier," as present in popular military shooters), commander (mostly in strategy games) or a rebel (e.g., *Homefront* [2011], a first-person shooter set in an alternate reality during a conflict between the United States and Korea). They typically do not go beyond simple power fantasies and the theme of "winning the war," with the indirect, nonmilitary aspects of conflicts mostly omitted.

It is worth noticing that such homogeneity is not present in film, literature, or comic books. Dozens of works revolve around themes that are rare or nonexistent in video games, such as mass murder (in *Maus*, a graphic novel), rape (in *Róża*, a Polish film), the absurdity of war (in *Catch-22*, a novel) and PTSD (in *Waltz With Bashir*, an animated documentary film). The survival of civilians is an especially well-covered topic, with laudable examples from many different media; e.g., *The Pianist* (2002; film), *Grave of the Fireflies* (1988; animated film), and *DMZ* (Wood 2005–12; a seventy-two-issue comic book series set during a fictional civil war that has turned the island of Manhattan into a demilitarized zone).

Describing *This War of Mine*

This War of Mine acknowledges the lack of thematic diversity in war video games. It is introduced with a trailer video that first shows soldiers fighting but then quickly switches to civilians hiding in a demolished building.[2] This approach is also emphasized by the game's tagline: "In war, not everyone is a soldier."

The experience of "normal people's struggle to survive the war" lies at core of *TWoM* and defines its gameplay. Therefore, early on the designers decided not to depict any specific genre, but to choose elements from different genres that would reinforce this experience. We used features of strategy and tactical games (resource management), roguelikes (permanent death), sims (characters), stealth games (danger avoidance) and adventure games (world-interaction). Moreover, we did not want it to be a plot-driven game, and so we relied more on game mechanics, a high level of player freedom, and randomized content in order to create emergent stories.

Is *This War of Mine* even a wargame? It occurs in a war setting and it incorporates strategy elements; however, it does not reflect military operations, a plausible requirement in the common understanding of "wargame." Here I would like to refer to Wikipedia's entry on wargaming, which uses "conflict simulator" as a synonym for "wargame." It also states: "Although there may be disagreements as to whether a particular game qualifies as a wargame or not, a general consensus exists that all such games must explore and represent some feature or aspect of human behavior directly bearing on the conduct of war, even if the game subject itself does not concern organized violent conflict or warfare."

Under this definition, *TWoM* qualifies as a wargame, since it simulates a particular aspect of the conflict and represents features of human behavior related to it, although it does not concern warfare directly.

Figure 58.1

A still image from the game's trailer. This view appears right after an image of soldiers fighting on the battlefield and is followed by the tagline, "In war not everyone is a soldier."

Building the City at War

The initial inspiration for the game was the article "One Year in Hell,"[3] whose anonymous author allegedly survived a year in a city under siege during the Bosnian War (which ran from April 6, 1992, to December 14, 1995). We realized that this subject never appeared in video games, although interactive media seemed to be especially suitable to deliver a message about real-life survival. However, this delicate subject had to be taken in a serious, realistic manner, so we decided to conduct broad research of various conflicts throughout history, focusing especially on city sieges and how they affect the lives of the residents.

During the early phase of the research, we considered basing the game on an actual historical conflict, but this idea was quickly abandoned, so as not to create the impression that the game was speaking about that specific event exclusively. So it was decided to create a fictional city under siege that would contain elements of the various conflicts that we researched. The difficulty of the task lay in the balance between making the setting interesting yet unspecific.

The most useful information was drawn from events in Bosnia, Kosovo (February 28, 1998–June 11, 1999), Chechnya (December 11, 1994–August 31, 1996 and August 26, 1999–April 15, 2009), Libya (January 5–October 23, 2011) and Syria (March 15, 2011–present). We decided mostly to rely on modern conflicts because of how well they are documented and to let the audience more easily identify with the events. However, to some extent we were also inspired by events further in the past. As our studio is located in Warsaw, Poland, we are strongly influenced by the stories about the Powstanie Warszawskie (Warsaw Uprising: August 1–October 2, 1944) and the Robinson Crusoes of Warsaw.[4]

But the biggest inspiration for *This War of Mine* was the siege of Sarajevo (April 5, 1992–February 19, 1996), the longest modern siege at almost four years, in which approximately 14,000 people died. We studied books about the fates of the people during the siege, such as Barbara Demick's *Logavina Street: Life and Death in a Sarajevo Neighborhood* (2012) and Zlata Filipović's *Zlata's Diary* (1993), as well as numerous other interviews and articles. We were also in contact with a person who lived in besieged Sarajevo as a child, Emir Cerimovic. He played an early version of the game and provided valuable advice as to how to improve its believability.

For the purpose of the development we created a very detailed description of the country where the game takes place and of the historical timeline that led to the conflict the players experience, starting a few centuries in the past. In brief, *TWoM* takes place during a civil war in a city at the center of events that has been under siege for a few years. Most of the buildings are damaged, the streets are empty, and there are shortages of food, water, and electricity. The common people are trapped between the military and the separatists, belonging to neither of the belligerent sides. The game starts at a moment when it is claimed that the war will soon be over, but at the same time the fights are intensifying and the shortages becoming even more severe.

Our goal was to make the city feel real, so even though its significance is meant to be universal, we decided to use subtle cultural touches, mostly inspired by Eastern Europe (including Poland) and the Balkans, for instance in the architecture and the names of the characters.

It is important to emphasize that the detailed story was not created to be a stand-alone feature of the game, but as a way for the team to keep the game-world consistent and to create a basis for events during the game. The player is not required to understand the reasons for the conflict nor the history of the region; however, if they are curious, some of the details can be learned through game content such as character speeches or location-specific notes. This approach reflects how war is often seen by the people whose stories we came across: they did not understand all of the underlying reasons behind the situation they were caught in; what mattered was their day-to-day survival.

Studying the source material, we quickly identified a particular survival strategy that contradicted some of our intuitive assumptions: the importance of a group. Survivors' stories usually spoke about the joint effort of family, friends, or neighborhood. At the same time, divisions often intensify; close groups become even closer, but distrust or even aversion intensifies between different groups.

We were determined to reflect this in the game design. Therefore, from the beginning we rejected the idea of a single protagonist in favor of managing a group. A similar principle was applied to the nonplayable characters (NPCs); the player often encounters other groups similar to the one he or she is responsible for.

The individuals in the player's group are mostly common people such as a teacher, a fireman, a pensioner, and a student. Some of them may stand out, like a deserter or a celebrity, but none is capable of surviving on his own. The case is similar with the NPCs: the player encounters families and groups of friends and neighbors, rarely gangs or the military. The goal was to create a basic simulation of a real city during the conflict.

We came across a huge amount of real human stories—stories of loss, theft, and murder, but also about the will to live, the kindness of strangers and unimaginable relief—and decided to incorporate them into the game's narrative. For example, one of the player characters is a football player, who tells a story of how an amateur football match boosted morale during the war; this is inspired by a particular part of Barbara Demick's *Logavina Street* (1996). Another character was loosely based on the story of Delila Lacevic, described in the same book (see also Demick 2012). She lost her parents in Sarajevo, and her younger brother was evacuated to the United States; her biggest motivation during the war was a plan also to move to the United States.

Figure 58.2
Looking for supplies in remote locations is an important part of the game. One of them is an abandoned supermarket that is said to be often visited by soldiers.

Of course, our inspirations were not limited to stories from Sarajevo. There are references to the Warsaw Uprising, such as the notes that can be discovered in some of the locations; during the uprising there was a custom of preparing brief notes to relatives and friends that were often delivered by the Boy Scouts.

A whole game mechanic was designed around the notion of neighborhood solidarity. In the game, the player's shelter is often visited by neighbors—for instance, a person who needs medicine for a relative, or someone who wants to share the firewood he got from chopping trees in his garden.

Ultimately, our most important conclusion from the research was that people act very similarly no matter when or where a conflict takes place. But when fundamental human needs are in question, people tend to change, and many of the social rules applicable during peace are suspended.

Designing the Civilian Struggle

We determined early on not to present every atrocity we could think of. We avoided delving into certain details, knowing that they might not only fail to support the main theme, but might even distract from it. For instance, we were often asked by the media if we were going to include specific kinds of violence. "Will you see a rape in this game? Can you kill a child? Can you eat another person?"—those are some questions we encountered. Internally, these kinds of controversial subjects were frequently debated in order to specify where the line should be drawn. Some of those topics were rejected just because our research failed to prove them truthful; in this way, we decided not to include cannibalism, for instance.

However, the decision was not so simple with topics such as rape or the suffering of children. Ultimately, we decided that the game did not need to be explicit in order to deliver its message, and so we did not choose to include literal sexual violence, gore, or the killing of children. On the other hand, we came up with more subtle ways of handling some of those subjects so that their importance is maintained, such as including them in character dialogue or creating offscreen scenes.

We were trying to find gameplay means that would represent aspects common to many conflicts, avoiding those that might create the impression that the game is only speaking about a particular event. One of the most visible of these decisions, reflecting the lifestyles of people during the conflicts we researched, was the clear division of the game into two phases, day and night.

During the day the player manages a group of survivors, usually three to four, each distinctive, often with particular skills usable for the group. At the beginning of the game, they have just found a shelter, a ruined building where they plan to stay until the war is over. They are not leaving it during the day for fear of the military presence, especially snipers. The game image in this phase is two-dimensional, showing the building and the characters from the side. The player selects characters and appoints tasks in real time.

This phase is mostly dedicated to the characters' basic needs: eating, treating wounds, and resting. In game design terms, it is a resource management phase, in which the resources are the characters, the items possessed (such as food, medication, or bandages), and time. The other important daily activity is improving the building, which at the beginning is very ill-equipped. The characters can use gathered materials to build various items, such as beds, stoves, or heating sources. In the morning, as well, the group may be visited by another character, such as a neighbor in need of help or offering an opportunity to barter.

The choice of activities available for the player during this phase reflects how the lives of people during such events is frequently reduced to minimal, primitive forms, where even satisfying basic human needs becomes a challenge.

The night phase starts in a different mode, a single menu screen from which nightly tasks for the group are chosen. Characters can sleep, but someone can also be assigned to guard the place in case of the arrival of aggressive groups. A special kind of assignment is sending a person to visit a chosen place in the city; this decision results in switching again to two-dimensional real-time mode to allow the player to control a chosen character in a remote location such as another house, a public building, a ruin, or other city location.

The most important task during such a trip is to find usable items such as food, medication, or building components. There are many methods to acquire these, including trading, extracting from the ruins, stealing, killing, or being rewarded for helping others. The freedom to make those kinds of decisions is an important feature of the game, and I will elaborate on this later in the chapter.

This part of the game is probably the most difficult. Each time a character goes in search of supplies

he can be wounded or even killed, and he might not be able to bring home anything useful. This phase is strongly influenced by the stories of real survivors struggling to find basic supplies, sometimes being forced to act in ways they would not accept during peacetime.

A freedom to make one's own decisions is an essential part of the game experience and affects most of its aspects. The player decides whose needs come first among the group. They choose the places to visit for supplies and the way in which they acquire them. It is possible to approach other characters in a variety of ways, including trading, violence, scaring them off, helping them, or just ignoring them. The game does not prompt the player to do one thing instead of another.

On a mechanical level, the interactions between player characters and NPCs are simple and clear, relying mostly on action instead of dialogue. Invading a stranger's house with a weapon will most likely make him run away or try to expel the player character. Showing him one's own goods might convince him to trade. When assaulted, he can call for help from the other inhabitants. Many of these behaviors are the emergent result of a complex AI system, arising from the interaction of place (e.g., private house or abandoned ruin), character (e.g., civilian or soldier), and player behavior.

The consequences of these decisions vary. The player can visibly affect not only the lives of the characters they control, but also the NPCs. An attacked person may fight back, killing someone may cause his family to collapse from grief, stealing food can cause someone to starve. On the other hand, the player can save lives, help people in need, or just rely on the simple exchange of goods and favors.

One particular mechanic is extremely important in the decision system: the characters' conscience mechanic. Each character has a predefined personality type and reacts differently to different events. Most people, for example, are not comfortable with hurting another person; doing so will deeply affect their mood and may even lead to depression, which causes instability and the lack of will to perform tasks. On the other hand, there are particularly empathetic people who gain additional motivation from helping others, even when they do so at their own cost. So making decisions that are consistent with or opposed to the character's personality introduces another type of consequence, one that lies within characters' psyche and is manifested by the ways in which they speak and act. This mechanic reflects how war forces people to make uncomfortable decisions and how they face their outcomes.

In the real world, some people change forever by being forced to make hard decisions during wartime, and the same can happen to characters in *TWoM*. A character's psyche is a complex system that in extreme cases can experience trauma. A traumatized character can act in unexpected and unpredictable ways, hurting himself or others, leaving the group, or even experiencing a permanent personality change—for example, an empathetic person can become

Figure 58.3
A view of the shelter, where the player characters are living. Here the player manages supplies, taking care of the characters' needs and crafting items using gathered materials.

indifferent to events that would normally move him or her.

These sorts of character changes are examples of the sort of irreversible factors that can lead to the player's failure. *This War of Mine* is structured in a similar way to many "roguelike" games; early on, we decided that the game should be hard and unforgiving in order to worthily represent the subject of wartime hardship. If all the player characters die, the game is over, without the option to use an "extra life" or go back to a previous saved game. On the other hand, each playthrough is noticeably different, with different groups of survivors, other locations to visit, and other opposing groups. Each time the game begins, it builds a new war scenario that requires a different approach and generates dozens of new emergent stories.

The Message

Since the game was announced, the team has often been asked why we decided to create such a game. The answer is that the game acknowledges war as an ever-present sociocultural phenomenon, saying to the audience that "It could happen to *you*" and asking the question, "What would *you* do in this situation?" Not as a hero-soldier, not as a commander or a rebel—as *you*, an ordinary person within a violent conflict. Every step of the design process described in this chapter is focused on this question, and the goal of creating a credible war situation populated with real people, on the behalf of whom players can make their own decisions and draw their own conclusions.

But there is also a message on another level, a meta-message about video games as a medium. *This War of Mine* attempts to prove that the game industry is already mature enough to expand the thematic spectrum and raise subjects that were not present in games before. Games are not only capable of doing so, but they also have the potential to do it better than other media. The basic ability to let members of the audience make their own choices is a powerful narrative tool that can induce emotions not available in passive media. Guilt, pride, remorse, or zeal, to name a few, can be utilized to provide experiences exclusively found in interactive media.

In recent years numerous games have been released that successfully use the medium to raise serious, mature subjects: *Papers, Please* (2013), about an immigration officer in a totalitarian regime; *Dear Esther* (2012), about loss of a loved one; *To the Moon* (2011), about dealing with death. Other games besides *TWoM* also speak of war in a nontrivialized way, such as *Valiant Hearts: The Great War* (2014), which focuses on the characters' personal stories instead of the warfare, or *Sunset*, an upcoming exploration game that lets the player, as an ordinary housekeeper, influence the course of a revolution. *Spec Ops: The Line* (2012) is superficially a military shooter, but it surprises with thematic depth and an underlying critique of the genre.

The announcement of *This War of Mine* met with a powerful response from audiences and the media, often provoking discussion about the role of video games in modern culture and the tropes of popular wargames. In this context, it was mentioned by *The Guardian* (Stuart 2014), *The Verge* (Webster 2014), *Edge*

(Wordsworth 2014), and *Kotaku* (Totilo 2014a and 2014b). Some of the comments were especially interesting and insightful, particularly those appearing on Kotaku. To our relief, most of the commenters understood our unusual approach and expressed their support:

Reader Ellen J. Miller: "There's a rich field out there for powerful marriages of game design and the realities of war. The possibilities of something based around Dragon of Bosnia Street, Sarajevo for instance as you try and go about your daily business even when that has to take you through Sniper Alley."

Reader Solidus: "I only recently watched 'The Pianist' and after the credits rolled I couldn't help but imagine the possibilities of stories to be told. Real or fiction, putting the gamer in a miserable time of death and destruction with a gun pointed at him, not in his hand, would give a new perspective. I'm so sick of the average hero american soldier for war games."

A minority of comments expressed lack of interest or disapproval. Some commenters honestly admitted that they are not looking for such an experience in a game, like the reader dubbed Lobomobile, who wrote: "I play war games to have fun." We do not condemn this attitude. Since the inception of the idea, we assumed it would not be a game for everyone, and we were prepared to face criticism. However, the general support and understanding of the public strengthened us and inspired further development.

One particular Kotaku commenter, John Keyser (classykeyser) had a particularly big impact on the game. He began by saying: "As a veteran of Operation Phantom Fury, the 2004 assault on the city of Fallujah, I commend 11 Bit Studios for having the balls to develop something like this. Just the concept of this game is profound. It's a sad state of affairs when the idea that war affects real human lives is an innovative one." Later, John shared his story on our website (Keyser 2014) and became a tester and consultant for us. He was impressed with how the game handles emotions and found similarities to his own experience.

Personally, as a game developer, I feel genuine pride that my work reaches beyond sheer entertainment and helps develop a new perception of the medium. And as a gamer, I like to believe that *This War of Mine* is a part of a larger movement that has yet to flourish.

Afterword: The Reception

The game was released on November 14, 2014, primarily on Steam. The reception proved to be much better than expected, with the game recouping its budget in only two days. Both critic and user reviews are mostly positive (at the time of writing, Metacritic shows 82 and 8.4 respectively), and the game was featured outside gaming media, with much focus on its novelty and cultural importance (e.g., in *Wired*, the *Washington Post*, and *Zeit*). Matt Peckham wrote in *Wired*: "The scenarios *This War of Mine* engages are less antiwar than they are actual war stories, and that, I think, is the point: This is what unflinching war looks like from the standpoint of those powerless to stop it, the ones caught in the teeth of the machine without catchy operational monikers to rally behind or celebrated by politicians to usher them home as heroes. The ones whose war this isn't" (Peckham 2014).

Moreover, we were glad to see how well the game was understood by the players and that the design decisions described in this chapter succeeded in inducing the intended experience. The biggest success, in my opinion, is that many players really empathize with the characters and consider the situations emerging in the game in narrative terms, not just as gameplay events. There are countless of such descriptions among Steam reviews; for example, the user Alamist concludes his review with his interpretation of the moment when his character saved a girl from an aggressor:

> Making eye contact with me, the girl screams "Please! Help me!"

To which the man immediately turns and sprays my chest full of lead.

As I lie dying, gasping my final breaths, I see the girl climb up onto some broken carts and jump over the fence. She had escaped. As I fade into darkness, I smile: knowing that that girl will go on to live another day (Alamist 2014).

This kind of reception confirms to me how capable gaming media can be as a narrative device—that the games can be used not only to tell stories, but to let players tell *their* stories. I hope that the success of *This War of Mine* will encourage more creators to explore those capabilities.

About the Author

Mostly a game designer, but sometimes a writer, producer, and programmer, Kacper Kwiatkowski currently co-runs Vile Monarch game studio and works as a game design teacher at Warsaw Film School. With 11 bit studios, he co-created *This War of Mine* (as senior game designer and writer) and *Sleepwalker's Journey* (as project lead and game designer).

Before that, he worked on a number of mobile games for Nawia Games. He was one of the organizers of 2012 and 2013 WGK conferences, held in Gdańsk, Poland. Besides gaming, he is interested in film, music, photography and fitness. <https://twitter.com/TheMimizu>.

Notes

1. Not the very first video game, although it is generally considered the first video game to garner significant recognition.

2. View at <http://youtu.be/pH_tYB_Ntlg>.

3. We could not verify the article's authenticity, but later we compared it with confirmed survivor accounts, which convinced us that its content is believable.

4. The people still hiding in the demolished Warsaw after the failure of the uprising. The most famous of them was Władysław Szpilman, whose story was depicted in the film *The Pianist* (2002).

59 PRACTICING A NEW WARGAME

Mary Flanagan

It seems that games have long been a form of conflict simulation. Some of humanity's oldest games—chess, Go, the Olympic Games—are all ways of modeling and mediating conflict. In contemporary times, computer games were developed right on the very machines used to calculate secret war codes and bombing trajectories. But what if wargames could be something else?

As a kid, I was fascinated with wargames. My cousin was in the US Marine Corps, and when on leave he would describe the wargames that his platoon would play against other platoons and, indeed, against other national militaries from around the world.[1] Call them demos, field exercises, full-scale rehearsals, schemes, maneuvers, simulations, call them costume play in full military getup, these wargames were enacted by troops who meant business. Teams Red and Blue were part of a continuing saga that sounded more exciting than *Star Wars*. Hearing all about such games, I desperately wanted to play too. I pined to track the villains on maps, ferret out perpetrators of espionage, plan sweeps around the periphery, and try my hand at leading the team to a surprise victory with unconventional maneuvers that no one would see coming. I guess that's what you get if you grow up a gamer

and learn of such amazing, all-encompassing play spaces.

I am glad I followed a different path and now make games that have very different aims. But I am still avidly curious about wargaming. I stop by the massive miniatures-ridden battle scenes at GenCon to see tabletop armageddons that would make H. G. Wells envious. I am interested in historical, sci-fi, fantasy, and even hypothetical conflict simulations and have attended wargame role-playing groups and conferences.

I am also engaged in systems design, and surely military simulations are ideal domains for such types of thinking. A few years ago, a friend described the wargames at a nuclear plant, in which she took part as a member of the military. She had to defend the controls at a nuclear reactor while others at her base took on the defense of the layers leading up to this inner sanctum. My friend was stationed on the inside, while the various groups set up their campaign around her. In this scenario, the nuclear reactor was supposed to be under attack by an invading army. The simulation planners did not think to model the situation using lone warrior terrorists, differently trained teams, or individuals with something to prove—instead, the simulation focused on a massive invading army, complete with tanks and even a front line.

Through the course of our conversation it became clear that what was modeled was truly an outdated mode of conflict. The nuclear plant warzone sounded much like the description of the British redcoats lined up in the field during the US Revolutionary War. Rules of engagement change through time, and this example represents a wargame at its "gamey-est"—it didn't resemble practice for any possible real world event.

The nuclear plant attack scenario makes it clear that whatever we think of wargaming, such games are always tied to highly imagined scenarios and speculative events, and are therefore, at best, power-ful fictions. This is their strength, and also the root of their problem.

We are only as brilliant as the tool sets we have; as the old adage goes, if one has a hammer, then every problem looks like a nail.[2] Surgeons, for example, tend to see answers to health problems through the lens of surgery. Likewise, soldiers are trained using wargames. Wargaming is about negotiating power, about systems modeling, about strategy. The scenar-ios we provide in our games, and the possible out-comes we permit, show us the ways in which we are *capable of thinking*. Thus, if we train our military primarily on two-sided, violence-based conflict sce-narios with one winner, we will tend to frame most conflicts as such, and similarly, we will create cir-cumstances that mirror that training, leading to unresolvable contemporary situations and an out-of-date military.

Indeed, more broadly, through repeated witness to global conflict, military leaders, politicians, and even the public may come to think that armed con-flict is an appropriate (and perhaps the only) answer

to difficult and seemingly unsolvable problems. For war is what we have seen before in the news, it's what we read about in our history books, and it turns out it's what we play in our games.

There are many models for wargames across digi-tal, board game, tabletop, and enacted platforms. I would like to briefly focus on a few that are not easily categorized and perhaps not as well known. For example, there are myriad versions of the classic game of chess.[3] Fans of wargames are perhaps famil-iar with the *Play It by Trust* piece, an interactive chess-board created by provocateur artist and pacifist Yoko Ono. Since its first 1966 iteration, the *Play It by Trust* series of installations has continued to stimulate pro-vocative conversations about wargaming. The prem-ise of her work is simple. All of the pieces are white, as are all the squares on the board. Instructions for players are slim: we are to play as long as we can remember where our pieces lie. Ono's all-white chess erases the distinction between sides and asks the player to approach the game in a different manner from a typical antagonistic stance. It is a model for play that lends itself to thoughts about commonali-ties, not difference. As players reflect on similarities, they are, at least for an instant, part of the whole of humanity; distinctions based on nation-state, race, religion, or language seems to drift away. Perhaps, as Ono's work suggests, the time for taking "sides" is over.

Artist Takako Saito exhibited *Liquid Chess/Smell Chess* in 1975. The game was created from a group of scented vials that players had to smell in order to understand which piece was which scent, then make a move. Saito's scented board game was part of a number of works by Saito and others involved in the Fluxus movement that used multiple senses and emphasized aesthetics and the changeable nature of games, for how long could someone remember a position and a scent?

A quarter-century later, Ruth Catlow developed the digital game *Rethinking Wargames: Three Player Chess* (2003), in response to the Western war against Iraq. Catlow was inspired by street protests in London, in which the "little people," the people on the streets, were saying no to the war. In her version of chess, Catlow crafted a three-player variant in which one player plays as white royals, a second player plays as black royals, and a third player plays as all of the pawns, both black and white. White and black aim to annihilate each other, but the pawns place themselves at risk and attempt to stop the fighting, or at least slow down the violence, so that negotiation might take place. After five nonviolent rounds, the pawns will have won by reducing retaliatory behavior, thus allowing the battlefield to become overgrown with grasses, masking the checkerboard and effectively stopping war. Catlow's *Rethinking Wargames* provides an alternative model of a wargame that introduces a new interested party, the pawns, who know they will bear the brunt of any war in terms of military service, economic challenge, and sacrifice. The mechanics in Catlow's new chess game demonstrate that peace can only come if the "little people" reinvent their role in the peacemaking process, with a balanced effort between all sides.

I make special note of these projects knowing full well that in a volume specifically crafted to document and analyze wargaming, there is the definite risk that you, the reader, might think that these examples aren't "real wargames" at all. They stand out as almost contradictions to stereotypical notions of war play. But think twice before dismissing these atypical games that may make us, as players, feel uncomfortable—we would be wise to take these alternate styles of simulation very seriously. These are not jokes, nor annoying interferences with "real" models of war. The wargames proposed by Ono, Takako, and Catlow are legitimate conflict resolution models that engage players in new ways and should be studied by the wargaming community for modeling new approaches to old problems.

Alternate wargames express the different ways we might begin to see contemporary global challenges, incorporating different modes of problem solving, aesthetics, and nonviolent conflict resolution. It is possible not only to teach such principles, but also to practice them and enact them in our games, making these principles available and repeatable to a wider audience. Such alternative chess examples may provide perhaps the only real solutions that are humane, civilized, and sustainable.

I have not played many wargames in which players literally stop conflict by having a moving aesthetic experience that changes their worldview. I have not played a wargame in which the public acts as a real player in the game, and surprises the powers-that-be with an effective pacifist move.[4] Our models for wargames need to continue to evolve using unusual, creative solutions to problem solving. For example, perhaps games could model negotiations on urban violence and crime with the highly unorthodox and creative strategies used by Antanas Mockus Šivickas, former mayor of Bogotá, Colombia. In the 1990s, he was able to radically change the city and cut crime. He did so through rather untraditional and effective means: he hired mimes to shame drivers at certain lawless intersections, stirring dramatic prosocial behavior shifts and changing the city through these nonviolent, creative tactical performances. He asked his citizens to pay extra voluntary taxes, and, surprisingly, they did: in 2002, the city collected more than three times the revenue it had in 1990. He distributed 350,000 "thumbs up" and "thumbs down" visual cards that the public could use to peacefully show support or discourage antisocial public behavior (Caballero 2004).

Such unusual conflict strategies might be a welcome surprise to wargaming culture. Wargaming has been criticized for using mainstream techniques and for having an overwhelmingly white male player base. It has often modeled quintessential notions of power, domination, nationalism, binary truths, and a sense of correctness or self-righteousness in communicating a single story of history to mirror "true" conflict.

We must look to transcend old conflict models, or we risk perpetuating the damaging myth that there are limited ways of resolving conflicts. If games in some way are a practice for the real world, for rehearsing a way of thinking, we are ill-prepared to solve conflicts in creative ways given the current state of the art that wargaming offers.

Are classic wargaming models popular because they simplify the world? Probably. Are they romanticized and distant from the horrors that real warfare brings? Most certainly. I loved the idea of wargames when I was young because planning tactics, outsmarting the enemy, and "destroying them all" is a fantasy that engages us with human history and myth. Such tales have indeed been a part of the human condition, but so have many others. Finding and fostering alternative models for conflict resolution using social norms or aesthetics is a surprisingly difficult challenge. But ultimately, I don't want to live in a world where there only can be victors lording over the slaughtered, defeated other. I doubt most of us truly do. So how do we find new models?

What will wargames look like with different kinds of rules, with new expectations, with radical strategies and consensus built in? What if their simulation of conflict isn't so much about war as it is about critical thinking and critique from an outsider status? We know that games can change over time.[5] It is vital that game scholars, makers, and players see these familiar models on a continuum of change, so new play forms that model new solutions to our problems can be invented. Our games are constantly evolving, and this means we all have an opportunity, even a responsibility, to evolve with them and push ourselves to model the world we wish to create.

About the Author

Mary Flanagan directs the internationally acclaimed game research laboratory Tiltfactor, the theory/ practice laboratory she founded in 2003. Her books include *reload: rethinking women + cyberculture* (2002), *re:SKIN* (2007), *Critical Play* (2009), and *Values at Play in Digital Games* (2014) with Helen Nissenbaum. Flanagan created the first Internet adventure game for girls and researches and creates socially conscious games and software at Tiltfactor. With collaborator Helen Nissenbaum, she has investigated how games, interactive systems, and online activities can be redesigned to prioritize human values; in this work, they have proven that using humanist principles to shape software development and guide the game design process is a process of innovation. Flanagan is the Sherman Fairchild Distinguished Professor in Digital Humanities at Dartmouth College.

Notes

1. I have changed my personal relationships to those mentioned in this chapter to ensure their privacy.

2. For the debate on the origin of this axiom, visit the "Quote Investigator" website (O'Toole 2014); Gary O'Toole maps quite a lengthy attribution record for this handy expression.

3. I chose chess here as an approachable example. There are many more games beyond chess mods, of course, that can be highly influential new models for wargaming. In particular, I would refer players to Nordic LARPs that position players as prisoners of war or victims of human trafficking, simulations that also question the traditional logic of wargaming. In these, the ideas of binary conflict, taking sides, good and evil, loyalty, and the physical embodied experiences of war become the subject of extreme focus.

4. Surprisingly, these things have happened in real life. Recall instances where the singing of Christmas carols temporarily halted a war (World War I) or where massive peace demonstrations changed a nation (1930s India).

5. As we know now, rules for chess have been much altered through the centuries, with the queen introduced in medieval Europe and changing its power status over time (Yalom 2004).

ACKNOWLEDGMENTS AND PERMISSIONS

Pat and Matthew would like to thank all of the contributors to this book, who gave generously of their time and ideas; also Doug Sery, Susan Buckley, and everyone at MIT Press; Raiford Guins and Henry Lowood for inducting this book into their "Game Histories" series; our editorial assistant, Jacques Plante, for her invaluable eye for detail; Timothy Wilkie for the transcription of Thomas Schelling's speech; and Nathan Dize for translating Laurent Closier's chapter.

Matthew would also like to thank Kari Kraus for lovingly supporting his gaming (and game collection); as well as everyone who has ever rolled dice with him—you know who you are.

Pat would like to thank his playtesters: Paul Bachleitner, Jon Cazares, Hetal Dalal, Amanda Kudalis, T. J. Kudalis, Allana Olson, J. J. Plude, Zvie Razieli, Joseph Scrimshaw, Tim Uren, Nathan Wardrip-Fruin, and of course, Carrie Rainey.

Unless otherwise noted, all images are used by permission of the author of the associated chapter, or are reprinted under fair use practice. Images from the following games are reprinted by permission of GMT Games: *Combat Commander: Pacific*, *Empire of the Sun*, *Here I Stand*, *Operation Dauntless*, *Paths of Glory*, *Sekigahara*, *Twilight Struggle*, *Virgin Queen*, *Wing Leader*. The *A Most Dangerous Time* map is reprinted by permission of Multi-Man Publishing. In Elizabeth Losh's chapter, figure 1 is reprinted with permission of Getty Images, figure 2 with permission of the Milton Caniff estate, and figure 3 with permission of the RAND Corporation, which are the original source and copyright holder. In John Prados's chapter, the *Third Reich* photo is by Matthew Kirschenbaum.

Alexander R. Galloway's "Debord's Nostalgic Algorithm" originally appeared in *Culture Machine* 10 (2009): 131–156, and is reprinted by permission of the author.

Thomas Schelling's chapter was originally presented as the 2014 Connections conference keynote address. The video of the speech can be seen at <https://www.copy.com/s/ZtjO7awE6KZk>. It has been slightly reworked for this volume.

Jenny Thompson's "War Re-created: Twentieth-Century War Reenactors and the Private Event" is adapted from her book *War Games: Inside the World of Twentieth-Century War Reenactors* (Washington, DC: Smithsonian Books, 2004) and is reprinted by permission of the author. The photographs in this chapter are by Jenny Thompson.

REFERENCES

Abt, Clark. (1970). *Serious Games*. New York: Viking.

Ackerman, Spencer. (2011). Eye Spy: Monocle Gives Commandos Drone Vision. *Wired*, May 19, 2011, accessed January 19, 2015. <http://www.wired.com/2011/05/eye-spy-monocle-gives-commandos-drone-vision>.

Ackerman, Spencer. (2012). After Taking SEALs Hollywood, Navy Slams Commandos for Videogame. *Wired*, November 9, 2012, accessed January 19, 2015. <http://www.wired.com/dangerroom/2012/11/seal-video-game>.

Ackerman, Spencer, and Noah Shachtman. (2012). Almost 1 in 3 U. S. Warplanes Is a Robot. *Wired*, January 9, 2012, accessed January 19, 2015. <http://www.wired.com/2012/01/drone-report>.

Ackoff, Russell L. (1977). The Corporate Rain Dance. *The Wharton Magazine* (Winter): 36–41.

Adamson, John. (2003). England Without Cromwell. In *Virtual History: Alternatives and Counterfactuals*, edited by Niall Ferguson, 91–124. London: Pan.

Advanced Training Methods Research Unit. (2004). *Symposium on PC-Based Simulations and Gaming for Military Training*. RP 2005–01, ARI, October.

Agamben, Giorgio. (2002). Difference and Repetition: On Guy Debord's Films. In *Guy Debord and the Situationist International: Texts and Documents*, edited by Tom McDonough, 313–319. Cambridge, MA: MIT Press.

Agamben, Giorgio. (2006). Repetition and Stoppage—Debord in the Field of Cinema. In *Girum Imus Nocte et Consumimur Igni—The Situationist International (1957–1972)*, edited by Stefan Zweifel, Juri Steiner, and Heinz Stahlhut, 36–38. Basel, Switzerland: Museum Tingley.

Alamist (2014). Reviews: This War of Mine. *Steam*, last modified December 6, 2014. <http://steamcommunity.com/id/alamist/recommended/282070>.

Albert, Jason. (2014). In the World of Role-playing War Games, Volko Ruhnke Has Become a Hero. *The Washington Post*, January 10, 2014 <http://www.washingtonpost.com/lifestyle/magazine/in-the-world-of-role-playing-war-games-volko-ruhnke-has-become-a-hero/2014/01/10/a56ac8d6-48be-11e3-bf0c-cebf37c6f484_story.html>.

Allen, John. (1977). The Use of Simulators: A New Thrust in the Technology Base. *Defense Management Journal* 13 (January): 30–32.

Allen, Myron. (1962). *Morphological Creativity: The Miracle of Your Hidden Brain Power: A Practical*

Guide to the Utilization of Your Creative Potential. Englewood Cliffs, NJ: Prentice-Hall.

Allen, Robertson. (2011). The Unreal Enemy of America's Army. *Games and Culture* 6 (1): 38–60.

Allen, Thomas. (1987). *War Games: The Secret World of the Creators, Players, and Policy Makers Rehearsing World War III Today.* New York: McGraw-Hill.

Allen, William H. (1956). Audio-Visual Materials. *Review of Educational Research* 26 (2): 125–156.

Allison, Graham, and Phillip Zelikow. (1999). *Essence of Decision: Explaining the Cuban Missile Crisis.* New York: Longman.

Allison, Tanine. (2010). The World War II Video Game, Adaptation, and Postmodern History. *Literature Film Quarterly* 38 (3): 183–193.

Alt, Jonathan K., Leroy A. Jackson, David Hudak, and Stephen Lieberman. (2009). The Cultural Geography Model: Evaluating the Impact of Tactical Operational Outcomes on a Civilian Population in an Irregular Warfare Environment. *Journal of Defense Modeling and Simulation* 6 (4): 185–199.

Alter, Robert. (1987). Sterne and the Nostalgia for Reality. In *Laurence Sterne's Tristram Shandy: Modern Critical Interpretations*, edited by Harold Bloom, 87–105. New York: Chelsea House.

Anderson, Craig, Douglas Gentile, and Katherine Buckley. (2007). *Violent Video Game Effects on Children and Adolescents: Theory, Research, and Public Policy.* Oxford: Oxford University Press.

Anderson, Jon R. (2013). "America's Army: Proving Grounds" out Today. *Army Times*, August 29, 2013, accessed January 19, 2015. <http://www.armytimes.com/article/20130829/OFFDUTY02/308290054>.

Andlinger, G. R. (1958a). Business Games—Play One! *Harvard Business Review* 36 (2): 115–125.

Andlinger, G. R. (1958b). Looking Around: Evolution in Which Business Gaming Finds Itself Today. *Harvard Business Review* 36 (July–August): 147–148.

Anker, Peder. (2007). Buckminster Fuller as Captain of Spaceship Earth. *Minerva* 45:428–430.

Antley, Jeremy. (2012). Going Beyond the Textual in History. *Journal of Digital Humanities* 1 (2): 57–63.

Antley, Jeremy. (2013). *Thoughts from the Peasant Muse.* Amazon Digital Services, Inc.

Aoi, Chiyuki, Cedric de Coning, and Ramesh Thakur. (2007). *Unintended Consequences of Peacekeeping Operations.* Tokyo: United Nations University.

Apperley, Tom. (2014). Modding the Historians' Code: Historical Verisimilitude and the Counterfactual Imagination. In *Playing with the Past: Video Games and the Simulation of History*, edited by Matthew Wilhelm Kapel and Andrew B. R. Elliot, 185–196. New York: Bloomsbury.

Appleget, Jeff. (2011). *PSOM Overview and Peacekeeping Operations Assessment Using PSOM.* Monterey, CA: US Naval Postgraduate School, accessed December 19, 2014. <https://calhoun.nps.edu/handle/10945/30745>.

Aristotle. (1998). *Nicomachean Ethics.* Oxford: Oxford University Press.

Arkin, Ronald. (2010). *The Case for Ethical Autonomy in Unmanned Systems.* Atlanta: Georgia Institute of Technology, accessed January 11, 2015. <http://hdl.handle.net/1853/36516>.

Armed Forces Management. (1963). The Growing Role of Simulators. *Armed Forces Management* 9 (8): 47–48.

Arnspiger, V. C. (1936). The Educational Talking Picture. *Journal of Educational Sociology* 10 (3): 143–150.

Arquilla, John, and David F. Ronfeldt. (1997). *In Athena's Camp: Preparing for Conflict in the Information Age.* Santa Monica, CA: RAND Corporation.

Arvold, Alan R. (n.d.). A Comprehensive Index to PanzerBlitz, accessed January 13, 2015. <http://grognard.com/info1/pbartrev.html>.

Atari. (1983). *APX/Atari Program Exchange Product Catalog: Fall Edition 1983. Internet Archive,* accessed January 13, 2015. <https://archive.org/details/Atari_Program_Exchange_catalog_Fall_1983>.

Attig, J. C. (1967). Use of Games as a Teaching Technique. *Social Studies* 58 (January): 25–29.

Autesserre, Séverine. (2014). *Peaceland: Conflict Resolution and the Everyday Politics of International Intervention.* Cambridge: Cambridge University Press.

Avalon Hill. (1964). Midway—Newest Battle Game! *GEN* 1 (3): 1–2.

Avalon Hill. (1965). General McAuliffe Added to Advisory Staff. *GEN* 1 (6): 1–2.

Avalon Hill. (1967a). The Avalon Hill Philosophy—Part 3. *GEN* 4 (1): 2–4.

Avalon Hill. (1967b). Cover Story. *GEN* 4 (1): 2.

Avalon Hill. (1970). Avalon Hill Philosophy—Part 24: Why PanzerBlitz? *GEN* 7 (4): 2–3.

Avalon Hill. (1976). Avalon Hill Philosophy—Part 53. *GEN* 12 (5): 2.

Avalon Hill. (1980). The General: Index and Company History, 1952–1980. Volume 1-Volume 16. Baltimore, MD: Avalon Hill.

Avalon Hill. (1988). The Ultimate Wargame. *GEN* (Special Issue): 59.

Avedon, Elliot M., and Brian Sutton-Smith, eds. (1971). *The Study of Games.* New York: John Wiley and Sons.

Aylward, Frank. (1993). Nominations for Allied Combat Commander of the GWA. *On the Wire* 4: 5.

Bacevich, Andrew J. (2005). *The New American Militarism: How Americans are Seduced by War.* Oxford: Oxford University Press.

Bacevich, Andrew. (2013). *The New American Militarism: How Americans Are Seduced by War. Updated edition.* Oxford: Oxford University Press.

Bacon, Reginald. (1940). *From 1900 Onward.* London: Hutchinson.

Bandry-Scubbi, Anne, and Peter de Voogd, eds. (2013). *Hilarion's Asse: Laurence Sterne's Tristram Shandy.* Newcastle upon Tyne, UK: Cambridge Scholars Publishing.

Banks, Iain M. (1987). *Consider Phlebas.* London: Macmillan.

Banks, Iain M. (1988). *The Player of Games.* London: Macmillan.

Banks, Iain. (1993). *Complicity.* London: Little, Brown.

Banks, Iain. (2007). *The Steep Approach to Garbadale.* London: Little, Brown.

Barbrook, Richard (2014). *Class Wargames: Ludic Subversion against Spectacular Capitalism.* New York: Minor Compositions/Autonomedia.

Barker, P. (1979). *Wargame Rules for Armoured Warfare at Company and Battalion Battle Group Level 1950–1985.* Worthing, UK: WRG Ltd., Flexiprint Ltd.

Barnes, D. S. (1963). A Decade of Missile Control Simulation. *Flight International* 83 (March): 437.

Barringer, Richard, and Barton Whaley (1965). The MIT Political-Military Gaming Experience. *ORBIS: A Journal of World Affairs* 9 (2): 437–458.

Barron, Frank. (1963). *Creativity and Psychological Health*. Princeton, NJ: D. Van Nostrand.

Barthes, Roland. (1985). The Reality Effect. In *The Rustle of Language*, translated by R. Howard, 141–148. New York: Farrar, Straus & Giroux.

Barton, Keith C., and Linda S. Levstik. (2004). *Teaching History for the Common Good*. Mahwah, NJ: Lawrence Erlbaum.

Barzun, Jacques. (1960). The Cults of "Research" and "Creativity." *Harper's* 221 (1325): 69–74.

Bauer, Richard. (1970a). Thoughts on *Strategy I*—Part 1. *S&T Supplement* 3: 7–11.

Bauer, Richard. (1970b). More Thoughts on *Strategy I*. *S&T Supplement* 4: 18–22.

Bassford, Christopher. (1993). Jomini and Clausewitz: Their Interaction. *The Clausewitz Homepage*, accessed August 31, 2013. <www.clausewitz.com/readings/Bassford/Jomini/JOMINIX.htm>.

Baudry, A. (1914). *The Naval Battle*. London: Hugh Rees Ltd.

Bayer, Martin. (2006). Virtual Violence and Real War: Playing War in Computer Games: The Battle with Reality. In *Cyberwar, Netwar and the Revolution in Military Affairs*, edited by Edward F. Halpin, Philippa Trevorrow, David Webb, and Steve Wright, 31. New York: Palgrave Macmillan.

Beal, Scott A., and Richard E. Christ. (2004). *Training Effectiveness Evaluation of the [ICT] Full Spectrum Command Game*. TR 1140, ARI, January.

Becker, Jo, and Scott Shane. (2012). Secret "Kill List" Proves a Test of Obama's Principles and Will. *New York Times*, May 29, 2012, accessed January 11, 2015. <http://www.nytimes.com/2012/05/29/world/obamas-leadership-in-war-on-al-qaeda.html?pagewanted=all>.

Becker-Ho, Alice, and Guy Debord. (2006). *Le Jeu de la Guerre: Relevé des Positions Successives de Toutes les Forces au Cours d'une Partie*. Paris: Gallimard.

Becker-Ho, Alice, and Guy Debord. (2007). *A Game of War*. Translated by D. Nicholson-Smith. London: Atlas Press.

Beebe, James. (2001). *Rapid Assessment Process: An Introduction*. Lanham, MD: AltaMira Press.

Beesly, Patrick. (1983). *Room 40: British Naval Intelligence 1914–18*. London: Hamish Hamilton.

Belanich, James, Daragh E. Sibley, and Kara L. Orvis. (2004). *Instructional Characteristics and Motivational Features of a PC-Based Game*. RR 1822, ARI, April.

Bell, Daniel. (1964). Twelve Modes of Prediction, a Preliminary Sorting of Approaches in the Social Sciences. *Daedalus* 93 (3): 845–880.

Belletto, Steven. (2011). *No Accident, Comrade: Chance and Design in Cold War American Narratives*. Oxford: Oxford University Press.

Bennett, Peter G., and Michael R. Dando. (1979). Complex Strategic Analysis: A Hypergame Study of the Fall of France. *Journal of the Operational Research Society* 30: 23–32.

Berg, Richard, James Dunnigan, David Isby, Stephen Patrick, and Redmond Simonsen. (1977). *Wargame Design: The History, Production and Use of Conflict Simulation Games. Strategy & Tactics Staff Study Number 2.* New York: Simulations Publications Incorporated.

Berkun, Mitchell. (1964). Performance Decrement Under Psychological Stress. *Human Factors* 6 (1): 21–30.

Berman, Eli, Michael Callen, Joseph Fletre, and Jacob Shapiro. (2011). Do Working Men Rebel? Insurgency and Unemployment in Afghanistan, Iraq, and the Philippines. *Journal of Conflict Resolution* 55:4.

Bettner, Steven M. (1994). Simulation: Past, Present, and Future. *Defense Electronics* 26 (11): 74–75.

Biddle, Stephen. (2004). *Military Power: Explaining Victory and Defeat in Modern Battle.* Princeton: Princeton University Press.

Bizzocchi, Jim, and Josh Tanenbaum. (2011). Well Read. In *Well Played 3.0: Video Games, Value and Meaning,* edited by Drew Davidson. Pittsburgh, PA: ETC Press.

Black, Jeremy. (2008). *What If? Counterfactualism and the Problem of History.* London: Social Affairs Unit.

Blackett, Patrick Maynard Stuart. (1962). *Studies of War: Nuclear and Conventional.* New York: Hill and Wang.

Blackmore, Tim. (2005). *War X: Human Extensions in Battlespace.* Toronto: University of Toronto Press.

Blair, Clay, Jr. (1996). *Hitler's U-Boat War: The Hunters, 1939-1942.* New York: Modern Library.

Blair, Clay, Jr. (1998). *Hitler's U-Boat War: The Hunted, 1942-1945.* New York: Modern Library.

Blank, J. A. (1991). A Remote Underwater Closure of Kerr Hollow Quarry. Paper presented at the Fourth Topical Meeting on Robotics and Remote Systems, Albuquerque, NM, February 25–27, 1991.

Bloomberg. (2014). Games Workshop Group Plc (GAW: London). *Bloomberg Business Week,* June 30, 2014, accessed June 30, 2014. <http://investing.businessweek.com/research/stocks/snapshot/snapshot.asp?ticker=GAW:LN>.

Bloomfield, Lincoln, and Norman Padelford. (1959). Teaching Note: Three Experiments in Political Gaming. *American Political Science Review* 53:4.

Body, Howard, and Colin Marston. (2011). The Peace Support Operations Model: Origins, Development, Philosophy, Support. *Journal of Defense Modeling and Simulation* 8:2.

Boehm, William R. (1954). *Evaluation of the US Naval Academy Educational Television System as a Teaching Aid.* Annapolis, MD: US Naval Academy.

Bogost, Ian. (2006). *Unit Operations: An Approach to Videogame Criticism.* Cambridge: MIT Press.

Bogost, Ian. (2007). *Persuasive Games: The Expressive Power of Videogames.* Cambridge, MA: MIT Press.

Bolaño, Roberto. (2008). *The Savage Detectives.* Reprint edition. Translated by N. Wimmer. New York: Picador.

Bolaño, Roberto. (2009). *2666.* Reprint edition. Translated by N. Wimmer. New York: Picador.

Bolaño, Roberto. (2012). *The Third Reich.* Translated by N. Wimmer. New York: Farrar, Straus and Giroux.

Bomba, Tyrone. (1981). Origins 1981 Report. *Campaign* 105.

Boocock, Sarane. (1967). Games Change What Goes on in Classroom. *Nation's Schools* 80 (October): 94–95.

Boocock, Sarane, and E. O. Schild, eds. (1968). *Simulation Games in Learning.* Beverly Hills, CA: Sage Publications.

Boot, Max. (2003). The New American Way of War. *Foreign Affairs* 82 (4): 41–58.

Boulding, Kenneth. (1964). *The Meaning of the Twentieth Century: The Great Transition.* New York: Harper & Row.

Bourriaud, Nicholas. (2002). *Relational Aesthetics.* Dijon: Les Presses du Réel.

Bourseiller, Christophe. (1996). *Les Maoïstes: La Folle Histoire des Gardes Rouges Français.* Paris: Plon.

Bowden, Mark. (1999). *Black Hawk Down: A Story of Modern War.* New York: Grove Atlantic.

Box, George E. P., and Norman R. Draper. (1987). *Empirical Model-Building and Response Surfaces.* New York: John Wiley & Sons.

Boyer, Mark. (2011). Simulation in International Studies. *Simulation & Gaming* 42 (6): 685–689.

Bracken, Len. (1997). *Guy Debord: Revolutionary.* Venice, CA: Feral House.

Brand, Stewart, ed. (1968–1972). *The Whole Earth Catalogue.* Sausalito, CA: Whole Earth.

Brandt, Marisa. (2014). From the Ultimate Display to the Ultimate Skinner Box: Virtual Reality and the Future of Psychotherapy. In *Media Studies Futures,* edited by Kelly Gates, 518–539. London: Wiley-Blackwell.

Brathwaite, Brenda, and Ian Schreiber. (2008). *Challenges for Game Designers.* New York: Delmar.

Breuer, Johannes, Ruth Festl, and Thorsten Quandt. (2011). In the Army Now—Narrative Elements and Realism in Military First-person Shooters. Paper presented at *DiGRA 2011: Think Design Play,* Utrecht, NL, Utrecht School of the Arts, September 14–17, 2011. <http://www.digra.org/wp-content/uploads/digital-library/11307.54018.pdf>.

Breuer, Johannes, Ruth Festl, and Thorsten Quandt. (2012). Digital War: An Empirical Analysis of Narrative Elements in Military First-person Shooters. *Journal of Gaming & Virtual Worlds* 4 (3): 215–237.

Brewer, Garry D., and Martin Shubik. (1979). *The War Game: A Critique of Military Problem Solving.* Cambridge, MA: Harvard University Press.

Brey, Philip. (1999). The Ethics of Representation and Action in Virtual Reality. *Ethics and Information Technology* 1 (1): 5–14.

Brightman, Hank J., and Melissa K. Dewey. (2014). Trends in Modern War Gaming: The Art of Conversation. *US Naval War College Review* 671:18–30.

Broderick, Damien, and Paul Di Filippo. (2012). *Science Fiction: The 101 Best Novels 1985–2010.* New York: Nonstop Press.

Brooks, John. (2006). *Dreadnought Gunnery and the Battle of Jutland.* London: Routledge.

Brooks, Richard. (1997). *Fred T. Jane: An Eccentric Visionary.* Coulsdon, UK: Jane's Information Group.

Broyles, William, Jr. (1984). Why Men Love War. *Esquire,* May 23, 2014. <http://www.esquire.com/_mobile/blogs/news/why-men-love-war>.

Brynen, Rex. (2010). (Ending) Civil War in the Classroom. *PS, Political Science & Politics* 43 (1): 145–149.

Brynen, Rex. (2012). Connections 2012 AARs. *Wargaming Connection,* July 27, 2012. <https://wargamingcommunity.wordpress.com/2012/07/27/connections-2012-aars>.

Brynen, Rex. (2013a). The "Fuzzy Edges of Wargaming"? Exploring Non-kinetic Conflict Dynamics. *PAXsims,* August 28, 2013. <http://paxsims.wordpress.com/2013/08/28/the-fuzzy-edges-of-wargaming-exploring-non-kinetic-conflict-dynamics>.

Brynen, Rex. (2013b). Reflections on a Humanitarian Policy Simulation. *PAXsims,* April 30, 2013. <https://paxsims.wordpress.com/tag/humanitarian-simulation>.

Brynen, Rex. (2013c). Student Interactive Simulation-writing in Political Science. *PAXsims,* May 8, 2013. <http://paxsims.wordpress.com/2013/05/08/student-interactive-simulation-writing-in-political-science>.

Brynen, Rex. (2014a). Connections 2014—A First Report. *PAXsims,* August 5 2014. <http://paxsims.wordpress.com/2014/08/05/connections-2014-a-first-report>.

Brynen, Rex. (2014b). Teaching About Peace Operations. *International Peacekeeping* 21:4.

Brynen, Rex. (2014c). Viking 14 Peacekeeping Exercises. *PAXsims,* April 12, 2014. <http://paxsims.wordpress.com/2014/04/12/viking-14-peacekeeping-exercise>.

Brynen, Rex, and Gary Milante. (2013). Peacebuilding with Games and Simulations. *Simulation & Gaming* 44 (1): 27–35.

Budiansky, Stephen. (2013). *Blackett's War: The Men Who Defeated the Nazi U-Boats and Brought Science to the Art of Warfare.* New York: Knopf.

Bumiller, Elisabeth. (2010). We Have Met the Enemy and He is PowerPoint. *New York Times*, last modified April 26, 2010. <http://www.nytimes.com/2010/04/27/world/27powerpoint.html?_r=0>.

Burne, Alfred Higgins. (1950). *Battlefields of England.* London: Methuen.

Burns, Shawn, ed. (2013). *War Gamers' Handbook: A Guide for Professional Gamers.* Newport, RI: Defense Automated Printing Office.

Butcher, Jim. (2000). *The Dresden Files* [series]. New York: Penguin.

Butcher, Jim. (2004–9). *Codex Alera* [series]. New York: Ace Books.

Bynum, Terrell Ward. (2006). Flourishing Ethics. *Ethics and Information Technology* 8:157–173.

Caballero, María Cristina. (2004). Academic Turns City into a Social Experiment. *Harvard Gazette*, March 11, 2004. <http://news.harvard.edu/gazette/2004/03.11/01-mockus.html>.

Caillois, Roger. (1961). *Man, Play and Games.* New York: Free Press.

Call, Morris (1997). Small Survey. WWII newsgroup, September 23, 1997.

Call of Duty. (2012). Documentary—Official Call of Duty Black Ops II. *YouTube*, May 2, 2012, accessed January 19, 2015. <http://www.youtube.com/watch?v=Gm5PZGb3OyQ&feature=youtube_gdata_player>.

Call of Duty Franchise Game Sales Statistics. (2014). *Statistic Brain*, February 19, 2014, accessed January 9, 2015. <http://www.statisticbrain.com/call-of-duty-franchise-game-sales-statistics>.

Campbell, Ann. (2006). Tristram Shandy and the Seven Years' War: Beyond the Borders of the Bowling-green. *Shandean* 17:106–120.

Campbell (HumRRO), Charlotte H, Bruce W. Knerr and Donald R. Lampton. (2004). *Virtual Environments for Infantry Soldiers.* Special Report 59, ARI, May.

Campbell, John. (1998). *Jutland: An Analysis of the Fighting.* London: Conway.

Card, Orson Scott. (1985). *Ender's Game.* New York: Tor Books.

Card, Orson Scott. (1989). Gameplay. *Compute (Greensboro)* 104 (January): 12.

Cardullo, Bert. (1995). Enter Dramaturges. In *What Is Dramaturgy?* edited by Bert Cardullo, 3–11. New York: Peter Lang.

Carey, Jacqueline. (2003). *Kushiel's Dart.* New York: Tor Books.

Carley, Kathleen M. (1999). On the Evolution of Social and Organizational Networks. In *Research in the Sociology of Organizations,* Vol. 16: *Networks in and Around Organizations,* edited by Steven B. Andrews and David Knoke, 3–30. Greenwich, CT: JAI Press, Inc.

Carley, Kathleen M., Jeffrey Reminga, Jon Storrick, and Matt De Reno (2009). *ORA User's* Guide 2009: Carnegie Mellon University, School of Computer Science, Institute for Software. *Research, Technical Report CMU-ISR-09-115.* Pittsburgh, PA: Institute for Software Research, School of Computer Science, Carnegie Mellon University.

Carlson, Elliot. (1967). Games in the Classroom. *Saturday Review* 50 (15): 62–64.

Carmack, John. (2002). Re: Definitions of terms. *Slashdot,* January 2, 2002, accessed January 13, 2015. <http://slashdot.org/comments.pl?sid=25551&cid=2775698>.

Carpenter, Clarence. (1953). A Theoretical Orientation for Instructional Film Research. *AV Communication Review* 1 (Winter): 38–52.

Carroll, Lewis. (1871). *Through the Looking Glass.* London: Macmillan.

Carter, Marcus, Martin Gibbs, and Mitchell Harrop. (2014a). Drafting an Army: The Playful Pastime of Warhammer 40,000. *Games and Culture* 9 (2): 122–147.

Carter, Marcus, Mitchell Harrop, and Martin Gibbs. (2014b). The Roll of the Dice in Warhammer 40,000. *Digra: Transactions of the Digital Games Research Association* 1:3. <http://todigra.org/index.php/todigra/article/view/20/31>.

Castells, Manuel. (2001). *The Internet Galaxy: Reflections on the Internet, Business, and Society.* Oxford, New York: Oxford University Press.

Catagnus, E. J., Sgt., Cpl. Edison, B. Z., LCpl. Keeling, J. D., and LCpl. Moon, D. A. (2005). Lessons Learned: Infantry Squad Tactics in Military Operations in Urban Terrain During Operation Phantom Fury in Fallujah, Iraq. *Marine Corps Gazette* 89 (September): 9.

Cavagnaro, Catherine, and John Tiller. (2011). Tipping Points and Models. *International Journal of Intelligent Games and Simulation* 6:5–11.

Cebrowski, Arthur K., and John H. Garstka. (1998). Network-Centric Warfare—Its Origin and Future. *Proceedings Magazine* 124:139. <http://www.usni.org/magazines/proceedings/1998-01/network-centric-warfare-its-origin-and-future>.

Center for Naval Analyses. (1985). *Annual Report 1984.* Alexandria, VA: Center for Naval Analyses.

Center for Naval Analyses. (1986). Systems Analysis in Perspective. In *Annual Report 1986.* Alexandria, VA: Center for Naval Analyses.

Chamayou, Grégoire. (2013). *Théorie du drone.* Paris: La Fabrique.

Chaplin, Heather, and Aaron Ruby. (2005). *Smartbomb: The Quest for Art, Entertainment, and Big Bucks in the Videogame Revolution.* Chapel Hill, NC: Algonquin Books of Chapel Hill.

Chapman, Gary. (2003). An Introduction to the Revolution in Military Affairs. *XV Amaldi Conference on Problems in Global Security, Helsinki, Finland,* September 2003, accessed January 11, 2015. <http://www.lincei.it/rapporti/amaldi/papers/XV-Chapman.pdf>.

Chapman, Robert L., John L. Kennedy, Allen Newell, and William Biel. (1959). The Systems Research Laboratory's Air Defense Experiments. *Management Science* 5 (3): 250–269.

Charles, Cheryl L., and Ronald Stadsklev, eds. (1973). *Learning with Games: An Analysis of Social Studies Educational Games and Simulations.* Boulder, CO: The Social Science Education Consortium and The ERIC Clearinghouse for Social Studies/Social Science Education.

Cherryholmes, Cleo. (1966). Some Current Research on Effectiveness for Educational Simulations. *American Behavioral Scientist* 10 (2): 4–7.

Childers, P. B., E. H. Hobson, and J. A. Mullin. (1998). *Articulating: Teaching Writing in a Visual World.* Portsmouth, NH: Heinemann.

Chomsky, Noam, and Edward S. Herman. (2010). *Manufacturing Consent: The Political Economy of the Mass Media.* New York: Random House.

Christiansen, Peter. (2013). Technoscience in Virtual Worlds. *Play the Past,* accessed September 4, 2013. <http://www.playthepast.org/?p=4053>.

Chupin, Dominique. (2011). 1680. *Battles Magazine* 6:59–61.

Church, Joseph. (1952). *A Survey of Literature Bearing on Perceptual Aspects of the Effectiveness of Visual Aids.* HRRL Memo Report No. 16, US Air Force, Human Resources Research Laboratories, Bolling Air Force Base, January.

Churchill, Winston. (2005). *The Second World War,* vol. 2, *Their Finest Hour.* London: Penguin Classics.

Cianciolo, Anna T. (Global Information Systems Technology, Inc.), and William R. Sanders. (2006). *Wargaming Effectiveness: Its Conceptualization and Assessment.* TR 1178, ARI, March.

Clancy, Tom. (1984). *The Hunt for Red October.* Annapolis, MD: US Naval Institute Press.

Clancy, Tom. (1986). *Red Storm Rising.* New York: Putnam.

Clark, Kate. (2011). The Takhar Attack: Targeted Killings and the Parallel Worlds of U.S. Intelligence and Afghanistan. *Afghan Analysts Network,* May 2011, accessed January 11, 2015. <http://www.afghanistan-analysts.net/uploads/20110511KClark_Takhar-attack_final.pdf>.

Clark, Richard E., and D. F. Feldon. (2005). Five Common but Questionable Principles of Multimedia Learning. In *Cambridge Handbook of Multimedia*

Learning, edited by R. E. Mayer, 97–117. Cambridge, UK: Cambridge University Press.

Clark, Richard E., K. Yates, S. Early, and K. Moulton (2010). An Analysis of the Failure of Electronic Media and Discovery-Based Learning: Evidence for the Performance Benefits of Guided Training Methods. *Handbook of Training and Improving Workplace Performance, Volume I: Instructional Design and Training Delivery,* edited by K. H. Silber and R. Foshay, 263–287. Silver Spring, MD: International Society for Performance Improvement.

Clarke, Adele, and Joan H. Fujimura. (1992). *The Right Tools for the Job: At Work in Twentieth-Century Life Sciences.* Princeton: Princeton University Press.

Clausewitz, Carl von. (1832). *Vom Kriege.* Berlin: bei Ferdinand Dümmler.

Clausewitz, Carl von. (1976). *On War.* Edited and translated by M. Howard and P. Paret. Princeton: Princeton University Press.

Clausewitz, Carl von. (1993). *On War.* Edited by Peter Paret and Michael Howard. Translated by P. Paret. London: Knopf Doubleday Publishing Group.

Clausewitz, Carl von. (1995). *The Campaign of 1812 in Russia.* Cambridge, MA: Da Capo Press.

Cline, Ernest. (2011). *Ready Player One.* New York: Random House.

Clover, Carol. (1992). *Men, Women and Chainsaws: Gender in the Modern Horror Film.* Princeton: Princeton University Press.

Cohen, William S. (2000). *Annual Report to the President and the Congress.* Washington, DC: Department of Defense.

Coleman, James S. (1967). Learning Through Games. *NEA Journal* 56 (January): 69–70.

Collings, Ellsworth. (1931). Social Foundations of Project Teaching. *Journal of Educational Sociology* 5 (1): 5–42.

Collins, Randall. (2007). Turning Points, Bottlenecks, and the Fallacies of Counterfactual History. *Sociological Forum* 22 (3): 247–269.

Conley, Brian. (2007). *Miniature War in Iraq.* Installation. Las Vegas Games Expo.

Conley, Brian. (2010). *Miniature War in Iraq . . . and Now Afghanistan.* New York City: Installation.

Conrad, Joseph. (1990). *Heart of Darkness Unabridged.* New York: Dover Publications, Inc.

Conrad, Peter. (1978). *Shandyism: The Character of Romantic Irony.* New York: Harper & Row.

Constant, Nieuwenhuys. (2001). A Conversation with Constant. In *The Activist Drawing: Retracing Situationist Architectures from Constant's New Babylon to Beyond,* edited by Catherine de Zegher and Mark Wigley, 15–26. Cambridge, MA: MIT Press.

Cooper, Helene, and Thom Shanker. (2014). Pentagon Plans to Shrink Army to Pre–World War II Level. *The New York Times,* February 23, 2014, accessed January 19, 2015. <http://www.nytimes.com/2014/02/24/us/politics/pentagon-plans-to-shrink-army-to-pre-world-war-ii-level.html?hp&_r=0>.

Corbeil, Pierre. (2011). History and Simulation/Gaming: Living with Two Solitudes. *Simulation & Gaming* 42 (4): 418–422.

Corbett, E. P. (1919). Selling Goods by Illustrated Lectures. *Reel and Slide* (February): 9.

Cornell, Tim, and Thomas Allen, eds. (2002). *War and Games*. Rochester, NY: Bordell.

Costikyan, Greg. (1996). A Farewell to Hexes. *Internet Archive*, accessed January 13, 2015. <http://web.archive.org/web/20040212100739/http:/www.costik.com/spisins.html>.

Costikyan, Greg. (2006). The Revolution Began with Paper. *The Escapist*, April 26, 2006 <http://www.escapistmagazine.com/articles/view/video-games/issues/issue_42/253-The-Revolution-Began-With-Paper>.

Costikyan, Greg. (2007). Games, Storytelling and Breaking the String. In *Second Person: Role-Playing and Story in Games and Playable Media*, edited by Pat Harrigan and Noah Wardrip-Fruin, 5–14. Cambridge, MA: MIT Press.

Costikyan, Greg. (2011). Board Game Aesthetics. In *Tabletop: Analog Game Design*, edited by Greg Costikyan and Drew Davidson, 179–184. Pittsburgh, PA: ETC Press.

Coulmas, Florian. (1991). *The Writing Systems of the World*. Hoboken, NJ: Wiley-Blackwell.

Craddock, David L. (2013). *Stay Awhile and Listen: How Two Blizzards Unleashed Diablo and Forged a Video-Game Empire, Book I*. Kindle edition.

Cramer, Christopher. (2010). *World Development Report 2011: Unemployment and Participation in Violence*, accessed December 19, 2014. <https://openknowledge.worldbank.org/bitstream/handle/10986/9247/WDR2011_0022.pdf>.

Crary, Jonathan. (1999). *Suspensions of Perception*. Cambridge, MA: MIT Press.

Crawford, Chris. (1981). The Future of Computer Wargaming. *Computer Gaming World* 1 (1): 3–7.

Crawford, Chris. (1982a). *The Art of Computer Game Design*. Berkeley: McGraw-Hill.

Crawford, Chris. (1982b). *Eastern Front: A Narrative History*. *Creative Computing* 8 (8): 100–107.

Crogan, Patrick. (2008). Wargaming and Computer Games: Fun with the Future. In *The Pleasures of Computer Gaming: Essays on Cultural History, Theory and Aesthetics*, edited by Melanie Swalwell and Jason Wilson, 147–166. Jefferson, NC: McFarland and Company.

Crogan, Patrick. (2011). *Gameplay Mode: War, Simulation and Technoculture*. Minneapolis, MN: University of Minnesota Press.

Crookall, David, and Warren Thorngate. (2009). Acting, Knowing, Learning, Simulating, Gaming. *Simulation & Gaming* 40 (1): 8–26.

Cuban, Larry. (1986). *Teachers and Machines: The Classroom Use of Technology Since 1920*. New York: Teachers College Press.

Cummings, Larry. (1965). Organizational Climates for Creativity. *Academy of Management Journal* 8 (3): 220–227.

Curry, John. (2008a). *The Fred Jane Naval Wargame (1906), including the Royal Navy's Wargaming Rules (1921)*. Bristol, UK: The History of Wargaming Project.

Curry, John. (2008b). *Verdy's Free Kriegspiel, including the Victorian Army's 1896 War Game*. Bristol, UK: The History of Wargaming Project.

Curry, John. (2008c). *Dunn Kempf: The Tactical Wargame of the American Army (1977-1997)*. Bristol, UK: The History of Wargaming Project.

Curry, John. (2011a). *Tacspiel: The American Army's War Game of the Vietnam War (1966)*. Bristol, UK: The History of Wargaming Project.

Curry, John. (2011b). *The Wargaming Pioneers, including Little Wars by H.G. Wells, The War Game for Boy Scouts and The War Game by Captain Sachs 1898-1940* (Early Wargames Vol. 1). Bristol, UK: The History of Wargaming Project.

Curry, John. (2012a). *Fletcher Pratt's Naval Wargame: Wargaming with Model Ships 1900-1945*. Bristol, UK: The History of Wargaming Project.

Curry, John. (2012b). *Innovations in Wargaming Vol. 1: Developments in Professional and Hobby Wargames*. Bristol, UK: The History of Wargaming Project.

Curry, John. (2014). *Early Naval Wargaming*. Bristol, UK: The History of Wargaming Project.

Curry, John, and Tim Price, MBE. (2013). *Dark Guest: Training Games for Cyber Warfare Volume 1: Wargaming Internet Based Attacks*. Bristol, UK: The History of Wargaming Project.

Curry, John, and Tim Price, MBE. (2014). *Matrix Games for Modern Wargaming: Developments in Professional and Education Wargames Volume 2*. Bristol, UK: The History of Wargaming Project.

Daer, Alice J. (2010). This Is How We Do It: A Glimpse at Gamelab's Design Process. *E-Learning and Digital Media* 7 (1): 108–119.

Dale, A. G., and C. R. Klasson. (1962). *Business Gaming: A Survey of American Collegiate Schools of Business*. Austin: Bureau of Business Research, University of Texas.

Dannhauer, General der Infanterie Z.D. (1874). Das Reisswitzsche Kriegsspiel von seinen Beginn bis zum Tode des Erfinders, 1827 (The Reisswitz Wargame from the Beginning to the Death of Its Inventor, 1827, unpublished translation by William Leeson). *Militair Wochenblatt* 56.

Darley, Andrew. (2000). *Visual Digital Culture: Surface Play and Spectacle in New Media Genre*. London: Routledge.

D'Arn, Gigi. (1982). A Letter from Gigi. *Different Worlds* 24:46.

de Jomini, Antoine-Henri. (2010). [1862]. *The Art of War*. Translated by Thomas Cleary. London: Dodo Press.

De Landa, Manual. (1991). *War in the Age of Intelligent Machines*. New York: Zone Books.

Debord, Guy. (1981). Report on the Construction of Situations and of the International Situationist Tendency's Conditions of Organisation and Action. In *Situationist International Anthology*, edited by Ken Knabb, 17–25. Berkeley, CA: Bureau of Public Secrets.

Debord, Guy. (1991). *Panegyric*. vol. 1. London: Verso.

Debord, Guy. (1993). *Panégyrique, Tome Premier*. Paris: Gallimard.

Debord, Guy. (1999). *In Girum Imus Nocte et Consumimur Igni*. Paris: Gallimard.

Debord, Guy. (2005). *Correspondance, Volume V: janvier 1973-Décembre 1978*. Paris: Librairie Arthème Fayard.

Debord, Guy. (2006a). *Correspondance, Volume VI: Janvier 1979–décembre 1987*. Paris: Librairie Arthème Fayard.

Debord, Guy. (2006b). *Oeuvres*. Paris: Gallimard.

Debord, Guy. (2007). The State of Spectacle (Preface to the fourth Italian edition of *The Society of the Spectacle*). In *Autonomia: Post-political Politics*, edited by Sylvere Lotringer & Christian Marazzi, 96–99. New York: Semiotext(e).

Debord, Guy, and Gianfranco Sanguinetti. (1985). *The Veritable Split in the International: Public Circular of the Situationist International*. London: B. M. Chronos.

DefenseAerospace.com. (2011a). DARPA Kicks off Mind's Eye program, accessed January 23, 2015. <http://www.defense-aerospace.com/articles-view/release/3/121450/darpa-kicks-off-mind%E2%80%99s-eye-program.html>.

Deleuze, Gilles. (1977). Nous Croyons au Caractère Constructiviste de Certaines Agitations de Gauche. *Recherches* 30:149–150.

Deleuze, Gilles. 2003. *Deux Régimes de Fous: Textes et Entretiens 1975-1995*. Paris: Les Éditions de Minuit.

Delwiche, Aaron. (2007). From *The Green Berets* to *America's Army*: Video Games as a Vehicle for Political Propaganda. In *The Players' Realm: Studies on the Culture of Video Games and Gaming*, edited by J. Patrick Williams and Jonas Heide Smith, 91–109. Jefferson, NC: McFarland.

Demick, Barbara. (1996). *Logavina Street: Life and Death in a Sarajevo Neighborhood*. Kansas City, MO: Andrews McMeel Publishing.

Demick, Barbara. (2012). Life and death on my street in Sarajevo. *The Guardian,* April 3, 2012. <http://www.theguardian.com/books/2012/apr/03/life-and-death-in-sarajevo>.

Dench, Ernest A. (1917). *Motion Picture Education*. Cincinnati, OH: The Standard Publishing Company.

Der Derian, James. (2001). *Virtuous War: Mapping the Military-Industrial-Media-Entertainment Network*. Boulder, CO: Westview Press.

Der Derian, James. (2009). *Virtuous War: Mapping the Military-Industrial-Media-Entertainment Network*. 2nd ed. New York: Routledge.

Descargues, Madeleine. (2006). *Tristram Shandy* and the Appositeness of War. In *Laurence Sterne's Tristram Shandy: A Casebook*, edited by Thomas Keymer, 240–258. Oxford: Oxford University Press.

Dewey, John. (1925). *Experience and Nature*. Chicago: Open Court Publishing.

Dick, Philip K. (1962). *The Man in the High Castle*. New York: Putnam.

Dill, W. R., and N. Doppelt. (1963). The Acquisition of Experience in a Complex Management Game. *Management Science* 10 (1): 30–46.

Dorner, Dietrich. (1996). *The Logic of Failure: Recognizing and Avoiding Error in Complex Situations*. Cambridge, MA: Perseus Books.

Dorosh, Michael. (2008). Tactical Game 3. *The Tactical Wargamer,* accessed January 13, 2015. <http://www.tacticalwargamer.com/boardgames/panzerblitz/tacgame3.htm>.

Dorris, Anna Verona. (1928). *Visual Instruction in the Public Schools*. Cambridge, UK: Ginn & Company.

Dougherty, Jeff. (2014). Updating *Persian Incursion*. *The Naval SITREP* 46.

Downes-Martin, Stephen. 2013. Adjudication: The *Diabolus in Machina* of War Gaming. *US Naval War College Review* 66 (3): 67–80.

Drucker, Peter. (1968). *The Age of Discontinuity*. New York: Harper and Row.

Duel on a Dutch Levee. (1996). World War II private reenactment event announcement, sponsored by Tim Castle, Chesapeake, MD, June 6, 1996.

Duke, Richard D. (1974). Toward a General Theory of Gaming. *Simulation & Gaming* 5 (2): 135–136.

Duncum, Paul. (2004). Visual Culture Isn't Just Visual: Multiliteracy, Multimodality and Meaning. *Studies in Art Education* 45 (3): 252–264.

Dunnigan, James, F. (1967). The Fletcher Pratt Naval War Game. *Strategy & Tactics* 1: 7.

Dunnigan, James F. (1970). Designer's Notes: The Game is a Game. *Strategy & Tactics* 22: XS3.

Dunnigan, James F. (1980). *The Complete Wargames Handbook*. New York: Morrow.

Dunnigan, James F. (1992a). *The Complete Wargames Handbook: How to Play, Design and Find Them*. Revised edition. New York: William Morrow.

Dunnigan, James. (1992b). *The Complete Wargames Handbook: How to Play, Design and Find Them*. 2nd ed. New York: Quill.

Dunnigan, James F. (2000a). *Wargames Handbook, Third Edition: How to Play and Design Commercial and Professional Wargames*. Lincoln, NE: Writers Club Press. Kindle e-book.

Dunnigan, James F. (2000b). *Wargames Handbook: How to Play and Design Commercial and Professional Wargames*. San Jose, CA: Writers Club Press.

Dunnigan, James F. (n.d.). Transition: S&T Change Publishers. *Strategy & Tactics. Book IV: Nrs. 16–18*, inside covers.

Dunnigan, James F., and Albert A. Nofi. (1990). *Dirty Little Secrets of the Vietnam War*. New York: St. Martin's Press.

Dunnigan, James F., and Raymond M. Macedonia. (1993). *Getting It Right: American Military Reforms After Vietnam to the Gulf War and Beyond*. New York: William Morrow & Co.

Dunnigan, James F., and Redmond Simonsen. (1969). The Blitzkrieg Module System. *Strategy & Tactics* 19: 17–24.

Dupuy, T. N. (1979). *Numbers, Predictions & War*. Indianapolis: Bobbs-Merrill.

Dyer-Witherford, Nick, and Greig De Peuter. (2009). *Games of Empire: Global Capitalism and Video Games*. Minneapolis: University of Minnesota Press.

Earle, David M. (2009). *Re-covering Modernism: Pulps, Paperbacks, and the Prejudice of Form*. Burlington, VT: Ashgate Publishing Company.

Earle, David M. (2012). Pulp Magazines and the Popular Press. In *The Oxford Critical and Cultural History of Modernist Magazines, Vol. 2: North America 1894-1960*, edited by Peter Brooker and Andrew Thacker, 197–216. Oxford: Oxford University Press.

Edwards, John. (1970). Stalingrad: Australian Style. *S&T Supplement* 3: 12–18.

Edwards, John. (1978). Interview: John Edwards. *GEN* 15 (1): 16–17.

Edwards, Paul. (1996). *The Closed World: Computers and the Politics of Discourse in Cold War America.* Cambridge, MA: MIT Press.

Edwards, Ron. (2001). GNS and Other Matters of Role-Playing Theory, Chapter 2. *The Forge,* October 14, 2001, accessed December 12, 2014. <http://www .indie-rpgs.com/articles/3>.

Electronic Arts. (2013). Medal of Honor Warfighter. *EA,* accessed January 19, 2015. <http://www.ea.com/ medal-of-honor-warfighter>.

Eliot, Charles. (1913). *The Tendency to the Concrete and Practical in Modern Education.* Boston: Houghton Mifflin.

Elliott, Carlson. (1966). The Versatile Business Game; its Growing use in Industry. *Wall Street Journal,* July 8: 1–2.

Ellis, Don Carlos, and Laura Thornborough. (1923). *Motion Pictures in Education.* New York: Thomas Y. Cromwell Company.

Esposito, Vincent J., ed. (1995). *The West Point Atlas of American Wars, vol. 1., 1689–1900.* New York: Henry Holt and Company.

Evans, Richard. (2014). *Altered Pasts: Counterfactuals in History.* London: Little, Brown and Company.

Ewalt, David. (2013). *Of Dice and Men: The Story of Dungeons & Dragons and the People Who Play It.* New York: Scribner.

Faden, Lisa Y. (2014). The Story of the Nation in Wartime: World War II in US and Canadian Secondary History Classes. In *(Re)Constructing Memory: School Textbooks, Identity, and the Pedagogies and Politics of Imagining Community,* edited by J. H. Williams, 191–218. Rotterdam: Sense.

Faidutti, Bruno. (2007). On *Mystery of the Abbey.* In *Second Person: Role-Playing and Story in Games and Playable Media,* edited by Pat Harrigan and Noah Wardrip-Fruin, 95–98. Cambridge, MA: MIT Press.

Farrow, Daniel W, IV. (2005). Avalon Hill Games, 1952–1998. Personal website, accessed January 13, 2015. <http://users.rcn.com/dwfiv/games/ avalonhillgames.html>.

Featherstone, Donald. (1962). *War Games.* London: Stanley Paul.

Featherstone, Donald. (1965). *Naval War Games.* London: Stanley Paul. Second edition (2009) reprinted as *Donald Featherstone's Naval War Games: Wargaming with Model Ships.* Bristol, UK: The History of Wargaming Project.

Feist, Raymond, and Janny Wurts. (1987–1992). *The Empire Trilogy* [series]. New York: Doubleday.

Ferguson, Niall, ed. (2000). *Virtual History: Alternatives and Counterfactuals.* New York: Basic Books.

Ferguson, Niall. (2003). Introduction. Virtual History: Towards a 'Chaotic' Theory of the Past. In *Virtual History: Alternatives and Counterfactuals,* edited by Niall Ferguson, 1–90. London: Pan.

Fields, A. Belden. (1988). *Trotskyism and Maoism: Theory and Practice in France and the United States.* New York: Autonomedia.

Filewod, Alan. (2012). Warplay: Spectacle, Performance, and (Dis) Simulation of Combat. In *Bearing Witness: Perspectives on War and Peace from the Arts and*

Humanities, edited by Sherrill Grace, Patrick Imbert and Tiffany Johnstone, 17–27. Montreal: McGill-Queen's University Press.

Filipović, Zlata. (1993). *Zlata's Diary: A Child's Life in Wartime Sarajevo*. London: Penguin.

Fine, Gary. (1979). Small Groups and Culture Creation: The Idioculture of Little League Baseball Teams. *American Sociological Review* 44: 733–745.

Fine, Gary. (1983). *Shared Fantasy: Role-playing Games as Social Worlds*. Chicago: Chicago University Press.

Foley, John A. (2007). *Combat Commander*—Developer's Notes: Up Close and Personal. *C3i Magazine* 19.

Fortun, M., and S. Schweber. (1993). Scientists and the Legacy of the World War II: The Case of Operations Research. *Social Studies of Science* 23 (4): 595–642.

Fossheim, Hallvard, and Tarjei Mandt Larsen. (2012). *The Philosophy of Computer Games*. Dordrecht: Springer.

Foster, Aroutis N., and Punya Mishra. (2009). Games, Claims, Genres & Learning. In *Handbook of Research on Effective Electronic Gaming in Education*, vol. III. Edited by Richard E. Ferdig, 33–50. Hershey, PA: Information Science Reference.

Foxhall, Lin. (2013). Can We See the "Hoplite Revolution" on the Ground? Archaeological Landscapes, Material Culture and Social Status in Early Greece. In *Men of Bronze: Hoplite Warfare in Ancient Greece*, edited by Donald Kagan and Gregory F. Viggiano, 194–221. Princeton: Princeton University Press.

Frank, Anders. (2012). Gaming the Game: A Study of the Gamer Mode in Educational Wargaming. *Simulation & Gaming* 43 (1): 118–132.

Frank, Richard B. (1990). *Guadalcanal: The Definitive Account of the Landmark Battle*. New York: Penguin Books.

Fredericks, P. G. (1958). And Now—"Wide-Screen" Warfare. *New York Times Sunday Magazine*, December 7: 96.

Freeman, Frank N. (1924). *Visual Education: A Comparative Study of Motion Pictures and Other Methods of Instruction*. Chicago: University of Chicago Press.

Friedman, Norman. (2011). *Naval Weapons of World War One*. Annapolis: Naval Institute Press.

Fryer-Biggs, Zachary. (2014). Cyber Spending Rare Bright Spot in Budget. *Defense News,* March 2, 2014, accessed January 9, 2015. <http://www.defensenews.com/article/20140302/DEFREG02/303020017/Cyber-Spending-Rare-Bright-Spot-Budget>.

Frost and Sullivan. (1980). *The Military and Aerospace Trainer and Simulator Market*. New York: Frost and Sullivan.

Frost, Holloway. (1936). *The Battle of Jutland*. Annapolis: Naval Institute Press.

Fuller, Buckminster. (1969a). *Utopia or Oblivion: The Prospects for Humanity*. New York: Bantam Books.

Fuller, Buckminster. (1969b). *Operating Manual for Spaceship Earth*. Chicago: Southern Illinois University Press.

Gaddis, John Lewis. (2002). *The Landscape of History: How Historians Map the Past*. Oxford: Oxford University Press.

Gadomski, Christopher. (1980). The Great Pretenders: Simulators and Training Devices in Today's Defense Environment. *Sea Power* 23 (12): 38–42.

Gaffney, Helen, and Alasdair Vincent. (2011). Modeling Information Operations in a Tactical-level Stabilization Environment. *Journal of Defense Modeling and Simulation* 8:2.

Gagnon, Frédérick. (2010). Invading Your Hearts and Minds: *Call of Duty* and the (Re)Writing of Militarism in US Digital Games and Popular Culture. *European Journal of American Studies* 5 (3): document 3.

Galloway, Alexander R. (2006). *Gaming: Essays on Algorithmic Culture*. Minneapolis: University of Minnesota Press.

Games Workshop Group PLC. (2000–2014a). The Games Workshop Hobby. *Games Workshop* 2000–2014, accessed January 6, 2014. <http://investor.games-workshop.com/the-games-workshop-hobby>.

Games Workshop Group PLC. (2000–2014b). Our Business Model. *Games Workshop* 2000–2014, accessed June 30, 2014. <http://investor.games-workshop.com/our-business-model>.

Games Workshop Group PLC. (2006). *Chairman's Preamble: Annual Report 2005-06*. <http://investor.games-workshop.com/chairmans-preamble-annual-report-2005-06>.

Games Workshop Group PLC. (2014). *Annual Report 2013-14*. <http://investor.games-workshop.com/2014/07/29/annual-report-2013-14>.

Gardner, Luke. (1993). Fourth Armored Unit, Company A, 51st Armored Infantry Battalion newsletter, December, 1993.

Gardner, Luke. (1994). Warning Order [to 4th Armored unit members].

Gardner, Marvin. 1975. John E. Koontz to Marvin Gardner, 11 June. Box 33, folder 8. In *Marvin Gardner Papers. SC647*. Stanford University Libraries.

Garamone, Jim. (2010). Alexander Details U. S. Cyber Command Gains. *American Forces Press Service, September 24, 2010*, accessed January 19, 2014. <http://www.defense.gov/news/newsarticle.aspx?id=61014>.

Gascoigne, Marc, and Nick Kyme. (2007). *The Art of Warhammer*. Nottingham: The Black Library.

Gates, Robert. (2014). *Duty: Memoirs of a Secretary at War*. New York: Knopf.

Gay, R. C. (1937). Teacher Reads the Comics. *Harvard Educational Review* (March): 198–209.

Geertz, Clifford. (1972). *The Interpretation of Cultures*. New York: Basic Books, Inc.

General Accounting Office. (1980). *GAO Report PAD-80-21. Models, Data, and War: A Critique of the Foundation for Defense Analysis*. Washington, DC: General Accounting Office.

Gerbaudo, Paolo. (2012). *Tweets and the Streets: Social Media and Contemporary Activism*. London: Pluto.

Gertler, Jeremiah. (2012). *U. S. Unmanned Aerial Systems*. Washington, DC: Congressional Research Service. <http://fas.org/sgp/crs/natsec/R42136.pdf>.

Ghamari-Tabrizi, Sharon. (2005). *The Worlds of Herman Kahn: The Intuitive Science of Thermonuclear War*. Cambridge, MA: Harvard University Press.

Ghamari-Tabrizi, Sharon. (n.d.). US Wargaming Grows Up: A Short History of the Diffusion of Wargaming in the Armed Forces and Industry in the Postwar Period up to 1964. *Strategy Page*. <http://

www.strategypage.com/articles/default.asp?target=Wgappen.htm>.

Ghamari-Tabrizi, Sharon. (2005). *The Worlds of Herman Kahn*. Cambridge, MA: Harvard University Press.

Ghamari-Tabrizi, Sharon. (2012). Cognitive and Perceptual Training in the Cold War Man-Machine System. In *Uncertain Empire: American History and the Idea of the Cold War*, edited by Joel Isaacs and Duncan Bell, 267–293. Oxford: Oxford University Press.

Gibson, James, ed. (1947). *Motion Picture Testing and Research: Report No. 7*. Washington DC: Army Air Forces Aviation Psychology Program Research Reports.

Gile, Robert H. (2004). *Global War Game: Second Series 1984-1988*. Newport, RI: Naval War College.

Gilman, Don. (2012). *Harpoon Timeline*. Accessed May, 2014. <http://www.h3milsim.net/timeline>.

Gilman, Don, and Larry Bond. (2006). *Harpoon*: An Original Serious Game. Paper presented at the Serious Games Conference, Arlington, VA, October 2006.

Gilman, Robert. (1971). *The Navigator of Rhada*. London: Gollancz.

Glick, Stephen, and Ian Charters. (1983). War, Games and Military History. *Journal of Contemporary History* 18 (4): 567–582.

Godfrey, Eleanor. (1967). *The State of Audiovisual Technology, 1961–1966*. Washington, DC: National Education Association.

Goldhamer, Herbert. (1954). *Toward a Cold War Game*. Santa Monica, CA: RAND Corporation.

Goldhamer, Herbert, and Hans Speier. (1959). Observations on Political Gaming. *World Politics* 12:1.

Gooderson, Ian. (1998). *Air Power at the Battlefront: Allied Close Air Support in Europe 1943-45*. London: Routledge.

Gordon, Andrew. (1996). *The Rules of the Game: Jutland and British Naval Command*. London: John Murray.

Gordon, Alice Kaplan. (1970). *Games for Growth*. Palo Alto, CA: Science Research Associates, Inc.

Gordon, William J. J. (1956). Operational Approach to Creativity. *Harvard Business Review* 34 (6): 41–51.

Gouglas, Sean, Mihaela Ilovan, Shannon Lucky, and Silvia Russell. (2014). Abort, Retry, Pass, Fail: Games as Teaching Tools. In *Pastplay: Teaching and Learning History with Technology*, edited by Kevin Kee, 121–138. Ann Arbor: University of Michigan Press.

Graham, R. G., and C. F. Gray. (1969). *Business Games Handbook*. New York: American Management Association.

Graham, Thomas, and Robert Allyn Dick. (1996). Tactical awareness monitoring and direct response system. Google patent, filed April 17, 1996. <http://www.google.com/patents/US5971580>.

Grant, Tom. (2005–14). Insurgency and Terrorism. *BoardGameGeek,* accessed January 13, 2015. <http://boardgamegeek.com/geeklist/6478/insurgency-and-terrorism>.

Grant, Tom. (2012). Episode 38: Jerry Taylor. *I've Been Diced*. Podcast audio. August 6, 2012. <http://ivebeendiced.blogspot.com/2012/08/ive-been-diced-episode-38-jerry-taylor.html>.

Graubard, Morlie, and Carl Builder. (1980). *RAND's Strategic Assessment Center: An Overview of the Concept, N-1583-DNA*. Santa Monica, CA: RAND Corporation.

Greenwood, Don [interviewed by Rex A. Martin] (1986). Staff Briefing: An Interview with Don Greenwood. *The General* 22: 6.

Greenwood, Don, John Hill, and Hal Hock. (1978). Design Analysis—Game Design: Art or Science (An Evaluation of the *Squad Leader* Game Design). *The General* 14: 5.

Gregory, Derek. (2011a). Lines of Descent. *openDemocracy*, November 8, 2011, accessed January 11, 2015. <http://www.opendemocracy.net/print/62494>.

Gregory, Derek. (2011b). From a View to a Kill: Drones and Late Modern War. *Theory, Culture & Society* 28 (7–8): 188–215.

Gregory, Derek. (2014). The God Trick and the Administration of Military Violence. *Geographical Imaginations: War, Space and Security*, April 26, 2014, accessed January 11, 2015. <http://geographicalimaginations .com/2014/04/26/the-god-trick-and-the -administration-of-military-violence>.

Grossman, Dave. (2009). *On Killing: The Psychological Cost of Learning to Kill in War and Society*. New York: Little, Brown and Co.

Grosvenor, Ian. (2012). Back to the Future or Towards a Sensory History of Schooling. *History of Education* 41 (5): 675–687.

Grusin, Richard A. (2010). *Premediation: Affect and Mediality after 9/11*. New York: Palgrave Macmillan.

Guattari, Felix. (2013). Balance Program for Desiring-Machines. In *The New Media and Technocultures Reader*, edited by Seth Giddings and Martin Lister, 129–138. New York: Routledge.

Guetzkow, Harold, Chadwick F. Alger, Richard A. Brody, Robert C. Noel, and Richard C. Snyder. (1963). *Simulation in International Relations*. Englewood Cliffs, NJ: Prentice-Hall.

Gunning, Tom. (1990). The Cinema of Attraction: Early Film, Its Spectator, and the Avant-Garde. In *Early Cinema: Space Frame Narrative*, edited by Thomas Elsaesser and Adam Barker, 56–62. London: British Film Institute Publishing.

Gunning, Tom. (1993). Now You See It, Now You Don't: The Temporality of the Cinema of Attractions. *Velvet Light Trap* 32 (Fall): 3–12.

Gunning, Tom. (1994). The Whole Town's Gawking: Early Cinema and the Visual Experience of Modernity. *Yale Journal of Criticism* 7 (2): 189–201.

Gunzinger, Mark. (2013). *Shaping America's Future Military toward a New Force Planning Construct*. Washington, DC: Center for Strategic and Budgetary Assessments.

Guy, Emmanuel, and Laurence de Bras. (2013). *Guy Debord: Un Art de la Guerre*. Paris: Bibliothèque Nationale de France/Gallimard.

Gysin, Fritz. (1983). *Model and Motif in Tristram Shandy*. Bern: Francke Verlag.

Haefele, John W. (1962). *Creativity and Innovation*. New York: Reinhold Publishing Co.

Haigh, Thomas. (2001). Inventing Information Systems: The Systems Men and the Computer, 1950–1968. *Business History Review* 75 (1): 15–61.

Haldon, John, Bart Craenen, Georgios Theodoropoulos, Vinoth Suryanarayanan, Vincent Gaffney, and Philip Murgatroyd. (2010). Medieval Military Logistics: A Case for Distributed Agent-based Simulation. In *SIMUTools 10: Proceedings of the 3rd International ICST Conference on Simulation Tools and Techniques*. Brussels:

Institute for Computer Sciences, Social-Informatics and Telecommunications Engineering.

Halter, Ed. (2006). *From Sun Tzu to XBox: War and Video Games.* New York: Thunder's Mouth Press.

Hamburger, W. (1955). *Monopologs: an Inventory Management Game. RM-1579.* Santa Monica, CA: RAND Corporation.

Hamer, John. (2005). History Teaching and Heritage Education: Two Sides of the Same Coin, or Different Currencies? In *The Politics of Heritage: The Legacies of Race*, edited by Jo Littler and Roshi Naidoo, 159–168. London: Routledge.

Hamilton, Kirk. (2013). *Spec Ops* Writer on Violent Games: 'We're Better Than That.' *Kotaku*, accessed May 5, 2013. <http://kotaku.com/spec-ops-writer -on-violent-games-were-better-than-th-460992384>.

Hanley, Nathan, and Helen Gaffney. (2011). The Peace Support Operations Model: Modeling Techniques Present and Future. *Journal of Defense Modeling and Simulation* 8:2.

Hanson, Victor Davis. (2013). The Hoplite Narrative. In *Men of Bronze: Hoplite Warfare in Ancient Greece*, edited by Donald Kagan and Gregory F. Viggiano, 256–276. Princeton: Princeton University Press.

Harding, Tucker, and Mark Whitlock. (2013). Leveraging Web-based Environments for Mass Atrocity Prevention. *Simulation & Gaming* 44:1.

Hardy, Thomas. (1908). *The Dynasts.* London: Macmillan.

Harmon, Robert D. (1974). Beyond Situation 13. *GEN* 11 (4): 7–12.

Harrigan, Pat, and Noah Wardrip-Fruin. (2011). *Twilight Struggle* and Card-Driven Historicity. In *Table-*

top: Analog Game Design, edited by Greg Costikyan and Drew Davidson, 159–166. Pittsburgh, PA: ETC Press.

Harris, Chester, and Louise Buenger. (1955). Relation Between Learning by Film and Learning by Lecture. *AV Communication Review* 3 (Winter): 29–34.

Harris, Derrick. (1999). Unit Count, WWII Newsgroup, January 9, 1999.

Harrop, Mitchell, and Martin Gibbs. (2013). Everyone's a Winner at Warhammer 40K (or, at least not a loser). *Marcus Carter*, August 2013, accessed July 6, 2014. <http://marcuscarter.com/wp-content/ uploads/2013/08/harrop-warhammer.pdf>.

Harvey, Giles. (2012). *The Third Reich* by Roberto Bolaño. *The Guardian*, January 27, 2012, accessed October 14, 2014. <http://www.theguardian.com/ books/2012/jan/27/third-reich-roberto-bolano -review>.

Hausrath, Alfred. (1971). *Venture Simulation in War, Business, and Politics.* New York: McGraw-Hill.

Hawley, Judith. (2009). Tristram Shandy, Learned Wit, and Enlightenment Knowledge. In *The Cambridge Companion to Laurence Sterne*, edited by Thomas Keymer, 34–48. Cambridge: Cambridge University Press.

Hay, Bud, and Bob Gile. (1993). *Global War Game: The First Five Years.* Newport, RI: Naval War College.

Heims, Steve J. (1993). *Constructing a Social Science for Postwar America: The Cybernetics Group 1946–1953.* Cambridge, MA: MIT Press.

Heist, Paul. (1968). *Education for Creativity.* San Francisco, CA: Jossey-Bass.

Heller, Joseph. (1961). *Catch-22.* New York: Simon & Schuster.

Heller, Major Charles E. (1984). *Chemical Warfare in World War I: The American Experience, 1917–1918.* Leavenworth Papers No. 10. Fort Leavenworth, KS: Combat Studies Institute.

Helmer, Olaf. (1967). *Methodology of Societal Studies. P-3611.* Santa Monica, CA: RAND Corporation.

Hemingway, Graham, Himanshu Neema, Harmon Nine, Janos Sztipanovits, and Gabor Karsai. (2011). Rapid Synthesis of High-level Architecture-Based Heterogeneous Simulation: A Model-Based Integration Approach. *Simulation,* March 17: 1–16.

Henry, Mark. (1993). Nominations for Central Powers Combat Commander of the GWA. *On the Wire* 4: 5.

Herbert, Frank. (1965). *Dune.* Philadelphia: Chilton.

Herken, Gregg. (1985). *Counsels of War.* New York: Knopf.

Herman, Mark, Mark Frost, and Robert Kurz. (2009). *Wargaming for Leaders: Strategic Decision Making from the Battlefield to the Board Room.* New York: McGraw-Hill.

Hickman, Tracy and Margaret Weis. (1984–2009). *Dragonlance* [series]. New York: Random House.

Hill, John. (1977). A *Squad Leader* Preview—The Building of *Squad Leader. GEN* 14:2.

Hill, John. (2010). *The 2 Half-Squads,* February 26, 2010, podcast audio. <http://www.the2halfsquads.com/2010/02/episode-32-view-from-hill.html>.

Hill, Joseph E., and Derek Nunner. (1971). *Personalizing Educational Programs Utilizing Cognitive Style Mapping.* Bloomfield Hills, MI: Oakland Community College Press.

Hitch, Charles J., and Roland N. McKean. (1960). *The Economics of Defense in the Nuclear Age.* Cambridge, MA: Harvard University Press.

Hitchens, Michael, Bronwin Patrickson, and Sherman Young. (2014). Reality and Terror, the First-Person Shooter in Current Day Settings. *Games and Culture* 9 (1): 3–29.

Hoare, Andy. (2011). Rick Priestley Interview. *Tales from the Maelstrom,* September 25, 2011, accessed January 6, 2015. <http://talesfromthemaelstrom.blogspot.com.au/2011/09/rick-priestley-interview.html>.

Hoarn, Steven. (2013). SOCOM Seeks TALOS (Tactical Assault Light Operator Suit). *Defense Media Network,* May 18, 2013, accessed January 19, 2013. <http://www.defensemedianetwork.com/stories/socom-seeks-talos-tactical-assault-light-operator-suit>.

Hoban, Charles F., Jr. (1946). *Movies that Teach.* New York: The Dryden Press.

Hoban, Charles F., Jr., and Edward Van Ormer. (1950). *Instructional Film Research, 1918–1950. SDC 269-7-19.* Port Washington, NY: Special Devices Center, Department of the Army and Department of the Navy.

Hockaday, David, Daniel Barnhardt, James Staples, Pamela Sitko, and Odile Bultan. (2013). *Simulating the Worst to Prepare the Best: A Study of Humanitarian Simulations and their Benefits. Emergency Capacity Building Project.* <http://www.ecbproject.org/resource/18416>.

Hocking, Clint. (2007). Ludonarrative Dissonance in *Bioshock:* The Problem of What the Game Is About. *Click Nothing,* last modified October 7, 2007. <http://clicknothing.typepad.com/click_nothing/2007/10/ludonarrative-d.html>.

Hofer, Margaret. (2003). *The Games We Played: The Golden Age of Board and Table Games.* Princeton, NJ: Princeton Architectural Press.

Höglund, Johan. (2008). Electronic Empire: Orientalism Revisited in the Military Shooter. *Game Studies* 8:1.

Hollis, A. P. (1926). *Motion Pictures for Instruction.* New York: The Century Company.

Hooper, Richard. (1969). A Diagnosis of Failure. *AV Communication Review* 17 (3): 245–264.

Hound, Carl, Arthur Lumsdaine, and Fred Sheffield. (1949). *Experiments on Mass Communication, Studies in Social Psychology in World War II.* vol. 3. Princeton: Princeton University Press.

House, Daniel. (2012). The Viability of Commercial Sub-Orbital Spacecraft for Military Strike Missions. M.A. thesis, American Public University System.

Huizinga, Johan. (1950). *Homo Ludens: A Study of the Play Element in Culture.* Boston: Beacon Press.

Human Rights Watch. (2010). Open Letter to President Obama: Targeted Killings and Unmanned Combat Aircraft Systems (Drones). *Human Rights Watch,* December 7, 2010, accessed January 11, 2015. <http://www.hrw.org/news/2010/12/07/letter-obama-targeted-killings>.

Huntemann, Nina B. (2009). Playing with Fear: Catharsis and Resistance in Military-Themed Video Games. In *Joystick Soldiers: The Politics of Play in Military Video Games,* edited by Nina B. Huntemann and Matthew Thomas Payne, 223–236. New York, London: Routledge.

Huntemann, Nina, and Matthew Thomas Payne. (2010). *Joystick Soldiers: The Politics of Play in Military Video Games.* New York: Routledge.

Hurd, Archer Willis. (1945). Do You Learn to Do by Doing? *Journal of Educational Sociology* 19 (2): 83–86.

Hussey, Andrew. (2001). *The Game of War: The Life and Death of Guy Debord.* London: Jonathan Cape.

Hussey, Thomas. (2014). Potential Impact of Civilian Wargames on the Military. Submitted manuscript.

Hyde, Henry. (2013). *The Wargaming Compendium.* Barnsley, UK: Pen & Sword.

Illingworth, David. (2007). Allusive, Ludicrous, Illusive: Games in and with *Tristram Shandy. Shandean* 18:40–55.

Institute for Creative Technologies. (2012). BiLAT Bilateral Negotiation Trainer, accessed December 19, 2014. <http://ict.usc.edu/wp-content/uploads/overviews/BiLAT_Overview.pdf>.

Institute for Creative Technologies. (2015). ICT Overview. *USC Institute for Creative Technologies,* accessed August 28, 2014. <http://ict.usc.edu/about>.

Institute of Contemporary Art. (1957). *Conference on Motivating the Creative Process.* Harriman, NY, Arden House, May 7–10, 1957.

Interdisciplinary Symposia on Creativity, Michigan State University. (1959). *Creativity and Its Cultivation: Addresses,* edited by Harold H. Anderson. New York: Harper & Row.

International Committee of the Red Cross. (2013). Video Games and Law of War, accessed December 19, 2014. <http://www.icrc.org/eng/resources/documents/film/2013/09-28-ihl-video-games.htm>.

Iraq Body Count. (2014). Documented Civilian Deaths from Violence, accessed December 19, 2014. <https://www.iraqbodycount.org/database>.

Italian Campaign 1944. (1998). World War II event announcement.

Jacka, Benedict. (2013). *Chosen.* London: Ace Books.

Jackson, J. R. (1959). Learning from Experience in Business Decision Games. *California Management Review* 1 (2): 92–107.

Jackson, Robert. (1952). *Visual Principles for Training by Television. SDC 20-TV-2.* Port Washington, NY: Special Devices Center, Department of the Army and Department of the Navy.

Jafnakol, Orlygg. (2013). The Mighty Avenger: An Interview with Bryan Ansell. *Realm of Chaos 80s,* February 16, 2013, accessed June 6, 2014. <http://realmofchaos80s.blogspot.co.uk/2013/02/the-mighty-avenger-interview-with-bryan.html>.

Jafnakol, Orlygg. (2014). The Grand Master Returns: A Second Interview with Tony Ackland. *Realm of Chaos 80s,* January 25, 2014, accessed June 6, 2014. <http://realmofchaos80s.blogspot.co.uk/2014/01/the-grandmaster-returns-second.html>.

Jane, Fred. (1898) *Jane's All the World's Fighting Ships.* New York: Little, Brown and Company.

Jappe, Anselm. (1999). *Guy Debord.* Berkeley: University of California Press.

Jay, E. S., and R. L. McCornack. (1960). Information-Processing under Overload Conditions. *American Psychologist* 15 (7): 21–30.

Jensen, Kurt, and Lars M. Kristensen. (2009). *Coloured Petri Nets: Modelling and Validation of Concurrent Systems.* Berlin: Springer-Verlag.

Johnson, Burt (1996). Referees. World War II newsgroup, November 18, 1996.

Johnson, Roy Ivan. (1938). The Experience Curriculum in Action. *English Journal* 27 (3): 229–235.

Johnson, Stuart, Rita Johnson, and the Regional Education Laboratory for the Carolinas and Virginia. (1970). *Developing Individualized Instructional Materials.* Palo Alto, CA: Westinghouse Learning Press.

Johnson, Walter. (2003). On Agency. *Journal of Social History* 37: 113–124.

Johnson, William H. (1927). *Fundamentals in Visual Instruction.* Chicago: The Educational Screen, Inc.

Joint Chiefs of Staff (1987–2013). *JP 1-02. DOD Dictionary of Military and Associated Terms.* Washington, DC: Department of Defense.

Jones, Joshua. (2012). Necessary (Perhaps) But Not Sufficient: Assessing Drone Strikes Though a Counterinsurgency Lens. *Small Wars Journal,* August 28, 2012, accessed January 11, 2015. <http://smallwarsjournal.com/blog/necessary-perhaps-but-not-sufficient-assessing-drone-strikes-through-a-counterinsurgency-lens>.

Jones, Phillip N., and Thomas Mastaglio (MYMIC LLC). (2006). *Evaluating the Contributions of Virtual Simulations to Combat Effectiveness.* Study Report 2006–04, ARI, March.

Jones, William. (1985). *RAND Corporation Research Note N-2322-RC: On Free-Form Gaming,* accessed December 19, 2014. <http://www.rand.org/content/dam/rand/pubs/notes/2007/N2322.pdf>.

Jordan, A. M. (1937). Use of Motion Pictures in Instruction. *High School Journal* 20 (5): 188–193.

Jordan, Robert. (1990–2007). *The Wheel of Time* [series]. New York: Tor Books.

Jordan, Robert, and Brandon Sanderson. (2007–13). *The Wheel of Time* [series]. New York: Tor Books.

Juul, Jesper. (2011). *Half-Real: Video Games between Real Rules and Fictional Worlds*. Cambridge, MA: MIT Press.

Kagan, Donald, and Gregory F. Viggiano. (2013). The Hoplite Debate. In *Men of Bronze: Hoplite Warfare in Ancient Greece*, edited by Donald Kagan and Gregory F. Viggiano, 1–56. Princeton: Princeton University Press.

Kahn, Herman. (1960). *On Thermonuclear War*. Princeton: Princeton University Press.

Kahn, Herman. (1964). *Thinking about the Unthinkable*. New York: Horizon Press.

Kahn, Herman, and Anthony Weiner. (1961). *The Year 2000*. New York: Macmillan.

Kahn, Herman, Daniel Bell, and Anthony Wiener. (1968). *The Year 2000: A Framework for Speculation on the Next 33 Years*. New York: Macmillan.

Kanner, Joseph, Richard Runyon, and Otello Desiderato. (1954). *Television in Army Training: Evaluation of Television in Army Basic Training*. Technical Report 14. Washington, DC: George Washington University, Human Resources Research Office.

Kant, Immanuel. (2003). *The Critique of Pure Reason*, translated by J.M.D. Meikeljohn. Project Gutenberg Ebook #4280. <http://www.gutenberg.org/files/4280/4280-h/4280-h.htm>.

Kapell, Matthew Wilhelm, and Andrew B. R. Elliott. (2013). *Playing with the Past: Digital Games and the Simulation of History*. New York: Bloomsbury.

Kaplan, Wendy, ed. (2011). *California Design, 1930–1965: Living in a Modern Way*. Cambridge, MA: MIT Press.

Karsai, Gábor, Miklos Maroti, Ákos Lédeczi, Jeff Gray, and Janos Sztipanovits. (2004). Composition and Cloning in Modeling and Meta-Modeling. *IEEE Transactions on Control Systems Technology* 12 (2): 263–278.

Katz, Leon. (1995). The Compleat Dramaturg. In *What Is Dramaturgy?* edited by Bert Cardullo, 13–16. New York: Peter Lang.

Kaufman, Vincent. (2006). *Guy Debord: Revolution in the Service of Poetry*. Minneapolis: University of Minnesota Press.

Kebritchi, Mansureh, and Atsusi Hirumi. (2008). Examining the Pedagogical Foundations of Modern Educational Computer Games. *Computers & Education* 51: 1729–1743.

Kee, Kevin, ed. (2014). *Pastplay: Teaching and Learning History with Technology*. Ann Arbor: University of Michigan Press.

Keegan, John. (1976). *The Face of Battle: A Study of Agincourt, Waterloo, and the Somme*. London: Jonathan Cape.

Kelly, Henry. (2005). Games, Cookies and the Future of Education. *Issues in Science and Technology*, last modified on November 27 2013, accessed January 9, 2015. <http://issues.org/21-4/kelly>.

Kelly, Henry. (2008). Continuous Improvement in Undergraduate Education: A Possible Dream. *Innovations: Technology, Governance, Globalization* 3 (3): 133–151.

Kemp, Peter K., ed. (1960). *The Papers of Admiral Sir John Fisher* [2 vols.]. London: Naval Records Society.

Kendler, Howard, and John Cook. (1951). *Implications of Learning Theory for the Design of Audio-Visual Aids.* HRRL Memo Report No. 12(a). Washington, DC: US Air Force, Human Resources Research Laboratories, Headquarters Command, Bolling Air Force Base.

Keogh, Brendan. (2013). *Killing is Harmless: A Critical Reading of Spec Ops: The Line. Stolen Projects.* Kindle Edition.

Kessel, John. (2004). Creating the Innocent Killer: *Ender's Game*, Intention and Morality. *Foundation, the International Review of Science Fiction* 33: 90, accessed October 14, 2014. <http://johnjosephkessel.wix.com/kessel-website#!creating-the-innocent-killer/ce5s>.

Keymer, Thomas. (2006). Sterne and the "New Species" of Writing. In *Laurence Sterne's Tristram Shandy: A Casebook*, edited by Thomas Keymer, 50–75. Oxford: Oxford University Press.

Keyser, John. (2014). The Letter from John. *11 bit studios,* last modified March 27, 2014. <http://www.11bitstudios.com/blog/en/16/this-war-of-mine/23/the-letter-from-john.html>.

Kibbee, J. M. (1959). Dress Rehearsal for Decision-Making: The Growing Use of Business Games. *Management Review* 48 (February): 4–8.

Kibbee, J. M., C. J. Craft, and B. Nanus. (1961). *Management Games.* New York: Reinhold.

Kilcullen, David. (2010). *Counterinsurgency.* New York: Oxford University Press.

Kiell, Norman. (1961). The Myth of Fun. *Journal of Educational Sociology* 35 (1): 1–10.

Kim, James. (2007). "Good cursed, bouncing losses": Masculinity, Sentimental Irony and Exuberance in *Tristram Shandy. Eighteenth Century (Lubbock, Tex.)* 41 (1): 3–24, 93.

Kim, John H. (2008). The Threefold Model. *Darkshire.* <http://www.darkshire.net/~jhkim/rpg/theory/threefold>.

Kipp, Jacob (1985). Lenin and Clausewitz: the Militarisation of Marxism, 1914-1921. *Military Affairs* 49: 4 (October): 184–191.

Kirschenbaum, Matthew. (2009). War Stories: Board Wargames and (Vast) Procedural Narratives. In *Third Person: Authoring and Exploring Vast Narratives*, edited by Pat Harrigan and Noah Wardrip-Fruin, 357–371. Cambridge, MA: MIT Press.

Kirschner, P. A., J. Sweller and Richard E. Clark. (2006). Why Minimal Guidance During Instruction Does Not Work: An Analysis of the Failure of Constructivist, Discovery, Problem-Based Experiential and Inquiry-Based Teaching. *Educational Psychologist* 41 (2): 75–86.

Kittel, Charles. (1947). The Nature and Development of Operations Research. *Science* 105 (2719): 150–153.

Klabbers, Jan. (2009). Terminological Ambiguity: Game and Simulation. *Simulation & Gaming* 40 (4): 446–463.

Knerr, Bruce W. (2007). *Immersive Simulation Training for the Dismounted Soldier.* Study Report 2006–1 ARI, February.

Kohn, Alfie. (1986). *No Contest: The Case Against Competition.* Boston: Houghton Mifflin.

Kraft, Ivor. (1966). The Cult of Creativity. *Teachers College Record* 67 (8): 618–622.

Kraft, Ivor. (1967). Pedagogical Futility in Fun and Games. *NEA Journal* 56: 71–72.

Krentz, Peter. (2013). Hoplite Hell: How Hoplites Fought. In *Men of Bronze: Hoplite Warfare in Ancient Greece*, edited by Donald Kagan and Gregory F. Viggiano, 134–156. Princeton: Princeton University Press.

Krepinevich, Andrew. (1992). *The Military-Technical Revolution: A Preliminary Assessment*. Washington, DC: Office of Net Assessment.

Kuenne, Robert. (1965). *The Attack Submarine: A Study in Strategy*. New Haven: Yale University Press.

Kumar, Radha, ed. (2009). *Negotiating Peace in Deeply Divided Societies: A Set of Simulations*. New Delhi: SAGE Publications India.

LaGrone, Sam. (2013). Interview: Larry Bond on Tom Clancy. *USNI News,* October 8, 2013, accessed October 14, 2014. <http://news.usni.org/2013/10/08/interview-larry-bond-tom-clancy>.

Lamb, Jonathan. (1981). The Comic Sublime and Sterne's Fiction. *ELH* 1:110–143.

Lamb, Jonathan. (1989). *Sterne's Fiction and the Double Principle*. New York: Cambridge University Press.

Lampton, Donald R., Daniel P. McDonald, Mar E. Rodriguez, James E. Cotton, Christina S. Morris, James Parsons, and Glenn Martin. (2001). *Instructional Strategies for Training Teams in Virtual Environments*. TR 1110, ARI, March.

Lanchester, F. W. (1916). *Aircraft in Warfare: The Dawn of the Fourth Arm*. London: Constable and Company, Ltd.

Langner, Ralph. (2013). Stuxnet's Secret Twin. *Foreign Policy*, November 19, 2013, accessed July 29, 2015. <http://foreignpolicy.com/2013/11/19/stuxnets-secret-twin>.

Lanham, Michael J., Geoffrey P. Morgan, and Kathleen M. Carley. (2014). Social Network Modeling and Agent-Based Simulation in Support of Crisis De-escalation. *IEEE Transactions on Human-Machine Systems* 44 (1): 103–140.

Lanham, Richard A. (1973). *Tristram Shandy: The Games of Pleasure*. Berkeley: University of California Press.

Lanier, Jaron. (n.d.). No title. *Jaron Lanier,* accessed July 28, 2010. <www.jaronlanier.com/lecture.html>.

Lawrence, Philip K. (1997). *Modernity and War: The Creed of Absolute Violence*. London: Macmillan Press.

Lean, Jonathan, Jonathan Moizer, Michael Towler, and Caroline Abbey. (2006). Simulations and Games: Use and Barriers in Higher Education. *Active Learning in Higher Education* 7 (3): 227–242.

Learning Federation. (2003). *Component Roadmap: Question Generation and Answering Systems R&D for Technology-Enabled Learning System*s. Federation of American Scientists, Washington DC, October. <http://www.fas.org/programs/ltp/publications/roadmaps.html>.

Lebow, Ned. (2010). *Forbidden Fruit: Counterfactuals in International Relations*. Princeton: Princeton University Press.

Ledwidge, Frank. (2011). *Losing Small Wars*. New Haven: Yale University Press.

Leed, Eric J. (1979). *No Man's Land: Combat and Identity in World War I*. Cambridge: Cambridge University Press.

Leeson, William. (1988). *The Reisswitz Story: Five Articles from the Militair Wochenblatt.* Self-published.

Lemne, Bengt. (2010). March numbers for XBLA. *Game Reactor*, last modified April 27, 2010, accessed September 29, 2014. <http://www.gamereactor.eu/news/3557/March+numbers+for+XBLA>.

Lenoir, Tim. (2000). All But War Is Simulation: The Military-Entertainment Complex. *Configurations* 8 (3): 289–335.

Lenoir, Tim. (2002). Fashioning the Military Entertainment Complex. *Correspondence: An International Review of Culture and Society* 10 (Winter/Spring): 14–16.

Lenoir, Tim. (2003). Programming Theaters of War: Gamemakers as Soldiers. In *Bombs and Bandwidth: The Emerging Relationship between IT and Security*, edited by Robert Latham, 175–198. New York: New Press.

Lenoir, Tim, and Henry Lowood. (2003). Theatres of War: The Military-Entertainment Complex. In *Kunsthammer, Laboratorium, Bühne-Schauplätze des Wissens im 17. Jahrhundert/ Collection, Laboratory, Theater*, edited by Jan Lazardzig, Helmar Schramm, and Ludger Schwarte, 432–464. Berlin: Walter de Gruytcr.

Lenoir, Tim, and Henry Lowood. (2005). Theaters of War: The Military-Entertainment Complex. In *Collection-Laboratory-Theater: Scenes of Knowledge in the 17th Century*, edited by Jan Lazardsiz, Ludger Schwarte and Helmar Schramm, 427–465. New York: Walter de Gruyter Publishing.

Levine, Robert, Thomas Schelling, and William Jones. 1991. Crisis Games for Adults and Others. In *Crisis Games 27 Years Later: Plus C'est Déja Vu. P-7719* [reprint of 1964 internal RAND document]. Santa Monica, CA: RAND Corporation.

Levinthal, David. (2009). *I.E.D. War in Afghanistan and Iraq.* New York: Powerhouse Books.

Levinthal, David, and Garry Trudeau. (1977). *Hitler Moves East: A Graphic Chronicle, 1941-43.* Kansas City, MO: Sheed, Andrews & McMeel.

Levis, Alexander H. (2005). Executable Models of Decision Making Organizations. In *Organizational Simulation*, edited by William B. Rouse and Ken Boff, 369–388. NY: Wiley-Interscience.

Levis, Alexander H., and A. Abu Jbara. (2013). Multi-Modeling, Meta-Modeling and Workflow Languages. In *Theory and Application of Multi-Formalism Modeling*, edited by Marco Gribaudo and Mauro Iacono, 56–80. Hershey, PA: IGI Global.

Levis, Alexander H., S. K. Kansal, A. E. Olmez, and A. M. AbuSharekh. (2008). Computational models of Multi-national Organizations. In *Social Computing, Behavioral Modeling and Prediction*, edited by Huan Liu, John Salerno, Michael J. Young, 57–68. Berlin: Springer-Verlag.

Levis, Alexander H., Abbas K. Zaidi, and Mohammed F. Rafi. (2012). Multi-modeling and Meta-modeling of Human Organizations. In *Proceedings of the Fourth International Conference on Applied Human Factors and Ergonomics: AHFE2012*, San Francisco, CA, July 2012.

Lewin, Christopher George. (2012). *War Games and their History.* Stroud: Fonthill Media.

Lexington. (2014). Medals for Drone Pilots? *The Economist,* March 29 2014, accessed January 19, 2015. <http://www.economist.com/news/united

-states/21599785-fraught-debate-over-how-honour-cyber-warriors-medals-drone-pilots>.

Lindeman, Eduard C. (1948). The Dynamics of Recreational Theory. *Journal of Educational Sociology* 21 (5): 263–269.

List, Steve. (1970). Game Design: Down Highway 61, Through State Farm 69, Around Tactical Game 3, and into *PanzerBlitz*. *Strategy & Tactics* 22 14, XS3.

Little, W. McCarty. (1912). The Strategic Naval War Game or Chart Maneuver. *Proceedings of the US Naval Institute*, 1219–1220.

Loomis, Rick. (1970). Opponents Wanted. *GEN* 7 (5): 16.

Losh, Elizabeth. (2009). Regulating Violence in Virtual Worlds: Theorizing Just War and Defining War Crimes in World of Warcraft. *Pacific Coast Philology* 44 (2): 159–172.

Losh, Elizabeth. (2010). A Battle for Hearts and Minds: The Design Politics of ELECT BiLAT. In *Joystick Soldiers: The Politics of Play in Military Video Games*, edited by Nina Huntemann and Matthew Thomas Payne, 160–177. London: Routledge.

Loveridge, Mark. (1983). *Laurence Sterne and the Argument about Design*. Totowa, NJ: Barnes and Noble Books.

Lowenfeld, V. (1957). *Creativity and Mental Growth*. New York: Macmillan.

Lowood, Henry. (2009). Game Counter. In *The Object Reader*, edited by Fiona Candlin and Raiford Guins, 466–469. Abingdon, UK: Routledge.

Lowood, Henry. (2014). Game Engines and Game History. *Kinephanos* History of Games International Conference Proceedings special issue (January 2014), accessed January 13, 2015. <http://www.kinephanos.ca/2014/game-engines-and-game-history>.

Lumbry, E. W. R., ed. (1970). *Policy and Operations in the Mediterranean 1912-14*. London: Navy Record Society.

Lumsdaine, Arthur. (1953). Audio-Visual Research in the US Air Force. *AV Communication Review* 1 (Spring): 76–90.

Lupton, Christina, and Peter McDonald. (2010). Reflexivity as Entertainment: Early Novels and Recent Video Games. *Mosaic* 43 (4): 157–173.

Luttwak, Edward. (1987). *Strategy: The Logic of War and Peace*. Cambridge, MA: Harvard University Press.

Lynch, Scott. (2007). *Red Seas Under Red Skies*. London: Gollancz.

Lynn, William J, III. (2010). Defending a New Domain: The Pentagon's Cyberstrategy. *Foreign Affairs* 89 (5): 97–108.

McAneny, Larry. (1976). *PanzerBlitz*: Hex by Hex. *GEN* 12 (5): 3–13, 34.

MacCombe, Leonard (1959). Valuable Batch of Brains: An Odd Little Company Called RAND Plays Big Role in U.S. Defense. *LIFE*, May 11: 101–7.

MacGillivray, Alan. (1996). The Worlds of Iain Banks. *The Association for Scottish Literary Studies,* September 30, 2013, accessed October 14, 2014. <http://www.arts.gla.ac.uk/scotlit/asls/Laverock-Iain_Banks.html>.

MacGowan, Rodger B. (1987). 20 Years Later and 10 Years After Squad Leader. *Fire & Movement* 53: 34–37.

MacKinnon, Donald. (1961). Fostering Creativity in Students of Engineering. *Journal of Engineering Education* 52 (3): 129–142.

Madeja, Victor. (1965). Midway, D-Day, Tactics II, Stalingrad Re-worked. *GEN* 1 (5): 3.

Malcolm, D. G. (1959). *A Bibliography of the Use of Simulations in Management Analysis. SP-126*. Santa Monica, CA: System Development Corporation.

Malone, T. W., and M. R. Lepper. (1987). Making Learning Fun: A Taxonomy of Intrinsic Motivations for Learning. In *Aptitude, Learning, and Instruction, Vol. 3: Conative and Affective Process Analyses*, edited by R. E. Snow and M. J. Farr, 223–253. Hillsdale, NJ: Erlbaum.

Manstein, Erich. (1983). *Verlorene Siege* [*Lost Victories*]. Munich: Bernard & Graefe.

Mantello, Peter. (2012). Playing Discreet War in the US: Negotiating Subjecthood and Sovereignty through Special Forces Video Games. *Media, War, & Conflict* 5 (3): 269–283.

Marcus, Greil. (1989). *Lipstick Traces: A Secret History of the Twentieth Century*. London: Secker & Warburg.

Marder, Arthur J., ed. (1952). *The Making of an Admiral, 1854-1904. vol. I. Fear God and Dread Nought: The Correspondence of Admiral of the Fleet Lord Fisher of Kilverstone*. London: Jonathan Cape.

Marder, Arthur J., ed. (1956). *Years of Power, 1904-1914. vol. II. Fear God and Dread Nought: The Correspondence of Admiral of the Fleet Lord Fisher of Kilverstone*. London: Jonathan Cope.

Marder, Arthur J. (1961). *From Dreadnought to Scapa Flow* [5 vols.]. London: Oxford University Press.

Marien, Michael. (1970). *Essential Reading for the Future of Education. A Selected and Critically Annotated Bibliography*. Washington, DC: National Center for Educational Research and Development.

Martin, David. (2012). 7 Navy SEALs Disciplined for Role with Video Game. *CBS*, November 8, 2012, accessed January 19, 2015. <http://www.cbsnews.com/news/7-navy-seals-disciplined-for-role-with-video-game>.

Martin, George R. R. (1996). *A Song of Ice and Fire* [series]. London: Voyager Books.

Martin, Mike. 2014. *An Intimate War: An Oral History of the Helmand Conflict*. Oxford: Oxford University Press.

Martin, Rex. (2001). Cardboard Warriors: The Rise and Fall of an American Wargaming Subculture, 1958-1998. Ph.D. dissertation, Pennsylvania State University.

Martino, John. (2012). Video Games and the Militarisation of Society: Towards a Theoretical and Conceptual Framework. In *ICT: Critical Infrastructures and Society*, edited by M. David Hercheui, D. Whitehouse, W. McIver Jr., and J. Phahlamohlaka, 264–273. New York and Heidelberg: Springer.

Marty, Martin. (1969). *The Search for a Usable Future*. New York: Harper and Row.

Marx, Karl, and Friedrich Engels. (1929). *Marx/Engels Collected Works*. vol. 40. London: Progress Publishers.

Mason, Bill. (1997). Small Survey. WWII newsgroup, September 23, 1997.

May, Hope. (2010). *Aristotle's Ethics: Moral Development and Human Nature*. New York: Continuum.

May, Mark. A. (1937). Educational Possibilities of Motion Pictures. *Journal of Educational Sociology* 11 (3): 149–160.

Mazzetti, Mark. (2014). Intelligence Chief Condemns Snowden and Demands Return of Data. *The New York Times,* January 29, 2014, accessed January 19, 2015. <http://www.nytimes.com/2014/01/30/us/politics/intelligence-chief-condemns-snowden-and-demands-return-of-data.html?partner=rss&emc=rss>.

McAlinden, Ryan, Paula Durlach, H. Chad Lane, Andrew Gordon, and John Hart. (2008). UrbanSim: A Game-based Instructional Package for Conducting Counterinsurgency Operations. In *Proceedings of the Twenty-Sixth Army Science Conference.* Orlando, FL, 2008, accessed December 19, 2014. <http://people.ict.usc.edu/~gordon/publications/ASC08.PDF>

McAllister, Gillen. (2012). Interview with Walt Williams, E3 2012. *Gamereactor,* last modified June 21, 2012. <http://www.gamereactor.eu/news/33921/Spec+Ops%3AThe+Line+GRTV+Interview>.

McCabe, June. (2013). Review of the Canadian Humanitarian and Disaster Response Training Program SimEx 2013. *PAXsims,* August 3, 2013. <http://paxsims.wordpress.com/2013/08/03/review-of-the-canadian-humanitarian-and-disaster-response-training-program-simex-2013>.

McCall, Jeremiah. (2011). *Gaming the Past: Using Video Games to Teach Secondary History.* New York: Routledge.

McCarty, Willard. (2004). Modeling: A Study in Words and Meanings. In *A Companion to Digital Humanities*, edited by Susan Schreibman, Ray Siemens and John Unsworth, 254–269. Oxford: Wiley-Blackwell.

McChrystal, Stanley A. (2011). It Takes a Network: The New Front Line of Modern Warfare. *Foreign Policy,* February 21, 2011, accessed July 29, 2015. <http://www.foreignpolicy.com/articles/2011/02/22/it_takes_a_network>.

McConnell, Mike. (2010). "Mike McConnell on How to Win the Cyber-War We're Losing." *The Washington Post,* February 28, 2010, accessed January 19, 2015. <http://www.washingtonpost.com/wp-dyn/content/article/2010/02/25/AR2010022502493.html?sid=ST2010031901063>.

McCloskey, Joseph F. (1987). British Operational Research in World War II. *Operations Research* 35 (3): 453–470.

McCown, Margaret (2005). Strategic Gaming for the National Security Community. *Joint Forces Quarterly* 39.

McCue, Brian. (2008). *U-Boats in the Bay of Biscay: An Essay in Operations Analysis.* Xlibris Corporation.

McDonald, John, and Frank Ricciardi. (1958). The Business Decision Game. *Fortune* 57 (3): 140–142.

McDonough, Tom. (2006). Guy Debord, or the Revolutionary Without a Halo. *October* 115: 39–45.

McDuffee, Allen. (2014). At Last, a Google Glass for the Battlefield. *Wired,* February 24, 2014, accessed January 19, 2015. <http://www.wired.com/dangerroom/2014/02/battlefield-glass>.

McGonigal, Jane. (2011). *Reality Is Broken: Why Games Make Us Better and How They Can Change the World.* London: Jonathan Cape.

McGuire, Michael. (1976). The Wargamer as Nigger. *Fire & Movement* 3: 20–23.

McHugh, Francis J. (1968). *Fundamentals of War Gaming.* Newport, RI: US Naval War College.

McLaughlin, Fran. (1967). New Circuits or Short Circuits? *Educators' Guide to Media & Methods* 4 (3): 18–21.

McLeroy, Carrie. (2008). History of Military Gaming. *Soldiers Magazine* (September): 4–6.

McConnell, Mike. (2010). Mike McConnell on How to Win the Cyber-War We're Losing. *The Washington Post,* February 28, 2010, accessed January 19, 2015. <http://www.washingtonpost.com/wp-dyn/content/article/2010/02/25/AR2010022502493.html?sid=ST2010031901063>.

McLuhan, Marshall. (1960). Classrooms Without Walls. In *Explorations in Communication,* edited by Marshall McLuhan and Edmund Carpenter, 1–3. Boston: Beacon Press.

McLuhan, Marshall. (1961). Inside the Five Sense Sensorium. *Canadian Architect* 6 (6): 49–54.

McLuhan, Marshall, and Edmund Carpenter. (1957). Classroom without Walls. *Explorations* 7: 22–26.

McLuhan, Marshall, and George B. Leonard. (1967). The Future of Education: The Class of 1989. *Look* 30 (4): 23–25.

McLuhan, Marshall, and Harley Parker. (1968). *Through the Vanishing Point: Space in Poetry and Painting.* New York: Harper & Row.

McNeil, David. (1990). *The Grotesque Depiction of War and the Military in Eighteenth-Century Fiction.* Newark: University of Delaware Press.

McRaven, William H. (2012). *Posture Statement of Admiral William H. McRaven, USN, Commander, United States Special Operations Command before the 112th Congress Senate Arms Services Committee.* Washington, DC: USSOCOM.

Mead, Corey. (2013). *War Play: Video Games and the Future of Armed Conflict.* New York: Houghton Mifflin Harcourt.

Meadows, Donella, Dennis Meadows, Jorgen Randers, and William Behrens, III. (1972). *The Limits to Growth.* New York: Universe Books.

Medal of Honor: Warfighter. (2014). *Medal of Honor Wiki,* accessed January 19, 2015. <http://medalofhonor.wikia.com/wiki/Medal_of_Honor:_Warfighter#Weapons>.

Meilinger, Phillip S. (2003). *Airwar: Theory and Practice.* Portland, OR: Frank Cass.

Menninger, William C. (1948). Recreation and Mental Health. *Recreation* 42 (November): 340–346.

Menn, Joseph. (2013). SPECIAL REPORT—U. S. Cyberwar Strategy Stokes Fear of Blowback. *Reuters,* May 10, 2013, accessed January 19, 2015. <http://in.reuters.com/article/2013/05/10/usa-cyberweapons-idINDEE9490AX20130510>.

Merrifield, Andy. (2005). *Guy Debord.* London: Reaktion Books.

Metz, Steven, and James Kievit. (1995). *Strategy and the Revolution in Military Affairs: From Theory to Policy.* Carlisle, PA: Strategic Studies Institute, U.S. Army War College. <http://www.strategicstudiesinstitute.army.mil/pubs/download.cfm?q=236>.

Michael, Donald N. (1968). *The Unprepared Society: Planning for a Precarious Future.* New York: Basic Books.

Milante, Gary. (2009). Carana. *PAXsims,* January 27, 2009. <http://paxsims.wordpress.com/2009/01/27/carana>.

Miles, John, and Charles Spain. (1947). *Audio-Visual Aids in the Armed Services*. Washington, DC: Commission on Implications of Armed Services Educational Programs, American Council on Education.

Miller, James Grier. (1960). Information Input Overload and Psychopathology. *American Journal of Psychiatry* 116 (8): 695–704.

Miller, James Grier. (1964). The Information Explosion: Implications for Teaching. *Journal of the National Association of Women Deans & Counselors* 27: 54–59.

Miller, Walter M. (1960). *A Canticle for Leibowitz*. Philadelphia: J. B. Lippincott & Co.

Mirowski, Philip. (1999). Cyborg Agonistes: Economics Meets Operations in Mid-Century. *Social Studies of Science* 29 (5): 685–718.

Mockenhaupt, Brian. (2010). SimCity Baghdad. *The Atlantic*, January/February 2010, accessed July 29, 2015. <http://www.theatlantic.com/magazine/archive/2010/01/simcity-baghdad/307830>.

Moizer, Jonathan, Jonathan Lean, Michael Towler, and Caroline Abbey. (2009). Simulations and Games: Overcoming the Barriers to their Use in Higher Education. *Active Learning in Higher Education* 10 (3): 207–224.

Moore, L. B. (1958). Experiencing Reality in Management Education. *Journal of the Academy of Management* 1 (October): 7–14.

Morgan, Gary C. (1990). Wargaming and the Military. *Fire & Movement: The Forum of Conflict Simulation* 66 (June/July): 31–36.

Morie, Jacquelyn Ford. (2013). *Enhancing Sexual Harassment Training for the 21st Century Military*. Playa Vista, CA: USC Institute for Creative Technologies.

Morison, Elting E. (1977). *From Know-How to Nowhere*. New York: Mentor.

Morris, Errol. (2014). The Certainty of Donald Rumsfeld (Part 4). *The New York Times*, March 28, 2014, accessed January 19, 2015. <http://opinionator.blogs.nytimes.com/2014/03/28/the-certainty-of-donald-rumsfeld-part-4>.

Morse, Philip M., and George E. Kimball. (1946). *OEG Report 54. Methods of Operations Research*. Washington, DC: Operations Evaluation Group, Office of the Chief of Naval Operations.

Morse, Philip M., and George E. Kimball. (1951). *Methods of Operations Research*. Revised 1st edition. Cambridge, MA: MIT Press.

Morse, Philip M., and George E. Kimball. (1956). How to Hunt a Submarine. In *The World of Mathematics*, edited by James R. Newman, 2160–2181. New York: Simon and Schuster.

Morse, Philip, and George Kimball. (1959). *Methods of Operations Research*. Revised edition. Cambridge, MA: MIT Press.

Morschauser, Joe. (1962). *How to Play War Games in Miniature*. New York: Walker and Company.

Mukherjee, Souvik. (2010). Shall We Kill the Pixel Soldier? Perceptions of Trauma and Morality in Combat Video Games. *Journal of Gaming and Virtual Worlds* 2 (1): 39–51.

Mullan, John. (1988). *Sentiment and Sociability: The Language of Feeling in the Eighteenth Century*. Oxford: Clarendon Press.

Mulvey, Laura. (1975). Visual Pleasure and Narrative Cinema. In *Issues in Feminist Film Criticism*, edited by Patricia Erens, 28–71. Bloomington, IN: Indiana University Press.

Munn, C., S. Wales, and A. Beach. (July 2, 1859). Chess-Playing Excitement. *Scientific American* 9, accessed October 14, 2014. <http://books.google.co.uk/books?id=90hGAQAAIAAJ>.

Murdock, Clark A. (1974). *Defense Policy Formation: A Comparative Analysis of the McNamara Era.* Albany: State University of New York Press.

Murray, H. J. R. (1913). *A History of Chess.* Oxford: Oxford University Press.

Murray, H. J. R. (1952). *A History of Board-games Other Than Chess.* Oxford: Clarendon Press.

Myers, David. (1990). Chris Crawford and Computer Game Aesthetics. *Journal of Popular Culture* 24 (2): 17–32.

Nakashima, Ellen. (2010). War Game Reveals U.S. Lacks Cyber-Crisis Skills. *The Washington Post*, February 17, 2010, accessed January 19, 2015. <http://www.washingtonpost.com/wp-dyn/content/article/2010/02/16/AR2010021605762.html>.

Nakashima, Ellen. (2012). U.S. Accelerating Cyberweapon Research. *The Washington Post*, March 18, 2012, accessed January 19, 2015. <http://www.washingtonpost.com/world/national-security/us-accelerating-cyberweapon-research/2012/03/13/gIQAMRGVLS_story.html>.

Nannini, Christopher, Jeffrey Appleget, and Alejandro Hernandez. (2012). Game for Peace: Progressive Education in Peace Operations. *Journal of Defense Modeling and Simulation* 10:3.

Nasar, Sylvia. (1998). *A Beautiful Mind: A Biography of John Forbes Nash, Jr., Winner of the Nobel Prize in Economics, 1994.* New York: Simon & Schuster.

Nash, Jay B. (1948). A Philosophy of Recreation in America. *Journal of Educational Sociology* 21 (5): 257–263.

National Research Council (US), and Committee on Modeling and Simulation: Opportunities for Collaboration Between the Defense and Entertainment Research Communities. (1997). *Modeling and Simulation: Linking Entertainment and Defense.* Washington, DC: National Academy Press.

Negri, Antonio. (1998). Reviewing the experience of Italy in the 1970s. *Le Monde diplomatique*, September 1998.

Nelson, Theodor H. (1974). *Computer Lib/Dream Machines.* Self-published.

New London Group. (1996). A Pedagogy of Multiliteracies: Designing Social Futures. *Harvard Educational Review* 66: 60–92.

Newbould, M.-C. (2006). For the Good of the Nation: "Unkle" Toby and Corporal Trim. *Shandean* 17:85–92.

Nofi, Albert A. (2010). *To Train the Fleet for War: The US Navy Fleet Problems, 1923–1940.* Newport, RI: Naval War College Press.

Nofi, Albert A. (2012). Some Lessons from History about Wargaming and Exercises. In *Peter Perla's The Art of Wargaming*, edited by John Curry, 288–309. Bristol, UK: The History of Wargaming Project.

Nordling, Elias. (2009). Really Small. *Battles Magazine* 1: 35–39.

Nottelman, Dirk. (2014). From Ironclads to Dread-noughts: The Development of the German Navy, 1864–1918. *Warship International* 51 (1): 43–91.

Odessa '97. (1997). World War II private reenactment event announcement, sponsored by Fusilier Kompanie 272 and W2HPG, New York, 1997.

Odlyzko, Andrew. (2010). Social Networks and Mathematical Models Electronic Commerce: A Research Commentary on 'Critical Mass and Willingness to Pay for Social Networks' by J. Christopher Westland. *Research and Applications* 9 (1): 26–28.

One Year In Hell ... Surviving a Full SHTF Collapse in Bosnia. (2013). *Silver Doctors*, May 13, 2013. <http://www.silverdoctors.com/one-year-in-hellsurviving-a-full-shtf-collapse-in-bosnia>.

Onians, John. (1989). War, Mathematics, and Art in Ancient Greece. *History of the Human Sciences* 4 (2): 39–62.

Orbanes, Philip E. (2004). *The Game Makers.* Cambridge, MA: Harvard Business School Press.

O'Reilly, Bill. (2012). Talking Points Memo: Is Traditional America Gone for Good? *Fox News Insider,* last modified November 13, 2012. <http://foxnewsinsider.com/2012/11/13/talking-points-memo-is-traditional-america-gone-for-good>.

Organisation for the Prohibition of Chemical Weapons. (2005). *Chemical Weapons Convention: Convention on the Prohibition of the Development, Production, Stockpiling and Use of Chemical Weapons and on Their Destruction.* <www.opcw.org/chemical-weapons-convention>

Osbourne, Lloyd. (1898). Stevenson at Play. *Scribner's Magazine* 24:709–719.

O'Toole, Gary. (2014). If Your Only Tool Is a Hammer Then Every Problem Looks Like a Nail. *Quote Investigator*, last modified May 8, 2014. <http://quoteinvestigator.com/2014/05/08/hammer-nail>.

Ottenberg, Michael. (2008). Algernon Wargame. In *Seventy-sixth Annual Symposium of the Military Operations Research Society.* <http://oai.dtic.mil/oai/oai?verb=getRecord&metadataPrefix=html&identifier=ADA490233>.

Ottosen, Rune. (2009). The Military-Industrial Complex Revisited: Computer Games and War Propaganda. *Television & New Media* 10 (1): 122–125.

Overy, Richard. (2010). The Historical Present. *Times Higher Education,* April 29, 2010: 30–34.

Owens, William A. (1996). The Emerging U. S. System-of-Systems. *National Defense University, Institute for National Strategic Studies* 63 (February). <http://www.dtic.mil/cgi-bin/GetTRDoc?AD=ADA394313>.

Page, Susan. (2014). Panetta: "30-Year War" and a Leadership Test for Obama. *USA Today,* October 6, 2014, accessed January 19, 2015. <http://www.usatoday.com/story/news/politics/2014/10/06/leon-panetta-memoir-worthy-fights/16737615>.

Paletta, Anthony. (2012). Wargames: On Roberto Bolaño's *The Third Reich. The Millions,* February 10, 2012, accessed October 14, 2014. <http://www.themillions.com/2012/02/war-games-on-roberto-bolanos-the-third-reich.html>.

Palmer, Nicholas. (1977). *The Comprehensive Guide to Board Wargaming.* New York: McGraw-Hill.

Pape, Robert A. (1996). *Bombing to Win.* Ithaca, NY: Cornell University Press.

Parker, L. E., and M. R. Lepper. (1992). Effects of Fantasy Contexts on Children's Learning and Motivation—Making Learning More Fun. *Journal of Personality and Social Psychology* 62 (4): 625–633.

Parkin, Simon. (2013). Shooters: How Video Games Fund Arms Manufacturers. *Eurogamer,* January 31, 2013, accessed January 19, 2015. <http://www .eurogamer.net/articles/2013-02-01-shooters-how -video-games-fund-arms-manufacturers>.

Parks, Lisa. (2011). *Coverage: Media Spaces and Security after 9/11.* London: Routledge.

Parlett, David. (1999). *The Oxford History of Board Games.* Oxford: Oxford University Press.

Parnes, Sidney. (1963). Education and Creativity. *Teachers College Record* 64 (4): 331.

Parrott, Marvin. (1963). $600 Tanks Embattle. *Army* 13 (6): 48–50.

Parsons, Henry McIlvaine. (1972). *Man-Machine System Experiments.* Baltimore, MD: Johns Hopkins University Press.

Patrick, Stephen B. (1977a). The History of Wargaming. In *Strategy & Tactics Staff Study Nr. 2: Wargame Design,* 1–29. New York: Hippocrene.

Patrick, Stephen B. (1977b). Notes on Game Design. In *Strategy & Tactics Staff Study Nr. 2: Wargame Design,* 78–106. New York: Hippocrene.

Patterson, A. Temple, ed. (1966). *The Jellicoe Papers.* vol. I. London: Naval Records Society.

Paulson, Ronald. (1998). *Don Quixote in England: The Aesthetics of Laughter.* Baltimore, MD: Johns Hopkins University Press.

PAXsims (2015). AFTERSHOCK. <https://paxsims. wordpress.com/aftershock/>.

Payne, Matt, and Nina Huntemann. (2009). *Joystick Soldiers: The Politics of Play in Military Video Games.* New York: Routledge.

Payne, Matthew Thomas. (2014). War Bytes: The Critique of Militainment in Spec Ops: The Line. *Critical Studies in Media Communication* 31 (4): 265–282.

Peck, Michael. (2011). Confessions of an Xbox General. *Foreign Policy,* last modified September 28, 2011. <http://www.foreignpolicy.com/articles/2011/ 09/28/Xbox_general>.

Peckham, Matt. (2014). A War Survival Videogame That Shows You the Real Horrors of Fighting. *Wired,* November 14, 2014. <http://www.wired.com/2014/ 11/this-war-of-mine>.

Perica, Jon. (1964). Putting More Realism into Tactics II. *GEN* 1 (4): 7–12.

Perla, Peter P. (1990). *The Art of Wargaming: A Guide for Professionals and Hobbyists.* Annapolis, MD: Naval Institute Press.

Perla, Peter P. (1991). A Guide to Navy Wargaming. In *War Gaming Anthology,* edited by Mel Chaloupka, Joseph Coelho and Linda Lou Borges-DuBois, 2–3. Newport, RI: Naval War College, Center for Naval Warfare Studies, Advanced Concepts Department, Naval Reserve Project.

Perla, Peter P., and Ed McGrady. (2011). Why Wargaming Works. *Naval War College Review* 64 (3): 111–128.

Perla, Peter, and Edsel D. McGrady. (2009). *Systems Thinking and Wargaming.* Arlington, VA: Center for Naval Analysis.

Perla, Peter, and Michael Markowitz. (2009). *Conversations with Wargamers*. Arlington, VA: Center for Naval Analyses.

Peterson, Jon. (2012). *Playing at the World: A History of Simulating Wars, People and Fantastic Adventures, from Chess to Role-Playing Games*. San Diego, CA: Unreason Press.

Philbin, Tobias. (2014). *The Battle of Dogger Bank*. Indianapolis: Indiana University Press.

Phillies, George. (1975). Phillies on *Dungeons & Dragons*. *American Wargamer* 2 (8): 8.

Phillies, George. (2014). *Designing Wargames—Introduction. Studies in Game Design Book 5*. Amazon Digital Services.

Pickering, Andy. (1995). Cyborg History and the World War Two Regime. *Perspectives on Science: Historical, Philosophical, Social* 3 (1): 1–48.

Pimper, Jeff. (1977). *All the World's Wargames: 1953–1977. With addenda by George Phillies, including 1978–1982, 1983–1989, and 1990–1995*. Livermore, CA: American Wargaming Association.

Platt, John. (1969). What We Must Do. *Science* 166 (3909): 1115–1121.

Pleban, Robert J., and Jena Salvetti. (2003). *Using Virtual Environments for Conducting Small Unit Dismounted Mission Rehearsals*. RR 1806, ARI, June.

Power, Marcus. (2007). Digitized Virtuosity: Video War Games and Post-9/11 Cyber-Deterrence. *Security Dialogue* 38:2.

Pratchett, Terry. (2004). *Going Postal*. London: Doubleday.

Pratchett, Terry. (2005). *Thud!* London: Doubleday.

Prensky, Marc. (2001). *Digital Game-Based Learning*. New York: McGraw-Hill.

Price, Martin. (1987). Art and Nature: the Duality of Man. In *Laurence Sterne's Tristram Shandy: Modern Critical Interpretations*, edited by Harold Bloom, 23–30. New York: Chelsea House.

Public International Law and Policy Group. (n.d.). Negotiation Simulations, accessed December 19, 2014. <http://publicinternationallawandpolicygroup.org/library/negotiation-simulations>.

Pussy Riot. (2012). Punk Prayer. You Tube, accessed August 31, 2013. <www.youtube.com/watch?v=ALS92big4TY>.

Rabinovitz, Lauren. (2004). More Than the Movies: A History of Somatic Visual Culture through Hale's Tours, IMAX, and Motion Simulation Rides. In *Memory Bytes: History, Technology, and Digital Culture*, edited by Lauren Rabinovitz and Abraham Geil, 99–125. Durham, NC: Duke University Press.

Rabinovitz, Lauren. (2006). From Hale's Tours to Star Tours. In *Virtual Voyages: Cinema and Travel*, edited by Alexandra Schneider, Jeffrey Ruoff, Amy J. Staples and Dana Benelli, 42–60. Durham, NC: Duke University Press.

Rabinovitz, Lauren. (2012). *Electric Dreamland: Amusement Parks, Movies, and American Modernity*. New York: Columbia University Press.

Radford, Elaine. (2007). Ender and Hitler: Sympathy for the Superman (20 Years Later). *Peachfront Speaks*, March 26, 2007, accessed October 14, 2014. <http://peachfront.diaryland.com/enderhitlte.html>.

RAND Corporation. (2000a). GAMING (pre-1960): A Bibliography of Selected RAND Publications SB-1050. May 2000.

RAND Corporation. (2000b). GAMING (1970-1984): A Bibliography of Selected RAND Publications SB-2050. May 2000.

RAND Corporation. (2001). RAND Hosts Army Science Board Tour of Innovative Modeling and Simulation Techniques, accessed November 21, 2014. <http://www.rand.org/natsec_area/products/ictvisit.html>.

RAND Corporation. (2004a). GAMING (1985-2004): A Bibliography of Selected RAND Publications SB-3050. May 2004.

RAND Corporation. (2004b). Microworld Simulations: A New Dimension in Training Army Logistics Management Skills, accessed November 21, 2014. <http://www.rand.org/pubs/research_briefs/RB3037/index1.html>.

Rasmussen, Frederick N. (2010). Charles S. Roberts, Train Line Expert, Dies at 80. *Baltimore Sun*, August 28, 2010.

Rau, Erik. (2000). The Adoption of Operations Research in the United States During World War II. In *Systems, Experts, and Computers. The Systems Approach in Management and Engineering, World War II and After*, edited by Agatha Hughes and Thomas Hughes, 57–92. Cambridge, MA: MIT Press.

Ray, Herbert. (1966). Air Defense Simulation Through the Years. *Air University Review (United States Edition)* 17 (September-October): 62–70.

Reddoch, Russell. (1970). Comments on Module *Blitzkrieg*. *S&T Supplement* 2: 9–11.

Rehkop, J. (1957). *Experience with the Management-Decision Simulation Game: Monopologs. P-1131.* Santa Monica, CA: RAND Corporation.

Reiber, L. P. (1996). Seriously Considering Play. *Educational Technology Research and Development* 44 (2): 43–58.

Reichenbach, Harry. (1931). *Phantom Fame: The Anatomy of Ballyhoo.* New York: Simon & Schuster.

Reisswitz, Georg Heinrich Rudolf Johann von (1824). *Anleitung zur Darstellung Militairischer Manöver mit dem Apparat des Kriegs-Spieles [Instructions for the Representation of Military Maneuvers with the War Game Apparatus].* Berlin: Trowitzsch.

Remington, Roger. (2003). *American Modernism: Graphic Design 1920–1960.* New Haven: Yale University Press.

Rhea, John. (1980). Military Simulators: Total Training. *National Defense* 64 (2): 32–35, 64–64.

Rhyne, R. F. (1972). Communicating Holistic Insights. In *Fields Within Fields Within Fields: The Methodology of Pattern.* vol. 5. Edited by Julius Stulman, 93–104. New York: The World Institute Council.

Ricciardi, Frank. (1957). Business War Games for Executives: A New Concept in Management Training. *Management Review* 46 (May): 45–55.

Richfield, Paul. (2011). Intell Video Moves to a Netflix Model. *Government Computer News: Technology, Tools and Tactics for Public Sector IT,* March 29, 2011, accessed January 23, 2015. <http://gcn.com/articles/2011/03/29/c4isr-1-battlefield-full-motion-video.aspx>.

Riff, David. (2012). A Representation which is Divorced from the Consciousness of Those Whom It Represents is No Representation. What I do not know, I do not worry about. *Chto Delat?,* accessed August 31, 2013. <http://chtodelat.org/b8-newspapers/12-38/david-riff-a-representation-which-is-divorced-from

-the-consciousness-of-those-whom-it-represents-is -no-representation-what-i-do-not-know-i-do-not -worry-about/>.

Riza, M. Shane. (2013). *Killing Without Heart: Limits on Robotic Warfare in an Age of Persistent Conflict.* Washington, DC: Potomac Books.

Roark, M. L. (1925). Is the Project Method a Contribution? *Peabody Journal of Education* 2 (4): 197–204.

Robb, Tim. (1996). Enlightenment for the GWA Vice President. *On the Wire* 7.

Robbins, Reece. (2014). Bay Area Open 2014 Warhammer 40000 Championships Format. *Frontline Gaming,* June 10, 2014, accessed January 6, 2015. <http://www .frontlinegaming.org/2014/06/10/bay-area-open -2014-warhammer-40000-championships-format>.

Roberts, Adam. (2013). Iain M Banks' *The Player of Games* (1988). *Sibilant Fricative,* May 18, 2013, accessed October 14, 2014. <http://sibilantfricative.blogspot. co.uk/2013/05/iain-m-banks-player-of-games-1988. html>.

Roberts, Andrew, ed. (2004). *What Might Have Been.* London: Orion.

Roberts, Charles S. (1983). Charles S. Roberts: In His Own Words. *Charles S. Roberts Awards,* accessed January 3, 2015. <http://www.alanemrich.com/CSR _pages/Articles/CSRspeaks.htm>.

Roberts, R. M., and L. Strauss. (1975). Management Games in Higher Education 1962–1974—An Increasing Acceptance. In *North American Simulation and Gaming Association*, edited by J. Elliott and R. McGinty, 381–385. Los Angeles: University of Southern California Press.

Robinson, James. (1966). Simulation and Games. In *The New Media and Education*, edited by Peter Rossi and Bruce Biddle, 93–135. Chicago: Aldine Publishing Company.

Rock, Robert, James Duva, and John Murray. (1952). *The Comparative Effectiveness of Instruction by Television, Television Recordings, and Conventional Classroom Procedures.* NAVEXOS P-850–2. Port Washington, NY: Special Devices Center, Department of the Army and Department of the Navy.

Roeder, Oliver. (2014). Designing the Best Board Game on the Planet. *Fivethirtyeight.com*, December 31, 2014. <http://fivethirtyeight.com/features/designing-the -best-board-game-on-the-planet/>.

Rogers, Carl. (1954). Toward a Theory of Creativity. *ETC: A Review of General Semantics* 11: 249–260.

Ross, Ian Campbell. (2001). *Laurence Sterne: A Life.* Oxford: Oxford University Press.

Rowland, David. (2006). *The Stress of Battle: Quantifying Human Performance in Combat.* London: The Stationery Office.

Rowling, J. K. (1997). *Harry Potter and the Philosopher's Stone.* London: Bloomsbury.

Rubel, Robert. (2006). The Epistemology of Wargaming. *Naval War College Review* 59 (2): 108–128.

Rucker, Rudy, R.U. Sirius, and Queen Mu. (1992). *Mondo 2000: A User's Guide to the New Edge.* New York: Harper Perennial.

Rumsfeld, Donald. (2002). *Annual Report to the President and Congress.* Washington, DC: Department of Defense.

Rushing, John, and John Tiller. (2011). Rule Learning Approaches for Symmetric Multiplayer Games. Paper presented at the Sixteenth International Conference on Computer Games: AI, Animation, Mobile, Educational and Serious Games (CGAMES 2011), Louisville, KY, July 27–30, 2011.

Saberhagen, Fred. (1981). *Octagon.* New York: Ace Books.

Sabin, Philip. (2002). Playing at War: The Modern Hobby of Wargaming. In *War and Games*, edited by Tim Cornell and Thomas Allen, 193–230. Rochester, NY: Bordell.

Sabin, Philip. (2007). *Lost Battles: Reconstructing the Great Clashes of the Ancient World.* London: Hambledon Continuum.

Sabin, Philip. (2011). The Benefits and Limits of Computerisation in Conflict Simulation. *Literary and Linguistic Computing* 26 (3): 323–328.

Sabin, Philip. (2012). *Simulating War: Studying Conflict through Simulation Games.* New York: Continuum.

Sabin, Philip. (2013). The Hollywood Syndrome: Accuracy vs Drama in Wargame Design. *Battles Magazine* 9: 59–61.

Sabin, Philip. (2014). *Simulating War: Studying Conflict Through Simulation Games.* Reprint Edition. New York: Bloomsbury.

Sadd, Dave. (2012). *Spec Ops: The Line* Made Me a Bad Person. *Pixels or Death,* last modified September 7, 2012. <pixelsordeath.com/features/spec-ops-the-line-made-me-a-bad-person>.

Saettler, Paul. (2004). *The Evolution of American Educational Technology.* 2nd ed. Englewood, CO: Information Age Publishing.

Salter, Mark B. (2011). The Geographical Imaginations of Video Games: *Diplomacy, Civilization, America's Army* and *Grand Theft Auto IV. Geopolitics* 16 (2): 359–388.

Samuel, William. (1997). Small Survey. WWII newsgroup, September 23, 1997.

Sanger, David E. (2012). Obama Order Sped Up Wave of Cyberattacks Against Iran. *New York Times,* June 1, 2012, accessed January 19, 2015. <http://www.nytimes.com/2012/06/01/world/middleeast/obama-ordered-wave-of-cyberattacks-against-iran.html?pagewanted=all&_r=0>.

Sargent, Robert G. (2005). Verification and Validation of Simulation Models. In *Proceedings of the 2005 Winter Simulation Conference, Orlando, FL, December 2005*, edited by M. E. Kuhl, N. M. Stieger, F. B. Armstrong, and J. A. Jones, 130–143. Piscataway, NJ: Institute of Electrical and Electronics Engineers.

Sarudy, Barbara Wells. (2013). The Bowling Green and the Machine in the Garden. *Early American Gardens,* September 7, 2013. <http://americangardenhistory.blogspot.com/2013/09/bowling-greens-machine-in-garden.html>.

Savage, Sean. (2006). The Eye Beholds: Silent Era Industrial Film and the Bureau of Commercial Economics. M.A. thesis, New York University.

Saxenian, AnnaLee. (1994). *Regional Advantage: Culture and Competition in Silicon Valley and Route 128.* Cambridge, MA: Harvard University Press.

Shachtman, Noah. (2013). This Pentagon Project Makes Cyberwar as Easy as *Angry Birds. Wired,* May 28, 2013, accessed January 19, 2015. <http://www.wired.com/dangerroom/2013/05/pentagon-cyberwar-angry-birds/all>.

Schechter, Joel. (1976). American Dramaturgs. *Drama Review* 20 (2): 88–92.

Schelling, Thomas. (1960). *The Strategy of Conflict.* Oxford: Oxford University Press.

Schelling, Thomas. (1987). The Role of War Games and Exercises. In *Managing Nuclear Operations*, edited by Ashton Carter et al. Washington, DC: The Brookings Institution.

Schmitt, Eric. (2014). U. S. Strategy to Fight Terrorism Increasingly Uses Proxies. *New York Times*, May 28, 2014, accessed January 19, 2015. <http://www.nytimes.com/2014/05/30/world/africa/us-strategy-to-fight-terrorism-increasingly-uses-proxies.html>.

Schorske, Carl. (1998). *Thinking With History: Explorations in the Passage to Modernism.* Princeton: Princeton University Press.

Schrieber, A. N. (1958). Gaming: A New Way to Teach Business Decision-Making. *University of Washington Business Review* 17 (April): 18–29.

Schrock, S. L. (1989). A DOE SUCCESS: Underwater Environmental Restoration Activities at Quarry, Kerr Hollow, accessed April 1, 2014. <www.rim.doe.gov/KHQ.pdf>.

Schulzke, Marcus. (2010). Defending the Morality of Violent Video Games. *Ethics and Information Technology* 12 (2): 127–138.

Schulzke, Marcus. (2013a). Rethinking Military Gaming America's Army and Its Critics. *Games and Culture* 8 (2): 59–76.

Schulzke, Marcus. (2013b). Ethically Insoluble Dilemmas in War. *Journal of Military Ethics* 12 (2): 95–110.

Schwartz, Mattathias. (2014). "We're at Greater Risk": Q. & A. with General Keith Alexander. *The New Yorker*, May 15, 2014, accessed January 19, 2015. <http://www.newyorker.com/online/blogs/newsdesk/2014/05/were-at-greater-risk-q-a-with-general-keith-alexander.html?utm_source=www&utm_medium=tw&utm_campaign=20140515>.

Scott, James C. (1990). *Seeing Like a State: How Certain Schemes to Improve the Human Condition Have Failed.* New Haven: Yale University Press.

Sears, Stephens. (2001). A Confederate Cannae and Other Scenarios. In *What If? Military Historians Imagine What Might Have Been*, edited by Robert Cowley, 239–258. London: Pan.

Seixas, Peter. (2004). *Theorizing Historical Consciousness.* Toronto: University of Toronto Press.

Shaftel, Fannie R., and George Shaftel. (1967). *Role-Playing for Social Values.* Upper Saddle River, NJ: Prentice-Hall.

Shalett, Sidney. (1943). Navy Trainees Put Under "Air Attack." *New York Times,* May 9, 1943: 25.

Shaw, Ian Graham Ronald. (2010). Playing War. *Social & Cultural Geography* 11 (8): 789–803.

Shimer, Eric R. (1965). Meanwhile—Back at Tactics II. *GEN* 1 (5): 11.

Shirts, Garry R. (1970). Games Students Play. *Saturday Review* (May 16), 81–82.

Shlapak, David, David Orletsky, and Barry Wilson, and the RAND Corporation. (2000). *Dire Strait? Military Aspects of the China-Taiwan Confrontation and Options for US Policy.* Washington, DC: RAND Corporation.

Showalter, Dennis, and Harold Deutsch, eds. (2010). *If the Allies Had Fallen: Sixty Alternate Scenarios of World War II*. London: Frontline.

Shrader, Charles R. (2006). *The History of Operations Research in the United States Army, Volume 1: 1942-1962*. Washington, DC: Office of the Deputy Under Secretary of the Army for Operations Research, United States Army.

Shubik, Martin. (2002). Game Theory and Operations Research: Some Musings 50 Years Later. *Operations Research* 50 (1): 192–196.

Sicart, Miguel. (2009). *The Ethics of Computer Games*. Cambridge, MA: MIT Press.

Sicart, Miguel. (2013). *Beyond Choices: The Design of Ethical Gameplay*. Cambridge, MA: MIT Press.

Simeone, Nick. (2014). Hagel: Proposed Defense Budget Tailored to Meet Future Threats. *American Forces Press Service,* June 18, 2014, accessed January 19, 2015. <http://www.defense.gov/news/newsarticle.aspx?id=122497>.

Simon, Herbert A. (1956). Rational Choice and the Structure of the Environment. *Psychological Review* 63 (2): 129–138.

Simonsen, Redmond A. (1973). Physical Systems Design in Conflict Simulations. *Moves* 7: 22–24.

Simonsen, Redmond A. (1977). Image and System: Graphics and Physical Systems Design. In *Wargame Design: The History, Production and Use of Conflict Simulation Games,* edited by the staff of *Strategy & Tactics,* 45–77. New York: Hippocrene.

Singer, Michael J., Jason P. Kring, Roger M. Hamilton. (2006). 2006–01 *Instructional Features for Training in Virtual Environments*. TR 1184, ARI, July.

Sirlin, David. (2008a). Balancing Multiplayer Games, Part 1: Definitions. *Sirlin.net,* October 17 2008, accessed January 6, 2015. <http://www.sirlin.net/articles/balancing-multiplayer-games-part-1-definitions>.

Sirlin, David. (2008b). Balancing Multiplayer Games, Part 3: Fairness. *Sirlin.net,* October 17, 2008, accessed January 6, 2015. <http://www.sirlin.net/articles/balancing-multiplayer-games-part-3-fairness>.

Sloyan, Patrick J. (2002). What Bodies? *The Digital Journalist*, November 1, 2002, accessed January 19, 2015. <http://digitaljournalist.org/issue0211/sloyan.html>.

Slye, John. (2012). Federal Cybersecurity Market to Grow amid Challenges. *The Washington Post*, November 9, 2012, accessed January 19, 2015. <http://www.washingtonpost.com/business/capitalbusiness/federal-cybersecurity-market-to-grow-amid-challenges/2012/11/09/c2807218-251f-11e2-9313-3c7f59038d93_story.html>.

Smelser, Ronald, and Edward Davies. 2008. *The Myth of the Eastern Front: The Nazi-Soviet War in American Popular Culture*. New York: Cambridge University Press.

Smith, Frederick James. (1913). The Evolution of the Motion Picture. *New York Dramatic Mirror*, July 9, 1913: 24.

Smith, Kinsley, and Edward Van Ormer. (1949). *Learning Theories and Instructional Film Research. SDC 269-7-6. Instructional Film Research Program, Pennsylvania State College*. Port Washington, NY: Office of Naval Research, Special Devices Center.

Smith, Perry M. (2007). *Assignment Pentagon: How to Succeed in a Bureaucracy*. Dulles, VA: Potomac Books, Inc.

Smith, Roger. (2009). *Military Simulation and Serious Games: Where We Came From and Where We are Going.* Orlando, FL: Modelbenders Press.

Smith, Ryan. (2012). Partners in Arms. *The Gameological Society*, August 13, 2012, accessed January 19, 2015. <http://gameological.com/2012/08/partners-in -arms>.

Snider, Mike. (2012). Interview: "Black Ops II" Consultant Peter Singer. *USA Today* May 2, 2012, accessed January 19, 2015. <http://content.usatoday.com/ communities/gamehunters/post/2012/05/ interview-black-ops-ii-consultant-peter-singer/1#. UZwk1iuc7yd>.

Sones, W. W. D. (1944). The Comics and Instructional Method. *Journal of Educational Sociology* 18 (4): 232–240.

Sorkin, Roger, Sut Jhally, Leigh Alexander, Craig Anderson, Andrew J. Bacevich, Nina Huntemann, Elizabeth Losh, Matthew Thomas Payne, K. C. Thompson, and Media Education Foundation. (2013). *Joystick Warriors: Video Games, Violence & Militarism.* Northhampton, MA: Media Education Foundation.

Soud, Stephen. (1995). "Weavers, Gardeners, and Gladiators": Labyrinths in *Tristram Shandy. Eighteenth-Century Studies* 28 (4): 397–411.

Specht, Robert D. (1957). War Games. RAND Report P-1041, March 18, 1957, accessed January 13, 2015. <http://www.rand.org/content/dam/rand/pubs/ papers/2005/P1041.pdf>.

Specht, Robert. (1958). War Games. In *Operational Research in Practice: Report of a NATO Conference,* edited by Max Davies and Michel Verhulst, 144–152. New York: Pergamon Press.

Spick, Mike. (1978). *Air Battles in Miniature.* Cambridge: Patrick Stephens Limited.

Spiegelman, Art. (1991). *Maus.* New York: Pantheon Books.

SRI International. (1977). *Proceedings.* vol. I. Theater-Level Gaming and Analysis Workshop for Force Planning. Menlo Park, CA: SRI International. <http:// oai.dtic.mil/oai/oai?verb=getRecord&metadataPrefi x=html&identifier=ADA101846>.

Stahl, Roger. (2006). Have You Played the War on Terror? *Critical Studies in Media Communication* 23 (2): 112–130.

Stahl, Roger. (2009). *Militainment, Inc.: War, Media, and Popular Culture.* New York: Routledge.

Stahl, Roger. (2010a). *Militainment, Inc.: War, Media, and Popular Culture.* Reprint edition. New York: Routledge.

Stahl, Roger. (2010b). *Militainment, Inc: War, Media and Popular Culture.* New York: Routledge. Stanford International Human Rights & Conflict Clinic and the Global Justice Clinic of New York University (2012). *Living Under Drones,* accessed January 11, 2015. <http://www.livingunderdrones.org/wp-content/ uploads/2013/10/Stanford-NYU-Living-Under -Drones.pdf>.

Stanney, Kay, Ronald Mourant, and Robert Kennedy. (1998). Human Factors Issues in Virtual Environments: A Review of the Literature. *Presence* 7 (4): 327–351.

Stallabrass, Julian. (1999). *High Art Lite: British Art in the 1990s.* London: Verso.

Starr, Paul. (1994). Seductions of Sim: Policy as a Simulation Game. *American Prospect* 17: 19–29.

Staves, Susan. (1989). Toby Shandy: Sentiment and the Soldier. In *Approaches to Teaching Tristram Shandy*, edited by Melvyn New. New York: MLA Publications.

Stelek (2013). 40K Is Competitive? *Yes The Truth Hurts,* October 29, 2013, accessed December 12, 2014. <http://yesthetruthhurts.com/2013/10/40k-is-competitive>.

Sterne, Laurence. (1940). *The Life and Opinions of Tristram Shandy, Gentleman.* Edited by James Aiken Work. New York: The Odyssey Press.

Sterne, Laurence. (1967). *A Sentimental Journey Through France and Italy by Mr. Yorick.* Berkeley: University of California Press.

Sterne, Laurence. (2003). *The Life and Opinions of Tristram Shandy, Gentleman: The Florida Edition.* Edited by Melvyn New and Joan New. New York: Penguin Books.

Sterne, Theodore. (1966). War Games: Validity and Interpretation. *Army* 16 (4): 64–68.

Sternstein, Aliya. (2013). White House's $14 Billion Cyber Spending Claim Is Squishy. *Nextgov,* November 8, 2013, accessed January 19, 2015. <http://www.nextgov.com/cybersecurity/cybersecurity-report/2013/11/white-houses-14-billion-cyber-spending-claim-squishy/73475>.

Sterrett, James. (2014). Review: This War of Mine. *PAXsims,* November 27, 2014. <https://paxsims.wordpress.com/2014/11/27/review-this-war-of-mine>.

Stiegler, Bernard. (1998). *Technics and Time 1: The Fault of Epimetheus.* Translated by R. Beardsworth and G. Collins. Palo Alto, CA: Stanford University Press.

Stiegler, Bernard. (2009). *Technics and Time 2: Disorientation.* Translated by S. Barker. Palo Alto, CA: Stanford University Press.

Stiegler, Bernard. (2011). *Technics and Time 3: Cinematic Time and the Question of Malaise.* Translated by S. Barker. Palo Alto, CA: Stanford University Press.

Stimson Center. (2014). Recommendations and Report of the Task Force on US Policy. <http://www.stimson.org/images/uploads/task_force_report_final_web_062414.pdf>.

Stockfish, J. A. (1973). *Plowshares into Swords: Managing the American Defense Establishment.* New York: Mason & Lipscomb.

Stockfisch, J. A. (1975). *Models, Data, and War: A Critique of the Study of Conventional Forces.* R-1526-PR. Santa Monica, CA: RAND Corporation.

Stoll, Clarice, and Samuel Livingston. (1973). *Simulation/Gaming: An Introduction for Social Studies Teachers.* New York: Free Press.

Strong, Paul. (2011). The Peace Support Operations Model: Strategic Interaction Process. *Journal of Defense Modeling and Simulation* 8: 2.

Stuart, Keith. (2014). War Games—Developers Find New Ways to Explore Military Conflict. *The Guardian,* July 15, 2014. <http://www.theguardian.com/technology/2014/jul/15/war-games-developers-military-conflict>.

Sumida, Jon. (1993). *In Defence of Naval Supremacy: Financial Limitation, Technological Innovation and British Naval Policy, 1889-1914.* New York: Routledge.

Svenson, Elwin V., and Paul H. Sheats. (1950). Audio-Visual Aids in Adult Education. *Review of Educational Research* 20 (3): 216–223.

Swanson, Mark. (1976). Games Computers Play. *American Wargamer* 4 (2): 12.

Talbot, Oliver, and Noel Wilde. (2011). Modeling Security Sector Reform Activities in the Context of Stabilization Operations. *Journal of Defense Modeling and Simulation* 8: 2.

Taleb, Nassim Nicholas. (2007). *The Black Swan: The Impact of the Highly Improbable*. New York: Random House.

Tapscott, Mark. (1993). Paradigm Changing from Simulators to Simulation. *Defense Electronics* 25 (10): 33.

Tarr, Ronald W., Christina S. Morris, and Michael J. Singer. (2002). *Low-Cost PC Gaming and Simulation: Doctrinal Survey*. RN 2003-03, ARI, Army Research Institute for the Behavioral and Social Sciences, Ft. Belvoir, VA. October.

Taylor, A. J. P. (1974). *An Illustrated History of the First World War*. London: Penguin.

Taylor, Calvin Walker. (1959). The 1955 and 1957 Research Conferences: The Identification of Creative Scientific Talent. *American Psychologist* 14 (2): 100–102.

Taylor, Calvin Walker, and F. E. Williams, eds. (1966). *Instructional Media and Creativity*. New York: John Wiley.

Taylor, Calvin Walker, and Frank Barron. (1963). *Research Conference on the Identification of Creative Scientific Talent*. New York: John Wiley.

Taylor, Giles. (2013). A Military Use for Widescreen Cinema. *Velvet Light Trap* 72 (1): 17–32.

Test Series Games. (1969). *S&T Supplement* (December 1969-January 1970): 24.

Thomas, Clayton. (1961). Military Gaming. In *Progress in Operations Research*. vol. I. Edited by Russell Ackoff, 421–465. New Jersey: John Wiley and Sons.

Thomas, Douglas, and John Seely Brown. (2011). *A New Culture of Learning: Cultivating the Imagination for a World of Constant Change*. Charleston, SC: CreateSpace.

Thomas, Jim, and Chris Dougherty. (2013). *Beyond the Ramparts: The Future of U. S. Special Operations Forces*. Washington, DC: Center for Strategic and Bugetary Assessments.

Thomson, Nicholas. (2013). Roberto Bolaño's Playful Obsession: The Third Reich. *PopMatters,* February 21, 2013, accessed October 14, 2014. <http://www.popmatters.com/review/168372-the-third-reich-by-roberto-Bolaño>.

Tilden, Steve. (1997). Small Survey. WWII newsgroup, September 24, 1997.

Toffler, Alvin. (1970). *Future Shock*. New York: Bantam Books.

Tolstoy, Leo. (1982). *War and Peace*. London: Penguin.

Tooby, John. (2012). Nexus Causality, Moral Warfare, and Misattribution Arbitrage. In *This Will Make You Smarter: New Scientific Concepts to Improve Your Thinking*, edited by John Brockman, 33–36. New York: Harper Perennial.

Torrance, Paul E. (1965). *Rewarding Creative Behavior; Experiments in Classroom Creativity*. New Jersey: Prentice-Hall.

Totilo, Stephen. (2014a). The War Video Game That We Need May Finally Be On Its Way. *Kotaku*, March 12, 2014. <http://kotaku.com/the-war-video-game-that-we-need-may-finally-be-on-its-w-1542406407>.

Totilo, Stephen. (2014b). The Making of a Very Different Kind of War Video Game. *Kotaku*, last modified April 8, 2014. <http://kotaku.com/the-making-of-a-very-different-kind-of-war-video-game-1560735762>.

Train, Brian. (2011). Gaming Military Coups. *PAXsims*, August 12, 2011. <http://paxsims.wordpress.com/2011/12/08/gaming-military-coups>.

Trimble, Stephen. (2011). REPORT: RQ-170 Spied over Osama Bin Laden's Bed Last Night. *Flightglobal: Aviation Connected*, May 2, 2011, accessed January 19, 2015. <http://www.flightglobal.com/blogs/the-dewline/2011/05/report-rq-170-spied-over-osama>.

Tsouras, Peter, ed. (2002). *Third Reich Victorious: Alternate Decisions of World War II*. London: Greenhill.

Turkle, Sherry. (1997). Seeing through Computers. *American Prospect* 31:76–82.

Turkle, Sherry. (2009). *Simulation and Its Discontents*. Cambridge: MIT Press.

Turse, Nick. (2012). *The Changing Face of Empire: Special Ops, Drones, Spies, Proxy Fighters, Secret Bases, and Cyberwarfare*. Chicago: Haymarket Books.

Turse, Nick. (2014). Washington's Back-to-the-Future Military Policies in Africa: America's New Model for Expeditionary Warfare. *TomDispatch*, March 13, 2014, accessed January 19, 2015. <http://www.tomdispatch.com/blog/175818/tomgram%3A_nick_turse,_american_proxy_wars_in_africa>.

Tuttle, F. P. (1938). Educative Value of the Comic Strip. *American Childhood* (March): 14–15.

Ubisoft Entertainment. (2005). Ghost Recon Advanced Warfighter. *Ubisoft*, accessed January 19, 2015. <https://web.archive.org/web/20061210061138/http://www.ubi.com/UK/Games/Info.aspx?pId=4258>.

UK War Office. (1884). *Rules for the Conduct of the War-Game*. London: Stationery Office.

Unique Simulator for SAC Crews. (1967). *Air Force Times*, November 15, 1967: 28.

United States Institute of Peace. (n.d.). Simulations, accessed December 19, 2014. <http://www.usip.org/simulations>.

Unsworth, L. (2001). *Teaching Multiliteracies Across the Curriculum: Changing Contexts of Text and Image in Classroom Practice*. Berkshire: Open University Press.

US Air Force. (2009). *US Air Force's Unmanned Aircraft Systems Flight Plan 2009–2047*, accessed January 11, 2015. <http://www.fas.org/irp/program/collect/uas_2009.pdf>.

US Air Force. (2011). *Air Force Doctrine Document 1* <http://www.au.af.mil/au/cadre/aspc/l004/pubs/afdd1.pdf>.

US Army. (2006). *FM 3-24: Counterinsurgency*. Washington, DC: Department of the Army.

US Army. (2008). *FM 3-07: Stability Operations*. Washington, DC: Department of the Army.

US Army. (2014). *FM 3-24: Insurgencies and Countering Insurgencies*. Washington, DC: Department of the Army.

US Department of Defense. (1997). *Quadrennial Defense Review Report*. Washington, DC: Department of Defense.

US Department of Defense. (2001). *Quadrennial Defense Review Report*. Washington, DC: Department of Defense.

US Department of Defense. (2006). *Quadrennial Defense Review Report.* Washington, DC: Department of Defense.

US Department of Defense. (2010). *Quadrennial Defense Review Report.* Washington, DC: Department of Defense.

US Department of Defense. (2010). Milgaming—Supporting Games for Training, accessed December 19, 2014. <https://milgaming.army.mil>.

US Department of Defense. (2014a). *Quadrennial Defense Review Report.* Washington, DC: Department of Defense.

US Department of Defense. (2014b). *Joint Publication 1-02: Department of Defense Dictionary of Military and Associated Terms, 8 November 2010 (As Amended Through 15 March 2014),* accessed January 11, 2015. <http://www.dtic.mil/doctrine/dod_dictionary>.

US Joint Chiefs of Staff. (1969). *Joint War Gaming Manual. JWCA-167-69.* Washington, DC: Joint Chiefs of Staff.

US used white phosphorus in Iraq. (2005). *BBC News Online,* last modified November 16, 2005. <http://news.bbc.co.uk/2/hi/middle_east/4440664.stm>.

Van Creveld, Martin. (2008). *The Culture of War.* New York: Ballantine.

Van Creveld, Martin. (2013). *Wargames: From Gladiators to Gigabytes.* New York: Cambridge University Press.

Vane, Russell R. (2000). Using Hypergames to Select Plans in Competitive Environments. Ph.D. dissertation, George Mason University.

Vaneigem, Raoul. (1999). *A Cavalier History of Surrealism.* Edinburgh: AK Press.

Vanore, John J. (1988). Interview: Charles S. Roberts—Founder of the Avalon Hill Game Company and Founding Father of Board Wargaming. *Fire & Movement* 56: 17–18.

Van Wees, Hans. (2013). Farmers and Hoplites: Models of Historical Development. In *Men of Bronze: Hoplite Warfare in Ancient Greece,* edited by Donald Kagan and Gregory F. Viggiano, 222–255. Princeton: Princeton University Press.

Van Zwieten, Martijn. (2011). Danger Close: Contesting Ideologies and Contemporary Military Conflict in First-person Shooters. Paper presented at *DiGRA 2011: Think Design Play,* Utrecht, NL, Utrecht School of the Arts, September 14–17, 2011. <http://www.digra.org/wp-content/uploads/digital-library/11312.17439.pdf>.

Various (2001–). "*Advanced Squad Leader* player rating comments," accessed November 14, 2014. <http://boardgamegeek.com/collection/items/boardgame/243/page/1?rated=1>.

Vela, Larry. (2013). Academic Study of Tabletop Wargamers: The Results Are In! Part 4: Player Political Preferences. *Bell of Lost Souls,* last modified July 14, 2013. <http://www.belloflostsouls.net/2013/07/academic-study-of-tabletop-wargamers-the-results-are-in-part-4-player-political-preferences.html>.

Venturini, Georg. (1797). *Beschreibung und Regeln eines neuen Krieges-Spiels zum Nutzen und Vergnügen, besonders aber zum Gebrauche in Militairschulen* [Description and Rules for a New Wargame, both for Pleasure and Instruction, Especially for Use in Military Schools]. Schleswig: J. G. Röhss.

Verbeek, Peter Paul. (2007). *What Things Do. Philosophical Reflections on Technology, Agency, and Design.* University Park: Pennsylvania State University Press.

VGChartz. (2014). Game Database. *VGChartz*, accessed September 15, 2014. <http://www.vgchartz.com/gamedb/>.

Viggiano, Gregory F. (2013). The Hoplite Revolution and the Rise of the Polis. In *Men of Bronze: Hoplite Warfare in Ancient Greece*, edited by Donald Kagan and Gregory F. Viggiano, 112–133. Princeton: Princeton University Press.

Virilio, Paul. (1976). *Essai sur l'insécurité du territoire*. Paris: Editions Stock.

Virilio, Paul. (2000). *The Information Bomb*. New York: Verso.

Virilio, Paul, and Sylvère Lotringer. (1997). *Pure War*, revised edition, translated by M. Polizzotti and B. O'Keeffe. New York: Semiotext(e).

von Hase, Georg. (1921). *Kiel and Jutland*. London: Skeffington & Son, Ltd.

Von Hilgers, Philipp. (2012). *War Games: A History of War on Paper*. Translated by B. Ross. Cambridge, MA: MIT Press.

Von Neumann, John, and Oskar Morgenstern. (1944). *Theory of Games and Economic Behavior*. Princeton: Princeton University Press.

von Reisswitz, Georg Heinrich Rudolf Johann. (1824). *Anleitung zur Darstellung Militairischer Manöver mit dem Apparat des Kriegs-Spieles [Instructions for the Representation of Military Maneuvers with the War Game Apparatus]*. Berlin: Trowitzsch.

W2HPG (n.d.). Rules.

Wackerfuss, Andrew. (2013). "This Game of Sudden Death": Simulating Air Combat of the First World War. In *Playing with the Past: Digital Games and the Simulation of History*, edited by Andrew E.R. Elliott and Matthew Wilhelm Kappell, 233–246. New York: Bloomsbury.

Waddington, David I. (2007). Locating the Wrongness in Ultra-violent Video Games. *Ethics and Information Technology* 9 (2): 121–128.

Wagner, Christopher. (n.d.) Background on S&T Nrs. 16 & 17. *Strategy & Tactics. Book IV: Nrs. 16–18*, inside front cover.

Wajcman, Judy. (2004). *TechnoFeminism*. Cambridge, MA: Polity.

Waldman, Thomas. (2013). *War, Clausewitz and the Trinity*. London: Ashgate.

Waldron, Arthur. (2001). China Without Tears: If Chiang Kai-shek Hadn't Gambled in 1946. In *What If? Military Historians Imagine What Might Have Been*, edited by Robert Cowley, 377–392. London: Pan.

Waller, Fred. (1946). The Waller Flexible Gunnery Trainer. *Journal of the Society of Motion Picture Engineers* 47 (1): 73–87.

Wansbury, Timothy, John Hart, Andre Gordon, and Jeff Wilkinson. (2010). UrbanSim: Training Adaptable Leaders in the Art of Battle. In *Interservice/Industry Training, Simulation, and Education Conference*, accessed December 19, 2014. <http://ict.usc.edu/pubs/UrbanSim-%20Training%20Adaptable%20Leaders%20in%20the%20Art%20of%20Battle%20Command.pdf>.

Wardrip-Fruin, Noah, and Pat Harrigan. (2004). *First Person: New Media as Story, Performance, and Game*. Cambridge, MA: MIT Press.

Ware, Willis H. (2008). *RAND and the Information Evolution: A History in Essays and Vignettes*. Santa Monica, CA: RAND Corporation.

Wark, McKenzie. (2008). *50 Years of Recuperation: The Situationist International 1957-2007*. Princeton: Princeton Architectural Press.

Wark, McKenzie. (2011). *The Beach Beneath the Street: The Everyday Life and Glorious Times of the Situationist International*. London: Verso.

Warren, Gemma, and Patrick Rose. (2011). Representing Strategic Communication and Influence in Stabilization Modeling. *Journal of Defense Modeling and Simulation* 8: 2.

Watts, Evan. (2011). Ruin, Gender, and Digital Games. *WSQ: Women's Studies Quarterly* 39 (3/4): 247–265.

Webb, Richard. (2014). The Copper Promise. *Goodreads*, last modified February 13, 2014, accessed October 14, 2014. <https://www.goodreads.com/book/show/18667112-the-copper-promise>.

Weber, Joseph John. (1928). *Picture Values in Education: A Complete Record of an Experimental Investigation*. Chicago: The Educational Screen, Inc.

Webster, Andrew. (2014). Beyond "Battlefield": These Games Show the Dark Reality of War. *The Verge*, June 19, 2014. <http://www.theverge.com/2014/6/19/5824114/these-games-show-the-dark-reality-of-war>.

Weiland, William J., John Deato, Charles A. Barba, and Thomas P. Santarelli. (CHI Systems, Inc.) (2003). *Virtual Environment Cultural Training for Operational Readiness: VECTOR*. ARI Research Note 2003–10, ARI, April.

Weisgerber, Robert A., ed. (1971). *Perspectives in Individualized Learning*. Itasca, IL: F. E. Peacock Publishers.

Wells, H. G. (1913). *Little Wars*. Originally published in Windsor Magazine, December 1912-January 1913. London: Frank Palmer.

Wells, H. G. (1914). *The World Set Free*. New York: E. P. Dutton & Company.

Wells, H. G. (2004). *Little Wars*. Springfield, VA: Skirmisher.

Wentworth, Donald, and Darrell R. Lewis. (1973). A Review of Research on Instructional Games and Simulations in Social Studies Education. *Social Education* 37 (5): 432–440.

Wild, Lorraine. (2007). Formal, Cool, Dense: Graphic Design in Los Angeles at Midcentury. In *Birth of the Cool: California Art, Design, and Culture at Midcentury, Exhibition Catalogue, Orange County Museum of Art*, edited by Elizabeth Armstrong and Michael Boyd, 151–172. New York: Prestel Publishing.

Williams, Jen. (2014). *The Copper Promise*. New York: Hodder Headline.

Williams, Raymond. (1976). *Keywords: A Vocabulary of Culture and Society*. New York: Oxford University Press.

Williams, Walt. (2013). We Are Not Heroes: Contextualizing Violence Through Narrative. Paper presented at the Game Developers Conference, March 27, 2013. Gamasutra, accessed May 1, 2013. <http://www.gamasutra.com/view/news/188964/Video_Spec_Ops_The_Line_contextualizes_violence_through_story.php>.

Wills, Sandra, Elyssebeth Leigh, and Albert Ip. (2011). *The Power of Role-Based E-learning*. New York: Routledge.

Wilson, Andrew. (1968). *The Bomb and the Computer: A Crucial History of War Games.* New York: Delacorte Press.

Wilson, Andrew. (2014). *The Bomb and the Computer: The History of Professional Wargaming 1780–1968*, edited by John Curry. Bristol, UK: History of Wargaming Project.

Wilson, Howard E. (1928). Cartoons as an Aid in the Teaching of History. *School Review* 36 (3): 192–198.

Wilson, Johnny L. (1991). The History of Computer Games. *Computer Gaming Weekly* 88: 16.

Wineburg, Sam. (2001). *Historical Thinking and Other Unnatural Acts: Charting the Future of Teaching the Past.* Philadelphia: Temple University Press.

Withers, Samuel. (1961). Creativity in English: A Dissent. *Phi Delta Kappan* 42 (7): 311–314.

Witty, Paul A. (1944). Some Uses of Visual Aids in the Army. *Journal of Educational Sociology* 18 (4): 241–249.

Wood, Brian. (2005–12). *DMZ.* New York: Vertigo.

Woods, Stewart. (2012). *Eurogames: The Design, Culture and Play of Modern European Board Games.* Jefferson, NC: McFarland.

Woolsey, R. James. (1980). *The Uses and Abuses of Analysis in the Defense Environment: A Conversation with R. James Woolsey.* Washington, DC: American Enterprise Institute.

Wordsworth, Richard. (2014). *This War of Mine:* A Civilian Survival Story That Is 11 Bit Studios' "Most Important Work Ever." *Edge,* last modified April 14, 2014. <http://www.edge-online.com/features/this-war-of-mine-a-civilian-survival-story-that-is-11-bit-studios-most-important-work-ever>.

World War II Historical Preservation Federation. (1996). To all reenactors and veterans of the Battle of the Bulge from the Federation Staff Officers. Memo, January 26, 1996.

Wynn, Kenneth. (1997). *Career Histories, U1–U510.* vol. 1. U-Boat Operations of the Second World War. Annapolis: Naval Institute Press.

Wynn, Kenneth. (1998). *Career Histories, U511–UIT25.* vol. 2. U-Boat Operations of the Second World War. Annapolis, MD: Naval Institute Press.

Yalom, Marilyn. (2004). *The Birth of the Chess Queen.* New York: Harper Collins.

Yoder, Christian. (2012). Anonymous Retaliates for Villainous Portrayal in Activision Game. *The Daily Dot,* May 9, 2012, accessed January 19, 2015. <http://www.dailydot.com/news/anonymous-activision-call-duty-black-ops>.

Young, A. L. (1926). Teaching with Motion Pictures. *Peabody Journal of Education* 3 (6): 321–326.

Zagal, José P. (2009). Ethically Notable Videogames: Moral Dilemmas and Gameplay. Paper presented at *DiGRA 2009: Breaking New Ground: Innovation in Games, Play, Practice and Theory.* Uxbridge, UK, Brunel University, September 2009. <http://www.digra.org/wp-content/uploads/digital-library/09287.13336.pdf>.

Zamoyski, Adam. (2004a). *1812: Napoleon's Fatal March on Moscow.* London: Harper.

Zamoyski, Adam. (2004b). Napoleon Triumphs in Russia. In *What Might Have Been: Imaginary History from Twelve Leading Historians*, edited by Andrew Roberts, 79–91. London: Phoenix.

Zbylut, Michelle L. and Jason N. Ward. (2004). *Think Like a Commander—Excellence in Leadership: Educating Army Leaders with the [ICT] Power Hungry Film.* RP 2004-01, ARI, April.

Zedong, Mao. (1971). On Protracted War. In *Six Essays on Military Affairs* by Mao Zedong, 195–339. Beijing: Foreign Languages Press.

Zocchi, Lou. (2007). Gettysburg. In *Hobby Games: The 100 Best*, edited by James Lowder. Seattle: Green Ronin.

Zorbaugh, Harvey, ed. (1944). Bibliography. *Journal of Educational Sociology* 18 (4): 250–255.

Zuber, Terence. (2002). *Inventing the Schlieffen Plan: German War Planning 1871-1914.* Oxford: Oxford University Press.

2KTV. (2012). *Spec Ops: The Line*: The Official Walt Williams Video Interview. *2KTV*, last uploaded February 9, 2012. <https://www.youtube.com/watch?v=qRyAfmVQOZU>.

References: Games

1000 Days of Syria. (2014). Mitch Swenson <https://onethousanddaysofsyria.squarespace.com>.

1914. (1967). James F. Dunnigan; Avalon Hill.

1989: Dawn of Freedom. (2012). Ted Torgerson and Jason Matthews; GMT Games.

Advanced Dungeons & Dragons Dungeon Master's Guide. (1979). Gary Gygax; TSR.

Advanced Dungeons & Dragons Monster Manual. (1977). Gary Gygax; TSR.

Advanced Dungeons & Dragons Players Handbook. (1978). Gary Gygax; TSR.

Advanced Squad Leader. (1985). Don Greenwood; Avalon Hill.

Afrika Korps. (1964). Charles S. Roberts; Avalon Hill.

Aftermath! (1981). Paul Hume and Robert N. Charrette; Fantasy Games Unlimited.

AFTERSHOCK: A Humanitarian Crisis Game. (2015). T Fisher's Games.

Age of Empires. (1997–). Ensemble Studios; Big Huge Games; Robot Entertainment.

Age of Empires III. (2005). Greg Street; Ensemble Studios.

Age of Renaissance. (1996). Jared Scarborough; Avalon Hill.

Air & Armor. (1986). Bruce S. Maxwell; West End Games.

Air Superiority. (1987). J. D. Webster; Game Designer's Workshop.

Air War. (1977). David C. Isby; SPI.

Algeria: The War of Independence 1954-62. (2000). Brian Train; Microgame Design Group.

Amber Diceless Roleplaying Game. (1991). Erick Wujcik; Phage Press.

Ambush! (1983). John Butterfield; Victory Games Inc.

America's Army. (2002–). Michael Zyda; Sega Studios San Francisco, US Army.

The Ancient Art of War. (1984). Brøderbund.

Andean Abyss: Insurgency and Counterinsurgency in Colombia (COIN Series, Volume I). (2012). Volko Ruhnke; GMT Games.

Anleitung zum Kriegsspiel. (1862). Wilhelm von Tschischwitz. Translated by Captain E. Baring as *Rules for the Conduct of the War-Game*.

Anleitung zur Darstellung militairischer Manöver mit dem Apparat des Kriegs-Spieles. (1824). Georg Heinrich Rudolf Johann von Reisswitz. Translated by William Leeson and published as *Von Reisswitz Kriegsspiel* (1989).

Anzio Beachhead. (1970). Dave Williams; Poultron Press.

ARMA: Armed Assault. (2006). Bohemia Interactive.

Arms Law. (1980). Coleman Charlton, Pete Fenlon, Kurt Fischer, and Bruce Shelley; Iron Crown Enterprises.

Atomic Bomber. (1946). International Mutoscope.

Axis & Allies. (1981). Larry Harris, Jr.; Milton Bradley, Nova Games, Jedko and PewterCraft.

Azhanti High Lightning. (1980). Frank Chadwick and Mark W. Miller; GDW.

Balance of Power. (1985). Chris Crawford; Mindscape.

Balkan Hell. (1995). Ty Bomba; XTR Corp.

Battle for Baghdad. (2009). Joseph Miranda; MCS Group.

Battle of the Bulge. (1964). Larry Pinsky and Tom Shaw; Avalon Hill.

Battle Over Britain. (1983). John H. Butterfield; TSR.

Battlefield 2. (2005). Electronic Arts.

Battlefield 3. (2011). Electronic Arts.

Battlefield 4. (2013). Lars Gustavsson; EA Digital Illusions.

Battlefield: 1942. (2002). Romain de Waubert de Genlis; EA Digital Illusions.

Battlefront. (1986). Roger Keating and Ian Trout; Strategic Studies Group.

Battleship. (1931). Clifford von Wickler; Original Publisher Unknown.

Battleship. (1967). Milton Bradley.

BCT Command Kandahar. (2013). Joseph Miranda; MCS Group.

Beirut '82: Arab Stalingrad. (1989). Thomas Kane; World Wide Wargames.

Beyond Valor. (1985). Don Greenwood, Charles Kibler, Rex A. Martin, Bob McNamara, and Jon Mishcon; Avalon Hill and Multi-Man Publishing.

Bioshock. (2007). Feral Interaction; 2K Games.

Bird of Prey: Air Combat in the Jet Age. (2008). Philip A. Markgraf and Tony Valle; Ad Astra Games.

Blitzkrieg. (1965). Larry Pinsky; Avalon Hill.

Blitzkrieg. (1970). James F. Dunnigan; Avalon Hill, 1970. Formerly *Tactical Game 3*, published by Poutron Press (1969).

The Blitzkrieg Module System. (1969). James F. Dunnigan and Redmond Simonsen; Poultron Press.

Blood Reef: Tarawa—ASL Historical Module 5. (1999). Steven Dethlefsen and Eddie Zeman; Heat of Battle, Multi-Man Publishing.

Bonaparte at Marengo. (2005). Bowen Simmons; Simmons Games.

Boom Beach. (2014). Supercell Oy.

Brynania. (2014). McGill University.

Call of Cthulhu. (1981). Sandy Petersen; Chaosium.

Call of Duty. (2003). Activision.

Call of Duty: Black Ops. (2010). Activision.

Call of Duty: Black Ops II. (2012) Activision.

Call of Duty: Modern Warfare 2. (2009). Activision.

Call of Duty: Modern Warfare 3. (2011). Activision.

Call of Duty: World at War. (2008). Activision.

Call of Duty 2. (2005). Activision.

Call of Duty 3. (2006). Activision.

Call of Duty 4: Modern Warfare. (2007). Activision.

Campaign for North Africa. (1979). Richard Berg; Simulations Publications, Inc.

Carrier. (1990). Kevin Boylan, Jon Southard; Victory Games.

Chad: The Toyota Wars. (1991). Richard Davis; Decision Games.

Chainmail. (1971; 2nd edition 1972). Gary Gygax and Jeff Perren; Guidon Games.

Champions. (1981). Steve Peterson, George MacDonald, Bruce Harlick, and Ray Greer; Hero Games.

Civilization. (1980). Francis Tresham; Hartland Trefoil; 1981 edition published by Avalon Hill.

Civilization. (1991). Sid Meier; MicroProse.

Civilization IV. (2005). Sid Meier; Firaxis Games.

Clash of Clans. (2013). Supercell Oy.

Claw Law. (1982). Terry Amthor, Coleman Charlton, Leonard Cook, Pete Fenlon, and Brice Neidlinger; Iron Crown Enterprises.

Cloudships & Gunboats. (1989). Frank Chadwick; GDW.

Cobra. (1977). Brad Hessel; Simulations Publications, Inc.

Code of Bushido: ASL Module 8. (1991). Bob McNamara and Rick Troha; Avalon Hill.

Combat Commander: Europe. (2006). Chad Jensen; GMT Games.

Combat Commander: Mediterranean. (2007). Chad Jensen; GMT Games.

Combat Commander: Pacific. (2006). Chad Jensen; GMT Games.

Combat Commander: Resistance! (2011). Chad Jensen; GMT Games.

Combat Mission: Shock Force. (2007). Paradox Interactive.

Command & Colors: Napoleonics. (2010). Richard Borg; GMT Games.

Command & Colors: Napoleonics Expansion #2—The Russian Army. (2013). Richard Borg; GMT Games.

Commandos: Behind Enemy Lines. (1998). Pyro Studios; Eidos Interactive.

Command: Modern Air/Naval Operations. (2013). Matrix Games, Warfare Sims.

Company of Heroes. (2006). Relic Entertainment; THQ; Sega.

Computer Bismarck. (1980). Strategic Simulations, Inc.

Cortex. (2005). Jamie Chambers; Margaret Weis Productions.

Cosmic Encounter. (1977). Eon.

Country X. (2009). Columbia University.

Crescendo of Doom. (1979). Don Greenwood; Avalon Hill.

Crisis 2000. (1997). Joseph Miranda; One Small Step.

Crisis 2020. (2007). Joseph Miranda; Victory Point Games.

Cross of Iron. (1978). John Hill (I); Avalon Hill.

Crusader Kings II. (2012). Paradox Interactive.

The Crusades. (1978). Richard H. Berg; Simulations Publications, Inc.

Cuba Libre: Castro's Insurgency (COIN Series, Volume II). (2013). Volko Ruhnke and Jeff Grossman; GMT Games.

Cybernaut. (1996). Joseph Miranda; One Small Step.

Cyberwar XXI. (Forthcoming). Joseph Miranda. Hexagon Interactive.

DAK. (1997). Dean Essig; The Gamers.

Dark Nebula. (1980). Marc W. Miller; GDW.

A Day of Heroes. (2008). Tom Herrschaft and Mark H. Walker; Lock 'n Load Publishing.

D-Day. (1961). Charles S. Roberts; Avalon Hill.

Dear Esther. (2012). The Chinese Room.

Decision Iraq. (2013). Joe Miranda; Decision Games.

Defense Grid. (2008–10). Hidden Path Entertainment.

Dien Bien Phu. (1973). Guy Hail; Flying Buffalo.

Diplomacy. (1959). Allan Calhamer. Original prepublication manuscript as *The Game of Realpolitik* (1958).

A Distant Plain: Insurgency in Afghanistan (COIN Series, Volume III). (2013). Volko Ruhnke and Brian Train; GMT Games.

Dixie. (1976). Redmond A. Simonsen; Simulations Publications, Inc.

Doom. (1993). Shawn C. Green, Sandy Petersen and John Romero; id Software, Inc.

Downtown. (2004). Lee Brimmicombe-Wood; GMT Games.

Drang nach Osten. (1973). Frank Chadwick; Game Designers Workshop.

Drive on Stalingrad. (1977). Brad Hessel; Simulations Publications, Inc.

Dune. (1979). Avalon Hill.

Dune II: The Building of a Dynasty. (1992). Aaron E. Powell and Joseph Bostick; Westwood Studios, Inc.

Dungeons & Dragons. (1974). Gary Gygax and Dave Arneson; Tactical Studies Rules.

Dungeons & Dragons Basic Set. (1977). Dave Arneson, Gary Gygax, and J. Eric Holmes; TSR.

Eagles of the Empire: Borodino. (1994). Brien J. Miller, Arron J. Monroe and Mark E. Searle; Games USA.

Eagles of the Empire: Friedland. (1995). Brien J. Miller and Arron J. Monroe; Games USA.

Eagles of the Empire: Preussisch-Eylau. (1999). Brien J. Miller, Arron J. Monroe and Mark E. Searle; Avalanche Press Ltd.

Eagles of the Empire: Spanish Eagles. (2008). Stephen C. Jackson and Brien J. Miller; Compass Games LLC.

Eastern Front (1941). (1981). Chris Crawford; Atari Program Exchange.

Empire. (1971). Walter Bright; noncommercial product.

Empire. (1973). PLATO system.

Empire of the Sun. (2005). Mark Herman; GMT Games.

Encyclopedia of War: Ancient Battles. (1988). Robert Smith; CCS.

England Expects. (Forthcoming). Charles Vasey.

Europa Universalis. (2000). Paradox.

Europa Universalis II. (2001). Paradox Development Studio.

Fate. (2003). Fred Hicks and Rob Donoghue; Evil Hat Productions.

Feng Shui. (1996). Robin Laws; Daedalus Entertainment.

Fiasco. (2009). Jason Morningstar; Bully Pulpit Games.

Field of Glory. (2009). Slitherine Ltd.

Fierce Fight! Stalingrad Blitzkrieg. (2013). Tetsuya Nakamura; Game Journal 47.

Fifth Corps. (1980). Jim Dunnigan; Simulations Publications, Inc.

Fifth Frontier War. (1981). John Astell, Frank Chadwick, and Marc W. Miller; GDW.

Fight in the Skies. (1968). Mike Carr; War Game Inventors Guild.

Fire in the Lake: Insurgency in Vietnam (COIN Series, Volume IV). (2014). Mark Herman and Volko Ruhnke; GMT Games.

Fire in the Sky. (2005). Tetsuya Nakamura; Multi-Man Publishing.

Fleet Admiral. (1987). Jack Greene; Quarter Deck Games.

Fleet Admiral II. Forthcoming. Jack Greene; publisher TBD.

Fletcher Pratt's Naval War Game. (1943). Fletcher Pratt; Harrison-Hilton.

For the People. (1998). Mark Herman; Avalon Hill.

Force on Force. (2011). Shawn and Robby Carpenter; Osprey Publishing & Ambush Alley Games.

France 1940. (1972). James F. Dunnigan; Avalon Hill Game Company.

The Franco-Prussian War. (1992). Joseph Miranda; Decision Games.

Freedom in the Galaxy. (1979). Howard Barasch and John Butterfield; SPI Games.

Galaga. (1981). Midway.

The Game of War. (1977). Guy Debord; Champ Libre.

Gamma World. (1978). James M. Ward and Gary Jaquet; TSR.

Gary Grigsby's War in the East. (2010). 2 By 3 Games.

Gary Grigsby's War in the Pacific. (2004). 2 By 3 Games.

Gary Grigsby's World at War. (2005). Joel Billings, Keith Brors & Gary Grigsby; 2 By 3 Games.

Generic Universal RolePlaying System (*GURPS*). (1986). Steve Jackson; Steve Jackson Games.

Gettysburg. (1958). Charles S. Roberts; Avalon Hill Game Company.

Gettysburg. (1961). Charles S. Roberts; Avalon Hill.

Ghost Recon (Tom Clancy's) [series] (2001–2014). Ubisoft.

Ghost Recon: Advanced Warfighter (Tom Clancy's). (2006). Ubisoft.

GI: Anvil of Victory. (1982). Don Greenwood; Avalon Hill.

Global Challenge: The Game of International Peacekeeping. (2001). Identity Games International.

Golem Arcana. (2014). Hairbrained Scheme.

Greek Civil War. (2014). Brian Train; Decision Games.

Grenadier: Company Level Combat 1700–1850. (1971). James F. Dunnigan; Simulations Publications, Inc.

Group of Soviet Forces Germany. (2003). Ty Bomba; Decision Games.

Gung-Ho. (1992). Don Greenwood and Bob McNamara; Avalon Hill.

The Guns of Gettysburg. (2013). Bowen Simmons; Mercury Games.

Hammer of the Scots. (2002). Jerry Taylor; Columbia Games.

Harpoon (a.k.a. *Paper Harpoon, Paper Rules*). (1981). Larry Bond; Adventure Games.

Harpoon. (1989). Larry Bond; Three-Sixty Pacific, Inc.

Harpoon [series]. (1981–2013). Larry Bond; Various publishers, e.g., Three-Sixty Pacific (1981) and Matrix Games (2013).

Harpoon, third edition. (1987). Larry Bond; Game Designer's Workshop.

Harpoon I. (1989). Larry Bond; Three Sixty Pacific, Alliance Interactive, iMagic, Advanced Gaming Systems Inc., Matrix Games.

Harpoon II. (1994). Larry Bond; Three-Sixty Pacific.

Harpoon III. (2001). Jesse Spears.

Harpoon IV. (1997). Larry Bond and Chris Carlson; Clash of Arms Games.

Harpoon 3: Advanced Naval Warfare. (2007). Matrix Games. Originally called Harpoon 3.

Harpoon 3 Professional [*H3MilSim*]. (2009). Matrix Games; Renamed H3 MilSim in 2010 and then H3Pro in 2013.

Harpoon Ultimate Edition. (2011). Matrix (Stuttgart, Germany).

Hearts and Minds: Vietnam 1965–1975. (2010). John Poniske; Worthington Games.

Hearts of Iron. (2002). Henrik Fåhraeus, Joakim Bergqwist and Johan Andersson; Paradox Entertainment.

Here I Stand: Wars of the Reformation 1517–1555. (2006). Ed Beach; GMT Games.

Hitler's War. (1981). Keith Gross; Metagaming.

Holy War: Afghanistan. (1991). Joseph Miranda; Decision Games.

Homefront. (2011). Kaos Studios; THQ/Spike (Japan).

Imperium. (1977). Frank Chadwick, John Harshman, and Marc W. Miller; GDW.

Insurgency. (1979). Blake Smith; Battleline Games.

Invasion: Earth. (1981). John Astell, Frank Chadwick, and Marc W. Miller; GDW.

Invasion Orion. (1979). Automated Simulations.

Ironclads and Ether Flyers. (1990). Frank Chadwick; GDW.

Jagged Alliance 2. (1999). Ian Currie, Linda Currie and Shaun Lyng; Sirtech Canada, Ltd.

Joust. (1982). Williams Entertainment.

Jutland. (1967). James F. Dunnigan; Avalon Hill.

Jutland: Fleet Admiral II. (2016). Jack Greene; Comsim Press.

Kharkov. (1978). Stephen B. Patrick; Simulations Publications, Inc.

Killer Angels. (1984). Helena Rubinstein; West End Games.

Kingmaker. (1974). Andrew McNeil; Avalon Hill.

Kosovo: The Television War. (2014). Ty Bomba; Decision Games.

Kriegsspiel. (1803). Johann Christian Ludwig (Ludewig) Hellwig.

Labyrinth: The War on Terror, 2001–? (2010). Volko Ruhnke; GMT Games.

Last Battle. (1989). Tim Ryan; GDW.

L'Attaque [Stratego]. (1910). Mme. Hermance Edan; Au Jeu Retrouvé.

La Bataille de la Moscowa. (1975). Laurence A. Groves; Marshall Enterprises.

La Conquête du Monde. (1957). Albert Lamorisse. Miro.

League of Legends. (2009). Tom Cadwell, Rob Garrett, Christina Norman, Steve Feak; Riot Games.

Liberia: Descent into Hell. (2008). Ben Madison and Wes Erni; Fiery Dragon Productions.

Luftwaffe. (1971). Lou Zocchi; Avalon Hill.

Mage Knight. (2000). WizKids.

Magic: The Gathering. (1993). Richard Garfield; Wizards of the Coast.

Map Maneuvers. (1908). Farrand Sayre; Staff College Press.

Masters of the World: Geo-Political Simulator 3. (2013). Eversim.

Mayday. (1978). Mark W. Miller; GDW.

Medal of Honor. (1999). Electronic Arts.

Medal of Honor. (2010). Electronic Arts.

Medal of Honor: Warfighter. (2012). Electronic Arts.

Midway. (1964). Lindsley Schutz and Larry Pinsky; Avalon Hill.

Mississippi Banzai. (1990). Ty Bomba; XTR Corp.

Modern Air Power. (2014). John Tiller Software.

Modern Battles: Four Contemporary Conflicts. (1975). Howard Barasch, Edward Vurran, Jim Dunnigan, J.A. Nelson; SPI.

Modern War in Miniature. (1966). Michael F. Korns; M & J Research.

The Morrow Project. (1980). Kevin Dockery, Robert Sadler, and Richard Tucholka; TimeLine, Ltd.

A Most Dangerous Time. (2009). Tetsuya Nakamura; Multi-Man Publishing.

The Napoleonic Wars. (2002). Don Greenwood, Ben Knight, and Mark McLaughlin; GMT Games.

Napoleon's Triumph. (2007). Bowen Simmons; Simmons Games.

New World Order Battles: Kiev. (Forthcoming). Joseph Miranda; Decision Games.

The Next War. (1978). Jim Dunnigan; SPI.

Nicaragua. (1988). Joseph Miranda; 3W (World Wide Wagames).

Nightfighter. (2011). Lee Brimmicombe-Wood; GMT Games.

Nuclear Destruction. (1970). Rick Loomis; Flying Buffalo.

OGRE. (1977). Steve Jackson; Metagaming Concepts.

The Operational Art of War I: 1935-1955. (1998). TalonSoft.

The Operational Art of War II: Flashpoint Kosovo. (1999). TalonSoft.

The Operational Art of War II: Modern Battles 1956-2000. (1999). TalonSoft.

The Operational Art of War III. (2006). Matrix Games.

Operation Dauntless: The Battles for Fontenay and Rauray, France, June 1944. (2015). Mark Mokszycki; GMT Games.

Order of Arms [series]. (2015). Brien J. Miller and Matthew Kirschenbaum; Compass Games.

Over the Edge. (1992). Robin Laws and Jonathan Tweet; Atlas Games.

Pacific War. (1985). Mark Herman; Victory Games.

PanzerBlitz. (1970). James F. Dunnigan; Avalon Hill.

Panzergruppe Guderian. (1976). James F. Dunnigan; Simulations Publications, Inc.

Panzer Leader. (1974). Avalon Hill.

Papers, Please. (2013). Lucas Pope.

Paths of Glory. (1999). Ted Racier; GMT Games.

Peace Operations Support Model. (2006). UK Defense Science and Technology Laboratory.

Peloponnesian War. (1991). Mark Herman; Victory Games.

Persian Incursion. (2010). Larry Bond, Chris Carlson and Jeff Dougherty; Clash of Arms.

Phantom Fury. (2011). Laurent Closier; Nuts! Publishing.

Phoenix Command. (1986). Barry Nakazono and David McKenzie; Leading Edge Games.

Plants vs. Zombies. (2009–2013). Pop Cap Games.

The Plot to Assassinate Hitler. (1976). James Dunnigan; SPI.

Point of Attack 2. (2004). Scott Hamilton; HPS Simulations.

PRISM: Guard Shield. (2008). US Army National Guard.

Quake. (1996). American McGee, Sandy Petersen, John Romero and Tim Willits; id Software, Inc.

Quebec 1759. (1972). Steve Brewster, Tom Dalgliesh and Lance Gutteridge; Columbia Games.

RAF. (1986). John H. Butterfield; West End Games.

Rainbow Six (*Tom Clancy's*). (1998). Brian Upton; Majesco Entertainment, Red Storm Entertainment.

Rampart. (1990). John Salwitz; Atari Games.

Red Barricades: ASL Historical Module 1. (1990). Charles Kibler; Avalon Hill.

Rethinking Wargames: Three Player Chess. (2003). Ruth Catlow; furtherfield.org. <http://www.furtherfield .org/rcatlow/rethinking_wargames/docs/ 3playerchess.htm>.

Richard III: The Wars of the Roses. (2009). Jerry Taylor and Tom Dalgliesh; Columbia Games.

Richthofen's War. (1972). Randall C. Reed; Avalon Hill.

Rise and Decline of the Third Reich. (1974). John Prados; Avalon Hill.

Risen 2: Dark Waters. (2012). Deep Silver, Ubisoft.

Risk: The Game of Global Domination. (1959). Parker Brothers.

Road to the Rhine. (1979). Frank Chadwick; Game Designers' Workshop.

RoleMaster. (1980). Coleman Charlton, John Curtis, Pete Fenlon, and Steve Marvin; Iron Crown Enterprises.

Rome: Total War. (2004). The Creative Assembly.

RuneQuest. (1978). Steve Perrin, Ray Turney, Steve Henderson, Warren James, and Greg Stafford; Chaosium.

The Russian Campaign. (1974). John Edwards; Jedko.

The Russian Campaign. (1976). John Edwards and Don Greenwood; Avalon Hill.

Savage Worlds. (2003). Shane Lacy Hensley; Pinnacle Entertainment Group.

Schach-oder König-Spiel. (1616). Gustavus Selenus (Augustus, Duke of Brunswick-Lüneburg).

Second Life. (2003). Philip Rosedale; Linden Lab.

Sekigahara: The Unification of Japan. (2011). Matt Calkins; GMT Games.

September 12th: A Toy World. (2002). Newsgaming.

Shining Path. (1995). Brian Train; Microgame Design Group.

Shogun: Total War. (2000). Michael Simpson; The Creative Assembly; Electronic Arts.

Sid Meier's Civilization: The Board Game. (2002). Eagle Games.

Sid Meier's Civilization V. (2010). Firaxis Games.

Sid Meier's Civilization V: Gods and Kings expansion pack (2012). Firaxis Games.

Silent War: The United States' Submarine Campaign Against Imperial Japan. (2005). Brien J. Miller and Stephen C. Jackson; Compass Games.

SimCity. (1989). Maxis.

Six Days in Fallujah. (Unpublished). Konami/Atomic Games.

Snapshot. (1979). Marc W. Miller; GDW.

Sniper! (1973) James F. Dunnigan; Simulations Publications, Inc.

Somali Pirates. (2012). Joseph Miranda; Decision Games.

Somalia Interventions. (1998). Brian Train; Shutze Games.

Sorcerer. (1975). Redmond A. Simonsen; Simulations Publications, Inc.

South Africa. (1977). Irad Hardy; Simulations Publications Incorporated.

South Park Let's Go Tower Defense Play! (2009). Doublesix; Xbox Live Productions; South Park Digital Studios.

Space: 1889. (1988). Frank Chadwick; GDW.

Space Hulk. (1989). Richard Halliwell; Games Workshop.

Spacewar! (1962). Steve Russell et al.

Spec Ops: The Line. (2012). Yager Development; 2K Games.

Squad Leader. (1977). John Hill; Avalon Hill.

Stalingrad. (1963). Charles S. Roberts, Lindsley Schutz, and Thomas N. Shaw; Avalon Hill.

Star Fleet Battles. (1979). Steven V. Cole; Task Force Games.

Star Fleet Battles: Captain's Edition Basic Set. (1999). Steven V. Cole; Amarillo Design Bureau, Inc.

Star Fleet Battles: Advanced Missions. (1999). Steven V. Cole; Amarillo Design Bureau, Inc.

Starcraft. (1998). Blizzard Entertainment, Inc.

Starfleet Orion. (1978). Automated Simulations.

Starweb. (1976). Flying Buffalo.

Steel Wolves: The German Submarine Campaign Against Allied Shipping – Vol. 1. (2010). Brien J. Miller and Stephen C. Jackson; Compass Games.

Stonewall Jackson's Way. (1992). Joseph M. Balkoski; Avalon Hill.

Stonkers. (1983). Imagine Software.

Storm over Stalingrad. (2006). Tetsuya Nakamura; Multi-Man Publishing.

Stratego. (1961). Milton Bradley.

Strategos: The American Game of War. (1880). Charles A. L. Totten.

Streets of Stalingrad. (2003). Dana Lombardy and Art Lupinacci; L2 Design Group.

Striker. (1981). Frank Chadwick; Games Designers' Workshop (GDW).

The Sun King. (Forthcoming). Charles Vasey; Publisher TBD.

Sunset. (2015). Tale of Tales.

Sword & Sorcery. (1978). Greg Costikyan; Simulations Publications, Inc.

The Sword and the Flame (first edition). (1979). Larry V. Brom; Yaquinto Publications.

The Sword and the Flame (second edition). (1984). Larry V. Brom; Greenfield Hobby Distributors.

The Sword and the Flame, Twentieth Anniversary Edition. (1999). Larry V. Brom; And That's The Way It Was.

The Sword and the Flame, Twentieth Anniversary Edition Update. (2008). Larry V. Brom; Sergeants 3.

Tac Air. (1987). Gary C. Morgan, S. Craig Taylor; Avalon Hill.

Tactical Game 3. (1970). James F. Dunnigan; Poultron Press.

Tactics. (1952). Charles S. Roberts; Avalon Game Company.

Tactics II. (1958). Charles S. Roberts; Avalon Hill Company.

Taktisches Kriegs-Spiel oder Anleitung zu einer mechanischen Vorrichtung um tactische Manoeuvres sinnlich darzustellen. (1812). Georg Leopold Reiswitz.

Tank. (1974). Kee Games; Atari Inc.

Tanktics: Computer Game of Armored Combat on the Eastern Front. (1978). Chris Crawford; Microcomputer Simulations.

Tanktics. (1981). Chris Crawford; Avalon Hill.

Third Lebanon War. (2014). Brian Train; BTR Games.

This War of Mine. (2014). 11 bit studios.

Thud! (2002). Trevor Truran; The Cunning Artificer.

The Tigers Are Burning. (1988). Ty Bomba; World Wide Wargames.

Titan. (1980). Gorgonstar.

To the Moon. (2011). Kan Gao; Freebird Games.

Top Secret. (1980). Merle M. Rasmussen; TSR.

Total War: Rome II. (2013). Michael M. Simpson; The Creative Assembly, Ltd.

Toy Soldiers. (2010). Signal Studios.

Traveller. (1977). Marc W. Miller; GDW.

Traveller: 2300. (1986). Marc W. Miller, Timothy B. Brown, Lester W. Smith, and Frank Chadwick. GDW.

Trillion Credit Squadron. (1981). John Astell, Frank Chadwick, John Harshman, Stefan Jones, and Marc W. Miller; GDW.

Tropico 5. (2104). Kalypso Media.

Tunnels and Trolls. (1975). Ken St. Andre; Flying Buffalo.

Tupamaro. (1996). Brian Train; Strategy Gaming Society.

Twilight Struggle: The Cold War, 1945–1989. (2005). Ananda Gupta and Jason Matthews; GMT Games.

UFO: Enemy Unknown [marketed in the US as *X-COM: UFO Defense*]. (1994). Julian Gollop; Mythos Games.

UMS: The Universal Military Simulator. (1987). Ezra Sidran; Rainbird Software.

Unity of Command. (2011). 2x2 Games.

The Universal Military Simulator. (1987). Rainbird Software.

Unknown Armies. (1998). John Tynes and Greg Stolze; Atlas Games.

Up Front. (1983). Courtney Allen; The Avalon Hill Game Company.

Uplink: Hacker Elite. (2003). Chris Delay; Introversion Software.

UrbanSim. (2010). Institute for Creative Technologies and US Army.

Valiant Hearts: The Great War. (2014). Ubisoft.

Vampire: The Masquerade. (1991). Mark Rein-Hagen; White Wolf Games.

Versuch eines aufs Schachspiel gebauten taktischen Spiels von zwey und mehrern Personen zu spielen. (1780). Johann Christian Ludwig Hellwig.

Victory in the Pacific. (1977). Richard Hamblen; Avalon Hill Game Company.

A Victory Lost. (2006). Tetsuya Nakamura; Multi-Man Publishing.

Viet Nam. (1965). Phil Orbanes; Gamescience.

Vietnam 1965–1975. (1984). Nick Karp; Victory Games.

Virgin Queen: Wars of Religion 1559–1598. (2012). Ed Beach; GMT Games.

Virtual Battlespace. (2002). Bohemia Interactive, Coalescent Technologies.

Virtual Battlespace 2. (2007). Bohemia Interactive.

Virtual Battlespace 3. (2014). Bohemia Interactive.

Warcraft: Orcs & Humans. (1994). Blizzard Entertainment, Inc.

Warcraft 3: Reign of Chaos. (2002). Rob Pardo; Capcom, Blizzard Entertainment, Sierra Entertainment.

Wargame Construction Set. (1986). Roger Damon; Strategic Simulations, Inc.

Wargame Construction Set II: Tanks! (1994). Strategic Simulations, Inc.

Wargame Construction Set III: Age of Rifles 1846–1905. (1996). Strategic Simulations, Inc.

Warhammer. (1983). Bryan Ansell, Richard Halliwell, and Richard Priestly; Games Workshop.

Warhammer Book 2: Battle Magic. (1984). Bryan Ansell, Rick Priestley, and Richard Halliwell; Games Workshop.

Warhammer 40,000: Rogue Trader. (1987). Rick Priestly; Games Workshop.

Warhammer 40,000: Codex: Tyranids. (1995). Andy Chambers; Games Workshop.

Warhammer 40,000: Codex: Orks. (2008). Phil Kelly; Games Workshop.

Warhammer 40,000 (seventh edition). (2014). Games Workshop.

War in Europe. (1976). James F. Dunnigan; Simulations Publications, Inc.

War of the Ring. (1977). Howard Barasch and Richard Berg; Simulations Publications, Inc.

War of Wizards. (1975). M.A.R. Barker; Tactical Studies Rules.

We Must Tell the Emperor. (2010). Steve Carey; Victory Point Games.

We the People. (1994). Mark Herman; Avalon Hill.

Wellington's Victory: Battle of Waterloo. (1976). Frank Davis; Simulations Publications, Inc.

West of Alamein. (1988). Bob McNamara; Avalon Hill.

Whistling Death. (2003). J.D. Webster; Clash of Arms Games.

White Bear and Red Moon. (1975). Greg Stafford; Chaosium.

White Death. (1979). Frank Chadwick; Game Designers' Workshop.

Wing Leader: Victories 1940–1942. (2015). Lee Brimmicombe-Wood; GMT Games.

World of Tanks. (2011). Wargaming.net, Inc.

World of Warcraft. (2005–). Blizzard.

World War I. (1975). Jim Dunnigan; Simulations Publications, Inc.

INDEX

Note: Page numbers followed by "n" indicate endnotes. Italicized titles are game titles unless otherwise indicated.